D1233922

THE LEGAL IMAGINATION

Studies in the Nature of Legal Thought and Expression

JAMES B. WHITE

Professor of Law
University of Colorado

Little, Brown and Company
Boston 1973 Toronto

LIBRARY OF CONGRESS CATALOG CARD NO. 72–13324

Published simultaneously in Canada
by Little, Brown & Company (Canada) Limited

PRINTED IN THE UNITED STATES OF AMERICA

Since this page cannot legibly accommodate all the requisite permissions to reprint, the following pages constitute an extension of the copyright page.

I should like to acknowledge the permissions kindly granted to reprint the selections indicated below. Other acknowledgments appear on pages xxvi–xxx.

Thomas Y. Crowell — for the selection from *King Solomon's Ring* by Konrad Z. Lorenz. Copyright 1952 by Thomas Y. Crowell Company, New York, Publishers, and reprinted with their permission.

Doubleday & Company, Inc. — for the selection from *Tolstoy* by H. Troyat. Copyright © 1967 by Doubleday & Company, Inc. Reprinted by permission of Doubleday & Company, Inc.

E. P. Dutton — for the selection from the book *Nigger: An Autobiography* by Dick Gregory with Robert Lipsyte. Copyright © 1964 by Dick Gregory Enterprises, Inc. Published by E. P. Dutton & Co., Inc. and used with their permission.

Harcourt Brace Jovanovich, Inc. — for selections from the following works: "Shooting an Elephant" in *Shooting an Elephant and Other Essays* by George Orwell, copyright 1945, 1946, 1949, 1950 by Sonia Brownell Orwell. Reprinted by permission of Harcourt Brace Jovanovich, Inc. *Aspects of the Novel* by E. M. Forster, copyright, 1927, by Harcourt Brace Jovanovich, Inc.; copyright, 1955, by E. M. Forster. Reprinted by permission of the publisher.

Harper & Row, Publishers, Inc. — for the selection from pp. 610–615 of *An American Dilemma* by Gunnar Myrdal. Copyright, 1944, 1962, by Harper & Row, Publishers, Inc. By permission of the publishers.

The Harvard Law Review Association — for "With The Editors," 84 *Harvard Law Review*, No. 2, by permission of the Harvard Law Review. Copyright 1970 by The Harvard Law Review Association.

Holt, Rinehart and Winston, Inc. — for "The Figure a Poem Makes" from *Selected Prose of Robert Frost* edited by Hyde Cox and Edward Connery Lathem. Copyright 1939, © 1967 by Holt, Rinehart and Winston, Inc. Reprinted by permission of Holt, Rinehart and Winston, Inc. "Design," "Directive," and "The Road Not Taken" from *The Poetry of Robert Frost* edited by Edward Connery Lathem. Copyright 1916, 1947, © 1969 by Holt, Rinehart and Winston, Inc. Copyright 1936, 1944, by Robert Frost. Copyright © 1964 by Lesley Frost Ballantine. Reprinted by permission of Holt, Rinehart and Winston, Inc. The selection from *Life Under the "Peculiar Institution": Selections from the Slave Narrative Collection* by Norman R. Yetman. Copyright © 1970 by Holt, Rinehart and Winston, Inc. Reprinted by permission of Holt, Rinehart and Winston, Inc.

Hutchinson & Co. — for the selections from *The Frying-Pan* by Tony Parker, published by Hutchinson & Co. (Publishers) Ltd., 178–202 Great Portland Street, London, W.1. Reprinted by permission.

International Universities Press — for the selection from "*The Treatment of a Dying Patient*," by Janice Norton, published by International Universities Press, Inc. and reprinted with permission. Copyright, 1963, International Universities Press, Inc.

Little, Brown and Co. — for selections from *Of a Fire on the Moon* by Norman Mailer, by permission of Little, Brown and Co. Copyright © 1969, 1970 by Norman Mailer. Three poems from *Complete Poems of Emily Dickinson* (Johnson ed.).

New Directions Publishing Corporation — for the selection from *The Autobiography of William Carlos Williams*. Copyright 1951 by William Carlos Williams. Reprinted by permission of New Directions Publishing Corporation. Two poems by Dylan Thomas, *Collected Poems*. Copyright 1946 by New Directions Publishing Corporation. Reprinted by permission of New Directions Publishing Corporation.

Random House, Inc. and Alfred A. Knopf, Inc. — for passages by Proust, Ransom, Frost, Stevens, and Tolstoy, as follows: Copyright 1929, renewed 1957 by Random House, Inc. From *Remembrance of Things Past*, by Marcel Proust, translated by C. K. Scott Moncrieff. Reprinted by permission of the publisher. Copyright 1925, renewed 1953 by Random House, Inc. From *Remembrance of Things Past*, by Marcel Proust, translated by C. K. Scott Moncrieff. Reprinted by permission of the publisher. Copyright 1927 by Alfred A. Knopf, Inc., renewed 1955 by John Crowe Ransom. From *Selected Poems*, Third Edition, Revised and Enlarged, by John Crowe Ransom. Reprinted by permission of the publisher. Copyright 1946 by Random House, Inc. From *The Poems of Robert Frost*, by Robert Frost. Reprinted by permission of the publisher. From *The Necessary Angel* by Wallace Stevens. Copyright 1942, 1944, 1947, 1948, 1949, 1951 by Wallace Stevens. Published by Alfred A. Knopf, Inc. and Random House, Inc., and reprinted with their permission. From *The Letters of Wallace Stevens*, edited by Holly Stevens. © Copyright 1966 by Holly Stevens. Published by Alfred A. Knopf and reprinted with their permission. From *The Collected Poems of Wallace Stevens* by Wallace Stevens, Copyright 1923, 1931, 1935, 1936, 1937, 1942, 1943, 1944, 1945, 1946, 1947, 1948, 1949, 1950, 1951, 1952, 1954, by Wallace Stevens. All rights reserved under International and Pan-American Copyright Conventions. Published by Alfred A. Knopf and reprinted with their permission. From *War and Peace* by L. Tolstoy (Garnett trans.) published by Random House.

Scott Meredith Literary Agency — for selections from *Of a Fire on the Moon* by Norman Mailer, Copyright © 1969, 1970 by Norman Mailer. Reprinted by permission of the author and his agents, Scott Meredith Literary Agency, Inc., 580 Fifth Avenue, New York, N.Y. 10036.

The Viking Press — for selections from the following works: *A Portrait of the Artist as a Young Man* by James Joyce. Copyright 1916 by B. W. Huebsch, renewed 1944 by Nora Joyce. Reprinted by permission of The Viking Press, Inc. *The Short Stories of Saki* by H. H. Munro. All rights reserved. Reprinted by permission of The Viking Press, Inc. *Women In Love* by D. H. Lawrence. Copyright 1920, 1922 by D. H. Lawrence, renewed 1947, 1949 by Frieda Lawrence Ravagli. All rights reserved. Reprinted by permission of The Viking Press, Inc. *The Letters of D. H. Lawrence* edited by Aldous Huxley. Copyright 1932 by The Estate of D. H. Lawrence, © 1960 by Angelo Ravagli and C. M. Weekly, Executors of The Estate of Frieda Lawrence Ravagli. Reprinted by permission of The Viking Press, Inc.

Lieber-Atherton, Inc. — from Freund, "Rationality in Judicial Decisions." Reprinted by permission of the publisher, Lieber-Atherton, Inc. Copyright © 1964. All rights reserved.

To My Friend and Teacher
Theodore Baird

The difference of men is very great, you wou'd scarce thinke them to bee of the same species. And yet it consists more in the affection then in the Intellect, for as in the strength of the body two men shall bee of an equall strength, yet one shall appeare stronger then the other, because hee Exercises and putts out his strength, the other will not stirr nor straine himself, so 'tis in the strength of the Braine, the one endeavours, straines, labours & studies, the other sitts still & is idle, & takes no paines, & therefore hee appear^{e}s soe much the Inferiour.

John Selden, *Table Talk*

Does it seem incongruous to you that a Middlemarch surgeon should dream of himself as a discoverer?

George Eliot, *Middlemarch*

CONTENTS

CHAPTER 2. THE LIMITS AND RESOURCES OF LEGAL LANGUAGE: AN INTRODUCTION TO YOUR LITERARY CIRCUMSTANCES

CHAPTER 4. RULES AND RELATIONSHIPS

APPENDIX: SUPPLEMENTARY WRITING ASSIGNMENTS

PREFACE

The task of telling the reader what sort of book he has in his hand is unusually difficult in this case, for this book does not fit easily into any existing category. Since it might be said to have as its purpose the definition of a new subject, or at least a new way of addressing one, it cannot be classified by identifying its subject matter in traditional terms, and any introductory remarks can be at best only suggestive. In what follows, I try to give some idea of how the book can be used to teach a course, but it is also my hope that one can be interested simply in reading it through.

I have sometimes said that this is a course in reading and writing, but the pretense that such a phrase clarifies the subject is at least mildly ironic, since, as you shall see, in my view "reading and writing" could be said to cover the whole of one's education. Perhaps the title points the way as well as anything might do: what can we learn and say about the legal imagination? What are the ways in which lawyers and judges traditionally conceive of and talk about experience, and how can these modes of thought and expression be mastered — and perhaps modified — by an individual mind? What are the consequences of learning to function in these ways? We shall look at the literature of the law as a literature of the imagination of which such questions can be asked, both directly and by comparing it with other literatures. But we do not stop there, since the student is asked how he can contribute to this literature of the law — to this world of thought and expression — and in doing so, how he defines his profession and himself. For one of our premises is that one is responsible for what one does and writes.

Another way to put it might be to say that the question upon which the course proceeds is this: "What does it mean to learn to think and speak like a lawyer?" The readings and the writing assignments can be said to elaborate and complicate that question. In the course of the book the student is asked to write as lawyer, judge, and legislator, and to reflect as a mind and a person on what he has done, to speak in his own voice about his experience of writing and thinking. He is asked to see what the lawyer does as a literary activity, as an enterprise of the imagination, with respect to which both success and failure — if he can define them — are possibilities for him. He must judge for himself what these possibilities are. The demand is upon his imagination, his ability to make sense out of what he does by looking beyond it.

As you look at the readings, you will notice that in selecting them I have drawn heavily upon my own reading of literature.* Of course I hope that others will find this material and the lines of thought to which it gives rise of interest, but my purpose is not to claim that a literary education is the only one for a lawyer or for this course: it is to establish a way of looking at the law from the outside, a way of comparing it with other forms of literary and intellectual activity, a way of defining the legal imagination by comparing it with others. The non-legal readings are meant to give us a common sense (if an incomplete one) of what legal literature leaves out, of what others do that the law does not, and to define a context out of which judgments can begin to be drawn and against which they can be tested. In the notes and questions I bring to both sorts of literature some of the concerns of the literary critic, but I hope I do so in a way that the general reader can easily follow. The aim is not to make a systematic comparison between law and literature, to articulate a general theory of literary analysis or anything like it, but to bring to life by the contrast a set of loosely related questions about language and imagination, to open up diverse and competing lines of thought among which choices can be made by the student or other reader. The activity which I mean to encourage in defining as I do the lawyer as writer is an enterprise of the independent intelligence and imagination.

What might appear to be something of an eccentric diversity in the selection of passages has a real purpose: it is a way of urging the student to bring together the various elements of his own education (however disparate they may seem to be), a way of claiming that nothing is irrelevant until it is shown to be. One who knows about biology or mathematics or music ought to be able to draw connections between these activities and the law similar to those I draw between law and literature. The idea is that the law should be compared not just with literature but with anything that the reader knows, that it should be seen as a part of a larger individual and intellectual life. Accordingly, there is one other resource upon which the student is constantly encouraged to draw: his own experience of social and personal life. Again and again he is asked to talk about his life as a lawyer by comparing it with his life as a person, to connect what he is doing with what he knows.

The student, then, is asked to speak out of an awareness of four sorts

* In fact, as later notes will make clear, I ask the student to read Shakespeare's *Troilus and Cressida* in connection with his work in Chapter 1; and in connection with Chapter 3, Jane Austen's *Pride and Prejudice* and Euripides' *Alcestis.*

of material: the literature of the law, the introduction to literary criticism this book is meant to afford, his intellectual activity outside the law, and his ordinary experience of life. The premise upon which we operate is that the activity called the law can be seen as an activity of the imagination, an activity that creates and uses a literature which we are interested in assessing — what is the state of the legal imagination in America? — and to which the student is asked to contribute, feeling free to bring into play anything that he knows or is. The questions and assignments in this book, therefore, do not ask for answers of the sort that the questions in a property book might be said to call for, but rather are meant as occasions for the play of the individual mind and imagination, as invitations to talk. The student is addressed and asked to speak not as a student but as an independent mind.

Although many of the issues with which this book deals — what it means to speak in a language of rules, how the judicial mind connects the particular and the general, and so on — are sufficiently familiar to lead one to the supposition that this is really a jurisprudence book in disguise, I trust you can see why I am reluctant to call it that. Such a name would make claims that I want to avoid — and which would indeed not be warranted — and in any event, the focus of this course is far from the center of usual philosophical discourse. The effort of the book is not to reach conclusions, even tentative ones, but to define responsibilities. The hope is not that a systematic view of life will be exposed, but that the student will come to some new awareness of his place in the world, of his powers and obligations. In every paper he defines himself as a mind, and you might say that this act of self-expression is our real subject. Not a legal writing course, then, but a course in writing.

It might be summed up by saying that the student or other reader is asked to turn and look back on his life and talk about it, to take a position from which he can say that his whole education (including his legal education to date) lies within his ken, and ask: "Where do I go now?" He is asked to collect himself for the moment and imagine his future.

"How is this book to be used?" you may properly ask. In the Introduction to the Student, I say that each student is charged with the responsibility of making his own course out of these materials; and although the questions are meant to provide some direction, the same goes for the teacher too. The course is inevitably different each time it is taught, as different personalities, interests, and capacities find expression in it.

But it may be of interest if I say something of what I have usually done. I have the students write a paper each week (due two days before our two-hour class), usually on one of the writing assignments given in the text. I duplicate portions of these papers without the writers' names, and it is mainly out of these that we make our class discussion. Another teacher might prefer to run a class that meets several times a week, and the emphasis could be on the readings and questions in the book rather than on the papers. Indeed it need not be taught as a writing course at all; and as I say above, I hope the book can be read outside any formal course of instruction.

I have included more writing assignments than can reasonably be done in a semester. This should permit the exercise of the individual teacher's choice and some variety from year to year.* In addition, I do not hesitate to make a writing assignment out of one of the questions not originally intended for written response, or to combine two or more assignments for the same week, or even to have different students write on different questions. And of course another teacher might want to work out his own writing assignments to replace some or all of those included here. Another practice of mine, for what it is worth, is to tell the student that if for any reason he does not wish a particular paper or portion of one to be duplicated, he need only indicate that when he hands the paper in. And since the major purpose of this course is to encourage him to form and work with his own interests, to make his own questions, I begin the course on the understanding that he is free to disregard any assignment if he wishes and hand in a paper on some other topic instead. I also agree to read any writing of any kind that he does during the semester. Not a great many students take advantage of these possibilities, but I am usually pleased when they do. One warning: to build a class around the writing of students is to subject their egos and emotions to considerable strain, especially where the recurring questions are perplexing and important ones — what sort of life can I make for myself as a lawyer? how do I define myself and my future in what I write? — and a class taught this way can work only if its members trust each other, if there is a sense of shared interest and concern. Partly for this reason I encourage the students to talk matters over outside of class and to feel free to read and criticize each other's papers while they are in the process of composition. If the class is too large for the teacher to read every paper, I recommend the practice of having the students exchange papers for written comments before handing them in. This ensures that every paper has a reader, and of course the process of criticism is itself of value. But most of all, it may help create the sense that we are all colleagues here. I do not think this course lends itself to teaching by competitive methods.

* But the book is intended to have a real structure, to carry its reader from one situation to another, and I think it would probably be a mistake to omit Chapters 1 or 6.

From time to time the materials include alternative and (in the Appendix) supplementary writing assignments. The purpose is to increase the choices available to the teacher, student, and other reader, and to make some variation possible from year to year. The distinction between alternative and supplementary writing assignments, while not rigid, is this: alternative assignments might suitably be substituted for the main writing assignments; the supplementary assignments should probably be done in addition to the main assignments, rather than instead of them, because they usually raise questions that are specialized or peripheral to the lines of thought traced out in the text and excerpts.

The book is addressed to the individual student, not to the usual anonymous reader. I find this form of address congenial, in part because it seems to me to be itself a way of teaching: to address someone as an ideal student, as if he were someone he is not (and you are not), is a way of expressing a view of what you are trying to do, of what you wish you both were, and it may exert some pressure in the right direction. That my own voice is somewhat more personal here than is usually the case is a reflection of an attempt to define a candid relationship with the student, not a claim for the value of my own idiosyncrasies. The hope is that the student will respond in kind, that he will be less timid about exposing his own individuality. I hope other teachers will not be inhibited by my tone from exposing their own intellectual personalities, in similar ways, in courses that they teach using this book. One of my purposes is to encourage the student to make a life of his own in the law, to resist the pressures to conform to the expectations of others. I try to record here something of my own attempt to do that as a way of urging him to assert himself boldly. The teacher will have to be prepared to assert his interests and capabilities too, but I think it best not to hide that fact by a pretended objectivity of voice. All I can do is urge him to make a course of his own out of these materials, treating them with no more respect than he thinks they deserve.

I have included many more questions and notes than is typical of the traditional legal casebook, primarily on the grounds that both teacher and student can rightfully ask for more than the usual assistance in working through a book which departs so markedly from the familiar. Also, since one hope is that the student can be asked to read each section of the book on his own with enough understanding and critical judgment to respond well to the writing assignments, it is important for him, as well as for the ordinary reader, that this be a self-teaching book, and the questions are an attempt to make that possible. There is obviously nothing sacred about the lines of questioning I set up, and all readers are encouraged to create and pursue their own, but I do hope that the questions I suggest will prove to be of some interest and assistance.

Although the particular audience addressed by this book is a student who has at least some experience of legal education, I think the book also can be used as an introduction to law either in law school or before. To see how law students are addressed here might be of some educational value to undergraduate students, conceivably even affecting their expectations of their own futures. I also hope that the book may be read by students of literature, who may be interested by the claim implicit here that the activities of the literary critic, his distinctions and concerns, may have significance for the professional lives of practical people.

I would be most interested in receiving any suggestions or criticisms that readers of this book might have, especially those who use it in the classroom.

ACKNOWLEDGMENTS

In this book I try to establish connections between the law and other intellectual activities, and in doing so I necessarily draw heavily on my own education in classics and literature, a debt impossible to acknowledge in detail because it is owed to the experience of class work and conversation with several fine teachers, rather than to any body of published material. I do not try to trace every idea or perception to its source, since the attempt would be both pretentious and impossible, but I would like to acknowledge in general terms my debts to the following teachers, any one of whom should be able to recognize some of his ideas here: Wendell Clausen, Thomas Gould, and the late John Moore, all at one time members of the Classics Department at Amherst College; Reuben Brower, William Alfred, Richard Poirier, and Edgar Rosenberg, all at one time members of the English Department at Harvard; John H. Finley, Jr., of the Classics Department at Harvard; Joseph Epstein of the Philosophy Department at Amherst College; Albert Sacks and Samuel Thorne of the Harvard Law School. In some instances the debt can be stated with more particularity: my reading of Mark Twain and *Walden,* and much of my understanding of the novel, can be traced to Richard Poirier; and I owe to Edgar Rosenberg my introduction to Edward Hyde, Earl of Clarendon. I should thank as well my teachers at Groton School, especially John Crocker, Melvin Mansur, James Waugh, Norris Getty, Russell Young, and the late Malcolm Strachan, who introduced me to the intellectual world in the finest way. My best teachers in the law have been my colleagues on the *Harvard Law Review,* especially Michael Boudin; my associates at Foley, Hoag, and Eliot in Boston, especially Hans F. Loeser, Esq.; and my colleagues at the University of Colorado School of Law, especially Homer H. Clark, Jr. Many of the students who have taken this course have helped enormously, but it perhaps is not invidious to say that the ideas of James Scarboro have found their way into the book in great numbers. My colleague Alfred T. McDonnell read and criticized the manuscript, and has given me useful ideas. This book would not have been written without the encouragement and criticism of Homer Clark, who has assisted in every possible way.

There remains this to say: anyone who knows Theodore Baird of Amherst College will instantly see that this book is the direct result of his teaching, full of his ideas and imitative of his style; and to such a one, nothing here that may please or instruct will be new or unfamiliar. If I were asked to be particular, I would say that he taught me what writing is and how to ask a question, but that is just another way of saying that to him everything is owed.

I should like to acknowledge the permissions kindly granted to reprint the selections indicated below. Other acknowledgments appear on the copyright page.

George Allen & Unwin Ltd. — for the selection from *Nigger: An Autobiography* by Dick Gregory. Published by George Allen & Unwin Ltd. and used with their permission.

W. H. Allen and Co., Ltd. — for the selection from *Tolstoy* by Henri Troyat, by permission of W. H. Allen and Co., Ltd.

American Bar Association — for the selection from the *Code of Professional Responsibility.*

The American Council on Education — for the selection from *Growing Up in the Black Belt* by Charles Johnson, published by The American Council on Education in 1941.

The American Law Institute — for the selections from *Model Penal Code,* Tentative Draft No. 4. Copyright 1955. Reprinted with the permission of The American Law Institute.

Edward Arnold (Publishers) Limited — for selections from *Aspects of the Novel* by E. M. Forster.

The Associated Press — for a dispatch printed in the Boulder (Colo.) Daily Camera.

Atheneum — for the selection from *Tristes Tropiques,* by Claude Lévi-Strauss, published by Atheneum and reprinted with their permission. English translation Copyright © by Hutchinson & Co. All rights reserved. Selections from *The Soul of the Ape* by Eugene Marais, published by Atheneum and reprinted with their permission. Copyright © 1969 by Human and Rousseau Publishers Ltd.

Athlone Press of the University of London — for the selection from *An Introduction to the Principles of Morals and Legislation* by Jeremy Bentham.

Atlantic, Little, Brown — for the selection from *Whereas — A Judge's Premises* by Charles E. Wyzanski, Jr.

Basil Blackwell & Mott Ltd. — for the selection from *Philosophical Investigations* by L. Wittgenstein.

M. Block — for the selection from *The Art of Summation,* edited by M. Block and reprinted with his permission.

Bowes and Bowes — for the selection from *Slavery in America,* by Barnett Hollander. Published by Bowes & Bowes Publishers Ltd.

Calmann-Levy and Georges Borchardt — for the selection from Camus, *Reflections on the Guillotine* by permission of Calmann-Levy and Georges Borchardt, Inc. Translation by Richard Howard, reprinted by his permission.

Jonathan Cape Ltd. — for the selection from *A Portrait of the Artist as a Young Man* by James Joyce, by permission of the Executors of the James Joyce Estate. "Design," "Directive," and "The Road Not Taken," by Robert Frost, from *The Poetry of Robert Frost,* edited by Edward Connery Lathem. By permission of The Estate of Robert Frost. Published in Britain by Jonathan Cape, Ltd.

A. James Casner — for the selection from *Estate Planning* (third edition, 1972 Supplement) by A. James Casner. Reprinted by permission.

Cassell and Company Ltd. — for the selections from Emily Post, *Etiquette.*

Center for Applied Linguistics — for the selection from "On the Use of Negro Dialect in the Teaching of Reading," by W. Stewart, published in *Teaching Black Children to Read,* pages 170–172 (J. Baratz and R. Shuy, eds.) by the Center for Applied Linguistics, Washington, D.C. 1969.

Chatto and Windus — for the selection from *Experiments* by Norman Douglas, published by Chatto and Windus and reprinted by their permission and that of the Author's Literary Estate, and for selections from *Remembrance of Things Past* by Marcel Proust in the translation of George Scott Moncrieff. By permission.

The Clarendon Press, Oxford — for selections from the following works: *The Works of Thomas Malory* edited by Eugene Vinaver (2d ed. 1967) reprinted by permission of The Clarendon Press, Oxford; *Children's Games in Street and Playground* by Iona and Peter Opie (1969) reprinted by permission of The Clarendon Press, Oxford; *Modern English Usage* by H. W. Fowler (2d ed. revised by Sir Ernest Gowers 1965) reprinted by permission of The Clarendon Press, Oxford; *The Oxford Translation of Aristotle* edited by W. D. Ross, by permission of The Clarendon Press, Oxford; *The Study of Instinct* by N. Tinbergen, by permission of The Clarendon Press, Oxford.

J. M. Dent & Sons Ltd. — for two poems by Dylan Thomas.

Federal Probation — for selections from "The Sentencing Problem," by S. Glueck, reprinted by his permission and that of *Federal Probation;* and from "Institutional Innovations in Juvenile Corrections," by R. Gerard, reprinted by his permission and that of *Federal Probation.*

The Foundation Press, Inc. — for the selection from *Criminal Process* by Lloyd L. Weinreb. Copyright © 1969 by The Foundation Press, Inc., and reprinted by permission of The Foundation Press, Inc.

Lon Fuller — for the selection from *The Forms and Limits of Adjudication* by L. Fuller. Reprinted with permission.

Funk and Wagnalls Publishing Company, Inc. — for the selection from *Emily Post's Etiquette*, Copyright © 1969 by the Emily Post Institute. With permission of the publisher, Funk & Wagnalls Publishing Company, Inc.

Hart Publishing Company — for the selection from *Summerhill: A Radical Approach to Child Rearing*, by A. S. Neill, copyright 1960 Hart Publishing Company, New York.

Harvard University Press — for selections reprinted by permission of the publishers from *Herman Melville's Billy Budd*, edited by Frederick Barron Freeman and corrected by Elizabeth Treeman, Cambridge, Mass.: Harvard University Press, Copyright 1948, 1956 by the President and Fellows of Harvard College.

Hendricks House — for the selection from *Utopia* by More, published by Hendricks House in F. White, *Famous Utopias*.

Hill and Wang — for the selection from *The Theatre* by Stark Young. Published by Hill and Wang and reprinted with their permission.

H.M.S.O. — for the selections from *Report of the Commission on the Third London Airport*, with permission of the Controller of Her Britannic Majesty's Stationery Office.

Houghton Mifflin — for the selections from *The Education of Henry Adams*, by Henry Adams, published by Houghton Mifflin and reprinted by their permission.

Johns Hopkins University Press — for the selection from *Law and Psychiatry* by Shelden Glueck, published by The Johns Hopkins Press and reprinted with their permission. Copyright © 1962 by the Johns Hopkins University Press.

William Labov — for the selection from his article "The Logic of Nonstandard English."

Levitt and Sons — for the selection from *Homeowner's Guide* by Levitt and Sons, reprinted by permission of Levitt and Sons.

Lieber-Atherton, Inc. — for the passage from *On Law and Justice* by Paul A. Freund.

Macmillan — for the selection from Donnelley, Goldstein & Schwartz, *Criminal Law* published by The Macmillan Company and reprinted with their permission. Copyright © 1962 by The Free Press of Glencoe, Inc.

Macmillan, London — for the selection from *The Endless Adventure* by F. S. Oliver, reprinted by permission of the publisher, Macmillan London Limited. Selections from *Life* by Zeno, by permission of Macmillan, London and Basingstoke.

Methuen & Co., Ltd. — for the selection from K. Lorenz, *King Solomon's Ring*.

M.I.T. Press — for the selection from *Language, Thought, and Reality* by B. L. Whorf, published by the M.I.T. Press and reprinted with their permission.

The New Statesman — for the article, "Lawyers at Play," by Timothy Hilton, reprinted from the *New Statesman*, London, by permission.

Penguin Books — for the selections from Theophrastus: *Characters*, translated by Philip Vellacott. Copyright © Philip Vellacott, 1967. Published by Penguin Books Ltd., and reprinted by their permission.

Laurence Pollinger — for *Janet Waking* by John Crowe Ransom, published by Eyre & Spottiswoode. Also by permission of Alfred A. Knopf Inc. and Random House, Inc. Selections from the *Autobiography of William Carlos Williams,* published by MacGibbon and Kee Ltd. Also by permission of New Directions Publishing Corporation. The selection from *Women in Love* by D. H. Lawrence, by their permission and that of the Estate of the late Mrs. Frieda Lawrence.

Princeton University Press — for the selection from *The Art of Persuasion in Greece* by G. Kennedy. Copyright © 1963 by Princeton University Press.

Routledge & Kegan Paul Ltd. — for the selection from Boulton, *The Language of Politics in the Age of Wilkes and Burke.*

Secker & Warburg — for the selection from *Shooting an Elephant* by George Orwell. Also by permission of Mrs. Sonia Brownell Orwell.

The Selden Society — for the selections from John Selden, *Table Talk* (F. Pollock ed. 1927) by permission of the Selden Society.

Stein and Day — for the selections from the book *Life* by Zeno. Copyright © 1968 by Zeno. Reprinted with permission of Stein and Day Publishers.

Sweet and Maxwell — for the selections from *Criminal Law Review,* published by Sweet & Maxwell, with permission of the publisher.

Trial Magazine — for an interview with M. Abram published in *Trial Magazine,* by permission of author and publisher.

The University of Chicago — for the selection from *The Iliad of Homer* translated by Richmond Lattimore and published by the University of Chicago Press. Copyright 1951 by The University of Chicago. All rights reserved. Reprinted by permission. The selection from *Aeschylus I: Oresteia* translated by Richmond Lattimore and published by the University of Chicago Press. © 1953 by The University of Chicago. All rights reserved. Reprinted by permission.

University of Toronto Press — for the selection from Boulton, *The Language of Politics in the Age of Wilkes and Burke.*

J. L. Van Schaik (Pty) Ltd. — for the selections from *The Soul of the White Ant* by Eugene Marais, published by Methuen & Co. Ltd. and J. L. Van Schaik (Pty) Ltd., and reprinted by permission of E. N. Marais Jnr. and J. L. Van Schaik (Pty) Ltd.

Wall Street Journal — for "Wall Street's Hippies: Long-Haired Couriers Make Financial Scene," by M. Bralove, reprinted with permission of *The Wall Street Journal.*

George Weidenfeld and Nicholson — for the selection from *Commandant of Auschwitz* by Rudolf Hoess.

World Publishing Co. — for the selection from Hoess, *Commandant of Auschwitz:* reprinted by permission of The World Publishing Company from *Commandant of Auschwitz* by Rudolph Hoess. English translation copyright © 1959 by George Weidenfeld & Nicolson Ltd.

Yale University Press — for the selection from *The Nature of the Judicial Process* by B. Cardozo, published by Yale University Press and reprinted by their permission.

INTRODUCTION TO THE STUDENT

I want to begin by calling this an advanced course in reading and writing, a study of what lawyers and judges do with words. You may at first feel that reading and writing is a subject proper not for graduate school but for primary school, and that you already know how to read and write very well indeed or you would not be where you are. If this feeling exists, I hope it will change during the course, for to the lawyer these are not easy matters; to say that he is a literary man, that virtually everything he does — counselling, arguing, brief-writing, negotiating — is done with words, is to define a life (as I hope you will see) of genuine difficulty. At every stage the lawyer speaks to experience and in doing so defines anew the limits and capacities of his own imagination, defines himself as a person and a mind. Ask yourself how satisfactory your own moot court briefs and arguments have been.

To ask how to read and write well is to ask practically everything, one might say, and indeed a legal education could be defined by saying that one learns to read and write the professional language of the law, to master a set of special ways of thinking and talking. Your central question in the course could then be put this way: what does it mean to give yourself such an education, to learn to think and speak like a lawyer? You will see that the question so stated has two obvious branches: how do you do it, in what does the lawyer's art consist? And what does it signify to have mastered that art — what have you gained, what lost?

In asking such questions of you as one engaged in the process, this course takes as its subject your own intellectual life in the law. The idea is not to train you in a skill that will make you a verbal wizard (although I hope your writing will be the better for what you do here), but to ask you to come to terms with your own experience and write about it. The focus of our thinking will not be upon the law as a great purposive system of rule-making and administration — which it is, or could be said to be — but upon what it is that individual persons in the law in fact do (in particular, what they do with words) and how you regard your future so defined. Frequently we shall compare what is said by people in the law with what other people have found it possible to say, in similar circumstances or on similar subjects; in this way we hope to expose some unexpressed assumptions or characteristics of legal discourse, to uncover the special circumstances of the writer who is a lawyer. We shall examine the lawyer speaking as counselor, advocate, legislator, and judge, and in the writing assignments you yourself will be asked to speak in each of these roles as well as to talk in your own voice about what lawyers do. The questions asked by the assignments do not have answers as mathematical questions might, but call upon you to form your own sort of response, to make up your own course as you go along. The question asked of what you write will not be how well you have answered an assignment, but what you have managed to make for yourself out of what it offers. Our subject is obviously not capable of complete analysis and expression — as Samuel Johnson said, life is not the object of science — but this course can be taken as an invitation to you to explore your own interests in the law, to form and to hold to statements of your own creation. You are here asked to express the workings of your own imagination.

Another way to explain what this course is about is to say that its ultimate question is how an intelligent and educated person can possibly spend his life working with the law, when life is short and there is so much else to do. This question will obviously be answered differently by different people, and one object of the course is to give you a chance to arrive at and express your own answer. For me, at least, the first step towards an answer is talk not about the importance of the law in the world, but about its interest. That is, I think that one can regard the law as a subject that can command the attention of independent and curious minds entirely aside from the importance it may have to society. It is not from society's point of view (whatever way that might be defined) that I encourage you to look at the law, but from your own. The language that so commonly appears at the beginning of law books, by which law is characterized as a "tool of social control" or a "science of social problem-solving," no doubt has its value, but it does not point towards what interests me in the law, and I suspect the same may be true of you. One may express the importance of the law by saying that it is the cement that holds society together, or that it is a great machine for social improvement, or that it is essential to the rational expression of a society's values, without saying why the law is interesting. To be important — as the law undoubtedly is, and for reasons dimly expressed in that series of metaphors — is not necessarily to be interesting. If you ask a businessman why what he does is important, he may say because the economy depends upon enterprises such as his, and because the whole of society depends upon a healthy economy. That is perfectly true, of course, but if you try to find out what interests him about his job, you may find that he talks less about his sense of importance than about the challenge of doing a difficult job, or the excitement of exercising certain skills, or the meaning of the human relationships through which he must work — matters on which you can imagine yourself questioning him intensely. He may say, "The name of the game is written on the bottom line," but I should think that that figure expresses the life of the businessman as little as the score tells the story of a football game.

This course, then, is about what makes the law and the life of the lawyer interesting. Of course you will not be interested by exactly the same matters that I am, and the course is not designed to make you pretend that you are, but we do operate on the premise that to study what lawyers do with language makes room for the pursuit of virtually any interest you may have in the life of the lawyer. And I hope it does make sense to you that our problems should invite you to explore, for yourself and to your own satisfaction, your life with the law and your interest in it, that your focus is upon your curiosity, not your sense of importance. You might say that the course is idiosyncratic for you as well as for your teacher, in that you are encouraged to express the peculiarity, the individuality, of your own intellectual and emotional experience as a lawyer. Your concern will be less with what makes a good law than what will make you a good lawyer, what will yield a life of interest and value for you.

Two of my own experiences may help define a point of view from which you may wish to regard this course. I was led to go to law school by many things, including a desire to participate in the great social life of our world and a desire to do good, but what probably closed the decision for me was the experience of watching a moot court case involving abstruse questions of Georgia sales tax law and administrative law. Obviously it was not the rule of law at issue or its social implications or its effectiveness as a tool of social control or the reasons behind the rule that interested me. It was the kind of altercation that I saw. I was shown that in the law even such matters could be made the topic of argument and intellectual confrontation of a most exciting and challenging kind. The resolution of the question seemed to call upon every intellectual skill and insight. Why this seemed so, I cannot say, but it still does today: one has the feeling about a legal argument that it involves everything. The moment arrives when the law will act upon life, will declare its final simplification and pass on. What choices of argument has the lawyer, what of explanation has the judge? Of all that could be said about what has happened, what will each in his brief half-hour choose to say? This sense that the life of the lawyer somehow involves everything, and that much of it is never stated or even talked about, may be taken as a starting point for this course.

The second experience was the new impression of law practice that I obtained when I finally arrived at a position from which I could observe lawyers at work. There seem to be two distinct ways in which law firms try to educate their younger lawyers: some firms establish detailed procedures for the treatment of problems, supervising young people very closely and assuring themselves that each step has been mastered completely before permitting the young lawyer to go on to the next. Typically this leads to rather narrow specialization. At its best, the system produces an institutional style of caution and assured competence. No mistakes: do it the way it has been done. The opposite technique is to encourage the development of individual characteristics and abilities, on the theory that a finely tooled training process stifles the ingenuity and the sense of confident individuality that are essential to first-rate legal practice. The assumption is that in any situation there is no single right response at which we would like every member of the firm to arrive by the same steps, but that there are a great many different right responses (depending upon the talents of the particular lawyer and what he intends to do next) to be arrived at in a great many different ways. One person can rightly run a risk — of litigation, say, or of antagonizing another lawyer or his client — that another would wisely avoid. This produces, at its best, not an institutional style but a cluster of individual styles.* So viewed, the law is one of the few activities where you can recognize and live with your peculiarities of skill and weakness, and take pride in managing them, where your job is to find or create a style of your own, a way of doing things that seems right to you. And the activities in which a lawyer is given the opportunity to excel cover nearly the whole range of human experience, from the exercise of pure logic to sensitivity to the emotional qualities of a human relationship.

To what extent can you give yourself — can you demand and take — a life in the law that does express your individuality of mind and character? To what extent, if you are to be a really fine lawyer, must your mind be cast in a mold set by others? Without trying to answer these questions (which of course only you can do), this course urges you not to give up but to make the most insistent demands for a life of self-expression that you can. You will discover for yourself what limits there may be upon your freedom.

I want you to begin this course, then, by trying to imagine as fully as possible how it might be said that law is not a science — at least not the

* Perhaps I should add that what I say here about differences of attitude in private law firms could be said of public legal agencies as well — of the offices of the prosecutor or public defender or legal aid attorney. And one could find offices of both kinds, public and private, in which no teaching of any kind is felt to go on, where law is viewed not as a chance for an education, but as a trade or an unimportant and uninteresting game.

"social science" some would call it — but an art. And this course is directed to you as an artist. There is no body of rules expressing the art of the lawyer any more than that of the sculptor or painter. You are as free as they, and as responsible for what you do. It is true that one of the mediums of the lawyer's art is rules, and the lawyer must know rules, and the other materials of the law, as the sculptor must know clay and the painter paint and canvas. You must know what they are and how they work, before you can work with them. But what you must ultimately learn is what to do with rules and judicial opinions and all the other forms of expression that are the working stuff of a lawyer's life, just as the sculptor must learn what to do with clay and marble. You may feel that you are constrained by your material, as indeed you are. But compare the pianist, who is told what notes to play, in what order, how long and how loud; yet art is surely possible there. In asking you to define for the moment the lawyer as writer, to regard yourself in that way, I am asking you not to follow direction and example but to trust and follow your own curiosity; to work out in your imagination various future possibilities for yourself, defined by the real and imagined performances of your mind at its best; and to subject what you discover to criticism and speculation.

THE LEGAL IMAGINATION

CHAPTER 1

THE LAWYER AS WRITER

A. LEARNING THE LANGUAGE OF THE LAW

Our attempt to define the lawyer as a special sort of writer might most naturally begin with a double effort: to try to locate and define his professional language, and to draw a line between what he does with that language and whatever else he does. But these are far from simple matters, and we should not look for a clarity we shall not find. For example, it is so obvious that the lawyer uses words at every stage of his professional life that we might slip into thinking that a full description of his use of words would fully describe his life as a lawyer, that there is no other side. But a moment's thought will show that a lawyer's professional experience and even his professional uses of language are not confined to the use of words. He talks in nonverbal ways as well, all the time — think of the shifts of demeanor the skillful attorney displays in arguing to a jury, negotiating a contract, or cross-examining an expert witness; and behind all his languages, verbal and nonverbal, is a world of feeling, thought, and judgment that is never expressed at all.[1] The trial lawyer will tell you that it is his "instinct" that tells him when to object and when to be silent, or whether he should ask that last question on cross-examination; a business lawyer will tell you that "judgment" is the most important quality in a lawyer.

If you have difficulty in imagining what I mean by the experience that

1. Compare the following remarks on the languages of the theater: "The tempo and the tone are languages quite as the word is, sometimes one of the three is more important to the idea, sometimes another. The plain word *no* means simply negation or refusal, but by tempo and vocal tone other meanings are added. When a character asks, Are you certain of his guilt? and another answers *no*, he is speaking two languages, one the language of the word, which in this case remains the same; the other of music, by which the meaning can be changed at will. If he says *no* at once in a clear tone, *no* fifty seconds after the question and in a shrill tone, *no* one minute after the question in an angry tone, and so on, he is plainly saying different things, things of which the word is only a small part. The gradations and values of sound in the theatre are in their way as infinite and inexhaustible as music is." Stark Young, *The Theatre* 24 (1958).

is never expressed, it might be helpful for you to make a diagram of a relatively simple case — say, one where a person recovers $5000 for personal injury caused by negligent driving — in which you show the structure of the legal process, dividing verbal from nonverbal experience. You might start with the accident, or perhaps the moment just before (when everyone was leading some other life, not even thinking of such a thing), or perhaps when the driver had decided against his better judgment to stay a little longer at the party. How much of all that could ever be expressed? How much will ever be expressed in the lawsuit? To look at the final statement the law makes, the conclusory legal description of the event, there is a judgment for $5000 and perhaps the delivery and deposit of a certified check, with corresponding bookkeeping entries. That is one way, and the final way, in which the law expresses the meaning of the accident. But of course a great deal preceded that statement; the people of the law have already had a great deal to say about the meaning of the event. Who has described the event and in what languages has he spoken? What of his experience did each express and what remains unstated? What part of what was said was expressed verbally and what part nonverbally? In your diagram, indicate not only what has been said, but also the experience that was never expressed at all. Think of the experience of the accident itself, the sudden terror, the pain, the misery of hospital life; of the interviews, the anxieties, and speeches and arguments; the letters and conferences and phone calls; the emotions of lawyers and clients, moving across the spectrum from elation to despair as the events of the trial proceed; the several witnesses each saying what he now remembers that he saw or felt; and the unexpressed experience of the deciders of the question: the judge shifting his weight from ham to ham, the drowsy juror studying the varnished bench, the feelings aroused and dispelled as the words flow by. All this time there is the internal experience, partly verbal, partly not, which will finally be expressed in the single sentence of the verdict. To what sorts of experience, expressible in what sorts of language, can you trace the history of this single sentence? How much of the experience of the juror and judge — of listening to witnesses and argument, of reaching tentative and then final conclusions — is an experience of language and how much is something else? What part of such experience can be expressed and what part cannot? How long could this description go on? See how elaborate your diagram quickly becomes, and how uncertain are its categories; for there is no bright line between language and behavior, between thought and sympathy.

Although the final legal statement is a judgment for one side or the other, the case itself — as it is worked out, tried, and decided — is made by the lawyers and the judge to involve much more than this. They give it meanings of other kinds, they put much at stake in it. Partly this is a consequence of the fact that the argument of the lawyers takes a thousand forms, as they dispute points of procedure, offer and object to evidence, propose instructions, and so on, speaking with respect to every issue as if this case were critical to the integrity of a whole body of law and to future cases innumerable. But this is not all. One has a feeling that what any case really involves is rather different from anything expressed in argument, something not even expressed in the summation to the jury. Is it the constant pressure of a sense of justice? One might put it this way: the jury is always asked to imagine events from competing points of view, to imagine what life has been like for both the plaintiff and the defendant, to see, as it were, what can never be seen: the whole of an event. And both the jury and the judge are constantly subject to a threatened tension between fidelity to duty and their own sense of what is right. The lawyers' technical and legal argument is directed to these matters of imagination and feeling, to getting a sense of the meaning of things and of one's relationship to them, as well as to ends more clearly articulated. When the trial closes, more has happened than the reaching of a verdict. The verbal side of what occurs is rich and complicated, with depths as well as surface. Your study of what the lawyer does with words can be regarded as the study of the rhetoric (in the ancient sense of that term) of the language of the law.

The lawyer is a user of words; but like all such people, he must use them in a world of unexpressed and inexpressible experience. The description of an event can go on forever and still be incomplete. What is said is only part of what happens. The new lawyer sees this as soon as he finds that he must tell a real story and discovers that it can never be done, that there is always more to say, always a qualification to be drawn. We shall return again and again to the line that separates the expressed from the unexpressed, what can be said from what cannot.

When we turn to the lawyer's use and experience of language and ask how that side of his life can be characterized, we open up a fundamental and perplexing question: do such peculiarities as we observe reside in the existence of a discrete professional language, with its own vocabulary and syntax? Or in habits of mind and ways of working that find expression in whatever verbal language the lawyer uses, even when he is talking, say, to his client or to a jury in ordinary English? And most serious of all: what relationship can the lawyer establish with these patterns of thought and language that he uses? Can he simply learn to use and master them without being somehow affected — perhaps controlled — by what he has learned? To put the question in even larger terms: what is the relationship between the lawyer's language and his mind? What can you hope to make that relationship in your own case?

In what now follows, then, we shall be trying to do two things: first, to understand and characterize the language or languages that the lawyer uses, which we all learn as lawyers; and then to ask what it means, both generally and in one's own case, to learn such a language. What possibilities — what risks, what hopes — can you define? Or is it all very simple: one learns a language that one can use as a tool; it is all gain, no loss? Can we talk about language in a way that recognizes the context of inexpressible experience in which its use always occurs?

To start with the more manageable possibility, it is almost possible to describe the legal system of language as a linguistically separate dialect, with a peculiar vocabulary and peculiar constructions. This is one purpose of Professor Mellinkoff's interesting book, *The Language of the Law* (1963), an analytic account of legal terms and legal habits of speech, with a few suggestions for reform (e.g., do not say "null and void"),[2] based upon the appealing premise that legal language should not be different from ordinary English without good reason.

An even clearer example of the technical language of the law is law French, the separate tongue spoken in the English law courts in the late Middle Ages and Renaissance. This language is described by Maitland in some detail in his introduction to volume 17 of the Selden Society Reprints, including a brief grammar and glossary. Here he describes one consequence of the highly technical nature of this language:

> When the history of English law is contrasted with the history of its next of kin, the existence of law French is too often forgotten. It is forgotten that during the later middle age English lawyers enjoyed the inestimable advantage of being able to make a technical language. And a highly technical language they made. To take one example, let us think for a moment of "an heir in tail rebutted from his formedon by a lineal warranty with descended assets." Precise ideas are here expressed in precise terms, every one of which is French: the geometer or the chemist could hardly wish for terms that are more exact or less liable to have their edges worn away by the vulgar. Good came of this and evil. Let us dwell for a moment on an important consequence. We have known it put by a learned foreigner as a paradox that in the critical sixteenth century the national system of jurisprudence which showed the stoutest nationalism was a system that was hardly expressible in the national language. But is there a paradox here? English law was tough and impervious to foreign influence because it was highly technical, and it was highly technical because English lawyers had been able to make a vocabulary, to define their concepts, to think sharply as the man of science thinks. It would not be a popular doctrine that the Englishry of English law

2. This sort of advice is needed more acutely than one might realize. I once drafted a complaint in which I alleged that the defendant had committed "many and numerous" breaches of a contract.

was secured by "la lange francais qest trope desconue"; but does it not seem likely that if English law had been more homely, more *volksthümlich*, Romanism would have swept the board in England as it swept the board in Germany?*

As lawyers, we still speak an inherited and traditional language with marked peculiarities of vocabulary and construction. Much of what we say is as thoroughly unintelligible to the layman as the phrase used by Maitland would be. The existence of such a professional language — almost a secret way of talking — has most complex consequences, which we can only begin to trace in this book. For one thing, it gives us the sense that we are part of the past, the true intellectual conservatives, talking now as lawyers did centuries ago. (I once heard a lawyer say of the popular inter vivos trust device for the avoidance of probate that it "violated the Statute of Wills.") One might generalize and say that your mastery of the literature of the law gives you a way of connecting what people have said and done in the past with what you and your clients say and do today, a way of learning from the experience of others and of using what you learn. It is in part the special legal language that defines that literature and makes it still intelligible to us.

But the sort of legal language Maitland describes has a more obvious characteristic, which is of considerable importance to us because it still exists and is the subject of a great deal of foolish talk. Much legal language can be said to be a "technical language" in which "precise ideas" are expressed in "precise terms." What, you may ask, is the difficulty with that? Who could possibly regard that as anything but a merit?

QUESTIONS

1. *Maitland says of the precision of legal language that "good came of this and evil." What evil could possibly have come from the use of a precise language to express precise ideas?*
2. *It is apparently a premise of much literary education that the rules of grammar, diction, and style can be reduced without much loss to a single forceful command: "Be clear and precise." The function of language is to communicate ideas, and the task of the writer is to be sure that the words he chooses communicate precisely the ideas he has in mind and no other. Language is a machine, efficiency its virtue. It is a moving belt that conveys ideas from mind to mind. Efficiency in the operation of the machine is especially important for lawyers: "The power of Clear Statement is the Great Power at the Bar," said Daniel Webster, or so one is told. Clarity and precision are the sum of good writing.*

   One purpose of this course is to complicate beyond recognition that

* Page xxxvi (1903).

sense of how language works and of what good writing is. The following questions may be taken as a start in this direction.

a. *What is the most precise language you know? Why has that language not been universally adopted for all purposes?*

b. *Obviously there are limits upon what can be said in a language of mathematics or physics, in the language of "the chemist or geometer." What are these limits and how do they work?*

   (1) *Can you explain why you cannot say in the language of mathematics all that you wish to say in your life?*

   (2) *Is the answer really very simple: "There is no word for love in mathematics"? (If you are tempted by that suggestion, let me propose that we agree that from now on the number "3" shall mean "love.")*

c. *To restate the question slightly: the system of legal language is not uniformly technical and precise; why, at the very least, do we not reform this professional language to meet the standards of precision in fact achieved only in limited sections of it, such as those dealing with tax and real property? Exactly why is most of the Constitution – our most important document – not written in a "precise language expressing precise ideas"? What are the "limits" on what can be said in technical legal language and how do they work?*

d. *I have spoken here as if clarity and precision are synonymous. Is that always true? Can you draft a precise statement that is not clear, or a clear statement that is not precise?*

To consider how the legal language system works as a technical language is, as you can see, to open up several lines of inquiry. But we should perhaps recognize that we can talk about the legal language system in a more comprehensive way, to include not only peculiar and technical phrases but habits of thought and conditions of mind, for it is language that demonstrates the condition of the imagination. To take a historical example, one might conclude from Clarendon's *History of the Rebellion* that Oliver Cromwell's failure to build new and lasting institutions was a failure to find new ways of talking and thinking about the public world. Clarendon shows him as one who accepted an inheritance of political language and habits of thought and the old forms of government they implied, with the consequence, fatal to the permanence of his revolution, that the only expressible difference between his and royal rule was legitimacy.[3] In a similar way one could say that lawyers think and talk in distinct ways which we could hardly imagine being changed,

3. Edward Hyde, First Earl of Clarendon, *The History of the Rebellion and Civil Wars in England*, Books 14 and 15 (1702; Macray ed. 1888). Compare Maine's discussion of the effect that intellectual context had upon the nature of the claims to empire made by Charlemagne, in H. Maine, *Ancient Law* 101–102 (1861; Beacon ed. 1963). In *Oliver Cromwell* 21 (1968), Professor Christopher Hill says that Cromwell's difficulty lay in his dependence upon the army, which made it risky to shift the power to another, less autocratic institution. Is this inconsistent with the view I have attributed to Clarendon?

for good or ill. What are these ways and how are we bound by them? If you refuse to be bound by them, how do you plan to make your refusal stick — except perhaps by never really learning them? To put it somewhat differently, we can sometimes identify a remark or question as lawyerlike even where there is no use of a special vocabulary. How do we do that? What are the lawyer's questions, his remarks, his habitual processes of mind? What sorts of explanation does he demand or accept? Can you regard yourself with a cold enough eye to see what the infuriated layman at the cocktail party means when he explodes at you for being "legalistic" or "talking like a lawyer again"? Or to be more positive, what do your teachers mean when they characterize their goal for you as "thinking like a lawyer"?

The ambiguous relationship between mind and language leads to another uncertainty: once it is recognized that lawyers do see things differently from other people, that their minds work differently — that they themselves are different — it becomes important to ask what it means to become a lawyer oneself. Is being a lawyer something you can put on and take off like a suit of clothes, or does it somehow change you beyond repair? Who is in control of whatever process of change goes on, who determines what you gain or lose? The difficulty is that there are, of course, ways in which you are pleased to see yourself change as you get a legal education—you want to have the perceptions and capacities for which people call upon lawyers, you want a legal mind; yet it would be possible to describe as typically lawyerlike certain casts of mind, habits of thought, which you would not want to see in yourself. The very idea of an education, if it means anything, means a process of change — of self-improvement, it is hoped — but what can one mean by that in one's own case? Your question, which the course as a whole is meant to elaborate, is this: how will you, you personally, as an independent mind, respond to and attempt to control the pressure of your training in the law?

These questions can be regarded as a critical part of this course. I hope they are alive for you, for it is no small thing to subject yourself to training in a system of thought and expression that in turn affects you and your mind. Think for a moment of the dangers of the life of the salesman. What might it do to you to sell encyclopedias for the next three years? Surely you know some salesmen on whom such a way of life has made a deep impression. Perhaps you have received a telephone call marked by a forced and embarrassed joviality from an old college friend who now wants you as his customer, or perhaps you have even tried selling and know from experience what it can do. What sorts of relationships does the salesman seek to establish with other people, and what is the place in those relationships of what you would call friendliness? How does he describe the world of material objects, and what do the words "true" and "false" mean to such a mind? Do you see that what happens to the salesman could be expressed by identifying the forms of thought and speech in which he engages? You could certainly tell if someone started talking like a salesman to you, and would blame him for it if the occasion did not warrant it. You might draft a speech from a play or novel in which you show the salesman's mind at work and express his way of regarding experience.

Would you choose to subject yourself to training as a salesman? If not, are you sure that your legal education will not be equally destructive? Can you explain why it will not? To be specific, how does a jury speech differ, if at all, from a sales pitch?

What does a similar attempt to draw a caricature of a lawyer produce? What is meant when your friend at the cocktail party calls you "legalistic" and gives up in disgust? Can you stand outside the legal language system and look at it? Can you stand far enough back from your legal education to ask, "What am I becoming?"

Here is a passage in which one man looks back on his professional education and tries to say something of what it has meant to him.

LIFE ON THE MISSISSIPPI*

Mark Twain

[Twain, an apprentice pilot, has just explained to Mr. Bixby why he suddenly changed course: to avoid a bluff reef.]

"No, it wasn't a bluff reef; there isn't one within three miles of where you were."

"But I saw it. It was as bluff as that one yonder."

"Just about. Run over it!"

"Do you give it as an order?"

"Yes. Run over it!"

"If I don't, I wish I may die."

"All right; I am taking the responsibility."

I was just as anxious to kill the boat, now, as I had been to save it before. I impressed my orders upon my memory, to be used at the inquest, and made a straight break for the reef. As it disappeared under our bows I held my breath; but we slid over it like oil.

"Now, don't you see the difference? It wasn't any thing but a *wind* reef. The wind does that."

"So I see. But it is exactly like a bluff reef. How am I ever going to tell them apart?"

"I can't tell you. It is an instinct. By and by you will just naturally

* Chapter 8 (1883).

know one from the other, but you never will be able to explain why or how you know them apart."

It turned out to be true. The face of the water, in time, became a wonderful book — a book that was a dead language to the uneducated passenger, but which told its mind to me without reserve, delivering its most cherished secrets as clearly as if it uttered them with a voice. And it was not a book to be read once and thrown aside, for it had a new story to tell every day. Throughout the long twelve hundred miles there was never a page that was void of interest, never one that you could leave unread without loss, never one that you would want to skip, thinking you could find higher enjoyment in some other thing. There never was so wonderful a book written by man; never one whose interest was so absorbing, so unflagging, so sparklingly renewed with every reperusal. The passenger who could not read it was charmed with a peculiar sort of faint dimple on its surface (on the rare occasions when he did not overlook it altogether); but to the pilot that was an *italicized* passage; indeed, it was more than that, it was a legend of the largest capitals, with a string of shouting exclamation points at the end of it, for it meant that a wreck or a rock was buried there that could tear the life out of the strongest vessel that ever floated. It is the faintest and simplest expression the water ever makes, and the most hideous to a pilot's eye. In truth, the passenger who could not read this book saw nothing but all manner of pretty pictures in it, painted by the sun and shaded by the clouds, whereas to the trained eye these were not pictures at all, but the grimmest and most dead-earnest of reading matter.

Now when I had mastered the language of this water, and had come to know every trifling feature that bordered the great river as familiarly as I knew the letters of the alphabet, I had made a valuable acquisition. But I had lost something, too. I had lost something which could never be restored to me while I lived. All the grace, the beauty, the poetry, had gone out of the majestic river! I still kept in mind a certain wonderful sunset which I witnessed when steamboating was new to me. A broad expanse of the river was turned to blood; in the middle distance the red hue brightened into gold, through which a solitary log came floating, black and conspicuous; one place a long, slanting mark lay sparkling upon the water; in another the surface was broken by boiling, tumbling rings, that were as many-tinted as an opal; where the ruddy flush was faintest, was a smooth spot that was covered with graceful circles and radiating lines, ever so delicately traced; the shore on our left was densely wooded, and the somber shadow that fell from this forest was broken in one place by a long, ruffled trail that shone like silver; and high above the forest wall a clean-stemmed dead tree waved a single leafy bough that glowed like a flame in the unobstructed splendor that was flowing from the sun. There were graceful curves, reflected images, woody heights, soft distances; and over the whole scene, far and near, the dissolving lights drifted steadily, enriching it every passing moment with new marvels of coloring.

I stood like one bewitched. I drank it in, in a speechless rapture. The world was new to me, and I had never seen anything like this at home. But as I have said, a day came when I began to cease from noting the glories and the charms which the moon and the sun and the twilight wrought upon the river's face; another day came when I ceased altogether to note them. Then, if that sunset scene had been repeated, I should have looked upon it without rapture, and should have commented upon it, inwardly, after this fashion: "This sun means that we are going to have wind to-morrow; that floating log means that the river is rising, small thanks to it; that slanting mark on the water refers to a bluff reef which is going to kill somebody's steamboat one of these nights, if it keeps on stretching out like that; those tumbling 'boils' show a dissolving bar and a changing channel there; the lines and circles in the slick water over yonder are a warning that that troublesome place is shoaling up dangerously; that silver streak in the shadow of the forest is the 'break' from a new snag, and he has located himself in the very best place he could have found to fish for steamboats; that tall dead tree, with a single living branch, is not going to last long, and then how is a body ever going to get through this blind place at night without the friendly old landmark?"

No, the romance and the beauty were all gone from the river. All the value any feature of it had for me now was the amount of usefulness it could furnish toward compassing the safe piloting of a steamboat. Since those days, I have pitied doctors from my heart. What does the lovely flush in a beauty's cheek mean to a doctor but a "break" that ripples above some deadly disease? Are not all her visible charms sown thick with what are to him the signs and symbols of hidden decay? Does he ever see her beauty at all, or doesn't he simply view her professionally, and comment upon her unwholesome condition all to himself? And doesn't he sometimes wonder whether he has gained most or lost most by learning his trade?

QUESTIONS

1. *Here Twain compares the pilot's landscape with the passenger's landscape. Can you imagine a legal landscape? What would a legal representation of your home town look like? Draw a diagram of a landscape in which you show its legal elements.*
2. *Twain expresses something of what learning to be a pilot meant for him, and laments his loss. Does this passage speak also for your legal education,*

have you lost something in learning to speak and think like a lawyer, are the romance and beauty gone from the river?

a. *What is it that you have lost?*

b. *Does it trouble you that you can say of your education, and that Twain can say of his, that it has entailed a loss, that learning has not been pure gain? How do you explain this paradox? And what causes the loss? Can it be traced to new sorts of nonverbal experience — steering a riverboat or exposure to the world of conflict and greed — or to the experience of learning a language?*

c. *Or do you want to say that your education, unlike Twain's, has entailed no loss, that you are better off in every way? If that is the response most natural to you at present, can you imagine making a different one years from now, when your professional life has begun to take shape?*

3. *Read this passage again. What has Twain really lost: the poet's view of the world and the river, or the sentimentalist's? Can this passage be read as the story of growing out of a childish way of thinking and talking?*
4. *Suppose another pilot told Twain, "I think that's a lot of nonsense — I can perceive the beauty of the sunset and the river as well as ever." What would you expect Twain to say to or about such a person?*
5. *Twain's feelings are inconsistent, of course. At one time he says that all the "grace, the beauty, the poetry" had left the river, never to be restored, and all for the sake for knowing every "trifling feature" of the river; at another, he tells us he has learned to read a wonderful book, more absorbing, sparkling, and unflagging than any ever written by man, one that tells him the hidden truth, at the slight cost of no longer seeing "all manner of pretty pictures." The book as a whole is written to celebrate the life of the pilot, especially the process of learning the job, and he sees plenty of romance in that life, to say the least. But by the time of writing, Twain has put that behind him too; his loss is double. What has he gained at the end?*

AMERICAN NOTES*
Charles Dickens

[Here is another description of a Mississippi River sunset.]

But what words shall describe the Mississippi, great father of rivers, who (praise be to Heaven) has no young children like him! An enormous ditch, sometimes two or three miles wide, running liquid mud, six miles an hour: its strong and frothy current choked and obstructed everywhere by huge logs and whole forest trees: now twining themselves together in great rafts, from the interstices of which a sedgy, lazy foam works up, to float upon the water's top; now rolling past like monstrous bodies, their tangled roots showing like matted hair; now glancing singly by like giant leeches; and now writhing round and round in the vortex of some small whirlpool, like wounded snakes. The banks low, the trees

* Chapter 12 (1842).

dwarfish, the marshes swarming with frogs, the wretched cabins few and far apart, their inmates hollow-cheeked and pale, the weather very hot, mosquitoes penetrating into every crack and crevice of the boat, mud and slime on everything: nothing pleasant in its aspect, but the harmless lightning which flickers every night upon the dark horizon.

For two days we toiled up this foul stream, striking constantly against the floating timber, or stopping to avoid those more dangerous obstacles, the snags, or sawyers, which are the hidden trunks of trees that have their roots below the tide. When the nights are very dark, the look-out stationed in the head of the boat, knows by the ripple of the water if any great impediment be near at hand, and rings a bell beside him, which is the signal for the engine to be stopped: but always in the night this bell has work to do, and after every ring, there comes a blow which renders it no easy matter to remain in bed.

The decline of day here was very gorgeous; tingeing the firmament deeply with red and gold, up to the very keystone of the arch above us. As the sun went down behind the bank, the slightest blades of grass upon it seemed to become as distinctly visible as the arteries in the skeleton of a leaf; and when, as it slowly sank, the red and golden bars upon the water grew dimmer, and dimmer yet, as if they were sinking too; and all the glowing colours of departing day paled, inch by inch, before the sombre night; the scene became a thousand times more lonesome and more dreary than before, and all its influences darkened with the sky.

QUESTIONS

1. *Here a visitor tells you what he saw when he looked at the river, and I suppose it is no surprise to you that it is very different from what Twain tells you he once saw. Each person sees things his own way, of course.*
   a. *But is this true of the pilot? Would not any good pilot looking upon the same river see very much what Twain, the pilot, saw?*
   b. *Do good lawyers not see very much the same things when they look as lawyers upon the same events? Do they not ask of the client's half-told story very much the same questions?*
   c. *Is it fair to say, then, that at least one strain in a professional education works against the purposes of one's liberal education: not to foster individuality and diversity, but to train into sameness?*
2. *How, if at all, can the Dickens and the Twain passages be related? Does it help you to be told that when Dickens visited the river Samuel Clemens was a seven-year-old boy in Hannibal, living the life from which he was later to fashion Tom Sawyer and Huckleberry Finn?*
3. *Can you bring Dickens and Twain closer together in your imagination? Suppose, for example, that Twain had been the pilot of the steamboat in which Dickens "toiled up this foul stream." What would these two men have been to each other as they passed on the deck? If they had stopped to talk, what might they have said?*

a. *To Twain, Dickens would have been a passenger, and about that status he had feelings that were partly nostalgic. On what matters would he have been interested in hearing Dickens's views?*
b. *How would Dickens have regarded the pilot of his boat? As being, for example, in what respects different from a London hackdriver or a railroad engineer? On what matters would he have been interested in hearing the pilot's views?*
c. *In this imaginary meeting, who would have been condescending to whom?*
d. *Is the mutual obliviousness of this imagined relationship a constant characteristic of relationships between professionals and others? What can the patient know of the doctor? As you give yourself a legal education, do you give yourself a mind increasingly unknowable to those around you?*

4. *In what other ways could you imagine the Mississippi River being described? Imagine what might have been said in the last century by an Indian, for example, or a railroad magnate, or what might be said today in a social studies class or environmentalists' meeting.*
5. *The meaning of the landscape has been a consistent preoccupation of American writers. If you are interested in how the "same" thing – nature in America – can be made to mean such different things, you might wish to read some of the following: J. H. St. J. Crevecoeur, Letters from an American Farmer (1782); J. F. Cooper, The Deerslayer (1841) or The Prairie (1827); H. D. Thoreau, Walden (1854); Frances Trollope, Domestic Manners of the Americans (1832); F. Parkman, La Salle and The Discovery of the Great West (1879); The Journals of Lewis and Clark (B. DeVoto ed. 1953).*

   This subject is intelligently discussed in L. Marx, The Machine in the Garden (1964). The story of the exploration of the West is told with imagination and feeling in W. H. Goetzmann, Exploration and Empire (1966).
6. *In what terms might a legal document speak of the Mississippi?*

LA SALLE AND THE DISCOVERY OF THE GREAT WEST*

Francis Parkman

[La Salle, the first European to do so, has made his way from Canada to the mouth of the Mississippi.]

La Salle, in a canoe, coasted the marshy borders of the sea; and then the reunited parties assembled on a spot of dry ground, a short distance above the mouth of the river. Here a column was made ready, bearing the arms of France, and inscribed with the words,

LOUIS LE GRAND, ROY DE FRANCE ET DE NAVARRE, RÈGNE
LE NEUVIÈME AVRIL, 1682.

The Frenchmen were mustered under arms; and while the New England Indians and their squaws looked on in wondering silence, they

* Chapter 20 (1879).

chanted the *Te Deum,* the *Exaudiat,* and the *Domine salvum fac Regem.* Then, amid volleys of musketry and shouts of *Vive le Roi,* La Salle planted the column in its place, and, standing near it, proclaimed in a loud voice:

"In the name of the most high, mighty, invincible, and victorious Prince, Louis the Great, by the grace of God King of France and of Navarre, Fourteenth of that name, I, this ninth day of April, one thousand six hundred and eighty-two, in virtue of the commission of his Majesty, which I hold in my hand, and which may be seen by all whom it may concern, have taken, and do now take, in the name of his Majesty and of his successors to the crown, possession of this country of Louisiana, the seas, harbors, ports, bays, adjacent straits, and all the nations, peoples, provinces, cities, towns, villages, mines, minerals, fisheries, streams, and rivers, within the extent of the said Louisiana, from the mouth of the great river St. Louis, otherwise called the Ohio . . . as also along the river Colbert, or Mississippi, and the rivers which discharge themselves thereinto, from its source beyond the country of the Nadouessioux . . . as far as its mouth at the sea, or Gulf of Mexico, and also to the mouth of the River of Palms, upon the assurance we have had from the natives of these countries, that we are the first Europeans who have descended or ascended the said river Colbert; hereby protesting against all who may hereafter undertake to invade any or all of these aforesaid countries, peoples, or lands, to the prejudice of the rights of his Majesty, acquired by the consent of the nations dwelling herein. Of which, and of all else that is needful, I hereby take to witness those who hear me, and demand an act of the notary here present."

Shouts of *Vive le Roi* and volleys of musketry responded to his words. Then a cross was planted beside the column, and a leaden plate buried near it, bearing the arms of France, with a Latin inscription, *Ludovicus Magnus regnat.* The weather-beaten voyagers joined their voices in the grand hymn of the *Vexilla Regis:*

> "The banners of Heaven's King advance,
> The mystery of the Cross shines forth;"

and renewed shouts of *Vive le Roi* closed the ceremony.

On that day, the realm of France received on parchment a stupendous accession. The fertile plains of Texas; the vast basin of the Mississippi, from its frozen northern springs to the sultry borders of the Gulf; from the woody ridges of Alleghanies to the bare peaks of the Rocky Mountains — a region of savannahs and forests, sun-cracked deserts and grassy prairies, watered by a thousand rivers, ranged by a thousand warlike tribes, passed beneath the sceptre of the Sultan of Versailles; and all by virtue of a feeble human voice, inaudible at half a mile.

QUESTIONS

1. *In what other ways might the law speak of the Mississippi River?*
2. *Twain tells us how his professional education affects the way he defines himself and his relation to the river, the way he "sees" the river. Is it only professional training that has such consequences, or might an academic education present similar dangers?*

TRISTES TROPIQUES*

Claude Lévi-Strauss

I was reading for a philosophy degree — not because I had any true vocation for philosophy, but because I had sampled other branches of learning and detested them, one and all. I had begun my philosophy classes with a vague liking for a form of rationalistic monism. This I meant to justify and reinforce, and to this end I pulled every string to get put up to the teacher who was reputedly the most "advanced" in his views. Gustave Rodrigues was, as a matter of fact, an active member of the S.F.I.O.; but as far as philosophy was concerned his mixture of Bergsonism and neo-Kantianism was a sad disappointment to me. Arid and dogmatic as he was, he advanced his views with great fervour from the first lecture to the last, gesticulating the while like a man possessed. Never have I seen such skimpy intellectual processes put forward with such ingenuous conviction. He killed himself in 1940 when the Germans entered Paris.

It was then that I began to learn how any problem, whether grave or trivial, can be resolved. The method never varies. First you establish the traditional "two views" of the question. You then put forward a commonsense justification of the one, only to refute it by the other. Finally you send them both packing by the use of a third interpretation, in which both the others are shown to be equally unsatisfactory. Certain verbal manoeuvres enable you, that is, to line up the traditional "antitheses" as complementary aspects of a single reality: form and substance, content and container, appearance and reality, essence and existence, continuity and discontinuity, and so on. Before long the exercise becomes the merest verbalizing, reflection gives place to a kind of superior punning, and the "accomplished philosopher" may be recognized by the ingenuity with which he makes ever-bolder play with assonance, ambiguity, and the use of those words which sound alike and yet bear quite different meanings.

Five years at the Sorbonne taught me little but this form of mental gymnastics. Its dangers are, of course, self-evident: the mechanism is so

* Pages 54–56 (Atheneum ed. 1967).

simple, for one thing, that there is no such thing as a problem which cannot be tackled. When we were working for our examinations and, above all, for that supreme ordeal, the *leçon* (in which the candidate draws a subject by lot, and is given only six hours in which to prepare a comprehensive survey of it), we used to set one another the bizarrest imaginable themes. I brought myself to the point at which, given ten minutes' preparation, I could lecture for an hour on the respective merits of the tramway and the omnibus and miss not one of the arguments for either side. The method, universal in its application, encouraged the student to overlook the many possible forms and variants of thought, devoting himself to one particular unchanging instrument. Certain elementary adjustments were all that he needed: it was as if music could be reduced to one single tune, as soon as he realized that it was played sometimes in G Major and sometimes in F. From this point of view philosophy, as taught at the Sorbonne, exercised the intelligence but left the spirit high and dry.

It seems to me even more dangerous to confuse the advance of knowledge with the growing complexity of intellectual organization. We were invited to bring into being a dynamic synthesis in which we would start from the least adequate of philosophical systems and end by appraising the subtlest among them. But at the same time (and because all our teachers were obsessed with the notion of historical development) we had to explain how the latter had gradually grown out of the former. Philosophy was not *ancilla scientiarum,* the handmaid and auxiliary of scientific exploration: it was a kind of aesthetic contemplation of consciousness by consciousness. We watched self-consciousness in its progress through the ages — elaborating constructions ever lighter and more audacious, resolving problems of balance and implication, inventing refinements of logic; and the more absolute the technical perfection, the more complete the internal coherence, the "greater" was the system in question. It was as if the student of art-history had been taught that Gothic was necessarily better than Romanesque, and flamboyant Gothic better than primitive Gothic, without stopping to wonder what was beautiful and what was not. The signification was what mattered, not the thing signified: nobody connected the one with the other. Know-how had taken the place of the passion for truth. After spending several years on exercises of this sort I found myself still falling back, when alone, on unsophisticated convictions which I had held, more or less, since I was a boy of fourteen. I was better able, perhaps, to see where they fell short of my needs; but at least they were instruments adapted to my purpose, and I was in no danger either of being deluded by their internal complication or of forgetting, in the excitement of watching the marvellous machinery go round, that it was meant to serve practical ends.

QUESTIONS

1. *Does the lawyer learn an intellectual method of universal application similar to that described above? Present a caricature of that method. Think of: abstracting a case; taking an examination; teaching a law class by the Socratic method; responding to questions asked in such a class; and so on.*
2. *Are the legal methods of thought you have just described as sterile as those described by Levi-Strauss? In calling these methods sterile you accept the possibility of some other sort of thought and speech, say fertile or creative or fecund. Can you explain what you mean by sterile and its opposite?*
3. *Notice that question two presents the very danger Levi-Strauss points to, of falling into a thesis-antithesis pattern of speech and thought: "sterile" is opposed to "fertile," both to be supplanted perhaps by a third term. Our tendencies to think in such a pattern are very deep. How are they to be resisted? (Indeed, are they to be resisted? If, as it is often said, the hearing is the heart of the legal process, does it not proceed by thesis and antithesis? How, if at all, is the legal hearing different from the sterile philosophical disquisition described above?)*
4. *To what extent can the terms by which Levi-Strauss characterizes this method be fairly applied to the law? Does a legal education encourage one to "overlook the many possible forms and variants of thought" in favor of one "unchanging instrument"? Can you say of the law that "know-how" takes the place of the "passion for truth"? Does the law ever recognize such a thing as a "problem that cannot be tackled"? When and how?*
5. *Is it a sign of a failure of education that one falls back in the end upon "unsophisticated convictions" one has had since a boy? Or is that what one properly seeks — like Twain — to keep alive? What place do such convictions have in your present intellectual life as a lawyer?*

OF A FIRE ON THE MOON*
Norman Mailer

He went on to talk of star sightings and the powered ascent from the moon — that moment when, having landed successfully and reconnoitered the moon ground, they would be back in the Lem and ready to ascend — would the motor ignite or did the moon have a curse? Aldrin spoke of this as a "new item," then of rendezvous with the Command Module, which would return them to earth, of "various contingencies that can develop," of "a wider variety of trajectory conditions" — he was talking about not being able to join up, wandering through space, lost forever to life in that short eternity before they expired of hunger and thirst. Small hint of that in these verbal formulations. Even as the Nazis and the Communists had used to speak of mass murder as

* Pages 25, 273–274 (1970).

liquidation, so the astronauts spoke of possible personal disasters as "contingency." The heart of astronaut talk, like the heart of all bureaucratic talk, was a jargon which could be easily converted to computer programming, a language like Fortran or Cobol or Algol. Anti-dread formulations were the center of it, as if words like pills were there to suppress emotional symptoms. . . .

This endless preciosity of specification was necessary. In relation to their equipment, the trip was not unique, but merely another store of information in the continuing line of missions from the past which would lead toward expeditions in the future. So everything was important — the malfunctions in the oxygen transducer, and the glare from the foil wrappings of the Lem, the time it took the waste-water cloud to disperse, and the hours they slept, the unexpected reactions of the computer. Everything was important. After a while everything began to seem equally important, even the crumpling of the food bags. Like narcissists, like children, like old people, the astronauts all exhibited a single-minded emphasis on each detail which arrived before them, large or small. . . . Embarked on a heroic vault and subjected to a monotonous round of monitoring and mechanical housekeeping in relation to objects they could never comprehend sufficiently well, they existed in capsule like the real embodiments they were of technological man, forever engaged in activities whose controls he wields until he controls them no more, powerful, expert, philosophically naive, jargon-ridden, and resolutely divorced from any language with grandeur to match the proportions of his endeavor.

QUESTIONS

1. *This account of the consequences of an education into a particular sort of language and thought is described from the outside, and perhaps therefore less authentically than might otherwise be the case, but I suspect there is a ring of truth here for you. We all know people who have been affected in one way or another by the language of systems analysis, by the jargon of social organization, not least in the world of the school and university. Much could be said on the subject, but I want now to raise only one series of questions:*
   a. *Is legal language just another language of systems analysis, not so moronically inexpressive as computer talk, perhaps, but sharing its essential characteristics: rigid, mechanical, quantitative, dead? If it differs, exactly how does it do so?*
   b. *Does the law also use terms and locutions that hide the truth, that serve as "anti-dread formulations"?*
   c. *What other languages similar to these can you identify in the world around you? Examine especially the language of education, as you see it in catalogs, reports on the curriculum, and the like; and the language*

of current politics, as you see it in your campus newspaper and in other forums of such discussion.

d. *Does the lawyer — or the educator, or the politician — have a language "with a grandeur to match the proportions of his endeavor"? Find or make up samples for which such claims might be made.*

2. *What do you suppose the effects of learning and using the language of the astronauts, or some other computer talk, would be upon the mind so engaged? Could one simply go home at the end of a day or a year or a decade of such conversation and be the same old fellow one always was?*
3. *In considering what the effect of language on the mind can be, you might think of your own experience of learning and using a real language. French, for example, can be learned in the classroom as an intellectual system, into which more or less life can be breathed by a good teacher or an imaginative student, but which never really lives until one uses it as one uses other languages: to say something one wants to say to another person, to serve a real purpose. If you have traveled from one country to another, you know that one undergoes a process of adjustment to a new language, trying to forget French phrases and recall German ones, for a split second tongue-tied even in English by one's concentration on a foreign language, even one of which one is almost wholly ignorant. And I am told that people brought up to speak two languages may speak neither comfortably and well. One can apparently live without any but the most basic sort of language. Compare George Orwell's invention of Newspeak in Nineteen Eighty-Four (1949).*
4. *Compare what Henry Adams said of the effects of learning the language of diplomacy: "He never labored so hard to learn a language as he did to hold his tongue, and it affected him for life. The habit of reticence — of talking without meaning — is never effaced." The Education of Henry Adams, Chapter 8 (1918).*
5. *You have just seen a representation of what a debased language may do to human experience. Below is a different sort of response to a destructive way of talking.*

HUCKLEBERRY FINN*

Mark Twain

[Huck and Jim, Miss Watson's escaped slave, are floating down the river on a raft.]

. . . Jim said it made him all over trembly and feverish to be so close to freedom. Well, I can tell you it made me all over trembly and feverish, too, to hear him, because I begun to get it through my head that he *was* most free — and who was to blame for it? Why, *me*. I couldn't get that out of my conscience, no how nor no way. It got to troubling me so I couldn't rest; I couldn't stay still in one place. It hadn't ever come home to me before, what this thing was that I was doing. But now it did; and it stayed with me, and scorched me more and more. I tried to

* Chapter 16 (1884).

make out to myself that *I* warn't to blame, because *I* didn't run Jim off from his rightful owner; but it warn't no use, conscience up and says, every time, "But you knowed he was running for his freedom, and you could 'a' paddled ashore and told somebody." That was so — I couldn't get around that no way. That was where it pinched. Conscience says to me, "What had poor Miss Watson done to you that you could see her nigger go off right under your eyes and never say one single word? What did that poor old woman do to you that you could treat her so mean? Why, she tried to learn you your book, she tried to learn you your manners, she tried to be good to you every way she knowed how. *That's* what she done."

I got to feeling so mean and so miserable I most wished I was dead. I fidgeted up and down the raft, abusing myself to myself, and Jim was fidgeting up and down past me. We neither of us could keep still. Every time he danced around and says, "Dah's Cairo!" it went through me like a shot, and I thought if it *was* Cairo I reckoned I would die of miserableness.

Jim talked out loud all the time while I was talking to myself. He was saying how the first thing he would do when he got to a free state he would go to saving up money and never spend a single cent, and when he got enough he would buy his wife, which was owned on a farm close to where Miss Watson lived; and then they would both work to buy the two children, and if their master wouldn't sell them, they'd get an Ab'litionist to go and steal them.

It most froze me to hear such talk. He wouldn't ever dared to talk such talk in his life before. Just see what a difference it made in him the minute he judged he was about free. It was according to the old saying, "Give a nigger an inch and he'll take an ell." Thinks I, this is what comes of my not thinking. Here was this nigger, which I had as good as helped to run away, coming right out flat-footed and saying he would steal his children—children that belonged to a man I didn't even know; a man that hadn't ever done me no harm.

I was sorry to hear Jim say that, it was such a lowering of him. My conscience got to stirring me up hotter than ever, until at last I says to it, "Let up on me — it ain't too late yet — I'll paddle ashore at the first light and tell." I felt easy and happy and light as a feather right off. All my troubles was gone. I went to looking out sharp for a light, and sort of singing to myself. By and by one showed. Jim sings out:

"We's safe, Huck, we's safe! Jump up and crack yo' heels! Dat's de good ole Cairo at las', I jis knows it!"

I says:

"I'll take the canoe and go and see, Jim. It mightn't be, you know."

He jumped and got the canoe ready, and put his old coat in the bottom for me to set on, and give me the paddle; and as I shoved off, he says:

"Pooty soon I'll be a-shout'n' for joy, en I'll say, it's all on accounts o' Huck; I's a free man, en I couldn't ever ben free ef it hadn' ben for Huck; Huck done it. Jim won't ever forgit you, Huck; you's de bes' fren' Jim's ever had; en you's de *only* fren' ole Jim's got now."

I was paddling off, all in a sweat to tell on him; but when he says this, it seemed to kind of take the tuck all out of me. I went along slow then, and I warn't right down certain whether I was glad I started or whether I warn't. When I was fifty yards off, Jim says:

"Dah you goes, de ole true Huck; de on'y white genlman dat ever kep' his promise to ole Jim."

Well, I just felt sick. But I says, I *got* to do it — I can't get *out* of it. Right then along comes a skiff with two men in it with guns, and they stopped and I stopped. One of them says:

"What's that yonder?"

"A piece of a raft," I says.

"Do you belong on it?"

"Yes, sir."

"Any men on it?"

"Only one, sir."

"Well, there's five niggers run off to-night up yonder, above the head of the bend. Is your man white or black?"

I didn't answer up prompt. I tried to, but the words wouldn't come. I tried for a second or two to brace up and out with it, but I warn't man enough — hadn't the spunk of a rabbit. I see I was weakening; so I just give up trying, and up and says:

"He's white."

"I reckon we'll go and see for ourselves."

"I wish you would," says I, "because it's pap that's there, and maybe you'd help me tow the raft ashore where the light is. He's sick — and so is mam and Mary Ann."

"Oh, the devil! we're in a hurry, boy. But I s'pose we've got to. Come, buckle to your paddle, and let's get along."

I buckled to my paddle and they laid to their oars. When we had made a stroke or two, I says:

"Pap 'll be mighty much obleeged to you, I can tell you. Everybody goes away when I want them to help me tow the raft ashore, and I can't do it by myself."

"Well, that's infernal mean. Odd, too. Say, boy, what's the matter with your father?"

"It's the — a — the — well, it ain't anything much."

They stopped pulling. It warn't but a mighty little ways to the raft now. One says:

"Boy, that's a lie. What *is* the matter with your pap? Answer up square now, and it 'll be the better for you."

"I will, sir, I will, honest — but don't leave us, please. It's the — the — Gentlemen, if you'll only pull ahead, and let me heave you the headline, you won't have to come a-near the raft — please do."

"Set her back, John, set her back!" says one. They backed water. "Keep away, boy — keep to looard. Confound it, I just expect the wind has blowed it to us. Your pap's got the smallpox, and you know it precious well. Why didn't you come out and say so? Do you want to spread it all over?"

"Well," says I, a-blubbering, "I've told everybody before, and they just went away and left us."

"Poor devil, there's something in that. We are right down sorry for you, but we — well, hang it, we don't want the smallpox, you see. Look here, I'll tell you what to do. Don't you try to land by yourself, or you'll smash everything to pieces. You float along down about twenty miles, and you'll come to a town on the left-hand side of the river. It will be long after sun-up then, and when you ask for help you tell them your folks are all down with chills and fever. Don't be a fool again, and let people guess what is the matter. Now we're trying to do you a kindness; so you just put twenty miles between us, that's a good boy. It wouldn't do any good to land yonder where the light is — it's only a wood-yard. Say, I reckon your father's poor, and I'm bound to say he's in pretty hard luck. Here, I'll put a twenty-dollar gold piece on this board, and you get it when it floats by. I feel mighty mean to leave you; but my kingdom! it won't do to fool with smallpox, don't you see?"

"Hold on, Parker," says the man, "here's a twenty to put on the board for me. Good-by, boy; you do as Mr. Parker told you, and you'll be all right."

"That's so, my boy — good-by, good-by. If you see any runaway niggers you get help and nab them, and you can make some money by it."

"Good-by, sir," says I; "I won't let no runaway niggers get by me if I can help it."

They went off and I got aboard the raft, feeling bad and low, because I knowed very well I had done wrong, and I see it warn't no use for me to try to learn to do right; a body that don't get *started* right when he's little ain't got no show — when the pinch comes there ain't nothing to back him up and keep him to his work, and so he gets beat. Then I thought a minute, and says to myself, hold on; s'pose you'd 'a' done right and give Jim up, would you felt better than what you do now? No, says I, I'd feel bad — I'd feel just the same way I do now. Well, then, says I, what's the use you learning to do right when it's troublesome to do right and ain't no trouble to do wrong, and the wages is just the same? I was stuck. I couldn't answer that. So I reckoned I wouldn't bother no more about it, but after this always do whichever come handiest at the time.

QUESTIONS

1. When Huck says that he will just do what comes handiest at the time, what does he mean by "handy"? Is this a statement of pure hedonism, moral whimsicality, total unconcern for what sort of person he is, or what?

2. In what terms would you characterize the course of action that Huck here calls the "handiest," the one that "ain't no trouble"? Why does Huck not perceive it as you do and describe it in the terms you would use?

3. Can you think of any modern parallels to this scene? One student suggested the situation of a young man raised in an old-fashioned patriotic home and drafted to serve in the Viet Nam war. But that is not really a modern parallel, because the person who suggests it assumes that what is confusing to the young man is of course clear to all of us. Can you imagine any situations in which you or I might talk in a confused way about right and wrong, any matters on which your views or mine might sound as confused as Huck's last paragraph — or worse? Or can one never perceive that sort of confusion in oneself?

4. One might say that Huck's situation is really not so difficult after all, that all he had to do was state the abolitionist position, which he so unaccountably found impossible. Why do you suppose he found that impossible?

a. One view might be that what Huck struggles with here is not bad language but bad ideas, bad values.

(1) What view of language is implicit in such a remark: that it is a simple and frictionless machine for conveying ideas from mind to mind? A transparent vessel for holding visible values? An instrument for pointing to things and ideas in the real world, the true and only realities, plainly observable to all?

(2) Does Huck appear to you to value slavery and to approve of its social and other implications? If not, why does he not see what we see, and say what we would say?

b. The view that one's values exist outside of and unaffected by one's language disregards the experience of being brought up to say "nigger," and ignores the effect of such a word on human relationships. Such a word, defining such a relationship, is a real fact of existence with which one must in some way come to terms. Compare G. Sykes, Society of Captives, Chapter 5 (1958), *in which he concludes that the best way to describe the social world of the prison is by defining terms in its argot: "fag," "punk," "wolf," and so on.*

c. It may help you to see Huck's position if you ask what else he could have called Jim than "nigger." Exactly what other word in the language he was given might he have used? To say "my best friend, Jim" would have been an absurdity — "slave" and "friend" cannot go to-

gether that way, because "slave" means "chattel." It could only be understood in some peculiar or metaphorical way like "my best friend, Lassie" or "my best friend, IBM." Huck makes no verbal response when Jim calls him the "bes' fren' Jim's ever had," though he is deeply affected and it is clear the friendship goes both ways. To say something directed to the general social situation, such as "slaves are really our equals," would be to attack an institution central to society, imbued with all the values of property, regularity, productivity, the necessary order of things; to speak against it would be to incite to anarchy. As Huck rightly saw, the idea of slavery was intimately tied to the most fundamental ideas of right and wrong, and the untangling was beyond his capacities.

d. If Huck had stated the abolitionist position, to whom would he have stated it? In exactly what words? What would have happened next?

5. What was called for in Huck's situation was nothing less than a new way of imagining human relationships and a new way of expressing one's imagination. Huck achieves the first – the experience of the boy and the slave on the raft is a genuine discovery – but he fails to do the second and retreats into silence: at the end of the book he "lights out for the territories." In this passage, Twain does achieve a new way of expressing a newly imagined relationship, but even he has his difficulties.

a. Twain's crisis of imagination might become clearer if you pretend you are Twain, having written the passage you have just read. What will the rest of your novel be like: what will Huck and Jim do and say next, whom will they meet and on what terms? What will they talk about and how? Can you imagine a friendship between these two people expressed in their actual lives in the world? Or will they have to stay on the raft forever?

You may be interested to know that Twain in fact stopped writing this book at this point for several years, apparently stuck, not knowing how to go on. Many critics think that the rest of the novel fails to live up to what was achieved here, that at this point the imagination collapses. See R. Poirier, A World Elsewhere 193–194 (1966).

b. Are there matters as to which we are situated somewhat like Huck or Twain? At first glance it would seem that anything at all can be said in our society, that we live in a time of change in which every social premise is open to examination. This may be true if you view American society as a whole, but it is doubtful if you consider the particular social groups in which people live: the university, the bar, the job, the golf club. Think for example of what you could say or expect to hear in different groups about the following topics: the Viet Nam war; the environment; population control; gun controls; and so on. Can you say anything other than clichés on any of these subjects, anything of the slightest interest or value, anything that expresses a hard truth? Or does the actual freedom you feel to reject or accept anything not include a liberty to carry on intelligent conversation on some subjects?[4]

4. Compare Edmund Burke, *Reflections on the Revolution in France*, in III *Works* 352 (1790; Beaconsfield ed. 1901): "It has been the misfortune (not, as these gentlemen think it, the glory) of this age, that everything is to be discussed. . . ." Selden says: "In troubled water you cann scarce see your face, or see

6. *These remarks could be seen as putting two connected questions, which will be considered more fully later on: what are the conditions that make good talk on a particular subject possible? How, if at all, does the law concern itself with making possible good conversation on new topics?*
7. *Below is a final account of what learning a language may involve.*

THE LOGIC OF NONSTANDARD ENGLISH*

William Labov

I would like to contrast two speakers dealing with roughly the same topic — matters of belief. The first is Larry H., a 15-year-old core member of the Jets, being interviewed by John Lewis. Larry is one of the loudest and roughest members of the Jets, one who gives the least recognition to the conventional rules of politeness. For most readers of this paper, first contact with Larry would produce some fairly negative reactions on both sides: it is probable that you would not *like* him any more than his teachers do. Larry causes trouble in and out of school; he was put back from the eleventh grade to the ninth, and has been threatened with further action by the school authorities.

JL: What happens to you after you die? Do you know?
Larry: Yeah, I know.
JL: What?
Larry: After they put you in the ground, your body turns into — ah — bones, an' shit.
JL: What happens to your spirit?
Larry: Your spirit — soon as you die, your spirit leaves you.
JL: And where does the spirit go?
Larry: Well, it all depends . . .
JL: On what?
Larry: You know, like some people say if you're good an' shit, your spirit goin' t'heaven . . . 'n' if you bad, your spirit goin' to hell. Well, bullshit! Your spirit goin' to hell anyway, good or bad.
JL: Why?
Larry: Why? I'll tell you why. 'Cause, you see, doesn' nobody really know that it's a God, y'know, 'cause I mean I have seen black gods, pink gods, white gods, all color gods, and don't nobody know it's really a God. An' when they be sayin' if you good,

---

it very little till the water bee quiett & stand still; so in troubled times you cann see little truth, when times are quiett & settled then truth appeares." *Table Talk* (Truth, 3) (1689).

* Pages 12–18 (Monograph Series on Languages and Linguistics No. 22, 1969).

> you goin' t-heaven, tha's bullshit, 'cause you ain't goin' to no heaven, 'cause it ain't no heaven for you to go to.

Larry is a paradigmatic speaker of nonstandard Negro English (NNE) as opposed to standard English (SE). His grammar shows a high concentration of such characteristic NNE forms as negative inversion [*don't nobody know* . . .], negative concord [*you ain't goin' to no heaven* . . .], invariant *be* [*when they be sayin'* . . .], dummy *it* for SE *there* [*it ain't no heaven* . . .], optional copula deletion [*if you're good* . . . *if you bad* . . .], and full forms of auxiliaries [*I have seen* . . .]. The only SE influence in this passage is the one case of *doesn't* instead of the invariant *don't* of NNE. Larry also provides a paradigmatic example of the rhetorical style of NNE: he can sum up a complex argument in a few words, and the full force of his opinions comes through without qualification or reservation. He is eminently quotable, and his interviews give us many concise statements of the NNE point of view. One can almost say that Larry *speaks* the NNE culture.

It is the logical form of this passage which is of particular interest here. Larry presents a complex set of interdependent propositions which can be explicated by setting out the SE equivalents in linear order. The basic argument is to deny the twin propositions

(A) If you are good, (B) then your spirit will go to heaven.
(−A) If you are bad, (C) then your spirit will go to hell.

Larry denies (B), and asserts that *if* (A) *or* (−A), *then* (C). His argument may be outlined as follows:

(1) Everyone has a different idea of what God is like.
(2) Therefore nobody really knows that God exists.
(3) If there is a heaven, it was made by God.
(4) If God doesn't exist, he couldn't have made heaven.
(5) Therefore heaven does not exist.
(6) You can't go somewhere that doesn't exist.
(−B) Therefore you can't go to heaven.
(C) Therefore you are going to hell. . . .

This hypothetical argument is not carried on at a high level of seriousness. It is a game played with ideas as counters, in which opponents use a wide variety of verbal devices to win. There is no personal commitment to any of these propositions, and no reluctance to strengthen one's argument by bending the rules of logic as in the (2-5) sequence. But if the opponent invokes the rules of logic, they hold. In John Lewis' interviews, he often makes this move, and the force of his argument is always acknowledged and countered within the rules of logic. In this case, he pointed out the fallacy that the argument (2-3-4-5-6) leads to (−C) as well as (−B), so it cannot be used to support Larry's assertion (C):

JL: Well, if there's no heaven, how could there be a hell?
Larry: I mean — ye-eah. Well, let me tell you, it ain't no hell, 'cause this is hell right here, y'know!
JL: This is hell?
Larry: Yeah, this is hell right here!

Larry's answer is quick, ingenious and decisive. The application of the (3-4-5) argument to hell is denied, since hell is here, and therefore conclusion (C) stands. These are not ready-made or preconceived opinions, but new propositions devised to win the logical argument in the game being played. The reader will note the speed and precision of Larry's mental operations. He does not wander, or insert meaningless verbiage. The only repetition is (2), placed before and after (1) in his original statement. It is often said that the nonstandard vernacular is not suited for dealing with abstract or hypothetical questions, but in fact speakers from the NNE community take great delight in exercising their wit and logic on the most improbable and problematical matters. Despite the fact that Larry H. does not believe in God, and has just denied all knowledge of him, John Lewis advances the following hypothetical question:

JL: . . . But, just say that there is a God, what color is he? White or black?
Larry: Well, if it is a God . . . I wouldn' know what color, I couldn' say, — couldn' nobody say what color he is or really *would* be.
JL: But now, jus' suppose there was a God —
Larry: Unless'n they say . . .
JL: No, I was jus' sayin' jus' suppose there is a God, would he be white or black?
Larry: . . . He'd be white, man.
JL: Why?
Larry: Why? I'll tell you why. 'Cause the average whitey out here got everything, you dig? And the nigger ain't got shit, y'know? Y'understan'? So — um — for — in order for *that* to happen, you know it ain't no black God that's doin' that bullshit.

No one can hear Larry's answer to this question without being convinced that they are in the presence of a skilled speaker with great "verbal presence of mind," who can use the English language expertly for many purposes. Larry's answer to John Lewis is again a complex argument. The formulation is not SE, but it is clear and effective even for those not familiar with the vernacular. The nearest SE equivalent might be: "So you know that God isn't black, because if he was, he wouldn't have arranged things like that."

The reader will have noted that this analysis is being carried out in standard English, and the inevitable challenge is: why not write in NNE, then, or in your own nonstandard dialect? The fundamental reason is, of course, one of firmly fixed social conventions. All communities agree that SE is the "proper" medium for formal writing and public communication. Furthermore, it seems likely that SE has an advantage over NNE in explicit analysis of surface forms, which is what we are doing here. We will return to this opposition between explicitness and logical statement in sections 3 and 4. First, however, it will be helpful to examine SE in its primary natural setting, as the medium for informal spoken communication of middle-class speakers.

Let us now turn to the second speaker, an upper-middle-class, college-educated Negro man being interviewed by Clarence Robbins in our survey of adults in Central Harlem.

CR: Do you know of anything that someone can do, to have someone who has passed on visit him in a dream?

Chas. M.: Well, I even heard my parents say that there is such a thing as something in dreams some things like that, and sometimes dreams do come true. I have personally never had a dream come true. I've never dreamt that somebody was dying and they actually died, (Mhm) or that I was going to have ten dollars the next day and somehow I got ten dollars in my pocket. (Mhm). I don't particularly believe in that, I don't think it's true. I do feel, though, that there is such a thing as — ah — witchcraft. I do feel that in certain cultures there is such a thing as witchcraft, or some sort of *science* of witchcraft; I don't think that it's just a matter of believing hard enough that there is such a thing as witchcraft. I do believe that there is such a thing that a person can put himself in a state of *mind* (Mhm), or that — er — something could be given them to intoxicate them in a certain — to a certain frame of mind — that — that could actually be considered witchcraft.

Charles M. is obviously a "good speaker" who strikes the listener as well-educated, intelligent and sincere. He is a likeable and attractive person — the kind of person that middle-class listeners rate very high on a scale of "job suitability" and equally high as a potential friend. His language is more moderate and tempered than Larry's; he makes every effort to qualify his opinions, and seems anxious to avoid any misstatements or over-statements. From these qualities emerge the primary characteristic of this passage — its *verbosity*. Words multiply, some modifying and qualifying, others repeating or padding the main argument. The first half of this extract is a response to the initial question on dreams, basically:

(1) Some people say that dreams sometimes come true.
(2) I have never had a dream come true.
(3) Therefore I don't believe (1).

Some characteristic filler phrases appear here: *such a thing as, some things like that, particularly.* Two examples of dreams given after (2) are afterthoughts that might have been given after (1). Proposition (3) is stated twice for no obvious reason. Nevertheless, this much of Charles M.'s response is well-directed to the point of the question. He then volunteers a statement of his beliefs about witchcraft which shows the difficulty of middle-class speakers who (a) want to express a belief in something but (b) want to show themselves as judicious, rational and free from superstitions. The basic proposition can be stated simply in five words:

But I believe in witchcraft.

However, the idea is enlarged to exactly 100 words, and it is difficult to see what else is being said. In the following quotations, padding which can be removed without change in meaning is shown in brackets.

(1) "I [do] feel, though, that there is [such a thing as] witchcraft." *Feel* seems to be a euphemism for "believe."

(2) "[I do feel that] in certain cultures [there is such a thing as witchcraft.]" This repetition seems designed only to introduce the word *culture,* which lets us know that the speaker knows about anthropology. Does *certain cultures* mean "not in ours" or "not in all"?

(3) "[or some sort of *science* of witchcraft.]" This addition seems to have no clear meaning at all. What is a "science" of witchcraft as opposed to just plain witchcraft? The main function is to introduce the word "science," though it seems to have no connection to what follows.

(4) "I don't think that it's just [a matter of] believing hard enough

that [there is such a thing as] witchcraft." The speaker argues that witchcraft is not merely a belief; there is more to it.

(5) "I [do] believe that [there is such a thing that] a person can put himself in a state of *mind* . . . that [could actually be considered] witchcraft." Is witchcraft as a state of mind different from the state of belief denied in (4)?

(6) "or that something could be given them to intoxicate them [to a certain frame of mind] . . ." The third learned word, *intoxicate,* is introduced by this addition. The vacuity of this passage becomes more evident if we remove repetitions, fashionable words and stylistic decorations:

> But I believe in witchcraft.
> I don't think witchcraft is just a belief.
> A person can put himself or be put in a state of mind that is witchcraft.

Without the extra verbiage and the O.K. words like *science, culture,* and *intoxicate,* Charles M. appears as something less than a first-rate thinker. The initial impression of him as a good speaker is simply our long-conditioned reaction to middle-class verbosity: we know that people who use these stylistic devices are educated people, and we are inclined to credit them with saying something intelligent. Our reactions are accurate in one sense: Charles M. is more educated than Larry. But is he more rational, more logical, or more intelligent? Is he any better at thinking out a problem to its solution? Does he deal more easily with abstractions? There is no reason to think so. Charles M. succeeds in letting us know that he is educated, but in the end we do not know what he is trying to say, and neither does he.

QUESTIONS

1. *Here an expert in linguistics shows us a person imprisoned by his language, but this time the language that paralyzes or destroys is not computerese or legal jargon, but Standard English, our ordinary language. Charles M. speaks SE, but at the apparent price of having nothing to say, of losing all force and directness in speech and thought.*
   a. *Can language possibly so affect the mind? Or should we attribute the differences in speech between Charles and Larry to differences in intelligence or interest?*
   b. *Does this passage define a danger for you, who are also a speaker of SE, or do you regard yourself as utterly different from Charles M.? Before you answer, you might compare what he says with a paragraph taken at random from a term paper you have recently written.*

2. If NNE can be so much more forceful and direct than SE, why should its use not be encouraged for all purposes, at least by those for whom it is a natural language? Professor Labov says it is partly a matter of "convention" and partly because SE is better for "explicit analysis of surface forms."
   a. What weight should be given the universal convention in favor of SE? Who are parties to this convention? See generally D. Lewis, Convention (1969).
   b. Why should legal argument, for example, not be carried on in NNE? What would be the effect of the introduction of a mind like Larry's, expressed as his is expressed, to the processes of the courtroom? Does the inhospitability of the law to such a language cost it anything, or is it pure gain, in rationality and decorum?
   c. One response might be that the law is preeminently a matter of "explicit analysis of surface forms" of the kind to which SE, and its subdivisions such as legal language, are so well suited. How would you expect that argument to be met by a proponent of NNE in the courtroom?
3. By what standards does Professor Labov explicate and evaluate the statements he analyzes here? What other standards might one bring to these passages?
   a. He shows how Larry's statements are surprisingly logical in structure. Would you agree that the strength of Larry's speech is its logic and efficiency, or would you find its excellence in something else?
   b. Examine again the speech of Charles M. and Professor Labov's analysis of it. Is there anything else to be said about what you see here? Can you find another way to characterize that speech, to explain its qualities?
      (1) Suppose you begin by asking what Charles M. is trying to achieve here. What is he doing? Does his use of SE help him succeed? Do you ever use language for similar purposes?
      (2) Here is one possible account of Charles's remarks: Charles is being polite here, making a civil response to what is (certainly in the eyes of the interviewer and the author) a foolish question. The question really is, "Are you superstitious like other black people?" and Charles might well have been insulted. Instead he responds politely, saying essentially nothing at all, with skill a politician could envy.
      (3) Here is another possibility: to the extent that Charles regards this as a serious question about which he has real views, one may read his response as a refusal to talk, as a claim of privacy.
      (4) Could Charles have achieved what he does here, on either of these readings, if he had been speaking NNE? Exactly how might he have done so?
4. Professor Labov criticizes Charles for his "verbosity," for his use of "O.K. words" to gain credit with his audience, and so on. Might one not say of Professor Labov's defense of Larry's speech that it too is verbose, meant to gain credit with an audience impressed by academic talk, logical analyses, schematic representations, and O.K. words? Might one say of both Charles M. and Labov that they talk down to their audiences in similar ways and even for similar (perhaps quite legitimate) purposes? Does a lawyer ever do what these two writers do here?

WRITING ASSIGNMENT 1: A Variety of Languages

Part One

• Draft three paragraphs about the same real or imaginary death, each written in a different language system. One statement should be written at least in part in legal language, the others in whatever other languages you choose.

The languages you choose may be defined by the occupation of the speaker — reporter, priest, camp counselor, chemist, novelist — or in any way you wish, but each language should be clearly identifiable. The reader should know who is talking, and should recognize the language right away.

Your passages may be short, but try to make them live. This is not an exercise in lexicography, in piecing together a dead language from strange words, but an invitation to express what you hear when you listen to other people talk. You should form statements — of course they can be questions, or reflections, or exclamations, as well as descriptions — that you can actually imagine someone wanting to make, statements as close to living speech as you can manage.

You should write in direct discourse; that is, you should represent each person actually speaking to another or to himself in his own words, and not merely describe or characterize what he would say. Perhaps it would be helpful to conceive of yourself as writing a series of speeches from a play. How fully can you define the character you create, both as a person and as a professional, in what he says? Of course it is hard to define character in direct discourse, but that is how playwrights have always proceeded, and how lawyers do too whenever they put a witness on the stand, and indeed whenever they speak themselves. The strain is upon your imagination, your capacity to understand and express how someone else thinks and speaks about his experience.

In each instance try to express a mind that is both individual and typical. Each speaker should be identifiable both by reference to his role or profession or whatever it is that defines his language, and in some other way. That is, you should not simply represent what any lawyer or doctor or priest would say, but try to imagine and express as completely as you can an individual personality in the situation you present. Perhaps it would be helpful to ask yourself what a particular lawyer or doctor or priest you actually know would be likely to say.

Try to show these people — or this person, in case you wish to show one person speaking three ways — functioning and behaving in ways you can respect and admire. It is no trick to represent an utter fool, a caricature. Try to define each speaker as someone who interests you, whom you can respect. This is especially true of the lawyer: as novelists have always known, it is easy to despise and make fun of the lawyer, but you will probably not want to confine yourself to that response, since in what you write here you define a possibility for your own future. Can you show a lawyer at work in a way that interests and attracts you?

You may feel that you have not been told in sufficient detail what is meant by the term "language system," but that is deliberate: part of your task is how to decide what is significant about the ways people talk, and to reflect that decision in what you write. Some questions meant to help you think about this matter follow soon, but the basic idea is simple enough: to try to record three distinguishable ways of talking, one of which pertains particularly to the lawyer. If you are troubled by what "language system" might mean, it might be instructive to try to write one of your passages in ordinary English, in no special language at all. Is it possible, do you think?

This assignment, like all the assignments in this book, is designed not with an ideal answer in mind which you are meant to approximate, but as an invitation for you to exercise your own mind, to finish off the question in a way that interests you. The question that will be asked of what you write is not how well you have "answered the question," but what you have been able to make of it. Accordingly, these instructions are not meant as binding directions, but as suggestions for your consideration. You are the one who is responsible for what you write.

(The reason that you are asked to write about a death here, rather than about some other topic, is that Chapter 2 contains a lengthy anthology on that subject, to which your own paper may perhaps be seen as contributing.)

Part Two

• Now write a fourth paragraph in which you explain what defines each of the language systems you have used, what sets it off from the others.

You are asked here to attend to what you hear in the passages you have written and to explicate the differences you perceive. The matter of defining language systems is the subject of a set of questions that follows shortly, and you may want to consider them in working out this portion of the assignment.

Part Three

• In an additional paragraph or two, explain what inferences might be drawn about the life of a lawyer from the example of legal speech and thought you have given us. What possibilities, what risks, do you perceive here? Does this passage — by showing what a lawyer says and does on one occasion — define an activity of promise, of interest to you?

The use of the word "inference" is meant to leave you free to choose your own direction, to say what interests you about the moment of legal life you have shown us. The idea is that you have reported a sample of legal life and in doing so have defined a possibility for your own future. How do you regard that future so defined: with elation, despair, or what? Can you rewrite the paper in a way that gives the activity you define more appeal? A set of questions on drawing inferences of this kind follows soon and may give you some assistance with this part of your paper.

But first, an alternative version of this assignment is set forth below; you may prefer to do it instead of this one. The suggestions and explanations made above apply to it as well as the main assignment.

WRITING ASSIGNMENT 1, ALTERNATIVE A: What Do Different Speakers Want to Know?

Part One

• Assume that there has been a stabbing in a barroom brawl. What more does each of the following speakers want to know about this event? How does he frame his questions, and what responses does he expect?

a. the doctor called to the scene
b. the assailant's priest
c. the brother of the stabbed man
d. the lawyer for the defendant

• Draft passages in which you show each of these people framing the questions he would ask about this event. Take special care in framing the questions each would ask about the degree of drunkenness of the two men.

Part Two

• In an additional paragraph or two, explain how each speaker differs from the others. What defines his language, what sets it off from the others?

Part Three

• Now explain what inferences might be drawn about the life of a lawyer from the example of legal speech and thought you have shown us. What possibilities, what risks do you perceive here? Does this passage — by showing what a lawyer says and does on one occasion — define an activity of promise, of interest to you?

QUESTIONS: Defining a Language System

1. Look at the paragraphs you have written. How can you identify each of the language systems you have used?
   a. Does each language system have its own vocabulary? No doubt there are technical words in some languages, and legal language certainly has them, but is this true of the language of the reporter or the novelist? Yet you can almost always distinguish between a paragraph from a novel and one from a newspaper. How do you do so?

      Even where a language system does have a special vocabulary, do you want to define the language as that vocabulary, without more? Or as a way of using that vocabulary? What might you mean by "ways of using" a vocabulary?
   b. One might try to identify a language by identifying the speaker. If it is spoken by a lawyer acting as a lawyer, it is legal speech. But in the passage you have prepared, how do we know that the speaker is a lawyer or other legal speaker? And if you can tell us that, how do we know he is "acting as a lawyer" rather than, say, as a voter or fisherman or husband? Is it more sensible to say that the speaker is defined, for the moment at least, by the language he uses, rather than the other way around?
   c. Another way we might try to identify a language is by the audience it seems to address. We can identify legal speech when we see that it is addressed to a legal audience. But how do we know that, except by examining the credentials of the people in the room? And certainly one can address nonlegal remarks — after-dinner jokes or political speeches, for example — to a roomful of lawyers. Or is the audience defined by the language too?

      What is it about a statement that "defines" its speaker and its audience?
   d. Is what we are trying to define perhaps neither the speaker nor the audience but the relationship between them that is created by or expressed in the statement we are examining? He may be a lawyer addressing a client, or golfer addressing his partner, or passenger addressing the bus driver — and in each case remain the same man. Perhaps the first step in discerning the relationship would be to imagine the statement in question as part of a conversation, and ask what the rest of the conversation would be like, how it would go. You might actually do this with the passages you have drafted. Here are some questions that may help you characterize the language or relationship:
      (1) What does the speaker seem to expect or want his audience to do? How is this expectation expressed in his language?
      (2) So far as you can judge from the speaker's apparent assumptions, why is the audience listening to him at all? What knowledge does the speaker claim to have, and what knowledge does he expect

his audience to have? What are their mutual interests and concerns? What is the speaker good at doing with words?

(3) Is this just a way of saying that we can identify the language of a passage by asking what issue it addresses? "This is medical speech because it addresses a medical issue." But can all statements be said to address an issue? Think of a lament, an evasion, an expression of delight, a threat or challenge, a teasing remark. Are any of those activities done by a lawyer in legal language or in special legal ways? How, in particular instances, can the legal quality of such activities be identified?

2. As you go through life, you say many things in many languages. Can you pick one language and say anything you wish in that, or is there some innate connection between the language and what is said? One way to define a starting point for this course might be to say that we pretend that your only language is the language of law. What would life under these conditions be like? Just difficult, or impossible? How, for example, could you state a medical issue in legal terms?

   One might say that technical languages are shorthand expressions for what could easily be said in plain English, and that while one cannot say everything in the languages of law or medicine, one can translate into plain English everything that is said in a technical language. If this statement appeals to you, imagine an appellate argument in a tax case carried on in plain English. If it stills appeals to you, write out some of the argument.

3. One reason language is hard to talk about is that it is always a social as well as an intellectual activity. It is not merely a way of communicating information but a way of expressing and managing relations between people. Whether a particular statement pertains to the social and intellectual relationship it affects is a matter about which we are naturally sensitive and constantly make judgments in our ordinary social life. After all, what do you suppose is meant by the word "impertinent"? One can err in a thousand ways, of course, but literary misjudgments of this social kind could be said to fall into two main classes: a remark can make the wrong assumptions about what the audience knows or cares about (as to the proper issue of the conversation) or about the nature of the relationship between two individuals (at its crudest, as to who has the upper hand). Think of what you mean by "patronizing" or "obsequious," for example.

   a. The expressed sense of the relationship, as it is or as the speaker hopes it will be, can be called the tone of voice. What tones of voice can you identify in the passages you have written? In various legal statements you can think of? Consider the statute; the will; the negotiating session; the complaint; an opinion letter; and how fatal it might be for a writer to adopt the wrong tone of voice in any of these documents. Are there tones of voice that are peculiar to the lawyer?

   b. The phrase "tone of voice" can apply to qualities of spoken as well as written speech. We are all sensitive to variations of this kind and what they mean. Consider: "The Tone in preaching does much in workeing upon the peoples affeccon. If a man should make love in an ordinary tone his Mistress would not regard him, & therefore hee must whine.

If a man should cry fire or Murther in an ordinary Voice no body would come out to helpe him." John Selden, Table Talk (Preaching, 6) (1689). What are the tones of voice, in this auditory sense, that the lawyer must master?

c. *I hope that out of your thinking about these questions comes a sharpened sense of the difficulties you will face in your life as a lawyer, and that to conceive of the lawyer as writer is a complication for you. When the heart of a passage can be said to be the relationship it expresses between speaker and audience, the management of speech becomes critical to one who, like you, must live and work through his relationships with others. Think of the mistakes one might make: you can easily imagine a lawyer addressing a judge in a manner appropriate for the jury, for example, or a client in a manner suitable for argument to a judge, with disastrous consequences. You could correct such an error if the lawyer in question were your junior: "That's jury talk, not judge-talk" or "your opinion letter sounds like a brief." What sorts of mistakes in managing social relations, perhaps less obvious and less easily correctible than these, can you imagine? Probably it would be best not to try to answer that question in general terms but to imagine and analyze particular events: the collapse of a negotiating session, for example, or the client walking out in a huff. To what extent is the management of such relations a matter of controlling language, and to what extent something else?*

d. *As you work over such imagined events in your mind, you will no doubt come to a complication that you may have sensed already: to say that language expresses a relationship is a distorting simplification, because language does more: it helps shape the relationship for the future. The writer not only meets the expectations of his audience, he states expectations of his own and, by doing so, makes claims and demands that will have to be accepted or resisted. Management of these expectations, of the social implications of language, is an activity of the most demanding kind, and I hope you recognize it as part of the lawyer's art.*

e. *Look now at the paragraphs you have written. What are the social relationships of which each is a part, and how does each paragraph affect its relationship? If you want to say that a particular paragraph has no social implications, what kind of writing is that?*

QUESTIONS: Drawing Inferences from Speech

When you are asked what inferences can be drawn from the sample of legal expression you have produced, nothing mysterious is meant. We all draw inferences from what people say and do all the time; and we constantly and consciously define ourselves in what we say, in the way we write. You have read letters to the editor that impressed or surprised you, as well as plenty that were dull and boring. One writer you would be interested to meet, the other you would just as soon leave where he is. Yet all that you know of either is what he writes. And you have drafted letters of application for a job or a scholarship with the greatest care, knowing that your reader would draw inferences from this document and that from your performance as a writer he would judge as well as he could your capacities and qualities of mind.

The writer defines himself in what he writes; he performs, and the performance is a part of himself just as his other behavior – say, a choice of right and wrong – is part of himself. He shows what he can make of experience and in doing so creates an identity for himself. One might borrow from the health food people and say, "You are what you write."

Of course, the process of drawing inferences, of tracing how a person defines himself in his writing, is in some ways a tentative one. Every shortstop misses some grounders, every businessman makes some mistakes in judgment, every teacher asks some hopelessly misguided questions. But that sort of qualification does not change one's judgment of the performance in question, whether it is by oneself or another. Part of an education is learning to be mortified by what one has just done, and it is only through a process of unsparing criticism of his own work that an athlete, a carpenter, a writer, a pianist, or a lawyer can make himself what he wants to be. One of the great things about the law is that it is an enterprise of writing, a constant opportunity for self-definition and self-improvement: how often one comes away bedraggled from a negotiation or an argument, asking why and how it went wrong, trying to see how one can make oneself different, someone who could do with language what one just failed to do.

Fortunately, some judgments can be less tentative: when one sees a great infield play, or hears a remarkable piano performance, or perceives a mind at work in writing in an original or forceful way, the performer has momentarily set himself off from all others; he has defined himself as having possibilities of his own, and one can be confident in one's admiration.

In this course you will be asked to draw inferences from your writing in a double way: first, you will be asked to look at the portion of a paper in which you show a lawyer – yourself? another? – functioning and talking as a lawyer, and to draw what inferences you can about the possibilities of legal life there defined. Then you will be asked to turn to the part of your paper written in your own voice, as an independent mind, and ask how you define yourself there. The ultimate question, of course, is what connection you can establish between these two sorts of performance, these two kinds of writing, these two selves that you define.

In a sense the whole rest of the course is devoted to working out these problems. At this stage, perhaps you will find the following questions helpful in figuring out what inferences might be drawn from your writing.

1. *Ask of the passage you have written for the lawyer, "Who talks this way? What voice do I hear? Is this the voice of a person with feelings, for example, or the voice of a machine? Can I see an independent or creative mind at work?"*
2. *If this were the only evidence you had of what a lawyer does and who he is, would you want to be a lawyer?*
3. *If you want to say that the inferences drawn from this passage would be misleading or not representative of the lawyer's life, of the life you hope to make for yourself as a lawyer, explain why that is so. Can you rewrite this passage to make it more nearly true to your own experience or hopes?*
4. *Look at your last paragraph, written as an independent mind, and ask the same questions: who is speaking here and to whom? How does he define himself and his audience and the relationship between them? Is there any life or interest in this paragraph?*

5. *Another approach might be to ask of each of the paragraphs you have written, "Would anyone, given any choice in the matter, want to read this paragraph? Why?" The skeptical question every reader asks of everything he reads (except for a teacher reading term papers) is, "Why should I pay any attention at all to what this person writes?" How do you as a writer attempt to provide your reader with an answer to that question?*
6. *It may help you criticize your own writing to look at a passage by someone else. Below, a writer expresses a conflict between law and life. How does he define himself in the way he states that conflict and his response to it?*

WITH THE EDITORS

84 Harv. L. Rev., No. 2, vii (1970)

Each Sunday from early spring to early fall, hundreds of young people gather in the Cambridge Commons. It is a varied group in appearance and mood. Bright and outlandishly romantic costumes are set against drab proletarian outfits, smiles of companionship juxtaposed with wan, blank faces. A band plays; there is some marijuana; sailing frisbees define the perimeter of the group.

Here in Gannett House — across Massachusetts Avenue — work proceeds as usual. An editor and an author dispute the most effective way of countering a troublesome argument: drop it to a note or meet it head on in text? A quick glance at the Sunday *Times*; a cold Pepsi at eleven in the morning; a glance out the window into the Commons. And back to work.

Cambridge Sundays are a plain metaphor of the gulf between law and life which deeply disturbs many of us. The eight to ten years in which a young person attends law school and makes his way into the partnership ranks of a firm have heretofore been years of intense and virtually exclusive involvement in acquiring the lawyer's skills of rationality and judgment. Perhaps prior generations of young lawyers felt no isolation in these olympian confines because they knew where they wished to be at the end of the long hard road of legal apprenticeship. Most wanted to be practitioners. Many could confidently postpone the integration of law with life until security had been assured and the burden of total devotion passed along to the newer, and younger, men in the firm.

But the sacrifices inherent in a diligent apprenticeship grow increasingly difficult to make. Few of us know where we are headed, and even fewer believe that the slow seepage of personal vibrancy which follows from single-minded devotion to legal studies is worth whatever additional skills may be exercisable upon "arrival" at the unknown point of aspiration. Not only is there no sharp vision of future reintegration to sustain us, but we also wonder whether it will ever be possible fully to reawaken our esthetic and emotional dimensions after they have fallen into disuse during the long period of legal development.

Legal institutions are responding to the need of young lawyers to find moral worth in their professional activities, but there is little indication of sensitivity to the more subtle discontent we describe. Nor are we so lucky that the remedies for one malady will alleviate the other. The gulf between law and life cannot be cured by sprinkling an appealingly modern seasoning into the law school curriculum, so long as total devotion to things legal and analytical are the stuff around which even the newer courses are built. More flexible selection processes for legal journals will not explain to newly chosen editors why they must become library fixtures at the age of twenty-two. And the law firms will not satisfy the yearnings of our generation through collateral mechanisms, however praiseworthy,[1] for promoting the public good. For conscience, after all, is very different from spirit.

Of course, we will be here this Sunday, hammering away at a legal conundrum and hoping that we shall better equip ourselves to play a constructive role in the affairs which interest us. We confess that most of us would not be content to abandon this intense way of life for a home on the Commons. Sundays, though, will never be the same.

QUESTIONS

1. *This writer observes what he calls a "gulf" between law and life, and what he sees distresses him. Exactly what is his complaint? Does he wish that he had not made Law Review, for example, or that he were able to leave Gannett House and join the others on the Common? Does he see his study of law destroying what he values in himself and others? If so, why does he keep on?*
2. *One way to start to analyze this passage would be to ask how this writer defines the "life" that has such appeal for him and the "law" whose separation from that life so distresses him. And how does he define his own role in addressing this conflict?*
   a. *Make a list of the various words and phrases used by this writer to characterize the two sides of his life and to express his feelings and attitudes towards the conflict he perceives; then ask what inferences can be drawn from his choices. Why does he use this word or figure of speech instead of another? How else might this have been put? How does he define himself as a mind and person in the way he writes? Here are a few examples of what I mean:*
      (1) *So far as you can tell from this passage, exactly what goes on in Gannett House? In what terms is the life of the Law Review expressed here?*
      (2) *What are we told here of the "skills of rationality and judgment" that are acquired in law school and the early years of practice? From what is said here, why would anyone want them? And how are they "acquired": by drudgery, payment in time and personality, or how?*

1. See generally Note, "Structuring the Public Service Efforts of Private Law Firms," 84 *Harv. L. Rev.* 410 (1970).

(3) *Make a list of the terms and phrases that define the life that this passage admires: does this statement express your own aspirations? So far as you can tell from this passage, if this writer had everything he wanted, what would he spend his time doing?*

(4) *What metaphors can you discover in the language that is used to define the writer and those for whom he speaks? Of whom might one say, for example, that he had "yearnings" that might or might not be "satisfied" by someone else? And who has "discontents" that are "subtle," or "maladies" upon which no "remedies" will work?*

(5) *One way to expose the implications of a particular sentence or phrase is to recast it in different terms, and examine the choices of language and form you have thus identified. For example, what happens when the phrase "seepage of personal vibrancy" is put into the form of a declarative sentence: who is doing what to whom? Another technique is to imagine carrying on where the writer left off: for example, how would you as president of the Harvard Law Review respond to a "newly chosen editor" when he asked you to explain why he "must become a library fixture at the age of twenty-two"?*

(6) *What are the differences between this writer and the "prior generations" of young lawyers of whom he speaks? Exactly why is it that "so few of us know where we are headed"?*

(7) *According to the writer, who is responsible for the deplorable state of affairs described here, and what should be done about it?*

b. *What does the writer do at the end of the passage, and why does he do it?*

c. *How would you characterize this passage in a single phrase: is it a firm protest, a howl of rage, an attempt to persuade, an analysis of a current problem, a letter from the heart, a cry of injured innocence, or what?*

d. *How would you compare what this person finds it possible to say about his professional education with what Twain said about his?*

3. *How would you respond to a paper assignment that asked you to address yourself to the relationship between law and life?*

WRITING ASSIGNMENT 1, ALTERNATIVE B: What Has It Meant for You to Learn the Legal Language System?

The question stated in this assignment could be said to be the subject of the whole course, and I do not mean that you should make any final statement on the matter now. But you can begin an inquiry into the experience of your own legal education. The question is one of tentative self-definition: who are you now?

Certainly you are different from the person who came to law school not so long ago, and very different indeed from people who have never been to law school. You may find it disturbing or elating, but your experience of education, if it is anything at all, must be an experience of change. Yet in meeting students from other law schools you may have noticed great similarities in your experience. Law students somehow manage to find each other at vacation parties and ruin the occasion for everyone else. What is it that you have in common? How can you express your sense of difference from those who do not go to law school, your present sense of what it means to be giving yourself a legal education?

Part One

• Imagine that a friend from your home town, who is now a sophomore in college, tells you that he wants to become a lawyer, and asks for your advice. In particular he wants to know what to expect when he gets to law school, so that he can prepare for it by choosing the right courses and so on. What do you tell him?

Here are some questions that may complicate what might at first seem, through its frequency, to be a simple event.

1. What on earth does your friend mean when he says he wants to be a lawyer? Does he know what a lawyer is? How can he possibly want to be one, then? What do you think a person who says that really does want?

2. Once you yourself decided that you wanted to be a lawyer, or at least that you wanted to go to law school, without knowing any more about it than your friend does now. It may be helpful for you to draft a brief account of that process of decision, as it seemed to you then and as it seems now.

3. Is the difficulty one of imagining the person who does not know what you know, the mind with which conversation as you usually engage in it is impossible? Consider how you would respond if someone said something like this to you: " 'I am not yet willing,' said the prince, 'to suppose that happiness is so parsimoniously distributed to mortals; nor can believe but that, if I had the choice of life, I should be able to fill every day with pleasure. I would injure no man, and should provoke no resentment: I would relieve every distress, and should enjoy the benedictions of gratitude. I would choose my friends among the wise, and my wife among the virtuous; and therefore should be in no danger of treachery, or unkindness.' " Samuel Johnson, Rasselas, Chapter 12 (1759).

In analyzing the difficulties you face in addressing the young person who wants to be a lawyer, you may wish to look into some of the existing literature of that kind. Most of it is unbelievably bad — think of the usual law school catalog — but some of it does have interest. Three books worth looking at are: T. Smith, Lawyer (1961); D. Lunt, The Road to the Law (1932); A. Harris, Letters to a Young Lawyer (1912). An interesting specimen of a different sort of book is H. Seligson, Building a

Practice (1955). Compare K. Colby, *A Primer for Psychotherapists* (1951).

Part One (Alternative)

• *Give a brief account (in two or three pages at most) of a conversation between a legal and a nonlegal mind.*

As the main assignment asks you to define three different sorts of speech, this alternative asks that you imagine and portray a conversation between minds to which different sorts of speech are congenial. Exercise your imagination as fully as you can to envision the differences between the minds you present and use every art you have to express them. It may help to consider two sorts of conversations that lawyers have with laymen all the time:

1. The layman asks you a question framed in theoretical terms to which he thinks an answer can easily be given — "Are Mexican marriages valid in Colorado?" "Am I liable if a guest at my party slips and hurts himself?" — when in fact he has given you none of the information upon which a conclusion will ultimately depend. You question him and question him, and at last, reluctantly, he agrees to tell you his story as it happened. As you listen to the story, certain things seem to you to be missing, and you ask more questions on many points until the story at last seems complete to you. Why does the story seem incomplete to you when to the other person everything has been said? To what do you trace your sense of what is missing, this sense that is so critical, that keeps you going? How do you know when the story is complete?

2. The layman wants to talk about a case, usually a Supreme Court case, of which he approves or disapproves — say, Miranda v. Arizona, 384 U.S. 436 (1966), or one of the sit-in or school desegregation cases. He talks as if he understands the case and can judge the result even if he does not understand all the background, all the technicalities. Is this true? What does such a person understand?

It is not a confidence that he can decide cases perfectly well that is missing in the layman or first-year law student, is it? What, then?

Part Two

• *Based upon your response to Part One of this assignment, what is it that distinguishes the legal mind, that sets it apart from others?*

Here you are asked to tell us what distinguishes the lawyer's mind: is it a special sort of knowledge, say, of rules? A special capacity or set of capacities? To put it somewhat differently, ask what characterizes your education: the layman would think you had picked up the knowledge of a set of more or less self-explanatory rules, and a jargon of self-serving obscurity. You know that does not explain it. What is it that sets you apart, then? If you want to say it is the mastery of a special language, be sure to explain what that means and how it has affected you.

Here are some questions designed to help you think this matter through.

1. Consider exactly how you would respond to a proposal to adopt the following amendment to your state constitution: "Every person of good moral character, being a voter, shall be entitled to admission to practice law in all courts of justice." Ind. Const. art. 7, §21 (in effect from 1851 to 1933).

2. As you work on this assignment, it may be helpful to consider how other professional people seem to differ from you, what it is they have that you lack: the dentist, doctor, engineer, auto mechanic, detective, and so on. What distinguishes their minds, so far as you can judge? Here you need to think by analogy from your own prior experience of learning, and it would probably be valuable if you wrote out a paragraph or two in which you tried to express what it has meant for you actually to have learned something you now know: how to fix a car, to speak French, to run the mile. How were you different, before, from what you are now? Consider specific examples: compare looking under the hood as a child and seeing — what? a mass of metal? a mystery? — and doing so now as one who knows how to clean spark plugs or adjust the idling mechanism, but not much more. Or take a football game: what does the child see at a football game? The experienced suburban football fan? The scout? Of course it is exactly the same football game. How do you express the differences among the minds that see it? How do you explain these differences? Is it a matter of knowing different languages?

3. To what extent does language define the mind? Can you even imagine, for example, what it would be like to think and speak only in Chinese? Or what the experience of translating from Chinese into Urdu and back would consist of? Or is that wholly out of your universe? Perhaps you can put such a conversation into your world by saying that you know people who know Chinese and therefore some sense could conceivably be made of it for you. But take the case of the Minoan trader, from Crete, speaking a lost language, talking with an Etruscan merchant, speaking a different lost language: do not those minds and their experience absolutely elude your imagination?

One classic work on the relationship between language and the mind is B. L. Whorf, Language, Thought, and Reality (1956), a collection of articles in which the author tries to show how certain American Indian languages entail ways of looking at the world that are missing from and foreign to the European languages. Ideas of time among the Hopi, for example, are utterly unlike anything we know. In Shawnee the two sentences we would phrase as "I pull the branch aside" and "I have an extra toe on my foot" are identical except for two syllables. Compare F. Boas, Handbook of American Indian Languages, introduction (1911), on the same subject. Boas speaks here of the enormous Eskimo vocabulary for different sorts and conditions of snow; of classifications built into the very structure of languages of a kind that we can make in English only by special locutions (a language might always tell us whether an object is animate or inanimate, for example, or moving or at rest, or round or not-round); of the use of tense to locate nouns as well as verbs in time, found in English only in such phrases as "her late husband" or the "future president"; and so on. In one language you cannot say "that house": the language compels you to say whether it is visible or invisible, near or far. But we make some distinctions in English that other languages do not: some languages ordinarily make no distinction between plural and singular, for example.

Can you imagine what it might involve to try to learn Eskimo or Hopi? How do you compare what it has meant to learn the language of the law?

QUESTION: Who Will You Become?

You have just been asked to look back from your position as an educated person upon the ignorant. Here you are asked to look forward from your position of ignorance, to state your expectations of the future. You were perhaps troubled, as you considered what has happened to you in your legal education, by the fact that you have exercised very little control over the process. Have you resolved to do differently in the future? How will you manage that? As you educate yourself increasingly in the ways of the lawyer, what will you lose, what gain, and what choices in this matter do you have?

You are not asked to do a writing assignment on this question, but you ought to consider it. Look at the people you know who are lawyers: do you want to end up like that? What do you now have that they lack — and will you lose it?

It might be worthwhile for you to draft a paragraph or two in which you define, in the style of Dickens perhaps, the sort of lawyer you do not want to be: the caricature of the stuffy senior partner, constantly conscious of his success; or the sanctimonious self-styled idealist who does well by doing good; or the academic operator. Then ask yourself: how can you prevent it in your case? It may be too easy for you to think that you can see the dangers of the life of the corporation lawyer (What do you really know about it? Is this just a cliché for you?) and altogether too easy to meet the problem by saying you plan to do something else anyway. I hope you can imagine ways in which the life even of the representative of the poor and downtrodden, the custodian of our liberties, the firebrand for justice, has dangers of its own that may be not so different from those of Wall Street. For example, do you suppose that the lawyer who represents those who refuse to join the army represents only the moral and just?

Following is a final word on the future.

THE ART OF FICTION*

Henry James

It is equally excellent and inconclusive to say that one must write from experience; to our supposititious aspirant such a declaration might savour of mockery. What kind of experience is intended, and where does it begin and end? Experience is never limited, and it is never complete; it is an immense sensibility, a kind of huge spiderweb of the finest silken threads suspended in the chamber of consciousness, and catching every airborne particle in its tissue. It is the very atmosphere of the mind; and when the mind is imaginative — much more when it happens to be that of a man of genius — it takes to itself the faintest hints of life, it converts the very pulses of the air into revelations. The young lady living in a village has only to be a damsel upon whom nothing is lost to make it quite unfair (as it seems to me) to declare to her that she shall have nothing to say about the military. Greater miracles have been seen than that, imagination assisting, she should speak the truth about some of these gentlemen. I remember an English novelist, a woman of genius, telling me that she was much commended for the impression she had managed to give in one of her tales of the nature and way of life of the French Protestant youth. She had been asked where she learned so much about this recondite being, she had been congratulated on her peculiar opportunities. These opportunities consisted in her having once, in Paris, as she ascended a staircase, passed an open door where, in the household of a *pasteur*, some of the young Protestants were seated at table round a finished meal. The glimpse made a picture; it lasted only a moment, but that moment was experience. She had got her direct personal impression, and she turned out her type. She knew what youth was, and what Protestantism; she also had the advantage of having seen what it was to be French, so that she converted these ideas into a concrete image and produced a reality. Above all, however, she was blessed with the faculty which when you give it an inch takes an ell, and which for the artist is a much greater source of strength than any accident of residence or of place in the social scale. The power to guess the unseen from the seen, to trace the implication of things, to judge the whole piece by the pattern, the condition of feeling life in general so completely that you are well on your way to knowing any particular corner of it — this cluster of gifts may almost be said to constitute experience, and they occur in country and in town, and in the most differing stages of education. If experience consists of impressions, it may be said that impressions *are* experience,

* In *Partial Portraits* (1888).

just as (have we not seen it?) they are the very air we breathe. Therefore, if I should certainly say to a novice, "Write from experience and experience only," I should feel that this was rather a tantalising monition if I were not careful immediately to add, "Try to be one of the people on whom nothing is lost!"

B. SUCCESS FOR THE LAWYER AND WRITER: ESTABLISHING THE RIGHT RELATIONSHIP WITH HIS LANGUAGE

When we ask the question, "What does it mean to give oneself a legal education?" we quickly stumble upon an obtrusive difficulty: it must mean something different for everyone. In our most unsettled moments we may think that some wish it otherwise, but it is fair to say that as lawyers we are not the products of a mass-production, assembly-line educational system, identical little lawyers lined up in a row. For some people, law leads to an ever duller and more restrictive life, to drudgery and routine; for others, to a life by comparison free and self-expressive, which seems to yield and form itself to the controlling intelligence or imagination. To ask what marks the difference between success and failure of this kind is necessarily to ask what marks it for oneself, or for one particular other person, not generally, for what bears down on one person liberates another. One of the demands of this course is that you state a response for yourself, that you express something of your own situation as you see it. Henry James tells you with magnificent vagueness to be one of those upon whom nothing is lost; very well, you say, I shall be such a one. But how? And what can my choices have to do with it? What do I do next?

From this point one might move in any of several directions, for success could obviously be defined in many ways: in a language of psychology, for example, or of religion or politics, or in some expression of personal values and goals. This section begins an examination of success defined rather differently, as a matter of one's relationship with language. The passages you read here will exemplify a variety of relationships with language, some successful, others less so, for you to examine and compare with your own experience.

This is not as specialized or narrow an inquiry as one might at first suspect. Most people would agree that to say of a lawyer that he had mastered the legal language system, or that he could be counted upon to say the right thing at the right time, would go a fair way towards defining success for him. But there is more to his relationship with language than mastering it as a professional instrument, as the carpenter masters his tools; there is a possibility of success or failure of a different kind, in the way he talks about and conceives of his work. For even one who does not use words in his work (say, the carpenter again) does use words to talk about himself and what he does, even if to express displeasure, even if he sees in his work no meaning or a meaning highly qualified. He finds himself called upon to express just the right relationship with what he does, to define himself as different from his purely professional role, and to do this requires an art of language. One might say that the really unfortunate person is not the one with meaningless work (we could all end up that way) but the one whose language is so constructed of cliché or otherwise inadequate that no judgment on his situation can be expressed, no intelligible and true statement uttered even of rage or disappointment.

For you as a lawyer, the matter of achieving the "right relationship" with a language is thus enormously complex. For not only like the workingman must you find a satisfactory way to describe your place in the universe, to express your sense of what you do, your work itself is a literary activity and you must master the special ways that lawyers talk. That is, you must establish the right relationship with this language — a sense that you are saying the right thing in the right way — both from outside your professional life, as you look at what it means to you and to others, and from inside it, as you try to do your job well. And you may take it as a hypothesis for your examination that these two relationships are themselves related: that perhaps the most satisfying claim you can make for what you do is that it is the work of an artist.

There is a further complication to your mastery of legal language: in this course, at least, you are asked not only to become a master but to explain your mastery: to become a critic as well as a writer. Part of your task is fashioning a language of criticism in which to define and express your perceptions of success and failure in yourself and others.

In the rest of this section you will be asked to read a play by Shakespeare, passages from other nonlegal literature, and a series of notes and questions, all of which are meant to help you analyze various relationships that writers and speakers can establish with languages they use. The aim is to begin to define some general notions of success and failure that can be of value to us as writers in the law. You will be asked in a writing assignment to produce examples of legal writing of both kinds and to explain why you regard one as "successful" and the other as not. I think you will find that as a writer in the law you cannot simply imitate the successes you see in the passages that follow — indeed, I make the argument that the lawyer is so situated that the most common and effective ways of controlling language systems are denied him — but I hope that what you read here will help you arrive at a new sense of what success might mean for a writer and a new appreciation of the special difficulties the lawyer faces.

1. *Defining the Relationship Between Self and Language: Troilus and Cressida*

Please read Shakespeare's *Troilus and Cressida* with great care. This is a difficult play written in difficult language. To understand it you will need to reread the play (parts of it many times, no doubt) and spend a considerable time thinking about it. It is important that you work hard on this. If we can arrive at a common understanding of this play, it will give us a way of talking about problems of reading and writing that will carry us a fair way towards an understanding of the lawyer's literary circumstances and how they might be addressed.

The questions that follow are meant to help you work through this play and to connect it with the concerns of this course.

QUESTIONS

1. *In Writing Assignment 1, you used and analyzed at least three language systems. As you read this play, ask yourself how many language systems you can find here. Make a list of them with reference to particular speeches in which they are used.*
   a. *It will probably not be possible for you to classify the languages of this play by referring to the profession or business of the speaker, as you could classify, say, legal and medical speech. How can you classify or otherwise speak about the language systems then?*
   b. *While professions may not be represented in this play with their technical language and jargon, there are identifiable differences in the way different characters speak. There are roles, relationships, and attitudes that have their own languages, and you are able to characterize them. For example, look at the speeches of Troilus in act 1, scene 1: you know what kind of talk that is, you have heard that voice before. Draft one sentence in which you tell how Troilus is defined by his speeches. What kind of person talks that way?*
   c. *Now look at the speech of Agamemnon at the beginning of act 1, scene 3. You know that is not Troilus speaking. How do you know that? In the same way that you distinguished medical from legal talk?*
   d. *Here are some other speeches to consider. (References are to act, scene, and line.)*

      Hector, 4.5.119
      Thersites, 5.1.15
      Pandarus, 1.2.215
      Ajax, 2.1.1
      Nestor, 1.3.31

      If these were read aloud, you could attribute them to the proper characters. In fact, that is probably true of nearly any speech in the entire play. (Try it with a friend and see.) How are these voices defined so thoroughly? Differentiation of voice in this way is a most important part of Shakespeare's art, since that is how he creates character – a fact not without significance for you.

Study these or some other representative passages with care. Exactly how are the languages made so different? Is it the vocabulary? The definition of speaker or audience? The kind of "issue" that is stated, what it is that is seen as worth saying? The substance of the view that is expressed?

As you make your list of different voices you may notice that while each character has his own distinctive voice, the speeches can be grouped by subject matter into two main categories: talk about love (or sex) and the public talk about government and war. Two generally different kinds of discourse are defined, in each of which various characters engage, each in his own way: several characters speak on only one sort of subject (Pandarus or Agamemnon, for example); others speak in some fashion on both (Troilus, Diomedes, and Thersites).

2. You are now asked to look at the play as a whole and ask what Shakespeare does with these disparate materials. How, if at all, does he put them together into a composition, an organization of speech? What connections can be drawn between the talk about love and the talk about war? What relations exist among these characters? The usual idea of a play is that characters who talk differently talk to each other. Is that so here? What conversation can you imagine between Pandarus and Agamemnon, for example? You would have difficulty imagining a coherent universe in which they both fit. How can the same person say what Troilus says about love and what he says about war? If you find that Thersites and Diomedes alone manage to express consistent personalities in both sorts of discourse, that they alone can unite the two worlds, you may take it that Shakespeare did not do that by accident but meant something by it.

A drastic lack of cohesion exists within each kind of discourse as well as between them. How differently Hector and Ajax talk about war for example, or Troilus and Pandarus about love. The inconsistencies of attitude are so marked that the only conversation one could easily imagine between such characters would have as its subject the very fact of inconsistency ("How can you talk in that disgusting – or naive or dishonest or romantic or cynical – way?") but the inconsistencies go generally unrecognized. Pandarus talks as if his view of sex were the only possible one, and so does Troilus, and so does Diomedes – each as if he spoke to an unquestioned tradition. And when they meet in the Greek camp (act 4, scene 5), Hector and Achilles are able to converse about warfare only on a false basis, with Achilles simply cheating, trying to get Hector drunk to be easier prey on the morrow.

It is important to emphasize that this social and intellectual disorganization is not the automatic result of such differences of view and language. One could write a play of which the subject was an irreconcilable difference of view expressed in the language of the characters. Sophocles' Antigone and Philoctetes are such plays, and so in their way are Antony and Cleopatra and Romeo and Juliet. But in this play the recognition that others talk differently, that there is any other way to talk, is exactly what is missing.

This obliviousness of character to character has consequences for the life and structure of the play. It means that the characters do not learn and change, but continue in set patterns of speech and behavior – "he beats me and I rail at him." One might say that what is missing here is the shift of voice, the expression of learning, that often gives a play its central meaning: Lear at the end could not be imagined imperious again, nor Oedipus serenely confident. Now consider Pandarus: does he ever talk in any other way than the way he begins? Does Ajax? Thersites? Hector? Troilus does move from expressing love to expressing rejection, but he expresses no sense of having changed or learned from experience, and in a sixth act he could easily be shown saying about another woman precisely the things he said in act 1 about Cressida. Cressida does in fact change, but no one can make sense of it; in this world, to these characters, change is an inconceivable event.

This is, then, the drama not of the collapse or disintegration of social or intellectual order, but of the failure to meet and respond, the failure to organize around differences and similarities of view. The universe is in pieces at the beginning as well as at the end of the play. This utter fragmentation is expressed by having most of the characters each speak only one way, with no recognition of other possibilities.

3. *Read the speeches of Troilus with particular care. He has only the formal language of love with which to respond to the events of the play, and it is wholly inadequate even as a means of establishing and expressing a relationship with Cressida. For example, the decision to send Cressida to the Greeks is made without argument or dissent from him. When Cressida asks whether she must indeed go – "Is't possible?" – Troilus does not answer her, but gives instead a Beautiful Farewell Speech: "And suddenly, where injury of chance. . . ." At the end of it she asks: "I must then to the Grecians?" "No remedy." (Act 4, scene 4.) He then falls into a language of lover's cliché, persistently telling Cressida to be true, which is, in the circumstances, incredibly insulting and received as such. "I true? How now? What wicked deem is this?" The poetry of love and parting and sorrow and eternal fidelity goes on and on, but what the scene makes clear is that no decent relationship can be built upon or expressed in such a language. Troilus says at the end:*

The moral of my wit
Is "plain and true"; there's all the reach of it.
Welcome, Sir Diomed! Here is the lady
Which for Antenor we deliver you.

How is Troilus defined by what he says here, when the love-speeches he knows how to make are over? Isn't he a little like an actor who yawns in the wings when his fiery scene is at an end? What you see here is what it means to have only one resource for expression, and how impossible it proves in any situations but those few to which it (by its nature) is directed. Troilus is defined so wholly by the formal talk of love that his conduct is impossible – cruel, stupid, brutal – except where he is playing that particular role. The rest of what he says is unaffected by his talk of love, beautiful and poetic though it is.

Do you see this as pathetic? Do you know any lawyers (or law teachers) who are defined by a single language in a similarly pathetic way? If one who talks only one way has lost control of his language, how do you plan to establish a different relationship, one of control, with the legal language that you will use all day every day?

4. *In contrast to most of the others, Cressida clearly does talk more than one way. Her response to Pandarus' obvious over-praise of Troilus is, "What sneaking fellow comes yonder?" and the comedy of that scene is her mockery of a foolish use of a foolish language. But she loves him, and in what way can she express that? Her complex relationship to the language of love is first defined at the end of that scene, when she says she will hide her actual feelings. "Then though my heart's content firm love doth bear, Nothing of that shall from my eyes appear." Does Troilus ever talk about his actual feelings as anything different from what he says? It seems fair to say that Troilus is wholly defined by the formal language of love, with no indication of any unexpressed or private life, while Cressida is defined as standing outside the language of love, which she treats as inadequate to express her private experience. "But more in Troilus thousandfold I see Than in the glass of Pandar's praise may be." (Act 1, scene 1.)*

   One might go further and draw an analogy to this course: our purpose is to define and take a position with respect to legal language like Cressida's with respect to love language: outside it and skeptical of it.

5. *Cressida is clearly not expressed by the formal language of love (in fact, she begins by debunking it); Troilus as clearly is. Is the tragedy of this play her attempt to do the impossible, to use this language to express herself, to allow herself to be defined in a way she – alone – can see is inadequate? She sees it coming; having declared her love, having expressed herself in this language, she says, "Why have I blabb'd? Who shall be true to us When we are so unsecret to ourselves?"*

   In fact, her use of the language of love is even more subtle. She first expresses her love not in the flowery and formal speech of Troilus, but in a very direct and simple way: "Prince Troilus, I have lov'd you night and day For many weary months." But she is unable to maintain this sort of speech under the pressure of Troilus' rhetoric, and that scene concludes with a formal posturing: "As true as Troilus," "as false as Cressida," and so forth.

   Does this enactment of what it means to try to express oneself in a single formal language define a problem for you as a lawyer?

6. *Some of the characters are fully expressed by one sort of speech, such as Pandarus ("How go maidenheads?"), Thersites ("No, no! I am a rascal, a scurvy railing knave, a very filthy rogue"), Hector ("Mine honor keeps the weather of my fate"), or Ajax ("I do hate a proud man as I hate the engend'ring of toads"). Cressida stands outside as long as she can, but finally becomes the victim of the language she uses. There is one other who stands outside the languages he uses, with very different results. Ulysses does not fail, he succeeds: he is the master of rhetoric, the great persuader.*

   Ulysses wears down the resistance of Achilles by staging a snub and making a long speech whose premise is that honor is defined as reputation, which must be maintained or lost. "Perseverance, dear my lord, Keeps honor bright." While Achilles was at the beginning of the speech open to such a line of argument, he was not without some sense of his merit apart from its recognition by others: "I do enjoy At ample point all that I did possess Save these men's looks . . ." Of course the rhetoric of Ulysses is false, and the idea of honor that gives this speech its persuasive force will be defined, by the ending of the play, as absurd. In the famous "Degree" speech (1.3.75), Ulysses persuades Agamemnon by a rhetoric very different but equally absurd. No one could possibly think that this play creates an ordered working universe in which everyone and everything has a proper place, yet Ulysses moves Agamemnon into action by just such a claim. And at the end of act 2 he manages the brutish Ajax by the most exaggerated flattery.

Ulysses can thrive in the world created by the play because he stands outside all of the different languages and can use them to gain his ends. He can speak many ways, not just one, and instead of falling prey to the weakness of those who can speak only one way, he preys upon them. By manipulating their language he manipulates them. The secret of his success is that he never makes the mistake that Cressida did once, of trying to use language to express himself, of trying to tell the truth.

Is Ulysses the model lawyer in this play? Is this the sort of success to which you can at best look forward?

7. *Some of the characters who can talk only one way are seen as utter fools, like Pandarus or Ajax. Their one language is obviously inadequate to any valuable experience or purpose. But with respect to others the situation is not so simple. Look at Troilus' language: however impossible as a sole resource, it is beautiful. (See, e.g., 4.4.32.) You might say that Romeo and Juliet was a play founded on just this sort of language. And Hector: at the end of act 2, scene 2, when they are debating whether to return Helen to the Greeks and stop the war, he faces a conflict between morality and glory, a dilemma of honor, that could serve as the subject of a play. But here this language and the behavior which belongs to it are defined as impossible. When Troilus upbraids Hector for releasing defeated Greeks, Hector says, "'Tis fair play"; Troilus replies, "Fool's play, by heaven, Hector." Act 5, scene 3. Hector is taken unarmed by Achilles and slaughtered. The morality and glory whose conflict presented such a moral crisis were real to him alone.*[5]

   Does the tragedy of this play arise less from the use of foolish languages than from the foolish use of excellent languages?
8. *One might recast that suggestion and say that the tragedy of this play is the tragedy of overconfidence in language. One language — love, honor, or war — is used by a character as a complete expression of all life; each character (except Cressida and Ulysses) can be defined by the language system he uses, and as to which he expresses no doubts whatever. This*

5. If you analyze Hector's speeches with care, I think you will find that he expresses no consistent and firm notions either of morality or of glory, that honor receives no definition sharp enough to make this dilemma live for the reader. His is the mind that tried to think that way but without the context that could give support and substance to his claims. This is perhaps the subtlest way in which Shakespeare enacts disorganization in this play. Compare the heroic plays of Corneille, which create a most highly ordered heroic context against which such a dilemma can be defined with real precision.

leads to an impossible world in which no social relations can be maintained except those of manipulation and exploitation. When Cressida behaves in the Greek camp as a person, not as a part of a love poem, Troilus has no language except that of rejection with which to respond. Achilles can be manipulated by talk of individual glory; Agamemnon can be aroused by very different talk of the importance of social order and degree; both of these languages are shown in this play to be as impossible as Troilus' talk of love or Hector's of honor.

Think now about the world around you. Do you know people who put a similar confidence in a single language? Surely you know some people who seem almost to be caricatures, so complete is their confidence in the language, say, of religion or politics or romantic love, or perhaps in a somewhat more complex language, say, that of psychology or sociology or systems analysis or economics. They see things and talk about them in only one way; they recognize no other. This sort of overconfidence in a single language, and in one's mastery of it, makes one a know-it-all and a bore: what other consequences may it have? Consider again the parting scene discussed above.

Now think about people you know in the law: what relationships do they have with the language of the law? How do these relationships affect their relationships with people? You must know one or two who seem to be lawyers and nothing else. Think of lawyers you know who are your friends' fathers: do some of them not exhibit an overconfidence in this language and the attitudes it entails, do they not seem sometimes to be utterly certain that it is a sufficient means of life and expression? Surely we all know some lawyers we might call stuffy; in exactly what does their stuffiness consist? We perhaps know as well, or have heard of, some who are knaves, who use the language of the law without regard for the truth of what is said, with no concern for the purposes for which this instrument of civilization has been designed. Your friend at the cocktail party would have something to say here. He would know some lawyers to whom he would hesitate to take a real problem. Do you know any law teachers of whom similar things could be said? Any law students? Or are the dangers pointed to here simply insubstantial and unreal to the young lawyer of the modern breed who knows how foolish all prior generations of men have been, who bears within himself the sure knowledge of his superiority to circumstance?

The question that has been posed for you is this: what relationship will you – can you, dare you – have with the habits of thought and speech that define your profession? How, in what language, will you express that relationship and to whom? How do you articulate to yourself the dangers and the possibilities you perceive? How can you control the language of the law, and what will you have achieved when you have done so?

2. *Traditional Ways of Controlling a Language*

In *Troilus and Cressida* you see at least three relationships between speaker and language: the language system wholly expresses the speaker (Troilus); it does not, and the speaker loses control as she tries to use it to tell the truth (Cressida); it does not, and the speaker maintains control, but does not tell the truth (Ulysses). On the basis of this play, would you conclude that it is just not possible to use a language system to tell the truth and still maintain control over it? *Troilus and Cressida* expresses the tragedy of the failure to control the use of language. It is about the wrong relationship between a person and his language. What is the right relationship, and how do you attain it?

You will see that such a question states the goal of an education and a life. All literary art, including the lawyer's, must respond to it. No formulaic or other answer can be given. You should now have a clearer idea of what I meant when I said that this course addresses you as an artist, and you should see that the question points you in a direction in which you must make your own way, both as a writer and as a critic.

Having studied a play about failure, in the brief excerpts that follow we shall look at some successes. We shall examine some ways in which these writers exert control over the languages they use, some ways in which they master the implication of confidence that the very use of a language involves. This is obviously a subtle business, and it is only fair to alert you now to the fact that the terms we have been using to express one aspect of the writer's success — his "control" of his language and his avoidance of "overconfidence" — are too crude to be more than the barest beginning of a critical vocabulary. But perhaps they can be used to mark out some large notions at least.

There are I think three principal ways in which writers have traditionally sought to maintain control over the language they use: metaphor, irony, and ambiguity. Metaphor and irony are sometimes called figures of speech, and I suppose ambiguity could be called that too, but I prefer to think of these as relationships a writer establishes with a language.

For fairly obvious reasons the lawyer cannot often establish such relationships with legal language: one would think that the lawyer had to say, not suggest, what he meant; that he had to say it directly, not ironically; and that ambiguity was no merit for him. But to analyze how others have controlled their language may help the lawyer when he struggles with his own. And these specific relationships are not wholly absent from the law: our Constitution is certainly ambiguous, and irony is often heard in the courtroom.

a. Metaphor

One way to control a language is to use it as a metaphor — "saying one thing and meaning another," as Robert Frost characterized it. This is a way of making a language mean more than it seems to. Here is a brief example:

THE SICK ROSE
William Blake

O Rose, thou art sick!
The invisible worm
That flies in the night,
In the howling storm,

Has found out thy bed
Of crimson joy;
And his dark secret love
Does thy life destroy.

Here the poet talks about a sick rose, but it should be apparent that he means something else, something that could not possibly be restated in the language of horticulture. Whether that meaning can be fully stated in plain English, or in any other form than this poem, is a difficult question, familiar to all readers of literature, the dogma of today being that the poem cannot be so translated. "A poem should not mean but be." (For an intelligent elaboration of how this poem works, see the introductory chapter to R. Brower, *The Fields of Light* (1951).) Of course while this poem seems to describe only a sick rose, it does not confine itself to, and in fact barely uses, the language of the gardener. It is the deliberate use of other languages — of disease and sex and storm and spirits — that creates the metaphorical meaning. Is such a tension between languages essential to metaphor? To any control of language?

Another example of metaphorical writing is Melville's use of the language of whaling in *Moby Dick*, which you may have read. What does the white whale mean in that book? To Ahab? To the reader? However you answer that, the whale is clearly more than a potential source of whale oil.[6] Another example, perhaps a closer parallel to a way you might imagine yourself writing, is Joseph Conrad's *Mirror of the Sea* (1906), an autobiography in which he uses the world and language of the sailor to say what he wants to say about life. Can you imagine so using the world and language of the lawyer?

Can you see legal language as a metaphor? I assume that in some sense you can and do — surely you see some unexpressed meaning in what you do — but it may be that you can do this only as a person, not as a lawyer. As he works on an antitrust case or a criminal appeal, the

6. The use of metaphor in *Moby Dick* is analyzed well in J. Guetti, *The Limits of Metaphor* (1967).

lawyer may say to himself that what he is doing and saying really means something else, to him and, if his ego is sufficient to the claim, to the world: order, or reason, or balance in the affairs of men, or justice, or some such thing. The activity of law can be spoken of in other terms. "What does the carefully prepared financial exhibit really mean?" one might ask, and be told that it means something very different from what it says: it says one thing and means another. But that meaning may not be expressible in lawyers' ways at all.

Here experience tells youth, with splendid vagueness, to make a claim of this kind:

> However a man feels about his work nature is likely to see to it that his business becomes his master and an end in itself, so that he may find that he has been a martyr under the illusion of self-seeking. But we rank men partly at least by the nature of their dominant interests, and we think more highly of those who are conscious of ulterior ends — be those ends intellectual ideals, to see the universal in the particular, or the sympathetic wish to help their kind. For your sake I hope that when your work seems to present only mean details you may realize that every detail has the mystery of the universe behind it and may keep up your heart with an undying faith.*

As a young person addressed in such a way, one might wish to ask exactly where behind the details one can find the mystery of the universe, and expect to be told that one must find that out for oneself. Some never do. Wallace Stevens, the poet and executive, wrote his daughter: "But take my word for it that making your living is a waste of time. None of the great things in life have anything to do with making your living; and I had hoped that little by little, without now being able to say how, you would find the true field for your intelligence and imagination in something that was at least a part of one of the great things of life."†

But for William Carlos Williams, the poet and doctor, poetry and medicine were "nearly the same thing," and medicine was "the very thing that made it possible for me to write. Was I not interested in man?"‡ You can take this passage as one possible response to Twain's query whether the doctor has not lost more than he has gained in learning his trade:

> Forget writing, it's a trivial matter. But day in day out, when the inarticulate patient struggles to lay himself bare for you, or with nothing more than a boil on his back is so caught off balance that he reveals some secret twist

* O. W. Holmes, Jr., Letter to Charles E. Wyzanski, Jr., in C. Wyzanski, Jr., *Whereas — A Judge's Premises* 289–290 (1965).

† *Letters of Wallace Stevens* 426 (H. Stevens ed. 1966).

‡ W. C. Williams, *Autobiography* 286, 357 (1948).

of a whole community's pathetic way of thought, a man is suddenly seized again with a desire to speak of the underground stream which for a moment has come up just under surface. It is just a glimpse, an intimation of all that which the daily print misses or deliberately hides, but the excitement is intense and the rush to write is on again. It is then we see, by this constant feeling for a meaning, from the unselected nature of the material, just as it comes in over the phone or at the office door, that there is no better way to get an intimation of what is going on in the world.

We catch a glimpse of something, from time to time, which shows us that a presence has just brushed past us, some rare thing — just when the smiling little Italian woman has left us. For a moment we are dazzled. What was that? We can't name it; we know it never gets into any recognizable avenue of expression; men will be long dead before they can have so much as ever approached it. Whole lives are spent in the tremendous affairs of daily events without even approaching the great sights that I see every day. My patients do not know what is about them among their very husbands and children, their wives and acquaintances. But there is no need for us to be such strangers to each other, saving alone laziness, indifference and age-old besotted ignorance.

So for me the practice of medicine has become the pursuit of a rare element which may appear at any time, at any place, at a glance. It can be most embarrassing. Mutual recognition is likely to flare up at a moment's notice. The relationship between physician and patient, if it were literally followed, would give us a world of extraordinary fertility of the imagination which we can hardly afford. There's no use trying to multiply cases, it is there, it is magnificent, it fills my thoughts, it reaches to the farthest limits of our lives.*

This sort of claim to metaphorical meaning can be made of course for practically any sort of activity, whether verbal itself or not: the football coach sees perseverance and courage on the field, the policeman feels himself a guardian against evil, and so on.

But how in a given case is the metaphor to be justified, the claim of meaning to be defended? Holmes gives us very little, Williams a great deal more. Here Conrad tells us of the meaning he finds in sailing: how adequately does he support his claims of significance, and by what art does he do so?

THE MIRROR OF THE SEA†

Joseph Conrad

The sailing and racing of yachts has developed a class of fore-and-aft sailors, men born and bred to the sea, fishing in winter and yachting in summer; men to whom the handling of that particular rig presents no

* W. C. Williams, *Autobiography* 359–360 (1948).

† Chapter 8 (1906).

mystery. It is their striving for victory that has elevated the sailing of pleasure craft to the dignity of a fine art in that special sense. As I have said, I know nothing of racing and but little of fore-and-aft rig; but the advantages of such a rig are obvious, especially for purposes of pleasure, whether in cruising or racing. It requires less effort in handling, the trimming of the sail-planes to the wind can be done with speed and accuracy; the unbroken spread of the sail-area is of infinite advantage; and the greatest possible amount of canvas can be displayed upon the least possible quantity of spars. Lightness and concentrated power are the great qualities of fore-and-aft rig. . . .

For racing, a cutter; for a long pleasure voyage, a schooner; for cruising in home waters, the yawl; and the handling of them all is indeed a fine art. It requires not only the knowledge of the general principles of sailing, but a particular acquaintance with the character of the craft. All vessels are handled in the same way as far as theory goes, just as you may deal with all men on broad and rigid principles. But if you want that success in life which comes from the affection and confidence of your fellows, then with no two men, however similar they may appear in their nature, will you deal in the same way. There may be a rule of conduct; there is no rule of human fellowship. To deal with men is as fine an art as it is to deal with ships. Both men and ships live in an unstable element, are subject to subtle and powerful influences, and want to have their merits understood rather than their faults found out.

It is not what your ship will *not* do that you want to know to get on terms of successful partnership with her; it is, rather, that you ought to have a precise knowledge of what she will do for you when called upon to put forth what is in her by a sympathetic touch. At first sight the difference does not seem great in either line of dealing with the difficult problem of limitations. But the difference is great. The difference lies in the spirit in which the problem is approached. After all, the art of handling ships is finer, perhaps, than the art of handling men.

And, like all fine arts, it must be based upon a broad, solid sincerity, which, like a law of Nature, rules an infinity of different phenomena. Your endeavour must be single-minded. You would talk differently to a coal-heaver and to a professor. But is this duplicity? I deny it. The truth consists in the genuineness of the feeling, in the genuine recognition of the two men, so similar and so different, as your two partners in the hazard of life. Obviously, a humbug, thinking only of winning his little race, would stand a chance of profiting by his artifices. Men, professors or coal-heavers, are easily deceived; they even have an extraordinary knack of lending themselves to deception, a sort of curious and inexplicable propensity to allow themselves to be led by the nose with their eyes open. But a ship is a creature which we have brought into the world, as it were on purpose to keep us up to the mark. In her handling a ship will not put up with a mere pretender, as, for instance, the public will do with Mr. X, the popular statesman, Mr. Y, the popular scientist, or Mr. Z, the popular — what shall we say? — anything from a teacher of high morality to a bagman — who have won their little race. But I would like (though not accustomed to betting) to wager a large sum that not one of the few first-rate skippers of racing yachts has ever been a humbug. It would have been too difficult. The difficulty arises from the fact that one does not deal with ships in a mob, but with a ship as an individual. So we may have to do with men. But in each of us there lurks some particle of the mob spirit, of the mob temperament. No matter how earnestly we strive against each other, we remain brothers on the lowest side of our intellect and in the instability of our feelings. With ships it is not so. Much as they are to us they are nothing to each other. Those sensitive creatures have no ears for our blandishments. It takes something more than words to cajole them to do our will, to cover us with glory. Luckily, too, or else there would have been more shoddy reputations for first-rate seamanship. Ships have no ears, I repeat, though, indeed, I think I have known ships who really seemed to have had eyes, or else I cannot understand on what ground a certain 1000-ton barque of my acquaintance on one particular occasion refused to answer her helm, thereby saving a frightful smash to two ships and to a very good man's reputation. I knew her intimately for two years, and in no other instance either before or since have I known her to do that thing. The man she had served so well (guessing, perhaps, at the depths of his affection for her) I have known much longer, and in bare justice to him I must say that this confidence-shattering experience (though so fortunate) only augmented his trust in her. Yes, our ships have no ears, and thus they cannot be deceived. I would illustrate my idea of fidelity as between man and ship, between the master and his art, by a statement which, though it might appear shockingly sophisticated, is really very simple. I would say that a racing-yacht skipper who thought of nothing else but the glory of winning the race would never attain to any eminence of reputation. The genuine masters of their craft — I say this confidently from my experience of ships — have thought of nothing but of doing their very best by the vessel under their charge. To forget one's self, to surrender all personal feeling in the service of that fine art, is the only way for a seaman to the faithful discharge of his trust.

Such is the service of a fine art and of ships that sail the sea. And therein I think I can lay my finger upon the difference between the seamen of yesterday, who are still with us, and the seamen of to-morrow, already entered upon the possession of their inheritance. History repeats itself, but the special call of an art which has passed away is never reproduced. It is as utterly gone out of the world as the song of a destroyed wild bird. Nothing will awaken the same response of pleasurable emotion or conscientious endeavour. And the sailing of any vessel afloat is an art whose fine form seems already receding from us on its way to the overshadowed Valley of Oblivion. The taking of a modern steamship about the world (though one would not minimize its responsibilities) has not the same quality of intimacy with nature, which, after all, is an indispensable condition to the building up of an art. It is less personal and a more exact calling; less arduous, but also less gratifying in the lack of close communion between the artist and the medium of his art. It is, in short, less a matter of love. Its effects are measured exactly in time and space as no effect of an art can be. It is an occupation which a man not desperately subject to sea-sickness can be imagined to follow with content, without enthusiasm, with industry, without affection. Punctuality is its watchword. The incertitude which attends closely every artistic endeavour is absent from its regulated enterprise. It has no great moments of self-confidence, or moments not less great of doubt and heart-searching. It is an industry which, like other industries, has its romance, its honour, and its rewards, its bitter anxieties and its hours of ease. But such sea-going has not the artistic quality of a single-handed struggle with something much greater than yourself; it is not the laborious, absorbing practice of an art whose ultimate result remains on the knees of the gods. It is not an individual, temperamental achievement, but simply the skilled use of a captured force, merely another step forward upon the way of universal conquest.[7]

The justification of metaphor, the claim to special meaning in what seems ordinary and dull, is the subject of George Eliot's *Middlemarch* (1871–1872). This novel is about what English provincial life can be made to mean by an ardent and aspiring person. Dorothea Brooke, in her glowing eagerness to lead a life imbued with meaning, misunderstands everything and agrees to marry a cold-hearted, half-dead antiquarian much older than she. In planning her life, she makes her claim: "There would be nothing trivial about our lives. Every-day things would mean the greatest things." Her melancholy marriage ends with his death, and she can start anew, with chastened expectations. In a similar effort the idealistic Dr. Lydgate comes to the provincial town to try to forge a life of moral and medical significance for himself: "Does it seem incongruous to you that a Middlemarch surgeon should dream of himself as a discoverer?" From the beginning he is frustrated by the surpris-

7. What would Mark Twain say to these assertions about the limited possibilities for art in the management of steam vessels?

ing complexity and intractability of life: "For the first time Lydgate was feeling the hampering threadlike pressure of small social conditions, and their frustrating complexity." The aspirations are not small — "She longed for work that would be directly beneficent, like the sunshine and the rain" — and the motion of the novel is one of adjustment to failure, of coming to comprehend, in part at least, one's mistaken view of the social relations in which and through which one has lived, and of forming new and more realistic expectations of life. This process of learning is its own sort of success for Dorothea, and "her finely touched spirit had still its fine issues, though they were not widely visible." The claims for heroic life are not utterly lost at the end though, as Eliot says, the new St. Theresa cannot reform conventual life, the new Antigone will not dare all for the sake of a brother's burial, "the medium in which their ardent deeds took shape is forever gone." One cannot by a simple act of decision be what one will: "For there is no creature whose inward being is so strong that it is not greatly determined by what lies outside it." The process is one of claiming a meaning and then seeking, always imperfectly, to justify it, of coming to terms with the tension between imagination and reality.

I hope you have such a sense of living a metaphor, and that you repeatedly ask yourself whether what you say or do sustains the meaning you try to give it. T. S. Eliot said in a famous phrase of *Hamlet* that it failed as a play because Shakespeare never found an "objective correlative" in the world of dramatic action that was adequate to his meaning. And we all know people who make noble claims for the meaning of what they do, which we regretfully find unsustained. It isn't there, we say. In fact, to return to *Moby Dick*, it can be said that Ahab fails utterly in his attempt to make the white whale a metaphor for something else, that he cannot sustain his attempt to give it meaning, and that the book is really about this failure of meaning.

But whatever metaphor you claim to live, whatever the ultimate meaning you give to legal language, is there any way you can express this while talking and acting as a lawyer? Or is that side of your life silent in these critical respects? If so, is this situation intolerable for you, or have you the self-sufficiency to live with it? You need not answer such questions now, of course, but you will be given several opportunities to write about them, starting with your next writing assignment.

b. Irony

Irony is another way of controlling a language. It is a way of saying one thing and meaning, not just another, but its opposite. One could call it a special kind of metaphor. Here is Thoreau's gently ironic use of the legal notions and language of property, in which he claims that he gets the best possession and title by refusing them.

WALDEN*
H. D. Thoreau

At a certain season of our life we are accustomed to consider every spot as the possible site of a house. I have thus surveyed the country on every side within a dozen miles of where I live. In imagination I have bought all the farms in succession, for all were to be bought, and I knew their price. I walked over each farmer's premises, tasted his wild apples, discoursed on husbandry with him, took his farm at his price, at any price, mortgaging it to him in my mind; even put a higher price on it, — took everything but a deed of it, — took his word for his deed, for I dearly love to talk, — cultivated it, and him too to some extent, I trust, and withdrew when I had enjoyed it long enough, leaving him to carry it on. This experience entitled me to be regarded as a sort of real-estate broker by my friends. Wherever I sat, there I might live, and the landscape radiated from me accordingly. What is a house but a *sedes*, a seat? — better if a country seat. I discovered many a site for a house not likely to be soon improved, which some might have thought too far from the village, but to my eyes the village was too far from it. Well, there I might live, I said; and there I did live, for an hour, a summer and a winter life; saw how I could let the years run off, buffet the winter through, and see the spring come in. The future inhabitants of this region, wherever they may place their houses, may be sure that they have been anticipated. An afternoon sufficed to lay out the land into orchard, wood-lot, and pasture, and to decide what fine oaks or pines should be left to stand before the door, and whence each blasted tree could be seen to the best advantage: and then I let it lie, fallow perchance, for a man is rich in proportion to the number of things which he can afford to let alone.

My imagination carried me so far that I even had the refusal of several farms, — the refusal was all I wanted, — but I never got my fingers burned by actual possession. The nearest that I came to actual possession was when I bought the Hollowell place, and had begun to sort my seeds, and collected materials with which to make a wheelbarrow to carry it on or off with; but before the owner gave me a deed of it, his wife — every man has such a wife — changed her mind and wished to keep it, and he offered me ten dollars to release him. Now, to speak the truth, I had but ten cents in the world, and it surpassed my

* Pages 73–76 (1854; Modern Library ed. 1950).

arithmetic to tell, if I was that man who had ten cents, or who had a farm, or ten dollars, or all together. However, I let him keep the ten dollars and the farm too, for I had carried it far enough; or rather, to be generous, I sold him the farm for just what I gave for it, and, as he was not a rich man, made him a present of ten dollars, and still had my ten cents, and seeds, and materials for a wheelbarrow left. I found thus that I had been a rich man without any damage to my poverty. But I retained the landscape, and I have since annually carried off what it yielded without a wheelbarrow. With respect to landscapes, — "I am monarch of all I *survey*, My right there is none to dispute."

I have frequently seen a poet withdraw, having enjoyed the most valuable part of a farm, while the crusty farmer supposed that he had got a few wild apples only. Why, the owner does not know it for many years when a poet has put his farm in rime, the most admirable kind of invisible fence, has fairly impounded it, milked it, skimmed it, and got all the cream, and left the farmer only the skimmed milk. . . .

Old Cato, whose "De Re Rusticâ" is my "Cultivator," says, — and the only translation I have seen makes sheer nonsense of the passage, — "When you think of getting a farm turn it thus in your mind, not to buy greedily; nor spare your pains to look at it, and do not think it enough to go round it once. The oftener you go there the more it will please you, if it is good." I think I shall not buy greedily, but go round and round it as long as I live, and be buried in it first, that it may please me the more at last.[8]

Compare this passage by Thoreau with the passage from Twain's *Life on the Mississippi* you have already read. In both cases the poet's way of viewing the world is compared with someone else's — the pilot's or farmer's way. Do you see how the precise position each writer takes, what he says, is expressed by the relationship he establishes between two ways of talking? Thoreau uses the farmer's or owner's language, only to reject it in favor of the poet's way of looking at the landscape. Since he says little that affirmatively describes the poet's life, one might say that he expresses his own view mainly by rejecting another, by telling us what his is not. His claim for the meaning and value of his own life must lie in the wit and energy with which the farmer's is rejected. He controls the languages of property and farming by rejecting them. Twain poses the two ways of talking side by side, and is more ambivalent in his attitudes: to learn to be a pilot opens a wonderful book to

8. Richard Poirier gives an account of this passage in which he brings to life a persistent comedy one might miss: what does it mean to "walk over the premises," for example? Or to "cultivate the farmer"? See *A World Elsewhere* 85–89 (1966).

him, a life rich with knowledge and activity, but it entails a real loss as well. Sometimes the loss seems greater than the gain, sometimes the reverse; the balance is not struck, satisfaction and longing remain mingled. Perhaps his real compensation is to be a poet, one who (unlike the enraptured passenger) can see and talk both ways at once: whatever his loss, there is a gain of fuller understanding. Twain gives recognition to the inconsistencies of life and to his own uncertainties of attitude, and in this way qualifies both languages as he uses them. Thoreau makes a heroically unqualified rejection, a claim to live a life of ineffable but obvious meaning. His life becomes, as he says when speaking of his own farming, a parable:

> When my hoe tinkled against the stones, that music echoed to the woods and the sky, and was an accompaniment to my labor which yielded an instant and immeasurable crop. It was no longer beans that I hoed, nor I that hoed beans; and I remembered with as much pity as pride, if I remembered at all, my acquaintances who had gone to the city to attend oratorios. . . . Not that I wanted beans to eat, because I am by nature a Pythagorean, so far as beans are concerned, whether they mean porridge or voting, and exchanged them for rice; but, perchance, as some must work in the fields if only for the sake of tropes and expression, to serve a parable-maker one day.*

c. *Ambiguity*

While irony and metaphor are used differently by different writers — the artist's statement must be personal to himself — both could be said to be methods of control that involve talking two ways, saying one thing and meaning another. This is how "more" is recognized or an "opposite" expressed. As you can see from the Twain passage, when a language is used either metaphorically or ironically there may be considerable ambiguity as to the extent to which it is accepted or rejected, the reader being led to do both at once, and often being left at last in doubt. Another example of this sort of ambiguity in the use of metaphor is the meaning of the white whale in *Moby Dick*. The book begins with more than eighty brief extracts from other writers on the subject of whales, defining as it were the universe of talk about whales and showing that it is filled with various and inconsistent meanings. This opening makes insistent the question of choice of language: how should whales, and this whale, be talked about? Melville talks about the white whale in many different languages as the book proceeds: the commercial, in which he is viewed as a source of oil; the biological, in which

* H. D. Thoreau, *Walden* 143, 146 (1854; Modern Library ed. 1950).

sperm whales as a class are compared with others; the mystical, in which he is talked about as the emblem of evil or of good; the psychological, in which he is regarded as the object of Ahab's fixation; and so on. No one meaning is settled upon for the whale and Ahab's pursuit of him; it may mean this and it may mean that, but the pursuit goes on with a significance that is no less intense for being uncertain. Melville creates a universe in which the inherited systems of thought and language that give meaning to events no longer work — no language can explain what occurs — but in which we are made to feel that events have meaning of an intense, immensely important, kind. Perhaps one of these ways of talking (say, the diabolic) is true? The ambiguity is a way of stating such a fear. And more than that: this structural ambiguity at once induces the reader to concentrate on the whale as the repository of some final meaning and frustrates him in his efforts to discover and state that meaning. Melville involves the reader directly in the disorganization of language that is the center of this book by challenging him to devise or choose a language in which to say what needs to be said about the whale — in which to express the significance of his own experience as a reader — and by then proving the inadequacy of every possibility. The reader's search for meaning is a direct parallel to Ahab's similar search.

There are other kinds and degrees of ambiguity of course, used with a great variety of purpose. It would be a life's work to try to analyze ambiguity as a phenomenon. Certainly, for example, "The Sick Rose" is an ambiguous poem — you would have a hard time even saying what it was "about." Is there a sense in which you can say that your inability to claim a clear meaning for the poem, one that you could paraphrase, is no loss — indeed, could you say that this ambiguity is part of the point, as it certainly is in *Moby Dick?* The passage from Thoreau is extremely clear in its claim for the private meaning of his relationship to the landscape, and in its rejection of the language of private property as a way of talking about it. This is about as direct and plain as ironic statement can be; yet where does it leave you? The claim is that the language of property does not work, yet it is not clear what does. Thoreau uses the very language he rejects to make his statement, with a simple negative to turn it his way. May it be that ambiguity here becomes total, itself uncontrolled? It may help you see the consequences of this sort of attempt to get on in the world if you ask how long someone could keep it up.[9]

Here is a famous poem, ambiguous in a somewhat different way:

9. The implications of Thoreau's way of imagining and talking about experience are the subject of Baird, "Corn Grows in the Night," 4 *Massachusetts Review* 93 (1962).

THE ROAD NOT TAKEN

Robert Frost

Two roads diverged in a yellow wood,
And sorry I could not travel both
And be one traveler, long I stood
And looked down one as far as I could
To where it bent in the undergrowth;

Then took the other, as just as fair,
And having perhaps the better claim,
Because it was grassy and wanted wear;
Though as for that, the passing there
Had worn them really about the same,

And both that morning equally lay
In leaves no step had trodden black.
Oh, I kept the first for another day!
Yet knowing how way leads on to way,
I doubted if I should ever come back.

I shall be telling this with a sigh
Somewhere ages and ages hence:
Two roads diverged in a wood, and I —
I took the one less traveled by,
And that has made all the difference.

Perhaps in your first reading you did not think this was an ambiguous statement, but a simple, really quite childish one. That is what I thought until someone asked this question: did the choice make "all the difference"? Did it make any difference at all? The poet says it did — or does he? What he says is that sometime, ages and ages hence, looking back on his life, he will sigh and say that it did. And what can actually be said of the choice about which he will have such emotions? As described in the first three stanzas it can have hardly any significance at all, certainly no meaning as a moral matter or as the expression of character. As advice on making choices, say from the old to the young, the poem would be simply no good. Is the poem perhaps not about choices at all, but about one's capacity for making fatuous remarks? The narrator looks back on a meaningless event, is tempted to describe it in a sentimental phrase (choosing the way "less traveled by") and catches himself just in time, just barely ("Though as for that, the passing there Had worn them really about the same"). He realizes that sometime he will not catch himself, that he will succumb to the temptation to look back and sigh, a foolish fond old man. The poet's use of this sentimental language — a cliché of his own invention — is ambiguous indeed, at once rejecting it and recognizing its seductive appeal. The recognition of weakness, the self-depreciation is a severely qualified claim of control: "I know something at least of my tendencies towards the foolish."

Below is a final and somewhat lengthy example of deliberate ambiguity. Billy Budd, in Melville's story of that name, is the model of a perfect sailor in every way: competent, strong, handsome, admired by the crew, and so known for his cheerful ability to make men forget their hatreds and troubles that he is known as the peacemaker. In a time shortly following two serious mutinies in the British fleet, he is falsely accused of conspiring to mutiny by Claggart, an officer who is the very ideal of evil, as Billy is of innocence. When accused and asked to answer, a speech impediment renders him silent; he fells Claggart with a fatal blow. He is being tried for this offense, by the captain and three officers, who have retired to make their decision.

BILLY BUDD*

Herman Melville

The marine — the same who had been the sentinel without the cabin-door at the time that the foretopman followed by the master-at-arms, entered it — he, standing by the sailor throughout their judicial proceedings, was now directed to take him back to the after compartment originally assigned to the prisoner and his custodian. As the twain disappeared from view, the three officers as partially liberated from some inward constraint associated with Billy's mere presence, simultaneously stirred in their seats. They exchanged looks of troubled indecision, yet feeling that decide they must and without long delay. For Captain Vere [was] for the time standing unconsciously with his back towards them, apparently in one of his absent fits, gazing out from a sashed porthole to windward upon the monotonous blank of the twilight sea. But the court's silence continuing, broken only at moments by brief consultations in low earnest tones, this seemed to assure him and encourage him. Turning, he to-and-fro paced the cabin athwart; in the returning ascent to windward, climbing the slant deck in the ship's lee roll; without knowing it symbolizing thus in his action a mind resolute to surmount difficulties even if against primitive instincts strong as the wind and the sea. Presently he came to a stand before the three. After scanning their faces he stood less as mustering his thoughts for expression, than as one inly deliberating how best to put them to well-meaning men not intellectually mature, men with whom it was necessary to

* Pages 242–248, 264–266 (1924; Freeman and Treeman ed. 1956). Footnotes are omitted.

demonstrate certain principles that were axioms to himself. Similar impatience as to talking is perhaps one reason that deters some minds from addressing any popular assemblies.

When speak he did, something both in the substance of what he said and his manner of saying it, showed the influence of unshared studies modifying and tempering the practical training of an active career. This, along with his phraseology now and then was suggestive of the grounds whereon rested that imputation of a certain pedantry socially alleged against him by certain naval men of wholly practical cast, captains who nevertheless would frankly concede that His Majesty's navy mustered no more efficient officers of their grade than "*Starry Vere.*"

What he said was to this effect: "Hitherto I have been but the witness, little more; and I should hardly think now to take another tone, that of your coadjutor, for the time, did I not perceive in you — at the crisis too — a troubled hesitancy, proceeding, I doubt not from the clashing of military duty with moral scruple — scruple vitalized by compassion. For the compassion how can I otherwise than share it. But, mindful of paramount obligation I strive against scruples that may tend to enervate decision. Not, gentlemen, that I hide from myself that the case is an exceptional one. Speculatively regarded, it well might be referred to a jury of casuists. But for us here acting not as casuists or moralists, it is a case practical and under martial law practically to be dealt with.

"But your scruples: do they move as in a dusk? Challenge them. Make them advance and declare themselves. Come now: do they import something like this: If, mindless of palliating circumstances we are bound to regard the death of the master-at-arms as the prisoner's deed, then does that deed constitute a capital crime whereof the penalty is a mortal one. But in natural justice is nothing but the prisoner's overt act to be considered? How can we adjudge to summary and shameful death a fellow-creature innocent before God, and whom we feel to be so? — Does that state it aright? You sign sad assent. Well, I too feel that, the full force of that. It is Nature. But do these buttons that we wear attest that our allegiance is to Nature? No, to the King. Though the ocean, which is inviolate Nature primeval, though this be the element where we move and have our being as sailors, yet as the King's officers lies our duty in a sphere correspondingly natural? So little is that true, that in receiving our commissions we in the most important regards ceased to be natural free-agents. When war is declared, are we the commissioned fighters previously consulted? We fight at command. If our judgments approve the war, that is but coincidence. So in other particulars. So now. For suppose condemnation were to follow these present proceedings. Would it be so much we ourselves that would condemn as it would be martial law operating through us? For that law and the rigor of it, we are not responsible. Our vowed responsibility is in this: That however pitilessly that law may operate, we nevertheless adhere to it and administer it.

"But the exceptional in the matter moves the heart within you. Even so too is mine moved. But let not warm hearts betray heads that should be cool. Ashore in a criminal case will an upright judge allow himself off the bench to be waylaid by some tender kinswoman of the accused seeking to touch him with her tearful plea? Well, the heart, sometimes the feminine in man, here is [as] that piteous woman. And hard though it be, she must here be ruled out."

He paused, earnestly studying them for a moment; then resumed.

"But something in your aspect seems to urge that it is not solely that heart that moves in you, but also the conscience, the private conscience. But tell me whether or not, occupying the position we do, private conscience should not yield to that imperial one formulated in the code under which alone we officially proceed?"

Here the three men moved in their seats, less convinced than agitated by the course of an argument troubling but the more the spontaneous conflict within. Perceiving which, the speaker paused for a moment; then abruptly changing his tone, went on.

"To steady us a bit, let us recur to the facts. — In war-time at sea a man-of-war's-man strikes his superior in grade, and the blow kills. Apart from its effect the blow itself is, according to the Articles of War, a capital crime. Furthermore — "

"Ay, Sir," emotionally broke in the officer of marines, "in one sense it was. But surely Budd purposed neither mutiny nor homicide."

"Surely not, my good man. And before a court less arbitrary and more merciful than a martial one that plea would largely extenuate. At the Last Assizes it shall acquit. But how here? We proceed under the law of the Mutiny Act. In feature no child can resemble his father more than that Act resembles in spirit the thing from which it derives — War. In His Majesty['s] service — in this ship indeed — there are Englishmen forced to fight for the King against their will. Against their conscience, for aught we know. Though as their fellow-creatures some of us may appreciate their position, yet as Navy Officers, what reck we of it? Still less recks the enemy. Our impressed men he would fain cut down in the same swath with our volunteers. As regards the enemy's naval conscripts, some of whom may even share our own abhorrence of the regicidal French Directory, it is the same on our side. War looks but to the frontage, the appearance. And the Mutiny Act, War's child, takes after the father. Budd's intent or non-intent is nothing to the purpose.

"But while, put to it by those anxieties in you which I cannot but respect, I only repeat myself — while thus strangely we prolong proceedings that should be summary — the enemy may be sighted and an engagement result. We must do; and one of two things must we do — condemn or let go."

"Can we not convict and yet mitigate the penalty?" asked the junior Lieutenant here speaking, and falteringly, for the first.

"Lieutenant, were that clearly lawful for us under the circumstances consider the consequence of such clemency. The people" (meaning the ship's company) "have native sense; most of them are familiar with our naval usage and tradition; and how would they take it? Even could you explain to them — which our official position forbids — they, long moulded by arbitrary discipline have not that kind of intelligent responsiveness that might qualify them to comprehend and discriminate. No, to the people the foretopman's deed, however it be worded in the announcement will be plain homicide committed in a flagrant act of mutiny. What penalty for that should follow, they know. But it does not follow. *Why?* They will ruminate. You know what sailors are. Will they not revert to the recent outbreak at the Nore? Ay, they know the well-founded alarm — the panic it struck throughout England. Your clement sentence they would account pusillanimous. They would think that we flinch, that we are afraid of them — afraid of practicing a lawful rigor singularly demanded at this juncture lest it should provoke new troubles. What shame to us such a conjecture on their part, and how deadly to discipline. You see then, whither prompted by duty and the law I steadfastly drive. But I beseech you, my friends, do not take me amiss. I feel as you do for this unfortunate boy. But did he know our hearts, I take him to be of that generous nature that he would feel even for us on whom in this military necessity so heavy a compulsion is laid."

How do you characterize what you read here? The captain is said to have a "mind resolute to surmount difficulties even if against primitive instincts as strong as the wind and sea." Are those primitive instincts good or bad? Is the resolution to surmount them a noble overcoming of soft-hearted weakness, or the insanely rigid application of law against every notion of justice? What does Melville tell you? How does he tell you? What is meant by the sentence: "But let not warm hearts betray heads that should be cool"? And where does Melville stand on the question whether the "private conscience" should not "yield to the imperial one"? If there will be acquittal at the "Last Assizes," why not at this trial? Is this the story of a wise but painful administration of justice in an imperfect world, where necessity takes its toll, or is it the example of a radical injustice speciously rationalized? If Melville does not answer these questions, why does he not? Is it that he is a bad writer? Or does a deliberate ambiguity as to both languages — of private conscience and the imperial one — enable Melville to make some other kind of statement?

Billy Budd is convicted, of course, and sentenced to hang. If you were writing the book, in what language might you consider describing the execution? Consider what Melville chose to do in the passage that follows. What language does he use to describe this death? Is the use of that language ironic, ambiguous, or perfectly direct?

The night so luminous on the spar-deck but otherwise on the cavernous ones below, levels so like the tiered galleries in a coalmine — the luminous night passed away. But, like the prophet in the chariot disappearing in heaven and dropping his mantle to Elisha, the withdrawing night transferred its pale robe to the breaking day. A meek shy light appeared in the East, where stretched a diaphanous fleece of white furrowed vapor. That light slowly waxed. Suddenly *eight bells* was struck aft, responded to by one louder metallic stroke from forward. It was four o'clock in the morning. Instantly the silver whistles were heard summoning all hands to witness punishment. Up through the great hatchways rimmed with racks of heavy shot, the watch below came pouring overspreading with the watch already on deck the space between the mainmast and foremast including that occupied by the capacious *launch* and the black booms tiered on either side of it, boat and booms making a summit of observation for the powder-boys and younger tars. A different group comprising one watch of topmen leaned over the side of the rail of that sea-balcony, no small one in a seventy-four, looking down on the crowd below. Man or boy none spake but in whisper, and few spake at all. Captain Vere — as before, the central figure among the assembled commissioned officers — stood nigh the break of the poop-deck facing forward. Just below him on the quarter-deck the marines in full equipment were drawn up much as at the scene of the promulgated sentence.

At sea in the old time, the execution by halter of a military sailor was generally from the fore-yard. In the present instance for special reasons the main-yard was assigned. Under an arm of that weather or lee [?] yard the prisoner was presently brought up, the Chaplain attending him. It was noted at the time and remarked upon afterwards, that in this final scene the good man evinced little or nothing of the perfunctory. Brief speech indeed he had with the condemned one, but the genuine Gospel was less on his tongue than in his aspect and manner towards him. The final preparations personal to the latter being speedily brought to an end by two boatswain's-mates, the consummation impended. Billy stood facing aft. At the penultimate moment, his words, his only ones, words wholly unobstructed in the utterance were these — "God bless Captain Vere!" Syllables so unanticipated coming from one with the ignominous hemp about his neck — a conventional felon's benediction directed aft towards the quarters of honor; syllables too delivered in the clear melody of a singing-bird on the point of launching from the twig, had a phenomenal effect, not unenhanced by the rare personal beauty of the young sailor spiritualized now through late experiences so poignantly profound.

Without volition as it were, as if indeed the ship's populace were the vehicles of some vocal current electric, with one voice from alow and aloft, came a resonant sympathetic echo — "God bless Captain Vere!" And yet at that instant Billy alone must have been in their hearts, even as he was in their eyes.

At the pronounced words and the spontaneous echo that voluminously rebounded them, Captain Vere, either through stoic self-control or a sort of momentary paralysis induced by emotional shock, stood erectly rigid as a musket in the ship-armorer's rack.

The hull deliberately recovering from the periodic roll to lee-ward was just regaining an even keel, when the last signal the preconcerted dumb one was given. At the same moment it chanced that the vapory fleece hanging low in the East, was shot through with a soft glory as of the fleece of the Lamb of God seen in mystical vision and simultaneously therewith, watched by the wedged mass of upturned faces, Billy ascended; and ascending, took the full rose of the dawn.

In the pinioned figure arrived at the yard-end, to the wonder of all no motion was apparent save that created by the ship's motion, in moderate weather so majestic in a great ship ponderously cannoned.

Now you know all. How is Billy Budd's death defined? What does Melville's ambiguity on this point enable him to say? One possible meaning is that this is a reenactment of the great Christian sacrifice, in which the innocent dies for the imperfections of others, righting a moral imbalance in the world. This is a Holy Event. Much of the language of course supports this meaning, and indeed we seem to be told that Billy and the captain both regard it as such.[10] Another possibility is that this is a barbaric, cruel, hypocritical, and unjust killing, an event without meaning in a universe without meaning. Melville does not seem to make his position clear on this central question: how can his silence possibly be explained? Can one regard Melville's refusal to take a position as essential to his point? One could say that as he dramatized the failure of meaning in *Moby Dick*, where it was first Ahab and secondarily the

10. For the view that Vere's solution to his moral dilemma is "at once unanswerable, dignified, and profound," see Y. Winters, *In Defense of Reason* 231 (Swallow ed. 1947).

reader who could not sustain the meaning that he tried to give the whale and his pursuit, here he forces the problem directly upon the reader. There can be no doubt about the enormous moral importance of the event, whatever view one takes of it — an innocent young man is deliberately put to death — but there is permanent doubt as to what it means. Melville not only creates a fictional world where events command attention by their importance and their dubiety of significance; he forces the reader to share the doubt as to meaning by keeping him in doubt of the one thing a reader can usually count on: the view of the author. Here a world is created like the one we live in: events are critically important, but no one can explain them with certainty. Language is made to break down and the burden is shifted to you.

We shall have occasion later in the course to explore somewhat more fully the ideas of metaphor, irony, and ambiguity. But what can now be said is that these are all ways of controlling a language by standing outside it and pointing to something else, something the language does not state. These are ways of talking two ways at once. The writer uses a language and at the same time expresses a recognition of what it leaves out.[11] Can you find a way to live and work within the language system of the law and be ironic or ambiguous about what you do? As a person speaking to others or to yourself, you may be able to express this sort of relationship with the law; but while acting as a lawyer, how can it be done? Is it possible to use legal language in a way that points to or recognizes what the law leaves out? You might say that that is exactly what Captain Vere finds he cannot do. Is this a paradigm for the whole of your experience of law? Must we say with Thoreau: "I must not lose any of my freedom by being a farmer or landholder. Most who enter on any profession are doomed men. The world might as well sing a dirge over them forthwith."

d. The Power of the Language Maker

As the course proceeds, you will be asked again and again to write as a lawyer, and I hope that as you do so you can bring to bear the reading you have just done. How will you control the legal language system, what success and mastery can you hope for? I have suggested that the lawyer suffers from disadvantages from which the poet and novelist are

11. Is this a general characteristic of all good writing? Even in the natural or social sciences a good piece of work will put forth a line of argument and criticize it at the same time, it will assert and doubt at once. See, e.g., Zimring, "The Medium Is the Message: Firearm Caliber as a Determinant of Death From Assault," 1 *J. Legal Studies* 97 (1972). And one could say that the most difficult task of one who plans to use the languages of systems analysis, economics, or accounting is to know with some sureness what each is good for and what not, that the essence of control is an understanding of limits, perceived from outside.

free, that he cannot simply adopt their traditional techniques for his own use. But the lawyer has one advantage that others often lack: he is one who makes the language system he uses. If he does not like what he sees his language system to be doing, he can argue for its change; if he is a judge or legislator, he may be able to decree its change. The lawyer can help fashion the language that limits him, he is its artificer. This relationship is denied the ironic artist, who always says of the language he uses that it is in some way no good. It is difficult to see how the roles of maker and mocker can easily be united with respect to the same language.

And the powers and satisfactions of a maker of a language are not minor:

> It is difficult to disconnect the idea of ships' anchors from the idea of the ship's chief mate — the man who sees them go down clear and come up sometimes foul; because not even the most unremitting care can always prevent a ship swinging to winds and tide, from taking an awkward turn of the cable round stock or fluke. Then the business of "getting the anchor" and securing it afterwards is unduly prolonged, and made a weariness to the chief mate. He is the man who watches the growth of the cable — a sailor's phrase which has all the force, precision, and imagery of technical language that, created by simple men with keen eyes for the real aspect of the things they see in their trade, achieves the just expression seizing upon the essential, which is the ambition of the artist in words. Therefore the sailor will never say, "cast anchor," and the shipmaster aft will hail his chief mate on the forecastle in impressionistic phrase: "How does the cable grow?" Because "grow" is the right word for the long drift of a cable emerging aslant under the strain, taut as a bow-string above the water. And it is the voice of the keeper of the ship's anchors that will answer: "Grows right ahead, sir," or "Broad on the bow," or whatever concise and deferential shout will fit the case.*

Who else makes a language or contributes to its creation? Think of people in various trades and professions and the languages they have made: the carpenter, the doctor, the architect, the mechanic. Can the law in your hands be a professional language of such a kind?

WRITING ASSIGNMENT 2: Controlling a Language System[12]

Part One

• *Write or find a brief passage in which you show a person expressing himself in legal language and exhibiting a dangerous overconfidence in*

* Joseph Conrad, *The Mirror of the Sea,* Chapter 6 (1906).

12. Supplementary assignments exploring additional aspects of the issues raised in the text are collected in the Appendix.

that language. In an additional paragraph, explain clearly and specifically how your speaker is overconfident.

In order to do this, you will have to decide what you mean by "overconfidence." This requires you to begin to make up your own language of critical judgment. The statement you use can be that of lawyer, judge, legislator, or even layman, but its language should be legal.

Part Two

• Write or find a brief passage in which you show a person using legal language and controlling it. Explain what you mean by "control" and what, if any, relationship there is between this form of control and the traditional forms discussed earlier in this section.

WRITING ASSIGNMENT 2 (ALTERNATIVE): Good Writing

Part One

• Find a passage of legal or nonlegal literature which you consider good writing. It should be a passage of some importance or significance — its excellence should be difficult, not easy — though of course it can be amusing or comic. Try to find a passage that could be a source of real satisfaction and pleasure to the writer and the reader.

Part Two

• Explain your judgment of this passage. In doing so, be sure to explain and support your language of criticism as well.

Part Three

• Look at your response to part two: Is that good writing as you have defined it? Can you rewrite it so that it is?

If there is one assignment that sets the problem of the whole course, this is it. Like the assignment on conversations (Appendix, Supplementary Writing Assignment 2-1), it could hardly be repeated too often.

You may feel that you ought to be given more guidance with this question, and in fact some proposed approaches follow shortly. But the essential uncertainty in this and many of the other assignments in this book is deliberate: it is my hope to ask questions that are incomplete, that do not imply an answer, that ask you to finish making the question as you work out your response to it. You are not being asked, that is, to approximate some answer I have in mind, or to write along any set lines *at all; instead of telling you what to do, these questions are meant to push you off to make your own way in your own direction. A considerable measure of the energy upon which the course proceeds must come from you. This is an invitation to talk about the writer's excellence in any way that interests you. If you feel at a loss as to how to proceed, the following suggestions may help.*

Proposal One

• *Is success in this passage a matter of writing more than one way, of using more than one language or speaking in more than one voice? If you wish to say so, identify the different ways of speaking and the relationship the writer establishes between or among them.*

Proposal Two

• *Draft a paraphrase of your passage, converting it to a version in plain English and making a statement of its message or meaning. Now compare the paraphrase with the original and explain what the paraphrase leaves out. What does it fail to do that the original achieves? Why would anyone write the original, or read it, instead of the paraphrase?*

This proposal asks you to examine the common talk about language which assumes that it is simply a way of communicating information, and that its greatest virtues are accordingly efficiency and accuracy. Often, of course, language is used for these purposes, but often it is not, and in such cases this view of what a writer does is hopelessly misleading. The suggestion is that you ask of your passage what purposes the writer has beyond the communication of information; then ask how he tries to achieve them and how well he succeeds. This is meant to be a way of asking, "Is this good writing? Why?" without inviting an answer that says it conveys thoughts clearly or uses precise terms. You are urged to see the document you read as a part of life, not as an exercise, and when you ask yourself what purposes the writer has, do not limit yourself to intellectual purposes: he may be trying to weasel out of something, or to tease or challenge his reader, or to give a false impression of his intentions or of the facts, or to make someone feel angry or at ease or any of the things that we do every day.

Proposal Three

• *Using your passage as an example of what the good writer can do, how would you teach good writing? Can you figure out principles of good writing that can be articulated for the guidance of aspiring writers? If not, what can you possibly do for those who seek your advice?*

Here is a passage on good writing which may be of interest: "It is the fault of some excellent writers — DeQuincey's first impressions on seeing London suggest it to me — that they express themselves with too great fullness and detail. They give the most faithful, natural, and lifelike account of their sensations, mental and physical, but they lack moderation and sententiousness. They do not affect us by an ineffectual earnestness and a reserve of meaning, like a stutterer; they say all they mean. Their sentences are not concentrated and nutty. Sentences which suggest far more than they say, which have an atmosphere about them, which do not merely report an old, but make a new, impression; sentences which suggest as many things and are as durable as a Roman aqueduct; to frame these, that is the art of writing. Sentences which are expensive, towards which so many volumes, so much life, went; which lie like boulders on the page, up and down or across; which contain the seed of other sentences, not mere repetition, but creation; which a man might sell his grounds and castles to build. If DeQuincey had suggested each of his pages in a sentence and passed on, it would have been far more excellent writing. His style is nowhere kinked and knotted up into something hard and significant, which you could swallow like a diamond, without digesting." H. D. Thoreau, Journal Aug. 22, 1851.

Can you make any sense of this view of good writing? How does it apply to the lawyer? You might be tempted to look on this as an obstinate and perverse statement by a transcendentalist crank, one who says that good sentences are not those that give a "faithful, natural and lifelike account" but those that are "nutty," or like an aqueduct or boulder, or are kinked and knotted up into something hard and indigestible. The good writer is like a stutterer? An impossible view! But as you look at your own sentences, is this passage one that you can disregard?

CHAPTER 2

THE LIMITS AND RESOURCES OF LEGAL LANGUAGE: AN INTRODUCTION TO YOUR LITERARY CIRCUMSTANCES

In this chapter we begin with what we worked out in the first: the sense that to speak in an inherited and formal language is a dangerous enterprise, and that for one who engages in it, as the lawyer does, the management of just the right relationship with that language is critical to his success, both in the exercise of his art and in the claims he makes for the meaning of what he does. I have suggested the barest beginnings of a way to talk about such a relationship: that the writer wishes to "control" the language he has been given, so that it is he and not it that determines the shape and meaning of what he says; and that an essential part of this control is a qualification of the confidence — or overconfidence — in a particular language that its use normally entails. While the traditional means of controlling a language — by metaphor, irony, and ambiguity — are likely to be of little use to us as lawyers, or of use only in special ways, we may be able to learn much from them, especially since they share an essential characteristic: in each case the writer asserts control over a language by taking a position outside it, from which he may use it to say, or at least to recognize, more than the language in other hands would be made to say, more than it seems to want to say, something new and different. The writer, that is, speaks two ways at once: using a language and at the same time recognizing what it leaves out. He is defined less by the language he uses than by the relationship with it that he can establish and maintain, less by his material than by his art.

But part of any art is knowing one's materials well, and in this chapter we shall begin to examine the legal language system as it exists, as it comes down to you, made by others for your use. It is the stuff upon which you will work as a lawyer and writer, it is your marble and canvas: what are its peculiar limits and resources, its strengths and weaknesses? To what purposes is it readily adaptable, to what not? What are the implications of its traditional forms, and how can they be managed? The nature of your inherited language shapes your task as a writer much as marble or steel shapes that of the sculptor — perhaps even more, since you cannot choose (as he can) among various materials, and since the language imposed upon you has, beyond its inherent limitations, the quality of defining the habitual expectations, the cast of mind, of the audience with which you will necessarily deal. How are you to come to understand this language that is given you, its secret failings and capacities? How are you to master it, or remake it for the future? What success can you fashion for yourself, as a lawyer and a writer?

This is, of course, the major question of the book as a whole, and you are not expected to produce a definitive response in seven days. The present chapter approaches the matter in three sets of readings and writing assignments, each operating in its own way: in Sections B and C you will be asked to write as lawyer and legislator, respectively, in response to particular problems that will be set for you, and to examine the limits of what you can do with your professional language in those situations; Section A is more general and diffuse both in purpose and form. It consists of a series of contrasting passages, legal and nonlegal, meant to invite the most open and wide-ranging consideration of how it is that lawyers think and speak — to place legal language in a universe of languages — and to begin a process of comparative reading and thinking that will go on throughout the book. (It is as a mark of the particular qualities of this section that I call it an anthology.) This set of passages and questions is not meant to reflect an analytic scheme (though I hope there is some sense to their arrangement) nor to build to a particular point, but to raise what might be called a series of first and second questions, to define the beginnings of several lines of inquiry (some of which we shall pursue, others not). A line of questioning may, for example, be begun with respect to one set of passages, then dropped in favor of another approach in the next set (though it may very well reappear in a later chapter). The passages chosen are meant to be sufficiently rich and provocative that a class or a writing assignment could be based on almost any one of them, and this means that what you do with them is mainly your responsibility, not mine or your teacher's. The anthology is not meant to exemplify a particular theory of the lawyer's use of language, but to begin some tentative lines of inquiry, to invite you to make and work on some questions of your own. We are still making a beginning here.

I can suggest some questions, however, that might help you draw connections among these rather disparate passages. As you read these samples of legal and nonlegal speech, for example, keep asking yourself this: of all that might be said about an event, or as part of one, what do the people of the law find it possible to say? What does their system of speech and thought include, what does it leave out? What can people achieve that way, and what not? How do your responses to these questions define the activity we call law and the people who give themselves to it? The anthology is meant to encourage you to start making what might be called a literary criticism of the law, a way of defining and assessing particular failures and successes. Again and again you will be asked what seems to you to be worth saying about a particular passage — to work out your own sense of what you admire, of what you deplore, and why. In working out your answers you will define an art, and this will be our subject.

It may be best to read this anthology through once carefully and slowly, in a sitting or two, and then go back and worry hard over some passages or questions that especially interest you.

A. *YOUR LANGUAGE IN A UNIVERSE OF LANGUAGES — A COMPARATIVE ANTHOLOGY ON DEATH*

The passages in this section all deal with the same topic, death, which is meant to provide a common subject for the comparison of different language systems at work. Death is a universal experience about which many people have had much to say, expressing their thoughts and feelings in a literature of extraordinary intensity and diversity. More than that: it is a literature of great importance, for death — we are told by the psychiatrists — is perhaps the fact of existence most difficult and important to come to terms with. It might be a test of a person's emotional health to ask how he deals with the fact of death; here we ask that question of the law and its language.

You might say that this anthology is meant to examine, perhaps in exaggerated terms, the sense we have all had of the defective expressiveness of the legal language system, of its incompleteness as a system of expression. Suggest to a nonlawyer friend that legal language is an imperfect medium of speech, that it does not permit one to say all that needs to be said about an event, and I imagine you will be greeted with warm agreement. In fact, you may be told that it is dry, technical stuff that has no relation to the human experiences it describes and regulates, that its complex logic is heartless and irrational. Without going that far, I think you can see there is a problem here; and if you consider what proportion of everything you say in your lifetime will be said in the language of the law, the problem should take on quite a personal significance. You would not want said of you what Dickens said of Mr. Tulkinghorn in *Bleak House*, that "he never converses, when not professionally consulted."

It might put you in the right frame of mind for the readings that follow to ask what sort of novel you could make out of the materials of the law: what sorts of characters would people it? What events would occur? What could be said in this language about the most important events of human life? I hope the comparison of legal and nonlegal speech will establish for us some common understanding of what the law leaves out, a sense of possibilities that seem never to have been considered. You are looking at your own future in the law from the outside here, and it may help to ask again this general question: given the other alternatives, why would anyone want to spend his time reading and writing the language of the law?

One final word: the occasions for and kinds of legal speech on the subject of death are too numerous and varied for a collection such as this to be any more than suggestive. Only a few examples are given, and you are urged to supply others from your own reading and imagination.

1. *What the Law Leaves Out: The Law Among Other Possibilities for Expression*

a. *The Georgetown Hospital Case: A Paradigm of Legal Speech?*

APPLICATION OF THE PRESIDENT AND DIRECTORS OF GEORGETOWN COLLEGE, INC.
331 F.2d 1010 (D.C. Cir. 1964)

PER CURIAM. Upon consideration of a pleading styled "Petition for Rehearing En Banc" in the above-entitled matter and an opposition thereto, it is

Ordered by the court en banc that said petition is denied.

MILLER, J. (dissenting): . . . On September 17, 1963, two attorneys appeared at the chambers of District Judge Edward A. Tamm and tendered the following order, which they requested him to sign:

ORDER

United States District Court for the District of Columbia Civil Division

In re: Application of the President and Directors of Georgetown College, Inc., a Body Corporate

This cause having come on to be heard upon application of The President and Directors of Georgetown College, Inc., a body corporate, owning and operating Georgetown University Hospital, and it being represented by counsel for the applicant that a Mrs. Jesse [*sic*] E. Jones is presently a patient at Georgetown University Hospital and that she is in extremis and it being further represented that the physician in attendance, the chief resident at Georgetown Hospital, Edwin Westura, is of the opinion that blood transfusions are necessary immediately in order to save her life and it being further represented by the applicant that consent to the administration thereof can be obtained neither from the patient nor her husband; it is therefore

ORDERED that the applicant acting through its duly accredited and licensed physicians in attendance may administer such transfusions as are in the opinion of the physicians in attendance necessary to save her life.

Although the proposed order was styled "Application of The President and Directors of Georgetown College, Inc., a Body Corporate," there was no such proceeding pending in the District Court; there had been no complaint, petition or formal written application filed. The only "application" was the oral request of the attorneys that the tendered order be signed and entered. To this day, there is nothing on file in the District Court Clerk's office with reference to this "application." Judge Tamm endorsed on the paper the word "Denied," which of course meant that he was denying the oral application for the order. It is plain, I think, that at the very least Judge Tamm's denial was based on the fact that there was nothing before him upon which he could act, that the jurisdiction of the District Court had not been properly invoked, and that there was no pending case or controversy.

About 4:00 p.m. on September 17 the same attorneys appeared, unannounced, at the chambers of a judge of this court and requested an immediate review of Judge Tamm's action denying the application for authority to administer a transfusion to a patient at the hospital, said to be in imminent danger of death from loss of blood. They did not file a written petition for review of Judge Tamm's refusal to sign the order but merely orally requested a single judge to take the action which Judge Tamm had just refused to take. The appellate judge spoke by telephone with the hospital's chief resident physician who confirmed the representations made by counsel and thereupon the judge proceeded to the hospital. There he spoke to the husband of the patient who advised that, on religious grounds, he would not approve a blood transfusion for his wife. The judge advised the husband to obtain counsel immediately but, after brief consideration, the husband declined to do so. The judge then called at the patient's room and repeated to her what the doctors had said. Her only reply audible to him was, "Against my will."

Then, at 5:20 p.m. on September 17, at Georgetown Hospital, the appellate judge signed the order which Judge Tamm had declined to sign and then signed the following additional order, which was filed by our Clerk the same day:

The applicant having appeared before me for the issuance of a writ permitting the applicant to administer such transfusions as are in the opinion of the physicians in attendance necessary to save the life of Mrs. Jesse [*sic*] E. Jones and it appearing that on September 17, 1963, the District Court denied such application; and a hearing having been conducted before me at which all the interested parties were present and upon due consideration had thereon, I signed, pursuant to the provisions of Section 1651, Title 28, United States Code, the attached order granting such relief which counsel had presented to the District Court Judge and which had been denied by him, it is therefore

ORDERED that the Clerk of this court is hereby directed to file this memorandum order and attachment.

The blood transfusion was accomplished immediately after the order was signed.

On September 19 the appellate judge filed a memorandum concerning his action, in which he said inter alia:

It was obvious that the woman was not in a mental condition to make a decision. I was reluctant to press her because of the seriousness of her condition and because I felt that to suggest repeatedly the imminence of death without blood *might place a strain on her religious convictions.* I asked her whether she would oppose the blood transfusion if the court allowed it. She indicated, as best I could make out, that it would not then be her responsibility. [Emphasis added.]

And on September 20 — three days after the transfusion had been accomplished — the hospital filed affidavits by four physicians to the effect that the transfusion had been necessary.

On October 14, 1963, Jessie E. Jones, the patient, filed a petition for a rehearing en banc and for an order vacating and quashing the order of September 17 which authorized the transfusion. The petition states the question presented as follows: "The question is whether a free adult citizen of the United States can be forced against her will to accept medical treatment to which she objects on both religious and medical grounds. . . ."

I am not now concerned, however, with the substantive questions presented by the petition for rehearing; I am disturbed by the procedural aspects of the situation. In the description of the nature of the proceedings the petition for rehearing says: "The procedure by which the matter came before this Court is not clear to counsel, but no issue is raised on the point at this time." It seems clear to me, however, that the matter did not properly come before this court and that, had it been duly presented on appeal, one judge of this court was not authorized to make a summary disposition of the matter on the merits. These procedural defects are, therefore, fatal to the validity of the purported orders entered September 17 by a single judge when no appeal had actually been filed. Argument that a court is justified, in physical circumstances such as were present here, in ordering blood transfusions against the will of an adult patient necessarily presupposes a properly constituted court and an action actually filed and pending before it. Such argument, no matter how extensive and persuasive, cannot validate the action which was taken here because it cannot destroy the basic facts which make the purported orders mere nullities: that no action was filed in the District Court and that no appeal was filed in this court; and that, had there been an actual appeal, a single appellate judge was not authorized to act. . . .

Under Article III, Section 2, of the Constitution of the United States, the judicial power extends only to cases and controversies. Although this Section defines and limits judicial power, it does not prescribe the particular method by which that power may be invoked. The method of invoking it is provided by Rule 3 of the Federal Rules of Civil Procedure, which reads: "A civil action is commenced by filing a complaint with the court." As has been shown, there was no complaint filed here, so a civil action was not commenced and the power of the District Court was not properly invoked. I do not understand that one may institute a civil action merely by entering the chambers of a district judge and asking him to sign a proffered order; nor that an appeal from his refusal may be taken by orally requesting a single circuit judge to review it.

Even when a case or controversy is properly presented to a Court of Appeals, one judge thereof is not empowered to take the decisive action which was taken here. The determination of such matters is committed to a division of three judges, of which two constitute a quorum, or to the court en banc. . . .

I think that, instead of merely denying the petition for rehearing, we should dismiss it on the ground that there was no case or controversy presented or determined and that consequently there is nothing to rehear. But, whether the petition for rehearing be denied or dismissed, the purported orders of September 17 should be expunged so there would be nothing in our records which could be cited as a precedent for future similar action by a single appellate judge. We have inherent power to take that action sua sponte.

I do not mean to impugn the motives of our colleague who signed these orders. He was impelled, I am sure, by humanitarian impulses and doubtless was himself under considerable strain because of the critical situation in which he had become involved. In the interval of about an hour and twenty minutes between the appearance of the attorneys at his chambers and the signing of the order at the hospital, the judge had no opportunity for research as to the substantive legal problems and procedural questions involved. He should not have been asked to act in these circumstances.

BURGER, J. . . . It is at the periphery of the boundaries of power where the guidelines are less clear that an appealing claim presents difficult choices, but this is precisely the area in which restraint is called for in light of the absolute nature of our powers and the finality which often, as here, attends our acts. But we should heed Cardozo's counsel of restraint and reconcile ourselves to the idea that there are myriads of problems and troubles which judges are powerless to solve; and this is as it should be. Some matters of essentially private concern and others of enormous public concern, are beyond the reach of judges.

[Here is what Judge Wright, the single judge who had ordered the transfusion, had to say at the end of his separate opinion, 331 F.2d 1000, 1009: "The final, and compelling, reason for granting the emergency writ was that a life hung in the balance. There was no time for research and reflection. Death could have mooted the cause in a matter of minutes, if action were not taken to preserve the status quo. To refuse to act, only to find later that the law required action, was a risk I was unwilling to accept. I determined to act on the side of life."]

QUESTIONS

1. *To say that the single circuit judge should not have made the order that saved the woman's life, on the grounds that no complaint or petition had been properly filed and that the court lacked a quorum, seems to carry sterile formalism to its ultimate limits: what sort of blinders permit one to say of the judge in such a case that "there was nothing before him"? Or of the absence of legal power to act, that "this is as it should be"? Indeed, these opinions may seem so obviously wrong to you that it seems unfair to use them as examples of legal expression, especially when they are minority opinions.*
   a. *If this is your view, draft a brief opinion sustaining the order, in which you define the circumstances in which a trial court may act without the filing of a petition or complaint, and in which an appellate judge may act without a quorum of his court: in what classes of case, in what sorts of emergency? Can you imagine circumstances in which one would wish to make exceptions to your rule? Should a judge waiting for the subway be able to order two brawlers to stop, and hold them in contempt when they refuse? Or decide with legal force a dispute between two neighbors over a boundary line? Why not? (A case on whether a judge has acted as a judge: Havey v. Kropp, 458 F.2d 1054 (6th Cir. 1972).)*
   b. *Does Judge Miller's opinion perhaps reflect a basic truth: that a court must act formally or not at all, that the very idea of a judge (as opposed to a man) is a formal notion? He is a judge rather than a man, that is,*

only when the conditions to his jurisdiction exist; under our rule of law, he has no power as an individual, in himself, but only the power of an office, by whose definition alone he exists as a judge. He cannot act outside the limits of his official role as an official but only as a usurper, illegally. There is no way for him to qualify the supreme confidence expressed by the law in the lines it has drawn, no way to recognize what the law leaves out, because as a judge he is the creature of that language. The judge then is like one of the characters in Shakespeare's Troilus and Cressida: wholly defined by his language, able to speak only one way. Is there any way out of this situation for him, any way he can deal with it?

2. *The obvious justification for the single judge's extraordinary conduct here is that he acted to save a life. Was he right to do so? How would you go about deciding that question?*

   The usual way in which a judge decides what he ought to do is by an established procedure, formal and adversary in nature, by which the judge is given the opportunity to hear every side of the question, to look up the law, and to compare this case with earlier ones. This process is generally approved. Here it was not used. Can we say that the reason it was not used is that it could not have worked, that the judge threw out the procedure to save that for which it exists, namely, the right result?

   If you think the answer is a simple affirmative, recall that many old people have a terrible fear that they will be kept artificially alive for unnecessary months and years, miserable and at great expense. And this woman seems to have had an even greater repugnance to transfusions. She was heard to say, "Against my will." Who was the judge to disregard her will?

   How would you have acted in his place, and why?

3. *Notice that the judge does give an explanation for what he did in a sort of legal language: he acted "to preserve the status quo." Was his response to the emergency therefore not inconsistent with but actually justified by the procedural system he seems to disregard? Or is his remark a specious use of legal language?*
4. *How do you suppose Melville would portray contrasting views of what the judge should have done in this case? You might draft a passage from an imaginary Melville novel on this subject.*
5. *Is the lawyer likewise defined procedurally — by the rules and practices of an institution of which he is a part — or is he a free and independent soul? Is he ever told by forces outside of himself that he may not speak to certain matters or, if he is to speak, how he must do so?*

b. *One Way the Lawyer Speaks About Death: The Will*

WILL OF RICHARD HARRY BLACK III*

FOURTH: Under the will of my late mother, who died in 1953, a trust was established for my benefit with the Old Line Trust Company,

* A. J. Casner, *Estate Planning* 1267, 1273–1276 (3d ed. 1961; Supp. 1972).

of Boston, Massachusetts, as trustee. On my death the trustee is directed to distribute the principal to, or for the benefit of, any one or more of the limited class consisting of my wife, my issue then living or born thereafter, spouses of my issue and charities in such amounts and proportions and for such estates and interests and upon such terms, trusts, conditions and limitations and generally in such manner as I shall appoint by will. I hereby exercise said power of appointment by directing the said trustee to hold or dispose of the principal of said trust as follows:

1. If my children, Richard Harry Black IV and Margaret Black Logan, both survive me, to pay the principal in equal shares to my said children.

2. If only one of my said children survives me and the one who predeceases me leaves no issue who survive me, to pay the principal to the child of mine who survives me.

3. If only one of my said children survives me and the one who predeceases me leaves issue who survive me, to pay one half of the principal to the child who survives me and to hold one half of the principal in trust for the issue of my deceased child in accordance with the provisions of Section 7 of this Article FOURTH.

4. If neither of my said children survives me and only one of my said children leaves issue who survive me, to hold the principal in trust for the issue of my deceased child in accordance with the provisions of Section 7 of this Article FOURTH.

5. If neither of my said children survives me but each of my said children leaves issue who survive me, to hold one half of the principal in trust for the issue of one deceased child of mine and to hold the other half of the principal in trust for the issue of my other deceased child in accordance with the provisions of Section 7 of this Article FOURTH.

6. If no issue of mine survives me, to pay the net income to my said wife for her life and on the death of my said wife, or on my death if my said wife does not survive me, to pay the principal to THE BLACK FAMILY FOUNDATION created by indenture of trust dated.......... , 19......,[177] if it is then in existence, and appointment to it is permissible, otherwise to ....[178]

7. The trustee is directed as follows with respect to the trust for the issue of a deceased child of mine:

(a) The trustee shall divide the trust property into as many equal shares as there are children of such deceased child of mine who survive me and deceased children of such deceased child of mine who leave issue who survive me. The trustee shall pay one of such equal shares to

177. Insert the date when the indenture of trust was executed.
178. Insert the name of a charity.

the issue of a deceased child of such deceased child of mine, such issue to take *per stirpes*; and the trustee shall hold in a separate trust one of such equal shares for each living child of such deceased child of mine as follows:

(i) If such child has attained the age of thirty (30) years, the trustee shall pay the trust fund to such child.

(ii) If such child has not attained the age of thirty (30) years then the trustee shall accumulate the income until such child attains the age of thirty (30) years, or until twenty-one (21) years after the death of the survivor of myself and my children,[178a] or until such child dies, whichever event first occurs, provided that if the event first to occur occurs within nine (9) years and one day after my death, then the income shall be accumulated until nine (9) years and one day after my death.[179] When the period of accumulation designated in the preceding sentence has come to an end, the trustee shall pay to such child the principal and accumulated income; if such child is not then living, the trustee shall pay the principal and accumulated income to such child's issue then living, such issue to take *per stirpes*; if such child is not then living and no issue of such child is then living, the trustee shall pay the principal and accumulated income to the issue then living of such deceased child of mine, such issue to take *per stirpes*, provided always, however, that if an issue of such deceased child of mine who would be entitled to a share is one for whom another share is then being held in trust under this Section 7, the share of such issue shall be added to the share being held in trust for such issue and henceforth administered accordingly; if such child is not then living and no issue of such child is then living and no issue of such deceased child of mine is then living, the trustee shall pay the principal and accumulated income to my issue then living, such issue to take *per stirpes*, provided always, however, that if an issue of mine who would be entitled to a share is one for whom

178a. It must be kept in mind that Mr. Black III is exercising a power of appointment given him under the will of his mother, who died in 1953. Thus the measuring lives must be persons alive when his mother died. Mr. Black's present children were both alive in 1953, and if he does not have another child before he dies, the measuring lives referred to will keep any interests created by the exercise of the power from violating the rule against perpetuities. If he has another child before he dies, the result should be the same because his reference to "my children" in the context clearly refers to his son and daughter named earlier in the Article. [Supp. 1972.]

179. The nine-year period is inserted to take advantage of 1954 I.R.C. §665(b)(4), quoted infra page 1368. Is this nine-year period essential in view of the fact that the trust created by the exercise of the power is a continuation of the trust created under the will of the testator's mother, who died in 1953? — Ed.

The nine-year period has no significance in relation to the operation of the throwback rule under the Tax Reform Act of 1969. See the discussion of that Act supra Supp. page 742, note 104. [Supp. 1972.]

another share is then being held in trust under this Section 7, the share of such issue shall be added to the share being held in trust for such issue and henceforth administered accordingly; if such child is not then living and no issue of such child is then living and no issue of such deceased child of mine is then living and no issue of mine is then living and my said wife is not then living, the trustee shall pay the principal and accumulated income to THE BLACK FAMILY FOUNDATION created by indenture of trust dated ...., 19......,[180] if it is then in existence, and appointment to it is permissible, otherwise to ....;[181] if such child is not then living and no issue of such child is then living and no issue of such deceased child of mine is then living and no issue of mine is then living but my said wife is then living, the trustee shall hold the principal and accumulated income in trust as follows:

(aa) To pay the net income therefrom to my said wife for her life.

(bb) On the death of my said wife, to pay the entire trust fund to THE BLACK FAMILY FOUNDATION, created by indenture of trust dated ...., 19......,[182] if it is then in existence, and appointment to it is permissible, otherwise to.............................[183]

QUESTIONS

1. *What is the death of his children made to mean in Mr. Black's will?*
   a. *Is this what the death of your children would mean to you?*
   b. *Would you ever write this way? When and why?*
2. *Notice that Mr. Black is a fictional person and that the will is a form, not a real will. This form defines the death of his children as meaning exactly the same thing for each testator who uses it. This is not a normal assumption about human life and emotion: why should the law and lawyer make it, then? Is the use of forms in this sense a fundamental characteristic of legal speech?*
3. *You may be inclined to say that while the will is of course not a complete statement of a response to an anticipated death, it is a perfectly appropriate and highly intelligent form of speech: technical language serving technical ends.*
   a. *If that is your view, draft a paragraph setting it forth, in which you define "technical language," "technical ends," and "appropriate."*
   b. *To say that this is a legitimate form of technical speech is not to say that it has any interest for reader or writer, however. Does this writing have any interest for you, or is it just an engineer's manual?*

180. Insert the date when the indenture of trust was executed.
181. Insert the name of a charity.
182. Insert the date when the indenture of trust was executed.
183. Insert the name of a charity.

c. Can you imagine how one might read or write such a passage with real interest, how this might be an activity in which you would want to engage?

4. We have here traced out two fundamental questions. First you have been asked how a particular sort of legal speech, which at first seems dead or drastically inadequate, can be explained and justified, if at all. The most common response is to say that the law is not meant to be a way of saying all that one wishes to say in one's life, but to serve particular ends, and that it is to be approved if it is suited to these. The second question grants all that, and shifts the burden to you: are these ends, these purposes, worthy activities for you in your life, or have you just defined a kind of living and writing in which you can have no interest? This question may carry you back to the first one with a new sense of its complexities, of what it puts at stake.

5. Look now at the will as a piece of writing, as an intellectual and literary performance, and see if you can discover the art and life that lie behind it.
   a. Do you see a mind actively controlling a language system here, recognizing what it leaves out, forcing it to operate in an original fashion?
   b. Or is legal language here controlled in the lawyer's way, by being remade to say exactly what the lawyer wishes to say?
   c. It may help you work out a sense of the art of this writing to ask if you are competent to judge it, to approve or disapprove the clauses you read. If the answer is no, how do you explain why that is so? What would you need to know or do if you were to judge the quality of this writing?
   d. If you are inclined to regard this instrument as dead writing, of no interest whatever, ask yourself what litigation over the meaning or legality of its clauses might involve. Would that be a simple, dead process too? Does the existence of that possibility define an art for the draftsman?

6. It may be that there is a life of difficulty and complexity behind this instrument, an art required for its construction, but what do these activities have to do with the death with which they deal? The art is not an art by which death is faced and addressed, not a way of claiming a meaning (or no meaning) for that event, but something else entirely. Into what does the law convert this future death?

7. Here is an agonizing statement from Milam v. Stanley, 33 Ky. 783, 111 S.W. 296 (1908). Do you suppose the law gives this letter any significance at all? If so, what?

"My Dear Loving Daughters:

"I guess my last hope is gone. I don't want you all to grieve after me for I think I will be better off than to be in jail, for I think I am prepared to go and want to ask one thing of you all is to meet me in heaven. Jennie, Lula and Bettie and Mary, I want you to understand that I am as innocent of the charge which I have to die for as an angel in heaven, and it does me good to know that God knows that I am not guilty. Jennie, tell John to see that my body is taken home and buried in our own graveyard, and get Stinson to preach my funeral. Tell him I am at rest. I want to make you and Lula a deed to that house and lot, and I don't want you and her to ever have any trouble over it. Jennie, I don't do this because

I think more of you and Lula than I do of Mary and Bettie, but I do it because you both attended to your dear old mother so good. I hope to soon meet her in heaven. Jennie, Mary has got enough of my money to bury me, I guess. So this is from your loving father,

"W. R. Fletcher.

"To Jennie and Lula, may God bless you all, is my prayer.

"Yours,
"W. R. F."

8. *As you read the will that follows, ask in what ways it is similar to Mr. Black's will and in what ways different from it.*

WILL OF EDMUND BURKE*

If my dear Son & friend had survived me, any Will would have been unnecessary but since it has pleased God to call him to himself before his Father, my duty calls upon me to make such a disposition of my worldly affairs as seems to my best Judgment most Equitable and reasonable; therefore, I, Edmund Burke, of the parish of Saint James, Westminster, though suffering under sore and inexpressible affliction being of sound and disposing Mind and not affected by any bodily infirmity, do make my last will and Testament, in manner following; First, according to the Ancient good and laudable Custom of which my Heart & understanding recognizes the propriety, I bequeath my soul to God, hoping for his Mercy thro' the only Merits of our Lord and Saviour Jesus Christ; my Body I desire, if I should die in any place very convenient for its Transport thither (but not otherwise), to be buried in the Church at Beaconsfield near to the Bodies of my dearest Brother & my dearest Son, in all Humility praying that as we have lived in perfect Amity together we may together have a part in the Resurrection of the Just; I wish my Funeral to be (without any Punctiliousness in that respect) the same as that of my brother and to exceed it as little as possible in point of Charge, whether on Account of my Family or of any others who would go to a greater expence, & I desire in the same manner and with the same Qualifications that no Monument beyond a Middle-sized Tablet with a small and simple inscription on the Church Wall or on the Flagstone be erected; I say this because I know the Partial kindness to me of some of my Friends, but I have had in my life time but too much of noise and compliment: as to the rest it is uncertain what I shall leave after the Discharge of my Debts which when I write this are very great. Be that as it may, my Will concerning my worldly substance is short. As my entirely beloved, Faithful & affectionate Wife did during the whole time in which I lived most happily with her take on her the charge & Management of my affairs, assisted by her son,

* In V. Harris, *Ancient, Curious, and Famous Wills* 261 (1911).

whilst God was pleased to lend him to us, did conduct them (often in a state of much derangement and embarrassment) with a patience and prudence which probably have no example, & thereby left my Mind free to prosecute my publick duty or my Studies or to indulge in my relaxations or to cultivate my friends at my pleasure; so on my Death I wish things to continue as substantially they have always been. I therefore by this my last and only Will devise, leave & bequeath to my entirely beloved and incomparable Wife, Jane Mary Burke, the whole real Estate of which I shall die seized, whether Lands, Rents or Houses, in absolute Fee simple; as also all my Personal Estate, whether Stock, Furniture, Plate, Money or Securities for Money Annuities for lives or Years, be the said Estate of what nature, Quality, extent or description it may be, to her sole uncontrolled Possession & disposal, as her property in any manner which may seem proper to her to possess or to dispose of the same (whether it be real Estate or Personal Estate) by her last will or otherwise; it being my intention that she may have as clear and uncontrolled a right and Title thereto and therein as I possess myself as to the use, expenditure, Sale or devise. I hope these Words are sufficient to express the absolute and unconditioned, unlimited right of compleat Ownership. I mean to give to her the said Lands and Goods and I trust that no words of surplusage or ambiguity may vitiate this my clear intention; there are no persons who have a right or I believe a disposition to complain of this bequest which I have only weighed and made on a proper consideration of my Duties and the relations in which I stand. I also make my wife, Jane Mary Burke, aforesaid, my sole Executrix of this my last Will, knowing that she will receive advice and assistance from her and my excellent Friends Dr. Walker King & Dr. Lawrence, to whom I recommend her & her concerns, though that perhaps is needless, as they are as much attached to her as they are to me. I do it only to mark my special Confidence in their affection, Skill and Industry. . . . In the Political World I have made many connections and some of them amongst persons of high rank: their Friendship from political became personal to me and they have shewn it in a manner more than to satisfie the utmost demands that could be made from my love & sincere attachment to them. They are the worthiest people in the Kingdom; their intentions are excellent, and I wish them every kind of success. . . . In speaking of my Friends to whom I owe so many obligations I ought to name specially Lord Fitzwilliam, the Duke of Portland and the Lord Cavendishes with the D. of Devonshire the worthy head of that Family. If the intimacy which I have had with others has been broken off by a Political Difference on great Questions concerning the State of things existing and impending, I hope they will forgive whatever of general human Infirmity or of my own particular Infirmity has entered into that contention. I heartily entreat their forgiveness. I have nothing Further to say. Signed & Sealed as my last Will and Testament this 11th day of August, 1794 being written all with my own hand. Edm. Burke — in the presence of — Dupont — William — Webster — Walker & King.

In reading over the above Will I have nothing to add or essentially to alter but one point may want to be perfected & explained. In leaving my Lands and Heredits to my wife I find that I have omitted the Words which in Deeds Create an Inheritance in Law. Now tho' I think them hardly necessary in a Will yet to obviate all doubts I explain the matter in a Codicil which is annexed to this — (sic) 22 1797. — Edm. Burke.

The reason of my making this will or Codicil to my former Will is from my having omitted in devising by that Will my Lands and Heredits to my Wife aforesaid, the full and absolute Property thereof & therein I have omitted the legal Words of Inheritance. Now tho' I think those words however necessary in a Deed are not so in a Will, yet to prevent all Question, I do hereby devise all my Lands Tenements and Heredits as well as all other property that may be subject to a strict Rule of Law in Deeds & which would pass if left undevised to my Heirs. I say I do devise the same Lands tenements and Hereditaments to my Wife, Jane Mary Burke, and her Heirs for ever in pure absolute and unconditional Fee simple.

QUESTIONS

1. *This is a different sort of document from the will of Mr. Black, written not only to ensure the desired devolution of property but as a statement of attitude and feelings in the face of death.*
   a. *Can you imagine wishing to make your own last will and testament the occasion for speech of this kind?*
   b. *Suppose a client indicated a wish to speak in a similar vein in a will you were preparing for him. What would you say to him? What would you do on his behalf?*
   c. *Does the personal quality of this statement have any significance for the law or lawyer, or is it just irrelevant and embarrassing surplusage?*
   d. *For the rare view that estate planning is a process charged with emotional and psychological significance, see T. Shaffer, Death, Property, and Lawyers (1970). Compare B. Partridge, Country Lawyer 160 et seq. (1939).*
2. *Consider the codicil in which Burke substitutes for the declaration of his intent and feelings in plain English the legal phrase, "to my wife, Jane Mary Burke, and her heirs." Can this act of translation, of literary conversion by formula, serve as a paradigm of the lawyer's life?*
3. *The will is, of course, only one way in which the law describes or responds to a death. What other ways can you think of, and how are they different? Later in this section we shall examine the literature of the death penalty, and in the last section of this chapter, the law of wrongful death. But first we shall look at some nonlegal materials.*

A REFUSAL TO MOURN THE DEATH, BY FIRE, OF A CHILD IN LONDON

Dylan Thomas

Never until the mankind making
Bird beast and flower
Fathering and all humbling darkness
Tells with silence the last light breaking
And the still hour
Is come of the sea tumbling in harness

And I must enter again the round
Zion of the water bead
And the synagogue of the ear of corn
Shall I let pray the shadow of a sound
Or sow my salt seed
In the least valley of sackcloth to mourn

The majesty and burning of the child's death.
I shall not murder
The mankind of her going with a grave truth
Nor blaspheme down the stations of the breath
With any further
Elegy of innocence and youth.

Deep with the first dead lies London's daughter,
Robed in the long friends,
The grains beyond age, the dark veins of her mother,
Secret by the unmourning water
Of the riding Thames.
After the first death, there is no other.

QUESTIONS

1. *Thomas here says that he refuses to write an elegy because that kind of poetic writing does not do justice to experience; an elegy converts a living reality into a literary event and makes an intolerable truth manageable by fitting it into a pattern of stock emotions. "I shall not murder The mankind of her going with a grave truth." He calls the elegy a blasphemy.*
   a. *What then do you imagine he would say of the language of the estate plan? Of the language of the wrongful death action?*
   b. *The elegy is only a form of words, of course, not an actual force of destruction in the real world. Is Thomas's concern for its inadequacy merely academic or literary pretentiousness, a sort of poet's complaint*

not to be taken seriously by serious people? Or can it be seen to have some bearing on our concerns? Should a lawyer likewise express a recognition that his forms of speech and thought convert life into literature, that they are similarly untrue to experience? How can he do so?

c. *To go even further, should the lawyer find a way to demonstrate his awareness that to choose one statement rather than another is always to be partly false, that writing always reduces and changes experience, that justice — in this literary sense — can never be done?*

2. *Does Thomas really refuse to write an elegy? What does he do? Can you imagine controlling the language of the estate plan in a similar way?*
3. *What do you imagine Thomas would say to Judge Burger's view that "restraint is called for" when "guidelines are less clear"? Would he simply have failed to see the judge's problem?*
4. *Compare the two following poems.*

JANET WAKING
John Crowe Ransom

Beautifully Janet slept
Till it was deeply morning. She woke then
And thought about her dainty-feathered hen,
To see how it had kept.

One kiss she gave her mother.
Only a small one gave she to her daddy
Who would have kissed each curl of his shining baby;
No kiss at all for her brother.

"Old Chucky, old Chucky!" she cried,
Running across the world upon the grass
To Chucky's house, and listening. But alas,
Her Chucky had died.

It was a transmogrifying bee
Came droning down on Chucky's old bald head
And sat and put the poison. It scarcely bled,
But how exceedingly

And purply did the knot
Swell with the venom and communicate
Its rigor! Now the poor comb stood up straight
But Chucky did not.

So there was Janet
Kneeling on the wet grass, crying her brown hen
(Translated far beyond the daughters of men)
To rise and walk upon it.

And weeping fast as she had breath
Janet implored us, "Wake her from her sleep!"
And would not be instructed in how deep
Was the forgetful kingdom of death.

THE LAST NIGHT THAT SHE LIVED

Emily Dickinson

The last Night that She lived
It was a Common Night
Except the Dying — this to Us
Made Nature different

We noticed smallest things —
Things overlooked before
By this great light upon our Minds
Italicized — as 'twere.

As We went out and in
Between Her final Room
And Rooms where Those to be alive
Tomorrow were, a Blame

That Others could exist
While She must finish quite
A Jealousy for Her arose
So nearly infinite —

We waited while She passed —
It was a narrow time —
Too jostled were Our Souls to speak
At length the notice came.

She mentioned, and forgot —
Then lightly as a Reed
Bent to the Water, struggled scarce —
Consented, and was dead —

And We — We placed the Hair —
And drew the Head erect —
And then an awful leisure was
Belief to regulate —

QUESTIONS

1. How do the three preceding poems differ from the legal literature about death you have read in this course or elsewhere? This sets up an enormously complex comparison, of course, which you could spend a lifetime working out, but these questions may suggest some lines of approach.
   a. Draft a paraphrase of one of the poems and of one of the legal passages. Is it harder to paraphrase the poem?
   b. What does the poem say or do that your paraphrase omits? Why, for example, would anyone read it rather than your paraphrase?
   c. What does the legal original say or do that your paraphrase omits? Why would anyone read it rather than your paraphrase? You know that you sometimes read cases, not just the headnotes: why do you do so and under what circumstances? (You can see that while there are differences here, one cannot simply assert that poetry is living speech, and that legal speech is dead.)
2. Notice that the poems each express an experience of learning, and that one function of the writing is to bring the reader to share it: Janet learns despite her refusal, her father learns what he has known and forgotten; Thomas has learned once and maintains that his change is permanent; Dickinson moves into a new position from which she must reflect anew. The process of change essential to each of these poems has two sorts of effect: first, it is this that enables the poem to be a way of working directly on the reader (moving him from one way of seeing things to another), that makes the poem an activity and not a mere statement. Second, it operates as a qualification of both positions, even the concluding one; for to show how you came to a particular way of seeing things is to recognize something outside it, as well as the possibility that you may once more move on. This is a way of writing two ways at once, of giving life and movement to what one writes.
   a. Does any of the legal statements you have read concern itself with an experience of change or learning? Can you perceive or imagine such an experience lying behind these statements?
   b. Another way to put it might be this: the speaker in each of the poems is self-regarding, self-critical – the contemplator becomes the contemplated. Can the same be said of either legal passage reproduced above? Of any legal passage you know?
   c. Can you imagine that any legal statement could be thought of as an activity as complex and significant as a poem?[1]

c. *Versions and Conversions of Experience: Imagining What the Law Would Do*

Here we shall continue our comparative examination of legal language, but in a slightly different way: as you read the following six passages, each of which gives an account of a death in a nonlegal lan-

1. See Chapter 6, Section A: Is the Judge Really a Poet?

guage, you will be asked to imagine what versions of these events might be given in legal language. Pretend that there is a lawsuit about them and that a lawyer is advising his client or arguing to a judge, or that the judge is asking questions of the lawyer or explaining his own decision of the case; what can such people so situated actually say about the events before them? What is the range of possibilities for legal speech? How might the law convert this experience into a statement of its own, and what would such a version leave out? You are called upon here to exercise your legal imagination, as well as your knowledge of the law. (You might also ask: in what ways and with what effect might a legislature speak to this situation?)

THE STORY OF BURNT NJAL*

[This passage is from an early Icelandic saga. Njal's enemies, led by Flosi, have surrounded his house and now set it afire. Helgi, Skarphedinn, and Grim are sons of Njal; Bergthora is his wife; Kari is a friend of his sons.]

Then Flosi and his men made a great pile before each of the doors, and then the women folk who were inside began to weep and to wail.

Njal spoke to them and said, "Keep up your hearts, nor utter shrieks, for this is but a passing storm, and it will be long before ye have another such; and put your faith in God, and believe that he is so merciful that he will not let us burn both in this world and the next."

Such words of comfort had he for them all, and others still more strong.

Now the whole house began to blaze. Then Njal went to the door and said —

"Is Flosi so near that he can hear my voice."

Flosi said that he could hear it.

"Wilt thou," said Njal, "take an atonement from my sons, or allow any men to go out."

"I will not," answers Flosi, "take any atonement from thy sons, and now our dealings shall come to an end once for all, and I will not stir from this spot till they are all dead; but I will allow the women and children and house-carles to go out."

Then Njal went into the house, and said to the folk —

"Now all those must go out to whom leave is given, and so go thou out Thorhalla Asgrim's daughter, and all the people also with thee who may."

Then Thorhalla said —

"This is another parting between me and Helgi than I thought of a

* Chapter 128 (Dasent trans. 1861).

while ago; but still I will egg on my father and brothers to avenge this manscathe which is wrought here."

"Go, and good go with thee," said Njal, "for thou art a brave woman."

After that she went out and much folk with her.

Then Astrid of Deepback said to Helgi Njal's son —

"Come thou out with me, and I will throw a woman's cloak over thee, and tire thy head with a kerchief."

He spoke against it at first, but at last he did so at the prayer of others.

So Astrid wrapped the kerchief round Helgi's head, but Thorhilda, Skarphedinn's wife, threw the cloak over him, and he went out between them, and then Thorgerda Njal's daughter, and Helga her sister, and many other folk went out too.

But when Helgi came out Flosi said —

"That is a tall woman and broad across the shoulders that went yonder, take her and hold her."

But when Helgi heard that, he cast away the cloak. He had got his sword under his arm, and hewed at a man, and the blow fell on his shield and cut off the point of it, and the man's leg as well. Then Flosi came up and hewed at Helgi's neck, and took off his head at a stroke.

Then Flosi went to the door and called out to Njal, and said he would speak with him and Bergthora.

Now Njal does so, and Flosi said —

"I will offer thee, master Njal, leave to go out, for it is unworthy that thou shouldst burn indoors."

"I will not go out," said Njal, "for I am an old man, and little fitted to avenge my sons, but I will not live in shame."

Then Flosi said to Bergthora —

"Come thou out, housewife, for I will for no sake burn thee indoors."

"I was given away to Njal young," said Bergthora, "and I have promised him this, that we would both share the same fate."

After that they both went back into the house.

"What counsel shall we now take," said Bergthora.

"We will go to our bed," says Njal, "and lay us down; I have long been eager for rest."

Then she said to the boy Thord, Kari's son —

"Thee will I take out, and thou shalt not burn in here."

"Thou hast promised me this, grandmother," says the boy, "that we should never part so long as I wished to be with thee; but methinks it is much better to die with thee and Njal than to live after you."

Then she bore the boy to her bed, and Njal spoke to his steward and said —

"Now shalt thou see where we lay us down, and how I lay us out, for

I mean not to stir an inch hence, whether reek or burning smart me, and so thou wilt be able to guess where to look for our bones."

He said he would do so.

There had been an ox slaughtered and the hide lay there. Njal told the steward to spread the hide over them, and he did so.

So there they lay down both of them in their bed, and put the boy between them. Then they signed themselves and the boy with the cross, and gave over their souls into God's hand, and that was the last word that men heard them utter.

Then the steward took the hide and spread it over them, and went out afterwards. Kettle of the Mark caught hold of him, and dragged him out, he asked carefully after his father-in-law Njal, but the steward told him the whole truth. Then Kettle said —

"Great grief hath been sent on us, when we have had to share such ill-luck together."

Skarphedinn saw how his father laid him down, and how he laid himself out, and then he said —

"Our father goes early to bed, and that is what was to be looked for, for he is an old man."

Then Skarphedinn, and Kari, and Grim, caught the brands as fast as they dropped down, and hurled them out at them, and so it went on a while. Then they hurled spears in at them, but they caught them all as they flew, and sent them back again.

Then Flosi bade them cease shooting, "for all feats of arms will go hard with us when we deal with them; ye may well wait till the fire overcomes them."

So they do that, and shoot no more.

Then the great beams out of the roof began to fall, and Skarphedinn said —

"Now must my father be dead, and I have neither heard groan nor cough from him."

QUESTIONS

1. *What versions of this story might be given in legal language? What would those versions leave out?*
   a. *One way to work this out would be to imagine a legal proceeding about these events. What might be said on such an occasion, by lawyer, judge, or witness, and in what form or forms? What voices heard in the saga would be missing in the courtroom? What new voices, missing here, would be heard there?*
   b. *Another approach would be to look at the speeches given above, one by one, and ask of each whether it can be redrafted into some sort of legal statement. If these characters had been made to speak the language of the law, what could they have said, what would they have been unable to say?*

2. What sorts of reasoning and expression do these characters engage in? How can these kinds of thought and speech be compared with what one finds in the law? Ask yourself, for example, why Njal refuses to leave, and why Bergthora and Thord stay with him. Does the law ever recognize such a moment, such motives? What processes of mind and spirit produced the remark, "Our father goes early to bed," and what place have they in the law?
3. Can you imagine a legal language in which much of what you read here would be a part?
4. If the law leaves out much of what you can see in this passage, this passage seems to leave out the law. No one so much as mentions the legal consequences of conduct, no one makes any appeal to a legal system of meaning. Is that a defect?
5. You may ask how you can talk about the omission of legal speech here without knowing what the relevant legal speech is, assuming that there is any law at all in this world. That defect in your knowledge can be remedied in part by a reading of the whole of this saga, which I warmly recommend. The heroic age of Iceland, in which these events occurred, was a very legal one indeed: litigation of a highly formal kind and the sort of warfare you see here were alternative modes of carrying on a dispute, often proceeding at the same time. Two systems of thought, language, and action existed side by side, apparently with equal validity.

   Chapters 135 to 144 give an account of a lawsuit brought against Flosi for this burning, which he won by procedural devices. A general battle then ensued until a settlement was negotiated, under which Flosi was exiled. If you look at the saga as a whole, then, it does not leave out the law, nor should the legal parts be read as failing to recognize the possibility of events such as these. The law does not seem to have made the claim that it was the ultimate way of talking, the only way that really counted. Legal and other ways of speaking and acting exist side by side and may even work together. The final reconciliation between Flosi and Kari was the work partly of law, partly of religion, and partly of temperament and circumstance.

   Can you take a similar attitude towards the relationship between the law and other kinds of speech and thought you see around you? Is it important for a lawyer to be able to do this?

   For two other passages that express a particularly Icelandic attitude towards death, see the death of Eyvind in "Hrafnkel the Priest of Frey" and the death of Bjarni Grimolfsson in "Eirik the Red," in Eirik the Red and Other Icelandic Sagas, 120, 157 (Gwyn Jones ed. 1961).

LE MORTE DARTHUR*
Thomas Malory

[Sir Gawain, whose implacable hatred for Lancelot has led to the destruction of the Round Table, has been wounded in a battle with Mordred.]

So whan thys batayle was done, kynge Arthure let serche hys people

* In *Works* 1230–1232 (Vinaver ed. 1967).

that were hurte and dede. And than was noble sir Gawayne founde in a greate boote, liynge more than halff dede. Whan kyng Arthur knew that he was layde so low he wente unto hym and so fownde hym. And there the kynge made greate sorow oute of mesure, and toke sir Gawayne in hys armys, and thryse he there sowned. And than whan he was waked, kyng Arthur seyde,

"Alas! sir Gawayne, my syster son, here now thou lyghest, the man in the worlde that I loved moste. And now ys my joy gone! For now, my nevew, sir Gawayne, I woll discover me unto you, tha[t] in youre person and in sir Launcelot I moste had my joy and myne affyaunce. And now have I loste my joy of you bothe, wherefore all myne erthely joy ys gone fro me!"

"A, myn uncle," seyde sir Gawayne, "now I woll that ye wyte that my deth-dayes be com! And all I may wyte myne owne hastynes and my wy[l]fulnesse, for thorow my wylfulnes I was causer of myne owne dethe; for I was thys day hurte and smytten uppon myne olde wounde that sir Launcelot gaff me, and I fele myselff that I muste nedis be dede by the owre of noone. And thorow me and [my] pryde ye have all thys shame and disease, for had that noble knyght, sir Launcelot, ben with you, as he was and wolde have ben, thys unhappy warre had never ben begunne; for he, thorow hys noble knyghthode and hys noble bloode, hylde all youre cankyrde enemyes in subjeccion and daungere. And now," sayde sir Gawayne, "ye shall mysse sir Launcelot. But alas that I wolde nat accorde with hym! And there[fore], fayre unkle, I pray you that I may have paupir, penne, and inke, that I may wryte unto sir Launcelot a letter wrytten with myne owne honde."

So whan pauper, penne and inke was brought, than sir Gawayne was sette up waykely by kynge Arthure, for he was shryven a lytyll afore. And than he toke hys penne and wrote thus, as the Freynshe booke makith mencion:

"Unto the, sir Launcelot, floure of all noble knyghtes that ever I harde of or saw be my dayes, I, sir Gawayne, kynge Lottis sonne of Orkeney, and systirs sonne unto the noble kynge Arthur, sende the gretynge, lattynge the to have knowlecche that the tenth day of May I was smytten uppon the olde wounde that thou gaff me afore the cité of Benwyke, and thorow that wounde I am com to my dethe-day. And I woll that all the worlde wyte that I, sir Gawayne, knyght of the Table Rounde, soughte my [*sic*] dethe, and nat thorow thy deservynge, but myne owne sekynge. Wherefore I beseche the, sir Launcelot, to returne agayne unto thys realme and se my toumbe and pray som prayer more other les for my soule. And thys same day that I wrote the same sedull I was hurte to the dethe, whych wounde was fyrste gyffyn of thyn honde, sir Launcelot; for of a more nobelar man myght I nat be slayne.

"Also, sir Launcelot, for all the love that ever was betwyxte us, make no taryyng, but com over the see in all the goodly haste that ye may, wyth youre noble knyghtes, and rescow that noble kynge that made the knyght, for he ys full straytely bestad wyth an false traytoure whych ys my halff-brothir, sir Mordred. For he hath crowned hymselff kynge, and wolde have wedded my lady, quene Gwenyver; and so had he done, had she nat kepte the Towre of London with stronge honde. And so the tenth day of May last paste my lorde kynge Arthur and we all londed uppon them at Dover, and there he put that false traytoure, sir Mordred, to flyght. And so hit there mysfortuned me to be smytten uppon the strooke that ye gaff me of olde.

"And the date of thys lettir was wrytten but two owrys and an halff afore my dethe, wrytten with myne owne honde and subscrybed with parte of my harte blood. And therefore I requyre the, moste famous knyght of the worlde, that thou wolte se my tumbe."

And than he wepte and kynge Arthur both, and sowned. And whan they were awaked bothe, the kynge made sir Gawayne to resceyve hys sacrament, and than sir Gawayne prayde the kynge for to sende for sir Launcelot and to cherysshe hym aboven all othir knyghtes.

And so at the owre of noone sir Gawayne yelded up the goste. And than the kynge lat entere hym in a chapell within Dover castell. And there yet all men may se the skulle of hym, and the same wounde is sene that sir Launcelot gaff in batayle.

QUESTIONS

1. *Ask of this passage the questions asked of Burnt Njal: what versions of these events could be given in legal language? Of what you see here, what might be included in such versions, and what left out?*
2. *Can you imagine a legal system to which the words of Gawain would be relevant?*
   a. *While the Morte Darthur has little of what we would call law in it (at least if law is regarded as the command of a sovereign), its central value is the sense of chivalric honor expressed in the conduct and talk of the knights. It celebrates a chivalric ideal, the expression of a civilization, and this passage gives some sense of how it does so.*

      Could a code of chivalry operate as a legal system, or as part of one? Why or why not? It would be interesting to inquire what the chivalric code leaves out, for example, and to compare this system with a legal system.
   b. *Gawain's dying speech would presumably be relevant to any account of this event expressed in the language of Christianity. (If this is a genuine repentance, he will be forgiven.) How can the operation of formal Christian doctrine be compared with the law as a way of organizing experience, as a way of claiming meaning for events? What does Christianity leave out?*

THE HISTORY OF THE REBELLION AND CIVIL WARS IN ENGLAND*

Edward Hyde, First Earl of Clarendon

[This history of the civil wars is written by one of the councilors of King Charles. Lindsey is loyal to the king; Essex is a rebel general, and his side is ultimately victorious.]

The earl of Lindsey was a man of a very noble extraction, and inherited a great fortune from his ancestors; which though he did not manage with so great care as if he desired much to improve, yet he left it in a very fair condition to his family, which more intended the increase of it. He was a man of great honour, and spent his youth and vigour of his age in military actions and commands abroad; and albeit he indulged to himself great liberties of life, yet he still preserved a very good reputation with all men, and a very great interest in his country, as appeared by the supplies he and his son brought to the King's army; the several companies of his own regiment of foot being commanded by the principal knights and gentlemen of Lincolnshire, who engaged themselves in the service principally out of their personal affection to him. He was of a very generous nature, and punctual in what he undertook and in exacting what was due to him; which made him bear that restriction so heavily which was put upon him by the commission granted to prince Rupert, and by the King's preferring the prince's opinion in all matters relating to the war before his. Nor did he conceal his resentment: the day before the battle he said to some friends, with whom he used freedom, that "he did not look upon himself as general; and therefore he was resolved when the day of battle should come that he would be in the head of his regiment as a private colonel, where he would die." He was carried out of the field to the next village; and if he could then have procured surgeons, it was thought his wound would not have proved mortal. And it was imputed to the earl of Essex's too well remembering former grudges that he neither sent any surgeon to him nor performed any other offices of respect towards him; but it is most certain that the disorder the earl of Essex himself was in at that time, by the running away of the horse, and the confusion he saw the army in, and the plundering the carriages in the town where the surgeons were to attend, was the cause of all the omissions of that kind. And as soon as the other army was composed by the coming on of the night, the earl of Essex about midnight sent sir William Balfore and some other officers to see him, and to offer him all offices, and meant himself to have visited him. They found him upon a little straw in a poor house, where

* Book 6, para. 90 (1702; Macray ed. 1888).

they had laid him in his blood, which had run from him in great abundance, no surgeon having been yet with him; only he had great vivacity in his looks, and told them he was sorry to see so many gentlemen, some whereof were his old friends, engaged in so foul a rebellion: and principally directed his discourse to sir William Balfore, whom he put in mind of the great obligations he had to the King; how much his majesty had disobliged the whole English nation by putting him into the command of the Tower; and that it was the most odious ingratitude in him to make him that return. He wished them to tell my lord of Essex, "that he ought to cast himself at the King's feet to beg his pardon; which if he did not speedily do, his memory would be odious to the nation;" and continued this kind of discourse with so much vehemence that the officers by degrees withdrew themselves, and prevented the visit the earl of Essex intended him, who only sent the best surgeons to him; who in the very opening of his wounds died before the morning, only upon the loss of blood. He had very many friends and very few enemies, and died generally lamented.

QUESTIONS

1. *What versions of these events might be given in legal language? Into what sorts of statement might the law convert what you read here?*
2. *Suppose, for example, that Lindsey has survived and that his side has won the civil war. Essex and Balfore are to be tried for treason.*
   a. *Imagine an indictment drafted by Lindsey: what would it say? What would it leave out? If he said just what he says here, how much could be struck as surplusage?*
   b. *Imagine Lindsey as a witness: how much of what he says here would he be able to say on the stand? (Do you see that this might be a legal question itself, the subject of argument by opposing counsel?)*
   c. *Imagine Lindsey as judge: how much of what he says here would he be able to say in expressing his judgment of guilt or innocence? What do you think he would say, how would he talk?*
   d. *Would Lindsey be able to speak more nearly as he speaks here if he were explaining, as a judge, the sentence he had imposed? If he were a lawyer arguing to a jury?*
   e. *How do you explain the limits and demands of these various legal roles? Why should one not simply state the truth as one sees it, whatever one's role? Why should lawyer, judge, and witness all speak so differently, according to different forms and different expectations?*
3. *There is another event of potential legal significance here as well: can you imagine how lawyers, witnesses, and judges would talk about the question whether Essex's failure to supply surgeons more quickly was culpable or not? How would these various statements differ from the one that Clarendon makes?*
4. *One alternative in the next writing assignment asks you to draft a pleading and to explain what happens when a claim of legal meaning is made*

for an event in this way. Perhaps it would be helpful to redraft Lindsey's speech several times, each approaching more nearly what a pleading would say. Then imagine the most formal and perfect pleading, something from a form book perhaps, and imagine how you might redraft it to include something of what is omitted. Is the art of drafting a pleading an art of writing two ways?

AGAMEMNON*

Aeschylus

[Clytemnestra has just killed Agamemnon, her husband, upon his victorious return from the Trojan War.]

Much have I said before to serve necessity,
but I will take no shame now to unsay it all.
How else could I, arming hate against hateful men
disguised in seeming tenderness, fence high the nets
of ruin beyond overleaping? Thus to me
the conflict born of ancient bitterness is not
a thing new thought upon, but pondered deep in time.
I stand now where I struck him down. The thing is done.
Thus have I wrought, and I will not deny it now.
That he might not escape nor beat aside his death,
as fishermen cast their huge circling nets, I spread
deadly abundance of rich robes, and caught him fast.
I struck him twice. In two great cries of agony
he buckled at the knees and fell. When he was down
I struck him the third blow, in thanks and reverence
to Zeus the lord of dead men underneath the ground.
Thus he went down, and the life struggled out of him;
and as he died he spattered me with the dark red
and violent driven rain of bitter savored blood
to make me glad, as gardens stand among the showers
of God in glory at the birthtime of the buds.

These being the facts, elders of Argos assembled here,
be glad, if it be your pleasure; but for me, I glory.
Were it religion to pour wine above the slain,
this man deserved, more than deserved, such sacrament.
He filled our cup with evil things unspeakable
and now himself come home has drunk it to the dregs.

* Lines 1372–1398 (Lattimore trans. 1953).

QUESTIONS

1. What significance might a legal system – our own, for instance – give to this speech?
2. Here a woman exults over the killing of her husband. Is such an emotion foreign to the law? Does the law ever take satisfaction in a death?
3. After this killing, Orestes, the son of Agamemnon and Clytemnestra, is under conflicting obligations: to avenge the murder, and not to harm his mother.
   a. How would you characterize these obligations? How do they differ from what we think of as legal obligations?
   b. Orestes, with great uncertainty and apparently only because he regards it as the higher duty, kills his mother.
      (1) He then steps forth and speaks about his conduct. What do you expect Aeschylus will have him say about it?
      (2) How else do you suppose his conduct might have been characterized? If you remember the play, you should ask yourself how else it is characterized by other people in the play and how the inconsistencies between these versions of the event are reconciled.
   c. Can you compare, as a general matter, the process by which the competition between inconsistent versions of experience goes on in the drama and in the law?
4. Some other works in which death is defined in ways that might interest you are: Bede, A History of the English Church and People (731) (e.g., Book 4, Chapter 24); Hemingway, "The Short Happy Life of Francis Macomber" (1938); W. Cather, Death Comes for the Archbishop (1927); L. Van der Post, Venture to the Interior 152–155 (1951); and the Icelandic Egil's Saga (Jones trans. 1960).
5. Below are two more passages about death. Of each, ask what death is made to mean and by what art or feat of language that meaning is established. What might the law have to say about these events, and what would such a statement leave out?

THE EDUCATION OF HENRY ADAMS*

Henry Adams

He had been some weeks in London when he received a telegram from his brother-in-law at the Bagni di Lucca telling him that his sister had been thrown from a cab and injured, and that he had better come on. He started that night, and reached the Bagni di Lucca on the second day. Tetanus had already set in.

The last lesson — the sum and term of education — began then. He had passed through thirty years of rather varied experience without having once felt the shell of custom broken. He had never seen Nature — only her surface — the sugar-coating that she shows to youth. Flung suddenly in his face, with the harsh brutality of chance, the terror of the blow stayed by him thenceforth for life, until repetition made it

* Chapter 19 (1918).

more than the will could struggle with; more than he could call on himself to bear. He found his sister, a woman of forty, as gay and brilliant in the terrors of lockjaw as she had been in the careless fun of 1859, lying in bed in consequence of a miserable cab-accident that had bruised her foot. Hour by hour the muscles grew rigid, while the mind remained bright, until after ten days of fiendish torture she died in convulsions.

One had heard and read a great deal about death, and even seen a little of it, and knew by heart the thousand commonplaces of religion and poetry which seemed to deaden one's senses and veil the horror. Society being immortal, could put on immortality at will. Adams, being mortal, felt only the mortality. Death took features altogether new to him, in these rich and sensuous surroundings. Nature enjoyed it, played with it, the horror added to her charm, she liked the torture and smothered her victim with caresses. Never had one seen her so winning. The hot Italian summer brooded outside, over the market-place and the picturesque peasants, and, in the singular color of the Tuscan atmosphere, the hills and vineyards of the Apennines seemed bursting with mid-summer blood. The sick-room itself glowed with the Italian joy of life; friends filled it; no harsh northern lights pierced the soft shadows; even the dying woman shared the sense of the Italian summer, the soft, velvet air, the humor, the courage, the sensual fulness of Nature and man. She faced death, as women mostly do, bravely and even gaily, racked slowly to unconsciousness, but yielding only to violence, as a soldier sabred in battle. For many thousands of years, on these hills and plains, Nature had gone on sabring men and women with the same air of sensual pleasure.

THE HISTORY OF ENGLAND FROM THE ACCESSION OF JAMES II*

T. B. Macaulay

[Monmouth's attempt to win the crown by arms from the Catholic James II has failed, and he has been sentenced to death.]

The hour drew near; all hope was over; and Monmouth had passed from pusillanimous fear to the apathy of despair. His children were brought to his room that he might take leave of them, and were followed by his wife. He spoke to her kindly, but without emotion. Though she was a woman of great strength of mind, and had little cause to love him, her misery was such that none of the by-standers could refrain from weeping. He alone was unmoved.

It was ten o'clock: the coach of the lieutenant of the Tower was ready. Monmouth requested his spiritual advisers to accompany him to

* Chapter 5 (1848).

the scaffold, and they consented; but they told him that, in their judgment, he was about to die in a perilous state of mind, and that, if they attended him, it would be their duty to exhort him to the last. As he passed along the ranks of the guards he saluted them with a smile, and mounted the scaffold with a firm tread. Tower Hill was covered up to the chimney tops with an innumerable multitude of gazers, who, in awful silence, broken only by sighs and the noise of weeping, listened for the last accents of the darling of the people. "I shall say little," he began. "I come here, not to speak, but to die. I die a Protestant of the Church of England." The bishops interrupted him, and told him that, unless he acknowledged resistance to be sinful, he was no member of their Church. He went on to speak of his Henrietta. She was, he said, a young lady of virtue and honor. He loved her to the last, and he could not die without giving utterance to his feelings. The bishops again interfered, and begged him not to use such language. Some altercation followed. The divines have been accused of dealing harshly with the dying man; but they appear to have only discharged what, in their view, was a sacred duty. Monmouth knew their principles, and, if he wished to avoid their importunity, should have dispensed with their attendance. Their general arguments against resistance had no effect on him; but when they reminded him of the ruin which he had brought on his brave and loving followers, of the blood which had been shed, of the souls which had been sent unprepared to the great account, he was touched, and said, in a softened voice, "I do own that. I am sorry that it ever happened." They prayed with him long and fervently; and he joined in their petitions till they invoked a blessing on the king. He remained silent. "Sir," said one of the assistants, "do you not pray for the king with us?" Monmouth paused some time, and after an internal struggle, exclaimed "Amen." But it was in vain that the prelates implored him to address to the soldiers and to the people a few words on the duty of obedience to the government. "I will make no speeches," he exclaimed. "Only ten words, my lord." He turned away, called his servant, and put into the man's hand a toothpick-case, the last token of ill-starred love. "Give it," he said, "to that person." He then accosted John Ketch, the executioner, a wretch who had butchered many brave and noble victims, and whose name has, during a century and a half, been vulgarly given to all who have succeeded him in his odious office. "Here," said the duke, "are six guineas for you. Do not hack me as you did my Lord Russell. I have heard that you struck him three or four times. My servant will give you some more gold if you do the work well." He then undressed, felt the edge of the ax, expressed some fear that it was not sharp enough, and laid his head on the block. The divines in the mean time continued to ejaculate with great energy, "God accept your repentance; God accept your imperfect repentance."

The hangman addressed himself to his office; but he had been disconcerted by what the duke had said. The first blow inflicted only a slight wound. The duke struggled, rose from the block, and looked reproachfully at the executioner. The head sank down once more. The stroke was repeated again and again; but still the neck was not severed, and the body continued to move. Yells of rage and horror rose from the crowd. Ketch flung down the ax with a curse. "I can not do it," he said; "my heart fails me." "Take up the ax, man," cried the sheriff. "Fling him over the rails," roared the mob. At length the ax was taken up. Two more blows extinguished the last remains of life; but a knife was used to separate the head from the shoulders. The crowd was wrought up to such an ecstasy of rage that the executioner was in danger of being torn in pieces, and was conveyed away under a strong guard.

In the mean time many handkerchiefs were dipped in the duke's blood, for by a large part of the multitude he was regarded as a martyr who had died for the Protestant religion. The head and body were placed in a coffin covered with black velvet, and were laid privately under the communion-table of St. Peter's Chapel in the Tower. Within four years the pavement of that chancel was again disturbed, and hard by the remains of Monmouth were laid the remains of Jeffreys. In truth, there is no sadder spot on the earth than that little cemetery. Death is there associated, not, as in Westminster Abbey and Saint Paul's, with genius and virtue, with public veneration and with imperishable renown; not, as in our humblest churches and church-yards, with every thing that is most endearing in social and domestic charities, but with whatever is darkest in human nature and in human destiny, with the savage triumph of implacable enemies, with the inconstancy, the ingratitude, the cowardice of friends, with all the miseries of fallen greatness and of blighted fame. Thither have been carried, through successive ages, by the rude hands of jailers, without one mourner following, the bleeding relics of men who had been the captains of armies, the leaders of parties, the oracles of senates, and the ornaments of courts. Thither was borne, before the window where Jane Grey was praying, the mangled corpse of Guilford Dudley. Edward Seymour, duke of Somerset, and protector of the realm, reposes there by the brother whom he murdered. There has moldered away the headless trunk of John Fisher, bishop of Rochester and Cardinal of Saint Vitalis, a man worthy to have lived in a better age, and to have died in a better cause. There are laid John Dudley, duke of Northumberland, Lord High Admiral, and Thomas Cromwell, earl of Essex, Lord High Treasurer. There, too, is another Essex, on whom nature and fortune had lavished all their bounties in vain, and whom valor, grace, genius, royal favor, popular applause, conducted to an early and ignominious doom. Not far off sleep two chiefs of the great house of Howard, Thomas, fourth Duke of

Norfolk, and Philip, eleventh Earl of Arundel. Here and there, among the thick graves of unquiet and aspiring statesmen, lie more delicate sufferers; Margaret of Salisbury, the last of the proud name of Plantagenet, and those two fair queens who perished by the jealous rage of Henry. Such was the dust with which the dust of Monmouth mingled.

d. A Primary Distinction in Talk About Death: Humanity and Inhumanity in Speech

As the course proceeds we shall draw many rather complex and subtle distinctions among various forms of speech, pushing to its limit our capacity to understand the implications of language. But it is worth making some primary, almost primitive, distinctions as well, especially since "fundamental" does not necessarily mean "easy."

How do you respond to the following letter? Can you explain how it goes wrong?

LETTER TO COLONEL WALTON*

Oliver Cromwell

Dear Sir, — It's our duty to sympathize in all mercies; and to praise the Lord together in chastisements or trials, that so we may sorrow together.

Truly England and the Church of God hath had a great favor from the Lord, in this great Victory given unto us, such as the like never was since this War began. It had all the evidences of an absolute Victory obtained by the Lord's blessing upon the Godly Party principally. We never charged but we routed the enemy. The Left Wing, which I commanded, being our own horse, saving a few Scots in our rear, beat all the Prince's horse. God made them as stubble to our swords. We charged their regiments of foot with our horse, and routed all we charged. The particulars I cannot relate now; but I believe, of twenty thousand the Prince hath not four thousand left. Give glory, all the glory, to God. —

Sir, God hath taken away your eldest Son by a cannon-shot. It brake his leg. We were necessitated to have it cut off, whereof he died.

Sir, you know my own trials this way: but the Lord supported me with this, That the Lord took him into the happiness we all pant for and live for. There is your precious child full of glory, never to know sin or sorrow any more. He was a gallant young man, exceedingly gracious. God give you His comfort. Before his death he was so full of comfort that to Frank Russel and myself he could not express it, "It was so great

* July 5, 1644, in Thomas Carlyle, *Oliver Cromwell's Letters and Speeches* (1845).

above his pain." This he said to us. Indeed it was admirable. A little after, he said, One thing lay upon his spirit. I asked him, What that was? He told me it was, That God had not suffered him to be any more the executioner of His enemies. At his fall, his horse being killed with the bullet, and as I am informed three horses more, I am told he bid them, Open to the right and left, that he might see the rogues run. Truly he was exceedingly beloved in the Army, of all that knew him. But few knew him; for he was a precious young man, fit for God. You have cause to bless the Lord. He is a glorious Saint in Heaven; wherein you ought exceedingly to rejoice. Let this drink up your sorrow; seeing these are not feigned words to comfort you, but the thing is so real and undoubted a truth. You may do all things by the strength of Christ. Seek that, and you shall easily bear your trial. Let this public mercy to the Church of God make you to forget your private sorrow. The Lord be your strength: so prays

Your truly faithful and loving brother,
Oliver Cromwell.

My love to your Daughter, and my Cousin Perceval, Sister Desborow and all friends with you.

QUESTIONS

1. *I assume you agree that there is much wrong in this letter, that it is one you would like neither to have written nor received. Can you explain what is wrong? (Or, if you take the opposite view, how nothing is?)*

   Our questioning takes a turn here, from identifying differences among languages and passages, to working out a way of judging what a writer does. As you talk about your response to this letter and to the passages that follow these questions, ask this: do the defects you find here have any parallels or analogs in the law?

   a. *Here is one familiar question with which we might begin: what inferences can you draw from this letter about the sort of person Cromwell was? How do you justify those inferences?*
   b. *In particular, do you think he was being honest or dishonest? If honest, what conversation can you imagine having with a mind so defined? If dishonest, what do you think he would have said had he been honest?*
   c. *Why do you think he wrote this way?*
2. *How does Cromwell define the death of Walton's son in the way he writes here? How does he define the deaths of the soldiers of the prince?*
3. *Can you find a way of stating what is wrong here in general terms, in a critical vocabulary that has a general validity?*
   a. *Do you want to say that there is an inappropriate "leaving out" here? What more could Cromwell have said? Draft an improved letter that goes on from where Cromwell left off.*
   b. *Or is it the very language of the letter and not its message that "leaves out"? Can you rewrite the letter in a different language, so that it puts in what is now left out?*

c. Or is it the writer's relationship with his language that is wrong?
d. Might you generalize this way: what is wrong here is the conversion of life into fiction, the literary destructiveness that troubled Dylan Thomas? To test this, one might ask what claims Cromwell makes about the meanings of these deaths, and whether they are substantiated or qualified in any way. Is this all an impossible sort of pretending?

4. Everyone knows that a sympathy letter is hard to write, and perhaps you do not look upon your own efforts in that way with any satisfaction. Are the following passages improvements on the Cromwell letter? How can you express your sense of how they differ from what Cromwell wrote?
   a. "You lost your brother at about the same time that I lost my sister, the last member of my family, so that we are in a position to exchange sympathy. She died in Philadelphia within less than 24 hours after being taken to the hospital. While things of this kind are blows, my own feeling is that, at your age and mine, the best thing for us to do is to try to feel about it as if it was something that had happened long ago." Wallace Stevens to Henry Church, Mar. 2, 1943, in Letters of Wallace Stevens 440 (H. Stevens ed. 1966). Stevens was in his early sixties at the time he wrote this letter.
   b. "You have, as I find by every kind of evidence, lost an excellent mother; and I hope you will not think me incapable of partaking of your grief. I have a mother, now eighty-two years of age, whom therefore I must soon lose, unless it please God that she rather should mourn for me. I read the letters in which you relate your mother's death to Mrs. Strahan, and I think I do myself honour, when I tell you, that I read them with tears; but tears are neither to you, nor to me, of any farther use, when once the tribute of nature has been paid. The business of life summons us away from useless grief, and calls us to the exercise of those virtues, of which we are lamenting our deprivation.

      "The greatest benefit which one friend can confer upon another, is to guard, and excite, and elevate his virtues. This your mother will still perform, if you diligently preserve the memory of her life, and of her death: a life, so far as I can learn, useful, wise, and innocent; and a death resigned, peaceful, and holy. . . .

      "There is one expedient, by which you may, in some degree, continue her presence. If you write down minutely what you remember of her from your earliest years, you will read it with great pleasure, and receive from it many hints of soothing recollection, when time shall remove her yet farther from you, and your grief shall be matured to veneration. To this, however painful for the present, I cannot but advise you, as to a source of comfort and satisfaction in the time to come. . . ." Samuel Johnson to James Elphinstone, Sept. 25, 1750.

5. Can you explain the differences you perceive among these letters of condolence?
6. I have suggested that they may be examples of a primary distinction between decent and indecent, between humane and inhumane. Do you agree? Can you explain what you mean by such terms, can you point to manifestations of either attitude in the languages, or the uses of language, in the passages you have read?
7. Following are two more passages on topics related to death. Can you articulate what is wrong with them? Or a way of claiming that nothing is?

SHAREHOLDERS REPORT*

Boyertown Burial Casket Company

To the shareowners of
BOYERTOWN BURIAL CASKET COMPANY

Your Board of Directors declared a quarterly dividend of thirty cents per share on the $10 par Capital Stock of the Company, payable March 1, 1969 to shareowners of record at the close of business on February 18, 1969. This represents an increase of five cents over the amount previously paid. Check for amount due you is enclosed.

Sales for the six months thru December 31, 1968 increased 16% over the corresponding period of last year. Casket unit sales increased 10.5%. Mortality in the areas served by the Company increased 3.6%.

The Company is continuing its policy of purchasing its shares when offered by shareowners. At December 31, 1968 such total purchases amounted to 44,923 shares.

The flu epidemic which swept the country during November and December and thru January added greatly to the already elevated demand for our product. Sales in both units and dollars reached record levels for each month and for the six months period to December 31, 1968.

Sales for the second half of our fiscal year are expected to exceed those of the same period last year. Because of strong sales in the second half of last year, we anticipate the increase will not be as pronounced which will provide a levelling effect on the year's results.

The interim financial summary submitted below is subject to year end adjustments and audit by public accountants.

INTERIM FINANCIAL SUMMARY

	Six months ended December 31	
	1968	*1967*
Sales	$8,189,848	$7,055,339
Earnings before taxes	641,575	335,203
Earnings after taxes	314,075	177,203
Earnings per share, on average number of shares outstanding during respective periods	1.23	.67
Dividends paid per share	.50	.50

PLEASE CASH YOUR DIVIDEND CHECK PROMPTLY

* Boyertown, Pa. (March 1, 1969).

MANUAL OUTLINES "PERFECT SNIPER"*

WASHINGTON (AP) — The ability to go for long periods without food or water, to control emotions and to kill "calmly and deliberately" and without remorse are the main qualifications of a good sniper, says a proposed Marine Corps manual.

In effect, it adds, the sniper cannot be made — he must be born.

The 240-page manual is being circulated through Marine commands for comment and has not yet been adopted.

Written by Maj. Robert A. Russell of Vista, Calif., who commanded early pickup sniper teams in Vietnam, it lays out the first formal training program on the subject since World War II.

The document says that candidates for sniper training should undergo psychiatric screening to make sure they have "certain essential mental qualities."

"A sniper . . . must kill calmly and deliberately, shooting carefully selected targets," the manual says.

"He must not be susceptible to emotions of anxiety or remorse."

The manual says "a proper mental condition cannot be taught or instilled by training."

Russell, now retired, told newsmen at the time he completed the manual more than a year ago that sniping is a "very personal kind of fighting — you can see the look on people's faces" when they are shot.

By this, he meant that a telescopic sight brings the face of the often unsuspecting victim close to the eye of the sniper, even from a thousand yards away.

"It's different than spraying lead all over a hill," Russell said.

His manual says a sniper must be highly intelligent, because he must learn a wide variety of skills such as ballistics, radio operation, adjustment of artillery fire, map reading and military intelligence collection and reporting.

Sniper teams, generally two men, must operate for long periods by themselves and this means, the manual says, the sniper must display decisiveness and self-reliance.

Stressing coolness, the document says that "even an instant of uncontrolled emotion can be fatal."

"The sniper must possess true equanimity, a perpetual self-possession and serenity which fosters maturity and patience," the manual says.

QUESTIONS

1. *This newspaper article talks in what you may regard as a surprising way: about the process of deliberate killing, but in a familiar language of praise*

* *Boulder* (Colo.) *Daily Camera,* July 17, 1968, at 19.

("decisiveness and self-reliance," "highly intelligent," "essential mental qualities"). Is this a form of control, a kind of art? One that you wish to imitate?

2. *Do you want to say of the preceding two passages – and perhaps of the Cromwell letter as well – that the writer talks about people as things, that he does not recognize their humanity? What does it mean to "recognize the humanity" of a person, or to express such a recognition in one's speech and language? Does the law ever "recognize the humanity" of a litigant, a witness, a judge, or a lawyer?*

COMMANDANT OF AUSCHWITZ*
Rudolf Hoess

I had to see everything. I had to watch hour after hour, by day and by night, the removal and burning of the bodies, the extraction of the teeth, the cutting of the hair, the whole grisly, interminable business. I had to stand for hours on end in the ghastly stench, while the mass graves were being opened and the bodies dragged out and burned.

I had to look through the peephole of the gas chambers and watch the process of death itself, because the doctors wanted me to see it.

I had to do all this because I was the one to whom everyone looked, because I had to show them all that I did not merely issue the orders and make the regulations but was also prepared myself to be present at whatever task I had assigned to my subordinates.

The Reichsführer SS sent various high-ranking Party leaders and SS officers to Auschwitz so that they might see for themselves the process of extermination of the Jews. They were all deeply impressed by what they saw. Some who had previously spoken most loudly about the necessity for this extermination fell silent once they had actually seen the "final solution of the Jewish question." I was repeatedly asked how I and my men could go on watching these operations, and how we were able to stand it.

My invariable answer was that the iron determination with which we must carry out Hitler's orders could only be obtained by a stifling of all humans [*sic*] emotions. Each of these gentlemen declared that he was glad the job had not been given to him.

Even Mildner and Eichmann, who were certainly tough enough, had no wish to change places with me. This was one job which nobody envied me.

I had many detailed discussions with Eichmann concerning all matters connected with the "final solution of the Jewish question," but without ever disclosing my inner anxieties. I tried in every way to discover Eichmann's innermost and real convictions about this "solution."

Yes, every way. Yet even when we were quite alone together and the

* Pages 171–176 (1959).

drink had been flowing freely so that he was in his most expansive mood, he showed that he was completely obsessed with the idea of destroying every single Jew that he could lay his hands on. Without pity and in cold blood we must complete this extermination as rapidly as possible. Any compromise, even the slightest, would have to be paid for bitterly at a later date.

In the face of such grim determination I was forced to bury all my human considerations as deeply as possible.

Indeed, I must freely confess that after these conversations with Eichmann I almost came to regard such emotions as a betrayal of the Führer.

There was no escape for me from this dilemma.

I had to go on with this process of extermination. I had to continue this mass murder and coldly to watch it, without regard for the doubts that were seething deep inside me.

I had to observe every happening with a cold indifference. Even those petty incidents that others might not notice I found hard to forget. In Auschwitz I truly had no reason to complain that I was bored.

If I was deeply affected by some incident, I found it impossible to go back to my home and my family. I would mount my horse and ride, until I had chased the terrible picture away. Often, at night, I would walk through the stables and seek relief among my beloved animals.

It would often happen, when at home, that my thoughts suddenly turned to incidents that had occurred during the extermination. I then had to go out. I could no longer bear to be in my homely family circle. When I saw my children happily playing, or observed my wife's delight over our youngest, the thought would often come to me: how long will our happiness last? My wife could never understand these gloomy moods of mine, and ascribed them to some annoyance connected with my work.

When at night I stood out there beside the transports or by the gas chambers or the fires, I was often compelled to think of my wife and children, without, however, allowing myself to connect them closely with all that was happening.

It was the same with the married men who worked in the crematoriums or at the fire pits.

When they saw the women and children going into the gas chambers, their thoughts instinctively turned to their own families.

I was no longer happy in Auschwitz once the mass exterminations had begun.

I had become dissatisfied with myself. To this must be added that I was worried because of anxiety about my principal task, the never-ending work, and the untrustworthiness of my colleagues.

Then the refusal to understand, or even to listen to me, on the part of my superiors. It was in truth not a happy or desirable state of affairs. Yet everyone in Auschwitz believed that the commandant lived a wonderful life.

My family, to be sure, were well provided for in Auschwitz. Every wish that my wife or children expressed was granted them. The children could live a free and untrammeled life. My wife's garden was a paradise of flowers. The prisoners never missed an opportunity for doing some little act of kindness to my wife or children and thus attracting their attention.

No former prisoner can ever say that he was in any way or at any time badly treated in our house. My wife's greatest pleasure would have been to give a present to every prisoner who was in any way connected with our household.

The children were perpetually begging me for cigarettes for the prisoners. They were particularly fond of the ones who worked in the garden.

My whole family displayed an intense love of agriculture and particularly for animals of all sorts. Every Sunday I had to walk them all across the fields, and visit the stables, and we might never miss the kennels where the dogs were kept. Our two horses and the foal were especially beloved.

The children always kept animals in the garden, creatures the prisoners were forever bringing them. Tortoises, martens, cats, lizards: there was always something new and interesting to be seen there. In summer they splashed in the wading pool in the garden, or in the Sola. But their greatest joy was when Daddy bathed with them. He had, however, so little time for all these childish pleasures. Today I deeply regret that I did not devote more time to my family. I always felt that I had to be on duty the whole time. This exaggerated sense of duty has always made life more difficult for me than it actually need have been. Again and again my wife reproached me and said: "You must think not only of the service always, but of your family too."

Yet what did my wife know about all that lay so heavily on my mind? She has never been told.

When, on Pohl's suggestion, Auschwitz was divided up, he gave me the choice of being commandant of Sachsenhausen or head of DI.

It was something quite exceptional for Pohl to allow any officer a choice of jobs. He gave me twenty-four hours in which to decide. It was really a kindly gesture in good will, a recompense, as he saw it, for the task I had been given at Auschwitz.

At first I felt unhappy at the prospect of uprooting myself, for I had become deeply involved with Auschwitz as a result of all the difficulties and troubles and the many heavy tasks that had been assigned to me there.

But then I was glad to be free from it all.

QUESTIONS

1. *I assume you agree that there is inhumanity, indecency, here. Can you show how those qualities are manifested in Hoess's language or uses of language? Or is what you respond to here simply his terrible behavior?*
2. *You might find it valuable to compare this passage with the passages from Huckleberry Finn and from the Harvard Law Review, supra pages 21 and 41, respectively.*
3. *Below is a passage where the law for once does seem to say what is called for, to say what a decent person would say. Here the law recognizes the humanity of the people it talks about; how does it do so? Why does it not always do so?*

PEOPLE v. SHERWOOD
271 N.Y. 427, 3 N.E.2d 581 (1936)

[New York Penal Law §1120 provided: "An act done by a person who is an idiot, imbecile, lunatic, or insane is not a crime. A person can not be tried, sentenced to any punishment or punished for a crime while he is in a state of idiocy, imbecility, lunacy, or insanity so as to be incapable of understanding the proceeding or making his defense.

"A person is not excused from criminal liability as an idiot, imbecile, lunatic, or insane person, except upon proof that, at the time of committing the alleged criminal act, he was laboring under such a defect of reason as:

"1. Not to know the nature and quality of the act he was doing; or

"2. Not to know that the act was wrong."]

CROUCH, J. The defendant stands convicted of murder in the first degree. On the date of the homicide she was twenty-seven years of age. The victim was her own infant son aged two years and three months. On August 20, 1935, under circumstances hereinafter to be stated, she put the child in his carriage, walked three and one-half miles from her lodging place to a secluded spot off the main highway, and, in a small pool of water eight inches deep, held his head under water until he was drowned.

The sole defense was that at the time of the crime she was laboring under such a defect of reason as not to know the nature and quality of the act or that the act was wrong. It is now urged that the verdict was against the weight of the evidence, and that it was rendered under misapprehension of the applicable law because of erroneous instructions.

We cannot say that the verdict was against the weight of the evidence. The defense and the prosecution each swore two qualified psychiatrists who expressed contrary opinions as to the mental state of the defendant in answer to hypothetical questions which were not substantially different. Under such circumstances, argument based upon scattered gleanings from the cross-examination of the People's experts, must fail in an appellate court to demonstrate that the weight of evidence on the issue of insanity was with the defense. The jury could accept or reject the opinion of any expert. (*Dougherty v. Milliken,* 163 N.Y. 527, 533.)

The serious question is whether the conclusion which was reached can or ought in justice to stand. Technical legal error there was in instructions to the jury, which may or may not have affected the result. Error also there was in an incident of the charge, which, whether it be called technical legal error or not, did almost beyond doubt affect the verdict. Under such circumstances we think the verdict should be set aside.

The claim of the defense was that the mother killed the child because she had become obsessed with a delusion that in death alone could there be safety and freedom from pain, suffering and misery for her son. The time has gone by when such a claim could seem fantastic, either to judge or juror. While we still — and rightly — accept the validity of such claims with the utmost caution, we nevertheless know now that they may be valid. The claim here rests upon evidence which, on the one hand, neither discloses nor even suggests any rational motive for the tragic act; and, on the other hand, does build up a personality which might well crack and crumble under the hard blows which fate, within a brief period, dealt it. Born of indifferent stock in a small western town, the defendant at nine years of age had lost her mother. For a time she was in an orphanage, and then for a period served her itinerant father and his successive wives as a household drudge. There followed a period of a few years when she lived at various places in the middle west with a succession of Salvation Army families, doing household and other work, and getting some scattered and interrupted schooling. Following that insecure and sorry young girlhood, she commenced when about sixteen years old to earn her own independent way. Shortly she went on the stage as a chorus girl with traveling companies. When she was nineteen years old she met and married her husband, a stage electrician, whose job, like her own, kept him moving from place to place. Within a year a baby girl was born. The couple finally came to rest in Newburgh on the Hudson, where the man secured a job with a moving picture house. After a period of comparative peace and security, what small prosperity had come to them was ended by the illness of the husband. Early in 1933 the boy baby was born. The evidence of the doctor who attended the defendant and of the nurse at a pre-natal clinic, shows clearly that the child was not an unwanted one. On the contrary it was desired, welcomed, and after birth was lovingly and carefully attended to and looked after. The husband's illness developed into tuberculosis. The home, the only one the defendant had ever known, was broken up. He went to a sanitarium, the little daughter was taken by the mother-in-law, and the defendant with the infant son went to a lodging house, the landlady of which looked after the child while the defendant, as her sole means of support, worked as a waitress in a restaurant. In April, 1935, her husband died. Several months later the defendant met a man who, after a time, offered to provide a home for her and her son, to marry her and to educate the boy. On a day fixed they were to leave Newburgh for a new home in the west. She gave up her job. She made ready to go. The day came but not the man. She waited until she realized she had been deceived. She tried to get work and failed. Without a job, without means, she and her little son were evicted by the landlady—though the latter denied that—and thereupon was committed the act for which her life is forfeit. A laconic statement made to the police the same day tells the story: "My husband, Fred Sherwood, died about four months ago, and since that time I have found it very difficult to make a living for myself and my two children, Dorothy, aged seven, and James, aged two. This afternoon, August 20th, 1935, shortly before twelve o'clock noon I took my younger child, James Sherwood, in a stroller down to Caesar's Lane at New Windsor, New York. There is a very shallow brook there and I let him wade in the brook until he seemed to get tired of it, and then I picked him up in my arms and held him under water for about half an hour. During this period of time his head was completely covered with water. I picked him up then, put a clean suit on him and held him in my arms for some time. . . . Later I walked up to the state road and was given a ride to the City of Newburgh. After I got into the City I walked into Police headquarters and told the lieutenant at the desk what I had done."

During the ride back to town she carried the dead child in her arms. In that fashion she entered police headquarters. The lieutenant of police in charge testifies: "In a low monotone voice she came up alongside of my desk and said to me, 'Here he is.' . . . I said, 'You killed him?' She said, 'Yes, I drowned him.' I said, 'Where did you drown him?' She said, 'In Caesar's Lane.' I said, 'What did you do that for?' She said, 'I couldn't take care of him any longer and I thought he would be better off dead.' "

At no time was there the slightest evidence of emotion, except for a moment when, taken back to the scene of the crime, she was "teary-eyed" at the sight of the wet, discarded baby clothes; nor was there ever the least sign of regret or of doubt that she had acted for the best, as she regarded it. That the defendant knew what she was doing — the nature and quality of the act — although perhaps a matter of small doubt to the lay mind, was still an issue because both experts called as witnesses by the defendant denied that she had such knowledge. That she knew it was wrong was, when the case went to the jury, open to serious and substantial doubt. (*People v. Schmidt*, 216 N.Y. 324, 338, 340.) It was of the utmost importance, therefore, that the law as respects criminal responsibility under section 1120 of the Penal Law, should have been made clear to the jury.

In the main charge it was not made clear that a defect of reason which inhibited a knowledge *either* of the nature and quality of the act *or* that the act was wrong, excused a person from criminal liability. At various points the two matters were referred to in the conjunctive, with the word "and" instead of the word "or." The error was called to the attention of the court at the close of the main charge, and the court said merely: "If I made that error, I so charge." Left in that way, the distinction might doubtfully be considered as having been made clear. But thereafter — and it was the court's last word before the jury retired — the court upon request charged that a mere false belief would not be sufficient to excuse her, "unless it was the result of some mental *disease* which prevented her from knowing the nature and quality of the act *and* that it was wrongful." Here was a repetition of the same error, complicated with a reference to "some mental disease," i.e., some pathological condition, instead of a "defect of reason," as the statute reads. No disease, no pathological condition, existed or was claimed to exist. It may be doubted whether the jury had a clear conception of when a person is or is not criminally liable under section 1120. . . .

The judgment of conviction should be reversed and a new trial ordered.

Crane, Ch. J., Lehman, Hubbs and Loughran, JJ., concur; O'Brien and Finch, JJ., dissent.

QUESTIONS

1. *This opinion seems to speak in a voice we can recognize as decent, expressing familiar and appropriate emotions. Does it leave something out, or is it a complete statement of what needs to be said about these events?*
2. *Here is one difficulty with this opinion as an example of successful legal expression: how can the court justify including anything in its opinion except the last paragraph? Is the telling of the real story, which is so important to the meaning of this case for any reader, in fact legally irrelevant? The judge talks two ways, but perhaps it is a violation of standards of legal expression for him to do so. The headnotes would contain the rule of law and nothing of what one finds important in the opinion. Is this opinion a paradigm for the lawyer and judge: he can say what really counts only by breaking the rules, just as the judge in the Georgetown Hospital*

case (at the beginning of this chapter) could do what really counted only by breaking the rules?

3. Could Judge Crouch say that he was not breaking the rules, on the grounds that the "real story" must be told in order to determine whether the error in the charge was harmful or harmless?
   a. Notice that here the jury in fact convicted Mrs. Sherwood of first-degree murder. Can you seriously believe that the use of "and" instead of "or" in the charge was responsible for that verdict?
   b. The existence of this verdict raises another possibility: that the court here does not tell the "real" story but only one side of it. Can you assess the honesty of the story told by Judge Crouch? How do you do so?
   c. How do you suppose Judges Finch and O'Brien would explain their dissents?
4. Compare the common judicial tactic of stating the brutal details of the crime, however irrelevant to any legal question, where the court wishes to affirm a conviction. See, e.g., Smith v. Texas, 395 F.2d 958 (5th Cir. 1968).
5. Other passages or books dealing with death that might be of some interest are: Plato, Crito and Phaedo; Matthew, Chapter 27; Chaucer, "The Knight's Tale," in Canterbury Tales; L. O'Flaherty, Famine (1937); B. Behan, The Quare Fellow (1956); James Agee, A Death in the Family (1957); V. Frankl, Man's Search for Meaning (1959); McGahern, The Barracks (1963). Medical and psychiatric books include: K. Eissler, The Psychiatrist and the Dying Patient (1955); E. Kubler-Ross, On Death and Dying (1969); A. Kutscher, Loss and Grief (1970).

e. *Justifying a Language by Its Special Purposes*

One response to what you have just read would be to say that the assumption of the questions (indeed, of the anthology) — that the law can profitably be compared with literature — is wrong. Of course experience is incompletely, often only technically, expressible in the language of the law; but whoever would have supposed otherwise? The law is a special language designed to serve special social and intellectual purposes, and was never intended as a way of saying much about life.

In some of the questions asked above, I have maintained that this sort of justification poses a dilemma for the lawyer: in relying on it, one defines one's professional life in a highly restricted way, and must then ask if one is prepared to live such a life. But is it fair to claim that just because there are matters that you do not express, which your literature fails to recognize, that you as a person or a lawyer must be blind to them? Why measure the life by what is expressed? As I put it earlier, does it really matter if we as lawyers fail to say what we want, so long as we can do what we want? Might it not be enough for us, like Ulysses, to use the language to achieve our goals, whatever they may be, even if we cannot use it to say all we would like to say about an event, to tell the truth? Such a relationship of control over the language — though manipulative and conceivably dishonest, one might call it — would leave us free to have whatever private sense of irony or ambiguity we might choose. A silent exercise of power would be ours. Is that enough? If you are attracted by the idea that your task as a writer is simply to make your language help you achieve what you want in the world, consider this question: exactly what goals would such a power enable you to attain?

These matters are, of course, complex and difficult. The proposed distinction between what a statement "says" and what it "does" may not bear analysis, although it would seem to lie behind the law school common-place that the "right result" in a case is of very little value unless the "right reasons" are expressed to support it. The distinction raises the question, which runs very deep in the law, of the importance of expressing what we do and why we do it. The whole notion of law seems to require that judges do that, and perhaps legislators; is the lawyer perhaps situated differently?

Another way to put it might be this: how does the lawyer properly decide when enough has been said, when a statement is complete? No statement says all that can be said about an event; one can always go on. All statements stop short of full expression; some seem incomplete and we want more to be said; some say too much; of others we have a feeling that the writer was right to stop where he did. How do we make this judgment? How, in particular, can various legal statements be evaluated in this respect? What are the forces that give shape to a statement in the law? How much of what the lawyer knows should he feel called upon to say?

Our attention has temporarily shifted from defining legal literature to criticizing it, and Section A2 will continue this enterprise. How does one sensibly evaluate a legal statement or a branch of legal literature? What merits and what defects can we expect, and how can we define them? What language of critical judgment can we make for ourselves? We shall study the death penalty as a sample for analysis. Can you find a way to express what is wrong with this literature? If you wish to say that it is inhumane or indecent — that it is like the literature of war and the concentration camp — can you explain what you mean by such terms? Is the death penalty an oddity, or is it representative of other branches of legal literature?

2. *Defining Viciousness in Language and Imagination: The Rhetoric of the Death Penalty*

An attempt will be made in the next few pages to work around a subject with some thoroughness, to carry a line of critical analysis to a sort of conclusion. The aim is to learn something both about the particular abuses of life and language that have been worked by the death penalty and about the process of critical judgment in which we are now engaged.[2] This is an exercise in explanation and complication.

It appears at the outset that this literature presents a very different sort of difficulty from the estate plan: no one would say that it is a technical language admirably suited to technical ends. In fact, you might say it is technical language used in a wholly inappropriate way, though you may find it hard to explain what you mean by that. For we really are not badly troubled by the language of the estate plan — though you might be hard pressed to explain exactly why not, and you might not want to devote your life to it — but nearly everyone has been troubled by the death penalty, and it is my view that part of what troubles us is its rhetoric, its way of talking. In what follows I want to suggest that the death penalty is not merely wrong in itself as a brutal practice, but that it is vicious as a literature, that it is a way of imagining and talking about experience that corrupts our minds and lives, and that it is perhaps representative of other literatures in the law and elsewhere.

To make such a suggestion is to state a problem for critical analysis and judgment: how can we define and express what we sense to be wrong with this way of talking? What might one mean by an "inappropriate" use of "technical" language, for example? Or how can one explain what one means when one calls this literature "inhumane" or "indecent"? To look back over some of the terms that have been used in this course, do we want to say that the law of the death penalty leaves out what it should include, that it raises false and unsubstantiated pretenses, that it talks only one way, that it is overconfident, or what? Or can we find some different terminology in which to express our sense of the wrongness of this language?

REPORT*

Royal Commission on Capital Punishment 1949–1953

Part III. Methods of Execution, Etc.
Chapter 12. The Sentence of Death

683. The traditional formula is well known. Its essential elements are of great antiquity. "The judgment against a man or woman for felony of death hath always been the same since the reign of Henry the First, viz.

2. Although the death penalty was held unconstitutional in *Furman v. Georgia*, 408 U.S. 238 (1972), many people strongly favor its reinstatement. As a practice and as a way of talking about experience, the death penalty is still urged upon us, and partial reinstatement is by no means impossible. For these reasons I speak here of the death penalty not in the past tense but the present.

* Pages 240–261 (1953).

that he or she be hanged by the neck till dead, which in the Roll is shortly entered thus, 'sus per coll'." A longer form of sentence was in regular use in the seventeenth century and remained virtually unchanged until 1948. This formula was revised by the Judges in 1903, after which it ran as follows: — "The sentence of the Court upon you is, that you be taken from this place to a lawful prison and thence to a place of execution and that you be hanged by the neck until you be dead; and that your body be afterwards buried within the precincts of the prison in which you shall have been confined before your execution." It has been usual to add the words "And may the Lord have mercy on your soul", which are followed by the chaplain's invocation "Amen".

684. It has long been customary for the Judge to put on the black cap before he pronounces sentence, although it appears that in recent years some Judges have, on occasion, not assumed it. The black cap, which is a square of black silk, is part of the judicial costume of the Judge and its use is not regulated by any statutory provision. . . .

697. As we have said, the wearing of the black cap is governed by custom. The Judges are under no obligation to assume it, and in England they have sometimes refrained from doing so when they felt that its use would be out of place. On the other hand all the Judges were in favour of retaining this custom. The Lord Justice General told us that, at any rate in Scotland, this was not only for sentimental reasons, but because the assumption of the black cap symbolised the fact that the Judge was not expressing a private judgment, but was merely an instrument of the State, and some Judges who have conscientious objections to the death sentence desired "to safeguard themselves by assuming the full cloak of judicial officialdom in pronouncing the sentence". We consider that this matter may well be left to the discretion of individual Judges and we therefore make no recommendation about it, or about the use in England of the words "And may the Lord have mercy on your soul" and of the chaplain's invocation, which are also governed only by tradition and custom. . . .

Hanging

711. In most of the English prisons equipped for execution the execution chamber adjoins the condemned cell. The chamber itself is a small room and the trap occupies a large part of the floor. The trap is formed of two hinged leaves held in position from below by bolts which are withdrawn when the lever is pulled, allowing the leaves to drop on their hinges. Above the trap a rope of a standard length is attached to a strong chain, which is fitted to the overhead beam in such a way that it can be raised and lowered and secured at any desired height by means of a cotter slipped into one of the links and a bracket fixed on the beam.

This enables the length of chain to be adjusted to make the drop accord with the height and weight of the prisoner.

712. The executioner and his assistant arrive at the prison on the afternoon before the execution. They are told the height and weight of the prisoner and are given an opportunity to see him from a position where they themselves cannot be seen. While the prisoner is out of his cell they test the apparatus to ensure that it is working satisfactorily. For this purpose they use a sack of approximately the same weight as the prisoner, having ascertained the proper drop from a table which gives the length appropriate to a prisoner's weight. Some adjustments in the length given in the table may be necessary to allow for other physical characteristics of the prisoner, such as age and build. . . .

713. On the morning of the execution a final check of the equipment is carried out. The rope is coiled, fitted to the chain, and secured in position by a piece of pack-thread which will be broken by the weight of the prisoner when he drops. Just before the time of execution the executioner and his assistant join the Under-Sheriff and the prison officials outside the door of the condemned cell. The Under-Sheriff gives the signal; the executioner enters the cell and pinions the prisoner's arms behind his back, and two officers lead him to the scaffold and place him directly across the division of the trap on a spot previously marked with chalk. The assistant executioner pinions his legs while the executioner puts a white cap over his head and fits the noose around his neck with the knot drawn tight on the left lower jaw, where it is held in position by a sliding ring. The executioner then pulls the lever. The medical officer carries out an immediate inspection to assure himself that life is extinct and the body is then left to hang for an hour before being taken down. Mr. Pierrepoint said that the time which elapses between the entry of the executioner into the cell and the pulling of the lever is normally between 9 and 12 seconds but may be 20 to 25 seconds in a few prisons where the condemned cell does not adjoin the execution chamber. Captain Williams of the Prison Commission stated that the periods in two recent executions which had been timed by stop-watch were 17 and 19 seconds.

COLORADO REVISED STATUTES (1963)

§39-11-2. The governing authority of the state penitentiary, at the expense of the state of Colorado, shall provide a suitable and efficient room or place, enclosed from public view, within the walls of the penitentiary, and therein construct, and at all times have in preparation all necessary appliances requisite for carrying into execution the death penalty by means of the administration of lethal gas. The punishment of death in each and every case of death sentence pronounced in this state, must be inflicted by the warden of the state penitentiary in the room or place, and with the appliances provided for inflicting the punishment of death by the administration of lethal gas.

§39-11-4. The particular day and hour of the execution of said sentence within the week specified in said warrant shall be fixed by said warden, and he shall be present thereat, or shall appoint the deputy warden or some other representative among the officials or officers of the penitentiary to be present in his place and stead. There shall also be present such guards and attendants from the penitentiary as the warden in his discretion shall deem necessary. The warden shall also invite to be present thereat the sheriff of the county wherein the conviction was had or a deputy appointed by him, the chaplain and physician of the penitentiary, two other duly licensed physicians, residents of the state, the spiritual adviser of the convict, if any, and in addition not less than six nor more than twelve reputable citizens of the state of full age, and said warden shall not permit any other person to be present at said execution. The time fixed by said warden for said execution shall be by him kept secret and in no manner divulged except privately to the persons herein provided to be present. Such persons who are to be present, or who are invited to be present, shall not before such execution divulge such fact to any person whomsoever, nor in any manner disclose the time of such execution.

§39-11-7. Any person who before the time of the execution of any death sentence shall divulge the time thereof to any person other than those specified in section 39-11-4, shall be guilty of a misdemeanor and, upon conviction thereof, be punished by a fine of not less than fifty dollars nor more than five hundred dollars, or by imprisonment in the county jail for not less than thirty days nor more than six months, or both.

§39-11-8. The warden or other person acting in his stead, who performs the duties imposed upon him by this article, shall be paid for his services out of the moneys provided for the maintenance of said state penitentiary, the sum of fifty dollars. The sheriff shall be paid for his services by the county where such conviction was had, the sum of twenty-five dollars, together with his mileage fees as provided by law.

REFLECTIONS ON THE GUILLOTINE*

Albert Camus

Instead of saying, "If you kill someone you will pay for it on the scaffold," would it not be more politic — if we are interested in setting an example — to say instead: "If you kill someone, you will be thrown

* In E. London (ed.), *The Law as Literature* 517–531 (Richard Howard trans. 1960).

into prison for months or even years, torn between an impossible despair and a constantly renewed fear, until one morning we will sneak into your cell, having taken off our shoes in order to surprise you in your sleep, which has at last overcome you after the night's anguish. We will throw ourselves upon you, tie your wrists behind your back, and with a pair of scissors cut away your shirt collar and your hair, if it should be in the way. Because we are perfectionists we will lash your arms together with a strap so that your body will be arched to offer unhampered access to the back of your neck. Then we will carry you, one man holding you up under each arm, your feet dragging behind you, down the long corridors, until, under the night sky, one of the executioners will at last take hold of the back of your trousers and throw you down on a board, another will make sure your head is in the lunette, and a third one will drop, from a height of two meters twenty centimeters, a blade weighing sixty kilograms that will slice through your neck like a razor."[1]

For the example to be even better, for the terror it breeds to become in each of us a force blind enough and powerful enough to balance, at the right moment, our irresistible desire to kill, we must go still further. Instead of bragging, with our characteristic pretentious ignorance, that we have invented a swift and humane[2] means of killing those condemned to death, we should publish in millions of copies, read out in every school and college, the eyewitness accounts and medical reports that describe the state of the body after execution. We should particularly recommend the printing and circulation of a recent communication made to the Academy of Medicine by Doctors Piedelièvre and Fournier. These courageous physicians, having examined, in the interests of science, the bodies of the condemned after execution, have considered it their duty to sum up their terrible observations thus: "If we may be permitted to present our opinion on this subject, such spectacles are horribly painful. The blood rushes from the vessels according to the rhythm of the severed carotids, then coagulates. The muscles contract and their fibrillation is stupefying. The intestine undulates and the heart produces a series of irregular, incomplete, and convulsive movements. The mouth tightens, at certain moments, into a dreadful grimace. It is true that the eyes of a decapitated head are immobile, the pupils dilated; fortunately, they cannot see, and if they exhibit no signs of disturbance, none of the characteristic opalescence of a cadaver, they at least have no capacity for movement: their transparency is that of life, but their fixity is mortal. All this may last minutes, even hours, in a healthy subject: death is not immediate. . . . Thus each vital element

1. A description of the actual procedure in French prisons. Cf. the movie *We Are All Murderers.* — Translator.

2. According to the optimistic Dr. Guillotine, the condemned man would feel nothing at all — at most a "slight coolness at the back of his neck."

survives decapitation to some extent. There remains, for the physician, the impression of a hideous experiment, a murderous vivisection followed by a premature burial."[3] . . .

I could cite many other eyewitness accounts as hallucinatory as these. But as for myself, I hardly need or know how to go further. After all, I make no claim that the death penalty is exemplary: indeed, this torture affects me only as what it is — a crude surgery practiced in conditions that deprive it of any edifying character whatsoever. Society, on the other hand, and the State (which has seen other tortures) can easily bear such details; and since they favor preaching examples, they might as well make them universally known so that a perpetually terrorized populace can become Franciscan to a man. For who is it we think we are frightening by this example constantly screened from view; by the threat of a punishment described as painless, expedient, and on the whole less disagreeable than cancer; by a torture crowned with all the flowers of rhetoric? Certainly not those who pass for honest (and some are) because they are asleep at such an hour, to whom the *great example* has not been revealed, and who drink their morning coffee at the hour of the premature burial, informed of the operation of justice, if they happen to read the newspapers, by a mealy-mouthed bulletin that dissolves like sugar in their memory. Yet these same peaceful creatures furnish society with the largest percentage of its homicides. Many of these honest men are criminals without knowing it. According to one magistrate, the overwhelming majority of the murderers he had tried did not know, when they shaved themselves that morning, that they were going to kill someone that night. For the sake of example and security alike, we should brandish rather than disguise the agonized face of our victim before the eyes of every man as he shaves himself in the morning.

This is not done. The State conceals the circumstances and even the existence of its executions, keeps silent about such reports and such accounts. It does not concern itself with the exemplary value of punishment save by tradition, nor does it trouble to consider the present meaning of its act. The criminal is killed because he has been killed for centuries, and furthermore he is killed according to a procedure established at the end of the eighteenth century. The same arguments that have served as legal tender for centuries are perpetuated as a matter of routine, contradicted only by those measures which the evolution of public sensibility renders inevitable. The law is applied without consideration of its significance, and our condemned criminals die by rote in the name of a theory in which their executioners no longer believe. If they believed in it, it would be known, and above all it would be seen. But such publicity, beyond the fact that it arouses sadistic instincts of

3. *Justice sans bourreau*, No. 2, June, 1956.

which the repercussions are incalculable and which end, one day or another, by satisfying themselves with yet another murder, also risks provoking the disgust and revolt of public opinion itself. It would become more difficult to execute by assembly line, as we do in France at this moment, if such executions were translated into the bold images of popular fantasy. The very man who enjoys his morning coffee while reading that justice has been done would certainly choke on it at the slightest of such details. . . .

Here again, when our official jurists speak of death without suffering, they do not know what they are talking about, and furthermore they betray a remarkable lack of imagination. The devastating, degrading fear imposed on the condemned man for months or even years[4] is a punishment more terrible than death itself, and one that has not been imposed on his victim. A murdered man is generally rushed to his death, even at the height of his terror of the mortal violence being done to him, without knowing what is happening: the period of his horror is only that of his life itself, and his hope of escaping whatever madness has pounced upon him probably never deserts him. For the man condemned to death, on the other hand, the horror of his situation is served up to him at every moment for months on end. Torture by hope alternates only with the pangs of animal despair. His lawyer and his confessor, out of simple humanity, and his guards, to keep him docile, unanimously assure him that he will be reprieved. He believes them with all his heart, yet he cannot believe them at all. He hopes by day, despairs by night.[5] And as the weeks pass, his hope and despair increase proportionately, until they become equally insupportable. According to all accounts, the color of his skin changes: fear acts like an acid. "It's nothing to know you're going to die," one such man in the Fresnes prison said, "but not to know if you're going to live is the real torture." At the moment of his execution Cartouche remarked, "Bah! a nasty quarter of an hour and it's all over." But it takes months, not minutes. The condemned man knows long in advance that he is going to be killed and that all that can save him is a reprieve which operates, so far as he is concerned, like the will of heaven itself. In any case he cannot intervene, plead for himself: he is no longer a man, but a thing waiting to be manipulated by the executioners. He is kept in a state of absolute

4. Roemen, condemned to death at the time of the Liberation, remained in chains for 700 days before being executed: a scandal. Those condemned by common law wait, as a general rule, three to six months until the morning of their death. Yet if one wishes to preserve their chances for reprieve, it is not advisable to shorten the delay. I can bear witness, moreover, that the examination leading to a recommendation of mercy is conducted in France with a gravity that does not exclude an evident willingness to reprieve to the full extent that law and public opinion will allow.

5. Since there are no executions on Sunday, Saturday night is always a good night in death row.

necessity, the condition of inert matter, yet within him is the consciousness that is his principal enemy.

When the officials whose trade is to kill such a man refer to him as "luggage," they know what they are saying: to be unable to react to the hand that moves you, holds you, or lets you drop — is that not the condition of some package, some *thing*, or better still, some trapped animal? Yet an animal in a trap can starve itself to death; the man condemned to death cannot. He is provided with a special diet (at Fresnes, diet No. 4 with *extras* of milk, wine, sugar, preserves, and butter); he is encouraged to eat well — if necessary he is forced to eat. The animal must be in good condition for the kill. The thing — the animal — has a right only to those corrupted privileges known as caprices. "You'd be surprised how sensitive they are!" declared one sergeant at Fresnes without a trace of irony. Sensitive? Unquestionably — how else recover the freedom and dignity of will that man cannot live without? Sensitive or not, from the moment the death sentence is pronounced, the condemned man becomes part of an imperturbable mechanism. He spends several weeks within the cogs and gears of a machine that controls his every gesture, ultimately delivering him to the hands that will lay him out on the last device of all. The luggage is no longer subjected to the operations of chance, the hazards that dominate the existence of a living being, but to mechanical laws that permit him to foresee in the minutest perspective the day of his decapitation.

His condition as an object comes to an end on this day. During the three-quarters of an hour that separates him from his extinction, the certainty of his futile death overcomes everything: the fettered, utterly submissive creature experiences a hell that makes a mockery of the one with which he is threatened. For all their hemlock, the Greeks were humane: they provided their criminals a relative liberty at least, the possibility of postponing or advancing the hour of their own death; and of choosing between suicide and execution. For reasons of security, we carry out our justice by ourselves. Yet there could not be real justice in such cases unless the murderer, having made known his decision months in advance, had entered his victim's house, tied him up securely, informed him he would be put to death in the next hour, and then used this hour to set up the apparatus by which his victim would be dispatched. What criminal has ever reduced his victim to a condition so desperate, so hopeless, and so powerless?

QUESTIONS

1. *Can you draft a statute authorizing the death penalty, or providing for its administration, that expresses what Camus would like it to? Try to do so.*

2. Is the vice of legal talk about the death penalty that it leaves out any statement of what the experience of death means to the convict, to his family, and to others? If so, where should that statement be made: in the statute? In the judge's sentencing opinion? In the charge to the jury, if the jury sentences the defendant? In the verdict of the jury, if that entails a sentencing?

   Imagine the end of a murder trial in which the jury is asked to decide the penalty.

   a. As lawyer for the defense, would you be able to say all you wanted to say about the death in question? Would the law impose any restrictions on you? (Your powers with language would of course do so.) Outline such an argument to the jury. You might want to read Clarence Darrow's famous summation in the Loeb-Leopold case reproduced in F. Hicks, Famous American Jury Speeches 992 (1925).
   b. As a judge would you be able, in your charge to the jury, to say about the death penalty what you thought was called for?
   c. As a juror could you say what was called for to the other jurors?

      Is there anything that should be said with respect to the experience of the death penalty that could not be said at trial or sentencing? If so, draft a statement in which you express what the law would exclude.

      Is it fair to say that there are virtually no restrictions on the lawyer here, that at least in jury argument the legal language system is identical with plain English? Are there any restrictions on the judge?

3. In any event, it is hard to say that the vice of this language is simply incompleteness of expression, since the literature of estate planning likewise leaves out virtually everything that a particular death might be said to mean, yet you presumably regard that way of talking as appropriate, although incomplete. How can you explain such a position? Is it just that you disapprove of the death penalty, or does your objection have something to do with defects in expression? Here are two possible explanations:

   a. "The difference is that in the estate plan the death is a given, over which the law has no control, and to which it merely attaches consequences, while in the operation of the death penalty the law actually causes a death, thereby incurring a vastly greater responsibility to explain what is really involved."

      If that is your view, tell us how to distinguish this situation: the law permits and encourages activities, such as building bridges or skyscrapers, that are certain to result in fatalities, yet it is absolutely silent with respect to those deaths (except perhaps for the Workmen's Compensation statutes, which are hardly full expressions of the experience). It is similarly silent about the deaths of sick persons whose lives could be extended if society provided at public cost some expensive treatment, such as kidney machines, which it refuses to do. See, e.g., D. Gould, "Deciding Who Shall Die," The New Statesman, Jan. 24, 1969.

   b. "What is left out of the literature of the death penalty is not an expression of the experience of death or of grief, but a justification of what the law is doing. We could call this a failure to give the event an intelligible legal significance, a failure to make and substantiate a claim to meaning." To examine this suggestion, consider the following:

(1) What language of justification for the death penalty can you imagine? Describe or give an example of this language of justification, as employed by a prosecutor, say, or a judge. How do you evaluate the statement you have drafted?
(2) Where should this justification appear? In the statute, the judicial opinion, the charge to the jury, the jury's verdict, or somewhere else?
(3) How do the proponents of the death penalty in fact justify or explain their position? What is the theoretical or doctrinal structure of which the death penalty is a part?
(4) Is the institution of noncapital punishment explained and justified more nearly to your satisfaction? Explain how.

4. Evaluate the following proposal for a Supreme Court opinion on the subject: "We do not decide that the death penalty is necessarily and in all cases constitutionally impermissible, but that the legal systems within our jurisdiction which wish to employ it have hitherto failed to make and express the sort of considered and rational judgment that must underlie the state's participation in any such brutal and drastic conduct. Accordingly we hold that the death penalty may not be imposed until the legal system seeking to employ it has justified its use by demonstrating with great specificity the necessity of this punishment. The state must show, with respect to every class of case for which the death penalty is proposed, that the death penalty has more social benefits and fewer social costs than any alternative. The classes of case for which the death penalty is proposed must of course be defined with great clarity and specificity."
   a. Would this be an effective way of forcing the state to declare the meaning it wishes to claim for the death it inflicts?
   b. How would a state meet such a burden? On the difficulties of making such classifications, see McGautha v. California, 402 U.S. 183, 204 (1971).
5. Below is another opinion on the death penalty. How do you evaluate what you read here?

FURMAN v. GEORGIA
408 U.S. 238, 405 (1972)

BLACKMUN, J., dissenting. I join the respective opinions of the Chief Justice, Mr. Justice Powell, and Mr. Justice Rehnquist, and add only the following, somewhat personal, comments.

1. Cases such as these provide for me an excruciating agony of the spirit. I yield to no one in the depth of my distaste, antipathy, and, indeed, abhorrence, for the death penalty, with all its aspects of physical distress and fear and of moral judgment exercised by finite minds. That distaste is buttressed by a belief that capital punishment serves no useful purpose that can be demonstrated. For me, it violates childhood's training and life's experiences, and is not compatible with the philosophical convictions I have been able to develop. It is antagonistic to any sense of "reverence for life." Were I a legislator, I would vote against the

death penalty for the policy reasons argued by counsel for the respective petitioners and expressed and adopted in the several opinions filed by the Justices who vote to reverse these convictions.

2. Having lived for many years in a State that does not have the death penalty, that effectively abolished it in 1911, and that carried out its last execution on February 13, 1906, capital punishment had never been a part of life for me. In my State, it just did not exist. So far as I can determine, the State, purely from a statistical deterrence point of view, was neither the worse nor the better for its abolition, for, as the concurring opinions observe, the statistics prove little, if anything. But the State and its citizens accepted the fact that the death penalty was not to be in the arsenal of possible punishments for any crime.

3. I, perhaps alone among the present members of the Court, am on judicial record as to this. As a member of the United States Court of Appeals, I first struggled silently with the issue of capital punishment in *Feguer v. United States,* 302 F.2d 214 (CA8 1962), cert. denied, 371 U.S. 872 (1962). The defendant in that case may have been one of the last to be executed under federal auspices. I struggled again with the issue, and once more refrained from comment, in my writing for an en banc court in *Pope v. United States,* 372 F.2d 710 (CA8 1967), vacated (upon acknowledgment by the Solicitor General of error revealed by the subsequently decided *United States v. Jackson,* 390 U.S. 570 (1968)) and remanded, 392 U.S. 651 (1968). Finally, in *Maxwell v. Bishop,* 398 F.2d 138 (CA8 1968), vacated and remanded, sua sponte, by the Court on grounds not raised below, 398 U.S 262 (1970), I revealed, solitarily and not for the panel, my distress and concern. 398 F.2d, at 153-154. And in *Jackson v. Bishop,* 404 F.2d 571 (CA8 1968), I had no hesitancy in writing a panel opinion that held the use of the strap by trusties upon fellow Arkansas prisoners to be a violation of the Eighth Amendment. That, however, was in-prison punishment imposed by inmate-foremen.

4. The several concurring opinions acknowledge, as they must, that until today capital punishment was accepted and assumed as not unconstitutional per se under the Eighth Amendment or the Fourteenth Amendment. This is either the flat or the implicit holding of a unanimous Court in *Wilkerson v. Utah,* 99 U.S. 130, 134-135, in 1879; of a unanimous Court in *In re Kemmler,* 136 U.S. 436, 447, in 1890; of the Court in *Weems v. United States,* 217 U.S. 349, in 1910; of all those members of the Court, a majority, who addressed the issue in *Louisiana ex rel. Francis v. Resweber,* 329 U.S. 459, 463-464, 471-472, in 1947; of Mr. Chief Justice Warren, speaking for himself and three others (Justices Black, Douglas, and Whittaker) in *Trop v. Dulles,* 356 U.S. 86, 99, in 1958; in the denial of certiorari in *Rudolph v. Alabama,* 375 U.S. 889, in 1963 (where, however, Justices Douglas, Brennan, and Goldberg

would have heard argument with respect to the imposition of the ultimate penalty on a convicted rapist who had "neither taken nor endangered human life"); and of Mr. Justice Black in *McGautha v. California,* 402 U.S. 183, 226, decided only last Term on May 3, 1971.

Suddenly, however, the course of decision is now the opposite way, with the Court evidently persuaded that somehow the passage of time has taken us to a place of greater maturity and outlook. The argument, plausible and high-sounding as it may be, is not persuasive, for it is only one year since *McGautha,* only eight and one-half years since *Rudolph,* 14 years since *Trop,* and 25 years since *Francis,* and we have been presented with nothing that demonstrates a significant movement of any kind in these brief periods. The Court has just decided that it is time to strike down the death penalty. There would have been as much reason to do this when any of the cited cases were decided. But the Court refrained from that action on each of those occasions.

The Court has recognized, and I certainly subscribe to the proposition, that the Cruel and Unusual Punishments Clause "may acquire meaning as public opinion becomes enlightened by a humane justice." *Weems v. United States,* 217 U.S., at 378. And Mr. Chief Justice Warren, for a plurality of the Court, referred to "the evolving standards of decency that mark the progress of a maturing society." *Trop v. Dulles,* 356 U.S., at 101. Mr. Jefferson expressed the same thought well.

My problem, however, as I have indicated, is the suddenness of the Court's perception of progress in the human attitude since decisions of only a short while ago.

5. To reverse the judgments in these cases is, of course, the easy choice. It is easier to strike the balance in favor of life and against death. It is comforting to relax in the thoughts — perhaps the rationalizations — that this is the compassionate decision for a maturing society; that this is the moral and the "right" thing to do; that thereby we convince ourselves that we are moving down the road toward human decency; that we value life even though that life has taken another or others or has grievously scarred another or others and their families; and that we are less barbaric than we were in 1879, or in 1890, or in 1910, or in 1947, or in 1958, or in 1963, or a year ago, in 1971, when *Wilkerson, Kemmler, Weems, Francis, Trop, Rudolph,* and *McGautha* were respectively decided.

This, for me, is good argument, and it makes some sense. But it is good argument and it makes sense only in a legislative and executive way and not as a judicial expedient. As I have said above, were I a legislator, I would do all I could to sponsor and to vote for legislation abolishing the death penalty. And were I the chief executive of a sovereign State, I would be sorely tempted to exercise executive clemency as Governor Rockefeller of Arkansas did recently just before he departed from office. There — on the Legislative Branch of the State or Federal Government, and secondarily, on the Executive Branch — is where the authority and responsibility for this kind of action lies. The authority should not be taken over by the judiciary in the modern guise of an Eighth Amendment issue.

I do not sit on these cases, however, as a legislator, responsive, at least in part, to the will of constituents. Our task here, as must so frequently be emphasized and re-emphasized, is to pass upon the constitutionality of legislation that has been enacted and that is challenged. This is the sole task for judges. We should not allow our personal preferences as to the wisdom of legislative and congressional action, or our distaste for such action, to guide our judicial decision in cases such as these. The temptations to cross that policy line are very great. In fact, as today's decision reveals, they are almost irresistible. . . .

7. I trust the Court fully appreciates what it is doing when it decides these cases the way it does today. Not only are the capital punishment laws of 39 States and the District of Columbia struck down, but also all those provisions of the federal statutory structure that permit the death penalty apparently are voided. No longer is capital punishment possible, I suspect, for, among other crimes, treason, 18 U.S.C. §2381; or assassination of the President, the Vice President, or those who stand elected to those positions, 18 U.S.C. §1751; or assassination of a Member or member-elect of Congress, 18 U.S.C. §351; or espionage, 18 U.S.C. §794; or rape within the special maritime jurisdiction, 18 U.S.C. §2031; or aircraft or motor vehicle destruction where death occurs, 18 U.S.C. §34; or explosives offenses where death results, 18 U.S.C. §§844(d) and (f); or train wrecking, 18 U.S.C. §1992; or aircraft piracy, 49 U.S.C. §1472(i). . . .

8. It is of passing interest to note a few voting facts with respect to recent federal death penalty legislation:

A. The aircraft piracy statute, 49 U.S.C. §1472(i), was enacted September 5, 1961. The Senate vote on August 10 was 92–0. It was announced that Senators Chavez, Fulbright, Neuberger, and Symington were absent but that, if present, all four would vote yea. It was also announced, on the other side of the aisle, that Senator Butler was ill and that Senators Beall, Carlson, and Morton were absent or detained, but that those four, if present, would vote in the affirmative. These announcements, therefore, indicate that the true vote was 100–0. 107 Cong. Rec. 15440. The House passed the bill without recorded vote. 107 Cong. Rec. 16849.

B. The presidential assassination statute, 18 U.S.C. §1751, was approved August 28, 1965, without recorded votes. 111 Cong. Rec. 14103, 18026, and 20239.

C. The Omnibus Crime Control Act of 1970 was approved January 2, 1971. Title IV thereof added the congressional assassination statute that is now 18 U.S.C. §351. The recorded House vote on October 7, 1970, was 341–26, with 63 not voting and 62 of those paired. 116 Cong. Rec. 35363–35364. The Senate vote on October 8 was 59–0, with 41 not voting, but with 21 of these announced as favoring the bill. 116 Cong. Rec. 35743. Final votes after conference were not recorded. 116 Cong. Rec. 42150, 42199.

It is impossible for me to believe that the many lawyer-members of the House and Senate — including, I might add, outstanding leaders and prominent candidates for higher office — were callously unaware and insensitive of constitutional overtones in legislation of this type. The answer, of course, is that in 1961, in 1965, and in 1970 these elected representatives of the people — far more conscious of the temper of the times, of the maturing of society, and of the contemporary demands for man's dignity, than are we who sit cloistered on this Court — took it as settled that the death penalty then, as it always had been, was not in itself unconstitutional. Some of those Members of Congress, I suspect, will be surprised at this Court's giant stride today.

9. If the reservations expressed by my Brother Stewart (which, as I read his opinion, my Brother White shares) were to command support, namely, that capital punishment may not be unconstitutional so long as it be mandatorily imposed, the result, I fear, will be that statutes struck down today will be re-enacted by state legislatures to prescribe the death penalty for specified crimes without any alternative for the imposition of a lesser punishment in the discretion of the judge or jury, as the case may be. This approach, it seems to me, encourages legislation that is regressive and of an antique mold, for it eliminates the element of mercy in the imposition of punishment. I thought we had passed beyond that point in our criminology long ago.

10. It is not without interest, also, to note that, although the several concurring opinions acknowledge the heinous and atrocious character of the offenses committed by the petitioners, none of those opinions makes reference to the misery the petitioners' crimes occasioned to the victims, to the families of the victims, and to the communities where the offenses took place. The arguments for the respective petitioners, particularly the oral arguments, were similarly and curiously devoid of reference to the victims. There is risk, of course, in a comment such as this, for it opens one to the charge of emphasizing the retributive. But see *Williams v. New York*, 337 U.S. 241, 248 (1949). Nevertheless, these cases are here because offenses to innocent victims were perpe-

trated. This fact, and the terror that occasioned it, and the fear that stalks the streets of many of our cities today perhaps deserve not to be entirely overlooked. Let us hope that, with the Court's decision, the terror imposed will be forgotten by those upon whom it was visited, and that our society will reap the hoped-for benefits of magnanimity.

Although personally I may rejoice at the Court's result, I find it difficult to accept or to justify as a matter of history, of law, or of constitutional pronouncement. I fear the Court has overstepped. It has sought and has achieved an end.

QUESTIONS

1. *If Justice Blackmun believes that the death penalty serves no useful purpose, that it violates childhood's training and life's experiences, and that it is abhorrent, why does he not vote against its constitutionality? If he rejoices at the Court's opinion, why does he not join it?*
2. *What would you have held, as a Supreme Court Justice asked to decide whether the death penalty is unconstitutional? How would you have explained your decision?*
3. *Following is another story of death and punishment, concerning Barnett Welansky, owner of the Cocoanut Grove nightclub where the terrible fire took place. What significance does the law give to his incarceration? To his death? To the deaths of the people killed in the fire through his fault?*

CRIMINAL LAW*
Donnelly, Goldstein, and Schwartz

Note 2. Welansky Petitions for Pardon

THE COMMONWEALTH OF MASSACHUSETTS

July 12, 1946

To His Excellency the Governor:

I, *Barnett Welansky* now confined under sentence in the State Prison Colony (at present in the Mass. General Hospital) at Norfolk on conviction of the crime of Manslaughter, do hereby petition for a pardon of said offence and a release from further imprisonment on said sentence, either absolute or upon such conditions and limitations as may be deemed proper.

[signed] *Barnett Welansky*

* Pages 596–600 (1962).

NOTE 3. RECOMMENDATION OF THE COMMISSIONER OF CORRECTION

THE COMMONWEALTH OF
MASSACHUSETTS

Department of Correction
State House, Boston 33

August 19, 1946

To His Excellency the Governor:

In Re: *PETITION FOR PARDON*

NAME	NUMBER	INSTITUTION
	6323	*State Prison Colony*
Barnett Welansky	*22121*	*State Prison*

Pursuant to the provisions of Chapter 127, Section 152 of the General Laws, as amended, I have the honor to transmit herewith the original petition for the pardon of the above named prisoner, and my recommendation.

RECOMMENDATION

The petitioner's request for a pardon is based upon the fact that he is seriously ill. An investigation by this Department has shown that a positive diagnosis of cancer of the lung and the trachea has been made by reputable medical authorities. A period of life expectancy not to exceed one year has been made.

In view of the medical findings and the fact that there is no hope of recovery in this case, I recommend that the petitioner's request for a pardon be granted. . . .

Respectfully yours,
J. Paul Doyle
Commissioner of Correction

Note 5. Recommendation of the Advisory Board of Pardons

THE COMMONWEALTH OF MASSACHUSETTS
ADVISORY BOARD OF PARDONS

State House, Boston
In the matter of *Barnett Welansky,*
(Applicant for Pardon)

Your Excellency:

The Advisory Board of Pardons, to whom has been referred the case of Barnett Welansky, under General Laws, Chapter 127, section 152, as amended, respectfully reports as follows: . . .

The petitioner is requesting a pardon, it having been found that he is suffering from cancer of the right lung and it has been predicted that the duration of his life will be approximately one year.

If the petitioner should be pardoned because he has a life expectancy of one year, and that seems to be the only grounds for the petition, it should follow that every other inmate with the same life expectancy or less, should be pardoned. That is not the case. Some inmates remain in prison until a few weeks of death and some even die in prison.

In view of all the circumstances of this case, the Advisory Board of Pardons cannot recommend a pardon at this time. It is respectfully recommended that the petition be denied without prejudice.

Respectfully submitted,
[signed] F. J. Bradlee, Jr.
Member
[signed] Harold Lundgren
Member

Matthew W. Bullock concurs in this recommendation, but is absent on vacation at the time of filing.
August 26, 1946

Note 6. Letter from a Friend of the Prisoner

FRANK G. LICHTENSTEIN

Attorney and Counsellor at Law
Boston, Mass.

September 3, 1946

Hon. Maurice J. Tobin
State House
Boston, Massachusetts

Dear Governor:

I desire to be recorded as being highly in favor of the petition for pardon of Barnett Welansky. Not only was I friendly with Mr. Welansky in years gone by, but I have known him somewhat intimately.

I have followed the accounts in the newspapers concerning the activities of the District Attorney and the Parole Board, who have recorded themselves against favorable action by Your Excellency on this pardon application.

An examination of the record at the trial and a study of all the facts, principally undisputed facts, would disclose, I am sure, that if Welansky was guilty of manslaughter in connection with the terrible deaths resulting from the Cocoanut Grove fire, then it was a technical guilt and nothing more. Certainly, in those circumstances, the sentence that was imposed upon him by the court was much too severe.

The newspaper accounts further state that reputable physicians and surgeons, after diagnosing his case from a health standpoint, give him but a very short time, probably a year, to live. The Parole Board, as I read the papers, refuses its consent on the ground that the man's health is not sufficient reason for a pardon. It may well be true that in appropriate cases, such as criminals whom the public would have a right to fear if they were released, that the criminal's health should not be taken into consideration, but in this particular case where there was no intention to do harm in the first place, but through a succession of misfortunes a man has been found guilty of manslaughter only from a technical point of view and not otherwise, certainly the reason given by the Parole Board can have no application to this case now before you.

Very sincerely yours,
Frank G. Lichtenstein

NOTE 7. FOR THE RECORD, FROM THE DISTRICT ATTORNEY

THE COMMONWEALTH OF
MASSACHUSETTS

District Attorney Suffolk District
Court House Pemberton Square
Boston

November 22, 1946

Hon. Maurice J. Tobin
Governor of the Commonwealth
State House, Boston, Mass.

Dear Sir:

. . . [T]he defendant deliberately failed to install firedoors called for on plans of the premises approved by the Municipal Building Department and deliberately failed to care for the safety of his patrons by providing proper exits, thereby causing death to five hundred persons and severe burns and suffering to hundreds of other patrons.

Previous to the granting of a pardon in a homicide case it has been the traditional procedure in this Commonwealth that an expression of opinion be obtained from the relatives of the victim. In August, 1946, I publicly expressed my opinion that a pardon should not be given to the petitioner, Barnett Welansky, until such an expression of opinion from the relatives of the five hundred victims in this case be obtained by the Committee on Pardons. From available information, no such expression of opinion has been obtained.

I, therefore, wish to be recorded that I take the same position now that I did in August of 1946 that this petition be denied.

Yours very truly,
[signed] William J. Foley
District Attorney.

Note 8. Letter from the Relative of a Victim

Maurice J. Tobin
Governor of Massachusetts

[N.D.]

Your Excellency:

I vehemently oppose any pardon for Barnett Welansky whose criminal re-construction of the Cocoanut Grove building sacrificed 492 human beings. I am a close relative of one of the victims. This horrible holocaust was a civic disgrace. It would become even more unspeakable were this man to be freed. In his petition for premature freedom, Welansky claims illness — says he wants to spend the rest of his days with his family. I recall 492 persons (one in particular) who wanted to live out their lives with their families. *They are dead.* He also disclaims guilt because he was at home the night of the fire.

Guiltless? He *accepted guilt* when he criminally flouted the building laws in callously renovating his night club and did *not* have the work done according to the plans which he had had okayed.

He evaded the law when he employed a young fellow to do some electrical wiring and *knew* that this worker did not have the proper license to do this work. Has it been *absolutely proven* that faulty wiring *did not* cause this fire? Although he was not present he *knew* that his illegally reconstructed club was open for public attendance the night of the fire.

Governor Tobin, consider the fact of locked exits in a place of public patronage. Hundreds died because a locked exit barred their way to the street's safety. These facts are public record. They also are hideous facts burning deeply into the hearts of hundreds of heartbroken families.

Of what avail are trials, findings of guilt and commitments to prison if they are contingent upon the convicted person's health. If Welansky's health is failing it should not cause sorrow in the City of Boston.

I was aghast as were countless others when I read that this man Welansky has been removed from prison to the Massachusetts General Hospital. In what way is he at present incarcerated? Massachusetts maintains hospital and medical care within the prisons for inmates becoming ill. Why has the above mentioned consideration been given to Welansky?

Governor Tobin, I am not a bloodthirsty creature seeking undue revenge but I am a decent citizen and a relative of one of the Grove victims demanding that Barnett Welansky remain in prison and that the justice meted out to him be sustained by our public officials.

I bitterly and irrevocably insist that even the suggestion of a pardon or parole is unthinkable not only to the relatives of more than 490 unnecessary dead but to all of our decent, law abiding citizens.

Katharine F. Denehy,
313 Boston Avenue,
Medford, Mass.

NOTE 9. THE GOVERNOR DECIDES

THE COMMONWEALTH OF
MASSACHUSETTS

Executive Department
State House, Boston

November 19, 1946

To the Honorable Council

Gentlemen:

Subject to your approval, I have fully and completely pardoned Barnett Welansky, sentenced April 15, 1943 in the Suffolk Superior Court to serve a term of 12 to 15 years in the State Prison for the crime of manslaughter.

Sincerely yours,
Maurice J. Tobin
Governor

QUESTIONS

1. *What significance did the law give the impending death of Barnett Welansky? What significance did Katharine Denehy think the law should have given it?*
2. *What significance did the law give to Barnett Welansky's punishment by incarceration? What significance did Katharine Denehy think it should have given it?*
3. *Suppose that Welansky had been sentenced to death instead of imprisonment; would he have been pardoned then, or executed, dying of cancer though he was? What could such a death possibly be said to mean? Compare People v. Sullivan, 111 Colo. 205, 139 P.2d 876 (1943), where the court ordered the execution of a forty-year-old retarded defendant.*
4. *One could call the impending death of Welansky pathetic. Does the law express that pathos? If so, does it do so directly – by saying "this is a pathetic case and therefore . . ." – or by indirection, by slipping in what is irrelevant?*

5. *The deaths at the Cocoanut Grove fire were not pathetic, perhaps, so much as terrible or horrifying. Does the law express that quality of those deaths? What significance does it give them?*
6. *Below is another story of death by capital punishment. What is it made to mean?*

A TALE OF TWO CITIES*

Charles Dickens

[His great devotion to Lucie Manette has led the wastrel Sydney Carton to take the place of her husband, Charles Darnay, upon the revolutionary guillotine.]

They said of him, about the city that night, that it was the peacefullest man's face ever beheld there. Many added that he looked sublime and prophetic.

One of the most remarkable sufferers by the same axe — a woman — had asked at the foot of the same scaffold, not long before, to be allowed to write down the thoughts that were inspiring her. If he had given an utterance to his, and they were prophetic, they would have been these:

"I see Barsad, and Cly, Defarge, The Vengeance, the Juryman, the Judge, long ranks of the new oppressors who have risen on the destruction of the old, perishing by this retributive instrument, before it shall cease out of its present use. I see a beautiful city and a brilliant people rising from this abyss, and, in their struggles to be truly free, in their triumphs and defeats, through long long years to come, I see the evil of this time and of the previous time of which this is the natural birth, gradually making expiation for itself and wearing out.

"I see the lives for which I lay down my life, peaceful, useful, prosperous and happy, in that England which I shall see no more. I see Her with a child upon her bosom, who bears my name. I see her father, aged and bent, but otherwise restored, and faithful to all men in his healing office, and at peace. I see the good old man, so long their friend, in ten years' time enriching them with all he has, and passing tranquilly to his reward.

"I see that I hold a sanctuary in their hearts, and in the hearts of their descendants, generations hence. I see her, an old woman, weeping for me on the anniversary of this day. I see her and her husband, their course done, lying side by side in their last earthly bed, and I know that each was not more honoured and held sacred in the other's soul, than I was in the souls of both.

"I see that child who lay upon her bosom and who bore my name, a

* Book 3, Chapter 15 (1859).

man winning his way up in that path of life which once was mine. I see him winning it so well, that my name is made illustrious there by the light of his. I see the blots I threw upon it, faded away. I see him, foremost of just judges and honoured men, bringing a boy of my name, with a forehead that I know and golden hair, to this place — then fair to look upon, with not a trace of this day's disfigurement — and I hear him tell the child my story, with a tender and a faltering voice.

"It is a far, far better thing that I do, than I have ever done; it is a far, far better rest that I go to than I have ever known."

QUESTIONS

1. The ending of A Tale of Two Cities is pathetic in a very different way from the death of Barnett Welansky. How is this pathetic? Is it simply that one man dies for another?

2. What meaning does Dickens claim for the death of Sydney Carton? It obviously is not deterrence or justified revenge, or even bitterness and confusion at such a miserable end to a human existence, but something quite different. One might say that Sydney Carton's death is not miserable at all, but a great moment, in which by dying nobly he can make others happy and grateful forever. This sacrifice enables him to atone for an imperfect life. This is a Happy Ending.

a. Could such a meaning be claimed for any actual death on the guillotine? For any other actual death?

b. Can any meaning of any kind be claimed for the death of a real person on the guillotine? For any other actual death? What would Camus say?

3. Consider again the selection from Billy Budd reproduced in Chapter 1 (page 70). Can you see this as a story about the failure of meaning of the death penalty? The claim that it means everything is balanced against the claim that it means nothing, and the reader is left uncertain on a point as to which uncertainty is as bad as knowing the worst.

4. Is the viciousness of the death penalty at least in part a viciousness of rhetoric, a corruption of language? The claim is made that the inflicted death can have a sort of moral meaning, a simplicity of significance, that it cannot have. The claim fails as utterly as Ahab's claim to give meaning to the white whale and Captain Vere's claim to give meaning to the death of Billy Budd. And the claim cannot be qualified, cannot be made partial — as the same sort of claim of the meaning of ordinary punishment can be qualified by a termination date, by parole possibilities, and by the well-meaning (however ineffectual) concern of some of the custodians for the prisoner's welfare.

To test this suggestion, you might draft a paragraph in the style of Dickens in which you give an account of an execution that expresses what you believe those who favor the death penalty think it means. Could this paragraph be true?

5. Perhaps still more can be learned from Dickens. In describing the meaning he claims for the death, we have not defined the pathos one feels at the end of the book. Does the pathos arise, not from the sadness of the events, but from our recognition that such happy and noble events with such blissful consequences cannot occur in the real world, and that we are turning the last page on a world where they can? The pathos lies in the fact that we are not purely moral beings with purely moral significance, and that we are leaving behind a make-believe world where such meaning is claimed. Even Jesus breaks the ritual of his sacrifice to express the despair and loneliness of a dying man.

What moral is there here for the law and the lawyer? Is the conversion of life into fiction – which can be said to be the heart of the rhetoric of the death penalty – a fundamental characteristic of legal speech? Does the law always talk about people as if they were purely moral, fictional beings? Think of the dying woman in the Georgetown Hospital case, of Mr. Black and his children, of the Reasonable Man, the Offeror, the Tort-feasor, even of Mrs. Sherwood.

6. *Study of the next passage might sum things up for you. What does this passage teach us about capital punishment, about other punishment, about legal language, about good writing? What does it teach us about humanity and decency, in speech and otherwise?*

SHOOTING AN ELEPHANT*

George Orwell

[Orwell, a British policeman in India, has been called to deal with an elephant that had gone temporarily berserk and killed a man.]

It was perfectly clear to me what I ought to do. I ought to walk up to within, say, twenty-five yards of the elephant and test his behaviour. If he charged I could shoot, if he took no notice of me it would be safe to leave him until the mahout came back. But also I knew that I was going to do no such thing. I was a poor shot with a rifle and the ground was soft mud into which one would sink at every step. If the elephant charged and I missed him, I should have about as much chance as a toad under a steam-roller. But even then I was not thinking particularly of my own skin, only the watchful yellow faces behind. For at that moment, with the crowd watching me, I was not afraid in the ordinary sense, as I would have been if I had been alone. A white man mustn't be frightened in front of "natives"; and so, in general, he isn't frightened. The sole thought in my mind was that if anything went wrong those two thousand Burmans would see me pursued, caught, trampled on and reduced to a grinning corpse like that Indian up the hill. And if that happened it was quite probable that some of them would laugh. That would never do. There was only one alternative. I shoved the cartridges into the magazine and lay down on the road to get a better aim.

* In *Shooting an Elephant and Other Essays* (1945).

The crowd grew very still, and a deep, low, happy sigh, as of people who see the theatre curtain go up at last, breathed from innumerable throats. They were going to have their bit of fun after all. The rifle was a beautiful German thing with cross-hair sights. I did not then know that in shooting an elephant one should shoot to cut an imaginary bar running from ear-hole to ear-hole. I ought therefore, as the elephant was sideways on, to have aimed straight at his ear-hole; actually I aimed several inches in front of this, thinking the brain would be further forward.

When I pulled the trigger I did not hear the bang or feel the kick — one never does when a shot goes home — but I heard the devilish roar of glee that went up from the crowd. In that instant, in too short a time, one would have thought, even for the bullet to get there, a mysterious, terrible change had come over the elephant. He neither stirred nor fell, but every line of his body had altered. He looked suddenly stricken, shrunken, immensely old, as though the frightful impact of the bullet had paralysed him without knocking him down. At last, after what seemed a long time — it might have been five seconds, I dare say — he sagged flabbily to his knees. His mouth slobbered. An enormous senility seemed to have settled upon him. One could have imagined him thousands of years old. I fired again into the same spot. At the second shot he did not collapse but climbed with desperate slowness to his feet and stood weakly upright, with legs sagging and head drooping. I fired a third time. That was the shot that did for him. You could see the agony of it jolt his whole body and knock the last remnant of strength from his legs. But in falling he seemed for a moment to rise, for as his hind legs collapsed beneath him he seemed to tower upwards like a huge rock toppling, his trunk reaching skyward like a tree. He trumpeted, for the first and only time. And then down he came, his belly towards me, with a crash that seemed to shake the ground even where I lay.

I got up. The Burmans were already racing past me across the mud. It was obvious that the elephant would never rise again, but he was not dead. He was breathing very rhythmically with long rattling gasps, his great mound of a side painfully rising and falling. His mouth was wide open — I could see far down into caverns of pale pink throat. I waited a long time for him to die, but his breathing did not weaken. Finally I fired my two remaining shots into the spot where I thought his heart must be. The thick blood welled out of him like red velvet, but still he did not die. His body did not even jerk when the shots hit him, the tortured breathing continued without a pause. He was dying, very slowly and in great agony, but in some world remote from me where not even a bullet could damage him further. I felt that I had got to put an end to that dreadful noise. It seemed dreadful to see the great beast lying there, powerless to move and yet powerless to die, and not even to be able to finish him. I sent back for my small rifle and poured shot after shot into his heart and down his throat. They seemed to make no impression. The tortured gasps continued as steadily as the ticking of a clock.

In the end I could not stand it any longer and went away. I heard later that it took him half an hour to die. Burmans were bringing dahs and baskets even before I left, and I was told they had stripped his body almost to the bones by the afternoon.

Afterwards, of course, there were endless discussions about the shooting of the elephant. The owner was furious, but he was only an Indian and could do nothing. Besides, legally I had done the right thing, for a mad elephant has to be killed, like a mad dog, if its owner fails to control it. Among the Europeans opinion was divided. The older men said I was right, the younger men said it was a damn shame to shoot an elephant for killing a coolie, because an elephant was worth more than any damn Coringhee coolie. And afterwards I was very glad that the coolie had been killed; it put me legally in the right and it gave me a sufficient pretext for shooting the elephant. I often wondered whether any of the others grasped that I had done it solely to avoid looking a fool.

3. *Complications: False Pretenses and Rhetorical Resources*

Having seen what may come from making a statement that gives rise to false pretenses, do you resolve never to allow yourself to do that, but always to tell the truth simply and plainly?

THE HISTORY OF THE DECLINE AND FALL OF THE ROMAN EMPIRE*

Edward Gibbon

While Julian struggled with the almost insuperable difficulties of his situation, the silent hours of the night were still devoted to study and contemplation. Whenever he closed his eyes in short and interrupted slumbers, his mind was agitated with painful anxiety; nor can it be thought surprising that the Genius of the empire should once more appear before him, covering with a funeral veil his head and his horn of abundance, and slowly retiring from the Imperial tent. The monarch started from his couch, and stepping forth, to refresh his wearied spirits with the coolness of the midnight air, he beheld a fiery meteor, which

* Chapter 24 (1776–1788).

shot athwart the sky, and suddenly vanished. Julian was convinced that he had seen the menacing countenance of the god of war; the council which he summoned, of Tuscan haruspices, unanimously pronounced that he should abstain from action: but, on this occasion, necessity and reason were more prevalent than superstition; and the trumpets sounded at the break of day. The army marched through a hilly country; and the hills had been secretly occupied by the Persians. Julian led the van, with the skill and attention of a consummate general; he was alarmed by the intelligence that his rear was suddenly attacked. The heat of the weather had tempted him to lay aside his cuirass; but he snatched a shield from one of his attendants, and hastened, with a sufficient reinforcement, to the relief of the rear-guard. A similar danger recalled the intrepid prince to the defence of the front; and, as he galloped between the columns, the centre of the left was attacked, and almost overpowered, by a furious charge of the Persian cavalry and elephants. This huge body was soon defeated, by the well-timed evolution of the light infantry, who aimed their weapons, with dexterity and effect, against the backs of the horsemen and the legs of the elephants. The Barbarians fled; and Julian, who was foremost in every danger, animated the pursuit with his voice and gestures. His trembling guards, scattered and oppressed by the disorderly throng of friends and enemies, reminded their fearless sovereign that he was without armour; and conjured him to decline the fall of the impending ruin. As they exclaimed, a cloud of darts and arrows was discharged from the flying squadrons; and a javelin, after razing the skin of his arm, transpierced the ribs, and fixed in the inferior part of the liver. Julian attempted to draw the deadly weapon from his side; but his fingers were cut by the sharpness of the steel, and he fell senseless from his horse. His guards flew to his relief; and the wounded emperor was gently raised from the ground, and conveyed out of the tumult of the battle into an adjacent tent. The report of the melancholy event passed from rank to rank; but the grief of the Romans inspired them with invincible valour and the desire of revenge. The bloody and obstinate conflict was maintained by the two armies, till they were separated by the total darkness of the night. The Persians derived some honour from the advantage which they obtained against the left wing, where Anatolius, master of the offices, was slain, and the præfect Sallust very narrowly escaped. But the event of the day was adverse to the Barbarians. They abandoned the field, their two generals, Meranes and Nohordates, fifty nobles or satraps, and a multitude of their bravest soldiers: and the success of the Romans, if Julian had survived, might have been improved into a decisive and useful victory.

The first words that Julian uttered, after his recovery from the fainting fit into which he had been thrown by loss of blood, were expressive of his martial spirit. He called for his horse and arms, and was impatient to rush into the battle. His remaining strength was exhausted by the painful effort; and the surgeons who examined his wound discovered the symptoms of approaching death. He employed the awful moments with the firm temper of a hero and a sage; the philosophers who had accompanied him in this fatal expedition compared the tent of Julian with the prison of Socrates; and the spectators, whom duty, or friendship, or curiosity, had assembled around his couch, listened with respectful grief to the funeral oration of their dying emperor. "Friends and fellow-soldiers, the seasonable period of my departure is now arrived, and I discharge, with the cheerfulness of a ready debtor, the demands of nature. I have learned from philosophy, how much the soul is more excellent than the body; and that the separation of the nobler substance should be the subject of joy, rather than of affliction. I have learned from religion, that an early death has often been the reward of piety; and I accept, as a favour of the gods, the mortal stroke that secures me from the danger of disgracing a character, which has hitherto been supported by virtue and fortitude. I die without remorse, as I have lived without guilt. I am pleased to reflect on the innocence of my private life; and I can affirm, with confidence, that the supreme authority, that emanation of the Divine Power, has been preserved in my hands pure and immaculate. Detesting the corrupt and destructive maxims of despotism, I have considered the happiness of the people as the end of government. Submitting my actions to the laws of prudence, of justice, and of moderation, I have trusted the event to the care of Providence. Peace was the object of my counsels, as long as peace was consistent with the public welfare; but, when the imperious voice of my country summoned me to arms, I exposed my person to the dangers of war, with the clear foreknowledge (which I had acquired from the art of divination) that I was destined to fall by the sword. I now offer my tribute of gratitude to the Eternal Being, who has not suffered me to perish by the cruelty of a tyrant, by the secret dagger of conspiracy, or by the slow tortures of lingering disease. He has given me, in the midst of an honourable career, a splendid and glorious departure from this world; and I hold it equally absurd, equally base, to solicit, or to decline, the stroke of fate. — Thus much I have attempted to say; but my strength fails me, and I feel the approach of death. — I shall cautiously refrain from any word that may tend to influence your suffrages in the election of an emperor. My choice might be imprudent, or injudicious; and, if it should not be ratified by the consent of the army, it might be fatal to the person whom I should recommend. I shall only, as a good citizen, express my hopes that the Romans may be blessed with the government of a virtuous sovereign." After this discourse, which Julian pronounced in a firm and gentle tone of voice, he distributed, by a military testament, the remains of his private fortune; and, making some inquiry why Anatolius was not present, he understood, from the answer of Sallust, that Anatolius was killed; and bewailed, with amiable inconsistency, the loss of his friend. At the same time he reproved the immoderate grief of the spectators; and conjured them not to disgrace, by unmanly tears, the fate of a prince who in a few moments would be united with heaven, and with the stars. The spectators were silent; and Julian entered into a metaphysical argument with the philosophers Priscus and Maximus, on the nature of the soul. The efforts which he made, of mind as well as body, most probably hastened his death. His wound began to bleed with fresh violence; his respiration was embarrassed by the swelling of the veins: he called for a draught of cold water, and, as soon he had drunk it, expired without pain, about the hour of midnight. Such was the end of that extraordinary man, in the thirty-second year of his age, after a reign of one year and about eight months from the death of Constantius. In his last moments he displayed, perhaps with some ostentation, the love of virtue and of fame which had been the ruling passions of his life.

QUESTIONS

1. *This passage is great literature, constituting a great resource for us, perhaps marking a stage in the progress of the imagination. But does it not give rise to false pretenses? It is as ideal in its way as the death of Sydney Carton or the legal literature on the death penalty. In the material on the death penalty I suggested that what was wrong with that writing was a falsity, a failure to be true to experience. I am now suggesting a complication: that some sort of falsity may lie at the heart of all literature, all rhetoric, that what we say or read or hear with greatest feeling may be no more than a pretense. "These our actors were all spirits, and are melted into air, into thin air." (Shakespeare, The Tempest, act 4, scene 1, line 148.) Can we root all falsity out of legal language? If so, at what cost?*
   a. *One response is to say that we can and must. The falseness in Gibbon's passage does no harm, for this is only literature, a kind of dreaming. But where one defines how a government is to run or when people are to die or be imprisoned or pay damages, then one simply must eliminate all false pretenses from one's speech and thought. Here one's words are not merely words but law. The literature of reality must meet standards different from those we apply to an attempt to distill in a few pages an ideal view of the world. As lawyers we must be ruthless in our insistence upon speaking directly and simply, without the slightest falsity or pretense.*
   b. *What happens when we try? We shall consider this matter at length later, but the suggestion that the law is imbued with fiction to its core*

will not surprise you. The literature of the law, it might be said, promises us an impossible order and happiness. What are the pretenses of a statute, for example? It gives an order in the sublime and innocent belief that it will be obeyed; or defines certain rights – say, civil rights – and provides remedies, without a single blushing reference to the obvious imperfections of the processes by which these ideals are expressed in people's lives. It may simply be impossible for the law to tell the truth.

What is perhaps even more troubling is the fact that some sorts of falsity, under some circumstances, are essential to our great purposes. Surely one purpose of the language of the Constitution is to inspire us, to express a hope or ideal; but to do these things the language must necessarily give rise to false pretenses. The statute seems to be a pipe dream of a different and more perfect world – but may that sort of speech not serve a purpose? And where would we be without wills, without corporations, without a law defining civil rights, and so on? In what ways does the falsity of legal language contribute to its value to us?

c. *It seems then that what is wrong with the death penalty is not that it leaves out too much (for the estate plan does that) nor that it creates a false pretense (for the Constitution does that), but something else. Somehow we must choose among ways of talking – each of which leaves out too much, each of which is based on false pretenses. How is one to do that: does the secret lie in some capacity for controlling one's language, defects and all? Under what principles, by what art, is one to control one's language?*

2. *Rhetoric of this kind is not a matter for fiction alone. The sort of meaning Gibbon claims for Julian's death can be claimed in real life as well, as shown by the following selections by and about David Hume.*

THE LIFE OF DAVID HUME, ESQ.*

David Hume

It is difficult for a man to speak long of himself without vanity; therefore I shall be short. It may be thought an instance of vanity that I pretend at all to write my life; but this narrative shall contain little more than the history of my writings; as, indeed, almost all my life has been spent in literary pursuits and occupations. The first success of most of my writings was not such as to be an object of vanity.

I was born the twenty-sixth of April, 1711, old style, at Edinburgh. I was of a good family, both by father and mother: my father's family is a branch of the earl of Home's, or Hume's; and my ancestors had been proprietors of the estate which my brother possesses, for several generations. . . .

* A preface to Hume's *History of England from Julius Caesar to 1688* (1778; Sampson ed. 1856).

In 1759, I published my history of the house of Tudor. The clamor against this performance was almost equal to that against the history of the two first Stuarts. The reign of Elizabeth was particularly obnoxious. But I was now callous against the impressions of public folly, and continued very peaceably and contentedly, in my retreat at Edinburgh, to finish, in two volumes, the more early part of the English history, which I gave to the public in 1761, with tolerable, and but tolerable, success.

But, notwithstanding this variety of winds and seasons, to which my writings had been exposed, they had still been making such advances, that the copymoney given me by the booksellers much exceeded any thing formerly known in England; I was become not only independent, but opulent. I retired to my native country of Scotland, determined never more to set my foot out of it; and retaining the satisfaction of never having preferred a request to one great man, or even making advances of friendship to any of them. As I was now turned of fifty, I thought of passing all the rest of my life in this philosophical manner; when I received, in 1763, an invitation from the earl of Hertford, with whom I was not in the least acquainted, to attend him on his embassy to Paris, with a near prospect of being appointed secretary to the embassy; and, in the mean while, of performing the functions of that office. This offer, however inviting, I at first declined; both because I was reluctant to begin connections with the great, and because I was afraid that the civilities and gay company of Paris would prove disagreeable to a person of my age and humor; but on his lordship's repeating the invitation, I accepted of it. I have every reason, both of pleasure and interest, to think myself happy in my connections with that nobleman, as well as afterwards with his brother, General Conway.

Those who have not seen the strange effects of modes, will never imagine the reception I met with at Paris, from men and women of all ranks and stations. The more I resiled from their excessive civilities, the more I was loaded with them. There is, however, a real satisfaction in living at Paris, from the great number of sensible, knowing, and polite company with which that city abounds above all places in the universe. I thought once of settling there for life.

I was appointed secretary to the embassy; and, in summer, 1765, Lord Hertford left me, being appointed lord lieutenant of Ireland. I was chargé d'affaires till the arrival of the duke of Richmond, towards the end of the year. In the beginning of 1766, I left Paris, and next summer went to Edinburgh, with the same view as formerly, of burying myself in a philosophical retreat. I returned to that place, not richer, but with much more money, and a much larger income, by means of Lord Hertford's friendship, than I left it; and I was desirous of trying what superfluity could produce, as I had formerly made an experiment of a competency. But in 1767, I received from Mr. Conway an invitation to be under-secretary; and this invitation, both the character of the person, and my connections with Lord Hertford, prevented me from declining. I returned to Edinburgh in 1769, very opulent, (for I possessed a revenue of one thousand pounds a year,) healthy, and though somewhat stricken in years, with the prospect of enjoying long my ease, and of seeing the increase of my reputation.

In spring, 1775, I was struck with a disorder in my bowels, which at first gave me no alarm, but has since, as I apprehend it, become mortal and incurable. I now reckon upon a speedy dissolution. I have suffered very little pain from my disorder; and what is more strange, have, notwithstanding the great decline of my person, never suffered a moment's abatement of my spirits; insomuch, that were I to name a period of my life which I should most choose to pass over again, I might be tempted to point to this later period. I possess the same ardor as ever in study, and the same gayety in company. I consider, besides, that a man of sixty-five, by dying, cuts off only a few years of infirmities; and though I see many symptoms of my literary reputation's breaking out at last with additional lustre, I know that I could have but few years to enjoy it. It is difficult to be more detached from life than I am at present.

To conclude historically with my own character: I am, or rather was, (for that is the style I must now use in speaking of myself, which imboldens me the more to speak my sentiments;) I was, I say, a man of mild disposition, of command of temper, of an open, social, and cheerful humor, capable of attachment, but little susceptible of enmity, and of great moderation in all my passions. Even my love of literary fame, my ruling passion, never soured my temper, notwithstanding my frequent disappointments. My company was not unacceptable to the young and careless, as well as to the studious and literary; and as I took a particular pleasure in the company of modest women, I had no reason to be displeased with the reception I met with from them. In a word, though most men, anywise eminent, have found reason to complain of Calumny, I never was touched, or even attacked, by her baleful tooth; and though I wantonly exposed myself to the rage of both civil and religious factions, they seemed to be disarmed in my behalf of their wonted fury. My friends never had occasion to vindicate any one circumstance of my character and conduct; not but that the zealots, we may well suppose, would have been glad to invent and propagate any story to my disadvantage, but they could never find any which they thought would wear the face of probability. I cannot say there is no vanity in making this funeral oration of myself, but I hope it is not a misplaced one; and this is a matter of fact which is easily cleared and ascertained.

LETTER TO WILLIAM STRAHAN*

Adam Smith

Dear Sir,

It is with a real, though a very melancholy pleasure, that I sit down to give you some account of the behavior of our late excellent friend, Mr. Hume, during his last illness.

Though, in his own judgment, his disease was mortal and incurable, yet he allowed himself to be prevailed upon, by the entreaty of his friends, to try what might be the effects of a long journey. A few days before he set out, he wrote that account of his own life, which, together with his other papers, he has left to your care. My account, therefore, shall begin where his ends.

He set out for London towards the end of April, and at Morpeth met with Mr. John Home and myself, who had both come down from London on purpose to see him, expecting to have found him at Edinburgh. Mr. Home returned with him, and attended him during the whole of his stay in England, with that care and attention which might be expected from a temper so perfectly friendly and affectionate. As I had written to my mother that she might expect me in Scotland, I was under the necessity of continuing my journey. His disease seemed to yield to exercise and change of air; and when he arrived in London, he was apparently in much better health than when he left Edinburgh. He was advised to go to Bath, to drink the waters, which appeared for some time to have so good an effect upon him, that even he himself began to entertain, what he was not apt to do, a better opinion of his own health. His symptoms, however, soon returned with their usual violence; and from that moment he gave up all thoughts of recovery, but submitted with the utmost cheerfulness, and the most perfect complacency and resignation. Upon his return to Edinburgh, though he found himself much weaker, yet his cheerfulness never abated, and he continued to divert himself, as usual, with correcting his own works for a new edition, with reading books of amusement, with the conversation of his friends; and, sometimes in the evening, with a party at his favorite game of whist. His cheerfulness was so great, and his conversation and amusements ran so much in their usual strain, that, notwithstanding all bad symptoms, many people could not believe he was dying. "I shall tell your friend, Colonel Edmonstone," said Dr. Dundas, to him one day, "that I left you much better, and in a fair way of recovery." "Doctor,"

* Nov. 9, 1776; in the preface to Hume's *History of England* (1778; Sampson ed. 1856).

said he, "as I believe you would not choose to tell any thing but the truth, you had better tell him that I am dying as fast as my enemies, if I have any, could wish, and as easily and cheerfully as my best friends could desire." Colonel Edmonstone soon afterwards came to see him, and take leave of him; and on his way home he could not forbear writing him a letter, bidding him once more an eternal adieu, and applying to him, as to a dying man, the beautiful French verses in which the abbé Chaulieu, in expectation of his own death, laments his approaching separation from his friend the marquis de la Fare. Mr. Hume's magnanimity and firmness were such, that his most affectionate friends knew that they hazarded nothing in talking or writing to him as to a dying man, and that so far from being hurt by this frankness, he was rather pleased and flattered by it. I happened to come into his room while he was reading this letter, which he had just received, and which he immediately showed me. I told him, that though I was sensible how very much he was weakened, and that appearances were in many respects very bad, yet his cheerfulness was still so great, the spirit of life seemed still to be so very strong in him, that I could not help entertaining some faint hopes. He answered, "Your hopes are groundless. An habitual diarrhoea of more than a year's standing, would be a very bad disease at any age; at my age it is a mortal one. When I lie down in the evening, I feel myself weaker than when I rose in the morning; and when I rise in the morning, weaker than when I lay down in the evening. I am sensible besides, that some of my vital parts are affected, so that I must soon die." "Well," said I, "if it must be so, you have at least the satisfaction of leaving all your friends, your brother's family in particular, in great prosperity." He said that he felt that satisfaction so sensibly, that when he was reading, a few days before, Lucian's Dialogues of the Dead, among all the excuses which are alleged to Charon for not entering readily into his boat, he could not find one that fitted him: he had no house to finish, he had no daughter to provide for, he had no enemies upon whom he wished to revenge himself. "I could not well imagine," said he, "what excuse I could make to Charon in order to obtain a little delay. I have done every thing of consequence which I ever meant to do; and I could at no time expect to leave my relations and friends in a better situation than that in which I am now likely to leave them: I, therefore, have all reason to die contented." He then diverted himself with inventing several jocular excuses, which he supposed he might make to Charon, and with imagining the very surly answers which it might suit the character of Charon to return to them. "Upon further consideration," said he, "I thought I might say to him, 'Good Charon, I have been correcting my works for a new edition.

Allow me a little time, that I may see how the public receives the alterations.' But Charon would answer, 'When you have seen the effect of these, you will be for making other alterations. There will be no end of such excuses; so, honest friend, please step into the boat.' But I might still urge, 'Have a little patience, good Charon: I have been endeavoring to open the eyes of the public. If I live a few years longer, I may have the satisfaction of seeing the downfall of some of the prevailing systems of superstition.' But Charon would then lose all temper and decency. 'You loitering rogue, that will not happen these many hundred years. Do you fancy I will grant you a lease for so long a term? Get into the boat this instant, you lazy, loitering rogue.' "

But, though Mr. Hume always talked of his approaching dissolution with great cheerfulness, he never affected to make any parade of his magnanimity. He never mentioned the subject but when the conversation naturally led to it, and never dwelt longer upon it than the course of the conversation happened to require; it was a subject indeed which occurred pretty frequently, in consequence of the inquiries which his friends, who came to see him, naturally made concerning the state of his health. The conversation which I mentioned above, and which passed on Thursday the eighth of August, was the last, except one, that I ever had with him. He had now become so very weak, that the company of his most intimate friends fatigued him; for his cheerfulness was still so great, his complaisance and social disposition were still so entire, that when any friend was with him, he could not help talking more, and with greater exertion, than suited the weakness of his body. At his own desire, therefore, I agreed to leave Edinburgh, where I was staying partly upon his account, and returned to my mother's house here at Kirkaldy, upon condition that he would send for me whenever he wished to see me; the physician who saw him most frequently, Dr. Black, undertaking, in the mean time, to write me occasionally an account of the state of his health.

On the twenty-second of August, the doctor wrote me the following letter: —

Since my last, Mr. Hume has passed his time pretty easily, but is much weaker. He sits up, goes down stairs once a day, and amuses himself with reading, but seldom sees any body. He finds that even the conversation of his most intimate friends fatigues and oppresses him; and it is happy that he does not need it, for he is quite free from anxiety, impatience, or low spirits, and passes his time very well with the assistance of amusing books.

I received, the day after, a letter from Mr. Hume himself, of which the following is an extract: —

23d August 1776

My Dearest Friend,

I am obliged to make use of my nephew's hand in writing to you, as I do not rise to-day. . . .

I go very fast to decline, and last night had a small fever, which I hoped might put a quicker period to this tedious illness; but unluckily it has, in a great measure, gone off. I cannot submit to your coming over here on my account, as it is possible for me to see you so small a part of the day; but Dr. Black can better inform you concerning the degree of strength which may from time to time remain with me. Adieu, etc.

Three days after, I received the following letter from Dr. Black: —

26th August 1776

Dear Sir,

Yesterday, about four o'clock, afternoon, Mr. Hume expired. The near approach of his death became evident in the night between Thursday and Friday, when his disease became excessive, and soon weakened him so much, that he could no longer rise out of his bed. He continued to the last perfectly sensible, and free from much pain or feelings of distress. He never dropped the smallest expression of impatience; but when he had occasion to speak to the people about him, always did it with affection and tenderness. I thought it improper to write to bring you over, especially as I heard that he had dictated a letter to you, desiring you not to come. When he became very weak, it cost him an effort to speak; and he died in such a happy composure of mind, that nothing could exceed it.

Thus died our most excellent and never to be forgotten friend; concerning whose philosophical opinions men will, no doubt, judge variously, every one approving or condemning them, according as they happen to coincide or disagree with his own; but concerning whose character and conduct there can scarce be a difference of opinion. His temper, indeed, seemed to be more happily balanced, if I may be allowed such an expression, than that perhaps of any other man I have ever known. Even in the lowest state of his fortune, his great and necessary frugality never hindered him from exercising, upon proper occasions, acts both of charity and generosity. It was a frugality founded not upon avarice, but upon the love of independency. The extreme gentleness of his nature never weakened either the firmness of his mind or the steadiness of his resolutions. His constant pleasantry was the genuine effusion of good nature and good humor, tempered with delicacy and modesty, and without even the slightest tincture of malignity, so frequently the disagreeable source of what is called wit in other men. It never was the meaning of his raillery to mortify; and therefore, far from offending, it seldom failed to please and delight, even those who were the objects of it. To his friends, who were frequently the objects of it, there was not perhaps any one of all his great and amiable qualities which contributed more to endear his conversation. And that gayety of temper, so agreeable in society, but which is so often accompanied with frivolous and superficial qualities, was in him certainly attended with the most severe application, the most extensive learning, the greatest depth of thought, and a capacity in every respect the most comprehensive. Upon the whole, I have always considered him, both in his lifetime and since his death, as approaching as nearly to the idea of a perfectly wise and virtuous man as perhaps the nature of human frailty will permit.

I ever am, dear sir,

Most affectionately yours,
Adam Smith

QUESTIONS

1. *For other attitudes towards the dying Hume's view of himself, see Boswell, The Life of Samuel Johnson, LL.D., II, 335 (1791; Glover ed. 1901), and Boswell in Extremes 1776–1778, at 11–15 (Weis and Pottle ed. 1970).*
2. *I have suggested that Hume's achievement here is one of the imagination, that what he does is to make and defend a claim of meaning, a pretense that is its own truth. Do you agree, or would you rather say that his achievement is one of actually living his life in such a way that his claims are simply and factually true? Or is that not a meaningful distinction?*
3. *We have been looking at literature as a way of defining what the law leaves out, what cannot be said in lawyers' ways. But the question can be turned upon literature as well: what does literature leave out? When you consider what is most important in your life as you live it, how much of that finds expression or reference in any literature at all? Think not only of your private relationships — where in what you read do you find expressed such relationships as those you have with your own spouse and children? — but of your feelings and expectations about yourself as you begin a career. What literature addresses itself in a way that you find interesting or useful to the young person choosing a career or setting forth on a job? Or think of your college and high school days: does anyone anywhere talk about that stage of life in any way you can recognize as having something to do with experiences you have had? How do you explain these extraordinary omissions from the world of literature?*
4. *The following three passages express various relationships between imagination and reality. How can you distinguish among them? Is what you read in these passages true or false? What lesson do you learn that can be applied to legal speech expressing a legal imagination?*

HISTORY OF THE PELOPONNESIAN WAR*
Thucydides

[Pericles is speaking at the funeral of Athenian soldiers.]

. . . We cultivate refinement without extravagance and knowledge without effeminacy; wealth we employ more for use than for show, and place the real disgrace of poverty not in owning to the fact but in declining the struggle against it. Our public men have, besides politics, their private affairs to attend to, and our ordinary citizens, though occupied with the pursuits of industry, are still fair judges of public matters; for, unlike any other nation, regarding him who takes no part in these duties not as unambitious but as useless, we Athenians are able to judge at all events if we cannot originate, and instead of looking on discussion as a stumbling-block in the way of action, we think it an indispensable preliminary to any wise action at all. Again, in our enterprises we present the singular spectacle of daring and deliberation, each carried to its highest point, and both united in the same persons; although usually decision is the fruit of ignorance, hesitation of reflexion. But the palm of courage will surely be adjudged most justly to those, who best know the difference between hardship and pleasure and yet are never tempted to shrink from danger. In generosity we are equally singular, acquiring our friends by conferring not by receiving favours. Yet, of course, the doer of the favour is the firmer friend of the two, in order by continued kindness to keep the recipient in his debt; while the debtor feels less keenly from the very consciousness that the return he makes will be a payment, not a free gift. And it is only the Athenians who, fearless of consequences, confer their benefits not from calculations of expediency, but in the confidence of liberality.

In short, I say that as a city we are the school of Hellas; while I doubt if the world can produce a man, who where he has only himself to depend upon, is equal to so many emergencies, and graced by so happy a versatility as the Athenian. And that this is no mere boast thrown out for the occasion, but plain matter of fact, the power of the state acquired by these habits proves. For Athens alone of her contemporaries is found when tested to be greater than her reputation, and alone gives no occasion to her assailants to blush at the antagonist by whom they have been worsted, or to her subjects to question her title by merit to rule. Rather, the admiration of the present and succeeding ages will be ours, since we have not left our power without witness, but have shown it by mighty proofs; and far from needing a Homer for our panegyrist, or other of his craft whose verses might charm for the

* Book 2 (Crawley trans. 1876).

moment only for the impression which they gave to melt at the touch of fact, we have forced every sea and land to be the highway of our daring, and everywhere, whether for evil or for good, have left imperishable monuments behind us. Such is the Athens for which these men, in the assertion of their resolve not to lose her, nobly fought and died; and well may every one of their survivors be ready to suffer in her cause.

HISTORY OF ENGLAND FROM THE FALL OF WOLSEY TO THE DEATH OF ELIZABETH*

J. A. Froude

[He is writing of the religious persecutions of the sixteenth century.] . . . England became the theatre of a war between two armies of martyrs, to be waged, not upon the open field, in open action, but on the stake and on the scaffold, with the nobler weapons of passive endurance. Each party were ready to give their blood; each party were ready to shed the blood of their antagonists; and the sword was to single out its victims in the rival ranks, not as in peace among those whose crimes made them dangerous to society, but, as on the field of battle, where the most conspicuous courage most challenges the aim of the enemy. It was war, though under the form of peace; and if we would understand the true spirit of the time, we must regard Catholics and Protestants as gallant soldiers, whose deaths, when they fall, are not painful, but glorious; and whose devotion we are equally able to admire, even when we cannot equally admire their cause. Courage and self-sacrifice are beautiful alike in enemy and friend.

ROMEO AND JULIET*

Shakespeare

[Romeo has just found Juliet in the tomb, apparently dead.]

How oft when men are at the point of death
Have they been merry! Which their keepers call
A lightning before death. O, how may I
Call this a lightning? O my love! my wife!
Death, that hath sucked the honey of thy breath,
Hath had no power yet upon thy beauty.
Thou art not conquer'd; beauty's ensign yet
Is crimson in thy lips and in thy cheeks,

* Chapter 9 (1856–1870).
* Act 5, scene 3.

And death's pale flag is not advanced there.
Tybalt, liest thou in thy bloody sheet?
O, what more favour can I do to thee,
Than with that hand that cut thy youth in twain
To sunder his that was thine enemy?
Forgive me, cousin! Ah, dear Juliet,
Why art thou yet so fair? Shall I believe
That unsubstantial Death is amorous,
And that the lean abhorred monster keeps
Thee here in dark to be his paramour?
For fear of that, I still will stay with thee,
And never from this palace of dim night
Depart again. Here, here will I remain
With worms that are thy chambermaids; O, here
Will I set up my everlasting rest,
And shake the yoke of inauspicious stars
From this world-wearied flesh. Eyes, look your last!
Arms, take your last embrace! and, lips, O you
The doors of breath, seal with a righteous kiss
A dateless bargain to engrossing death!
Come, bitter conduct, come, unsavoury guide!
Thou desperate pilot, now at once run on
The dashing rocks thy seasick weary bark!
Here's to my love! [*Drinks.*] O true apothecary!
Thy drugs are quick. Thus with a kiss I die. [*Dies.*]

4. Professional Attitudes: Uses and Effects of Professional Rhetoric

The artist, like the God of the creation, remains within or behind or beyond or above his handiwork, invisible, refined out of existence, indifferent, paring his fingernails.*

We have been studying some of the characteristics of legal language as an intellectual or literary system, as a way of thinking and talking. Now we return to a concern expressed earlier, and look at what is happening to us as we learn to use this language, to function on its terms. What does an education into a professional rhetoric, a mastery of a professional activity, mean for the one who engages in it? Here you are asked in a specific way whether the experience of the river pilot is a cautionary example for the lawyer.

What we asked before of particular languages and uses of language

* James Joyce, A *Portrait of the Artist as a Young Man* 215 (1916; Viking ed. 1964).

we ask here of conduct and feeling: what do we mean by decency and humanity, and how can they be achieved? What does it mean, for example, to treat another person as a person and not as a thing, and how does one do it? How does one recognize the humanity of another and not convert him into a fiction, a role, an idea? To what extent is success here a matter of feeling and physical conduct, and to what extent a matter of expression, an art of language?

A PORTRAIT OF THE ARTIST AS A YOUNG MAN*

James Joyce

[Stephen Daedalus is talking with his friend Lynch about tragedy.]

They lit their cigarettes and turned to the right. After a pause Stephen began:

— Aristotle has not defined pity and terror. I have. I say . . .

Lynch halted and said bluntly:

— Stop! I won't listen! I am sick. I was out last night on a yellow drunk with Horan and Goggins.

Stephen went on:

— Pity is the feeling which arrests the mind in the presence of whatsoever is grave and constant in human sufferings and unites it with the human sufferer. Terror is the feeling which arrests the mind in the presence of whatsoever is grave and constant in human sufferings and unites it with the secret cause.

— Repeat, said Lynch.

Stephen repeated the definitions slowly.

— A girl got into a hansom a few days ago, he went on, in London. She was on her way to meet her mother whom she had not seen for many years. At the corner of a street the shaft of a lorry shivered the window of the hansom in the shape of a star. A long fine needle of the shivered glass pierced her heart. She died on the instant. The reporter called it a tragic death. It is not. It is remote from terror and pity according to the terms of my definitions.

— The tragic emotion, in fact, is a face looking two ways, towards terror and towards pity, both of which are phases of it. You see I use the word *arrest*. I mean that the tragic emotion is static. Or rather the dramatic emotion is. The feelings excited by improper art are kinetic, desire or loathing. Desire urges us to possess, to go to something; loathing urges us to abandon, to go from something. These are kinetic emotions. The arts which excite them, pornographical or didactic, are therefore improper arts. The esthetic emotion (I use the general term)

* Pages 204–207 (1916; Viking ed. 1964).

is therefore static. The mind is arrested and raised above desire and loathing.

— You say that art must not excite desire, said Lynch. I told you that one day I wrote my name in pencil on the backside of the Venus of Praxiteles in the Museum. Was that not desire?

— I speak of normal natures, said Stephen. You also told me that when you were a boy in that charming carmelite school you ate pieces of dried cowdung.

Lynch broke again into a whinny of laughter and again rubbed both his hands over his groins but without taking them from his pockets.

— O I did! I did! he cried.

Stephen turned towards his companion and looked at him for a moment boldly in the eyes. Lynch, recovering from his laughter, answered his look from his humbled eyes. The long slender flattened skull beneath the long pointed cap brought before Stephen's mind the image of a hooded reptile. The eyes, too, were reptilelike in glint and gaze. Yet at that instant, humbled and alert in their look, they were lit by one tiny human point, the window of a shrivelled soul, poignant and self-embittered.

— As for that, Stephen said in polite parenthesis, we are all animals. I also am an animal.

— You are, said Lynch.

— But we are just now in a mental world, Stephen continued. The desire and loathing excited by improper esthetic means are really unesthetic emotions not only because they are kinetic in character but also because they are not more than physical. Our flesh shrinks from what it dreads and responds to the stimulus of what it desires by a purely reflex action of the nervous system. Our eyelid closes before we are aware that the fly is about to enter our eye.

QUESTIONS

1. *Do you agree that the death of the girl is not tragic? What do you mean by "tragic"? (What would the girl's fiancé or mother say about that death? About Stephen's remark?)*
2. *The artist dismisses that death. How would a lawyer respond to it? What would he do about it? He might do many different things, of course; upon what circumstances would his choices of action, or inaction, depend?*
   a. *Imagine a case in which the lawyer would "dismiss" it: what would the dismissal involve, how would it work? Is the process of the lawyer's dismissal like or unlike that of the artist? Compare the Georgetown Hospital case, supra page 84. What is the difference, if any, between saying "no tragedy" and saying "no cause of action"?*
   b. *Imagine a case in which it could be said that a lawyer does not dismiss the death but deals with it. What does he do when he deals with it?*

How, for example, would this story be told in a lawsuit over the liability of the manufacturer of the windshield? Or in a probate proceeding?

3. *Stephen justifies the apparent coldness of his view by saying "we are just now in a mental world." Is the law always "in a mental world" and is the lawyer always a Stephen Daedalus?*

REMEMBRANCE OF THINGS PAST*

Marcel Proust

We made our way back along the Avenue Gabriel, through the strolling crowd. I left my grandmother to rest on a seat and went in search of a cab. She, in whose heart I always placed myself when I had to form an opinion of the most unimportant person, she was now closed to me, had become part of the world outside, and, more than from any casual passerby, I was obliged to keep from her what I thought of her condition, to say no word of my uneasiness. I could not have spoken of it to her in greater confidence than to a stranger. She had suddenly handed back to me the thoughts, the griefs which, from the days of my infancy, I had entrusted for all time to her keeping. She was not yet dead. I was already alone. And even those allusions which she had made to the Guermantes, to Mme. de Sévigné, to our conversations about the little clan, assumed an air of being without point or occasion, fantastic, because they sprang from the nullity of this very being who to-morrow possibly would have ceased to exist, for whom they would no longer have any meaning, from that nullity, incapable of conceiving them, which my grandmother would shortly be.

"Well, Sir, I don't like to say no, but you have not made an appointment, you have no time fixed. Besides, this is not my day for seeing patients. You surely have a doctor of your own. I cannot interfere with his practice, unless he were to call me in for a consultation. It's a question of professional etiquette . . ."

Just as I was signalling to a cabman, I had caught sight of the famous Professor E——, almost a friend of my father and grandfather, acquainted at any rate with them both, who lived in the Avenue Gabriel, and, with a sudden inspiration, had stopped him just as he was entering his house, thinking that he would perhaps be the very person to advise my grandmother. But he was evidently in a hurry and, after calling for his letters, seemed anxious to get rid of me, so that my only chance of speaking to him lay in going up with him in the lift, of which he begged me to allow him to work the switches himself, this being a mania with him.

* Volume 1, pages 940–943 (1913–1928; Random House ed. 1934).

"But, Sir, I am not asking you to see my grandmother here; you will realise from what I am trying to tell you that she is not in a fit state to come; what I am asking is that you should call at our house in half an hour's time, when I have taken her home."

"Call at your house! Really, Sir, you must not expect me to do that. I am dining with the Minister of Commerce. I have a call to pay first. I must change at oncc, and to make matters worse I have torn my coat and my other one has no buttonholes for my decorations. I beg you, please, to oblige me by not touching the switches. You don't know how the lift works; one can't be too careful. Getting that buttonhole made means more delay. Well, as I am a friend of your people, if your grandmother comes here at once I will see her. But I warn you that I shall be able to give her exactly a quarter of an hour, nor a moment more."

I had started off at once, without even getting out of the lift which Professor E—— had himself set in motion to take me down again, casting a suspicious glance at me as he did so.

We may, indeed, say that the hour of death is uncertain, but when we say so we represent that hour to ourselves as situated in a vague and remote expanse of time, it never occurs to us that it can have any connexion with the day that has already dawned, or may signify that death — or its first assault and partial possession of us, after which it will never leave hold of us again — may occur this very afternoon, so far from uncertain, this afternoon every hour of which has already been allotted to some occupation. You make a point of taking your drive every day so that in a month's time you will have had the full benefit of the fresh air; you have hesitated over which cloak you will take, which cabman to call, you are in the cab, the whole day lies before you, short because you have to be at home early, as a friend is coming to see you; you hope that it will bc as fine again to-morrow; and you have no suspicion that death, which has been making its way towards you along another plane, shrouded in an impenetrable darkness, has chosen precisely this day of all days to make its appearance, in a few minutes' time, more or less, at the moment when the carriage has reached the Champs-Elysées. Perhaps those who are haunted as a rule by the fear of the utter strangeness of death will find something reassuring in this kind of death — in this kind of first contact with death — because death thus assumes a known, familiar guise of everyday life. A good luncheon has preceded it, and the same outing that people take who are in perfect health. A drive home in an open carriage comes on top of its first onslaught; ill as my grandmother was, there were, after all, several people who could testify that at six o'clock, as we came home from the Champs-Elysées, they had bowed to her as she drove past in an open carriage, in perfect weather. Legrandin, making his way towards the

Place de la Concorde, raised his hat to us, stopping to look after us with an air of surprise. I, who was not yet detached from life, asked my grandmother if she had acknowledged his greeting, reminding her of his readiness to take offence. My grandmother, thinking me no doubt very frivolous, raised her hand in the air as though to say: "What does it matter? It is not of the least importance."

Yes, one might have said that, a few minutes earlier, when I was looking for a cab, my grandmother was resting on a seat in the Avenue Gabriel, and that a little later she had driven past in an open carriage. But would that have been really true? The seat, for instance, to maintain its position at the side of an avenue — for all that it may be subjected also to certain conditions of equilibrium — has no need of energy. But in order that a living person may be stable, even when supported by a seat or in a carriage, there is required a tension of forces which we do not ordinarily perceive, any more than we perceive (because its action is universal) atmospheric pressure. Possibly if we were to be hollowed out and then left to support the pressure of the air we might feel, in the moment that preceded our extinction, that terrible weight which there was nothing left in us to neutralise. Similarly when the abyss of sickness and death opens within us, and we have no longer any resistance to offer to the tumult with which the world and our own body rush upon us, then to endure even the tension of our own muscles, the shudder that freezes us to the marrow, then even to keep ourselves motionless in what we ordinarily regard as nothing but the simple negative position of a lifeless thing requires, if we wish our head to remain erect and our eyes calm, an expense of vital energy and becomes the object of an exhausting struggle.

And if Legrandin had looked back at us with that astonished air, it was because to him, as to the other people who passed us then, in the cab in which my grandmother was apparently seated she had seemed to be foundering, sliding into the abyss, clinging desperately to the cushions which could barely arrest the downward plunge of her body, her hair in disorder, her eye wild, unable any longer to face the assault of the images which its pupil was not strong enough now to bear. She had appeared to them, although I was still by her side, submerged in that unknown world somewhere in which she had already received the blows, traces of which she still bore when I looked up at her a few minutes earlier in the Champs-Elysées, her hat, her face, her cloak left in disorder by the hand of the invisible angel with whom she had wrestled. I have thought, since, that this moment of her stroke cannot have altogether surprised my grandmother, that indeed she had perhaps foreseen it a long time back, had lived in expectation of it. She had not known, naturally, when this fatal moment would come, had never been certain, any more than those lovers whom a similar doubt leads alternately to found unreasonable hopes and unjustified suspicions on the fidelity of their mistresses. But it is rarely that these grave maladies, like that which now at last had struck her full in the face, do not take up their abode in the sick man for a long time before killing him, during which time they make haste, like a 'sociable' neighbour or tenant, to introduce themselves to him. A terrible acquaintance, not so much from the sufferings that it causes as from the strange novelty of the definite restriction which it imposes upon life. A woman sees herself dying, in these cases not at the actual moment of death but months, sometimes years before, when death has hideously come to dwell in her. The sufferer makes the acquaintance of the stranger whom she hears coming and going in her brain. She does not know him by sight, it is true, but from the sounds which she hears him regularly make she can form an idea of his habits. Is he a criminal? One morning, she can no longer hear him. He has gone. Ah! If it were only for ever! In the evening he has returned. What are his plans? Her specialist, put to the question, like an adored mistress, replies with avowals that one day are believed, another day fail to convince her. Or rather it is not the mistress's part but that of the servants one interrogates that the doctor plays. They are only third parties. The person whom we press for an answer, whom we suspect of being about to play us false, is life itself, and although we feel her to be no longer the same we believe in her still or at least remain undecided until the day on which she finally abandons us.

I helped my grandmother into Professor E——'s lift and a moment later he came to us and took us into his consulting room. But there, busy as he was, his bombastic manner changed, such is the force of habit; for his habit was to be friendly, that is to say lively with his patients. Since he knew that my grandmother was a great reader, and was himself one also, he devoted the first few minutes to quoting various favourite passages of poetry appropriate to the glorious summer weather. He had placed her in an armchair and himself with his back to the light so as to have a good view of her. His examination was minute and thorough, even obliging me at one moment to leave the room. He continued it after my return, then, having finished, went on, although the quarter of an hour was almost at an end, repeating various quotations to my grandmother. He even made a few jokes, which were witty enough, though I should have preferred to hear them on some other occasion, but which completely reassured me by the tone of amusement in which he uttered them. I then remembered that M. Fallières, the President of the Senate, had, many years earlier, had a false seizure, and that to the consternation of his political rivals he had returned a few days later to his duties and had begun, it was said, his preparations for a more or less remote succession to the Presidency of the Republic. My confidence in my grandmother's prompt recovery was all the more complete in that, just as I was recalling the example of M. Fallières, I was distracted from following up the similarity by a shout of laughter, which served as conclusion to one of the Professor's jokes. After which he took out his watch, wrinkled his brows petulantly on seeing that he was five minutes late, and while he bade us good-bye rang for his other coat to be brought to him at once. I waited until my grandmother had left the room, closed the door and asked him to tell me the truth.

"There is not the slightest hope," he informed me. "It is a stroke brought on by uraemia. In itself, uraemia is not necessarily fatal, but this case seems to me desperate. I need not tell you that I hope I am mistaken. Anyhow, you have Cottard, you're in excellent hands. Excuse me," he broke off as a maid came into the room with his coat over her arm. "I told you, I'm dining with the Minister of Commerce, and I have a call to pay first. Ah! Life is not all a bed of roses, as one is apt to think at your age."

And he graciously offered me his hand. I had shut the door behind me, and a footman was shewing us into the hall when we heard a loud shout of rage. The maid had forgotten to cut and hem the buttonhole for the decorations. This would take another ten minutes. The Professor continued to storm while I stood on the landing gazing at a grandmother for whom there was not the slightest hope. Each of us is indeed alone. We started for home.

QUESTIONS

1. *It may seem barbaric that a doctor should behave this way, but is it really surprising? One who spends his life in the presence of suffering cannot share it all; he must build defenses, adopt a professional attitude. Is there any other way?*
2. *You may in your own life have been talked to by a doctor in a similarly insincere way, pretending to treat you as a person while examining you as an organism. No doubt this is vexing; but exactly how would you prefer him to talk?*

THE TREATMENT OF A DYING PATIENT*

Janice Norton, M.D.

What follows is a detailed case summary of the last three and a half months of life of a gallant and articulate woman. The case report owes its existence to the fact that all those on whom we usually rely to spare us the necessity of listening to dying patients, family, clergy, friends,

* 1963 *The Psychoanalytic Study of the Child* 541.

other physicians, had already relinquished their roles and could not be induced to resume them. I was faced with the choice of allowing this patient to die a miserable and lonely death, possibly by suicide, or of trying to relieve her suffering in so far as I could.

CASE REPORT

Mrs. B., the thirty-two-year-old married mother of two sons, five and three, reluctantly came to see me at the urging of her sister, a social worker from a distant city. Her sister had been visiting and had become alarmed at Mrs. B.'s increasing depression and her hints at suicidal thoughts. While the patient frankly told me both were present, she herself felt no need to see a psychiatrist as both depression and a wish to commit suicide seemed to her to be entirely reasonable under the circumstances. She had substantial pain, cough, hemorrhagic tendencies, anemia, and increasing fatigue from metastatic breast cancer; she was losing weight and strength rapidly, had little appetite, slept poorly, and it was apparent to her that X-ray therapy, hormones, and repeated transfusions were having increasingly little effect in controlling the relentless progression of the disease toward her death. She was using very small doses of morphine, mostly at night, in a partial attempt to control the pain and in order to sleep, but had been told to use narcotics very sparingly because of the possibility of addiction. She felt it quite reasonable to wish to stop her suffering by suicide and also felt her suicide would considerably lessen the burden she was imposing on her parents, her sons, and her husband. She told me all this in a quite matter-of-fact way, underscoring the idea that she felt no need to see a psychiatrist and was only coming in once in order to please her sister. She felt she had the right to die as she pleased, had drugs readily available to her, and that her suicide could be made to look like death due to the disease if she took an overdose of morphine at some time when she was unusually sick. She had not confided this plan to anyone, although her statements about her wish to die without a prolonged terminal phase of pain and increasing incapacitation had alarmed her sister; the rest of the family had taken these to mean that she was sick and in pain but "just talking" at times when she felt most uncomfortable. . . .

. . . She presented everyone with a picture of a young woman visibly dying an early death who had a great need to come to terms with her feelings about this. As subsequent therapy with me bore out, listening had its problems as the entire situation was tragic. She was an appealing, attractive woman, warm, intelligent, well read, interested in many things, and capable of very intense feeling. One result of this was that all who loved her most and might have been expected to help her with her feelings about dying were intensely and understandably involved in grieving. Talking to others of her feelings about dying was virtually precluded by the intensity of the feelings she provoked in them. Her parents, both chronically ill and in their seventies, lived nearby and periodically cared for the children, but they could not bring themselves to see her because they "hated to cry" in her presence. Her husband, increasingly miserable at her impending death, busied himself with his work. Her doctors, increasingly frustrated at her lack of medical response to their various forms of treatment, became hearty and hollow; and her sister, frightened by the patient's obvious loneliness and despair, lived a great distance away and referred her to me. At the time I first saw her, her relationships with the two boys were about all that remained even relatively intact. She had not yet spent any protracted time in the hospital and was using what strength she had to continue to care for them as she always had, although this was becoming an increasing problem for her.

That this patient had remarkable ego strengths was immediately evident. She had faced surgery, pain, sickness, and the knowledge of her impending early death with impressive insistence on reality, and was doing her utmost to adapt to very adverse circumstances. She had continued her life as usual within the limits of her physical condition, did not resort to the drugs readily available to her, and the only demands she had made on those around her were that they allow her to share her experience with them. It was only when she became aware of their increasing withdrawal from her that she became suicidal. Her attitude toward her parents, her husband, and her doctors was essentially maternal, that she was protecting them from pain by not insisting that they listen and help her with her ever-increasing distress. At the same time she was well aware of her need for help and had done her utmost to find it.

All of this became apparent in my initial interviews with the patient and despite her superficial objections to psychiatric treatment, it was possible to get her to continue to see me on a regular basis by agreeing that she had no serious, long-standing psychiatric problems, that she was facing an extraordinarily painful reality situation with admirable courage, but that it might be of some help to her if we were to talk over her feelings about this. In addition, with the relieved consent of her surgeon, I took over the management of her narcotics and sedation so that very soon she became relatively free of pain and began to sleep at night. I explained this to her as essential both for her comfort and for her ability to care for the children as she wished to. She never did agree very wholeheartedly to the idea of seeing a psychiatrist and even in the last week of her life teased me about what an "unpsychiatric psychiatrist" I had been in that I had never lived up to her stereotype of what a psychiatrist should be, a silent, remote interpreter of dreams and of the oedipal situation. The implication was that she had not really had psychiatric treatment but had found someone with whom she could talk, who fortunately happened to be a physician and was, almost by unhappy accident, a psychiatrist as well. My initial treatment plan was to help her with her depression, prevent her suicide if at all possible, and to see if I could help the family to deal with the situation somewhat more effectively. By this time, however, both her husband and her parents had so decathected their relationship with the patient that it proved impossible for them to help; to them, in many respects she was already dead or had in any event delayed her dying too long. Her sister lived too far away to be of any immediate help although she did come to stay with the patient and care for her during the last three weeks of her life. As a result of this, my treatment goal was very rapidly changed to that of trying to make this patient's death less lonely and frightening. To this end, I saw her daily in my office, the hospital, or at her home, depending on her physical condition, for the last three and a half months of her life. I made it explicit that I would be available to her at any time, and would be for as long as she needed me. . . .

. . . I assured her that I was willing to help her in any way that I could and that this certainly included helping her with her feelings about dying. When she asked if this might not make me uncomfortable, I replied that I would try to help her in any event. She then began to discuss religion and philosophy with me, in large part I think to see whether I was really willing to help her with her feelings or would, like her parents and the minister, succumb to religious platitudes or withdraw out of my own discomfort. I did neither, and out of these discussions emerged several problems. She was afraid of dying alone, of becoming less and less attractive, "sick," and having people lose interest in her, a fear which was partially substantiated by the way her family had turned away from her. She also feared the gradually increasing sense of helplessness that her physical incapacitation was giving rise to and was in part using her intelligence to help to master this difficult situation. She was also using the philosophic discussions in an attempt to gain my approval of how "adult" she was being. Discussion of these problems gradually led to a diminution of her depression, complete absence of any talk of suicide, impressive absence of anxiety, and an increased sense of well-being and of hope which was quite at odds with her deteriorating physical condition. She was physically more comfortable during this period because of adequate medication. At this same time she asked to borrow some books of mine, which I loaned her, and she began to bring me poetry which she had written earlier. I quote one poem to illustrate her preoccupation with separation.

To die is such a lonely thing,
We cannot take one friend along.
To hold a hand would make it
Far less a frightening song.

With this she began to share with me her grief over dying, which to her essentially meant leaving those she loved best. Despite occasional interruptions by her worsening physical condition, mourning continued in one form or another until her final coma. She began by talking about the relationship to the minister and how hurt and angry she had been at his misunderstanding her need for him and his present avoidance of her. She told me in detail how they had met, the discussions they had had about her illness, and what they discussed during the times she was discouraged. She wept over his leaving her when she needed him most. She was very scornful of this kind of "religion," but also felt that he was to be pitied as he apparently did not have the strength to remain with her to help.

This led to her feelings about her husband's withdrawing from her. She understood that he was grieving himself, was hurt by his inability to help her with her feelings, but for the most part was protective about his feelings. Except for occasionally talking of feeling irritated by the lengthy hours he worked, she expressed little anger about him. She gradually told me about her marriage and relationship to her husband, of their courtship, honeymoon, the earlier happy times that they had had, his hopes and aspirations about his profession, and how she shared these. She was deeply grieved by the fact that she would not be around to continue to share his life with him; she hoped he would marry again, but preferred not to think about this. She discussed both pregnancies and her relationships with both sons in equal detail, again with emphasis on how sorely she would miss future participation in their lives. She allowed herself some daydreaming as to what she hoped their futures would be like. All of this seemed very much like working through in mourning, was accompanied by appropriate crying and by occasional denial, although the denial was almost always in the form of giving herself an extra year or so of life, not of being cured. Her ego never permitted her any convincing fantasies of a hereafter in which she might continue to be aware of the lives of those she loved. Death to her meant the end of these relationships and a separation from those she loved best. She was angry at the unfairness of her early death and talked with intense feeling of the impending loss of those she loved most and the experiences she would never have with them. She tried to console herself by reminding herself of the things she had already had, but until she was much sicker physically, she found little comfort in this. . . .

. . . While in the hospital she gradually became intermittently blind. She showed more severe anxiety about this than she had about any previous symptom. It was a concrete sign of the nearness of her death, of course, but to her this meant that she was about to be completely cut off from the people around her, by this time especially from me, and she was terrified of what she envisioned as a life in which she was mentally alert but remote from contact with people. . . .

During the first few days of her blindness I spent extra time with her and at her request visually described and identified for her hospital personnel and the details of her room; she was particularly interested in knowing what clothing I was wearing and was pleased when it was something familiar to her. I also did my utmost to demonstrate that while visual communication was seriously interfered with, we retained the equally important avenues of communication of talking and of touch. She likened these to the way a baby must feel, that feeling physical closeness and hearing the sound of mother's voice might be of as basic importance as seeing. I read to her — she particularly liked the 23rd and 121st Psalms — and I sat close enough that she could touch me or I her at any time. She often drowsed or fell asleep during these hours, and I had the impression that my physical presence and the tone of my voice were almost more important than the verbal content of what I said.

This outbreak of acute anxiety, in fact the only such outbreak during treatment, at a time when her relationship to me was threatened by blindness is an impressive illustration of the level of ego regression. By this time I had assumed for her many aspects of ego functioning. Her anxiety signaled the danger of ego disruption at the threatened loss of my supporting ego. This is, of course, an infantile form of separation anxiety. I responded to her anxiety with a marked increase in my availability to her and by "loaning" her my sight as well as by reassuring her that her loss of sight did not mean a disruption of our relationship. Her anxiety diminished with this. . . .

Three days before her death and a few hours before she became terminally comatose, we had a long conversation about her dying. She told me her only remaining fear was that dying was strange and unknown to her, that she had never done it before. Like birth, it was something that only happened once to any individual, and that similarly one might not remember what it was really like, only know that it had once happened. She no longer worried about what was to happen to her after death any more than an infant being born could worry about what his future life might be; she felt that she might be unnecessarily concerned with the actual process of death itself. She then asked me if I had been with other patients when they died and seemed relieved by my affirmative answer. One very comforting recurring thought to her was that throughout the centuries many people had died before her; more importantly, it had occurred to her that I would share this experience with her, although not at this time. I agreed that this was certainly so and added that I hoped I might equal her courage. She was pleased by this, and she then reminisced about our relationship. She recalled our first meeting and smiled in retrospect at her needless reluctance at seeing a psychiatrist. She thanked me for having helped her, particularly not to commit suicide, which she now felt would have been most difficult for her family, especially her sons. I was obviously moved by the finality of all this, and she chided me about being much more involved with her than doctors should be with their patients, and abruptly cried. Her regret was that we had known each other so briefly, that she was dying without ever knowing me really well. I said she had known me rather better than she might think, that I felt it a great privilege that she had shared this experience with me and that I, too, wished we had had more time together. She asked me if after her death I would wear for her a red dress she had bought just before she became too sick to have any fun — she wanted "the dress to have some fun." I agreed, thanked her, asked whether there was anything else I might do for her, and she asked that I again read the 23rd Psalm. In the midst of this she interrupted me by crying. She said she would miss me terribly but somehow knew I was "always there" and asked that I hold her hand while she fell asleep. I did, and this was the last time the patient was conscious except for very brief periods that afternoon. She became comatose later on in the day and died three days later without regaining consciousness.

QUESTIONS

1. *You see that another sort of professional attitude is possible at least for a doctor, at least part of the time. Where was the patient's lawyer all this time, and what was he doing?*
2. *Was Doctor Norton really acting as a professional woman here, or as a person? Or is she in the lucky position of feeling no conflict between those roles? Notice that the patient refused to regard her as a psychiatrist.*
3. *How do you reconcile the doctor's laconic remark that "listening had its problems" with such an observation as "I had assumed for her many aspects of ego functioning"? Is it not true that Dr. Norton, in a most skillful fashion, talks two ways here?*
4. *To ask of psychiatry what we have asked of law: what sort of possibilities does it offer? What does her education in psychiatry and her mastery of its language enable Dr. Norton to say or do that another could not do?*
5. *Can you think of any analog to this passage in the lawyer's life, any mo-*

ment where your legal education and your mastery of legal language will enable you to do what no one else can? You are asked to search for the unique, for the heroic, in your profession. What can you bear that another cannot?

6. Or to put it in more homely terms: at a party of musicians, you may be aware that (even if they do not do it) all the others can step to the piano and play and you cannot. What can you do that they cannot, what unexpressed power do you have?
7. To what extent is Dr. Norton's achievement here a matter of feeling and conduct, and to what extent a matter of the control of language? Is it in part an achievement of the imagination?

WRITING ASSIGNMENT 3: *Defining by Comparison the Literature of the Law*

Part One

• *Add one legal and one nonlegal passage to the anthology you have just read. They need not be on the subject of death, but they should invite an interesting contrast or comparison.*

I hope that to choose such passages and set them side by side is something you want to do, that you see possibilities here. What questions based upon your two passages can you ask about the nature of legal language, about the place of language in the life of the lawyer, or about the writer's art? About the nature of the legal imagination? How do you respond to the questions you pose?

Part Two

• *Explicate the contrast or comparison that interests you. How have you defined the life of the lawyer here — what possibilities, what risks, have you perceived and expressed?*

Your explication can take whatever form you wish, but I hope you see it as sensible to be asked to make for yourself in this way a definition of the rhetoric of the law. You may wish to consider once more the questions proposed on pages 78–80 in connection with the assignment on good writing — indeed, you might wish to consider this another version of that assignment.

Here is a question suggested by a student as a possible beginning for analysis: identify the fictions used in each statement and ask whether the writer recognizes that they are fictions, and if so, how he does so. If he does not recognize the fictions he uses, suggest how he might do so.

WRITING ASSIGNMENT 3, ALTERNATIVE A: The Law Controls the Speaker

Part One

• *Give an account of an occasion upon which the law controls the way a person talks: he is forced against his will to speak in one way rather than another, or not to speak at all. Make the occasion one of real importance to the speaker, a real frustration for him.*

Part Two

• *Should the law be rewritten to permit this person to say what he wants in the way he wants? (If possible, find an occasion to which your answer to this question is no.) Explain either how the law should be so rewritten or why it should not be.*

WRITING ASSIGNMENT 3, ALTERNATIVE B: Drafting a Complaint

Part One

• *Give an account of a death in some language other than legal language. Your account should not take the form of the "statement of facts" in a legal brief or judicial opinion, but should be a living statement of its own.*

Part Two

• *A. Draft a complaint, civil or criminal, based upon that event.*
• *B. Explain and evaluate what you have done as a writer of a complaint.*
• *C. Explain what sort of rhetorical resource the complaint affords. What interest or value has this sort of writing? What dangers?*

Here are some questions that may help you work this assignment out.

1. What sort of literature is the complaint? On what understanding is it to be read? Look at your complaint and ask what it has left out, what else might be said about these events. Imagine an answer to the complaint you have drafted: would that document complete the picture, exhaust the possibilities of legal speech, or might there still be something to be said? What would you think of a judicial opinion that simply adopted a complaint or answer?

2. To the layman the complaint may seem a conclusory, dead instru-

ment of no interest except as another example of the dishonest and nonsensical ways that lawyers speak. It is about the most partisan and artlessly exaggerated document one could imagine. Does it make sense, is it honest, to another audience, on some special understanding?

a. Examine your own complaint and ask how you have characterized the events you describe — with what specificity, what bias. What pretenses has your complaint made, and how do you justify them? What have you tried to hide? Consider in this connection both the portion of the complaint that sets forth the cause of action and the portion that seeks relief. You might go back and read once more the dying words of the Earl of Lindsey, supra page 108, and the questions that follow that excerpt. Is your complaint just a tissue of fictions, of lies? Who do you think you are kidding?

b. If you wish to say that the complaint must be understood as part of the process of trial, during which its false pretenses will be exposed and what is now left out will be put back in again, be sure to explain exactly how this process works, how it is that the trial saves the complaint.

c. By what process did you compose your complaint? What were the questions you faced? What inconsistent pressures did you try to accommodate, what tensions resolve? What experience lies behind this rather lapidary document?

3. The following passage may be a way of posing a question about the nature of the complaint.

"But how many kinds of sentence are there? Say assertion, question, and command? — There are countless kinds: countless different kinds of use of what we call 'symbols,' 'words,' 'sentences.' And this multiplicity is not something fixed, given once for all; but new types of language, new language-games, as we may say, come into existence, and others become obsolete and get forgotten. (We can get a rough picture of this from the changes in mathematics.)

"Here the term 'language-game' is meant to bring into prominence the fact that the speaking of language is part of an activity, or of a form of life.

"Review the multiplicity of language-games in the following examples, and in others:

Giving orders, and obeying them —
Describing the appearance of an object, or giving its measurements —
Constructing an object from a description (a drawing) —
Reporting an event —
Speculating about an event —

Forming and testing a hypothesis —
Presenting the results of an experiment in tables and diagrams —
Making up a story; and reading it —
Play-acting —
Singing catches —
Guessing riddles —
Making a joke; telling it —
Solving a problem in practical arithmetic —
Translating from one language into another —
Asking, thanking, cursing, greeting, praying.

" — *It is interesting to compare the multiplicity of the tools in language and of the ways they are used, the multiplicity of kinds of word and sentence, with what logicians have said about the structure of language.*" L. Wittgenstein, Philosophical Investigations ¶23 (3d ed. 1958).

Your question is this: how do you define and explain the language game of the legal complaint?

4. In the portion of your paper in which you explain what it is you have done when you have drafted a complaint, you will necessarily characterize a part of the lawyer's life. In what terms do you do so? What inferences about the lawyer's life could be drawn from your account of what you did? Consider in particular the metaphors you use, and ask whether they do justice to your experience: "start the machinery of the law," "screen out the irrelevant," use a "tool," and so on. Try to find a way to express as fully as you can what drafting the complaint involved for you.

5. The temptation is to look at this in mechanical terms: the writer is a selector, like a cranberry-grader or gravel-screen perhaps. But your writing has a real audience and real purposes. To whom are you writing, and what are you trying to achieve with this document? Does it help to conceive of the complaint as a threat, say, or a challenge, or a bid, or a wish?

6. You may wish to say that drafting a complaint is not an important or interesting part of a lawyer's life, that the main goal is to do it quickly. That is what form books are for. No valid inferences as to the nature of the lawyer's life can be drawn from this routine and boring activity. The interest of the lawyer's life lies elsewhere.

a. If you are inclined to take this position, you should not fail to ask yourself where the interest lies, then, in what it consists.

b. See Giordanello v. United States, 357 U.S. 480 (1958).

c. Was the task that faced the lawyers in the Georgetown Hospital case a boring and routine one?

7. Consider the following case and the complaint upon which it is based.

". . . As grounds for relief, petitioner states the following: 'Petitioner avers that on or about the night of July 18, 1970, petitioner was attacked and hit in the face, by another inmate, with a metal dust mop and his fist. This inmate also picked up a chair but, petitioner left the room before he could hit petitioner with the chair. Petitioner did not strike out at, or move to hit this other inmate at any time. Petitioner suffered cuts on the surface of his face and lacerations on the inside of the mouth. Petitioner has several witnesses to this fact. Furthermore: petitioner states that the other inmate and himself were placed in segregation on the same night, July 18, 1970. Before and during my stay in segregation I was not examined by a Doctor, Nurse, or M.T.A. for lacerations, abrasions, cuts, or broken bones. Petitioner feels this is negligence on the part of the staff here and demands 'show cause' by the Warden of this institution as to why petitioner should not seek Civil relief in this matter. Petitioner seeks punitive and actual relief in the amount of Two Hundred and Fifty Thousand Dollars each. Petitioner is a Diabetic (Brittle Diabetic) and can prove he has been one for 16 years or more. During petitioners stay in segregation he was sick twice with a diabetic reaction, and in both instances petitioner was not examined for urine test, blood sugar, etc., by a Doctor, Nurse, or M.T.A. This could have cost petitioner his life.'

"Treated as a proceeding for equitable relief, this cause must be dismissed. Only in exceptional circumstances which rise to the level of a constitutional deprivation will the courts undertake "to review the nature and conditions of a prisoner's otherwise lawful confinement." And, the allegations of petitioner's pleading indicate only a single, isolated incident rather than a continuing practice which might be violative of the Eighth Amendment prohibition against cruel and unusual punishment." Cummins v. Ciccone, 317 F. Supp. 342 (W.D. Mo. 1970).

a. How would you draft a complaint for this plaintiff? What else would you want to know? Is this activity of preparing such a complaint dull and routine, or has it some real interest for you? Why?

b. Notice that with respect to one serious charge — of inadequate medical examination — there was no death or injury. Does that bar recovery here? Would it do so elsewhere in the law?

8. Would you regard it as a mechanical exercise to redraft the following complaint?

". . .'On August 7th 1969 I was sent to the Chicago halfway house from Milan, Michigan. I stayed about a month and ran off I was mixed up. So I went to Kankakee, Ill. and committed a break in which is a felony I was out of my head by then. I was arrested Nov. 17th 1969 by the Kankakee Police and put in jail I seen a FBI agent the same day so he call D.C. and told them I had been caught. I stayed in jail 3 months *and then I went to court while I was in jail. The court had 2 mental doctors to see me after they seen me they told the court that I was mentally incompetent so the court committed me to the Illinois Mental Health and Walfare Department that was Feb 3 or 4, 1970, on Feb 5 1970 I was taken to the Kankakee State Hospital and was comitted. I was put on the intensive care ward because I was on medication 100 mg. thorozine that night at 8:00 P.M. the federal Marshals came in and took me out forcefully I was not released by any doctors for I was just committed. They took me 80 miles away to the county jail at Danville, Ill. I was there 5 days then sent to Terre Haute. Right now I am sitting in a cell in the Springfield Hospital. I am receiving no help at all and it is not because I don't want it. Its because this is not a mental hospital. I am only asking [to] go back to the Kankakee State Hospital and get help.' (sic)" Potter v. Ciccone, 316 F. Supp. 703 (W.D. Mo. 1970).*

9. Two other cases presenting interesting problems of pleading are: Huey v. Barloga, 277 F. Supp. 864 (N.D. Ill. 1967); People v. Jacoby, 304 N.Y. 33, 105 N.E. 2d 613 (1952).

WRITING ASSIGNMENT 3, ALTERNATIVE C: A Judicial Opinion in the Georgetown Hospital Case

- *Draft a judicial opinion expressing your view of how the Georgetown Hospital case (page 84 supra) should have been decided.*

If you wish, you may write an opinion for any other case that is of interest to you, perhaps Furman v. Georgia, for example (page 137 supra).

WRITING ASSIGNMENT 3, ALTERNATIVE D: The Lawyer's Conversations on Death

Part One

- *Give an account of a death in some language other than legal language. Your account should not take the form of the "statement of facts" in a legal brief or judicial opinion, but should be a living statement of its own. The death should be one which might give rise to a civil cause of action.*

Part Two

- *Imagine you are the lawyer to whom the spouse, child, or parent of the person who died has come. Give an account of the conversations you have:*

  a. with your client

b. with the lawyer on the other side
c. with the judge
d. with the jury

With respect to each conversation, ask yourself what you are trying to achieve. What limits, if any, are there upon your freedom to say what you want? How does the law shape and control these conversations — and how do you do so? Try to find a way to express your sense of the difficulties and opportunities each conversation presents, and how you would meet them.

• *The demand here is upon your imagination, your capacity to figure out ahead of time how things might go. Does the law add to your possibilities here as well as limiting them — is it a valuable resource for speech and thought?*

Here is another possible version: suppose a person comes to you who is dying of cancer, the result (his doctor says) of his working for five years in the uranium mines of Utah in the early 1960s. Give accounts of your conversations with him; with an opposing lawyer in a proceeding brought by you on his behalf; with the judge and jury if it is a civil suit; with the appropriate officials if you bring another sort of proceeding.

This version of the assignment combines the concerns of this section and the next, and if you choose to do this assignment you should read as far as page 195 before starting.

B. THE VOICES OF THE LAWYER, OR: WHAT CAN YOU SAY IN THE LANGUAGE OF THE LAW?

In Writing Assignment 4 you will be asked to pretend that you are a lawyer handling a particular case, the facts of which will be given you. Your assignment will be to describe the conversations you have, or imagine having, about the case with four different people — your client, the lawyer on the other side, the judge, and the jury. Your general question is this: how — in what ways, to what extent — does the legal language system control what you say? What limits are there, in each instance, upon your freedom to say what you want, and how do you address these limits? Do you find that the law in some ways actually enhances your possibilities of expression, that it has value as a rhetorical resource? To respond to such questions you will have to imagine as fully as you can what goes on in such conversations, or what might go on: in the conversation you imagine having with your client, for example, who is he and who are you in relation to him? How do you respond to the story he tells you, what do you ask and say? How does the legal language system shape your relationship and your conversation?

In your accounts of your conversations, do you show yourself in control of legal language, or does it control you? In the first chapter, I described the career of Cressida as turning upon the moment at which she succumbs to an inadequate language. Is this what happens to you? Or do you somehow master the situation — and if so, how do you do so? You may take it that you are invited to look, for the moment, at the lawyer as an artist in a certain sort of conversation. How do you define his art?

I have suggested that the traditional means of control — irony and so forth — are not normally available to you, at least with respect to legal language, but that you have your own peculiar advantage: you are one of the makers of the legal language system and to some extent can control it by making it over again, so that it says what you want it to say. The good lawyer is constantly at work, arguing for changes in the way the law talks about experience, for expansion to include what is left out, for the elimination of false pretenses, or for reshaping the language in other ways. As a lawyer you are always a tentative maker of the language that you use: but exactly how great is your power? What limits are there, in the legal system, in legal language, or in the nature of things, upon your power to make the law say what you want it to? You will see that the law imposes limits on what can be said not only by defining a language — a vocabulary and an intellectual structure — but by defining social roles, by giving to certain voices only certain sorts of speeches. How do you address the limits the law imposes upon you?

PROBLEM: THE SABBATARIAN AND THE MILITARY LAW

Harold Stein spoke with you yesterday on the phone, telling you the facts set forth below; at the end of the conversation you suggested that he come to your office to discuss the matter further. He is due this afternoon.

Stein said that he had just been served with an indictment and a summons, and needed a lawyer. The indictment was for refusing induction into the armed services. The reason he refused is that he is an extremely devout and scrupulous Orthodox Jew, who has always followed the dietary and other laws of his religion with exactitude, and he has been unable to satisfy himself that he could continue to do so in the army. When he was classified 1-A upon graduation from college, he asked the clerk of the local draft board if he would be given food in the army that met his dietary requirements and whether he would be able to observe Saturday as his Sabbath. The clerk said she did not know, so he called the army officer in charge of the local induction center, who said he did not know. Stein then called the army recruiting office in his home town and the office of the General Counsel of the Army in Washington, and was told that the army tried to make kosher food available but could not always do so, and that the commandants of large bases would frequently (but not always) permit those who so desired to be treated on Saturday the same way the rest of the soldiers were treated on Sunday. Stein told both the local recruiter and the lawyer in Washington that this was not satisfactory, and asked whether some special assurance could be made in his case. The answer in both instances was no.

He then requested classification as a conscientious objector, stating on the application that he was opposed to any sort of military service that involved interference with his right to exercise his religion, and that he would not serve unless he were guaranteed that his religious requirements with respect to dietary regulation and the Sabbath would be fully met. When his request was rejected, he followed all available administrative appeals without success. He received an order to report for induction. At the induction center he went through all stages of induction except the last, the "one step forward" into the army. Upon request by the officer in charge of the station, he signed a paper stating that he refused induction into the armed services for conscientious reasons.

Since his phone call you have done extensive research, uncovering the following materials, among others.

SELECTIVE SERVICE ACT OF 1967
50 U.S.C. App. (*1968*) (*as amended*)

§456(j) Nothing contained in this title shall be construed to require any person to be subject to combatant training and service in the armed forces of the United States who, by reason of religious training and belief, is conscientiously opposed to participation in war in any form. As used in this subsection, the term "religious training and belief" does not include essentially political, sociological, or philosophical views, or a merely personal moral code. Any person claiming exemption from combatant training and service because of such conscientious objection whose claim is sustained by the local board shall, if he is inducted into the armed forces under this title, be assigned to noncombatant service as defined by the President, or shall, if he is found to be conscientiously opposed to participation in such noncombatant service, in lieu of such induction, be ordered by his local board, subject to such regulations as the President may prescribe, to perform for a period equal to the period prescribed in section 4 (b) of this Appendix such civilian work contributing to the maintenance of the national health, safety, or interest as the local board pursuant to Presidential regulations may deem appropriate and any such person who knowingly fails or neglects to obey any such order from his local board shall be deemed, for the purposes of section 12 of this title to have knowingly failed or neglected to perform a duty required of him under this title.

§460(b)(3) . . . Such local boards, or separate panels thereof each consisting of three or more members, shall, under rules and regulations prescribed by the President, have the power within the respective jurisdictions of such local boards to hear and determine, subject to the right of appeal to the appeal boards herein authorized, all questions or claims with respect to inclusion for, or exemption or deferment from, training and service under this title, of all individuals within the jurisdiction of such local boards. The decisions of such local board shall be final, except where an appeal is authorized and is taken in accordance with such rules and regulations as the President may prescribe. . . . No judicial review shall be made of the classification or processing of any registrant by local boards, appeal boards, or the President, except as a defense to a criminal prosecution instituted under section 12 of this title, after the registrant has responded either affirmatively or negatively to an order to report for induction, or for civilian work in the case of a registrant determined to be opposed to participation in war in any form: *Provided,* That such review shall go to the question of the jurisdiction herein reserved to local boards, appeal boards, and the President only when there is no basis in fact for the classification assigned to such registrant. . . .

§462(a) Any member of the Selective Service System or any other person charged as herein provided with the duty of carrying out any of the provisions of this title, or the rules or regulations made or directions given thereunder, who shall knowingly fail or neglect to perform such duty, and any person charged with such duty, or having and exercising any authority under said title, rules, regulations, or directions who shall knowingly make, or be a party to the making, of any false, improper, or incorrect registration, classification, physical or mental examination, deferment, induction, enrollment, or muster, and any person who shall knowingly make, or be a party to the making, of any false statement or certificate regarding or bearing upon a classification or in support of any request for a particular classification, for service under the provisions of this title, or rules, regulations, or directions made pursuant thereto, or who otherwise evades or refuses registration or service in the armed forces or any of the requirements of this title, or who knowingly counsels, aids, or abets another to refuse or evade registration or service in the armed forces or any of the requirements of this title, or of said rules, regulations, or directions, or who in any manner shall knowingly fail or neglect or refuse to perform any duty required of him under or in the execution of this title, or rules, regulations, or directions made pursuant to this title or any person or persons who shall knowingly hinder or interfere or attempt to do so in any way, by force or violence or otherwise, with the administration of this title or the rules or regulations made pursuant thereto, or who conspires to commit any one or more of such offenses, shall, upon conviction in any district court of the United States of competent jurisdiction, be punished by imprisonment for not more than five years or a fine of not more than $10,000, or by both such fine and imprisonment, or if subject to military or naval law may be tried by court martial, and, on conviction, shall suffer such punishment as a court martial may direct. . . . Precedence shall be given by courts to the trial of cases arising under this title, and such cases shall be advanced on the docket for immediate hearing, and an appeal from the decision or decree of any United States district court or United States court of appeals shall take precedence over all other cases pending before the court to which the case has been referred.

§462(c) The Department of Justice shall proceed as expeditiously as possible with a prosecution under this section, or with an appeal, upon the request of the Director of Selective Service System or shall advise the House of Representatives and the Senate in writing the reasons for its failure to do so.

Among other things, you have learned that the scope of review in the statute is a codification of earlier cases establishing what has been called the "narrowest scope of review known to the law." See *Witmer v. United States,* 348 U.S. 375 (1955); *Estep v. United States,* 327 U.S. 114 (1946). The question whether there is a "basis in fact" for the classification has been held to be one for the court and not the jury, *Cox v. United States,* 332 U.S. 442 (1947). There is a summary of the statute and some case law in White, "Processing Conscientious Objector Claims: A Constitutional Inquiry," 56 *Calif. L. Rev.* 652 (1968). (Assume for the purposes of this problem that the classification complained of is secure against procedural attack: the local board was properly constituted and its meetings were regular, the defendant was called for service in proper order, the appeals procedure was followed to the letter both by Stein and the SSS, and the like.) Be sure you do whatever additional research is required to enable you to answer the questions in the writing assignment with confidence. This will require considerable time. The best general work is the Selective Service Law Reporter. Your judgment as to when you have done enough will be a measure of your present adequacy as a lawyer.

WRITING ASSIGNMENT 4: The Lawyer's Conversations[3]

Part One

• *Give an account of the conversations you have as Stein's lawyer with each of the following people.*

a. *your client*
b. *the lawyer representing the government*
c. *the jury*
d. *the judge*

Your account in each instance should include some passages of dialog in which you show how you meet the difficulties you face. What are you trying to achieve, and how do you make the attempt? To what extent does the law shape and control these conversations? What limits are there upon your freedom to say what you want?

• *Does the law add to your possibilities here, as well as perhaps limiting them — is it a valuable resource for speech and thought?*

You are free to approach this problem as you wish, but one way might be to ask of each conversation what the issues are. Exactly what questions do you address, and how are they chosen? When you have stated the issues of all the conversations, what is still left out?

Try to imagine as fully as you can how these conversations might actually proceed, and to reflect some sense of that in what you write: who you are, who the other person is, and so on. How does the nature of your language affect these matters of social and personal definition? In each instance you should try to define yourself and your interlocutor as both typical and individual. No one should be a caricature here.

Part Two

• *In your response to Part One, you have defined a set of possibilities for the life of the lawyer. How do you characterize these possibilities? How do you regard them? Do you show the life of the lawyer to be dull and mechanical (like the life of the student perhaps?) or full of life and interest, an activity you can admire?*

• *According to your accounts of these conversations, what arts and qualities of mind is the lawyer called upon to exercise? Can you express the fascination the law holds for you?*

Here are some questions that may help you work this assignment out.

1. What differences can you identify among the various voices with which you show yourself to speak? What similarities? Do you just say the same thing different ways?

3. A supplementary assignment is in the Appendix.

2. What relationship do you establish in each instance with the other party to the conversation? Are you telling, or asking, or begging, or threatening, or something else? To what extent does your tone of voice — the attitude you express towards the other person — depend on his official role as judge or lawyer or client, and to what extent on some assessment you make of him as a person? One would seldom, if ever, adopt an attitude towards a judge that had the slightest touch of bullying (for a number of reasons); but might one try to overbear an opposing lawyer by one's forceful and decisive manner? Or to induce a complaisant attitude by flattery? Can you imagine yourself doing these things? Do you really believe they would work?

3. It may help you see what is involved in this assignment if you pretend that you have objected to the introduction of some testimony in a case you are trying, and see how differently you would answer what appears to be exactly the same question — "Why did you object?" — when it is asked by the judge at trial, or afterwards by the opposing lawyer, by your junior counsel, by your client, or by yourself.

4. In articulating what you "want to say" and the limits that operate upon you, you will face the unresolved ambiguity we uncovered in Section A: if you can use legal language to achieve your goals, to get what you want, why do you care if it does not permit you to say all that you as a person would like to say about a situation? For example, find something that the law as you have recorded it leaves out in what was said about Stein. When you were acting as a lawyer, did you leave it out? Did the others with whom you spoke? Where was it then?

5. Draft a judicial opinion disposing of the Stein case. What are the limits, if any, upon your freedom to say all that you think should be said in the way you wish to say it?

6. Draft a statutory provision dealing with this sort of case. What are the limits, if any, upon your freedom to say all that you think should be said in the way you wish to say it?

7. Suppose all your arguments fail, and Stein is sentenced to jail; what then do you say to him? What do you say about him when you meet the district attorney for lunch to discuss another matter? When you speak to the judge at the bar association cocktail party? Has the legal disposition of Stein made him disappear for you, as a lawyer, the way it would not for a neighbor? The danger is that he has become to you not a person but a legal problem. Compare the passages by Proust and Dr. Norton, pages 170 and 174 supra.

8. Incidental notes:

a. In determining the sentence of such a person as Stein, what weight should be given the deliberate character of the offense? Is his behavior worse because deliberate and unlikely to change, or better because conscientious? How do you imagine argument on this point would go? See United States v. Dancis, 406 F.2d 729 (2d Cir. 1969).

b. In Barnett v. Rodgers, 410 F.2d 995 (D.C. Cir. 1969), it was held that Black Muslim prisoners were entitled to a pork-free meal in prison. Does this help Stein in the army?

c. Does the jury have the power to acquit Stein against the law? If so, is the defense entitled to an instruction to that effect? See United States v. Berrigan, 417 F.2d 1002 (4th Cir. 1969). What happens if the defense attorney advises them of their power and urges them to use it? How would you explain to a judge why you wanted a jury trial? See United States v. Davis, 413 F.2d 148 (4th Cir. 1969).

d. What state of mind is required for violation of the statute? See United States v. Rabbs, 394 F.2d 230 (3d Cir. 1968).

e. Is the statutory provision of an exemption "for those religiously opposed to one aspect of service and not for those religiously opposed to another aspect" an unconstitutional discrimination against one religion in favor of another? See Gillette v. United States, 401 U.S. 437 (1971); United States v. Carson, 282 F. Supp. 261 (E.D. Ark. 1968); United States v. Sisson, 297 F. Supp. 902 (D. Mass. 1969).

f. See Straut v. Calissi, 293 F. Supp. 1339 (D.N.J. 1968), dealing with a statute punishing those who urge people not to go in the army; and McFadden v. Selective Service System, 423 F.2d 1291 (9th Cir. 1970), which deals with the potential liability of draft counselors.

WRITING ASSIGNMENT 4, ALTERNATIVE A: The Voices of the Judge

Part One

- Imagine that you are the judge in the Stein case. Give an account of one or more of the conversations you have with the prosecutor, the defense attorney, the jury, or with Stein.

Part Two

- Draft a judicial opinion disposing of this case.

Part Three

- With respect both to the conversation and to the opinion, ask what you are trying to achieve, and what limits (if any) there are upon your freedom to say what you want. Try to define the difficulties you face here, and tell how you would meet them.

• *Does the law add to your possibilities here, as well as perhaps limiting them? Is it a valuable resource for speech and thought?*

WRITING ASSIGNMENT 4, ALTERNATIVE B: The Lawyer's Conversations on Death

This assignment is given at pages 186–187 supra.

C. ORGANIZING FUTURE EXPERIENCE AS A LAWMAKER — HOW A STATUTE WORKS

Lawyers, I know, cannot make the distinction for which I contend, because they have their strict rule to go by. But legislators ought to do what lawyers cannot; for they have no other rule to bind them, but only the great principles of equity and the sense of mankind.*

When you considered in the last writing assignment what you as a lawyer could say or do to affect the process by which law is brought to bear on life, you doubtless came to recognize all too quickly some special difficulties of your situation: the lawyer must master not one voice but a variety of voices, to be used in an enormous diversity of conversations; yet never does he seem to be free to speak directly and easily in his own way, to say what is actually on his mind. Faced with the unbudging uniqueness of things, he is engaged in a perpetual struggle with what others have said, with what the law has given him to work with; and it is no wonder if you conclude that he is bound by restraints of intolerable rigidity. To ask him whether he is able to say what he wants is to ask him to address a sea of difficulties, and it should not surprise you to be told by a particular lawyer that he chooses not to ask that question of himself.

But in the present section you will be asked to write as a legislator, it is you who will be responsible for the process by which law is applied to life. You are now the imagined maker of the legal language system, and the restrictions imposed by rules of law — under which you labored in the *Stein* case — are all gone: you will choose and articulate the rules that define how experience is to be talked about, the rules that determine the shape of future conversations. You are as free as the wind to say what you want in your own way. What limits, if any, now bear upon you? How can you characterize, how describe or explain, the art by which you address them? In your next writing assignment, you will be

* Edmund Burke, "Letter to the Sheriffs of Bristol" (1777), in *Works* II, 196 (Beaconsfield ed. 1901).

asked to draft a statute that creates a cause of action for wrongful death. When you have finished, compare it with the passages in the anthology in Section A, and ask what sort of literature you have now produced. What can be said and done in such a literature and what cannot? Here the law defines the very meaning of a death, facing it by redressing it. One might think that here if ever the law should speak fully, that here it should come to terms with the experience of ordinary people as it is ordinarily conceived and talked about. Is that what your statute will do? How will you explain or justify what you have done?

As you examine the statutes given below, and start to work out a sense of what can be done in this form and what cannot, try to find or fashion new ways of talking, new forms for the making of law. You should feel that you are an inventor as well as a student. Statutes are normally cast, for example, in the form we call the rule — a direction that must be general without being vague — and our attachment to that form is very deep-seated in all our thinking. (Indeed, many have thought that the secret to legal thought and speech lies in the use of that form.) But nothing compels us to use it. What can you think of that might replace the rule: the extremely general principle coupled with lots of examples? The requirement that the judge bring back cases difficult for you to decide? That he draft supplementary rules and bring them in for your approval? These devices have of course been used. What new ones can you invent? Do not be afraid to be innovative or revolutionary in devising ways for lawmakers to talk, though you may find that there are advantages in using the old forms and even an established vocabulary.

It may help you break down inherited patterns of expectation if you compare the statute with other forms of speech with which you are familiar in ordinary life and with which it has some similarities. For example, one could say that the statute is a kind of order or command (which is, as you know, how some philosophers have viewed it): in what other forms, addressed to what other situations, do you see orders given, and how can you compare what you see there with the statute? Think, for example, of parent speaking to child, sergeant to private, rider to horse, Houston to Apollo, boss to employee, and so on. How are such orders like or unlike statutory commands? Are they ever in the form of rules? In formal language of any kind? Think of a particular order from your own experience: what would it mean to translate it into the form of a statute?

Or one could say that the statute is a way of giving directions, perhaps a somewhat different language game from commanding. Think of different sorts of directions: how to get to the hot dog stand, how to assemble the amplifier, how to drive a car, how to pick a jury, how to take an exam, and so on. Consider some actual directions you have given or received, and ask if they take the same form as the statute. What happens when a set of directions is translated into that form? (What is the difference between giving orders and giving directions?)

Traditionally, at least, the statute takes the form of what we call a rule, and you should compare it with other uses and forms of the rule you have known: school rules, moral rules, safety rules, dietary rules, football rules, dress codes, rules of grammar or manners or religious observance, and so on. What differcnces among these kinds of rules can you observe? Is the statute a special kind of rule, and if so, can you define what sets it apart from other rules? Can you perhaps write a statute that is not a rule but something else?

All these activities are ways of organizing future experience, as the statute is too of course. What other ways of organizing future experience can you think of? Here is one: "Last one in is a rotten egg!" The game is a way of organizing experience that does depend upon rules, and is in that respect like the statute as usually written. Can you even imagine a game without rules? (What are the rules of the statute game?) What different kinds of game rules can you identify? For example, do the rules of all games simply give directions to be followed — or do they sometimes call for creation or invention? (Consider the rules of gymnastics, mumblety-peg, and bridge.) Which do statutory rules do? Ask whether a comparison can be drawn between drafting a statute and making rules for kick-the-can or poker.

There are other ways of arranging matters beforehand, of organizing future experience, as well as these. Think of Harvard University or the Roman Catholic Church or the Elks or G.M. or the Peace Corps or the State of Texas: can you tell us what an institution is? A game set up on a permanent basis?

It would be a good idea to begin to work out your responses to these questions on paper. On the basis of what you do here, how do you characterize the language game of giving orders? Of giving directions? Of speaking in rules? What is a game, and what is an institution? What connections can you draw among these various intellectual and social enterprises? To pursue these questions in detail would be a subject in itself, and you are not expected to do it now. But I hope that it does make sense to you to be asked to imagine the statute as a way of setting things up for the future, as a way of organizing future experience, and to compare it with other similar activities from your own experience. Your next writing assignment will in fact ask you to make such a comparison.

As you think out how these ways of organizing future experience actually work, you will see that they entail enormous social as well as intellectual differences, that implicit in the various activities of speech — language games, if you will — are various social activities as well. The one who organizes experience in language makes a claim for social as well as intellectual creation. For example, to use the general rule rather than a specific command to state an order or a direction is to say a good deal about what the speaker thinks of the person to whom it is addressed: the form defines the degree of trust. What are the social and intellectual relations implied in an agreement to play bridge? In the articles of a law partnership? In the statute as it is usually written? Who speaks this way, talking to whom, and how do you characterize the relationship so expressed? Here your archeological or literary imagination is called upon: what social universe can you reconstruct from this evidence? As a writer of statutes, how can you hope to manage the social and intellectual implications of what you write?

1. *The Statute as a Social Instrument: Establishing the Terms of Cooperation with Your Audience*

It is critical for any writer to know his audience as well as he can, to understand its capacities and interests, because only then can he begin the process of adjusting expectations and changing attitudes, of getting his audience to see things his way. To you as a legislator, your audience is even more important because you can do nothing without it. You only make the rules; it is others who will play the game. Unlike the lawyer, who addresses a single situation that confronts him, as a legislator you address countless future situations, none of which is before you and to which your words will be applied (if at all) by someone else. You will probably articulate standards of a general character, and it is no secret that your language will be more or less ambiguous, susceptible to various readings. You count absolutely upon your reader to resolve ambiguities wisely, to perceive and follow your purposes, to make what you write intelligible as law; and, what is more (unlike more elegant writers who can settle for one good reading out of fifty), you do so every time the use of your statute is considered. You are not trying to express a personal attitude to a handful of like-minded readers, but to provide a working direction that can be followed both consistently and well by a great variety of people with diverse capacities and qualities of mind. How can you control, or at least influence, the way your statute is used? One might say that your statute not only expresses your ideas, your wishes as to what will happen in the world, but that it establishes (at least tentatively) the terms upon which this process of cooperation between writer and audience will proceed. How will you try to recognize — to define and regulate — the powers of those who will apply your statute? What terms of cooperation will you seek to establish with your judges and lawyers, and how will you do so?

The answer to those questions must depend in part upon who your judges and lawyers are, and one purpose of this section is to give you some samples of the judicial mind at work. The study of the art of the statute is a study of the judicial mind as well.

Perhaps it would help you get a sense of what I mean by "managing the terms of cooperation" to draw an analogy to the relationship between cookbook and cook: the greatest cookbook in the world is no guarantee of a good dinner, and doubtless some recipes are so bad that even a fine cook cannot save the meal. The success of the dinner, with which they are both concerned, depends on the existence of some comprehensible process of cooperation between them. A particular cookbook will define its audience with some care — either it explains how to make a court bouillon, or it does not — and one should be able to tell rather quickly whether the book is directed to oneself or to someone else. Success for the cookbook depends very much on the establishment of a consistent and comprehensible relationship between the writer and his audience — each recipe should define the cook similarly with respect to expertise, dependence on detailed instructions, willingness to experiment, and so on. To make a fine cookbook requires excellence in writing as well as cooking. As with the statute, it is not enough to say that the art is one of precision in speech: it is the art of defining and managing an audience, the central art of using language as power. You might examine an actual cookbook directed to your own degree of culinary expertise, and ask of a particular recipe what it is that makes the cooperation comprehensible and workable. What has the writer chosen to tell you? Is it enough? How do you know and how does he?

A more complex analogy would be what happens during the planning and building of a house. Here there may be not one but two sets of instructions; imagine and compare, for example, a letter from an owner to an architect, asking for the preparation of plans for his summer house and explaining his own ideas on the subject, with the instructions from the architect to the builder. Why does the owner himself not tell the builder what he wants? He may have difficulty with builders' shoptalk, but surely the builder can understand ordinary English. What do you suppose an architect does when he receives such a letter as I describe? His task is not merely a matter of understanding and following someone else's ideas; he must do something with what he is given. Is the same true of the builder given a set of architect's plans, or do you suppose those plans answer every question? (Could you build a house from such plans?) How can one compare (a) what the architect, builder, or cook does with the instructions he receives and (b) what the lawyer and judge do with a statute? How might a writer of directions of each kind try to influence or control what his reader will do? To put it slightly differently, on what understandings do these people cooperate, and how are the terms of that cooperation established?

Still another comparison might be drawn: between the statute writer and the playwright. Like the writer of statutes, the playwright is theoretically in complete control, a despotic creator; but actually he is utterly dependent upon the cooperation of actors and director if his imagination is ever to find expression on the stage. How does a playwright attempt to establish and manage the terms of this process of cooperation? What directions does he give to his director and actors, and how does he do it? You might compare a play by G. B. Shaw, full of notes and explanations and directions, with one by Shakespeare, which has none, and ask: which writer exerts more effective control over the way his words are given life on the stage? How does he do so? Is there a lesson here for the writer of statutes?

Like the cookbook writer or architect or playwright, you have an audience to direct in an activity of great complexity and subtlety. How do you propose to do this? You can probably have no more than the roughest idea even of what your choices are, let alone how to make them, until you have thought in considerable detail about the activity you are hoping to control or influence. (Certainly it is no less delicate than cooking.) What we need is a legal analogy for the meal that is the joint product of the cook and cookbook (splendid when things work well, not so good when they do not), a working notion of how a statute operates. We need to understand how a statute is brought to bear on the events of someone's life in the first place (how its directives come to be seen as dispositive of a question or conflict) and how it is actually applied by the judge, or by the lawyer in anticipation of the judge (how it is that a statute actually disposes of something). When we have some notion of what the lawyers and judges do, we can try to figure out a way to tell them how to do it.

a. One Version of How the Statute Is Put to Work: Stating Issues and Defining Terms

Let us look at the evolution of a case: the client walks in the lawyer's door and tells his story; the lawyer begins the process of giving the narrative legal shape by asking questions, by forcing him to fill in omissions or to explicate what to the client seems clear and simple, but to the legal mind is obscure. As work on the case proceeds, the lawyer sees many legal questions, stating them first this way, then that, advancing a possibility only to drop it, constantly wondering if he has overlooked something, and so on. In his mind — and in conversation with his colleagues, with his client, with the opposing lawyer, and with the judge — he works out what seem to him the most important issues, those worth arguing on facts and law; and the case takes shape, ready for trial or settlement. Every case presents innumerable possibilities, and the articulation of certain issues in a brief (or in negotiation or in conversation with the client) is not a claim to have stated all the legal difficulties or to have exhausted all that might be said in legal ways, but is a statement of relative importances, a way of picking out what really counts. The complexities of life are pared down to a relatively small number of issues, and the case becomes manageable, capable of decision under a statute or other rule of law. The process of paring down can be a drastic one; it is not rare for an appeal to present a single substantial issue. Of course the lawyer never knows in advance which issue will prove critical (if the case in fact ever reaches the final stages of appellate decision), and he is constantly working over his material to see that each issue is stated in just the right way.

How does the statute get off the page and come to affect the lives of people? The first stage seems to be the determination by the lawyer that it indeed bears on the case and might possibly be dispositive of it: in a rough and tentative way the issue has been stated. But what does it mean to state a legal issue? One can regard a legal issue as a way of asking a question, a way of calling for the application of a legal rule. It must be stated in legal terms, in terms of the rule it invokes; and its resolution, if it ever is resolved, can be said to turn on the meaning of a term or phrase in the rule: was the instrument "negotiable," was the document "notarized," was there a "search," was there a "basis in fact" for the board's decision, and so on. The critical moment of judicial decision (which it is the lawyer's constant task to anticipate in his imagination and to imitate in cases which he does not push to their limit), the moment when the law gives meaning to life, occurs when the decisive issue has been stated at last and the term in the statute or other rule upon whose definition the case depends has been identified.

The lawyer's ultimate question, asked perhaps of hundreds of terms in a complex case, could then be said to take this form: "How shall this term be defined in this case?" According to this paradigm, the final judicial act is a definition of terms, a statement of meaning. The critical term is given meaning with respect to the particular facts of the case; "offer" is defined to include the letter of February 17, or not to include the statement of intention the defendants made here.

What I propose, then, as a legal analogy to the dinner with which the kitchen artists are concerned, or to the architect's building, is an account of the judicial process that divides it into two operations — stating the issue and defining terms — and when both are done, the job of decision is complete. Each of the two operations is complex, of course, and I do not mean to have made the judicial process seem simple; my hope rather is that this account of the process by which a statute is brought to bear on life, this version of the basic structure of the judicial process, may enable us to ask some useful and perplexing questions.

The sorts of questions I have in mind are these: how are these processes of stating the issue and defining the terms carried out in fact? How ought they be? What can you as statute maker have to do with them as they affect what you have written? For example, how can you possibly influence the process by which the issues are chosen, stated, and pared away? It is necessarily others who will decide when your words will be critical to someone's life and when not. How, if at all, can you affect their processes of judgment? But once the decision to bring your statute into play has been made, your powers increase: it is your statute that gives the ultimately decisive term its significance — it is important only because it is part of what you have written — and you should have something to say about how it is defined. How can you hope to do so? The following material is meant to provide the occasion for exploring further the relationship between the writer of a statute and his audience. Your questions are these: how can you describe and explain the phenomenon we call the use of a statute? How can you as a statute writer control this phenomenon? What happens when you do not control it: does chaos result — or does someone else control it, and if so, how does he do so?

The readings that follow are mainly about death, and can be regarded as a continuation of the anthology in Section A. How do you regard these legal versions of experience, these conversions of life into the material of the law? How might you compare them with other possibilities? What future do they define for you?

TOVEY v. GEISER
150 Kan. 149, 92 P.2d 3 (1939)

DAWSON, C. J. Leon Arthur Preston and Faye Vandaveer Preston, husband and wife, died of asphyxiation in their home in Osawatomie on December 6 or 7, 1936. They left no children or other descendants. Mrs. Preston died intestate. Mr. Preston left a will executed before his marriage. By its terms he devised all his property to the appellant Margaret Helen Tovey.

That his subsequent marriage to Mrs. Preston had the legal effect of reducing by one-half the extent of Mrs. Tovey's interest in Mr. Preston's estate, if Mrs. Preston survived her husband, is not controverted. . . .

Plaintiff claimed that Preston survived his wife. The defendants as heirs of Mrs. Preston claimed that she outlived her husband.

This issue was properly joined by pleadings, and the cause was tried before a jury which returned the following verdict: "We, the Jury empaneled and sworn in the above entitled case, do, upon our oaths, find that Leon Arthur Preston, the husband, died *before* the time of the death of Faye Vandaveer Preston, the wife."

At the same time the jury returned an answer to a special question thus: "[Question]: If you find that Leon Arthur Preston died *before* Faye Vandaveer Preston died, you will please state your reasons or grounds for so finding. Answer: Health, age, sex, and accustomed to gas."

Judgment was accordingly entered—decreeing that plaintiff Margaret Helen Tovey took an undivided one-half of Leon Arthur Preston's property by virtue of his will, and that as Faye Vandaveer Preston, his wife, survived him she took the other undivided one-half as his statutory heir; and that upon her death the same passed with all the rest of her individual property to her heirs, defendants herein.

Plaintiff appeals, not contending against the trial court's finding and judgment that she had failed to establish her own cause of action, but contending that there was not sufficient competent evidence to establish defendants' cross action — that Mrs. Preston had survived her husband.

. . . Mr. and Mrs. Preston lived in a five-room, one-story house. It had no basement but was heated by gas piped to two floor furnaces under the house. There was a vent pipe connected with the furnaces intended to carry off noxious gases. Three rooms, a kitchen, dining room, and parlor, were in line from north to south, and on the west were two bedrooms with a bath room between them. In the dining room which also served as a sitting room, and which was situated between the kitchen on the north and the parlor on the south, stood a sofa or davenport against its west wall. There was virtually no partition between the middle room and the parlor. In the floor near the west sides of these two rooms, and about the division line between them, was a floor register with a burner below which heated both rooms. In the parlor to the south of this floor register, was an overstuffed chair. The south end of the davenport standing against the west wall of the dining room was at some slightly greater distance from the floor register than the overstuffed chair in the parlor. Doors connected the two bedrooms with the dining room and parlor. There was an outside door on the north in the kitchen and an outside door on the south side of the parlor. There were windows on the east sides of the dining room and the parlor.

On December 6, 1936, the weather was very cold and a strong wind was blowing from the north. Mr. and Mrs. Preston had planned to go to Neodesha to visit Mrs. Preston's sister in the evening of that day. They did not come, and telephone calls failed to reach them that evening or the next morning. This prompted Mrs. Preston's sister in Neodesha to call the city officials of Osawatomie. The chief of police accompanied by a Mr. Samuels went to the Preston home. All the doors were locked. They broke a glass panel in the enclosed porch on the north, unbolted a door and entered. The whole house was suffocatingly hot. Fires were burning in all four of the burners of the kitchen range, both floor register burners were lit and so too was a burner in the bath room.

Passing from the kitchen to the dining room, the chief of police and Mr. Samuels saw Mrs. Preston sitting almost erect on the davenport at its south end near the floor register between the two rooms. She was dead but her body was still slightly warm. Next they noticed Mr. Preston lying on the floor on his left side. His face was about four or five inches from the south edge of the floor register, and the top of his head about twelve inches east of its west edge. He, too, was dead, and his body felt cooler than that of Mrs. Preston.

On further investigation the chief of police and the county coroner found that there were no regulators for the floor furnaces, but there was a vent pipe which extended under the floor and passed through the east foundation wall and which was designed to furnish an outlet for any noxious fumes generated by the gas burners. It was discovered that this vent pipe was choked and frozen with ice and snow — a fact which quite clearly revealed the cause of the fatal tragedy which befell the occupants of the house. . . .

A fact of some probative value was that a very hard wind was blowing from the north on December 6 and 7, 1936. Whatever draft penetrated the house would tend to deflect the noxious gases and fumes in the house toward the south, past where Mrs. Preston sat, and towards her husband who was south of the floor register from which some of the poisonous fumes must have issued.

There was circumstantial evidence which tended to show that her husband had been sitting in the overstuffed chair near to the floor register but south of it. Apparently he had vomited before he slipped or fell from this chair because there was vomit on the chair and on the sleeve of his shirt.

An expert witness whose qualifications were well established was asked to assume as true the locus in quo, the positions and relative proximity of the husband and wife to the floor register, the stiff north wind, the doors, windows and other pertinent matters shown in evidence, and then questioned:

[Question]: With that situation, if gas was coming out of this furnace grate, would there be any deflection of the gas in that room from one direction to another? A. There would be some deflection, in the direction the wind is blowing.

Q. From the direction the wind is blowing to the opposite direction? A. Yes sir.

Q. What would you say as to whether or not the presence of that draft would affect the probable concentration of the monoxide gas in that room in relation to the two subjects that were there breathing it. A. The one on the side . . . from which the drafts were coming from, would have the advantage.

Q. The one on the north would have the advantage? A. If the drafts were coming from the north, the one sitting on the north would have the advantage.

One feature of the evidence which tended to show whether the husband or wife died first was the comparative condition of their health. Mr. Preston was 47 years of age and had followed the occupation of a railway freight train conductor and brakeman but had been retired from active service on account of ill-health. For several years he had been forced to go back and forth to the railway hospital at St. Louis for occasional treatment and examination. He took medicine three times a day and breathed heavily whenever he walked or took any exercise. He had suffered one paralytic stroke on the right side of his body, one of his feet dragged, and he required a lot of rest. His entire physical, nervous and circulatory system had been weakened by syphilis, of which disease he was in the tertiary stage. His red blood count was below normal, hemoglobin 82%. Medical and scientific experts testified that a man in such condition would lack normal resistance to monoxide poisoning. One pathologist of many years' experience testified: "A man may have syphilis and have a damaged heart and when under those circumstances he contacted carbon monoxide, that his blood will pick up carbon monoxide just as quickly as anybody else's. But what I am trying to say to the court is this, that when it comes to the response of weakened organs, under those circumstances, that you can certainly expect a man with weakened organs to succumb quicker than a perfectly normal individual. And, furthermore, I would like to emphasize again my answer, that a person who has had syphilis for a number of years is not a normal individual." . . .

Contrasting Mrs. Preston's condition of health with that of her husband, she was 43 years of age and weighed between 150 and 160 lbs. The evidence tended to show that she was a robust, healthy woman, never known to be sick, active and quick in her movements, did her own housework and ready to help with the work when she visited with her mother, ready to go "anywhere on a picnic or swim, she was a great hand to swim."

There was some testimony that however well-regulated gas burners for domestic use may be there is some escape of carbon monoxide gas, but that a housewife and cook develops a certain resistance to its evil effects. . . .

There was also some testimony that a woman's chest capacity being less than a man's (which was the fact in this case), she would breathe into her lungs a less quantity of monoxide gas at each respiration and its deadly effect would thereby be delayed. To a hypothetical question formulated to include the questioner's summary of the evidential facts and circumstances, one expert, Dr. B. L. Phillips, testified:

> I think he [Mr. Preston] would die quicker under the exposure to the carbon monoxide poisoning — other conditions being fairly equal.
>
> Q. Would you say whether or not a man in that condition — in the condition I have assumed would be more or would be less susceptible to monoxide poisoning than an ordinarily healthy, robust individual.
>
> A. He would be more susceptible. . . .

It would serve no useful purpose to glean more minutely from the record other incidents of fact or opinion of some probative force. What we have summarized above, did, in our opinion, constitute sufficient evidence to take the case to the jury.

QUESTIONS

1. *Precisely what in the court's view is the decisive issue in this case? How does the court explain or justify its statement of the issue?*
2. *Upon the definition of what term or terms does the resolution of that issue depend?*
3. *How does this court go about the task of defining the critical term or terms: by what intellectual process, with reference to what premises, guides, or directions? How does it explain or justify the definition it reaches?*
4. *Notice that the court does not quote any statutory or other legally operative language, but merely says that it is "not controverted" that the disposition of the property depends upon "whether Mrs. Preston survived her husband." If you had represented Mrs. Tovey, would you have controverted that proposition? Exactly what would you have said to the court?*
   a. *How would you have proposed that the issue in this case be stated?*
   b. *What evidence would you have offered to support your view of how that issue should be resolved?*
5. *Could you draft a statute for this case that would increase the chances of a proper statement of the issue and of a proper definition of the critical term?*

YOUNG WOMEN'S CHRISTIAN HOME v. FRENCH
187 U.S. 401 (1902)

The will of Sophia Rhodes was executed at Washington, May 10, 1894, and read as follows:

"In the name of the bountiful Giver of all. Amen.

"I, Sophia Rhodes, of the city of Hutchinson, in the State of Kansas, temporarily residing at Washington, in the District of Columbia, being now of sound and disposing mind and memory, do make, publish and declare this my last will and testament, hereby revoking all former wills or testamentary dispositions of my property.

"I now dispose of the property and estate which it has pleased Almighty God to intrust to me, as follows, viz.:

"*Imprimis.* I will that all my just debts and funeral expenses shall be paid by my executor hereinafter named, out of the first money from my estate that shall come into his hands.

"*Item* 1. I give, devise and bequeath unto my husband Oliver Wheeler Rhodes, during his life one half (½) of the income from all my properties and estate in the next following item of this last will and testament disposed of, to be paid over to him from time to time by my executor hereinafter named, who, for this purpose, shall also act as trustee.

"*Item* 2. I now give, devise and bequeath unto my only and beloved son, Eugene Rhodes, all my property, real, personal and mixed, of whatsoever nature, kind or description, including moneys, credits and evidences of indebtedness of which I may be possessed at the time of my death, to be his absolutely, to hold and to dispose of as unto him may seem good and proper, and subject only to the provisions of item 1 of this last will and testament.

"*Item* 3. In the event of the death of my son, Eugene Rhodes, before the decease either of myself or of my husband, I then give, devise and bequeath all my property, everything I own on earth, as follows, viz.:

"1st. I give, devise and bequeath all my pictures and paintings to the Young Women's Christian Home, in the city of Washington, District of Columbia. It is my will that the said pictures and paintings may, so long as the said home shall exist, be the ornaments of the said home, with my name [as] the giver connected with them during that time.

"2d. All the rest and residue of my property, real, personal and mixed, I give, devise and bequeath to Michael H. Fitch, of Pueblo, Colorado, to have and to hold, in trust nevertheless, to invest the same to the best of his knowledge and experience, and to pay over the rents and profits arising therefrom to my husband, Oliver Wheeler Rhodes, during his, my said husband's life; and on the death of my said husband to turn over the said property, moneys, etc., with whatsoever accumulation thereon may be existing, to the Young Women's Christian Home, of Washington, in the District of Columbia, to be the property of the said home absolutely.

"*Item* 4. In the event of my becoming the survivor of both my husband, Oliver Wheeler Rhodes, and of my son, Eugene Rhodes, I then give, devise and bequeath all my property, real, personal and mixed, of whatsoever nature, kind or description, to the Young Women's Christian Home, of the city of Washington, in the District of Columbia, to have and to hold the same absolutely and forever, for the good of that institution. It is my will that my pictures and paintings shall be disposed of in this event as provided in paragraph 1st, of item 3, of this last will and testament.

"*Lastly.* I hereby constitute and appoint my only son, Eugene Rhodes, the sole executor and trustee of this my last will and testament; and it is my will that my said sole executor and trustee shall administer and execute this last will and testament without giving bond therefor."

The facts were stipulated, and may be shortly stated thus: Oliver Wheeler Rhodes died at Washington, January 27, 1895, at which time his wife, Sophia Rhodes, and their only child, Eugene Rhodes, were in Heidelberg, Germany. They sailed for home from Bremen on the steamship Elbe at three o'clock P.M. on Tuesday, January 29, 1895. About half-past five o'clock the next morning the Elbe collided with another steamship, and sank in about twenty minutes after the collision. Mrs. Rhodes was about fifty-two years old, corpulent, and short of breath, and her son was about twenty-three years old, a single man, and rather a good swimmer. His body came up in a fishing net off the coast of Holland some six weeks after the collision, but his mother's body was never recovered. Of the persons who survived the shipwreck, only two had any knowledge of the mother and son at the time of the disaster. One of them saw Mrs. Rhodes come out of her cabin just after the collision with a blanket over her night dress, and some minutes later saw her son. The other saw the mother and son on deck after the collision, the son endeavoring to put a shawl around his mother, and she with her arms thrown around her son's neck. This person was the last to get into the last boat to leave the ship, and, when it had gotten some distance away, the ship went down with a lurch and every one on board was drowned. He testified that "both of these parties died together, and, so far as this affiant was able to learn, after he saw these parties on the deck clasped in an embrace that would never be loosened until after death, no one else saw them."

QUESTIONS

1. *The next of kin of Mrs. Rhodes, the administrator of Eugene Rhodes, and the Young Women's Christian Home each claim the property of Mrs. Rhodes. If you were the judge deciding this case, how would you state the central issue presented by these facts? Upon the definition of what terms, in what statute or other document, would the resolution*

of that issue depend? If the question is not "who died first," what is it, and why do you say so?

2. *Could the court in Tovey have stated the issue in a similar way? Should it have done so?*
3. *How would you as judge in French go about defining the term or terms you find to be critical?*
4. *The French Court in fact said that nothing should follow from the testator's choosing to say, "If I survive my family, my property goes to the Home," instead of, "If my family fails to survive me, my property goes to the Home." Obviously, however, there is a plain difference, and it is at issue in this case: where death is simultaneous, neither survives. That is a matter of common sense and plain English. Do you agree with the Court's view then? How do you explain your position?*
5. *"Who died first – A or B?" Is that question, without more, intelligible? Not if the answer would vary depending upon the purpose for which it was asked, one might say. Is it the task of the judicial opinion to make the question intelligible in this sense, by articulating such purposes? Or is that the task of the statute?*
6. *You have been asked if you could have reached correct decisions in these cases, acting as judge. Could you as a legislator have written statutes that would have guaranteed such decisions, or at least have made them more likely?*
   a. *Could you solve the difficulties of these cases by the simple expedient of careful definition of the terms of the statute? Try drafting a statute that would ensure the correct decision of these cases. Is the critical problem the definition of "death"? Of "survival"? Of what, then?*
   b. *If you cannot control the process by which your words are applied to particular facts by defining terms yourself, can you write clear directions to your lawyers and judges, telling them how to engage in the process of definition? Draft a passage of such directions.*
   c. *Or should you just make plain the purposes for which your statute proposes that the critical questions should be asked?*
   d. *Which kind of correction – statutory definition, statutory direction, or declaration of statutory purpose – would more nearly ensure the proper statement of the issue in these cases?*
7. There is of course a body of learning directed to the interpretation of statutes, and you are familiar with some of it. Take the Canons of Construction, for example: eiusdem generis, expressio unius, in derogation of the common law, and so on. Of what assistance is all this to you? Consider Llewellyn, "Remarks on the Theory of Appellate Decision and the Rules or Canons About How Statutes Are To Be Construed," 3 Vand. L. Rev. 395 (1950); H. Hart and A. Sacks, The Legal Process 1221 (1958). In the Interpretation of Statutes (Law Commn. No. 21, June 9, 1969), the proposal is considered that Parliament should enact comprehensive and general directions to the reading of statutes: is that perhaps the best solution of all?
8. How are you taught as a will draftsman to define "simultaneous death" or "survival"?
9. Consider the solution to the problem provided by the Uniform Simultaneous Death Act (as amended 1953):

   "§1. Where the title to property or the devolution thereof depends upon priority of death and there is no sufficient evidence that the persons *have died otherwise than simultaneously, the property of each person shall be disposed of as if he had survived, except as provided otherwise in this act.*

"§6. This act shall not apply in the case of wills, living trusts, deeds, or contracts of insurance, or any other situation where provision is made for distribution of property different from the provisions of this act, or where provision is made for a presumption as to survivorship which results in a distribution of property different from that here provided."

Exactly how would this statute have affected the result in Tovey? In French? How do you know?

10. *Is the most sensible solution for the problem of simultaneous death a presumption that the younger survived? See In re Lindop, [1942] Ch. 377.*
11. *What presumption as to survival should be applied in a case where a couple is killed in a common accident, the man having no heirs or relatives, the woman having none except a child by a prior marriage? Assume that there are no wills and no adoption of the child by the stepfather. Is the answer the same if the child is that of the man by a prior marriage? Suppose in each case that the nonparent spouse has a brother: does that affect the decision as to what presumption is proper? What if, in addition, there is evidence that the nonparent spouse hated the child?*
    a. *Should the law simply not ask the question, "Who survived?" What should it do?*
    b. *Why is it not the most sensible suggestion for the judge to look at all the circumstances and to determine from them, and from the will if there is one, where the deceased owners of property would want their property to go? Draft a statute implementing that suggestion.*

b. Three Problems on Defining Terms and Stating Issues

These optional problems could be used as supplementary writing assignments or as the basis for class discussion.

PROBLEM: STATING THE ISSUE

You have received the following memorandum from a senior partner in your firm.

A young man named Tom Wilson came to the office today with the following problem which I would like you to handle.

His father and stepmother were killed in an automobile accident a few weeks ago. His father left very little, but there are apparently substantial assets on the stepmother's side. However, when he called her lawyer he was told that her will left him nothing at all. In fact, he was told, all her property had been left to the Red Cross and a distant cousin in equal shares.

This struck me as slightly odd, and Wilson candidly told me the following story. He is the son of his father, Thomas Wilson, Sr. and one Roberta Jones. His parents were not married at the time of his birth, because his mother's divorce decree from her first husband was not yet final. She died a month after his birth without ever marrying his father. This was twenty years ago, in the state of Clark. He lived with his father in Clark his entire childhood, and was treated as his son in every way. About three years ago, Wilson, Sr. and Selma Vann married and moved here to the state of King, where Tom finished high school and where he is now at the university.

Relations between the parents had deteriorated badly before the accident, and in fact Wilson, Sr. had filed a petition for divorce from Selma, alleging, among other grounds, adultery. I have seen Selma's will, a copy of which is attached. It seems valid in all respects, if the disinheriting of Wilson, Sr. and of Tom are valid. It makes no reference to them; the dispositive provision merely leaves "all my property in equal shares to the Red Cross Society and to my cousin Herbert Vann." Tom's relations with Selma had never been comfortable, and he frankly admits that he resented and disliked her, and is not surprised at her treatment of him. His father left no will and very little property. I asked him if the two people died at the same time, and he said he had been told by the doctor that Selma died at 2:30 in the afternoon, in the hospital, and Wilson, Sr. about half an hour later.

I have called Selma's lawyer, Martin, and he says that he thinks Tom has no claim against her estate. He said he drafted the will that way because Selma wrote him a letter instructing him to draft a will "that will leave my so-called husband and my so-called son without a nickel."

King has the following statutes, as well as all statutes of your own state not inconsistent therewith:

Section 101: The Uniform Simultaneous Death Act.

Section 150: A surviving spouse shall be entitled to one-half of the estate of a decendent spouse, if he so elects, notwithstanding the existence of any will.

Section 151: When a testator omits to provide in his will for any of his children, or for the issue of any deceased child, whether born or adopted before or after the execution of the will, unless it appears from the will that such omission was intentional, such child or issue succeeds to the same share of the testator as if he had died intestate.

Section 152: When a decendent dies intestate, his estate shall be distributed as follows: if he has no children, and no issue of any deceased child, the whole shall go to his spouse; if he has children, or issue of any deceased child, the spouse if he or she survive shall take half, and the children shall, as a class, take the remainder of the estate in equal shares per stirpes.

Section 200: Every illegitimate child is the heir of his mother and also of that person who in writing, and in the presence of competent witnesses, acknowledges himself to be the father.

Section 205: The father of an illegitimate child, by publicly acknowledging it as his own, receiving it as such, with the consent of his wife, if he is married, into his family, and otherwise treating it as if it were a legitimate child, thereby adopts it as such; and such child is thereupon deemed to be legitimate, for all purposes.

You do the necessary legal and factual research. You cannot find that Wilson, Sr. ever made the sort of formal, written acknowledgement outlined in §200. You discover the following statute of Clark: "§1-202: An illegitimate child shall become legitimate upon the marriage of his parents or upon a judicial decree authorizing his adoption by any person." The other relevant Clark law is a recent case holding that an illegitimate child does not inherit from his father, although he does from his mother. Martin files the will for probate; you appear on Tom's behalf to contest it, making whatever allegations seem to you appropriate. Martin files a motion to dismiss on the basis of the agreed statement of facts including all of the above.

The motion is to be argued this afternoon. You are both before the judge. He calls you to the bench and says to you, "I have looked at the papers here, but I have not had time to read the briefs. What does this case involve?"

Draft the beginning of your response, no more than one page in length. Then assume that you are cut off at that point by the judge, who says, "I get the general idea, but before I hear argument on specific issues, let me ask Martin the same question. What does this case involve?" Draft the beginning of his response, of similar length.

In what language or languages do you state what this case involves? What are the key terms you use, and how do you propose that they be defined by the court? In stating what the case "involves," do you state the "issue" or something else? State what you would consider to be the decisive issue in this case. What have you done when you have done so? Compare *Estate of Lund,* 26 Cal. 2d 472, 159 P.2d 643 (1945).

PROBLEM: ORGAN TRANSPLANT STATUTE

Draft a statute authorizing the removal of vital organs from dead people for the purpose of transplantation. Define "death" or "dead" for the purposes of this statute.

QUESTIONS

1. *You might want to argue that under your statute a person should be considered "dead" when he was dying, even though he was breathing and his heart was still beating. How can you define "dying" in such a statute? We are all dying, aren't we?*

Might you ever want to speak of a person as "alive," even though his heart and respiration had stopped?

2. *A committee of doctors has proposed that death for these purposes be defined by irreversible coma rather than by the traditional cessation of heartbeat. "A Definition of Irreversible Coma," 205 J.A.M.A. 337 (1968).*
3. *How should death be defined in the following case?*

   Mr. F. was gravely injured on Saturday morning in a waterfront accident and was taken directly to the hospital where he arrived at 10:47, unconscious and in critical condition. Directly upon learning of this his wife consulted a lawyer, who immediately prepared a complaint in the name of Mr. F., seeking damages for his injuries. The lawyer telephoned a deputy clerk of court and told him that an emergency had arisen and that immediate filing of a lawsuit was necessary. The clerk agreed to open the courthouse to receive the complaint. The attorney's messenger got to the courthouse at 12:15, where he waited until about 12:50 when the clerk got there and received the complaint, marking it "filed 1:00 P.M."

   Mr. F. had died at 12:20 P.M.

   Now, more than two years later, Mrs. F. seeks substitution of her name as plaintiff. The court says that this is permissible only if the suit was "commenced" within the meaning of Rule 3, during Mr. F.'s "lifetime." Rule 3 of the Federal Rules of Civil Procedure reads: "A civil action is commenced by filing a complaint with the court." What result? See Freeman v. Andrea, 36 U.S.L.W. 2630 (E.D. Pa. 1968).

   a. *Does the proper statement of the issue in this case turn on the definition of "lifetime"? Of "filing"? Are those two questions identical?*
   b. *Suppose the clerk had refused to open the courthouse on Saturday. Is it conceivable that a complaint filed Monday morning could be "filed" within the plaintiff's "lifetime"?*
   c. *Federal Rule of Civil Procedure 77 says that the court shall be "deemed" to be "always open" for the purpose of filing papers. What can that possibly mean?*
   d. *How would you decide this case and why?*

PROBLEM: DRAFTING AN ABORTION STATUTE

Draft model abortion and homicide statutes which you would recommend to your own state legislature. Do you use the terms "life," "death," "person," and "abortion"? If so, how do you define them?

It may help to consider the following problem.

Assume an abortion statute provides that a hospital board may "authorize the termination of a pregnancy at any time if it determines that continuation of the pregnancy would endanger the life of the mother" and of a pregnancy of less than fifteen weeks "if the mother is under sixteen years of age or the pregnancy is the result of forcible rape"; and that it is a felony punishable by a maximum of ten years in prison "to induce abortion" without the approval of a hospital board. The homicide statutes punish acts that willfully or negligently "cause the death of any person." A doctor is charged both with homicide and with committing an illegal abortion under the following circumstances: a woman patient had taken a drug which was known to produce a very high incidence of deformities in children when taken by pregnant women, and she was in an acute nervous state. The doctor feared that she would commit suicide either before or after the birth. He presented the case to his community hospital board, which refused to authorize the abortion. Twenty-two weeks after conception he injected a highly saline solution into the amniotic fluid surrounding the fetus, whose heart stopped within an hour. The woman went into labor and expelled the dead fetus.

1. What are the legal issues in this case?
2. Is one issue whether there was a death of a person? How should the law define "death" here? Or is the critical issue the definition of "person"?
3. If it is said that there was a "death" in this case, why should there not be a "death" and consequent homicide liability where a woman:
   a. uses a spermicidal douche that on contact brings to a halt all organic activity in the sperm cells;
   b. uses an intrauterine device that inhibits the attachment of a fertilized ovum to the uterine wall, thus preventing its development;
   c. uses a diaphragm that prevents fertilization of the ovum?
4. If there was no "death" here, how could there be a death if the baby were killed after a live birth — say, when it was found to be deformed?
5. If there is an "inducement of abortion" and criminal liability here, why are there not similar "inducements of abortion" in the situations described in questions 3 and 4?

In *People v. Belous,* 80 Cal. Rptr. 354, 458 P.2d 194 (1969); *United States v. Vuitch,* 305 F. Supp. 1032 (D.D.C. 1969); and *Babitz v. McCann,* 306 F. Supp. 400 (1969), 310 F. Supp. 293 (E.D. Wis. 1970), various criminal abortion statutes were held unconstitutionally vague. *Vuitch* was overruled by the Supreme Court, 402 U.S. 62 (1971). *People v. Barksdale,* 18 Cal. App. 3d 813, 96 Cal. Rptr. 265 (1971), held that a woman has a constitutional right to have an abortion up to the twentieth week of fetal existence.

QUESTIONS

1. If you conclude that the doctor in the problem given should not be held guilty of criminal homicide, how do you explain your decision? By saying a fetus is not a person? How would you decide a homicide case where the defendant kicked and beat a woman in a deliberate and successful attempt to kill her unborn child? See People v. Keeler, 2 Cal. 3d 619, 470 P.2d

617 (1970). And would you feel bound by your decision that a fetus is not a person if the question were recovery of damages for wrongful death under a statute creating a cause of action for the death of any "person"? See Estate of Powers v. City of Troy, 380 Mich. 160, 156 N.W. 2d 530 (1968).

2. *Is it important that such words as "life," "death," and "person" have the same meaning each time they are used in a particular statute? Each time they are used in the law?*
3. *If you conclude that definitions of such key terms can vary, especially in a single statute, do you not destroy the logical and theoretical consistency of the law, and at the same time its rationality and fairness?*
4. *If one principle emerges from this material, it is that words should be defined to serve the purposes of the general rule or other statement of which they are a part. Draft a clear statement of the purposes of your statute, by reference to which its terms can be defined.*
5. *In Roe v. Wade, 409 U.S. 817 (1973), and Doe v. Bolton, 409 U.S. 817, 909 (1973), the Supreme Court held certain abortion statutes unconstitutional. Examine those cases and ask of them these questions: what impact would these decisions have on the resolution of the problem given above? After these decisions, what statute (if any) regulating abortion would be constitutional? How do you evaluate the Court's attempt to resolve the difficulties of defining terms and articulating purposes, with which you have just been struggling?*

c. *The Process of Cooperation Between Writer and Reader: The Statute as a Way of Giving Structure to Conversations*

I have suggested that the process of stating issues and defining terms by which the statute operates is an inherently cooperative activity, and that accordingly an important part of the statute writer's art is the management of the relationship between him and his audience. But how is this to be achieved? Or to put it slightly differently — for our critical language is still largely unrefined — how is it to be spoken of? We need to find a new and effective way of talking about the statutory process that will expose the difficulties of the situation and the art by which they are addressed. While this question is directed ultimately to you — and you will have an opportunity to respond in your next writing assignment — I can perhaps suggest a way of looking at it, a sort of analogy, that may be of some assistance.

The suggestion is that we conceive of the statute as a way of setting up conversations among its users, as a way of giving structure to an activity of statement, question, response, and argument among the people of the law. That is, for conversation to go on at all, the discussion must have some form; the various propositions for and against must be seen to have some connection, and the statute can be regarded as a way of providing such a form. It is a way of organizing future experience by setting up discussions, by giving structure to conversations that occur within its ambit. To look at it this way — rather than, say, as an order that is obeyed or a principle that is applied — is to express an awareness of its extraordinary intellectual and social complexity, a recognition that it operates only by the cooperation of other minds, and that this cooperation is in no sense automatic, but a process of questioning and doubting. This is, perhaps, not how the statute is usually viewed, and it may help you to regard it in this way if you ask what other ways there are of giving form to conversation. Consider a particular conversation from your own experience — about religion, politics, medicine, or mathematics, for example — and ask what gave it shape, if anything did.

Often, of course, conversations simply fail, never really take any shape at all; this possibility is a special danger for the law, where the litigants and their lawyers are likely to be emotionally given to one version of events and unable to imagine others. One purpose of the statute is to provide a beginning with which speakers can work, a common proposition by which their disagreement can be defined, a first principle of organization. The hope is that legal argument will have a form and an intelligibility that is missing in political arguments, faculty debates, and other common forms of senseless disputation. But how does the statute achieve this? How can the writer ensure that his statute is brought into play only where it should be? How can he use it to shape the conversations upon which it is brought to bear?

There may, in addition, be argument on the question whether a proposition is in fact held in common, whether — in legal conversations — a statute or other rule does apply. How do arguments of this sort proceed in ordinary conversation and in the law? What can the writer of a statute do to influence their course?

The following questions may help you work these matters out.

QUESTIONS

1. *To give shape to a conversation, one must have a good idea who the participants are. How should the statute writer define his audience, what should he assume these people know and can do? Look at particular statutes given in the next set of readings, and at your own when you have drafted it, and ask how the audience is defined. Most obviously, perhaps, one does not reenact with every statute all the rules of procedure and evidence. Why not, and what other similarly crucial matters does one not enact? What must a person know or be able to do to understand your statute, to build a conversation out of it? Ask this question of the usual wrongful death statute, which takes this form: it establishes a "cause of action" in certain people for a death which has been "caused" by the "wrongful act or default" of the defendant. How does the use of these terms define the audience?*

   The statute is a general statement often as weak and useless as a cliché.

Does one count upon one's audience to save it, to make it one of those great sentences praised by Thoreau – like a Roman aqueduct – and if so, how and why? (See pages 79–80 supra.)

2. As you have seen, the special relationship between the legislator and his audience permits a great deal to be left unsaid. Somehow, it is assumed, the judge and lawyer will know how to read and talk about a statute which would make little sense to the layman. This is a consequence of a common professional education, and it entails an understanding of forms and purposes – of what a statute is and what the law attempts to do – and knowledge of professional and technical terms. I want now to ask about the latter: what is a technical language, anyway? And does it always serve to make speech more efficient, or does it have dangers of its own? How does one build conversations out of such a language? You might read again the passage from Maitland, page 6 supra, and the questions that follow it.
   a. When you look back upon the definition of terms such as "death" or "person" in the cases you have read, you see the making of what could be called a technical vocabulary, in which words are given special meanings for special purposes. We might say, for example, that the dying man is "dead," or that a paper is "filed" when the messenger shows up at the empty courthouse. This phenomenon, depending upon its degree, could be called the creation of a technical vocabulary, the use of legal fictions, or the fabrication of false pretenses, and it affects in important ways the conversations in which it appears. Your friend at the party will perhaps be even more frustrated by the lawyer's special uses of words he has heard before (for example, "negligence" or "equity") than he is by the – to him – meaningless jargon of "reversions" or the "Statute of Frauds." The law feels free to rearrange language even to the point of having a word mean its opposite, an event usually signaled by the use of our special term "constructive": when we say a person had "constructive notice," we mean that he had no notice but we will pretend that he did. To what extent is this practice of special definition desirable, and under what circumstances? How can it be controlled or limited or perhaps avoided? How is one to state an issue in such terms? What sort of conversation can be built out of a language like this?
   b. Another way to put the question might be this: are there any necessary connections between legal talk and plain English? Is the law free to define, say, "marriage," "income," "insanity," or "malice aforethought" in its own way without regard to the use of the term in plain English? How about "death" or "birth"? How about a word such as "remainder" or "reversion"? One view is that the law is a technical language free to make its own meanings. On the other hand, one might argue that the law should be reduced to plain English comprehensible to everyone. Would that make for more intelligent and intelligible conversation? Why do you suppose the makers of the law have not taken this obvious step?

3. One way in which you might attempt to control the conversations that your statute is meant to regulate is to use a vocabulary of great precision. To do so would restrict the portion of the task of lawmaking that is delegated to others and would impose a detailed structure upon the conversations that concern you. Could this possibly be bad?
   a. To return to the building analogy, would you do better to describe the

cabin you want built in general terms, or to give the architect precise plans – and why? Imagine his conversations with you and the builder, in either case. Compare the cookbook: is it a better direction to say that trout should be cooked "at 325 degrees for six minutes per pound," or "until tender throughout," or "until the flesh turns from translucent to white"? Which of those is the most precise instruction? Which is the most clear?

b. The partner asks the summer associate to give him a draft of a brief in a case. What else does he tell him and why? What does he want him to do? Do you suppose law offices prepare booklets on pleading, writing briefs, interviewing clients, and so on? Why or why not?

c. If you rely upon the judge to define your terms in the way you have meant – to perceive and articulate your purposes, to decide cases as you intend – why do you not take care of these things yourself? Put your question this way: why do you leave so much to be done, so much to be talked about, when your statute is finished?

It may assist your analysis of that question to ask what is meant by the word "mean" in the sentence "I trust them to see what I mean." What does the statute writer "mean" when he writes his statute? Why does he not tell us? Is he really saying that he can decide cases but cannot say how, that he doesn't know much about art but knows what he likes? Compare the sophomore who said he "wanted to be a lawyer."

d. Ask of your statute when you have finished it: what sort of conversations among lawyers and judges do you want to give rise to? What questions do you want these people to ask, what concerns do you want them to have? What have you done to ensure that what you want to happen will happen?

4. The basic question this much of your reading leaves you with, to be considered more fully in actually performing your assignment, is this: what sort of control can you have over the way your statute is put to use? Can you provide, as it were, a point of view from which your reader can see the same things you do, so that he will use your statute in the right way, resolving ambiguities correctly, perceiving and pursuing your purposes? Your task is to set up conversations in the future and to do all you can to ensure that they proceed in the right way, based upon the proper premises and asking the right questions. One particular matter you must face is the choice of vocabulary: will you write a statute with special terms and technical meanings, or can you find a way to make a comprehensive statement in plain English, one that can work in a direct and sensible way and not by the manipulation of fictions? Or can you perhaps devise some new form that does not have these difficulties? You are being asked how you will make what you write intelligible, how you will place it in a context (perhaps of your own creation) that will tell your reader what he needs to know, so that his conversation with himself and others will proceed in ways of which you approve.

2. *A Case and Some Statutes on Wrongful Death*

The following case and statutes on wrongful death illustrate how others have faced the difficulties we have been discussing. What terms of cooperation does the writer of each statute try to establish with his audience? What sorts of conversations do these statutes call for? How has the writer attempted to give them shape? I hope you can view these statutes as part of an activity of making law and deciding cases that is by its nature a cooperative one, as examples of a difficult and important literary art.

We shall also ask some new questions, beginning new lines of inquiry or elaborating old ones. For example, the statute is usually written in terms of general categories of a kind that seem to require that they be interpreted — at least on some occasions — to produce results inconsistent with the evident purposes of the statute in question. For example, these statutes commonly provide that when a man is wrongfully killed his "wife" can recover damages. But suppose she has left him for another man, and he has met another woman he hopes to marry? Who should recover then? How do you expect conversation on such a matter to proceed, and how will you in your own statute attempt to guide or control such a conversation? What sort of consistency or rationality do you hope for in your statute: a fidelity to your purposes, or to the categories and terms in which you express them? Or will you perhaps not use such categories at all, and simply state your purposes in a plain and direct way and expect them to be followed?

Another matter raised below is the question of relief: ask of each statute how it seems to direct that damages be measured and assessed. For what items can the plaintiff recover, and for what not? What is the judge or jury actually supposed to do in setting the amount, and what guidance does the statute provide? And why should damages be the remedy anyway? In drafting your own statute, you should consider other forms of relief as well as damages.

The following case holds that no civil action will lie for the death of a person. The first time the law was made, one might say, that was something left out. Legislatures have responded by passing statutes establishing in various ways a cause of action for wrongful death. How do you evaluate what you read here? How would you draft such a statute?

BAKER v. BOLTON
1 Camp. 492 (1808)

This was an action against the defendants as proprietors of a stage-coach, on the top of which the plaintiff and his late wife were traveling from Portsmouth to London, when it was overturned; whereby the plaintiff himself was much bruised, and his wife was so severely hurt, that she died about a month after in a hospital. The declaration besides other special damage, stated, that "by means of the premises, the plaintiff had wholly lost, and been deprived of the comfort, fellowship, and assistance of his said wife, and had from thence hitherto suffered and undergone great grief, vexation, and anguish of mind."

It appeared that the plaintiff was much attached to his deceased wife; and that, being a publican, she had been of great use to him in conducting his business.

Lord Ellenborough said, the jury could only take into consideration the bruises which the plaintiff had himself sustained, and the loss of his wife's society, and the distress of mind he had suffered on her account, from the time of the accident till the moment of her dissolution. In a civil Court, the death of a human being could not be complained of as an injury; and in this case the damages, as to the plaintiff's wife, must stop with the period of her existence.

Verdict for the plaintiff, with £100 damages.

QUESTIONS

1. *The law is often regarded as a system of thought and expression whose parts fit together more or less exactly to form a whole. Can you imagine or find a system of thought of which this sentence is a part: "The death of a human being cannot be complained of as an injury"? With what other propositions is that consistent?*
2. *Assume that it would be tortious for one to entice away a barmaid in violation of her long-term employment contract, and that the consequent economic losses would be recoverable. How could one conceivably then hold that there is no recovery when the barmaid is one's wife and is not enticed away but killed?*
3. *What is the place of consistency in the reasoning behind this judgment?*

AN ACT FOR COMPENSATING THE FAMILIES OF PERSONS KILLED BY ACCIDENTS (LORD CAMPBELL'S ACT)

9 & 10 Vict., c. 93 (1846)

Whereas no Action at Law is now maintainable against a Person who by his wrongful Act, Neglect, or Default may have caused the Death of another Person, and it is oftentimes right and expedient that the Wrongdoer in such Case should be answerable in Damages for the Injury so caused by Him: Be it therefore enacted by the Queen's most Excellent Majesty, by and with the Advice and Consent of the Lords Spiritual and Temporal, and Commons, in this present Parliament assembled, and by the Authority of the same, That whensoever the Death of a Person shall be caused by wrongful Act, Neglect, or Default, and the Act, Neglect, or Default is such as would (if Death had not ensued) have entitled the Party injured to maintain an Action and recover Damages in respect thereof, then and in every such Case the Person who would have been liable if Death had not ensued shall be liable to an Action for Damages, notwithstanding the Death of the Person injured, and although the Death shall have been caused under such Circumstances as amount in Law to Felony.

And be it enacted, That every such Action shall be for the Benefit of the Wife, Husband, Parent, and Child of the Person whose Death shall have been so caused, and shall be brought by and in the Name of the Executor or Administrator of the Person deceased; and in every such Action the Jury may give such Damages as they may think proportioned to the Injury resulting from such Death to the Parties respectively for whom and for whose Benefit such Action shall be brought; and the Amount so recovered, after deducting the Costs not recovered from the Defendant, shall be divided amongst the beforementioned Parties in such Shares as the Jury by their Verdict shall find and direct.

Provided always, and be it enacted, That not more than One Action shall lie for and in respect of the same Subject Matter of Complaint, and that every such Action shall be commenced within Twelve Calendar Months after the Death of such deceased Person.

QUESTIONS

1. *Is the effect of this statute to permit a cause of action for personal injuries to survive the death of the plaintiff, or is it to compensate his spouse, children, or parents for their losses occasioned by his death?*
   a. *How do you know? How would you expect conversation on this question to proceed?*
   b. *Would it ever matter what the theory was? When and why? See Michigan Central R.R. v. Vreeland, 277 U.S. 59 (1913).*
2. *Exactly what elements of damage are provable under this statute? How do you know, or how would you expect conversation on this matter to proceed?*
3. *It might help you imagine how these conversations might go if you ask yourself how you would decide these questions if you were a judge. Would you look for statutory definitions of terms, for some general theory of recovery from which to deduce answers to specific questions, or what? Would you be seeking consistency? If so, consistency with what?*
4. *Would it have been preferable for the legislature merely to have said "Baker v. Bolton is hereby overruled"? To have said "The death of a human being may be complained of as injury in a civil court"? What would have happened then? See the interesting material in H. Hart and A. Sacks, The Legal Process 798–818 (1958), on the different ways in which a legislature can overrule a case.*

GEORGIA CODE ANNOTATED (1968)

105-1302. A widow, or, if no widow, a child or children, minor or sui juris, may recover for the homicide of the husband or parent, the full value of the life of the decedent, as shown by the evidence.

105-1305. No recovery had under the provisions of section 105-1302 shall be subject to any debt or liability of any character of the deceased husband or parent.

105-1306. The husband and/or child or children may recover for the homicide of the wife or mother, and those surviving at the time the action is brought shall sue jointly and not separately, with the right to recover the full value of the life of the decedent, as shown by the evidence, and with the right of survivorship as to said suit, if either shall die pending the action.

105-1307. A mother, or, where no mother, a father, may recover for the homicide of a child, minor or sui juris, unless said child shall leave a wife, husband, or child. The mother or father shall be entitled to recover the full value of the life of said child.

105-1308. The full value of the life of the decedent, as shown by the evidence, is the full value of the life of the decedent without deduction for necessary or other personal expenses of the decedent had he lived.

QUESTIONS

1. *Georgia is said to measure damages for wrongful death by reference to the "loss to the estate" rather than the "loss to the beneficiaries."* Rose, "Foreign Enforcement of Actions for Wrongful Death," 33 Mich. L. Rev. 545, 589 (1938). *Is this the same distinction as that between survival and wrongful death statutes?*
2. *What is the "full value" of the life of a decedent? How do you expect conversation on this question to proceed?*
   a. *If you were a judge or juror, how would you determine the "full value" of the life of a decedent? What evidence would you want to hear? What would you do with it?*
   b. *Is the happiness that one spouse brings to the life of the other a part of the value of his life? Or is this statute concerned only with economic or pecuniary value? How do you know, or how would you decide?*
   c. *In any event, what justification can there be for omitting from the calculation of the impaired value of the estate the expenses that the decedent would have incurred had he lived? For rendering recovery immune from his creditors? Are these provisions consistent with the estate theory of the statute?*
   d. *If there are such inconsistencies in the statute, should they not be cured – for example, by changing the provisions just cited? If you say no, how do you explain your position? Logical consistency is the core of rationality, and surely you do not favor irrational statutes?*
3. *Compare:* "The human companionship thus afforded has a definite, substantial, and ascertainable pecuniary value and its loss forms a part of the 'value' of the life we seek to ascertain." Wycko v. Gnodtke, 361 Mich. 331, 105 N.W.2d 118 (1960).
4. *Would you as judge feel free to decide that there should be no recovery in a particular case because the decedent's life was worthless? We all*

know that an economic entity can have more liabilities than assets, a "negative value"; and is the same not true of a life? Imagine a case in which the judge said:

a. *"No recovery, because the decedent earned no money and was in fact a drain on the resources of the beneficiaries." In such a case, in fact, should not the tort-feasor be able to recover from the beneficiaries some portion of the benefit he conferred on them? Exactly why not? What is the place of theoretical consistency in your analysis of this problem?*
b. *Are there important differences between the "estate" and "beneficiaries" theories here? The aging relative, whose hospital expenses are rapidly eating away at his savings, would present a similar problem under both. But one might argue for a difference in the case of a child: under the estate theory, substantial damages might be awarded for his death since presumably he would sometime have a net worth; but not under the beneficiaries theory (if one is to be truly consistent), since the child is obviously a drain on the family finances and would presumably never benefit his parents, who would in all likelihood predecease him. Should the difference in theory have this difference in result? How do you expect conversation on this point to proceed? What is the place of consistency in your analysis of this question?*
c. *Here is another form of the "worthless life" argument: "No recovery, because the decedent was a vile and disgusting person, whose death is a benefit to his family and to the world. Good riddance." This might be true, and to some extent a matter susceptible of proof. Exactly why would you disapprove of a system of law which permitted that result?*

5. *What result if W sues for the death of H, and the defendant can show that at the time of death she was receiving no support from him and that they were separated? See Willitt v. Purvis, 276 F.2d 129 (5th Cir. 1960). Suppose she is living adulterously with someone else? Jones v. Massachusetts Bonding and Ins. Co., 55 So. 2d 88 (La. 1951). Or suppose, in a suit by the child, the defendant can show that the deceased parent disinherited him before he died. Would the result in these cases be different if the statute followed the "beneficiaries" rather than the "estate" theory? How do you know, or how would you decide?*
6. *Now consider the Georgia statute as a way of talking about people and their experience. How does it talk about the decedent and his family? Into what does it convert them? How will your statute talk about the people whose lives it affects?*

ILLINOIS ANNOTATED STATUTES (1959)

C. 70, §1. Whenever the death of a person shall be caused by wrongful act, neglect or default, and the act, neglect or default is such as would, if death had not ensued, have entitled the party injured to maintain an action and recover damages in respect thereof, then and in every such case the person who or company or corporation which would have been liable if death had not ensued, shall be liable to an action for damages, notwithstanding the death of the person injured, and although the death shall have been caused under such circumstances as amount in law to felony.

§2. Every such action shall be brought by and in the names of the personal representatives of such deceased person, and, except as otherwise hereinafter provided, the amount recovered in every such action shall be for the exclusive benefit of the widow and next of kin of such deceased person and in every such action the jury may give such damages as they shall deem a fair and just compensation with reference to the pecuniary injuries resulting from such death, to the wife and next of kin of such deceased person, not exceeding $20,000 where such death occurred prior to July 14, 1955, and not exceeding $25,000 where such death occurred on or after July 14, 1955 and prior to the effective date of this amendatory Act of 1957, and not exceeding $30,000 where such death occurs on or after the effective date of this amendatory act of 1957.

The amount recovered in any such action shall be distributed by the court in which the cause is heard or, in the case of agreed settlement, by the county or probate court, as the case may be, to each of the widow and next of kin of such deceased person in the proportion, as determined by the court, that the percentage of dependency of each such person upon the deceased person bears to the sum of the percentages of dependency of all such persons upon the deceased person.

QUESTIONS

1. *Does Illinois follow the "estate" or "beneficiaries" theory? How do you know, or how would you decide?*
2. *Illinois has answered the question of the disinherited child. City of Chicago v. Major, 18 Ill. 349 (1857).*
3. *Here are some questions on contributory negligence. How would you as judge decide them under the statutes you have been given? What would be the place of consistency in your reasoning?*
   a. *If the decedent were contributorily negligent, should that be a bar in Georgia? In Illinois? Why? See Dee v. City of Peru, 343 Ill. 36, 174 N.E. 901 (1931).*
   b. *Should the contributory negligence of the beneficiary be a bar in Georgia? In Illinois? Why? See Lorts v. MacDonald, 17 Ill. App. 2d 278, 149 N.E.2d 768 (1958).*
   c. *What if one beneficiary is contributorily negligent and the others are not? Does this bar them all, bar none of them, or bar only the negligent one? In Illinois, all are barred if one is negligent (Hozel v. Hoopeston-Daniel Motor Bus Co., 310 Ill. 38, 141 N.E. 392 (1923);[4] in Missouri, none are barred unless all are negligent (Herrell v. St. Louis-San Francisco Ry., 324 Mo. 38, 23 S.W.2d 102 (1929)). If only the*

4. This result has been changed by statute. See Ill. Ann. Stat. c. 70, §2 (Supp. 1972).

negligent one is barred, is his share divided among the others, or not recovered at all? See Cleveland, C.C. & St. L. Ry. v. Gramb, 103 Ohio St. 471, 134 N.E. 648 (1921). How would you decide these questions as a judge, and why?

4. *What theory justifies limiting the amount one can recover under this statute? Is that consistent with any possible theory?*
5. *In Massachusetts, the statute provides that damages shall be "assessed with reference to" the "degree of culpability" of the defendant. Mass. Gen. Laws c. 229, §2. Is this an improvement? How and why would you decide the contributory negligence questions under this statute?*

3. *The Rhetoric of the Statute: How Is Such a Language to Be Controlled?*

The following notes and questions will elaborate certain lines of questioning that were begun earlier in Section C.

a. The Fiction of Relief: Damages and Other Remedies

Each of the statutes given above responds to the death of one person by requiring another to pay money to his family or estate. Does this seem to you a sensible response? Is money what you would want if your child or spouse were killed by an intoxicated driver? How do you suppose these damages are measured and proved? As you probably know, the usual rule limits damages to "pecuniary" injuries, defined not to include emotional suffering and loss. Does this not seem a strange way for the law to behave? How else might damages be measured? What other forms of relief might be possible?

QUESTIONS

1. *Suppose you were a judge administering a wrongful death statute that was silent on the matter of remedy, or determining the question as a matter of common law. What forms of relief would you consider granting? If you did grant money relief, for what items of injury would you do so?*
2. *In Michigan Cent. R.R. v. Vreeland, 227 U.S. 59 (1913), the Supreme Court construed a federal wrongful death act to authorize damages for pecuniary injury only, in part on the grounds that the law should confine itself to giving damages for injuries that "are capable of being measured by a material standard." Do you agree? What injuries can be so measured?*
   a. *If a statute is construed to authorize recovery only for pecuniary injury, does that mean that parents cannot recover for the death of a child? What will your statute provide that parents may recover when a child is wrongfully killed, and why?*
   b. *Does the pecuniary injury theory mean that an employer can recover*

when a valued employee is killed? Or a partnership for the death of a partner? A merchant for the death of a customer?

3. What is the law doing when it says that damages can be given only for pecuniary injury? Do you believe what it says?
   a. Suppose you try to straighten the law out, so that it does what we all know it should do and does it directly. How can you do that? Should evidence of the quality of the emotional relationship between the parties be admissible and if so, under what standard? Some families are close, others distant; some spouses hate each other richly, and for others the world revolves around their relationship. Should these differences be reflected in the relief granted for wrongful death? How can that be achieved? Can you draft a statute authorizing recovery for emotional as well as pecuniary losses?

      Certainly this sort of remark needs correction: "The law does not allow compensation for the real damages suffered by these good parents – their grief, sorrow, and loss of companionship." Hernandez v. United States, 313 F. Supp. 349 (N.D. Tex. 1969). How can you correct it?
   b. One source of perplexity for us all is the sense of the impossibility or absurdity of putting a cash value on the life of a person wrongfully killed. In Estate of Powers v. City of Troy, 380 Mich. 160, 171, 156 N.W.2d 530, 533 (1968), Justice Brennan of the Michigan Supreme Court expressed the view that it is hard-hearted and mercenary, as well as irrational, to try to value a person, "like a horse or a mule . . . in greenback dollars. . . ." Do you share this view?

      Compare the following: "The plaintiff has suffered great disfigurement. She will carry her crippled and unsightly figure into every phase of life, her home, store, neighbors, and church. The ever-present halt in her gait is surely a ghastly burden. She is a female. The Almighty created beauty of form and face more specially for the female. Sadie Bell Ray (and no other woman of reasoned mind) would sell her natural attractiveness for any price. This court feels the necessity of being conservative and awards the amount of $10,000 for disfigurement. The amount cannot compensate, nor restore, but it is adjudged by this court to be a just figure under the circumstances." Ray v. United States, 277 F. Supp. 952 (D.S.C. 1968). How would you go about measuring damages in a case such as this?
   c. Obviously, measuring damages is a very imperfect business in almost all cases – how do you put a greenback value on an eye or a hand or an hour's pain? – so I suppose what is meant by those who maintain the impossibility of giving damages for what death really means is that the idea of "value" is significantly less precise here than in other cases. How much less precise is it? Take what would seem to be one of the easiest cases in which to determine value, the valuation of an economic enterprise. What is the value of a business? See J. Bonbright, The Valuation of Property, Chapter 2 (1938), where he suggests, among others, the following possible meanings of the term:
      (1) amount actually paid for assets, less depreciation
      (2) market value
      (3) normal market value
      (4) price at which the present owner would in fact be willing to sell

(5) price at which an actual buyer would in fact be willing to buy
(6) replacement cost
(7) capitalized earnings
(8) predicted growth of the business

A moment's reflection will show that each of those definitions of "value" – which could yield remarkably different conclusions in terms of dollars and cents – is itself highly ambiguous. And consider the valuation of particular sorts of assets: an employment contract with an executive; an FCC license, subject to possible nonrenewal; a patent; a noncompetition contract; and the like. And how would you go about setting a value on the control of a business? In International Harvester Co. v. Kentucky, 234 U.S. 216 (1914), a statute forbidding sales below or above "real value" was held unconstitutionally vague.

You will explore these and similar questions in your accounting courses. But they are relevant to our present inquiry because they permit us to ask: is "value" a less certain or more metaphorical term in the wrongful death context than in the business world? One can, after all, imagine staggering differences in valuing a business under various theories. Suppose you are drafting a statute authorizing condemnation of property by the state, or setting the proportion of debt to the value of the assets that a public utility might legally incur. What theory of value, if any, would you articulate? Should the courts evolve a consistent theory to be applied whenever the statute is silent?

How should the law ask judges and juries to determine the value of a life?

4. *Is any form of relief other than monetary damages a possibility here? If so, what fictions does it involve? Is this where you come out: that the very idea of "remedy" as the law uses it is inherently a fictional one?*

b. *Fictions II: The Intellectual Structure of the Statute*

You have just been examining one fiction that lies very near the center of much legal talk: the pretense that legal relief is adequate, that when the law has spoken the job has been done. We assume — or pretend to assume — that damages can "make whole" or "restore," that penal sanctions deter and reform, that an order to an agency to hold an impartial hearing will be obeyed, and so on. The law promises what it cannot give.

The subject of this note is another sort of fiction, a fiction that arises from what might be called the intellectual structure of the legal rule, from the very form the statute takes. On such a subject many beginnings would be possible, but let me suggest that we start with what we have noticed from the beginning of the course: the propensity of the law to make a language of special meanings. Somehow the legal rule seems always to be making a special or technical vocabulary, a language in which words mean something different from what they mean in plain English: the dying man is "dead," "pecuniary" includes emotional, and so on. And think what different meanings the following terms have for the lawyer and the layman: "offer" and "acceptance," "equity," "negligence," "contempt," etc. How and why do these words get their special meanings? Are they given technical definitions to start with, or does the way they are used somehow change them? Are we to regard the invention and use of such meanings as a valuable resource, as a useless fiction, or as something else? Or will the answer vary from instance to instance?

The obvious way to start to draw distinctions is to ask what purposes can possibly be served by such a language of special meanings. One purpose is identified by Maitland in the passage you have read on law French (page 6 *supra*): to establish definitions not used in ordinary speech, to express new and technical ideas. So it may be with property and tax terms, for example, and these may be considered a valuable addition to our resources of thought and language if their purposes are achieved. Perhaps even more fundamental inventions are the languages that make possible the trust, the corporation, and the constitution. Another purpose may be to refer not to a particular idea but to a professional history of thought and argument, to a set of questions the law has raised and not answered: "jurisdiction" and "equity" are such terms, as in a slightly different way "due process" and "unreasonable search and seizure" are too. These terms do not express precise ideas, but do practically the reverse: they point to enormously complex difficulties to which our education has introduced us, and they provide a beginning for argument and thought. We can approve a language that works in these ways. Finally, as the traditional work on legal fictions has shown, the fictional use of terms may be regarded as a stage in the working out of an idea, a symptom of imperfect but healthy thought, to be used until the truth is seen and then to be discarded.

But I think there is another sort of technical or fictional use of language in the law to which such explanations do not apply, one that arises from the very nature of the organization of speech we call the rule, one that is entailed in its form and function. There is a sense in which the very structure or syntax of the rule — the way it works — makes it a radically fictional expression. In this paragraph I shall mention the four characteristics of the statutory rule that seem to me to contribute most to this effect; the rest of the note will be given to their explication. First, as we have already seen, the rule reduces all that can be said about an event to a "legal issue," a question framed in legal terms demanding an answer "yes" or "no"; second, it works by a process of naming or labeling that has the false appearance of being a simple and easy operation, a falsity that seriously misleads many users of legal language; third, an apparent premise of the rule is that it shall always be applied consistently, so that its terms — its labels — shall always mean exactly the same thing (and as I think I can show, this premise is unworkable if true, dishonest if not); fourth, the legal rule is usually designed to have a sort of middle degree of generality, between the specific command and the vague ideal, and this form involves constant compromise and inaccuracy, as everyone knows who has ever said "no generalization can possibly be true." The language built up in this way is, to say the least, very hard to manage. What follows is meant to trace out the difficulties in greater detail, to define some of the troubles you will have to face as a writer of statutes.

Since the process by which the rule reduces what can be said about an event to the simple statement of an issue — a question that must be answered yes or no — has already been examined, we shall begin here with what I call the misleading pretense that the language of the rule is a language of description, not judgment.

(1) The Simple Process of Naming: A Language of Judgment or Description? Reduced to simplest terms, the rule can be said to operate this way: a label is applied to experience, and a consequence determined by the label is imposed. The rule seems to reduce all experience to a single descriptive term: one is or is not "married" or "domiciled in Nevada" or "inducted," and from this everything flows. We lawyers know that a great deal of thought and argument of a most interesting kind lies behind the statement of the issue and application of the label, but no hint of that appears in the rule itself. Rules such as "an arrest is valid where based upon probable cause" and "jurisdiction to divorce exists where either party is domiciled" seem to call for nothing more than a simple glance at reality to see if the name fits or not. We know — but are not told — how false that is. The process is in fact enormously difficult, but it is made to appear almost automatic. The phenomenon can perhaps best be stated by saying that the rule appears to be a language of description, one that works by a simple process of comparison, but it is in truth a language of judgment, working in ways that find no expression in the rule itself. The verbal surface of the law is in this respect simply not true to the complications and frustrations that the use of rules necessarily involves. Think of the labor and doubt you would go through in using either of the two rules just quoted, for example, in almost any case to which they might apply.[5]

How is this false appearance of simplicity to be explained, and how

5. Professor H. L. A. Hart, in an article I regrettably read only after this note was prepared, has drawn a distinction between languages of description and of what he calls "ascription," which is very close to what I mean by "judgment." "The Ascription of Responsibility and Rights," in *Logic and Language*, First Series 145 (Flew ed. 1955).

lived with? Can we somehow understand it and continue to use the language as it exists, or should a new verbal invention occur that does not involve such pretenses?

To begin with the explanation part, one might wish to trace this misleading usage to some congenital dishonesty or stupidity on the part of lawyers, but I think it is better regarded as one manifestation of a common misunderstanding of how language works: the view that all language always operates by naming, that what words do is stand for things or ideas in the world. Thus when I say, "Put the milk on the table," it might be said that I engage in a process of naming, and indeed naming is part of what I do. But you know very well that the notion of naming does not exhaust what can be done with language; it is only one language game out of many. The management of the relations among legislatures, judges, and lawyers with which you have just been concerned is a difficult art of language that does not work by naming. And what does the word "put" label in the sentence just quoted? Where are the labels in these sentences: "Whoops!" "I hope peace comes," "please," "good-bye"? Of course we could say that "put" labels a certain gesture, and "peace" an idea, and that "please" labels the asker and the asked in a particular way. But by that point the notion of labeling or naming has come a long way from "that is milk" or "here is a nail," and in the process it has lost whatever clarity it might have had as a way of characterizing a particular language game. Here are some legal statements that take the external form of naming, and their use can be made to sound as easy as pie, but ask yourself how sensible it is to conceive of them that way: we talk of "title" to property as though such a thing really existed, as if a verifiable relationship between man and thing actually existed in the world apart from some statement of legal conclusions; of "possession" as though it were a simple fact instead of a word pointing to a world of argument and judgment; of "First Amendment rights" as though they could be counted and examined; of a "trust" as though it could be picked up and handled — and one of the great instances of all time is *Palsgraf*'s rule that there must somehow "be" a "duty" before there can "be" any "negligence." The apparent syntax of the legal rule is a syntax of simple "naming," but this appearance is seriously misleading because it hides the truth that the use of the rule requires a process of judgment — of argument and thought — of a most difficult kind.[6] There are those, for example, who speak as if they be-

6. In "Definition and Theory in Jurisprudence," 70 *L.Q. Rev.* 37 (1954), Professor H. L. A. Hart examines in some detail the difficulties that arise from trying to define terms in legal rules (such as "corporation" or "domicile") in the same way that terms in biology or geology might be defined. He makes two points critical to our purposes: that the terms should be defined not in the abstract, as

lieve that what the Constitution requires is perfectly plain, and that deciding constitutional cases is simply a matter of looking and seeing; but such a view — whatever the merits of the proposed results in particular cases — can only debase the process by which constitutional decisions are made and explained.

Here is a rather simple example of what I mean: I once argued very strenuously that a certain administrative practice violated the constitution, and a friend kept asking me how I knew it was unconstitutional. I kept avoiding the question, feeling that the question put the issue wrongly but not knowing how to say so. It has since occurred to me that you never "know" that a practice is unconstitutional or that a right has been violated the way you know that the Dodgers won or that your bike is stolen; instead you decide that the practice is unconstitutional or that the right is violated and explain why, or you urge upon another the rightness of your proposed decision. The question "How do you know?" is a move from another game, a response to statements of description, not to statements of argument or decision. The question that should come next is "How do you reach that conclusion?" or "Why do you say so?"

Of course if "stolen" or "won" are terms of a rule, as they might be, then they are not descriptive but terms of judgment too. What counts is not what word is used but how it is used — whether the activity is one of description or of judgment. For this reason one simply cannot write rules in ordinary English instead of legal language; to write a rule is to write a language of judgment that looks like a language of description, and its syntax is foreign to ordinary speech. The rule is a special language that works in special ways, and it converts whatever terms it uses to serve its purposes.

"How can one use intelligently a language that makes this sort of misleading pretense?" is a question you must face in drafting your statute. Can you just assume that all lawyers realize that the rule is a language of judgment, not description, and keep on in traditional ways, using it as a conventional figure of speech that misleads no one? Perhaps that is best, but one can point to judges and lawyers who do not seem to know what you know. Your audience in fact does not seem to meet your highest expectations. Can you address them more precisely as they are,

---

single terms, but as parts of sentences that use them; and that we must recognize that sentences consisting of exactly the same words (say, "that letter was an acceptance") may be used in very different ways in the law — for example, as statements of binding legal decision by a judge, as arguments, or as explanations to a client. It is to this world of legal activity I wish to point — and which indeed it is the purpose of the course as a whole to explore — when I speak of a language of judgment or argument as opposed to a language of description.

or can you somehow show them what you are doing and change their minds? Do you maintain the pretense that the rule operates by a sort of simple naming, and use it in some metaphorical way, or do you reject it and expose the truth? When you draft your statute you will see that neither suggestion is easy of achievement.[7]

(2) *Consistency of Meaning: An Artificial Syntax.* As I suggested at the beginning of this note, the rule not only pretends that its operation is a simple process of naming, it works on an apparent assumption that each term or "name" must have the same meaning whenever it is used. That is, the legal rule seems to establish a closed system in which it is the case — or is pretended — that every term has exactly the same meaning in every instance in which the rule is used. One either is or is not married, and from that fact flows a host of consequences. One is not half-married or quarter-married or even married for some purposes and not for others, it appears. "Domicile" must apparently be defined in one case just as it is in another, and the same is true of "simultaneous death" or "survival." Of course the appearance of uniformity is often false in practice: is this falseness ever recognized in the law, and if so, how? If not, how can such a language be used intelligently? How can its use by the law be explained?

The expected response begins this way: the practice of uniform meanings of legal labels is compelled by fundamental assumptions of logic. For if a set of statements is to operate as an intelligible system, its terms must have consistent meanings. It is, I believe, an unquestioned premise of logic that for the purposes of a particular logical system each term can be applied to experience in the following way: a person (or thing or event) either is X — whatever X may be and however it may be defined — or is not. There is no middle ground. One either is or is not the wife of John; an object subject to duty either is or is not a "baseball glove";[8] one either has or has not been "inducted" into the armed

7. Another way to make much the same point is this: the legal rule has the appearance of the sort of rule we see in geometry, of a theorem or axiom, and one half-expects that it should be used as those rules are, deductively. And while there are cases so clear that no real argument is possible, every lawyer knows that the legal rule does not compel a single result but authorizes a wide range of logically permissible results, among which choices must be made and justified by lawyer and judge. It would be as deductive as it appears to be only if there were an exact and obvious correspondence between its labels and the real world, if there were no room for argument about the meaning of "marriage" or "domicile" or "search," if it were a language of simple description rather than an invitation to conversation and to judgment.

8. *New York Merchandise Co. v. United States,* 294 F. Supp. 971 (Cust. Ct. 1969), faced the question whether an inexpensive vinyl baseball glove was a "baseball glove" or a "toy" for duty purposes. How would you go about deciding such a question? Here is what the court said:

"We first consider the facts in the case as shown by the record. Initially, it is

services.[9] If it is to conform to the most basic logical standards, then, the law seems forced to admit no doubt, no third possibility, and its every term is to be applied with the greatest practicable consistency. How could rules work on any other basis?

But how sensible is this logical principle for the purpose of expressing real judgments in the real world? "However you wish to define 'raining,' the term must always be used for the purposes of your system such that it is always true that it either is or is not 'raining.'" This is a common example of the principle of logical consistency. But who in real life would ever take the position that it necessarily either was or was not raining? Suppose it is just foggy and wet? Obviously the answer to the question "Is it raining?" depends upon the purpose for which it is asked. Does your questioner want to know whether to wear a raincoat? To

---

to be noted that the glove in issue is similar in appearance to baseball gloves used by professional players, and has various features and characteristics of such gloves. Thus, like the professionals' baseball glove, it has a solid stitched webbing between the thumb and the forefinger; fingers laced with rawhide; a pocket with padding; and a welted seam. In other aspects, too, of design and feel, it is the same or similar to gloves used by professional baseball players.

"In construction, however, the imported glove is considerably less rugged than a professional baseball player's glove. For one thing, it is made of vinyl, whereas a professional's glove is made of leather to absorb perspiration. Beyond that, it is single-stitched; the thread is made of cotton; and the rawhide lacing — while substantial — is run through holes in the vinyl which lack eyelets to give it added strength. By contrast, the professional's glove is double-stitched; nylon thread is used; and it has eyelets around the holes. Nor is the glove in issue nearly as rugged as a vinyl glove in evidence which is conceded to be a baseball glove suitable for Little League play. For the latter glove is made of a far heavier vinyl; it is double-stitched; and it has eyelets around the holes for added strength.

"The imported gloves were displayed and offered for sale in plaintiff's showroom on a counter with plaintiff's 'other baseball gloves,' and were never displayed on any other counter in the showroom. The retail selling price of the imported glove was 98 cents. In comparison, a leading domestic sport goods manufacturer makes various baseball gloves which sell at retail at a price ranging from $4.00 to $42.00, with gloves suitable for Little League play being in the $4.00 to $7.00 range.

"The glove in issue, the record indicates, is suitable for use by children — particularly below the age of eight — in a regular or organized game of baseball. It does not appear be rugged enough for Little League play but could be used as a substitute for that purpose. The record further indicates (1) that during the period 1953 to 1956, children aged 7 to 11 played organized games of baseball in parks in the poorer districts of San Francisco using gloves similar to those involved in this case; and (2) that children in other neighborhoods of San Francisco used gloves like those here in issue to play a regular game of baseball.

"The evidence thus adduced establishes clearly that the imported gloves are not toys, but rather constitute baseball gloves, characteristic of the types of gloves commonly used in the game of baseball."

Compare *Norton Mfg. Corp. v. United States,* 288 F. Supp. 829 (N.D. Ill. 1968), where the court was faced with the question whether a fishing implement was a "pole" or a "rod."

9. Compare *Brown v. Resor,* 407 F.2d 281 (5th Cir. 1969), with *United States v. Norman,* 296 F. Supp. 1270 (N.D. Ill. 1969).

water the garden? To call off the picnic? To go out for a sunbath? The convention of ordinary speech is that critical terms are defined anew each time for the purposes of a particular conversation, not as part of an enduring system. (The logician might say that each conversation constitutes a different "system" in which the general principle of consistency must be applied — for example, if that question were followed by "Was it raining yesterday?" But that really does not help us as lawyers, for we are not free to have as many systems as we have cases.)

Suppose I am asked if it is raining, and I say "I don't know; you come to the window and decide." What sort of statement is that? Not "systematic" in the logical sense, but need either people or the law be that? But a decision not to decide is familiar enough to us as lawyers, and even as legislators.

Here is another example: think how one might respond in ordinary life if asked whether a man's act was "malicious," or whether a car had been "wrecked": one would talk around the event, explaining more and more fully what had happened, why one thought so, and so on — "Maybe not wrecked, but banged up pretty good"; "I think he meant to do it but not to hurt him" — and in the process would define one's terms for the purposes of the present conversation. Terms mean different things on different occasions, and no one feels that violence has been done to rationality. How differently the rule works: once the issue is stated — and you know how complex and unexplained that process is — the rule operates by labeling a person or event and then imposing a consequence determined by the label. The pretense or assertion that the law makes is always the same: that all people or events similarly labeled are in all relevant respects similar. It is the function and the glory of the rule to impose "like results in like cases." "All A shall be B."

What is special about conversations based upon rules, then, is that terms are defined not for the purposes of an immediate conversation but for a class of conversations, and these must (as a matter of fundamental assumption) be as consistent as possible. The idea is by making similar to connect conversations remote from each other in time and place. The distinctive characteristic of this form of speech is less the creation of a technical vocabulary — "offer" and "marriage" are common terms — than the use of the special syntax of the rule, which requires a way of thinking and talking very different from what we know in our ordinary speech. It often is not the case that the law creates a new meaning (as it does in "reversion") but that it limits a term to one of many already existing possibilities of meaning and does so with a rigidity incompatible with the conventions of ordinary English. In this sense, one creates a technical vocabulary whenever one makes a rule, no matter how ordinary its terms may be, because the operation of the rule itself involves an artificial way of giving meaning to words and events. In the operation of the rule, all experience is reduced to a single question — for example, whether the label "arrest" or "contract" applies to these facts — with no opportunity for what would be the most common response in our ordinary lives: to say that it does and it doesn't, or that it partially does, or that it depends on why you ask. Why should we not speak in the law, as we might in ordinary life, of half-arrests and partial contracts?[10] The form of the rule not only assumes that it makes sense to ask such a binary question — "either the label applies or it does not" — it must also assume that the process by which that question is seen as dispositive, by which the issue is stated, is simple and accurate; and whatever it may be, you know it is not that. This usage generates great pressure on the user of rules to be enormously simple-minded, to see things as a hornbook does, as if they really were as simple as the rule pretends. How is this pressure to be resisted, how can the rule be written or used in a way that recognizes the complexities its form seems to deny?

In these remarks I have not meant to exhaust what can be said about the rule and the apparently simple-minded labeling process by which it operates (in Chapter 3 we shall explore these matters in greater detail) but to point to a difficulty for you as a writer of rules. When you reflect upon the incredible diversity and variety of life, the countless possibilities, what sense does it make to have everything turn on the application of a single label claimed to have a single meaning? This use of language disregards the common experience of man, and to speak of its mastery defines an art of the greatest difficulty. How can you intelligently use a form of language — the rule — that makes promises of order and simplicity, of fairness and comprehensibility, that it cannot possibly keep? Is it tolerable to suggest that the very notion of uniform meaning of terms, of like results in like cases, is a hopeless and empty dream? What should the legislator do in the face of that fact?

As you consider the difficulties of a language made up of rules, do not forget to ask yourself where we should be without rules, what would happen if we had to carry on our legal business in plain English.

(3) *The General Category and the False Approximation.* Implicit in our notion of fairness is that the law shall be of general application, treating everybody equally; and for a rule to meet this standard, its labels and categories must not only be consistently defined, they must be general too. The lawmaker must then face his own version of the grade school paradox that while "no generalization is true," he — like the rest of us — is under great pressure to speak in general terms.

10. Is the Restatement of Contracts §90 just such a proposal? The idea of a partial arrest and a partial search was adopted by the Court in *Terry v. Ohio*, 392 U.S. 1 (1968).

What it means to use a general or categorical language may become clearer if you think of places outside the law, and aside from rules, where this form of speech is common. Consider sociological or political talk of the sort that makes a single characteristic all-important: when one talks about blacks or old people or students, one is asserting the existence and significance of a likeness that is necessarily only part of the story, and which in many instances gives rise to the falsest of inferences about the individual. Much the same is true of the natural sciences as well: do you suppose that every bird of the same species is exactly the same? Darwin's simple recognition that these discrete categories, defining thousands of different kinds of plants and animals, could be understood only by seeing that they were impermanent — constantly shifting and partially false — was one of the great shocks in the history of thought, resisted desperately.

When you write your statute, you will (if you do as others have done) write in a language of general labels to an audience that will expect you to mean or to pretend that each label should be applied uniformly, that fairness means defining the law as the same for everybody. How can you control these expectations? The law is nothing if not a regular and consistent conceptual system, and to be such, it must operate by uniform and general definitions. You will probably draft a statute that works this way and will presumably claim that the truth can be spoken in this form. Under the scheme you establish you will know that only part of the story can be told, but you will say that it is enough. How can you explain and justify what you do?

Perhaps the most obvious example of false generalization in the material you have read is the use of legally defined family relationships to determine who may recover. We imagine a typical example and say that we shall allow the wife to recover because she loved her husband, is grief-stricken at his death, and suffers a serious economic injury. Do we therefore articulate a rule that says the "wife" may recover? Or "one who is grief-stricken"? In the next case the spouses may hate each other cordially, and the truly injured one may be a mistress. Worse than that, even where there is only one woman in his life she may fail to recover if the marriage is invalid (say, because of a defective divorce or for failure to go through a ceremony in a state which does not recognize common law marriages). Thus the category "wife" errs both in what it includes and in what it excludes. And children typically recover without regard to their emotional or financial dependence upon the decedent. Should the legislature disregard these categories of wife and child, as approximations that are simply too false, and say that recovery should be measured by the quality of the emotional relationship terminated by the death? By the degree of emotional suffering the plaintiff can show? The degree of economic injury?

The general category, suspended between the most vaguely stated purposes of the law and the details of the particular case, is a category of convenience. If you use it in your statute, be prepared to justify what you do. Can you do without such categories entirely? Or can you use them intelligently in some way, perhaps by giving directions for their use so that they do not lead to stupid or wrong results? Could they perhaps be used only as presumptions, to be overridden where the greater purposes of the law require it?

One more comparison: in ordinary life the general rule is often the form in which the most meaningless sort of statement, the cliché, is cast. One thinks of proverbs, guides to life, parents speaking to children, and so on — "Be thou familiar, but by no means vulgar." Can the truth possibly be spoken in such a style? Think of (or better, actually read) a page chosen at random from *Corpus Juris Secundum* or *American Jurisprudence*. There you have the body of rules that are the law. You can find the law in these books. Yet, are these books not very nearly meaningless whether viewed as directions to judgment or rules to conduct? The possibility you are asked to face is that the general rule is necessarily a form of cliché, an impossible term even for the master. Perhaps you can remember your own first attempts to talk and write as a lawyer, in your moot court arguments or on exams: out tumble the rules, fully memorized, but somehow nothing is made of them, no intelligible and relevant position is expressed. Your judge or examiner keeps saying "So what?" This is doubtless no longer the case with you. What have you learned that enables you to use rules well as a lawyer? Do you see how a rule is like a cliché? As a legislator, how do you work with and control the clichés — the general rules — that are your professional tools?

Despite all of the difficulties the rule presents, you may conclude when you draft your own statute that this is the best we can do. Instead of speaking of "fictions," one could say that the law by using this form simplifies the intolerable complexities of life, that it reduces to comprehensibility the bewildering diversity of events. But whatever your view on this, do not be oblivious to the difficulties of the forms in which you give your directions.

The validity of the general label, of the category of convenience, has been the subject of constitutional adjudication. See, e.g., *Levy v. Louisiana*, 391 U.S. 68 (1968); *Labine v. Vincent*, 401 U.S. 532 (1971); *Weber v. Aetna Casualty and Surety Co.*, 406 U.S. 164 (1972); *Stanley v. Illinois*, 405 U.S. 645 (1972).

(4) *Degrees of Consistency and the Paradox of Logical Tightness.* I

have suggested that when the law is actually applied, its terms may not have the uniformity they seem to have, that its categories may in practice be bent to serve more general or more specific purposes. The absence of susceptibility to finer distinctions, to the sense and color of events, may be only apparent. For example, it is hardly possible that "malice" could be given a universally consistent meaning every time it is used, and think how variously "negligence" has been defined by judges and juries in the world of actual fact. But this suggestion is scarcely a comforting one, since we have no idea how, on what principles, the rigidity is made flexible. And this sort of "flexibility" erodes the fundamental premise of consistency for the sake of which the convention of uniform definitions might be accepted in the first place. Our most basic expectation is that there should be a fundamental intellectual consistency in a statute, that the particular should be determined by the general, that it should all hang together somehow. Certainly from the first day of law school you have been occupied with consistency, being trained to distinguish and reconcile apparent inconsistencies and to face with intrepid resolve the hard choices presented by real ones. And who would actually recommend inconsistency in the law: how could argument then go on? How could reasoned decisions be made? No one in the law ever asked to be told that consistency was the hobgoblin of little minds.

Yet you have seen how unsatisfactory the result would be if any of the theories you have so far encountered was followed to its limits — the pecuniary damages theory, for example, or the estate theory. But how can you adopt a theory and tell your reader to use it only part way? And the articulation of a theory meant to be followed consistently is of enormous value to the reader, for it gives him a way of resolving ambiguities and uncertainties in what you have written. Might you avoid these difficulties by articulating as your basic premise not a theory but a purpose or a set of purposes? What, in fact, will be the purposes of your wrongful death statute? What, if anything, remains to be done after you have stated them?

As I have suggested, one difficulty is that any consistency you achieve may be more apparent than real, especially if you use terms that are vague and ill-defined. The appearance of consistency in your statute may be belied in its application. How far is it your object to ensure consistency in the actual use of your statute, and how far may you properly wink at it? Is the appropriate attitude of the maker of rules a genial hypocrisy?

This question has another side: you may notice, as you fret over your statute, that the more you ensure its consistency — the more clear and precise and logical you make it — the more artificial it becomes, the more removed from what you are really trying to do, from what you think ought to be said. As what you write becomes more internally coherent, it becomes more mechanical, more technical — more removed from life, your friend at the cocktail party might say, and certainly more odious to him.

When you consider specific instances of statutory writing, you may uncover a paradox: that it is exactly when the law expresses least that we are most confident about its logical consistency and internal rationality. The tax laws, which focus only on a few narrow questions of economic life, and rigidly exclude the human content of the experience which they regulate, constitute a structure of marvelous complexity, the parts of which really do fit together into an operating and consistent whole (or at least are said to do so by those who know). This is reason at work. Yet in criminal law we cannot seem to get away from the vague words "knowing," "willful," "malicious," "unlawfully," "wrongfully," despite all the efforts of those who advise us to write precisely and clearly. We are unable to perfect the criminal law system as we apparently perfect the tax system. But while the language of criminal law is always unsatisfactorily vague and does not express very well the psychological facts with which we are concerned, it does at least point to or recognize the existence of a side of life that the other excludes entirely. Can you explain this paradox? When should the law speak one way, and when the other? When is perfect consistency in detail important and when not?

Historians have a similar dilemma. Either they try to write about history as a whole or perhaps the life of an age, in which case they wallow around in generalities of dubious meaning that cannot be tested, or they write monographs on narrow subjects in which higher scientific standards can be maintained, "but only at the expense of leaving out the greater part of what is known about the lives of the human beings whose histories are being recorded." Berlin, "The Concept of Scientific History," in *Philosophical Analysis and History* 23 (Dray ed. 1966). Berlin goes on to suggest that models, theories, or systems of language and thought can be most rigorous and most universal when most abstract. Procedurally, mathematics is the most satisfactory discipline; its statements either meet the highest possible standards or are rejected. Physics ignores all experience except that relating to the "very narrow group of characteristics which material objects possess in common." As one moves along the scale away from abstraction, the theoretical model of the activity becomes less rigorous, less quantitative, less scientific in its structure and logic. His analysis leaves history among the humane arts. In *Historical Inevitability* (1954) he explicitly rejects the form of history that tries to explain events in terms of general rules, on the grounds that rules cannot describe experience so various, complex, and subjective as that which history must describe. To use such rules, he suggests, is to engage in a pointless and pathetic fiction, to raise false pretenses and to make unsubstantiated claims; it is to avoid facing the limits of what can be truly said. The implications of such a theory for the maker of the law — who is in his own way writing history ahead of time, and who should be as unwilling as the historian to narrow his ultimate purposes — are dismaying. The heart of the problem is the same: rules cannot express what needs to be said about such various experience, and their use inspires a false confidence in whatever logical scheme is expressed. And the fictional quality of the logical scheme in either case increases as the rules become more precise. But to generalize is to obscure both fiction and inconsistency by a kind of silence.

The suggestion for your analysis, then, is that we are facing an essential paradox: the more technically and logically satisfactory the statements within a set of rules, the more those rules must fail to express what the situation thus regulated really holds. There is a scale, and every set of rules must find its place along it, between an inarticulate pointing to the whole of experience at one end and a mathematically precise failure to express anything that has to do with anything at the other. By what process of reasoning and judgment is one to choose a point along that scale in a particular case?

Of course there is one great difference in our favor: the historian explains, the lawmaker gives directions. Exactly how does this fact change the nature of the peril the lawyer faces when he starts to talk in rules? Can he count on his audience, those who use his rules, to rescue him? You know too much to answer that in a word. Perhaps the question is better put as the beginning of inquiry: how can the lawmaker best attempt to manage his audience so that it will do what he cannot?

WRITING ASSIGNMENT 5: Drafting a Statute on Wrongful Death[11]

Part One

- *Draft a statute addressed to the situation where one person dies by the wrongful act of another.*

Part Two

- *In a brief paper, tell what difficulties you faced. How — by what art — did you address them? In particular, what directions, if any, did you*

11. Supplementary assignments are in the Appendix.

give for the use of your statute? How did you attempt to manage the terms of cooperation between you and your readers?

Part Three

- Give an account, from your own experience, of an attempt to organize future experience in some way other than a statute. Did this attempt work well? Why or why not? What can a writer of statutes learn from this account? Explain how this way of organizing experience is different from or similar to a statute.

The way of organizing experience you choose to discuss in Part Three may have some things in common with the statute; for example, it may be an order, a rule, a game, or an institution of some kind. It might be especially interesting if it were a way of establishing and directing future conversations. As you work on your statute, review the reading in Section C and ask of what you write the questions asked there: how do you see to the definition of your terms? By defining them yourself, or giving directions, or what? How do you frame your statute so that its user will be most likely to state the issue in a proper way? Are your terms drawn from a technical vocabulary, each with a single unique meaning, or do you make room for the sort of shifts and complications of meaning usual in plain English? How can you do that if you write in rules? What categorical terms do you use, and how do you control their inherent fictions? What sort of relief do you authorize courts to grant, and do you acknowledge the metaphorical nature of this sort of talk? What degree of logical consistency and clarity do you achieve, and at the cost of what degree of artificiality? How do you address your judges, lawyers, and citizens, and how do you tell each one what is expected of him? As you look back over your work in Section C, what sort of rhetorical resource do you conclude that the statute affords?

When you have finished your statute and are satisfied that it is the best you can do, ask yourself: "How free am I as a legislator to say what I want?" Insofar as you find or claim to find limitations on your freedom, be prepared to identify them in class. To what extent do they arise from substantive rules of law? From the nature of the statutory form? From the nature of language? From your own inabilities?

Much has been written on how to draft statutes. See, e.g., the appropriate chapters in R. Cook, Legal Drafting (1951); F. Cooper, Writing in Law Practice (1963); F. Dickerson, The Fundamentals of Legal Drafting (1965); F. Newman and S. Surrey, Legislation (1955). The list could go on. It would repay you to look at one or more of these *books to discover what sort of help they can give you with your present problem.*

WRITING ASSIGNMENT 5 (ALTERNATIVE): Other Statutes

• *If you wish, you may modify the foregoing assignment by drafting your statute on some subject other than wrongful death. Here are two possibilities:*

• *A. Draft a statute establishing military conscription but providing for exemption of those conscientiously opposed to military duty.*

• *B. Draft a statute defining the circumstances under which policemen may arrest and search other citizens.*

CHAPTER 3

HOW THE LAW TALKS ABOUT PEOPLE — "WHO IS THIS MAN?"

And what is a novel if not a conviction of our fellow-men's existence strong enough to take upon itself a form of imagined life clearer than reality and whose accumulated verisimilitude of selected episodes puts to shame the pride of documentary history?*

You are asked to begin the next stage of your examination of what it means to think and speak like a lawyer by regarding the law as a sort of social literature, as a way of talking about people and their relationships. In Chapter 2 you studied the statute as social literature of a rather special kind — as a way of defining and managing relationships among officials, as a literature of professional cooperation — and the enormous complications inherent in the fact that legal language is constantly used for the purposes of defining and sharing power, of giving directions and delegating discretion, will be with us throughout the course. But at present our emphasis is somewhat different: you are asked to regard the law as a social literature of a different kind, as a way of talking about people rather than to them. We are continuing here a line of thought begun in Chapter 2, where we asked of the passages we read, "What way of talking about people is this?" Or, as we asked of the wrongful death statute, "Into what does this statute convert — to what does it reduce — the experience of the dead person and his family?" In what follows, we shall compare what we find in the law with other literatures that define character and personality, and your attention will be directed as well to your own experience of life. The aim is to discover something about the limits and resources of legal language and to explain what is found. We might use a question now familiar and ask: "Can you say what you want about people in the language of the law?"

The readings and questions in Section A are meant to provide some material with which you can begin to work out a response to that

* Joseph Conrad, A *Personal Record,* Chapter 1 (1912).

question. Our first concern will be to figure out what possibilities there are in general for the literary creation of character, for talking about people, and to arrive at some sense of what is at stake in the choice among them. What does the writer say about himself and his subject in the way he chooses to write? We shall repeatedly turn from legal to nonlegal passages and back again, asking particularly what possibilities are open to the lawyer and what seem to be the implications of his choices. The initial effort is to expose the difficulty of writing about another person as a general matter, and you will accordingly be asked in your next writing assignment to give an account of someone else's experience in which you express who he is, doing justice to his difference from yourself.

In Sections B to E we shall consider particular situations in which the effort of the law is to define a person: the insanity defense, which reduces what can be said about the defendant to a single label; the sentencing decision, where for once the law looks at the whole man; and the language of race, which involves a particularly intractable sort of labeling. In Chapter 4 we shall return to a line of thought begun in the wrongful death assignment and examine the rule as a way of defining and regulating social relationships among people. That is, having asked how the law talks about the person outside the system — the ordinary man — we shall there ask how it defines those who are part of it — the judge, administrator, lawyer, and so on.

It may help us get a sense of what it might mean to regard the law as a social literature if we ask a question raised earlier: what happens if you look at the world created by legal speech as if it were a novel? What sorts of characters inhabit it, engaged in what activities? How are people defined in this literature by their interests and concerns, by what they say or do? What voices do you hear? There is much intense activity, no doubt: how is it represented and defined? Think of or read a law case, imagine the characters freed from the page and alive in a storyland, and ask what their story would be like. It would not be like most novels you have read, although you might examine the stories of Edmund Gorey or Jane Austen's "Frederic and Elfrida" as possible parallels.[1] You are familiar, for example, with the ubiquitous personage of the law of torts, the Reasonable Man, and could write a story about him, I suppose: A Day in the Life of the Reasonable Man. Would such a story have any life or interest? Compare a similar effort on behalf of the Offeror, the Preferred Shareholder, or the Victim of Robbery. If you cannot imagine

1. "Frederic and Elfrida" is an early story and can be found in Volume 6 of the Oxford edition of the works (Chapman ed. 1954). An amusing example of reading as a novel a book meant otherwise is Edmund Wilson's article, "Books of Etiquette and Emily Post," reprinted in Wilson, *A Literary Chronicle: 1920–1950*, at 380 (Anchor ed. 1950).

that a novel built around characters defined in this way would have any interest for you, how can legal talk about the same characters, the same events, have any interest? Imagine or peruse a commercial contract and ask how the two parties are defined, how they have expressed the success they hope for, the failure they fear. Or look at a corporate charter or a wrongful death statute, and ask how human felicity receives its momentary definition in these documents. What range of human character and experience is here expressed? The same questions could be asked of the New York Domestic Relations Law or the California Criminal Code or of any judicial opinion. It would be illuminating to try to draft a page or two from a novel created out of the materials of legal literature, perhaps by piecing together actual passages, perhaps by placing its characters in another, imagined world.

Although there may be occasions where a deliberate restriction of view, a narrowing of concern, is entirely appropriate — talk about the Holder in Due Course, for example, could be said to be a "technical language suited to technical ends" — there are also occasions where the law must deal with matters of the greatest intensity and importance, where nothing should be excluded, occasions that make the most rigorous demands for full expression of the human personality. Two that we shall examine are the judgment of sanity in a criminal trial and the judgment made in sentencing a convicted defendant. In both, the whole person stands before the bar, and the very question the law must face is, "Who is this man?"

What possibilities are there in legal literature for responding to such a question? What direction and assistance are given to those who must judge and speak in legal terms about other people and their experience? As a way of helping you work out a response to these questions, you will be asked to look at what other writers — especially novelists and historians — have said and done. And you will be urged, as usual, to look to your life as well as your reading. Think, for example, of occasions in your own experience when it has been important to know and express what a person really is, to perceive the genuine identity that exists underneath the social exterior defined by his job, his habits, his manners and clothes. Such moments are perhaps most common in the life of the teen-ager, at an age when no one's identity is certain and when an exterior is especially likely to be impermanent or false. Uncertainty in one's own sense of self makes the process of knowing and describing others, and of establishing relations with them, especially intense. Do you not remember struggling and failing to say what you wanted about someone you knew, or his behavior? The establishment and expression of human relations has been for all of us at times a matter of crisis: how to talk to that girl (or boy) and seem to be what you want to be? How to explain strained or broken relations: "He is a . . ." This is a world filled with emotion and moral significance, in which the business of life is the process of social relation and social judgment; one is constantly trying to fix one's view of others, to do justice to one's emotions and one's judgments, but language always seems inadequate to express what one knows. This is a world that many people leave behind as they grow up. But it is with something like the feelings of the sixteen-year-old that you are urged to look at what can be said about people in the language of the law. Is this language fit only for half-dead obese men of business, whose sole concern is for things? Or is it — can it be made to be — something else? Can you use this language to say what you want about people and their experience?

In connection with your work in Section A, you are asked to read Euripides' *Alcestis.*

A. *POSSIBILITIES FOR THE DEFINITION AND EXPRESSION OF CHARACTER: THE LAW AMONG OTHERS*

One cannot make an exhaustive catalog of all possible ways of talking about people, but the questions and selections that follow will sketch some possibilities for us, enough at least to start an intelligible conversation on the subject. You will not be surprised to find that we examine particular passages of legal speech not only directly but by comparison with other kinds of literature. This is an attempt to establish some sense of the range of possibilities, to place the law within that range, and to work out a vocabulary of criticism in which to evaluate what we write and read.

I do not mean to suggest that all the possibilities of legal talk about people are exemplified in what follows; indeed the assumption is quite the reverse: that the possibilities are limitless, and that it is up to you to conceive of and pursue those of your own choosing. But we can perhaps identify certain more or less permanent characteristics of the lawyer's social speech. Some of these arise from the nature of his tasks, from the particular verbal and social activities in which he engages: arguing, negotiating, counseling, drafting, and so on. Others are inherent in the very structure of his language: the surface varies enormously of course, but at the center of nearly every legal conversation is a rule or set of rules, and you know how impossible that form is. As we saw in Chapter 2, it operates by reducing what can be said about experience to a series of questions cast in terms of legal conclusions ("legal issues") which must be answered simply "yes" or "no"; it maintains a false pretense that it can be used as a language of description or naming, when in fact it calls for a process of complex judgment, to which it seems to give no directions whatever; its terms are given (or appear to be given) rigidly uniform meanings of a kind radically inconsistent with the conventions of ordinary speech; and its crucial terms are almost always imperfect generalities. The language built upon this form seems to be either impossibly simple-minded or — to the extent that its requirements are evaded — dishonest. In addition, as you saw, the rule can be understood only when it is seen to operate through time, by the cooperation of several different minds, rather like music: the first stage is the statement of the rule, but the process is not complete until a final judgment has been reached by others, in litigation, negotiation, or planning. Imperfections in the understandings by which the cooperation proceeds can throw the whole enterprise out of kilter, and attempts to regulate the terms of cooperation are uncertain at best. You have already considered how difficult it is to use such a language as a legislator giving directions to lawyers and judges, talking to people whom you wish to see things your way and to behave accordingly, even in as simple a matter as a wrongful death statute. We shall now test this language from a different perspective by regarding it not as an instrument for the communication of directions, but as a way of talking about people, as a social literature of the kind the novel and drama are.

It is easy to see how one might go wrong with such a language. Is it conceivable that one might go right and if so, how? Such a question asks you what expectations you bring to talk about other people, and you are urged to reflect upon your own literary and social experience. How do you perceive and describe people in your ordinary life, how do you make and express judgments about them? How do you — or might you — give directions to others with respect to these matters? Look to your reading as well: can you find passages in which you think justice is done to a person talked about, and the reverse? As throughout this course, you are here asked to see law as an activity among your other activities, as a part of your life.

1. *Character and Caricature*

a. *Being True and False to Life*

Our attempt to identify and scrutinize some possibilities for the literary definition of character begins with the distinction, familiar in some form to us all, between character and caricature. Character is the successful rendition of the personality: believable, full, complex, living and breathing, and so on. Caricature is the reverse: it is a way of talking about people that reduces them to single exaggerated aspects, to labels, roles, moments from their lives; it is narrow, two-dimensional, unconvincing. It may be hard to carry the definition of these terms much further, but we all have some sense of the differences to which they point. Character is true to life; caricature, false to it. The obvious suggestion is that the law — especially in its basic form, the rule — is a literature of caricature; it pares away all that can be said about a person's life until nothing is left except the rule and the label. You might say that the application of the legal rule converts life into a little story, a narrative made up of the elements of the crime or cause of action, and this story tells us all we need to know about the person involved — either he did it, or he did not, and everything else is irrelevant. The question, "Who is this man?" is answered by telling us what he has done on a single occasion ("He is the one who on the fourteenth of March, 1971 . . .") rather than by telling us who he is or what he has done in his lifetime. We never hear his own voice. When this way of talking about people by reducing them to their roles in single transactions is compared with other possibilities, it seems even at its best to be nothing more than a cliché, a cheapening of thought and feeling. This is a sort of writing used elsewhere mainly for jokes.

As you read the passages in Section A, ask of each how you would describe and evaluate its creation or rendition of a human personality. In what terms, what language, do you explain the successes and failures you encounter? Ask whether the distinction between caricature and character is useful to you, or whether you can articulate another pair of opposites that will express your judgments more accurately. Or perhaps you will find that your judgments of success and failure cannot be expressed by points along a scale. If not that way, how? The following two passages from a professional literature about the creation of character may give you some assistance in finding a way to talk about these matters. You can see from the first that it is not only the lawyer whose characters may be untrue to life, and that even the novelist may have tendencies that way.

A PLEA FOR BETTER MANNERS*
Norman Douglas

[Douglas complains that D. H. Lawrence has given a false picture in a particular biography because he has used the "novelist's touch." Douglas now explains what this is.]

I spoke just now of the novelist's touch in biography. What is this touch? It consists, I should say, in a failure to realise the profundities

* In *Experiments* 223, 246 (1925).

and complexities of the ordinary human mind; it selects for literary purposes two or three facets of a man or woman, generally the most spectacular and therefore "useful" ingredients of their character, and disregards all the others. Whatever fails to fit in with these specially chosen traits is eliminated; must be eliminated, for otherwise the description would not hold water. Such and such are the data; everything incompatible with those data has to go by the board. It follows that the novelist's touch argues, often logically, from a wrong premise; it takes what it likes and leaves the rest. The facts may be correct so far as they go, but there are too few of them; what the author says may be true, and yet by no means the truth. That is the novelist's touch. It falsifies life.

QUESTIONS

1. *If this is the novelist's touch, what is the lawyer's or judge's touch?*
2. *Of course, the novelist may give a false picture of life and still entertain or instruct, but is it defensible on any grounds for the lawyer or judge to speak in a way that "falsifies life"? Remember that it was suggested that one particularly hideous and corrupting vice of the death penalty is that real people are spoken of as if they were fictional. Is this a universal characteristic of legal speech? How can it be corrected or controlled?*
3. *What alternative to "the novelist's touch" is there for the writer who talks about others? Can you think of any passage of any literature that does "realize the profundities and complexities" of another's mind and experience? Any passage of legal literature that does so?*
4. *E. M. Forster addressed the matter of characterization in Aspects of the Novel, where he quotes the passage from Douglas you have just read. He distinguishes between "flat" and "round" characters, and says that while flat characters have no place in a biography, "for no human being is simple," they do serve certain useful purposes in the novel; but he goes on to say that the greater achievement in fiction is, of course, the round character.*

ASPECTS OF THE NOVEL*
E. M. Forster

[Here Forster discusses Jane Austen's *Mansfield Park*, of which Fanny is the heroine. Financially dependent upon her relatives, the Bertrams, she is their superior in every other way.]

So now let us desert these two-dimensional people, and by way of transition to the round, let us go to *Mansfield Park*, and look at Lady Bertram, sitting on her sofa with pug. Pug is flat, like most animals in fiction. He is once represented as straying into a rose-bed in a cardboard kind of way, but that is all, and during most of the book his mistress

* Chapter 4 (1927).

seems to be cut out of the same simple material as her dog. Lady Bertram's formula is, "I am kindly, but must not be fatigued," and she functions out of it. But at the end there is a catastrophe. Her two daughters come to grief — to the worst grief known to Miss Austen's universe, far worse than the Napoleonic wars. Julia elopes; Maria, who is unhappily married, runs off with a lover. What is Lady Bertram's reaction? The sentence describing it is significant: "Lady Bertram did not think deeply, but, guided by Sir Thomas, she thought justly on all important points, and she saw therefore in all its enormity, what had happened, and neither endeavoured herself, nor required Fanny to advise her, to think little of guilt and infamy." These are strong words, and they used to worry me because I thought Jane Austen's moral sense was getting out of hand. She may, and of course does, deprecate guilt and infamy herself, and she duly causes all possible distress in the minds of Edmund and Fanny, but has she any right to agitate calm, consistent Lady Bertram? Is not it like giving pug three faces and setting him to guard the gates of Hell? Ought not her ladyship to remain on the sofa saying, "This is a dreadful and sadly exhausting business about Julia and Maria, but where is Fanny gone? I have dropped another stitch"?

I used to think this, through misunderstanding Jane Austen's method — exactly as Scott misunderstood it when he congratulated her for painting on a square of ivory. She is a miniaturist, but never two-dimensional. All her characters are round, or capable of rotundity. Even Miss Bates has a mind, even Elizabeth Eliot a heart, and Lady Bertram's moral fervour ceases to vex us when we realize this: the disk has suddenly extended and become a little globe. When the novel is closed, Lady Bertram goes back to the flat, it is true; the dominant impression she leaves can be summed up in a formula. But that is not how Jane Austen conceived her, and the freshness of her reappearances are due to this. Why do the characters in Jane Austen give us a slightly new pleasure each time they come in, as opposed to the merely repetitive pleasure that is caused by a character in Dickens? Why do they combine so well in a conversation, and draw one another out without seeming to do so, and never perform? The answer to this question can be put in several ways: that, unlike Dickens, she was a real artist, that she never stooped to caricature, etc. But the best reply is that her characters though smaller than his are more highly organized. They function all round, and even if her plot made greater demands on them than it does, they would still be adequate. Suppose that Louisa Musgrove had broken her neck on the Cobb. The description of her death would have been feeble and ladylike — physical violence is quite beyond Miss Austen's powers — but the survivors would have reacted properly as soon as the corpse was carried away, they would have brought into view new sides of their character, and though *Persuasion* would have been spoiled as a book, we should know more than we do about Captain Wentworth and Anne. All the Jane Austen characters are ready for an extended life, for a life which the scheme of her books seldom requires them to lead, and that is why they lead their actual lives so satisfactorily.

QUESTIONS

1. *How effectively do Douglas and Forster, respectively, explain their conceptions of success and failure in the literary definition of character? Construct from each passage a set of directions for fair and lifelike characterization. Could these be followed by a judge or lawyer?*
2. *Forster goes on to say, "The test of a round character is whether it is capable of surprising in a convincing way." Do characters in legal literature ever surprise you? Do they ever convince you? Are they ever "ready for an extended life"? Or is it in fact one function of legal literature to "sum up" people and their experiences "in a formula"? This question invites you to examine actual cases and statutes and arguments, and to imagine ones you do not know.*
3. *Consider your reading of the law. Does the distinction between caricature and character, between flat characters and round ones, help explain the successes and failures you see? One might say, for example, that both the estate plan and the death penalty reduce a person to "two or three facets" selected for special purposes, yet you presumably evaluate those two literatures differently. If caricature is sometimes successful writing, when is it — under what circumstances or upon what understandings? Can you find any legal writing about people that presents not caricature but character?*
4. *Ask of the following passage whether it creates a literature of character or of caricature, and whether it is a success or a failure. Are these the same questions?*

THE HISTORY OF ENGLAND FROM THE ACCESSION OF JAMES II*

T. B. Macaulay

[Macaulay speaks here of Charles II, restored to the English throne in 1660 when Cromwell's Protectorate had ended and no other system of government was found to be workable.]

The restored king was at this time more loved by the people than any of his predecessors had ever been. The calamities of his house, the heroic death of his father, his own long sufferings and romantic adventures, made him an object of tender interest. His return had delivered the country from an intolerable bondage. Recalled by the voice of both the contending factions, he was the very man to arbitrate between them; and in some respects he was well qualified for the task. He had received from nature excellent parts and a happy temper. His education

* Chapter 2 (1848).

had been such as might have been expected to develop his understanding, and to form him to the practice of every public and private virtue. He had passed through all varieties of fortune, and had seen both sides of human nature. He had, while very young, been driven forth from a palace to a life of exile, penury, and danger. He had, at the age when the mind and body are in their highest perfection, and when the first effervescence of boyish passions should have subsided, been recalled from his wanderings to wear a crown. He had been taught by bitter experience how much baseness, perfidy, and ingratitude may lie hid under the obsequious demeanor of courtiers. He had found, on the other hand, in the huts of the poorest, true nobility of soul. When wealth was offered to any who would betray him, when death was denounced against all who should shelter him, cottagers and servingmen had kept his secret truly, and had kissed his hand under his mean disguises with as much reverence as if he had been seated on his ancestral throne. From such a school it might have been expected that a young man who wanted neither abilities nor amiable qualities would have come forth a great and good king. Charles came forth from that school with social habits, with polite and engaging manners, and with some talent for lively conversation, addicted beyond measure to sensual indulgence, fond of sauntering and of frivolous amusements, incapable of self-denial and of exertion, without faith in human virtue or in human attachment, without desire of renown, and without sensibility to reproach. According to him, every person was to be bought. But some people haggled more about their price than others; and when this haggling was very obstinate and very skillful, it was called by some fine name. The chief trick by which clever men kept up the price of their abilities was called integrity. The chief trick by which handsome women kept up the price of their beauty was called modesty. The love of God, the love of country, the love of family, the love of friends, were phrases of the same sort, delicate and convenient synonyms for the love of self. Thinking thus of mankind, Charles naturally cared very little what they thought of him. Honor and shame were scarcely more to him than light and darkness to the blind. His contempt of flattery has been highly commended, but seems, when viewed in connection with the rest of his character, to deserve no commendation. It is possible to be below flattery as well as above it. One who trusts nobody will not trust sycophants. One who does not value real glory will not value its counterfeit.

QUESTIONS

1. *Does Macaulay here "realize the profundities and complexities" of another's mind and experience, or does he "falsify life"? Whatever he does, how does he do it?*

2. *Do lawyers ever talk about people this way? Give a name to the language game in which Macaulay engages here.*
3. *Do you admire the mind expressed in this passage? Do you dare regard it as trivial?*
4. *The foregoing questions should make this one complicated: is this characterization a success or a failure?*
5. *Here is a question to ask at least of those writers like the biographer, the historian, and the lawyer who talk about real people in the real world, and which I suggest you ask of the preceding passage: can what he says possibly be true? Compare the following passage by the same author.*

NOTES ON THE INDIAN PENAL CODE*
T. B. Macaulay

We conceive the general rule to be, that nothing ought to be an offence by reason of any harm which it may cause to a person of ripe age who, undeceived, has given a free and intelligent consent to suffer that harm or to take the risk of that harm. The restrictions by which the rule is limited affect only cases where human life is concerned. Both the general rule and the restrictions may, we think, be easily vindicated.

If Z., a grown man, in possession of all his faculties, directs that his valuable furniture shall be burned, that his pictures shall be cut to rags, that his fine house shall be pulled down, that the best horses in his stable shall be shot, that his plate shall be thrown into the sea, those who obey his orders, however capricious those orders may be, however deeply Z. may afterwards regret that he gave them, ought not, as it seems to us, to be punished for injuring his property. Again, if Z. chooses to sell his teeth to a dentist, and permits the dentist to pull them out, the dentist ought not to be punished for injuring Z.'s person. So if Z. embraces the Mahomedan religion, and consents to undergo the painful rite which is the initiation into that religion, those who perform the rite ought not to be punished for injuring Z.'s person.

The reason on which the general rule which we have mentioned rests is this, that it is impossible to restrain men of mature age and sound understanding from destroying their own property, their own health, their own comfort, without restraining them from an infinite number of salutary or innocent actions.

QUESTIONS

1. *Here Macaulay writes about an imaginary person whom he calls Z. What sort of writing about people is this? Have you seen anything like it before? (Is it a paradigm of legal writing?)*
2. *Is this really writing about a person, or some other kind of writing?*

* "Note B: On the Chapter of General Exceptions," in *Works*, VII, 449 (1866).

3. *Would you say of one who behaved as Z did that he was in "possession of all his faculties"? Why did Macaulay say it then?*
4. *Suppose you rewrote his second paragraph to give a different sort of example of consent to risk or injury, an example which you could imagine happening. Does your account still justify the proposed rule? What is the relation between your example and the rule?*
5. *Is Macaulay's proposed rule better supported by his example or by his reason?*
6. *Compare here the statement in Miranda v. Arizona, 384 U.S. 436 (1966), that after the famous warnings have been given there can be no questioning of a suspect unless there is an "intelligent, knowing, and voluntary waiver" of his rights to counsel and silence. Could there possibly be such a waiver? Tell the story of one.*
7. *Do the following two short stories contain caricatures or characters? Are they failures or successes?*

THE TALKING-OUT OF TARRINGTON

H. H. Munro [Saki]

"Heavens!" exclaimed the aunt of Clovis, "here's some one I know bearing down on us. I can't remember his name, but he lunched with us once in Town. Tarrington — yes, that's it. He's heard of the picnic I'm giving for the Princess, and he'll cling to me like a lifebelt till I give him an invitation; then he'll ask if he may bring all his wives and mothers and sisters with him. That's the worst of these small watering-places; one can't escape from anybody."

"I'll fight a rearguard action for you if you like to do a bolt now," volunteered Clovis; "you've a clear ten yards start if you don't lose time."

The aunt of Clovis responded gamely to the suggestion, and churned away like a Nile steamer, with a long brown ripple of Pekingese spaniel trailing in her wake.

"Pretend you don't know him," was her parting advice, tinged with the reckless courage of the non-combatant.

The next moment the overtures of an affably disposed gentleman were being received by Clovis with a "silent-upon-a-peak-in-Darien" stare which denoted an absence of all previous acquaintance with the object scrutinized.

"I expect you don't know me with my moustache," said the newcomer; "I've only grown it during the last two months."

"On the contrary," said Clovis, "the moustache is the only thing about you that seemed familiar to me. I felt certain that I had met it somewhere before."

"My name is Tarrington," resumed the candidate for recognition.

"A very useful kind of name," said Clovis; "with a name of that sort no one would blame you if you did nothing in particular heroic or remarkable, would they? And yet if you were to raise a troop of light horse in a moment of national emergency, 'Tarrington's Light Horse' would sound quite appropriate and pulse-quickening; whereas if you were called Spoopin, for instance, the thing would be out of the question. No one, even in a moment of national emergency, could possibly belong to Spoopin's Horse."

The new-comer smiled weakly, as one who is not to be put off by mere flippancy, and began again with patient persistence:

"I think you ought to remember my name — "

"I shall," said Clovis, with an air of immense sincerity. "My aunt was asking me only this morning to suggest names for four young owls she's just had sent her as pets. I shall call them all Tarrington; then if one or two of them die or fly away, or leave us in any of the ways that pet owls are prone to, there will be always one or two left to carry on your name. And my aunt won't *let* me forget it; she will always be asking 'Have the Tarringtons had their mice?' and questions of that sort. She says if you keep wild creatures in captivity you ought to see after their wants, and of course she's quite right there."

"I met you at luncheon at your aunt's house once — "broke in Mr. Tarrington, pale but still resolute.

"My aunt never lunches," said Clovis; "she belongs to the National Anti-Luncheon League, which is doing quite a lot of good work in a quiet, unobtrusive way. A subscription of half a crown per quarter entitles you to go without ninety-two luncheons."

"This must be something new," exclaimed Tarrington.

"It's the same aunt that I've always had," said Clovis coldly.

"I perfectly well remember meeting you at a luncheon-party given by your aunt," persisted Tarrington, who was beginning to flush an unhealthy shade of mottled pink.

"What was there for lunch?" asked Clovis.

"Oh, well, I don't remember that — "

"How nice of you to remember my aunt when you can no longer recall the names of the things you ate. Now my memory works quite differently. I can remember a menu long after I've forgotten the hostess that accompanied it. When I was seven years old I recollect being given a peach at a garden-party by some Duchess or other; I can't remember a thing about her, except that I imagine our acquaintance must have been of the slightest, as she called me a 'nice little boy,' but I have unfading memories of that peach. It was one of those exuberant peaches that meet you halfway, so to speak, and are all over you in a moment. It was a beautiful unspoiled product of a hothouse, and yet it managed quite successfully to give itself the airs of a compote. You had to bite it and imbibe it at the same time. To me there has always been something charming and mystic in the thought of that delicate velvet globe of fruit, slowly ripening and warming to perfection through the long summer days and perfumed nights, and then coming suddenly athwart my life in the supreme moment of its existence. I can never forget it, even if I wished to. And when I had devoured all that was edible of it, there still remained the stone, which a heedless, thoughtless child would doubtless have thrown away; I put it down the neck of a young friend who was wearing a very *décolleté* sailor suit. I told him it was a scorpion, and from the way he wriggled and screamed he evidently believed it, though where the silly kid imagined I could procure a live scorpion at a garden-party I don't know. Altogether, that peach is for me an unfading and happy memory — "

The defeated Tarrington had by this time retreated out of ear-shot, comforting himself as best he might with the reflection that a picnic which included the presence of Clovis might prove a doubtfully agreeable experience.

"I shall certainly go in for a Parliamentary career," said Clovis to himself as he turned complacently to rejoin his aunt. "As a talker-out of inconvenient bills I should be invaluable."

THE OPEN WINDOW

H. H. Munro [Saki]

"My aunt will be down presently, Mr. Nuttel," said a very self-possessed young lady of fifteen; "in the meantime you must try and put up with me."

Framton Nuttel endeavoured to say the correct something which should duly flatter the niece of the moment without unduly discounting the aunt that was to come. Privately he doubted more than ever whether these formal visits on a succession of total strangers would do much towards helping the nerve cure which he was supposed to be undergoing.

"I know how it will be," his sister had said when he was preparing to migrate to this rural retreat; "you will bury yourself down there and not speak to a living soul, and your nerves will be worse than ever from moping. I shall just give you letters of introduction to all the people I know there. Some of them, as far as I can remember, were quite nice."

Framton wondered whether Mrs. Sappleton, the lady to whom he was presenting one of the letters of introduction, came into the nice division.

"Do you know many of the people round here?" asked the niece, when she judged that they had had sufficient silent communion.

"Hardly a soul," said Framton. "My sister was staying here, at the rectory, you know, some four years ago, and she gave me letters of introduction to some of the people here."

He made the last statement in a tone of distinct regret.

"Then you know practically nothing about my aunt?" pursued the self-possessed young lady.

"Only her name and address," admitted the caller. He was wondering whether Mrs. Sappleton was in the married or widowed state. An undefinable something about the room seemed to suggest masculine habitation.

"Her great tragedy happened just three years ago," said the child; "that would be since your sister's time."

"Her tragedy?" asked Framton; somehow in this restful country spot tragedies seemed out of place.

"You may wonder why we keep that window wide open on an October afternoon," said the niece, indicating a large French window that opened on to a lawn.

"It is quite warm for the time of the year," said Framton; "but has that window got anything to do with the tragedy?"

"Out through that window, three years ago to a day, her husband and her two young brothers went off for their day's shooting. They never came back. In crossing the moor to their favourite snipe-shooting ground they were all three engulfed in a treacherous piece of bog. It had been that dreadful wet summer, you know, and places that were safe in other years gave way suddenly without warning. Their bodies were never recovered. That was the dreadful part of it." Here the child's voice lost its self-possessed note and became falteringly human. "Poor aunt always thinks that they will come back some day, they and the little brown spaniel that was lost with them, and walk in at that window just as they used to do. That is why the window is kept open every evening till it is quite dusk. Poor dear aunt, she has often told me how they went out, her husband with his white waterproof coat over his arm, and Ronnie, her youngest brother, singing, 'Bertie, why do you bound?' as he always did to tease her, because she said it got on her nerves. Do you know, sometimes on still, quiet evenings like this, I almost get a creepy feeling that they will all walk in through that window —— "

She broke off with a little shudder. It was a relief to Framton when the aunt bustled into the room with a whirl of apologies for being late in making her appearance.

"I hope Vera has been amusing you?" she said.

"She has been very interesting," said Framton.

"I hope you don't mind the open window," said Mrs. Sappleton briskly; "my husband and brothers will be home directly from shooting, and they always come in this way. They've been out for snipe in the marshes today, so they'll make a fine mess over my poor carpets. So like you men-folk, isn't it?"

She rattled on cheerfully about the shooting and the scarcity of birds, and the prospects for duck in the winter. To Framton it was all purely horrible. He made a desperate but only partially successful effort to turn the talk on to a less ghastly topic; he was conscious that his hostess was giving him only a fragment of her attention, and her eyes were constantly straying past him to the open window and the lawn beyond. It was certainly an unfortunate coincidence that he should have paid his visit on this tragic anniversary.

"The doctors agree in ordering me complete rest, an absence of mental excitement, and avoidance of anything in the nature of violent physical exercise," announced Framton, who laboured under the tolerably wide-spread delusion that total strangers and chance acquaintances are hungry for the least detail of one's ailments and infirmities, their cause and cure. "On the matter of diet they are not so much in agreement," he continued.

"No?" said Mrs. Sappleton, in a voice which only replaced a yawn at the last moment. Then she suddenly brightened into alert attention — but not to what Framton was saying.

"Here they are at last!" she cried. "Just in time for tea, and don't they look as if they were muddy up to the eyes!"

Framton shivered slightly and turned towards the niece with a look intended to convey sympathetic comprehension. The child was staring out through the open window with dazed horror in her eyes. In a chill shock of nameless fear Framton swung round in his seat and looked in the same direction.

In the deepening twilight three figures were walking across the lawn towards the window; they all carried guns under their arms, and one of them was additionally burdened with a white coat hung over his shoulders. A tired brown spaniel kept close at their heels. Noiselessly they neared the house, and then a hoarse young voice chanted out of the dusk: "I said, Bertie, why do you bound?"

Framton grabbed wildly at his stick and hat; the hall-door, the gravel-drive, and the front gate were dimly noted stages in his headlong retreat. A cyclist coming along the road had to run into the hedge to avoid imminent collision.

"Here we are, my dear," said the bearer of the white mackintosh, coming in through the window; "fairly muddy, but most of it's dry. Who was that who bolted out as we came up?"

"A most extraordinary man, a Mr. Nuttel," said Mrs. Sappleton; "could only talk about his illnesses, and dashed off without a word of good-bye or apology when you arrived. One would think he had seen a ghost."

"I expect it was the spaniel," said the niece calmly; "he told me he had a horror of dogs. He was once hunted into a cemetery somewhere on the banks of the Ganges by a pack of pariah dogs, and had to spend the night in a newly dug grave with the creatures snarling and grinning and foaming just above him. Enough to make any one lose their nerve."

Romance at short notice was her speciality.

QUESTIONS

1. *Are Clovis, Vera, and the others caricatures or characters? Why do you say so? Are they capable of "surprising in a convincing way"? Certainly you would not say that they are true to life, but you would probably not want to call this literature a failure either. How do you explain this circumstance, and has your explanation any lesson for the law?*
2. *What would you say to someone who, upon reading these stories and finding them delightful, behaved at the next opportunity in the manner of Clovis or Vera? What would such a person not understand? Imagine how you would explain such behavior to your four-year-old child.*
3. *You may think that Saki's way of talking about others has nothing to do with the law and the way it talks. Compare the following passage, which gives an actual example (of sorts) of the law talking.*

LAWYERS AT PLAY*
Timothy Hilton

Here is an instructive story:

Henry occupies an unfurnished flat in Herbert's house. Herbert serves on Henry an invalid note to quit and when Henry refuses to go Herbert decides to eject him by force. He approaches Henry's front door in the company of a private detective and begins to break it down with a pickaxe, whereupon Henry shoots him with a revolver, intending to incapacitate him. The detective then puts his hand inside his overcoat and Henry, thinking that the detective is about to draw on him, aims a second shot at the detective but this time he misses. Gangrene sets in in Herbert's foot and a few months later he dies. What offence or offences, if any, has Henry committed?

If Henry doesn't know he will no doubt find out about the exact significance of his behaviour from someone who has been trained in the law and taken the Council for Legal Education's exams, from which papers I have taken this pugnacious vignette. A collection of the questions set

* *New Statesman* (London), Jan. 26, 1968, at 117.

in the last few years makes disturbing reading: the above is actually a mild example of the things that people get up to in this particular world. It all takes place in a region variously referred to as Ruritania, Urbania, Imperia and, be it noted, *Proletania.* With weird consistency a mad dystopia is created, whose citizens are exclusively involved in horrible crimes and complex litigation. The names, *Volpone*-like, narrow character to some quintessentially lawless quality. We have Messrs Shady, Lustful, Lusty and Playboy. Mr Lightfingers cashes bad cheques under the assumed name of Goldbags. The ladies are Miss Flighty or Miss Tattle. A "musical group" known as the Scorpions is involved with a critic called Scathing. These citizens keep pet jackals. They argue violently with the proprietors of Indian restaurants. They impersonate world-famous conjurors. "By way of a joke," they are given to releasing their neighbours' horses at dead of night. They are often the worse for drink. They are usually armed, but often with such objects as bicycle pumps, which might or might not be construed as dangerous weapons. At football matches, the stands always collapse beneath them. Whenever possible, they leave their money via invalid and hotly contested wills to lunatic illegitimate daughters. Watching other citizens fighting, they exhort them to greater efforts with stilted old-fashioned phrases like "Go to it, lads!" People invited to dinner are shown sketch maps of how to get to the rendezvous which lead them to drive over ravines. Public services are untrustworthy, all transport uninsured. The man reading the electricity is in reality an undischarged bankrupt. "Dr Jekyll" has sexual intercourse with a woman patient with her consent under the pretence that he is performing a surgical operation which will cure her of whooping cough ("has he committed an offence?"). Careful of that seemingly friendly neighbour; really he is intent on planting a grove of fast-growing Lombardy poplars in your front garden. Can this be a microcosm of society, or just the brilliant imagination of some grave gentleman in the Inns of Court? One would like to think that these putative situations do really mirror that certain waywardness, crankiness, often detected on the frontiers where cold legislation has to deal with unstoppable human oddity—and were the surrealists so wrong to think that England might be a spiritual home from home?

QUESTIONS

1. *In what ways is a law school exam like a story by Saki?*
2. *The characters in this and other law school exams are caricatures by any measure. Is this nevertheless a successful literature? If so, why, on what understanding?*
3. *One response is to say that because neither the examination nor the Saki story is about real people, caricature is perfectly appropriate. Something like this is what Norman Douglas would presumably say. Saki pretends*

to talk about real people, but we know he is talking directly to us about our social expectations. The law school exam pretends to be about the lives of real people, but we know it is really about the casebook and lectures and work that was done during the term.

a. *If the law school exam indeed presents only a pretended problem, an intellectual exercise, this has severe consequences for the quality of legal education. Surely we should not continue to give examinations of this unrealistic kind. What kind of examinations should we give? Give an example.*
b. *In any event, this justification of the examination — that it is all make-believe — is no defense of the use of caricature in actual legal talk about real people. Can you identify in some legal literature any real talk about real people in the real world — a kind of literature demonstrably different from the examination — or is the law always "at play"? To put it in terms of the New Statesman article, is the law incurably surrealistic? At whose expense? Think here of the estate plan; the Georgetown Hospital case; the wrongful death statute; and the complaint (all found in Chapter 2).*

4. *How do you describe and judge the character-writing in the following passage?*

MIRANDA v. ARIZONA
384 U.S. 436, 448 (1966)

WARREN, C.J. . . . Interrogation still takes place in privacy. Privacy results in secrecy and this in turn results in a gap in our knowledge as to what in fact goes on in the interrogation rooms. A valuable source of information about present police practices, however, may be found in various police manuals and texts which document procedures employed with success in the past, and which recommend various other effective tactics. These texts are used by law enforcement agencies themselves as guides. It should be noted that these texts professedly present the most enlightened and effective means presently used to obtain statements through custodial interrogation. By considering these texts and other data, it is possible to describe procedures observed and noted around the country.

The officers are told by the manuals that the "principal psychological factor contributing to a successful interrogation is *privacy* — being alone with the person under interrogation." The efficacy of this tactic has been explained as follows:

> If at all practicable, the interrogation should take place in the investigator's office or at least in a room of his own choice. The subject should be deprived of every psychological advantage. In his own home he may be confident, indignant, or recalcitrant. He is more keenly aware of his rights and more reluctant to tell of his indiscretions or criminal behavior within the walls of his home. Moreover his family and other friends

are nearby, their presence lending moral support. In his own office, the investigator possesses all the advantages. The atmosphere suggests the invincibility of the forces of the law.

To highlight the isolation and unfamiliar surroundings, the manuals instruct the police to display an air of confidence in the suspect's guilt and from outward appearance to maintain only an interest in confirming certain details. The guilt of the subject is to be posited as a fact. The interrogator should direct his comments toward the reasons why the subject committed the act, rather than court failure by asking the subject whether he did it. Like other men, perhaps the subject has had a bad family life, had an unhappy childhood, had too much to drink, had an unrequited desire for women. The officers are instructed to minimize the moral seriousness of the offense, to cast blame on the victim or on society. These tactics are designed to put the subject in a psychological state where his story is but an elaboration of what the police purport to know already — that he is guilty. Explanations to the contrary are dismissed and discouraged. . . .

The manuals suggest that the suspect be offered legal excuses for his actions in order to obtain an initial admission of guilt. Where there is a suspected revenge-killing, for example, the interrogator may say:

> Joe, you probably didn't go out looking for this fellow with the purpose of shooting him. My guess is, however, that you expected something from him and that's why you carried a gun — for your own protection. You knew him for what he was, no good. Then when you met him he probably started using foul, abusive language and he gave some indication that he was about to pull a gun on you, and that's when you had to act to save your own life. That's about it, isn't it, Joe?

Having then obtained the admission of shooting, the interrogator is advised to refer to circumstantial evidence which negates the self-defense explanation. This should enable him to secure the entire story. One text notes that "Even if he fails to do so, the inconsistency between the subject's original denial of the shooting and his present admission of at least doing the shooting will serve to deprive him of a self-defense 'out' at the time of trial."

When the techniques described above prove unavailing, the texts recommend they be alternated with a show of some hostility. One ploy often used has been termed the "friendly-unfriendly" or the "Mutt and Jeff" act:

> . . . In this technique, two agents are employed. Mutt, the relentless investigator, who knows the subject is guilty and is not going to waste any

time. He's sent a dozen men away for this crime and he's going to send the subject away for the full term. Jeff, on the other hand, is obviously a kindhearted man. He has a family himself. He has a brother who was involved in a little scrape like this. He disapproves of Mutt and his tactics and will arrange to get him off the case if the subject will cooperate. He can't hold Mutt off for very long. The subject would be wise to make a quick decision. The technique is applied by having both investigators present while Mutt acts out his role. Jeff may stand by quietly and demur at some of Mutt's tactics. When Jeff makes his plea for cooperation, Mutt is not present in the room.

The manuals also contain instructions for police on how to handle the individual who refuses to discuss the matter entirely, or who asks for an attorney or relatives. The examiner is to concede him the right to remain silent. "This usually has a very undermining effect. First of all, he is disappointed in his expectation of an unfavorable reaction on the part of the interrogator. Secondly, a concession of this right to remain silent impresses the subject with the apparent fairness of his interrogator." After this psychological conditioning, however, the officer is told to point out the incriminating significance of the suspect's refusal to talk:

Joe, you have a right to remain silent. That's your privilege and I'm the last person in the world who'll try to take it away from you. If that's the way you want to leave this, O.K. But let me ask you this. Suppose you were in my shoes and I were in yours and you called me in to ask me about this and I told you, "I don't want to answer any of your questions." You'd think I had something to hide, and you'd probably be right in thinking that. That's exactly what I'll have to think about you, and so will everybody else. So let's sit here and talk this whole thing over.

Few will persist in their initial refusal to talk, it is said, if this monologue is employed correctly. . . .

From these representative samples of interrogation techniques, the setting prescribed by the manuals and observed in practice becomes clear. In essence, it is this: To be alone with the subject is essential to prevent distraction and to deprive him of any outside support. The aura of confidence in his guilt undermines his will to resist. He merely confirms the preconceived story the police seek to have him describe. Patience and persistence, at times relentless questioning, are employed. To obtain a confession, the interrogator must "patiently maneuver himself or his quarry into a position from which the desired objective may be attained." When normal procedures fail to produce the needed result, the police may resort to deceptive stratagems such as giving false legal advice. It is important to keep the subject off balance, for example, by trading on his insecurity about himself or his surroundings. The police then persuade, trick, or cajole him out of exercising his constitutional rights.

QUESTIONS

1. *This account of interrogation practices presents both the policeman and the suspect as caricatures. Draft an account of a single real or imaginary interrogation in which you express them as characters, not caricatures. How does your account differ from this one?*
2. *Can this use of caricature by the Supreme Court be justified in any way? Or is it perhaps someone else who is responsible for this use of caricature? (If the Court was presented with a literature of caricature written by someone else, what should it have done with it?)*
3. *Assuming that this account of common police practices is or could be true, of what conceivable relevance is it to the decision of a particular case? Is not the proper inquiry in this case what happened in Miranda's interrogation, and not what happens elsewhere? If the Court had engaged in that inquiry, do you think it less likely that it would have produced a literature of caricature?*
4. *Notice that question three can be recast this way: why does the Court feel obliged to make a legislative rule (requiring the warnings in every case) based upon an assessment of general probabilities, instead of deciding the particular case under general constitutional principles? Implicit here is a suggestion that to speak as a legislator – or to speak in rules – is to create caricature, not character. Can the judge generally speak otherwise? If so, how and why?*
5. *The materials given above raise the suggestion that what we call caricature may be appropriate to certain forms of literature – Saki stories, examinations – which everyone knows are not about people at all, and are quite inappropriate in any literature about the real world, such as history, a judicial opinion, or the death penalty. Caricature falsifies life and should not be used to describe it.*

   But is caricature always false, or does it sometimes tell the truth about people? The literature of protest against social exploitation, for example, frequently claims that people can actually be turned into caricatures – perhaps into human machines in the factory or in the data-processing center, perhaps into bosses or salesmen identifiable solely by their institutional roles – by the forces of an inhumane and materialistic society. Caricature is seen as a serious real-life threat to the human personality. Is it a danger of this sort with which Miranda was (or should have been) concerned? Compare H. Marcuse, One-Dimensional Man (1964); Charles Dickens, Hard Times for These Times (1854); J. Ruskin, Unto This Last (1862). Erving Goffman, in Asylums (1961), describes in a most painstaking and credible way the process by which inmates at total institutions – prisons, hospitals, boarding schools, convents, armies, mental hospitals, and the like – are each stripped of his own identity and given instead a role in a system, a place in a routine, a new institutional identity that could only be expressed as caricature. The personality of the inmate can indeed be "summed up in a formula." Caricature here falsifies not what life is but what it should be. Another example follows.

LITTLE DORRIT*
Charles Dickens

"You and me," said the turnkey, one snowy winter's night when the lodge, with a bright fire in it, was pretty full of company, "is the oldest inhabitants. I wasn't here myself, above seven year before you. I shan't last long. When I'm off the lock for good and all, you'll be the Father of the Marshalsea."

The turnkey went off the lock of this world, next day. His words were remembered and repeated; and tradition afterwards handed down from generation to generation — a Marshalsea generation might be calculated as about three months — that the shabby old debtor with the soft manner and the white hair, was the Father of the Marshalsea.

And he grew to be proud of the title. If any impostor had arisen to claim it, he would have shed tears in resentment of the attempt to deprive him of his rights. A disposition began to be perceived in him, to exaggerate the number of years he had been there; it was generally understood that you must deduct a few from his account; he was vain, the fleeting generations of debtors said.

All new-comers were presented to him. He was punctilious in the exaction of this ceremony. The wits would perform the office of introduction with overcharged pomp and politeness, but they could not easily overstep his sense of its gravity. He received them in his poor room (he disliked an introduction in the mere yard, as informal — a thing that might happen to anybody), with a kind of bowed-down beneficence. They were welcome to the Marshalsea, he would tell them. Yes, he was the Father of the place. So the world was kind enough to call him; and so he was, if more than twenty years of residence gave him a claim to the title. It looked small at first, but there was very good company there — among a mixture — necessarily a mixture — and very good air.

It became a not unusual circumstance for letters to be put under his door at night, inclosing half-a-crown, two half-crowns, now and then at long intervals even half-a-sovereign, for the Father of the Marshalsea. "With the compliments of a collegian taking leave." He received the

* Volume 1, Chapter 6 (1857).

gifts as tributes, from admirers, to a public character. Sometimes these correspondents assumed facetious names, as the Brick, Bellows, Old Gooseberry, Wideawake, Snooks, Mops, Cutaway, the Dogs-meat Man; but he considered this in bad taste, and was always a little hurt by it.

In the fulness of time, this correspondence showing signs of wearing out, and seeming to require an effort on the part of the correspondents to which in the hurried circumstances of departure many of them might not be equal, he established the custom of attending collegians of a certain standing, to the gate, and taking leave of them there. The collegian under treatment, after shaking hands, would occasionally stop to wrap up something in a bit of paper, and would come back again calling "Hi!"

He would look round surprised. "Me?" he would say, with a smile.

By this time the collegian would be up with him, and he would paternally add, "What have you forgotten? What can I do for you?"

"I forgot to leave this," the collegian would usually return, "for the Father of the Marshalsea."

"My good sir," he would rejoin, "he is infinitely obliged to you." But, to the last, the irresolute hand of old would remain in the pocket into which he had slipped the money, during two or three turns about the yard, lest the transaction should be too conspicuous to the general body of collegians.

QUESTIONS

1. *Here Dickens sums up the process by which a person becomes reduced to a role, a set of habitual responses, a partial person who denies most of his own knowledge of life and of himself. The rest of the novel complicates and expands the reader's sense of this process: Dorrit inherits a vast sum and leaves the Marshalsea, but he does not leave behind his false pride, his fantastic pretentiousness and self-deception, his ability to obliterate portions of his experience he dislikes; and he finds that the status-conscious world of the middle classes in which he then lives is as much a prison as the Marshalsea. As he travels through the world, we see that other prisons work on other people with similar effect: the world of high finance; the expatriate society of Venice; the convent of St. Bernard; the Circumlocution Office; the house of an old lady consumed by hate; and so on. Caricature is the expression of a threat to the self, to the springs of life; it is one of the great facts of the real world as Dickens imagines it.*
2. *Look now at the world around you. Do you know any people who seem to be subject to pressures to become caricatures? Do you know any lawyers of whom this is true? Draft a fair but comic caricature of a modern lawyer. Does it state a genuine threat?*
3. *What is there in the life of the lawyer that tends to make him a caricature?*

THE APPLE FALLS CLOSE TO THE TREE*

James Dempsey

Now, as to children. It seems to me that there is a very definite approach because the hardest thing in the world is to establish the value of the life of a child to a bereaved family. A two year old child; five year old child; ten or twelve year old child — the jury is supposed to assess pecuniary damages when they know, of course, that at that age the child is a financial liability.

So, I suggest this kind of an approach. "There is an old saying — and bear in mind that you cannot see, you never have seen and you never will see this child. The law forbids me to introduce into evidence the photograph of this child. Yet, you are called upon to find damages for the loss of this child, who to you is an unknown individual. The old saying is this, 'the apple falls close to the tree.' What does that mean? You have seen the mother; you have seen the father and although you will never see this child, by seeing the mother and the father you can get some estimate of the blood that was in this child's veins before the child died.

"There are people who put their money in the bank; there are people who put their money into property; into stocks, into bonds; but there are other people who put their money into their children. Their savings, the results of their sacrifice, the result of their every living thought, they put that into their children. Not that they expect ever to get anything back from their children, not that they are concerned with money received but because they are their children.

"In the early morning of life from the time that the child gets out of the crib and first begins his faltering steps across the floor, from the time the child rises from the crib and endeavors to walk, whose strong sustaining hand lifts that child to its feet and helps the child across the living room floor? The hand of the father, the hand of the mother, that is the strong hand, the hand of the parents that starts the child out in the pathway of life. But as life goes on, the morning sun goes to sunset, and at that time in life, the father, the mother has come to the evening tide of their days and at that point, when the steps of the father and the mother are faltering and heavy, what hand goes out to help them? The hand of that child, grown to manhood, at the time the parents need the help of the child, the hand of that child is there.

"Well, these parents will not have that hand. It is up to you to decide. You must realize that in the days of their extremity they will not have the help of this boy whose life has been lost at this tragic time."

* In M. Block, *The Art of Summation* 101–102 (1963).

QUESTIONS

1. *The child and his parents in this story are "flat" characters indeed, and one could easily say of this argument that it "falsifies life." A novel built out of this material would not have much interest for you.*
   a. *Is this sort of argument good advocacy nonetheless?*
   b. *Is it conceivable that this argument could have been made in a way that recognized the "complexities and profundities" of the experience of the individual people whose lives it concerned? Draft such an argument. Is that an example of good advocacy?*
2. *Notice that this argument can be used in nearly every death-of-a-child case, that it is a form much as the will is a form. Is it this quality of legal speech that is responsible for its use of caricature?*
3. *Look at this speech as a lawyer: what difficulty was the lawyer trying to meet in this argument? How did he attempt to do so, and how do you evaluate his attempt? Is this successful writing?*
4. *Now look at the speech as a reader of literature: how does the lawyer define himself in the way he talks here, what sort of mind and personality does he express? How would you argue in the situation he describes, and how would your argument define you?*

   Is the activity of engaging in this sort of speech likely to have any enduring effect on the speaker himself — on how he speaks and acts at other moments, in other relationships — or is this a voice one can turn on and off at will? Imagine how the lawyer might speak about this child's death with his law partner; with the lawyer on the other side; with his wife; with the child's parents.
5. *In the following passage you see two lawyers at work. How do you evaluate the creation or rendition of character in which they engage?*

PEOPLE v. HANEY*

Opening Statement on Behalf of the People

Mr. Miller: If the Court please.

The Court: Mr. Miller.

Mr. Miller: Ladies and gentlemen of the jury: It now becomes my duty as prosecutor on behalf of the People to make what is known as an Opening Statement.

In this case, as in all criminal cases in Michigan, there has been an Information drawn up. I have in my hand what is known as a General Information, drawn up by the Prosecutor of the County of Wayne, which is in effect the same thing as an indictment. I am not going to read it to you now because the Court will read it to you and it is rather

* Aug. 24, 1959. Printed in H. Norris, *Casebook of Complete Criminal Trials* 13 (1965).

lengthy. But in this indictment the elements are set up, the elements in this case being common law rape; that is, the Defendant is charged with having carnal knowledge of this woman by force and against her will. I want you to listen carefully to the testimony as it comes from the witness stand because you will have to make a determination as to whether or not this crime occurred and whether or not the elements contained in that Information have all been proven by the People.

To be more specific the People claim and will offer testimony from the witness stand to prove that on Saturday, January 31, 1959, at approximately five-fifty P.M., the complainant, Nancy Boytor, left her place of employment and —

OFFICER BOYTOR: Mr. Miller, I am not the complainant; Mrs. Jones is the complainant.

MR. MILLER: Oh, I am sorry. I mean the complainant Mary Jones. I am sorry. Nancy Boytor is the policewoman. I am sorry.

The complainant, Mrs. Jones, left her place of employment at the Wrigley Super Market store on Joy and Mendota. She will testify that she made a left turn on Joy, from Mendota, and was driving West between Meyers and Schaefer when this defendant, Clarence Tom Haney, pulled alongside of her and motioned her to the curb.

He parked behind her and came up to her and told her he was a police officer, off duty and that she should get a ticket. She apologized for what she might have done and drove on. Now remember, this was a complete stranger, this woman, to the defendant. They didn't know each other.

At the intersection of Westwood and Meyers, I believe — anyway, it was still in the City of Detroit — she was driving on Meyers and came to the vicinity of Westwood and he then forced her over again to the curb and came up to her car. He told her that she had ran [*sic*] an amber light and that he wanted to see her driver's license and so forth. He said he was going to give her a ticket. He sat in his car at first and she in hers, as you have seen many times police officers do when they pull somebody over to give them a ticket.

After a few minutes he rolled the window down and had her come back, asked her to come back to his car. He then told her to get in, while he finished writing the ticket. Believing this was a police officer writing her a ticket she sat down in his car and left the door open, but he slammed the door shut. Then he asked her some more questions about her marital status, how many children, and so forth, and told her that he would have to take her into the Schaefer Station.

Testimony will show then that he drove a few blocks and parked, told her she could get ten days for running a light, an amber light. Then he told her his name was "Officer Parker" or "Officer Barker," something of that nature. Then there was some more conversation about the ticket. He started the motor up then and drove east and again north and parked somewhere — she will testify between the National Biscuit Company and the Ditzler Color Division, which is on Fitzpatrick, east of Warren. Now some of you west-siders will be familiar with that neighborhood. But that is where the testimony will show that this act took place.

The testimony will also show that while parked in this car he pushed her down in the seat, used force on her. She began to cry. She raised her head, tried to get away from him. He grabbed her and pushed her down in the seat, and first he committed an act of oral perversion on her body. Then still holding on to her, still using force, he took sufficient of her clothing off and his clothing off that he could have an act of sexual intercourse with her, which he did, all the time holding her, threatening her, frightening her, and doing this against her will.

Now, without going into further minute details, which will be brought out in the testimony, she went home and thought about this all night, worried about it, and told her husband the following morning. After telling her husband about it they went to the police.

Now, those roughly are the facts of what the People will show in this case, and again I want to ask you to listen carefully to the testimony as it comes from the witness stand and be governed by that, and by that alone. Thank you.

Opening Statement on Behalf of the Defendant

Mr. Smith: May it please the Court, ladies and gentlemen of the jury, you have just heard Mr. Miller outline to you the People's theory of these facts in this case. The Defense also has a theory, different considerably from that given to you by Mr. Miller, which is the reason we are here today. Substantially, though, Mr. Miller outlined the facts to you which at least in their incidence are substantially true. Just what happened between Clarence Tom Haney and Mary Jones, who will appear on the witness stand shortly as a witness, — what happened between them in this automobile on this particular night, is where the questions arise.

We acknowledge the fact that the two of them did happen to meet as each were driving their own vehicles west on Joy Road. They stopped once and conversed. Some two and a half miles further west there was a second time when they stopped and conversed. They wound up around the corner. She wound up in his car, and wound up in the dark parking lot, and then what happened is a matter of two different stories told by two different people.

We will introduce, ladies and gentlemen of the jury, evidence showing the character of this defendant. We will introduce evidence showing our theory of the case. That this man did not use any force and violence in having intercourse with this woman. That he had intercourse with her we will admit; but whether there was force and violence we will emphatically deny.

We will deny, further, that there was any misrepresentation in this. He was identified, the defendant, and is in this court standing trial. He did not misrepresent his identity to the extent that he could not be located on very short notice.

We will show, too, that a woman who has a panty-girdle on in the winter months and the weather cold enough to require a continuity of clothing to keep warm, in an automobile, in the front seat of an automobile, can not be so easy a victim to a man's advances unless she of course had some inclination along his line of thinking.

But, again, as Mr. Miller said, this is what you are here to listen to. You will be the sole judges of the facts. It will be for you to determine whose story is to receive the greatest credence.

QUESTIONS

1. *Are the characters in either argument "round"? Are they made "round" by the juxtaposition of two "flat" passages?*
2. *Might caricature have been avoided in these arguments? Draft a descriptive or narrative passage (not an argument) giving an account of this event in which you do not reduce the people to caricatures, to the sort of formal cliche you see here, but do justice to their experience as you imagine it. Feel free to add whatever facts and flavor you wish. Can you make the characters round? Why do you suppose the lawyers did not do so?*
   a. *Now put your account in the form of an argument. Is this a good argument? (Does it depend which side you represent?)*
   b. *Assuming that the full account you have given of these events is a true one, how would you make an opening statement as lawyer for the prosecution? For the defense?*
3. *How and to whom are these characters made "round," if at all, during this trial?*
4. *You can take the preceding three passages as defining a danger for the writer of caricature, and a serious one it is. But look again at the Saki stories, and ask how he defines himself in what he writes. Can a writer make and use a literature of caricature without becoming one himself? How can he do so?*
5. *Do you expect characters to be more — or less — "round" in a judicial opinion than in an argument? Why? By what art are they made round?*

HOFFA v. UNITED STATES
385 U.S. 293, 317 (1967)

WARREN, C.J., (dissenting): . . . But I consider both *Lewis* and *Osborn* to be materially, even fundamentally, different from this *Hoffa* case. Here, Edward Partin, a jailbird languishing in a Louisiana jail under indictments for such state and federal crimes as embezzlement, kidnapping, and manslaughter (and soon to be charged with perjury and assault), contacted federal authorities and told them he was willing to become, and would be useful as, an informer against Hoffa who was then about to be tried in the Test Fleet case. A motive for his doing this is immediately apparent — namely, his strong desire to work his way out of jail and out of his various legal entanglements with the State and Federal Governments. And it is interesting to note that, if this was his motive, he has been uniquely successful in satisfying it. In the four years since he first volunteered to be an informer against Hoffa he has not been prosecuted on any of the serious federal charges for which he was at that time jailed, and the state charges have apparently vanished into thin air.

Shortly after Partin made contact with the federal authorities and told them of his position in the Baton Rouge Local of the Teamsters Union and of his acquaintance with Hoffa, his bail was suddenly reduced from $50,000 to $5,000 and he was released from jail. He immediately telephoned Hoffa, who was then in New Jersey, and, by collaborating with a state law enforcement official, surreptitiously made a tape recording of the conversation. A copy of the recording was furnished to federal authorities. Again on a pretext of wanting to talk with Hoffa regarding Partin's legal difficulties, Partin telephoned Hoffa a few weeks later and succeeded in making a date to meet in Nashville where Hoffa and his attorneys were then preparing for the Test Fleet trial. Unknown to Hoffa, this call was also recorded and again federal authorities were informed as to the details.

Upon his arrival in Nashville, Partin manifested his "friendship" and made himself useful to Hoffa, thereby worming his way into Hoffa's hotel suite and becoming part and parcel of Hoffa's entourage. As the "faithful" servant and factotum of the defense camp which he became, he was in a position to overhear conversations not directed to him, many of which were between attorneys and either their client or prospective defense witnesses. Pursuant to the general instructions he received from federal authorities to report "any attempts at witness intimidation or tampering with the jury," "anything illegal," or even "anything of interest," Partin became the equivalent of a bugging device which moved with Hoffa wherever he went. Everything Partin saw or heard was reported to federal authorities and much of it was ultimately the subject matter of his testimony in this case. For his services he was well paid by the Government, both through devious and secret support payments to his wife and, it may be inferred, by executed promises not to pursue the indictments under which he was charged at the time he became an informer. . . .

I do not say that the Government may never use as a witness a person of dubious or even bad character. In performing its duty to prosecute crime the Government must take the witnesses as it finds them. They may be persons of good, bad, or doubtful credibility, but their testimony may be the only way to establish the facts, leaving it to the jury to determine their credibility. In this case, however, we have a totally different situation. Here the Government reaches into the jailhouse to employ a man who was himself facing indictments far more serious (and later including one for perjury) than the one confronting the man against whom he offered to inform. It employed him not for the purpose of testifying to something that had already happened, but rather for the purpose of infiltration to see if crimes would in the future be committed. The Government in its zeal even assisted him in gaining a position from which he could be a witness to the confidential relationship of attorney and client engaged in the preparation of a criminal defense. And, for the dubious evidence thus obtained, the Government paid an enormous price. Certainly if a criminal defendant insinuated his informer into the prosecution's camp in this manner he would be guilty of obstructing justice. I cannot agree that what happened in this case is in keeping with the standards of justice in our federal system and I must, therefore, dissent.

QUESTIONS

1. *How else might this story have been told? Draft possible versions (a) by a prosecutor and (b) by another judge.*
2. *Can we connect the reading we have done on caricature with our work on the death penalty and say that the use of caricature entails an essential and corrupting inhumanity, for it teaches us that others are not to be spoken of as people?*
   a. *If caricature has this implication, how can it be used — as it must, by lawyers, all the time — yet somehow controlled?*
   b. *What ways for talking about people other than by caricature can be found or devised?*
3. *The readings and questions given above set up several lines of questioning which the rest of Section A will pursue in a rather more leisurely way. But first, an example of caricature that may sum things up for you:*

THE PRAISE OF CHIMNEY-SWEEPERS*

Charles Lamb

I like to meet a sweep; understand me, — not a grown sweeper, (old chimney-sweepers are by no means attractive,) but one of those tender novices, blooming through their first nigritude, the maternal washings not quite effaced from the cheek: such as come forth with the dawn, or somewhat earlier, with their little professional notes sounding like the *peep peep* of a young sparrow; or liker to the matin lark should I pronounce them, in their aërial ascents not seldom anticipating the sunrise? I have a kindly yearning toward these dim specks — poor blots — innocent blacknesses.

I reverence these young Africans of our own growth, — these almost clergy imps, who sport their cloth without assumption; and from their little pulpits, (the tops of chimneys,) in the nipping air of a December morning, preach a lesson of patience to mankind.

When a child, what a mysterious pleasure it was to witness their operation! to see a chit no bigger than one's-self, enter, one knew not by what process, into what seemed the *fauces Averni,* — to pursue him in imagination, as he went sounding on through so many dark stifling caverns, horrid shades! — to shudder with the idea that "now, surely, he must be lost for ever!" — to revive at hearing his feeble shout of discovered day-light — and then (O fulness of delight!) running out of doors, to come just in time to see the sable phenomenon emerge in safety, the brandished weapon of his art victorious like some flag waved over a conquered citadel! I seem to remember having been told that a bad sweep was once left in a stack with his brush, to indicate which way the wind blew. It was an awful spectacle certainly; not much unlike the old stage direction in Macbeth, where the "Apparition of a child crowned, with a tree in his hand, rises."

Reader, if thou meetest one of these small gentry in thy early rambles, it is good to give him a penny. It is better to give him twopence. If it be starving weather, and to the proper troubles of his hard occupation a pair of kibed heels (no unusual accompaniment) be superadded, the demand on thy humanity will surely rise to a tester.

b. The "Alcestis" of Euripides — A Play About Character and Caricature

You are asked now to read Euripides' *Alcestis,* a play that can be said to be about the subject of this chapter: how to talk and think about people. Its structure is based upon two distinctly different ways of creat-

* From *Essays of Elia* (1823).

ing character in drama — one of which is startlingly like legal speech — which the play contrasts and compares, exposing the consequences of each way of talking.

You remember the plot: when Admetus' time for death has come, his wife, Alcestis, agrees to die in his stead — an arrangement made possible by the intervention of Apollo in return for a favor once done him by Admetus — and is herself rescued by Heracles, who wrestles her away from Death.

This is not an easy play, and most readers have found it frustrating. There are marvelous moments, but the pieces of the play do not fit easily together into an intelligible and organized whole. It is hard to explain much of what we see. What sort of characters are Death and Apollo, for example, with whom the play begins? How are we supposed to take the business of Heracles wrestling with Death: as a joke, a miracle, or what? Is this a realistic or unrealistic world? What sort of relationship is there, or could there possibly be, between Admetus and Alcestis?

In their search for ways of putting this play together, readers have usually given it one of two readings: either this is a Greek equivalent of the Christian myth of sacrifice and redemption (Alcestis dies for and saves her husband), or it is the story of virtue rewarded (the virtue being Admetus' remarkable hospitality to Apollo and Heracles). Whatever incongruities remain are explained by the fact that this play is in some technical matters the descendant of the satyr play, a sort of buffoonery, neither tragedy nor comedy. But it is hard to imagine this play being acted on either of the usual readings.

What happens if we look at this as a play about different ways of talking about people? To start at the beginning, ask yourself how Admetus is defined by the way he is spoken of in the first scene. What do you know about him? You know — as its original audience did, from the familiar myth on which the play is based — that he was once hospitable and generous to Apollo, who appeared as a stranger in need of help. But do you know what his life is like, or what it would mean to be Admetus? To have him for a husband or a son? And what sort of characters are Death and Apollo? It seems that they are merely elements in the situation, and the play begins as a situation comedy with Death as the fall guy. We best know this sort of characterless narrative form in musical comedy, or perhaps the fairy tale. The characters are defined by a single narrative in which they have one identity. They are labels — Admetus is "the man who befriended Apollo" — not voices. They are merely parts of a problem. They have no insides. This is the sort of writing about people that jokes engage in, from the short stories of Saki to ethnic jokes.

In the myths that everyone knew, however, Admetus had two identities: he was not only the Good Friend, he was the one whose wife died for him. Euripides sees these two identities as posing a problem, the problem the play explores.

At the beginning, the reader is invited to have the sort of attitude towards this play that one does towards a modern comedy, relaxed, inattentive, waiting for an elaborate joke to be set up. Against such a background, the first speech of the maid comes as a shock: it portrays Alcestis, the one who is about to die, not as a mere label, a narrative identity like that of Apollo, or like that of Tarrington in Saki's story, but as a complex and living person — willing to die, but only as the lesser of two painful evils, and miserable with her lot. When Alcestis herself appears, she utters the agonized cries of one about to die, distracted by fear and misery. We do not know how to take this: she seems to belong in another world, to be a character from a different sort of play. Is this all part of some joke? If so, it seems a bad one. The incompatibility of characterization throws the reader into doubt as to what sort of play this can be, and makes him attend with great intensity to what next occurs. He especially wants to know what Admetus will be like when he appears: will he be a character like Alcestis, or a caricature like Death and Apollo?

With respect to this matter, at least, we are left not long in doubt: Admetus appears with his wife, bemoaning his fate and begging her not to leave him. "Sorrow for all who love you, most of all for me;" "Do not be so harsh as to leave me, leave your children forlorn." He is defined here by his role in a single situation: he is the Bereaved Husband and nothing more. There are no connections between his experiences; he lacks even the memory that would tell him that this is all his fault, that she is dying because he asked her to. This is, in its way, very funny writing indeed, but we are uneasy because we are led to take Alcestis' suffering seriously. We cannot make sense of the play as a whole, we do not know how to take what we see. The experience of the reader becomes one almost of embarrassment.

Alcestis treats Admetus as a child, not bothering to respond to the offensiveness of his behavior but insisting upon a promise that he will not remarry. Her speech defines her situation: she has chosen to die, but reluctantly, for the sake of the children; she fears it, but thinks it the best of her unhappy possibilities. This is the voice of one who has made an impossibly difficult judgment with every recognition of its difficulties, and is suffering from the strain of inconsistent emotions. No simple remark will do for her situation as she perceives it. Admetus, on the other hand, swept up by his emotions of the moment, seems to enjoy his imminent position as Bereaved Husband; he even looks forward with a certain relish to the period of mourning. How fine it will be, he seems to say, to lose such a Noble Wife, to mourn sadly for a year, a lifetime. Admetus can see only one fact, speak only one way.

No sooner has Alcestis died, however, than Admetus is presented with the sort of problem that we face every day, and which he is unable to imagine. Heracles arrives and asks to be entertained, as in ordinary circumstances he had the right to do according to the custom of hospitality in the ancient world. With a little difficulty Admetus puts off his label of Bereaved Husband and puts on that of Good Friend: he admits Heracles to the house, hiding the fact of Alcestis' death. He is still defined by his role in a single relationship, a single social moment, but the relationship is a new one and defines an identity inconsistent with the person he has just seemed to be.

The reader is still perplexed by this play: its direction is still unclear, and he asks, "How can Euripides possibly put this play together?" One possibility would be for the play to trail off into chaos, as *Troilus and Cressida* does, with no change, as an expression of the meaninglessness of life lived on terms such as these. As it is, the next stage is Admetus' period of mourning, the poetic and self-indulgent grief to which he has looked forward; but it quickly appears that Admetus is finding that being a Bereaved Husband is not what he had looked forward to. Some recognition of his real condition seems to be expressed in his speeches: "What have I gained by living?" Although this seems to be a moment of self-revelation, the reader cannot be sure; what Admetus is best at, after all, is acting. There is real uncertainty here about what we perceive, an uncertainty of the kind Admetus has never admitted. This is a critical moment in the play: Admetus can move either way — back to the world of labels and roles, or on to something else.

At this point Heracles, who had learned the truth from a servant and left in a hurry, comes back with the rescued and disguised Alcestis, and asks Admetus to keep this "serving-girl" for him. He makes a direct claim to his hospitality. But this time Admetus asks him to go elsewhere. He does not put off the identity of Bereaved Husband and put on that of Good Friend. When he explains why he cannot, he speaks out of a larger experience than the present moment. He is no longer definable as an element in a situation, a part of a problem; he speaks out of more than one relationship. He has learned from his experience and in doing so has moved from the caricature world of musical comedy into a drama of character. The play fits together, but only at the end: there are two plays, two kinds of character, and Admetus moves from one to the other. The two kinds of writing define radically different sorts of character, two kinds of identity, and the moral and psychological implications of these differences are enormous. The movement of Admetus from one way of seeing and expressing himself to another is a growth, as if from infancy to maturity, or from disease to health: the play is about salvation but it is Admetus, not Alcestis, who is saved.

Why should a law student be asked to read such a play? The short answer is that this play is a dramatization of what it means to talk about people in a language of label or caricature. This shows us what the world would be like if such a language told the truth and if we were fully expressed by a single label, relationship, or experience. But labels, names, and other statements of identity are not properly to be conceived as operating in an "either-or" way; they overlap in immensely complicated and unstable patterns, and the tension among them is part of the life of the person. I asked at the beginning of this chapter what a novel would be like that was peopled with the characters of the law; Euripides gives us something very much like that. This is a demonstration of what it means to talk only one way, out of only one relationship or identity.

Another way to state the purpose of this assignment is to ask: is there any place for an Alcestis in the law? Will you as a lawyer always talk about an Alcestis as though she were an Admetus, denying the possibility of a voice and experience like the one she expresses here? If this is the way your language tends, how can you master it? How can you find a way to express or recognize what your language leaves out?

c. *The Uses of Caricature*

His neck was long and thin; his eyelids were red; rare hairs hung about his jaws; his shoulders were peaked and drooped like the broken wings of a bird; all his left side was caked with mud which showed that he had lately slept in a wet ditch. He had saved his inefficient carcass from violent destruction by running away from an American ship where, in a moment of forgetful folly, he had dared to engage himself; and he had knocked about for a fortnight ashore in the native quarter, cadging for drinks, starving, sleeping on rubbish-heaps, wandering in sunshine: a startling visitor from a world of nightmares. He stood repulsive and smiling in the sudden silence. This clean white forecastle was his refuge; the place where he could be lazy; where he could wallow, and lie and eat – and curse the food he ate; where he could display his talents for shirking work, for cheating, for cadging; where he could find someone to wheedle and someone to bully – and where he would be paid for doing all this. They all knew him. Is there a spot on earth where such a man is unknown, an ominous survival testifying to the eternal fitness of lies and impudence?*

We have seen that caricature may be used appropriately enough in certain forms of fiction (in jokes at least) and in the literature of reality to express a threat to the personality. In what other ways can caricature

* Joseph Conrad, *The Nigger of the "Narcissus,"* Chapter 1 (1897).

be used well, for what other purposes can it be considered a valuable resource of language?

ASPECTS OF THE NOVEL*
E. M. Forster

One great advantage of flat characters is that they are easily recognized whenever they come in — recognized by the reader's emotional eye, not by the visual eye, which merely notes the recurrence of a proper name. In Russian novels, where they so seldom occur, they would be a decided help. It is a convenience for an author when he can strike with his full force at once, and flat characters are very useful to him, since they never need reintroducing, never run away, have not to be watched for development, and provide their own atmosphere — little luminous disks of a pre-arranged size, pushed hither and thither like counters across the void or between the stars; most satisfactory.

A second advantage is that they are easily remembered by the reader afterwards. They remain in his mind as unalterable for the reason that they were not changed by circumstances; they moved through circumstances, which gives them in retrospect a comforting quality, and preserves them when the book that produced them may decay. The Countess in *Evan Harrington* furnishes a good little example here. Let us compare our memories of her with our memories of Becky Sharp. We do not remember what the Countess did or what she passed through. What is clear is her figure and the formula that surrounds it, namely, "Proud as we are of dear papa, we must conceal his memory." All her rich humour proceeds from this. She is a flat character. Becky is round. She, too, is on the make, but she cannot be summed up in a single phrase, and we remember her in connection with the great scenes through which she passed and as modified by those scenes — that is to say, we do not remember her so easily because she waxes and wanes and has facets like a human being. All of us, even the sophisticated, yearn for permanence, and to the unsophisticated permanence is the chief excuse for a work of art. We all want books to endure, to be refuges, and their inhabitants to be always the same, and flat characters tend to justify themselves on this account.

QUESTIONS

1. *We can take it for granted that lawyers and judges in their writing and speaking make at least some use of characters that Forster would call flat.*

* Chapter 4 (1927). *Evan Harrington* is by George Meredith (1860); Becky Sharp appears in Thackeray's *Vanity Fair* (1848).

Do they do it, so far as you can tell, to gain the advantages Forster sees in that kind of writing, or for some other reason? Find specific examples in the law and ask this question of them.

2. Does the judge or lawyer ever address an audience that "yearns for permanence," that seeks a "refuge" where people are "always the same"? Give an example, legal or not, of writing that seems to be directed to such an audience; or of an expression of desires of this kind by a member of such an audience.
   a. How would you be disposed to address an audience with desires such as these?
   b. Might you ever try to gratify these desires while speaking as a lawyer? a judge? a law teacher? Look back at the passages from judicial opinions and legal arguments above, and ask whether those writers seem to be attempting to gratify such desires.
3. Suppose you were arguing a case against a lawyer who tried to satisfy these yearnings in his jury or judge. How would you go about meeting his argument? Consider the actual jury arguments in the Haney case, and how you would have argued Miranda.
4. In an essay on Pride and Prejudice (a novel you will be asked to read in Section C), Professor Reuben Brower has observed that many of Jane Austen's characters are what we would call caricatures. He gives examples, and goes on to suggest that these "fixed characters make up a set of certainties against which more intricate exhibitions of pride and prejudice are measured. They are the 'fools' which James says are almost indispensable for any piece of fiction." R. Brower, "Light and Bright and Sparkling: Irony and Wit in Pride and Prejudice," in The Fields of Light 164, 174 (Galaxy ed. 1962).
   a. Would a lawyer ever use caricature to set the poles of possibility between which more "intricate exhibitions" might take place and be "measured"? Can you find or imagine an example?
   b. Is there a sense in which "fools" are indispensable to the lawyer trying a case or writing a brief, as well as to the novelist?
   c. What other purposes might the use of caricature serve?
5. Compare the following three passages:

   "The puppet is the actor in his primitive form. Its symbolic costume, from which all realistic and historically correct impertinences are banished, its unchanging [stare], petrified (or rather lignified) in a grimace expressive to the highest degree attainable by the carver's art, the mimicry by which it suggests human gesture in unearthly caricature — these give to its performance an intensity to which few actors can pretend, an intensity which imposes on our imagination like those images in immovable hieratic attitudes on the stained glass of Chartres Cathedral, in which the gaping tourists seem like little lifeless dolls moving jerkily in the draughts from the doors, reduced to sawdusty insignificance by the contrast with the gigantic vitality in the windows overhead." G. B. Shaw, "Note on Puppets," in M. von Boehn, Dolls and Puppets 5 (1932).

   "Than hym semed there com oute of the Oryent a grymly beare, all blak, in a clowde, and his pawys were as byg as a poste. He was all torongeled with lugerande lokys, and he was the fowlyst beste that ever ony man sye." Thomas Malory, Morte Darthur, in Works 196 (Vinaver ed. 1967).

THE PARDONER'S TALE*

Geoffrey Chaucer

Thise ryotoures three, of whiche I telle,
Longe erst er pryme rong of any belle,
Were set hem in a taverne for to drinke;
And as they satte, they herde a belle clinke
Biforn a cors, was caried to his grave;
That oon of hem gan callen to his knave,
"Go bet," quod he, "and axe redily,
What cors is this that passeth heer forby;
And look that thou reporte his name wel."
"Sir," quod this boy, "it nedeth never-a-del.
It was told, er ye cam heer, two houres;
He was, pardee, an old felawe of youres;
And sodeynly he was y-slayn to-night,
For-dronke, as he sat on his bench upright;
Ther cam a privee theef, men clepeth Deeth,
That in this contree al the peple sleeth,
And with his spere he smoot his herte a-two,
And wente his wey with-outen wordes mo.
He hath a thousand slayn this pestilence:
And, maister, er ye come in his presence,
Me thinketh that it were necessarie
For to be war of swich an adversarie:
Beth redy for to mete him evermore.
Thus taughte me my dame, I sey na-more."
"By seinte Marie," seyde this taverner,
"The child seith sooth, for he hath slayn this yeer,
Henne over a myle, with-in a greet village,
Both man and womman, child and hyne, and page.
I trowe his habitacioun be there;
To been avysed greet wisdom it were,
Er that he dide a man a dishonour."
"Ye, goddes armes," quod this ryotour,
"Is it swich peril with him for to mete?
I shal him seke by wey and eek by strete,
I make avow to goddes digne bones!
Herkneth, felawes, we three been al ones;
Lat ech of us holde up his hond til other,

* *Complete Works of Geoffrey Chaucer,* IV, 310–313 (Skeat 2d ed. 1900).

And ech of us bicomen otheres brother,
And we wol sleen this false traytour Deeth;
He shal be slayn, which that so many sleeth,
By goddes dignitee, er it be night."
  Togidres han thise three her trouthes plight,
To live and dyen ech of hem for other,
As though he were his owene y-boren brother.
And up they sterte al dronken, in this rage,
And forth they goon towardes that village,
Of which the taverner had spoke biforn,
And many a grisly ooth than han they sworn,
And Cristes blessed body they to-rente —
"Deeth shal be deed, if that they may him hente."
  Whan they han goon nat fully half a myle,
Right as they wolde han troden over a style,
An old man and a povre with hem mette.
This olde man ful mekely hem grette,
And seyde thus, "now, lordes, god yow see!"
  The proudest of thise ryotoures three
Answerde agayn, "what? carl, with sory grace,
Why artow al forwrapped save thy face?
Why livestow so longe in so greet age?"
  This olde man gan loke in his visage,
And seyde thus, "for I ne can nat finde
A man, though that I walked in-to Inde,
Neither in citee nor in no village,
That wolde chaunge his youthe for myn age;
And therfore moot I han myn age stille,
As longe time as it is goddes wille.
  Ne deeth, allas! ne wol nat han my lyf;
Thus walke I, lyk a restelees caityf,
And on the ground, which is my modres gate,
I knokke with my staf, bothe erly and late,
And seye, 'leve moder, leet me in!
Lo, how I vanish, flesh, and blood, and skin!
Allas! whan shul my bones been at reste?
Moder, with yow wolde I chaunge my cheste,
That in my chambre longe tyme hath be,
Ye! for an heyre clout to wrappe me!'
But yet to me she wol nat do that grace,
For which ful pale and welked is my face.
  But, sirs, to yow it is no curteisye

To speken to an old man vileinye,
But he trespasse in worde, or elles in dede.
In holy writ ye may your-self wel rede,
'Agayns an old man, hoor upon his heed,
Ye sholde aryse;' wherfor I yeve yow reed,
Ne dooth un-to an old man noon harm now,
Na-more than ye wolde men dide to yow
In age, if that yc so longc abyde;
And god be with yow, where ye go or ryde.
I moot go thider as I have to go."
"Nay, olde cherl, by god, thou shalt not so,"
Seyde this other hasardour anon;
"Thou partest nat so lightly, by seint Iohn!
Thou spak right now of thilke traitour Deeth,
That in this contree alle our frendes sleeth.
Have heer my trouthe, as thou art his aspye,
Tel wher he is, or thou shalt it abye,
By god, and by the holy sacrament!
For soothly thou art oon of his assent,
To sleen us yonge folk, thou false theef!"
"Now, sirs," quod he, "if that yow be so leef
To finde Deeth, turne up this croked wey,
For in that grove I lafte him, by my fey,
Under a tree, and ther he wol abyde;
Nat for your boost he wol him no-thing hyde.
See ye that ook? right ther ye shul him finde.
God save yow, that boghte agayn mankinde,
And yow amende!" — thus seyde this olde man.
And everich of thise ryotoures ran,
Til he cam to that tree, and ther they founde
Of florins fyne of golde y-coyned rounde
Wel ny an eighte busshels, as hem thoughte.
No lenger thanne after Deeth they soughte,
But ech of hem so glad was of that sighte,
For that the florins been so faire and brighte,
That doun they sette hem by this precious hord.

QUESTIONS

1. *Shaw said that the puppet – a physical caricature – has an intensity no human actor can match. Does the lawyer ever strive for this sort of intensity? Does caricature help him achieve it?*

2. *Is a heightened intensity what Chaucer achieves in the passage about the old man and the rioters? If not that, what does he achieve?*
3. *The reasons given by Forster and Professor Brower for the use of caricature are not exactly exhilarating to the lawyer; these characters are useful as background, because they are memorable, for the creation of fools, and so on. Shaw suggests that caricature has a special intensity, but the intensity he speaks of is that of exaggeration. Does Chaucer point out another possibility for the use of what might be called caricature? What uses will you as a lawyer make of this kind of writing, and how can what you do be explained or justified?*
   a. *It is plain that one will often use caricature in legal argument. This is a way of making someone seem impossibly good or evil or banal, of creating a fool perhaps, of flooding the scene with a strong light from the single point of view one is engaged to represent. But how can this usage be justified? Is this a mature and sensible way to carry on argument, to talk about others?*
   b. *One sort of justification is familiar: like Ulysses in Troilus and Cressida, one says, one does not care whether one does justice to experience, whether one says what a decent person would say, but only whether one can use language to achieve one's goals. Does this argument satisfy you?*
   c. *To whatever extent the argument just made might satisfy you as a lawyer working within the system of language and behavior we call the law, does it satisfy you as a judge or legislator, as one who is responsible for the system as a maker of it?*
   d. *Do you imagine that as an arguing lawyer you will ever seek to do justice to the complexities and profundities of the experience of another, that you will ever use a literature of character, not caricature? When and why? What does your answer say about the activity of legal argument?*
   e. *One might say that in legal argument, especially jury argument, there is this constant tension: each side is trying to represent his client as "one of us," as a person of the sort the jury and the lawyer are, and the adversary as "one of them," as outside the pale of humanity. Is this a tension between caricature and character, or between two sorts of caricature? Does the competition between these versions result in a sort of justice being done to the humanity of the litigants and to the actuality of their experience?*
   f. *Does the Chaucer passage suggest another possibility, another justification, for caricature? Do the following passages do so?*

THE CHARACTERS*

Theophrastus

The Boor

Boorishness I would define as uncivilized ignorance.

The boor is the sort of man who drinks barley-brew before going into

* Pages 29–30, 52–53 (Penguin ed. 1967).

the Assembly; who asserts that garlic smells as sweet as any perfume; wears shoes too big for his feet; and can't talk without bellowing. He won't trust his friends and relations, but he'll consult his slaves about his most important business; and he'll retail all the affairs of the Assembly to the labourers he employs on his farm. He sits down with his clothes hitched above the knee, exposing his nakedness. In the streets, other sights arouse in him no interest or surprise whatever, but if he sees a cow or a donkey or a goat he stops and inspects it. He can't fetch a bit of food from the cupboard without nibbling at it on the way; he drinks his wine neat. He quietly tries to rumple the bakery-maid, after he's helped her to do the grinding for the whole household, himself included. He feeds his horses while still eating his own breakfast. He answers the front door himself; and calls his dog and takes hold of it by the nose, and says, "This fellow guards the house and the whole place." When he has been paid by someone with a silver coin, he rejects it, saying it is worn too smooth, and takes another instead. If he has lent his plough, or a basket, or a sickle, or a bag, he remembers it as he lies awake and goes to ask for it in the middle of the night. On his way down to town he asks anyone he meets what price hides of bloaters were fetching, or whether the new-moon festival is being held today. And in the same breath he tells you he's going down to get his hair cut; and while he's passing that way he means to call at Archias's for some fish. He sings in the public bath; and he drives hobnails into his shoes.

Love of Evil

By "love of evil" I mean a partiality for the criminal character.

The "lover of evil" is the sort of man who contacts those who have lost lawsuits or been found guilty in criminal cases, and reckons that by associating with them he will become more experienced and more formidable. If someone is referred to as honest, he adds, "To all appearance", and goes on to say that there is no such thing as an honest man; that all men are alike; indeed he uses the phrase "What a good man" as a joke. A criminal type he will describe as "Independent-minded, if you look at him fairly. Many of the things people say of him," he admits, "are true; but there are some things they don't know. He's naturally talented; he sticks to his friends; and he's no fool." He insists emphatically that he has never met a more capable person. He will take the side of a man who is making his defence in the Assembly, or on trial in a lawcourt; and he will probably tell the jury that "They must judge the case and not the man." He will describe the defendant as a "watchdog of the people, one who keeps his eye on wrongdoers. Unless we value such men," he says, "we shall have no one left who cares what goes wrong in public life." He can't resist championing worthless men; on a jury he organizes a pressure-group in a bad cause; when judging a case he takes the statements of the opposed parties in the worst sense.

FICTION AND REALITY IN TALK ABOUT PEOPLE: THE TRUTH OF GENERALIZATION

Theophrastus' book goes on in this vein about several dozen different types of character. None of them could be real, of course. They have a certain affinity with Macaulay's "Z," the impossible fellow who burned his house, gave away his plate, and so on (page 253 *supra*). Why do you suppose Theophrastus might write such a book, or another might read it?

Here is one possible explanation suggested in the questions following the Saki stories (page 259 *supra*): the characters of Theophrastus, Chaucer, and the others are not real people nor meant to be like real people. They are part of a literature that is intended not to be "true to life" but something else, a way of arousing certain feelings, of articulating general truths, or — in the case of the joke or parody — of amusing the audience. We can read a Saki story as a joke because we know the people are not real. The characters of Theophrastus and Chaucer and Dickens are not people but ways of talking. Thus it is that Sophocles can be reported to have said that "Euripides portrayed men as they are; I as they ought to be;" that Thucydides can say of the speeches he records that he did not write down exactly what was said, but what the situation "called for" or what ought to have been said; that Coleridge can say, in praise of *King Lear*: "In *Lear* old age is itself a character — its natural imperfections being increased by lifelong habits of receiving a prompt obedience. Any addition of individuality would have been unnecessary and painful . . ."* And Ben Jonson in *Volpone* and Molière in *The Miser* give us portrayals not of people but of what avarice and miserliness really mean.

But to explain the use of caricature in fiction in this way is to say very little for the law, especially for its endemic use of caricature. For the law is a literature of reality and it always talks about real people, or at least legal talk always bears on the lives of real people, and it would seem that this justification of literary caricature will simply not work for the law.

Or can the distinction between the literature of truth and that of fiction be blurred? Although the Theophrastus "characters" are obviously fictional, and in their own way caricatures, they constitute a somewhat different sort of resource from Macaulay's "Z" or Saki's Clovis; one feels, of the Boor or the Lover of Evil, that one "knows people like that." Indeed, is there any spot on earth where such a man is unknown?

* Quoted in Shakespeare, *King Lear* 61 n.7 (Furness variorum ed. 1880).

Consider the following passage. Does Pope here describe a literature of character or caricature? Of truth or fiction? Can the law become a literature of the kind he describes?

*PREFACE TO THE ILIAD**
Alexander Pope

We come now to the *Characters* of [Homer's] Persons, and herc we shall find no Author has ever drawn so many with so visible and surprizing a Variety, or given us such lively and affecting Impressions of them. Every one has something so singularly his own, that no Painter could have distinguish'd them more by their Features, than the Poet has by their Manners. Nothing can be more exact than the Distinctions he has observ'd in the different degrees of Virtues and Vices. The singe Quality of *Courage* is wonderfully diversify'd in the several Characters of the *Iliad*. That of *Achilles* is furious and intractable; that of *Diomede* forward, yet list'ning to Advice and subject to Command: That of *Ajax* is heavy and self-confiding; of *Hector*, active and vigilant: The Courage of *Agamemnon* is inspirited by Love of Empire and Ambition, that of *Menelaus* mix'd with Softness and Tenderness for his People: We find in *Idomeneus* a plain direct Soldier, in *Sarpedon* a gallant and generous one. Nor is this judicious and astonishing Diversity to be found only in the principal Quality which constitutes the Main of each Character, but even in the Under-parts of it, to which he takes care to give a Tincture of that principal one. For Example, the main Characters of *Ulysses* and *Nestor* consist in *Wisdom*, and they are distinct in this; that the Wisdom of one is *artificial* and *various*, of the other *natural*, *open*, and *regular*. But they have, besides, Characters of *Courage*; and this Quality also takes a different Turn in each from the difference of his Prudence: For one in the War depends still upon *Caution*, the other upon *Experience*. It would be endless to produce Instances of these Kinds.

QUESTIONS

1. *Is this, then, where you come out: "Whenever one generalizes about life – whether in telling a story with general significance, reaching historical conclusions, or in making and applying rules, whether of judgment or description – one creates a literature of caricature. There is a sense in which every statement of meaning is a fiction. And at the end of any such piece of writing, the pressures towards caricature are increased still further: when the novel or drama comes to a close, when the trial is over, the characters – like Mrs. Bertram (page 249 supra) and perhaps like your client Mr. Stein (page 188) – fade into flatness. We regard them in the*

* *The Complete Poetical Works of Alexander Pope* 253 (Boynton ed. 1903).

light of conclusions that have been reached and stated, and to do so is to deny some of the complexity and profundity of their lives as they have been represented. "Caricature is the price we pay for any attempt to make sense of life." Can you disagree with this statement?

2. *Is the lawyer really then to regard himself as a sort of novelist or dramatist, writing a language of general significance? (How would you explain that view to a client?)*
3. *Perhaps this is the way to look at it: how one talks about another person is really a question of degree, not kind, and the possibilities range from a gargoylelike exaggeration at one end to some imaginary rendition of the whole person at the other. The task of the writer is to choose his place along that scale with some real understanding of what the choice entails and an awareness of why he made that choice rather than another. The question can then be put this way: how and why are such choices to be made? What ways of talking about people should the lawyer master, and by what art can he do so?*
4. *Are there analogs in the world of social behavior to what we have called caricature? What is a ritual, for example – or perhaps better, what sorts of ritual are there – and how does ritual define character? What place has ritual in the law? Compare the following two passages.*

THE FORM OF SOLEMNIZATION OF MATRIMONY*

Then they shall give their troth to each other in this manner. The Minister, receiving the Woman at her father's or her friend's hands, shall cause the Man with his right hand to take the Woman by her right hand, and to say after him as followeth.

I N. take thee N. to my wedded Wife, to have and to hold from this day forward, for better for worse, for richer for poorer, in sickness and in health, to love and to cherish, till death us do part, according to God's holy ordinance; and thereto I plight thee my troth.

CHILDREN'S GAMES IN STREETS AND PLAYGROUND*

I. and P. Opie

The best version of this acting game was collected in Swansea. The characters are a Mother, her Children, and an Old Man. The Old Man goes off and secretes himself in some suitably dark and mysterious place which is designated "the well". Thereupon a set dialogue takes place.

Children to Mother: "Please, mother, can we have a piece of bread and butter?"

Mother: "Let me see your hands."

The children hold out their hands for inspection.

* Protestant Episcopal Church, *Book of Common Prayer* (1952).
* Page 305 (1969).

Mother: "Your hands are very dirty. Go to the well and wash them."

The children go to the well, where they spy the Old Man crouching down. They rush back to the Mother screaming: "Mother! Mother! There's an Old Man in the well."

Mother: "Don't be silly, children. There isn't an Old Man in the well."

Children: "But we saw him."

Mother: "It's only your father's under-pants. I hung them out to dry. Go again."

The children go again, see the Old Man, and again come back screaming: "Mother! Mother! There's an Old Man in the well."

The Mother again reassures them (repetition is a feature of these playlets), and they go to the well perhaps twice or three times more, until they persuade the Mother to come herself. She sends one of the children to fetch a candle (a twig), lights it, and goes to the well with the children. When they reach the well, and she is about to look in, the Old Man blows the candle out.

Mother to child nearest her: "What did you want to blow out my candle for?" She cuffs the child who sets up a howl.

The Mother relights the candle, holds it over the well, and the Old Man blows it out again. Mother to another child: "What did you want to blow out my candle for?" A second child is cuffed and sets up a howl. This happens three or four times, so that three or four children, or perhaps all of them, are crying at once, which gives a fine opportunity for dramatics.

Eventually the Mother manages to look in the well. The Old Man jumps up with a horrible shriek and gives chase. Whoever he catches is the next Old Man.

2. *Other Possibilities for the Rendition of Character: Complication, Inconsistency, and Detail*

The Nurse is one of the characters in which the author has delighted; he has, with great subtlety of distinction, drawn her at once loquacious and secret, obsequious and insolent, trusty and dishonest.*

In the passages in this chapter, you have seen what we have called caricature used both well — perhaps best in the comic writing such as the Saki stories — and badly, worst of all probably in the judicial opinions. What possibilities other than caricature are there for the literary creation or rendition of character? If your criticism of the literature of

* Samuel Johnson, *General Observations on the Plays of Shakespeare* (1765), in *Works*, V, 145, 164 (Lynam ed. 1825).

caricature is that it is somehow false to life — that it is a hopeless oversimplification to write that way, that life is not so easy — you will presumably be expected to show that you, or someone, can be true to life, and that justice can be done to the variety and difficulty of experience. How will you do so? What possibilities are there?

Forster's account of Mrs. Bertram (page 249 *supra*), who becomes for the moment "round" and then subsides into flatness again, may give us some help, and his proposed test for "round" characters gives even more: that they are capable of "surprising in a convincing way." In the discussion of *Alcestis* it was suggested that what distinguished Alcestis from Admetus, Apollo, and Death was the expression of inconsistent emotions and thoughts: her voice was made lifelike, it seemed, by its inconsistency. Is inconsistency then the key to making a character true to life? One might draw that conclusion also from the passage by Samuel Johnson on Shakespeare's Nurse, but a moment's thought shows that the response is still incomplete: Admetus is the soul of inconsistency; in Forster's terms, he "surprises" us but not in a "convincing way." Is the question, then, what it is that "convinces"?

Perhaps something can be learned from the practice and experience of novelists, since one of the apparent assumptions of their art is that their writing shall be as much like life as possible. How do novelists create characters who are true to the "profundities and complexities" of life, if they do, and against what pressures? The English novel of the eighteenth and nineteenth centuries provides an especially interesting comparison with the law, for in its central tradition it was a social literature about the lives of individuals in a highly organized society, a society with clearly articulated and understood values, manners, and roles by which the characters could be defined (rather than, say, about the lives of individuals alone with themselves, with nature, or with God). In writing about characters in this way, the novelist had to come to terms with their social identities, their external definitions, much as a lawyer has to come to terms with the way his characters are defined by his only slightly more rigid intellectual and social system. English society was so finely ordered and complex, in fact, that one could well imagine a novel written about characters defined solely by their roles, much as legal characters are defined: Poor Curate, Insolent Lord, Rich Banker, Pretty Chambermaid, and so on. Especially in the early novels, characters were often representative figures, even being given generic names: one thinks of Squire Allworthy and Squire Western in Fielding's *Tom Jones,* for example, or the parties of the wealthy Mr. Merdle, attended by Bench, Bar, Bishop, and Treasury, in Dickens's *Little Dorrit.* R. S. Surtees could write a whole novel, *Mr. Sponge's Sporting Tour,* about different sorts of foxhunts. The fully expressed social world is one of the achievements of the English novel, but it presents the danger that the individual character shall become a type, a part of the social world and no more. The full expression of the social world seems to threaten the full expression of the individual mind and personality. How have English novelists responded to this danger, to the risk that they would end up writing about society rather than people, writing caricature rather than character?

The answer may seem obvious to you, but it was not to the writers. You may recall one example: George Eliot's *Middlemarch* takes as its subject the tension between the social identity of a young provincial woman and her sense of some other, deeper, self. The novel is brought to life by showing how the possibility of caricature, of definition by a social role, is a real threat for a person living in such a society as well as for a writer writing about it. For both George Eliot and Dorothea, the question is what sort of life for the individual can be imagined in such a world. The novel expresses a tension between the socially ascribed self and the inner self; both are true, neither is sufficient. One way of defining character — by place and role in society — is controlled by the expression of what it leaves out, what it does not recognize. A realization of "complexity and profundity" is achieved by expressing the self in a state of tension and uncertainty. The pressure towards caricature becomes one subject of the book, and paradoxically it makes possible — by its negation — the definition of character of another sort. The heart of this way of writing about people is (not to your surprise) writing two ways at once. Could writing of this sort go on in the novel today? Or is our society so disorganized that it does not impose identities upon us, or at least not identities of sufficient clarity and force to make our resistance to them significant? Whatever the case may be with the modern novelist, can the lawyer learn from George Eliot and write about people as she does? When and how?

Below you are told how another writer, a Russian, made his characters live.

TOLSTOY*
H. Troyat

In spite of the monumental dimensions of the book, this preoccupation with detail never deserts Tolstoy for one moment. When he shows the surgeon coming out of the operating tent, he notes that "he held his cigar carefully, between thumb and little finger, for fear of staining it"; Kutuzov, talking to the tsar, has "a trembling of his upper lip"; when

* Pages 307–309 (1967).

Anatol talks to Princess Marya, he "slides one finger through the buttonhole of his uniform." Minor characters are identified by some external feature that recurs whenever they appear. The first thing the author notes about the little Princess Bolkonsky is "her short upper lip, slightly down-shadowed." This "short lip" is mentioned four or five times, and after the young woman's death the angel on the monument over her grave is also given "an imperceptibly raised upper lip." The lovely Elena, Pierre's wife, always appears with "her smile," "her plump hand," "her marble shoulders and throat." Dolokhov is identified by his light blue eyes and the lines of his mouth, the upper lip of which "came down far over the large lower lip, forming an acute angle." Vereshagin, a Moscow merchant turned over to the mob by Rostopchin has for distinguishing marks his "fox fur jacket," his "shaved skull," his "long thin neck" and "frail hands." Bilibin the diplomat is noteworthy for the mobility of his face: "Sometimes his brow would be grooved by broad wrinkles and his eyebrows would rise, and sometimes they lowered and deep furrows formed in his cheeks."

One must not conclude that Tolstoy freezes his characters into immobility by this process. On the contrary, believing that human personality is multiple, dynamic and changing, he contrives to show his people in different lights according to their surroundings. Prince Andrey is not the same in "society" as when he is alone with Pierre, or with Bilibin the diplomat, or among the officers of his regiment, or in his father's presence, or escorting his sister, or with Natasha. Each time we see him through the eyes of the people with him, and discover a new side of his character. But these psychological fluctuations do not affect the rock on which the individual's entire personality is built, always perceptible beneath the waves that occasionally engulf it. Even when the foundation contradicts itself, it does not cease to exist. What gives so much life to the protagonists in *War and Peace* is that they are all defined in terms of each other.

"Returning to Moscow from the army," writes Tolstoy, "Nicholas Rostov was welcomed *by his close relatives* as the best of sons, a hero, the irreplaceable Nikolenka; *by the other members of his family* as a pleasant, easy-going and well-mannered young man; *by his friends* as a good-looking lieutenant of hussars, a first-rate dancer and one of the most eligible young men in Moscow."

Prince Andrey, on the other hand, is much sought-after by the high society of St. Petersburg: "*The pro-reform party* opened their doors wide to him — first, because he was noted for his intelligence and culture, and then, because by freeing his serfs he had acquired the reputation of being a liberal. *The discontented old men* sought his favor because, for them, he was first and foremost his father's son and as such, they thought, he must disapprove of the reformers. *The ladies* welcomed him with open arms because he was an eligible bachelor, rich, notorious and surrounded by an aura of romance because he had been thought dead at the front and had just lost his wife."

Among Kutuzov's staff officers, "Prince Andrey had *two conflicting reputations*. Some — a minority — realized that he was an unusual person and expected great things from him, listened to him, admired and imitated him. . . . Others — a majority — did not like him and considered him insufferably haughty, cold and unfriendly."

Through a thousand observations of this type Tolstoy creates a definite atmosphere around each of his characters. Each one is caught up in an extremely subtle net of sympathies and antipathies. His slightest gesture resounds in several other consciousnesses. Prince Andrey, Pierre, Natasha and Princess Marya are not flat images, always seen from the same side; the reader moves around them and feels their interdependence with all the other characters. They all obey the law of relativity.

QUESTIONS

1. *The multiplication of possibilities through what Troyat calls the law of relativity – through multiplying points of view – is a way of complicating the imagined characters by constantly asking the reader to adjust to new facts about them. Is this simply a matter of defining people and events in the greatest possible detail? Or is there another principle here, and if so, is it the principle of inconsistency, or something else? What Troyat describes here amounts to a process of raising and then meeting uncertainties in the reader, of stating and resolving ambiguities. The principle is perhaps not one of inconsistency, but of threatening consistency and then reestablishing it. This sort of writing would give both the* "surprise" *and the* "convincing way." *Can the lawyer ever write this way?*
2. *There follows next a passage which presents an altogether different possibility for the creation of character. Here D. H. Lawrence, like George Eliot, reflects an inconsistency between the way his characters are defined by the social order of wealth, status, and power and their true selves. But – coming at a later stage in the development of the novel or the disintegration of society – he finds it both easier and less significant to do this, and you will see him moving back and forth with great (almost contemptuous) facility between social definitions of his characters and other ways of defining them. The pressure towards social definition is greatly relaxed, and less can be achieved by author or character in resisting it. Lawrence's main concern is accordingly with experiences and relationships that find no expression whatever in that order, not even by negation; his definition of the true self goes beyond a statement that it is more than or different from the social self, and he tries to express it directly. How does he attempt to do this? Is this, at last, writing that realizes the* "profundity and complexity" *of experience, that is true to life?*

WOMEN IN LOVE*
D. H. Lawrence

[Ursula and Gudrun are sisters.]

Turning, they passed down the high-road, that went between high banks towards the church. There, in the lowest bend of the road, low under the trees, stood a little group of expectant people, waiting to see the wedding. The daughter of the chief mine-owner of the district, Thomas Crich, was getting married to a naval officer.

"Let us go back," said Gudrun, swerving away. "There are all those people."

And she hung wavering in the road.

"Never mind them," said Ursula, "they're all right. They all know me, they don't matter."

"But must we go through them?" asked Gudrun.

"They're quite all right, really," said Ursula, going forward. And together the two sisters approached the group of uneasy, watchful common people. They were chiefly women, colliers' wives of the more shiftless sort. They had watchful, underworld faces.

The two sisters held themselves tense, and went straight towards the gate. The women made way for them, but barely sufficient, as if grudging to yield ground. The sisters passed in silence through the stone gateway and up the steps, on the red carpet, a policeman estimating their progress.

"What price the stockings!" said a voice at the back of Gudrun. A sudden fierce anger swept over the girl, violent and murderous. She would have liked them all annihilated, cleared away, so that the world was left clear for her. How she hated walking up the churchyard path, along the red carpet, continuing in motion, in their sight.

"I won't go into the church," she said suddenly, with such final decision that Ursula immediately halted, turned round, and branched off up a small side path which led to the little private gate of the Grammar School, whose grounds adjoined those of the church.

Just inside the gate of the school shrubbery, outside the churchyard, Ursula sat down for a moment on the low stone wall under the laurel bushes, to rest. Behind her, the large red building of the school rose up peacefully, the windows all open for the holiday. Over the shrubs, before her, were the pale roofs and tower of the old church. The sisters were hidden by the foliage.

Gudrun sat down in silence. Her mouth was shut close, her face averted. She was regretting bitterly that she had ever come back. Ursula

* Chapter 1 (1920).

looked at her, and thought how amazingly beautiful she was. flushed with discomfiture. But she caused a constraint over Ursula's nature, a certain weariness. Ursula wished to be alone, freed from the tightness, the enclosure of Gudrun's presence.

"Are we going to stay here?" asked Gudrun.

"I was only resting a minute," said Ursula, getting up as if rebuked. "We will stand in the corner by the fives-court, we shall see everything from there."

For the moment, the sunshine fell brightly into the churchyard, there was a vague scent of sap and of spring, perhaps of violets from off the graves. Some white daisies were out, bright as angels. In the air, the unfolding leaves of a copperbeech were blood-red.

Punctually at eleven o'clock, the carriages began to arrive. There was a stir in the crowd at the gate, a concentration as a carriage drove up, wedding guests were mounting up the steps and passing along the red carpet to the church. They were all gay and excited because the sun was shining.

Gudrun watched them closely, with objective curiosity. She saw each one as a complete figure, like a character in a book, or a subject in a picture, or a marionette in a theatre, a finished creation. She loved to recognise their various characteristics, to place them in their true light, give them their own surroundings, settle them for ever as they passed before her along the path to the church. She knew them, they were finished, sealed and stamped and finished with, for her. There was none that had anything unknown, unresolved, until the Criches themselves began to appear. Then her interest was piqued. Here was something not quite so preconcluded.

There came the mother, Mrs. Crich, with her eldest son Gerald. She was a queer unkempt figure, in spite of the attempts that had obviously been made to bring her into linc for the day. Her face was pale, yellowish, with a clear, transparent skin, she leaned forward rather, her features were strongly marked, handsome, with a tense, unseeing, predative look. Her colourless hair was untidy, wisps floating down on to her sac coat of dark blue silk, from under her blue silk hat. She looked like a woman wih a monomania, furtive almost, but heavily proud.

Her son was of a fair, sun-tanned type, rather above middle height, well-made, and almost exaggeratedly well-dressed. But about him also was the strange, guarded look, the unconscious glisten, as if he did not belong to the same creation as the people about him. Gudrun lighted on him at once. There was something northern about him that magnetised her. In his clear northern flesh and his fair hair was a glisten like sunshine refracted through crystals of ice. And he looked so new, unbroached, pure as an arctic thing. Perhaps he was thirty years old, perhaps more. His gleaming beauty, maleness, like a young, good-humoured, smiling wolf, did not blind her to the significant, sinister stillness in his bearing, the lurking danger of his unsubdued temper. "His totem is the wolf," she repeated to herself. "His mother is an old, unbroken wolf." And then she experienced a keen paroxysm, a transport, as if she had made some incredible discovery, known to nobody else on earth. A strange transport took possession of her, all her veins were in a paroxysm of violent sensation. "Good God!" she exclaimed to herself, "what is this?" And then, a moment after, she was saying assuredly, "I shall know more of that man." She was tortured with desire to see him again, a nostalgia, a necessity to see him again, to make sure it was not all a mistake, that she was not deluding herself, that she really felt this strange and overwhelming sensation on his account, this knowledge of him in her essence, this powerful apprehension of him. "Am I *really* singled out for him in some way, is there really some pale gold, arctic light that envelopes only us two?" she asked herself. And she could not believe it, she remained in a muse, scarcely conscious of what was going on around.

The bridesmaids were here, and yet the bridegroom had not come. Ursula wondered if something was amiss, and if the wedding would yet all go wrong. She felt troubled, as if it rested upon her. The chief bridesmaids had arrived. Ursula watched them come up the steps. One of them she knew, a tall, slow, reluctant woman with a weight of fair hair and a pale, long face. This was Hermione Roddice, a friend of the Criches. Now she came along, with her head held up, balancing an enormous flat hat of pale yellow velvet, on which were streaks of ostrich feathers, natural and grey. She drifted forward as if scarcely conscious, her long blanched face lifted up, not to see the world. She was rich. She wore a dress of silky, frail velvet, of pale yellow colour, and she carried a lot of small rose-coloured cyclamens. Her shoes and stockings were of brownish grey, like the feathers on her hat, her hair was heavy, she drifted along with a peculiar fixity of the hips, a strange unwilling motion. She was impressive, in her lovely pale-yellow and brownish-rose, yet macabre, something repulsive. People were silent when she passed, impressed, roused, wanting to jeer, yet for some reason silenced. Her long, pale face, that she carried lifted up, somewhat in the Rossetti fashion, seemed almost drugged, as if a strange mass of thoughts coiled in the darkness within her, and she was never allowed to escape.

QUESTIONS

1. *Are Ursula and Gudrun "flat" or "round"? Are they capable of "surprising in a convincing way"?*

2. Does the life of these characters come from a tension between different ways of talking — an inconsistency between different identities expressible in different languages — or is it expressed directly?
3. The daughter of Mr. Crich is defined in social terms: "The daughter of the chief mineowner of the district, Thomas Crich, was getting married to a naval officer." How is Mr. Crich's son defined? How is Hermione defined?
4. Do you want to say that this literature is true to life, or that it is nonsense? Would any person you know ever wonder if there were "some pale gold, arctic light that envelops only us two"?
5. Here is what Lawrence himself had to say about his creation of character. He is speaking here of The Rainbow, a novel that preceded Women in Love.

   "You mustn't look in my novel for the old stable ego of the character. There is another ego, according to whose action the individual is unrecognizable, and passes through, as it were, allotropic states which it needs a deeper sense than any we've been used to exercise, to discover are states of the same single radically-unchanged element. (Like as diamond and coal are the same pure single element of carbon. The ordinary novel would trace the history of the diamond — but I say, "Diamond, what! This is carbon." And my diamond might be coal or soot, and my theme is carbon.) You must not say my novel is shaky — it is not perfect, because I am not expert in what I want to do. But it is the real thing, say what you like. And I shall get my reception, if not now, then before long. Again I say, don't look for the development of the novel to follow the lines of certain characters: the characters fall into the form of some other rhythmic form, as when one draws a fiddle-bow across a fine tray delicately sanded, the sand takes lines unknown." Letter to Edward Garnett, June 5, 1914, in Letters of D. H. Lawrence 199 (Huxley ed. 1932).

   Does Lawrence tell us (and show us) how to do justice to the profundity and complexity of a human being, or is this writing just romantic and disorganized?
6. There is a danger that one might take this series of observations about successful and less successful literary renditions of character as a sort of formula: you need only to mix together the proper amounts of inconsistency, detail, tension, the right degree of conflict between competing identities, raise and meet uncertainties in the reader, and there you have it — literature that is true to life. Of course there can be no recipe in such matters, though those phrases do identify some important elements of some successes. But how do you explain the following one?

   In Shakespeare's Antony and Cleopatra, Antony chooses Egypt over Rome, life with Cleopatra over life as one of three rulers of the world. As this choice is regarded over and over through the play, the opposites are defined: pleasure, fertility, richness and variety, feeling, inventiveness, the world of woman; and order, discipline, logic, force, achievement, the world of man. But how are we to regard the choice so characterized — as a tragic fall or a great movement of the spirit? Is it good or bad? Who is this Antony: "The triple pillar of the world transform'd Into a strumpet's fool"? Or one who discovers and lives a life of "infinite variety"? He is spoken of in constantly shifting terms — now as the good soldier ruined, then as one who gives up all for love, and then the focus shifts again. Cleopatra likewise is by turns adventurer, genius, virago, original and *touching person, traitor. Antony is engaged in a pursuit of an imagined self, a process of making his own life and character through his claims to meaning. There is no single true view of him or Cleopatra; the truth shifts constantly as they define themselves anew, for the moment. The play entertains the most enormous possibilities for both, and what we perceive at the end is not the death of an understood or comprehended man, but the extinction of a world of possibilities.*

ANTONY AND CLEOPATRA*
William Shakespeare

Antony: I am dying, Egypt, dying.
Give me some wine and let me speak a little. . . .
The miserable change now at my end
Lament nor sorrow at; but please your thoughts
In feeding them with those my former fortunes,
Wherein I liv'd the greatest prince o' th' world,
The noblest; and do now not basely die,
Not cowardly put off my helmet to
My countryman — a Roman by a Roman
Valiantly vanquish'd. Now my spirit is going.
I can no more.
Cleopatra: Noblest of men, woo't die?
Hast thou no care of me? Shall I abide
In this dull world, which in thy absence is
No better than a sty? O, see, my women. [*Antony dies.*]
The crown o' th' earth doth melt. My lord!
O, wither'd is the garland of the war,
The soldier's pole is fall'n! Young boys and girls
Are level now with men. The odds is gone,
And there is nothing left remarkable
Beneath the visiting moon. [*Faints.*]
. . .
I dreamt there was an Emperor Antony —
O, such another sleep, that I might see
But such another man!
Dolabella: If it might please ye —
Cleopatra: His face was as the heav'ns; and therein stuck
A sun and moon, which kept their course and lighted
The little O, the earth.
Dolabella: Most sovereign creature —
Cleopatra: His legs bestrid the ocean; his rear'd arm
Crested the world. His voice was propertied

* Act 4, scene 15; act 5, scene 2.

As all the tuned spheres, and that to friends;
But when he meant to quail and shake the orb,
He was as rattling thunder. For his bounty,
There was no winter in't; an autumn 'twas
That grew the more by reaping. His delights
Were dolphin-like: they show'd his back above
The element they liv'd in. In his liv'ry
Walk'd crowns and crownets. Realms and islands were
As plates dropp'd from his pocket.
Dolabella: Cleopatra —
Cleopatra: Think you there was or might be such a man
As this I dreamt of?
Dolabella: Gentle madam, no.
Cleopatra: You lie, up to the hearing of the gods!
But, if there be or ever were one such,
It's past the size of dreaming. Nature wants stuff
To vie strange forms with fancy; yet, t'imagine
An Antony were nature's piece 'gainst fancy,
Condemning shadows quite.

3. *The Way Institutions Talk About People — A Fundamental Paradox for the Law*

As you look over your own experience you may find that the most exaggerated caricatures, the most excessive clichés in character-writing, can be found in the literature by which institutions set themselves up and operate in the world. Think of the view that has been taken of you by the army, the law school, or your bank, for example. The law of course is an institution too, and you are here asked to bring to your reading of legal literature your experience of other institutional languages.

One could describe institutions as separate ways of organizing experience through language (different language systems, if you will), each of which defines experience and people in its particular way. Earlier I spoke of the institution as a game set up on a permanent basis; and a simple definition of roles is typical of institutions, as it is of games. Each institution seems to use its particular labels or identities without regard to other possible ways of talking about people. To the post office each of us is an address and a zip code and nothing more; to the social security administration, a serial number connected with some other numbers — all that remains of one's working life — reflecting probable government liability; to the actuarial department of a life insurance company we are merely statistics, and if the company wishes us a long life we know why.

You must have wondered what grades and class rank really say about your education. Each person is talked about as if only a particular aspect of his nature mattered at all, as if there were nothing else to be said. Can you think of any institutions that do not take this incredibly simple view of the human personality? To the Elks, I suppose, you are an Elk and only an Elk; to the church you are first and last a member or not, a good one or not; to the business corporation you are a salesman who produces well or badly, or a financial officer whose figures can be trusted or not; to the football team you are always and only a center or an end, a good one or a bad one.

The institutional way of talking about people is not simply a matter of the use of excessively abstract characteristics such as the social security number; sometimes, in fact, the institution's concern is with a very wide range of capacities and experience, as in the navy's idea of the good officer or the corporation's idea of a good president. What does seem central to all institutional speech is that the institution recognizes no other way of talking. Think of the language of the charter of your college fraternity or sorority, the manual for officer candidates, the pamphlets handed out at the church door, an annual report of IBM, and so on: these languages make a common and mutually exclusive claim to universal sufficiency.[2]

Find a passage of institutional talk and pretend that a person is speaking that way. How would his tone of voice define himself and you? Think of the literature of institutions you have actually known: the school, the college, the army, the fraternity or sorority, the political organization, the law, and so on. What tones of voice do you hear? How would you respond if a human being addressed you in such a way? We seem to live in a world in which the propriety of this patently impossible institutional talk is unquestioned. Is it conceivable that the language of a particular institution could be rewritten a different way, that we could have an anti-institutional institution? If not, how can this language be controlled?

To begin a response with the experience of ordinary life, we do not in fact take these institutional labels as seriously as one might think if one saw only the official documents of institutions — the constitution, by-laws, minutes, rules, regulations, banquet speeches, and the like. While the official speech of an institution may single out only a small part of your identity as relevant, the people who participate in the institution all know, or should know, better. One would worry about someone who

2. What happens when a single institution does take complete control of the lives of its people is the grim subject of Goffman, *Asylums* (1961). This account of the social reality shows that the implications of institutional language pointed out above are not exaggerated.

saw himself and others solely as members of the Democratic party, IBM, Sigma Chi, the National Organization of Women, or the law school. The ordinary person comes to see that the official institutional views of mankind are impossible, and does not take them with complete seriousness. Yet he does not utterly reject them, and one might say that an important ingredient of maturity is the ability to live with institutions without ending up sounding like one. How does one achieve this? How can a lawyer do so? You certainly cannot just chuck out legal language as impossible and remain a lawyer, but you cannot use it undiluted without being absurd. How can you find a way of using the language without taking it too seriously, a way of expressing or exercising a sense of your own distance from this system? What do you know that enables you to use the languages of institutions in an intelligent way?

One thing you know is that as a fortunate matter of social fact, we belong to a great many institutions at once, and this helps us resist the claims of any one institution over our lives. The social theory which favors the existence of many competing institutions and centers of power is called pluralism. There is no one great institution that runs us all, although (and perhaps because) there are many avid competitors for that position. This conflict among competitors yields a certain surprising freedom even beyond the assurance that none will grow too great: not only are you not straitjacketed into a single identity, the composite picture of all your institutional identities and labels does not add up to some sort of final and complete identity upon which any person or institution can act. The conflict among institutions leaves room for something else, for something not expressed in institutional ways at all. But while this knowledge might help you keep your sanity as a citizen who must live in such a society, how does it help you in your activities of writing and managing institutional language as a lawyer? The benefits of pluralism could easily be seen as a result of our social structure for which the law can take no credit; in fact, the law might be seen as one of the competing institutions that most needs checking by others, or even as the superinstitution we hoped to avoid. And where in the law is there any recognition of the sides of life that find no institutional expression?

Here we come to the paradox: if the first point is that we do not have to take institutional ways of talking at face value, the second is that sometimes we want to do just that, and not in spite of their limitations but because of them. Sometimes it is desirable in every way to use institutional identities, narrow as they are and partly because they are narrow. For example, we are glad that the post office does not concern itself with more than it does. And in more personal experience, think of the relationship between salesman and customer: as a customer you no doubt wish to have everything except technical discussion left out. How do you like a salesman who talks to you as a friend, and asks about your wife and children and tells you about his, on the theory that the spirit of camaraderie that this sincere interest inspires will make you more ready to buy whatever he is selling? What is the word for this sort of behavior? It is "rudeness," isn't it?

But the paradox can be stated even more strongly: institutional language may be more than a way of regulating and limiting our intrusions upon each other, more than a system of manners: it may be an expression of the imagination, a resource for thinking and living. Surely the institutional languages of religion have been that, and to a lesser degree the languages of political and legal institutions as well — one thinks of the United States Constitution, the Communist Manifesto, the Supreme Court of the United States, the United Nations, and so on.

There is a genre of literature that has concerned itself with the paradox of institutional speech, with the tension between the life of the self and the institutional statement and regulation of life. From its beginnings, this has been one concern of the epic, and we shall look briefly at three very different examples.

Homer's *Iliad,* which tells a small segment of the story of the fall of Troy, is about a critical episode in the life of Achilles, whose "wrath" is the express subject of the poem. In the Greek society represented in the *Iliad,* that of the Achaeans, the great activity of life was warfare, and the great reward was the acquisition of prizes — the booty won by prowess — which was, far beyond its material value, the mark of that honor and respect which was the goal of life. Achilles is deprived by Agamemnon (his chief) of a prize fairly won, a slave girl; this is what sets off his wrath. He nearly kills Agamemnon, then withdraws from the battle. The war from that time goes very badly for the Achaeans, who finally send an embassy to his tent to beg his pardon, restore his prizes manyfold, and seek his aid. He refuses. Having withdrawn because of an outrage within the system of warfare and prizes, he now rejects that system. His refusal to meet the institutional expectations of the Achaeans utterly perplexes them; he can seem no less than mad. When his friend Patroclus is killed, Achilles does return to the battle and saves the war for the Achaeans — not for the prizes and honor he can win, not for the old heroic reasons, but out of a new and personal fury at the loss of his friend. At the close, he emerges as perhaps the first existential hero, cut off from his society and responsible for his own destiny.

Vergil's *Aeneid* is quite different. This is the story of the founding of Rome by Aeneas, a fugitive from fallen Troy. To found the city, he must undergo the most lengthy and exhausting voyages and suffer the loss of his wife and many friends. He forbids himself the peace he longs for, and forces himself to go through an endless series of terrible battles in Italy. He leaves the sanctuary and affection offered him by Dido, queen of Carthage. The cost of the founding of Rome is total to Aeneas: he sacrifices himself. This poem can be read as the highly qualified celebration of an institutional event, the founding of Rome. The institution that will at last bring peace, the *pax Romana,* is established by brutality. The glory is foreseen, but the cost is almost unbearable. The heroism of Aeneas lies in the resolute paring away of all aspects of identity other than that of the founder of Rome. He makes himself, as it were, an institutional identity. His sacrifice is that he becomes a "label" of the kind we have discussed.

A still different sort of expression is found in the third epic I want to mention (if it is right to classify it as such): Malory's *Morte Darthur.* This retelling of the old chivalric tales of King Arthur's court is the story of the creation of an institution: the Knights of the Round Table, who in a world of brutality and lawlessness are inspired by a sense of duty and bound by a code of honor. This is the creation of a civilization out of barbarity. But when Lancelot and Gawain quarrel and the company of knights fall into dissension (as we have seen in the passage reproduced in Chapter 2, page 104 *supra*), the institution falls; this civilization dies and is, by the close of the book, merely a part of the past. For once the institution is not greater than the men who created and sustained it. This is a unique view, in my reading, and a complete repudiation of the usual, and artificial, claims of institutional permanence. The law, the church, the nation, and the club each speaks as though whatever else might happen, it will never falter or fail. Malory's writing completely rejects the claim of an institution to be somehow greater than its men. An identity is admitted to exist between the people and the institution, but it is the former, not the latter, who dominate.[3]

This note has been meant to complicate our sense of the paradox of institutional speech by suggesting that the very "institutional" qualities that we have seen to be so dangerous give the language great value when it works as a system of manners or social regulation; and even beyond that, that the grand claims of institutional speech, its impossibilities, and even its caricatures contribute to making it an imaginative and verbal resource essential to any understanding of ourselves as members of a community. The tension between one's view of oneself and the

3. Two other great epics concern themselves with a special form of the institutional identity, the tension between a man's view of himself and his place in a universe run by God. In the *Divine Comedy,* Dante again and again leads the reader to admire those whom God has damned; this is a way of stating both a threat and a faith that God is right and man — including the reader and the author — wrong. Milton's *Paradise Lost* begins with Satan presented as a Renaissance hero, and part of the reader's experience is the purification of his initial admiration for Satan, and the reader's own adjustment to what is portrayed as the great institutional truth of Puritan Christianity.

recognition of one's place in a larger system of life seems fundamental to human experience. The good and bad possibilities of institutional language are intimately related, and the language of the law is institutional if any is. How is such a language to be understood and controlled? That question does not call for an answer in words, of course, but in the way one responds as writer and speaker to the difficulties one perceives.

4. Real Talk About Real People: Is There Someone Out There?

We come now to the problem of expressing what a real person's experience is like — the subject of your next writing assignment. One place to begin to explore the difficulties of this task might be your own sense of who you are: how would you try to express that? Of course you could describe your family, what you have done and suffered, your social roles and habits, and you could tell stories about yourself. But would all that express the real you? Suppose all the conditions of your life changed totally, and you found yourself in an alien society (perhaps even in a concentration camp or a prison, or forced to do meaningless labor); how would you express the essential person who remained?[4] Can you tell us who you really are?

The first passage reproduced below is from the all-time great attempt to respond to that question, Proust's *Remembrance of Things Past.* This book is the record and expression of the author's search for himself in his own past. Proust conceives of the search for oneself as being like the search for another, and much of his book concerns such social quests. Swann, in love with Odette; St.-Loup with Rachel; Proust with Albertine and Gilberte — each fails in his attempt to understand the one he loves, to grasp even the most simple facts about her. Concentration increases impossibility: at last, Proust says, Albertine ceased to be a person to him, she had become a series of incomprehensible events.

As for the internal self, Proust repeatedly uses the image that we are not one but a great many people, constantly shifting, being born, and dying; to meet a stranger is to be forever changed. When Albertine dies, each one of the many people Proust is, as he emerges, must be told the news, and each time it is fresh; so too, it is not one but a thousand Albertines he must mourn, one at a time. To recapture the past is to become for a moment a person one once was but is no longer. It is the memory that permits the imagination to work upon life. It is not because our friend is dead that our affections for him grow faint, but because we ourselves are dying.

4. See V. Frankl, *Man's Search for Meaning* (1959), for one account of such a shock to the identity.

REMEMBRANCE OF THINGS PAST*
Marcel Proust

More than that, a thing we saw at a certain period, or a book we once read, does not remain forever associated solely with what was about us at that time; they are attached quite as faithfully to what we then were and they can be lived through again only by the conglomerate of sensations, the person, we then were. In this library, if I pick up *François le Champi* again, even in thought, there immediately rises within me a child who takes my place and alone has the right to read that title, *François le Champi,* and who reads it as he did years ago, with the same impression of the weather out in the garden, the same dreams as he dreamed that day about far-away lands and life, the same anguish about the morrow. But let me see some object from another bygone time and a different young man will arise within me. And my inner self of today is merely an abandoned quarry which believes that all the marble it contains is uniform and monotonous, but out of which each remembrance, like a Greek sculptor, carves innumerable statues. I purposely said "some object," for books act in this respect the same as objects, and the way a book used to open, or the grain of the paper, may have retained as keen a remembrance of what I imagined Venice to be like, for instance, and my longing to go there, as the sentences themselves. Even keener, for the latter are sometimes a hindrance, like photographs of a person, which prevent one from recalling him as well as if one were satisfied merely to think about him. It is true, with many books of my childhood (and, alas, even with some of Bergotte's) if I happened to pick them up some evening when I was tired, I did it, I must admit, only as I might have taken a train, in the hope of resting my spirit with the sight of different objects and a breath of air from olden times. But it happens also that the much-desired recalling of things past is actually hampered by a prolonged reading of the book. There is one book by Bergotte (the copy in the Prince's library bore an extremely fawning and platitudinous inscription) which I read all through in one winter's day long ago, when I could not see Gilberte, and now I cannot manage to find the pages I loved so much. Certain words here and there make me think it might be those pages, but that is impossible, for where then, can be the beauty I thought I found there? But the snow that covered the Champs-Elysées the day I read that book still lies upon it; I can see it still. And that is why, if I had been tempted to be a book collector, as the Prince de Guermantes was, I would have been one of a very peculiar sort, seeking that beauty which is independent of the "value" of a book, properly

* Volume 2, pages 1005–1007 (1913–1928; Random House ed. 1934).

speaking, and which it possesses for booklovers because of their knowing the libraries it has passed through, or that it was given to this or that famous man by this or that sovereign on the occasion of some special event, and through their having followed it from sale to sale throughout its career; this historic beauty of a book, so to speak, would not be lost for me. But I would more gladly extract it from the history of my own life than merely as a connoisseur and for me it would often reside, not in one specific copy, but in the work itself, as in this *François le Champi*, which I had contemplated for the first time in my little room at Combray during what was, perhaps, the sweetest and the saddest night of my life (when I had, alas — at a time when the mysterious Guermantes seemed to me very inaccessible — obtained from my parents the initial abdication, from which I can date the decline in my health and my will power and the daily increasing habit of postponing a difficult task) and rediscovered today in the Guermantes library on the most beautiful day of my life, as it happened, when a great light suddenly shone, not only on the old gropings of my thought, but even on the purpose of my life and, perhaps, of art itself. As for the individual volumes themselves, I would, by the way, have been able to take an interest in them, but only by giving living meanings to the terms. The first edition of a work would have been more precious to me than the others, but I would have understood by that the edition in which I read it for the first time. I would look for original editions, by which I mean editions from which I received an original impression. For the later impressions are no longer original. I would seek for the novels old-fashioned bindings, of the time when I read my first novels, in those days when my father used so often to say to me, "Stand up straight." Like the dress in which we saw a woman for the first time, they would help me recapture the love that filled me then, the first beauty, on which I have superposed so many images, less and less dear, trying to recapture the first one when I am not the "I" who saw them and must give place to the "I" which I was at that time in order that he may call forth the thing he knew, which my present self does not know at all. And the library I would build up in this way would be even more precious, for the books I read in years past in Combray, in Venice, now enriched by memory with vast illuminations representing the church of Saint-Hilaire, the gondola tied fast at the foot of San Giorgio Maggiore on the Grand Canal encrusted with sparkling sapphires, would have become worthy of those old illustrated books, those Bibles in story form, which the booklover never opens in order to read the text but to charm himself again with the colours added to it by some rival of Fouquet, which give the volume all its value. And yet, after all, not to open the books one read in earlier days except to look at illustrations with which they were not embellished at that time would still seem to me so dangerous that I would not be tempted to be a book collector even in the sense I have described, the only one I could understand. I know too well how easily the pictures left by the mind can be effaced by the mind. For the old ones it substitutes new ones which do not have the same power of resurrection. If I still possessed the copy of *François le Champi* which Mamma one evening took out of the package of books my grandmother was to give me for my birthday, I would never look at it; I would be too afraid of inserting in it little by little my impressions of today, covering completely those of former years; I would be too afraid of seeing it become so completely a thing of the present that, when I asked it to call forth again the child who spelled out its title in the little room at Combray, not recognising its voice, he might not respond any longer to its call and might remain forever buried in oblivion.

QUESTIONS

1. *Can you, in similar fashion, express what you see when you look into your own internal life? Try it, giving an account of one event in your internal life.*
2. *If you cannot do that, how can you — or anyone — hope to do justice to the experience of someone else?*
3. *There follows a series of passages in which two writers talk about real people. How is this literature like or unlike the literature of fictional characterization you have been reading? Do these writers find ways to do justice to the complexity and foreignness of the experience of others, or do they write a sort of fiction of their own? Here you are asked to face squarely, for the first time, the problem of what legitimate expectations one brings to talk by one real person about another.*

THE HISTORY OF THE REBELLION AND CIVIL WARS IN ENGLAND*

Edward Hyde, First Earl of Clarendon

Character of Essex (vi, 402)

The earl of Essex hath been enough mentioned before; his nature and his understanding have been described; his former disobligations from the Court, and then his introduction into it, and afterwards his being displaced from the office he held in it, have been set forth; and there will be occasion hereafter to renew the discourse of him; and therefore it shall suffice in this place to say, that a weak judgment, and a little vanity, and as much of pride, will hurry a man into as unwarrantable

* (1702; Macray ed. 1888). Roman numbers represent books; arabic numbers, paragraphs.

and as violent attempts as the greatest and most unlimited and insatiable ambition will do. He had no ambition of title, or office, or preferment, but only to be kindly looked upon and kindly spoken to, and quietly to enjoy his own fortune: and, without doubt, no man in his nature more abhorred rebellion than he did, nor could he have been led into it by any open or transparent temptation but by a thousand disguises and cozenages. His pride supplied his want of ambition, and he was angry to see any other man more respected than himself, because he thought he deserved it more, and did better requite it. For he was in his friendships just and constant, and would not have practised foully against those he took to be enemies. No man had credit enough with him to corrupt him in point of loyalty to the King whilst he thought himself wise enough to know what treason was. But the new doctrine and distinction of allegiance, and of the King's power in and out of Parliament, and the new notions of ordinances, were too hard for him, and did really intoxicate his understanding, and made him quit his own to follow theirs who he thought wished as well and judged better than himself. His vanity disposed him to be *His Excellence*, and his weakness to believe that he should be the general in the Houses as well as in the field, and be able to govern their counsels and restrain their passions as well as to fight their battles; and that by this means he should become the preserver, and not the destroyer, of the King and kingdom. And with this ill-grounded confidence he launched out into that sea where he met with nothing but rocks and shelves, and from whence he could never discover any safe port to harbour in.

Hampden's Skill (iii, 31)

Mr. Hambden was a man of much greater cunning, and it may be of the most discerning spirit and of the greatest address and insinuation to bring any thing to pass which he desired of any man of that time, and who laid the design deepest. He was a gentleman of good extraction and a fair fortune, who from a life of great pleasure and license had on a sudden retired to extraordinary sobriety and strictness, and yet retained his usual cheerfulness and affability; which, together with the opinion of his wisdom and justice and the courage he had shewed in opposing the ship-money, raised his reputation to a very great height, not only in Buckinghamshire where he lived but generally throughout the kingdom. He was not a man of many words, and rarely began the discourse, or made the first entrance upon any business that was assumed; but a very weighty speaker, and, after he had heard a full debate and observed how the House was like to be inclined, took up the argument, and shortly and clearly and craftily so stated it that he commonly conducted it to the conclusion he desired; and if he found he could not do that, he never was without the dexterity to divert the debate to another time, and to prevent the determining any thing in the negative which might prove inconvenient in the future. He made so great a show of civility and modesty and humility, and always of mistrusting his own judgment and of esteeming his with whom he conferred for the present, that he seemed to have no opinions or resolutions but such as he contracted from the information and instruction he received upon the discourses of others, whom he had a wonderful art of governing and leading into his principles and inclinations whilst they believed that he wholly depended upon their counsel and advice. No man had ever a greater power over himself or was less the man that he seemed to be, which shortly after appeared to every body when he cared less to keep on the mask.

Coventry's Skill (i, 99)

He had, in the plain way of speaking and delivery, without much ornament of elocution, a strange power of making himself believed, the only justifiable design of eloquence: so that though he used very frankly to deny, and would never suffer any man to depart from him with an opinion that he was inclined to gratify when in truth he was not, (holding that dissimulation to be the worst of lying,) yet the manner of it was so gentle and obliging, and his condescension such, to inform the persons whom he could not satisfy, that few departed from him with ill will and ill wishes.

Goring and Wilmot (viii, 169)

Goring, who was now general of the horse, was no more gracious to prince Rupert than Wilmott had been; and had all the other's faults, and wanted his regularity and preserving his respect with the officers. Wilmott loved debauchery, but shut it out from his business; and never neglected that, and rarely miscarried in it. Goring had much a better understanding and a sharper wit, (except in the very exercise of debauchery, and then the other was inspired,) a much keener courage, and presentness of mind in danger: Wilmott discerned it farther off, and because he could not behave himself so well in it, commonly prevented or warily declined it, and never drank when he was within distance of an enemy: Goring was not able to resist the temptation when he was in the middle of them, nor would decline it to obtain a victory, and in one of those fits had suffered the horse to escape out of Cornwall; and the most signal misfortunes of his life in war had their rise from that uncontrollable license. Neither of them valued their promises, professions, or friendships, according to any rules of honour or integrity; but Wilmott violated them the less willingly, and never but for some great benefit or convenience to himself: Goring without scruple, out of humour, or for wit sake, and loved no man so well but that he would cozen him, and then expose him to public mirth for having been cozened; and therefore he had always fewer friends than the other, but more company, for no man had a wit that pleased the company better. The ambitions of both were unlimited, and so equally incapable of being contented; and both unrestrained by any respect to good-nature or justice from pursuing the satisfaction thereof: yet Wilmott had more scruples from religion to startle him, and would not have attained his end by any gross or foul act of wickedness: Goring could have passed through those pleasantly, and would without hesitation have broken any trust, or done any act of treachery, to have satisfied an ordinary passion or appetite; and, in truth, wanted nothing but industry (for he had wit and courage and understanding and ambition, uncontrolled by any fear of God or man) to have been as eminent and successful in the highest attempt in wickedness of any man in the age he lived in or before. And of all his qualifications dissimulation was his master-piece; in which he so much excelled, that men were not ordinarily ashamed, or out of countenance, with being deceived but twice by him.

QUESTIONS

1. *Are these characters "flat" or "round"? Are they capable of "surprising in a convincing way"? To what extent does Clarendon express or recognize the foreignness of another's experience? How does he do so?*
2. *Perhaps you wish to answer that question differently for the different characters. Here are two comparisons that may help you work this through:*
   a. *Compare Clarendon on Hampden with Macaulay on Charles II (page 251 supra).*
   b. *Compare Clarendon on Goring and Wilmot with Theophrastus on the lover of evil (page 285 supra).*
3. *This writing puts much at stake. The tone of the Essex passage is one of remarkable fairness in judgment, even to one's enemies. Essex's decency is made clear, and he is carefully positioned with respect to the other rebels. This statement of credit enables Clarendon to get away with "did really intoxicate his understanding" and makes the final image of the battered pilot a complex one, expressing both patronizing respect for his motives and pity for his foolishness. But notice how this writing defines not only a person but the world in which he lives. This brief chronicle of the decent man led into moral destruction by a little weakness and vanity defines a world of peril, one in which a good heart is not enough, and this world is the real world in which Clarendon lived. This sort of writing is a way of posing a question to which the History as a whole is directed: how can one live and act in such a world? In Chapter 6 we shall examine*

in detail Clarendon's way of putting and responding to that question. For the moment it is enough to see that the way a person is written about can have implications such as these.

THE EDUCATION OF HENRY ADAMS*

Henry Adams

[Adams has become friendly with Badeau, who has written a life of President Grant.]

. . . Badeau, who had come to Washington for a consulate which was slow to reach him, resorted more or less to whiskey for encouragement, and became irritable, besides being loquacious. He talked much about Grant, and showed a certain artistic feeling for analysis of character, as a true literary critic would naturally do. Loyal to Grant, and still more so to Mrs. Grant, who acted as his patroness, he said nothing, even when far gone, that was offensive about either, but he held that no one except himself and Rawlins understood the General. To him, Grant appeared as an intermittent energy, immensely powerful when awake, but passive and plastic in repose. He said that neither he nor the rest of the staff knew why Grant succeeded; they believed in him because of his success. For stretches of time, his mind seemed torpid. Rawlins and the others would systematically talk their ideas into it, for weeks, not directly, but by discussion among themselves, in his presence. In the end, he would announce the idea as his own, without seeming conscious of the discussion; and would give the orders to carry it out with all the energy that belonged to his nature. They could never measure his character or be sure when he would act. They could never follow a mental process in thought. They were not sure that he did think.

In all this, Adams took deep interest, for although he was not, like Badeau, waiting for Mrs. Grant's power of suggestion to act on the General's mind in order to germinate in a consulate or a legation, his portrait gallery of great men was becoming large, and it amused him to add an authentic likeness of the greatest general the world had seen since Napoleon. Badeau's analysis was rather delicate; infinitely superior to that of Sam Ward or Charles Nordhoff.

Badeau took Adams to the White House one evening and introduced him to the President and Mrs. Grant. First and last, he saw a dozen Presidents at the White House, and the most famous were by no means the most agreeable, but he found Grant the most curious object of study among them all. About no one did opinions differ so widely. Adams had no opinion, or occasion to make one. A single word with Grant satisfied

* Chapter 17 (1918).

him that, for his own good, the fewer words he risked, the better. Thus far in life he had met with but one man of the same intellectual or unintellectual type — Garibaldi. Of the two, Garibaldi seemed to him a trifle the more intellectual, but, in both, the intellect counted for nothing; only the energy counted. The type was pre-intellectual, archaic, and would have seemed so even to the cave-dwellers. Adam, according to legend, was such a man.

In time one came to recognize the type in other men, with differences and variations, as normal; men whose energies were the greater, the less they wasted on thought; men who sprang from the soil to power; apt to be distrustful of themselves and of others; shy; jealous; sometimes vindictive; more or less dull in outward appearance; always needing stimulants, but for whom action was the highest stimulant — the instinct of fight. Such men were forces of nature, energies of the prime, like the *Pteraspis,* but they made short work of scholars. They had commanded thousands of such and saw no more in them than in others. The fact was certain; it crushed argument and intellect at once.

Adams did not feel Grant as a hostile force; like Badeau he saw only an uncertain one. When in action he was superb and safe to follow; only when torpid he was dangerous. To deal with him one must stand near, like Rawlins, and practice more or less sympathetic habits. Simple-minded beyond the experience of Wall Street or State Street, he resorted, like most men of the same intellectual calibre, to commonplaces when at a loss for expression: "Let us have peace!" or, "The best way to treat a bad law is to execute it"; or a score of such reversible sentences generally to be gauged by their sententiousness; but sometimes he made one doubt his good faith; as when he seriously remarked to a particularly bright young woman that Venice would be a fine city if it were drained. In Mark Twain, this suggestion would have taken rank among his best witticisms; in Grant it was a measure of simplicity not singular. Robert E. Lee betrayed the same intellectual commonplace, in a Virginian form, not to the same degree, but quite distinctly enough for one who knew the American. What worried Adams was not the commonplace; it was, as usual, his own education. Grant fretted and irritated him, like the *Terebratula,* as a defiance of first principles. He had no right to exist. He should have been extinct for ages. The idea that, as society grew older, it grew one-sided, upset evolution, and made of education a fraud. That, two thousand years after Alexander the Great and Julius Caesar, a man like Grant should be called — and should actually and truly be — the highest product of the most advanced evolution, made evolution ludicrous. One must be as commonplace as Grant's own commonplaces to maintain such an absurdity. The progress of evolution from President Washington to President Grant, was alone evidence enough to upset Darwin.

Two passages you should reread at this point are the account of Hume's death and the article by Janice Norton, *supra* pages 160 and 174.

Although this section has asked specifically how the writer can talk about real people, it is worth considering that one response to the puzzle of life may be to write fiction. Take Joseph Conrad, for example, British sea captain of Polish birth: after fifteen years of the life of the sea, he took up a pen to write a novel. Why on earth did he do so, what can possibly have possessed him? He says, "Till I began to write that novel I had written nothing but letters and not very many of these." *A Personal Record*, Chapter 4 (1912). In *Almayer's Folly* (1895) he told the story of a man he had known in the East, a European who lived in the bush, a man of inexplicable ideals and expectations. Out of a sense of being European, this defunct trader disowns his daughter when she marries a native prince; she goes off to a life of rich possibility as queen of a tropical island; he returns to his house in the mud, his broken business, his isolation. He could have gone with her but refused. Conrad says, "He governed his conduct by considerations removed from the obvious, by incredible assumptions, which rendered his logic impenetrable to any reasonable person." *A Personal Record*, Chapter 4. Conrad's testimony — for what it is worth — is this: "If I had not got to know Almayer pretty well it is almost certain that there never would have been a line of mine in print." *Ibid.*

5. *Defining Character in Your Own Life and Relationships*

Here is a series of old and new questions that ask you to think about your own private and social experience and how it can be expressed.

1. Draft a passage in which you express the real you, the ultimate personality or identity that exists behind your external attributes (behind your physical characteristics, social relations and habits, incidents of conduct, and the like). If you cannot, explain why you cannot.

2. Think now of your relations with others. Do you recognize that each person you deal with has the sort of ultimate self you have just tried to express? Consider first the formal relations you have had — say, with superiors or inferiors in the army, or with lifeguards, bus drivers, customers, and so on. Now think of relations with your parents, with your children (if you have any), with your social friends. Have you ever perceived and communicated with the ultimate and true identity of any person? How great is the difference between formal and intimate rela-

tionships? Here are two specific questions that examine aspects of these matters:

a. It is frequently said that what is wrong with modern education is that "kids are not treated as people." What is meant by that remark? Viktor Frankl describes a very successful talk he once gave to the prisoners at San Quentin, and explains his success by saying, "I had simply taken them as human beings and not mistaken them for mechanisms to repair." *The Will to Meaning* 7 (Plume ed. 1970). What do you suppose his speech was like? How, with what words or manners, did he "take them as human beings"?

Give an account of a real or imaginary occasion on which one person treats another as a person, not as a thing. Express how he does what he does. Could you now give someone else directions to this process?

b. How do you get on with your teachers: do you treat them as people, do they treat you that way? Do you approve or disapprove of what you see yourself and others doing? Give an account of a teacher treating a student as a person. Is this what the Socratic method achieves?

You should see that these questions have parallels in the relations between a lawyer and others: client, judge, juror, another lawyer, and so on. In the light of your responses to the preceding questions, do you think we should strive single-mindedly to cut through the artificiality and falseness of formal relations and treat each other simply and directly as people on every occasion? How could any other view possibly be maintained?

3. Much of our ordinary conversation about life assumes that sympathy (or empathy) is the ideal mode of human relationship. We do not often approach the ideal, of course, but perfect humanity would be perfect sympathy: chords that vibrate to the joys and sufferings of others. A sense of common humanity, rarely glimpsed, is the highest moment of life.

a. Do you share this view? Consider an occasion on which another person sympathized with you. Were you being treated like a person? Or were you being patronized?

b. Consider what you do when a friend suffers — say, from the loss of a spouse or child, from the knowledge of his own impending death, or on less serious occasions by a professional setback, sickness, or material loss. How do you sympathize, and how do you express your sympathy? Do you tell him you know how he feels? Draft an account of an occasion on which you gave sympathy, and one on which you received it.

4. In defining another person in speech or writing, you define yourself and your relationship with him as well. In doing this, for what excellence shall you strive?

WRITING ASSIGNMENT 6: Talking About Others

Part One

• *Give an account of an event in the life of another person, real or fictional, in which you show him or her to be different from yourself.*

You are here asked to express your sense of what it would be like to be someone else, to engage in the literary creation or rendition of character. How do you do it? In particular, how do you combat the natural tendency of the writer to reduce experience to caricature? You should attempt here to "realize the complexity and profundity" of another's experience; to find a way to express a self of your own; and to make clear the essential difference between yourself and the other person, between observer and observed.

Part Two

• *In an additional paragraph, explain whether your writing is true or false to life, and why.*

Part Three

• *Would you as a lawyer ever write about someone else in the way you do here? Explain when you would do so, or why you would not.*

You may find it helpful in answering Part Three to give another account of the event in Part One, this one in some form of legal speech.

WRITING ASSIGNMENT 6, ALTERNATIVE A: A Letter of Recommendation

Alternatives A and B are somewhat more sharply focused than Assignment 6, but have the same purpose: to ask you to imagine and express the life of another.

Part One

• *Draft a letter of recommendation for a law student you actually know to an employer who has asked you for your views. The employer in question may be whoever you choose — a private firm, the government, a law school faculty, a poverty law office — but write to a specific audience, if possible to a real one, rather than to "whom it may concern."*

Part Two

• *Explain the character-writing you have just engaged in. Is your student flat or round? Have you created caricature or something else? Have you done justice to the reality and foreignness of his experience, or have you made him seem an extension of your own mind?*

WRITING ASSIGNMENT 6, ALTERNATIVE B: Problems for a Prosecutor

"On the same morning three shoplifters are apprehended by a store detective for a large department store and brought to the office of the district attorney for the filing of a complaint:

"(i) A college sophomore, who was observed slipping a sweater worth $15 into her purse. She is well-dressed and comes from a comfortable home. She is embarrassed and contrite. She explains that on the previous night she had a quarrel with her boyfriend and was unable to sleep. She had gone to the department store rather than go to classes in order to forget about the quarrel. The sweater is not of a kind that she would ordinarily wear. She states that she has been in no prior trouble with the law. Final examinations will be held at the college during the following week. The girl is accompanied by a lawyer.

"(ii) A girl of nineteen, who was observed slipping a pocketbook worth $20 into a shopping bag. She is married and has a child. She works part time as a counter girl in a luncheonette and receives welfare payments. Her husband does not live with her and contributes little to her or her children's support. She did not complete high school education. She offers no explanation for her act. So far as anyone knows, she has been in no prior trouble with the law.

"(iii) A woman of sixty, who was observed taking a bead necklace worth $2 into the ladies' washroom; the necklace was found in her pocketbook by the store detective as the woman was about to walk out of the store. The detective states that she had seen the woman do the same thing with other items of small value on many previous occasions and, despite the store's general policy of ignoring occasional acts of this kind by well-to-do patrons, had decided to arrest the woman if she did it again. The woman is wealthy and an 'established' member of the community. She indignantly denies any intention to steal; she states that she had gone into the washroom to look at the necklace in a mirror and had absent-mindedly put it in her pocketbook. She threatens to sue the store for false arrest. She states that she has been in no prior trouble with the law. She is accompanied by a lawyer.

"How should the assistant district attorney who is in charge of the complaint desk respond to the three cases?" Weinreb, The Criminal Process 401–402 (1969).

Part One

• On the basis of these stories, can you tell what you would decide to do as prosecutor? If not, what else would you need to know, and how would you express it?

Part Two

• On the basis of these stories, can you tell what you would decide to do as sentencing judge? If not, what else would you need to know, and how would you express it?

Part Three

• If your answers to Parts One and Two are different, explain the difference.

Part Four

• Draft a narrative of one of these stories in which you express what is missing that would enable you to be confident in your judgment as prosecutor or judge.

A. Is the story as you have written it one that could possibly be true, or is it like Macaulay's tale of Mr. Z.(page 253 supra)?

B. In your final draft, try to ensure that your story realizes the "profundities and complexities of the ordinary human mind."

Part Five

• What do you conclude about the way that the prosecutor or the judge talks about people?

B. TALKING ABOUT PEOPLE IN A LANGUAGE OF LABELS: THE INSANITY DEFENSE

How copious and precise the botanical language to describe the leaves, as well as the other parts of a plant! Botany is worth studying if only for the precision of its terms — to learn the value of words and of system. It is wonderful how much pains has been taken to describe a flower's leaf, compared for instance with the care that is taken in describing a psychological fact. Suppose as much ingenuity (perhaps it would be needless) in making a language to express the sentiments! We are armed with language adequate to describe each leaf in the field, or at least to distinguish it from each other, but not to describe a human character. With equally wonderful indistinctness and confusion we describe men. The precision and copiousness of botanical language applied to the description of moral qualities!*

In Section A you saw how difficult or impossible it is to talk about a real person in a way that does justice to what he is, to his difference from oneself, even when one is free to use any literary resource one can devise or invent. Of course those who make and manage the legal system are not so free, and in this section you are asked to face the consequences of the fact that legal talk about people takes place in a language whose central form is the rule, which operates by affixing unitary labels to people and their experience. How can sensible talk about people possibly go on in such a language?

Our principal effort will be to analyze the application of the label "insane" in criminal cases. What process of judgment and thought lies behind the application of that label, and what directions (if any) does the law give to that process? Your assignment at the end of this section will be to draft a simple statement of what "insanity" should be said to mean for the purposes of the criminal law — to draft your own insanity test, together with such additional instructions and explanations as you think appropriate. You will then be asked to evaluate the literature you have created as a way of talking about people: do your explanations and instructions, your directions for use, somehow save this language from the dangers of the label and rule? Does the context you give it make it intelligible and usable, and if so, how? If not, what then? If you conclude that the task is impossible you will be asked to explain the source and nature of the impossibility you face.

To put it in terms of the preceding section, one might say that the various existing statements of the insanity defense all talk about people as caricatures, not as characters. Your first question is whether the insanity defense can be rewritten to do justice to the full personalities, the real identities, of the people it talks about. If not, can its use of caricature be controlled somehow? Or is it conceivable that, on a proper understanding, its use of caricature can be regarded as an advantage, as a means of control? To respond to these questions you will have to figure out for yourself as thoroughly as you can just what the language-game of the insanity defense should be.

* H. D. Thoreau, *Journal*, Aug. 20, 1851.

You may find this problem frustrating, but it cannot be shrugged off unless you wish to say that in no case should the defendant's insanity be a defense to his criminal liability. This is not an instance in which one can easily justify an artificially limited way of talking about another person on the grounds that one's purposes are carefully and narrowly defined. The issue you address is as solemn as any faced by the law: whether a defendant is to be held responsible for his conduct, convicted, and punished, or to be excused as one not responsible for what he does. Here the law must face the problems of individual responsibility and guilt that have always perplexed mankind. The whole person is before the court, and the very question to be decided is what sort of person he is. The law here has an opportunity and an obligation to speak in the most comprehensive and understanding way about the human personality, to leave nothing out that a decent person would consider. Can you see that it does speak this way?

General works of some relevance to your consideration of this problem are: A. Goldstein, *The Insanity Defense* (1967); Goldstein and Katz, "Abolish the Insanity Defense: Why Not?" 72 *Yale L.J.* 853 (1963); H. Packer, *The Limits of the Criminal Sanction* (1968); M. Foucault, *Madness and Civilization* (1965); R. D. Laing, *Sanity, Madness, and the Family* (1964), and *The Divided Self* (1960).

1. *Proposals and Practices*

Below is a tentative draft of the Model Penal Code in which three alternative formulations of an insanity test are proposed. It is followed by a brief explanation by the reporter which makes reference to other tests, and by a proposal by Professor Glueck for yet another test. As you read this material, ask how you would characterize this sort of talk about people. Would you ever talk this way? How would you like it if someone talked this way about you? Do these tests invite or permit the lawyers and others who use them to do justice to the full personality of the defendant? Who do you suppose ever began to talk this way and why?

MODEL PENAL CODE*
American Law Institute

Article 4. Responsibility

Section 4.01. Mental Disease or Defect Excluding Responsibility.

(1) A person is not responsible for criminal conduct if at the time of such conduct as a result of mental disease or defect he lacks substantial

* Tent. Draft No. 4 (1955).

capacity either to appreciate the criminality of his conduct or to conform his conduct to the requirements of law.

(2) The terms "mental disease or defect" do not include an abnormality manifested only by repeated criminal or otherwise anti-social conduct.

Alternative formulations of paragraph (1).

(a) A person is not responsible for criminal conduct if at the time of such conduct as a result of mental disease or defect his capacity either to appreciate the criminality of his conduct or to conform his conduct to the requirements of law is so substantially impaired that he cannot justly be held responsible.

(b) A person is not responsible for criminal conduct if at the time of such conduct as a result of mental disease or defect he lacks substantial capacity to appreciate the criminality of his conduct or is in such state that the prospect of conviction and punishment cannot constitute a significant restraining influence upon him.

THE PROBLEM OF DEFINING THE CRITERIA OF IRRESPONSIBILITY*

1. No problem in the drafting of a penal code presents larger intrinsic difficulty than that of determining when individuals whose conduct would otherwise be criminal ought to be exculpated on the ground that they were suffering from mental disease or defect when they acted as they did. What is involved specifically is the drawing of a line between the use of public agencies and public force to condemn the offender by conviction, with resultant sanctions in which there is inescapably a punitive ingredient (however constructive we may attempt to make the process of correction) and modes of disposition in which that ingredient is absent, even though restraint may be involved. To put the matter differently, the problem is to discriminate between the cases where a punitive-correctional disposition is appropriate and those in which a medical-custodial disposition is the only kind that the law should allow.

2. The traditional *M'Naghten* rule resolves the problem solely in regard to the capacity of the individual to know what he was doing and to know that it was wrong. Absent these minimal elements of rationality, condemnation and punishment are obviously both unjust and futile. They are unjust because the individual could not, by hypothesis, have employed reason to restrain the act; he did not and he could not know the facts essential to bring reason into play. On the same ground, they are futile. A madman who believes that he is squeezing lemons when he chokes his wife or thinks that homicide is the command of God is plainly beyond reach of the restraining influence of law; he needs re-

* *Id.* at 156 (Reporter's Commentary on Article Four).

straint but condemnation is entirely meaningless and ineffective. Thus the attacks on the *M'Naghten* rule as an inept definition of insanity or as an arbitrary definition in terms of special symptoms are entirely misconceived. The rationale of the position is that these are cases in which reason can not operate and in which it is totally impossible for individuals to be deterred. Moreover, the category defined by the rule is so extreme that to the ordinary man the exculpation of the persons it encompasses bespeaks no weakness in the law. He does not identify such persons and himself; they are a world apart.

Jurisdictions in which the *M'Naghten* test has been expanded to include the case where mental disease produces an "irresistible impulse" proceed on the same rationale. They recognize, however, that cognitive factors are not the only ones that preclude inhibition; that even though cognition still obtains, mental disorder may produce a total incapacity for self-control. The same result is sometimes reached under *M'Naghten* proper, in the view, strongly put forth by Stephen, that "knowledge" requires more than the capacity to verbalize right answers to a question, it implies capacity to function in the light of knowledge. Stephen, *History of English Criminal Law*, vol. 2, p. 171. See also Jerome Hall, *Principles of Criminal Law* (1947) 518 et seq. In modern psychiatric terms, the "fundamental difference between verbal or purely intellectual knowledge and the mysterious other kind of knowledge is familiar to every clinical psychiatrist; it is the difference between knowledge divorced from affect and knowledge so fused with affect that it becomes a human reality." Zilboorg, Misconceptions of Legal Insanity, 9 *Am. J. Orthopsychiatry* 540, 552. See also Wertham, *The Show of Violence* (1949) 86. The application of *M'Naghten* has been mitigated somewhat, especially in England, by accepting evidence couched in these terms. Cf. *Rex v. True*, 16 Cr. App. R. 164, 167 (1922).

3. The draft accepts the view that any effort to exclude the non-deterrables from strictly penal sanctions must take account of the impairment of volitional capacity no less than of impairment of cognition; and that this result should be achieved directly in the formulation of the test, rather than left to mitigation in the application of *M'Naghten*. It also accepts the criticism of the "irresistible impulse" formulation as inept in so far as it may be impliedly restricted to sudden, spontaneous acts as distinguished from insane propulsions that are accompanied by brooding or reflection. See e.g., Royal Commission on Capital Punishment, *Report* (1953) par. 314, p. 110.

Both the main formulation recommended and alternative (a) deem the proper question on this branch of the inquiry to be whether the defendant was without capacity to conform his conduct to the requirements of law. Compare the test for proceedings in courts-martial: "whether the accused was, at the time of the alleged offense, so far free from mental defect, disease, or derangement as to be able, concerning the particular acts charged, to distinguish right from wrong and to adhere to the right." *Manual for Courts-Martial, United States,* 1951, paragraph 120b; *United States v. Smith,* 17 CMR 314, 320. The application of the principle will call, of course, for a distinction between incapacity, upon the one hand, and mere indisposition on the other. Such a distinction is inevitable in the application of a standard addressed to impairment of volition. We believe that the distinction can be made.

Alternative (b) states the issue differently. Instead of asking whether the defendant had capacity to conform his conduct to the requirements of law, it asks whether, in consequence of mental disease or defect, the threat of punishment could not exercise a significant restraining influence upon him. To some extent, of course, these are the same inquiries. To the extent that they diverge, the latter asks a narrower and harder question, involving the assessment of capacity to respond to a single influence, the threat of punishment. Both Dr. Guttmacher and Dr. Overholser considered the assessment of responsiveness to this one influence too difficult for psychiatric judgment. Hence, though the issue framed by the alternative may well be thought to state the question that is most precisely relevant for legal purposes, the Reporter and the Council deemed the inquiry impolitic upon this ground. In so far as non-deterrability is the determination that is sought, it must be reached by probing general capacity to conform to the requirements of law. The validity of this conclusion is submitted, however, to the judgment of the Institute.

4. One further problem must be faced. In addressing itself to impairment of the cognitive capacity, *M'Naghten* demands that impairment be complete: the actor must *not* know. So, too, the irresistible impulse criterion presupposes a complete impairment of capacity for self-control. The extremity of these conceptions is, we think, the point that poses largest difficulty to psychiatrists when called upon to aid in their administration. The schizophrenic, for example, is disoriented from reality; the disorientation is extreme; but it is rarely total. Most psychotics will respond to a command of someone in authority within the mental hospital; they thus have some capacity to conform to a norm. But this is very different from the question whether they have the capacity to conform to requirements that are not thus immediately symbolized by an attendant or policeman at the elbow. Nothing makes the inquiry into responsibility more unreal for the psychiatrist than limitation of the issue to some ultimate extreme of total incapacity, when clinical experience reveals only a graded scale with marks along the way. . . .

We think this difficulty can and must be met. The law must recognize that when there is no black and white it must content itself with different shades of gray. The draft, accordingly, does not demand *complete* impairment of capacity. It asks instead for *substantial* impairment. This is all, we think, that candid witnesses, called on to infer the nature of the situation at a time that they did not observe, can ever confidently say, even when they know that a disorder was extreme.

If substantial impairment of capacity is to suffice, there remains the question whether this alone should be the test or whether the criterion should state the principle that measures how substantial it must be. To identify the degree of impairment with precision is, of course, impossible both verbally and logically. The recommended formulation is content to rest upon the term "substantial" to support the weight of judgment; if capacity is greatly impaired, that presumably should be sufficient. Alternative (a) proposes to submit the issue squarely to the jury's sense of justice, asking expressly whether the capacity of the defendant "was so substantially impaired that he can not justly be held responsible." Some members of the Council deemed it unwise to present questions of justice to the jury, preferring a submission that in form, at least, confines the inquiry to fact. The proponents of the alternative contend that since the jury normally will feel that it is only just to exculpate if the disorder was extreme, that otherwise conviction is demanded, it is safer to invoke the jury's sense of justice than to rest entirely on the single word "substantial," imputing no specific measure of degree. The issue is an important one and it is submitted for consideration by the Institute.

5. The draft rejects the formulation warmly supported by psychiatrists and recently adopted by the Court of Appeals for the District of Columbia in *Durham v. United States,* 214 F.2d 862 (1954), namely, "that an accused is not criminally responsible if his unlawful act was the product of mental disease or defect." . . .

The difficulty with this formulation inheres in the ambiguity of "product." If interpreted to lead to irresponsibility unless the defendant would have engaged in the criminal conduct even if he had not suffered from the disease or defect, it is too broad: an answer that he would have done so can be given very rarely; this is intrinsic to the concept of the singleness of personality and unity of mental processes that psychiatry regards as fundamental. If interpreted to call for a standard of causality less relaxed than but-for cause, there are but two alternatives to be considered: (1) a mode of causality involving total incapacity or (2) a mode of causality which involves substantial incapacity. See Wechsler, The Criteria of Criminal Responsibility, 22 *U. of Chi. L. Rev.* 367 (1955). But if either of these causal concepts is intended, the formulation ought to set it forth.

The draft also rejects the proposal of the majority of the recent Royal Commission on Capital Punishment, namely, "to leave to the jury to determine whether at the time of the act the accused was suffering from disease of the mind (or mental deficiency) to such a degree that he ought not to be held responsible." *Report* (1953) par. 333, p. 116. While we agree, as we have indicated, that mental disease or defect involves gradations of degree that should be recognized, we think the legal standard ought to focus on the *consequences* of disease or defect that have a bearing on the justice of conviction and of punishment. The Royal Commission proposal fails in this respect.

6. Paragraph (2) of section 4.01 is designed to exclude from the concept of "mental disease or defect" the case of so-called "psychopathic personality." The reason for the exclusion is that, as the Royal Commission put it, psychopathy "is a statistical abnormality; that is to say, the psychopath differs from a normal person only quantitatively or in degree, not qualitatively; and the diagnosis of psychopathic personality does not carry with it any explanation of the causes of the abnormality." While it may not be feasible to formulate a definition of "disease", there is much to be said for excluding a condition that is manifested only by the behavior phenomena that must, by hypothesis, be the result of disease for irresponsibility to be established. Although British psychiatrists have agreed, on the whole, that psychopathy should not be called "disease", there is considerable difference of opinion on the point in the United States. Yet it does not seem useful to contemplate the litigation of what is essentially a matter of terminology; nor is it right to have the legal result rest upon the resolution of a dispute of this kind.

LAW AND PSYCHIATRY*
S. Glueck

. . . [I suggest] the following formulation as perhaps more realistic and more in harmony with expanding psychiatric knowledge than either *M'Naghten* alone or *M'Naghten* supplemented by irresistible impulse, or the American Law Institute's formulation, or the *Currens* decision. I shall put the test in terms of instructions to the jury. While it is understood that the prosecution must prove every element, including sanity, beyond a reasonable doubt, I am deliberately omitting reference to burden of proof in spelling out the test because I think this should be separately charged, in order to reduce the chance of confusing the jury. It will be noted that I include a provision for a mid-verdict of partial responsibility.

The proposed test is as follows:

If you are convinced that the defendant, at the time of the crime, was suffering from mental disease or defect which impaired his powers of

* Pages 105–107 (1962).

thinking, feeling, willing or self-integration, *and* that such impairment probably made it impossible for him to understand or control the act he is charged with as the ordinary, normal person understands and controls his acts, you should find him *Not guilty on the ground of insanity.*

If you are convinced that the defendant, at the time of the crime, was suffering from mental disease or defect which impaired his powers of thinking, feeling, willing or self-integration, *but you doubt* whether such impairment probably made it impossible for him to understand or control the act he is charged with as the ordinary, normal person understands and controls his acts, you should find him only *Partially responsible.*

If you are convinced that the defendant was *not* suffering from mental disease or defect at the time of the crime, you should find him *Guilty.*

There is a difference of opinion as to whether the jury should be told what the consequence of their verdict will be. I am convinced that this is desirable; and, if it is, I suggest the following addition to the charge:

If you find the defendant *Not Guilty on the ground of insanity,* he will be committed to a public mental hospital for supervision and treatment until such time as the superintendent will certify, and a court will thereafter find, that he is no longer criminally dangerous. If you find him *Partially responsible* he will be committed to a public mental hospital until such time as the superintendent will certify, and a court will thereafter find, that he is no longer criminally dangerous, and thereupon he will be transferred to the jurisdiction of the correctional and paroling authorities to be dealt with in accordance with the sentencing and paroling provisions, taking account of his former status of partial responsibility. If you find him *Guilty,* he will receive the punishment provided by law.

QUESTIONS

1. Here you see several tests proposed and choices among them explained and defended. Do you think it would really matter in a particular case what test was chosen? Or is this literature a prime example of useless academic disputation?

Remember the question asked of the Sherwood case (page 122 supra): whether it was conceivable that the jury found Mrs. Sherwood guilty of first-degree murder because the judge had used an "and" instead of an "or" in his charge. Judges themselves have expressed doubts: in United States v. Shapiro, 383 F.2d 680 (7th Cir. 1967), holding that the Model Penal Code test should thereafter be used in place of the earlier test used in the trial court's charge, a substantial minority of the bench thought that there should be no reversal in the particular case, on the grounds that the use of one charge rather than another was not prejudicial error. R. Simon, The Jury and the Defense of Insanity 213 et seq. (1967), does report empirical studies showing that the Durham rule produces more insanity verdicts than the M'Naghten rule; but except in your role as prosecutor or defense attorney, what can you conclude from that? Does that fact tell you as judge or legislator which test to adopt?

2. *Is the reality behind this language that we send the issue of insanity to the jury without any real controls at all? If so, should we explicitly recognize that fact? Compare Model Penal Code §4.01, Alternative (a), which takes a step in that direction, making part of the question whether the defendant can justly be held responsible. Does this not seem sensible to you? In fact, why should that ultimate question not be the only question the jury is asked? You can view your next writing assignment as asking what you would say to the jury in addition to such a charge. In what you say, how do you define their task? What assistance do you give them?*
3. *The various tests seem to be competing descriptions of the state of mind or heart believed to be undeserving of punishment. Are these statements really descriptions or are they something else? If they are not descriptive statements, what kind of meaning are they intended to have?*
   a. *How would you know, for example, whether a defendant's "capacity to appreciate the criminality of his conduct" was substantially "impaired"? Where is this "capacity"? What does it look like and how does it operate? How could you tell whether it was "impaired" or "unimpaired"?*
   b. *What exactly is a "mental disease or defect," and how would you distinguish it from, say, an abnormality, an imperfection, or a malfunction? (How, indeed, would you explain why the insanity tests all limit the defense to those who are suffering from "mental disease or defect" in the first place? To put it in terms of the M'Naghten rule, why should we punish someone who did not know the nature and quality of his act, whether or not he was also suffering from a "mental disease or defect"?)*
   c. *Of course, you may say that these are terms not of description but of judgment, and the statements containing them are not meant to be verifiable as descriptive statements are. We made that distinction in Chapter 2, at page 229. But to say this, while it may cut off some fruitless sorts of disputation, opens up fundamental and unanswered questions of its own: what is the process of judgment that these terms are meant to invoke, and what purposes does it serve? How can it be described and guided?*
4. *While adding to it and trying to improve upon it, the Model Penal Code seems to accept the basic premise of the M'Naghten rule that we should not punish a person who, through mental illness, does not know that what he is doing is wrong. Does this premise accord with your own notions of responsibility and psychology?*

   In your experience, does anyone ever do anything that he recognizes is wrong? If so, what do you think of and how do you characterize such conduct? Of course, one may know that behavior is wrong generally, or that it would be blamed by others if known. But is it not an integral part of a normal psychology that one always has an excuse or justification, some reason why the general rule does not apply to oneself? The wife-killer says, "No one could put up with what I have faced; anyone would have done the same." The thief says that the rules of property are inherently unjust — "property is theft" — or that they apply only to those who have been fairly treated by the system; "Others get it free by inheritance, why not I by stealing? And no one is hurt when I take money from a bank." Or if someone is hurt, one may say that people get hurt all the time, that's the breaks, or that the temptation was more than anyone could resist. Such a process of rationalization is a familiar part of the moral life of every person, I suppose.[5]

To complete the picture, what do you conclude about a person who does what he knows and feels to be wrong while he does it? "I know that drugs are destroying me, that I have no excuse, yet I keep on." "I have killed, knowing it wrong, with nothing to mitigate my crime, and loathing myself."

Which one is insane? Which deserves punishment as an example to others and a corrective to himself? Is it the truth that the M'Naghten test is 180 degrees off, that we should give special treatment to the person who does know what he is doing is wrong, and leave for punishment the one who does not, who always has an excuse?

You undoubtedly know the story of Faust, and I recommend that you read or reread Marlowe's Doctor Faustus. This is a story of damnation — not irrelevant, I should think, to one who is preparing to establish a system for condemnation. It is sometimes talked about as an instance of early atheism, which always surprises me: the atheist may break all the rules of church and religion, on the grounds that there is no God, no Heaven or Hell; but when to such a one — deliberately setting out on such a course, offering to sell his soul to the devil — there appears in his study, in a puff of smoke and with the odor of brimstone, the devil himself (or his majordomo), there is no longer any atheism about it. In that play there is never the slightest hint that Faustus expects anything except destruction; he blasphemes a God he knows to exist and to be omnipotent. He is presented as knowing as fully as one could that what he is doing is wrong, and at the last moment before death he is offered a chance to repent, which he rejects. Is this the criminal or the insane mind? The theological answer is his damnation. The answer of the play seems to be that such a damnation is a hideous wrong. This is not a play in which the author says he disbelieves in God, but that he hates him.

5. We have asked about the view the law expresses of the people subject to its regulations, particularly as that view involves the application and use of "labels." There is another, equally important question: what view does the law express of the people who operate and manage the legal system? What process of cooperation does it seek to establish among them?
   a. What attitudes towards the judge and jury do the insanity tests given or referred to above express? How are these people defined by the tasks they are given and the terms in which they are stated?
   b. Would you like to be a juror asked to apply one of the insanity tests given above? Would you feel flattered? Insulted? Why?
   c. Would you like to be a judge asked to frame jury instructions explaining how the M'Naghten or the Model Penal Code test should be applied? Draft a model instruction for one of those tests.
6. If you were a judge or juror charged with the task of making a judgment as to the defendant's sanity in a criminal case, what questions would you ask yourself about the defendant? About the process of judgment in which you were engaged?

5. See Samuel Johnson, *Rambler* No. 76 (Dec. 8, 1750), for a classic account of man's capacity for such rationalization.

2. *Talk About the Mind: The Fact of Difference*

You are well acquainted with what is involved in an attempt to express in words the experience of another. We are now concerned with a special aspect of this difficulty: how to talk about the internal experience of someone else — about his mind, his heart, whatever it is one cannot see — in a systematic way, in a way that relates his experience to everyone else's. What we call explaining behavior requires a certain kind of generalization: I tell you what someone did by describing his mind, and we all have minds, so you understand his experience and can compare it with your own experience and the described experience of others. The pressure to keep unfolding the unique is resisted in favor of an explanation that connects, that makes experience common. So it is that we have theories of psychology and morality, images or models that enable us to speak of the normal mind and the abnormal. In what such ways does the law talk about the mind? The language of the Model Penal Code and the M'Naghten rule seems hopelessly mechanical and false: it pretends that we each have a "capacity to appreciate wrongfulness" which can be found to be impaired or in good working order, like a carburetor or typewriter. The basic metaphor is that of a machine: the mind has certain functions — cognition, volition, self-integration, and so on — which can be found to be either in whack or out of whack. This is the science of the mind. The defendant has impulses that are either resistible or irresistible, and it is our business to find out which they are.

What other metaphors or models or theoretical constructs of the mind do you know? We are familiar with the traditional Christian view of man's makeup: he consists of soul and body; he has reason to discern right from wrong and free will to choose the right; the process of choice both reflects and determines the state of his soul, which must be his main concern; sometimes his reason or will or both will fail, but by divine grace this failure is not permanently damning so long as he maintains the attitude of repentance. The Freudians slice up experience quite differently: a person consists of superego, ego, and id, and remarkably little choice exists in the matter of desire or behavior. There is no clear division between mind and body.

You might make a list of other systematic ways of talking about the mind (especially if you have training in psychology) and identify the key terms of each. How are these languages normally used: as descriptions of reality, hypotheses to be checked against experience, forms of technical shorthand, ways of pointing to common experiences, or what? Do you find in their use any recognition of their false pretenses, of what they leave out? What fundamental metaphors can you uncover? The languages of psychology are so familiar that it may seem strange to be asked to regard them as metaphorical rather than as plain description, but I think it is true that any such language is an invented one, rooted in an act of the imagination. What new psychological languages — what metaphors — can you invent: the mind is like a flower, like the ocean, like a solar system, like a snail? To try to invent your own language for talking about the mind — even an extravagant one — may help you to regard the more common languages as inventions too.

One might reply that the existing psychological languages are perfectly fine. We are used to talking about the will and the emotions just as we are about chairs and trees, as if they were matters we all could see, and we find that way of talking useful. Psychologists and psychiatrists are valuable people who seem to know what they are talking about. Why fret so over the kind of approximation that any language on this sort of subject must have? There are two lines of response. For one thing, while our ordinary languages of psychology are adequate for many sorts of statements in many sorts of circumstances, we do not use them to decide whether someone should be sent to jail, to the hospital, or set free. There is a world of difference between saying as a parent of a three-year-old child that he did not know something was wrong (say, playing with the electric cord or taking a toy away from a friend) and saying the same thing as a juror of a multiple murderer. Much the same is true of the professional language of psychology as well: a diagnosis for the purpose of choosing treatment (say, to decide whether chemotherapy or analysis is more promising) is a far cry from a diagnosis to determine whether a person should be treated or punished. We are in a different game now, and the language by which we explain why someone is to go to jail or not is subject to stresses both greater than and different from our usual explanations of the conduct of others.

The other line of response to what seems to be the obvious adequacy of psychological language is to stare at the familiar until it becomes strange. There follows a series of passages about conduct and minds very different from your own, and I think you will see how tentative any psychological language must be in these situations. How much more certain can it be in the criminal courtroom? As you read these passages, ask what is happening in the mind portrayed. How do you know? In what language can you describe or explain how this mind works?

THE SOUL OF THE WHITE ANT*

Eugene Marais

The well-known yellow South African weaver bird, there are many kinds, but any kind may be used for this experiment, plaits a wonderful

* Pages 32–33 (1938).

little nest at the extreme tip of a flexible branch, generally over water. You often see their nests at the end of the thin drooping twigs of the graceful weeping willow, but have you ever taken the trouble of watching to discover how the very first piece of grass is tied to the twig and what kind of knot the little bird uses? The full-grown bird is a seed eater, but the little ones are fed on worms until it is nearly time for them to leave the nest. Remember these two instinctive memories:

1. How to build the nest, and
2. How to feed the fledglings.

I hatched the eggs of the yellow weaver under canaries, for four generations. The new birds were forced to lay eggs each time without being able to build their characteristic nest. This is the most difficult part of the experiment, but it can be done. Every time these eggs were hatched under canaries, the young ones were fed on a synthetic diet and were never allowed to see a worm or an insect. Nor did they ever see a piece of grass which might be utilized for building. Then I took this fourth generation and provided them with everything which they would need in their normal environment. Remember now that for four generations they have not seen a plaited nest or tasted a worm. From personal experience the bird cannot possibly know what to do. There can be no question of individual memory. I expected at least that there would occur *some* deviation from normal behaviour, but it was not so. When the time arrived for nesting, the birds began plaiting vigorously. They made more nests than they required. This often happens in nature as a means of protection. The eggs were hatched and the young ones were fed on worms!

QUESTIONS

1. *What sort of question is this: "Why does the weaver bird build his nest this way?" What responses does it invite, what language-game is it part of? Imagine different responses and analyze them. Does it make sense to say that he does this for protection against tree-climbing predators? That he does it because he wishes to? Or is he a machine, who cannot help what he does? Ask yourself whether it makes sense to say that this mind has the "functions" of "cognition and volition." In what language can you talk sensibly about this mind and conduct?*
2. *Can you imagine what it would be like to be a weaver bird? Compare Thoreau's Journal (Nov. 16, 1850): "A truly good book is something as wildly natural and primitive, mysterious and marvellous, ambrosial and fertile, as a fungus or a lichen. Suppose the muskrat or beaver were to turn his views to literature, what fresh views of nature would he present! The fault of our books and other deeds is that they are too humane. I want something speaking in some measure to the condition of muskrats and skunk-cabbage as well as of men . . ."*

3. *Following are some more events described by Marais. How do you explain or describe the minds you see portrayed here?*

THE SOUL OF THE WHITE ANT*

Eugene Marais

If you ask scientists what the psychological difference is between a baboon and an otter, nine out of ten will say that the baboon possesses powers of reasoning and intelligence, which the otter lacks. It would be just as clear if they said the baboon is a baboon and the otter is an otter. Neither answer takes you very far. Another scientist may say that a baboon can learn new habits more easily than an otter. This is more enlightening but does not help us a great deal. . . . Once in the Waterberg during a drought which lasted for four years and when all the streams became stagnant, you would find otters all over the veld adjacent to the big waterways. There were still pools of water, but these contained no fish or crabs. The otter is a nimble creature, and you can teach him to catch birds and other small land animals in the same way as a cat does. But he cannot teach himself to do this. Hundreds of these wild otters died in the midst of plenty. At this time I managed to get hold of a pair of newly born otters. One of these I sent to Springbokvlakte, thirty miles from the nearest running water. As he was dug out of the nest shortly after birth, he had never seen a river. A bitch reared him with her own litter. He never saw or was given food other than raw meat, birds and other land animals, and he never saw water except when it was given to him in a dish to quench his thirst.

At the same time I took a newly born baboon from the mountains to the plain and reared him with a feeding-bottle. Afterwards he was fed on food which was not his natural diet. No opportunity was given him of catching or eating a living insect. When both these animals were three years old they were taken for the first time to their own natural environments, the otter to Sterk river, whence he originally came, and the baboon to the Dubbele Mountains where his mother had been shot. Both were starved for a short while previously. Here I had a wonderful opportunity of observing the great difference in behaviour of these two creatures. The otter just hesitated for a moment or two, then plunged into the water, and within half an hour had caught a crab and a large carp and devoured them on the rocks.

The baboon, on the contrary, was completely lost. He was in the midst of a plenitude of natural food yet, although starving, he obviously knew nothing of turning over stones and catching the living insects which hide beneath them. There is no doubt he would have died of

* *Id.* at 40–43.

hunger if he had been left alone. When I turned up a stone for him, he retreated from the wriggling insects, and showed signs of fear and horror. With the greatest difficulty I succeeded in persuading him to taste a dead scorpion, from which I had removed the sting and the poison gland, and at last he was induced to catch a living one, with the result that he was immediately stung on the finger. He chose, amongst other things, to eat a wild mountain fruit which is deadly poison and his life perforce had to be saved. Such accidents never happen to wild baboons. They have learnt. Our tame baboon also eventually understood all these things, but he had to learn by painful experience.

THE SOUL OF THE APE*

Eugene Marais

A nest of a small species of Namaqua partridge (*Pterocles*) was found on the Springbok Flats and its position indicated by three inconspicuous marks, all at long distances from the nest. Anyone knowing the marks, and with the assistance of a signaller, could find the nest. Without these aids it seemed humanly impossible ever to discover the nest again after one had gone any distance away from it. The country is so absolutely level that it can hardly be said to possess a watershed. It is in addition quite trackless, without a single conspicuous natural feature, and is covered with shrubs and grass all monotonously unvarying. Three eggs had been hatched just after the nest was found. The female bird was on different occasions disturbed at the nest. She invariably flew straight away at great speed until she vanished in the distance. The direction in which she flew was determined by the side on which the nest was approached. It seemed impossible that she could ever find the nest again by any of the ordinary psychic processes that a human being employs. Generally within half an hour she returned, flying swiftly and in an apparently straight line to the nest. After the duration of her absences had been ascertained, she was trapped and temporarily blinded. She was then taken a distance of three hundred paces from the nest, liberated and watched for about two hours. During this time she kept "calling" at intervals and made three short flights, but not once in the direction of the nest. She was then caught and taken a distance of seven miles to a settlement where she could not have been before. Here her sight was restored and she was liberated. She flew straight back to the nest.

A number of different men and boys all long resident on the Flats and experienced hunters were then tested in the following manner:

Each one was taken to the nest and allowed to study the surroundings for as long and as carefully as he liked. He was then taken in a straight

* Pages 167–169 (1969).

line away from the nest a distance of two hundred yards and again at right angles to this line for another hundred yards. He was then told to find the nest. Out of five individuals thus tested, not one even came near the place. One, after wandering for some time — he admitted becoming gradually more confused — struck his own original spoor and so found his starting-point. But it was quite evident that no one could have found the nest by his sense of locality alone.

A boy of fourteen, born on the Flats and known to possess a high sense of locality, was then tested in the same manner. In three trials he never succeeded in getting near the correct locality. He was then hypnotised at the nest and led a long distance away while every device was adopted to obliterate his sense of direction. About a mile from the nest he was stopped and told to go back. He unhesitatingly did so in a perfectly straight line. It was ascertained that his ability to find the nest was not in any way affected by the distance he was taken away, nor by the nature of the route. Even where a series of circles were described, and numberless zigzags and angled courses, he was never in the least doubt as to the exact direction in which the nest lay. When he was led away blindfolded and the same methods of mystification were adopted, the moment his eyes were opened he invariably turned and walked in the right direction. If, however, he was led away blindfolded even a short distance and told to find the nest still blindfolded, he not only could not do it but as often as not walked directly away from it. And the same result followed if he was led away open-eyed for a short distance and then told to go back blindfolded.

QUESTIONS

1. *Why did the otter plunge with little hesitation into the water and begin to hunt skillfully for food? Why did the baboon behave so incompetently? How did the bird and the hypnotized boy find their way back to the nest?*
2. *How would you characterize the questions asked in question one: what sort of responses do they invite, what language-games are they part of? In what languages, based upon what metaphors, do you respond to them?*

THE STUDY OF INSTINCT*

N. Tinbergen

One of the first things that impresses the student of animal behaviour is the fact that the working of the animal's sense organs is not the same as ours. For instance, many animals, like starfish, snails, flies, are completely deaf. Others are blind, or nearly so, etc. But, on the other hand, some animals are able to hear sounds that are inaudible to us

* Page 16 (1951).

(locusts, bats) or may smell odours that are entirely imperceptible to us (many mammals, moths). A careful study of sensory capacities reveals that almost no two species have exactly the same capacities. Von Uexkull (1921) has emphasized this by saying that each animal has its own *Merkwelt* (perceptual world) and that this world is different from its environment as we perceive it, that is to say, from our own *Merkwelt*.

QUESTIONS

1. The frontispiece of Tinbergen's book shows a male stickleback fish standing on its nose in front of a mirror. What sort of question is it to ask, "Why does he do that?" Is this question like or unlike the same question asked about people? We are told that this is a "threat posture." Do you want to say that he is threatening other fish, warning them off, defending his territory, or what? Elsewhere the author speaks of a locust that is "willing to mate."

2. Could one say of a weaver bird that it was "mentally ill" or "abnormal"? Of an otter, a baboon, or stickleback? Of a man? What might be meant by such a remark in each case? If nothing can ever be known of the mind of another, does that mean that terms such as "abnormal" or "diseased" can be meaningfully applied only to behavior, not to mental and emotional processes? What are the consequences of such a view for the insanity defense in the criminal law?

3. You may wish to say that this talk about birds and baboons and sticklebacks has nothing to do with our current problem, which is how to talk about the mind of man. We are men, and we know from our own experience what it is to be one. We can talk about men out of a direct knowledge. Compare the attempt of Lévi-Strauss to express an understanding of a kind of mind very different from that of the modern European man, in The Savage Mind *(1962). He finds that at what is usually called a primitive stage of existence many cultures have achieved an astonishingly rich and diverse intellectual life, consisting largely of classifying and arranging what is perceived around one into patterns of meaning. At this stage of development occurred the great neolithic inventions of the wheel, weaving, pottery, and the like; but development then stopped for a long time before a different kind of mind, capable of different sorts of thought, came into existence and modern scientific civilization was begun. Lévi-Strauss tries to imagine what it would be like to have a primitive mind, he tries to discover something of what man in his progress has left behind him. He draws a modern parallel between the "bricoleur" or handyman who makes do with whatever lies at hand, as a sort of creative genius of the surface world, and the engineer who figures out in an abstract way forces and strengths that lie beneath the surface.*

The attempt is to imagine what another's life is like, and the differences are enormous. Take knowledge of plants, for example: how many different sorts of plant can you name at sight? A single Seminole informant could identify 250 plants, and at least 500 are known to the Navaho. Elenore Smith Bowen, as an anthropologist just arrived in an African village, made the mistake of trying to commence good relations by learning the names of common plants; she was completely bewildered, unable to perceive differences perfectly obvious to everyone else. E. Smith Bowen, Return to Laughter 14 (Anchor ed. 1964). What would it be like to perceive so much more of the animal and vegetable world than you do? The ultimate concern of Lévi-Strauss is to discover what meanings people have perceived in these systems of simplification and classification, what connections they have seen among their various experiences – why, in fact, this sort of classification goes on – and he attempts to elucidate what he calls magical as opposed to scientific thought. For Lévi-Strauss, the mysteriously strong appeal of art (painting, music, narrative) is to what remains of the primitive mind. You can see that he does not regard the primitive mind as an inferior one.

Is it perhaps only a failure of imagination that makes us believe that the man in the dock has a mind that is directly comprehensible, that it has workings that can be measured and tested? How much more confidently can you speak of it than of the muskrat, the baboon, or the cat?

In what language, for example, could you hope to explain the mind and conduct expressed in the following passage? What questions would you want to ask, of whom, and inviting what responses?

FERRIN v. PEOPLE
164 Colo. 130, 433 P. 2d 108 (1967)

Stephen was one of seven children residing with his family in the small mountain community of Basalt, Colorado. He was an average student, well behaved and quiet. He was reared in the Mormon faith and attended church and Sunday school regularly. He had a close and affectionate relationship with David, who was two years younger.

On the date of the homicide, Stephen and David were at a neighbor's ranch to visit with a playmate, Roger Sharp, aged thirteen. The Ferrin brothers accompanied Roger who had some irrigating to be done. Stephen carried with him a .22 single shot rifle. The irrigation chore took about 45 minutes, and after it was completed the three boys started back to the ranch house area intending to play baseball. Roger and David were in front, and as they passed through a gate on the Sharp property, Stephen ordered them to come back through the gate. The boys did not respond to the "command" and Stephen fired a shot near David's feet. David responded, "I told you I am invulnerable just like Superman. . . . There is really nothing you can do to me." Stephen then fired a second shot which hit David causing him to fall screaming. Defendant then ordered Roger to return through the gate, which Roger did. Then Stephen fired a third shot at David.

Roger was ordered to strip down. Then Stephen marched Roger, sans pants, up the road about an eighth of a mile. Roger remarked to the defendant to the effect "You are a Mormon boy." Defendant then threw down his gun and started to cry "real loud." Roger recovered his trousers and went to a neighbor's house and called the authorities. Defendant continued to lay on the ground and cry incessantly. He was still crying at the house when the authorities arrived; and was in such an emotional state that he was taken to a doctor.

Roger testified that prior to the shooting there was no quarrel or disagreement between the brothers. He said that after the shooting defendant's face was "different" and that it "looked real serious."

At the arraignment on the information charging that Stephen "did feloniously, willfully and of his malice aforethought kill and murder" David, pleas of not guilty and not guilty by reason of insanity were entered.

A BIRD CAME DOWN THE WALK (1862)

Emily Dickinson

A Bird came down the Walk —
He did not know I saw —
He bit an Angleworm in halves
And ate the fellow, raw,

And then he drank a Dew
From a convenient Grass —
And then hopped sidewise to the Wall
To let a Beetle pass —

He glanced with rapid eyes
That hurried all around —
They looked like frightened Beads, I thought —
He stirred his Velvet Head

Like one in danger, Cautious,
I offered him a Crumb
And he unrolled his feathers
And rowed him softer home —

Than Oars divide the Ocean,
Too silver for a seam —
Or Butterflies, off Banks of Noon,
Leap, plashless as they swim.

3. *Mental Illness: A Medical Problem for Medical Experts?*

There are experts who classify and explain behavior, treat and sometimes cure those who are mentally or emotionally ill, and so on. Should the law turn the insanity defense over to them?

WASHINGTON v. UNITED STATES
390 F.2d 444 (D.C. Cir. 1967)

Bazelon, C.J.: Appellant was convicted by a jury of rape, robbery, and assault with a deadly weapon. His major defense was insanity. On appeal, he contends that the trial judge should have entered a judgment of acquittal by reason of insanity.

I

. . . In *Durham v. United States,* [214 F.2d 862 (D.C. Cir. 1954)], we announced a new test for insanity: "An accused is not criminally responsible if his unlawful act was the product of a mental disease or defect." We intended to widen the range of expert testimony in order to enable the jury "to consider all information advanced by relevant scientific disciplines."

This purpose was not fully achieved, largely because many people thought *Durham* was only an attempt to identify a clearly defined category of persons — those classified as mentally ill by the medical profession — and excuse them from criminal responsibility. In fact, the medical profession has no such clearly defined category, and the classifications it has developed for purposes of treatment, commitment, etc., may be inappropriate for assessing responsibility in criminal cases. Since these classifications were familiar, however, many psychiatrists understandably used them in court despite their unsuitability. And some psychiatrists, perhaps unwittingly, permitted their own notions about blame to determine whether the term mental illness should be limited to psychoses, should include serious behavior disorders, or should include virtually all mental abnormalities. To ensure that the views of the experts would not bind the fact-finder, we decided to give mental illness a legal definition independent of its medical meaning. We announced in *McDonald v. United States* [312 F.2d 847 (D.C. Cir. 1962)] that mental illness "includes any abnormal condition of the mind which substantially affects mental or emotional processes and which substantially impairs behavior control." . . .

In insanity cases today, the jury must be prepared to hear evidence concerning diverse aspects of defendant's life and then to make difficult judgments regarding the impairment of behavioral processes and controls. By their very nature these judgments cannot be precise. Thus, within the confines of the *Durham-McDonald* standard, the jury must be allowed a wide latitude in its task. A judgment of acquittal by reason of insanity is appropriate only when a jury verdict of guilty would clearly violate the law or the facts.

We cannot say that this was the situation in Washington's case. The district court did not err in its refusal to enter a judgment of acquittal by reason of insanity.

II

. . . The testimony of the defense psychiatrist, Dr. Adland, was based solely on a one hour and fifteen minute interview with defendant. Dr. Adland did not administer electroencephalogram, neurological, or physical tests, and did not have the benefit of reports of the tests given at Saint Elizabeth's Hospital. He requested permission to see them, but permission was denied.

Since the defendant was at Saint Elizabeth's Hospital for two months, the two Government psychiatrists had an opportunity for more prolonged observation. Yet both Dr. Owens and Dr. Hamman testified that they had seen Washington for approximately the same amount of time as Dr. Adland. Of course, they did have the benefit of the testing and observations performed by others at the Hospital. As Dr. Owens explained:

> When a patient is under constant observation, the examinations that were conducted in St. Elizabeth's by the psychiatrists, laboratory studies, psychological examinations, social service, interviews with relatives, all of this was part of the basis of my opinion that I rendered and the examination which I conducted at the medical staff conference on November 16, 1965 . . . By [constant observation] I mean 24 hours a day, and reports are submitted to the physicians as to their behavior, actions or activity while on the ward.

Unfortunately, except for brief references to a Rorschach test, none of this information was presented to the jury. The Government psychiatrists claimed to have based their conclusions on these studies, but they told the jury only the conclusions without any explanation of the studies themselves, what facts the studies uncovered, and why these facts led to the conclusions.

There was other available information, as well, which the jury was not told about. When Washington was twelve or thirteen, he was committed to Cedar Knolls, the District of Columbia School for Children. Apparently the records of that institution contained a lengthy history of Washington's childhood. At first, defense counsel moved them into evidence, but later he withdrew that request, perhaps because he thought it would be tactically unwise to make the jury read such a long report. Whatever the reason, the jury was forced to make its decision without any historical background on the defendant.

The omission of significant underlying information was one defect in the testimony. Another was that the jury was often subjected to a confusing mass of abstract philosophical discussion and fruitless disputation between lawyer and witness about legal and psychiatric labels and jargon. Dr. Hamman's entire testimony on direct examination was that Washington did not have a "passive-aggressive personality," did not suffer from any "personality trait disturbance," did not have "an irresistible impulse," was "not mentally ill," and was not "abnormal from the standpoint of psychiatric illness." A substantial part of Dr. Owens' testimony was similar. He was familiar with the defendant, had participated in a staff conference at which the defendant was discussed, and had formed an opinion about him.

Q. All right. And what was that opinion?
A. It was my opinion that he did not have a mental disease or mental defect. . . .

He testified also that the defendant did not have "an irresistible impulse" to rape, did not have a "passive-aggressive personality," and that in any event someone with a "passive-aggressive personality" was not necessarily "mentally ill."

Even if these labels had meaning for the witnesses, the testimony was useless unless that meaning was communicated to the jury. Explanation was attempted but it was often more confusing than clarifying. Dr. Owens explained that a "passive-aggressive personality"

is a type of personality that an individual has, that is, everybody has some-type of personality. We all have a type of personality. I mean no one has no personality. We have some type. Well, you may say schizoid personality, or compulsive personality, but speaking of the one that you ask, such [as] the passive aggressive personality, these are broken down into two different categories.

One is passive and one is aggressive. Usually in these people the aggressive type acts out in an aggressive manner, to either major or minor stressful situations, they maneuver under close confinement or under strict rules and regulations except maneuvering into a psychosis.

It is generally considered that the passive type or the aggressive type frequently or sometimes an aggressive personality will also behave in a passive manner.

This is where we get the term "passive-aggressive." This is more a classification of the type of personality that the individual has. . . .

We all have a type of personality. For example, physicians are generally considered to be compulsive personalities. That is, they are very meticulous to details and work things out or [*sic*] in a very orderly and organized fashion.

Generally speaking lawyers are considered to be aggressive or to have an aggressive personality. If they are not, they cannot be real passive [*sic*] and really do an expert job.

They have to be aggressive. Everybody has a type of personality. I mean, you have to be categorized somewhere.

Other explanations cast serious doubt upon the basis for many of the experts' conclusions as expressed in their labels. For example, Dr. Owens did not think the defendant had an "impulse to rape." Here is his explanation: "I think it was not an impulse to rape. It was an impulse to have sexual relations with a lady and if she did not agree with it, why, they forced her." Dr. Hamman agreed that Washington did not have an irresistible impulse to rape. But here is what "irresistible impulse" meant to Dr. Hamman:

Q. Isn't this almost irresistible, this antisocial act when he is in this situation with the urge?
A. Not from the way I understand irresistible impulse. An irresistible impulse means to me that there is a conflict and the unwanted behavior breaks through. I do not think there is a conflict in Mr. Washington.
Q. But, without the theory of conflict, without the conflict, isn't it a fact that he is in the situation with the urge for sexual contact, he cannot stop?
A. Well, he will just do it. He has no desire to stop.
Q. He has no power to stop?
A. That is correct.
Q. And, doctor, isn't it a fact that he has no power to stop an irresistible impulse?
A. Not as I understand it.
Q. And you understand it from a legal terminology?
A. I understand it both from legal terminology and from a psychiatric terminology.

Dr. Owens testified also that Washington's difficulty in controlling his sexual impulses did not affect his "voluntary controls."

Q. Didn't this impulse to have sexual relations affect his voluntary behavior controls?
A. No, I would not think so. I think, had a policeman, or witnesses or say, if he and two or three men had been going to rape a lady and there had been thirty other men present, where their force would not overpower the woman, that they would have backed off for another lady somewhere else to have raped.

I think when I say it impairs his voluntary control, I would say that it did not.

Dr. Hamman thought that Washington was "psychiatrically normal." Then he added, "The best definition of normal I have ever heard is the person is not too neurotic." . . .

Again and again the jury was diverted from evidence of the defendant's underlying mental and emotional difficulties by the emphasis on conclusory phrases. After defense counsel vigorously cross-examined Dr. Owens and brought out some facts which indicated that Washington's mental and emotional processes of control may have been impaired, the prosecuting attorney rehabilitated his witness as follows:

Q. Notwithstanding that history, doctor, and after that thorough study of Mr. Washington, you are of the opinion that he was not suffering with a mental illness on August 9, is that correct?
A. That is correct.

In this regard Dr. Hamman's testimony epitomized the whole trial. At times his testimony was more favorable to the defendant than the defense psychiatrist's testimony. According to Dr. Hamman, Washington had a twelve or thirteen year history of aggressive behavior. He has "very little regard for . . . people. And when he wants something, he takes it." "He has a tendency to be withdrawn, does not relate to people, tends to stay by himself." "He acts out his impulses." "Mr. Washington [does not have] much control." "He is a very aggressive individual." Dr. Hamman agreed that Washington "does not have any brakes, things that stop him from doing antisocial acts" and that "he has no power to stop." But these underlying facts were muddied by disputes and conclusions about medical and legal terminology — about whether a person is "normal" if he is not "too neurotic," about whether Washington was suffering from a "neurosis," about whether he has a "schizoid personality" as opposed to "traits of a schizoid nature," about whether "he has sociopathic symptomology," or whether instead "he has aggressive antisocial activity," about whether he was a "sociopath," had "personality difficulty," "personality disorder," or merely "personality problems," about whether he suffered from "irresistible impulses," about whether his aggression indicated that he had a "character disorder," and about whether his aggressive acts were caused by a "personality pattern the way he reacts, rather than [a personality] disorder."

Whatever opportunity the jury may have had to focus upon the underlying information provided by Dr. Hamman, this opportunity was materially diminished by a series of redirects and recrosses which dealt entirely with labels. The prosecutor asked on redirect examination:

Q. Now, the mere fact that this defendant has somewhat of a weird background according to what has come out here, and a very interesting sexual

background, do you feel — I mean, as a result of all of this information you have assembled concerning him, is it still your opinion that this defendant was not suffering with a mental illness on August 9, 1965?
A. That is correct. I do not think he was.

The defense attorney responded on recross:

Q. Doctor, he still has this behavior problem and the control problem with these sexual urges, right?
A. I am hesitating because I want to condense this as much as possible. He has problems in society. He does not have a problem with himself, and I think mental illness — it is my opinion that mental illness is one of the problems between he [*sic*] and himself. He may act it out and he may not. But I do not think he has much problem with himself about this. He takes what he wants.
Q. He is an emotional cripple, is he not?
A. Yes.

. . .

Q. Doctor, wouldn't you say, based upon the history that Mr. Washington is chronically ill?
A. No. I do not think he is ill.
Q. You do not think he is ill at all?
A. No.
Q. He just cannot control what he is doing?
A. Well, now, again when you say "can't," you imply that he would like to, and has a conflict. I don't think he wants to.

And finally, on redirect:

Q. . . . The mere fact that he is emotionally crippled, does that mean he is mentally ill?
A. No.

. . .

Q. Now, I will ask you this. You have been asked, or in reply to a question you indicated that this defendant will take what he wants.
A. Yes.
Q. Well, now, the mere fact that he will take what he wants even if it is in the field of sex, does that mean he is mentally ill?
A. No.[15]

It seems clear to Judge Robinson and me that the persistent use of conclusory labels may have hindered the jury in getting to the underlying facts. But we think that the jury obtained enough concrete information to preclude us from disturbing the verdict. The defense psychiatrist

15. Both lawyers aggravated the confusion by emphasizing the conflict of labels in their arguments to the jury. This seems to be the usual practice.

and, on cross-examination, the Government psychiatrists gave some meaningful descriptions of defendant's mental and emotional processes as emphasized in Judge Fahy's concurring opinion herein. Moreover, we recognize that, taken as a whole, the testimony in this case was, if anything, a little better than that in most insanity cases. Under these circumstances, reversal seems inappropriate. We conclude, therefore, that the conviction should be affirmed.

III

We all agree that more effort is needed in future cases to ensure that the issue of responsibility is decided upon sufficient information. Unfortunately, we have no easy solution. The history of the insanity defense in this jurisdiction shows that the misuse of conclusory labels has always been a central concern. The *M'Naghten* test, which we have quoted above, had two major defects. First, it encouraged psychiatrists to say whether the defendant knew "right" from "wrong," terms which have no particular medical meaning. Consequently, because the psychiatrist's attention was focused on these judgments and not on the medical facts, the jury was diverted from and perhaps even deprived of his expert knowledge. Second, and perhaps more important, the right-wrong test required psychiatrists to make a moral judgment about the defendant. It has often been argued that in the guise of an expert, the psychiatrist became the thirteenth juror, and unfortunately the most important one. Thus, the labels of "right and wrong" precluded the jury from considering all the relevant information and also encouraged the psychiatrist to impose his moral judgment upon the jury.

In Part I we described the steps taken in *Durham* and *McDonald* to enable the jury to consider all the relevant information about the defendant. *Durham* and *McDonald* were also attempts to clarify the respective roles of the expert and the jury by reducing the emphasis on conclusory labels. We thought the new test announced in *Durham* would allow the expert to testify in *medical* terms familiar to him and to his profession. The jury would no longer be forced to focus on the conclusory labels used by the expert. . . .

. . . [I]n *McDonald v. United States* we gave the terms "disease" and "defect" a *legal* definition independent of their medical meanings.

> . . . Our purpose now is to make it very clear that neither the court nor the jury is bound by ad hoc definitions or conclusions as to what experts state is a disease or defect. What psychiatrists may consider a "mental disease or defect" for clinical purposes, where their concern is treatment, may or may not be the same as mental disease or defect for the jury's purpose in determining criminal responsibility. Consequently, for that purpose the jury should be told that a mental disease or defect includes

any abnormal condition of the mind which substantially affects mental or emotional processes and substantially impairs behavior controls. Thus the jury would consider testimony concerning the development, adaptation and functioning of these processes and controls. . . .

We clearly separated the legal and moral question of culpability from the medical-clinical concept of illness. We hoped thereby to separate the roles of the psychiatrist and the jury, with the former stating medical-clinical facts and opinions and the latter making the judgments required by the legal and moral standard. Also, we hoped that the expert's conclusion would not be so heavily weighted in the jury's minds if we made plain that the expert and the jury had different judgments to make. . . .

With the relevant information about defendant, and guided by the legal principles enunciated by the court, the jury must decide, in effect, whether or not the defendant is blameworthy. Undoubtedly, the decision is often painfully difficult, and perhaps its very difficulty accounts for the readiness with which we have encouraged the expert to decide the question. But our society has chosen not to give this decision to psychiatrists or to any other professional elite but rather to twelve lay representatives of the community. The choice was not made on a naive assumption that all jurors would be fully capable of dealing with these difficult questions or with the underlying information. Nonetheless, this decision, along with many equally difficult ones in other areas, ranging from negligence to antitrust, was given to a jury.[28] As long as this is our system, we should try to make it work.

The trial judge should limit the psychiatrists' use of medical labels — schizophrenia, neurosis, etc.[29] It would be undesirable, as well as diffi-

28. The phrase "mental disease or defect" has been criticized for not giving enough guidance to the jury. In this regard the phrase is similar to other conclusory labels in the law. For example, "negligence" is a vague label given content primarily by the conclusions for which it stands. A person is "negligent" if he is at "fault" (blameworthy?), or if he has not exercised "due care," or if he has not met some standard of reasonable conduct. We are comfortable with a concept like negligence because we understand that it is a conclusion based on other considerations. Similarly, we can accept the term "mental disease or defect" if we understand what it represents.

29. The Department of Defense has directed medical officers to avoid "the use of scientific jargon" in court martial proceedings. "The witness should use the approximate lay equivalents, or, if technical terms are unavoidable, should define them." Moreover, the expert witness is instructed that it is his "obligation to make his method and techniques intelligible to the court" and that he "should never hesitate to admit before a court the limitations of his medical knowledge and experience." Department of Defense, *Psychiatry in Military Law* 35, 37 (approved draft 1967).

In the Soviet Union, courts reject psychiatric reports which employ too many technical and evaluative terms. Berman, Justice in the U.S.S.R. 322–323 (rev. ed. 1963).

cult, to eliminate completely all medical labels, since they sometimes provide a convenient and meaningful method of communication. But the trial judge should ensure that their meaning is explained to the jury and, as much as possible, that they are explained in a way which relates their meaning to the defendant.[30] . . .

A strong minority of this court has consistently advocated that psychiatrists be prohibited from testifying whether the alleged offense was the "product" of mental illness, since this is part of the ultimate issue to be decided by the jury. We now adopt that view. The term "product" has no clinical significance for psychiatrists. Thus there is no justification for permitting psychiatrists to testify on the ultimate issue. Psychiatrists should explain how defendant's disease or defect relates to his alleged offense, that is, how the development, adaptation and functioning of defendant's behavioral processes may have influenced his conduct. But psychiatrists should not speak directly in terms of "product," or even "result" or "cause."

It can be argued that psychiatrists should also be prohibited from testifying whether the defendant suffered from a "mental disease or defect," since this too is part of the ultimate issue. But unlike the term "product," the term "mental disease or defect" may have some clinical significance to the psychiatrist. . . .

Affirmed.

. . .

FAHY, J. (concurring specially in affirmance). . . .

30. A diagnosis of the defendant's condition, while involving conclusions of a kind, is admissible even though a jury is not bound by a diagnosis or a particular diagnostic label on a mental disorder. The jury wants and needs help from the expert, but it does not help a jury of laymen to be told of a diagnosis limited to the esoteric and swiftly changing vocabulary of psychiatry. Every technical description ought to be "translated" in terms of "what I mean by this," followed by a down-to-earth concrete explanation in terms which convey meaning to laymen. A psychiatrist who gives a jury a diagnosis, for example, of "psychoneurotic reaction, obsessive compulsive type" and fails to explain fully what this means, would contribute more to society if he were permitted to stay at his hospital post taking care of patients.

It is at this point where trial counsel's responsibility comes into play. It is for him to elicit, either by direct or cross-examination, "the material from which [the psychiatric] opinion is fashioned" and the steps by which the raw material of the tests, observations and other data led to the diagnosis and opinion. The value of an expert opinion can rise no higher than the facts and premises on which it is based. But it is only a rare medical witness who is so skilled in the forensic art that he can present testimony adequately even where there is inept interrogation by counsel. If trial counsel fail in their role the trial judge would be well advised to urge them, out of the presence of the jury, to explore and develop the subject so that the witness can translate all of his medical observations to the jury. This is the area in which the deterioration if not breakdown of the trials of these "insanity" cases is to a large extent the fault of the trial counsel. If lawyers want the views of the experts to be accepted by lay jurors their first duty is to draw out expert testimony in terms which are intelligible and meaningful.

Part II

As to Part II of the opinion I too would have welcomed fuller information about the defendant. I do not feel justified, however, in joining in the court's appraisal of the testimony on the issue of defendant's mental condition. It is true that labels were used by the psychiatrists but the record I think discloses rather full explanations of their medical terminology.

In addition to the opinion's excerpt from Dr. Owens' explanation of "passive-aggressive personality," which seems to me to clarify his views, the doctor went further in explanation. I dislike to burden the opinion with lengthy quotations from his testimony, but do need to be indicative. Thus, the following appears during his examination:

Q. Now, doctor, do you feel that Mr. Washington has any personality defect?
A. Not in the sense of "defect." I would prefer to say he has personality problems, that is a difficulty in getting along or adjusting, that probably the difficulties that he experiences in relating adequately to other people are more severe or more extreme than the average person has.
Q. Is it accurate to say that he has a personality disorder?
A. I generally would prefer not to say "disorder," because when you say "disorder," this denotes that you mean something is wrong, that is a disease or an illness or some disorder. I would prefer to say that he has a personality, a type of personality.
Q. What type of personality do you think he has?
A. My opinion would be that he was generally or would generally be described as somewhat schizoid, that is, he has difficulty relating to people.
He gets angry if he does not have his way. He tends at times to spend his time alone, or has difficulty relating to people with some aggression when he does not — when things do not go exactly his way, he acts out in an aggressive manner.
. . .
Q. Doctor, do you believe, based upon the examination of Mr. Washington and the records that he would be classified with this terribly ambiguous term "normal" — is he normal?
A. Well, a lot depends, if you mean by "normal," that he has no mental illness, then he would be normal in my opinion.
However if you mean normal by his behavior, being socially acceptable, then he would not be normal.

This was pursued still further in ordinary language of explanation.

When the doctor used the term "sociopathic symptomology" he was asked its meaning and replied:

A. By sociopath, we mean an individual who is antisocial. That is a type of personality who acts out in an anti-social way, has little control over his desires and his needs.
He is constantly repetitiously being involved in criminal activity. He has little guilt. He does not feel that things are wrong. The only time he feels it is wrong is when he gets caught.
Q. Little anxiety?
A. Very little. They usually act out, behave in an anti-social manner before they get anxiety.
Q. Rape is consistent with a sociopathic personality, is not that correct?
A. Any crime would be consistent with it. There are sociopaths who commit crimes and sociopaths who do not.

During Dr. Hamman's testimony for the United States he was asked, "Could you tell us in psycho-dynamic terms how you analyze Mr. Washington's personality?" He responded:

A. I think he is an individual, it is my opinion that he is an individual who does have impulses. He does have drives. Who has very little regard for the people. And when he wants something, he takes it.
Q. He will act out these impulses?
A. Yes.
Q. The impulses, if they are strong, he will act strongly?
A. Yes.
. . .
Q. Psychiatrically considering this picture of Mr. Washington, don't you think he has a personality difficulty or personality disorder?
A. No. I think he has personality problems. But I don't think they are marked to the extent that I would call them character neurotic.
Q. I don't understand what you mean, doctor. Would you explain?
A. Well, he is not the best adjusted person in the world.
. . .
A. He is a very aggressive individual, there is no question about that. But I do not think he has a mental illness. I do not think he has — I do not think he shows symptoms that would justify a diagnosis of a character disorder, personality disorder, or a neurosis.
Q. Doctor, isn't it all a question of degree in reaching your diagnostic impression?
A. Absolutely right.
. . .
Q. And isn't this behavior, which is this aggressive behavior, directly caused by this personality problem which is of a sociopathic nature?
A. It is caused — no.
Q. No?
A. Look, anything that any of us do is caused by our personality, by our character. I would not know whether you want to call this illness or not.

It seems to me the witnesses' explanations of their opinions were understandable. One might not be persuaded by them, but that is a different matter. Doctors Owens and Hamman, both witnesses for the Government, readily conceded impulsive conduct by defendant, his "lack of brakes" in his sexual urge; but in their opinion this was not due to mental disease and they explained in understandable language the situation as they saw it. I think it was fairly put to the jury on the evidence to decide whether defendant's weakness in sexual matters amounted to mental disease excusing him from criminal responsibility, or, on the other hand, was a character or personality weakness which did not absolve him of such responsibility. I agree with the court that we should seek improvement, and that the witnesses should inform the jury clearly of the meaning of their medical terms, and of the basis for their opinions; but I do not feel justified in saying that the use of labels, when considered with all the testimony, left the jury confused in this case.

QUESTIONS

1. Examine the testimony of the psychiatrists with particular care.

a. Do you think that they could have said anything either (1) in their professional language or (2) in legal language that would have helped the jury decide what it had to decide? Could they have done so in ordinary English?

b. Exactly what is their difficulty, so far as you can tell? Is it that they are not permitted to speak their own language, that they are not able to translate what they have to say into legal language, or what? These really are extraordinary conversations, and one can understand the court's impatience. Yet the doctors and lawyers are presumably conscientious and intelligent men. Can you explain why these doctors have such difficulties?

2. The court disapproves of the quality of testimony in this case, saying that it is not adequate to permit a jury to make a judgment in which they or anyone else can have much confidence. The major deficiency is that there is inadequate information about the "mental and emotional processes" and "makeup" of the defendant, too much bickering over conclusory labels and not enough in the way of "underlying facts."

a. What does the court mean by the phrase "underlying facts"? At one point it refers to reports of examinations made at St. Elizabeth's by other psychiatrists and psychologists, of interviews with relatives, and of laboratory studies. Would it have helped if these had been introduced into evidence? Imagine documents of this kind, and ask how they would help a jury decide what to do with the defendant.

b. Or is the idea that this material would have helped the defendant's lawyer in his cross-examination? Why do you think it was not obtained and used for this purpose, then?

c. Elsewhere the following phrases of testimony are referred to as "underlying facts": he has "very little regard for other people. And when he wants something he takes it"; "he has a tendency to be withdrawn, does not relate to people, tends to stay by himself"; "he is a very aggressive individual"; he does not have "any brakes, things that stop him from doing antisocial acts," and he "has no power to stop." Do you agree that these are underlying facts or are they conclusory labels? How would they help the jury decide what it is asked to decide here? What other sorts of "facts" would you want if you were a juror in this case?

d. Or is the main fact that interests you as a juror the conclusion of the doctor as to whether the defendant has a "mental disease or defect"?

e. Look at the testimony of Doctor Hamman. What should he have said that he does not say here? Redraft his testimony to make it satisfactory to the court. Does it now express the true condition of the defendant?

3. Do you think that after this opinion was handed down the psychiatric testimony in the District of Columbia suddenly began to meet the standards expressed here? Why not? What difficulties remain?

   a. In footnote 28 the court says that the label "mental disease or defect" is like the label "negligence" and that we can accept it if we "understand what it represents." Draft a brief statement in which you explain what it represents. If you cannot, tell us how you would go about learning what it represents.

   b. Footnote 30 contains some very specific advice: "Every technical description ought to be 'translated' in terms of 'what I mean by this,' followed by a down-to-earth concrete explanation in terms which convey meaning to a layman." It sounds very simple. Do you believe that it is? Why is it not simple, what exactly is the nature of the difficulty here?

4. The basic premise of the opinion is that the doctors should "state the medical-clinical facts and opinions" and the jury should make the "judgment required by the moral and legal standard." We should bow to the expertise of the psychiatrist and let him talk about the defendant just as he would with his family or other colleagues, at least so long as he can do so without going beyond the clinical facts into matters of legal and moral judgment. Is this suggestion workable? Why not? Let us begin by asking what his expertise really consists of, what he is good at doing.

   a. Is the psychiatrist's an ability to classify and label, to call names, to describe? It certainly seems so: if a doctor is to treat a disease, he must diagnose it first, and diagnosis is a form of classification by label. If this is so, it would indeed be possible for him simply to state the clinical facts and let the jury make its legal-moral judgment about them. What is wrong with this version of psychiatric expertise?[6]

   b. How else might you possibly define the psychiatrist's expertise? If it is not in diagnosing and labeling — in stating clinical facts — what is it? What do people pay him to do?

5. How would you respond to a suggestion that a panel of doctors be established to decide whether or not a defendant is insane for the purposes of the insanity defense? This would mean that experts could not only talk freely in their professional way, but that they could decide this question that lies squarely within their expertise.

   Here is the opposite suggestion: with respect to the matters that really

6. See "The Psychoanalytic Concept of Cure," 18 *Psychoanalytic Study of the Child* 456 (1963).

concern the law here, we are all experts and should be able to give our opinions as to the sanity of the defendant. The landlady, the bus driver, the golfing partner, the girl friend could all give both "underlying facts" and their opinions as to the defendant's insanity to the jury. Do you agree?

One suggestion assumes this is "really" a medical problem; the other that it is "really" a question of blameworthiness: the court thinks it is partly one and partly the other; what sort of question do you think the insanity defense presents? Who should respond to it, and on the basis of what factual inquiries?

6. We have talked about what the jury should do, what the doctors should do, and what the lawyers should do; the answers all depend in part upon what they are good at. Look at the Washington opinion again and ask (as it is here defined) what the task of the judge is, what he is good at. How does the court define itself in the way it writes?

7. In Powell v. Texas, 392 U.S. 514 (1968), the question arose whether the disease of chronic alcoholism was a constitutional defense to the crime of public drunkenness. The state court held it was not, in spite of its findings: "(1) That chronic alcoholism is a disease which destroys the afflicted person's will power to resist the constant, excessive consumption of alcohol. (2) That a chronic alcoholic does not appear in public by his own volition but under a complusion symptomatic of the disease of chronic alcoholism. (3) That Leroy Powell, a defendant herein, is a chronic alcoholic who is afflicted with the disease of chronic alcoholism."

The Supreme Court affirmed in an opinion written by Justice Marshall, which seemed to make and rely upon the following points, among others: (a) alcoholism is not a disease, or at least, we do not know what it means to say that alcoholism is a disease; (b) some alcoholics in fact can control their drinking; and the lower court did not in its findings distinguish among the various categories of alcoholics, and determine whether this defendant had the kind of alcoholism which deprived him of all control over his drinking.

On the basis of this account, how do you evaluate this opinion? How would you have decided this case and why?

8. Consider the following proposal: "The labels of disease, insanity, and alcoholism, and the lesser labels by which varieties of these phenomena are categorized, have no meaning at all for the legal system. Perhaps doctors can usefully employ them, but judges, juries, and lawyers cannot. They do not and cannot serve the purposes of the law. Therefore, we propose that they be dispensed with entirely. The half-step taken in alternative (a) to §4.01 of the Model Penal Code should become a whole step: the jury should simply be told to acquit if justice requires it."
   a. Can you explain why these labels can serve medical purposes but not legal purposes?
   b. Can you define "justice" in the proposed test in a way which would make it a real standard the jury could rationally apply? Where would you look for the idea of justice and ways to express it? Do you find yourself using the familiar insanity tests?
   c. Can you perhaps continue to use the familiar tests but in a more intelligible way — by first telling the jury that their basic standard is "justice," and then stating not one test but all of them, as examples

of ways in which justice has been defined in the past by those who have thought about it? This might disrupt the tendency to treat these terms as descriptive, yet give the jury some assistance in making its judgment. What other assistance might you give it?

9. *As you examine the way the law talks about insanity, think about other literature you may have read on this subject.*
   a. *Is Captain Ahab in Melville's Moby Dick insane? What does his insanity consist of?*
   b. *Is Raskolnikov in Dostoevsky's Crime and Punishment insane? What do you mean by "insane"?*
   c. *We all know that Hamlet pretends to be insane and that Ophelia is insane. How do we know that? What does "insane" mean here?*
   d. *Is Clovis Sangrail (page 254 supra) insane? What do you mean by "insane" here? Surely you would never behave or talk that way.*
   e. *Reread People v. Sherwood, page 122 supra. Was Mrs. Sherwood insane? What do you mean by "insane"? What relationship can you establish between the facts of her condition and the law of insanity?*

4. *Using Labels by Following Purposes: The Living Language of the Criminal Law*

Perhaps the enormous difficulties we perceive in the use of the insanity label are in part due to our having gone about things in the wrong way. Any term in a rule — any label — can of course be given a wide variety of meanings, and in the great majority of cases can be construed to come out for either side. To stare at the words in a rule as if they carried in themselves the clue to their use, and to examine and weigh the different "tests" for insanity, is futile, producing more uncertainty than clarification. The way to determine how a label should be used in a particular case is to ask what purposes we are following and which interpretation will best serve those purposes.[7] What is essential to the proper working of the insanity test, then, is not a dictionary definition of "insanity" but a clear statement of our fundamental purposes.

a. *The Purposes of the Insanity Defense*

What are the purposes of the insanity defense? You will quickly see that to respond to this question one must consider what the purposes

7. This is a greatly simplified statement of the thesis advanced by Hart and Sacks in *The Legal Process* (1958) that the law should always be viewed as a purposive process, and decisions made in ways that further our purposes. With respect to interpreting statutes, they make the suggestion that the process take two stages: first to determine what range of meanings is linguistically tolerable, what meanings the language will bear; then to choose among those meanings by asking which most fully serves the purposes of the statute. To try to determine what a word means without asking why you care is foolish, of course. But how would you decide what range of meanings a term might have? And what are your purposes in establishing an insanity defense?

are of the institution to which it is an exception, the criminal law. Here you deal with matters of choice and policy, not questions of fact, and in your writing assignment you will have to come to your own conclusions in your own way.

QUESTIONS

1. *If an individual has actually committed a crime, having done the prohibited acts with the requisite state of mind, why should he be released from criminal liability merely because he has one sort of mental illness or another? To punish him would, after all, still deter others, even if he were insane. If you wish to say that it is "not fair" to punish such a one, explain what you mean by "fair," including a statement of why it is fair to punish those who are not insane.*
2. *It has been suggested by Professor H. L. A. Hart that it is a fundamental principle of justice that it is unfair to punish those who could not help doing what they did.*[8] *Do you agree? Is the implication of this principle that the insanity test should consist simply of asking the jury whether the defendant could help doing what he did? There is considerable support in Powell v. Texas, 392 U.S. 514 (1968), for the view that this "can't help" defense is constitutionally required. Is the "can't help" defense the perfect form of the insanity defense?*
3. *The choice the jury makes when insanity is pleaded is almost always between two sorts of institutional disposition, penal and nonpenal, rather than between jail and freedom. One sort of disposition serves to restrain the individual from further wrongdoing and attempts to rehabilitate him, to improve his behavior – or such, at least, is the theory. The other sort of disposition serves both of those purposes and an additional one: it punishes the individual, not for his own good – presumably that sort of punishment would fall under the heading of rehabilitation and might occur even in a mental hospital – but to deter others, to warn them not to follow his deplorable example. How can a choice between these two sorts of disposition rationally be made? Imagine clear cases each way, and ask what it is that makes them clear.*
4. *Would the choice of disposition be more intelligible if it were regarded solely as a matter of sentencing? That is, suppose there were no insanity defense available at trial, but the defendant's mental condition were considered relevant to his disposition after conviction: on what basis might one sensibly and fairly choose which sort of disposition was appropriate?*
5. *For the view that the insanity defense should be abolished entirely, see N. Morris and G. Hawkins, The Honest Politician's Guide to Crime Control 174–201 (1970).*
6. *Does the following statute say all that needs to be said on the subject of insanity?*

MENTAL HEALTH ACT, 1959

[Chapter 72; Part V.]

60. — (1) Where a person is convicted before a court of assize or

8. See H. Hart, *Punishment and Responsibility* 181–183 (1963).

quarter sessions of an offence other than an offence the sentence for which is fixed by law, or is convicted by a magistrates' court of an offence punishable on summary conviction with imprisonment, and the following conditions are satisfied, that is to say —

(a) the court is satisfied, on the written or oral evidence of two medical practitioners . . .

(i) that the offender is suffering from mental illness, psychopathic disorder, subnormality or severe subnormality; and

(ii) that the mental disorder is of a nature or degree which warrants the detention of the patient in a hospital for medical treatment, or the reception of the patient into guardianship under this Act; and

(b) the court is of opinion, having regard to all the circumstances including the nature of the offence and the character and antecedents of the offender, and to the other available methods of dealing with him, that the most suitable method of disposing of the case is by means of an order under this section, the court may by order authorise his admission to and detention in such hospital as may be specified in the order or, as the case may be, place him under the guardianship of a local health authority or of such other person approved by a local health authority as may be so specified.

(2) Where a person is charged before a magistrates' court with any act or omission as an offence and the court would have power, on convicting him of that offence, to make an order under subsection (1) of this section in his case as being a person suffering from mental illness or severe subnormality, then, if the court is satisfied that the accused did the act or made the omission charged, the court may, if it thinks fit, make such an order without convicting him.

QUESTIONS

1. *It may help you work out the purposes of your insanity defense if you consider the following question: under what circumstances, if any, should insanity be a defense to a strict or absolute liability crime? One possibility is to say never: since such a crime requires no culpable state of mind, an abnormal state of mind is irrelevant. But this view regards the insanity defense as merely another form of the general rule that to commit a crime one must have the state of mind required by statute. What other way to regard the insanity defense is there?*

   The same question could be asked of negligence crimes, since by hypothesis the negligent (as opposed to the reckless) person fails to perceive a risk he is running. Psychologically speaking, negligence is another form of absolute liability. In fact, how should insanity bear on "recklessness" crimes?

   Here is a related question: is insanity ever a defense to a juvenile delinquency adjudication? When and why? See In re H. C., 106 N.J. Super. 583, 256 A.2d 322 (1969).

2. *Why do you suppose the prosecutor is not permitted to put the defendant's sanity in issue over his objection? See Lynch v. Overholser, 369 U.S. 705 (1962).*
3. *Why is it generally held that an insane person cannot be executed?*
4. *The following subsection concerns the relationship between label and purpose in the criminal law. This study may help you figure out what the proper purposes of the insanity defense are and how to employ them as grounds for decision in particular cases.*

b. The Relation Between Label and Purpose in the Criminal Law: Malice Aforethought

Consider how the label "malice" is employed in the following case, and ask what relationship you can perceive between the label and its purposes.

PEOPLE v. CONLEY
64 Cal. 2d 310, 411 P.2d 911 (1966)

TRAYNOR, C.J. Defendant appeals from a judgment of conviction entered on jury verdicts finding him guilty on two counts of first degree murder, finding him sane at the time of the commission of the crimes, and fixing the penalty on each count at life imprisonment. He contends that the court erred in instructing the jury on the elements of murder and in refusing to give requested instructions on manslaughter . . .

Defendant shot and killed Clifton and Elaine McCool on Sunday, July 19, 1964, in Ukiah. The victims, who were married and the parents of three children, had recently reconciled after a period of separation and were preparing to move to the State of Washington. They occupied cabin No. 7 of a bungalow court near the home of defendant's sister, Goldie Haley, with whom defendant was living at the time of the killings. While the McCools were separated, Elaine became romantically involved with defendant and told him that she would get a divorce and marry him.

Defendant injured his back in an industrial accident several months before the killings and had no regular employment since that accident. On July 15, the Wednesday before the shooting, he received two compensation checks and, as was his habit when he had funds, began a prolonged period of steady drinking. He and several other witnesses testified that he drank whiskey, vodka, and finally wine continually for over three days before the homicides. Defendant also testified that he had been taking medication to relieve the pain of his back injury and an ulcer. A medical expert testified that some of the medication prescribed for defendant could have increased the effect of alcohol.

On Thursday, July 16, the defendant took Elaine and the McCool children on an outing and apparently engaged in intimate relations with Elaine. When he brought her and the children back to their cabin, she told him that she had decided to return to her husband.

On Sunday, July 19, defendant purchased a .30-.30 rifle and early that evening tried it out with two friends at a nearby dump. His friends testified that on their way back defendant said that he ought to kill the McCools, but they dismissed the remark as "just the booze talking" and changed the subject. Thereafter, defendant went to his sister's home and drank wine until about 9:00 p.m. He then went to cabin No. 3 of the bungalow court and told other friends who lived there that he was going to kill the McCools because, "I have been hurt by three different women before. I can't take any more. She promised to marry me." They attempted to dissuade him, but he said he had made up his mind. Once again, however, he was not taken seriously and his friends allowed him to leave with his rifle.

A few minutes later, four shots rang out. Upon hearing the first shots, the occupants of cabin No. 1 went to their front porch and saw defendant shoot Elaine as she was running from him. Defendant walked back to cabin No. 3, told his friends that he had killed the McCools, and then went to his sister's house and told her what he had done. He left and was found two hours later in a nearby field.

Defendant testified that he did not intend to kill the McCools and remembered nothing from the time he was drinking at his sister's house until his arrest. The results of a blood alcohol test given about three hours after the shooting showed that his blood then contained .21 per cent alcohol. A medical expert testified that this alcohol level would be sufficient to impair fine muscular coordination and judgment in the average individual and that if defendant had consumed no food or alcohol between 9:00 p.m. and midnight, the blood alcohol level at 9:00 p.m. could have been .27 per cent, but that it might have been even less than .21 per cent.

A defense psychologist testified that in his opinion defendant was in a dissociative state at the time of the killings and because of personality fragmentation did not function with his normal personality.

Both sides requested manslaughter instructions. The court ruled that even if initially there had been adequate provocation to reduce the killing from murder to manslaughter, a sufficient cooling period had elapsed as a matter of law to preclude consideration of the crime as having been committed in the heat of passion. The court suggested that if either party could present an evidentiary theory upon which a manslaughter instruction could be based it would be given but ultimately refused any such instruction, although diminished capacity and intoxication were both suggested as theories upon which instructions on manslaughter were required. This refusal was prejudicial error.

It has long been settled that evidence of diminished mental capacity, whether caused by intoxication, trauma, or disease, can be used to show that a defendant did not have a specific mental state essential to an offense. Seventeen years ago, in *People v. Wells*, 33 Cal. 2d 330, 202 P.2d 53 [1949], we held that evidence must be admitted that shows that at the time a defendant committed an overt act he did or did not have a specific mental state such as malice aforethought. . . . We concluded . . . that evidence of an accused's abnormal mental condition that was relevant to malice aforethought was admissible, for malice aforethought was a "particular purpose, motive, or intent" essential to the crime charged.

We thus clearly recognized that malice aforethought is a specific mental state and that a defendant may show that he lacked that mental state when it is an essential element of the offense of which he stands accused. . . .

In the present case the jury was instructed that "You should find Mr. Conley guilty of first degree murder if you are convinced beyond a reasonable doubt that any shooting of either of the McCools was deliberate and premeditated as [the court has] defined those terms and that Mr. Conley was conscious of the shooting at the time." The jury was not advised that malice was also an essential element of murder. Defendant's plea of "not guilty" to the charge of first degree murder put in issue the existence of the mental states that are elements of that offense, namely, intent, deliberation, wilfulness, premeditation, and malice aforethought. . . .

Hoping to gain complete exculpation, defendant based his defense in part on a theory of unconsciousness. In support of that defense he introduced evidence of intoxication and mental illness and testified that he had no recollection of the shootings and did not intend to kill the McCools. Implicit in such a defense is also the defense of diminished capacity. The jury could well reject the claim of complete unconsciousness and yet believe that the evidence introduced to establish unconsciousness was sufficient to indicate that defendant's mental capacity was substantially reduced. Counsel for both sides made known to the court defendant's reliance on the defense of diminished capacity. Since the jury was not advised that diminished capacity could negate the existence of malice and that if malice were absent the offense could not be murder, a material issue was withheld from its consideration. . . .

The Attorney General contends, however, that the jury necessarily determined this issue under the instructions given by finding defendant guilty of first rather than second degree murder. There is no merit in this contention, for the issue of malice aforethought was not presented to the jury. . . . In returning a verdict of first degree murder, the jury found that defendant's act was intentional, voluntary, deliberate, and premeditated. They did not necessarily find, however, that defendant acted with malice aforethought.

We have previously noted the difficulty of formulating a comprehensive definition of malice aforethought that will serve to distinguish murder and manslaughter. Penal Code, section 188 provides that malice "may be express or implied. It is express when there is manifested a deliberate intention unlawfully to take away the life of a fellow creature. It is implied, when no considerable provocation appears, or when the circumstances attending the killing show an abandoned and malignant heart." These provisions create a presumption of malice when the commission of a homicide by the defendant has been proved and place the burden on him to raise a reasonable doubt in the minds of the jurors that malice was present. . . .

The mental state constituting malice aforethought does not presuppose or require any ill will or hatred of the particular victim. . . . When a defendant "with wanton disregard for human life, does an act that involves a high degree of probability that it will result in death," he acts with malice aforethought. This mental state must be distinguished from that state of mind described as "wilful, deliberate, and premeditated," however. The latter phrase encompasses the mental state of one who carefully weighs the course of action he is about to take and chooses to kill his victim after considering the reasons for and against it. . . . A person capable of achieving such a mental state is normally capable also of comprehending the duty society places on all persons to act within the law. If, despite such awareness, he does an act that is likely to cause serious injury or death to another, he exhibits that wanton disregard for human life or antisocial motivation that constitutes malice aforethought. An intentional act that is highly dangerous to human life, done in disregard of the actor's awareness that society requires him to conform his conduct to the law is done with malice regardless of the fact that the actor acts without ill will toward his victim or believes that his conduct is justified. . . .

Thus, one who commits euthanasia bears no ill will toward his victim and believes his act is morally justified, but he nonetheless acts with malice if he is able to comprehend that society prohibits his act regardless of his personal belief. If because of mental defect, disease, or intoxication, however, the defendant is unable to comprehend his duty to govern his actions in accord with the duty imposed by law, he does not act with malice aforethought and cannot be guilty of murder in the first degree. . . . [I]n the present case, the jury could have found that although defendant deliberated and premeditated the killings, his intoxication and mental disorder precluded malice aforethought. In finding him guilty of first degree murder under the instructions given it therefore did not necessarily determine that he acted with malice aforethought.

QUESTIONS

1. *The court says that "malice" is a "specific mental state" and that a person who "intentionally kills" may be "incapable of harboring malice aforethought" because of mental disease, defect, or intoxication. The court goes on to explain what "malice" is and how it is different from "intention to kill" and "premeditation."*
   a. *Does it make sense to speak of the statutory phrase "malice aforethought" as referring to a state of mind?*
   b. *Can you, with the court's aid, define that state of mind?*
   c. *How would you tell whether that state of mind existed in a particular case?*[9]
2. *If "malice" is a state of mind, should not a psychiatrist be permitted to testify that a defendant lacked the capacity "to harbor malice aforethought"? Imagine the processes through which a psychiatrist would go in making his judgment on that matter and how he could expect to be cross-examined. What result if similar testimony were offered with respect to "premeditated and deliberate"? See People v. Castillo, 70 Cal. 2d 264, 449 P.2d 449 (1969).*
3. *The Conley opinion is hardly satisfactory. It relies completely upon fictional talk of "malice" as a "specific mental state" that can be found to exist or not, talk which must bewilder a jury especially when it is told in addition that a killing can be intentional, voluntary, and deliberate, and still be without "malice." Moreover, without explaining why it does so, the court limits the diminished responsibility defense to cases of intoxication or mental disease or defect. Why should we not have a general notion of diminished responsibility not dependent upon these particular conditions? How would such a defense be defined and explained?*
4. *Should the phrase "malice aforethought" properly be viewed not as a term of description but as one of judgment? Under the Conley opinion it seems to operate as a largely uncontrolled grant of authority to the jury to convict a defendant of manslaughter rather than murder whenever the jury so chooses, and for whatever reasons the jury wishes.*
   a. *Is such a grant of authority desirable?*
   b. *If the phrase "malice aforethought" is such a grant, should that be made clear to the jury? Draft an instruction making that clear. (How could one possibly justify not making that clear to the jury?)*
5. *There is another possibility: the term "malice" is properly viewed not as an uncontrolled grant of power to the jury but as a controlled one. Their judgment is to be guided by the law. They are to apply the label "malice" or "no malice" by asking which result will better serve the purposes of the*

9. For one proposed statutory solution to the difficulties presented by the term "malice," see Purver, "The Language of Murder," 14 *U.C.L.A.L. Rev.* 1306 (1967).

criminal law. For this suggestion to work, they must of course be told what these purposes are. Draft a statement to the jury, telling them what purposes they should conceive of themselves as following in applying this label.

How, if at all, does your instruction on "malice" differ from an "insanity" instruction? Both labels are intended to serve the same purposes, so both are to be used exactly the same way? Or do you define their purposes differently?

6. Compare People v. Hood, 1 Cal. 3d 444, 462 P.2d 370 (1969). Here defendant was prosecuted for assault with a deadly weapon upon a peace officer, whom he had shot in a brawl when the police answered his battery victim's call for help. Defendant was drunk at the time. What instruction is he entitled to, with respect to his intoxication?
   a. "He is entitled to no instruction, because intoxication is a defense only to crimes one of whose elements is a specific intent — such as 'premeditated' or 'malice' — not crimes of general intent. Assault, assault with a deadly weapon, and assault upon a peace officer are all general intent crimes." Such is the expectable response.
   b. But how do we decide whether a crime is one of general or specific intent? As a matter of plain English, all three charges could as easily be called "specific" as "general" intent crimes. Surely that distinction must be designed to serve intelligible purposes, and should not the jury be able to decide whether those purposes are served in this case?
   c. To put it another way: why should the jury in Hood not be given an instruction like the one suggested for Conley, that the "assault" label should be applied by asking what purposes the criminal law of assault is meant to serve and whether conviction of this man of this crime under these circumstances would serve them? Suppose the jury finds that the elements of assault are made out, but that convicting the defendant will not serve any of the purposes of the criminal law: not deterrence, or rehabilitation, or restraint. Should he not be acquitted?
   d. Or should the jury's power to act upon what it perceives the purposes of the law to require properly be limited to judgments of grading — choosing between a less and a more serious crime — and not allowed with respect to judgments of guilt and innocence? Why should that be?
7. The assumption of the foregoing question is that one can apply legal labels by looking to the purposes they are meant to serve. If one can use an understanding of purpose in that direct way, why do we ever need labels?
   a. One response is to say that the label does have some descriptive function. However illusory this claim may prove to be in a statute turning upon the existence of "malice," it makes some sense in an assault case. The defendant must have done something to the victim; that much must be shown. The use of labels is closely related to the requirement that the defendant have "committed the crime" before he is convicted, to our basic idea of the rule of law.
   b. But what purpose does this requirement serve, or is it just an outdated remnant of an earlier era? If the jury can follow the purposes of the criminal law in cases in which it is asked to determine whether a killing is "malicious," why can it not do so as an original matter, disposing

of the defendant less on the basis of what he did (thus avoiding descriptive labels) than who he is, asking whether the purposes of the criminal law require that he be punished? Do you see that the question has become: what purposes are served by the trial stage — as opposed to the sentencing stage — of the criminal process? Is there any reason why a disposition of a defendant in the criminal process should turn on a definition of him by simple narrative identity ("he is the one who assaulted") rather than his real identity as a person and a member of society? Does the law here unnecessarily speak of a defendant as though he were an Admetus (see page 274 supra)?

One is often told that in criminal trials in civil law countries the evidence is not limited to what the defendant did on one occasion but is meant to give a complete understanding of the whole man. See the account of a criminal trial in Camus, The Stranger *(1942; trans. 1946). Why should we not adopt the same system, or the even stronger form just suggested, which would do away with the requirement that the defendant have violated the law? See Lady Wootton,* Crime and the Criminal Law *(1963). You are being asked here whether the deliberate use of caricature, the reduction of a person to a role in a story, should be dispensed with. Or, short of that, can its use be controlled somehow? Or is it in fact a valuable way for the law to speak, is caricature itself a form of control of legal language?*

WRITING ASSIGNMENT 7: *The Insanity Defense*[10]

Part One

• *Draft your own statement of the insanity defense. This should probably take the form of a rule, followed by whatever additional instructions or explanations are required to make clear to a jury what you expect of them. Indicate whether your defense is available against strict liability and negligence crimes, and whether it is available in juvenile delinquency proceedings, and explain why.*

Part Two

• *Give an account of a real or imaginary event in which you think someone was insane or close to it. Does your proposed test permit the expression in the courtroom of this event as you really see it?*

Here you are asked to evaluate your proposed test as a way of talking about people. What connections can you draw between what you have the law say and the way you actually regard insanity — or the possibility of it — in yourself and others? In your insanity defense, have you created a literature of character or caricature?

This is a frustrating and difficult job. People have always been per-

10. A supplementary assignment is in the Appendix.

plexed by abnormal behavior, by irrationality in others and themselves, and no comprehensive and clear way of talking about insanity has emerged. Is the difficulty that we have not invented a language to describe the mind that is as "copious and precise" as botanical language, or does the trouble lie in what the form of the rule does to whatever terms it uses? Or is it something else? Macaulay says that "the most copious and precise of human languages furnish but a very imperfect machinery to the legislator." Introductory Report Upon the Indian Penal Code (1837), in Works, VII, 416 (1866). What do you suppose he means by that? You may conclude that the assignment is impossible. If you come to that conclusion, what do you think the law should do then? Abolish the insanity defense? Abolish the criminal law?

Part Three

• Explain what your difficulties were in drafting your insanity test and how you faced them. How do you evaluate the literature you have created?

One likely source of difficulty is that you probably stated your test in the form of a rule, and we know something of the problems that presents. But you were also asked to give explanations and instructions — directions for use — that would make your statement intelligible and enable your reader to act sensibly and confidently in conformity with your purposes. Did this effort succeed? If so, how, and if not, why not?

It might help you understand what kind of literature you have created if you ask how a trial in which it was used might proceed. Would there be expert witnesses, for example, and if so, what qualifications should they have? What would you expect direct and cross-examination of these witnesses to be like? Would everyone experience the sort of frustration evident in the Washington case (page 337 supra), or would your proposal lead to an intelligible conversation, in which people spoke directly and plainly to their audiences, in which the witnesses could say what was on their minds and the judge and jury could get answers to their questions?

Look at what you have done as a way of talking about people: is this a literature of character or caricature? Into what will the law (as you have made it) convert the people with whom it deals?

One final question: judgments about mind and character can be drawn, as you well know, from how a person speaks and behaves: if a person spoke and behaved as you in your proposal make the law speak and behave, what judgment would you make about that person's intelligence and humanity? About his sanity?

WRITING ASSIGNMENT 7, ALTERNATIVE A: Purposes of People and of the Law

This assignment is meant to help you get a clearer sense of what the criminal process involves and what purposes it actually serves. You may then be in a better position to propose instructions to a jury and to make argument to a court based upon these purposes rather than upon the labels used in particular rules. This assignment may also clarify for you the purposes you wish to pursue in proposing your own insanity defense.

Part One

• In a single paragraph, tell briefly the story of a real or imaginary crime from the point of view of the person who committed it. Try to express something of what this person is like and how he sees things. Your account should express some understanding of why your imagined criminal did what he did.

Part Two

• Now draft a series of short paragraphs showing how real or imaginary individuals in each of the following roles would regard the event described above, or some aspect of it.

a. policeman
b. prosecutor
c. defense lawyer
d. psychiatrist
e. juror
f. sentencing judge
g. legislator

You may add to this list in any way you wish.

In working over these paragraphs, feel free to add whatever facts each official would be likely to want to know. Notice that some paragraphs leave out facts critical to the others. Try to write in direct discourse, representing the words or thoughts of the official directly rather than descriptively. It is hoped that this will lead you to imagine most fully a mind and a situation different from your own. You might present an internal conversation — showing the thoughts of the official as he works towards a conclusion — or an external one between the official and someone else who either argues or agrees with him.

Part Three

• Based upon Part Two of your paper, what do you see as the purposes of the criminal law, in light of which its rules and labels can most intelligently be used?

WRITING ASSIGNMENT 7, ALTERNATIVE B: Drafting Instructions

Here you are asked to draft instructions to a jury, telling them how to apply a particular term in a way most suited to the purposes of the law.

Part One

• Draft an instruction to the jury in the Conley case, telling them how to decide whether the defendant had the state of mind called "malice." Then draft an instruction in the Hood case, telling the jury how to decide whether or not there had been an assault with a deadly weapon upon a peace officer.

Part Two

• What relationship do you establish, in each case, between the label in the rule and the purposes the rule is intended to advance? Explain any differences between the two cases in this regard.

Part Three

• Have you, by speaking plainly and directly of your purposes, succeeded in removing the artificial and the fictional from the criminal law? Why or why not?

C. JUDGMENT WITHOUT LABELS — THE SENTENCING DECISION

They knew that in the beginning and in the end a man stands alone, his soul is alone in itself, and all attributes are nothing — and this curious final knowledge preserved them in simplicity.*

* D. H. Lawrence, *Sea and Sardinia* (1921).

Pontiac had been an old friend of [François] Baby; and one evening, at an early period of the siege [of Detroit], he entered his house, and, seating himself by the fire, looked for some time steadily at the embers. At length, raising his head, he said he had heard that the English had offered the Canadian a bushel of silver for the scalp of his friend. Baby declared that the story was false, and protested that he would never betray him. Pontiac for a moment keenly studied his features. "My brother has spoken the truth," he said, "and I will show that I believe him." He remained in the house through the evening, and, at its close, wrapped himself in his blanket, and lay down upon a bench, where he slept in full confidence till morning.†

We are still engaged in an attempt to find an occasion where the law addresses the human personality fully and directly, where a legal speaker does justice to the complexity and profundity of the experience of another. One might have thought that the determination of sanity for the purposes of the criminal law was such a moment; but, as you have seen, attention is there focused upon the choice among verbal formulas, upon competing "tests," to such a degree that the purposes of the enterprise are never stated with clarity (and seem hardly to be considered) and the person himself is nearly forgotten. It is not surprising that the result is a language inadequate to the experiences with which it deals.

Sentencing should be different. Here the entire individual stands before the judge, and the very question to be decided is, "Who is this man?" The judge is free to express his response in whatever way he wishes; no rules or conceptual schemes hedge him in. He should seek to understand the defendant and his act as fully as possible, from every point of view. No way of talking about the man and his crime should be considered irrelevant, and the defendant should be free to characterize himself in any terms he chooses. For to determine the sentence, it is not enough to put a label on the defendant's conduct: the punishment, we say, should fit the criminal, not the crime. The law looks beyond the single transaction that gives it jurisdiction, it looks to the whole man. It permits the judge to recognize that the person before him has a past and a future, to speak of him as a complete character rather than a caricature; and if the story of his life has a meaning, it can be expressed or recognized by the law. This is what we have been waiting for. In the insanity defense assignment (Sec. B) you were bound by the label; in the wrongful death assignment (Ch. 2, Sec. C), by the statutory rule; in the Stein assignment (Ch. 2, Sec. B), by your role as a lawyer; but in imagining yourself responsible for sentencing decisions you are as free as one might ask to be. What will you do with your freedom?

† Francis Parkman, *The Conspiracy of Pontiac*, Chapter 12 (1851).

This is your question. In the next writing assignment you will be asked to explain how you have made judgments about other people in your own life, to propose a wise and rational system for making sentencing judgments, and to explain what connections you can draw between your experience and your proposal. The first part of the assignment asks you what you do; the second part asks you to tell others how to do it.

For this assignment you are also asked to read Jane Austen's *Pride and Prejudice* (1813), and a note connecting that book with the problems of sentencing appears below at pages 401–407.

1. *What Do We Do with Our Freedom? — Existing Law and Practice*

Here is an actual statute that charges the jury, or in some cases the judge, with the duty of setting a sentence. How does this statute operate as a set of directions to that process of judgment?

PENNSYLVANIA STATUTES (1963)

Title 18, §4701.

All murder which shall be perpetrated by means of poison, or by lying in wait, or by any other kind of willful, deliberate and premeditated killing, or which shall be committed in the perpetration of, or attempting to perpetrate any arson, rape, robbery, burglary, or kidnapping, shall be murder in the first degree. All other kinds of murder shall be murder in the second degree. The jury before whom any person indicted for murder shall be tried, shall, if they find such person guilty thereof, ascertain in their verdict whether the person is guilty of murder of the first or second degree. If such person is convicted by confession, the court shall proceed, by examination of witnesses, to determine the degree of the crime, and to give sentence accordingly.

Whoever is convicted of the crime of murder of the first degree is guilty of a felony and shall be sentenced to suffer death in the manner provided by law, or to undergo imprisonment for life, at the discretion of the jury trying the case, which shall, in the manner hereinafter provided, fix the penalty. In the trial of an indictment for murder, the court shall inform the jury that if they find the defendant guilty of murder in the first degree, it will be their further duty to fix the penalty therefor, after hearing such additional evidence as may be submitted upon that question. Whenever the jury shall agree upon a verdict of murder of the first degree, they shall immediately return and render the same, which shall be recorded, and shall not thereafter be subject to reconsideration by the jury, or any member thereof. After such verdict is recorded and before the jury is permitted to separate, the court shall proceed to receive such additional evidence not previously received in the trial as may be relevant and admissible upon the question of the penalty to be imposed upon the defendant, and shall permit such argument by counsel, and deliver such charge thereon as may be just and proper in the circumstances. The jury shall then retire and consider the penalty to be imposed and render such verdict respecting it as they shall agree upon. A failure of the jury to agree upon the penalty to be imposed, shall not be held to impeach or in any way affect the validity of the verdict already recorded, and whenever the court shall be of opinion that further deliberation by the jury will not result in an agreement upon the penalty to be imposed, it may, in its discretion, discharge the jury from further consideration thereof, in which event if no retrial of the indictment is directed, the court shall sentence the defendant to life imprisonment upon the verdict theretofore rendered by the jury, and recorded as aforesaid. The court shall impose the sentence so fixed as in other cases. In cases of pleas of guilty, the court where it determines the crime to be murder of the first degree, shall, at its discretion, impose sentence of death or imprisonment for life. . . .

QUESTIONS

1. *Does this statute express the view that the defendant is a complete human being and that every aspect of his experience, every possible way of talking about him, is relevant to the sentencing process? What view of him does it express?*
2. *What view does this statute express of the jury? As a juror, would you be pleased to be addressed in such a way? Insulted? If you were a judge, would your response be the same or different, and why?*
3. *Would you know in either case how you were meant to sentence a defendant under this statute, and if so, how would you know? Flipping a coin would be an exercise of "discretion," but presumably it would be improper. How do you know that?*
4. *Would it be improper under this statute to refuse, on conscientious grounds, to sentence anyone to death? To sentence every first-degree murderer to death, out of a firm belief in the deterrent force of capital punishment? If one adopted no absolute rule, but somehow every case came out the same way, would that be preferable? Why?*
5. *One might say that the heart of the rule of law is the idea that like cases should be treated alike. How does this statute attempt to achieve that result? Or does it simply disregard that value, and if so, why does it do so?*
6. *One argument is that the statute does not intend to give directions to the sentencing process, it does not mean to make sentencing law: that task is delegated to the courts. If so, it follows that the judge has the responsibility of explaining his sentencing judgments in a rational and coherent way, or, where appropriate, of giving a jury rational and coherent instructions to the sentencing process.*

a. *Should the statute give him more assistance in this task than it does? How might it do so?*
b. *Under this statute, how would you as a judge begin to explain a sentencing judgment, or frame instructions to a jury?*

COMMONWEALTH v. RITTER
13 Pa. D. & C. 285 (1930)

STERN, P.J., March 27, 1930. — The defendant, Willard A. Ritter, pleaded guilty to an indictment charging murder. The case is before the court to determine the degree of the crime, and, under the provisions of the Act of May 14, 1925, P. L. 759, to fix the penalty if it should appear that the defendant committed murder of the first degree.

[The defendant left his wife for Mrs. Kennard, with whom he lived for a time. He was an alcoholic. On December 29, 1929, he quarreled violently with Mrs. Kennard at his room at the Patchels' boarding-house.]

. . . Mr. Patchel stated that after the quarrel the defendant looked like a man completely deranged, and Mrs. Patchel said that he looked like a man who had suddenly lost his reason. He told Mr. Patchel that he loved Mrs. Kennard better than his life, that he could not live without her, that he was no good, and that he "might as well finish it;" he also kept saying that he would kill her. He refused to dine with the Patchels that evening, telling them that he could not eat and that his nerves were all gone, and that as a matter of fact he had not eaten for four days.

That night the defendant tried repeatedly to reach Mrs. Kennard on the telephone, but without success. He spent the evening at the home of his wife; although, as above stated, she had divorced him, he seems to have continued to some extent friendly relations with her, and they were then living in the same house. Mrs. Ritter testified that he was very much upset, and at his request she gave him veronal tablets in order that he might sleep. On Monday evening, Dec. 30th, the defendant again tried to get Mrs. Kennard on the telephone at her home, and he seems to have prowled around there on the porch. On Tuesday, Dec. 31st, he sought Mrs. Kennard at her place of employment, a department store at 8th and Market Streets, and also kept telephoning to her during the day. That afternoon he told Mrs. Patchel that he loved Mrs. Kennard better than his life, but that he thought she had somebody else. Mrs. Patchel says that when the conversation turned on the subject of Mrs. Kennard, he seemed to go into a frenzy. Meanwhile, at about half-past 2 o'clock in the afternoon, he visited a pawnshop, where he had pawned a revolver some three months before, and obtained it out of pawn by pledging in its stead his overcoat and a ring. He then bought some bullets at another store, which bullets did not exactly fit the revolver, but, unfortunately, as the sequel shows, were sufficient for the purpose intended. He came to the department store in the late afternoon and had a verbal quarrel with Mrs. Kennard. He was overheard to say that he would give her five minutes to make up her mind. She started to call one of the store authorities, whereupon the defendant shot her, the first shot apparently striking her in the back. She then ran away from him, down some steps to a mezzanine floor, and he followed her. She fell and he leaned over her and fired two more shots into her body. As the store employees, who were attracted by the occurrence, began closing in on him, and one of them held him from the rear, he fired two shots into his own body, one into the chest, which was later extracted from in back of his arm; the other bullet entered below the lowest rib, tore four holes in his liver, struck a rib, by which it was deflected, and was later extracted from the right side of his body. . . .

These are the essential facts, and from a consideration of them the court has no hesitation in arriving at the conclusion, as it does, that the murder of Mrs. Kennard by the defendant was wilful, deliberate and premeditated and constitutes murder of the first degree.

The real question for the determination of the court is as to the penalty to be inflicted. . . .

It will be noticed that this statute leaves the penalty entirely to the discretion of the jury, or, in case of a guilty plea, to the court, and that it prescribes no rules for guidance in the exercise of such discretion, nor does it give any indication as to what was in the legislative mind as to the basis upon which such discretion was to be exercised. Of course, it is certain that the decision on this point, either by a jury or a court, is not to rest upon any conscientious scruple or objection to capital punishment in general. . . .

What then should be the punishment inflicted upon the defendant in this particular case? What considerations should weigh in the matter? It must be assumed that the discretion given by the act is to be exercised by the jury or by the court, as the case may be, on some rational basis, and not in an arbitrary, capricious or whimsical manner. The law, however, furnishes no precedents upon which any theory of determination of the question is to be sought. Indeed, it is obvious that the problem is not one of law at all, but only of penology.

In the present case, the court is acting really as a jury, and for that reason is not called upon to express the reasons by which it arrives at a conclusion. And since, as above pointed out, an opinion could have no authority as a precedent, or as laying down any legal principle of value in such cases, there is perhaps nothing to be gained from a judicial standpoint by a formal statement of the reasoning upon which the court's conclusion is based. Since, however, the district attorney has earnestly urged upon the court that the death penalty should be imposed in this case, and counsel for the defendant have argued vigorously to the contrary, and since the life of the defendant is at stake, it would seem to be in order for the court to give some expression to the views which have guided it in its consideration of the important question involved. At least, by so doing, there will be obviated any suspicion that the findings reached by the court are casual or emotional, rather than guided by intellectual processes. As a matter of fact, while in murder cases there is frequent reference to "mitigating" or "extenuating" circumstances, no tribunal, as far as I know, has ever attempted to express the reasoning which leads to a conclusion as to just what such circumstances consist of, or, generally, as to what factors in such cases should incline a jury or a court to imposition of the one penalty as against the other. The entire subject seems to be one of an uncharted sea, and, therefore, even the expression of an individual opinion may be a slight contribution toward some rationalized penology. . . .

. . . [W]e come to the crucial question underlying this and similar cases, namely, what is the purpose or object at which the law aims in the sentencing of those convicted of crime? . . .

Generally speaking, there have been advanced four theories as the basis upon which society should act in imposing penalties upon those who violate its laws. These are: (1) To bring about the reformation of the evil-doer; (2) to effect retribution or revenge upon him; (3) to restrain him physically, so as to make it impossible for him to commit further crimes; and (4) to deter others from similarly violating the law.

Let us briefly consider these in order:

1. As far as the principle of reformation is concerned, however important it may be in the general run of cases, it obviously has little or no application to such a case as the present. Whichever be the penalty here inflicted, the defendant will not again be in contact with society, and since secular law is concerned with one's relation to the community and not primarily with his inward moral development, the spiritual regeneration of a defendant is not, in such a case as this, a dominant factor. In other words, it would not be a practical consideration weighing in favor of life imprisonment that thereby the defendant might be susceptible of moral reformation, whereas the opportunity for this would be denied to him if the death penalty were inflicted.

2. The second theory which has been urged as a basis for the imposition of penalties is that of retribution. [The court rejects this theory.]

3. Rejecting, therefore, the theory of retribution as a proper basis upon which to impose the penalty of law, we come to the third prin-

ciple which has been advocated, namely, the restraint of the wrong-doer in order to make it impossible for him to commit further crime. Here we arrive not only at a justifiable basis for action but at one which is vital to the protection of society. To permit a man of dangerous criminal tendencies to be in a position where he can give indulgence to such propensities would be a folly which no community should suffer itself to commit, any more than it should allow a wild animal to range at will in the city streets. If, therefore, there is danger that a defendant may again commit crime, society should restrain his liberty until such danger be past, and, in cases similar to the present, if reasonably necessary for that purpose, to terminate his life. Admittedly, restraint by imprisonment can never be as wholly effectual as execution, and there are, from time to time, cases where imprisonment may not be sufficient for the protection of society. It is on this ground that it is pertinent to take testimony in regard to the history of a defendant and of the circumstances attending his commission of crime. If his record shows that he is of a dangerous type, or that he habitually commits grave crimes, or that he has a homicidal tendency, or that he is hopelessly depraved, or that he has a savage nature, or that he has committed murder under circumstances of such atrocity and inhuman brutality as to make his continued existence one of likely danger to society, then, in my opinion, the sentence of death is both justifiable and advisable. The community may not be safe with such a man in existence even though he be serving a term of life imprisonment; he may again commit murder within the prison walls, or may escape and again make innocent victims his prey, or may even, by cunning simulation of repentance, obtain a pardon from governmental authorities.

Examining the record of the present case from this point of view, in order to determine whether the defendant's continuation in life would be a lurking menace to society, I find nothing in the evidence which would lead to that conclusion. . . .

4. This brings us to the final and what must be fairly regarded as one of the most important objectives of punishment, namely, the element of deterrence — the theory which regards the penalty as being not an end in itself but the means of attaining an end, namely, the frightening of others who might be tempted to imitate the criminal. From this angle a penalty is a cautionary measure, aimed at the prevention of further crime in the community. . . .

My own opinion is that the extreme penalty of death works a deterrent effect, and, therefore, should be aimed against cases where a murder is committed from what might be called a mental, rather than an emotional, impulse — in other words, where the murder is deliberately planned from a sordid motive or where the likelihood of its occurring is callously ignored by those who commit some other crime which may well give rise to it. Typical examples would be cases of highway robberies, burglaries and robberies committed by raids on banks, stores and the like, murders committed by poisoning or other means in order to collect life insurance or to attain some other mercenary end. To my mind, it would be reasonable and proper in such cases, generally speaking, to impose the penalty of death. Where, however, a murder is committed under the impulse of some frenzy or strong passion, or where it results from a mind weakened by long brooding over a social entanglement, or by alcoholism or the like, such a person is not likely to be deterred by the example of a death penalty imposed upon those who committed similar offenses. Such murders are not the result of reasoning or of weighing considerations for or against the intended crime, and, therefore, they are not apt to be repressed by the force of example.

In the present case, the nature of the crime and the psychology of the criminal are clear. For several years the defendant, although a man of mature age, long married and the father of five children, had been embroiled in a love passion for a woman who was not his wife. She, of approximately the same age, and the mother of three children, apparently entered with him upon an illicit relationship. Having, by his business ability, succeeded in achieving a fair degree of material prosperity, he squandered large sums of money upon the woman who had thus come into his life. He developed an extreme jealousy in regard to her and what seems to have been a constant terror that she would desert him, especially when he had arrived at the end of his financial means. He took more and more to drinking and enfeebled his health and mentality to a point where he was obliged to go to a medical institution on two successive occasions a year apart. Finally, he reached so low a depth in the matter of his finances that in order to obtain the very pistol with which he committed the murder he was obliged to pawn his overcoat. He continually haunted the woman, besieging her with visits and telephone calls at her place of employment. For the few days immediately preceding the murder he was in a condition of tremendous excitement and agitation, even to the extent of doing without food. Immediately after the shooting he tried to commit suicide, firing two bullets into vital parts of his body, and it seems miraculous that although one of the bullets caused four perforations in his liver, his attempt to destroy himself was unsuccessful. Although he shot with the intention of killing his victim, and expressed the hope that he had done so, in the same breath he was solicitous about her photograph, for which he had a sentimental affection, and he expressed himself to the effect that, she being gone, he cared nothing about himself and was not concerned about his fate. The very afternoon of the murder he had told the proprietress of his lodging-house that he loved the woman better than his life. In short, the case was plainly one of a frenzied and jealous passion on his part, working on a man destroyed by drink and desperate by reason of the fact that he had come to the end of his resources. For the reasons already stated, it is not believed that the death penalty in a case such as this would have any effect of deterrence on persons who might commit similar crimes, because offences of this nature are not the result of calm and thoughtful planning or of rationalized deliberation. . . .

The court, therefore, adjudges the defendant to be guilty of murder of the first degree, and imposes upon him the penalty of imprisonment for and during the term of his natural life.

QUESTIONS

1. *Here Judge Stern undertakes to explain how he makes a sentencing decision: he looks to the purposes of the criminal law and asks what sentence would serve them most fully. Is this an adequate explanation of his process of judgment? An adequate guide to others who must make such judgments?*
   a. *You yourself have tried to use the purposes of the criminal law as guides to the application of the insanity label. On the basis of that experience, can you explain why it is of very little help to be told what the purposes of the criminal law are and that you should set the sentence by following them? Is the difficulty that while the judge tells you what the purposes are, he does not tell you how to use them? Or is it deeper than that?*
   b. *Does this statement of his reasoning process tell us what Judge Stern actually did when he decided what sentence to give Mr. Ritter? Or does some other part of the opinion (say, the narrative) provide a more genuine explanation and justification of his judgment?*
   c. *Judge Stern says that the deterrent purposes of the law would not be served by the imposition of the death penalty in this case. Why does he say so? Do you agree? How would you have sentenced Mr. Ritter, and why?*
2. *Notice that Judge Stern had "no hesitation" in finding that the murder was "willful, deliberate, and premeditated, and constitutes murder in the first degree." Is this consistent with his sentencing judgment? To repeat a familiar question: why should the judge not "follow the purposes" of the criminal law as well in applying the labels of the guilt stage – "premeditated," "malice," "assault" – as in determining the sentence at the disposition stage? Or do we look to "purposes" only as a last resort, when the legislature has made no law and given us no categories, and we are at our wit's end?*
3. *Judge Stern does try to explain the reasons for his judgment here, and (as he says) that is rarely done. Certainly the rule of law can hardly be said to apply to sentencing decisions unless they are explained, and*

preferably published and subjected to critical scrutiny. Why do you suppose judges normally do not explain them, then?

4. Judge Stern hoped that his opinion would be a contribution to the development of a rational penology. Can you figure out from this opinion what Judge Stern meant by a "rational penology"? Or what he meant when he said that sentencing is not a problem "of law at all, but only of penology"?
5. Judge Stern explains what he is doing by saying that the sentencing discretion must be exercised on some "rational basis"; his explanation is meant to dispel any suspicion that his decision is "casual and emotional, rather than guided by intellectual processes." "Of course," he says, the decision may not rest on any "conscientious scruple or objection to capital punishment."
   a. Does this psychological language – drawing a line between the casual, emotional, conscientious, and scrupulous on the one hand, and the rational and intellectual on the other – accord with your experience of yourself? Are your intellectual processes never casual? (Look at one of your own term papers or exams, chosen at random.) Do you value your capacities for intellectual activity more than your conscientious scruples? A judgment that can be explained and defended as perfectly rational more than one you sense to be right?
   b. The proper place of emotion and scruple in judicial judgment is a most difficult matter. No matter how fully you may recognize that your own processes of judgment cannot be expressed as wholly rational, you may prefer that judges (including yourself) pretend that they are. To do otherwise would be inconsistent with the rule of law. Consistency is essential to fairness, and rationality is a way of approaching consistency. To recognize the value of the process of judgment by feeling or scruple would be to invite overt inconsistency in the law. Does this add up to the conclusion that the very idea of rationality in the law excludes or hides the single most important kind of judgment?
   c. Compare the following instruction: [I]n this part of the trial the law does not forbid you from being influenced by pity for the defendants and you may be governed by mere sentiment and sympathy for the defendants in arriving at a proper verdict in this case; however, the law does forbid you from being governed by mere conjecture, public opinion or public feeling . . . [Y]ou are entirely free to act according to your own judgment, conscience, and absolute discretion. That verdict must express the individual opinion of each juror." McGautha v. California, 402 U.S. 183, 189–190 (1972).
6. How would you express the ultimate goal of a rational sentencing system: is it that the law should provide a process and a language to ensure that like offenders are treated alike? What could such a phrase possibly mean? See the ABA Standards Relating to Sentencing Alternatives and Procedures (1967); Report of the Pilot Institute on Sentencing, 26 F.R.D. 231 (1959); National Council on Crime and Delinquency, Guides for Sentencing (1957); Institute of Judicial Administration, Disparity in Sentencing of Convicted Defendants (1954). See also E. Green, Judicial Attitudes in Sentencing (1961), and the reports of sentencing

institutes at 30 F.R.D. 185 and 401 (1961). For an explanation of the Model Penal Code draft provisions, see Wechsler, "Sentencing, Corrections, and the Model Penal Code," 109 U. Pa. L. Rev. 465 (1961).

For one definition of the possible rationality of sentencing, see N. Walker, Sentencing in a Rational Society (1969).

7. Suppose every sentencing judgment were subject to review by an appellate court. Would this increase the uniformity, fairness, and rationality of sentences? Exactly how might such a process of review operate, by what rules or principles? See Thomas, "Appellate Review of Sentences and the Development of Sentencing Policy: The English Experience," 20 Ala. L. Rev. 193 (1968); American Bar Association, Standards Relating to Appellate Review of Sentences (1967); Note, "Appellate Review of Primary Sentencing Dispositions: A Connecticut Case Study," 69 Yale L.J. 1453 (1960). Two important federal cases: United States v. Weston, 448 F.2d 626 (9th Cir. 1971); United States v. Daniels, 446 F.2d 967 (6th Cir. 1971).

   What would we be saying about the sentencing process if we concluded that rational appellate review was possible? If we concluded that it was impossible?

8. In Principles of Sentencing (1970), D. A. Thomas describes British sentencing practice. As he puts it, the primary decision the court makes is whether to sentence the defendant on the principle of "individualization" – according to which the major question is what disposition is needed by the particular individual and will most nearly ensure his social rehabilitation – or to sentence him under what Thomas calls the "tariff," that is, the system of fitting the punishment to the seriousness of the crime, with the goals of deterring others and of satisfying a desire that a proportionate punishment be exacted. Where the crime is serious, the former is much to the defendant's advantage; where trivial, the latter sometimes is. How would you, as a judge, go about making the choice between these two types of disposition in particular cases? What questions would you ask about the defendant and his conduct?
   a. Would you conclude, for example, that certain types of conduct are so dangerous or reprehensible that a term of imprisonment is always called for, whatever the special circumstances of the individual before you? Examples might be crimes of violence or deliberation, such as rape or blackmail or tax fraud.
   b. Or would you look first at the individual, on the grounds that certain types of defendants (such as the very young) ought never to be imprisoned, and that certain others (such as the hardened professionals) ought always to be imprisoned, without much regard to the nature of the particular offense?
   c. It would be instructive to take the time now to draft a rule defining categories of offenses and offenders that would enable one to carry out either of the suggestions made above, or perhaps some compromise between them.

9. It is a real question for all of us to what extent we are defined by our conduct on a single occasion, whether it be conduct of which we are proud or ashamed. Will you always be the one who stole ten dollars from your employer or the one who won the football game with a famous

pass? The law faces this problem directly in the sentencing decision, since, as you have seen, there is almost always a competition between two ways of talking about the defendant: one tells us "what he did," the other "who he is."

In Lord Jim (1900), Conrad deals with this matter from the point of view of the actor: Jim is never able to come to terms with the fact that he once committed a flagrant and inexcusable violation of the laws of the sea and morality — though the narrator is careful to repeat, again and again, that he is "one of us." In Oedipus at Colonus, Sophocles presents Oedipus at the end of his life, twenty years after he has blinded himself in guilt and shame at the discovery of what he had done. He is at last able to face and judge himself, and he concludes that he is innocent of any wrong, that his conduct does not define him.[11]

On the other hand, it is a part of our sense of morality that conduct affects character, that we work out an identity for ourselves in what we do. When Tito, the charming and spoiled youth in George Eliot's Romola (1863), decides not to search for his missing father but to take as his own the money that might have saved him, "he had made it impossible that he should not from henceforth desire it to be the truth that his father was dead." (Chapter 9.) And much later, when he sees his father among some prisoners and in an act of instinct pretends not to know him, George Eliot says: "Tito was experiencing that inexorable law of human souls, that we prepare ourselves for sudden deeds by the reiterated choice of good or evil that gradually determines character." (Chapter 23.)

10. Compare another difficulty that faces judge and narrative artist alike: in what sense can it be said that the man before me is the same one who committed the crime, and the same one who will walk out of prison eight years from now? In what sense is my hero in chapter 50 the same character with which I began? Surely we have all asked ourselves whether the six-year-old child in our memory has any more connection with who we are now than does any other six-year-old child. Consider one of the great scenes in the Iliad, Hector's farewell to Andromache: together they foresee his death and her slavery, and lament their future. It is with great reluctance, with a real recognition of the costs of war, that he returns to the battle. But once it is joined, and the Trojans are driving the Achaeans to their ships, there is no man more ferocious, more relentless, than Hector. The experience — the sense of self — of the early scene has been replaced with another identity. "How can one who has seen what he has seen act as he is acting?" we ask. Is that just poor writing, or is it extremely realistic?

How is the judge to go about addressing the question, "Who is this man before me?" What connection can there be between him and what he has done?

What can we mean when we say that the judge's judgment should be a rational one?

11. An interesting essay on character definition and change in the drama and in law is Rosenberg, "Character Change in the Drama," in *The Tradition of the New* 135 (1960).

THE SENTENCING PROBLEM*

S. Glueck

A fixed punishment provision expresses the legislature's views as to the relative gravity or harmfulness of the crime in question. It stresses the criminal act rather than the makeup of the offender or his chances of reform or recidivism. While the statutory indeterminate sentence also expresses the legislature's view regarding the relative gravity of different crimes by providing varied minimum and/or maximum limits, the basic aim of the indefinite sentence system is to provide that the actual sentence in the individual case, taking account of the makeup and situation of each offender, can be tailored by the judge (and to some extent by the parole board) within the framework of a maximum or a minimum limit, or of both. The theory is that although, for instance, a burglary is always a burglary, not all burglars are alike in the motivations of their crime, in their mental and emotional makeup, social background, probability of recidivism and other such circumstances which are certainly every bit as relevant to the aim of protecting society as is the crime itself, if not more so. Such factors, to some extent, make each crime a unique event and each criminal a unique individual. . . .

How will the court individualize the sentence? This fundamental question has been all too lightly treated in the literature, the statutes, and penologic congresses. It has just been assumed that, given an investigation report on the particular offender before him for sentence, the judge will, by his learning and experience, or by some sort of super-jurisprudential magic, be able to decide the exact penal or correctional measure suited to the particular person undergoing sentence and the length of time the offender needs to be subjected to such treatment in order to reform or be rendered nondangerous.

But to "individualize" the sentence in the case of any specific offender means, first, to differentiate him from other offenders in personality, character, sociocultural background, the motivations of his crime and his particular potentialities for reform or recidivism and, secondly, to determine which, among a range of punitive, corrective psychiatric and social measures, is best adapted to solve the individualized set of problems presented by that offender in such a way as materially to reduce the probability of his committing crimes in the future. . . .

Disparities in Sentencing

Some time ago, an analysis was made of over 7,000 sentences imposed by six judges over a 9-year period in a county in New Jersey. Each of

* 20 *Fed. Prob.* No. 4, 15 (1956). Footnotes are omitted.

these judges dealt with such crimes as larceny, robbery, burglary, embezzlement, assault and battery, rape, etc. Since there was no special assignment of cases to any particular judge, each judge received cases in which, considering them as a whole and over a long period of time, the felonies were committed under similar circumstances, and the offenders, as groups, did not vary in general personal makeup and social background. Yet the study disclosed that while Judge A imposed sentences of imprisonment in 36 percent of his cases and Judge B in 34 percent of his, Judges C, D, E, and F imposed such sentences in 53, 58, 45 and 50 percent, respectively, of their cases. Thus an offender convicted of a serious crime had but 3 chances out of 10 of going to prison under Judges A and B, and 5 out of 10 if sentenced by Judges C, D, E, or F. Allowing the defendant to remain free in the community on probation, instead of sending him to prison, ranged, among the various judges, from 20 to 32 percent; suspension of sentence, from 16 to 34 percent. Other American studies have shown similar discrepancies in courts of different states.

Although sentencing practices in the federal courts have improved in recent years, there are still evidences of erraticism. Thus, in the 1955 Report of the Federal Bureau of Prisons, the average sentence for all offenses to federal institutions during the fiscal year ended June 30, 1955, was 25 months. While in the Third Circuit as a whole the average was 24.4 months, looking at the picture by Districts, the average sentence in Delaware was 13.7 months, in New Jersey 20.8 months, Pennsylvania Eastern 21.6 months, Pennsylvania Middle 53 months, Pennsylvania Western 25.7 months. The sentences for individual crimes also varied with the different Districts. There are similar divergencies in other Circuits.

In the important choice between imprisonment and probation there is also considerable disparity. True, in the Third Circuit the proportion of persons placed on probation in the different Districts is remarkably uniform, ranging from 48 percent in Pennsylvania Western to 54.6 percent in Pennsylvania Middle; but such consistency does not exist in a number of the other Circuits. For example, in the First Circuit, the total percentage of probation is 61.8 percent, or almost twice that of the 34.5 percent norm throughout the federal system; in Maine it is 39.6 percent, while in New Hampshire it rises to 84.2 percent. So also in the Second Circuit, the total proportion of probationers is 41 percent; but in Connecticut it is 53.3 percent while in the Northern District of New York it is only 29.1 percent and in the Eastern it is 37 percent. The percentages of probationers received from the courts by the federal probation system for the year ended June 30, 1955, ranged in the Fourth Circuit from 25.5 percent in Maryland to 62 percent in North Carolina Eastern; in the Fifth Circuit from 8.4 percent in Texas Western to 67 percent in Mississippi Southern; in the Sixth Circuit from 8.5 percent in Tennessee Western to 39.5 percent in Michigan Eastern; in the Seventh Circuit from 19.9 percent in Indiana Southern to 46 percent in Wisconsin Eastern; in the Eighth Circuit from 28.1 percent in Missouri Eastern to 52.3 percent in Arkansas Eastern; in the Ninth Circuit from 5.5 percent in Arizona to 51.2 percent in Oregon; in the Tenth Circuit (omitting territories) from 29.9 percent in Wyoming to 67.9 percent in Utah. . . .

Some Devices for Achieving Uniformity

There are several ways of doing this. The familiar one is to permit sentence revision by some appellate body. But such a twice-removed tribunal could not greatly improve on the original sentencing practices, or at best could only bring about a superficial uniformity of sentence. The basic problem — the proper exercise of creative discretion at the sentencing and releasing stages — cannot be met in this way.

Another device is detailed legislative prescription of criteria to be applied by the judge in assessing the length and nature of the sentence. The difficulty here is that the legislature may surround the judge with so clumsy an apparatus of control as to permit of but a poor counterfeit of scientific individualization. An illustration of a legislative attempt to cabin and confine judicial discretion is the Italian penal code project of the late Professor Enrico Ferri. . . . Is it not possible to have a less mechanical system which will still guide judges in the process of individualization?

This is attempted in the sentencing provisions of the Model Penal Code which the American Law Institute is in process of drafting. Section 7.01, for example, provides "Criteria for Withholding Sentence of Imprisonment and for Placing Defendant on Probation." I quote:

(1) The Court may deal with a person who has been convicted of a crime without imposing sentence of imprisonment if, having regard to the nature and circumstances of the crime and to the history and character of the defendant, it deems that his imprisonment is unnecessary for protection of the public, on one or more of the following grounds:

(a) The defendant does not have a history of prior delinquency or criminal activity, or having such a history, has led a law abiding life for a substantial period of time before the commission of the present crime;

(b) The defendant's criminal conduct neither caused nor threatened serious harm;

(c) The defendant did not contemplate that his criminal conduct would cause or threaten serious harm;

(d) The defendant's criminal conduct was the result of circumstances unlikely to recur;

(e) The defendant acted under the stress of a strong provocation;
(f) The victim of the defendant's criminal conduct consented to its commission or was largely instrumental in its perpetration;
(g) The imprisonment of the defendant would entail excessive hardship because of his advanced age or physical condition;
(h) The character and attitudes of the defendant indicate that he is unlikely to commit another crime.
(2) When a person who has been convicted of a crime is not sentenced to imprisonment, the Court shall place him on probation if he is in need of supervision, guidance or direction that it is feasible for the probation service to provide.

The Model Code provides other criteria to be taken into account in the imposition of fine and for sentence of imprisonment. For example, among the criteria for a sentence of "extended term" of imprisonment which the court may impose on a person convicted of a felony are:

(1) The defendant is a persistent offender whose commitment for an extended term is necessary for protection of the public . . .
(2) The defendant is a professional criminal whose commitment for an extended term is necessary for protection of the public . . .
(3) The defendant is a dangerous, mentally abnormal person whose commitment for an extended term is necessary for protection of the public . . .
(4) The defendant is a multiple offender whose criminality was so excessive that a sentence of imprisonment for an extended term is warranted . . .

Judges tend, at present, to take into consideration the type of criteria included in the draft code; but the spelling of them out should be helpful in reminding judges to consider, systematically, various matters deemed relevant by the legislature and the public. Freedom of judicial discretion remains unhampered; but the listing of the considerations to be taken into account should, in the long run, bring about greater uniformity of treatment.

But even such a device is insufficient. For the judge has no way of knowing how closely related such criteria as the Law Institute Code provides are to various types of postsentence behavior. The criteria do not largely derive from followup investigations that have related traits and factors in the makeup and background of various types of offenders to their actual postcorrectional conduct. The question presented is whether there is available, for the purposes of scientific differentiation of treatment, an instrument that can aid the judge in determining which factors have been shown, by systematic analysis of past experience, to be *truly relevant to the expectable behavior of various offenders, and how much weight to give such factors in the particular case before the judge for sentence.*

Predictive Tables

This brings me to a striking yet usually overlooked aspect of the history of penology and code drafting; namely, that all the reform devices of the present century — the juvenile court, probation, the indeterminate sentence, classification within institutions, parole — depend for their efficiency on the *reasonable predictability of human behavior under given circumstances.* Yet all these forward looking additions to the apparatus of criminal justice were adopted long before this indispensable basis for their success — predictability — was available, and they still ignore or minimize the crucial element of predictability.

Since scientific individualization of justice promises to reduce recidivism, it is desirable. But cannot it be more efficiently brought about than by merely supplying the judge with a set of criteria which he should more or less take into account without knowing their relative weights in terms of expectable behavior, and which most dedicated and intelligent judges nowadays actually do take into account anyhow?

Some American and a few foreign criminologists believe that the answer lies in the prognostic instrument known as the prediction table. In several followup researches which have checked on the posttreatment careers of various classes of ex-prisoners, Mrs. Glueck and I have constructed a series of prognostic instruments which give reasonable promise of bringing about better sentencing practices and treatment results than are achieved at present. . . .

In our first study, *500 Criminal Careers*, we thoroughly investigated the preinstitutional life histories of 500 former inmates of the Massachusetts Reformatory for young-adult felons, during a 5-year postparole "test period" following their discharge from that institution. Some 50 factors in the constitution, social background, and behavior of these offenders, from childhood through the parole and postparole periods, were explored and analyzed. By means of correlation tables, *the degree of relationship between each of these biologic and social factors and the postparole behavior of the men was determined.* To give one example, in respect to their prereformatory *industrial* habits the men were subclassified into "good worker," "fair worker" and "poor worker." By correlating each of these industrial categories with the criminal behavior of the men during the 5-year test period, it was found that of the *good* workers, 43 percent continued to commit crimes during the postparole test period; among the *fair* workers, 59 percent recidivated; of the *poor* workers, 68 percent were criminalistic. These percentages we call "*failure-scores*," because they indicate the proportion of the different subclasses of the men who *failed to reform*, considered from the point of view of their status in respect to such a factor as prereformatory industrial habits.

Similar correlations were established between each of the 50 biologic and sociologic factors, on the one hand, and the actual postparole behavior, on the other, with the result that many factors were found to bear very little relation to recidivism, while some showed a very high association therewith. In addition to *industrial habits preceding entrance to reformatory*, the following five factors, among those of greatest relationship to postparole conduct, were then employed in the construction of a table which judges could use in the sentencing of offenders: (1) *Seriousness and frequency of prereformatory crime;* (2) *Arrest for crimes preceding the offense for which sentence to the Reformatory had been imposed;* (3) *Penal experience preceeding Reformatory incarceration;* (4) *Economic responsibility preceding sentence to the Reformatory*, and (5) *Mental abnormality*.

By adding all the *lowest* percentages of failure (recidivism) associated with the various subcategories of these six factors, on the one hand, and all the *highest*, on the other, the two possible limits of "total failure-scores" were determined. These turned out to be 244 as the lowest, and 396 (or more) as the highest. Within this range of lowest and highest total failure-scores, the following subclasses of total failure-scores were then established: 224-295, 296-345, 346-395, 396 and over. Finally, all 500 cases were distributed in a table according, on the one hand, to each offender's total failure-score on all six predictive factors and, on the other, according to whether, so far as postparole behavior is concerned, he turned out to be a success, partial failure, or failure.

	Status Regarding Postparole Criminality		
	Percentage of —		
Total Score on Six Factors	Success	Partial Failure	Total Failure
244-295	75.0	20.0	5.0
296-345	34.6	11.5	53.9
346-395	26.2	19.1	54.7
Over 395	5.7	13.7	80.6
All cases	20.0	15.6	64.4

From such a table, a judge who is considering whether or not to sentence any particular offender to a reformatory can, with reasonable accuracy, determine the advisability of such disposition of the case before him, provided he has reliable information as to that offender's status in respect to the six simple predictive factors upon which this prognostic instrument is based. A prisoner scoring as low as 244 to 295 on these six factors which have been found (by comparison of factors with outcomes in hundreds of cases) to be *relevant to the question of reform or recidivism,* belongs to a class that has 7½ in 10 chances (75:100) of turning out a success; i.e., of not committing crimes during the postparole period. On the other hand, one with as high a failure-score as 396 or over has but half a chance in 10 (5.7:100) of succeeding under this type of penocorrectional treatment. The first man also has 2 in 10 chances (20:100) of failing only partially, and only half a chance in 10 (5:100) of turning out a total failure. The second has only 1½ chances in 10 (13.7:100) of partial failure and the high probability of 8 out of 10 chances (80.6:100) of turning out to be a complete failure.

Since this first table was published, we have improved and refined many predictive tables, have prepared them for each of the existing forms of correction which the laws place at the disposal of judges, have prepared instruments for predicting success or failure when offenders reach various ages, and for success or failure during a 15-year followup span.

QUESTIONS

1. *Exactly what do the statistics on sentencing disparities show? Are you surprised?*
2. *If uniformity were the goal, that would be easy to achieve, would it not? Explain how.*
   a. *How would you respond to the suggestion that all bookmakers and runners be sentenced to one year in jail? That all such defendants be sentenced by the same judge? These solutions would both tend to produce uniformity, but in State v. DeStasio, 49 N.J. 247, 229 A.2d 636 (1967), a defendant complains because all gambling defendants are sentenced by the same judge. Here he actually argues for less uniformity. What do you suppose "rational sentencing" would mean in the argument made by his lawyer?*
   b. *In that case the court said that judges often fail "to see beyond the individual they are sentencing." What else might one argue they should see?*
3. *Professor Glueck's basic premise is that "although a burglary is always a burglary, not all burglars are alike." But apparently all those who receive similar scores on a prediction table are "alike." Do you agree? How would you define "alike"?*
   a. *If you were a criminal defendant, would you feel the truth as to your situation and character were better expressed by the burglary label, or by the prediction table score you achieved?*
   b. *If you were a burglary victim, which criterion would express more accurately the truth of the situation as you saw it?*

c. *Is there some system for defining the actor and his act upon which both victim and defendant might agree?*

4. *If the critical facts for an assessment of dangerousness can be adequately expressed in a prediction table, why do we not dispense with the "burglary," "rape," and "theft" labels, and base the entire criminal process upon prediction tables? Why, that is, do we need a "guilt" stage of the criminal process at all?*

5. We have seen that there is a reality behind every legal label that the label or conclusion fails to express. Is Professor Glueck's purpose to express that reality? Does he succeed? Will his prediction table tell you what is really going on, or what really should be going on? At the end of Donnelly, Goldstein and Schwartz, Criminal Law (1962), there is a section which reexamines the criminal law "in terms of groups," such as racial, age, and economic groups. This is apparently meant to be a first step in an inquiry as to what is really going on beneath the surface of artificial rationality and fairness that the law presents. Can such an examination tell you what is really going on? What purpose can it serve?

6. In Nagel, "Disparities in Criminal Procedure," 14 U.C.L.A.L. Rev. 1272 (1967), a report is given of a study of disparities in various stages of criminal procedure, not just sentencing. The empirical study is said to "indicate" the existence of "substantial disparities" based upon the economic class, race, sex, age, and education of the defendant.
   a. Suppose the issue is the granting of probation: is it a "disparity" to grant probation more often to young people? Rich people? Women? White people? Educated people?
   b. What if the issue is the granting of a preliminary hearing?
   c. What if the issue is determination of guilt? (How could the existence of such a disparity be established?)
   d. The study shows that Negroes convicted of larceny are much more likely to receive sentences than white people convicted of larceny, but that the sentences are likely to be much shorter. What can you conclude from this?
   e. Suppose "disparity" is defined as a difference in result in similar cases that has no rational basis. What does "similar" mean in that sentence? How do you know when two cases are similar? What does "rational" mean there? How do you know when a difference in result has a rational basis? A difficult case in which racial bias in jury sentencing is alleged is Maxwell v. Bishop, 398 F.2d 138 (8th Cir. 1968).

7. Suppose you were asked by Congress to conduct an exhaustive study to determine whether like offenders were being treated alike in the determination of sentence, and given a million dollars with which to carry on the necessary research. How would you determine whether like offenders were being treated alike?
   a. Exactly what information would you collect and from whom? What questions would you have to ask and answer as necessary preliminaries to carrying on the study?
   b. Could such a study provide information that could be of use to judges in sentencing future defendants? To a legislature or state supreme court in fashioning rules for sentencing decisions? Exactly what information would be needed, and exactly how could it be used?

8. Professor Glueck quotes a provision from a tentative draft of the Model Penal Code which, somewhat revised, was the basis for the final provision

in the code and for the corresponding provision in the National Commission on Reform of Federal Criminal Law, Proposed New Federal Criminal Code, Chapter 31 (1971).[12] *The provision does not set forth a*

12. The major difference between the provision quoted by Professor Glueck and the current proposals is that both of the latter express a presumption that imprisonment is not to be imposed unless the judge is satisfied that the safety of the public — measured by the listed factors — warrants or requires it.

Here is the provision from the *Proposed New Federal Criminal Code* (published in *Hearings Before the Subcomm. on Criminal Laws and Procedures of the Senate Comm. on the Judiciary*, 92d Cong., 1st Sess., pt. 1, at 430 (1972)):

"Chapter 31. Probation and Unconditional Discharge

§3101. Criteria for Utilizing Chapter.

"(1) Eligibility. A person who has been convicted of a federal offense may be sentenced to probation or unconditional discharge as provided in this Chapter.

"(2) Criteria. The court shall not impose a sentence of imprisonment upon a person unless, having regard to the nature and circumstances of the offense and to the history and character of the defendant, it is satisfied that imprisonment is the more appropriate sentence for the protection of the public because:

(a) there is undue risk that during a period of probation the defendant will commit another crime;

(b) the defendant is in need of correctional treatment that can most effectively be provided by a sentence to imprisonment under Chapter 32; or

(c) a sentence to probation or unconditional discharge will unduly depreciate the seriousness of the defendant's crime, or undermine respect for law.

"(3) Factors to be Considered. The following factors, or the converse thereof where appropriate, while not controlling the discretion of the court, shall be accorded weight in making determinations called for by subsection (2):

(a) the defendant's criminal conduct neither caused nor threatened serious harm to another person or his property;

(b) the defendant did not plan or expect that his criminal conduct would cause or threaten serious harm to another person or his property;

(c) the defendant acted under strong provocation;

(d) there were substantial grounds which, though insufficient to establish a legal defense, tend to excuse or justify the defendant's conduct;

(e) the victim of the defendant's conduct induced or facilitated its commission;

(f) the defendant has made or will make restitution or reparation to the victim of his conduct for the damage or injury which was sustained;

(g) the defendant has no history of prior delinquency or criminal activity, or has led a law-abiding life for a substantial period of time before the commission of the present offense;

(h) the defendant's conduct was the result of circumstances unlikely to recur;

(i) the character, history and attitudes of the defendant indicate that he is unlikely to commit another crime;

(j) the defendant is particularly likely to respond affirmatively to probationary treatment;

(k) the imprisonment of the defendant would entail undue hardship to himself or his dependants;

(l) the defendant is elderly or in poor health;

(m) the defendant did not abuse a public position of responsibility or trust; and

(n) the defendant cooperated with law enforcement authorities by bringing other offenders to justice, or otherwise.

"Nothing herein shall be deemed to require explicit reference to these factors in a presentence report or by the court at sentencing."

rule, or guiding purposes, but a set of factors to be considered in determining whether to grant probation or to sentence to prison. It is a sort of checklist, perhaps. Is this a better structure for a language in which to tell others how to make sentencing judgments than the rule or statement of purpose would be? Is it a better language for expressing judgments made? Consider these questions again when you come to your next writing assignment.

9. Of course the judge is not the only person who participates in the sentencing decision. Under our system another agency, usually called the parole board, has the power to release the prisoner well in advance of the maximum sentence imposed by the judge, and in some states it has virtually complete control over his disposition. The idea is that this judgment will be based on vastly better information than the judge's can possibly be: while the judge must guess at future conduct, the correctional and parole officials make their judgment on the basis of the prisoner's actual response to prison life. And the possibility of a discretionary release may act as a real incentive to good behavior and a cooperative attitude towards correctional efforts.
   a. Are you persuaded? How would you qualify or challenge this view of the relative excellence of the parole judgment?
   b. Can you make an argument that it is unconstitutional to place the release decision in the hands of a parole board rather than those of a judge, or of judge and jury? How would you meet the argument that the parole board had a special expertise in these matters? See Bennett v. California, 406 F.2d 36 (9th Cir. 1969).
   c. Must the process by which the parole judgment is made meet the requirements of due process established for criminal trials? For judicial sentencing decisions? How would you expect these matters to be argued? Does revocation of parole present a different situation in these respects from the decision to grant or withhold parole as an initial matter? See Morrissey v. Brewer, 408 U.S. 471 (1972).
   d. Could one also make the opposite argument, that it would be unconstitutional to imprison someone for a fixed term of years without the possibility of discretionary release before the end of his term? Or that the judgment as to discretionary release must be made by correctional experts, not by a judge?

10. In McGautha v. California, 402 U.S. 183 (1971), the Supreme Court held that it was not unconstitutional to give the jury the task of deciding whether the death penalty should be imposed, even where the jury was not given any standards or criteria by which to make the judgment. The Court said: "To identify before the fact those characteristics of criminal homicides and their perpetrators which call for the death penalty, and to express those characteristics in language which can be fairly understood and applied by the sentencing authority, appear to be tasks which are beyond present human ability."
   a. Do you agree?
   b. Can the same observation be made about all sentencing judgments, or is the death penalty unique in this regard?
   c. In the light of your responses to these questions, what should the law do about sentencing?

TALK ABOUT PEOPLE IN TERMS OF GROUPS

One problem with the use of general rules and criteria to operate and review the sentencing process is the inherent falseness of any talk that assumes that people can be defined by the groups they belong to. The social generalization may be useful for some purposes, but it cannot be used with confidence in particular cases. Suppose you know that there is an 80 per cent chance that an individual with the psychological and social characteristics of the defendant will continue his pattern of criminal behavior if placed on probation. You thereby also know that one out of every five of the defendants with these characteristics who appears before you will respond to probation — so of what value is the generalization, unless you simply sacrifice the 20 per cent? If you are willing to do that, what will you do when you are told that there is an 80 percent chance that the defendant will respond favorably to probation? Of what value is the general prediction in such a case? And here you have been asked to assume as knowledge what can only be guessed at, and you have not been asked to consider what the realities of prison life might do to either class of prisoner.

This sort of generalization in talk about sentencing is a special case of a very widespread practice or language game of talking about people as members of groups. We do this all the time, especially in our talk about history and society: we talk about the middle class and blue-collar workers, about whites and blacks and browns, about women and students and the poor and hippies and so on, as though society as a whole consisted of groups and its life was their interaction — their formation, conflict, realignment, gaps, and so on. (But how many groups do you belong to?) This is a sort of talk that must go on, of course — but upon what understandings, what premises? In what ways can this sort of speech properly be used and in what not?

Here is an example of talk about people in terms of groups. This passage describes the Special Group Program adopted by the faculty of an American law school:

The Director, in consultation with the Special Group Program Committee, is in charge of the operations of the Program and is responsible for:

(a) Making recommendations to the faculty relating to the basic operations and policies of the Program.

(b) Maintaining a program designed to identify prospective law students who appear to have the intellectual ability to graduate from this law school but would not otherwise be eligible for admission under normal admission standards, and who are members of identifiable groups which have not had adequate educational and cultural opportunities available to them and which are seriously under-represented in the legal profession. It is understood that Negroes, Mexican-Americans and American Indians are such groups, members of which may be expected to constitute most if not all the participants in this program. It is not intended, however, to preclude participation by members of other identifiable groups which are shown to fit within the standards set forth in the first sentence of this subparagraph (b).

Does this seem to you an intelligent way to talk about people? Why should it matter whether a person is a member of a "group" that has been denied "adequate educational and cultural opportunities," so long as he himself has been denied those things? And what if his "group" has been denied them, but he has not? How does this faculty talk about its students?

Writers of many different kinds have been perplexed by their own desires to talk about people as members of groups. This simplification is intensely attractive at every level; one wants to believe one thing about one's countrymen, another about one's foreign adversaries or allies. Travelers return from summer trips to Europe and tell us all about the character of the English, the French, the Danes and so on. The novelist is not free from the temptation: as you have seen, many of his characters are types. In *The Republic*, Book 8, Plato describes four types of government and the kind of person who is analogous to each: timocracy, oligarchy, tyranny, and democracy. He tries to define a form of government that corresponds to the wisest and best man, and he thinks of both in terms of types or models. Compare the following:

The vulgar are apt to carry all *national characters* to extremes; and, having once established it as a principle that any people are knavish, or cowardly, or ignorant, they will admit of no exception, but comprehend every individual under the same censure. Men of sense condemn these undistinguishing judgments; though, at the same time, they allow that each nation has a peculiar set of manners, and that some particular qualities are more frequently to be met with among one people than among their neighbors. The common people in Switzerland have probably more honesty than those of the same rank in Ireland; and every prudent man will, from that circumstance alone, make a difference in the trust which he reposes in each. We have reason to expect greater wit and gaity in a Frenchman than in a Spaniard, though Cervantes was born in Spain. An Englishman will naturally be supposed to have more knowledge than a Dane, though Tycho Brahe was a native of Denmark.

. . . A *soldier* and a *priest* are different characters, in all nations, and all ages; and this difference is founded on circumstances whose operation is eternal and unalterable.

The uncertainty of their life makes soldiers lavish and generous, as well as brave: their idleness, together with the large societies which they form in camps or garrisons, inclines them to pleasure and gallantry: by their frequent change of company, they acquire good breeding and an openness of behaviour: being employed only against a public and an open enemy, they become candid, honest, and undesigning: and as they use more the labour of the body than that of the mind, they are commonly thoughtless and ignorant.

It is a trite, but not altogether a false maxim, that *priests of all religions are the same;* and though the character of the profession will not, in every instance, prevail over the personal character, yet it is sure always to predominate with the greater number. For as chemists observe, that spirits, when raised to a certain height, are all the same, from whatever materials they be extracted; so these men, being elevated above humanity, acquire a uniform character, which is entirely their own, and which, in my opinion, is, generally speaking, not the most amiable that is to be met with in human society. It is, in most points, opposite to that of a soldier; as is the way of life from which it is derived.*

This passage is brilliant, we say; but how could it be used in deciding whether to trust a particular soldier or a priest?

It may help you connect this section with what has gone before if you evaluate this suggestion: that the sort of caricature we see in Hume and in other literature of social description is perfectly appropriate on the understanding, expressed by Hume, that this is a literature of generalization and approximation; it is not appropriate as a way of making and articulating judgments about individual people. "Men of sense condemn these undistinguishing judgments." The difficulty for the law is that it must function both as a system of approximation — a set of general rules — and as a system for particular judgments. How is the tension between these two sorts of judgment, expressible in different languages, to be expressed and addressed? Is there any conceivable way it can be resolved?

2. *Expressing Judgments of Others: The Sentencing Problem as a Problem of Writing*

I hope you see the readings in the first part of Section C as posing a problem of extraordinary difficulty. How are judges to make and explain sentencing decisions? How can they give directions to others who must make similar decisions? What expectations should we bring to these activities, what critical standards can we employ?

You can readily enough see the pressures at work and watch the courts respond. To have each crime carry a fixed sentence is "uniform"

* David Hume, "Of National Characters," in *Essays Moral, Political, and Literary* 202 (1741; World's Classics ed. 1963).

all right, but it seems arbitrary and irrational when one considers the enormous variety of character and circumstance that would thus be treated in a uniform way. So the courts are given discretion to adjust the sentence to the needs and blameworthiness of the individual criminal. But how is a judge to make these judgments? What purposes is he serving when he does so? In practice, most sentencing judgments are made silently, without explanation. We simply do not know what is going on. The silence is partially invaded by new systems invented for making, explaining, guiding, and evaluating sentences — policies with respect to particular crimes, prediction tables, lists of factors and criteria. These are artificial, as other legal labels are, and are thus usually so subject to exception and qualification that they lack even the limited virtue a closed system can have, namely, internal consistency. And in any event they admit a margin of doubt which means they do not change the essence of the situation; it comes down at last to one man judging another without a language adequate to explain or justify what he has done. It is hard to see how the word "rational," or any other term of praise, can be applied to what we observe here. Can you imagine a sentencing system which you could approve, which you could call wise or rational?

In the readings and questions that follow, we shall look briefly outside the law to see how judgments are made and talked about in other contexts. You will not be surprised to find that we start with you: how do you in your ordinary life make and explain judgments about others? You say of another: "He is an honest man." What lies behind those words? Find an instance in your own experience in which you concluded that a person was honest or dishonest, or courageous or cowardly. What can you say about the process of judgment in which you engaged? Try to express what you did as fully as possible, preferably in writing. Is it important to you to be able to express what making that judgment involved — how you did it, what doubts you had, and how you faced them — or do you say that what matters is whether the judgment is right or wrong, not whether it is explained? (If it is not explained, how do you know whether it was right or wrong?)

What other judgments about people have you made? You have voted; chosen a roommate; chosen a doctor; said of yourself that you can become a lawyer and a good one; decided never to play cards with that person again; and the like. Think of some actual instances, and ask yourself what you did and how you can express it. In making these judgments did you use rules and labels? Refer to and follow purposes? Did you identify certain factors and criteria as the relevant ones and disregard the rest? This poses a challenge to your ability to talk about your own mind, to find or make a language to express what you did. Do you have a language that is sufficiently "copious and precise"? If not, how do you face and respond to that fact?

To look to the second part of the problem: how can you tell others how to judge? Take two or three instances of situations in which you have made judgments about other people. How would you tell another, situated now as you were then, to make such judgments? Say, your younger brother or sister. Draft a paragraph in which you give such directions in an actual situation. Do you use rules, labels, criteria, factors? What do you do?

There follow now several passages in which judgments about people are expressed. What can you learn from this literature about making and expressing judgments about people? Ask of each judgment, "Is that the sort of judgment I would make? The sort of explanation?" What directions to judgment can you construct out of these statements, and how do you evaluate them? Try to locate judgments and expressions of which you approve and disapprove. How do you explain your approval and disapproval in each case?

Ask of each passage: what does this tell me about the writer?

WALL STREET'S HIPPIES: LONG-HAIRED COURIERS MAKE FINANCIAL SCENE*

Mary Bralove

SOME WORRY ABOUT LOSS OF STOCKS, BUT OTHERS FIND YOUTHS FAST AND PLEASANT

NEW YORK — Daniel Smith is an easygoing teen-ager who forgets to collect his paycheck almost as often as he decides today isn't the day to get a haircut. His frayed bell-bottom trousers, beads and navy pea coat flap in the wind as he motorcycles through Wall Street, seemingly oblivious to the goings-on of the financial world around him.

Eighteen-year-old Dan Smith, along with a growing number of other young men who affect similar styles, has become an important cog in the operations of Wall Street. Messenger services, feeling the pinch of a labor shortage, are hiring hippies to carry millions of dollars in securities, important contracts and other commercial paperwork from one office to another in the financial district.

The psychedelic shirts and dangling beads of this new breed of messenger have some Wall Street nerves on edge. "A guy like that might pick up $100,000 worth of securities and stop because he sees a man strumming a guitar," worries Alan Kluger, managing partner of the brokerage firm of Kluger, Ellis & Mann. "Or he might stop for a hot dog and leave the package on the counter."

* *Wall Street Journal*, Nov. 5, 1969, at 1.

Indeed, tales of lost securities and misplaced merger documents are almost as numerous as the estimated 25,000 messengers who move about the city — mostly by foot and subway rather than by motorcycle. Last July a messenger from Empire State Messenger Service Corp. jumped off a pier in a suicide attempt with his satchel at his side. Another Empire messenger is said to have wandered off with news releases for an hour or two during a marijuana "high."

A Rose for the Client

In contrast to the crusty oldsters — often retired police and firemen — who traditionally do the bulk of Wall Street's messenger work, the hippie messengers generally have a reputation for being good-natured. One known as the "Twirler" is renowned for doing a pirouette before and after picking up a package. Many of the young men from Cosmic Messenger Service Inc. offer clients a smile and a rose.

The hippie messenger phenomenon may pass as quickly as it came. Hippie messengers, who usually earn about $65 a week, say the job is simply a way to keep themselves in bell-bottoms and bread for a while. Some are students, and still others aspire to be artists and singers. John Bernd, a 20-year-old Cosmic messenger, says he will quit the business when he starts making enough money from his rock and roll group, in which he plays lead guitar.

Some messenger outfits still refuse to hire hippies. Israel Kaver, assistant manager of Wall Street District Messenger Co., says his firm won't hire hippie messengers because, he asserts, their appearance would give the concern a bad image.

But the labor pinch is making it difficult for many other messenger services to be so choosy. "We hire anybody with two arms and legs — that's how hard it is," says Saul Gittelman, treasurer of Empire, which employs 250 hippies.

"A More Mature Type"

Messenger services blame higher welfare payments and increased Social Security benefits for the labor shortage. "If the situation were ever to turn around, we would eliminate the hippies as quickly as they were put on," Mr. Gittelman says emphatically.

Because messenger services are being forced to hire so many hippies, some disapproving prospective clients are hiring their own messengers or using office personnel to run errands. "We like the more mature type," says a partner of L. F. Rothchild & Co., a brokerage house that refuses to employ hippies. "That's the way it's been for years and years, and that's the way it will always be."

Such antipathy makes many hippie runners unsure of their reception. "Some of our messengers have trouble on Wall Street," says David

Lawner, co-owner of Cosmic, which employs hippies exclusively. "Elevator operators won't let them in without a coat and tie." On the other hand, when Robert Mertens, a Cosmic messenger, walked into the apartment of a conservative stockbroker to deliver some law books, the service supervisor heard about it. The broker's wife told the supervisor exactly what she thought of this "weird-looking" messenger. She said she found him delightful, well-mannered, and wonderfully knowledgeable about her favorite interest — Oriental rugs.

Barbara Levine, a receptionist for a brokerage house, agrees. She says that her firm employs the long-haired runners because "they're intelligent and fast. They just don't hang around and go to sleep." Still, she tries to hustle the messengers out as fast as she can, because occasionally a partner will see one and exclaim, "My God, my wife has shorter hair!"

Although hippie messengers are raising some eyebrows, cries of outright indignation are rare. Alfred J. Shuman, executive vice president of First Devonshire Corp., explains why: "There are too many people around here who are themselves parents of hippies."

QUESTIONS

1. *This passage expresses or points to a great many different judgments about people. How many such judgments can you find here? How do you evaluate them and their expression?*
2. *Mr. Kluger says that "a guy like that" might stop to hear a guitar, or leave a bundle of securities at a hot dog stand. Is that the sort of remark you might make? What does that remark tell you about Mr. Kluger?*
3. *Barbara Levine says that the "long-haired runners" are "intelligent and fast." Is that the sort of remark you might make? What does it tell you about Barbara Levine?*
4. *Would "psychedelic shirts and dangling beads" put your "nerves on edge"? What would they do to you? How do you respond to such apparel, and how would you respond if you were a judge? (Is it an answer to say: "This is no problem for me; I wear beads and long hair myself"?)*
5. *What judgments does Mary Bralove make, and how fully are they expressed? What does her writing tell you about her? (Look especially at the last sentence.)*
6. *There is one sort of judgment in which you must be an expert by now. How do you judge your teachers? How do you express your judgment of them? Consider the following passage taken from the 1968 Seer, the University of Colorado student guide to teachers and courses. Here one receives the collective judgment of hundreds of students. What does it tell you?*

   "Without question Professor ——— must be considered one of the finest teachers, not only in the ——— department but in the University

itself . . . An extraordinary man teaching an extremely valuable course.

"Professor —— is without question a truly outstanding teacher at this University. Everyone who commented about him had nothing but praise and awe for the inspiring teaching capabilities displayed by this man. He shows exceptional talent and rapport with students and receives the Seer's strongest endorsement as one of the finest instructors at this University."

7. What does that statement tell you about that professor? If you were president of the university, would you instantly give him a large raise? What does it tell you about The Seer?
8. Go back to your reading of Alcestis (see page 274 supra). Does this passage from The Seer create and define a character like Alcestis or like Admetus? Do you know what it would be like to take Professor ——'s course? Do you have any idea? Does this make you want to sign up for it?
9. If you were a student at that university, you would no doubt want to know who Professor —— is. Why? So you could laugh uproariously at this statement?
10. What sorts of judgments do you yourself make about your teachers, and how do you express them?
11. As you are doubtless ready and eager to say, there is another side to this coin.
    a. What sorts of judgments do your teachers make about you, and how do they express them? Are you satisfied with this process? If not, can you explain your dissatisfaction? How does your response define your idea of an education?
    b. What sorts of judgments do you think teachers should make about you, and how should they be expressed? You are being asked here to propose a rational grading system, and I hope you see that this has something to do with your eventual assignment to propose a rational sentencing system.
    c. In your ideal grading system, would there be any place for an unfavorable judgment? Or do you believe that to understand all is to forgive all? (The same result in your sentencing system?)
    d. One problem with the grading system is that it is purely comparative. You are given numbers that rank you. But by what standard or standards? What does this all say about the real you? Would you prefer to have individual comments in ordinary English by your teachers? Before you say yes, imagine from your experience what those comments would probably say. Would you rather have a 96 or a statement that "I have nothing but praise for and awe for the inspiring learning abilities displayed by this student"?
12. Before going on, come to some conclusion (preferably in writing) as to what is wrong with the passage from The Seer. You may wish to compare it with the following summary of a student survey evaluating teachers and courses at the Stanford Law School:

    "Torts, as a subject, found few fans among the first year class. Many thought the whole area 'absurd,' with little consistency or rationale, and that the law of torts was generally in a 'shambles.' Students felt that this situation had more or less forced otherwise competent teachers to emphasize questions rather than answers in their classes."

THE HISTORY OF THE REBELLION AND CIVIL WARS IN ENGLAND*

Edward Hyde, First Earl of Clarendon

[England is embroiled in civil war. The Duke of Hamilton, upon his return to England from Scotland, where his mission on the King's behalf has failed, is suspected of disloyalty and imprisoned. He is kept in the Castle of Pendennis in Cornwall. When he hears that the Prince has come to Cornwall he eagerly seeks to see him to try to persuade him of his innocence, but it is decided that the Prince will not receive him. Clarendon, as Lord Chancellor, is sent instead to hear what he has to say.]

. . . He [the duke] told him that he had very much desired to speak with him, that he might make a proposition to him, which he thought for the King's service; and he desired if it seemed so to him, that he [Clarendon] would find means to recommend it to his majesty, and to procure his acceptance of it. Then he told him that he was an absolute stranger to the affairs of both kingdoms, having no other intelligence than what he received from gentlemen whom he met in the next room at dinner; but he believed by his majesty's late loss at Naseby that his condition in England was very much worse than his servants hoped it would have been, and therefore that it might concern him to transact his business in Scotland as soon as might be: that he knew not in what state the lord Mountrose was in that kingdom, but he was persuaded that he was not without opposition. He said he was confident that if he had his liberty, he could do the King considerable service, and either incline that nation powerfully to mediate a peace in England, or positively to declare for the King and join with Mountrose. He said he knew it was believed by many that the animosity was so great from him to Mountrose, (who indeed had done him very causeless injuries,) that he would rather meditate revenge than concur with him in any action: but he said he too well understood his own danger if the King and monarchy were destroyed in this kingdom, to think of private contention and matters of revenge when the public was so much at stake; and he must acknowledge, how unjust soever the lord Mountrose had been to him, he had done the King great service; and therefore protested, with many execrations, he should join with him in the King's behalf as with a brother; and if he could not win his own brother from the other party, he would be as much against him. He said he could not apprehend that his liberty could be any way prejudicial to the King, for he would be a

* Book 9, para. 153 (1702; Macray ed. 1888).

prisoner still upon his parole; and would engage his honour that if he found that he could not be able to do his majesty that acceptable service which he desired, (of which he had not the least doubt,) he would speedily return, and render himself a prisoner again in the place where he then was. In this discourse he made very great professions and expressions of his devotion to the King's service, of his obligations to him, and of the great confidence he had in this particular of being useful to him.

After he made some pause in expectation of what the Chancellor would say, he [the Chancellor] told him he doubted not but he was very able to serve the King both in that and in this kingdom, there being very many in both who had a principal dependence upon him: that he heard the King was making some propositions to the Scotch army in England, and that it would be a great instance of his affection and fidelity to the King, if, by any message from him to his friends and dependents in the Scots' army then before Hereford, or to his friends in Scotland, his brother being the head or prime person of power there that opposed Mountrose, they should declare for the King, or appear willing to do him service; and that, he having free liberty to send through the Parliament's army to London or into Scotland, he might as soon do the King this service as receive a warrant for his enlargement; which he presumed he knew could not be granted but by the King himself.

He [the duke] replied, that he expected that answer, but that it was not possible for him to do any thing by message or letter, or any way but by his presence: first, that they in whom he had interest would look upon any thing he should write, or any message he should send, as the result of distress and compulsion, not of his affection or judgment. Besides, he said, he looked upon himself as very odious to that nation, which was irreconciled to him for his zeal to the King, and thought this a just judgment of God upon him for not adhering to them. And, he said, for his own brother, who he heard indeed had the greatest influence upon their counsels, he had no reason to be confident in him at that distance; for, besides the extreme injury he did to him in making an escape from Oxford, by which both their innocencies were to be suspected, and for which he should never forgive him, he was the heir of the house and family, and he believed would be well content that he [himself] should grow old and die in prison: whereas, if he were at liberty and amongst them, he was confident some for love, and others for fear, would stick to him; and he should easily make it appear to those who were fiercest against the King, that it concerned their own interest to support the King in his just power. However, he concluded, that the worst that could come was his returning to prison, which he would not fail to do. So the discourse ended for that night.

The next day he entered again into the same argument, with much earnestness that the Chancellor would interpose upon that ground for his liberty; who told him that he was so ill a courtier that he could not dissemble to him: that he was not satisfied with his reasons, and could not but believe he had interest enough at that distance to make some real demonstration of his affection to the King, by the impression he might make upon his dependents and allies: and therefore that he could not offer any advice to the King to the purpose he desired. He told him that he had been present at the Council-table when the King communicated that business which concerned him to the Board; and that he gave his opinion fully and earnestly for his commitment, being satisfied, upon the information that was given concerning him, that his affection to the King was very questionable; and that it appeared that he had been earnestly pressed, by those persons of honour in that kingdom upon whom his majesty relied, to declare himself, and that if he could have been induced so to do, having promised the King he would, and having authority to that purpose from him, they might very easily have suppressed that rebellion in the bud: but that his lordship and his brother were so far from opposing it, that the very proclamation which had issued out there for the general insurrection (which proclamation was perused at Council-table when he was committed) was not only set forth in his majesty's own name but sealed with his signet, which was then in the custody of the earl of Lanricke his brother, he being Secretary of State in that kingdom. That those who were the principal informers against him, and who professed that they could do no service if he were at liberty, had since his restraint, being armed with no more authority than he had at his last being there when the kingdom was in peace, upon all disadvantages imaginable, when that kingdom was totally lost to the King, reduced the greatest part of it again to his obedience; and therefore, whether it was his lordship's misfortune or his fault, since things prospered so well in his absence, he could not as a councillor advise the King, without the privity and consent of the lord Mountrose, or without some such testimony of his service as he had before proposed, to give him his liberty: and that any ill success, which possibly might have no relation to that act, would yet be imputed to that counsel, and my lord Mountrose have at least a just or probable excuse for any thing that should happen amiss.

The duke thanked him for the freedom he had used towards him, and said, upon the information which was given against him he must acknowledge the proceedings to be very just, but he was confident, whenever he should be admitted to a fair hearing, he should appear very innocent from the allegations which had been given.

QUESTIONS

1. *In this passage a man explains a judgment he has passed on another. Study it carefully: how is this explanation of a judgment to be compared with Judge Stern's opinion in the Ritter case (page 367 supra)? With the judgment expressed in The Seer? With the judgments about the long-haired messenger boys reported in the Wall Street Journal?*
2. *What does each writer tell you about himself in the way he explains his judgment?*
3. *Insofar as you can judge from the Clarendon passage, do you have confidence in his judgment? Here is a brief passage with which Clarendon prefaced the account you have just read:*

   ". . . It is at large set down in the former book what proceedings there had been at Oxford against duke Hambleton, and how he had been first sent prisoner to Bristol, and from thence to Pendennis Castle in Cornwall. And since we shall hereafter meet him acting a great part for the King, and general in the head of a great army, it would be very incongruous, after having spent so much time in Cornwall without so much as naming him, to leave men ignorant what became of him, and how he obtained his liberty; which he employed afterwards with so much zeal for the King's service, to the loss of his life, by which he was not only vindicated in the opinion of many honest men from all those jealousies and aspersions which he had long suffered under, but the proceeding that had been against him was looked upon by many as void of that justice and policy which had been requisite; and they conclude by what he did after a long imprisonment how much he might have done more successfully if he had never been restrained. Without doubt, what he did afterwards, and what he suffered, ought to free his memory from any reproaches for any errors or weakness of which he had before been guilty."
4. *If you were convicted of a crime, would you rather be judged by Clarendon, by Mr. Kluger, or by The Seer? Why?*
5. *Consider the following expression of a judgment, following a hearing on both guilt and sentencing. In this case the defendant was tried on a five-count indictment, alleging various Selective Service law violations, including refusing induction:*

   "I am going to adjudicate him guilty — and there are two offenses I can find him on — I am going to give him five years on the first and I will give him five years on the second, making a total of $10,000.00, no making a total of $20,000.00 and ten years in prison. We can't fool around with people like that. We are in a War and a man who is a citizen of this country ought to act as such and with that you can prepare the proper order."

   Exactly how should an appellate court respond to that judgment? See Haywood v. United States, 393 F.2d 780 (5th Cir. 1968).
6. *Let us now look at the convicted defendant from a different point of view. Suppose you lived or worked in a prison, surrounded by people who had been sentenced for what they had done. How would you go about*

making judgments about them? What questions would you be likely to ask yourself about them? Of what importance to you would be the crime an individual had committed?

Below an intelligent man tells you about some prison judgments. How many judgments can you identify? How are they made?

LIFE*

"Zeno"

I think of the others in the library. Of old "Pop," nearly seventy years old, and doing five years for a fraud into which he drifted in his retirement. I think of Derek, an ex-colonel, serving an eighteen month sentence for a crime that involved money. That is all I know of it, and although I like Derek very much that is all I want to know. It is surprising how little I am interested in the crimes of my fellows. This is a genuine lack of interest, and I am not alone in feeling it. It is something which creeps up on one as the years pass. There is no intellectual commitment to disregard the offence in judging the man — it just happens. One arrives at the stage where one is no longer curious about another's past. If interest there is to be, it is in what the man is whom you know, not in what the police, or the prosecution, or the judge said about him at the time of his trial.

When I go back for my coffee in a minute or so, I shall be able to sit down alongside Derek, and we shall talk, perhaps about prison, but this is unlikely. We have so much in common, and particularly our years in the army. I am going to miss Derek when he goes out in six months' time.

I squeeze out my cigarette and stand up, realising that at this moment in time I could be in any rose garden, anywhere; that there are moments in prison when being imprisoned is of no consequence, that for whole minutes at a time prison is irrelevant, for the situation and the circumstances might exist anywhere. In the Central Prison we have showers, and I think of how I stand under one of them in the evenings with my eyes closed, and how, with the sometimes hot water running over my shoulders and down my body I might be taking a shower in some other place. At home, in an hotel, in any army mess.

A man comes round the corner. He is wearing the patched uniform of the "escapee," and he is closely followed by a screw. I turn towards the library, frowning to myself. Today is not the day, and now is not the time for men on the "special watch" list to change their books. I make the door a few paces ahead of the two men and signal quickly to Derek behind the counter. The coffee jug is out of sight and Derek is reading a book as the screw follows the man on special watch through the door.

* Pages 104–105, 142–143 (1968).

The screw wanders round the library, looking idly at the shelves, and I turn to attend to the man in the patched suit.

He stands quietly, looking across the counter, and as I pick up fresh cards to make out for him I am conscious of a serenity in his face that is completely at variance with the normal look of the newly convicted.

I pick up a pen, pull the card towards me, smile up at him and say "Number and name?"

I have written the number he has given me, and my pen has made the first, downward stroke of his name before the impact of what he has said strikes me.

He said, "Blake." It is George Blake, sentenced a week ago to forty-two years' imprisonment. I complete the card and hand it over to him, and for a second our eyes meet. I turn away and point out to him where he will find fiction, and where biographies, and where travel books, and I am wondering what he is thinking as the oft repeated words fall parrot-like from my lips.

He turns away with the smile to which I am to grow accustomed, and moves over to the shelves. I watch him.

I see now that what I took to be serenity is taut control, for his smooth, unlined cheeks just miss the complete relaxation of acceptance. He is a dapper figure, smart in his new suit, and he moves swiftly and surely, yet without hurry, from shelf to shelf. He has a polished air, and I wonder whether this is the veneer of the diplomat or the camouflage cloak of the secret agent. It could be either, for he was both.

Watching him, I think of his sentence. Forty-two years. With full remission he must serve twenty-eight. He is thirty-eight now. He will be sixty-six if he lives to see the date of his discharge. What *can* he be thinking about? What must he have thought about while he was on remand awaiting trial? What did he think about during the past week while he was under observation in the prison hospital to see how he would take the impact of the vicious sentence which has been passed on him? What will he think about as the years pass?

I turn to where Derek is reading at table and surreptitiously sipping his coffee below the level of the counter. I touch his shoulder. He looks up, and I speak quietly.

"That's George Blake." . . .

Nearly two more years have passed. Two years of monotony, withdrawal, and work. But this period of my imprisonment seems to be coming to an end. Part of its ending will be due to my own wish, but most of it will be due to the friendship and giving of another. It is late in the year 1965. I have served seven and a half years of my sentence, and for the first eighteen months of the last two years I walked very much alone.

In October 1962, Loy Kwi went on to the hostel scheme; he was discharged in July 1963, but to all intents and purposes I saw no more of him after October '62; Dick joined him in 1964, and from that day onwards I played no more bridge. I told myself that this was because I was not prepared to spend another two years training a novice up to a reasonable standard, but that was only part of the truth. The real reason was that I was not prepared to take on another responsibility in prison.

Kurt went out at about the same time as Dick, and Big George had returned to the States years before. With the departure of these three, Loy Kwi, Dick, and Kurt, I felt very much alone: the only two real friends remaining to me were Hugh and George Blake — two very different men. I admire both, but they have hardly a thing in common. George I admire for the depth and breadth of his tolerance and generosity, but both virtues are so all-embracing that I cannot enjoy the conceit of a particular place in his affections, and I am unable to accept this without a feeling of regret. The fact that apart from his wife, his mother, his children, and his sister — his immediate family — no one has probably got closer to him than I have is not in itself sufficient to outweigh my regret. I believe that George, for a number of reasons, is incapable of the type of friendship which most of us understand so clearly.

Somebody once said or wrote that if he had to choose between a friend and his country he prayed that he would have the strength to come down on the side of his friend. Hugh, Loy Kwi and Dick, I feel, would always do this. George has no deep-rooted loyalty to either nation or friend. He betrayed not one country but several: national boundaries mean nothing to him; his betrayal was of one ideology for another. Apart from his family, individuals are only important to him in so far as they are part of the human race to which he feels himself passionately committed. But his commitment is not emotional: he is not blind to the shortcomings of communism, and nor does he see it as the great panacea which will solve all human problems within a few years, but he is convinced that on balance communism holds the promise of a better, fuller life for the vast majority of mankind. Perhaps it is this particular viewpoint which will always stand between us, for I cannot accept the enslavement of people by the State for any reason at all, and even if I were convinced that the world would ultimately benefit, I should still be of the opinion that it is possible to pay too high a price for gold.

But despite the qualifications of our friendship, I spend many hours of each week in George's company. I have found it an enriching experience, and I am enjoying a protracted intellectual relationship of a kind that is new to me. But had I not met him under these conditions I doubt whether I should have been much taken with him, for I should have taken him to be a diplomat, and this would have created in me the mistrust I have always felt instinctively for men of this profession.

I have spent many hours thinking around our friendship, searching for factors and views we have in common; trying to put my finger on the particular points where our thinking coincides, endeavouring to discover what it is that draws me to him.

I killed one man, he betrayed the whole of the western world, and yet we both believe that we love our fellow men.

QUESTIONS

1. *How does Zeno make the judgments of others that he expresses here? What is the place of the criminal event – the narrative identity – in his judgment of his acquaintances and friends?*
2. *How does Zeno's account of these judgments define his qualifications as a judge? If you were the chief judge of a court, would you rather have as a colleague him or the writer of The Seer?*
3. *A parole board also makes judgments about people in prison. How would you compare a typical parole board judgment with what you read here? Suppose you yourself were a member of a parole board: how and why would your processes of judgment differ from Zeno's?*
4. *From what you have read in this section and before, it is plain that when a person gives an account of a judgment he has made he expresses a partial definition of himself as a judge. Some people recommend themselves to us as judges in what they write, others do not. The perceivable differences in quality are enormous. Would it be wise to require that every sentencing judgment be explained by the judge, and then subjected to the sort of scrutiny that you have been giving passages in this course? How would you explain the process of scrutiny: what would you be looking for? How would you know when you had found it?*
5. *This brings us to another question: is there a hopeless inconsistency between the activities of expressing a judgment fully and of telling another how to judge? We know that we ourselves do not judge in terms of labels and generalities and rules, and a full expression of our judgments would not pretend that we did. But how can an expression in any other terms serve as a guide to another? When you try to tell another person how to judge, do you not find yourself using rules, labels, factors, and criteria all over again? What other possibility is there? Can you simply say that the good judge must be a good writer? And how will you define good writing?*

   The following note may help you work out a connection between good judging and good writing.

JANE AUSTEN'S *PRIDE AND PREJUDICE*: WRITING ABOUT JUDGMENT

I hope to suggest in this note how this story of nineteenth-century courtship might be read in such a way as to shed light on the problems of the sentencing judge. Accordingly, let me recommend that you read this book, as you have recently been reading the literature of the law, as a work about the processes of making and explaining judgments about people and of building social relationships upon those judgments. Here are some questions for you to keep in mind: what sorts of judgments about people (perhaps "characters" would be the better word) are expressed in this book? How are the various characters shown to judge each other and to express their judgments? How do you in turn judge the characters, or — putting it more accurately, since the characters do not exist as people in your world to be judged — how do you understand what Jane Austen, in writing this novel in the way she does, is trying to tell you? How do you respond to what she writes? What must you do, or be, to read this book well? By its demands upon you, how does it define you? Finally: how do you compare this literature with the literature of the law?

Imagine yourself, for example, a judge asked to make a sentencing judgment with respect to Darcy or Wickham: how different would such a process of judgment be from that with which this novel is concerned? One man is good, the other bad, and nothing could be more important to know; yet how does one "know," whether judge or young lady? How would you tell another how to make this judgment? What does Jane Austen tell you?

In assessing the way this novel defines the process of social life, you might begin by asking what judgments the various characters make about one another, and how they are expressed. I suggest that you make a list of several and study them. Now how would you give directions for making judgments in such a world? The questions that follow are meant to open up this matter for you; I hope that as you work through them, new questions of your own will come to light.

1. You will probably think first of the judgments at the center of the book — Elizabeth's judgments of Darcy and Wickham, for example — but there are other simpler judgments that you should not fail to consider.

For example, by what process does Mrs. Bennett judge Bingley? Who is he in her eyes? How does she judge Wickham and Darcy? Her conclusions shift drastically at different moments in the narrative. By what principle can these apparently inconsistent estimates of worth be reconciled? (See the first sentence of the book.)

As you examine instances of judgment in this book, ask how the character in question explains, or would explain, his judgment of another. How does the explanation define the character who is judging? What sorts of directions to the making of judgments would this character give and how would they work? Ask these questions of the following judgments, and be prepared to tell:

how Lady Catherine judges Elizabeth. In her eyes, who is Elizabeth?

how Lydia judges Wickham.

how Charlotte Lucas judges Mr. Collins. (Notice that she does give directions to the making of judgments. See volume I, chapter 6.)

how Mr. Collins judges everybody.

In each case you will see that there is no great difficulty in characterizing the process of judgment. The criteria of judgment, like the goals of life, by which these characters are defined are so incredibly simple that they can serve only as caricatures — as comic figures, or perhaps as sources of fear (for there is a real threat in Mr. Collins and Lady Catherine). They could not possibly support the whole novel. They are capable only of a single response or a very narrow range of responses to experience, however varied, and are without any capacity for growth or change. They seem to lack the slightest perception of what every ordinary decent person must perceive about other people: that each is different from oneself and entitled to claims and interests of his own. Taken together, these characters do not form a social world of a kind that you recognize from your own life, as you do recognize the relationship between Jane and Elizabeth, for example. They define a world in which conversation is impossible. Can you imagine or find a conversation, for example, between Mr. Collins and Mrs. Bennett: on what terms could it possibly proceed? What hopes, except of comedy, would you have of such a colloquy? When Mr. Collins asks Elizabeth's hand, she is unable to make him perceive the simple fact that she is refusing him; what she asks is what he cannot give her, nor she him, for opposite reasons: to be considered "a rational creature speaking the truth from her heart."

For our present purposes, what is most significant about these judgments is how they define the judge. These characters see clearly and judge firmly, but in doing so define themselves as fools. Is that possibility a real one for the judge or lawyer? For you or me? How does one guard against such a danger, or even know when it is too late?

Another value these characters may have for us is that they can be said to dramatize (as Admetus also does) what it means in human and social terms to reduce experience to a narrow range of responses, to impose rigid and flat identities upon oneself and others — to speak, that is, as the law seems to speak.

2. One has no difficulty knowing how to read the caricatures — the reader's judgment is made with clarity and certitude — but the novel contains another set of characters, the understanding of whose imagined life requires every skill and art, whose experience defines uncertainties for us as well as for them. It is Elizabeth and Jane, not Mr. Collins or Lydia, who concern us. How, for example, is Elizabeth to judge Darcy and Wickham? When Darcy and Wickham meet by chance on the street and each changes color and shows emotion, Elizabeth asks herself: "What could be the meaning of it? It was impossible to imagine; it

was impossible not to long to know." And how is Jane to judge Miss Bingley? And what is she to make of the behavior of Mr. Bingley? This is a social world of the greatest difficulty and uncertainty. How can the process of judgment that is necessary to survival in it be explained and guided? How can behavior be fitted to judgment, so that one expresses the degree of doubt, acceptance, or reserve — of warmth or coolness — that the situation seems to call for? Here is a series of questions about judgments of this sort:

a. One might say that these judgments are merely social, of trifling importance when compared with the judgments with which the law is concerned; this novel deals with refinements that the law is right to disregard. But what would have been the consequences had Elizabeth made and acted upon an erroneous judgment of Wickham? You will notice that she did make such a mistaken judgment but, through his avarice, did not have the opportunity to act upon it. Is *Pride and Prejudice* a comic version of a story whose other telling would be tragic?

Slightly more subtle is this danger: if she had accepted Darcy's hand the first time it was offered, what would her future have been?

b. To what extent can the difficulties of judging and acting be met by suspending judgment, by refusing to act? To make assurance doubly sure would be the prudent course? The short answer is to ask what the future of Elizabeth or Jane as a spinster would have been. Charlotte Lucas is the one who looks with clear eyes upon that fate and expresses its quality rather clearly by preferring to it a life as Mrs. Collins. And such a course would lead to a position outside the social world which is the metaphor for life in this novel. Look at Mr. Bennett, whose judgment of other people is not in question, but who never himself builds any relationships. When to his great delight he interviews Mr. Collins — "May I ask whether these pleasing attentions [to Lady Catherine] proceed from the impulse of the moment, or are the results of previous study?" — his enjoyment is complete. Except for a few glances at Elizabeth during dinner, he required "no partner in his pleasure." He is a detached observer rather than a participant in the social life of this world.

c. Granting the importance and necessity of judging rightly, how is one to proceed? What directions can be given for right judging in this world? To dispose of a possibility that obviously has no place in this book, one familiar answer is that the virtuous heart always succeeds, or that one need only be a good girl and do as one has been told. What character proves the foolishness and pointlessness of unalloyed virtue? Whose speeches are true but boring? If Lady Catherine, Mr. Collins, and the like are embodiments of the vices inherent in talking through a limited number of stock responses or labels, Mary might be taken as an embodiment of the idiocy of the cliché, and it is not irrelevant to our concerns that Mary's clichés take the form of rules, or could at least be recast in that form. (Of how much of what Elizabeth says is that true?)

If virtue alone is not enough, how about decency and perception? There is at least one perceptive and decent character who fails in the end. What then is called for, to succeed?

d. Are there any models of excellence in judgment to whom we can look? Elizabeth and Jane disagree about Darcy and Miss Bingley: Jane's charitable nature makes her right in one case and wrong in another; Elizabeth's preconceptions make her wrong about both Darcy and Wickham. And even the eminently sensible Mrs. Gardiner misjudges Wickham. There seems to be no one whom we can use as a model.

e. Consider a related point: adjusting one's behavior to fit one's judgments. To take the easy case, assume that a favorable judgment has been made, and one seeks to please. How is that done? By being accomplished? No; Mary's accomplished singing gives far less pleasure than Elizabeth's lively but imperfect voice. By being agreeable? No; it is Elizabeth's impertinence that first demonstrates her quality. By being perfectly well-mannered? No; Jane's decorum is so perfect that both Bingley and Darcy fail to see any encouragement to Bingley there. And how about the reverse: is the power to please itself connected with any virtue, even honesty? No; Mr. Bingley's sisters could be pleasing when they wished.

f. How then is one to get on in this world? What does one need? In what way does Jane Austen answer this question?

3. There is one success we can look to — not as a model of perfect judgment perhaps, but it is a genuine success. Darcy's judgment of Elizabeth is at first impeded by a stupid, if explicable, pride that leads him into a gross rudeness to Elizabeth; her judgment (not unaffected, one might suppose, by Darcy's remark) is apparently discolored by a prejudice against Darcy that leads her to misinterpret his behavior and misjudge his qualities, and indeed blinds her usually acute critical sense with respect to Wickham. When Darcy finally does ask for her hand, it is in the most patronizing way; her rejection is sufficiently violent, one might imagine, to close off the future entirely. How is it, then, that they come together at the end? What do they have that overcomes their own misjudgments, that leads to success at last?

a. An obvious and important part of the answer is this: each has the capacity to move to a new position from which the old self can be regarded and rejected. Judgments not only of others but of oneself can be discarded. (See especially their conversation, looking back, in chapter 16 of volume 3.) What do you call that process? Does the sentencing judge have any need of it? Do you?

b. Another contributor to their success is Elizabeth's masterful social control. She, it seems, can do anything, and it is her brilliance and power that first penetrate Darcy's sensibility. The great scenes are the early ones. Reread chapter 10 of volume 1: when Darcy, a little too heavily, reproves Bingley for what Darcy calls his false humility, embarrassing even that cheerful man, Elizabeth turns the conversation neatly upon Darcy ("Would Mr. Darcy then consider the rashness of your original intention atoned for by your obstinancy in adhering to it?") so effectively that even Bingley feels free to engage in a pleasantry at Darcy's expense. The roles have been reversed; Darcy is now the game. As soon as he has recovered, Darcy suggests with great ambiguity that they have a reel. Elizabeth refuses, telling him that he is trying to manipulate her into exhibiting what he regards as the familiar and contemptible taste of a young lady for a dance (exemplified to an exaggerated degree by Elizabeth's younger sisters), and expressing her awareness that he is trying to get her to accept the relationship on his terms (he is rich, she poor; it must be she who wants to dance with him), which she rejects, concluding: "And now despise me if you dare." Darcy's response is a marvelous expression of a sudden perception: "Indeed, I do not dare."

c. But Elizabeth has something else, which is the most important quality of all: a strength to be herself at any cost. When Darcy asks for her hand in an offensive way, her response is clear and forceful enough to be a real shock to him, supplying energy for his new look at himself. (Chapter 11 of volume 2.) "I have never sought your good opinion" is strong medicine indeed. "You could not have made me the offer of your hand in any possible way that would have tempted me to accept it." In chapter 14 of volume 3, in the interview with Lady Catherine, Elizabeth betrays a boldness that is certainly imprudent and possibly dangerous: though Darcy has not repeated his offer, she claims the right to marry him if he does, notwithstanding Lady Catherine's opposition. If she had been wrong, and Darcy had not been ready to ask, think how presumptuous, ill-bred, and mercenary she would have been made to seem to all of Lady Catherine's acquaintance. As it is, what happens? It is Lady Catherine's report of this scandalous conversation that brings Darcy down immediately to ask her hand.

In the light of these remarks, one might look at the opening scenes somewhat differently. We have supposed that Elizabeth's prejudice was an impediment to the establishment of this relation; but might it not be that her irritation, expressed by her wit at Darcy's expense, was a critical first step? If she had been quite as well-mannered and distant as one would expect her to be with a slightly disagreeable stranger, would there have been any notice on either side? And her prejudice flowed from his rudeness; is that then the source of all their happiness? I do not think that it is fruitful to psychoanalyze characters as though they were real people, but it does seem to me that the unseemliness and rudeness of his refusal to ask her to dance is an excessive rejection of the possibility that he could be attracted to her, sufficiently excessive to express the rejected fact to us and to her. And certainly Elizabeth's needling and teasing of Darcy in the early scenes (justifiable and proper if expressing hostility, otherwise too forward) and her almost violent rejection of his offer of marriage likewise express the reverse of what they say.

What do Elizabeth and Darcy have that enables them to succeed at last? Notice that Jane and Bingley do not have it; their success is achieved only by the intervention of Darcy.

What is the source of the energy upon which their relationship is founded? Is it curiosity? Sexuality? Hunger for truth? Elizabeth asks at the end: "Now be sincere; did you admire me for my impertinence?"

What is the analog to that energy in the life of a judge?

4. We have asked what it takes for a character to survive in the world created by Jane Austen. Now bring the question home: what does it take to be her reader? Do you see how this book, in making the demands it does upon one who wishes to read it well, offers its reader an education? Can the same be said of any legal literature you know?

5. As you try to compare this book with the literature of the law, ask: what would a legal description of the events of this novel be like? Then reverse direction: what would a Jane Austen novel about the events of a legal case — say, a criminal trial, including sentencing — be like? How would she write about the sentencing judgment?

6. To return to your imminent writing assignment: can your sentencing system express or recognize something of the truth that would be expressed in such a novel? You should be prepared to tell what good judgment is, where it comes from, and how you tell someone else about it.

WRITING ASSIGNMENT 8: *Sentencing Judgments — Explanations and Directions*

When a man is sentenced, the judge normally has a wide range of possible dispositions among which he can choose. His choice will be based upon his understanding of who the defendant is — not what he has done on one occasion or another, not what social or psychological labels can be applied to him, but who he really is. The defendant is not reduced to a narrative identity, defined by the story of his crime, but is given his true one, so far as the judge can perceive it. How does this process of judgment work? How should it work? What directions, if any, can be given to those who must participate in it? Notice that the lawyers may well have something to say about the true character of the defendant. What do you suppose these arguments would sound like? You are asked to approach these questions by comparing what the law does with what you yourself have done in your life.

Part One

• Give an account of a judgment you once made of another person, and explain what you did. Was your judgment right or wrong? In what you write here, how do you define your own qualifications as judge?

Part Two

• Give a set of directions to another person faced with the task of making a judgment similar to yours.
• What language have you used to explain and evaluate what you did when you judged another? What terms and forms did you employ in stating your directions for judgment? Did you speak in rules, and if so, how did you attempt to control them?

Part Three

• Propose a wise and rational sentencing system. If you find this task impossible, explain why it is impossible and what the law should do in the face of that fact.

Here you are asked to solve the sentencing problem, or at least indicate the way society should solve it. Ideally, you will draft a statute or rule of court which in meaningful terms tells judges how to sentence defendants. That is, the judges should be able to understand the rule (or rules), and should be supplied with reasonably adequate means for determining whether or not they are following it. Lawyers, appellate courts, and the public should likewise be able to tell whether your rule is at work in sentencing decisions, and to determine with reasonable accuracy whether it is being followed. If you find you cannot formulate such a statute or rule, you should explain why you cannot. In addition, you should describe any further information of any kind that might help you fashion such a rule. Here you must be precise: explain exactly what information you want, how it could be obtained, and how it would be relevant to making a rule governing sentencing decisions. If you find that no conceivable information would permit the formulation of such a rule, you should explain why, and ask yourself whether this impossibility has any consequences for the legal and penal systems.

Be sure to explain in your paper what it is that makes your system a rational one. What do you mean by "rational"?

Part Four

- *What connections can you draw between your account of your judgment of another person and your sentencing proposal? What connections can be drawn between the directions you would give for these two activities?*
- *In what you have written, how have you defined your own qualifications as a judge? What relationship can you see — or do you assert — between good judging and good writing?*

In your account of the judgment made in your own life, do you show yourself functioning by applying rules, by identifying and evaluating factors — operating, that is, as a lawyer or a judge operates? Does your sentencing system allow for the sort of judgments you make about others when you are acting at your best? If not, why not?

I have suggested a way of trying to bring what we know and do in ordinary life into the law of sentencing; namely, by requiring that the judge explain every judgment in an opinion that would then be subjected to the sort of scrutiny we have been giving papers and passages in this course. Does this suggestion have appeal for you? How can you define the sort of scrutiny that the opinions will receive, and who will do the scrutinizing? To what scrutiny will his work in turn be subjected?

What would you do if a sentencing judge made every case seem perfectly simple?

Here is a further complication of the relationship between good judging and good writing: it is a premise of this course that to be a good judge, as to be a good lawyer, requires what might be called an education, an education defined again and again in whatever one writes. This is a premise of Pride and Prejudice *as well, where you see each character defined by the way he makes and expresses his judgments of others. This much is familiar, but the discussion of that book suggests another step: the writing engaged in here is not only that of the characters but of the author, and its purpose is not merely to define a set of minds, to express various views of the world, but to offer an education to its reader. To read that book well requires an education which the book, to the attentive, supplies. The second reading will be different from the first. Can good writing in a sentencing judgment similarly offer as well as define an education? To whom is the education offered, and by what means?*

Two further remarks: as you in your proposal define the proper place of the defendant's conduct in the judgment as to his disposition, you at the same time define the function of the trial stage of the criminal process. That is, insofar as you give weight to the nature of the particular crime, you justify or validate the determination of guilt or innocence; insofar as you disregard the particular crime in favor of an inquiry into something else — the true nature of the defendant as a person, say — you make that stage of the criminal process correspondingly irrelevant, and you should be prepared to ask whether you think it serves any useful function. If the sentencing judgment is to be made by asking about the whole man, why should we ever ask whether he has on a particular occasion actually committed a crime?

The second point is this: your inquiry into the way judgments about others are to be made, expressed, and regulated has relevance far beyond the sentencing of criminal defendants. Think back to the alternative assignment in the insanity section, for example, where the student is asked to show how various people judge a particular event (page 362); or think of the process by which a police officer decides that he does or does not have probable cause to make an arrest or a search; or of the moment at which a justice department attorney decides that he should or should not prosecute a tax or antitrust case.

QUESTIONS: Cases on Sentencing

1. Should a court be free to ask a defendant whether he is guilty? See LeBlanc v. United States, 391 F.2d 916 (1st Cir. 1968).
2. In a hearing to determine whether or not his client should receive probation, should a lawyer be free to state his opinion that probation should or should not be granted? Would it be proper for the judge to ask his opinion? Consider not only the effect of various answers on the freedom of client communications in general, and the effect on other defendants, but exactly what kind of judgment or opinion the lawyer is asked for here. The lawyer can bring witnesses — the mother, the girl friend, the defendant himself — to tell the judge what they told him. Indeed, he could make available to the judge all the evidence upon which his judgment was based. So what is he being asked for?
3. Should evidence seized illegally be admissible at the sentencing stage? Why? See Verdugo v. United States, 402 F.2d 599 (9th Cir. 1968), cert. denied sub nom. Turner v. United States, 397 U.S. 925 (1970). How about a voluntary statement made after inadequate Miranda warnings? Or prior convictions that were themselves unconstitutional? See United States v. Tucker, 404 U.S. 443 (1972).
4. Suppose a jury is instructed to return a verdict only concerning guilt and to disregard the sentencing question. It gives a verdict of guilty, with a a recommendation of leniency. How should the legal system respond to this situation? See Pollock v. United States, 36 U.S.L.W. 3093 (2d Cir. 1967).
5. May a court properly give lighter sentences to those who plead guilty, on the grounds that this demonstration of contrition merits consideration?

See Scott v. United States, 419 F.2d 264 (D.C. Cir. 1969); United States v. Wiley, 184 F. Supp. 679 (E.D. Ill. 1960). Suppose a defendant appeals a conviction and sentence, wins, and is retried: may his sentence after the second trial exceed the sentence imposed at the first? See North Carolina v. Pearce, 395 U.S. 711 (1969).

6. *Has a defendant the right to see and respond to the probation report and other material upon which the judge bases his sentence? See Williams v. New York, 337 U.S. 241 (1949); United States v. Humphreys, 457 F.2d 242 (7th Cir. 1972); United States v. Dockery, 447 F.2d 1178 (D.C. Cir. 1971); United States v. Bryant, 442 F.2d 775 (D.C. Cir. 1971).*
7. *Below are excerpts from two case reports. How would you sentence each of these people, and why? If you would want more information, explain what information you would want, how you would get it, and what you would do with it.*

   In the first case the defendant explains his refusal to be inducted. How would you sentence this man?

UNITED STATES v. LEWIS
275 F. Supp. 1013 (E.D. Wis. 1967)

The defendant submitted the following written statement to the Local Board on April 17, 1967, after he was indicted, which reflects in essence the views that he has had since December 1965:

"Milwaukee Co. Local Bd. 44
Selective Service System
135 West Wells Street
Milwaukee, Wis.

"For me to be a member of the United States Army means that I, a black man, would have to defend and perpetuate the political, social, and economic system of this country. It means that I, a black man, would have to defend and perpetuate the "American way of life." This is an atrocious paradox.

"Why should I defend a country that kidnapped my people from their homeland brought them to this country, enslaved and oppressed them, raped them, beat them, and tried to rob them of their basic humanity? Would you if you were black? Why should I, a black man, defend a country that continues to oppress black people, rape black people, beat black people, and tries to make black people believe that they are inferior? Would you?

"Why should I defend a system that on one hand says that all men are created equal and that all citizens have the same rights, and on the other hand allows a red neck sheriff and his deputies to put you in jail and beat you when you try to exercise these rights? Why should I defend a system that allows the white population of a town to stomp your picket line into the ground while men from the Justice Department and the F.B.I. stand around and watch and say that all they can do is take notes? Why should I defend a system that teaches black people that everything black is bad and worthless, and everything white is good and virtuous?

"Realizing all along that some of these acts could be interpreted as individual acts by individual people, the mere fact that these individuals are allowed to commit these acts against black people and get away with them means that they have the sanction of the system.

"Would you defend a system that talked about freedom, justice, and equality for all men and then waited two hundred years before it said that people could sit at the same lunch counter or ride anywhere on a bus, and then acted as if full equality had been achieved? Would you defend a system where people had to be beat, killed, and put in jail before it could be prodded into making even these token gestures?

"What would you do if you lived in a system that had been crushing you, warping you, and lying to you for over three hundred [years] and then this system said that you had to put yourself in a position to kill another human being, or possibly be killed yourself, in order for that system to continue to prosper and grow? Because I am a black man in America I very conscientiously object, in fact I absolutely refuse, to defend this very racist society and system of government."

R. v. POWER
[1971] *Crim. L. Rev. (Eng.)* 432

Edmund Davies L.J., Karminski L.J. and Melford Stevenson J.: March 22, 1971. *Age:* 26 (m.). *Facts:* convicted of manslaughter having been indicted for murder. He returned home drunk to his second-floor flat. He quarrelled with wife and she left the building. He went onto the balcony of the flat and picked up his two-year-old son and shouted to his wife that he would throw the child if she did not come back. He leant over the balcony and threw the child in the air and caught him as he came down. He threw the child up again but this time failed to catch him and he fell to the ground and was killed. He said he had done it to frighten his wife. Sentenced to six years' imprisonment. *Previous convictions:* four for damage and drunkenness, six for dishonesty: discharge, fined, probation, prison terms up to nine months. *Special considerations:* he was a good father and there was no evidence of ill treatment of his children. He was reconciled with his wife. *Decision:* he had rightly been convicted of causing the child's death by gross negligence but there was no question of having deliberately thrown or dropped the child. The sentence was excessive and the court's duty to the public would be served by reducing it to three years.

WRITING ASSIGNMENT 8 (ALTERNATIVE): The Judge Defines Himself

Part One

- *Find and reproduce two passages in which a writer expresses a judgment about another person: one in which the writer recommends himself to you as a judge in the way he writes, the other in which he does the reverse. These need not be legal passages.*

Part Two

- *Explain your judgment of these passages.*

D. THE LANGUAGE OF INSTITUTIONAL DISPOSITION — INSANITY, SENTENCING, AND OTHERS

The work you have done on insanity and sentencing has exposed not a single kind or set of difficulties but a web of very different and only partially connected problems, all of which must be dealt with in every case. One of these is that the purposes of the insanity adjudication and the sentencing process have never been established and articulated — indeed, so far as they can be discerned, they are internally inconsistent — and without a coherent set of purposes, it is hard to see how either process can be anything but haphazard. Another difficulty arises from the incompatibility between appearance and reality in the language of judgment: certainty in judging another person is of course impossible, and a well-grounded confidence is rare, yet the language that defines the task of judgment seems to pretend that it is not only possible but easy. There is little or no recognition in the language of legislator, judge, or lawyer of what the process of judgment really involves. A third fundamental difficulty, or set of difficulties, is entailed in the fact that the law is not merely a system for expressing judgments but for telling others how to judge, for giving directions. You have seen how immensely uncertain that process is, yet it too is spoken of as easy.

There is still another difficulty that the insanity and sentencing judgments share, one which in fact works its way through much of the law: the language by which the judgment is expressed, the language of institutional disposition, is hopelessly and obviously fictional; yet it is most unclear what might be done instead. A person is sentenced to the penitentiary on the theory that rehabilitation will take place and that he will be restrained from exercising his criminal propensities; actually, we can hardly call the experiences of penitentiary life we read about reformative, and it is clear that there is even greater freedom and incentive to engage in some sorts of criminal behavior in prison than out. These pretenses are partially recognized from time to time: in *In re Gault*, 387 U.S. 1 (1967), the Supreme Court held that procedural protections generally available to criminal defendants could not be denied juveniles on the grounds that the reform school was really a school rather than a prison. And in *Holt v. Sarver*, 309 F. Supp. 362 (E.D. Ark. 1970), *aff'd*, 442 F. 2d 304 (8th Cir. 1971), the entire prison system of Arkansas was held unconstitutional, on the basis of prisoners' actual experiences, not the pretenses or claims of the institution. Insanity adjudications are similar: the commitment until "well" or "cured" or "no longer dangerous to self or others" makes a claim for the institution as a place of treating and curing (and indeed for the possibility of treatment and cure) that is often hopelessly false.

Similar pretenses seem to be involved in all institutional talk: an inquiry into the relationship between pretense and reality could be made of your own school, college, and law school; the U.S. Army; a center for advanced study; the research and development division of an automobile company; the United States courts; a children's summer camp; and so on.

But the difficulty has another side: these languages are false, perhaps, but what could we do without them? They constitute what we earlier called a valuable resource. How do they do so? What sorts of expression do they invite, what activities do they make possible? The question for you as a lawyer is how you can control or remake these institutional languages. Can you invent a new sort of institutional talk that does not raise such false pretenses (or not such flagrant ones), or can you find some technique for controlling the pretenses that are raised? What does your mastery of institutional language consist of, and what does it enable you to achieve?

Below is a lengthy description of one institution. What do you learn from it? How would you seek to learn more about this institution?

INSTITUTIONAL INNOVATIONS IN JUVENILE CORRECTIONS*

R. Gerard

The closing of the Bureau of Prisons' obsolete National Training School for Boys in Washington, D.C., provided an opportunity to which all correctional practitioners look forward — the chance to build

* 34 *Fed. Prob.* No. 4, 37 (1970).

a new institution based on the latest ideas in correctional design and treatment; an institution that would "graduate" law-abiding young citizens instead of potential recidivists.

Planning to replace the 100-year-old National Training School was actively begun in 1961. Morgantown, West Virginia, was selected as the site of the institution, the newest in the Federal Prison System.

One of three federal facilities serving youthful offenders, the Center is the first in which architecture was especially designed to facilitate treatment for a youthful population. Opened January 14, 1969, the $10,250,000 Center is located in a natural amphitheater formed by the Appalachian foothills. It is less than a mile from Morgantown and about 3 miles from West Virginia University. The Center maintains close ties with the University faculty and students. The University has made its computer available to help keep track of a vast amount of data and records necessary to the operation of the institution's innovative treatment programs.

A minimum custody facility, the institution resembles a modern college campus and is a self-sufficient community. Four cottages, housing 55 youths each and two housing 30 in each, accommodate almost all of the Center's population. An additional cottage is used as a prerelease facility.

The housing units are grouped informally around a "community square" which includes the dining room, school and library, hospital, auditorium, gymnasium, chapel, vocational shops, and other service buildings. This complex of units contains most of the Center's formal training and re-education programs.

The treatment approach used at the Center differs considerably from traditional correctional philosophy. The accent is on the individual, his needs and his potential. An "open" institution, the Center has no bars and no fences. The cottages' large, ceiling-high windows frame a peaceful vista of hilltops, trees and grass. In this relaxed atmosphere, tensions and pressures are eased. The Center's programs are open-ended; a youth can begin at his own level of capability and go as far as his determination will take him.

There are no external fences at the Center, neither are there the traditional internal barriers between inmates and staff. The students, as they are called, learn to communicate openly and freely and find that others, particularly the staff, will listen.

The institution's programs are designed to find new ways to reshape the behavior of delinquent youths. The techniques used are experimental in nature, but are based on carefully researched theoretical concepts. Potential commitments are screened to select those boys most likely to respond to the innovative programs. All designations to the

Center are made at the Bureau of Prisons' headquarters in Washington, D.C.

The 300 federal offenders who comprise the Center's population are 16 to 20 years old and generally come from the eastern part of the country. More than two-thirds are committed for driving a stolen car across a state line. Others are committed for forging government checks, stealing from the mails, "moonshining," and other federal offenses.

The program on which each new student embarks is individualized and flexible to meet his changing needs. It is carefully planned, however. Every possible area of institutional life is integrated and directed toward the treatment objective.

Differential Treatment

The Center's correctional approach is based on the philosophy of "differential treatment." Under this concept, treatment programs developed for youths vary according to the boys' behavioral characteristics, maturity level, and psychological orientation. To evaluate these factors, the Center uses a typological technique developed by Dr. Herbert C. Quay, of Temple University, and first used experimentally at the National Training School.

The methodology developed by Dr. Quay and his associates has been validated as statistically reliable. It identifies four dimensions of deviant behavior: (1) inadequate-immature, (2) neurotic-conflicted, (3) unsocialized-aggressive or psychopathic, and (4) socialized or subcultural delinquency.

Dr. Quay points out that these same dimensions occur not only in delinquent populations but also with "emotionally disturbed" and "normal" persons. The difference among these groups is quantitative — the "normal" individual either has lower scores on these dimensions or is more successful in controlling his undesirable tendencies.

The methodology for classifying offenders under a given behavioral category uses three thoroughly researched instruments developed by Dr. Quay: (1) a 44-item checklist of behavioral problems, completed by correctional officer/counselors who observe the boy as he interacts with his environment, (2) a 100-item true-false questionnaire filled out by the boy himself, and (3) a 36-item checklist on the boy's life history, completed by a counselor from the presentence report.

The cottage staff plays a key role in the differential treatment approach. An employee is assigned through a technique of "staff matching" to the cottage program in which by temperament and personality he can be most effective. Another Quay instrument, the "Correctional Preference Survey," is used to help make the assignment.

Dimensions of Delinquency

The discussion which follows outlines briefly the characteristics of youths placed in each of the behavior categories, the type of employee most effective as a treatment agent, and the major treatment objective for each category:

BC-1: *Inadequate-immature.* — These students are described as being preoccupied, reticent, lazy, inattentive individuals who behave in childish and irresponsible ways. They are resentful and/or dependent in their relationships with adults and are easily threatened by peers. Treatment agents for the BC-1 youth are selected for their ability to be instructive, patient, reassuring and supportive. The major program objective is to establish a secure, nonthreatening environment in which "growing up" can be stressed.

BC-2: *Neurotic-conflicted.* — This youth demonstrates anxiety, depression, feelings of inferiority and guilt. He readily verbalizes his problems and shows some understanding of his behavior. He often is sorry for what he has done but is likely to do it again anyway. The treatment agent should be perceptive, sensitive, able to become personally involved with the youth, and provide understanding support while emotional conflicts are being resolved. Treatment emphasis is on helping the youth to increased self-understanding of his limitations, strengths, and potential.

BC-3: *Unsocialized aggressive or psychopathic.* — This group consists of aggressive, untrustworthy, manipulative individuals. They have a high need for excitement, reject authority, and frequently become the institution "troublemakers." The treatment agent should be tough-minded, direct, and able to avoid being manipulated and to enforce strict adherence to rules. BC-3 youths need a highly controlled environment with a lively activities program to absorb their destructive energy. The behavioral objective is to teach them to conform, to accept responsibility for their own acts and to develop genuine, meaningful relationships with others.

BC-4: *Socialized or subcultural delinquency.* — This student has been involved in gang activities and adheres to the values and code of his delinquent peer group. He presents no serious personality problems and can make a suitable adjustment in the institution. However, he will support the gang position in any confrontation with institution authority.

BC-4 treatment agents must adhere strictly to a strong personal code to earn the respect of these students. They also must exercise firm control and be alert to the group's attempts at manipulation. The treatment objective is to help the youth change his gang-influenced value system and to teach him how to meet status and material needs in ways acceptable to society.

BC-5: *Subcultural-immature.* — During the institution's first few months, the research staff noted that some youths scored equally high on two behavior categories (BC-1 and BC-4). The staff's clinical judgment was that these youths shared more traits among themselves than with any other group. This, coupled with an administrative need for more equal distribution of population, led to establishment of the BC-5 behavior category. As with the other groups, they have their own cottage and their own treatment program.

The BC-5 youth presents a mixture of the behavioral problems of the BC-1 and BC-4. Somewhat socially inept and inadequate, the BC-5 youth seeks to meet his need for direction through attachment to a gang. However, he is not necessarily loyal to his peer group. The family of the BC-5 youth usually is severely disorganized, accounting for his distrust of authority figures.

"Strong" but flexible individuals who enjoy working with adolescents seem to work best with the BC-5 group. The youth should recognize the counselor as one who is interested in him as an individual and who is helping him to set limits rather than to restrict or punish him. Treatment programs for the BC-5 youths emphasize the development of positive, trusting relationships with adults and overcoming social learning deficits.

A youth admitted to the Center is assigned initially to the Admission and Orientation Unit of the Reception Cottage. There he is given extensive diagnostic tests to evaluate his educational, vocational, and medical requirements. After he has been under observation for about 2 weeks, the Behavioral Problem Checklist is completed by the Unit's specially trained Correctional Counselors. A youth who is difficult to categorize by the Quay tests, because of similar scores in two areas, will be assigned to a category on the basis of the clinical judgment of the psychologist who interviewed him.

Cottage Staff

The Center operates a cottage-based treatment program. Each cottage is staffed by a cottage supervisor, an assistant cottage supervisor, two or more correctional officer/counselors and enough correctional officers to provide 24-hour coverage.

The positions of the cottage supervisor and his immediate assistant can be filled interchangeably by a caseworker or a correctional supervisor, depending on the experience of the personnel available. Customarily the caseworker is the cottage supervisor and the correctional supervisor is his assistant.

A shortage of professional caseworkers plus the extra casework services required for younger offenders led the Bureau of Prisons to train correctional employees as counselors, with gratifying results. At the Center correctional counselors are the prime treatment agents. They work under the supervision of the cottage supervisor and a professional consultant (psychiatrist or psychologist) attached to each cottage.

Correctional officers assigned to the cottages also counsel and train the youths and are important members of the treatment team. The officers rotate to assignments in other areas (control center, patrol, etc.) and must be highly trained and flexible.

Case Management

The Center uses a decentralized case management approach to treatment programming. This assigns most decision-making concerning students to the cottage staff who are in the best position to make knowledgeable and timely judgments.

The responsibility for developing and implementing appropriate treatment strategies rests with the Cottage Committee (treatment team). The committee is made up of the cottage supervisor, the student's counselor, and an educational specialist. They determine such matters as educational and counseling goals, work assignments, and how soon the student is to be reviewed for parole.

Misconduct also is handled at the cottage level rather than by one central committee. The emphasis is on positive behavior, which is encouraged by rewards for good performance rather than punishment for lapses. Disciplinary measures available range from fines and loss of privileges to transfer to another institution. Action taken is related, not to the offense, but to the individual involved.

Responsibility for overall operation of the institution's cottage programs rests with the supervisor of case management. He is chairman of a Program Management Committee that also includes the supervisor of education, chief psychologist, and chief correctional supervisor. The group meets weekly to develop and interpret program guidelines and to review matters referred by the cottage committees.

Each youth at the Center is involved in responsibility for planning his own future. He is considered a full member of his treatment team and is expected to participate actively in designing his institutional program. Specific goals are established for the student by the Cottage Committee in three areas: education-vocational, cottage life, and work. The goals may vary from completing a course of study or qualifying for a high school equivalency certificate to staying out of some specific difficulty over a given period of time. The student also helps set the dates for periodic review of his progress and the setting of new goals.

Behavior Modification Techniques

Underlying the retraining approach at the Center is a procedure by which positive behavior is reinforced through use of external rewards. Reinforcement strategies are built into almost every student activity. The basic reinforcement devices are the class level system and token economy.

The class level system has proved to be one of the institution's most highly effective motivators of good behavior. By achieving progressively higher goals set by the cottage committee, youths can earn advancement from Trainee to Apprentice to Honor student. Living accommodations, work assignments, pay, clothing, and recreation improve with each class level.

Students usually progress from Trainee to Apprentice in 3 to 5 months and reach Honor status in from 5 to 8 months. They usually are ready for release in 10 to 12 months.

A second major reinforcer of positive behavior is the token economy system. While this approach to retraining has been used successfully in other areas (mental health, retardation, emotional disturbance), its application in corrections has been limited. Consequently, its institutionwide use at the Center represents one of the more ambitious undertakings of this nature in the field of corrections to date.

Under the token economy, students earn points (1 point equals 1 cent) as they meet goals set in each program area (school, work, cottage life). The students use the points to "buy" a wide variety of goods and services available at the institution.

Each youth receives a weekly pay check, in points, based on staff ratings of his daily performance. The pay check again reflects the distinction made between class levels. Apprentices earn points at a rate higher than Trainees, and Honor students earn at a rate higher than Apprentices. A student also may earn "bonus" points, awarded on the spot for certain kinds of positive behavior.

A student's institution expenses, including room rent, are deducted from his pay check. Trainees pay the least and Apprentices and Honor students pay more for their more desirable quarters. Fines, which are few, also are deducted from the pay check. Here, again, discipline is differentiated. A student in BC-1 may be fined 15 points for fighting while one in BC-3 may be fined 75 points for the same misbehavior. A fine for an Honor student may be up to three times that assessed a Trainee.

Students also can use their points to buy commissary, snack bar goods, and civilian clothing, and to participate in recreational activities. Points are not transferable from one student to another. They can spend only what they themselves earn. In effect, the point system teaches youths that if they want something, they must work for it.

Prerelease Program

A month to 6 weeks before release, Honor students can graduate to the Prerelease Cottage. This unit, which is primarily self-governing, houses youths from all five behavioral categories, brought together under the same cottage program for the first time since admission. Prerelease students are given the greatest measure of self-responsibility as a test of whether they are ready for release to the community. They do, however, retain some ties with their "home" cottage program, frequently serving as counselor-helpers with the newer students.

Counseling Program

Counseling is an essential ingredient in the Center's approach to reshaping behavior. While it is an ongoing feature of the daily cottage program, the most intensive counseling takes place during the evening and weekend hours.

The type of individual and group counseling provided varies with each behavior category.

The BC-1 student needs consistent daily contact with the counselor. Individual counseling sessions, which are held frequently, are short, casual, and usually relate to problem-solving. Transactional Analysis is being introduced into this cottage as the primary treatment strategy.

Each week each BC-2 student is involved in a minimum of two group sessions, one individual counseling session and one Cottage Forum (Town Meeting). Role-playing also is used to explore conflicts and behavior problems.

Individual counseling is of limited use with the BC-3 student. Therapy programs involve the whole group and are action-oriented to supply the novelty and excitement sought by these youths. "Directed sociodrama" is conducted twice a week, with emphasis on making the youth aware of the effects his behavior has on others. A Town Meeting is held once a week.

The counselor holds short individual sessions with the BC-4 student at least once a week, working to instill pro-social values and attitudes. BC-4 students participate in Reality Therapy group sessions three times a week, and a 1-hour Town Meeting once a week.

Heavy emphasis is given to individual counseling for BC-5 youths to help them overcome immature behavior. Group involvement takes the form of role-playing (Modeling). A large group meeting and several small-group sessions are held weekly. The group approach stresses problem-solving within the environment of the cottage to replace "acting-out" behavior.

Educational-Vocational Program

For 6 hours a day, 5 days a week, the student is in school. The Center's vocationally oriented instructional program is designed to give every student basic educational skills, entry-level proficiency in a trade, and supportive academic and social education. Courses at the Center are ungraded and the student progresses at his own pace. The institution uses the "integrated curriculum" approach in which education and trade training are coordinated so that a youth may achieve the equivalent of a high school education as he gains vocational skills.

The center offers several general areas of academic instruction: remedial and intermediate reading and mathematics, general equivalency development preparation, and courses in social, cultural, intellectual and physical improvement (SCIP).

All programs in the Education Department are structured toward the achievement of performance objectives. However, expectations and teaching techniques vary with each behavior category.

The Cottage Committee and the student set educational and vocational priorities, based on the youth's needs and abilities. Specific, measurable objectives are agreed upon in writing, along with estimated completion dates. Here, again, the student finds that good performance pays. When he completes an objective, he is awarded a predetermined number of points.

An evaluation of 47 students on the California Achievement Test at the time of admission to the Center showed that their average median score was 8.7. At the time of release, less than a year later, their average median score was 10.1, reflecting a gain of 1.4 grades. In recent months, precision teaching was introduced in the basic mathematics area. Preliminary evaluation of this approach indicates that general mathematical ability can be raised four grades in a 6-week period for the average student.

Each youth at the Center completes an introductory course in each of the Center's three vocational clusters: Aerospace, Graphics and Electronics. He then trains in depth in the specific technology he has selected (for example, power, wood and plastics, or metals, in the Aerospace cluster). At the same time, he attends academic classes designed to help him understand the technical language in his books.

The Center uses the Modular Concept in its vocational training program. This system breaks down the complex study units into small segments which, when mastered by the student, come together to form a total learning experience. The student signs a contract with his instructor for each segment to be learned and receives points for successful performance.

Religious Program

The Center has two full-time chaplains and a modern, uniquely designed chapel that readily lends itself to the requirements of all faith groups. People from the local community come to the ecumenical Sunday services, which feature folk masses and contemporary music. The chapel is at the geographic center of the campus and the focal point of much student activity.

Community volunteers have become an essential feature of the Center's treatment program. Recruited by the chaplains, more than 150 volunteers visit the cottages each week in what is called the "Life School Program." Over 70 percent of the volunteers are women and many are students from West Virginia University. All volunteers are screened and matched to the BC cottage they can work with best. About 95 percent of the cottage population are involved in a Life School activity.

The Life School Program has produced multiple benefits. Students retain their identity with the free community, learn social skills, and learn to form positive, trusting relationships. The community is becoming more involved in the Center's programs. Local businessmen sponsor a student Kiwanis Key Club, a Jaycee Chapter, and an Explorer Scout program.

WRITING ASSIGNMENT 9: *Telling the Truth About an Institution*

Part One

• *Give an account of some aspect of life at a real or imaginary institution — say, school, college, prison, army, hospital, or law school. Try to tell the truth about that institution in such a way that your reader can come to an accurate understanding of what goes on there.*

Part Two

• *Now give an account — in the language of that institution — of the events or experiences that you have just told us about. Speak as an administrator, board member, press agent, catalog writer, or in any other institutional voice.*

Part Three

• *Can you rewrite the language of that institution so that it tells the truth about itself? Can you either do away with the pretenses and fictions of institutional language or subject them to your control?*

WRITING ASSIGNMENT 9, ALTERNATIVE A: Discovering the Truth About an Institution

Here you are asked to compare your own experience of an actual institution with the institution's description of itself. You have been a student, of course, and perhaps a soldier, and no doubt you have memories of dealings with religious institutions, summer camps, the government, your law school, and so on. The questions are asked in terms of your college, but you should feel free to respond with respect to some other institution.

Part One

• Your choice of college was no doubt carefully made. Give an account of the process by which you chose your college. How does this account define you? What did you know or believe about that institution? Where did you get that belief or information?

Part Two

• Think of an actual experience you had in college, and give a brief account of it.
• A. What connection can you draw between that experience and your expectations before you arrived at college?
• B. Tell how your college described — or might have described — that event.
• C. Based on this experience, what advice or directions would you give a person who was in the process of choosing a college? How would you choose one yourself?

Part Three

• Suppose you wished to discover the truth about the prison system in your state. How would you go about doing that? Compare the value of each of the following.

a. statements the prison makes about itself in its brochures, etc.
b. statements made by prisoners serving time or who have been released
c. statements made by sociologists and psychologists who have studied prisons
d. your own firsthand fact-finding tour

The literature of prison life is not a simple one. Compare, for example, the following works: G. Jackson, Soledad Brother (1970); E. Knight, Black Voices From Prison (1970); E. Cleaver, Soul On Ice (1968); Zeno, Life (1968); Malcolm X, Autobiography (1964); T. Parker, The Courage of His Convictions (1962); B. Behan, Borstal Boy (1958). The best sociologist's study I know is G. Sykes, The Society of Captives (1958).

WRITING ASSIGNMENT 9, ALTERNATIVE B: Right to Treatment

• Some courts and legislatures have established a "right to treatment" in a mental hospital, according to which the power to detain involuntarily is conditioned upon actual treatment. Draft a full statement of one's "right to treatment" as you would like to see it established with respect to a mental hospital, jail, or college.

See United States v. McNeil, 434 F.2d 502 (D.C. Cir. 1970); Rouse v. Cameron, 373 F.2d 451 (D.C. Cir. 1966), appeal after remand, 387 F.2d 241 (D.C. Cir. 1967); Dobson v. Cameron, 383 F.2d 519 (D.C. Cir. 1967); Covington v. Harris, 419 F.2d 617 (D.C. Cir. 1969); Wyatt v. Stickney, 325 F. Supp. 179 (M.D. Ala. 1971); D.C. Code §21–562; Malmquist, "Right to and Adequacy of Treatment," 40 Am. J. Orthopsychiatry 388 (1970); Note, "Civil Restraints, Mental Illness, and the Right to Treatment," 77 Yale L.J. 87 (1967).

QUESTIONS

1. Suppose a principle were adopted that wherever possible an individual would not be placed in an institution that would assume total responsibility for his experience, but would be allowed to continue some form of ordinary life in the ordinary world, where he would be subject to some extent to other institutions and, indeed, to his own choices. Would this reduce the pressures on the inherently fictional languages of law and penology? See Advisory Council on the Penal System, Non-Custodial and Semi-Custodial Penalties (1970).
2. Next you hear three voices from a modern psychiatric prison in Britain. What do they tell you about what a system of criminal law and penology should do?

THE FRYING-PAN*
T. Parker

[*Archie:*] — Oh, to me when I'm out crime is a way of life, a profession. At times it can be exciting, at times it can be something you're

* Pages 36–38, 41–42, 58–59 (1970).

quite proud of. Not you personally of course, you couldn't, because you're not a criminal, at least not in society's eyes. You work for your living, and what you do is socially acceptable; and for all I know, where you live, in your own community, you might have a certain amount of prestige.

It's difficult for people like you to understand that I too, in my own community or what's the word, *milieu* is it — in that setting, I too have a certain amount of prestige. What's more, I don't want to lose it, anymore than you would yours. If you were caught embezzling the local cricket-club funds or whatever it was you were connected with, you'd take a sudden drop; people would look sideways at you when you went in the local for a drink, your friends wouldn't send you Christmas cards, even your wife would get the cold-shoulder. Because suddenly you'd no longer be considered reliable. Exactly the same thing would happen to me, in my world, if — well, let's be quite frank about it, even if it was generally known for instance that I was prepared to sit here like this and talk to you. It wouldn't matter how much or how little I was actually telling you: the mere fact that we were acquaintances would start doubts in people's minds. The code is that you don't mix with straight people. It's a very necessary law too, for self-preservation, my own and everyone else's. No matter what happens, what goes on, you don't know anything and you don't talk.

If it's a big robbery that six of us have pulled off, say, and there's been just one small error somewhere which brings the Law round to see me, the other five know — they have to know — that not only am I not going to let out a word about having anything to do with it, but even if by some incredible misfortune I'm so stuck with it that I'm obviously going to get ten years, I'll never so much as hint with a pause who the others were who were in it too. "Joe Smith?" "No, I don't know him." "Sam Brown?" "I've never heard of him." "Jack Jones — you can't say you don't know him, he's married to your sister." "Is he really? That's funny, I've not heard from her for five years."

You see, this is the only thing the criminal fraternity have got. It is a fraternity, though of course it doesn't operate down among the petty larcenists and what you might call the thoughtless one-man crooks who never plan anything. But amongst the firms, amongst the teams who work on a large scale and plan everything down to the last detail, which is what you have to do if you're after the big money, it does. Because all the other advantages are on the side of the Law. The radio-controlled cars, the forensic scientists, the squads of fifty or a hundred men on call at any one time, the legal experts, the barristers, even the judicial system — they're on the side of straight society. So the only thing we've got when it comes to the show-down is this absolute certainty, one with another, of a hundred-percent reliability. While you're planning a job, you won't talk one word about it to anyone, not even your own mother. And if one of you gets caught, the other five don't need to lose even a minute's sleep at night wondering about whether you might grass.

And if you haven't got that reputation, you're finished: you won't be asked to join in, you won't get a proposition, you won't even know a job's under consideration. The first you'll hear about it is when you read about it in the papers after it's over, like everyone else.

That's the number one thing: reliability. It's expected of you while you're outside prison — and just as much while you're in. Things get around fast: there's a man up in Durham prison now, I've never met him, and I don't know him except by name. But he was one of the boys — until about three months ago. He wanted to get his parole, so he passed-on a bit of information to the prison authorities: something quite trivial, a prisoner had got something in his cell he wasn't supposed to have. That man now, he's finished for the rest of his life: there's not one respectable criminal, inside or out, who'll ever trust him, take him in on a job with them, recommend him to someone else, or would even point out a sixpence to him if they saw it lying in the gutter.

The second thing is violence. By this I don't mean you spend your time looking for fights, in fact anyone of that sort would be considered a menace likely to cause trouble for everyone concerned. But it's necessary to have the reputation of being prepared to use it. A certain amount of brains and intelligence is needed, ability to think things out, to plan and avoid stupidity; but on top of that you need to be known as someone who can, and will, use physical force without hesitation if the jobs calls for it, who isn't going to have attacks of conscience all of a sudden if, well for example, if a woman's involved.

Yes. I'd hit a woman, I have. A young one or an old one, if it's got to be done, either to get what we want or to pull out of a difficulty. You'll occasionally come across one who doesn't think you mean what you say — "If you keep quiet I won't hurt you." Instead she starts yelling her head off. Well, you did warn her: she's only herself to blame if you belt her to shut her up. I don't reckon myself a sadist, I don't get pleasure out of hurting people. But I can't say I lose any sleep about what I've done either.

[*Bert:*] I suppose what it amounts to, to be honest, is that I must have lost my bottle; somehow when you get over thirty you begin to start and think what's the use, what's the point of fighting any more. I've got a couple of kids, they're growing up, the boy's nine or ten, something like that: when my wife brings him on a visit he sits at the table with us in the visiting-room, he says, "What's behind that door, daddy?" One time he got up, he tried to come through it with me when the visit was over, I felt terrible. All the bird I've done, all the time I've spent in these places, fighting and rioting, generally creating trouble, not buckling under, geeing-up screws, making myself a nuisance whenever I got the opportunity just to keep my spirits alive — I used to enjoy it, it made me feel terrific, it was wonderful to be locked-up in solitary on bread-and-water. They weren't beating me, that was what life was about — smashing yourself up against authority, fighting the whole lousy system. Same as when you were outside, you made your own rules you didn't give a fuck for the whole of the rotten lousy poxy society at all.

Other people had the money, and it was up to you to use what you'd got to get it off-of them. Size, strength, the ability to terrorise people. Me and another bloke, we were always the heavy mob in any firm we were with; we were the ones who went steaming-in first, after the wages-bag or whatever it was. Big leather gloves on like those old-fashioned motoring-gloves, leather-overcoats, guns, pick-axe handles, — we was the first ones in, laying-about, spinning blokes round, smashing them down. And it was, it was terrific.

No, you didn't wait to see if the bloke would give up without you hitting him, you hit him first. Your two principles were first that you always made sure that you outnumbered the opposition, if they had four in the wages-van you had six on your team; and second, when you went in, you started putting the stick about right away, never mind whether they were going to give you a fight or not. Last time I was in court, they read-out how one bloke had needed sixteen stitches, another one was still in hospital and nearly died, the third was going to be off work for three months. I'll tell you, I couldn't help it, in court I was laughing. I really thought it was funny. They didn't, of course: they thought it was diabolical, which I suppose it was in a way from their point of view.

I was saying about my boy, wasn't I, how he tried to see through the door and come with me? After that visit I thought "Jesus, what's the point of it all, the kid's growing-up, I've hardly seen him yet and he's ten years old, I've only been out once for a few months in the whole of his life so far; what's it going to do to him, how's he going to grow up, what sort of person will he be?"

Mind you, that's only an excuse, I know that; I say I'm thinking of packing it in for the sake of the kids, but I'm making-up an excuse for myself, that's all. My best mate, at the moment, he's doing fourteen years on the Moor, and I know I ought to be down there with him fighting the screws, plotting the next break, working on another tunnel like the one we did a few years back. Me and Archie and a couple of others, that's what we ought to be doing here.

But I'm bird-happy, that's my trouble. I've done too much of it, I'm getting old, I can't fight any more. Even agreeing to come here in the first place, that was treachery on my part; I thought I could do it without compromising myself. But it was a mistake: you shouldn't give an iota, not one little crack. You shouldn't give people even a sign there's any decent side to you at all, not "decent" by their standards, that is. I think society's one enormous big trick, the rich and the powerful and the educated will pull every stroke they can to get you round to their way of thinking, to accepting things as they are — that they're the ones who matter, and the rest of you have got to put up with your lot.

[A *correctional officer*:] It makes me sick, the hypocrisy of this place. These men in here, officially everyone's supposed to talk about them as "inmates" or "patients." To me sir, they're not patients, they're criminals. They're convicted felons who've committed an offence, been given a fair trial according to the laws of the country, and been found guilty and sent to prison quite rightly as a punishment. I agree with all that business about them being sent *as* a punishment and not *for* punishment: I don't believe they should be mishandled or knocked-about or ill-treated while they're inside, not unless they're the ones who start any trouble themselves. But I do think they should be treated firmly, and while they're here they should do exactly as they're told. They know they haven't got the same rights as ordinary citizens outside; their liberty's restricted, they can't indulge in business, or vote, or any of those things. And that's quite right: they've offended against society, and the Judge in his wisdom has sent them to prison for it. One of the penalties of prison is that you're not a free agent any longer: that's exactly why we have prisons. To give them the idea when they get here that they're important, their only trouble is they're misunderstood, they need sympathy: well to me, quite frankly that just seems plain ridiculous. They get more attention paid to them here, more mollycoddling, more listening-to than they've ever had in their whole lives outside. It makes them feel, it can't help it, that they're not really bad people at all: it's everyone else outside who's wrong, not them.

That wasn't why I came in the prison service, to encourage people to that sort of way of looking at things. I came into it to teach them they were offenders, and that whether they liked it or not, they'd have to toe the line until they went out. That's no idle phrase, either: in the previous prison I was at, when a prisoner put in an application to see the Governor about something, he was stood in the queue in the corridor on the flag-stones with all the others. When I was in charge of applications I'd say to each man "Right, 4372 Jones, you stand there with your toes on that crack, and you don't move until I tell you it's your turn to go in. That's what prison's for, son, to train you to keep your toes on the line."

E. HOW SHOULD THE LAW USE THE LANGUAGE OF RACE? THE LEGAL USE OF SOCIAL LABELS

Our exploration of the law as a way of organizing social relations, of talking about people, now takes a turn: instead of examining a special professional language made up (or made over) for legal purposes, we look here at the law's use of a language that has been made by other people to serve their own, possibly quite different, purposes. That is, the central operation of racial discourse is an irrational "labeling" process not unlike what you have seen in the law, but it has its origins elsewhere. Our question accordingly is not whether the law should invent and use such a language, but how it should respond to the existence of this social and verbal fact in the world. Here is an abuse of language and life that the law, let us assume, cannot be blamed for. But what should it do about it?

Any response must be based upon an understanding of what racial language is and how it works, of why it is such an abuse; and much of what follows is directed to that matter. You no doubt have the feeling that this is an impossible and destructive language, you have felt at least some of the frustration it generates; but can you explain exactly what is wrong with it? Turn back to the passage from *Huckleberry Finn*, *supra* page 21, and the questions that follow it, and try to explain why Huck's situation — and Twain's — is so impossible. Part of the discussion there speaks of what it means to be brought up to say "nigger": can you explain what that means, or what it means to be brought up to say "Negro" or "black" instead? While these different terms express different attitudes, each seems to invite the creation of what we have called a literature of caricature, not character, and the question for you is what to do about these ways of talking: can you discard them in favor of some new language for talking about race, one that does not reduce people to caricature? Or can you use one of the existing vocabularies and somehow subject it to your control, or can you perhaps avoid talking about race altogether? Think here of what you actually do in your own life when you are confronted with the fact of race.

Consider the *Huckleberry Finn* passage once more. Was this situation impossible for the law as well as for Huck and Twain, or should the law have been able to do what Twain could not: to go on with the story beyond the experiences of the raft, to bring Huck and Jim, related as they were, into the actual society of their time? Does the complete incompatibility between life on the raft and life on the riverbank point to an impossibility for the law, or does it define a problem the law should have solved? Think here of particular steps the law might have taken to abolish slavery and all that it meant. To do this, you will have to imagine what the social and legal world of slavery must have been like. What legal literature could possibly be expressive of such a way of life, of such relations among people? How would you expect this legal literature to be like and unlike your own? How might it have been rewritten to put an end to slavery? When you turn from slave-holding America to the present, do you find that the problem of race still constitutes an impossibility for the law, or has everything changed in some way to make this part of our social life amenable to legal regulation and control? If you see race as a problem that the law should solve, how do you express and define that problem? And exactly what should the law do about it? You no doubt feel that race presents great difficulties for you both as a person and a lawyer, and this section is meant to connect these two sides of your life: in one of its two writing assignments, you will be asked to give an account of an occasion in your own life when you responded to the fact of race and to explain whether the law can do what you did, or what you now see you should have done.

Such are the questions this section will ask, and such is their rough order. As you may have inferred, behind them all is another, which might be put this way: what connections can be drawn between what the law says and what the world is? For your judgment as to how we should proceed in the matter of race depends in large part upon your sense of the possible relationships between the commands of law and the life of society. For example, one ideal solution might be to outlaw racial language and all behavior based upon perceived racial distinctions, but obviously this is impossible. What is possible then, and how do we know that? What effects can we sensibly expect to flow from a judicial or legislative declaration, and how do we frame these expectations? No doubt the powers of the law over life vary enormously from topic to topic, perhaps from age to age; but for what reasons, according to what principles? Nothing less is involved here than the formation of our expectations as to what a legal system can actually achieve in people's lives.

Notice that the question has another side: exactly what can properly be inferred about the life of a society from its laws? We assume that the happy country is the land with good laws. How sensible is this assumption? Upon what else might we base our judgments of social felicity and misery?

What follows is meant to keep these inquiries alive. Our beginning is historical: we compare legal talk about race in America before the Civil War with the way the law talks today. Racial language is of enormous importance in both worlds, but the law has shifted from supporting to opposing a system of social classification based on race. Are its powers to do one greater than the other? What has happened in these years?

One provocative book on slavery is S. Elkins, *Slavery* (1959), which includes good bibliographical material. Its arguments are the subject of A. Lane (ed.), *The Debate Over Slavery: Stanley Elkins and His Critics* (1971). A more complicated treatment appears in C. Degler, *Neither White nor Black* (1971). Two somewhat more general histories are W. D. Jordan, *White Over Black* (1968), and J. H. Franklin, *From Slavery to Freedom* (rev. ed. 1956). Of special interest to lawyers: H. Catteral, *Judicial Cases Concerning American Slaves and the Negro* (1932), and a series of treatises recently republished by the Negro Universities Press, the best of which are J. Hurd, *The Law of Freedom and Bondage in the United States* (1858); J. Wheeler, *A Practical Treatise on the Law of Slavery* (1837); T. Cobb, *An Inquiry Into the Law of Negro Slavery* (1858). For one account of the origins of slavery, see Handlin, "Origins of the Southern Labor System," 7 *Wm. and Mary Q.* (3d ser.) 199–222 (1950). For firsthand reports of life under slavery, see B. Botkin, *Lay My Burden Down* (1945), and N. Yetman, *Life Under the "Peculiar Institution"* (1970). For what can be said in favor of slavery, see *The Pro-Slavery Argument* (1852) (reprinted by the Negro Universities Press), and E. McKittrick (ed.), *Slavery Defended* (1963). For what happened later, see R. Current (ed.), *Reconstruction* (1965); C. S. Johnson, *Shadow of the Plantation* (1934); and *Growing Up in the Black Belt* (1941). Most of the modern works cited are in paperback.

1. *The Old Days: The Vicious Use of Racial Language*

As you read the legal literature of our slave society, you will find that much of it is terrible, evil beyond your comprehension. Can this be our own legal system, managed by lawyers like ourselves? What connection can possibly be drawn between the past and present stages of our legal world?

We begin with the constitutional structure within which slavery flourished. The Constitution spoke on the subject of "involuntary servitude" as follows: "No person held to service or labor in one State, under the laws thereof, escaping into another, shall, in consequence of any law or regulation therein, be discharged from such service or labor, but shall be delivered up on claim of the party to whom such service or labor may be due." (Art. IV, §3.) As you see, slavery was not merely tolerated; all the states were bound to recognize it, at least to the point of returning runaway slaves. If you had been a representative of Massachusetts during the time of the Constitutional Convention, would you have agreed to such a provision? If not, what would you have proposed instead? (Notice that it does not speak in racial terms; can you explain why?)

Under the Fugitive Slave Act, 1 Stat. 392 (1793), the machinery of the United States courts was available to force the return of runaway slaves, and interference with the process of arrest and return was made a crime. *Prigg v. Pennsylvania,* 41 U.S. (16 Pet.) 539 (1842) held, per Story, J., that a Pennsylvania statute punishing those who took Negroes or mulattoes out of the state against their will to a condition of slavery was unconstitutional as applied to a master who recaptured a runaway slave.[13]

There were two other questions to which the federal government responded in a legal fashion. One was the slave trade from Africa, which was prohibited by the Act of March 2, 1807, 2 Stat. 426. This statute prohibited the importation of "any negro, mulatto, or person of color" with intent to hold, sell, or dispose of as a slave, "or to be held in service or labor." Why do you suppose this statute was cast in racial terms?[14] The other question was that of the extension of slavery to the territories, which was the subject of the Missouri Compromise, the Lincoln-Douglas debates, and the Civil War.

How do you describe the way the United States government talked about slaves? About race? What other possibilities do you suppose there were?

As you work out various alternatives, consider this one: the Constitution might have defined certain basic rights which even slaves should have, and a system for enforcing them; or at least provided that the duty of one state to deliver a slave to a master from another would exist only when that slavery system met certain minimal requirements of decency and fairness. Why do you suppose such a compromise was not adopted?

We shall soon look at some statutes and cases from the slave-holding states, but first an important piece of background information:

13. It is not clear how far that case would go. For example, would it prevent Pennsylvania from punishing a master from Alabama who upon finding his slave in Pennsylvania whipped him as authorized by his own law? How would you expect that question to be argued and decided? Cf. the Alabama statutes reproduced at pages 439–443 *infra.*

Is the situation constitutionally different if the slave is not a runaway but is brought by his master to the free state? For the view that it is, see Commonwealth v. Aves, 35 Mass. (18 Pick.) 193 (1836); Jackson v. Bulloch, 12 Conn. 39 (1837).

14. The present laws against slavery and the slave trade can be found in 46 U.S.C. §§1351–1364 and 18 U.S.C. §§1581–1588.

Census 1860. Total population of the U.S. 31,443,321. States seceding, 11.

	Total population	*Slaves*
Alabama	964,201	435,080
Arkansas	435,450	111,115
Florida	140,424	61,745
Georgia	1,057,286	462,198
Louisiana	628,279	331,726
Mississippi	791,305	436,631
North Carolina	992,622	331,059
South Carolina	703,708	402,406
Tennessee	1,109,801	275,719
Texas	604,215	182,566
Virginia	1,596,318	472,494
Total	9,023,609	3,502,739

Note: Four slave states remained loyal to the United States – Delaware, Maryland, Missouri and Kentucky. (Kentucky was the place of birth of both Abraham Lincoln and Jefferson Davis.)

Slave Growth, 1790 *to* 1860 (to nearest 1,000)

1790	698,000	1834 [*sic*]	2,000,000
1800	894,000	1840	2,487,000
1810	1,191,000	1850	3,204,000
1820	1,538,000	1860	3,954,000

(In July 1958 the population of the United States of America was 174,064,000, of which the number of non-whites was 19,269,000.) *

Below are some examples of legal talk about race and slavery from the slave states. As you read this material, ask yourself: (1) How does this literature define the slave? The Negro? The slave-owner? How would you describe each of the characters this literature creates? (2) How does this literature define its authors? What sort of person would have written this way? (3) What does this material tell you about the society that produced it?

LOUISIANA CIVIL CODE (1838) †

Art. 35. — A slave is one who is in the power of a master to whom he belongs. The master may sell him, dispose of his person, his industry

* B. Hollander, *Slavery in America* 19 (1962).

† Upton and Jennings authorized edition.

and his labor: he can do nothing, possess nothing, nor acquire any thing but what must belong to his master.

Art. 36. — Manumitted persons are those who, having been once slaves, are legally made free.

Art. 37. — Slaves for a time, or statu liberi, are those who have acquired the right of being free at a time to come, or on a condition which is not fulfilled, or in a certain event which has not happened, but who, in the mean time, remain in a state of slavery.

Art. 38. — Freemen are those who have preserved their natural liberty, that is to say, who have the right of doing whatever is not forbidden by law.

Art. 173. — The slave is entirely subject to the will of his master, who may correct and chastise him, though not with unusual rigor, nor so as to maim or mutilate him, or to expose him to the danger of loss of life, or to cause his death.

Art. 174. — The slave is incapable of making any kind of contract, except those which relate to his own emancipation.

Art. 175. — All that a slave possesses, belongs to his master; he possesses nothing of his own except his peculium, that is to say, the sum of money, or movable estate, which his master chooses he should possess.

Art. 176. — They can transmit nothing by succession or otherwise; but the succession of free persons related to them which they would have inherited had they been free, may pass through them to such of their descendants as may have acquired their liberty before the succession is opened.

Art. 193. — The slave who has acquired the right of being free at a future time, is from that time, capable of receiving by testament or donation. Property given or devised to him must be preserved for him, in order to be delivered to him in kind, when his emancipation shall take place. In the mean time it must be administered by a curator.

Art. 194. — The slave for years cannot be transported out of the State. He can appear in court to claim the protection of the laws in cases where there are good reasons for believing that it is intended to carry him out of the State.

Art. 195. — If the slave for years dies before the time fixed for his enfranchisement, the gifts or legacies made him revert to the donor or to the heirs of the donor.

Art. 196. — The child born of a woman after she has acquired the right of being free at a future time, follows the condition of its mother, and becomes free at the time fixed for her enfranchisement, even if the mother should die before that time.

Art. 3510. — If a master suffer a slave to enjoy his liberty for ten years, during his residence in the State, or for twenty years while out of it, he shall lose all right of action to recover possession of the slave, unless the slave be a runaway or fugitive.

QUESTIONS

1. What do you want to know about slavery that the Louisiana Civil Code does not tell you? Consider, for example:
   a. How would you know who was slave and who was free in Louisiana?
   b. How did one become a slave in Louisiana? Could a white person be a slave? How do you know?
   c. What other questions does this code leave unanswered? How do you explain its silence?

2. To put the question slightly differently, we can ask how this statute defines its audience: what does the ideal reader to which this literature is addressed know and understand that you do not? What experience, what expectations, what habits and capacities of mind is he assumed to have?

3. Slavery, it is often said, treated people as property. Does this statute define the slave as a person or a thing? Look especially at his capacity to contract; the rights of a slave who has the right to become free at some future time; the role of the slave in intestate succession; and the statutes of limitations.

4. Article 196 defines the status of a child born to a slave woman after the time at which she has acquired a right to her future freedom. Is this the obviously correct result? The Virginia court reached the opposite result in Maria v. Surbaugh, 23 Va. (2 Rand.) 228 (1824). By what process of reasoning, referring to what principles of law and what axioms of life, do you suppose such a question was decided? Imagine the arguments on each side before the Virginia court and before the Louisiana legislature, and be prepared to outline them. How would the legislative argument differ from the judicial?

   What was the status of her children born before such time? How do you suppose that issue was argued?

5. What was the status in Louisiana of a child born to a slave man after he had acquired a right to future freedom, and why?

6. Here is another question of statutory interpretation: a slave woman, given in 1840 her freedom as of 1850, died in 1848. Would her child, born in 1845, receive whatever donations had been made to her or would they revert to the donors? By what process of reasoning do you attempt to answer such a question?

7. The Louisiana statute does not speak in racial terms; why do you suppose it does not? (Would it be harder to justify a slave system that was based upon race than one that was not? Why?)

8. Here you have seen the structure of slavery described in legal terms. What do you expect the rest of the literature of slavery to look like? This question calls upon your imagination, your capacity to trace out implications in what you read, and to multiply possibilities.

LAWS OF MISSISSIPPI (1840)*

CHAPTER 92

An act, to reduce into one the several acts concerning Slaves, free negroes and mulattoes. [Passed June 18, 1822.]

Sec. 44. No cruel or unusual punishment shall be inflicted on any slave within this state. And any master, or other person, entitled to the service of any slave, who shall inflict such cruel or unusual punishment, or shall authorize or permit the same to be inflicted, shall, on conviction thereof, before any court having cognizance, be fined according to the magnitude of the offence, at the discretion of the court, in any sum not exceeding five hundred dollars, to be paid into the treasury of the state, for the use and benefit of the literary fund.

Sec. 54. When any negro or mulatto slave shall be convicted of any felony, not punishable with death, such negro or mulatto slave, shall be burnt in the hand by the sheriff, in open court, and suffer such other corporal punishment as the court shall think fit to inflict, except where he or she shall be convicted of a second offence of the same nature, in which case such negro or mulatto slave shall suffer death.

Sec. 59. If any negro or mulatto shall be found, upon due proof made to any county or corporation court of this state, to have given false testimony, every such offender shall, without further trial, be ordered by the said court, to have one ear nailed to the pillory, and there to stand for the space of one hour, and then the said ear to be cut off, and thereafter the other ear nailed in like manner, and cut off at the expiration of one other hour, and moreover to receive thirty-nine lashes on his or her bare back, well laid on, at the public whipping post, or such other punishment as the court shall think proper, not extending to life or limb.

Sec. 105. *Be it enacted, &c.*, That all and every free negro or mulatto in this state, under the age of fifty years, and over the age of sixteen years, shall, within ninety days after the passage of this act, remove and quit the state, and shall not return within the limits of the same, under any pretence whatsoever. And if any such free negro or mulatto, as aforesaid, shall not so remove and quit the state, within the time herein prescribed, or having removed, shall return within the limits of the same, all and every such free negro or mulatto, so offending, shall be considered taken, and committed to jail in the same manner as runaway slaves now are, by the act to which this is an amendment; and all and every such free negro or mulatto, so taken and committed to jail, as

* Alden and Van Hosen ed.

aforesaid, shall be sold, for the term of five years, within thirty days after such commitment by the sheriff or jailor of the proper county, upon giving fifteen days public notice, by advertisement, in the manner of other sales, by the sheriff of the proper county, under an execution; and the money arising from any such sale or sales, after paying all charges and expenses, shall be paid by the said sheriff or jailor, one half into the county treasury, for county purposes, and the other half into the state treasury, for the use of the state: *Provided,* That this section shall not apply to any free negro or mulatto who shall apply to the county and probate court of the county wherein said free negro or mulatto shall reside, for permission to remain and reside in this state, and shall prove to the satisfaction of such court, that he or she is of good character and honest deportment; and if such court shall be of opinion that said free negro or mulatto is of good character and honest deportment, and that it is expedient and proper that such free negro or mulatto shall remain in this state, such court shall have power to grant to such free negro or mulatto, a license to remain in this state; which license shall contain a particular description of the stature and complexion of such free negro or mulatto, together with the name, age and sex of the same; and shall be entered and recorded on the minutes of said court, at the time of granting the same, and the clerk of said court shall, upon the application of any free negro or mulatto, to whom any such license may be granted, as aforesaid, make out and deliver to said free negro or mulatto, a true copy of said license, upon parchment, and certify the same, under his official signature, and the seal of said court: which copy, so made out and certified, shall be a sufficient permit to authorise the said free negro or mulatto to travel through any part of this state: *Provided, however,* That any county court, where said free negro or mulatto may be, in this state, shall have full power to revoke any such license so granted, whenever any such court shall be of opinion that it is necessary to do so; and any such free negro or mulatto whose license shall be revoked, as aforesaid, shall within twenty days thereafter, remove and quit the state, on pain of incurring the penalty hereinbefore prescribed; and the said clerk shall be entitled to receive for his services under this section of this act, the sum of three dollars for each negro or mulatto to whom such license shall be granted, to be paid by such free negro or mulatto, at the time of rendering the same.

QUESTIONS

1. *Does the law of Mississippi treat the slave as a person or as a thing?*
   a. *In particular, how do you explain the provision that slaves who violate the law are to be punished with corporal punishment or death? Why do you suppose they are not to be imprisoned?*

b. *How is the slave defined by the provision for extremely atrocious punishment for perjury? By provision for any punishment for any crime?*
c. *How is the slave defined by the protection against cruel and unusual punishment by the master? (Notice the punishment imposed upon a master who violates this statute.)*

2. *The statute provides that no free Negro shall remain in the state without a license from the state, upon pain of being sold into a five-year slavery. How does this last section of the statute regard the free Negro — as property or as a person?*
3. *The old laws of Mississippi do give us some real evidence of what life was like in that particular state. Do these provisions arise necessarily from the institution of slavery, or can you imagine a slave society in which slaves were treated decently by the law (say, next door in Louisiana)?*

LAWS OF ALABAMA (1843)*

Slaves, and Free Persons of Color

§1. The general assembly shall have no power to pass laws for the emancipation of slaves, without the consent of their owners, or without paying their owners, previous to such emancipation, a full equivalent in money for the slaves so emancipated.

§3. Any person, who shall maliciously dismember or deprive a slave of life, shall suffer such punishment as would be inflicted in case the like offence had been committed on a free white person, and on the like proof, except in case of insurrection of such slave.

§5. No slave shall go from the tenement of his master or other person with whom he lives, without a pass, or some letter or token, whereby it may appear that he is proceeding by authority from his master, employer, or overseer; if he does, it shall be lawful for any person to apprehend and carry him before a justice of the peace, to be by his order punished with stripes, or not, at his discretion, not exceeding twenty stripes.

§6. If any slave shall presume to come and be upon the plantation of any person whatsoever, without leave in writing from his or her owner or overseer, not being sent upon lawful business, it shall be lawful for the owner or overseer of such plantation, to give or order such slave ten lashes on his or her bare back, for every such offence.

* *A Digest of the Laws of the State of Alabama: Containing All the Statutes of a Public and General Nature in Force at the Close of the Session of the General Assembly, in February, 1843* (Clay authorized ed. 1843). This compilation is arranged by topic rather than by chapter. Sections 1 and 3 under "Slaves and Free Persons of Color" are contained in the Alabama Constitution then in force. The other provisions were passed by the Alabama legislature at various times. The compilation gives references to the appropriate session laws for each provision.

§8. And to prevent the inconveniences arising from the meeting of slaves: *Be it enacted,* That if any master, mistress, or overseer of a family shall knowingly permit or suffer any slave not belonging to him or her, to be and remain in or about his or her house or kitchen, or upon his or her plantation, above four hours at any one time, without leave of the owner or overseer of such slave, he or she, so permitting, shall forfeit and pay ten dollars for every such offence; and every owner or overseer of a plantation, who shall so permit or suffer more than five negroes or slaves, other than his or her own, to remain upon his or her plantation or quarter at any one time, shall forfeit and pay ten dollars for each negro or slave above that number, which said several forfeitures shall be to the informer, and recoverable with costs, before any justice of the peace of the county or corporation where such offence shall be committed: *Provided,* That nothing, herein contained, shall be construed to prohibit the negroes or slaves of one and the same owner, though seated at different quarters, from meeting with their owner's or overseer's leave upon any plantation to such owner belonging, nor to restrain the meeting of slaves, on their owner's or overseer's business, at any public mill; nor to prohibit their meeting on any other lawful occasion, by license in writing from their owner or overseer, nor their going to church, and attending divine service on the Lord's day, and between sunrising and sunsetting.

§10. If any white person, free negro or mulatto, shall at any time be found in company with slaves, at any unlawful meeting, such person, being thereof convicted before any justice of the peace, shall forfeit and pay twenty dollars for every such offence, to the informer, recoverable with costs before such justice.

§16. All slaves are hereby prohibited from keeping dogs, under any pretence or consideration whatsoever; and the slave or slaves so offending, upon complaint thereof before any justice of the peace, shall be punished with not exceeding twenty-five stripes for every such offence, and the master or owner, who shall permit his slaves to keep dogs contrary to this law, shall forfeit and pay the sum of five dollars for each dog so kept, to the use of the person complaining; and moreover, shall make good all damages done by dogs appertaining to, or kept by any of his or her slaves.

§17. No slave shall be allowed to own any horse, mare, gelding, or mule; and if any slave shall actually own such property, the same shall be forfeited and sold under the direction of the court of the county where such property shall be so owned; one moiety of the proceeds for the use of the state, and the other moiety to any person who will sue for the same. It is also forbidden to slaves to keep hogs running at large, or to keep in enclosures more than they can conveniently maintain, the number of which to be regulated by the several owners, and be distinctly marked, and register thereof made, for the inspection of any person who shall require to see the same.

§18. All slaves emancipated shall be liable to be taken by execution to satisfy any debt contracted by the person emancipating them, before such emancipation is made.

§21. It shall not be lawful for any free negro or mulatto . . . to retail any kind of spiritous liquors within this state.

§23. Any free negro or mulatto, who shall violate the provisions of this act, after having been once convicted and fined, shall, in addition to the fine imposed by this act, receive for every offence, such corporal punishment on his or her bare back, not exceeding twenty-five stripes, as may be ordered by the court trying the same: *Provided,* That this act shall not affect any free negro, mulatto, or other person, who, by the treaty between the United States and Spain, became a citizen of the United States, or the descendants of any such person.

§24. Any person or persons, who shall attempt to teach any free person of color, or slave, to spell, read, or write, shall, upon conviction thereof by indictment, be fined in a sum not less than two hundred and fifty dollars, nor more than five hundred dollars.

§35. If any slave or free person of color shall preach to, exhort, or harangue any slave or slaves, or free persons of color, unless in the presence of five respectable slave-holders, any such slave or free person of color, so offending, shall, on conviction before any justice of the peace, receive, by order of said justice of the peace, thirty-nine lashes for the first offence, and fifty lashes for every offence thereafter; and any person may arrest any such slave or free person of color, and take him before a justice of the peace for trial: *Provided,* That the negroes, so haranguing or preaching, shall be licensed thereto, by some regular body of professing Christians immediately in the neighborhood, and to whose society or church such negro shall properly belong.

§36. Slaves shall be competent witnesses, in all cases where free persons of color are charged with any offence against the laws of the state.

§37. Whenever the owner or owners of any slave or slaves shall be desirous of emancipating such slave or slaves, such owner or owners shall make publication in some newspaper, printed within the county where such slave or slaves reside, (or if there be no paper printed in said county, then in the nearest paper thereto,) for at least sixty days previous to the making application, in which shall be set forth the time and place that such application will be made, together with the names and description of the slave or slaves sought to be emancipated; and, at the time appointed, the judge of the said county court may, upon petition filed, proceed to hear and determine upon the application so made, and if, in his opinion, the said slaves should be emancipated, in consideration of long, faithful and meritorious services performed, or for other good and sufficient cause shown, the said judge may proceed to emancipate and set free such slave or slaves; . . . *Provided,* That such slave or slaves shall remove without the limits of this state, within twelve months after such emancipation, never more to return; and that such emancipation shall not take effect, until after such removal.

Slave Trade

§1. Any slave or slaves, brought or imported into this state, contrary to the laws of the United States . . . shall be condemned by any superior court of this state . . . and shall be sold by the proper officer of the court to the highest bidder, at public auction, for ready money, after advertising the time and place of such sale, in some newspaper in this state, at least fifteen days previous thereto.

Penal Code

Chapter 6: Of Offences Against the Public Morals

§1. No cruel or unusual punishment shall be inflicted on any slave, and any master, or other person having charge of a slave, who shall be guilty of inflicting such punishment, or authorizing or permitting the same, shall be subject to indictment therefor, and, on conviction thereof, be punished by a fine not less than fifty and not exceeding one thousand dollars; and, in addition thereto, be required to give security for his good behavior, for the space of twelve months.

Chapter 15: Of Slaves and Free Negroes

§10. The trial of all slaves for capital offences shall be by the circuit court of the proper county, in the mode now provided by law for the trial of white persons; but, on such trial, the slave shall be allowed but twelve peremptory challenges, and the state but four, and at least two-thirds of the jury shall be slaveholders.

§13. If the owner of any slave should neglect or refuse to employ counsel to defend the prisoner, the court shall assign counsel for that purpose, who shall be authorized to demand from the owner ten dollars for this service; and, if any free negro be unable to employ counsel, the court shall assign counsel for his defence, who shall be entitled to a fee of ten dollars, to be paid out of the treasury of the state.

Patrols

§1. Every male owner of slaves, and all other persons below the rank of ensign, liable to perform military duty, are hereby declared liable to perform patrol duty, as hereinafter directed; but shall be at liberty to send a substitute to perform said duty in their stead.

§2. It shall be the duty of each patrol detachment, to visit all negro quarters, all places suspected of entertaining unlawful assemblies of slaves or other disorderly persons unlawfully assembled; and, upon finding such disorderly person or persons, to take him, her, or them, if free, before the nearest justice of the peace of such county, or make report thereof to said justice, so that he, she, or they, may be dealt with according to law; and if any slave or slaves shall be found so assembled, or strolling without a pass, or some token from his or her owner or overseer, the said patrol may give any such slave any number of lashes, not exceeding fifteen; and if there be reason to suspect any such slave or slaves to be runaway from his or her owner, they shall take such slave or slaves before the nearest justice of the peace for such county, to be dealt with according to law, and be allowed and paid by the owner, for all runaway slaves so taken up, the sum of ten dollars, and shall also be entitled to receive all other fines to which parties may be liable, which they may bring before any jurisdiction having cognizance thereof.

§5. If any of the patrols as aforesaid, under this act, should receive any information of any person or persons harboring any negro or negroes, or slaves, belonging to any other person or persons whatsoever, they shall immediately, on receiving any such information, summon together their patrols, and go immediately in search of said negroes, and if found, take them forthwith to the nearest justice of the peace: and if no owner comes and claims said slave or slaves, it shall be the duty of said justice to commit such slave or slaves to the common jail of the county.

§7. It shall be the duty of justices of the peace, to appoint and regulate patrol detachments in their respective beats throughout this state; and it shall be the duty of the justices of the peace in each beat, to meet once in each and every year, (which shall be done within the first week of March of each year,) and make a complete list of all male owners of slaves, of every age, and all other persons liable to patrol duty; which list they shall divide into patrol detachments, consisting of not less than three, nor more than five men, beside their leader — appointing some discreet person as leader of each detachment; and the detachments, so appointed, shall be compelled to perform patrol duty according to the patrol laws now in force in the state, but shall have the privilege of sending a substitute.

QUESTIONS

1. *How does the law of Alabama define the slave? The Negro? Can you make up a composite picture of the slave or the Negro from these materials?*
2. *The slave cannot be taught to read, cannot keep weapons, dogs, or hogs, cannot leave the plantation without a pass; but one who kills or maims him is to be punished exactly as if the victim were free and white, and in criminal cases slaves are entitled to counsel paid by the state. On what*

theory or view of life can these provisions of law be reconciled? Does this set of laws express a coherent view of the world it regulates?

3. How are white people defined by this law? A master cannot, without judicial approval, emancipate his slave or permit him to carry weapons or emancipate him to the detriment of his creditors, or teach him to read. And the master is subject to military draft for the purpose of patrols. How then does the law of Alabama define freedom?

   And why do you suppose the laws limiting what the slave could do were ever passed? These matters might, after all, have been left to private regulation under a general statute subjecting the slave in all things to the will of his master.

4. Alabama had a prohibition against the slave trade. How does the law manage to prohibit the trade, yet maintain the institution without exposing a glaring inconsistency?

5. How do you describe the society defined by these laws? What future would you predict for it? What, so far as you can tell from these laws, is the central principle of Alabama life? Is there any other possibility for a slave society?

6. Can you imagine being a judge or lawyer in such a world? For example, how would you as a judge go about deciding whether or not a showing had been made of "long, faithful, and meritorious services performed," or of "other good and sufficient cause" for emancipation? How would you expect argument on such questions to proceed? Begin by asking yourself why the law thus limited the master's power to emancipate; and why it permitted emancipation at all.

7. In a state that prohibited emancipation absolutely, would a devise of slaves to a Quaker Meeting be valid? "The individuals composing this society believe it to be repugnant to their religious principles to become the owners of slaves, and will not employ their labor to the advantage of themselves or of the society. The trustees were to act as guardians to the slaves, and to hold them for the benefit of the slaves themselves, who were to receive the surplus of the profits of their labor for their own emolument, and ultimately to emancipate them whenever it could be done consistently with the laws of the State." Trustees of the Quaker Society of Contentnea v. Dickenson, 12 N.C. 118, 120 (1827). The heirs contend the devise is void. How would you expect argument to proceed in such a case? What result is most consistent with the idea that the slave is property?

   The dissenting judge wrote: "I do not understand from that statement that they are averse from holding a title to slaves, or from being considered as having a right to the use of them, but that in point of law they may have the legal title, and a right to the use, but they claim the right of disposing of that use in any way they may think proper, provided that disposition does not conflict with the laws of the land; that they may gratify their thirst for gain with it, or render it subservient to the gratification of any other desire not prohibited by law; that the enjoyment of the use consists in the freedom of disposing of it; that it is optional with them to build churches, employ preachers or give it away in charity or in any other way their conscience approve of." Id. at 124.

8. Here we can ask this general question: what do you suppose were the effects of slavery upon the ways that judges and lawyers thought, argued,

and explained themselves, upon the legal system itself? We are shocked to see the materials of our law – statutes and judicial opinions – put to such uses, yet no doubt contemporaries would have claimed for their legal system (as a whole) many of the same purposes and hopes that you would claim for yours. Is the institution of slavery just an unfortunate imperfection, or does it strike to the heart of what we mean by law? Do our notions of what law is and how it operates express a view of life and man with which slavery is so thoroughly incompatible that its existence would infect and destroy the whole? Is this a way of defining an "internal morality" of law? See L. Fuller, The Morality of Law (1969).

Compare what the effect of the following amendment to the Constitution would be: "A confession obtained by physical coercion shall not on that ground be inadmissible in evidence."

REVISED CODE OF NORTH CAROLINA (1855)*

Chapter 107: Slaves and Free Negroes

27. In case any slave who shall appear not to have been properly clothed and fed, shall be convicted of stealing any corn, cattle, hogs, or other goods whatsoever, from any person not the owner of such slave, such injured person may maintain an action on the case, against the possessor of such slave, for his damages.

29. No slave shall go at large as a free man, exercising his own discretion in the employment of his time; nor shall any slave keep house to him or herself as a free person, exercising the like discretion in the employment of his or her time: and in case the owner of slave [*sic*] consent to the same, or connive thereat, he shall be deemed guilty of a misdemeanor, and on conviction be fined not exceeding one hundred dollars. *Provided, however,* that any person may permit his slave to live or keep house upon his land, for the purpose of attending to the business of his master.

31. It shall not be lawful for any slave to be insolent to a free white person; nor to utter mischievous and slanderous reports about any free white person; nor to wilfully trespass on his property or person; nor to intermarry or cohabit with any free person of color; nor for any male slave to have sexual intercourse, or indulge in any grossly indecent familiarities with a white female; nor to produce any forged free pass or certificate of freedom; nor to go from off the plantation or seat of land, where such slave may be appointed to live, without a certificate of leave in writing from his master, or manager; nor to raise any horses, cattle, hogs, or sheep; nor to teach, or attempt to teach, any other slave or free negro to read or write, the use of figures excepted; nor to sell any

* Moore and Biggs authorized edition.

spiritous liquor or wine; nor to play at any game of cards, dice, or nine pins, nor to play at any game of chance, hazard, or skill, for any money, liquor, or any kind of property, whether the same be staked or not; nor to set fire to any woods, except in such manner as is allowed by statute; nor to preach or exhort in public, or in any manner officiate as a preacher or teacher, at any prayer-meeting or other association for worship, where slaves of different families are collected together; nor to traffic with another slave, by buying of, or selling to him, any articles of property, forbidden absolutely, or forbidden, except by written permission, to be the subject of traffic between white persons and slaves; nor to traffic with any other person, by buying of, or selling to him, any article of property, unless such other person may lawfully buy of, or sell the same to, said slave.

QUESTIONS

1. *Section 27 makes the master liable if his slave steals from hunger. How does that provision define the slave: as a person? A thing? An animal?*
2. *Section 31 sets forth a set of rules governing the behavior of slaves. Do these rules mark the beginning of the rule of law in the life of the slave?*
   a. *For example, is a slave entitled to do whatever is not prohibited by law?*
   b. *How do these rules operate if the slave cannot be taught to read? Are they really rules at all? What are they then, and who is their audience?*
3. *As you compare the statutes from these four different states, what differences do you see among them? Ask yourself in which state you would rather be a slave; a Negro; a white person; a judge. Or are the states really all the same? Is there some other evidence you would want before choosing a state to live in? Where could you find it?*
4. *You have seen slaves defined as things, as animals, and as people. (Defenders of slavery said that the slave was regarded as a child, but are we to believe that they treated their actual children this way?) These are, to say the least, inconsistent identities. What principle determines which definition shall be used? What does this inconsistency, explicable only by reference to such a principle, tell you about this legal and social system? You might say this language leaves out a great deal of the experiences it regulates, but it expresses rather fully the minds and characters of its authors.*
5. *Let us take up here a question we have touched on before: how do you think a judge would interpret and apply the laws of slavery, by reference to what ideals and values, what fundamental maxims? To what principles and standards, to what commonplaces, would legal argument appeal?*
   a. *Would you expect the courts to define slaves as things, as children, as animals, or as people? Or sometimes one way, sometimes another? When would a judge know which way to define a slave? How would argument on this matter proceed?*
   b. *The judicial opinion is the judge's explanation of why he is exercising his power the way he is. Does the institution of the judicial opinion*

itself define in some way the people whose lot it affects? How? If slaves really were thought of as things or animals, would there ever be judicial opinions, except in disputes as to ownership?

c. *The judicial opinion is a moment at which a civilization is expressed. The statutes are only part of the material that goes into it. The judge must himself define the issues and create a system for explaining and resolving them. It is every judge's goal to create a system of wisdom, intelligence, and humanity. How could a decent judge possibly deal with a case in which the raw facts of slavery were critical? What assistance could he expect from his lawyers?*

6. *Suppose a white man has deliberately killed a slave. Of course he should pay the owner for the destruction of his property, but what notice (if any) should the criminal law take of this conduct? How would you decide that question as a judge, and how would you explain yourself?*

STATE v. JONES

2 Miss. (Walker) 83 (1820)

CLARKE, J. Because individuals may have been deprived of many of their rights by society, it does not follow, that they have been deprived of all their rights.

In some respects, slaves may be considered as chattels, but in others, they are regarded as men. The law views them as capable of committing crimes. This can only be upon the principle, that they are men and rational beings. . . . It has been determined in Virginia, that slaves are persons. In the constitution of the United States, slaves are expressly designated as "persons." In this state, the Legislature have considered slaves as reasonable and accountable beings and it would be a stigma upon the character of the state, and a reproach to the administration of justice, if the life of a slave could be taken with impunity, or if he could be murdered in cold blood, without subjecting the offender to the highest penalty known to the criminal jurisprudence of the country. Has the slave no rights, because he is deprived of his freedom? He is still a human being, and possesses all those rights, of which he is not deprived by the positive provisions of the law, but in vain shall we look for any law passed by the enlightened and philanthropic legislature of this state, giving even to the master, much less to a stranger, power over the life of a slave. Such a statute would be worthy [of] the age of Draco or Caligula, and would be condemned by the unanimous voice of the people of this state, where, even cruelty to slaves, much less the taking away of life, meets with universal reprobation. By the provisions of our law, a slave may commit murder, and be punished with death; why then is it not murder to kill a slave? can a mere chattel commit murder, and be subjected to punishment? Villeins, in England, were more degraded than our slaves. It is true, that formerly, the murder of a villein was not punished with death, but neither was the murder of a freeman then so punished. The only difference between the freeman and the slave, was in the magnitude of the fine. In England, killing a villein was as much murder, as killing a lord. Yet villeins were then the most abject slaves, and could be bought and sold as chattels, but because slaves can be bought and sold, it does not follow that they can be deprived of life. . . . Is not the slave a reasonable creature, is he not a human being, and the meaning of this phrase reasonable creature is a human being, for the killing [of] a lunatic, an idiot, or even a child unborn, is murder, as much as the killing [of] a philosopher, and has not the slave as much reason as a lunatic, an idiot, or an unborn child? . . .

At one period of the Roman history, a history written in the blood of vanquished nations, slaves were regarded as captives, whose lives had been spared in battle, and the savage conqueror might take away the life of the captive, and therefore he might take away the life of the slave. But the civil law of Rome extirpated this barbarous privilege, and rendered the killing [of] a slave a capital offence.

When the northern barbarians overran Southern Europe, they had no laws but those of conquerors, and conquered, victors, and captives, yet even by this savage people, no distinction was recognized between the killing in cold blood, [of] a slave or a freeman. And shall this court, in the nineteenth century, establish a principle, too sanguinary for the code even of the Goths and Vandals, and extend to the whole community, the right to murder slaves with impunity?

The motion to arrest the judgment must be overruled.

The defendant was sentenced to be hung on the 27th July 1821.

QUESTIONS

1. *Does Judge Clarke's opinion speak of the slave as person, thing, or animal?*
2. *Analyze this opinion with care and extract from it the basic principles, assumptions, or purposes upon which it rests. Now ask: is this opinion consistent with the premises of slavery as you understand them?*
3. *Compare the following opinion.*

STATE v. HOOVER
20 N.C. 500 (1839)

The prisoner was put upon his trial at Iredell, on the last Circuit, before his Honor, Judge Dick, for the murder of his own female slave, a woman named Mira. The witnesses called on the part of the State, testified to a series of the most brutal and barbarous whippings, scourgings and privations, inflicted by the prisoner upon the deceased, from about the first of December, to the time of her death in the ensuing

March, while she was in the latter stages of pregnancy, and afterwards, during the period of her confinement and recovery from a recent delivery. . . . The reasons assigned by the prisoner to those who witnessed his inhuman treatment of the deceased, were, at one time, that she stole his turnips and sold them to the worthless people in the neighborhood, and that she had attempted to burn his barn, and was disobedient and impudent to her mistress; at another, that she had attempted to burn his still-house, and had put something in a pot to poison his family. There was no evidence except her own confessions, extorted by severe whippings, that the deceased was guilty of any of the crimes imputed to her; nor did it appear that she was disobedient or impertinent to her master or mistress; on the contrary, she seemed, as some of the witnesses testified, to do her best to obey the commands of her master, and that when she failed to do so, it was from absolute inability to comply with orders to which her condition and strength were unequal. The prisoner offered no testimony.

His Honor charged the jury, "that they must be satisfied beyond a reasonable doubt, that the prisoner killed the deceased; that he intended to kill her, and that he had no legal provocation at the time of killing her, before they would bc justified in finding him guilty of murder; that if they doubted on any of those points, they ought not to find him guilty of murder." He charged the jury further, "that if the deceased attempted to burn the barn, still-house, or kitchen of the defendant, or if she put poison in a pot to poison the family, or stole turnips, or disobeyed the orders of her master, these were all acts of legal provocation; and if the defendant killed the deceased, upon the discovery of any of the aforesaid offences, or in so short a time thereafter that the passion of the defendant had not a reasonable time to subside, the slaying would be manslaughter, and not murder.

RUFFIN, C.J. With deep sorrow we have perused the statement of the case as it appeared upon the evidence; and we can not surmise a ground on which the prisoner could expect a venire de novo. Indeed, it seems to us, that the case was left hypothetically to the jury, much more favorably for the prisoner than the circumstances authorized. A master may lawfully punish his slave; and the degree must, in general, be left to his own judgment and humanity, and can not be judicially questioned: *State v. Mann*, 2 Dev. 263. But the master's authority is not altogether unlimited. He must not kill. There is, at the least, this restriction upon his power: he must stop short of taking life.

If death unhappily ensue from the master's chastisement of his slave, inflicted apparently with a good intent, for reformation or example, and with no purpose to take life, or to put it in jeopardy, the law would doubtless tenderly regard every circumstance which, judging from the conduct generally of masters towards slaves, might reasonably be supposed to have hurried the party into excess. But the acts imputed to this unhappy man do not belong to a state of civilization. They are barbarities which could only be prompted by a heart in which every humane feeling had long been stifled; and indeed there can scarcely be a savage of the wilderness so ferocious as not to shudder at the recital of them. Such acts can not be fairly attributed to an intention to correct or to chastise. They can not, therefore, have allowance, as being the exercise of an authority conferred by the law for the purposes of the correction of the slave, or of keeping the slave in due subjection.

The court is at a loss to comprehend how it could have been submitted to the jury that they might find an extenuation from provocation. There is no opening for such an hypothesis. There was no evidence of the supposed acts, which, it was thought, might be provocations. But if they had been proved, this court could not have concurred in the instructions — given, doubtless, from abundant caution and laudable tenderness of life. We could not have concurred, because however flagrant the provocation, the acts of the prisoner were not perpetrated in sudden heat of blood, but must have flowed from a settled and malignant pleasure in inflicting pain, or a settled and malignant insensibility to human suffering. There was none of that brief fury to which the law has regard, as an infirmity of our nature. On the contrary, without any consideration for the sex, health, or strength of the deceased, through a period of four months, including the latter stages of pregnancy, delivery, and recent recovery therefrom, by a series of cruelties and privations in their nature unusual, and in degree excessive beyond the capacity of a stout frame to sustain, the prisoner employed himself from day to day in practicing grievous tortures upon an enfeebled female, which finally wore out the energies of nature and destroyed life. He beat her with clubs, iron chains, and other deadly weapons, time after time; burnt her; inflicted stripes over and often, with scourges, which literally excoriated her whole body; forced her out to work in inclement seasons, without being duly clad; provided for her insufficient food; exacted labor beyond her strength, and wantonly beat her because she could not comply with his requisitions. These enormities, besides others too disgusting to be particularly designated, the prisoner, without his heart once relenting or softening, practiced from the first of December until the latter end of the ensuing March; and he did not relax even up to the last hours of his victim's existence. In such a case, surely, we do not speak of provocation; for nothing could palliate such a course of conduct. Punishment thus immoderate and unreasonable in the measure, the continuance, and the instruments, accompanied by other hard usage and painful privations of food, clothing, and rest, loses all character of correction in foro domestico, and denotes plainly that the prisoner must have contemplated the fatal termination, which was the natural consequence of such barbarous cruelties.

By Court. Judgment affirmed.

QUESTIONS

1. *Would a different result have been possible in Hoover? Outline an opinion supporting a different result.*
2. *What are the fundamental principles expressed in this opinion, and are they consistent with the premises of the law of slavery? Or has Judge Ruffin put himself in a position like Huck's on the raft, unable to go on in his society? What do you think he would say to such a suggestion? Compare his opinion in the following case.*

STATE v. MANN
13 N.C. 263 (1828)

The defendant was indicted for an assault and battery upon Lydia, the slave of one Elizabeth Jones.

On the trial it appeared that the defendant had hired the slave for a year; that during the term the slave had committed some small offense, for which the defendant undertook to chastise her; that while in the act of so doing the slave ran off, whereupon the defendant called upon her to stop, which being refused, he shot at and wounded her.

His Honor, Judge Daniel, charged the jury that if they believed the punishment inflicted by the defendant was cruel and unwarrantable, and disproportionate to the offense committed by the slave, that in law the defendant was guilty, as he had only a special property in the slave.

A verdict was returned for the State, and the defendant appealed.

Ruffin, J. A Judge cannot but lament when such cases as the present are brought into judgment. It is impossible that the reasons on which they go can be appreciated, but where institutions similar to our own exist and are thoroughly understood. The struggle, too, in the Judge's own breast between the feelings of the man and the duty of the magistrate is a severe one, presenting strong temptation to put aside such questions, if it be possible. It is useless, however, to complain of things inherent in our political state. And it is criminal in a Court to avoid any responsibility which the laws impose. With whatever reluctance, therefore, it is done, the Court is compelled to express an opinion upon the extent of the dominion of the master over the slave in North Carolina.

The indictment charges a battery on Lydia, a slave of Elizabeth Jones. Upon the face of the indictment, the case is the same as *S. v. Hall*, 9

N.C., 582. No fault is found with the rule then adopted; nor would be, if it were now open. But it is not open; for the question, as it relates to a battery on a slave by a stranger, is considered as settled by that case. But the evidence makes this a different case. Here the slave had been hired by the defendant, and was in his possession; and the battery was committed during the period of hiring. With the liabilities of the hirer to the general owner for an injury permanently impairing the value of the slave no rule now laid down is intended to interfere. That is left upon the general doctrine of bailment. The inquiry here is whether a cruel and unreasonable battery on a slave by the hirer is indictable. The Judge below instructed the jury that it is.

He seems to have put it on the ground that the defendant had but a special property. Our laws uniformly treat the master or other person having the possession and command of the slave as entitled to the same extent of authority. The object is the same — the services of the slave; and the same powers must be confided. In a criminal proceeding, and indeed in reference to all other persons but the general owner, the hirer and possessor of a slave, in relation to both rights and duties, is, for the time being, the owner. This opinion would, perhaps, dispose of this particular case; because the indictment, which charges a battery upon the slave of Elizabeth Jones, is not supported by proof of a battery upon defendant's own slave; since different justifications may be applicable to the two cases. But upon the general question whether the owner is answerable criminaliter for a battery upon his own slave, or other exercise of authority or force not forbidden by statute, the Court entertains but little doubt. That he is so liable has never yet been decided; nor, as far as is known, been hitherto contended. There have been no prosecutions of the sort. The established habits and uniform practice of the country in this respect is the best evidence of the portion of power deemed by the whole community requisite to the preservation of the master's dominion. If we thought differently we could not set our notions in array against the judgment of everybody else, and say that this or that authority may be safely lopped off. This had indeed been assimilated at the bar to the other domestic relations; and arguments drawn from the well-established principles which confer and restrain the authority of the parent over the child, the tutor over the pupil, the master over the apprentice, have been pressed on us. The Court does not recognize their application. There is no likeness between the cases. They are in opposition to each other, and there is an impassable gulf between them. The difference is that which exists between freedom and slavery — and a greater cannot be imagined. In the one, the end in view is the happiness of the youth, born to equal rights with that governor, on whom the duty devolves of training the young to usefulness in a station which he is afterwards to assume among freemen. To such an end, and with such a subject, moral and intellectual instruction seem the natural means; and for the most part they are found to suffice. Moderate force is superadded only to make the others effectual. If that fail it is better to leave the party to his own headstrong passions and the ultimate correction of the law than to allow it to be immoderately inflicted by a private person. With slavery it is far otherwise. The end is the profit of the master, his security and the public safety; the subject, one doomed in his own person and his posterity, to live without knowledge and without the capacity to make anything his own, and to toil that another may reap the fruits. What moral considerations shall be addressed to such a being to convince him what it is impossible but that the most stupid must feel and know can never be true — that he is thus to labor upon a principle of natural duty, or for the sake of his own personal happiness, such services can only be expected from one who has no will of his own; who surrenders his will in implicit obedience to that of another. Such obedience is the consequence only of uncontrolled authority over the body. There is nothing else which can operate to produce the effect. The power of the master must be absolute to render the submission of the slave perfect. I most freely confess my sense of the harshness of this proposition; I feel it as deeply as any man can; and as a principle of moral right every person in his retirement must repudiate it. But in the actual condition of things it must be so. There is no remedy. This discipline belongs to the state of slavery. They cannot be disunited without abrogating at once the rights of the master and absolving the slave from his subjection. It constitutes the curse of slavery to both the bond and free portion of our population. But it is inherent in the relation of master and slave.

That there may be particular instances of cruelty and deliberate barbarity where, in conscience, the law might properly interfere, is most probable. The difficulty is to determine where a Court may properly begin. Merely in the abstract it may well be asked, which power of the master accords with right? The answer will probably sweep away all of them. But we cannot look at the matter in that light. The truth is that we are forbidden to enter upon a train of general reasoning on the subject. We cannot allow the right of the master to be brought into discussion in the courts of justice. The slave, to remain a slave, must be made sensible that there is no appeal from his master; that his power is in no instance usurped; but is conferred by the laws of man at least, if not by the law of God. The danger would be great, indeed, if the tribunals of justice should be called on to graduate the punishment appropriate to every temper and every dereliction of menial duty. No man can anticipate the many and aggravated provocations of the master which the slave would be constantly stimulated by his own passions or the instigation of others to give; or the consequent wrath of the master, prompting him to bloody vengeance upon the turbulent traitor — a vengeance generally practiced with impunity by reason of its privacy. The Court, therefore, disclaims the power of changing the relation in which these parts of our people stand to each other.

We are happy to see that there is daily less and less occasion for the interposition of the Courts. The protection already afforded by several statutes, that all-powerful motive, the private interest of the owner, the benevolences towards each other, seated in the hearts of those who have been born and bred together, the frowns and deep execrations of the community upon the barbarian who is guilty of excessive and brutal cruelty to his unprotected slave, all combined, have produced a mildness of treatment and attention to the comforts of the unfortunate class of slaves, greatly mitigating the rigors of servitude and ameliorating the condition of the slaves. The same causes are operating and will continue to operate with increased action until the disparity in numbers between the whites and blacks shall have rendered the latter in no degree dangerous to the former, when the police [*sic*] now existing may be further relaxed. This result, greatly to be desired, may be much more rationally expected from the events above alluded to, and now in progress, than from any rash expositions of abstract truths by a judiciary tainted with a false and fanatical philanthropy, seeking to redress an acknowledged evil by means still more wicked and appalling than even that evil.

I repeat that I would gladly have avoided this ungrateful question. But being brought to it the Court is compelled to declare that while slavery exists amongst us in its present state, or until it shall seem fit to the legislature to interpose express enactments to the contrary, it will be the imperative duty of the Judges to recognize the full dominion of the owner over the slave, except where the exercise of it is forbidden by statute. And this we do upon the ground that this dominion is essential to the value of slaves as property, to the security of the master, and the public tranquility, greatly dependent upon their subordination; and, in fine, as most effectually securing the general protection and comfort of the slaves themselves.

PER CURIAM. Reversed and judgment entered for defendant.

QUESTIONS

1. *Suppose a slave was being severely beaten by an overseer and, in fighting back, stabbed him with a knife. Has he committed a crime? What else do you need to know in order to answer that question? By reference to what basic principles would you expect such a question to be argued and decided?*
2. *Imagine that you are a judge asked to decide the case: how does your opinion define the slave, the overseer, and yourself?*

DAVE v. STATE
22 Ala. 23 (1853)

GIBBONS, J. — In the relation of master and slave, the master is entitled to the absolute dominion and control over the slave. The slave owes absolute and unconditional submission to the master. The master has the right to chastise and punish the slave in order to enforce his obedience, and to compel him to the performance of his duties. If the slave throws off the authority of the master, puts himself in a hostile attitude towards him, resists his dominion and control by physical force, evincing by his acts, while in a personal conflict with the master, a design to make that resistance effectual in escaping from his dominion and authority, the master has the right to employ such means, and so much force, to any extent, as will be effectual to subdue him. But if the slave is not resisting the master by physical force, or by hostile acts, but is simply in a state of disobedience, without personal violence towards the master, then the latter can only administer such punishment as is appropriate to the case, without endangering life or limb.

The slave, in common with all human beings, undoubtedly has certain natural rights, and among these, is that of self-protection or self-defence; but in order to avail himself of these natural rights, for the justification of his acts, he must not himself be a wrong-doer. If, in the perpetration of a wrong, he does an act which he might justify if he was in the right, the law will no more protect him on the ground of natural right than it will any other wrong-doer.

The charge of the court below as given to the jury, when tested by these principles, we think contains no error. The first proposition which it asserts is, that if the defendant had neglected to perform his duty, and the overseer was proceeding to chastise him for his disobedience, and the defendant thereupon resisted him, the latter had the right to use so much force as was necessary to overcome such resistance; and if the defendant in this conflict between the overseer and him, drew his knife and stabbed the overseer with the intent to kill him, then he was guilty. This proposition as thus stated is undoubtedly correct. The court in its charge limited the right of the overseer in the employment of force, to overcome the resistance of the defendant, to the point "short of taking life or limb." The charge would have been correct even without that qualification. For we have already above stated that, if the slave, is in open hostile rebellion against the master, and is resisting his legal authority by physical force, the master has the right to employ so much force as shall be sufficient to overcome such resistance. . . .

The next proposition asserted by the charge is, that if the defendant, when the overseer ordered another negro to knock him in the head with an axe, was so much alarmed that his reason was dethroned, and he then made the cuts without any intention at all, or with the intention of cutting himself loose, he was not guilty. We see no error in this proposition of which the defendant can complain. It may be conceded, that the intention to cut himself loose was confined in the charge to the state of mind when the reason was dethroned; still there would be no error in the charge of which the defendant could complain, because there is nothing contained in it against him. It is entirely for him, as far as it goes. The objection is, that it does not go far enough, and announce to the jury the full extent of the defendant's rights. But this objection we cannot here consider. It was the privilege of the defendant to have called for a fuller charge upon this point, and if he neglected to do so we cannot aid him. The sole question for us is, whether the charge contains error against the defendant? We are clear that it does not.

QUESTIONS

1. *With this opinion compare State v. Caesar, 31 N.C. 391 (1849), especially Judge Ruffin's dissent.*
2. *How would you expect a court to respond to a slave's argument that he is property, not a person, and thus unable to commit a crime? See State v. Dick, 4 La. 182 (1849).*
3. *A master dies, leaving his female slave and concubine her freedom. Held: the legacy is annulled under a statute voiding legacies to concubines. What argument for the legatee on appeal? See Vail v. Bird, 6 La. 223 (1851).*
4. *The attitudes of southern courts towards the slave defendant are compared with southern judicial attitudes towards black defendants in the early decades of this century in Nash, "A More Equitable Past? Southern Supreme Courts and the Protection of the Antebellum Negro," 48 N.C.L. Rev. 197 (1970).*
5. *You have been asked to imagine how a court could decide questions arising under the laws of slavery in ways that were consistent both with that institution and with the fundamental values implicit in our legal system. The strain is evident. But there were those who supported slavery as an original matter, who declared it to be the economic and social system most consistent with the values of Western civilization. Can you imagine how such a position might have been expressed, or does this absolutely elude your imagination?*

MEMOIR ON SLAVERY*

Governor Harper

President Dew has shewn that the institution of Slavery is a principal cause of civilization. Perhaps nothing can be more evident than that it is the sole cause. If anything can be predicated as universally true of

* In *The Pro-Slavery Argument* 1, 3, 26 (1852; Negro Universities Press 1968).

uncultivated man, it is that he will not labor beyond what is absolutely necessary to maintain his existence. Labor is pain to those who are unaccustomed to it, and the nature of man is averse to pain. Even with all the training, the helps and motives of civilization, we find that this aversion cannot be overcome in many individuals of the most cultivated societies. The coercion of Slavery alone is adequate to form man to habits of labor. Without it, there can be no accumulation of property, no providence for the future, no tastes for comfort or elegancies, which are the characteristics and essentials of civilization. He who has obtained the command of another's labor, first begins to accumulate and provide for the future, and the foundations of civilization are laid. We find confirmed by experience that which is so evident in theory. Since the existence of man upon the earth, with no exception whatever, either of ancient or modern times, every society which has attained civilization, has advanced to it through this process.

Will those who regard Slavery as immoral, or crime in itself, tell us that man was not intended for civilization, but to roam the earth as a biped brute? That he was not to raise his eyes to heaven, or be conformed in his nobler faculties to the image of his Maker? Or will they say that the Judge of all the earth has done wrong in ordaining the means by which alone that end can be obtained? . . .

. . . Slave labor can never be so cheap as what is called free labor. Political economists have established as the natural standard of wages in a fully peopled country, the value of the laborer's existence. I shall not stop to inquire into the precise truth of this proposition. It certainly approximates the truth. Where competition is intense, men will labor for a bare subsistence, and less than a competent subsistence. The employer of free laborers obtains their services during the time of their health and vigor, without the charge of rearing them from infancy, or supporting them in sickness or old age. This charge is imposed on the employer of slave labor, who, therefore, pays higher wages, and cuts off the principal source of misery — the wants and sufferings of infancy, sickness, and old age. Laborers too will be less skilful, and perform less work — enhancing the price of that sort of labor. The poor laws of England are an attempt — but an awkward and empirical attempt — to supply the place of that which we should suppose the feelings of every human heart would declare to be a natural obligation — that he who has received the benefit of the laborer's services during his health and vigor, should maintain him when he becomes unable to provide for his own support. They answer their purpose, however, very imperfectly, and are unjustly and unequally imposed. There is no attempt to apportion the burden according to the benefit received — and perhaps there could be none. This is one of the evils of their condition.

In periods of commercial revulsion and distress, like the present, the distress, in countries of free labor, falls principally on the laborers. In those of slave labor, it falls almost exclusively on the employer. In the former, when a business becomes unprofitable, the employer dismisses his laborers, or lowers their wages. But with us it is at the very period at which we are least able to dismiss our laborers; and if we would not suffer a further loss, we cannot reduce their wages. To receive the benefit of the services of which they are capable, we must provide for maintaining their health and vigor. In point of fact, we know that this is accounted among the necessary expenses of management.

LETTERS ON SLAVERY*

Chancellor Hammond

Now I affirm, that in Great Britain the poor and laboring classes of your own race and color, not only your fellow-beings, but your *fellow-citizens*, are more miserable and degraded, morally and physically, than our slaves; to be elevated to the actual condition of whom, would be to these, *your fellow-citizens*, a most glorious act of *emancipation*. And I also affirm, that the poor and laboring classes of our older free States would not be in a much more enviable condition, but for our Slavery. One of their own Senators has declared in the United States Senate, "that the repeal of the Tariff would reduce New-England to a howling wilderness." And the American Tariff is neither more nor less than a system by which the slave States are plundered for the benefit of those States which do not tolerate Slavery.

To prove what I say of Great Britain to be true, I make the following extracts from the Reports of Commissioners appointed by Parliament, and published by order of the House of Commons. I can make but few and short ones. But similar quotations might be made to any extent, and I defy you to deny that these specimens exhibit the real condition of your operatives in every branch of your industry. There is of course a variety in their sufferings. But the same incredible amount of toil, frightful destitution, and utter want of morals, characterize the lot of every class of them.

Collieries. — "I wish to call the attention of the Board to the pits about Brampton. The seams are so thin that several of them have only two feet headway to all the working. They are worked altogether by boys from eight to twelve years of age, on all-fours, with a dog belt and chain. The passages being neither ironed nor wooded, and often an inch or two thick with mud. In Mr. Barnes' pit these poor boys have to drag the barrows with one hundred weight of coal or slack sixty times a day sixty yards, and the empty barrows back, without once straightening

* In *The Pro-Slavery Argument* 99, 135, 169 (1852; Negro Universities Press 1968).

their backs, unless they choose to stand under the shaft, and run the risk of having their heads broken by a falling coal." — *Report on Mines*, 1842, p. 71. "In Shropshire the seams are no more than eighteen or twenty inches." — *Ibid*, p. 67. "At the Booth pit," says Mr. Scriven, "I walked, rode, and crept eighteen hundred yards to one of the nearest faces." — *Ibid*. "Chokedamp, firedamp, wild fire, sulphur and water, at all times menace instant death to the laborers in these mines." "Robert North, aged 16: Went into the pit at seven years of age, to fill up skips. I drew about twelve months. When I drew by the girdle and chain my skin was broken, and the blood ran down. I durst not say anything. If we said anything, the butty, and the reeve, who works under him, would take a stick and beat us." — *Ibid*. "The usual punishment for theft is to place the culprit's head between the legs of one of the biggest boys, and each boy in the pit — sometimes there are twenty — inflicts twelve lashes on the back and rump with a cat." — *Ibid*. "Instances occur in which children are taken into these mines to work as early as four years of age, sometimes at five, not unfrequently at six and seven, while from eight to nine is the ordinary age at which these employments commence." — *Ibid*. "The wages paid at these mines is from two dollars fifty cents to seven dollars fifty cents per month for laborers, according to age and ability, and out of this they must support themselves. They work twelve hours a day." — *Ibid*.

In Calico Printing. — "It is by no means uncommon in all the districts for children five or six years old to be kept at work fourteen to sixteen hours consecutively." — *Report on Children*, 1842, p. 59.

I could furnish extracts similar to these in regard to every branch of your manufactures, but I will not multiply them. Everybody knows that your operatives habitually labor from twelve to sixteen hours, men, women, and children, and the men occasionally twenty hours per day. In lace-making, says the last quoted report, children sometimes commence work at two years of age.

Destitution. — It is stated by your Commissioners that forty thousand persons in Liverpool, and fifteen thousand in Manchester, live in cellars; while twenty-two thousand in England pass the night in barns, tents, or the open air. "There have been found such occurrences as seven, eight, and ten persons in one cottage, I cannot say for one day, but for whole days, without a morsel of food. They have remained on their beds of straw for two successive days, under the impression that in a recumbent posture the pangs of hunger were less felt." — *Lord Brougham's Speech*, 11th July, 1842. A volume of frightful scenes might be quoted to corroborate the inferences to be necessarily drawn from the facts here stated. I will not add more, but pass on to the important enquiry as to

Morals and Education. — "Elizabeth Barrett, aged 14: I always work without stockings, shoes, or trowsers. I wear nothing but a shift. I have to go up to the headings with the men. *They are all naked there.* I am got used to that." — *Report on Mines.* "As to illicit sexual intercourse it seems to prevail universally, and from an early period of life." "The evidence might have been doubled, which attest the early commencement of sexual and promiscuous intercourse among boys and girls." . . .

We have often been taunted for our sensitiveness in regard to the discussion of Slavery. Do not suppose it is because we have any doubts of our rights, or scruples about asserting them. There was a time when such doubts and scruples were entertained. Our ancestors opposed the introduction of slaves into this country, and a feeling adverse to it was handed down from them. The enthusiastic love of liberty fostered by our revolution strengthened this feeling. And before the commencement of the abolition agitation here, it was the common sentiment that it was desirable to get rid of Slavery. Many thought it our duty to do so. When that agitation arose, we were driven to a close examination of the subject in all its bearings, and the result has been an *universal conviction* that in holding slaves we violate no law of God, — inflict no injustice on any of his creatures — while the terrible consequences of emancipation to all parties and the world at large, clearly revealed to us, make us shudder at the bare thought of it. The slaveholders are, therefore, indebted to the abolitionists for perfect ease of conscience, and the satisfaction of a settled and unanimous determination in reference to this matter.

ON SLAVERY*

T. Dew

Let us now look a moment to the slave, and contemplate his position. Mr. Jefferson has described him as hating, rather than loving his master, and as losing, too, all that *amor patriæ* which characterizes the true patriot. We assert again, that Mr. Jefferson is not borne out by the fact. We are well convinced that there is nothing but the mere relations of husband and wife, parent and child, brother and sister, which produce a closer tie, than the relation of master and servant. We have no hesitation in affirming, that throughout the whole slaveholding country, the slaves of a good master are his warmest, most constant, and most devoted friends; they have been accustomed to look up to him as their supporter, director and defender. Every one acquainted with southern slaves, knows that the slave rejoices in the elevation and prosperity of his master; and the heart of no one is more gladdened at the successful debut of young master or miss on the great theatre of the world, than

* In *The Pro-Slavery Argument* 287, 457, (1852; Negro Universities Press 1968).

that of either the young slave who has grown up with them, and shared in all their sports, and even partaken of all their delicacies — or the aged one who has looked on and watched them from birth to manhood, with the kindest and most affectionate solicitude, and has ever met from them all the kind treatment and generous sympathies of feeling, tender hearts.

QUESTIONS

1. *When you look back over the literature of slavery, you no doubt feel that it defines a world of nightmare, that it works the ultimate perversion of every decent value. It is inconceivable to us that such a system could have been tolerated by men with claims to decency, but we know that it was. Is it conceivable that in the future others will look back with similar horror on the world you inhabit, and see similarly incomprehensible evils? In addition to the residual effects of slavery and other instances of racial prejudice, think of the institution of war; the way women are treated and talked about in our society; the institution of private capital; the treatment of the poor and the "mentally ill." To what viciousness of whose heart can the continued existence of such things be traced? Are these not problems that the law should speedily solve? Keep these questions in mind as you watch the law at work solving the problem of slavery.*
2. *Apparently our slave system was much worse than others have been. The slave system in the Catholic countries of South America, for example, was not nearly so terrible as ours: the slave had legal rights, especially to marry and to remain with his family, to hold property, and to buy his freedom; emancipation was universally favored; racial distinctions were far less severe; and he was generally treated more as an unlucky person than as a beast. How can it be that the Roman Catholic Church and the most backward legal system in Europe — the Spanish — could do for the slave what the genius of the common law, inspired by Anglo-Saxon traditions of decency and liberty, could not? See S. Elkins, Slavery 52-81 (1959); H. Klein, Slavery in the Americas (1967); C. Degler, Neither White nor Black (1971).*
3. *What was the role of race in American slavery? Originally it seems that there was no absolute distinction between black slaves and white bonded servants. For example, in 1659 the Massachusetts legislature authorized the treasurers of the several counties to sell into slavery certain Quakers, who refused to pay fines, "to any of the English Nation at Virginia and Barbadoes." J. Hurd, Law of Freedom and Bondage, I, 261 (1858). But, as you can see, by the middle of the nineteenth century the system was racial at its heart. (Indeed, it appears that whiteness diminished the value of a slave, since it made escape more feasible. H. Catterall, Judicial Cases Concerning the American Slave and the Negro, I, 278 (1932).) One version of the early history is given in Handlin, "Origins of the Southern Labor System," 7 Wm. and Mary Q. (3d ser.) 199–222 (1950). An interesting case on the racial characteristics of the slave system is Hudgins v. Wright, 11 Va. (Hen. & M.) 133 (1808).*
4. *One final document defining relations between the races in the mid-nineteenth century now follows.*

ADDRESS ON COLONIZATION TO A DEPUTATION OF COLORED MEN*

Abraham Lincoln

Having all been seated, the President, after a few preliminary observations, informed them that a sum of money had been appropriated by Congress, and placed at his disposition, for the purpose of aiding the colonization in some country of the people, or a portion of them, of African descent, thereby making it his duty, as it had for a long time been his inclination, to favor that cause. And why, he asked, should the people of your race be colonized, and where? Why should they leave this country? This is, perhaps, the first question for proper consideration. You and we are different races. We have between us a broader difference than exists between almost any other two races. Whether it is right or wrong I need not discuss; but this physical difference is a great disadvantage to us both, as I think. Your race suffer very greatly, many of them, by living among us, while ours suffer from your presence. In a word, we suffer on each side. If this is admitted, it affords a reason, at least, why we should be separated. You here are freemen, I suppose?

A voice: Yes, sir.

The President: Perhaps you have long been free, or all your lives. Your race is suffering, in my judgment, the greatest wrong inflicted on any people. But even when you cease to be slaves, you are yet far removed from being placed on an equality with the white race. You are cut off from many of the advantages which the other race enjoys. The aspiration of men is to enjoy equality with the best when free, but on this broad continent not a single man of your race is made the equal of a single man of ours. Go where you are treated the best, and the ban is still upon you. I do not propose to discuss this, but to present it as a fact with which we have to deal. I cannot alter it if I would. It is a fact about which we all think and feel alike, I and you. We look to our condition. Owing to the existence of the two races on this continent, I need not recount to you the effects upon white men, growing out of the institution of slavery.

I believe in its general evil effects on the white race. See our present condition — the country engaged in war — our white men cutting one another's throats — none knowing how far it will extend — and then consider what we know to be the truth. But for your race among us there could not be war, although many men engaged on either side do not care for you one way or the other. Nevertheless, I repeat, without

* Aug. 14, 1862, in *Complete Works of Abraham Lincoln,* VIII, 1–3 (Nicolay and Hay ed. 1894) [hereinafter cited as *Works*].

the institution of slavery, and the colored race as a basis, the war could not have an existence. It is better for us both, therefore, to be separated. I know that there are free men among you who, even if they could better their condition, are not as much inclined to go out of the country as those who, being slaves, could obtain their freedom on this condition. I suppose one of the principal difficulties in the way of colonization is that the free colored man cannot see that his comfort would be advanced by it. You may believe that you can live in Washington, or elsewhere in the United States, the remainder of your life as easily, perhaps more so, than you can in any foreign country; and hence you may come to the conclusion that you have nothing to do with the idea of going to a foreign country.

This is (I speak in no unkind sense) an extremely selfish view of the case. You ought to do something to help those who are not so fortunate as yourselves. There is an unwillingness on the part of our people, harsh as it may be, for you free colored people to remain with us. Now, if you could give a start to the white people, you would open a wide door for many to be made free. If we deal with those who are not free at the beginning, and whose intellects are clouded by slavery, we have very poor material to start with. If intelligent colored men, such as are before me, would move in this matter, much might be accomplished. It is exceedingly important that we have men at the beginning capable of thinking as white men, and not those who have been systematically oppressed. There is much to encourage you. For the sake of your race you should sacrifice something of your present comfort for the purpose of being as grand in that respect as the white people. It is a cheering thought throughout life, that something can be done to ameliorate the condition of those who have been subject to the hard usages of the world. It is difficult to make a man miserable while he feels he is worthy of himself and claims kindred to the great God who made him. In the American Revolutionary war sacrifices were made by men engaged in it, but they were cheered by the future. General Washington himself endured greater physical hardships than if he had remained a British subject, yet he was a happy man because he was engaged in benefiting his race, in doing something for the children of his neighbors, having none of his own.

2. *Amelioration and Abolition*

Having studied what was, we ask now the lawyer's question: what might have been. How would you have proposed to ameliorate or abolish slavery? We start with an examination of a code proposed by

Edmund Burke to govern colonial slavery pending its abolition. How do you compare this proposal with the actual legal materials set out above?

SKETCH OF A NEGRO CODE (1792)*
Edmund Burke

IV. And whereas the condition of persons in a state of slavery is such that they are utterly unable to take advantage of any remedy which the laws may provide for their protection and the amendment of their condition, and have not the proper means of pursuing any process for the same, but are and must be under guardianship: and whereas it is not fitting that they should be under the sole guardianship of their masters, or their attorneys and overseers, to whom their grievances, whenever they suffer any, must ordinarily be owing:

1. Be it therefore enacted, that his Majesty's Attorney-General for the time being successively shall, by his office, exercise the trust and employment of protector of negroes within the island in which he is or shall be Attorney-General to his Majesty, his heirs and successors; and that the said Attorney-General, protector of negroes, is hereby authorized to hear any complaint on the part of any negro or negroes, and inquire into the same, or to institute an inquiry ex officio into any abuses, and to call before him and examine witnesses upon oath, relative to the subject-matter of the said official inquiry or complaint: and it is hereby enacted and declared, that the said Attorney-General, protector of negroes, is hereby authorized and empowered, at his discretion, to file an information ex officio for any offences committed against the provisions of this act, or for any misdemeanors or wrongs against the said negroes, or any of them.

3. And be it enacted, that the said Attorney-General, protector of negroes, shall appoint inspectors, not exceeding the number of ——, at his discretion; and the said inspectors shall be placed in convenient districts in each island severally, or shall twice in the year make a circuit in the same, according to the direction which they shall receive from the protector of negroes aforesaid; and the inspectors shall and they are hereby required, twice in the year, to report in writing to the protector aforesaid the state and condition of the negroes in their districts or on their circuit severally, the number, sex, age, and occupation of the said negroes on each plantation; and the overseer or chief manager on each plantation is hereby required to furnish an account thereof within [ten days] after the demand of the said inspectors, and to permit the in-

* In *The Writings and Speeches of the Right Honorable Edmund Burke*, VI, 262 et seq. (Beaconsfield ed. 1901). With this proposal, compare An Act for the Abolition of Slavery Throughout the British Colonies, 3 & 4 Wm. 4, c. 73 (1833).

spector or inspectors aforesaid to examine into the same; and the said inspectors shall set forth, in the said report, the distempers to which the negroes are most liable in the several parts of the island.

4. And be it enacted, that the said protector of negroes, by and with the consent of the governor and chief judge of each island, shall form instructions, by which the said inspectors shall discharge their trust in the manner the least capable of exciting any unreasonable hopes in the said negroes, or of weakening the proper authority of the overseer, and shall transmit them to one of his Majesty's principal secretaries of state; and when sent back with his approbation, the same shall become the rule for the conduct of the said inspectors. . . .

18. And be it enacted, that for every two districts a school shall be established for young negroes to be taught three days in the week, and to be detained from their owner four hours in each day, the number not to be more or fewer than twenty males in each district, who shall be chosen, and vacancies filled, by the minister of the district; and the said minister shall pay to the owner of the said boy, and shall be allowed the same in his accounts at the synod, to the age of twelve years old, three-pence by the day, and for every boy from twelve years old to fifteen, five-pence by the day.

19. And it is enacted, that, if the president of the synod aforesaid shall certify to the protector of negroes, that any boys in the said schools (provided that the number in no one year shall exceed one in the island of Jamaica, and one in two years in the islands of Barbadoes, Antigua, and Grenada, and one in four years in any of the other islands) do show a remarkable aptitude for learning, the said protector is hereby authorized and directed to purchase the said boy at the best rate at which boys of that age and strength have been sold within the year; and the said negro so purchased shall be under the entire guardianship of the said protector of negroes, who shall send him to the Bishop of London for his further education in England, and may charge in his accounts for the expense of transporting him to England; and the Bishop of London shall provide for the education of such of the said negroes as he shall think proper subjects, until the age of twenty-four years, and shall order those who shall fall short of expectation after one year to be bound apprentice to some handicraft trade; and when his apprenticeship is finished, the Lord Mayor of London is hereby authorized and directed to receive the said negro from his master, and to transmit him to the island from which he came, in the West Indies, to be there as a free negro, subject, however, to the direction of the protector of negroes, relatively to his behavior and employment.

20. And it is hereby enacted and provided, that any planter, or owner of negroes, not being of the Church of England, and not choosing to

send his negroes to attend divine service in manner by this act directed, shall give, jointly or severally, as the case shall require, security to the protector of negroes that a competent minister of some Christian church or congregation shall be provided for the due instruction of the negroes, and for their performing divine service according to the description of the religion of the master or masters, in some church or house thereto allotted, in the manner and with the regulations in this act prescribed with regard to the exercise of religion according to the Church of England: provided always, that the marriages of the said negroes belonging to Dissenters shall be celebrated only in the church of the said district, and that a register of the births shall be transmitted to the minister of the said district.

21. And whereas a state of matrimony, and the government of a family, is a principal means of forming men to a fitness for freedom, and to become good citizens: Be it enacted, that all negro men and women, above eighteen years of age for the man and sixteen for the woman, who have cohabited together for twelve months or upwards, or shall cohabit for the same time, and have a child or children, shall be deemed to all intents and purposes to be married, and either of the parties is authorized to require of the ministers of the district to be married in the face of the church.

22. And be it enacted, that, from and after the ——— of ———, all negro men in an healthy condition, and so reported to be, in case the same is denied, by a surgeon and by an inspector of negroes, and being twenty-one years old, or upwards, until fifty, and not being before married, shall, on requisition of the inspectors, be provided by their masters or overseers with a woman not having children living, and not exceeding the age of the man, nor, in any case, exceeding the age of twenty-five years; and such persons shall be married publicly in the face of the church.

23. And be it enacted, that, if any negro shall refuse a competent marriage tendered to him, and shall not demand another specifically, such as it may be in his master's power to provide, the master or overseer shall be authorized to constrain him by an increase of work or a lessening of allowance.

24. And be it enacted, that the minister in each district shall have, with the assent of the inspector, full power and authority to punish all acts of adultery, unlawful concubinage, and fornication, amongst negroes, on hearing and a summary process, by ordering a number of blows, not exceeding———, for each offence; and if any white person shall be proved, on information in the supreme court, to be exhibited by the protector of negroes, to have committed adultery with any negro woman, or to have corrupted any negro woman under sixteen years of age, he shall be fined in the sum of ———, and shall be forever disabled

from serving the office of overseer of negroes, or being attorney to any plantation.

25. And be it enacted, that no slaves shall be compelled to do any work for their masters for [three] days after their marriage.

26. And be it enacted, that no woman shall be obliged to field-work, or any other laborious work, for one month before her delivery, or for six weeks afterwards.

27. And be it enacted, that no husband and wife shall be sold separately, if originally belonging to the same master; nor shall any children under sixteen be sold separately from their parents, or one parent, if [only] one be living.

28. And be it enacted, that, if an husband and wife, which before their intermarriage belonged to different owners, shall be sold, they shall not be sold at such a distance as to prevent mutual help and cohabitation; and of this distance the minister shall judge, and his certificate of the inconvenient distance shall be valid, so as to make such sale unlawful, and to render the same null and void.

29. And be it enacted, that no negro shall be compelled to work for his owner at field-work, or any service relative to a plantation, or to work at any handicraft trade, from eleven o'clock on Saturday forenoon until the usual working hour on Monday morning.

30. And whereas habits of industry and sobriety, and the means of acquiring and preserving property, are proper and reasonable preparatives to freedom, and will secure against an abuse of the same: Be it enacted, that every negro man, who shall have served ten years, and is thirty years of age, and is married, and has had two children born of any marriage, shall obtain the whole of Saturday for himself and his wife, and for his own benefit, and after thirty-seven years of age, the whole of Friday for himself and his wife: provided that in both cases the minister of the district and the inspector of negroes shall certify that they know nothing against his peaceable, orderly, and industrious behavior.

31. And be it enacted, that the master of every plantation shall provide the materials of a good and substantial hut for each married field negro; and if his plantation shall exceed——— acres, he shall allot to the same a portion of land not less than ———: and the said hut and land shall remain and stand annexed to the said negro, for his natural life, or during his bondage; but the same shall not be alienated without the consent of the owners.

32. And be it enacted, that it shall not be lawful for the owner of any negro, by himself or any other, to take from him any land, house, cattle, goods, or money, acquired by the said negro, whether by purchase, donation, or testament, whether the same has been derived from the owner of the said negro, or any other.

35. And be it enacted, that no blows or stripes exceeding thirteen

shall be inflicted for one offence upon any negro, without the order of one of his Majesty's justices of peace.

36. And it is enacted, that it shall be lawful for the protector of negroes, as often as on complaint and hearing he shall be of opinion that any negro hath been cruelly and inhumanly treated, or when it shall be made to appear to him that an overseer hath any particular malice, to order, at the desire of the suffering party, the said negro to be sold to another master.

37. And be it enacted, that, in all cases of injury to member or life, the offences against a negro shall be deemed and taken to all intents and purposes as if the same were perpetrated against any of his Majesty's subjects; and the protector of negroes, on complaint, or if he shall receive credible information thereof, shall cause an indictment to be presented for the same; and in case of suspicion of any murder of a negro, an inquest by the coroner, or officer acting as such, shall, if practicable, be held into the same.

38. And in order to a gradual manumission of slaves, as they shall seem fitted to fill the offices of freemen, be it enacted, that every negro slave, being thirty years of age and upwards, and who has had three children born to him in lawful matrimony, and who hath received a certificate from the minister of his district, or any other Christian teacher, of his regularity in the duties of religion, and of his orderly and good behavior, may purchase, at rates to be fixed by two justices of peace, the freedom of himself, or his wife or children, or of any of them separately, valuing the wife and children, if purchased into liberty by the father of the family, at half only of their marketable values: provided that the said father shall bind himself in a penalty of ——— for the good behavior of his children.

39. And be it enacted, that it shall be lawful for the protector of negroes to purchase the freedom of any negro who shall appear to him to excel in any mechanical art, or other knowledge or practice deemed liberal, and the value shall be settled by a jury.

40. And be it enacted, that the protector of negroes shall be and is authorized and required to act as a magistrate for the coercion of all idle, disobedient, or disorderly free negroes, and he shall by office prosecute them for the offences of idleness, drunkenness, quarrelling, gaming, or vagrancy, in the supreme court, or cause them to be prosecuted before one justice of peace, as the case may require.

QUESTIONS

1. *This is a different world indeed. Here we have the odious institution of slavery still, but one does not have quite the same sense that one is read-*

ing the literature of nightmare. Why not? How is the Burke proposal different from the slave-holding reality?

a. How are slaves defined in this statute? As things, children, animals, or people? Are they talked about in a consistent manner?

b. How does the literature define its author? The society which might adopt it?

c. Could you imagine being able to act as a judge in this legal world and still maintain and express the basic attitudes you think you could now express as a judge? Why or why not? Exactly how would the judge's position under Burke's proposal differ from what it would be, say, in slave-holding Alabama?

d. The real slave statutes seemed to be founded upon inconsistency. Does this statute share that defect? What inconsistencies do you find here?

2. *Would you have approved the passage of this act in prewar Mississippi?*
3. *Here is how Burke, in a prefatory letter, explained the premises upon which he proceeded in drafting this code:*

"Whenever, in my proposed reformation, we take our point of departure from a state of slavery, we must precede the donation of freedom by disposing the minds of the objects to a disposition to receive it without danger to themselves or to us. The process of bringing free savages to order and civilization is very different. When a state of slavery is that upon which we are to work, the very means which lead to liberty must partake of compulsion. The minds of men, being crippled with that restraint, can do nothing for themselves: everything must be done for them. The regulations can owe little to consent. Everything must be the creature of power. Hence it is that regulations must be multiplied, particularly as you have two parties to deal with. The planter you must at once restrain and support, and you must control at the same time that you ease the servant."

4. *Burke's proposal is very different from the actual abolition statutes passed in America. The usual pattern was to provide for gradual abolition: the Pennsylvania act of 1780, for example, provided that no person born thereafter should be a slave, but that Negroes and mulattoes born thereafter should serve as indentured servants for twenty-eight years. Later statutes provided that persons then slaves should lose that status with the passage of a certain number of years. Apparently the reason for gradualism was tenderness towards the economic interests of the owners, and I cannot find that any steps were taken to design the process of liberation to advance the interests of the slaves themselves.*
5. *Burke's proposal expressly tended towards the gradual abolition of slavery, and for this reason would probably have been unacceptable to Southern slave-holders. Could his proposal have been used to ameliorate slavery without leading to its abolition? Try to redraft it so that it has such an effect. What do you have when you are done?*
6. *Based upon your analysis of Burke's proposal and on your reading of the actual slave literature, prepare a response to this suggestion: "A legal system of the kind we lawyers can recognize and work with has at its heart certain fundamental principles, ideals, and values which are utterly inconsistent with the premises of slavery. The law as we know it is not a neutral tool for the expression of the will of the powerful but an actual force for justice in the world. This is demonstrated by the fact that as*

a slave system is more fully expressed in the law, either it becomes less and less a slave system or the more obvious it is that the 'legal' system bears little resemblance to any we know, that it is no system of law at all. Either the rights of slaves as people are recognized – and the first step is taken towards the sort of labor legislation we have today – or the hypocrisy of any claim to principle is exposed for what it is. If slavery is to exist, it must be as the sole concern of the society, subordinating every other value and interest. This institutional truth explains why the South became at last hysterical, why its intellectual, social, and moral order fell into chaos. It was a totalitarian system founded upon a principle that destroyed every other, including the fundamental principles of legality."

a. Do you concur? If so, explain (with reference to specific fact situations, cases, and rules) how it is that the law is by its nature an "actual force for justice." Can you explain why this should be so? What are the fundamental principles, ideals, and values of our legal system, and where do you find them? You might ask whether you can think of any other institutions that are similarly incompatible with the premises of law; consider the laws of war, for example, or those governing the treatment of soldiers in the army, or prisoners of war, or domestic prisoners, or inmates in mental hospitals. What happens as the experience of such people finds fuller expression in the law? Compare the effect that the Viet Nam war has had on American public and legal life. Given all these modern parallels to slavery, how do you suppose we manage to keep a legal system going?

b. In the suggestion quoted above, has anything more been said than that the law is here being used for purposes the speaker regards as very bad?

7. We shall soon move to a very different world, the humane, rational world of modern America, where we all agree that slavery and other racial injustice is bad and where the law uses racial labels no longer for vicious but for benign purposes. But ask yourself this question first: what is your relation to the world of slavery? Perhaps one or more of your own ancestors was a slave or slave-owner. What does that mean to you? Obviously no one alive today can be blamed for maintaining the system of slavery, and virtually no one alive today was ever a slave. So what is your relationship to that world, as a person? As a lawyer?

8. Your own attitude towards slavery is, no doubt, utterly clear: for once we have an issue as to which moral absolutes apply simply and directly, and only one position is conceivable. Below is a nineteenth-century voice expressing such a view; is this an adequate statement of the situation and what it means, or not? Explain your response.

"The object of these sketches is to awaken sympathy and feeling for the African race, as they exist among us; to show their wrongs and sorrows, under a system so necessarily cruel and unjust as to defeat and do away the good effects of all that can be attempted for them, by their best friends, under it.

"In doing this, the author can sincerely disclaim any invidious feeling towards those individuals who, often without any fault of their own, are involved in the trials and embarrassments of the legal relations of slavery.

"Experience has shown her that some of the noblest of minds and hearts are often thus involved; and no one knows better than they do, that *what may be gathered of the evils of slavery from sketches like these, is not the half that could be told, of the unspeakable whole.*

"In the northern states, these representations may, perhaps, be thought caricatures; in the southern states are witnesses who know their fidelity. What personal knowledge the author has had, of the truth of incidents such as here are related, will appear in its time.

"It is a comfort to hope, as so many of the world's sorrows and wrongs have, from age to age, been lived down, so a time shall come when sketches similar to these shall be valuable only as memorials of what has long ceased to be." Harriet Beecher Stowe, "Preface," in Uncle Tom's Cabin 6 (1852; Dolphin ed. 1962).

9. *A final complication: we generally assume that slavery either exists or does not, that there can be no middle ground. But as Stephen A. Douglas points out in a speech reproduced infra page 823, there was quite a variety of attitudes towards race and slavery in the Northern states. Following are some extracts from the laws of Illinois, the state of Douglas and Lincoln.*

ILLINOIS REVISED STATUTES (1845)

Chapter 74: Negroes, Mulattoes, etc.

Section 1. No black or mulatto person, shall be permitted to reside in this State, until such person shall produce to the county commissioners' court where he or she is desirous of settling, a certificate of his or her freedom; which certificate shall be duly authenticated in the same manner that is required to be done, in cases arising under the acts and judicial proceedings of other States. And until such person shall have given bond, with sufficient security, to the people of this State for the use of the proper county, in the penal sum of one thousand dollars, conditioned that such person will not, at any time, become a charge to said county, or any other county of this State, as a poor person, and that such person shall, at all times, demean himself or herself, in strict conformity with the laws of this State, that now are or hereafter may be enacted; the solvency of said security shall be appproved by said clerk. . . .

Sec. 2. If any person shall harbor such negro or mulatto as aforesaid, not having such certificate, and given bond, and taken a certificate thereof, or shall hire, or in anywise give sustenance to such negro or mulatto, not having such certificate of freedom, and of having given bond, [he] shall be fined in the sum of five hundred dollars, one-half thereof to the use of the county, and the other half to the party giving information thereof: *Provided,* This section shall not affect any negro or mulatto who is now a resident of this State.

Sec. 5. Every black or mulatto person who shall be found in this State, and not having such a certificate as is required by this chapter, shall be deemed a runaway slave or servant, and it shall be lawful for any inhabitant of this State, to take such black or mulatto person before some justice of the peace, and should such black or mulatto person not produce such certificate as aforesaid, it shall be the duty of such justice to cause such black or mulatto person to be committed to the custody of the sheriff of the county, who shall keep such black or mulatto person, and . . . it shall be the duty of the sheriff to hire him out for the best price he can get, after having given five days previous notice thereof, from month to month, for the space of one year; and if no owner shall appear and substantiate his claim before the expiration of the year, the sheriff shall give a certificate to such black or mulatto person, who, on producing the same to the next circuit court of the county, may obtain a certificate from the court, stating the facts, and the person shall be deemed a free person, unless he shall be lawfully claimed by his proper owner or owners thereafter.

Sec. 9. If any slave or servant shall be found at a distance of ten miles from the tenement of his or her master, or the person with whom he or she lives, without a pass, or some letter or token, whereby it may appear that he or she is proceeding by authority from his or her master, employer or overseer, it shall and may be lawful for any person to apprehend and carry him or her before a justice of the peace, to be by his order punished with stripes, not exceeding thirty-five at his discretion.

Sec. 10. If any slave or servant shall presume to come and be upon the plantation, or at the dwelling of any person whatsoever, without leave from his or her owner, not being sent upon lawful business, it shall be lawful for the owner of such plantation, or dwelling house, to give or order such slave or servant ten lashes on his or her bare back.

Sec. 12. If any person or persons shall permit or suffer any slave or slaves, servant or servants of color, to the number of three or more, to assemble in his, her or their out-house, yard or shed, for the purpose of dancing or revelling, either by night or by day, the person or persons so offending shall forfeit and pay the sum of twenty dollars with costs, to any person or persons who will sue for and recover the same by action of debt or by indictment, in any court of record, proper to try the same.

Sec. 14. In all cases of penal laws, where free persons are punishable by fine, servants shall be punished by whipping, after the rate of twenty lashes for every eight dollars, [but no servant shall receive more than forty lashes at any one time] unless such offender can procure some person to pay the fine.

Sec. 15. No person shall buy, sell, or receive of, to or from any servant or slave, any coin or commodity, without leave or consent of the master or owner of such slave or servant, and any person so offending shall forfeit and pay to the master or owner of such slave or servant four times the value of the thing so bought, sold or received, to be recovered with costs of suit, before any court having cognizance of the same.

Sec. 16. Any such servant being lazy, disorderly, guilty of misbehavior to his master or master's family, shall be corrected by stripes, on order from a justice of the county wherein he resides; or refusing to work, shall be compelled thereto in like manner, and moreover shall serve two days for every one he shall have so refused to serve, or shall otherwise have lost, without sufficient justification. All necessary expenses incurred by any master for apprehending and bringing home any absconding servant, shall be repaid by further services, after such rates as the circuit court of the county shall direct, unless such servant shall give security, to be approved by the court, for the payment in money within six months after he shall be free from service, and shall accordingly pay the same.

Sec. 17. All contracts between masters and servants, during the time of service, shall be void.

Sec. 18. The benefit of any contract of service shall be assignable by the master to any person being a citizen of this State, to whom the servant shall, in the presence of a justice of the peace, freely consent that it shall be assigned, the said justice attesting such free consent in writing; and shall also pass to the executors, administrators and legatees of the master.

Sec. 19. No negro, mulatto or Indian, shall at any time purchase any servant, other than of his own complexion; and if any of the persons aforesaid shall nevertheless, presume to purchase a white servant, such servant shall immediately become free, and shall be so held, deemed and taken.

Sec. 20. Servants shall be provided by the master with wholesome and sufficient food, clothing and lodging, and at the end of their service, if they shall not have contracted for any reward, food, clothing and lodging, shall receive from him one new and complete suit of clothing, suited to the season of the year, to-wit: a coat, waistcoat, pair of breeches and shoes, two pair of stockings, two shirts, a hat and blanket.

Sec. 21. If any servants shall at any time bring in goods or money during the time of their service, [or] shall by gift or other lawful means, acquire goods or money, they shall have the property and benefit thereof to their own use; and if any servant shall be sick or lame, and so become useless or chargeable, his or her master or owner shall maintain such servant until his or her time of service shall be expired; and if any master or owner shall put away any lame or sick servant, under pretence of freedom, and such servant becomes chargeable to the county, such master or owner shall forfeit and pay thirty dollars to the overseers of the poor of the county wherein such offence shall be committed, to the use of the poor of the county, recoverable with costs, by action of debt, in any circuit court; and moreover, shall be liable to the action of the said overseers of the poor at the common law for damages.

Sec. 22. The circuit court of every county shall, at all times, receive the complaints of servants, being citizens of any of the United States of America, who reside within the jurisdiction of such court, against their masters or mistresses, alleging undeserved or immoderate correction, insufficient allowances of food, raiment or lodging or any failure in the duties of such master or mistress as prescribed in this chapter, and the said circuit court shall hear and determine complaints of masters and mistresses against their servants, for desertion without good cause, and may oblige the latter, for loss thereby occasioned, to make restitution by further services after the expiration of the time for which they had been bound.[15]

WRITING ASSIGNMENT 10: *The Abolition of Slavery*

We now address a matter that has no doubt been on your mind throughout this section: the only decent response to slavery is to abolish it. How is that to be done?

- *Assume that you are special counsel to President Lincoln. You are asked to draft or outline whatever legal documents you think necessary or appropriate to secure the abolition of slavery. Explain the proposals you make.*

You can of course say "slavery is hereby abolished," but what effect would that statement have on the Mississippi of 1870? Of 1970? What else can you do?

You may learn something from Burke's proposal and from your own knowledge of the legal steps that were taken to abolish slavery. The most important recent step to abolish the effects of slavery was probably Brown v. Board of Education, 347 U.S. 483 (1954), and your familiarity with that case and its successors may be useful to you. In addition, there follow some largely self-explanatory extracts (through page 488) that may be of interest or assistance in working out this assignment.

LIFE UNDER THE "PECULIAR INSTITUTION"*

N. Yetman

THE STORY OF MARY ANDERSON

Sunday was a great day on the plantation. Everybody got biscuits, Sundays. The slave women went down to Marster's for their Sunday

15. It was held in Illinois that a registered servant could be sold on execution to satisfy the debts of the master. *Nance v. Howard,* 1 Ill. (Breese) 242 (1828).

* Pages 15–18 (1970).

allowance of flour. All the children ate breakfast at the Great House and Marster and Missus gave out fruit to all. The slaves looked forward to Sunday as they labored through the week. It was a great day. Slaves received good treatment from Marster and all his family.

The slave children all carried a mussel shell in their hands to eat with up to the Great House. The food was put on large trays and the children all gathered around and ate, dipping up their food with their mussel shells which they used for spoons. Those who refused to eat or those who were ailing in any way had to come back to the Great House for their meals and medicine until they were well.

Marster had a large apple orchard in the Tar River low grounds and up on higher ground and nearer the plantation house there was on one side of the road a large plum orchard and on the other side was an orchard of peaches, cherries, quinces, and grapes. We picked the quinces in August and used them for preserving. Marster and Missus believed in giving the slaves plenty of fruit, especially the children.

Marster had three children, one boy named Dallas, and two girls, Bettie and Carrie. He would not allow slave children to call his children "Marster" and "Missus" unless the slave said "Little Marster" or "Little Missus." He had four white overseers, but they were not allowed to whip a slave. If there was any whipping to be done he always said he would do it. He didn't believe in whipping, so when a slave got so bad he could not manage him, he sold him.

Marster didn't quarrel with anybody; Missus would not speak short to a slave, but both Marster and Missus taught slaves to be obedient in a nice quiet way. The slaves were taught to take their hats and bonnets off before going into the house, and to bow and say, "Good mornin' Marster Sam and Missus Evaline." Some of the little Negroes would go down to the Great House and ask them when it was going to rain, and when Marster or Missus walked in the grove the little Negroes would follow along after them like a gang of kiddies. Some of the slave children wanted to stay with them at the Great House all the time. They knew no better, of course, and seemed to love Marster and Missus as much as they did their own mother and father. Marster and Missus always used gentle means to get the children out of their way when they bothered them and the way the children loved and trusted them was a beautiful sight to see.

Patterrollers were not allowed on the place unless they came peacefully, and I never knew of them whipping any slaves on Marster's place. Slaves were carried off on two horse wagons to be sold. I have seen several loads leave. They were the unruly ones. Sometimes he would bring back slaves; once he brought back two boys and three girls from the slave market.

We were allowed to have prayer meetings in our homes and we also went to the white folks' church. But they would not teach any of us to read and write. Books and papers were forbidden. Marster's children and the slave children played together. I went around with the baby girl Carrie to other plantations visiting. She taught me how to talk low and how to act in company. My association with white folks and my training while I was a slave is why I talk like white folks.

The War was begun and there were stories of fights and freedom. The news went from plantation to plantation and while the slaves acted natural and some even more polite than usual, they prayed for freedom.

Then one day I heard something that sounded like thunder and Marster and Missus began to walk around and act queer. The grown slaves were whispering to each other. Sometimes they gathered in little gangs in the grove. Next day I heard it again, boom, boom, boom. I went and asked Missus, "Is it going to rain?" She said, "Mary, go to the icehouse and bring me some pickles and preserves." I went and got them. She ate a little and gave me some. Then she said, "You run along and play."

In a day or two everybody on the plantation seemed to be disturbed and Marster and Missus were crying. Marster ordered all the slaves to come to the Great House at nine o'clock. Nobody was working and slaves were walking over the grove in every direction. At nine o'clock all the slaves gathered at the Great House and Marster and Missus came out on the porch and stood side by side. You could hear a pin drop everything was so quiet. Then Marster said, "Good morning," and Missus said, "Good morning, children." They were both crying. Then Marster said, "Men, women, and children, you are free. You are no longer my slaves. The Yankees will soon be here." Marster and Missus then went into the house; got two large arm chairs and put them on the porch facing the avenue and sat down side by side and remained there watching.

In about an hour there was one of the blackest clouds coming up the avenue from the main road. It was the Yankee soldiers. They finally filled the mile long avenue reaching from Marster's house to the main Louisburg Road and spread out over the mile square grove. The mounted men dismounted. The footmen stacked their shining guns and began to build fires and cook. They called the slaves, saying, "You are free."

Slaves were whooping and laughing and acting like they were crazy. Yankee soldiers were shaking hands with the Negroes and calling them Sam, Dinah, Sarah, and asking them questions. They busted the door to the smokehouse and got all the hams. They went to the icehouse and got several barrels of brandy: such a time! The Negroes and Yankees were cooking and eating together. The Yankees told them to come on and join them, they were free. Marster and Missus sat on the porch and they were so humble no Yankee bothered anything in the Great House.

The slaves were awfully excited. The Yankees stayed there, cooked, ate, drank, and played music until about night. Then a bugle began to blow and you never saw such getting on horses and lining up in your life. In a few minutes they began to march, leaving the grove which was soon silent as a graveyard. They took Marster's horses and cattle with them and joined the main army and camped just across Cypress Creek one and one-half miles from my marster's place on the Louisburg Road.

When they left the county, [a] lot of the slaves went with them and soon there were none of Marster's slaves left. They wandered around for a year from place to place, fed and working most of the time at some other slave owner's plantation and getting more homesick every day.

The second year after the surrender our Marster and Missus got on their carriage and went and looked up all the Negroes they heard of who ever belonged to them. Some who went off with the Yankees were never heard from again. When Marster and Missus found any of theirs they would say, "Well, come on back home." My father and mother, two uncles and their families moved back. Also Lorenze Brodie and John Brodie and their families moved back. Several of the young men and women who once belonged to him came back. Some were so glad to get back they cried, 'cause fare had been mighty bad part of the time they were rambling around and they were hungry.

When they got back Marster would say, "Well, you have come back, have you?" And the Negroes would say, "Yes, Marster." Most all spoke of them as "Missus" and "Marster" as they did before the surrender, and getting back home was the greatest pleasure of all. We stayed with Marster and Missus and went to their church, the Maple Springs Baptist Church, until they died.

Since the surrender I married James Anderson. I had four children, one boy and three girls.

REPLY TO A COMMITTEE FROM THE RELIGIOUS DENOMINATIONS OF CHICAGO, ASKING THE PRESIDENT TO ISSUE A PROCLAMATION OF EMANCIPATION*

Abraham Lincoln

What good would a proclamation of emancipation from me do, especially as we are now situated? I do not want to issue a document that the whole world will see must necessarily be inoperative, like the

* Sept. 13, 1862, in *Works,* VIII, 30–31 (1894).

Pope's bull against the comet. Would my word free the slaves, when I cannot even enforce the Constitution in the rebel States? Is there a single court, or magistrate, or individual that would be influenced by it there? And what reason is there to think it would have any greater effect upon the slaves than the late law of Congress, which I approved, and which offers protection and freedom to the slaves of rebel masters who come within our lines? Yet I cannot learn that that law has caused a single slave to come over to us. And suppose they could be induced by a proclamation of freedom from me to throw themselves upon us, what should we do with them? How can we feed and care for such a multitude? General Butler wrote me a few days since that he was issuing more rations to the slaves who have rushed to him than to all the white troops under his command. They eat, and that is all; though it is true General Butler is feeding the whites also by the thousand, for it nearly amounts to a famine there. If, now, the pressure of the war should call off our forces from New Orleans to defend some other point, what is to prevent the masters from reducing the blacks to slavery again? For I am told that whenever the rebels take any black prisoners, free or slave, they immediately auction them off. They did so with those they took from a boat that was aground in the Tennessee River a few days ago. And then I am very ungenerously attacked for it! For instance, when, after the late battles at and near Bull Run, an expedition went out from Washington under a flag of truce to bury the dead and bring in the wounded, and the rebels seized the blacks who went along to help, and sent them into slavery, Horace Greeley said in his paper that the government would probably do nothing about it. What could I do?

PRELIMINARY EMANCIPATION PROCLAMATION*

Abraham Lincoln

I, Abraham Lincoln, President of the United States of America, and commander-in-chief of the army and navy thereof, do hereby proclaim and declare that hereafter, as heretofore, the war will be prosecuted for the object of practically restoring the constitutional relation between the United States and each of the States, and the people thereof, in which States that relation is or may be suspended or disturbed.

That it is my purpose, upon the next meeting of Congress, to again recommend the adoption of a practical measure tendering pecuniary aid to the free acceptance or rejection of all slave States, so called, the people whereof may not then be in rebellion against the United States, and which States may then have voluntarily adopted, or thereafter may voluntarily adopt, immediate or gradual abolishment of slavery within

* Sept. 22, 1862, in *Works*, VIII, 36–38 (1894).

their respective limits; and that the effort to colonize persons of African descent with their consent upon this continent or elsewhere, with the previously obtained consent of the governments existing there, will be continued.

That on the first day of January, in the year of our Lord one thousand eight hundred and sixty-three, all persons held as slaves within any State or designated part of a State the people whereof shall then be in rebellion against the United States, shall be then, thenceforward, and forever free; and the Executive Government of the United States, including the military and naval authority thereof, will recognize and maintain the freedom of such persons, and will do no act or acts to repress such persons, or any of them, in any efforts they may make for their actual freedom.

That the Executive will, on the first day of January aforesaid, by proclamation designate the States and parts of States, if any, in which the people thereof, respectively shall then be in rebellion against the United States; and the fact that any State or the people thereof, shall on that day be in good faith represented in the Congress of the United States by members chosen thereto at elections wherein a majority of the qualified voters of such State shall have participated, shall, in the absence of strong countervailing testimony, be deemed conclusive evidence that such State, and the people thereof, are not then in rebellion against the United States.

ANNUAL MESSAGE TO CONGRESS*

Abraham Lincoln

Our strife pertains to ourselves — to the passing generations of men; and it can without convulsion be hushed forever with the passing of one generation.

In this view I recommend the adoption of the following resolution and articles amendatory to the Constitution of the United States:

"Resolved by the Senate and House of Representatives of the United States of America in Congress assembled (two-thirds of both houses concurring), That the following articles be proposed to the legislatures (or conventions) of the several States as amendments to the Constitution of the United States, all or any of which articles when ratified by three fourths of the said legislatures (or conventions) to be valid as part or parts of the said Constitution, viz.:

"Article ———.

"Every state wherein slavery now exists which shall abolish the same therein at any time or times before the first day of January in the year of

* Dec. 1, 1862, in *Works,* VIII, 116–117 (1894).

our Lord one thousand and nine hundred, shall receive compensation from the United States as follows, to wit:

"The President of the United States shall deliver to every such State bonds of the United States, bearing interest at the rate of ——— per cent. per annum, to an amount equal to the aggregate sum of ——— for each slave shown to have been therein by the eighth census of the United States, said bonds to be delivered to such State by instalments, or in one parcel at the completion of the abolishment, accordingly as the same shall have been gradual or at one time within such State; and interest shall begin to run upon any such bond only from the proper time of its delivery as aforesaid. Any State having received bonds as aforesaid, and afterward reintroducing or tolerating slavery therein, shall refund to the United States the bonds so received, or the value thereof, and all interest paid thereon.

"Article ———.

"All slaves who shall have enjoyed actual freedom by the chances of the war at any time before the end of the rebellion, shall be forever free; but all owners of such who shall not have been disloyal shall be compensated for them at the same rates as are provided for States adopting abolishment of slavery, but in such way that no slave shall be twice accounted for.

"Article ———.

"Congress may appropriate money and otherwise provide for colonizing free colored persons, with their own consent, at any place or places without the United States."

LETTER TO GENERAL J. A. McCLERNAND*

Abraham Lincoln

My dear Sir:

Your interesting communication by the hand of Major Scates is received. I never did ask more, nor ever was willing to accept less, than for all the States, and the people thereof, to take and hold their places and their rights in the Union, under the Constitution of the United States. For this alone have I felt authorized to struggle and I seek neither more nor less now. Still, to use a coarse but an expressive figure, "broken eggs cannot be mended." I have issued the Emancipation Proclamation, and I cannot retract it. After the commencement of hostilities, I struggled nearly a year and a half to get along without touching the "institution"; and when finally I conditionally determined to touch it, I gave a hundred days' fair notice of my purpose to all the States and people, within

* Jan. 8, 1863, in *Works*, VIII, 181–183 (1894).

which time they could have turned it wholly aside by simply again becoming good citizens of the United States.

They chose to disregard it, and I made the peremptory proclamation on what appeared to me to be a military necessity. And being made, it must stand. As to the States not included in it, of course they can have their rights in the Union as of old. Even the people of the States included, if they choose, need not to be hurt by it. Let them adopt systems of apprenticeship for the colored people, conforming substantially to the most approved plans of gradual emancipation; and with the aid they can have from the General Government they may be nearly as well off, in this respect, as if the present trouble had not occurred, and much better off than they can possibly be if the contest continues persistently.

As to any dread of my having a "purpose to enslave or exterminate the whites of the South," I can scarcely believe that such dread exists. It is too absurd. I believe you can be my personal witness that no man is less to be dreaded for undue severity in any case.

If the friends you mention really wish to have peace upon the old terms, they should act at once. Every day makes the case more difficult. They can so act with entire safety, so far as I am concerned.

I think you had better not make this letter public; but you may rely confidently on my standing by whatever I have said in it. Please write me if anything more comes to light.

Yours very truly, A. Lincoln

PROCLAMATION OF AMNESTY AND RECONSTRUCTION*

Abraham Lincoln

I, Abraham Lincoln, President of the United States, do proclaim, declare, and make known to all persons who have, directly or by implication, participated in the existing rebellion, except as hereinafter excepted, that a full pardon is hereby granted to them and each of them, with restoration of all rights of property, except as to slaves, and in property cases where rights of third parties shall have intervened, and upon the condition that every such person shall take and subscribe an oath, and thenceforward keep and maintain said oath inviolate; and which oath shall be registered for permanent preservation, and shall be of the tenor and effect following, to-wit:

I, ———, do solemnly swear, in presence of almighty God, that I will henceforth faithfully support, protect, and defend the Constitution of the

* Dec. 8, 1863, in *Works*, IX, 219–222 (1894).

United States, and the union of the States thereunder; and that I will, in like manner, abide by and faithfully support all acts of Congress passed during the existing rebellion with reference to slaves, so long and so far as not repealed, modified, or held void by Congress, or by decision of the Supreme Court; and that I will, in like manner, abide by and faithfully support all proclamations of the President made during the existing rebellion having reference to slaves, so long and so far as not modified or declared void by decision of the Supreme Court. So help me God.

And I do further proclaim, declare, and make known that whenever, in any of the States of Arkansas, Texas, Louisiana, Mississippi, Tennessee, Alabama, Georgia, Florida, South Carolina, and North Carolina, a number of persons, not less than one tenth in number of the votes cast in such State at the presidential election of the year of our Lord one thousand eight hundred and sixty, each having taken the oath aforesaid and not having since violated it, and being a qualified voter by the election law of the State existing immediately before the so-called act of secession, and excluding all others, shall reestablish a State government which shall be republican, and in no wise contravening said oath, such shall be recognized as the true government of the State, and the State shall receive thereunder the benefits of the constitutional provision which declares that "the United States shall guaranty to every State in this Union a republican form of government, and shall protect each of them against invasion; and, on application of the legislature, or the executive (when the legislature cannot be convened), against domestic violence."

DOCUMENTARY HISTORY OF RECONSTRUCTION*
W. L. Fleming

Regulations for Freedmen in Louisiana

Whereas it was formerly made the duty of the police jury to make suitable regulations for the police of slaves within the limits of the parish; and whereas slaves have become emancipated by the action of the ruling powers; and whereas it is necessary for public order, as well as for the comfort and correct deportment of said freedmen, that suitable regulations should be established for their government in their changed condition, the following ordinances are adopted with the approval of the United States military authorities commanding in said parish, viz:

Sec. 1. *Be it ordained by the police jury of the parish of St. Landry,*

* Volume 1, pages 279–292 (1906).

That no negro shall be allowed to pass within the limits of said parish without special permit in writing from his employer. Whoever shall violate this provision shall pay a fine of two dollars and fifty cents, or in default thereof shall be forced to work four days on the public road, or suffer corporeal punishment as provided hereinafter.

Sec. 3. No negro shall be permitted to rent or keep a house within said parish. Any negro violating this provision shall be immediately ejected and compelled to find an employer; and any person who shall rent, or give the use of any house to any negro, in violation of this section, shall pay a fine of five dollars for each offence.

Sec. 4. Every negro is required to be in the regular service of some white person, or former owner, who shall be held responsible for the conduct of said negro. But said employer or former owner may permit said negro to hire his own time by special permission in writing, which permission shall not extend over seven days at any one time. Any negro violating the provisions of this section shall be fined five dollars for each offence, or in default of the payment thereof shall be forced to work five days on the public road, or suffer corporeal punishment as hereinafter provided.

Sec. 8. No negro shall sell, barter, or exchange any articles of merchandise or traffic within said parish without the special written permission of his employer, specifying the article of sale, barter or traffic. Any one thus offending shall pay a fine of one dollar for each offence, and suffer the forfeiture of said articles, or in default of the payment of said fine shall work one day on the public road, or suffer corporeal punishment as hereinafter provided.

Sec. 14. The corporeal punishment provided for in the foregoing sections shall consist in confining the body of the offender within a barrel placed over his or her shoulders, in the manner practiced in the army, such confinement not to continue longer than twelve hours, and for such time within the aforesaid limit as shall be fixed by the captain or chief of patrol who inflicts the penalty.

Mississippi Vagrant Law

Sec. 2. . . . All freedmen, free negroes and mulattoes in this State, over the age of eighteen years, found on the second Monday in January, 1866, or thereafter, with no lawful employment or business, or found unlawfully assembling themselves together, either in the day or night time, and all white persons so assembling themselves with freedmen, free negroes or mulattoes, or usually associating with freedmen, free negroes or mulattoes, on terms of equality, or living in adultery or fornication with a freed woman, free negro or mulatto, shall be deemed vagrants, and on conviction thereof shall be fined in a sum not exceeding, in the case of a freedman, free negro, or mulatto, fifty dollars, and a white man two hundred dollars, and imprisoned at the discretion of the court, the free negro not exceeding ten days, and the white man not exceeding six months.

Sec. 5. . . . All fines and forfeitures collected under the provisions of this act shall be paid into the county treasury for general county purposes, and in case any freedman, free negro or mulatto shall fail for five days after the imposition of any fine or forfeiture upon him or her for violation of any of the provisions of this act to pay the same, that it shall be, and is hereby, made the duty of the sheriff of the proper county to hire out said freedman, free negro or mulatto, to any person who will, for the shortest period of service, pay said fine and forfeiture and all costs: *Provided,* A preference shall be given to the employer, if there be one, in which case the employer shall be entitled to deduct and retain the amount so paid from the wages of such freedman, free negro or mulatto, then due or to become due; and in case said freedman, free negro, or mulatto cannot be hired out, he or she may be dealt with as a pauper.

Civil Rights of Freedmen in Mississippi

Sec. 5. . . . Every freedman, free negro, and mulatto shall, on the second Monday of January, one thousand eight hundred and sixty-six and annually thereafter, have a lawful home or employment, and shall have written evidence thereof as follows, to-wit: if living in any incorporated city, town, or village, a license from the mayor thereof; and if living outside of an incorporated city, town, or village, from the member of the board of police of his beat, authorizing him or her to do irregular and job work; or a written contract, as provided in section six in this act; which licenses may be revoked for cause at any time by the authority granting the same.

Sec. 7. . . . Every civil officer shall, and every person may, arrest and carry back to his or her legal employer any freedman, free negro, or mulatto who shall have quit the service of his or her employer before the expiration of his or her term of service without good cause. . . .

North Carolina "Black Code"

Chapter 5, section 3, of the revised code, as amended by this act, reads thus:

"The master or mistress shall provide for the apprentice diet, clothes, lodging, and accommodations fit and necessary; and such apprentice shall teach or cause to be taught to read and write, and the elementary rules of arithmetic; and at the expiration of every apprenticeship shall pay to each apprentice six dollars, and furnish him with a new suit of clothes, and a new Bible; and if upon complaint made to the court of pleas and quarter sessions it shall appear that any apprentice is ill-used, or not taught the trade, profession and employment to which he was bound, or that any apprentice is not taught reading, writing, and arithmetic as aforesaid, the court may remove and bind him to some other suitable person."

AN AMERICAN DILEMMA*
G. Myrdal

[Myrdal has started to describe what he calls the "etiquette of race relations" that exists in the American South. He says that its fundamental purpose is to establish the inferiority of the Negro and to prevent interracial sexual relations. The strongest taboos are accordingly against all forms of physical intimacy: actual sexual contact, flirtation, dancing, swimming or eating together, use of shared toilets and fountains, and so on.]

The conversation between whites and Negroes in the South is heavily regimented by etiquette. In *content* the serious conversation should be about those business interests which are shared (as when a white employer instructs his Negro employee or when there is a matter to be discussed concerning the welfare of the Negro community) or it should be polite but formal inquiry into personal affairs (either a white or a Negro person may inquire as to the state of the other's health or business). There can generally be no serious discussion — although there can be the banter of polite conversation or joking — about local or national politics, international relations, or "news," on the one hand, or about items connected with the course of daily life, such as the struggle for existence or the search for pleasure, on the other hand. There are exceptions, of course. Some white women use their Negro servants as sources of gossip and local news.

The conversation is even more regimented in *form* than in content. The Negro is expected to address the white person by the title of "Mr.," "Mrs.," or "Miss." The old slavery title of "Master" disappeared during Reconstruction entirely and was replaced by "Boss" or sometimes "Cap" or "Cap'n." From his side, the white man addresses the Negro by his first name, no matter if they hardly know each other, or by the epithets "boy," "uncle," "elder," "aunty," or the like, which are applied without regard to age. If he wishes to show a little respect without going beyond the etiquette, he uses the exaggerated titles of "doctor," "lawyer," "professor," or other occupational titles, even though the term is not properly applicable. The epithets "nigger" and "darky" are commonly used even in the presence of Negroes, though it is usually well

* Pages 610–615 (1944). Footnotes are omitted.

known that Negroes find them insulting. That there has been a slight tendency for this pattern to break down is shown by the use of the Negro's last name without title in many recent business relations. Too, a few salesmen will actually call Negroes by their titles of "Mr.," "Mrs.," and "Miss" in order to gain them as customers. Also significant is the fact that upper and middle class whites in the Upper South are beginning to call upper class Negroes by these titles.

Another aspect of the form of conversation between Negroes and whites is the rule that a Negro must never contradict the white man nor mention a delicate subject directly. That is, a good part of the Negro's conversation must be circumlocutory rather than direct. This is much less common now than formerly, but it has not disappeared. The *tone* of the conversation also was formerly fixed and still remains so to a certain extent: the Negro was to use deferential tones and words; the white man was to use condescending tones and words. If the white man became angry or violent in his speech, the Negro could not reciprocate.

The apparent purpose of this etiquette of conversation is the same as that of all the etiquette of race relations. It is to provide a continual demonstration that the Negro is inferior to the white man and "recognizes" his inferiority. This serves not only to flatter the ego of the white man, but also to keep the Negro from real participation in the white man's social life. Conversation with other people is the principal way to participate in the lives of those people, to understand each other completely. In the North, the caste etiquette of conversation does not exist. That is, whites do not expect it. When Southern Negroes act it out they usually embarrass the average Northerner more than they please him. Where Negroes and whites meet socially on the same class level in the North (which they do relatively seldom because of residential and institutional segregation) they actually may come to understand one another. Southern whites have a myth that they "know" their Negroes. This is largely incorrect, and in their franker moments white Southerners will admit that they feel that Negroes are hiding something from them. They cannot know Negroes as they know other human beings because in all their contacts Negroes must, or feel they must, pose in a framework of etiquette. "What the white southern people see who 'know their Negroes' is the role that they have forced the Negro to accept, his caste role." The racial etiquette is a most potent device for bringing persons together physically and having them cooperate for economic ends, while at the same time separating them completely on a social and personal level.

Closely allied to the forms of speech are the forms of bodily action when whites and Negroes appear before one another. For a Negro to sit down in the same room with a white person is not taboo, but it may be done usually only at the request of the white person. Since the invitation is often not extended, it frequently happens that Negroes are standing in the presence of whites, even those who are of the same or lower socio-economic status as themselves. In conferences and public places, Negroes sit down without invitation, but there is usually segregation: Negroes will sit at one end of the conference table, or in the rear of or on one side of a courtroom, or in the balcony or gallery of a theater which they are permitted to enter. In the North, Negroes, when they are allowed to enter, take seats much in the same manner that whites do. Whatever segregation in seating there is in the North would seem to have a voluntary or class basis rather than a strict caste basis as in the South. Many theaters in the North, however, refuse to let a Negro enter, or, if they are in a state with a civil rights law, they try to find some excuse to make him stay away voluntarily. Where seats are reserved, the management will often try to sell seats to Negroes in a special section. Changing seats on the part of individual whites also will sometimes isolate Negroes in a Northern theater.

In general, the American is a great and indiscriminate hand-shaker. The ceremony is to him a symbol of friendliness and basic human equality. The partial taboo against shaking hands with Negroes is, therefore, significant. Formerly there was practically no hand-shaking between members of the two races except for that occurring when a Negro house servant would greet his returning master. The taboo is much less strong now, but the relation — in so far as it exists — is, as we have mentioned, entirely one-sided: the white man in the South may offer to shake hands with the Negro, but the Negro may not offer his hand to the white man. A white woman practically never shakes hands with a Negro man. The greeting of the Negro has traditionally been a bow and a removal of thc hat. This, too, has become much less demanded. While talking, the traditional pattern was for the Negro to remain with hat off, with eyes directed on the ground, and with foot scraping the ground to "demonstrate" that he was incapable of standing and talking like a human being. This pattern, too, has rapidly been going into discard.

If he had to come into a white man's house, the rule was, and still is in most parts of the South, that the Negro must enter by the rear door. Since Negroes could plan this activity in advance they often avoided it by avoiding the need to talk to a white man in his house (by deliberately waiting until he came out to the street, or by going to his office, or by calling to him from the street or from the front yard). This etiquette form still exists for the most part, but many exceptions could be cited. Also, the increase in the number of houses without back doors is helping to break down the pattern. When a white man enters a Negro's house, he cannot be expected to show any signs of respect. He will enter without knocking; he will not remove his hat; he will not stand up when a Negro woman enters the room; he may even insist that the Negro occupants stand in his presence (the old-fashioned Negro will not presume to sit down anyway unless asked). There is little occasion for a white man to enter a Negro's house: if he wants to see a Negro he will send for him or call him on the telephone, or drive in his car to his house and blow the horn. White salesmen have found that they gained business if they showed Negroes some respect in their own homes, so they quite frequently violate the etiquette. Practically nothing of any phase of the etiquette of bodily action, or of that associated with entering the houses of members of the other race, exists in the North.

In an essential and factual sense the cumbersome racial etiquette is "un-American." American civilization has received its deepest imprints from immigrants from the lower classes in Europe who were not much versed in the intricacies and shibboleths of upper class ceremonial behavior in the old countries and who often consciously resented them on ideological grounds. The equalitarian Revolutionary *ethos* also endorsed simple and unaffected manners. Aristocratic travelers from England and other countries during colonial times complained about the Americans not caring about social distinctions of birth and breeding. This is part of the historical background for the European (and American) myth of the Americans as being particularly "materialistic." European observers with democratic leanings, from de Tocqueville on, have, on the contrary, found the lack of mannerisms of the typical American, his friendly, spontaneous, and equalitarian ways of meeting other human beings, a great charm of the new continent. The symbols a culture acquires are no accident and no forms are of more intrinsic importance than those of human contacts and relations. All these observers have, therefore, related this trait to the democratic and Christian *ethos* of the American Creed. When democratic European countries are said to become "Americanized," one of the positive elements in this change has commonly been recognized to be the throwing off of the inherited class etiquette, which is no longer functional in a modern democracy, and the breaking up of class isolation. Against this background, the caste etiquette in America stands out as a glaring contradiction. It indicates the split in the American's moral personality.

3. *These Days of Reform: The Benign Use of Racial Language*

One might consider that this has been an excursion into a region of our history that is little studied and, however tragic, of little relevance to current issues. That was all a hundred years and a Civil War ago; since that time we have amended the Constitution, passed various statutes protecting the rights of all irrespective of race, issued epoch-making judicial opinions — and this has changed it all. But you know that "abolition" is not an easy matter. Certainly the passage of statutes does not instantly eradicate patterns of discrimination and deprivation. See Justice Douglas's concurring opinion in *Jones v. Alfred H. Mayer Co.*, 392 U.S. 409, 444 (1968), for a catalog of existing discrimination. On the other hand, the legal and other work of the last century has had some effect. Very few people would say either that there has been no progress since 1840 or that the problem of race has now been met. What has been achieved, where are we now? You are asked to look at the laws of today as evidence from which to draw inferences about a society. How is racial language used by the law, with what purpose and effect? What characters does this literature create for the black man and the white man?

The final question will not surprise you: where do we go from here? Some nonlegal literature that may help you is listed.

For general background, see W. Cash, *The Mind of the South* (1941); C. Johnson, *Growing Up in the Black Belt* (1941); G. Myrdal, *An American Dilemma* (1944); Faulkner, *Absalom, Absalom!* (1936).

For current views, see G. Jackson, *Soledad Brother* (1970); E. Knight, *Black Voices from Prison* (1970); E. Cleaver, *Soul on Ice* (1968); Malcolm X, *Autobiography* (1965); D. Gregory, *Nigger!* (1964); J. Baldwin, *The Fire Next Time* (1963); J. Griffin, *Black Like Me* (1961); Moynihan et al., "*The Negro Family in America*," in L. Rainwater, *The Moynihan Report and the Politics of Controversy* (1967); C. Silberman, *Crisis in Black and White* (1964). See also C. Garry, *Minimizing Racism in Jury Trials: The Voir Dire Conducted by Charles R. Garry in People of California v. Huey P. Newton* (1969).

One can regard much of this literature as an enterprise in the discovery and definition of character. What ways can the black man find to talk about himself and the white man? How can the white man learn to talk about himself and the black man? You have no doubt read one or more of the books by Malcolm X, Knight, Baldwin, Cleaver, Gregory, Jackson, or other black writers and can ask of each how he defines himself in what he writes.

Here is how one scholar describes the way the black man was portrayed in the abolitionist literature of the nineteenth century:

> Notwithstanding the large amount written on the Negro, the authors were not too successful in their portrayal of the Negro as a character. In poetry and prose the Negro character appears more frequently as a puppet operated by strings than a flesh and blood personality. Stock characterizations became so much a part of the people of these stories that after

meeting a few of them, we know them all. The Negro maiden is usually beautiful without any specialized traits that set her off as an individual. The Negro male is one of heroic proportions, often more kin to the males of the heroic drama than to the males of Africa. Children are often used as characters, but their appeal is largely through sentimentality rather than characterization.*

Can you point to any literature you know of in which talk about the races has moved from caricature to character? There follows now a series of questions about modern legal literature which may elaborate that question.

QUESTIONS: Racial Talk in Modern Law

1. *In Green v. New Kent County, 391 U.S. 430 (1968), the Court held unconstitutional a "freedom of choice" plan for desegregation, under which each student could choose the school he would attend. There was no showing of coercion or intimidation, but very few black students had chosen to attend the white school, and no white student to attend the black school. There was no residential segregation, and students of both races lived all over the county. The Court did not say that freedom of choice could play no part in a valid plan, but held this plan invalid because it placed on the parents and children the responsibility for ensuring desegregation that Brown v. Board of Education (II), 349 U.S. 294 (1955), had placed "squarely on the School Board."*
   a. *How would you have decided this case and why? If you would need more information, indicate what that information is and how you would get it.*
   b. *So far as you can tell from the account given above, how does the Supreme Court define the black people it talks about in New Kent County? Does it talk about them as people? As things? As children?*
   c. *Is it conceivable to you that as a black parent you might prefer to have your child go to a black school? How does the Supreme Court treat the wishes of such people — and in doing so, how does it define them?*
   d. *As the Court says in New Kent County, the holding of Brown (I) was that segregated schools denied black children equal protection of the laws, even if the schools were equal by all objective or tangible criteria. "Does segregation of children in public schools solely on the basis of race, even though the physical facilities and other 'tangible' factors may be equal, deprive children of the minority group of equal educational opportunities? We believe that it does." Brown v. Board of Education (I), 347 U.S. 483, 493 (1954). "Separate education facilities are inherently unequal." Id. at 495. How does this sort of statement define the black child? The black community?*

      Can you imagine another ground for Brown (I) that would be less patronizing? On what basis, for example, do you suppose segregated schools were prohibited in the District of Columbia, to whose govern-

* J. Hopson, *Attitudes Towards the Negro as an Expression of English Romanticism* 332–333 (1948).

ment the equal protection clause does not apply? See Bolling v. Sharpe, 347 U.S. 497 (1954); cf. Hobson v. Hansen, 269 F. Supp. 401 (D.D.C. 1967).

e. New Kent County was a class action on behalf of all blacks deprived of racially integrated education. On what basis is it assumed that these plaintiffs represent all blacks? Could a white person thus represent all blacks? If not, why can a black? What way of talking about people is this? Compare Hicks v. Weaver, 302 F. Supp. 619 (E.D. La. 1969).

f. Notice that judicial action in New Kent County had to await a suit by a proper party. What assumptions about people, especially black people, underlie this practice? Are these assumptions consistent with those implicit in the holding of that case?

2. Suppose a school district, pursuant to a desegregation plan approved by the local federal court, closed down the black high school and sent the black children to school with the white children. It reassigned each black teacher to the integrated high school only if he was the most highly qualified applicant for a vacant position; otherwise it terminated his employment. Is that a proper practice? What standard applies to such reassignments, and where do you find it? Assuming the practice is improper, what relief is appropriate? See North Carolina Teachers Assn. v. Asheboro, 393 F.2d 736 (4th Cir. 1968). Compare Sparks v. Griffin, 460 F.2d 433 (5th Cir. 1972); Montgomery County v. Carr, 400 F.2d 1 (5th Cir. 1968); Brewer v. School Board of Norfolk, 397 F.2d 37 (4th Cir. 1968)

a. Is the danger against which the law should guard here that the teachers will be fired because they are black? How would you decide whether a teacher was fired because he was black?

b. Compare a situation in which a white teacher alleges arbitrary dismissal. What are the differences, if any, between an inquiry into "arbitrariness" and "racial motivation"? Is it simply that there is a different burden of proof? See Freeman v. Gould Special School District, 405 F.2d 1153 (8th Cir. 1969).

c. Or is it simply that the duty to achieve integration with all deliberate speed requires that black teachers be retained if they meet minimum standards of competence, whether or not they are the most qualified individuals available? Do you believe the Constitution should be held to require that result? Explain your position.

d. Suppose a school board on its own initiative adopted the policy of hiring and retaining competent black teachers without regard to the relative quality of white competitors for the same position. Would that policy be constitutional? Prepare an outline of an argument for a successful black applicant. How would you answer the argument that the white teachers had been fired, or not hired, "because they were white"? Now prepare an outline of an argument for a white teacher who is displaced by a black under such a system.

e. Suppose a school board promoted blacks to administrative positions in preference to better-qualified whites. Would this be constitutional? Desirable? See Porcelli v. Titus, 302 F. Supp. 726 (D.N.J. 1969).

3. The court in Asheboro seems to say what the law requires is that the same criteria of professional capability be applied to members of both races. If such criteria were applied, and the black teachers were found less well qualified, would any argument remain that their discharge was uncon-

stitutional? What might you argue on their behalf? Consider Gaston County v. United States, 288 F. Supp. 678 (D.D.C. 1968), aff'd, 395 U.S. 285 (1969), which held that it was illegal to use a literacy test for voter qualification purposes, however evenhandedly, in a community in which some people had received segregated (and hence constitutionally inferior) education. Would the same argument apply to ensure jobs to less qualified black teachers? See generally Fiss, "Gaston County v. United States: The Fruition of the Freezing Principle," 1969 Sup. Ct. Rev. 379.

Do you see the choice the law faces here as one between two different ways of talking about people? Compare your reading of Alcestis (see pages 274–278 supra).

4. Does it assist your analysis of the teacher appointment and retention cases to ask whose interest the constitutional law governing this matter should be meant to protect or advance?
5. To continue with the voting problem, suppose the federal legislature was convinced that registration technicalities were widely used in some states to prevent blacks from voting. Could it pass a statute providing that the following conditions to the voting privilege in state elections are invalid as applied to blacks: (a) any literacy test; (b) the requirement that one register prior to the day of the election; (c) the prohibition against taking advisers into the election booth?

   Suppose the law were even more radical: "All blacks of proper age resident in the voting district are assumed to have voted for whichever candidate a federal inspector certifies is the one most favorable to the black interest"? Or suppose all blacks were given two votes? How would such a benign statute talk about black people – as people, or things, or what?
6. Here are some more examples of the law talking about race.
   a. Can an employer who is subject to nondiscrimination laws use standard intelligence tests to assign and promote his employees if that results in blacks being grouped in the worst jobs? See Griggs v. Duke Power Co., 401 U.S. 424 (1971). Can a school district assign students to different schools or classes according to their I.Q. levels as determined by standard tests? See Stell v. Board of Public Education, 387 F.2d 486 (5th Cir. 1967); Larry P. v. Riles, 343 F. Supp. 1306 (N.D. Cal. 1972).
   b. Under what circumstances is the racial composition of the trial jury or grand jury a reason for reversing a conviction, and why? Is it enough that the panel from which the juries are drawn include blacks, or has a black the right to have members of his race actually on the jury, or perhaps a right to trial before a jury consisting entirely of blacks? How do you decide? See Witcher v. Peyton, 405 F.2d 725 (4th Cir. 1969). Is an Alabama statute providing for jury selection based upon "community esteem" automatically unconstitutional? If it is applied in a discriminatory way, who can complain, under what circumstances, and what relief can he obtain? See Carter v. Jury Commission of Greene County, 396 U.S. 320 (1970); Turner v. Fouche, 396 U.S. 346 (1970).

      How about the judge? Has a black defendant the right to a black judge? Must the relevant judiciary contain a proportionate number of blacks? What can "racial equality" mean here?

c. We are all acquainted with the gerrymander as a political weapon in this country. Suppose a Republican legislature reapportions legislative districts in such a way that a ward of Irish Catholic working-class Democrats is split, each half being attached to a suburban Republican ward. Is this unconstitutional? If the ward thus divided is largely black (and Democratic), is the problem different, and why? See Ince v. Rockefeller, 290 F. Supp. 878 (S.D.N.Y. 1968); Whitcomb v. Chavis, 403 U.S. 124 (1971); Gomillion v. Lightfoot, 364 U.S. 339 (1960).

d. Except in cases in which racial classifications are used to advance the interests of members of minority races, does the Constitution require officials to be color-blind? For example, can a police officer take the race of a suspect into account in determining whether he is in sufficient danger to warrant a "frisk" within the rule of Terry v. Ohio, 392 U.S. 1 (1968)? See Smith v. Swenson, 328 F. Supp. 747 (W.D. Mo. 1971); cf. Rollins v. Shannon, 292 F. Supp. 580 (E.D. Mo. 1968); Lankford v. Gelston, 364 F.2d 197 (4th Cir. 1966). Can race be used by a judge in making an estimate of probable recidivism at sentencing, assuming that there is empirical evidence of a correlation between race and recidivism? Is a witness in a criminal case prohibited from identifying people by race? See United States ex rel. Feldt v. Follette, 298 F. Supp. 1298 (S.D.N.Y. 1969). Is an employer prohibited from using arrest records in hiring, on the grounds that this is racially biased data? See Gregory v. Litton Systems, Inc., 316 F. Supp. 401 (C.D. Cal. 1970). Is race a factor that a moneylender can use to determine the trustworthiness of a borrower? See Local Finance Co. v. Massachusetts Commn. Against Discrimination, 355 Mass. 10, 242 N.E.2d 536 (1968). Is race a legitimate factor for a court or adoption agency to consider in placing children? See Fountaine v. Fountaine, 9 Ill. App. 2d 482, 133 N.E.2d 532 (1956).

e. Can black police officers be assigned on a regular and exclusive basis to patrol a black area? Can white officers be so assigned to black areas? See Baker v. St. Petersburg, 400 F.2d 294 (5th Cir. 1968); Allen v. City of Mobile, 331 F. Supp. 1134 (S.D. Ala. 1971).

f. The Internal Revenue Code provides various tax benefits to private educational institutions. If a private school excludes all but white pupils, are these tax benefits still available under that statute? If so, is the statute unconstitutional? See Green v. Connally, 330 F. Supp. 1150 (1971), aff'd sub nom. Coit v. Green, 404 U.S. 997 (1972); Bob Jones University v. Connally, 341 F. Supp. 277 (D.S.C. 1971).

g. Now ask yourself this general question: what does it mean to use the language of race, and how can that language be controlled? How should the law respond to the fact that people do use and act upon this language? Which of these two approaches is better: legal talk about the black person as a person, ensuring his rights to equal treatment; or legal talk about him as a racial entity, a thing to be moved around, sent to school, hired and promoted, in order to achieve a general social goal of integration? Which approach would mark a greater advance from the language and logic of slavery? Which would more effectively remove "badges of slavery"? Cf. Jones v. Alfred H. Mayer Co., 392 U.S. 409 (1968).

7. *Ask of the following case how the law here talks about people and in what respects this is an advance over the language of racial slavery.*

PEOPLE ex rel. ALTMAN v. BOARD OF EDUCATION
90 Ill. App. 2d 21, 234 N.E.2d 362 (1967)

Murphy, P.J.: This is a mandamus action, in which the relator seeks to compel the transfer of her daughter, Faye Diament, from the Hyde Park High School to the South Shore High School, because of emotional and psychological difficulties resulting from her attendance at Hyde Park. After a trial on the merits, the trial court denied the petition and the relator appeals.

The relator, Irene J. Altman, and her family live at 6921 Merrill Avenue, Chicago. Her daughter, Faye Diament, was a June 1964 graduate of the O'Keeffe Elementary School. In September 1964, Faye enrolled in the Hyde Park High School and commenced attending classes. At that time, 71st Street was the south boundary of Hyde Park High School and separated it from South Shore High School.

On April 15, 1965, the Board of Education, by resolution, established a new district [District 22] and extended the north boundary of the South Shore High School to 67th Street, which included the O'Keeffe school and the residence of the relator.

Subsequent to the adoption of the April 15, 1965, resolution, the relator, in person and in writing, requested a transfer of Faye to the South Shore High School. The transfer request was denied because of a Board policy and practice that assignment of elementary school pupils to high school affects future graduating classes only and does not retroactively apply to graduates of preceding years already enrolled in and attending high school.

The petition alleged the following reasons for the allowance of the transfer:

a. The Hyde Park High School is further away in distance and in a less safe area.

b. None of the girl classmates of her own race from the O'Keeffe elementary school now attend Hyde Park; most of them are at South Shore High School.

c. The only girl classmates of her own ethnic background in any of her classes at Hyde Park High School, live at the north end of that district and will be going to the new Kenwood High School next year.

d. That the South Shore High School is 3 or more blocks closer to relator's address than the Hyde Park High School and in a safer neighborhood; that the South Shore High School is an integrated school, whereas the Hyde Park High School is not, there being less than 10%

white in attendance there, and will be completely resegregated next year.

e. None of her present girl classmates live in her immediate neighborhood which deprives her of a traveling companion.

f. There are no students at Hyde Park with whom she can form a kinship, boys and girls of her peer group associated with her in social, religious, and cultural activities, mostly attend South Shore High School, none going to Hyde Park High School.

g. That with the graduation of her brother, her role at Hyde Park High School will be that of a "loner" which is not conducive to her best interests and will have an adverse effect on her development and psychological welfare, as set forth in a medical report sent to defendant, Margaret Clyne, at the suggestion of Mr. McKeag, an Assistant Superintendent on Dr. Willis' staff.

The petition included as an exhibit a letter dated July 15, 1966, from Curtis C. Melnick, District Superintendent, addressed to the relator, in which it is said:

"You have been told on at least four occasions involving personal conferences with the counseling staff at Hyde Park High School, Dr. Blyth, and myself that you have no grounds whatsoever to request a transfer of your daughter, Faye Diament, to South Shore High School. There is no justification for your continuing to phone and to write to change this situation. . . .

"In summary, there is no basis for granting a transfer to Faye to attend South Shore High School."

Another exhibit attached to the petition with a letter dated August 26, 1966, written by Dr. Eileen C. Stack, Associate Superintendent in charge of Administration, and addressed to the husband of the relator, in which it is said:

"I am sorry that it is not possible for Faye to attend South Shore, but I am sure you understand that the same principle must be applied to all students in a given grade level and to deviate would be to grant preferential treatment to some and not to others."

At the trial, the relator and her daughter, Faye Diament, testified in detail as to the reasons for the requested transfer. The testimony of the relator included: "My daughter comes from school at night on the CTA bus and walks. She doesn't have anyone to come home with. I drive her to school in the morning. Her classes are over at approximately two or three. Depending. I leave my job at quarter to five. As to whether either Faye or my son has been attacked in the Hyde Park area, to Faye, nothing has happened. My son has been beaten up."

Defendants' authorities cited to show "that the question of what school a pupil shall attend is for determination by the school officials and not for the courts," include *Board of Education etc., v. Board of Education*, 323 Ill. 152, p. 158, 153 N.E. 584, p. 586 (1926), . . . where the [Illinois] Supreme Court said:

"We have heretofore held . . . that it is not within the province of the courts to determine the question of what high school is the more convenient for high school pupils to attend, and there are many decisions to the effect that such a question is properly left by the legislature to the decision of a ministerial officer."

Conceding that the school a pupil shall attend is primarily a question for the determination of the school officials, we believe that the school authorities and the courts should be ever concerned with the "social and emotional problems" of the students to see that the students receive "a good common school education."

It is the rule that courts "will not use a writ of mandamus to compel a party to perform an act unless it is affirmatively made to appear that it is his clear duty to do so; the petitioner must establish every material fact necessary to show the plain duty of the respondent before courts will interfere. . . . No intendments will be indulged in to support the issuance of the writ." . . . If any reasonable doubt exists as to the question of discretion or want of discretion, the courts should hesitate to interfere, preferring to extend the benefit of the doubt in favor of the school officials. . . .

Examining this record in the light of the foregoing guidelines, we believe that the relator has failed to establish her right to have the writ issue, and the trial court was correct in denying the petition.

Affirmed.

4. What Is a Race?

Before deciding how the law should use racial language, we should ask what racial distinctions are perceived and expressed in our society. What differences among groups do these distinctions reflect, and for what purposes are they articulated? Skin color is not what people respond to; what do they respond to, and why?

In most of the questions so far I have spoken as if there were only two races in America, the white and the black. What other races are there? Go back to the cases and questions in Section E3 and ask if you would reach a different result if the case involved not a black but: an Oriental; a Mexican-American; a Puerto Rican; a Lithuanian immigrant; an American Indian; a white person in a community dominated by blacks. What is a "race" anyway?

HERNANDEZ v. TEXAS
347 U.S. 475 (1954)

WARREN, C.J., delivered the opinion of the Court.

The petitioner, Pete Hernandez, was indicted for the murder of one Joe Espinosa by a grand jury in Jackson County, Texas. He was convicted and sentenced to life imprisonment. The Texas Court of Criminal Appeals affirmed the judgment of the trial court. — Tex. Cr. R. —, 251 S.W.2d 531. Prior to the trial, the petitioner, by his counsel, offered timely motions to quash the indictment and the jury panel. He alleged that persons of Mexican descent were systematically excluded from service as jury commissioners, grand jurors, and petit jurors, although there were such persons fully qualified to serve residing in Jackson County. . . .

In numerous decisions, this Court has held that it is a denial of the equal protection of the laws to try a defendant of a particular race or color under an indictment issued by a grand jury, or before a petit jury, from which all persons of his race or color have, solely because of that race or color, been excluded by the State, whether acting through its legislature, its courts, or its executive or administrative officers. Although the Court has had little occasion to rule on the question directly, it has been recognized since *Strauder v. West Virginia*, 100 U.S. 303, that the exclusion of a class of persons from jury service on grounds other than race or color may also deprive a defendant who is a member of that class of the constitutional guarantee of equal protection of the laws. The State of Texas would have us hold that there are only two classes — white and Negro — within the contemplation of the Fourteenth Amendment. The decisions of this Court do not support that view. And, except where the question presented involves the exclusion of persons of Mexican descent from juries, Texas courts have taken a broader view of the scope of the equal protection clause.

Throughout our history differences in race and color have defined easily identifiable groups which have at times required the aid of the courts in securing equal treatment under the laws. But community prejudices are not static, and from time to time other differences from the community norm may define other groups which need the same protection. Whether such a group exists within a community is a question of fact. When the existence of a distinct class is demonstrated, and it is further shown that the laws, as written or as applied, single out that class for different treatment not based on some reasonable classification, the guarantees of the Constitution have been violated. The Fourteenth

Amendment is not directed solely against discrimination due to a "two-class theory" — that is, based upon differences between "white" and Negro.

Circumstances or chance may well dictate that no persons in a certain class will serve on a particular jury or during some particular period. But it taxes our credulity to say that mere chance resulted in there being no members of this class among the over six thousand jurors called in the past 25 years. The result bespeaks discrimination, whether or not it was a conscious decision on the part of any individual jury commissioner. The judgment of conviction must be reversed.

To say that this decision revives the rejected contention that the Fourteenth Amendment requires proportional representation of all the component ethnic groups of the community on every jury ignores the facts. The petitioner did not seek proportional representation, nor did he claim a right to have persons of Mexican descent sit on the particular juries which he faced. His only claim is the right to be indicted and tried by juries from which all members of his class are not systematically excluded — juries selected from among all qualified persons regardless of national origin or descent. To this much, he is entitled by the Constitution.

Reversed.

QUESTIONS

1. *The Court says that whether there exists a group whose exclusion from jury rolls should invalidate a conviction is a question of "fact." Is this a workable notion? How would you prepare evidence on this question?*
2. *Does a homosexual have a right to be tried by a jury from which homosexuals are not excluded? Does it depend upon whether his crime involves homosexuality? Does a hippie have a corresponding right? A drunk? A burglar?*
3. *Who can object to exclusion of members of a group from jury rolls: only defendants who are members of the group? If a white civil rights worker is tried, can the state exclude blacks from the jury? Is a run-of-the-mill white burglar entitled to blacks on his jury if he wants them? Is the victim entitled to insist upon inclusion of the minority if he thinks that would increase chances of conviction? See Peters v. Kiff, 407 U.S. 493 (1972).*
4. *Does the Hernandez case turn on the definition of a race or of something else?*
5. *Notice that throughout this section I have generally used the word "black" rather than the word "Negro." Does that distinction signify anything to anyone? What purpose does this distinction in racial language — between Negro and black — serve?*
6. *In the case of In re Middleton, 38 U.S.L.W. 2218 (N.Y.C. Civ. Ct.*

1969), a name change was denied to a black who wished to have an African name. What is the significance of this event?

7. To what activity or enterprise is the language of race suited?
   a. "Racial language marks off different groups with different cultural lives, each of which has its contribution to make to the American way of life. To keep alive these differences fosters diversity and variety. And the language of race can be used to ensure equal treatment for all groups." How do you respond? Compare Deloria, "The Great American White Wash," Denver Post, Feb. 21, 1971 (magazine section).
   b. Return to the problems of custody and adoption. Courts generally say race shall be just one factor of many bearing on the decision. Does that sort of statement make sense? One can see roughly how one might analyze competing homes for level of affection, stability, economic advantage, socially acceptable values, etc., and can imagine a scale of possibilities under each heading, with a scale of priorities among them. This may be a very crude way to make or talk about judgments but, one might say, it does tell us something. Where would you fit racial identity into such a pattern of thought and expression?
   c. Somehow race tends to count either for nothing or for everything. Why should this be? What is there about racial language which makes it take over any conversation in which it is used?
   d. The labels "guilty" and "insane" and "married" imply simple, binary systems, just like racial labels. One is or one is not what the label says, and everything hangs upon that. What is the difference, then, between such legal labels and racial labels? Here is a suggestion: "The essential difference is that labels expressing legal conclusions are the end product of inquiry and thought of a kind that may be very sophisticated indeed, and which may in practice reflect a great deal of what the labels and its language system seem to leave out. By contrast the racial labels are found, not invented and applied by the law. They really are as irrational and idiotic as legal labels seem to be."
   e. For a case in which a racial label is applied as a matter of legal judgment, see Greene v. New Orleans, 88 So. 2d 76 (La. App. 1956).
   f. Return now to the original question: to what activity or enterprise is racial language especially well suited?
8. Consider again Brown v. Board of Education. How would you decide that case today, and why?
   a. Suppose a county in Mississippi divided its school funds proportionately between white and black students, and provided that there should be a separate school system for each race, each system run by officials elected by the appropriate constituency. Would you hold such a system unconstitutional, and if so, why? Whose interest would you be protecting?
   b. Suppose the two school systems were established in this way, but individual students could attend whatever school they chose. Would you hold that system unconstitutional, and if so, why? Whose interest would you be protecting?
   c. Regard the matter now as an omnipotent legislator: what kind of schools should we have in this country? What reflection, if any, should be given to the "fact" of race?

NEGRO DIALECT IN THE TEACHING OF READING*

W. Stewart

In the latter part of 1965, I had decided to do a Negro-dialect translation of Clement Clarke Moore's famous Christmas poem "A Visit from St. Nicholas" (more widely known as "The Night Before Christmas") for Christmas greetings from the Urban Language Study of the Center for Applied Linguistics. In order to highlight the grammatical differences between nonstandard Negro dialect and standard English, I decided to retain standard-English word spellings in the nonstandard version wherever possible. Thus, I wrote *it's, the, night, before,* and *Christmas,* even though a child might be apt to pronounce /is/, /də/, /nay/,/bifów/, and /kísmɨs/. One modification I made in this rule was that, when the nonstandard pronunciation of a particular Negro-dialect word was better represented by the spelling of some standard-English word other than its direct functional equivalent, that spelling was used. Thus the Negro-dialect verb /fuw/, though equivalent to *fill* in standard English, was spelled *full* in the poem. In addition, the form and sequencing of the events in Moore's original version were recast to make the nonstandard version more in keeping with Negro discourse style and inner-city cultural reality. Some idea of what the result of this translation process looked like can be gotten from the first few lines, which went:

It's the night before Christmas, and here in our house,
It ain't nothing moving, not even no mouse.
There go we-all stockings, hanging high up off the floor,
So Santa Claus can full them up, if he walk in through our door.

For those who are not entirely familiar with this kind of dialect, I should probably point out that the Negro-dialect phrase *There go we-all stockings* does not mean "There go our stockings" in standard English. As often used by Negro children, the idioms *here go* and *there go* serve to point out something (not necessarily in motion) to the listener, and are thus equivalent to standard English *here is/are* and *there is/are,* or to French *voici* and *voilà.*

One evening, while I was working at home on the translation of the poem (a draft of which was in my typewriter, with the original version at the side), two inner-city children dropped by for a visit. While I was busy getting some refreshments for them from the refrigerator, Lenora (then about 12 years old) went over to play with the typewriter and found the draft of the nonstandard version of the poem in it. Lenora was one of the "problem readers" of the public schools; she read school

* In J. Baratz (ed.), *Teaching Black Children To Read* 170–172 (1969).

texts haltingly, with many mistakes, and with little ability to grasp the meaning of what she read. Yet, when she began to read the nonstandard version of the poem, her voice was steady, her word reading accurate, and her sentence intonation was natural (for her dialect, of course). This unexpected success in reading so surprised Lenora that she began to discuss the experience with her little brother. They decided that there was something different about the text, but were unable to tell exactly what it was. To compare, I then had Lenora read the standard English version of the poem, which was sitting beside the typewriter. When she did, all the "problem reader" behaviors returned.

WRITING ASSIGNMENT 11: *Using the Language of Race*

Part One

• *Give an account of an occasion in your life when you were confronted with the fact — is it a fact? — of race. How did you respond? What did you say and do? What language did you use and how did you control it? Did you create a literature of caricature or character, and why? Explain what you did.*

Part Two

• *Can the law do what you did or what you now see you should have done? Why?*

Part Three

• *Tell how the law should respond to the verbal and social fact of race. How should the law talk about race? Give an actual proposal for a statute or a judicial opinion in which you show what we should do. Do you propose the creation of a literature of caricature or character, and why? Explain what you propose.*

WRITING ASSIGNMENT 11, ALTERNATIVE A: *Race and the School System*

• *Pretend that you are an omnipotent legislator. Draft documents establishing a school system of which you would approve. What response do you make to the fact of race in our society? Do you use the language of race, and if so, how do you control it?*

Here you are asked to bring together several different lines of thought about schools: your responses to the questions about the New Kent

County and Asheboro cases, and your conclusion as to how Brown should have been decided (pages 490–492); your own experience of race; and whatever you can make of the Stewart and Labov passages (pages 500, 20). Necessarily involved as well are your general views on schools, your idea of what schools should be like entirely aside from any racial question, and your sense of what can be achieved by the law of race and education. Whose interests are you trying to advance or protect in what you propose?

ASSIGNMENT 11, ALTERNATIVE B: Race and the Law School

• *What response should your law school make to the fact of race in our society? Draft documents expressing a response of which you approve. Do you use the language of race, and if so, how do you control it?*

Consider in particular the following questions.

Suppose a state law school admits as students some members of minority races who do not meet the usual objective criteria for admission, and that this practice denies places to some white applicants who have better objective qualifications. See the "Special Group Program" described above, page 386.

1. Is this practice constitutional, or is it an illegal discrimination based on race? What would you argue on behalf of such a law school? On behalf of a rejected white applicant? See O'Neill, "Preferential Admissions: Equalizing the Access of Minority Groups to Higher Education," 80 Yale L.J. 699–767 (1971).

2. Suppose the members of the minority races receive preferential treatment economically, being given the first claim to scholarship and loan assistance. How would you defend or attack that practice?

3. Suppose the school thus favors only blacks, and an American Indian student is denied admission. What would you argue on his behalf? On behalf of the school?

4. Is the purpose of such a program to make up for social or educational deprivation, or something else? Is the racial label a meaningful one for these purposes? For example, compare the case of a white student from an unemployed family, who has accordingly suffered socially and educationally, with that of a middle class black with C– average from Princeton.

5. What standards should be used for graduating the students defined as special? People have suggested that students in such programs should be graduated from law school even if they do not meet the usual criteria, on the grounds that having some black or Indian or Mexican-American lawyers is better than having none. How do you respond to that suggestion? Do you see this as a problem in talking about people?

6. How does such a proposal define the special students? The teachers? The school? The other students? Are these ways of talking about people consistent with the assumptions that a law school normally makes about people? What happens to a law school that adopts such a program?

7. This is not a hypothetical problem. If you draft a program of this kind, be sure that it is one that you would want your own law school to adopt. Whose interest are you trying to protect or advance?

8. Are you trying to do the impossible here? If you think so, explain why it is impossible.

WRITING ASSIGNMENT 11, ALTERNATIVE C: Race in the Judicial Opinion

• *Draft a judicial opinion disposing of the New Kent County case, Gaston County, Brown v. Board of Education, or any other case involving race that seems to you to present a real difficulty.*

CHAPTER 4

RULES AND RELATIONSHIPS

Having looked at legal literature as a way of thinking about people, as a way of creating and defining character, we now shift our emphasis back to a line of inquiry begun in Chapter 2 and regard it as a way in which people talk to each other, as a way of planning and organizing social experience for the future. The focus moves, that is, from the moment of judgment about another — "How can I do justice to this man and his experience?" — to the establishment of relationships that are meant to work over time, to the process by which one person influences another. As before, we shall concern ourselves in large part with the limits and resources of the form we call the legal rule, for it is this more than anything else that gives structure to legal thought and expression; but in contrast to Chapter 2, our attention here will be upon what might be called the social or operational rather than the intellectual implications of that form. What sorts of relationships can be established in this way and how can they be managed? You are here asked what is implied in the use of the rule as a social instrument: who speaks this way, speaking to whom, and about what? What sort of social life does this form of expression make possible? What does it leave out? What does it mean to become — like you — a master of rules? Think of a group of people you actually know — say, family or friends, or people at school or church, or at the office or the hospital — and ask what it would mean (or has meant) for them to use rules to define and manage their relationships with each other. What other possibilities might there be? Our question might be put this way: what does it mean to say of a relationship or a side of life, "Let's have some rules around here?" And since rules work so differently in different hands, you are also being asked what the art of making rules — and of using them to organize and manage social relationships — consists of and how it is to be exercised. What can you hope to achieve as a maker of rules, against what pressures, and how shall you do it? The major writing assignment in this chapter (page 593) will ask you to respond to that question by drafting a portion of a set of rules for an institution and by explaining what you have done.

This is an enormously complex subject, of course — it really amounts to nothing less than a study of what makes good laws — and we shall have to approach it by stages. You will first be encouraged to look at your own experience of social life, asking how you see it organized and managed (especially in institutional settings) and what place the rule (or other formal statement) has in that process. What are the various ways by which one learns to behave in ordinary life, by which one figures out what is expected of oneself and what to expect of others? Exactly how, for example, does the new soldier in the army learn what it is that his superiors and his peers expect of him? By studying a rule book? There is no doubt that we influence one another's behavior all the time, and that social institutions actually function and social expectations can be managed; but how do these things happen? And what contribution to this activity can be made by a set of rules or other formal statements?

At this point our emphasis will be less upon the form we call the rule (as opposed to other sorts of official declarations) than upon the processes by which social expectations are created and manners formed, and upon the connections between such social experience and various ways of expressing and regulating it in language. Can you find or imagine, for example, a moment in someone's life where a rule or other direction to conduct actually operates, where it restrains or moves him, where it works on his behavior? Can you explain how this happens? In particular instances you can think of, what connections might be drawn between the ways people in fact learn to behave and some formal literature meant to tell them how to conduct themselves?

In the first portion of what follows (Section A1), you will be asked to pursue such questions with respect to particular moments and events in people's lives, both as they appear in various literatures and as you can reconstruct them from your experience or imagination. The next stage of the inquiry (Section A2) will take a turn and focus directly upon the form of legal speech we call the rule; not so specific as to be a mere command, not so general as to be too vague, the rule of the kind we lawyers understand and work with has a sort of middle generality. What are the social and intellectual implications of this form? How does one who speaks this way define himself and his audience? What can be done in this sort of speech, by what art, and what cannot? You will be given a writing assignment meant to test the limits of the rule as a way of organizing social life in specific situations.

In Section B you will be asked to draft part of a set of rules governing a complex institution and to explain what you have done. Here you must reckon with the ways in which rules, once articulated by the lawmaker, are used by others. Little seems to be said on this subject: as we saw in Chapter 2, rules themselves seldom refer to the process of cooperation upon which they depend for any effect they may have in the world. Can the processes by which they are brought to bear on life somehow be expressed and regulated, can the complex set of relationships which they entail be comprehended and controlled? A set of rules seems always to speak with an overconfidence of sublime proportions, as though their very statement achieved one's goals. Can you find a way to qualify this overconfidence, a way of expressing what you really know about the rules you write?

You can see that this assignment builds upon your work in drafting a wrongful death statute; and in connection with your work in this chapter you should perhaps look back at the readings in Chapter 2, Section C, and the paper you wrote for Writing Assignment 5. The task here is enormous, though it is only a beginning. But much is properly expected of you: rules are your field of expertise, and we expect you to know about rules the way the mechanic knows about engines and the farmer knows about grain. It is you to whom we turn as the one who knows what purposes rules are suited to, and what not, and how to discriminate among different kinds of rules. You are the one that can tell your society, your legislature, your court, or your client that it is reaching for the wrong kind of rule, or that it should not be reaching for a rule at all, and why. And it is your art, your understanding of the form, that can see to it that when rules are used they are kept in control, that they influence life in something like the way you hope they will. You are asked to perceive choices — including new ones of your own invention — and to judge among them with an awareness of the realities of social life and human behavior as you know them. The demand is upon your capacity to look at your social world with new eyes, to see the writing of rules (and other social instruments) as an act of the creative imagination.

A. *USING THE RULE TO ORGANIZE SOCIAL EXPERIENCE*[1]

1. *Learning How to Behave: The Formation and Management of Social Expectations, by Rules and Otherwise*

We begin our study of rules at work in the world by continuing a line of questions begun in the sections dealing with race and the language of

1. It is a pleasure to be able to say that both the general idea for this section and the particular passages from the Amherst College rules and from *Williamstown and Williams College, infra,* come directly from Theodore Baird's English 1–2 course at Amherst College.

institutions (Chapter 3, Sections D and E): what is the relationship between what the rule (or other social instrument) says and what the world is? Of course a set of rules never absolutely defines or controls any social situation, but equally obviously, rules are rarely without some effect in people's lives. Sometimes the most complex sets of expectations are formed without the articulation of any rules; on other occasions we see expressed rules actually changing and shaping conduct, filling a genuine need. How is the relationship between conduct and rules, between the fact of intelligible social expectations and their expression, to be understood and addressed in various situations? When, under what circumstances and by what authority, can rules work to change things and when not? The idea here is to urge you to examine and define for yourself your own sense of the context of social life — of how people learn to behave — within which any set of rules must work.

We begin with a passage on racial relations. Here is expressed a complex and highly ordered society; where do the expectations that make it orderly come from, and why are they so clear? Who makes these rules and how do they work?

GROWING UP IN THE BLACK BELT*

Charles S. Johnson

The two universally tabooed practices are intermarriage and interdancing. Interdining is generally prohibited in all counties, but occurs in minor instances in some. The exceptions are more significant in some than in other areas. In one county eating together is tolerated for a few at school exercises, in another county when whites are invited to a barbecue. Whites and Negroes play games together in semiprofessional baseball practice in Greene County, Georgia, and at dice in Bolivar County, Mississippi. Young children play together in any area, older ones occasionally in Macon County, Alabama, and Davidson County, Tennessee. Whites use "Mr." and "Mrs." only when as salesmen they are selling goods. Salesmen and department store clerks in Madison County, Alabama, selectively employ the titles when making sales or seeking patronage. The terms employed when titles are not used are "boy," "John," "Aunt," or "Uncle." Teachers and well-to-do Negro farmers and businessmen in Bolivar are sometimes addressed by their last names.

The exceptions in the case of entering white homes by the front door are business and professional calls, and when a Negro knows a white person personally. The practice depends upon the individual white man. Negroes and whites occasionally shake hands under a variety of condi-

* Pages 277–280 (1941).

tions: when a salesman is trying to sell goods, when a former employer meets a respected Negro who has worked for him, when whites are attending public programs or meetings of Negroes, and occasionally on the streets. The white man makes the first approach.

The following are, in general, the rules of racial etiquette in the eight counties studied as typical of the rural South.

Where taboos are rigid

1. Negroes may never marry whites in any of the counties studied.
2. Negroes may never dance with whites in any of the counties studied.
3. Negroes may never eat with whites in any of the counties except Bolivar and Coahoma (Mississippi), and Davidson (Tennessee).
4. Negroes may never play games with whites in any counties except Bolivar, Davidson, and Madison (Alabama).
5. Negroes must always use "Mr." and "Mrs." when addressing whites in all counties.
6. Whites never use "Mr." and "Mrs." when addressing Negroes in Bolivar, Coahoma, Johnston (North Carolina), Macon (Alabama), and Shelby (Tennessee).
7. Negroes never drink with whites in Madison and Shelby counties except occasionally among the lower classes.
8. Negroes never enter white people's houses by the front door in Coahoma and Johnston.
9. Negroes must give whites the right-of-way on the sidewalks in Bolivar and Madison.
10. Negro men must take off their hats in banks, stores, and so forth, where whites need not, in Madison.
11. Negroes cannot touch a white man without his resenting it in Bolivar and Madison.
12. Negroes must always say "Yes, sir," and "Yes, ma'am," when addressing whites in all counties except Davidson and Johnston.

Where the etiquette is relaxed

1. Negroes drink with whites sometimes in Bolivar, Coahoma, Davidson, Greene, Johnston, and Macon.
2. Negroes and whites shake hands sometimes in all counties.
3. Negroes enter white people's houses by the front door sometimes in Bolivar, Davidson, Greene, Madison, and Shelby.
4. Whites use "Mr." and "Mrs." sometimes in Davidson, Greene, and Madison when addressing Negroes.
5. Whites and Negroes play games together sometimes in Bolivar, Davidson, and Madison.

6. Negroes must use "Yes, sir," and "Yes, ma'am," sometimes in Davidson and Johnston.
7. Negroes may touch a white man without causing resentment in Davidson, Johnston, Macon, and Shelby.

Where the etiquette is confused

1. Negroes attend theaters patronized by whites in all counties but Madison.
2. Negroes can try on hats in all stores in all counties but Shelby.
3. Negroes can try on gloves in all stores in Bolivar, Davidson, Johnston, and Macon, and in no stores in Greene.
4. Negroes must occupy a separate section while being waited on in all stores in Coahoma, Macon, and Madison; in some stores in Davidson, Greene, Johnston, and Shelby; and in no stores in Bolivar.
5. Negroes may sit in all public parks in Bolivar, Coahoma, Greene, and Macon; in some parks in Davidson and Shelby; and in none in Johnston and Madison.
6. Negroes use hotels with whites in none of the counties.
7. Negroes use some restaurants with whites in Coahoma, Davidson, Madison, and Shelby only, and these are separated by partition.
8. Negroes serve on juries sometimes in Coahoma, Greene, and Shelby, never in Bolivar, Johnston, and Madison.
9. Negro lawyers may try cases in all counties except Madison.
10. Negroes are segregated in all courts except in Coahoma.
11. Whites work *for* Negroes sometimes in Bolivar, Davidson, Greene, Johnston, and Madison; never in Coahoma, Macon, and Shelby.
12. Whites work *with* Negroes usually in Coahoma and Greene; sometimes in Davidson, Johnston, and Madison; seldom if ever in Shelby.
13. Whites are served by Negro doctors in Davidson, Greene, Johnston, Madison, and Shelby; not in Bolivar, Coahoma, and Macon.
14. Negroes usually vote in Coahoma, Davidson, Johnston, Macon, and Shelby; sometimes in Greene and Madison.
15. Negroes and whites worship together sometimes in Coahoma, Davidson, Greene, Macon, and Madison; never in Bolivar, Johnston, and Shelby.
16. Negroes drink with whites in drug and liquor stores in Coahoma; at beer "joints" in Bolivar; when each party is about half drunk from whisky in Greene; and among the lower classes occasionally in all counties.

QUESTIONS

1. Go back and read again the description of racial relations in Myrdal's American Dilemma, supra page 485. Taken together, the Myrdal and Johnson passages describe a society that is highly ordered by a complex set of clear and universally intelligible rules. Everyone knows where he stands and what is expected of him. There seems to be very little social uncertainty here. Why is everything so certain? What kind of rules are these and how do they work? What connections can be drawn between these rules and the actual social life they describe or regulate?
   a. Where do these rules come from? Myrdal and Johnson are acting as reporters, not legislators, and presumably they do not have access to any written legislative code of racial etiquette; what are they reporting then, to what do they have access?
   b. Are these to be regarded as prescriptive or descriptive rules? That is, are they scientific generalizations about social behavior of the kind one would expect to find in the Kinsey reports, in a study of voting patterns, or in divorce statistics, or are they purposive declarations by those in control of society meant to serve as directions to conduct? How do you know?
   c. Does it matter whether the rules are descriptive or prescriptive? If a society is characterized by certain behavior, why should it matter — especially to the victims — whether there is a rule forbidding or requiring that particular behavior? You are asked, that is, how you might distinguish between a "social regularity" and a "rule." If the lawyer's task is prediction, as has often been maintained, does this distinction become meaningless, at least for him?

      Interesting material to examine in connection with these questions can be found in K. Llewellyn and E. Hoebel, The Cheyenne Way (1941), and M. Gluckman, Politics, Law, and Ritual in Tribal Society (1965).
   d. Is the distinction between prescriptive and descriptive rules an absolute one, or is it possible for a rule to be a sort of mixture of the two? To refer to the familiar old property case, how would you go about deciding whether a harpooned blackfish that had escaped from a fisherman, then died and washed ashore, belonged to the original fisherman or to the finder? Would you look to basic principles of possession and title, to cases dealing with property in wild beasts, to local custom, or somewhere else? How would you use whatever you looked to? Suppose the harpoon was still in the whale when it was found: what would determine the significance of that fact? See Ghen v. Rich, 8 F. 159 (D. Mass. 1881).
   e. Are these rules laws? How would you expect that question to be argued on both sides — or is this merely a matter of definition of terms about which no sensible person would ever care? See Douglas, J., concurring in Garner v. Louisiana, 368 U.S. 157, 176 et seq. (1961). Cf. Adickes v. S. H. Kress and Co., 398 U.S. 144 (1970).
   f. How do these rules work: by incentive? by deterrence? by appealing

to one's innate sense of what is right? Myrdal quotes the following brief story.

"The other day I saw a good-looking, modest-appearing, well-dressed, but frail colored woman with a child in her arms attempt to board a streetcar. She was about to fail. The conductor started to help her, then looked at the other passengers and desisted. His face was a study. Prejudice won; but it was a Pyrrhic victory." C. V. Roman, American Civilization and the Negro 58 (1921).

Can you explain what happened here? Is there anything more to be said than that "prejudice won"? Whose prejudice, and how did it win? See if you can imagine another way to tell that story.

g. Is it possible that the Negro has contributed in some way to the establishment of these rules? Notice that (according to Myrdal) he can turn them to his advantage, at least on some occasions.

2. Do these rules constitute an accurate and complete description of this aspect of social life in the South? How do you know? Put it this way: is there anything else to be said about what happens when a black man and a white man meet and greet each other on the street, or do these rules say it all?

a. The rules seem to express a sharply defined set of social expectations. Everyone seems to know what he should do. How are these expectations formed, and why are they so clear?

(1) Do you think a Negro or white person would need to be told the rule to know what was expected of him in this society? How would he learn it then?

(2) Could we hope that the social expectations defined by the criminal laws could be equally clear? Why or why not?

b. Are these rules really so clear after all?

(1) Notice that many of Johnson's rules use the word "sometimes" ("Negroes and whites sometimes shake hands"). How would you know whether this was one of those times? For such a relaxation of the rules to occur, someone has to take the first step; how would you know when to do that, or when someone else had done so?

(2) If you were a Negro man driving down a lonely road, would you be expected to stop to help a white woman whose car had broken down? Would you want to do so? You might be unclear about the meaning of the applicable social rule; what would you be clear about?

3. Why do you think these rules were not codified and published in a formal way?

a. Do you think that it would be impossible to express in such a way what everyone seems to know so clearly? How can that be? Or was formal codification just not necessary?

b. How might this society be changed if rules such as these were formally promulgated by: the state legislature; a high school principal; People United to Save Our Way of Life; a social scientist reporting his findings?

c. Suppose rules were promulgated by each of the foregoing, prohibiting such racially discriminatory behavior; how would that change things?

4. There follow two extracts from the rules of Amherst College at different eras of its existence. What differences can you perceive between them?

How do they variously define the college, the students, and the relationship between them?

THE RULES OF AMHERST COLLEGE (1874)

As it is the duty of the Faculty diligently to watch over the morals of the students, recommending to them both by precept and example a virtuous and blameless life, and a devout attention to the duties of religion, daily devotional exercises shall be conducted by the President or some one of the officers, in the Chapel, by reading a portion of Scripture and by prayer, with singing when convenient. . . .

The students shall constantly, seasonably and with reverence, attend these daily exercises, preserving silence and good order in the place of worship, and quietness and decorum in coming to and going from it. . . .

No student shall be absent from College in term time, without permission. . . .

Every student shall be required to observe all the laws of decency, order, neatness, cleanliness, and good breeding, in the arrangement and keeping of his room, and in the entry contiguous thereto; and the rooms shall be inspected, from time to time, by the Prudential Committee and the Faculty. . . .

The Government of this College earnestly desires that the students may be influenced to good conduct and literary exertion by higher motives than the fear of punishment, and it mainly relies for the success of the Institution, as designed for liberal education, on moral and religious principle, a sense of duty, and the generous feelings which belong to young men engaged in honorable pursuits; but when such motives fail, the Faculty will have recourse to friendly caution and warning, solemn admonition and official notice of delinquency to parents and guardians, reduction of the rank, refusal to grant privileges and indulgencies allowed to meritorious students, assignments of particular portions of study to be performed in vacation or at other times, withholding of honors which would otherwise be conferred; and, where the nature and circumstances of the case require it, to suspension, removal or expulsion. . . .

As every student will understand that crimes, vices, indecencies, dishonorable and ungentlemanly behavior, and conduct unbecoming a literary and Christian Institution cannot be allowed, extended statements of laws and duties will not be necessary; but among things specially reprehensible, all profane and impure language, all violence in word or deed against a fellow student or other person, all annoying or injurious treatment of classmates or members of other classes, all noisy gatherings by day or by night, disguises in dress, breaking of windows, using intoxicating liquors, gambling, destroying or injuring property, disturbing the quiet of the College or of the village, are strictly forbidden. . . .

Every student shall be answerable for all scandalous and immoral conduct during the several vacations or absences from College, in the same manner as in term time, or when present. . . .

If any student who has been removed from College should refuse to leave the town, or continue to associate with other students when forbidden, he may be expelled at the discretion of the Faculty. . . .

The students shall at all times treat the Faculty and every member thereof, and all other officers of the College, with the respect which becomes their relation to them, and their whole demeanor in their intercourse with each other, and with all other persons, must be conformable to the rules of decency and good breeding. Any insubordination or insolence of demeanor, in cases of discipline, will be regarded as specially reprehensible. No student shall receive an honorable dismission from College while under censure, nor until the Faculty are satisfied that he is worthy of it.

AMHERST COLLEGE BULLETIN*

Student Discipline

The officer in general charge of student discipline and conduct is the Associate Dean.

Conduct befitting a gentleman is expected at all times of students at Amherst College. It is assumed that undergraduates will understand what constitutes gentlemanly conduct without specific regulations forbidding particular actions.

The College reserves the right to exclude at any time students whose conduct or academic standing it regards as undesirable, and without assigning any further reason therefor; in such cases fees will not be refunded or remitted, in whole or in part, and neither the College nor any of its officers shall be under any liability whatsoever for such exclusion. . . .

Rooms and Board

All students, unless specifically excused by the Dean, are required to live either in the dormitories of the College or in fraternity houses. Dormitory rooms are equipped with bed, mattress, pillow, chiffonier, desk, chairs, and bookcase or shelves. Occupants furnish their own

* Catalog Issue 33–34 (1958–1959).

blankets, linen, and towels, and may provide extra furnishings if they wish, such as rugs, curtains, lamps, etc.; they may not add beds, sofas, lounges, or other furniture of such nature except under certain circumstances. More complete regulations for dormitory occupancy are contained in the Student Handbook. Room assignments are noted on the invoice from the Comptroller's Office.

All students are required to eat in Valentine Hall unless excused by the Dean. There are no rebates for absence from meals for any reason.

QUESTIONS

1. What inferences about life at Amherst College in 1874 and 1958 can you confidently draw from these rules?
   a. How does each set of rules define the college? Ask yourself what the purposes of the institution seem to be in each case and how they are expressed and pursued. How would you characterize the voice with which each set of rules speaks?
   b. How is the faculty defined? Based upon the official literature of his time, what meaning might a teacher at Amherst College in each era claim for his life?
   c. According to each set of rules, who is the student and what is he doing there? What meaning does the college claim for his experience?
   d. How is the relationship between the college and the student defined differently in each of these documents? What voices do you hear in each?

2. The lawyer's first question may be this: taken as a whole, which set of rules is more clear, and how can one explain its relative clarity?
   a. Which phrase is clearer to you: "dishonorable and ungentlemanly behavior" or "conduct befitting a gentleman"? Or are they the same?
   b. In which era, under which set of rules, do you think you as an Amherst student would be more confident that you knew what was expected of you? How do you explain the difference, especially when such a key term as "gentleman" remains exactly the same? What would a student in 1874 know that you would not?
   c. In which era do you think that the power of the college officials would be less subject to abuse? Or can't you tell? To respond, one must decide what an "abuse" of power should be taken to mean. Is it sensible to ask in which era you would more readily trust the dean to be fair, or is that necessarily a matter of individual character rather than rules? Is this perhaps the best way to put the question: in which social world would the idea of fairness — and hence of "abuse of power" — be more intelligible, and why do you say so?
   d. Imagine yourself a student newly arrived at Amherst College in each of the eras. How would you form your social expectations, and what place would the rules you have just read have in that process?

3. If it is the remaining portions of the rules of 1874 that make clear the references to gentlemanly and decent conduct and give definition to the vague terms of the general standards, why do you suppose there are no corresponding provisions in the rules of Amherst College in 1958? Of course the statements of 1874 would not apply to the modern college, but presumably a set of statements could be drafted that would express the college of today. Why has that not been done? What do you suppose such a set of statements would look like?

4. *Suppose Myrdal (page 485) or Johnson (page 507) were to study the Amherst College of 1958, or 1973, or your own undergraduate school as it exists today; what rules of life and behavior do you think they would report?*
5. *In neither era did Amherst College promulgate anything that could be called a clear and coherent set of rules of behavior. Why do you suppose this is so? Can a case be made that the very vagueness and uncertainty of the rules in either era served a valuable purpose?*
6. *Can you regard what has happened in this period of less than a hundred years as anything but the decay of social and institutional life, the partial collapse of civilization? If someone does not know what is expected of a gentleman, what can he know? Yet apparently none of us knows that.*
7. *Here is a later step in the organization of institutional relations at Amherst College: "It is the belief of Amherst College that its students want to take responsibility for setting, maintaining, and supporting moral and intellectual standards. With this in mind, the College has adopted an honor code. In a social and moral sense this honor code means the support of those standards which befit the conduct of a gentleman and which will reflect credit on the College, its students, and its guests." Amherst College Bulletin, Catalog Issue (1968–1969).*

   Assume that the honor code mentioned here deals only with intellectual dishonesty, and that this statement is the only declaration as to "social and moral standards." How do you compare Amherst College in 1968 with the same institution in the other two eras? Why does it here have an honor code setting forth specific rules governing intellectual dishonesty, but no similar code of social and moral rules? Is it because everyone is so clear about the latter that no rules are needed?
8. *We have looked only at the rules of this college and not at life as it was lived under them. How confident are you that life was different in 1874, and that it was different in ways that find expression in these rules? What differences are you most certain of?*

The next passage is about life not at Amherst College but at a similar institution.

WILLIAMSTOWN AND WILLIAMS COLLEGE*

A. L. Perry

Instead of attempting anything like an outline of Dr. Moore's character, which you can easily obtain from other sources, I take the liberty to comply with your request by stating an incident in his administration of the College, of which I was a witness, and which strikingly illustrated some of his most prominent characteristics.

The incident to which I refer, occurred in 1816, just after Dr. Moore

* Pages 396–398 (1899).

entered upon his duties as President of Williams College. It was not only a new field to him, but there were some circumstances that rendered his entrance upon it peculiarly embarrassing. His predecessor, Dr. Fitch, though in many respects an admirable man, did not always evince the highest degree of firmness; and hence, it had been common for the students, when his decisions were not in accordance with their wishes, to make an effort, and generally not an unsuccessful one, to procure their reversal. Dr. Moore came to the College when the three higher classes had been the subjects of this kind of training. In order to give governmental efficiency to the institution, he was instrumental in effecting a revision of its laws, and in introducing certain new regulations, which were designed to secure a more thorough and effective discipline. The new regulations took effect with the Sophomore class, of which I was a member. The class numbered twenty-one, among whom were several who have since attained to high distinction in the different walks of public usefulness. They felt as Sophomore classes are very apt to feel, a sufficiently deep sense of their own importance; and this was probably somewhat increased from the fact that the College was really in a tottering condition, and one in which it did not seem safe to enforce very stringent regulations.

A copy of the new code of laws was given to each pupil on his entrance into college, and soon afterwards he was summoned into the president's study, and questioned in the following manner: "Have you read the laws of the College?" "Do you approve of them?" "*Will you obey them?*" Of course an affirmative answer was returned. But to fix the matter more securely, he was then required to affix his name to his answer in a book prepared for that purpose. Two-thirds of the members of the class had passed through this ordeal, attesting their allegiance to the College government; but, in the meantime, this new regulation began to be talked about as an oppressive measure, especially in its application to the Sophomore class. The feeling that it was derogatory to their dignity began to run high, and, under the excitement, a class-meeting was called to decide upon the measures to be adopted to remedy the supposed oppression under which the class labored, and especially to vindicate its honor before the other classes. At this meeting speeches were made, which, in point of spirit were worthy of the times of '76. It was resolved to visit the president in a body, making a committee of twenty-one, with Selah Root Arms (now a highly respectable clergyman), for our chairman and chief speaker. The president received us politely, and almost immediately gave the chairman an opportunity to state the business of the committee. "Young gentlemen," said he, "what are your wishes? You must surely have some business of great importance to transact with me." "We have come, sir," replied the chairman, "for the purpose of getting our names expunged from that book," stepping forward at the same time a little in front of the row, and placing his feet squarely upon the floor. "Oh, indeed," said the president, "I am sorry for that; but you are no doubt willing to obey the laws of College." "Certainly, sir," said he; "but then our names are upon that book." "If that is all," answered the president, "you may be sure, that it will never hurt you." "But," replied the chairman, "we do not see why the Sophomore class should be singled out in this manner." "That," said the president, "is of little consequence, — you know we must begin somewhere; and you are only required to obey the laws of College, which you say you intend to do, and which all are required to do." "But," said the chairman, "our names are upon that book," — pointing to the very book on the table before the president, — "and it looks badly that we should be singled out in this way, when the Junior and Senior classes are allowed an exemption from the rule." "I repeat," says the president, "we must, as you well know, begin somewhere, and all the succeeding classes will be required to conform to the rule, so that your names will not stand alone upon that book." Suffice it to say, it was evident that no progress could be made, and the Doctor's manner carried more weight even than his words. It seemed to be tacitly admitted that our case was a hopeless one; and besides we had become quite cooled off in his presence. But our spokesman made another rally, coming directly to the point, — "Must we understand then that our names shall remain upon that book?" "*Certainly*," said the Doctor, — his benignant face becoming momentarily suffused with a deeper tint. We left his presence as quickly as possible, satisfied that no impression could be made upon his firmness; and his polite reception and gentle bearing had quite disarmed us of all personal hostility.

Dr. Moore was consistent in his measures for the government of the College, and this first occasion for the exercise of his firmness and moderation had its influence throughout the classes, and I do not know that he was afterwards called upon to exercise those admirable qualities in a similar manner.

QUESTIONS

1. *How do you explain what occurred here? Is this obedience to a rule?*
2. *One person has suggested that this is just the bald assertion of domination by one party and a corresponding acquiescence by the other – a common phenomenon in the human and animal world. The beaten wolf exposes its bare throat to the victor and is allowed to live. (See generally K. Lorenz, On Aggression (1963). Is that what happens here? What would you say of one who saw no more than that in this event?*

3. *Why did President Moore want the students to sign the book? What was the significance of that event in his eyes and theirs?*
4. *Why was the hostility of the young men "disarmed" by President Moore's "polite reception and gentle bearing"? How do you explain that event, and has it any parallel in the world around you? Why did the young men leave "as quickly as possible"?*
5. *Can you imagine a similar scene occurring in a college today? How and why would it be different?*
6. *There follows now a scene from life in the modern courtroom. Can you explain why it goes so differently from what you have just read?*

MAYBERRY *v.* PENNSYLVANIA
400 U.S. 455, 456–460, 462–463 (1971)

DOUGLAS, J. . . . (1) On the first day of the trial petitioner came to the side bar to make suggestions and obtain rulings on trial procedures. Petitioner said: "It seems like the court has the intentions [*sic*] of railroading us" and moved to disqualify the judge. The motion was denied. Petitioner's other motions, including his request that the deputy sheriffs in the courtroom be dressed as civilians, were also denied. Then came the following colloquy:

Mr. Mayberry: I would like to have a fair trial of this case and like to be granted a fair trial under the Sixth Amendment.

The Court: You will get a fair trial.

Mr. Mayberry: It doesn't appear that I am going to get one the way you are overruling all our motions and that, and being like a hatchet man for the State.

The Court: This side bar is over.

Mr. Mayberry: Wait a minute, Your Honor.

The Court: It is over.

Mr. Mayberry: You dirty sonofabitch.

(2) The second episode took place on the eighth day of the trial. A codefendant was cross-examining a prison guard and the court sustained objections to certain questions:

Mr. Codispoti: Are you trying to protect the prison authorities, Your Honor? Is that your reason?

The Court: You are out of order, Mr. Codispoti. I don't want any outbursts like that again. This is a court of justice. You don't know how to ask questions.

Mr. Mayberry: Possibly Your Honor doesn't know how to rule on them.

The Court: You keep quiet.

Mr. Mayberry: You ought to be Gilbert and Sullivan the way you sustain the district attorney every time he objects to the questions.

The Court: Are you through? When your time comes you can ask questions and not make speeches.

(3) The next charge stemmed from the examination of an inmate about a riot in prison in which petitioner apparently was implicated. There were many questions asked and many objections sustained. At one point the following outburst occurred:

Mr. Mayberry: Now, I'm going to produce my defense in this case and not be railroaded into any life sentence by any dirty, tyrannical old dog like yourself.

The Court: You may proceed with your questioning, Mr. Mayberry.

(4) The fourth charge grew out of an examination of another defense witness:

By Mr. Mayberry:

Q. I ask you, Mr. Nardi, is that area, the handball court, is it open to any prisoner who wants to play handball, who cares to go to that area to play handball?

A. Yes.

Q. Did you understand the prior question when I asked you if it was [a] freely open and accessible area?

The Court: He answered your question. Let's go on.

Mr. Mayberry: I am asking him now if he understands —

The Court: He answered it. Now, let's go on.

Mr. Mayberry: I ask Your Honor to keep your mouth shut while I'm questioning my own witness. Will you do that for me?

The Court: I wish you would do the same. Proceed with your questioning.

(5) The fifth charge relates to a protest which the defendants made that at the end of each trial day they were denied access to their legal documents — a condition which the trial judge shortly remedied. The following ensued:

Mr. Mayberry: You're a judge first. What are you working for? The prison authorities, you bum?

Mr. Livingston: I have a motion pending before Your Honor.

The Court: I would suggest —

Mr. Mayberry: Go to hell. I don't give a good God damn what you suggest, you stumbling dog.

Meanwhile one defendant told the judge if he did not get access to his papers at night he'd "blow your head off." Another defendant said he would not sit still and be "kowtowed and be railroaded into a life imprisonment." Then the following transpired:

Mr. Mayberry: You started all this bullshit in the beginning.
The Court: You keep quiet.
Mr. Mayberry: Wait a minute.
The Court: You keep quiet.
Mr. Mayberry: I am my own counsel.
The Court: You keep quiet.
Mr. Mayberry. Are you going to gag me?
The Court: Take these prisoners out of here. We will take a ten minute recess, members of the jury.

(6) The sixth episode happened when two of the defendants wanted to have some time to talk to a witness whom they had called. The two of them had had a heated exchange with the judge when the following happened:

Mr. Mayberry: Just one moment, Your Honor.
The Court: This is not your witness, Mr. Mayberry. Keep quiet.
Mr. Mayberry: Oh, yes, he is my witness, too. He is my witness, also. Now, we are at the penitentiary and in seclusion. We can't talk to any of our witnesses prior to putting them on the stand like the District Attorney obviously has the opportunity, and as he obviously made use of the opportunity to talk to his witnesses. Now —
The Court: Now, I have ruled, Mr. Mayberry.
Mr. Mayberry: I don't care what you ruled. That is unimportant. The fact is —
The Court: You will remain quiet, sir, and finish the examination of this witness.
Mr. Mayberry: No, I won't be quiet while you try to deny me the right to a fair trial. The only way I will be quiet is if you have me gagged. Now, if you want to do that, that is up to you; but in the meantime I am going to say what I have to say. Now, we have the right to speak to our witnesses prior to putting them on the stand. This is an accepted fact of law. It is nothing new or unusual. Now, you are going to try to force us to have our witness testify to facts that he has only a hazy recollection of, that happened back in 1965. Now, I believe we have the right to confer with our witness prior to putting him on the stand.
The Court: Are you finished?
Mr. Mayberry: I am finished.
The Court: Proceed with your examination.

(7) The seventh charge grew out of an examination of a codefendant by petitioner. The following outburst took place:

By Mr. Mayberry:
Q. No. Don't state a conclusion because Gilbert is going to object and Sullivan will sustain. Give me facts. What leads you to say that?

Later petitioner said:

Mr. Mayberry: My witness isn't being in an inquisition, you know. This isn't the Spanish Inquisition.

Following other exchanges with the court, petitioner said:

Mr. Mayberry: Now, just what do you call proper? I have asked questions, numerous questions and everyone [*sic*] you said is improper. I have asked questions that my adviser has given me, and I have repeated these questions verbatim as they came out of my adviser's mouth, and you said they are improper. Now just what do you consider proper?
The Court: I am not here to educate you, Mr. Mayberry.
Mr. Mayberry: No. I know you are not. But you're not here to railroad me into no life bit, either.
Mr. Codispoti: To protect the record —
The Court: Do you have any other questions to ask this witness?
Mr. Mayberry: You need to have some kind of psychiatric treatment, I think. You're some kind of a nut. I know you're trying to do a good job for that Warden Maroney back there, but let's keep it looking decent anyway, you know. Don't make it so obvious, Your Honor. . . .

These brazen efforts to denounce, insult, and slander the court and to paralyze the trial are at war with the concept of justice under law. Laymen, foolishly trying to defend themselves, may understandably create awkward and embarrassing scenes. Yet that is not the character of the record revealed here. We have here downright insults of a trial judge, and tactics taken from street brawls and transported to the courtroom. This is conduct not "befitting an American courtroom," as we said in *Illinois v. Allen*, 397 U.S. 337, 346; and criminal contempt is one appropriate remedy. Id., at 344-345.

QUESTIONS

1. *Why did the trial judge's evident firmness, politeness, and gentleness not disarm Mr. Mayberry and bring order into the courtroom?*
2. *What should the trial judge have said to establish the decorum he wanted? What would have worked?*
3. *Do you explain what you see happening here as the violation of a rule? How would you state that rule? Or is the trouble that there is just no rule at all?*
4. *Examine the last paragraph of Justice Douglas's opinion. Can you think*

of anything else that might have been said here? (What would you have said as counsel for Mayberry?)

5. *Below is an account of behavior in a time very different from our own. How do you describe and explain the conduct you read about here?*

ILIAD*
Homer

[Having returned to the battle after the death of his friend Patroclus, Achilles has at last killed Hector, the greatest Trojan warrior. The Achaeans have honored Patroclus with games at his funeral. The wrath of Achilles — the subject of the poem — is nearly spent, and we now move towards a moment of reconciliation. Priam, Hector's father, has with the assistance of a god come through the night to Achilles' tent to ask for the return of the body, so that he may see to its proper burial.]

. . . As when dense disaster closes on one who has murdered
a man in his own land, and he comes to the country of others,
to a man of substance, and wonder seizes on those who behold him,
so Achilleus wondered as he looked on Priam, a godlike
man, and the rest of them wondered also, and looked at each other.
But now Priam spoke to him in the words of a suppliant:
"Achilleus like the gods, remember your father, one who
is of years like mine, and on the door-sill of sorrowful old age.
And they who dwell nearby encompass him and afflict him,
nor is there any to defend him against the wrath, the destruction.
Yet surely he, when he hears of you and that you are still living,
is gladdened within his heart and all his days he is hopeful
that he will see his beloved son come home from the Troad.
But for me, my destiny was evil. I have had the noblest
of sons in Troy, but I say not one of them is left to me.
Fifty were my sons, when the sons of the Achaians came here.
Nineteen were born to me from the womb of a single mother,
and other women bore the rest in my palace; and of these
violent Ares broke the strength in the knees of most of them,
but one was left me who guarded my city and people, that one
you killed a few days since as he fought in defence of his country,
Hektor; for whose sake I come now to the ships of the Achaians
to win him back from you, and I bring you gifts beyond number.
Honour then the gods, Achilleus, and take pity upon me
remembering your father, yet I am still more pitiful;
I have gone through what no other mortal on earth has gone through;

* Book 24, lines 480–595 (Lattimore trans. 1951).

I put my lips to the hands of the man who has killed my children."
So he spoke, and stirred in the other a passion of grieving
for his own father. He took the old man's hand and pushed him
gently away, and the two remembered, as Priam sat huddled
at the feet of Achilleus and wept close for manslaughtering Hektor
and Achilleus wept now for his own father, now again
for Patroklos. The sound of their mourning moved in the house. Then
when great Achilleus had taken full satisfaction in sorrow
and the passion for it had gone from his mind and body, thereafter
he rose from his chair, and took the old man by the hand, and set him
on his feet again, in pity for the grey head and the grey beard,
and spoke to him and addressed him in winged words: "Ah, unlucky,
surely you have had much evil to endure in your spirit.
How could you dare to come alone to the ships of the Achaians
and before my eyes, when I am one who have killed in such numbers
such brave sons of yours? The heart in you is iron. Come, then,
and sit down upon this chair, and you and I will even let
our sorrows lie still in the heart for all our grieving. There is not
any advantage to be won from grim lamentation.
Such is the way the gods spun life for unfortunate mortals,
that we live in unhappiness, but the gods themselves have no sorrows.
There are two urns that stand on the door-sill of Zeus. They are unlike
for the gifts they bestow: an urn of evils, an urn of blessings.
If Zeus who delights in thunder mingles these and bestows them
on man, he shifts, and moves now in evil, again in good fortune.
But when Zeus bestows from the urn of sorrows, he makes a failure
of man, and the evil hunger drives him over the shining
earth, and he wanders respected neither of gods nor mortals.
Such were the shining gifts given by the gods to Peleus
from his birth, who outshone all men beside for his riches
and pride of possession, and was lord over the Myrmidons. Thereto
the gods bestowed an immortal wife on him, who was mortal.
But even on him the god piled evil also. There was not
any generation of strong sons born to him in his great house
but a single all-untimely child he had, and I give him
no care as he grows old, since far from the land of my fathers
I sit here in Troy, and bring nothing but sorrow to you and your children.
And you, old sir, we are told you prospered once; for as much
as Lesbos, Makar's hold, confines to the north above it
and Phrygia from the north confines, and enormous Hellespont,
of these, old sir, you were lord once in your wealth and your children.

But now the Uranian gods brought us, an affliction upon you,
forever there is fighting about your city, and men killed.
But bear up, nor mourn endlessly in your heart, for there is not
anything to be gained from grief for your son; you will never
bring him back; sooner you must go through yet another sorrow."
  In answer to him again spoke aged Priam the godlike:
"Do not, beloved of Zeus, make me sit on a chair while Hektor
lies yet forlorn among the shelters; rather with all speed
give him back, so my eyes may behold him, and accept the ransom
we bring you, which is great. You may have joy of it, and go back
to the land of your own fathers, since once you have permitted me
to go on living myself and continue to look on the sunlight."
  Then looking darkly at him spoke swift-footed Achilleus:
"No longer stir me up, old sir. I myself am minded
to give Hektor back to you. A messenger came to me from Zeus,
my mother, she who bore me, the daughter of the sea's ancient.
I know you, Priam, in my heart, and it does not escape me
that some god led you to the running ships of the Achaians.
For no mortal would dare come to our encampment, not even
one strong in youth. He could not get by the pickets, he could not
lightly unbar the bolt that secures our gateway. Therefore
you must not further make my spirit move in my sorrows,
for fear, old sir, I might not let you alone in my shelter,
suppliant as you are; and be guilty before the god's orders."
  He spoke, and the old man was frightened and did as he told him.
The son of Peleus bounded to the door of the house like a lion,
nor went alone, but the two henchmen followed attending,
the hero Automedon and Alkimos, those whom Achilleus
honoured beyond all companions after Patroklos dead. These two
now set free from under the yoke the mules and the horses,
and led inside the herald, the old king's crier, and gave him
a chair to sit in, then from the smooth-polished mule wagon
lifted out the innumerable spoils for the head of Hektor,
but left inside it two great cloaks and a finespun tunic
to shroud the corpse in when they carried him home. Then Achilleus
called out to his serving-maids to wash the body and anoint it
all over; but take it first aside, since otherwise Priam
might see his son and in the heart's sorrow not hold in his anger
at the sight, and the deep heart in Achilleus be shaken to anger;
that he might not kill Priam and be guilty before the god's orders.
Then when the serving-maids had washed the corpse and anointed it
with olive oil, they threw a fair great cloak and a tunic
about him, and Achilleus himself lifted him and laid him

on a litter, and his friends helped him lift it to the smooth-polished
mule wagon. He groaned then, and called by name on his beloved
companion:
"Be not angry with me, Patroklos, if you discover,
though you be in the house of Hades, that I gave back great Hektor
to his loved father, for the ransom he gave me was not unworthy.
I will give you your share of the spoils, as much as is fitting."

QUESTIONS

1. Why does Achilles return the body? Why does he not kill Priam?
   a. What are said to be his motives?
   b. How else might you account for or explain his behavior?
   c. Is he following a rule?
2. What differences can you find and express between this behavior and that reflected in the Mayberry trial transcript?
3. If you wished someone to behave in some respect as Achilles does, how would you attempt to see that he did so? Would you express your wishes in a rule of conduct?
4. What connections can you draw between this set of questions and your concerns as lawyer, judge, or legislator?
   a. Might one ask, for example, how the behavior of the policeman alone on the beat, or while questioning a suspect, is to be influenced? Or the sentencing judgment of a judge?
   b. Would you ever want such a one to behave in some respect as Achilles behaves? How would you attempt to see that he did so — by drafting a rule or other directions to conduct? If not that way, how?
5. Based on this introduction to the formation and management of social expectations, with what confidence and what hopes would you go about setting up an institution — say, a government or a prison or a school or a college? What purposes would you have and how would you seek to achieve them? How would you express, or otherwise reflect in what you did, the uncertainties you felt?
6. There follow now some passages on life at one institution, Rugby School as it existed under the headmastership of Thomas Arnold in the nineteenth century. The school had ten masters and about 300 boys, aged 9 to 18, arranged in ten classes or forms, of which the highest (through a peculiarity of numbering) was the sixth. Here is what Doctor Arnold had to say about one aspect of school government.

ON THE DISCIPLINE OF PUBLIC SCHOOLS (1835)*
Thomas Arnold

I now proceed to make a few remarks upon another part of the system of public schools, which is even less understood than the subject already considered, — I mean the power of fagging.

Now by "the power of fagging," I understand a power given by the

* In Findlay, *Arnold of Rugby* 222, 229–231 (1897).

supreme authorities of a school to the boys of the highest class or classes in it, to be exercised by them over the lower boys for the sake of securing the advantages of regular government amongst the boys themselves, and avoiding the evils of anarchy, — in other words, of the lawless tyranny of physical strength. This is the simple statement of the nature and ends of public school fagging — an institution which, like all other government, has been often abused, and requires to be carefully watched, but which is as indispensable to a multitude of boys living together, as government, in like circumstances, is indispensable to a multitude of men.

. . . It is idle to say that the masters form, or can form, this government; it is impossible to have a sufficient number of masters for the purpose; for, in order to obtain the advantages of home government, the boys should be as much divided as they are at their respective homes. There should be no greater number of schoolfellows living under one master than of brothers commonly living under one parent; nay, the number should be less, inasmuch as there is wanting that bond of natural affection which so greatly facilitates domestic government and gives it its peculiar virtue. Even a father with thirty sons, all below the age of manhood, and above childhood, would find it no easy matter to govern them effectually — how much less can a master govern thirty boys, with no natural bond to attach them either to him or to one another? He may indeed superintend their government of one another; he may govern them through their own governors; but to govern them immediately, and at the same time effectively, is, I believe, impossible. And hence, if you have a large *boarding*-school, you cannot have it adequately governed without a system of fagging.

Now, a government among the boys themselves being necessary, the actual constitution of public schools places it in the best possible hands. Those to whom the power is committed, are not simply the strongest boys, nor the oldest, nor yet the cleverest; they are those who have risen to the highest form in the school — that is to say, they will be probably at once the oldest, and the strongest, and the cleverest; and further, if the school be well ordered, they will be the most respectable in application and general character — those who have made the best use of the opportunities which the school affords, and are most capable of entering into its objects. In short, they constitute a real aristocracy, a government of the most worthy, their rank itself being an argument of their deserving. And their business is to keep order amongst the boys; to put a stop to improprieties of conduct, especially to prevent that oppression and ill-usage of the weaker boys by the stronger which is so often ignorantly confounded with a system of fagging. For all these purposes a general authority over the rest of the school is given them; and in some schools they have the power, like the masters, of enforcing this authority by impositions, that is, by setting tasks to be written out or learnt by heart for any misbehaviour. And this authority is exercised over all those boys who are legally subject to it, that is, over all below a certain place in the school, whatever be their age or physical strength; so that many boys who, if there were no regular fagging, would by mere physical force be exercising power over their schoolfellows, although from their idleness, ignorance, and low principle they might be most unfit to do so, are now not only hindered from tyrannizing over others, but are themselves subject to authority — a most wholesome example, and one particularly needed at school, that mere physical strength, even amongst boys, is not to enjoy an ascendancy. Meanwhile this governing part of the school, thus invested with great responsibility, treated by the masters with great confidence and consideration, and being constantly in direct communication with the head-master, and receiving their instruction almost exclusively from him, learn to feel a corresponding self-respect in the best sense of the term; they look upon themselves as answerable for the character of the school, and by the natural effect of their position acquire a manliness of mind and habits of conduct infinitely superior, generally speaking, to those of young men of the same age who have not enjoyed the same advantages.

QUESTIONS

1. *How do you suppose this system worked in practice? What dangers would you have anticipated if you were Dr. Arnold, and how would you have tried to forestall them?*
2. *Below is a fictional account of life in this school. As you read it, ask why the boys behave as they do. What rules or principles are articulated? Which ones can you see actually at work here?*

TOM BROWN'S SCHOOL DAYS*

Thomas Hughes

Matters were not so comfortable either in the house as they had been, for old Brooke left at Christmas, and one or two others of the sixth-form boys at the following Easter. Their rule had been rough, but strong and just in the main, and a higher standard was beginning to be set up; in fact, there had been a short foretaste of the good time which followed some years later. Just now, however, all threatened to return into darkness and chaos again. For the new praepostors were either small young boys, whose cleverness had carried them up to the top of the school, while in strength of body and character they were not yet fit for a share

* Pages 150–159 (1857; St. Martin ed. 1958).

in the government; or else big fellows of the wrong sort, boys whose friendships and tastes had a downward tendency, who had not caught the meaning of their position and work, and felt none of its responsibilities. So under this no-government the School-house began to see bad times. The big fifth-form boys, who were a sporting and drinking set, soon began to usurp power, and to fag the little boys as if they were praepostors, and to bully and oppress any who showed signs of resistance. The bigger sort of sixth-form boys just described soon made common cause with the fifth, while the smaller sort, hampered by their colleagues' desertion to the enemy, could not make head against them. So the fags were without their lawful masters and protectors, and ridden over rough-shod by a set of boys whom they were not bound to obey, and whose only right over them stood in their bodily powers; and, as old Brooke had prophesied, the house by degrees broke up into small sets and parties, and lost the strong feeling of fellowship which he set so much store by, and with it much of the prowess in games and the lead in all school matters which he had done so much to keep up. . . .

While matters were in this state, East and Tom were one evening sitting in their study. They had done their work for first lesson, and Tom was in a brown study, brooding, like a young William Tell, upon the wrongs of fags in general, and his own in particular.

"I say, Scud," said he at last, rousing himself to snuff the candle, "what right have the fifth-form boys to fag us as they do?"

"No more right than you have to fag them," answered East, without looking up from an early number of *Pickwick*, which was just coming out, and which he was luxuriously devouring, stretched on his back on the sofa.

Tom relapsed into his brown study, and East went on reading and chuckling. The contrast of the boys' faces would have given infinite amusement to a looker-on, the one so solemn and big with mighty purpose, the other radiant and bubbling over with fun.

"Do you know, old fellow, I've been thinking it over a good deal," began Tom again.

"Oh yes, I know, fagging you are thinking of. Hang it all, — but listen here, Tom — here's fun. Mr. Winkle's horse —"

"And I've made up my mind," broke in Tom, "that I won't fag except for the sixth."

"Quite right too, my boy," cried East, putting his finger on the place and looking up; "but a pretty peck of troubles you'll get into, if you're going to play that game. However, I'm all for a strike myself, if we can get others to join — it's getting too bad."

"Can't we get some sixth-form fellow to take it up?" asked Tom.

"Well, perhaps we might; Morgan would interfere, I think. Only," added East, after a moment's pause, "you see, we should have to tell him about it, and that's against School principles. Don't you remember what old Brooke said about learning to take our own parts?"

"Ah, I wish old Brooke were back again — it was all right in his time."

"Why, yes, you see, then the strongest and best fellows were in the sixth, and the fifth-form fellows were afraid of them, and they kept good order; but now our sixth-form fellows are too small, and the fifth don't care for them, and do what they like in the house."

"And so we get a double set of masters," cried Tom indignantly; "the lawful ones, who are responsible to the Doctor at any rate, and the unlawful — the tyrants, who are responsible to nobody."

"Down with the tyrants!" cried East; "I'm all for law and order, and hurra for a revolution."

"I shouldn't mind if it were only for young Brooke now," said Tom, "he's such a good-hearted gentlemanly fellow, and ought to be in the sixth — I'd do anything for him. But that blackguard Flashman, who never speaks to one without a kick or an oath —"

"The cowardly brute," broke in East, "how I hate him! And he knows it too, he knows that you and I think him a coward. What a bore that he's got a study in this passage! Don't you hear them now at supper in his den? Brandy punch going, I'll bet. I wish the Doctor would come out and catch him. We must change our study as soon as we can."

"Change or no change, I'll never fag for him again," said Tom, thumping the table.

"Fa-a-a-ag!" sounded along the passage from Flashman's study. The two boys looked at one another in silence. It had struck nine, so the regular night-fags had left duty, and they were the nearest to the supper-party. East sat up, and began to look comical, as he always did under difficulties.

"Fa-a-a-ag!" again. No answer.

"Here, Brown! East! you cursed young skulks," roared out Flashman, coming to his open door, "I know you're in — no shirking."

Tom stole to their door, and drew the bolts as noiselessly as he could; East blew out the candle.

"Barricade the first," whispered he. "Now, Tom, mind, no surrender."

"Trust me for that," said Tom between his teeth.

In another minute they heard the supper-party turn out and come down the passage to their door. They held their breaths, and heard whispering, of which they only made out Flashman's words, "I know the young brutes are in."

Then came summonses to open, which being unanswered, the assault commenced: luckily the door was a good strong oak one, and resisted the united weight of Flashman's party. A pause followed, and they heard a besieger remark, "They're in safe enough — don't you see how the door holds at top and bottom? so the bolts must be drawn. We should have forced the lock long ago." East gave Tom a nudge, to call attention to this scientific remark.

Then came attacks on particular panels, one of which at last gave way to the repeated kicks; but it broke inwards, and the broken pieces got jammed across, the door being lined with green baize, and couldn't easily be removed from outside: and the besieged, scorning further concealment, strengthened their defences by pressing the end of their sofa against the door. So, after one or two more ineffectual efforts, Flashman and Co. retired, vowing vengeance in no mild terms.

The first danger over, it only remained for the besieged to effect a safe retreat, as it was now near bed-time. They listened intently and heard the supper-party resettle themselves, and then gently drew back first one bolt and then the other. Presently the convivial noises began again steadily. "Now then, stand by for a run," said East, throwing the door wide open and rushing into the passage, closely followed by Tom. They were too quick to be caught, but Flashman was on the look-out, and sent an empty pickle-jar whizzing after them, which narrowly missed Tom's head, and broke into twenty pieces at the end of the passage. "He wouldn't mind killing one, if he wasn't caught," said East, as they turned the corner.

There was no pursuit, so the two turned into the hall, where they found a knot of small boys round the fire. Their story was told — the war of independence had broken out — who would join the revolutionary forces? Several others present bound themselves not to fag for the fifth-form at once. One or two only edged off, and left the rebels. What else could they do? "I've a good mind to go to the Doctor straight," said Tom.

"That'll never do — don't you remember the levy of the school last half?" put in another.

In fact, the solemn assembly, a levy of the school, had been held, at which the captain of the school had got up, and, after premising that several instances had occurred of matters having been reported to the masters; that this was against public morality and School tradition; that a levy of the sixth had been held on the subject, and they had resolved that the practice must be stopped at once; and given out that any boy, in whatever form, who should thenceforth appeal to a master, without having first gone to some praepostor and laid the case before him, should be thrashed publicly, and sent to Coventry.

"Well, then, let's try the sixth. Try Morgan," suggested another. "No use" — "Blabbing won't do," was the general feeling.

"I'll give you fellows a piece of advice," said a voice from the end of the hall. They all turned round with a start, and the speaker got up from a bench on which he had been lying unobserved, and gave himself a shake; he was a big loose-made fellow, with huge limbs which had grown too far through his jacket and trousers. "Don't you go to anybody at all — you just stand out; say you won't fag — they'll soon get tired of licking you. I've tried it on years ago with their forerunners."

"No! did you? Tell us how it was?" cried a chorus of voices, as they clustered round him.

"Well, just as it is with you. The fifth form would fag us, and I and some more struck, and we beat 'em. The good fellows left off directly, and the bullies who kept on soon got afraid."

"Was Flashman here then?"

"Yes! and a dirty little snivelling, sneaking fellow he was too. He never dared join us, and used to toady the bullies by offering to fag for them, and peaching against the rest of us."

"Why wasn't he cut then?" said East.

"Oh, toadies never get cut, they're too useful. Besides, he has no end of great hampers from home, with wine and game in them; so he toadied and fed himself into favour."

The quarter-to-ten bell now rang, and the small boys went off upstairs, still consulting together, and praising their new counsellor, who stretched himself out on the bench before the hall fire again. There he lay, a very queer specimen of boyhood, by name Diggs, and familiarly called "the Mucker." He was young for his size, and a very clever fellow, nearly at the top of the fifth. His friends at home, having regard, I suppose, to his age, and not to his size and place in the school, hadn't put him into tails; and even his jackets were always too small; and he had a talent for destroying clothes and making himself look shabby. . . .

[The boys carry out their strike, and there is a short but successful struggle with the fifth formers. Soon, as Diggs had told them, "all the better fellows in the fifth gave up trying to fag them, and public feeling began to set against Flashman and his two or three intimates, and they were obliged to keep their doings more secret."]

The storm had cleared the air for the rest of the house, and a better state of things now began than there had been since old Brooke had left; but an angry dark spot of thunder-cloud still hung over the end of the passage where Flashman's study and that of East and Tom lay.

He felt that they had been the first rebels, and that the rebellion had been to a great extent successful; but what above all stirred the hatred and bitterness of his heart against them was, that in the frequent collisions which there had been of late, they had openly called him coward and sneak, — the taunts were too true to be forgiven. While he was in the act of thrashing them, they would roar out instances of his funking at football, or shirking some encounter with a lout of half his own size. These things were all well enough known in the house, but to have his own disgrace shouted out by small boys, to feel that they despised him, to be unable to silence them by any amount of torture, and to see the open laugh and sneer of his own associates (who were looking on, and took no trouble to hide their scorn from him, though they neither interfered with his bullying or lived a bit the less intimately with him), made him beside himself. Come what might, he would make those boys' lives miserable. So the strife settled down into a personal affair between Flashman and our youngsters; a war to the knife, to be fought out in the little cockpit at the end of the bottom passage.

QUESTIONS

1. *Based on the passage from Tom Brown's School Days, explain how Rugby School was organized. Where did this organization come from, and how was it expressed? Read the passage over with great care, asking what rules, principles, standards, manners, and other formalities of social life you can discover.*
2. *How do you account for the following?*
   a. *Tom and East did not report the bullying to the faculty*
   b. *they did not report it to the sixth formers*
   c. *"toadies are never cut"*
   d. *the "better fellows in the fifth" gave up trying to fag them*
   e. *Diggs's conduct*
3. *To what do your explanations refer: rules, standards, principles, values, or what? How, for example, would you explain what "school principles" are and how they are different from rules? What can be meant when East says that the fifth formers have no "right" to fag the younger boys?*
4. *To what extent do you believe that Dr. Arnold understood how his school was organized and approved of it? To the extent he disapproved, why did he not change the rules and principles upon which it was based?*
5. *If you were the head of such a school, how would you attempt to organize it? What place would the rule have in what you did?*

   Here is what Arnold himself had to say: "Since I began this letter, I have had some of the troubles of school-keeping; and one of those specimens of the evil of boy-nature, which makes me always unwilling to undergo the responsibility of advising any man to send his son to a public school. There has been a system of persecution carried on by the bad against the good, and then, when complaint was made to me, there came fresh persecution on that very account; and divers instances of boys joining in it out of pure cowardice, both physical and moral, when if left to themselves they would have rather shunned it. And the exceedingly small number of boys, who can be relied on for active and steady good on these occasions, and the way in which the decent and respectable of ordinary life (Carlyle's 'Shams') are sure on these occasions to swim with the stream, and take part with the evil, makes me strongly feel exemplified what the Scriptures say about the strait gate and the wide one, — a view of human nature, which, when looking on human life in its full dress of decencies and civilizations, we are apt, I imagine, to find it hard to realize. But here, in the nakedness of boy-nature, one is quite able to understand how there could not be found so many as even ten righteous in a whole city. And how to meet this evil I really do not know; but to find it thus rife after I have been [so many] years fighting against it, is so sickening, that it is very hard not to throw up the cards in despair, and upset the table. But then the stars of nobleness, which I see amidst the darkness, in the case of the few good, are so cheering, that one is inclined to stick to the ship again, and have another good try at getting her about." Letter to Sir T. Pasley, in Findlay, Arnold of Rugby 111 (1897).

6. *Some other classic pieces of schoolboy life are George Orwell, "'Such, such were the Joys . . . ,'" in Collected Essays 9 (Anchor ed. 1954); Owen Johnson, The Varmint (1910), and his other stories of life at Lawrenceville.*
7. *In the next passage, people under circumstances of ultimate stress show what they are made of. How do you account for their behavior?*

SCOTT'S LAST EXPEDITION*

[The Scott expedition made its way to the South Pole only to discover that Amundsen, the Norwegian explorer, had got there first. On the way back, they met extremely bad weather. What follows is from Scott's diary, which was published as the first volume of this work.]

Saturday, March 10. — Things steadily downhill. Oates' foot worse. He has rare pluck and must know that he can never get through. He asked Wilson if he had a chance this morning, and of course Bill had to say he didn't know. In point of fact he has none. Apart from him, if he went under now, I doubt whether we could get through. With great care we might have a dog's chance, but no more. The weather conditions are awful, and our gear gets steadily more icy and difficult to manage. At the same time of course poor Titus is the greatest handicap. He keeps us waiting in the morning until we have partly lost the warming effect of our good breakfast, when the only wise policy is to be up and away at once; again at lunch. Poor chap! it is too pathetic to watch him; one cannot but try to cheer him up. . . .

This morning it was calm when we breakfasted, but the wind came from W.N.W. as we broke camp. It rapidly grew in strength. After travelling for half an hour I saw that none of us could go on facing such conditions. We were forced to camp and are spending the rest of the day in a comfortless blizzard camp, wind quite foul.

Sunday, March 11. — Titus Oates is very near the end, one feels. What we or he will do, God only knows. We discussed the matter after breakfast; he is a brave fine fellow and understands the situation, but he practically asked for advice. Nothing could be said but to urge him to

* Volume I (Being the Journals of Captain R. F. Scott, R.N., C.V.O.), pages 405–408 (L. Huxley ed. 1913).

march as long as he could. One satisfactory result to the discussion; I practically ordered Wilson to hand over the means of ending our troubles to us, so that anyone of us may know how to do so. Wilson had no choice between doing so and our ransacking the medicine case. We have 30 opium tabloids apiece and he is left with a tube of morphine. So far the tragical side of our story.

The sky completely overcast when we started this morning. We could see nothing, lost the tracks, and doubtless have been swaying a good deal since — 3.1 miles for the forenoon — terribly heavy dragging — expected it. Know that 6 miles is about the limit of our endurance now, if we get no help from wind or surfaces. We have 7 days' food and should be about 55 miles from One Ton Camp to-night, 6 × 7 = 42, leaving us 13 miles short of our distance, even if things get no worse. Meanwhile the season rapidly advances.

Monday, March 12. — We did 6.9 miles yesterday, under our necessary average. Things are left much the same, Oates not pulling much, and now with hands as well as feet pretty well useless. We did 4 miles this morning in 4 hours 20 min. — we may hope for 3 this afternoon, 7 × 6 = 42. We shall be 47 miles from the depôt. I doubt if we can possibly do it. The surface remains awful, the cold intense, and our physical condition running down. God help us! Not a breath of favourable wind for more than a week, and apparently liable to head winds at any moment.

Wednesday, March 14. — No doubt about the going downhill, but everything going wrong for us. Yesterday we woke to a strong northerly wind with temp. −37°. Couldn't face it, so remained in camp (R.54) till 2, then did 5¼ miles. Wanted to march later, but party feeling the cold badly as the breeze (N.) never took off entirely, and as the sun sank the temp. fell. Long time getting supper in dark. (R.55).

This morning started with southerly breeze, set sail and passed another cairn at good speed; half-way, however, the wind shifted to W. by S. or W.S.W., blew through our wind clothes and into our mits. Poor Wilson horribly cold, could not get off ski for some time. Bowers and I practically made camp, and when we got into the tent at last we were all deadly cold. Then temp. now midday down −43° and the wind strong. We *must* go on, but now the making of every camp must be more difficult and dangerous. It must be near the end, but a pretty merciful end. Poor Oates got it again in the foot. I shudder to think what it will be like to-morrow. It is only with greatest pains rest of us keep off frostbites. No idea there could be temperatures like this at this time of year with such winds. Truly awful outside the tent. Must fight it out to the last biscuit, but can't reduce rations.

Friday, March 16 or Saturday 17. — Lost track of dates, but think the last correct. Tragedy all along the line. At lunch, the day before yesterday, poor Titus Oates said he couldn't go on; he proposed we should leave him in his sleeping-bag. That we could not do, and induced him to come on, on the afternoon march. In spite of its awful nature for him he struggled on and we made a few miles. At night he was worse and we knew the end had come.

Should this be found I want these facts recorded. Oates' last thoughts were of his Mother, but immediately before he took pride in thinking that his regiment would be pleased with the bold way in which he met his death. We can testify to his bravery. He has borne intense suffering for weeks without complaint, and to the very last was able and willing to discuss outside subjects. He did not — would not — give up hope to the very end. He was a brave soul. This was the end. He slept through the night before last, hoping not to wake; but he woke in the morning — yesterday. It was blowing a blizzard. He said, "I am just going outside and may be some time." He went out into the blizzard and we have not seen him since.

I take this opportunity of saying that we have stuck to our sick companions to the last. In case of Edgar Evans, when absolutely out of food and he lay insensible, the safety of the remainder seemed to demand his abandonment, but Providence mercifully removed him at this critical moment. He died a natural death, and we did not leave him till two hours after his death. We knew that poor Oates was walking to his death, but though we tried to dissuade him, we knew it was the act of a brave man and an English gentleman. We all hope to meet the end with a similar spirit, and assuredly the end is not far.

I can only write at lunch and then only occasionally. The cold is intense, $-40°$ at midday. My companions are unendingly cheerful, but we are all on the verge of serious frostbites, and though we constantly talk of fetching through I don't think anyone of us believes it in his heart.

QUESTIONS

1. *How would you characterize the behavior of Oates and Scott? How do you account for it?*
2. *Are there rules of conduct at work here, and if so, what are they and where do they come from? Or must this conduct be traced to influences not expressible in such terms?*
3. *Notice that in this passage there is little evidence of deeply conflicting feelings, no expression of a sense that a rule or command is acting to restrain strong and contrary natural inclinations. Can it be that the conduct of Oates and Scott was really as inevitable, as natural, as it here appears to be?*

WRITING ASSIGNMENT 12: The Formation and Management of Social Expectations

• Give an account of a real or imaginary event in which you express how two or more people have organized their social relations. What expectations exist and how do they arise? If possible, choose a relationship or event to which some formal social instrument — such as a set of rules or directions or agreements — is directed, and demonstrate the relationship between that instrument and the social expectations it is intended to affect.

By "social expectations" I mean one's sense of what is expected of oneself as well as what one expects of others. By "social instrument" I mean any formal expression, written or not, that is intended to organize a relationship or a society. Your subject is the mystery of human conduct, of how we learn to behave as we do, how one person or group affects the conduct of another. You can do this assignment any way you choose, but here are some suggestions that may get you started:

1. You might show one person coming to terms with the expectations of others. Be sure to show where those expectations came from, how they were learned, and the place (if any) of rules in the process by which they were formed.

2. You might give an account of an event where a rule or other attempt to organize society — say by custom, manners, or direction — is actually at work, where it restrains someone or moves him to action. How successful is the attempt to organize social life that you portray? How was it — or might it have been — controlled by the maker or user? You might put it this way: can you show, in the particular instance you speak of, how a rule or other formality contributed to the creation or destruction of a relationship? Or how someone used the rule or formality to manage matters and achieve his ends? Or, finally, what it has actually meant for someone to say, "Let's have some rules around here"?

3. You might give an account of institutional identities at work in a relationship — say between teacher and student, doctor and patient, lawyer and client — in which you show how each party controls or fails to control the relationship. Consider, for example, formalities at work in the relationship between teacher and student. How would you describe, explain, and evaluate these? Why — to take the most obvious sort of index to the nature of a relationship — should students not at least call teachers by their first names and be addressed by them in the same way? No doubt the crude and artificial formality of "Mr." or "Ms." is an impediment to natural, warm, and genuine interpersonal relation-

ships. Can you conceive of a decent teacher not wanting to have such relationships with his students? Any decent student not wanting the same with his teachers?

The idea here is that you should exercise your social and literary imagination to visualize how people learn to live together. You should try to express as fully as possible the complex terms of an actual or imaginary relationship and demonstrate the place of rules — or formalities, manners, or customs — in that shared existence. What is the actual effect of the rule or formality? How do the people attempt to master it, and with what success? The use of any systematic statement to regulate or express a relationship, whether it takes the form of rules or not, changes things; it makes some things possible and interferes with others, and it is this tension that you are urged to address and explicate. The question might be said to have two parts: the place the rule (or other formality) has in forming social expectations; and how the intelligent person uses or evades the formality in managing his social environment. You have, no doubt, a great deal of experience to draw upon here: your life as a student or soldier, or in church or on a sports field. How have you in the past managed such formal relations? What has your mastery of the rule or other formal expression had to do with your successes and failures?

Please be careful in preparing this assignment not to fall into some sort of analytic or conclusory talk about how rules work, as though this were a political science essay. Your task is instead to express your own sense of how social life on one occasion was organized, and of the place of the rule (or other formality) in that organization. You may feel hesitation, uncertainty, and ambiguity as you look at your life; if such is your response, try to do justice to it in what you write.

2. *Vagueness, Specificity, and the Rule: The Implications of Form*

Here we shift our attention rather markedly, from how people form and manage their social expectations as a general matter to the implications of the particular form we call the rule. In Section A1 we were concerned with the social effect of any sort of formality, whatever its source and whatever its form; but here our concern is with the special form a rule must have to qualify as a valid rule in our legal system: it cannot be so specific as to be a mere command ("take the wood out back") nor can it be so general as to be too vague to operate as an intelligible guide to conduct ("be fair"). The form we call the rule is somewhere in between: "All A shall be B," or "When A occurs, B shall follow." The idea of the rule as somewhere in the middle, hovering between a specific order and a vague platitude, is fundamental to the way we think about law, and is indeed of constitutional significance: legislative rules that are too general are void for vagueness; if they are too specific they may be bad as attainders, special legislation, or for making unreasonable classifications. What are the implications and consequences of this form? Who speaks this way, talking to whom, and about what? What can be done in this language, what cannot, and why? How is it to be mastered?

a. What Happens As a Rule Changes Form?

We begin our study of the implications of form by tracing out what happens as one particular rule is recast in different ways. Our examples are drawn from past and present codes of legal ethics, beginning with old Canon 15, which has been supplanted by new provisions in the current Code of Professional Responsibility.

ABA CANONS OF PROFESSIONAL ETHICS (1908)

CANON 15

How Far a Lawyer May Go in Supporting a Client's Cause. Nothing operates more certainly to create or to foster popular prejudice against lawyers as a class and to deprive the profession of that full measure of public esteem and confidence which belongs to the proper discharge of its duties than does the false claim, often set up by the unscrupulous in defense of questionable transactions, that it is the duty of the lawyer to do whatever may enable him to succeed in winning his client's cause.

It is improper for a lawyer to assert in argument his personal belief in his client's innocence or in the justice of his cause.

The lawyer owes "entire devotion to the interest of the client, warm zeal in the maintenance and defense of his rights and the exertion of his utmost learning and ability," to the end that nothing be taken or be withheld from him, save by the rules of law, legally applied. No fear of judicial disfavor or public unpopularity should restrain him from the full discharge of his duty. In the judicial forum the client is entitled to the benefit of any and every remedy and defense that is authorized by the law of the land, and he may expect his lawyer to assert every such remedy or defense. But it is steadfastly to be borne in mind that the great trust of the lawyer is to be performed within and not without the bounds of the law. The office of attorney does not permit, much less does it demand of him for any client, violation of law or any manner of fraud or chicane. He must obey his own conscience and not that of his client.

QUESTIONS

1. *We lawyers expect and demand that rules of law be specific; if they are too vague, as you know, they may be held unconstitutional. Old Canon 15, however, is in most respects very vague indeed, and its vagueness cannot be excused on the grounds that it is an unimportant instrument – for lawyers, the canons had the force of law. How is this vagueness to bc explained?*
   a. *Why did the the authors of the canons not promulgate a set of specific, intelligible rules governing the conduct of attorneys? Do you think they were lazy? Or that they just did not know what they meant?*
   b. *How does the vagueness in this rule define its audience? What does it say about the relationship between the lawyer and those who made (and who would apply) this rule? About the relationship between the lawyer and his client?*
   c. *This canon does not answer the hardest problems – the client who lies on the witness stand, the escaped convict who decides not to take your advice to turn himself in, and so on. Why does it not do so? If it does not answer such questions, for what purposes can it possibly be used?*
2. *If a person were disbarred for violation of this canon, would he be entitled to relief in federal court on the ground that the canon is unconstitutionally vague? Why or why not?*
3. *In any event, this canon is now past history. The present Code of Professional Responsibility has rewritten this canon three ways: stating it as a canon, stating certain ethical considerations that one should take into account in following it, and stating certain disciplinary rules for violation of which an attorney may be disciplined. Below is a statement of the new canon followed by some of the Ethical Considerations and Disciplinary Rules.*

ABA CODE OF PROFESSIONAL RESPONSIBILITY AND CANONS OF JUDICIAL ETHICS (1970)

CANON 7

A Lawyer Should Represent a Client Zealously Within the Bounds of the Law

ETHICAL CONSIDERATIONS

EC 7-1 . . . The professional responsibility of the lawyer derives from his membership in a profession which has the duty of assisting members of the public to secure and protect available legal rights and remedies. In our government of laws and not of men, each member of our society is entitled to have his conduct judged and regulated in accordance with the law; to seek any lawful objective through legally permissible means; and to present for adjudication any lawful claim, issue or defense.

EC 7-4 The advocate may urge any permissible construction of the law favorable to his client, without regard to his professional opinion as to the likelihood that the construction will ultimately prevail. His conduct is within the bounds of the law, and therefore permissible, if the position taken is supported by the law or is supportable by a good faith argument for an extension, modification, or reversal of the law. However, a lawyer is not justified in asserting a position in litigation that is frivolous.

EC 7-10 The duty of a lawyer to represent his client with zeal does not militate against his concurrent obligation to treat with consideration all persons involved in the legal process and to avoid the infliction of needless harm.

EC 7-11 The responsibility of a lawyer may vary according to the intelligence, experience, mental condition or age of a client, the obligation of a public officer, or the nature of a particular proceeding. Examples include the representation of an illiterate or an incompetent, service as a public prosecutor or other government lawyer, and appearances before administrative and legislative bodies.

DISCIPLINARY RULES

DR 7-102 Representing a Client Within the Bounds of the Law.

(B) A lawyer who receives information clearly establishing that:

(1) His client has, in the course of the representation, perpetrated a fraud upon a person or tribunal shall promptly call upon his client to rectify the same, and if his client refuses or is unable to do so, he shall reveal the fraud to the affected person or tribunal.

(2) A person other than his client has perpetrated a fraud upon a tribunal shall promptly reveal the fraud to the tribunal.

DR 7-106 Trial Conduct.

(C) In appearing in his professional capacity before a tribunal, a lawyer shall not:

(1) State or allude to any matter that he has no reasonable basis to believe is relevant to the case or that will not be supported by admissible evidence.

(2) Ask any question that he has no reasonable basis to believe is relevant to the case and that is intended to degrade a witness or other person.

(3) Assert his personal knowledge of the facts in issue, except when testifying as a witness.

(4) Assert his personal opinion as to the justness of a cause, as to the credibility of a witness, as to the culpability of a civil litigant, or as to the guilt or innocence of an accused; but he may argue, on his analysis of the evidence, for any position or conclusion with respect to the matters stated herein.

(5) Fail to comply with known local customs of courtesy or practice of the bar or a particular tribunal without giving to opposing counsel timely notice of his intent not to comply.

(6) Engage in undignified or discourteous conduct which is degrading to a tribunal.

(7) Intentionally or habitually violate any established rule of procedure or of evidence.

QUESTIONS

1. What differences do you see among these various attempts to define the relationships the lawyer should have with his client and with the court?

2. One way to see what relationships are implied in these different forms might be to ask how you would draft rules for different kinds of people:

a. Suppose that you believed that every member of your community was a person of intelligence and good will who had a strong sense of obligation to do right. Would you, as omnipotent legislator, bother to make rules for them? On what matters and of what sorts?

(1) If you drafted rules, would they be specific or general in form, and why? Would the degree of generality be constant or would it vary from situation to situation? If there would be variations, explain the principles by which some rules would be made specific and others general in form.

(2) The suggestion is that great generality in the form of a rule expresses great trust in its audience. Why are trust and generality related in this way, if they are?

(3) Are the ethical implications of generality the same in all cases? Consider, for example, whether very detailed and precise parking and traffic rules express a lack of trust in the audience to which they are addressed, and why or why not.

(4) You would feel silly making rules for St. Francis or St. Benedict or even for those who wanted seriously to imitate such people. How then can you explain the existence of the monastic rules? Do you suppose they are written in general or specific terms? Or that their form varies with the subject matter? If the latter, according to what principles do you suppose the variation occurs? (A brief selection from The Rule of St. Benedict is reproduced infra page 584.)

b. Suppose you believed the reverse about your population: that everyone was utterly dishonest and self-interested. What sort of rules would you propose for them, with what sort of sanctions? Reproduced infra at pages 567–583 are some rules for prisoners, which can usefully be compared with the slave laws you have read (Chapter 3, Section E1) as examples of rules which might be thought to be of this kind.

c. How do you square your answers to these questions with Holmes's observation in "The Path of the Law," 10 Harv. L. Rev. 457, 459 (1897), that to understand the law you must look at it as a "bad man" would?

3. Does the vagueness of old Canon 15 express a high degree of trust in the attorney? In whom else might it be said to express a high degree of trust?

4. *Do you approve of the separation of the modern code into several different sorts of statement, each expressing a different set of relationships and attitudes?*
   a. *When the code states that discipline may be imposed for violation of the disciplinary rules but not for violations of the canons or ethical considerations, does this just amount to a liberal dose of ink eradicator on those portions of the code?*
   b. *Which instrument — the old canons or the new code — defines a profession of which you are more proud and in which you have more confidence? Under which set of rules do you think higher standards would be maintained and enforced? Or are the changes in the rules irrelevant to that question?*
5. *Compare these rules with those of Amherst College at the beginning of this chapter, and ask in each case why the maker of the rules might not wish to cast his directions in precise and detailed form. Is there in either case a conceivably proper reason?*
6. *Is the issue with respect to legal ethics really very simple: that moral rules are by their nature general in form, and when they are redrafted in more specific terms they lose that quality and become legalistic?*
   a. *Why should this be? Can you explain what there is about morality that requires generality, or what there is about generality that suits it to moral discourse? What does "moral" mean in propositions such as these?*
   b. *Could you argue that the fact that a set of rules is moral rather than legal should tend to make them more specific, not less so? In "Jewish Law and Morals," 75 Harv. L. Rev. 306, 320 (1961), Justice Silberg of the Israel Supreme Court explains the great formality and precision of traditional Jewish law in just that way. That law provides, for example, that when a pigeon has wandered fifty cubits from the cote, it belongs to the finder. We should today expect a rule cast in terms of "possession" defined by manifestation of control or of an attempt to control. Justice Silberg suggests that the difference can be explained by the fact that ours is a system for resolving conflicts between "man and man," while the traditional Jewish law is meant to be a "prospective ruling for moral behavior for each individual." It is exactly when the concerns are most moral or religious that certainty of obedience is most important and therefore that precision is most appropriate. How do you respond?*

WRITING ASSIGNMENT 13: The Form of Ethical Rules[2]

Part One

• *Give an account of an event in the life of a lawyer that presents a serious ethical problem. Explain why you regard this problem as serious.*

2. Four versions of assignment thirteen are given, here and at pages 545, 565, and 566 *infra*. They are somewhat shorter than the usual assignment, and it would be appropriate to ask each student to write on two or three of them.

Part Two

• *Draft a portion of a code of ethics that will tell lawyers how they should behave in the situation you have defined.*

Part Three

• *Explain what you have done. What form did your directions take, and why did you choose that form? What are the implications of the form you chose, and how do you control them in what you have written?*

b. The Constitutional Principle of Clarity — and the Practice

QUESTIONS

1. The principle that a law must not be too vague is part of our constitutional law. Precisely what purposes does this prohibition serve? Exactly what is wrong with a vague law? See generally Note, "The Void for Vagueness Doctrine in the Supreme Court," 109 U. Pa. L. Rev. 67 (1960).
2. Do these purposes require the invalidation of vague rules of civil liability as well as vague rules of criminal law? Vague mandates to administrative agencies and officers? Vague rules of professional ethics? Why do you say so?
3. Should all rules enforced by penal sanction be held to an identical standard of specificity? For example, is it unconstitutional or otherwise inappropriate that the terms of a convicted defendant's probation be that he lead a "clean, honest, and temperate life"? What are the social and intellectual implications of such a provision? See Escoe v. Zerbst, 295 U.S. 490 (1935); cf. Morrissey v. Brewer, 408 U.S. 471 (1972).
4. Evaluate the following arguments in favor of the probation terms described above.
   a. "We need discretionary power over this man in case he goes wrong."
   b. "If we do not have such discretionary powers, we shall be reluctant to grant probation."
   c. "It is appropriate for us to have this control because he has shown that he needs it."
   d. "He cannot complain about these terms, because we could perfectly properly have put him in jail. We are giving him a break and we are free to define the terms on which we do so. Probation is a privilege and not a right."
   e. "A special relationship exists here which justifies the vague terms: the grant of discretionary power to us is for his benefit."
   f. "This fellow is in no way injured by the vagueness of the standards, since by resolving every question as to his conduct in favor of socially approved behavior he can not only stay out of trouble but know he is doing so."

5. *Evaluate each of the arguments listed in question 4 with respect to the use of the same terms in a grant of parole. Do they have more or less force there, and why?*
6. *"Any commissioned officer, cadet, or midshipman who is convicted of conduct unbecoming an officer and a gentleman shall be punished as a court-martial may direct." 10 U.S.C. §933.*

   "Though not specifically mentioned in this chapter, all disorders and neglects to the prejudice of good order and discipline in the armed forces, all conduct of a nature to bring discredit upon the armed forces, and crimes and offenses not capital, of which persons subject to this chapter may be guilty, shall be taken cognizance of by a general, special, or summary court-martial, according to the nature and degree of the offense, and shall be punished at the discretion of that court." 10 U.S.C. §934.

   a. *In your opinion, are these statutory provisions constitutional?*
   b. *Would you so advise a client?*
7. *Here is a general question: when does the use of vague, ambiguous, or uncertain language in a rule serve a valuable purpose? Is it ever desirable to be vague? Consider again the various rules of Amherst College, supra, the probation standard set forth in question 3, and the various rules of legal ethics you have studied. See generally S. Surrey, Legislation 601–641 (1955); H. Hart and A. Sacks, The Legal Process 160–179 (1958).*

TWO SPECIAL KINDS OF LEGAL RULES

The Trust. One of the great creations of Anglo-Norman jurisprudence is the trust. The trust or fiduciary relationship permits one person to hold another's property not for his own benefit but for that of the beneficiary.

A special set of rules governs the fiduciary relationship, as you well know. How are these rules defined? How are they different from the rules governing other voluntarily assumed obligations? To what extent are they modifiable by contract? Are they general or specific? As they are usually stated, they seem very general indeed — almost as vague as moral obligations. Are they made specific by the cases that have defined trustees' duties in different factual situations? How heavily could you, as trustee faced with a problem of conduct, rely upon the decided cases, and how would you make that judgment? What social relationships are implied in the language of fiduciary obligation?

When does a fiduciary relationship, entailing this set of special rules, come into existence and why? How do you know one when you see it?

The Injunction. The injunction is an order of the court directed at a named individual telling him to do something, usually something specific: convey the real estate, return the heirloom, or the like.

What social relationship is implied by the use of the injunction? How is the defendant defined by this form of rule — or perhaps more accurately, by this sort of command? How is this different from the social relationship created by the law of fiduciary obligations? Note that they are both the peculiar resources of the equity court.

WRITING ASSIGNMENT 13, ALTERNATIVE A: Reconciling Constitutional Principles and Practices

The prohibition against vague statutes is a fine principle of our Constitution (which, thank heavens, is a written document and not a mystical airy nothing like the British Constitution) and a central element of the legal order.

But in what language is the vagueness rule itself expressed? One principal source is in the Fourteenth Amendment to the Constitution: "No State shall make or enforce any law which shall abridge the privileges and immunities of citizens of the United States; nor shall any State deprive any person of life, liberty, or property, without due process of law; nor deny to any person within its jurisdiction the equal protection of the laws."

• *Write a short paper in which you reconcile the constitutional principle of specificity with the constitutional practice of vagueness.* Explain why vague laws are bad but a vague constitution is not. If you are dissatisfied with the vagueness of our Constitution, draft a constitutional provision *setting forth in specific terms the prohibition against vagueness.*

It may help you to consider the following questions.

1. What do you think of this proposed amendment: "A criminal defendant shall always have the defense that he should not in good faith have known beyond a reasonable doubt that his conduct was prohibited." (Suggested by Gary Silverman.) To put it colloquially: "If the defendant's reading of the statute is a reasonable one, he wins."

2. In France, where ordinary courts do not have the power of judicial review, the courts do not hold a vague statute invalid but in a particular case will hold that a vague statute did not forbid the conduct in question. This is a nice solution: the legislative response that corrects the judicial decision must also cure the flaw in the statute. How do you evaluate this practice? Should our courts follow it? Would such a practice fully serve the purposes of the vagueness prohibition?

3. Is it really true that the language of the Bill of Rights is vague? For a view that much of it is perfectly clear see Black, "The Bill of Rights," 35 N.Y.U.L. Rev. 865 (1960); and Justice Black's opinions in New York Times v. Sullivan, 376 U.S. 254, 293 (1964), and Berger v. New York, 388 U.S. 41, 70 (1967).

4. On the assumption that you do indeed find this language of the Constitution to be vague, let me ask this: why do we bother to have such

an instrument at all? It seems little more than a set of platitudes or clichés; what can it possibly contribute to the hard problems of life?

c. *Rules and Happiness: An Impossible Combination?*

Our concern here is with what happens when people try to use rules to organize their relationships in a way that will increase their happiness. We start with one man's plan to set up society on a new basis.

LETTER TO RALPH WALDO EMERSON*

George Ripley

Our objects, as you know, are to insure a more natural union between intellectual and manual labor than now exists; to combine the thinker and the worker, as far as possible, in the same individual; to guarantee the highest mental freedom, by providing all with labor, adapted to their tastes and talents, and securing to them the fruits of their industry; to do away the necessity of menial services, by opening the benefits of education and the profits of labor to all; and thus to prepare a society of liberal, intelligent, and cultivated persons, whose relations with each other would permit a more simple and wholesome life, than can be led amidst the pressure of our competitive institutions.

To accomplish these objects, we propose to take a small tract of land, which, under skillful husbandry, uniting the garden and the farm, will be adequate to the subsistence of the families; and to connect with this a school or college, in which the most complete instruction shall be given, from the first rudiments to the highest culture. Our farm would be a place for improving the race of men that lived on it; thought would preside over the operations of labor, and labor would contribute to the expansion of thought; we should have industry without drudgery, and true equality without its vulgarity.

An offer has been made to us of a beautiful estate, on very reasonable terms, on the borders of Newton, West Roxbury, and Dedham. I am very familiar with the premises, having resided on them a part of last summer, and we might search the country in vain for anything more eligible. Our proposal now is for three or four families to take possession on the first of April next, to attend to the cultivation of the farm and the erection of buildings, to prepare for the coming of as many more in the autumn, and thus to commence the institution in the simplest manner, and with the smallest number, with which it can go into operation at all. It would thus be not less than two or three years, before we should be joined by all who mean to be with us; we should not fall to pieces by our own weight; we should grow up slowly and strong; and the

* In Warner, *George Ripley* 307–309 (1882).

attractiveness of our experiment would win to us all whose society we should want.

QUESTIONS

1. George Ripley now asks you in your capacity as a lawyer, as an expert in organizing social relationships and establishing institutions, to draw up whatever documents are in your judgment necessary or appropriate to the realization of his purposes. What do you tell him?

2. Below is an actual document meant to achieve this. How adequate is it?

CONSTITUTION OF BROOK FARM*

Articles of Agreement and Association between the members of the Institute for Agriculture and Education.

In order more effectually to promote the great purposes of human culture; to establish the external relations of life on a basis of wisdom and purity; to apply the principles of justice and love to our social organization in accordance with the laws of Divine Providence; to substitute a system of brotherly coöperation for one of selfish competition; to secure to our children, and to those who may be entrusted to our care, the benefits of the highest physical, intellectual and moral education in the present state of human knowledge, the resources at our command will permit; to institute an attractive, efficient and productive system of industry; to prevent the exercise of worldly anxiety by the competent supply of our necessary wants; to diminish the desire of excessive accumulation by making the acquisition of individual property subservient to upright and disinterested uses; to guarantee to each other the means of physical support and of spiritual progress, and thus to impart a greater freedom, simplicity, truthfulness, refinement and moral dignity to our mode of life, —

We, the undersigned, do unite in a Voluntary Association, to wit: —

Article 1. The name and style of the Association shall be "(The Brook Farm) Institute of Agriculture and Education." All persons who shall hold one or more shares in the stock of the Association, and shall sign the articles of agreement, or who shall hereafter be admitted by the pleasure of the Association, shall be members thereof.

Art. 2. No religious test shall ever be required of any member of the Association; no authority assumed over individual freedom of opinion by the Association, nor by any member over another; nor shall anyone be held accountable to the Association except for such acts as violate rights of the members, and the essential principles on which the Asso-

* Reproduced in J. Codman, *Brook Farm: Historic and Personal Memoirs* 11 (1894).

ciation is founded; and in such cases the relation of any member may be suspended, or discontinued, at the pleasure of the Association.

Art 4. The Association shall provide such employment for all of its members as shall be adapted to their capacities, habits and tastes, and each member shall select and perform such operation of labor, whether corporal or mental, as he shall deem best suited to his own endowments, and the benefit of the Association.

Art. 5. The members of this Association shall be paid for all labor performed under its direction and for its advantage, at a fixed and equal rate, both for men and women. This rate shall not exceed one dollar per day, nor shall more than ten hours in the day be paid for as a day's labor.

Art. 6. The Association shall furnish to all its members, their children and family dependents, house-rent, fuel, food and clothing, and all other comforts and advantages possible, at the actual cost, as nearly as the same can be ascertained; but no charge shall be made for education, medical or nursing attendance, or the use of the library, public rooms or baths to the members; nor shall any charge be paid for food, rent or fuel by those deprived of labor by sickness, nor for food of children under ten years of age, nor for anything on members over seventy years of age, unless at the special request of the individual by whom the charges are paid, or unless the credits in his favor exceed, or equal, the amount of such charges.

Art. 7. All labor performed for the Association shall be duly credited, and all articles furnished shall be charged, and a full settlement made with every member once every year.

Art. 8. Every child over ten years of age shall be charged for food, clothing, and articles furnished at cost, and shall be credited for his labor, not exceeding fifty cents per day, and on the completion of his education in the Association at the age of twenty, shall be entitled to a certificate of stock, to the amount of credits in his favor, and may be admitted a member of the Association.

Art. 9. Every share-holder in the joint-stock proprietorship of the Association, shall be paid on such stock, at the rate of five per cent, annually.

Art. 10. The net profits of the Association remaining in the treasury after the payments of all demands for interest on stock, labor performed, and necessary repairs, and improvements, shall be divided into a number of shares corresponding with the number of days' labor, and every member shall be entitled to one share for every day's labor performed by him.

Art. 11. All payments may be made in certificates of stock at the option of the Association; but in any case of need, to be decided by himself, every member may be permitted to draw on the funds of the treasury to an amount not exceeding the credits in his favor.

Art. 12. The Association shall hold an annual meeting for the choice of officers, and such other necessary business as shall come before them.

Art. 13. The officers of the Association shall be twelve directors, divided into four departments, as follows: first, General Direction; second, Direction of Agriculture; third, Direction of Education; fourth, Direction of Finance; consisting of three persons each, provided that the same person may be a member of each Direction at the pleasure of the Association.

Art. 14. The Chairman of the General Direction shall be presiding officer in the Association, and together with the Direction of Finance, shall constitute a Board of Trustees, by whom the property of the Association shall be managed.

Art. 15. The General Direction shall oversee and manage the affairs of the Association so that every department shall be carried on in an orderly and efficient manner. Each department shall be under the general supervision of its own Direction, which shall select, and, in accordance with the General Direction, shall appoint, all such overseers, directors and agents, as shall be necessary to the complete and systematic organization of the department, and shall have full authority to appoint such persons to these stations as they shall judge best qualified for the same.

Art. 16. No Directors shall be deemed to possess any rank superior to the other members of the Association, nor shall be chosen in reference to any other consideration than their capacity to serve the Association; nor shall they be paid for their official service except at the rate of one dollar for ten hours in a day, actually employed in official duties.

Art. 17. The Association may, from time to time, adopt such rules and regulations, not inconsistent with the spirit and purpose of the Articles of Agreement, as shall be found expedient and necessary.

[*This was signed by*]

Geo. Ripley,
Minot Pratt,
D. Mack,
Marianne Ripley,
Warren Burton,
Saml. D. Robbins,
Geo. C. Leach,
Leml. Capen,
Sophia W. Ripley,
Maria J. Pratt,
Nath. Hawthorne,
Mary Robbins.

QUESTIONS

1. *How adequate is this instrument to its purposes? Will it create the social world that Ripley has hoped for?*

a. *It may help if you put the question in these terms: what conduct will this document affect or give rise to, and how will it do so? What conversations will it occasion and how will they proceed? Exactly how will this document function in people's lives?*
b. *You may think that this document is only idealistic vaporizing. How does it differ in this respect from the Constitution of the United States?*

2. *This document recognizes that its expression of the ideal life of the Brook Farm society is incomplete: it authorizes additional rules and regulations. If you were asked by the Brook Farmers to assist them in drafting such rules, what would you tell them? On what particular subjects do you think they should consider having rules, and what alternatives as to form and substance do you see with respect to each subject?*
3. *Imagine the process of drafting such a set of bylaws, or a segment of them, and ask how the social relations defined by the official literature of Brook Farm would shift as you translated the constitutional ideals or principles into specific rules. How do you imagine the adoption of a specific set of rules would affect the hopes and lives of these good people?*
4. *Here is what one Brook Farmer had to say: "On the whole, it was a society such as has seldom met together; nor, perhaps, could it reasonably be expected to hold together long. Persons of marked individuality – crooked sticks, as some of us might be called – are not exactly the easiest to bind up into a fagot. But, so long as our union should subsist, a man of intellect and feeling, with a free nature in him, might have sought far and near without finding so many points of attraction as would allure him hitherward. We were of all creeds and opinions, and generally tolerant of all, on every imaginable subject. Our bond, it seems to me, was not affirmative, but negative. We had individually found one thing or another to quarrel with in our past life, and were pretty well agreed as to the inexpediency of lumbering along with the old system any further. As to what should be substituted, there was much less unanimity. We did not greatly care – at least, I never did – for the written constitution under which our millennium had commenced. My hope was, that, between theory and practice, a true and available mode of life might be struck out; and that, even should we ultimately fail, the months or years spent in the trial would not have been wasted, either as regarded passing enjoyment, or the experience which makes men wise." Nathaniel Hawthorne, The Blithedale Romance, Chapter 8 (1852).*
5. *Shift now from the literature of a Utopia to the reality of its life. How would you describe life in your own Utopian world? Would you do it in rules?*

UTOPIA (1516)*

Thomas More

Dishes are not served up to the whole table at first, but the best are first set before the old, whose seats are distinguished from the young, and

* In F. White, *Famous Utopias of the Renaissance* 58 (1955).

after them all the rest are served alike. The old men distribute to the younger any curious meats that happen to be set before them, if there is not such an abundance of them that the whole company may be served alike.

Thus old men are honored with a particular respect; yet all the rest fare as well as they. Both dinner and supper are begun with some lecture of morality that is read to them; but it is so short, that it is not tedious nor uneasy to them to hear it: from hence the old men take occasion to entertain those about them, with some useful and pleasant enlargements; but they do not engross the whole discourse so to themselves, during their meals, that the younger may not put in for a share: on the contrary, they engage them to talk, that so they may in that free way of conversation find out the force of every one's spirit, and observe his temper. They despatch their dinners quickly, but sit long at supper; because they go to work after the one, and are to sleep after the other, during which they think the stomach carries on the concoction more vigorously. They never sup without music; and there is always fruit served up after meat; while they are at table, some burn perfumes, and sprinkle about fragrant ointments and sweet waters: in short, they want nothing that may cheer up their spirits: they give themselves a large allowance that way, and indulge themselves in all such pleasures as are attended with no inconvenience. Thus do those that are in the towns live together; but in the country, where they live at great distance, every one eats at home, and no family wants any necessary sort of provision, for it is from them that provisions are sent unto those that live in the towns.

QUESTIONS

1. *More here describes part of life in a happy land. How do you explain the dullness of this Utopia (and of all others)? Is the problem that the very notion of a Utopia seems to suppose the disappearance of all the difficulties and troubles of life? For it can be argued that our main values and concerns take their life from adversity, and would have no meaning in such a world. See G. Kateb, Utopia and Its Enemies (1963), for a discussion of this problem familiar to every daydreamer. Referring back to a suggestion made in the section on race (Chapter 3, Section E) — would it really be ideal to abolish race, to live in a raceless world, or would that simply be a step towards dullness?*
2. *Or is this sort of dullness inherent in the rule itself (whether it be used to regulate or to describe experience), in its pretensions to do away with difficulties, its claims to solve the problems of life, its promises of an impossible and unattractive happiness?*
3. *There follows a Utopian world expressed even more completely in rules.*

HOMEOWNER'S GUIDE – SOME INFORMATION FOR RESIDENTS OF LEVITTOWN TO HELP THEM ENJOY THEIR NEW HOMES*

Levitt and Sons

Every fine residential community must have restrictions on property uses to insure the maintenance of its high standards. As a result, property values increase and greater enjoyment accrues to all homeowners. Here is a summary of the restrictions at Levittown. If you read them carefully, you will see that they have but one purpose: to protect you and your neighbors from practices that would be detrimental to your property. For that reason the restrictions will be strictly enforced.

(a) You may add an ATTACHED room or garage to your house. It must be similar in architecture, color and material to the original dwelling, and the addition must not project in front of the dwelling at all.

(b) On an interior lot, a rear addition may project up to 15 feet, provided that there is then left at least 20 feet of open rear yard. A side addition must leave at least 6 feet of open yard on each side, and a total of 13 feet on both sides.

(c) On a corner lot, each side of the house facing a street is considered a front. If your house fronts on two streets, a side or rear addition must leave at least 6 feet on one interior side and 20 feet on the other. If you bought one of the corner properties fronting on three streets, you must leave at least 6 feet on the interior side.

(d) Before you actually make any addition to your home, be sure to check the zoning ordinance and building code of the township. These, as well as the above property restrictions, must be complied with; and it may also be necessary for you to obtain a building permit from the township.

2. You may display a residence sign but it can't be more than one square foot in size. If you light it, don't use colored, flashing, unshielded or spot lighting. This could be very annoying to your neighbors.

3. You may keep not more than two domesticated household pets (dogs, cats, etc.) but no commercial breeding or harboring is allowed.

4. If you are a physician, dentist, chiropractor, chiropodist, optometrist, attorney, accountant or engineer, you may have your office in your home. But NO BUSINESS OF ANY KIND IS PERMITTED — the residential sections of Levittown must remain residential. No more than one family may occupy a house. Incidentally, no trucks or other commercial vehi-

* In J. Delafons, *Land-Use Controls in the United States* 77–79 (1962). These rules are summaries of the legal restrictions. They have in some respects been superseded.

cles may be garaged on the property except for the temporary servicing of the premises.

5. When you put your garbage out for collection make sure it is in a tightly closed metal container. Don't strew rubbish or garbage around your property.

6. You may plant a shrub or other growing fence BUT don't let it grow higher than 3 feet. NO FABRICATED FENCES (WOOD, METAL, ETC.) WILL BE PERMITTED. In designing the blocks and lots at Levittown we have achieved the maximum open and spacious appearance. Fences will cut this up into small parcels and spoil the whole effect no matter how good-looking the fence material itself may be — and some of it is or can become pretty terrible! This item is of prime importance.

7. Laundry must be hung *only* in the rear yard on a revolving portable type dryer which must be taken down when not actually in use. Old-fashioned clothes lines strung across the lawn or house look messy and are prohibited. And please don't leave laundry hanging out on Sundays and holidays when you and your neighbors are most likely to be relaxing on your rear lawn.

8. If your property backs on a road, the lot has been made at least 20 feet deeper than usual. This is so the rear 20 feet can be landscaped and screened, thereby protecting your privacy from passing automobiles and pedestrians. You must — and we're sure you'll want to — take care of this landscaping. With reasonable attention it will soon grow thick and high enough to give you complete privacy. This is the one and only place where shrub fencing is permitted to grow higher than 3 feet (see item 6 above).

9. Lawns must be mowed and weeds removed at least once a week between April 15th and November 15th. Nothing makes a lawn — and a neighborhood — look shabbier than uncut grass and unsightly weeds. A lot of thought, work and money has gone into the preparation of your lawn. It will flourish if you take care of it — but will quickly grow wild and unkempt if you don't.

10. If you live on a corner you cannot remove or add anything to the planting at the corner. Should anything die, you must replant the same items, if we don't. We go to special pains on corners and that's why we don't want them changed.

11. You or any other property owner in your section (as well as this Company) have the right to take legal steps to enforce these restrictions and eliminate violations by others.

12. The exterior material and color of each house have been carefully selected for pleasing and harmonious variety in the neighborhood. They must not be changed.

QUESTIONS

1. *Does this literature define a happy land? Can you redraft these rules so that they would do so, or do you conclude that rules can be used to define an unhappy land – here and in Myrdal (page 485 supra) and More – but not a happy land?*
2. *Exactly what is wrong with this attempt to achieve social felicity on earth? Are the rules wrongly chosen, or given the wrong form, or is there something wrong about the use of rules at all here?*
3. *What relationships among people are implied in this use of rules? Do the rules assume equality or inferiority in the audience? Trustworthiness, competence, and intelligence, or the opposite?*
   a. *Is the difficulty simply that these rules define a common taste that you do not share?*
   b. *Or is it worse: what is expressed by the existence of these rules is not the sense of a common taste, however odious, but a relentless determination not to tolerate idiosyncrasy and invention?*
4. *For a study of life as it is actually lived in Levittown, see H. Gans, The Levittowners (1967).*
5. *Next is described a Utopia that expressly casts off rules.*

THE TEMPEST*
William Shakespeare

[Alonso, King of Naples, and Sebastian, his brother, are shipwrecked on Prospero's magic island. Gonzalo is their faithful councilor. Traveling with them is Prospero's brother, Antonio, who has usurped from him the Dukedom of Milan.]

Gonzalo: Had I plantation of this isle, my lord —
Antonio: He'd sow't with nettle seed.
Sebastian: Or docks or mallows.
Gonzalo: And were the king on't, what would I do?
Sebastian: Scape being drunk, for want of wine.
Gonzalo: I' th' commonwealth I would by contraries
Execute all things; for no kind of traffic
Would I admit; no name of magistrate;
Letters should not be known; riches, poverty,
And use of service, none; contract, succession,
Bourn, bound of land, tilth, vineyard, none;
No use of metal, corn, or wine, or oil;
No occupation; all men idle, all;
And women too, but innocent and pure;
No sovereignty.

* Act 2, scene 1, lines 148 et seq.

Sebastian: Yet he would be king on't.
Antonio: The latter end of his commonwealth forgets the beginning.
Gonzalo: All things in common nature should produce
Without sweat or endeavor. Treason, felony,
Sword, pike, knife, gun, or need of any engine
Would I not have; but nature should bring forth
Of it [*sic*] own kind, all foison, all abundance,
To feed my innocent people.

QUESTIONS

1. *Can you imagine a serious claim being made that an actual legal system ought to do without rules? See O'Neil, "Research in East African Law," 3 East African L.J. 47, 67 (1967), and Tanner, "The Codification of Customary Law in Tanzania," 2 East African L.J. 105 (1966), for the somewhat tentative view that much customary and tribal law operates not by defining rights and wrongs but by establishing a process of negotiation or arbitration, and that to articulate rules defining clear sets of duties and rights would interfere with what is meant to be a process not of competition for victory but of reconciliation and compromise.*
2. *There follows here an account of a genuine society organized on the principle of no rules. How do you compare the world defined here with Rugby School and Amherst College?*

SUMMERHILL*
A. S. *Neill*

[Mr. Neill describes Summerhill as a truly democratic, self-governing school. Apparently any question can be raised and determined by a simple majority vote at the weekly school meeting. On one occasion, for example, Neill's proposal that no child under sixteen should be allowed to smoke was voted down. Interestingly a student proposal to prohibit smoking under twelve was passed, but the next week a boy under twelve proposed that smoking be universally allowed, saying, "We are all sitting in the toilets smoking on the sly just like kids do in a strict school, and I say it is against the whole idea of Summerhill." He prevailed. Individual punishments are meted out at these meetings as well, apparently in an ad hoc way. This works extremely well, says Neill: "No culprit at Summerhill ever shows any signs of defiance or hatred of the authority of his community." Neill generalizes as follows.]

At Summerhill we have proved, I believe, that self-government works. In fact, the school that has no self-government should not be called a progressive school. It is a compromise school. You cannot have freedom

* Pages 52–53 (1960). The subtitle is: *A Radical Approach to Child Rearing.*

unless children feel completely free to govern their own social life. When there is a boss, there is no real freedom. This applies even more to the benevolent boss than to the disciplinarian. The child of spirit can rebel against the hard boss, but the soft boss merely makes the child impotently soft and unsure of his real feelings.

Good self-government in a school is possible only when there is a sprinkling of older pupils who like a quiet life and fight the indifference or opposition of the gangster age. These older youngsters are often outvoted, but it is they who really believe in and want self-government. Children up to, say, twelve, on the other hand, will not run good self-government on their own, because they have not reached the social age. Yet at Summerhill, a seven-year-old rarely misses a General Meeting.

One spring we had a spate of bad luck. Some community-minded seniors had left us after passing their college entrance exams, so that there were very few seniors left in the school. The vast majority of the pupils were at the gangster stage and age. Although they were social in their speeches, they were not old enough to run the community well. They passed any amount of laws and then forgot them and broke them. The few older pupils left were, by some chance, rather individualist, and tended to live their own lives in their own groups, so that the staff was figuring too prominently in attacking the breaking of the school rules. Thus it came about that at a General School Meeting I felt compelled to launch a vigorous attack on the seniors for being not antisocial but asocial, breaking the bedtime rules by sitting up far too late and taking no interest in what the juniors were doing in an antisocial way.

QUESTIONS

1. *Does this account of Summerhill define a Utopia for school children? A Utopia you would like to make available to your own children?*
2. *Based upon what you learn from this passage, give an account of how Summerhill is really organized. How is it like and unlike Rugby School?*
   a. *One boy speaks of "the whole idea of Summerhill." How is that like or unlike the references to "school principles" in Tom Brown's School Days?*
   b. *What is the Summerhill term for those called "the wrong sort" or "thoroughly bad fellows" in the literature of Rugby School? Does Summerhill have its own version of the old-fashioned prefect system?*
   c. *Is it true that there are no rules imposed upon the children against their will, that they are free, that there is no boss?*
   d. *How do you compare and contrast the attitudes of Neill of Summerhill and Arnold of Rugby towards the social worlds for which each is responsible? Consider especially this sentence: "No culprit at Summerhill ever shows any signs of defiance or hatred of the authority of his community."*
3. *However incomplete its success, the idea of Summerhill that a community be organized without rules has a certain appeal. We have seen*

how destructive and deadening rules can be. Why do rules have this effect? Are there occasions and situations where rules do not have these consequences, but actually work well — are there occasions where they seem to be called for, to fill a need?

Consider, for example, the rules of a game — say, bridge or blackjack or golf. What are the characteristics of such rules, and how do they differ from rules of law? Is the rule somehow better adapted to the game than to the ordinary social relation, and if so, why?

a. Consider the suggestion that the unique characteristic of the rules of a game is that such rules do not regulate an activity, they constitute it. On the other hand, "the rules of law are followed and applied for reasons other than playing the law-game. The actions, decisions, and activities which are governed by legal rules are not exclusively defined by them." G. Gottlieb, The Logic of Choice 55 (1968). The author goes on to give the example of parking a car: one does not do this in order to follow rules about parking, and would in fact engage in the activity even if there were no rules.
    (1) Does one play blackjack in order to play "the blackjack game"? Are the activities governed by the rules of blackjack "exclusively defined" by those rules?
    (2) Consider the game of tennis. Do you play tennis in order to "follow rules about tennis," in order to "play the tennis game"? Are the activities of tennis "exclusively defined" by the rules of tennis? Is the tennis experience fully expressed in the rules that define it? (Wittgenstein observes that there are no rules in tennis about how high you throw the ball, or how hard. Philosophical Investigations ¶68 (2d ed. 1958).)
    (3) How about rules of poetry? Does one write poetry to play the "poetry game"? Yet Frost once said he would as soon write free verse as play tennis with the net down.

b. Now consider the rules of law and other social rules you have studied: can they be seen as defining and constituting a sort of game to be played and won? How do you distinguish in this respect the lawyer from the tennis player?
    (1) The tennis player has an experience of tennis, which is partly an experience of rules and their use, and partly something else. That is tennis. What experience does the lawyer have?
    (2) Do these questions show us what is wrong with all rules: that whatever the purposes of their makers and of much of the community, they can always be read and manipulated as the rules of a game, and that wherever there are rules, social life can be converted by a single person into a process of competition and argument?

4. Once a set of rules has been established for a relationship or an institution, it has a tendency to take over life and to dominate conversations, as you saw that the topic of race (once it is mentioned) is likely to do. When the law school dean or union officer or other bureaucrat is asked a question, he turns to a book of rules. Can you explain why this is so? What can be done about it?

5. The next version of your writing assignment will ask you to draft rules for a happy marriage and to explain what difficulties you face in trying to do so. What is there about rules that makes them unsuited to this

purpose? If they cannot be used in a relationship such as this, where there is affection and good will on both sides, where can they be used?

Consider McGuire v. McGuire, 157 Neb. 226, 59 N.W.2d 336 (1953), where a husband had a net worth of about $200,000 but gave his wife none of it to spend, keeping her at what amounted to a subsistence level. She was little more than an unpaid drudge, doing the chores, washing the clothes, and so on. She sued for more adequate support.

a. *How would you have decided this case and why? What relief would you have considered giving?*
b. *The court denied relief on the grounds that she was still living with her husband, indicating that she could recover if she moved out. Why do you suppose the court took this view? Because it did not believe it could draft rules for a happy marriage?*
c. *Can a marriage counselor draft such rules? If he can, why can a court not do likewise? If he cannot, what can he do?*
d. *Consider the following rules for marriage.*

RECONCILIATION AGREEMENT*
R. Pfaff

The aid of the Court having been requested to effect a reconciliation, or an amicable settlement of the controversy existing between the above named husband and wife, and a court conference having been held thereon in which it was indicated that certain conduct is deemed necessary to preserve the marriage or to implement the reconciliation of the parties, the parties hereby agree, each with the other and with the Court, as follows: . . .

SHARED INTERESTS:

Each party should make a deliberate effort to become interested in the work, hobbies and activities which the mate enjoys. Usually, this requires some "giving and taking" on the part of each. Married people should resolve to spend at least one half of their leisure time together, but still allow each other some freedom.

Successful marriages are those in which husband and wife plan together, work, play and laugh together, and suffer, sacrifice and pray together.

MUTUAL FRIENDS: . . .

Association by high-minded and essentially good people with persons of intemperate habits, of doubtful morals, or of vulgar or obscene speech can lead, little by little, to the dulling of fine sensibilities and to serious trouble.

We agree to strengthen our marriage through the making of mutual

* In R. Pfaff, *The Conciliation Court of Los Angeles County* (1963).

friends, new ones, if necessary, among happily married couples with responsibilities and problems akin to our own.

SOCIAL ACTIVITIES:

——— agrees to take out the ——— for dinner, entertainment, for a drive or outing, or for other social activities within the means of the family, at least ———.

RECOGNITION OF ACCOMPLISHMENTS:

Human beings are often in need of encouragement and recognition for their efforts, work and accomplishments. We agree to give each other such credit and encouragement; and, agree to accept suggestions without taking exception to them. . . .

LOVE AND AFFECTION:

Each party agrees to exert every effort to treat the other with consideration, love and understanding at all times.

TREATING MATE AS "BETTER HALF":

——— admits that in the past he has treated spouse like a child and has "punished" such spouse in various ways. He agrees hereafter to treat such spouse as a "better half", and not as a child.

TOLERANCE OF FRIENDS AND RELATIVES:

——— admits having been intolerant of spouse's relatives and friends. Therefore, such party agrees to accept such persons into the family home in a gracious manner; to carry on natural and normal conversation with them; and to treat them with respect, consideration and courtesy.

SPEAKING IN A NORMAL TONE OF VOICE:

Both parties agree that they will speak to each other in a normal tone of voice, and specifically agree not to speak in a loud or boisterous manner, or swear at, or call the other foul or obscene names, or use profane language in the presence of the children, or say anything derogatory of the members of the other's family.

SARCASTIC, BELITTLING REMARKS:

——— admits using sarcastic, cutting and belittling remarks to spouse and agrees to make every effort to avoid doing so in the future.

SILENT TREATMENT:

Each party agrees not to give the other the "silent treatment" by refusing to engage in normal conversation with the other for extended periods of time.

BEARING GRUDGES:

The parties agree that they will not harbor grudges against one another but on the contrary will air their grievances to each other before retiring for the night and make every effort to settle their differences by peaceful means. . . .

PRIVACY:

The parties agree to respect each other's right [of] privacy in such matters as personal mail. The return of either partner from an outing or visit should never be made the signal for a suspicious quizzing bee. Let each do the other the honor of reposing implicit trust in him; and let each so behave as to deserve that loyal trust by never doing anything to violate it. The parties should also learn to give each other freedom to be alone on occasions.

We agree to respect the right of privacy of one another. . . .

NAGGING:

"Nagging" is persistently annoying or fault finding. It is a tremendous contributor to marital discord and unhappiness.

The mere fact that the fault finding may be done for some justifiable reason does not excuse it. A nagging wife or husband is a most difficult person to live with. As a rule, nagging accomplishes nothing constructive; if anything, it merely gives the person being nagged an excuse for a very negative attitude.

——— admits having "nagged" spouse and agrees to make every effort to avoid doing so in the future. In return, spouse agrees to listen to the suggestions of the other and to discuss matters calmly, thereby doing away with any excuse for nagging. . . .

AN END TO THE DAY'S PROBLEMS:

Married people should acquire the habit of ending each day by calling a definite halt (as definite as the factory whistle) on the day's work and problems. Perhaps that halt might be when they close the door of their room at night. Once this time has been reached, they must resolutely keep out everything unpleasant (for their retirement hour is no place for such things). From then until sleep overtakes them, they should gladly give to each other the comfort, encouragement and loving solace they daily need, so that with strengthened hearts they can both face cheerfully the tasks and troubles of the morrow. That daily measure of mutual interest, support and love, is just as necessary for their happiness and welfare as their food and drink; and given this daily portion, they will be much less likely to forget and wound each other.

Such love, between husband and wife, is so strong a force for developing all that is good in human nature, that wise couples will not suffer their mutual attachment to become casual and commonplace under the spell of monotony, or to languish with neglect, or to degenerate into mere selfish passion; for they will realize that in this life they possess nature's most valued treasure — the loyal love of a human heart.

We promise that we will do our utmost to give each other the daily measure of interest, support and love required for a happy marriage and for a happy home for our children. . . .

SEXUAL INTERCOURSE:

Sexual intercourse provides a safe and healthy outlet of passion and preserves each party from temptations to infidelity, or to self-abuse. Moderation and considerateness should be observed in sexual relations. Moderation is simply the ability to manage one's self wisely, not allowing one's self to be carried away with passion; whether for food, drink, sex, or other pleasures.

The amount of sexual activity that constitutes moderation differs with persons, just as the amount of food they require likewise differs. To show selfishness in sexual matters brings on the offender the punishment of forfeiting respect and love. Love and consideration for the other partner will operate to find the right balance.

The parties agree that it should not be necessary for one to urge or insist that the other shall indulge in an act of sexual intercourse; because the other does not have the right to refuse, except for serious reasons. They further agree that it would be quite selfish and unjust for one to manufacture excuses or put difficulties in the way of granting the other's request. Mere inconvenience or disinclination are not sufficient reasons for refusing. The attitude of continual unwillingness or of reluctant and uncooperative acquiescence is a common cause of marital unhappiness. On the contrary, to anticipate the other's wishes — while sparing the other having to request — is proof of a love that is thoughtful, as well as genuine.

THE IMPORTANCE OF LOVE-MAKING:

The importance of "love-making" in the first stages of intercourse must not be ignored. Unfortunately, this occurs quite often between husband and wife after a few years of marriage. "Love-making", consisting of all those tender and gentle acts which are utilized to show affection and to give delight of mind and body, should not be rushed, but should be prolonged. The attentions given, however, must be such as to be agreeable and welcome — else they would repress desire, instead of arousing it.

"Lovemaking" as a prelude to sexual intercourse takes into account the difference in the nature of love in man and woman. In man, the physical or passion side is generally quickly and strongly aroused by the slightest stimulation and desire and by appropriate actions he quickly reaches the climax of physical satisfaction. In woman, it is the emotional and mental side that is most in evidence; for her, love is meaningless unless it be manifested in a profusion of loving attentions. Consequently, her passion side is slow to make its appearance, generally speaking, nor will it become strongly enough aroused except after an abundance of appropriate lovemaking. Physical union for her is out of the question until her physical desire is sufficiently aroused and her glandular processes have prepared her body for such union. Unless she has been properly prepared for it, the few minutes of union will not be sufficient to bring her to the necessary climax and consequent release of nerve tension.

If a husband and wife have quarreled, the husband will often suggest or even demand an act of sexual intercourse as a part of "making-up". Many husbands feel that this is the one big way to make up. This ignores the importance of a woman's mental attitude upon her participation in sexual union. It takes time for the wife to forget and forgive and to get herself mentally in hand so that she feels kindly and lovingly disposed toward her husband. The suggestion of intercourse, until this mental attitude has been adjusted, is generally very repulsive to her.

Repeated acts of intercourse which do not result in satisfaction for the wife become unpleasant. Under such conditions the evident satisfaction of the husband and his repeated requests must inevitably give the wife the impression of male selfishness. All the while, the ill-advised husband will come to blame her for not being interested in him — he will complain bitterly of her reluctance and her refusals — never realizing that he is himself responsible because of his own ineptness.

The wife agrees to respond to the husband's efforts in lovemaking and not to act like a patient undergoing a physical examination. For the husband to acquire proficiency in making intercourse pleasurable to the wife, he must learn to relax physically and to take his time. To do so, he should not be absorbed in himself, but rather in seeing to it that his wife is duly responding. The ultimate in his pleasure should be the realization that his wife also has enjoyed complete satisfaction.

In the event that any phase of intercourse is a cause of pain or discomfiture to either one, the parties agree to jointly discuss the matter with a competent physician; rather than to allow such a condition to continue until it becomes a real threat to the success of the marriage. . . .

HOUSEHOLD EXPENSES:

——— agrees to pay to the other party $——— per ——— out of which the latter will provide for the necessary food and clothing for the family and for the following items:

——— ———

——— ———

ALTERNATE PROVISION:

Parties agree that the ——— shall be the treasurer of the family partnership and that all pay checks shall be properly endorsed promptly upon receipt and delivered to said party. Said party shall apply the funds from such checks in payment of regular monthly bills and installment payments when due and provide necessary food, clothing and other necessities for the family. Any remaining balance shall be applied by said party only as agreed upon by husband and wife. Said party, as the family treasurer, shall maintain an accurate account of all receipts and payments in a permanent notebook which shall be available for inspection by the other party and by the court upon demand.

POCKET MONEY:

Parties further agree that there is to be deducted from each ——— check the sum of $——— as "pocket money" for the husband and $——— as "pin money" for the wife. Out of these sums the parties are to bear their own expenses for the following enumerated items as well as for the general purpose implied by the terms "pocket money" and "pin money".

ITEMS TO BE PAID OUT OF POCKET MONEY:	ITEMS TO BE PAID OUT OF PIN MONEY:
———	———
———	———

A PARTNERSHIP AGREEMENT:

Habits formed over a long period of time are not easily altered. Undoubtedly some of the provisions in this agreement will require considerable effort of the parties to this agreement. Many of the matters referred to in it may be forgotten unless it is used to refresh the memories of the parties from time to time. In times of stress, particularly, the parties should refer to it and calmly discuss it with one another, in an effort to see if its provisions are being fully complied with.

Business partnership agreements between individuals have provided the means whereby people of very different temperaments, experience and abilities have joined hands to accomplish a common objective. When difficulties arise between such partners they resort to the partnership agreement for the solution of those difficulties. If the problem is one which is new and has not been provided for in the agreement, and if they are unable to settle it between themselves, then the matter is referred to a third party or to the court to settle the dispute.

If the parties to this agreement will consider it in the nature of a partnership agreement between them and resort to it for the settlement of such disputes as may arise, it is believed that it will be of inestimable aid to them in preserving their marriage and in enabling them to discharge the obligations to one another and to the children of the marriage, which they assumed through the entering into of the marriage contract.

IT IS AGREED that the provisions of this agreement may be incorporated by the Court in a Court order. In making this agreement we and each of us hereby acknowledge that should either of us willfully fail to comply with such Court order, we shall be subject to being brought into court on a proceeding to show cause why we should not be found in contempt of court. . . .

DURATION OF AGREEMENT:

We, and each of us, hereby agree that this agreement and any order of the Court made pursuant hereto shall remain in full force and effect until further order of Court. Neither party shall take any further action in any pending divorce, separate maintenance, or annulment proceedings during the period of the conciliation proceedings and for such period of time thereafter when a Husband-Wife Agreement is in effect.

DATED: ———, 196—

———
PETITIONER

———
RESPONDENT

APPROVED

———
CONCILIATION COUNSELOR

WRITING ASSIGNMENT 13, ALTERNATIVE B: Rules for Marriage

Part One

- A young couple in your town, about to be married, have resolved upon the happiest life possible together and now come to you as the local expert in rules to ask you to draw up a set of rules for their marriage.
- Prepare a set of rules, or a portion of one, in response to that request. Consider the following questions:

1. What difficulties did you have in writing these rules? Are the rules general or specific? Do they have the essential elements of notice, sanctions, and adjudicability? Why or why not?

2. Would you recommend that your rules be enacted as laws for all married people? Why not?

No doubt you had a hard time reducing to rules what you and the young couple wanted to express. Why did you?

Part Two

- Explain what difficulties you faced and how you addressed them. If you found the task impossible, explain why it was so. If you cannot use rules to govern a marriage without destroying it, what hopes can you have for the use of rules in society at large? (Or does the law always concern itself with less important matters than marital happiness?)

It may be of interest to ask how the law talks about marriage. Think of marriage licensing laws, the doctrine of common law marriage, the law of support and community property, interspousal immunity, and so on. Perhaps the somewhat bizarre law of annulment (for fraud, impotence, incapacity, etc.) and the medieval law of divorce (for cruelty, adultery, etc.) constitute the most direct sort of legal statements about marriage — and odd you may find them, or at least foreign to your own experience or hopes of marriage. What does all that legal talk have to do with you or me? Does the law ever say anything about marriage that recognizes what it really means to the participants? Or is marriage one of the things the law just leaves out? See Schlesinger v. Schlesinger, 399 F.2d 7 (3d Cir. 1968).

Another way to state what marriage means is by the fact and language of a ceremony. See, for example, the passage from The Book of Common Prayer, supra page 288, and the marriage ritual that D. H. Lawrence in-

vented in The Plumed Serpent 343–345 (Penguin ed. 1961). The expression of marital understanding in Chapter 10 of Dickens, Our Mutual Friend (1864), may afford amusement.

d. What Are Rules Good For?

If rules are incompatible with happiness, if their very existence destroys a relationship, if they cannot be used to express our most important values and significant ideas, what are they good for? That is the subject of the last version of your assignment, which follows immediately.

WRITING ASSIGNMENT 13, ALTERNATIVE C: What Are Rules Good For?

Part One

- *Give an account of an occasion in your own experience when rules were at work in a way you approve, when they worked well.*

Part Two

- *Give an account of an occasion in your own experience when rules were at work in a way you disapprove, when they worked badly.*

Part Three

- *Explain the difference between these two occasions; and with specific reference to them, tell us what rules are good for.*

B. WHERE SEVERAL MUST COOPERATE — THE ART AND CRAFT OF MAKING RULES

In this section you will be asked to pull together much of your work in this course and to bring it to bear on the task of writing rules. In the first assigment you will be asked to draft a portion of a set of prison rules; in the second, a set of rules governing certain aspects of police behavior; and in both, to explain what you have done. These are difficult assignments that call upon your skills and knowledge as a lawyer as well as your understanding of how language works.

1. *Setting the Terms of a Complex System: The Prison as Example*

Below are collected some examples of rules governing an institution different from any we have yet studied, the prison. How does each set of rules define the institution of which it is part? Who is the prisoner here, and who are the officials? What relationships among people do these rules define and attempt to establish? What voices do you hear in these rules? Compare these rules with those of Amherst College (pages 512–514), the rules described by Myrdal and Johnson (485, 507), the Constitution of Brook Farm (547), the description of the Morgantown Center for youthful offenders (page 414), and the other rules you have read. Rules from four prisons are set forth, and you are asked to explicate the differences you see among them — and to judge whether these differences have any counterpart in the lives they are meant to regulate. The maker of rules must face as directly as he can the universal disparity between what the rule says and what the world is, between the intention and the reality. How can he respond to what he recognizes?

RULES AND REGULATIONS OF THE DIAGNOSTIC CENTER OF THE TEXAS DEPARTMENT OF CORRECTIONS (1968)

Preface

You are now in the custody of the Texas Department of Corrections.

We are required by law simply to feed you, house you, and clothe you. While you are with us, however, we shall endeavor to furnish you with experiences which will reduce the likelihood of your return to prison.

We would point out that no man was ever rehabilitated against his will. Whether you profit from the experiences here depends on you. You alone will ultimately determine whether your imprisonment is an ugly nightmare or a meaningful experience leading toward rehabilitation.

We also want to emphasize that most of the information regarding the Department of Corrections which you gathered while staying in a county jail is false and without foundation. We would suggest that you disabuse your mind of this information and rely on the instruction given you in the Diagnostic Center.

Finally, no one in this Department wants to keep you here any longer than the law demands. We are interested in getting men out of prison as fast as we legally can in order that they can enter upon productive living. Accordingly, we will aid in parole and in the earning of good time if you, by your conduct, allow us to help you.

George Beto, Ph.D.
Director.

QUESTIONS

1. *How does this preface define the prisoner it addresses?*
   a. *How, for example, does the statement that "We are required . . . simply to feed you, house you, and clothe you" define him? (Is that statement correct?)*
   b. *How about this statement: "We shall endeavor to furnish you with experiences which will reduce the likelihood of your return to prison"? How is the prisoner defined here? What would you expect those experiences to be?*
   c. *How does the instruction with respect to the information gathered in the county jail define the prison and the prisoner?*
   d. *What are the purposes of the social institution defined in this preface? Rehabilitation? Restraint? Reform? "We are interested in getting men out of prison as fast as we legally can in order that they can enter upon productive life." What can "productive life" mean in that sentence? What idea of law is implicit in this use of the word "legally"?*
   e. *How would you characterize the voice you hear in this passage?*
2. *If you were to draft an introduction to such a set of rules, what relationship would you seek to establish with the prisoner and how would you do it? Draft a paragraph from such an introduction.*
3. *Now that you have read this preface, what do you expect the rest of the rules to be like?*

RULES AND REGULATIONS OF THE DIAGNOSTIC CENTER OF THE TEXAS DEPARTMENT OF CORRECTIONS (1968)

TO ALL INCOMING INMATES:

The Diagnostic Center of the Texas Department of Corrections is designed specifically to receive all newly-committed inmates. Its primary function is to test and evaluate the individuals prior to their initial assignment.

While in the unit you will be processed through the Photo-Identification Division, Medical Department, Education Department, and Preliminary Consolidated Record Section. Upon completion of the various tests, you will appear before the sociologist for the final screening interview. The interview by the sociologist is perhaps the most important portion of your stay in the Diagnostic Center.

Upon completion of the final screening interview, you will be brought before the Classification Committee at which time you will receive your initial assignment in the Texas Department of Corrections. This assignment will be made in keeping with your medical and segregative classification and in line with your abilities. The entire processing will require from thirty to forty-five days.

Whether you are a recidivist or a first offender, it is to your advantage to maintain a clear record while in the Diagnostic Center. In the Texas Department of Corrections you must learn to respect authority; therefore, it is imperative that while in the Diagnostic Center you accept this fact.

Following is a list of rules and regulations with which you must comply. Violation of any of these will be cause for disciplinary action:

1. Upon arrival, examine your cell thoroughly to determine whether or not it contains items other than a mattress, pillow, sheet, blanket, and pillow case. Should your cell contain items other than those listed above, you should inform the officer on duty and he will make proper disposition. DO NOT, at any time, have anything in your possession or in your cell that is not issued to you by the Texas Department of Corrections, or that was not sold to you in the Diagnostic Center Commissary.

2. When speaking with an officer, stand and address him as "Mr. Smith," "Officer Smith," or "Sir." His name will be on his name plate on his right breast above the pocket.

3. Keep your cell clean at all times, and cooperate with the assigned personnel in sweeping and cleaning. Make your bed with the head to the cell door. In leaving your cell make sure that the bed is made, light is turned out and that all items are stored on the shelf.

4. Smoking is permitted in two areas only:
   A. In your cell.
   B. In the waiting room outside the Interview Section, second floor of Building "B."

There are sand urns in the above areas in which to throw cigarettes. Do not throw cigarettes or any type of litter on the floor. Do not smoke while going to and from the dining room or while you are in the dining room.

5. Do not mark, tear, or alter any clothing, shoes, or bedding issued to you.

6. Do not take to your cell from the dining room or any work area any items not in your possession when you left your cell.

7. Do not have in your possession, or make, or draw obscene pictures, literature, figures, etc.

8. Do not have in your possession playing cards, dominoes, or any material which may be used for gambling purposes.

9. Do not change places in the feed line. Remain in line when you walk from your cell block to the dining room and on return.

10. Do not waste food in the dining hall. You must eat all you take on your tray.

11. You will be required to take your seat in the dining room as directed by the officer in charge.

12. Talk in a sub-normal tone of voice while in the dining room.

13. Speak in a normal tone of voice at all times. Do not create any unnecessary disturbance or use abusive language.

14. You are only permitted two full sacks of Bull Durham in your cell or in your possession at any time. Do not stockpile it. If you don't smoke, don't take it.

15. You are permitted one towel and one pair of socks in your possession. Do not exceed the number permitted you.

16. Do not sell, give, or trade watches, rings, or any other personal possessions.

17. Always remain in the cell to which you are assigned. Do not enter anyone else's cell.

18. Fighting, scuffling, etc., will not be tolerated and violators will be punished.

19. Cursing, whether direct or indirect, will not be tolerated.

23. You will be required to obey officers at all times. Failure to do so will necessitate major disciplinary action.

24. Razors will be passed out for shaving on Monday, Wednesday and Friday nights. You will shave to include your sideburns and mustache and when razors are picked up you will stand in the cell door so the officer can see you.

25. You will remain dressed with all but the neck button of your coveralls buttoned between the hours of 7:00 AM and 5:00 PM, Mondays through Fridays and from 7:00 AM through 12:00 noon on Saturdays. When lying on your bed during the daytime, you must take your shoes off and keep them on the shelf.

If you have any questions concerning the rules and regulations, you may request information from an officer.

General Information

If you wish to discuss any matters personally with the Director of Classification or Assistant Warden, either write or speak to an officer, and he will relay the information.

We hope you will behave properly, adjust, and be eligible for release from the Department of Corrections in the shortest possible time. Good-time allowances in Texas are quite liberal. If you have to serve all your sentence you will do so in a much shorter time if you keep a good record. Your conduct will have a direct bearing on your eligibility for parole. We hope you will make a good beginning on your sentence by proper adjustment during the Diagnostic Center period.

QUESTIONS

1. *What assumptions about the prisoner are made by the preliminary statement of the function of the diagnostic center? What relationship does it seek to establish between him and his institution?*
2. *Why do you suppose the prisoner is told that the interview with the sociologist is especially important?*
3. *Now look at the rules themselves: how do they define the prisoner and his relationship with the institution? How do they define the purposes of the institution?*
4. *How is this legal literature like and unlike the literature of slavery you have read (in Chapter 3, Section E)? For example, is the prisoner entitled to do anything not expressly forbidden by the rules? If not, are these really rules of conduct or something else? What are they?*
5. *How is this literature like and unlike the various rules of Amherst College set out at the beginning of this chapter?*
6. *Which of these Texas rules, if any, do you think inappropriate in form or substance? How would you redraft this document?*

RULES OF THE COLORADO STATE PENITENTIARY (1967)[1a]

FOREWORD

Not many persons are pleased to go to prison. To most, a prison term is very painful. In spite of the fact a man may admit his guilt to himself, he has hoped throughout his trial that something may occur that will set him free.

A "GUILTY" verdict is always a heavy blow. This completely changes a man's future, disrupting his life. His spirits descend to a new low. Fear, anxiety and despair may dominate his thinking.

Aside from the possible loss of his family and friends, a man's loss means much in dollars and cents. These losses and others differ with each inmate entering prison. These losses may be offset with experiences that can be gained in prison and with what the inmate may learn "about himself and for himself". There are many ways in which the officer personnel and the officials can and will help you in this respect.

You are here because you failed to obey the laws that are acceptable to society. Due-process-of-law, in a District Court of the State of Colorado sent you here. Only by due-process-of-law will you be legally

1a. These rules are currently being revised.

released. Do not attempt to perform any action that will be detrimental to yourself, and to your obtaining that release.

Now that you ARE here, however, the administration, as well as the line officers, are responsible for your care, custody, and well being, which will be greatly improved with your cooperation. Your personal needs and comfort will be taken care of as required by the laws of the State of Colorado. A work, recreational and religious program and other privileges are maintained for your personal benefit as long as your conduct and behavior warrants these privileges.

In all communities there are certain laws and ordinances that control our conduct. There are certain institutional rules laid down to govern your conduct here, and are explained in this booklet. Strict adherence to the rules is expected and ignorance of them is no excuse for not conforming to them. Compliance with these rules will not only make your stay here easier, but may definitely shorten that stay. This is one of your prime concerns and really means the most to you.

"When can I expect to be released?" That depends entirely on you. You may wonder, "What kind of prison is this?" It is the kind of prison that you make it, and never forget that officials and line officers would like to help you make it a prison that will benefit you from having been in it.

QUESTIONS

1. *Compare this foreword with the preface to the Texas rules, and ask how each defines the prisoner it addresses.*
   a. *How does the Colorado prison define its obligation to the prisoner? How does it define the "experiences" that may be "gained in prison"?*
   b. *How does each define the prison official?*
   c. *How would you characterize the voice (or voices) you hear in this passage?*
2. *So far as you can figure out from this foreword, what are the purposes of this institution? How would you expect those purposes to be reflected in the rest of the rules?*

RULES OF THE COLORADO STATE PENITENTIARY (1967)

RULES AND REGULATIONS GOVERNING INMATES

Obey the Rules and Keep Your Privileges

Your attention is directed to the following rules and regulations. READ THEM CAREFULLY, and follow them to the letter.

Only by observing the rules and complying with them in every instance, can you maintain a good record as an inmate.

If you maintain a good record, have no reports against you, and do your work, duties and tasks assigned to you in a faithful, diligent and industrious manner, you will retain your privileges. You will receive due consideration when your case is considered by the Board of Parole.

Any breaking of the rules will subject you to penalties, forfeiture of privileges, loss of trusty and statutory-time, and other punishment as the officials may decide.

If you violate any rules, or if you fail to do your work, or if you are guilty of any misconduct, you MAY be subjected to solitary confinement or other disciplinary action. It will be entered on your record and will be taken into consideration when you apply for parole consideration, clemency, or other institutional privileges.

If an offense is of a minor nature, a Minor Report may be entered on your record. This type of report may affect your privileges, but will not affect your date of release. If the misconduct is of a major nature, you will forfeit some time as to your release date, as directed by the Disciplinary Board. You will be informed by the arresting officer that you are "on report" and the reason. Do not argue at the time of your arrest. You will be allowed to state your case at a hearing before the Disciplinary Board.

Maximum Security Division
General Rules

Rule 1. Your first duty is obedience to all the rules and regulations, and the orders of the officers of this institution.

Rule 2. Loud and boisterous talking, or shouting is strictly forbidden in any building of the institution. Whistling anywhere, at any time, is forbidden.

Rule 3. Respect yourself and all others. Be polite to the officers and to other inmates. If you wish to speak to an officer, approach him in the proper manner by addressing him as "Mr. . . . . . ," and confine your conversation to the business at hand. Insolence, in any form, to an officer is a serious offense and will call for a report.

Rule 4. Stealing, quarreling, fighting, insulting or assaulting any person is forbidden. (See rule on assault.)

Rule 5. If an argument arises between inmates, where they feel they must settle their differences by fighting, they are to obtain permission from the Midway Officer to settle their argument in the ring at the gymnasium under the supervision of an officer.

Rule 6. If any person shall pledge, solicit, or proposition a fellow inmate for [an] unnatural sex act, he will be guilty of a major rule violation.

Rule 7. Your work detail will have regular bath and haircut schedules. You are expected to keep yourself clean and shaved at all times. No mustaches or beards will be permitted. Inmates must be properly dressed at all times. Trousers are not to be worn low on hips. No cuffs are allowed on trousers. Shirts must be completely buttoned except the collar button. Long sleeve shirts may have the cuff turned up twice.

Rule 8. All outside wearing apparel and state issued clothing must be properly numbered.

Rule 9. Hands will not be allowed in pockets while talking to anyone or while walking anywhere in the Institution.

Rule 10. You must not write or carry notes or communicate by signs which involve a violation of any institutional rules.

Rule 11. Smoking will be permitted only in designated areas. There will be no smoking going to and from work nor any place in the yard while moving to or from such assignments.

Smoking tobacco, and matches are furnished to all. Only safety matches such as those issued by the institution are allowed. Lighters are permissible.

Rule 12. You must not speak to, give to, or receive from visitors, anything; except by the permission of the officer in charge. When visitors are being conducted through the prison grounds, you will not approach these visitors closer than five (5) paces at any time. Stand at attention until the visitors pass unless you are required to do otherwise in the performance of your duties.

Rule 13. Watches and rings will be allowed in the possession of inmates. The institution can assume no responsibility for jewelry items. This includes items mailed in to inmates from outside.

All Inmate Traffic Must Pass Through Midway

Rule 20. Yellow lines found throughout the institution grounds are warning lines. You are not to cross these lines without permission of the officer in charge of this area.

Keep in mind that [these] rules do not cover every contingency. Any deviation from good behavior or common decency will be considered as a rule violation even though it may not be specifically stated in the rules. Use your common sense and your good judgement. Other rules and regulations will be posted on bulletin boards from time to time.

Laws

You are advised that under the Statutes of the State of Colorado, there are penalties provided for punishment of inmates for escaping, attempting to escape, and/or for assaulting anyone with any weapon. These statutes are as follows:

The Colorado Revised Statutes, Volume 3, 1953, Chapter 105. Article 4, paragraph 6, provides that "Any inmate of the state penitentiary who escapes or attempts to escape will forfeit any good time earned to that date, both statutory and trusty."

Colorado Statutes, Annotated, 1935, Volume 2, Chapter 4g, Sec. 558: (b) "No prisoner confined in the State Prison and no prisoner under sentence to the State Prison who has escaped or attempted to escape from the prison or guards may be paroled or discharged until he has served at least two calendar years from and after the date of his return to the prison, whether such two years extended beyond his maximum sentence or not, and during such two years, such prisoner shall not be credited with any good time whatsoever." . . .

QUESTIONS

1. *Examine the passage just preceding the rules in the selection given above. How does this material define the inmate and the institution? Now examine the rules themselves: how do they do so? Do they express the attitude towards the prisoner implied in the foreword* (supra 571), *or are they just like the Texas rules all over again?*
2. *Why does this set of rules include the statutes governing escape? How does that inclusion define the prisoner it addresses?*
3. *Which of these Colorado rules, if any, do you think inappropriate in substancc or form? How would you redraft this document?*

WISCONSIN STATE PRISON RULES (1968)[1b]

General Rules of Conduct

In the interest of your protection and the protection of others, it is necessary that we have discipline and order in an institution of this size. You will get along well here by taking the attitude that you will respect the rights of others, cooperate with them, and govern your dealings with them by the principles of good sportsmanship.

If you refuse to cooperate with members of our staff, they will have no choice but to file a disciplinary report describing your misconduct. The report will be referred to the Disciplinary Committee for action and the results of the hearing, as well as the disciplinary report, will become a part of your record. Your attitude and frankness before the Disciplinary Committee will have much to do with the final outcome of the Committee action.

You will receive few disciplinary reports if you make some effort to "think first and act afterwards." If you follow the above rule, it will not

1b. The Wisconsin rules have been recently revised.

be difficult to avoid getting a disciplinary report, as is shown by the fact that many men who leave here have never received such a report.

Upon entering the prison, you will be placed in First Grade and entitled to all First Grade privileges.

For wilful violation of any of the following rules, in addition to punishment by solitary confinement on bread and water with loss of good time, or by recording a mark with loss of good time, or deprivation of privileges, the warden may, at his discretion, reduce the offender to Second or Third Grade.

You would not want others to be loud, insolent, or in any way annoy you to the point of getting you into trouble, so be considerate of others and avoid doing such things yourself.

No man shall sign any protest or petition in conjunction with other inmates. Each will make his own complaints or protests.

Trading or bartering between yourself and others is not allowed or wise without special permission of the warden or associate wardens.

Only items you have obtained through proper channels are permitted to be in your possession.

State magazines are subscribed to for your benefit. They are available to you on a loan basis. They are your magazines, so handle them with care so that as many as possible can get the benefit of them. No magazine cut-outs will be permitted in your cell for any reason, even though they may be from your own magazines.

Approach staff members in a respectful manner and use their last names, always with the title "Mr." If you don't know their last names, say "Sir."

You are not to try to become familiar with an employe nor to offer him any gift nor ask him to buy anything for or from you.

Any weapon, homemade or otherwise, found on your person or in your cell will be considered as evidence of intention to injure someone. This is a serious offense.

Cell House Rules

Keep your cell neat and clean. To draw, paint or paste pictures on the walls of your cell, or in any way to mark or mar the walls, floors, furniture, fixtures, or bed clothes, would not be good sportsmanship because when you leave that cell, someone else must move in. You will, of course, be expected to keep your wash basin and toilet clean.

So that men can study and rest, refrain from singing and whistling or making unnecessary noise. To talk or call to men in other cells would not be conducive to quiet and study.

When entering your cell, close the door quietly, and when leaving the cell, leave the door open. Whenever a count is being made, stand at the door with your hands on the bars.

Sleep with your feet towards the door.

Arise at the first gong signal in the morning — not before — and wash, dress, make your bed, sweep out your cell and be ready to march out.

Your cell hall Sergeant will instruct you as to when laundry, books, etc., are to be put out for exchange.

When you return to the cell hall, go at once to your cell. You should not remain in bed without permission after the signal to arise.

At the 10:00 P.M. signal, go to bed at once. Place your shoes at the door and the rest of your clothing on the chair next to the door. Sleep with your head uncovered or the officer will be forced to awaken you.

No smoking between 10:00 P.M. and 6:00 A.M. Smoking is permitted between the hours of 6:00 A.M. and 10:00 P.M. when you are in your cell and at authorized times and places outside of your cell.

Your door is not to be opened until the signal for your range is sounded.

Your clothing or shoes are not to be altered in any way. If your clothing or shoes do not fit or need repair, report the matter to your officer at your place of work.

Always be fully dressed when you leave your cell.

You must not have money, jewelry (other than hobby), or other valuables in your cell except approved wedding rings.

QUESTIONS

1. *How does this literature define the prisoner, the institution, and the relationship between them?*
   a. *Notice that punishment is said to follow only for "willful" violation of the rules; what is implied by this use of that term?*
   b. *The rules themselves are quite different in form from the others you have seen. Describe and explain the differences you see. Compare, for example, the following three rules:*
      (1) *Texas: "Speak in a normal tone of voice at all times. Do not create any unnecessary disturbance."*
      (2) *Colorado: "Loud and boisterous talking, or shouting is strictly forbidden in any building of the institution. Whistling anywhere, at any time, is forbidden."*
      (3) *Wisconsin: "So that men can study and rest, refrain from singing and whistling or making unnecessary noise. To talk or call to men in other cells would not be conducive to quiet and study."*

   What are the respective social implications of these rules? How confident are you in the accuracy of the implications you perceive?
2. *So far as you can tell from this literature, what are the purposes of Wisconsin State Prison? Are these purposes coherent and consistent with*

each other? Are the rules themselves written to promote those purposes, and if so, how? Or are these just the same old rules dressed up in a what is really a hypocritical way?

3. *Which of these Wisconsin rules, if any, is in your judgment inappropriate in form or substance?*
4. *Do these Texas, Colorado, and Wisconsin prison rules tell you all you need to know about social life in each institution? Imagine what other customs, practices, and formalities might exist in prison and how one would form expectations on these matters.*
5. *Below is one more document in which an institution addresses its inmates. What inferences can you confidently draw from this passage about life at Wisconsin Correctional Institution?*

RESPONSIBLE LIVING AT W.C.I. (1968)

Personal Responsibility

Your transfer to the Wisconsin Correctional Institution suggests your ability to adapt to community living and, hopefully, your desire to take advantage of opportunities on which a new life may be built under a combination training and treatment program. Maximum participation in these programs is expected. The program here contains many opportunities for education and vocational training, a variety of recreational offerings, religious services and counseling, medical care, and group and individual counseling. We place great emphasis on normal community living, stress personal responsibility and trust, and encourage the development of wholesome personal relationships. Although you may recognize the advantages of greater freedom and being encouraged to think things through and make decisions on your own, this calls for a correspondingly greater sense of personal responsibility and maturity on your part. In other words, you will have more freedom and privileges here, but you will also have greater responsibilities to yourself and to other inmates.

We would like to call attention to some of your responsibilities at the Wisconsin Correctional Institution. One important responsibility is the faith and trust that we place upon you in relation to the security of the institution. Rather than having high walls to prevent escapes, we place a high degree of trust upon you that you will not violate the security of the institution. In addition, escape is a felony offense and could add time to your present sentence. We will also expect you to do more "on your own" and accept a high degree of responsibility for your behavior 24 hours each day within the institution. Another important responsibility you will have at this institution is to be prompt and "on time" for counts, reporting for work and when attending school classes. Your responsibilities here are probably not too different from the responsibilities you have as a son, father, husband, employee, serviceman, or member of your community. Your confinement may very well represent your failure to fulfill your responsibilities in the past just as your ability and determination to meet your responsibilities will determine your future. We also feel you have the responsibility of exerting a maximum effort in your job or school program and all other activities of the daily program of the institution.

The staff here is interested in you and wants to help you. This is part of their job. They will show you consideration and they will in turn expect your attitude to be one of consideration for them. If you have any questions or problems, you are encouraged to ask any staff member for help. They will trust you and they will in turn expect you to act like an adult and not violate this trust. You will be expected to observe reasonable standards of language and conduct at all times and in all of your relationships. The program at the Wisconsin Correctional Institution is based on honest dealing with other men, respect for their dignity, and recognition of their right to make constructive use of their time. Your co-operation toward this end is strongly urged if you want to benefit from your stay here.

Negative Attitudes

There is a tendency among some inmates to be suspicious and resistive toward the administration of a correctional institution and some seem to have a need to oppose and criticize what anyone in authority tries to do for them. This is witnessed by the contrary attitudes of a few men toward treatment. Some have insulted or ridiculed other men who seem to want to get over being inmates all their lives. This so-called "Prison Code" not only handicaps the program as a whole but prevents many men from participating in activities which may lead to a better adjustment upon release. In addition, there may be obstacles to participation for some inmates because of their own suspicious and rejecting attitude. Other inmates may be so overcome by emotions such as anger, sorrow, or self pity, that they find it difficult to become strongly interested in a treatment program. At this institution, it is expected all inmates will participate in the treatment and training programs since these programs exist for your benefit and for no other reason.

2. *Drafting Institutional Rules*

Your next writing assignment will be to draft a portion of a set of rules for a prison. The questions and readings that follow are meant to help you work out a sense of what is at stake in the choices you will make in drafting such rules.

a. Increasing Confidence: Having Rules Work Both Ways

One reason why one might have little confidence in the inferences that one can draw from the prison rules presented above is that they work only one way — on the inmates and not on the institution. They are directed by an apparently omnipotent master to an abject population. What appear to be the more sensible and humane attitudes expressed in the rules may have or may not have any counterpart in institutional life. One cannot even be sure that the normal legal premise that "what is not forbidden is permitted" applies to these rules; in fact, one would probably guess it did not.

An obvious first step in drafting prison rules would then be to decide to include a set of rules going the other way — defining the rights the inmate has against his institution, rules the institution itself must follow. You will probably want to include such rules in your own draft. What matters should they cover? Against whom should they operate? By what procedures should they be enforced, and what sanctions should they invoke? Ask of this portion of your rules how it defines the prisoner, the official, and the relationship between them. What are the purposes of the institution defined here? Are these definitions of relationship and purpose consistent with those in the other portion of your rules, the portion that works on the inmates? Is it important that they be consistent?

Below is a set of rules that operate on behalf of the prisoner. How adequate are they? How might you supplement or change them?

ILLINOIS UNIFIED CODE OF CORRECTIONS (1973)

§1003-7-1. Administrative Regulations

The Department shall promulgate Rules and Regulations in conformity with this Code.

§1003-7-2. Facilities

(a) All institutions and facilities of the Department shall provide every committed person with access to toilet facilities, barber facilities, bathing facilities at least once each week, a library of legal materials, published materials including newspapers and magazines approved by the Director, and a radio or television system.

(b) All institutions and facilities of the Department shall provide facilities for every committed person to leave his cell for at least one hour each day unless the chief administrative officer determines that it would be harmful or dangerous to the security or safety of the institution or facility.

(c) All institutions and facilities of the Department shall provide every committed person with a wholesome and nutritional diet at regularly scheduled hours, drinking water, clothing adequate for the season, bedding, soap and towels and medical and dental care.

(d) All institutions and facilities of the Department shall permit every committed person to send and receive an unlimited number of uncensored letters, provided, however, that the Director may order that mail be inspected and read for reasons of the security, safety or morale of the institution or facility. Each week, the Department shall provide to every committed person postage for at least 3 first-class letters weighing one ounce or less.

(e) All of the institutions and facilities of the Department shall permit every committed person to receive visitors, except in case of abuse of the visiting privilege or when the chief administrative officer determines that such visiting would be harmful or dangerous to the security, safety or morale of the institution or facility. Clergy, religious chaplain and attorney visiting privileges shall be as broad as the security of the institution or facility will allow.

(f) All institutions and facilities of the Department shall permit religious ministrations and sacraments to be available to every committed person, but attendance at religious services shall not be required.

§1003-7-3. *Institutional Safety and Sanitation*

(a) Standards of sanitation and safety for all institutions and facilities shall be established and enforced by the Department. All buildings and facilities shall be cleaned regularly and properly maintained. Ventilation of air and heat adequate to the climate and season shall be provided.

(b) All new, remodeled and newly designated institutions or facilities shall provide at least 50 square feet of cell, room or dormitory floor space for each person.

§1003-7-4. *Protection of Persons*

The Department shall establish rules and regulations for the protection of the person and property of employees of the Department and every committed person.

§1003-8-7. *Disciplinary Procedures*

(a) All disciplinary action shall be consistent with this Chapter. Committed persons shall be informed of rules of behavior and discipline and such rules shall be posted or available to them.

(b) Corporal punishment and disciplinary restrictions on diet are prohibited. Disciplinary restrictions on clothing, bedding, mail, visitations, the use of toilets, washbowls, and showers shall be imposed only for abuse of such privileges or facilities. No person in the Adult Division may be placed in solitary confinement for disciplinary reasons for more than 15 consecutive days or more than 30 days out of any 45 day period except in cases of violence or attempted violence committed against another person or property when an additional period of isolation for disciplinary reasons is approved by the chief administrative officer. This paragraph shall not apply to segregation or isolation of persons for purposes of institutional control.

(c) Review of disciplinary action imposed under this Section shall be provided by means of the grievance procedure under Section 3-8-8. A written report of the infraction and the discipline imposed shall be filed with the chief administrative officer within 72 hours of the occurrence of the infraction or the discovery of it and such report shall be placed in the file of the institution or facility.

(d) All institutions and facilities of the Adult Division shall establish, subject to the approval of the Director, procedures for hearing disciplinary cases except those that may involve the imposition of disciplinary isolation; the loss of good time credit under Section 3-6-3 or eligibility to earn good time credit; or a change in work, education, or other program assignment of more than 7 days duration.

(e) In disciplinary cases which may involve the imposition of disciplinary isolation, the loss of good time credit or eligibility to earn good time credit, or a change in work, education, or other program assignment of more than 7 days duration, the Director shall establish disciplinary procedures consistent with the following principles:

(1) Any person or persons who initiate a disciplinary charge against a person shall not determine the disposition of the charge. The Director may establish one or more disciplinary boards to hear and determine charges. To the extent possible, a person representing the counseling staff of the institution or facility shall participate in determining the disposition of the disciplinary case.

(2) Any committed person charged with a violation of Department rules of behavior shall be given notice of the charge including a statement of the misconduct alleged and of the rules this conduct is alleged to violate.

(3) Any person charged with a violation of rules is entitled to a hearing on that charge at which time he shall have an opportunity to appear before and address the person or persons deciding the charge.

(4) The person or persons determining the disposition of the charge may also summon to testify any witnesses or other persons with relevant

knowledge of the incident. The person charged may be permitted to question any person so summoned.

(5) If the charge is sustained, the person charged is entitled to a written statement of the decision by the persons determining the disposition of the charge which shall include the basis for the decision and the disciplinary action, if any, to be imposed.

(6) A change in work, education, or other program assignment shall not be used for disciplinary purposes without prior review and approval under Section 3-8-3.

§1003-8-8. Grievances

(a) The Director shall establish procedures to review the grievances of committed persons. The Director may establish one or more administrative review boards within the Department to review grievances. A committed person's right to file grievances shall not be restricted. Such procedure shall provide for the review of grievances by a person or persons other than the person or persons directly responsible for the conditions or actions against which the grievance is made.

(b) Such procedures shall provide that a record of such grievance and any decision made with respect to it shall be preserved for a period of one year.

(c) Such procedures shall allow committed persons to communicate grievances directly to the Director or some person designated by the Director outside of the institution or facility where the person is confined.

(d) All committed persons shall be informed of the grievance procedures established by the Department and they shall be available to all committed persons.

(e) Discipline shall not be imposed because of use of the grievance procedure.

b. *Are There Any Limits upon the Principle That Rules Should Work Both Ways?*

Is the principle that rules should work both ways applicable to all institutions at all times, or are there proper limits upon its use? Look again at the various rules of Amherst College and imagine drafting a set of rules which a college must follow in its relations with its students. How would such a set of rules define the college, the students, and the relationship between them? Would you welcome such a set of rules at your own undergraduate college? At your law school?

Should we have similar sets of rules for institutions of all kinds: schools, hospitals, churches, clubs, labor unions, corporations? Should a group of law students get together right now and draft proposed codes of rights and duties for every institution in America? We lawyers have an urge to see that every part of life is expressed in legal terms, in rules and sanctions and judicial review. This is what is intelligible to us. Is there any conceivably legitimate argument to be made against such a pressure for universal lawmaking?

RULE OF SAINT BENEDICT
McCann trans. 1952

Chapter 23 Of Excommunication for Faults

If any brother shall be found contumacious, or disobedient, or proud, or a murmurer, or in any way despising and contravening the holy Rule and the orders of his superiors: let such a one, according to our Lord's commandment, be admonished secretly by his superiors for a first and a second time. If he do not amend, let him be rebuked publicly before all. But if even then he do not correct his life, let him suffer excommunication, provided that he understands the gravity of that penalty. If, however, he be perverse, let him undergo corporal punishment.

Chapter 44 How the Excommunicated Are to Make Satisfaction

Let this be the rule for one who for a serious fault is excommunicated from oratory and table. At the hour when the Work of God is being performed in the oratory, let him lie prostrate before the door of the oratory, saying nothing, but just lying there with his face to the ground at the feet of the brethren as they come out of the oratory. And let him continue to do this until the abbot judge that he has made satisfaction for his offence. When at the abbot's bidding he has come into the oratory, let him throw himself first at the abbot's feet and then before the rest of the brethren, asking them to pray for him. And then, if the abbot so order, let him be received into the choir, to the place which the abbot shall appoint. Nevertheless, he must not presume to intone psalm, or lesson, or anything else in the oratory, unless the abbot give that further permission. And at every Hour, at the end of the Work of God, let him cast himself on the ground in the place where he stands; and let him make such satisfaction until the abbot order him anew that he should desist from it. But those who for slight faults are excommunicated from the table only, shall make satisfaction in the oratory at the abbot's good pleasure. Let them do penance until he blesses them and says "That will do."

Would you propose a bill of rights for the Benedictine monk? Exactly why not? What differences are there among the monk, the prisoner, and the Amherst College student?

c. *Rules as a Way of Talking to People: Addressing One's Audience*

Your ultimate concern is with the way life is actually lived in your prison, and you no doubt hope to affect that reality somehow by your words. How can you do that? To expect that your commands will be obeyed universally and wholeheartedly is of course foolish, but it is equally foolish to think that what you say will have no effect at all. At the very least — as with the constitution of Brook Farm — you will establish a language in which certain conversations, internal and external, will go on. Your rules will set at least some of the terms of the complex activity or game of social life in your prison, if only by making some courses of conduct generally easier or less trouble than others. Inmates and officials alike will have to come to terms with what you write, though of course that is no guarantee that your purposes will be shared by anyone.

Can you find a way to address the gap between the pretenses your rules will undoubtedly raise and the reality of prison social life as you perceive or imagine it? What is the art that is called for here: writing the language of rules and at the same time recognizing what it leaves out? You can see that your attention is directed once more to the material on controlling a language system, with which the course began (Chapter 1, Section B2). Is the art of writing rules an art of writing two ways at once, of saying one thing and meaning another? What can that generalization mean in the specific instance you face?

Below are some specific questions that may help you work these matters out.

QUESTIONS

1. *How will you define the prisoner in the way you address him? How will you expect your directions to his behavior to operate? Perhaps the obvious and usual response is to say that prison rules are commands enforced by a threat of punishment. There can be no pretense of shared purposes here; the relation between institution and inmate is that between master and slave, involuntary at its heart. Accordingly, the primary merits of prison rules will be clarity of command and credibility of threat. Do you accept this view? What can you propose to replace it?*
2. *How do you define the guard in the way you address him? How do you expect your directions to his behavior to operate? Will the main virtue of your communication to him be clarity or something else? And will your directions operate by threat or on some other principle?*
3. *Put it this way: can you find a way to address either audience in a way that recognizes that both guards and prisoners are people like oneself? Or this way: can you create a literature of character, not caricature? With what voice or voices will your rules speak?*

4. *Think back to the literature of Amherst College and Rugby and Summerhill in Section A: has that any relevance to the maker of prison rules?*
   a. *Will there be any analogy in your prison to school principles or school spirit or "the whole idea of Summerhill"?*
   b. *Will there be any analogy to the praepostor of Rugby or the "community-minded senior" of Summerhill?*
   c. *Can you imagine a moment in the life of one of your inmates or guards like those moments you have been shown in the lives of Scott and Achilles (pages 533 and 522 supra)? Is there anything you can do to contribute to such an end?*

d. *Particular Difficulties That Prison Rules Must Face*

Here are some specific matters you will probably wish to address in your rules.

Sanctions. What are the appropriate sanctions for the violation of rules governing prisoner conduct? Consider the standard ones: reduction of "good time" (the acceleration of release date for trouble-free behavior); extending the period of sentence; loss of privileges pertaining to mail, visitors, exercise, movies, library, cigarettes, and so forth; detention in one's cell; segregation in a maximum security wing; solitary confinement. "Solitary" is of special interest because of its widespread use; should it be permitted at all, and if so, for how long and under what conditions?

May the prisoner be stripped, left in a room with a single light bulb permanently on, and fed an adequate but tasteless diet? Can he be denied the right to exercise and work? See *Wright v. McCann*, 321 F. Supp. 127 (N.D.N.Y. 1970); *Krist v. Smith*, 309 F. Supp. 497 (S.D. Ga. 1970), *aff'd*, 439 F.2d 146 (5th Cir. 1971); *Hancock v. Avery*, 301 F. Supp. 786 (M.D. Tenn. 1969); *Cunningham v. Wingo*, 443 F.2d 195 (6th Cir. 1971) (dictum). Cf. *Anderson v. Nosser*, 438 F.2d 183 (5th Cir. 1971).

What other sanctions can you think of?

Procedures for Punishment. How are the sanctions to be applied? By the decision of the individual guard, the chief guard, the warden, the court, or someone else? What procedures must be followed: must the prisoner have notice of charges, the opportunity to confront witnesses, to testify and introduce evidence, to have counsel, to receive a transcript, and to make an appeal? Are the same procedures required for every punishment — say, for loss of canteen privileges and for a month in solitary? For detention in isolation pending a full-scale hearing on a major charge? If the procedure varies with the nature of the offense, according to what principle does it do so? How do you decide such questions?

The following cases divide on these issues: *United States ex rel. Gallagher v. Daggett*, 326 F. Supp. 387 (D. Minn. 1971), holding that a prisoner has no right to an administrative hearing on alleged misconduct for which he is being transferred to a higher-security federal penitentiary; *Sostre v. Rockefeller*, 312 F. Supp. 863 (S.D.N.Y. 1970), *rev'd sub nom. Sostre v. McGinnis*, 442 F.2d 178 (2d Cir. 1971), *cert. denied*, 404 U.S. 1049 (1972); *Landman v. Royster*, 333 F. Supp. 621 (E.D. Va. 1971); *Bundy v. Cannon*, 328 F. Supp. 165 (D. Md. 1971); *Clutchette v. Procunier*, 328 F. Supp. 767 (N.D. Cal. 1971), holding that a prisoner has the right to seven days' notice of charges, may cross-examine and call his own witnesses, and has the right to counsel or "counsel substitute" where outcome of disciplinary proceeding may result in "grievous loss"; *Kritsky v. McGinnis*, 313 F. Supp. 1247 (N.D.N.Y. 1970). See *Haines v. Kerner*, 404 U.S. 519 (1972). Cf. *Baxstrom v. Herold*, 383 U.S. 107 (1966); *Matthews v. Hardy*, 420 F.2d 607 (D.C. Cir. 1969), *cert. denied*, 397 U.S. 1010 (1970); *United States ex rel. Schuster v. Herold*, 410 F.2d 1071 (2d Cir.), *cert. denied*, 396 U.S. 847 (1969); and *Shone v. Maine*, 406 F.2d 844 (1st Cir.), *vacated as moot*, 396 U.S. 6 (1969) — all dealing with procedures that must be followed in making transfers of prisoners to mental hospitals, or of juveniles to a prison. See also *Jackson v. Indiana*, 406 U.S. 715 (1973). *Thornton v. Corcoran*, 407 F.2d 695 (D.C. Cir. 1969), dealt with the rights of a prisoner committed for preindictment mental examination to representation at the hospital staff meeting concerning his diagnosis, and *Jones v. Robinson*, 440 F.2d 249 (D.C. Cir. 1971), with the procedures that a public mental hospital must use in placing a patient in its maximum security wing.

Use of Force. Under what circumstances is it appropriate for the officials to use force — fist, nightstick, tear gas, or lethal weapon — to compel a prisoner to obey a rule, instead of merely punishing him for noncompliance? See *Lake v. Lee*, 329 F. Supp. 196 (S.D. Ala. 1971); *Davis v. United States*, 316 F. Supp. 80 (E.D. Mo. 1970), *aff'd*, 439 F.2d 1118 (8th Cir. 1971); *Argentine v. McGinnis*, 311 F. Supp. 134 (S.D.N.Y. 1969).

A related question has arisen: when will a prisoner be entitled to relief on the grounds that his punishment is too severe for the offense he has committed? See *Fulwood v. Clemmer*, 206 F. Supp. 370 (D.D.C. 1962), holding that thirty days in solitary and two years in segregation is too severe a punishment for the offense of preaching racial incitement; *Roberts v. Pepersack*, 256 F. Supp. 415 (D. Md. 1966), *cert. denied*, 389 U.S. 877 (1967), holding that detention of the prisoner, naked, at about 40 degrees for twenty-seven hours was not too severe for circulating a letter advocating mass protest in the prison.

The Rule of Law. Must a prison regulation be stated with the clarity that we require of a penal statute? Or is there justification for punitive action under a vague rule prohibiting insubordination, insolence, indolence, uncleanliness, and the like? Refer again to the "catchall" rule (following Rule 20) in the Colorado State Penitentiary rules (page 574 *supra*). Would you allow punitive action to be undertaken for violation of such a standard?

How, if at all, should your rules regulate the discretion they give to particular officials — the guards, the warden, or others — to decide that violations have occurred and to set punishments?

Mail, Magazines, and Access to the Courts. How and why will you regulate incoming and outgoing mail? In particular, what will you do about letters coming to a prisoner from his lawyer, and those going from a prisoner to his lawyer, the courts, a publisher, or the news media? What limits will you impose on the magazines and books a prisoner may receive, and why? Cases dealing with these matters: *Nolan v. Fitzpatrick,* 451 F.2d 545 (1st Cir. 1971), holding that correspondence to the news media may be withheld by prison authorities only where it contains or concerns contraband or a plan for escape or other illegal conduct; *Berrigan v. Norton,* 451 F.2d 790 (2d Cir. 1971), dealing with the unsuccessful efforts of the Berrigan brothers to have their writings distributed for publication without review by the prison officials; *Sostre v. Otis,* 330 F. Supp. 941 (S.D.N.Y. 1971); *Peoples v. Wainwright,* 325 F. Supp. 402 (M.D. Fla. 1971); *Marsh v. Moore,* 325 F. Supp. 392 (D. Mass. 1971), enjoining the censorship of mail to and from the prisoners' attorneys; *Odell v. Wisconsin Department of Health and Social Services,* 319 F. Supp. 305 (W.D. Wis. 1970); *Fortune Society v. McGinnis,* 319 F. Supp. 901 (S.D.N.Y. 1970); *Palmigiano v. Travisono,* 317 F. Supp. 776 (D.R.I. 1970), enjoining censorship of correspondence critical of the institution and its officials between inmates awaiting trial and their attorneys, on First and Sixth Amendment grounds; *Carothers v. Follette,* 314 F. Supp. 1014 (S.D.N.Y. 1970); *Rhinehart v. Rhay,* 314 F. Supp. 81 (W.D. Wash. 1970).

Will you limit a prisoner's right to take correspondence courses? Should the subject matter of the course make a difference? See *Diehl v. Wainwright,* 419 F.2d 1309 (5th Cir. 1970). Should a prisoner be punished for refusing to disclose how he obtained letters from and photographs of his wife that had not gone through the prison censorship office? Would it matter if the photographs were pornographic? See *Rodriguez v. McGinnis,* 451 F.2d 730 (2d Cir. 1971). Can the authorities prohibit a prisoner from corresponding with his wife's sister with whom he has had an adulterous relationship? See *Morales v. Schmidt,* 340 F. Supp. 544 (W.D. Wis. 1972).

Library Privileges and Legal Advice. What rights will a prisoner have to access to a law library? To legal advice? See *Gilmore v. Lynch*, 319 F. Supp. 105 (N.D. Cal. 1970), *aff'd per curiam, sub nom. Younger v. Gilmore*, 404 U.S. 15 (1971); *Elkanich v. Alexander*, 315 F. Supp. 659 (D. Kan. 1970); *In re Harrell*, 2 Cal. 3d 675, 470 P.2d 640 (1970), *cert. denied*, 401 U.S. 914 (1971). See also *Johnson v. Avery*, 393 U.S. 484 (1969), for consideration of these matters by the Supreme Court.

Hygiene and Appearance. Will you require shaving? Short hair? See *Winsby v. Walsh*, 321 F. Supp. 523 (C.D. Cal. 1971); *Blake v. Pryse*, 315 F. Supp. 625 (D. Minn. 1970), *aff'd per curiam*, 444 F.2d 218 (8th Cir. 1971); *Brown v. Wainwright*, 419 F.2d 1376 (5th Cir. 1970).

Institutional Purposes. A prison should be a place of rehabilitation. Will you provide some relief for a prisoner who can show that his prison is in fact not rehabilitative? What relief? Compare here the "Right to Treatment" assignment, *supra* page 425. See *Holt v. Sarver*, 309 F. Supp. 362 (E.D. Ark. 1970), for the view that while one does not have a right to rehabilitation, conditions at a prison which tend to preclude rehabilitation may be unconstitutional. This opinion gives a clear account of incredibly foul prison conditions. Compare *Jones v. Wittenberg*, 323 F. Supp. 93 (N.D. Ohio 1971).

On these matters generally, see Turner, "Establishing the Rule of Law in Prison: A Manual for Prisoners' Rights Litigation," 23 *Stan. L. Rev.* 473 (1971); "Prisoners' Rights: Access to Court, Personal Security, and Restriction of Religious Practices," 42 *Colo. L. Rev.* 273 (1970).

Rules That Work on the Institution and Its Officials. What rules will you promulgate to control the actions of the institution and its officials, and how shall they be enforced? For example, suppose a guard beats a prisoner without cause and against a clear rule prohibiting that conduct; will you provide for his dismissal, for reduction in rank, for loss of vacation time, for a fine, or for damages? Or for some rehabilitative work such as one month on the garbage or latrine detail? And who shall enforce the rules — the warden, the officers' committee, the chief guard, the courts, or who?

Will your range of sanctions and procedures be uniform, or will they vary with the nature of the offense? Suppose, for example, that a guard is caught with his shirttail out or using an obscene word; what will happen to him? Who will decide this question? Should any or all of the prisoners ever be informed of the sanction that is applied in a particular case or kind of case?

e. *What Remains to be Done After Your Rules Have Been Formulated — Controlling the Terms of Cooperation*

Your job is not done when your standards have been articulated, for they are not self-executing, and some attention must be given to the processes by which they will be interpreted and applied. Is it important for you as a rule-maker to establish a procedural system by which your rules will work, or should you leave the decision of such matters to the prison officials, the lawyers, and the courts?

In setting up a procedural system — or in not doing so — you will delegate the task of deciding certain sorts of questions to various persons and agencies. How will you do this? It may be helpful to ask the following questions about each issue that you consider: who has any special competence or expertise to decide the question? Who can best acquire whatever information is needed to do it well? Whose decision will have the greatest legitimacy in the eyes of the parties and the public? Is there a provision for recourse to a higher authority, and what are that authority's qualifications? One way to begin to think these matters through would be to imagine the various practical and theoretical difficulties that would lie in the way of direct judicial enforcement of your rules if you made no specific provision for it. If someone calls upon the courts to enforce the rights defined by your prison rules (or related statutes), what arguments of what merit will he face?

Judicial Enforcement of Rules Governing Prisoner Conduct. When does the judiciary enforce rules that govern prisoner conduct? In the normal prison, never — or only when the prisoner commits a serious crime such as murder or aggravated assault. Otherwise the rules are interpreted and applied by the administration. Do you approve of this practice? Should we reverse it and make all questions of discipline justiciable? Or only some, and if so, on what principle? As you consider the possibilities, ask what other agencies might have a role here: say, a board consisting in part of prisoner representatives, or an administrative appeal board.

Who Can Challenge Institutional Action and When Can He Do So? Standing, Ripeness, and Exhaustion of Remedies. Suppose a practice exists in violation of your rules: solitary confinement is imposed without hearing, or prisoners are punished by beatings. Who can complain: any prisoner, or only one who has been injured? Can a prisoner's wife or mother complain? In *Cummins v. Ciccone,* 317 F. Supp. 342 (W.D. Mo. 1970), the prisoner alleged that his diabetic condition had been inadequately cared for and that this could have killed him. Has he standing to complain, or is the case moot? What remedy may he properly be given? Could another prisoner complain if he were also diabetic? If he were not? In *Cummins* the event complained of was not shown to be part of a policy or a regular practice, but an isolated event; how should that affect the complainant's chances of success? Compare *Church v. Hegstrom,* 416 F.2d 449 (2d Cir. 1969), holding that an allegation that prison officials knew of a prisoner's illness but did nothing about it, and that he died by reason of this neglect, fails to state a cause of action under 42 U.S.C. §1983.

Suppose a prisoner is threatened with a termination of necessary medical treatment if he persists in his intention to bring a civil action against one of the guards or the institution. Is that justiciable, or does he lack standing — or the case ripeness — because no injury has yet been suffered? See *Reynolds v. Swenson,* 313 F. Supp. 328 (W.D. Mo. 1970).

Suppose a prison is racially segregated and also practices racial discrimination in its employment of outside labor. Can black prisoners complain about both of these practices or only the former? How about white prisoners? See *Wilson v. Kelly,* 294 F. Supp. 1005 (N.D. Ga.), *aff'd per curiam,* 393 U.S. 266 (1968). Cf. *Peters v. Kiff,* 407 U.S. 493 (1972).

Is it a proper condition to a prisoner's right to bring a civil action that he have exhausted his administrative remedies? In what class of cases must a prisoner take his claim first to the warden or to an administrative board within the correctional system, and in what class may he seek judicial relief directly, and why? See *Wilwording v. Swenson,* 404 U.S. 249 (1971); *Houghton v. Shafer,* 392 U.S. 639 (1968). Cf. *Rodriguez v. McGinnis,* 450 F.2d 79 (2d Cir.), *cert. granted,* 407 U.S. 919 (1972). If the court is to be the ultimate arbiter, why should we ever require a person to go through the administrative processes first? On the other hand, assuming there is some reason for requiring exhaustion, why should it ever be excused? See *Quick v. Thompkins,* 425 F.2d 260 (5th Cir. 1970); *McNeal v. Taylor,* 313 F. Supp. 200 (W.D. Okla. 1970).

Here is the problem of exhaustion at its most dramatic: a diabetic prisoner is about to be sent to solitary for a week for repeated infractions of the dress code. He is told he can have no medicine when he is in solitary. He knows that two days without insulin will kill him. He overpowers the guards and escapes. He goes to the city hospital, where he identifies himself and gets his diagnosis and medical needs confirmed by his old doctor. He then turns himself in. What are the legal questions, and how should they be resolved? See *Dempsey v. United States,* 283 F.2d 934 (5th Cir. 1960); *United States v. Franklin,* 313 F. Supp. 43 (S.D. Ind. 1970). Of what relevance is the reasonableness of the beliefs upon which the prisoner acted? Of what relevance is their accuracy?

Compare *Wainwright v. New Orleans,* 392 U.S. 598 (1968), which raises but does not decide the question whether one has a constitutional right to resist an arrest that is unlawful under the Fourth Amendment; and *Molinaro v. New Jersey,* 396 U.S. 365 (1970), where the Court dismisses the appeal of a defendant who jumped bail pending appeal.

Scope of Review: Validity of Rules. How would you expect a court to go about deciding whether or not a rule adopted by a department of corrections was valid under a statute authorizing the department to "make appropriate rules and regulations" for the prison? Suppose the rule: prohibited beards; provided for the censorship of mail; limited access to the prison law library to two hours per week; removed the prison law library; provided for a medical doctor to be on the premises only one hour a day; established a solitary confinement system for punishment; permitted corporal punishment; required exhausting administrative remedies before seeking judicial relief; prohibited writing a court or lawyer without permission; and so on. What weight should be given the judgment of the corrections department that drafted the rules? By what standard would you determine their validity? How would you go about deciding what functions are appropriate, respectively, to the judiciary and to the administration?

Some courts have established what they call a "hands-off" policy with respect to all matters of prison administration. Does that policy meet with your approval? See, e.g., *Thogmartin v. Moseley*, 313 F. Supp. 158 (D. Kan. 1969), *aff'd mem.*, 430 F.2d 1178 (10th Cir.), *cert. denied*, 400 U.S. 910 (1970). But see *Haines v. Kerner*, 404 U.S. 519 (1972).

Scope of Review: Interpretation of Rules. Whatever weight you may give the judgment of the department of corrections in choosing and articulating a rule, what weight do you give an administrative interpretation of it and why? Is there any reason why the administrative judgment on that matter should not be conclusive, at least if the same body (say, the warden) that made the rules interprets them? Who is in the best position to say what the rules really mean?

Suppose a rule requires inmates to be "neat and orderly in appearance." In a disciplinary proceeding, the chief guard decides that sideburns below the ear violate this rule. What weight would you give that judgment and why? Would the weight depend upon the punishment provided for the violation? Why should that be?

Suppose a prison rule prohibits "all mass or collective protests or any action designed to support same." A prisoner circulates a note among several others saying, "Let's bitch about the lousy food." He is punished under the foregoing rule, which a prison hearing officer decides is applicable to this conduct. What weight would you give that judgment and why?

Scope of Review: Facts. What weight should be given the judgment of an administrative hearing officer on a disputed matter of fact? Suppose a prisoner has been beaten and the guard claims he acted in self-defense, which the prisoner denies. Each has several witnesses. The officer decides for the guard, and the prisoner is punished with ten days in solitary. What weight would you as a judge give the factual finding in a proceeding brought to restrain the imposition of that punishment? What facts not stated here would be relevant to your judgment?

Injunctions and Orders to Make Rules. In a case where the prison is fundamentally inadequate or where its rules are plainly unjust, two remedies are perhaps the most obvious: either the court can frame a set of rules governing institutional life and put them in injunctive form; or it can order the institution to make rules and submit them for court approval. How would you go about choosing between these two remedies? See *Sostre v. Rockefeller,* 312 F. Supp. 863 (S.D.N.Y. 1970), *rev'd sub nom. Sostre v. McGinnis,* 442 F.2d 178 (2d Cir. 1971), *cert. denied,* 404 U.S. 1049 (1972); *Payne v. Whitmore,* 325 F. Supp. 1191 (N.D. Cal. 1971); *Wright v. McMann,* 321 F. Supp. 127 (N.D.N.Y. 1970)—in all of which the prison or jail was ordered to draft rules and submit them for court approval; *Morris v. Travisono,* 310 F. Supp. 857 (D.R.I. 1970), in which the court adopted a set of rules negotiated between the parties and incorporated them in its order; *Holt v. Sarver,* 309 F. Supp. 362 (E.D. Ark. 1970), in which the court combined an injunction against certain practices with an order to prepare and submit rules. In *Valvano v. McGrath,* 325 F. Supp. 408 (E.D.N.Y. 1970), the court ordered a notice of the class action posted in the prison and enjoined the guards as individuals from taking any punitive action against any inmate coming forward with a complaint. Do you approve?

What other possible remedies can you think of? How about the appointment of a receiver with plenary powers over the institution? Cf. *Build of Buffalo, Inc. v. Sedita,* 441 F.2d 284 (2d Cir. 1971).

The significance of the questions we have just raised is that you must anticipate them, and others like them, in the rules you draft. You will either address them yourself or leave them to other hands; how will you decide which questions to deal with in your rules, and which to leave for others? To what extent can you, as omnipotent legislator, control the process of cooperation upon which your rules depend?

WRITING ASSIGNMENT 14: *Drafting Prison Rules*

Part One

- *Draft a portion of a set of rules governing life in a prison. These should be rules you would be happy to see your state department of corrections adopt under an act authorizing it to make "appropriate rules and regulations" for the prison.*

Part Two

• Explain what difficulties you faced and how you addressed them. Are you satisfied with the result? If not, explain why. If the reason is that you have inadequate time or information, explain what you would do with more time, and exactly what sort of information you would want and why.

Part Three

• Now give an account of an event within the prison upon which your rules bear. Try to show how in this instance law is related to life, how what the law says is connected to what the world is. Do not write as if the choice were a simple one between having things correspond precisely or not at all, between obedience and disobedience, but try to reflect in what you write what you actually know about social and institutional life. Show how your rules might actually work.

Ask of your rules the sorts of questions we have asked about the genuine rules: how do you define the prisoner and the guard in the way you address them? What relationships do you attempt to establish among these people? What purposes does your prison have, and how are these reflected in the rules you have drafted? With what voice or voices do your rules speak? You must come to terms with your estimate of the reality of prison life: what dangers do you guard against? What conflicts and tensions should you address? Do not try to draft a whole rule book, but your rules should be sufficiently complete so that the reader gets a real sense of how some aspect of prison life is regulated.

Here are some cases you can use to test your rules. Ask of each case what the legal questions are and how they would be resolved (first) under your rules and (second) in a judicial proceeding under an existing set of rules governing the conduct in question. By what procedures would these questions in each circumstance be raised and resolved?

a. A guard who has never had any training in the use of firearms is posted with a shotgun over a road crew. See Roberts v. Williams, 456 F.2d 819 (5th Cir. 1971) (addendum 1972), cert. denied, 404 U.S. 866 (1971).

b. A fire hose, mace, and clubs are used to quell a fight in the main yard. See Beishir v. Swenson, 331 F. Supp. 1227 (W.D. Mo. 1971).

c. The prison reduces sentence at a regular rate for those who do certain forms of unpaid manual labor, but not for others. Baldwin v. Smith, 316 F. Supp. 670 (D. Vt. 1970).

d. One prisoner alleges that the prison has failed to take adequate steps to protect him against homosexual attack; another, that he has been inadequately protected against revenge by inmates for his having acted as an informer. Williams v. Field, 416 F.2d 483 (9th Cir. 1969), cert. denied, 397 U.S. 1016 (1970). But cf. Perez v. Turner, 462 F.2d 1056 (10th Cir. 1972).

e. A prisoner is denied parole. He claims a right to a full hearing. The parole board takes the view that there is no need for a hearing beyond his right to appear and state his own view of his qualifications for parole, because there are no charges to be developed or defended. Menechino v. Oswald, 430 F.2d 403 (2d Cir. 1970). Cf. Morrissey v. Brewer, 408 U.S. 471 (1972).

WRITING ASSIGNMENT 14, ALTERNATIVE A: Rules for a College

The two alternative writing assignments raise difficulties similar to those of the prison rules assignment, but these may be more suited to the special interests and tastes of the student or teacher.

- *Draft a portion of a set of rules for a college. Be sure the rules "work both ways," that is, that they control the institution as well as the student. Explain what you have done and why. Be sure to study the questions raised above about the prison.*

WRITING ASSIGNMENT 14, ALTERNATIVE B: Labor Contract

- *Draft a portion of a collective bargaining agreement, with rules going "both ways." Explain what you have done and why.*

3. *How Should the Courts Speak to the Police? A Study in Institutional Relations*

In drafting the prison rules you were asked to act as a legislator, creating a self-contained institution over which you had complete power. Other agencies could act upon its affairs only when properly invoked under your rules or when authorized by the Constitution. Here, by contrast, you are asked to imagine yourself to be a court charged with the duty of deciding cases involving allegations of unconstitutional police behavior, and your situation is obviously very much changed: your powers are limited to those granted by the Constitution and the civil rights acts; and your relationship with the institution you affect —

the operating police force — is that not of creator but of outsider. The people you address are not under your command, but have loyalties running in other directions and engage in activities beyond your control or knowledge. How should you address this audience? Will you decide cases one by one under vaguely stated general principles, or will you make rules for the police to follow? If the latter, what form shall the rules take?

In this section, you will be asked to explore these questions in connection with two problems: (a) How should the courts — especially the Supreme Court — articulate and administer standards governing the admissibility of confessions in criminal trials? (b) When, if ever, should a court enforce the Fourth Amendment by an injunction against the police, and what form should such an injunction take?

a. Watts and Miranda: Finding Just the Right Way to Say "Involuntary"

Below are selections from two important cases governing the admissibility of confessions in state criminal trials. *Watts v. Indiana* applies the principle that the confession is inadmissible if it is "involuntary"; *Miranda v. Arizona* provides that confessions given by suspects in police custody are inadmissible unless the famous warnings have been given and the rights to counsel and silence validly waived. Of which of these cases do you more nearly approve and why?

You might start to work on that question by regarding each case as a way of talking about people, as a way of defining and managing social relations: each creates a social universe inhabited by the suspect, officer, trial court, and Supreme Court, a world in which a person is identified not by his character or personality but by the role he plays. In each case all officers are talked about the same way, and so are all suspects, though of course the personnel will be different every time. It is not who you are that counts, but the role that you play — and in *Miranda* some of the lines are even written for you. Which way of talking about people seems more sensible to you? Which recognizes more fully that one has some identity other than that created for him by the rule itself? In which does the Supreme Court address the policeman and the citizen more appropriately?

WATTS v. INDIANA
338 U.S. 49 (1949)

FRANKFURTER, J., announced the judgment of the Court and an opinion in which MURPHY and RUTLEDGE, JJ., join.

Although the Constitution puts protection against crime predominantly in the keeping of the States, the Fourteenth Amendment severely restricted the States in their administration of criminal justice. Thus, while the State courts have the responsibility for securing the rudimentary requirements of a civilized order, in discharging that responsibility there hangs over them the reviewing power of this Court. Power of such delicacy and import must, of course, be exercised with the greatest forbearance. When, however, appeal is made to it, there is no escape. And so this Court once again must meet the uncongenial duty of testing the validity of a conviction by a State court for a State crime by what is to be found in the Due Process Clause of the Fourteenth Amendment. This case is here because the Supreme Court of Indiana rejected petitioner's claim that confessions elicited from him were procured under circumstances rendering their admission as evidence against him a denial of due process of law.[2] 226 Ind. 655, 82 N.E.2d 846. The grounds on which our review was sought seemed sufficiently weighty to grant the petition for certiorari. 336 U.S. 917.

On review here of State convictions, all those matters which are usually termed issues of fact are for conclusive determination by the State courts and are not open for reconsideration by this Court. Observance of this restriction in our review of State courts calls for the utmost scruple. But "issue of fact" is a coat of many colors. It does not cover a conclusion drawn from uncontroverted happenings, when that conclusion incorporates standards of conduct or criteria for judgment which in themselves are decisive of constitutional rights. Such standards and criteria, measured against the requirements drawn from constitutional provisions, and their proper applications, are issues for this Court's adjudication. . . . Especially in cases arising under the Due Process Clause is it important to distinguish between issues of fact that are here foreclosed and issues which, though cast in the form of determinations of fact, are the very issues to review which this Court sits.

In the application of so embracing a constitutional concept as "due process," it would be idle to expect at all times unanimity of views. Nevertheless, in all the cases that have come here during the last decade from the courts of the various States in which it was claimed that the admission of coerced confessions vitiated convictions for murder, there has been complete agreement that any conflict in testimony as to what actually led to a contested confession is not this Court's concern. Such conflict comes here authoritatively resolved by the State's adjudication.

2. In the petitioner's statements there was acknowledgment of the possession of an incriminating gun, the existence of which the police independently established. But a coerced confession is inadmissible under the Due Process Clause even though statements in it may be independently established as true. See *Lisenba v. California*, 314 U.S. 219, 236–237.

Therefore only those elements of the events and circumstances in which a confession was involved that are unquestioned in the State's version of what happened are relevant to the constitutional issue here. But if force has been applied, this Court does not leave to local determination whether or not the confession was voluntary. There is torture of mind as well as body; the will is as much affected by fear as by force. And there comes a point where this Court should not be ignorant as judges of what we know as men. See Taft, C.J., in the *Child Labor Tax Case,* 259 U.S. 20, 37.

This brings us to the undisputed circumstances which must determine the issue of due process in this case. Thanks to the forthrightness of counsel for Indiana, these circumstances may be briefly stated.

On November 12, 1947, a Wednesday, petitioner was arrested and held as the suspected perpetrator of an alleged criminal assault earlier in the day. Later the same day, in the vicinity of this occurrence, a woman was found dead under conditions suggesting murder in the course of an attempted criminal assault. Suspicion of murder quickly turned towards petitioner and the police began to question him. They took him from the county jail to State Police Headquarters, where he was questioned by officers in relays from about 11:30 that night until sometime between 2:30 and 3 o'clock the following morning. The same procedure of persistent interrogation from about 5:30 in the afternoon until about 3 o'clock the following morning, by a relay of six to eight officers, was pursued on Thursday the 13th, Friday the 14th, Saturday the 15th, Monday the 17th. Sunday was a day of rest from interrogation. About 3 o'clock on Tuesday morning, November 18, the petitioner made an incriminating statement after continuous questioning since 6 o'clock of the preceding evening. The statement did not satisfy the prosecutor who had been called in and he then took petitioner in hand. Petitioner, questioned by an interrogator of twenty years' experience as lawyer, judge and prosecutor, yielded a more incriminating document.

Until his inculpatory statements were secured, the petitioner was a prisoner in the exclusive control of the prosecuting authorities. He was kept for the first two days in solitary confinement in a cell aptly enough called "the hole" in view of its physical conditions as described by the State's witnesses. Apart from the five night sessions, the police intermittently interrogated Watts during the day and on three days drove him around town, hours at a time, with a view to eliciting identifications and other disclosures. Although the law of Indiana required that petitioner be given a prompt preliminary hearing before a magistrate, with all the protection a hearing was intended to give him, the petitioner was not only given no hearing during the entire period of interrogation but was without friendly or professional aid and without advice as to his constitutional rights. Disregard of rudimentary needs of life — opportunities for sleep and a decent allowance of food — are also relevant, not as aggravating elements of petitioner's treatment, but as part of the total situation out of which his confessions came and which stamped their character.

A confession by which life becomes forfeit must be the expression of free choice. A statement to be voluntary of course need not be volunteered. But if it is the product of sustained pressure by the police it does not issue from a free choice. When a suspect speaks because he is overborne, it is immaterial whether he has been subjected to a physical or a mental ordeal. Eventual yielding to questioning under such circumstances is plainly the product of the suction process of interrogation and therefore the reverse of voluntary. We would have to shut our minds to the plain significance of what here transpired to deny that this was a calculated endeavor to secure a confession through the pressure of unrelenting interrogation. The very relentlessness of such interrogation implies that it is better for the prisoner to answer than to persist in the refusal of disclosure which is his constitutional right. To turn the detention of an accused into a process of wrenching from him evidence which could not be extorted in open court with all its safeguards, is so grave an abuse of the power of arrest as to offend the procedural standards of due process.

This is so because it violates the underlying principle in our enforcement of the criminal law. Ours is the accusatorial as opposed to the inquisitorial system. Such has been the characteristic of Anglo-American criminal justice since it freed itself from practices borrowed by the Star Chamber from the Continent whereby an accused was interrogated in secret for hours on end. . . .

. . . Under our system society carries the burden of proving its charge against the accused not out of his own mouth. It must establish its case, not by interrogation of the accused even under judicial safeguards, but by evidence independently secured through skillful investigation. "The law will not suffer a prisoner to be made the deluded instrument of his own conviction." 2 Hawkins, *Pleas of the Crown*, c. 46, §34 (8th ed., 1824). The requirement of specific charges, their proof beyond a reasonable doubt, the protection of the accused from confessions extorted through whatever form of police pressures, the right to a prompt hearing before a magistrate, the right to assistance of counsel, to be supplied by government when circumstances make it necessary, the duty to advise an accused of his constitutional rights — these are all characteristics of the accusatorial system and manifestations of its demands. Protracted, systematic and uncontrolled subjection of an accused to interrogation by the police for the purpose of eliciting disclosures or confessions is subversive of the accusatorial system. It is the inquisitorial system without its safeguards. For while under that system the accused is subjected to judicial interrogation, he is protected by the disinterestedness of the judge in the presence of counsel.

In holding that the Due Process Clause bars police procedure which violates the basic notions of our accusatorial mode of prosecuting crime and vitiates a conviction based on the fruits of such procedure, we apply the Due Process Clause to its historic function of assuring appropriate procedure before liberty is curtailed or life is taken. We are deeply mindful of the anguishing problems which the incidence of crime presents to the States. But the history of the criminal laws proves overwhelmingly that brutal methods of law enforcement are essentially self-defeating, whatever may be their effect in a particular case. Law triumphs when the natural impulses aroused by a shocking crime yield to the safeguards which our civilization has evolved for an administration of criminal justice at once rational and effective.

We have examined petitioner's other contentions and do not sustain them.

Reversed.

JACKSON, J., concurring in the result in No. 610 and dissenting in Nos. 76 and 107.[3]

These three cases, from widely separated states, present essentially the same problem. Its recurrence suggests that it has roots in some condition fundamental and general to our criminal system.

In each case police were confronted with one or more brutal murders which the authorities were under the highest duty to solve. Each of these murders was unwitnessed, and the only positive knowledge on which a solution could be based was possessed by the killer. In each there was reasonable ground to *suspect* an individual but not enough legal evidence to *charge* him with guilt. In each the police attempted to meet the situation by taking the suspect into custody and interrogating him. This extended over varying periods. In each, confessions were made and received in evidence at the trial. Checked with external evidence, they are inherently believable, and were not shaken as to truth by anything that occurred at the trial. Each confessor was convicted by a jury and state courts affirmed. This Court sets all three convictions aside.

The seriousness of the Court's judgment is that no one suggests that any course held promise of solution of these murders other than to take the suspect into custody for questioning. The alternative was to close the

3. No. 76 was *Harris v. South Carolina*, 338 U.S. 68; No. 107 was *Turner v. Pennsylvania*, 338 U.S. 62. Separate opinions were written by the Court for these cases; Justice Jackson wrote a single opinion for all three. — Ed.

books on the crime and forget it, with the suspect at large. This is a grave choice for a society in which two-thirds of the murders already are closed out as insoluble.

A concurring opinion, however, goes to the very limit and seems to declare for outlawing any confession, however freely given, if obtained during a period of custody between arrest and arraignment — which, in practice, means all of them.

Others would strike down these confessions because of conditions which they say make them "involuntary." In this, on only a printed record, they pit their judgment against that of the trial judge and the jury. Both, with the great advantage of hearing and seeing the confessor and also the officers whose conduct and bearing toward him is in question, have found that the confessions were voluntary. In addition, the majority overrule in each case one or more state appellate courts, which have the same limited opportunity to know the truth that we do.

Amid much that is irrelevant or trivial, one serious situation seems to me to stand out in these cases. The suspect neither had nor was advised of his right to get counsel. This presents a real dilemma in a free society. To subject one without counsel to questioning which may [bc] and is intended to convict him, is a real peril to individual freedom. To bring in a lawyer means a real peril to solution of the crime, because, under our adversary system, he deems that his sole duty is to protect his client — guilty or innocent — and that in such a capacity he owes no duty whatever to help society solve its crime problem. Under this conception of criminal procedure, any lawyer worth his salt will tell the suspect in no uncertain terms to make no statement to police under any circumstances.

If the State may arrest on suspicion and interrogate without counsel, there is no denying the fact that it largely negates the benefits of the constitutional guaranty of the right to assistance of counsel. Any lawyer who has ever been called into a case after his client has "told all" and turned any evidence he has over to the Government, knows how helpless he is to protect his client against the facts thus disclosed.

I suppose the view one takes will turn on what one thinks should be the right of an accused person against the State. Is it his right to have the judgment on the facts? Or is it his right to have a judgment based on only such evidence as he cannot conceal from the authorities, who cannot compel him to testify in court and also cannot question him before? Our system comes close to the latter by any interpretation, for the defendant is shielded by such safeguards as no system of law except the Anglo-American concedes to him.

Of course, no confession that has been obtained by any form of physical violence to the person is reliable and hence no conviction should rest upon one obtained in that manner. Such treatment not only breaks the will to conceal or lie, but may even break the will to stand by the truth. Nor is it questioned that the same result can sometimes be achieved by threats, promises, or inducements, which torture the mind but put no scar on the body. If the opinion of Mr. Justice Frankfurter in the *Watts* case were based solely on the State's admissions as to the treatment of Watts, I should not disagree. But if [the] ultimate quest in a criminal trial is the truth and if the circumstances indicate no violence or threats of it, should society be deprived of the suspect's help in solving a crime merely because he was confined and questioned when uncounseled?

We must not overlook that, in these as in some previous cases, once a confession is obtained it supplies ways of verifying its trustworthiness. In these cases before us the verification is sufficient to leave me in no doubt that the admissions of guilt were genuine and truthful. Such corroboration consists in one case of finding a weapon where the accused has said he hid it, and in others that conditions which could only have been known to one who was implicated correspond with his story. It is possible, but it is rare, that a confession, if repudiated on the trial, standing alone will convict unless there is external proof of its verity.

In all such cases, along with other conditions criticized, the continuity and duration of the questioning is invoked and it is called an "inquiry," "inquest" or "inquisition," depending mainly on the emotional state of the writer. But as in some of the cases here, if interrogation is permissible at all, there are sound reasons for prolonging it — which the opinions here ignore. The suspect at first perhaps makes an effort to exculpate himself by alibis or other statements. These are verified, found false, and he is then confronted with his falsehood. Sometimes (though such cases do not reach us) verification proves them true or credible and the suspect is released. Sometimes, as here, more than one crime is involved. The duration of an interrogation may well depend on the temperament, shrewdness and cunning of the accused and the competence of the examiner. But, assuming a right to examine at all, the right must include what is made reasonably necessary by the facts of the particular case.

If the right of interrogation be admitted, then it seems to me that we must leave it to trial judges and juries and state appellate courts to decide individual cases, unless they show some want of proper standards of decision. I find nothing to indicate that any of the courts below in these cases did not have a correct understanding of the Fourteenth Amendment, unless this Court thinks it means absolute prohibition of interrogation while in custody before arraignment.

I suppose no one would doubt that our Constitution and Bill of Rights, grounded in revolt against the arbitrary measures of George III and in the philosophy of the French Revolution, represent the maximum restrictions upon the power of organized society over the individual that are compatible with the maintenance of organized society itself. They were so intended and should be so interpreted. It cannot be denied that, even if construed as these provisions traditionally have been, they contain an aggregate of restrictions which seriously limit the power of society to solve such crimes as confront us in these cases. Those restrictions we should not for that reason cast aside, but that is good reason for indulging in no unnecessary expansion of them.

I doubt very much if they require us to hold that the State may not take into custody and question one suspected reasonably of an unwitnessed murder. If it does, the people of this country must discipline themselves to seeing their police stand by helplessly while those suspected of murder prowl about unmolested. Is it a necessary price to pay for the fairness which we know as "due process of law"? And if not a necessary one, should it be demanded by this Court? I do not know the ultimate answer to these questions; but, for the present, I should not increase the handicap on society.

QUESTIONS

1. *Justice Jackson suggests that the "ultimate quest" in criminal trials is for the "truth." Do you agree? What can be meant by "truth" in such a sentence? How, if at all, does Justice Frankfurter respond to this claim of Justice Jackson?*
2. *How can the Supreme Court decide any criminal case properly unless it both knows "the truth" and has decided what its "ultimate quest" is?*
3. *The Court says that the failure of the police to take Watts to a magistrate was a direct violation of Indiana law. Why is that fact itself not a sufficient reason to hold that the conviction based upon this confession violates the due process clause?*
4. *Why does the Supreme Court give great weight to the judgment of a state trial court in resolving disputes as to the primary facts and not to its judgment as to whether these facts constitute a "voluntary" or "involuntary" confession?*
5. *What, in fact, does the Court mean by the word "voluntary"? If a "confession by which life becomes forfeit" must be the "expression of free choice," what confessions will ever be valid? And what guidance does the Court give to an officer who wishes to carry on the interrogation of a suspect? Compare in these respects the following opinion.*

MIRANDA v. ARIZONA
384 U.S. 436 (1966)

WARREN, C.J., delivered the opinion of the Court. The cases before us raise questions which go to the roots of our concepts of American criminal jurisprudence: the restraints society must observe consistent with the Federal Constitution in prosecuting individuals for crime. More specifically, we deal with the admissibility of statements obtained from an individual who is subjected to custodial police interrogation and the necessity for procedures which assure that the individual is accorded his privilege under the Fifth Amendment to the Constitution not to be compelled to incriminate himself.

We dealt with certain phases of this problem recently in *Escobedo v. Illinois,* 378 U.S. 478 (1964). There, as in the four cases before us, law enforcement officials took the defendant into custody and interrogated him in a police station for the purpose of obtaining a confession. The police did not effectively advise him of his right to remain silent or of his right to consult with his attorney. Rather, they confronted him with an alleged accomplice who accused him of having perpetrated a murder. When the defendant denied the accusation and said "I didn't shoot Manuel, you did it," they handcuffed him and took him to an interrogation room. There, while handcuffed and standing, he was questioned for four hours until he confessed. During this interrogation, the police denied his request to speak to his attorney, and they prevented his retained attorney, who had come to the police station, from consulting with him. At his trial, the State, over his objection, introduced the confession against him. We held that the statements thus made were constitutionally inadmissible.

This case has been the subject of judicial interpretation and spirited legal debate since it was decided two years ago. Both state and federal courts, in assessing its implications, have arrived at varying conclusions. A wealth of scholarly material has been written tracing its ramifications and underpinnings. Police and prosecutor have speculated on its range and desirability. We granted certiorari in these cases, 382 U.S. 924, 925, 937, in order further to explore some facets of the problems, thus exposed, of applying the privilege against self-incrimination to in-custody interrogation, and to give concrete constitutional guidelines for law enforcement agencies and courts to follow.

We start here, as we did in *Escobedo,* with the premise that our holding is not an innovation in our jurisprudence, but is an application of principles long recognized and applied in other settings. We have undertaken a thorough re-examination of the *Escobedo* decision and the principles it announced, and we reaffirm it. That case was but an explication of basic rights that are enshrined in our Constitution — that "No person . . . shall be compelled in any criminal case to be a witness against himself," and that "the accused shall . . . have the Assistance of Counsel" — rights which were put in jeopardy in that case through official overbearing. These precious rights were fixed in our Constitution only after centuries of persecution and struggle. And in the words of Chief Justice Marshall, they were secured "for ages to come, and . . . designed to approach immortality as nearly as human institutions can approach it," *Cohens v. Virginia,* 6 Wheat. 264, 387 (1821). . . .

Our holding will be spelled out with some specificity in the pages which follow but briefly stated it is this: the prosecution may not use statements, whether exculpatory or inculpatory, stemming from custodial interrogation of the defendant unless it demonstrates the use of procedural safeguards effective to secure the privilege against self-incrimination. By custodial interrogation, we mean questioning initiated by law enforcement officers after a person has been taken into custody or otherwise deprived of his freedom of action in any significant way. As for the procedural safeguards to be employed, unless other fully effective means are devised to inform accused persons of their right of silence and to assure a continuous opportunity to exercise it, the following measures are required. Prior to any questioning, the person must be warned that he has a right to remain silent, that any statement he does make may be used as evidence against him, and that he has a right to the presence of an attorney, either retained or appointed. The defendant may waive effectuation of these rights, provided the waiver is made voluntarily, knowingly and intelligently. If, however, he indicates in any manner and at any stage of the process that he wishes to consult with an attorney before speaking there can be no questioning. Likewise, if the individual is alone and indicates in any manner that he does not wish to be interrogated, the police may not question him. The mere fact that he may have answered some questions or volunteered some statements on his own does not deprive him of the right to refrain from answering any further inquiries until he has consulted with an attorney and thereafter consents to be questioned.

QUESTIONS: Attitudes Towards the Police

1. Under Watts a confession is inadmissible if involuntary, admissible if voluntary. This seems to be a sensible and fair rule, expressing what a decent person would intend. Why do you suppose it was thought to be inadequate by the Miranda Court?

a. Is the problem that "voluntariness" is simply too vague to be used as a standard of behavior, that no one really knows what it means?

b. If you were an officer interrogating a suspect, could you confidently decide when your encouragement to confess was going so far that it might produce an "involuntary" confession? Suppose your suspect was: a sparring partner to the local boxer, suspected of a crime of violence; a pregnant woman suspected of killing her deserting husband; a thirteen-year-old child accused of shoplifting; a businessman charged with securities fraud. Are you confident of your ability to carry on each con-

versation without coercing the suspect? Would you behave differently in the different cases? If you were in doubt, what would you do?

c. *Would the seriousness of the crime and your assessment of the probability of the suspect's guilt affect the way you behaved towards him? Should they do so?*

d. *Under Watts, the officer's judgment was of course not final; the trial judge and the jury were given the task of deciding voluntariness for themselves after hearing the witnesses. Would you feel confident in making that determination as trial judge or juror? What would you do in cases of doubt?*

e. *If you were on the Supreme Court of the United States, would you feel confident that you could review judgments of voluntariness? What would you do in cases of doubt?*

f. *How does Watts define the officer and trial judge in assigning these tasks to them? How does Miranda define them in taking these tasks away? (Does it really take them away?)*

2. *Under Miranda, the suspect may of course waive the rights of which he is advised.*

   a. *Would you as an officer be able to tell whether such a waiver was voluntary? If the suspect were a thirteen-year-old boy? A prizefighter? A pregnant woman accused of murdering her spouse? What would you do in cases of doubt?*

   b. *As trial judge, would you be confident of your ability to review that judgment? What would you do in cases of doubt?*

   c. *How does Miranda define the officer and judge by assigning these tasks to them?*

   d. *Is Miranda then internally inconsistent? Ostensibly, the idea is to get away from the difficulties and uncertainties of a "voluntariness" test, partly because of lack of confidence in the officer and trial judge, partly because of an uneasy feeling that the question could not be satisfactorily reviewed — but does the Court not stick such a test right back in, to be administered by the same people and just as hard to review?*

      (1) *Or does Miranda facilitate both the initial judgment and review of it by providing an operational definition of "voluntary": if the warnings have been given, the waiver is automatically or presumptively voluntary?*

      (2) *A reverse argument could plausibly be made: no waiver of right to counsel could possibly be voluntary without the assistance of counsel to explain what the right may mean in practice.*

      (3) *Why does the Miranda Court not tell us which of these radically different conceptions of a voluntary waiver it intends to express? Or if some third conception, what that one is? One result of this fundamental ambiguity as to the meaning of "voluntary waiver" is that the judgment the officer must make under Miranda may be not easier but harder than that he must make under Watts.*

3. *At least aside from the waiver provisions, one might say, the Miranda rules are clear and specific and bring certainty into what had been a most unclear branch of the law.*

   a. *But what is the result under Miranda where the prosecution offers the following kinds of evidence?*

      (1) *Real evidence, e.g., a bloody handkerchief, obtained during an interrogation carried on without the warnings.*

(2) Real evidence obtained as a result of information revealed in such interrogation.
(3) Testimonial evidence obtained as a result of such interrogation, e.g., where the existence of a witness is disclosed by the suspect.
(4) A confession obtained as a result of such interrogation, but which is used only against a third party.

b. How is "custodial interrogation" defined under this rule? Is a person "in custody" if he believes he is restrained, even if he is in fact free to go? What if he in fact is secretly surrounded, but his interrogator in no way suggests that he is not free to leave? When a policeman stops a witness to ask what happened, must he give Miranda warnings? And even more basic: why limit the warning requirement to custodial interrogations in the first place?

c. Suppose a person is illegally arrested, is given the Miranda warnings, waives his rights, and confesses. Is his statement admissible against him?

d. These are difficult questions, as you readily perceive. How would you decide them, and how explain your decisions? Who is asked by Miranda to decide them in the first instance, and what directions or other assistance does Miranda give him? What weight will be given his initial judgment? How does Miranda define this person in assigning this task to him in the way it does?

e. Prepare to argue for and against the proposition that the Miranda rules make fundamentally inconsistent assumptions about the police who must administer them. How important is consistency here?

4. We can ask of Miranda a general question that might be asked of any of the rules the Supreme Court has promulgated to govern police behavior: are these rules to be conceived of as absolute requirements with an automatic sanction, or is evidence to be excluded only if the officer is to some extent at fault? For example, suppose an officer does not give the suspect the warnings, on the grounds that the latter is not "in custody." At trial the defendant persuades the court that he was "in custody" for purposes of the Miranda rules. Does it matter, for the purposes of excluding evidence, whether the officer's initial judgment was reasonable and in good faith?

One might say that the Court must here choose between two common sorts of rules relations:

a. The Miranda rules could be read like penal statutes, designed to control behavior through the use of the deterrent sanction of exclusion of evidence. If so, one might argue, it is sensible and fair to exclude evidence only when the police officer is at fault. Otherwise the common arguments against strict liability penal statutes would apply here.

b. They could be read as rules of law to be interpreted by the police as the initial lawmakers, the lowest rung in the ladder of the judiciary. A mistake of law is a mistake, and will be corrected on review no matter how reasonable it may have been; but no blame is implicit in such correction of a police officer any more than in the case of a lower court, and no deterrent sanction — no exclusion of evidence — is called for.

c. Is some combination of the two sorts of relationships possible? Is the choice that faces the Court between treating the officers as good guys or bad guys, or can a more complicated assumption be made? Consider the following: we shall have two sets of rules, depending upon the *reasonableness of the officer's behavior. If he was reasonable, we shall tell him he was wrong, if he was, and thus provide guidance to him and others in the future, but we shall exclude no evidence; if he was unreasonable or deliberate in his mistake, we shall exclude the evidence and perhaps punish him more directly as well. Would such a system be feasible? Is such a combination of rules "inconsistent" in the same way that Miranda could be said to be inconsistent?*

d. *One (unstated) purpose of the exclusionary rule may be to give a criminal defendant an incentive to litigate a question of the constitutionality of police conduct. Unless defendants are encouraged to raise such questions in this way, the Court will have very little opportunity to subject the police to the regulation of the Constitution. Would the proposal just made affect this aspect of the exclusionary rule? Is this a legitimate purpose of the exclusionary rule in the first place?*

e. *Here is another sort of rule for the police: would it make sense to use the principle of incentive rather than deterrence – say, by providing an award of $200 whenever a confession obtained by an officer is admitted in evidence? The same idea could be used to encourage legal searches and seizures. How does this proposal define the officer? How would it work in practice?*

QUESTIONS: Attitudes Towards the Suspect (I)

1. *What attitudes towards the suspect and his confession do these two cases express? You no doubt noticed that Watts, in leaving so much more to the judgment of the officer, makes allowance for differences among suspects of a kind that Miranda denies. What other differences can you find, and how do you explain them?*
2. *Both cases, but especially Miranda, seem to operate on the assumption that the confession of crime is necessarily against the suspect's best interests. How does this assumption define the suspect and his relationship to the officer and the court? What alternative might there be?*

ATTITUDES TOWARDS CONFESSION

Let us start with the psychiatric profession. How does a psychiatrist regard the act of confession? It seems to be a psychiatric truism that it is essential to the process of growth into maturity that a person recognize as fully and frankly as possible exactly what his position in the world is. This means recognizing the existence both of unlovely desires and of unpleasant behavior. All of us have inhibitions that to some extent prevent or hinder our conscious attempts to understand and express our true situation, and one of psychiatry's main tasks is to weaken or remove these inhibitions. People often repress their knowledge as well as their desires. Frequently a psychiatrist will show a patient that certain behavior or speech is really a way of talking about a repressed view of himself, and that what is apparently neutral talk or behavior is really a form of expression of what the conscious mind refuses to admit. Indeed, a psychiatrist will use carefully planned artifices and devices to nudge the patient towards full and free expression. Especially important is communicating to the patient that the psychiatrist is on his side, and that there are no secrets between them. The doctor will ask questions and make suggestions designed to lead the patient to "confess." The doctor might even use techniques such as those suggested by police manuals, e.g., expressing sympathy for the patient, treating very lightly the moral rules that the patient may have violated, condemning the victim (if there was one), and the like. See generally F. Inbau and J. Reid, *Criminal Interrogation and Confessions* (1967).

The therapeutic importance of confession is not destroyed, I suppose, by the unreliability of the confession as to particular events. Suppose the newspapers have been publicizing a sexual assault on a child. A patient, believed by the psychiatrist to have aggressive sexual tendencies, is encouraged by the psychiatrist to talk about this event. He does so by confessing to the attack. He might do so, even if he were innocent, as a way of confessing desires of which he was terribly ashamed and for which he felt guilty. A "confession" of the act might be the easiest way to express a recognition of a complex tangle of desire and inhibition whose elucidation could be the work of months or years. The value of the confession to the health of the patient might be considered to be very little impaired by the fact that, in the process of making the critically important confession of desires he did have, he said he had done something he had not done but only wished to do.[4]

The Christian tradition, of course, values confession very highly. Indeed, in some churches confession is a necessary part of the sacrament of penance, and the confession of wishes or desires is considered every bit as important as the confession of behavior. The priest, too, might use forms of pressure to help a person overcome his inhibitions to confession. In fact, it goes even deeper than that: if the psychiatrist says he cannot help the man who cannot face what he is, the Christian says that the man who cannot confess is damned. For literary representations of this sort of person, see Chaucer, *The Pardoner's Tale*; and Joyce, "A Painful Case," in *Dubliners*. In Dostoevsky's *Crime and Punishment*, Raskolnikov is brought to see that his own interest requires confession. Lady Macbeth's sleepwalking scene is usually read as an expression of the compulsion to confess.

Some systems of criminal law recognize such attitudes towards the

4. Some psychotherapy is of a very different kind. When the patient seems to be one who cannot stand the truth, the psychiatrist will help him maintain the illusions by which he gets along in the world. This is what Colby, in *A Primer for Psychotherapists* (1951), calls "covering therapy."

value of confession. In the People's Republic of China, for example, the criminal process involves informal sanctions ranging in seriousness from "criticism-education" by members of the local "power elite" to "struggle" or "speak-reason-struggle" which involves exhausting, humiliating, and vituperative criticism from peers and officials culminating in statements of confession and repentance. See Cohen, "The Criminal Process in the People's Republic of China," 79 *Harv. L. Rev.* 469, 490 (1966). This is seen as part of the general effort of that society to educate its members. Public education and self-criticism is one of the means by which that society is being remade. See generally K. S. Karol, *Mao's China* (1967); J. Myrdal, *Report from a Chinese Village* (1965). These techniques have been used for the purposes of "political education" or "brainwashing" of political prisoners. See J. Brown, *Techniques of Persuasion* (Penguin ed. 1963). The purpose is apparently to educate those who misunderstand themselves and their social environment; the emphasis in criminal law is accordingly not upon the "control of crime" nor upon ensuring procedural fairness, but upon a process of education of which the activity of confession is a central part. The conflict session is meant to be a learning experience which receives its ultimate expression in the confession.[5]

QUESTIONS: Attitudes Towards the Suspect (II)

1. *There seems to be widespread agreement that confession is essential to health, salvation, sanity, or whatever other ultimate personal value one may articulate. How then can you explain the rules of the Supreme Court which prevent public officials from trying to persuade men to confess even in the most gentle and noncoercive ways?*

   To put it slightly differently: one of the purposes of questioning and confession is the education of the one who confesses — but the Supreme Court says that the relationship between official and suspect can have no such element, it must be conceived of as purely hostile. How can this attitude be explained and justified?

   a. *Does the Court arrive at this conclusion merely because the penal system is so outmoded or vicious that it cannot possibly be in anyone's best interest to be subjected to it? Is that a possible basis for decision by the Supreme Court?*
   b. *If not, what reasons can you give for the result the Court reached in Miranda?*
   c. *Let us ask the same question of the lawyer. In his concurring opinion in Watts, Justice Jackson says that any lawyer "worth his salt" will advise a client under suspicion to refuse to talk to anyone. How can that uniform advice be justified?*
2. *Here is one line of explanation: the suspect is talked about by the in-*

5. Another society which honored confession was the Aztec. According to Prescott, confession and absolution were accepted instead of legal punishment, at least for a first offense. W. Prescott, *Conquest of Mexico*, Chapter 3 (1843).

stitution of the law in this highly unrealistic way as a way of protecting him from the institution itself. The artificiality and apparent stupidity of the law is a way in which the law limits itself. This is a special instance of the process we saw at work in the use of the label in criminal law, and in the correlative requirement of specificity in criminal statutes. We use the labels of the criminal law – "burglary," "theft," "rape," etc. – even though we know that they do not serve our purposes precisely. But to make rules in the language of those purposes – say, authorizing detention of those who are "demonstrably dangerous" – would put in the hands of prosecutors and judges and juries more power than any institution should have. The insistence upon an impossible form of speech – the label – is not accidental or stupid but deliberate, and it has the remarkable purpose of limiting the institution. The Miranda rule is in this tradition.

a. *Is law unique among institutions in that it is a self-limiting one?*
   (1) *What other institutions are self-limiting, and how do they establish such limits?*
   (2) *What other limits does the law set upon itself?*
b. *How does the process of self-limitation by the use of artificially specific rules, labels, and institutional identities actually work? To use the "theft" label rather than the "dangerousness" label expands as well as narrows the power of the law, since some people who commit theft would clearly present no abnormal danger of future criminal behavior. Is this the unfortunate price of clarity?*
c. *The idea seems to be that there is a control of legal speech very much like ironic control: the artificiality of the language is a way of recognizing what cannot be said directly. The law both affirms and denies by saying something which we all know cannot be sensible. This is a highly sophisticated use of an impossible language.*
d. *Try to find a passage in which the law (or other system of rules) seems to talk in a demonstrably foolish or incomplete way. Can you find a way to say that the defect is deliberate, that it amounts to a sort of control? Is the ultimate skill of the writer of rules akin to ironic wit?*
e. *Does this series of questions shed new light on the law's use of caricature?*

QUESTIONS: Attitudes Towards the Legislature — Choosing the Appropriate Form for a Rule

1. *The Miranda opinion seems to rest in substantial part upon the premise that certain coercive practices are widely used by the police in interrogating suspects, and it includes much factual material supporting that premise.*
   a. *Suppose the brief for the defendant included such material in support of its argument that the Miranda rules or some similar safeguards ought to be enacted by the Court. How would you expect a good lawyer for the state of Arizona to respond?*
   b. *One possible line of response is this: all that material and the conclusion it supports are irrelevant here because the only case before the Court is Miranda's, and the only proper question is how these*

police treated him, not how other police may have behaved in other cases.

(1) *How would you expect the defendant's attorney to respond to this argument?*

(2) *Was Miranda in fact the object of police practices which you would regard as unfair or abusive?*

2. *What do you suppose the Court saw at stake in the movement from Watts to Miranda?*

a. *In rejecting the "voluntariness" rule, did the Court mean that even voluntary confessions should be inadmissible? Or did they conceive themselves to be expressing the same idea in a different way?*

b. *Or is this the idea: we want all involuntary confessions to be excluded in practice as well as in theory; to achieve that goal in absolutely every case is impossible, but we shall adopt a rule which will approximate it, at the relatively small cost of excluding some confessions which happen to be voluntary, where the warnings were not given. Is this an appropriate way for the Court to proceed? How do you decide such a question?*

(1) *Suppose Congress wanted to overrule Watts; in what language might they do it? Can you imagine that such a statute would be held constitutional?*

(2) *Suppose Congress wanted to overrule Miranda; in what language might they do it? Can you imagine that such a statute might be held constitutional?*

"§3501. Admissibility of confessions

"(a) *In any criminal prosecution brought by the United States or by the District of Columbia, a confession, as defined in subsection* (e) *hereof, shall be admissible in evidence if it is voluntarily given.*" *18 U.S.C. §3501.*

(3) *Here there is a direct clash between the Court and Congress: unless specious techniques of interpretation are employed, one or the other must back down. See Note, "Title II of the Omnibus Crime Control Act: A Study in Constitutional Conflict," 57 Geo. L.J. 438* (1968). *How can you explain this clash? Is it simply that Congress and the Court want different results? How do you define "result" here?*

(4) *Actually, the Supreme Court has never addressed the conflict between Miranda and that statute. Why do you suppose it has not?*

3. *The argument could be put this way: when the legislature wishes to address an evil — for example, driving at excessive speeds — it may prohibit not only the precise evil with which it is concerned, but other conduct reasonably related to it, unless the other conduct is constitutionally protected. Thus it is illegal even for the highly skilled driver of a fine car to exceed the speed limit, and any offer of proof by him that what he did was safer than what is permitted by the statute would be rejected. The Supreme Court, on the other hand, at least when deciding constitutional questions, must concern itself with the ultimate evil alone, and may not make prophylactic rules of this kind. The reason is that the Supreme Court is striking a balance between competing interests of the greatest importance* (*such as the right not be abused by the police and the right of the state to protect its citizens against crime*), *and it must decide each case according to the interests actually at stake in that case, not by some general rule based upon an estimate of probabilities. It*

has no business excluding confessions that are in fact perfectly voluntary in order to advance some general purpose in other cases.

The suggestion, then, is that the Miranda rules are wholly misconceived: in order to advance or protect one constitutional interest, they promulgate a rule that unnecessarily sacrifices another. To say that the Court will ensure the exclusion of involuntary confessions by establishing and administering a practice that excludes other confessions as well is to make a claim for a power the Court does not and should not have.

a. Would the promulgation of the Miranda rules by Congress be equally inappropriate? By the Arizona legislature? Why?

b. Are not all rules of due process "legislative" the same way Miranda is? A person who is denied a hearing, a lawyer, or a jury is entitled to have one without showing that a different result is likely in his particular case; a search warrant is no good where the affidavit fails to set forth probable cause, even if the officer knew facts constituting probable cause; and so on. How would you expect this argument in support of the Miranda rules to be met by counsel for Arizona?

c. The difference between the Miranda rules and the traditional due process rules could be said to rest in this circumstance: one simply cannot ascertain as a factual matter whether a due process right – say, the right to a hearing or to a lawyer – was in a particular case necessary to protect the interests for which such rules exist without at the same time providing a redetermination of the dispute in which those rights are accorded. They are essential to any understanding of the facts and of the issues raised by the facts. For this reason it makes sense to require these due process rights in every case without asking whether their omission was harmful or harmless.

   (1) Does this argument suggest a way to delineate the proper scope of due process rights as a general matter? Or can some other justification be advanced for our practice of requiring certain procedural rights without inquiring as to their necessity or efficacy in a particular case?

   (2) How does this theory apply to the case where the officer has probable cause for a search but fails to express it in his application for a warrant?

   (3) In any event, could the Miranda rules be justified under such a theory?

d. Does the Constitution require a certain kind of rule-making from the Court? In particular, does it prohibit the sort of artificiality that we see in Miranda, which makes possible the sort of control we have called "ironic," involving as it does the controlled use of an impossible language? "The Supreme Court is not to be ironic: it must deal with the truth simply and directly." Does this mean it cannot speak a language of rules?

e. Is the entire analysis presented above mistaken as to a fundamental matter? Consider the suggestion that it is the function of the Miranda rules not only to apply new categories to events, to impose a new set of consequences on experience – but to change the very course of the events, to create a new set of experiences with which the law will deal. How would the lawyer for Arizona respond?

4. For an actual judicial opinion that asks questions similar to those suggested above (how does the proposed rule define the suspect, the officer,

and the other participants? are these assumptions factually sensible? what is their effect on the people involved, especially the officials? is this sort of rule proper to the Court?), see the opinion of Justice White in United States v. Wade, 388 U.S. 218, 250–259 (1967). For other suggested rules governing interrogation and confession, see the ALI Model Code of Prearraignment Procedure (Study Draft No. 1, 1968).

WRITING ASSIGNMENT 15: Rules for the Police

Part One

• As a justice of the Supreme Court of the United States, draft a statement of directions which you think the Court should issue to the police, governing some aspect of their relations with the public: search, arrest, interrogation, lineup, stop-and-frisk, wiretapping, eavesdropping, or any other matter of interest to you. Your directions need not be in the form of rules.

Part Two

• Explain what difficulties you faced and how you met them. In particular, explain why you chose to cast your statement in the form you did.

Here you have an opportunity to address as a lawmaker the difficulties we have been considering throughout this chapter. How will you talk to your police? What do you assume about them and the relationship between them and the Court? How do you decide which are proper matters for your decision, and which are to be left to others?

WRITING ASSIGNMENT 15, ALTERNATIVE A: The Exclusionary Rule

• You are an associate justice of the United States Supreme Court. The chief justice has just sent you the following memo: "You know I disapprove of the exclusionary rule as it has been developed and administered by this Court. It lets an intolerably large number of guilty people go free in return for highly speculative gains, and it brings the law and the Constitution into disrepute with ordinary people and officials everywhere. I am disposed to reject it entirely for the federal as well as the state system. What do you think? Please give me a proposal you support, with a full statement of your reasons."[6]

6. Compare the dissent of Chief Justice Burger in *Bivens v. Six Unknown Federal Narcotics Agents*, 403 U.S. 388, 411 (1971).

Another alternative for Writing Assignment 15 follows the next, very brief, set of readings.

b. When and How Should a Court Enforce the Constitution by an Injunction Against the Police?

In the readings and questions just completed, we have been studying how the Supreme Court ought to frame and enforce its directions to the police. Now the focus is on a single aspect of that question: when and how should a court issue an injunction against the police? Here is a case that will set this problem up for us.

WILSON v. WEBSTER
315 F. Supp. 1104, 1107-1108 (C.D. Cal. 1970)[7]

In applying to this court for an injunction, the plaintiffs in the prayer of their complaint ask that the officers be enjoined:

a. From breaking into any house, apartment or residence in Isla Vista, without warrant, in violation of the Fourth and Fourteenth Amendments to the Constitution of the United States;

b. From making illegal arrests under color of law;

c. From assaulting, beating, terrorizing, intimidating and inflicting summary and cruel punishment on members of plaintiffs' class, whether or not arrested, including denial of medical attention, phone calls, bail and legal assistance;

d. From using plastic and wire hand ties on human beings;

e. From requiring prisoners to furnish excessive bail;

f. From falsely imprisoning any member of this class or requiring him to remain in any courtroom, jail, or other form of custody under intimidation or threats of fear of death or otherwise, for any alleged "lack of authority" on the part of the individual deputy sheriffs or on any other pretext, after such person has posted bail in the amount legally required to obtain his release, or when such person has had all criminal charges against him dismissed in open court. . . .

A more serious issue, however, does appear in that the plaintiffs are seeking a permanent injunction of a kind and nature which this court cannot grant. For the most part, the police action complained of consists of conduct which is not illegal per se. Breaking into a private dwelling without a warrant may be justifiable and legal under certain circumstances, although illegal and improper under others. Beating a person over the head with a club, although brutal and excessive under

7. *Rev'd on other grounds,* 467 F.2d 1282 (9th Cir. 1972).

some circumstances, may in others be the only means by which an officer may subdue a recalcitrant offender. It would be improper for this court to enjoin all of such acts as this would amount to an unjustified interference with law enforcement officers of the state. Plaintiffs recognize this, and so they seek to enjoin only those acts when they are done in an unlawful manner.

But such an injunction would be unenforceable as it would lack the required specificity required by Rule 65(d) of the Federal Rules of Civil Procedure.[1] An injunction must be so clear and certain in its terms that a defendant may readily know what he is restrained from doing. *United States v. Vitasafe Corporation,* 345 F.2d 864 (3rd Cir. 1965). There it was held that an injunction prohibiting the distribution of literature containing certain specified statements and misrepresentations "or which is otherwise false or misleading," lacked the required specificity. This court holds, therefore, that the injunction which the plaintiffs seek would be unenforceable because of excessive vagueness.

QUESTIONS

1. *How would you argue on appeal against the reasoning advanced by this court to support its denial of an injunction?*
2. *Does this court mean that it is never appropriate to issue an injunction against the police in order to ensure compliance with the Fourth Amendment?*
3. *Suppose you represented the plaintiffs in this case; how would you have framed your proposed injunction against the police?*
4. Compare Morgan *v.* Rhodes, *456 F.2d 608 (6th Cir. 1972), cert. granted, 41 U.S.L.W. 3229 (Oct. 24, 1972), where the plaintiffs sought an injunction against a continuing pattern of inadequate training of National Guard troops resulting in a continual threat to the rights of free speech and assembly. As counsel for the plaintiffs, how would you have framed the order you sought?*

QUESTION: In What Circumstances Should a Court Issue an Injunction Against the Police?

Tradition maintains that the extraordinary relief of an injunction is available only in special circumstances; otherwise, why not simply issue an injunction to every policeman in the country to obey the law upon pain of contempt? And other less drastic remedies are already available: a civil suit for damages, a criminal prosecution, and the exclusion of illegally obtained evidence.

1. *Rule 65. Injunctions*

(d) *Form and Scope of Injunction or Restraining Order.* Every order granting an injunction and every restraining order shall set forth the reasons for its issuance; shall be specific in terms; shall describe in reasonable detail, and not by reference to the complaint or other document, the act or acts sought to be restrained; . . .

According to the traditional view, what will justify an injunction? Apparently the plaintiff must allege a pattern of misbehavior, not just isolated circumstances, and the misbehavior must be (a) flagrantly unlawful and (b) directed at him or people reasonably related to him. Lankford v. Gelston, *364 F.2d 197 (4th Cir. 1966). What such terms mean is, of course, not clear. For example, are threats of brutality enough, or must the plaintiff document a series of actual instances? Is racial identity enough to give a black man standing to protest practices of abusing blacks? Can a legal aid or public defender office raise the interests of its clients?*

One particularly important question is this: how specific must the allegations of misconduct be? Would those in the following case suffice?

HERNANDEZ v. NOEL

323 F. Supp. 779, 781 n.1 (D. Conn. 1970)

. . . The complaint alleges: "Said conduct includes, but is not limited to:

"1. Committing acts having no purpose or justification other than to humiliate, degrade, harass, intimidate, and discriminate against the Plaintiffs and the class they represent.

"2. Employing unnecessary deadly force and unnecessary physical force against Plaintiffs and the class they represent.

"3. Arresting Plaintiffs and the class they represent when no crime has been committed for the purpose of intimidation and harassment.

"4. Detaining and questioning Plaintiffs and the class they represent without arrest for the purpose of harassment and humiliation.

"5. Arresting Plaintiffs and the class they represent for the crime of loitering (Conn. Gen. Stats. §53-179) and threatening arrest for the said crime without cause or justification in an arbitrary, capricious, and discriminatory manner and for the sole purpose of discouraging and preventing Plaintiffs and the class they represent from exercising their constitutionally guaranteed rights to free speech and assembly.

"6. Denying Plaintiffs and the class they represent their right to remain silent in violation of the Fifth Amendment of the United States Constitution.

"7. Denying Plaintiffs and the class they represent their right to counsel as guaranteed by the Sixth Amendment of the United States Constitution.

"8. Subjecting Plaintiffs and the class they represent to fingerprinting when not required by law."

QUESTION: How Should an Injunction Be Framed?

Is the following injunction, in your judgment, appropriate in form? How would you go about redrafting it?

WHEELER v. GOODMAN
298 F. Supp. 935, 942 (W.D.N.C. 1969)

It is, therefore, ordered, adjudged and decreed, that the defendants and their officers, servants and agents and employees, pending further order of this court, be and they are ordered and directed:

1. To refrain from threatening or conducting or procuring the investigation, interrogation, detention, arrest or charge or prosecution of the plaintiffs or any other person under color of North Carolina General Statutes §14-336, the "vagrancy statute."

2. To refrain from arresting or charging the plaintiffs or other persons or threatening or conspiring to detain, arrest or search the plaintiffs or any other persons without legal probable cause or with any purpose to harass, intimidate or frighten plaintiffs or any other persons without legal probable cause so as to suppress, discourage, defeat, reduce or affect the constitutional rights of the plaintiffs or such persons, including their rights of free speech, peaceable assembly and freedom of association and their rights to be secure in their persons, in their homes and in their possessions, and against unreasonable searches and seizures.

3. To refrain from searching persons or property or seizing property except as incident to lawful arrest or under lawful warrant or when otherwise permitted by the Constitution.

4. To refrain from issuing or obtaining search warrants, or conducting searches under warrants, based only upon affidavits depending on "tips" from anonymous informers, reliable or otherwise, and not supported by affidavit as to other corroborating facts, detail and circumstances showing probable cause to believe the search will reveal evidence of crime.

5. To refrain from prosecution or threatened prosecution of plaintiffs or others except under valid statutes and with probable cause to believe that [a] crime has been committed and that its prosecution will be successful.

6. To return to the attorney for the plaintiffs the metal policeman and any other articles of personal property that may have been taken from the plaintiffs by the defendants at 216 East Kingston Avenue or at the police station.

7. To keep intact and sealed against any view, public or private (except upon order of this court), all records, notations, photographs and other writings dealing with plaintiffs and others who were arrested at 216 East Kingston Avenue on January 9, 1969.

8. To refrain from serving eviction notices, or attending while others serve such notices, except when ordered to do so by a court of law.

9. To refrain from ordering guests or tenants in private homes to depart and not return, upon threat of arrest.

QUESTIONS

1. People planning a peace demonstration seek an injunction requiring the police to provide adequate protection. They allege that at a demonstration two weeks earlier, the police had failed to protect them against the physical assaults of bystanders. As their lawyer, how would you ask that an injunction be framed? If your junior associate proposed the following, what would you tell him? See also Schnell v. City of Chicago, 407 F.2d 1084 (7th Cir. 1969); Hairston v. Hutzler, 334 F. Supp. 251 (W.D. Pa. 1971).

"It is now ordered that the defendants Howard R. Leary, Police Commissioner, City of New York, Inspector Harold Schryner, and all the other inspectors, captains, lieutenants, sergeants, and police officers of the City of New York be restrained from:

"(1) failing to protect plaintiffs and members of their class, while engaged in the peaceful and orderly exercise of their constitutional right to protest present Government war policies, from physical assaults and threat of physical assaults on May 29, 30, 31, 1970;

"(2) failing to guarantee to the plaintiffs and members of the class they represent proper and adequate police protection while said plaintiffs and members of their class are engaged in exercising their constitutional right to meet and assemble in a peaceful and orderly manner and protest against the Government's war policies on May 29, 30, and 31, 1970;

"(3) refusing or failing to take all reasonable precaution and means to protect plaintiffs and others similarly situated from acts of violence or other interference with the exercise of their right to peacefully assemble and protest present Government war policies on May 29, 30, and 31, 1970.

"It is further ordered that this order apply only to those demonstrations to be held on May 29, 30, 31, 1970 of which the Police Department has prior notice." Belknap v. Leary, 314 F. Supp. 574, 575 (S.D.N.Y.), rev'd, 427 F.2d 496 (2d Cir. 1970).

2. During a widespread manhunt for a black man suspected of killing a police officer, the Baltimore police carried out a series of raids on private homes without probable cause. These raids were invariably on black homes, occurred at all hours of the day and night, and were not gentle in manner. The suspect was caught in another town.

a. Should an injunction now issue? Against whom, and prohibiting what activities? How should it be framed?

b. The court did issue an injunction prohibiting "the Police Department" from conducting the search of any private house for the purpose of arresting a person not known to reside there, "where the belief that the person is on the premises is based only on an anonymous tip and hence without probable cause." Lankford v. Gelston, 364 F.2d 197 (4th Cir. 1966). Do the terms of this injunction just restate the law, or do they modify it? See the factual situation in Warden v. Hay-

den, 387 U.S. 294 (1967). How can any such modification of Constitutional law be justified?

3. *How does the issuance of an injunction alter the relationship between the court and the policeman? If there seems to be misconduct on both sides of a citizen-police dispute, might an injunction go both ways? Consider the following opinion.*

HOUSER v. HILL
278 F. Supp. 920, 928 (M.D. Ala. 1968)

In accordance with the foregoing and for good cause, it is the order, judgment and decree of this Court that Kenneth Hill and Norris Champion, as police officers for the City of Prattville, Autauga County, Alabama, and O. C. Thompson, as chief of police for the City of Prattville, Autauga County, Alabama, their agents, officers, employees, successors, and all persons in active concert and participation with them be and each is hereby enjoined from:

(1) Inflicting summary punishment upon Negro citizens for the purpose of and having the effect of deterring said citizens from the exercise of their legal and constitutional rights;

(2) Unlawfully interfering, through the use of force and intimidation, with the peaceful and lawful assemblies of Negro citizens in Prattville, Autauga County, Alabama;

(3) Failing to guarantee to and give these plaintiffs and members of the class they represent proper and adequate police protection while said plaintiffs and members of this class are engaged in exercising their constitutional right to meet and assemble in a peaceful and orderly manner;

(4) Arresting Negro citizens upon pretense and subterfuge for the purpose of deterring them from the exercise of their constitutional rights; and

(5) Allowing hostile white groups to gather and congregate for the purpose of committing acts of violence upon the plaintiffs and those similarly situated, or assaulting, threatening or intimidating them in the exercise of their constitutional rights, or otherwise impeding or interfering with the exercise of said rights.

It is further ordered that the plaintiffs (and defendants in counterclaim), Dan Houser and Sallie Hadnott, and the counterclaim defendants Student Nonviolent Coordinating Committee, an unincorporated association; Ulyssis Z. Nunnally, Will Henry Rogers, Charlie Levine, James Edward Harris, Santee Burnett, Doc Davis, and John Jackson, as agents of the Student Nonviolent Coordinating Committee; the Autauga County Voters Association, and the Autauga County Improvement Association, their agents, officers, employees, successors, and all persons in active concert and participation with them, be and each is hereby enjoined from:

(1) Sponsoring and arranging meetings and assemblies to be addressed by those who advocate violence through the use of weapons and other conduct designed to and tending to disrupt the peace and order of the community; and (2) Using violent means to protest and demonstrate.

It is further ordered that jurisdiction of this cause be and the same is hereby expressly retained.

QUESTIONS

1. *In Hughes v. Rizzo, 282 F. Supp. 881 (E.D. Pa. 1968), it was proved that the police had harassed "hippies" in Rittenhouse Square by ordering them about, threatening them with harm, actually arresting them, and on two occasions arresting them en masse – all without probable cause. The court ordered that all records of arrest be expunged and that all photographs be returned or destroyed. The court refused an injunction but "retained jurisdiction so that appropriate relief could be granted should the need arise." The court added in a footnote: "This is, of course, a two-way street, and includes intervention to abate a nuisance, for example, if plaintiffs' conduct should necessitate such action." Do you approve? Compare Gomez v. Wilson, 323 F. Supp. 87 (D.D.C. 1971).*
2. *What relief might a court grant to plaintiffs who have demonstrated that the police department has failed to pursue or respond to complaints of police misconduct? See Build of Buffalo, Inc. v. Sedita, 441 F.2d 284 (2d Cir. 1971).*
3. *One remedy even more drastic than the injunction would be the appointment of a receiver or other agent of the court with plenary powers over the police department. Does the court have the power to impose such a remedy? When (if ever) should it be exercised? Compare: why might a court, which has determined that a child should receive a blood transfusion over the objection of his parents, appoint a guardian for him rather than simply order that the transfusion take place? See State v. Perricone, 37 N.J. 462, 181 A.2d 751 (1962); Application of President and Directors of Georgetown College, Inc., 331 F.2d 1000 (D.C. Cir. 1964).*
4. *For an expert's view that police activity is a craft that cannot sensibly be governed by rules of any kind, see J. Q. Wilson, Varieties of Police Behavior 278–298 (1968).*

WRITING ASSIGNMENT 15, ALTERNATIVE B: *Enjoining the Police*

• *Assume that the plaintiffs in Wilson v. Webster (page 615 supra) have proven a deliberate police campaign to harass and abuse students and young people in Isla Vista. The police have beaten people up unneces-*

sarily, broken into houses and apartments without probable cause, held people incommunicado without judicial authority, and used abusive and insulting language in an attempt to incite disturbances. Draft an injunction directed to this situation which you would issue if you were the federal district (or appropriate California) judge. Explain what difficulties you faced and how you met them.

Two additional cases that might be of interest: *Miller v. United States*, 404 F.2d 611 (5th Cir. 1968), cert. denied, 394 U.S. 963 (1969); *Johnson v. Hackett*, 284 F. Supp. 933 (E.D. Pa. 1968).

CHAPTER 5

JUDGMENT AND EXPLANATION: THE LEGAL MIND AT WORK

Our emphasis in the last two chapters has been upon the law largely as a way of establishing relationships and constructing institutions — as a way of organizing future experience — and the frustrations and impossibilities of that process are no doubt familiar enough to you. One of our questions from the beginning has been whether the defects of the legal language system could be removed by changing it, by making it over again, but your attempts to rebuild it have undoubtedly been less than perfectly satisfactory to you. Now you are invited to shift your point of view to examine the law as it exists around you (made by others for your use), and to ask how an intelligent and responsible mind can deal with this material. Although such lines can never be adhered to with rigidity, our concern here will be less with trying to set things up for the future than with deciding cases, less with making rules than with using them. Your central questions are these: by what process does a good judge or lawyer, faced with a real difficulty in the real world, go about deciding what should be done? In what language or languages can he explain his judgment to himself and others? What place have legal rules in what he says and does, and how do they operate in his work? How can these rules be controlled by an active and creative mind? To put it in a single question: what is the art of making and explaining legal judgments?

Despite their differences in situation, I think these questions can sensibly be asked of judge and lawyer alike: while the lawyer does not have the judge's burden of deciding a case in an official way, of actually achieving justice if he can, he cannot discharge his responsibilities of counseling and arguing without reaching conclusions of his own, and an essential part of that process must be that he ask himself how an excellent judge would go about deciding his case. And if the judge need not convince other minds, need not speak to and persuade persons utterly different from himself, as the lawyer must constantly do, he is obliged to do something rather similar: he must always be ready to imagine other and better possibilities, to admire what at first seems strange, to recognize excellence in the uncongenial.

As I have suggested, the art of legal judgment is necessarily an art in the use — and perhaps in the avoidance — of rules. The lawyer or judge must address the rules that are directed to him and put them to work in his judgment. How does he do so? What relationship does the good judge or lawyer establish with the language of legal rules? How does he use them in making a judgment and in explaining what he has done? You will not expect these questions to prove simple or obvious, for you have seen that the rule is not an easy form to manage when it is used to organize relationships among people — for giving directions to judgment, for establishing social relations — and there is no reason to think that it will somehow be perfectly adapted to what the lawyer and judge do when arguing and deciding cases. The requirement that a legal rule be relatively specific, for example, has been seen to mean that it cannot be used to regulate the most important relationships, such as marriage and professional relations, and that it cannot be used to express our most important values; but its use of general or typical categories constantly produces results not required by and often inconsistent with its purposes — the wife recovers for the death of the husband, no matter how richly she may have hated him, no matter how unfaithful she may have been; the confession is excluded if the warnings were not given, no matter how fully the defendant may have known his rights and wished to confess; and so on. Thanks to the use of such "categories of convenience," rules not only leave out too much, they include too much. But we not only permit the use of the rule in our legal system, we require it and boast of the requirement — ours is a government founded upon the rule of law.

You yourself have experienced the frustration of acting as a legislator condemned to the use of such an impossible form, and I suspect that as you worked out your various proposals in detail — for a wrongful death action, for the insanity defense, for prison rules — you found yourself saying again and again that you had to rely upon the good sense and judgment of your lawyers and judges, assuming or hoping that at least some of the difficulties of your rules could be smoothed away by an audience who knew how to use them. That hope or assumption defines part of our present subject: what is the art of judging and lawyering upon which the rule-maker depends? How does one expect the user of a set of rules to try to establish a relationship of confident cooperation with their maker, and what will he do when he cannot? How, in either situation, is the language of legal rules to be controlled by the one who makes and explains a legal judgment in a particular case? We concern ourselves here with the crucial moment when law is translated into experience, the moment when by an act of judgment the law is brought to bear on life — finds its momentary expression in reality — and the world moves on. What can be said about the process by which such judgments are made or expressed? How can this art of the mind — of the will, of the imagination — be defined?

Such are your questions, and in what follows we shall put them several different ways. We shall begin with an ancient problem, the relation between rules and justice: can justice be done, as we seem to think, by the legal rule, or does the rule by its very nature work rather as a stumbling block to justice?

A. *THE PLACE OF THE RULE IN LEGAL JUDGMENT, OR: WHAT DOES THE GOOD JUDGE DO WITH THE LAW — CHEAT?*

Some Beauties yet, no Precepts can declare,
For there's a Happiness as well as Care.
Musick resembles Poetry, in each
Are nameless Graces which no Methods teach,
And which a Master-Hand alone can reach.
If, where the Rules not far enough extend,
(Since Rules were made but to promote their End)
Some Lucky LICENCE answers to the full
Th' Intent propos'd, that Licence is a Rule.
Thus Pegasus, a nearer way to take,
May boldly deviate from the common Track.
Great Wits sometimes may gloriously offend,
And rise to Faults true Criticks dare not mend;
From vulgar Bounds with brave Disorder part,
And snatch a Grace beyond the Reach of Art,
Which, without passing thro' the Judgment, gains
The Heart, and all its End at once attains.*

1. *Rules and Justice: Plato's View*

THE STATESMAN†
Plato

[The Stranger and the Younger Socrates (who is no relation to the great Socrates) are discussing the science of government. The Stranger

* Alexander Pope, *Essay on Criticism*, lines 141–157 (1711).
† Jowett translation.

says that this science is an art that can be exercised with laws or without laws, with consent of the ruled or without consent of the ruled, but only by one of the few who attain excellence in it. All other governments are merely imitations of government by such a one, by a master of the art. Socrates objects: how can there be good government without laws?]

Stranger. You have been too quick for me, Socrates; I was just going to ask you whether you objected to any of my statements. And now I see that we shall have to consider this notion of there being good government without laws.

Younger Socrates. Certainly.

Str. There can be no doubt that legislation is in a manner the business of a king, and yet the best thing of all is not that the law should rule, but that a man should rule, supposing him to have wisdom and royal power. Do you see why this is?

Y. Soc. Why?

Str. Because the law does not perfectly comprehend what is noblest and most just for all and therefore cannot enforce what is best. The differences of men and actions, and the endless irregular movements of human beings, do not admit of any universal and simple rule. And no art whatsoever can lay down a rule which will last for all time.

Y. Soc. Of course not.

Str. But the law is always striving to make one; — like an obstinate and ignorant tyrant, who will not allow anything to be done contrary to his appointment, or any question to be asked — not even in sudden changes of circumstances, when something happens to be better than what he commanded for some one.

Y. Soc. Certainly; the law treats us all precisely in the manner which you describe.

Str. A perfectly simple principle can never be applied to a state of things which is the reverse of simple.

Y. Soc. True.

Str. Then if the law is not the perfection of right, why are we compelled to make laws at all? The reason of this has next to be investigated.

Y. Soc. Certainly.

Str. Let me ask, whether you have not meetings for gymnastic contests in your city, such as there are in other cities, at which men compete in running, wrestling, and the like?

Y. Soc. Yes; they are very common among us.

Str. And what are the rules which are enforced on their pupils by professional trainers or by others having similar authority? Can you remember?

Y. Soc. To what do you refer?

Str. The training-masters do not issue minute rules for individuals, or give every individual what is exactly suited to his constitution; they think that they ought to go more roughly to work, and to prescribe generally the regimen which will benefit the majority.

Y. Soc. Very true.

Str. And therefore they assign equal amounts of exercise to them all; they send them forth together, and let them rest together from their running, wrestling, or whatever the form of bodily exercise may be.

Y. Soc. True.

Str. And now observe that the legislator who has to preside over the herd, and to enforce justice in their dealings with one another, will not be able, in enacting for the general good, to provide exactly what is suitable for each particular case.

Y. Soc. He cannot be expected to do so.

Str. He will lay down laws in a general form for the majority, roughly meeting the cases of individuals; and some of them he will deliver in writing, and others will be unwritten; and these last will be traditional customs of the country.

Y. Soc. He will be right.

Str. Yes, quite right; for how can he sit at every man's side all through his life, prescribing for him the exact particulars of his duty? Who, Socrates, would be equal to such a task? No one who really had the royal science, if he had been able to do this, would have imposed upon himself the restriction of a written law.

Y. Soc. So I should infer from what has now been said.

Str. Or rather, my good friend, from what is going to be said.

Y. Soc. And what is that?

Str. Let us put to ourselves the case of a physician, or trainer, who is about to go into a far country, and is expecting to be a long time away from his patients — thinking that his instructions will not be remembered unless they are written down, he will leave notes of them for the use of his pupils or patients.

Y. Soc. True.

Str. But what would you say, if he came back sooner than he had intended, and, owing to an unexpected change of the winds or other celestial influences, something else happened to be better for them, — would he not venture to suggest this new remedy, although not contemplated in his former prescription? Would he persist in observing the original law, neither himself giving any new commandments, nor the patient daring to do otherwise than was prescribed, under the idea that this course only was healthy and medicinal, all others noxious and heterodox? Viewed in the light of science and true art, would not all such enactments be utterly ridiculous?

Y. Soc. Utterly.

Str. And if he who gave laws, written or unwritten, determining what was good or bad, honourable or dishonourable, just or unjust, to the tribes of men who flock together in their several cities, and are governed in accordance with them; if, I say, the wise legislator were suddenly to come again, or another like to him, is he to be prohibited from changing them? — would not this prohibition be in reality quite as ridiculous as the other?

Y. Soc. Certainly. . . .

Str. . . . Is not this the true principle of government, according to which the wise and good man will order the affairs of his subjects? As the pilot, by watching continually over the interests of the ship and of the crew, — not by laying down rules, but by making his art a law, — preserves the lives of his fellow-sailors, even so, and in the self-same way, may there not be a true form of polity created by those who are able to govern in a similar spirit, and who show a strength of art which is superior to the law?

QUESTIONS

1. The major defects of the rule were clear enough in ancient Athens. The rule can only approximate the science or art of government, and is good enough only for the decidedly inferior man or government. True political wisdom – the art of knowing what is best for a society – cannot be expressed in rules any more than the art of the doctor or pilot can, and true judgment is superior to any rule.

a. Do you dispute what the Stranger says about the relationship between the rule and an art? Look back at the passage from Twain's Life on the Mississippi (page 10 supra): can you imagine a set of rules which, if thoroughly memorized, would enable you to pilot a steamboat from New Orleans to St. Louis?

b. What is the excellence by which the trainer or the doctor disregards his own rule, as in the examples given by Plato: an excellence in athletics or medicine, or an excellence in the use of rules? Or are these the same thing?

c. What is the excellence by which a good judge modifies or disregards a rule: an excellence in the art of government, or an excellence in the use of rules? Or are these the same thing?

2. How would you explain to the Stranger and the Younger Socrates why you think a city or state should be run by rules? What would you mean by such a proposition?

3. What view would Arnold of Rugby (page 525 supra) take of the issue that is the subject of this passage from The Statesman?

4. What, in Plato's view, would be the consequences of devoting one's life to the use and mastery of the materials of the law?

THEAETETUS*
Plato

Socrates. [Y]our remark recalls to my mind an observation which I have often made, that those who have passed their days in the pursuit of philosophy are ridiculously at fault when they have to appear and speak in court. How natural is this!

Theodorus. What do you mean?

Soc. I mean to say, that those who have been trained in philosophy and liberal pursuits are as unlike those who from their youth upwards have been knocking about in the courts and such places, as a freeman is in breeding unlike a slave.

Theod. In what is the difference seen?

Soc. In the leisure spoken of by you, which a freeman can always command: he has his talk out in peace, and, like ourselves, he wanders at will from one subject to another, and from a second to a third, — if the fancy takes him, he begins again, as we are doing now, caring not whether his words are many or few; his only aim is to attain the truth. But the lawyer is always in a hurry; there is the water of the clepsydra driving him on, and not allowing him to expatiate at will: and there is his adversary standing over him, enforcing his rights; the indictment, which in their phraseology is termed the affidavit, is recited at the time: and from this he must not deviate. He is a servant, and is continually disputing about a fellow-servant before his master, who is seated, and has the cause in his hands; the trial is never about some indifferent matter, but always concerns himself; and often the race is for his life. The consequence has been, that he has become keen and shrewd; he has learned how to flatter his master in word and indulge him in deed; but his soul is small and unrighteous. His condition, which has been that of a slave from his youth upwards, has deprived him of growth and uprightness and independence; dangers and fears, which were too much for his truth and honesty, came upon him in early years, when the tenderness of youth was unequal to them, and he has been driven into crooked ways; from the first he has practised deception and retaliation, and has become stunted and warped. And so he has passed out of youth into manhood, having no soundness in him; and is now, as he thinks, a master in wisdom. Such is the lawyer, Theodorus. . . .

[Socrates then describes the philosopher, to whom ordinary economic and political concerns are nothing and ultimate concerns of truth and justice everything. The Thracian handmaiden's jest at Thales, when he fell into a well while looking at the stars, properly applies to all philos-

* Jowett translation.

ophers: "He was so eager to know what was going on in heaven that he could not see what was before his feet." Of course he is at a loss in a lawcourt, and the lawyer can easily make him look foolish.]

Soc. But, O my friend, when he draws the other into upper air, and gets him out of his pleas and rejoinders into the contemplation of justice and injustice in their own nature and in their difference from one another and from all other things; or from the commonplaces about the happiness of a king or of a rich man to the consideration of government, and of human happiness and misery in general — what they are, and how a man is to attain the one and avoid the other — when that narrow, keen, little legal mind is called to account about all this, he gives the philosopher his revenge; for dizzied by the height at which he is hanging, whence he looks down into space, which is a strange experience to him, he being dismayed, and lost, and stammering broken words, is laughed at, not by Thracian handmaidens or any other uneducated persons, for they have no eye for the situation, but by every man who has not been brought up a slave. . . .

There are two patterns eternally set before them; the one blessed and divine, the other godless and wretched: but they do not see them, or perceive that in their utter folly and infatuation they are growing like the one and unlike the other, by reason of their evil deeds; and the penalty is, that they lead a life answering to the pattern which they are growing like. And if we tell them, that unless they depart from their cunning, the place of innocence will not receive them after death; and that here on earth, they will live ever in the likeness of their own evil selves, and with evil friends — when they hear this they in their superior cunning will seem to be listening to the talk of idiots.

Theod. Very true, Socrates.

Soc. Too true, my friend, as I well know; there is, however, one peculiarity in their case: when they begin to reason in private about their dislike of philosophy, if they have the courage to hear the argument out, and do not run away, they grow at last strangely discontented with themselves; their rhetoric fades away, and they become helpless as children.

QUESTIONS

1. *What can explain the differences that Plato observes between the lawyer and the philosopher: is it that the lawyer always works for a client, from whom he must take a view of the case (and perhaps directions for dealing with it as well)? Or that he must deal with every case in terms established by others, in the legal terms that define both his audience and his task? Or that he must bring to bear on every case a statement cast in the form of a legal rule, and claim that it says all that need be said? (Do you sup-*

pose these questions might be answered differently for the ancient and the modern lawyer?)

2. *However those questions are to be answered in detail, it does seem plain that we have been told off. We boast of a government that is subject to the rule of law, and we are told that this government is fit only for inferior communities and people, that it can only approximate a wise and just polity; proud of our profession, we are told that the lawyer is no better than a slave. And no doubt part of what Plato criticizes both in the government and in the lawyer is an excessive devotion to the form of the legal rule.*
   a. *How do you defend yourself and your profession against such remarks?*
   b. *Can you find a way to bring together the lawyer and philosopher in your own life, or are they, as Plato suggests, hopelessly incompatible identities?*
   c. *Or are you willing to say that you do not "love wisdom"?*
3. *Someone might actually adopt a form of that last suggestion, claiming that the philosopher may be a fine inspirational person but that he contributes very little to the task of facing real difficulties in the real world. The vaunted "freedom" of the philosopher is just an academic isolation from the actual problems of power and justice. "Wisdom" is a matter of personal value, like religion, and can have little to do with the work of the law, with justice as a practical matter — with the only genuine justice. How do you suppose Plato would respond?*
4. *To put the matter somewhat differently: what can be said about that art of the governor or judge (or lawyer) which, according to Plato, is like the art of the pilot and doctor and cannot be stated in or guided by rules? What is this art, and how does one go about acquiring it? Can it be defined as an art that somehow connects rules and justice?*
5. *How odd it may seem that law school does not begin with, or perhaps consist of, a course on the subject of justice: what it is and how it can be achieved. There follows the beginning of a Socratic dialog on this subject. Should law school take its shape from what you read here? What does this passage tell you about justice — about right judgment — and its relation to the truth? About the art of judgment?*

THE REPUBLIC*
Plato

[This dialog begins with a conversation between Socrates and Cephalus, a wealthy old man, about the advantages of age and wealth. Cephalus says that the greatest blessing of wealth is that one is under no temptation to defraud or deceive another, or otherwise to act unjustly, and that this contributes greatly to one's peace of mind as death approaches. To which Socrates responds: "Well said, Cephalus; but as concerning justice, what is it? — to speak the truth and pay your debts — no more? And even to this are there not exceptions? Suppose that a friend when in his right mind has deposited his arms with me and

* Book 1 (Jowett translation).

he asks for them when he is not in right mind, ought I to give them back to him?" With this Socrates begins the inquiry of the whole dialog, "What is justice?" Polemarchus suggests that it is giving each man his due, good to one's friends and evil to one's enemies. Socrates shows this to be an impossible position, because it cannot be the art of the just governor to do harm to his subjects any more than for the doctor to injure his patients; if he does these things he is acting in some other capacity, serving different standards. Polemarchus is silenced by this but Thrasymachus, a sophist, wishes to keep the argument going with his own definition of justice: he says it is "nothing else than the interest of the stronger." Socrates responds by questioning him.]

. . . Do you admit that it is just for subjects to obey their rulers?

I do.

But are the rulers of states absolutely infallible, or are they sometimes liable to err?

To be sure, he replied, they are liable to err.

Then in making their laws they may sometimes make them rightly, and sometimes not?

True.

When they make them rightly, they make them agreeably to their interest; when they are mistaken, contrary to their interest; you admit that?

Yes.

And the laws which they make must be obeyed by their subjects,— and that is what you call justice?

Doubtless.

Then justice, according to your argument, is not only obedience to the interest of the stronger but the reverse?

What is that you are saying? he asked.

I am only repeating what you are saying, I believe. But let us consider: Have we not admitted that the rulers may be mistaken about their own interest in what they command, and also that to obey them is justice? Has not that been admitted?

Yes.

Then you must also have acknowledged justice not to be for the interest of the stronger, when the rulers unintentionally command things to be done which are to their own injury. For if, as you say, justice is the obedience which the subject renders to their commands . . . is there any escape from the conclusion that the weaker are commanded to do, not what is for the interest, but what is for the injury of the stronger?

[Thrasymachus objects that he would not call a person "the stronger" at a time when he was mistaken. He explains himself:]

You argue like an informer, Socrates. Do you mean, for example, that he who is mistaken about the sick is a physician in that he is mistaken? or that he who errs in arithmetic or grammar is an arithmetician or grammarian at the time when he is making the mistake, in respect of the mistake? True, we say that the physician or arithmetician or grammarian has made a mistake, but this is only a way of speaking; for the fact is that neither the grammarian nor any other person of skill ever makes a mistake in so far as he is what his name implies; they none of them err unless their skill fails them, and then they cease to be skilled artists. No artist or sage or ruler errs at the time when he is what his name implies; though he is commonly said to err, and I adopted the common mode of speaking. But to be perfectly accurate, since you are such a lover of accuracy, we should say that the ruler, in so far as he is a ruler, is unerring, and, being unerring, always commands that which is for his own interest; and the subject is required to execute his commands; and therefore, as I said at first and now repeat, justice is the interest of the stronger.

[Socrates leads Thrasymachus to admit that every art has an interest outside of itself for which it must consider and provide. He goes on:]

Then medicine does not consider the interest of medicine, but the interest of the body?

True, he said.

Nor does the art of horsemanship consider the interests of the art of horsemanship, but the interests of the horse; neither do any other arts care for themselves, for they have no needs; they care only for that which is the subject of their art?

True, he said.

But surely, Thrasymachus, the arts are the superiors and rulers of their own subjects?

To this he assented with a good deal of reluctance.

Then, I said, no science or art considers or enjoins the interest of the stronger or superior, but only the interest of the subject and weaker?

He made an attempt to contest this proposition also, but finally acquiesced.

Then, I continued, no physician, in so far as he is a physician, considers his own good in what he prescribes, but the good of his patient; for the true physician is also a ruler having the human body as a subject, and is not a mere money-maker; that has been admitted?

Yes.

And the pilot likewise, in the strict sense of the term, is a ruler of sailors and not a mere sailor?

That has been admitted.

And such a pilot and ruler will provide and prescribe for the interest of the sailor who is under him, and not for his own or the ruler's interest?

He gave a reluctant "Yes."

Then, I said, Thrasymachus, there is no one in any rule who, in so far as he is a ruler, considers or enjoins what is for his own interest, but always what is for the interest of his subject or suitable to his art; to that he looks, and that alone he considers in everything which he says and does.

[Thrasymachus objects that the ultimate interest of the shepherd in fattening sheep, or of the horseman in training horses, is not their good but his own; and that the same is true of anyone who exercises an art for gain, and above all true of the master or ruler. The unjust man is the one who recognizes these facts and is by consequence both happier and stronger than the just; he cheerfully and profitably subjects everyone he can to his own dominion in his own interest. The person whom Socrates and others would call just, who acts otherwise than in his own interest, is (by contrast with the unjust man) weak, foolish, and unhappy. Socrates questions Thrasymachus, leading him first to admit that the fact that a person is paid for exercising his art proves the reverse of what Thrasymachus had claimed: if the pilot or doctor or ruler must be paid to perform his art, his art in itself must confer benefits not on him but on others. Socrates goes on:]

. . . [T]he truth is, that while the art of medicine gives health, and the art of the builder builds a house, another art attends them which is the art of pay. The various arts may be doing their own business and benefiting that over which they preside, but would the artist receive any benefit from his art unless he were paid as well?

I suppose not.

But does he therefore confer no benefit when he works for nothing?

Certainly, he confers a benefit.

Then now, Thrasymachus, there is no longer any doubt that neither arts nor governments provide for their own interests; but, as we were before saying, they rule and provide for the interests of their subjects who are the weaker and not the stronger — to their good they attend and not to the good of the superior. . . .

[The discussion turns to the second proposition advanced by Thrasymachus, that injustice is by its nature more profitable than justice.]

Well, then, Thrasymachus, I said, suppose you begin at the beginning and answer me. You say that perfect injustice is more gainful than perfect justice?

Yes, that is what I say, and I have given you my reasons.

And what is your view about them? Would you call one of them virtue and the other vice?

Certainly.

I suppose that you would call justice virtue and injustice vice?

What a charming notion! So likely too, seeing that I affirm injustice to be profitable and justice not.

What else then would you say?

The opposite, he replied.

And would you call justice vice?

No, I would rather say sublime simplicity.

Then would you call injustice malignity?

No; I would rather say discretion.

And do the unjust appear to you to be wise and good?

Yes, he said; at any rate those of them who are able to be perfectly unjust, and who have the power of subduing states and nations; but perhaps you imagine me to be talking of cutpurses. Even this profession if undetected has advantages, though they are not to be compared with those of which I was just now speaking.

I do not think that I misapprehend your meaning, Thrasymachus, I replied; but still I cannot hear without amazement that you class injustice with wisdom and virtue, and justice with the opposite.

Certainly I do so class them.

[Socrates then asks:] Does the just man try to gain any advantage over the just?

Far otherwise; if he did he would not be the simple amusing creature which he is.

And would he try to go beyond just action?

He would not.

And how would he regard the attempt to gain an advantage over the unjust; would that be considered by him as just or unjust?

He would think it just, and would try to gain the advantage; but he would not be able.

Whether he would or would not be able, I said, is not to the point. My question is only whether the just man, while refusing to have more than another just man, would wish and claim to have more than the unjust?

Yes, he would.

And what of the unjust — does he claim to have more than the just man and to do more than is just?

Of course, he said, for he claims to have more than all men.

And the unjust man will strive and struggle to obtain more than the unjust man or action, in order that he may have more than all?

True.

We may put the matter thus, I said — the just does not desire more than his like but more than his unlike, whereas the unjust desires more than both his like and his unlike?

Nothing, he said, can be better than that statement.

And the unjust is good and wise, and the just is neither?

Good again, he said.

And is not the unjust like the wise and good and the just unlike them?

Of course, he said, he who is of a certain nature, is like those who are of a certain nature; he who is not, not.

Each of them, I said, is such as his like is?

Certainly, he replied.

Very good, Thrasymachus, I said; and now to take the case of the arts: you would admit that one man is a musician and another not a musician?

Yes.

And which is wise and which is foolish?

Clearly the musician is wise, and he who is not a musician is foolish.

And he is good in as far as he is wise, and bad in as far as he is foolish?

Yes.

And you would say the same sort of thing of the physician?

Yes.

And do you think, my excellent friend, that a musician when he adjusts the lyre would desire or claim to exceed or go beyond a musician in the tightening and loosening the strings?

I do not think that he would.

But he would claim to exceed the non-musician?

Of course.

And what would you say of the physician? In prescribing meats and drinks would he wish to go beyond another physician or beyond the practice of medicine?

He would not.

But he would wish to go beyond the non-physician?

Yes.

And about knowledge and ignorance in general; see whether you think that any man who has knowledge ever would wish to have the choice of saying or doing more than another man who has knowledge. Would he not rather say or do the same as his like in the same case?

That, I suppose, can hardly be denied.

And what of the ignorant? would he not desire to have more than either the knowing or the ignorant?

I dare say.

And the knowing is wise?

Yes.

And the wise is good?

True.

Then the wise and good will not desire to gain more than his like, but more than his unlike and opposite?

I suppose so.

Whereas the bad and ignorant will desire to gain more than both?

Yes.

But did we not say, Thrasymachus, that the unjust goes beyond both his like and unlike? Were not these your words?

They were.

And you also said that the just will not go beyond his like but his unlike?

Yes.

Then the just is like the wise and good, and the unjust like the evil and ignorant?

That is the inference.

And each of them is such as his like is?

That was admitted.

Then the just has turned out to be wise and good and the unjust evil and ignorant.

Thrasymachus made all these admissions, not fluently, as I repeat them, but with extreme reluctance; it was a hot summer's day, and the perspiration poured from him in torrents; and then I saw what I had never seen before, Thrasymachus blushing. As we were now agreed that justice was virtue and wisdom, and injustice vice and ignorance, I proceeded to another point:

Well, I said, Thrasymachus, that matter is now settled; but were we not also saying that injustice had strength; do you remember? . . . I will repeat the question which I asked before, in order that our examination of the relative nature of justice and injustice may be carried on regularly. A statement was made that injustice is stronger and more powerful than justice, but now justice, having been identified with wisdom and virtue, is easily shown to be stronger than injustice, if injustice is ignorance; this can no longer be questioned by any one. But I want to view the matter, Thrasymachus, in a different way: You would not deny that a state may be unjust and may be unjustly attempting to enslave other states, or may have already enslaved them, and may be holding many of them in subjection?

True, he replied; and I will add that the best and most perfectly unjust state will be most likely to do so.

I know, I said, that such was your position; but what I would further consider is, whether this power which is possessed by the superior state can exist or be exercised without justice or only with justice.

If you are right in your view, and justice is wisdom, then only with justice; but if I am right, then without justice.

I am delighted, Thrasymachus, to see you not only nodding assent and dissent, but making answers which are quite excellent.

That is out of civility to you, he replied.

You are very kind, I said; and would you have the goodness also to inform me, whether you think that a state, or an army, or a band of robbers and thieves, or any other gang of evil-doers could act at all if they injured one another?

No indeed, he said, they could not.

But if they abstained from injuring one another, then they might act together better?

Yes.

And this is because injustice creates divisions and hatreds and fighting, and justice imparts harmony and friendship; is not that true, Thrasymachus?

I agree, he said, because I do not wish to quarrel with you.

How good of you, I said; but I should like to know also whether injustice, having this tendency to arouse hatred, wherever existing, among slaves or among freemen, will not make them hate one another and set them at variance and render them incapable of common action?

Certainly.

And even if injustice be found in two only, will they not quarrel and fight, and become enemies to one another and to the just?

They will.

And suppose injustice abiding in a single person, would your wisdom say that she loses or that she retains her natural power?

Let us assume that she retains her power.

Yet is not the power which injustice exercises of such a nature that wherever she takes up her abode, whether in a city, in an army, in a family, or in any other body, that body is, to begin with, rendered incapable of united action by reason of sedition and distraction; and does it not become its own enemy and at variance with all that opposes it, and with the just? Is not this the case?

Yes, certainly.

And is not injustice equally fatal when existing in a single person; in the first place rendering him incapable of action because he is not at unity with himself, and in the second place making him an enemy to himself and the just? Is not that true, Thrasymachus?

Yes.

And O my friend, I said, surely the gods are just?

Granted that they are.

But if so, the unjust will be the enemy of the gods, and the just will be their friend?

Feast away in triumph, and take your fill of the argument; I will not oppose you, lest I should displease the company.

Well then, proceed with your answers, and let me have the remainder of my repast. For we have already shown that the just are clearly wiser and better and abler than the unjust, and that the unjust are incapable of common action; nay more, that to speak as we did of men who are evil acting at any time vigorously together, is not strictly true, for if they had been perfectly evil, they would have laid hands upon one another; but it is evident that there must have been some remnant of justice in them, which enabled them to combine; if there had not been they would have injured one another as well as their victims; they were but half-villains in their enterprises; for had they been whole villains, and utterly unjust, they would have been utterly incapable of action. That, as I believe, is the truth of the matter, and not what you said at first. But whether the just have a better and happier life than the unjust is a further question which we also proposed to consider. I think that they have, and for the reasons which I have given; but still I should like to examine further, for no light matter is at stake, nothing less than the rule of human life.

Proceed.

[Thrasymachus agrees with Socrates that everything—horse, eye, ear, pruning-hook—has an end for which it is particularly intended, and an excellence insofar as it achieves that end.]

[A]nd has not the soul an end which nothing else can fulfil? for example, to superintend and command and deliberate and the like. Are not these functions proper to the soul, and can they rightly be assigned to any other?

To no other.

And is not life to be reckoned among the ends of the soul?

Assuredly, he said.

And has not the soul an excellence also?

Yes.

And can she or can she not fulfil her own ends when deprived of that excellence?

She cannot.

Then an evil soul must necessarily be an evil ruler and superintendent, and the good soul a good ruler?

Yes, necessarily.

And we have admitted that justice is the excellence of the soul, and injustice the defect of the soul?

That has been admitted.

Then the just soul and the just man will live well, and the unjust man will live ill?

That is what your argument proves.

And he who lives well is blessed and happy, and he who lives ill the reverse of happy?

Certainly.

Then the just is happy, and the unjust miserable?

So be it.

But happiness and not misery is profitable.

Of course.

Then, my blessed Thrasymachus, injustice can never be more profitable than justice.

QUESTIONS

1. Thrasymachus here maintains that justice is the interest of the stronger, and that if it is defined otherwise (as a traditional virtue, or as a way of recognizing the claims of others), it is of less advantage than injustice. Socrates claims the reverse: that justice is the interest of the weaker, that it is stronger and more profitable than injustice, and that the just man is happier than the unjust.

a. Has this argument any significance for the law of the twentieth century? For a modern judge or lawyer?

b. Explain what is at stake in this argument. How would you state the principal issue that divides the two speakers?

(1) Consider Socrates' famous assertion that even a band of thieves must recognize and operate by some principles of justice, since the purely evil would be incapable of common action; or the notion that the practitioner of an art or skill – whether shepherd, pilot, or governor – while acting in that capacity always serves the interest of another, not himself. What issue is Socrates addressing here? Can you put his argument in other and perhaps more modern terms? Can you adduce other examples?

(2) Or consider how Socrates shows that the "just" is "wise" and "good": he demonstrates that all three "desire more than their unlike but not more than their like." The ignorant and evil, by contrast, lay claim to "more than all other men." He gives examples from music, learning, and medicine. Does this argument persuade you, or do you regard it as meaninglessly abstract? Can you cast the argument in other terms, perhaps using other examples? What is the real issue Socrates addresses here, and what is his principal assertion with respect to it?

2. How does Socrates tell us what "justice" and "injustice" mean? Does he give an analysis or description of what those terms mean? Could justice as he conceives of it be expressed in a set of rules? If not that way, how might it be expressed?

3. Look at how Thrasymachus defines justice and injustice. He calls the "unjust" the "wise" and "good." This seems to us to be an impossible combination of terms. Why do you suppose he made it, then? Was he just showing off?

a. Can you imagine how a conversation about the rightness or wrongness of a particular act might proceed under the assumption that the "un-

just" is "wise" and "good"? How might a judicial argument proceed, for example?

b. *Suppose you rewrote what Thrasymachus says here, shifting the key terms slightly so that what he says about the "unjust" man was said instead about the "sensible" or "realistic" or "effective" or "pragmatic" man. Would you find such statements equally surprising?*

c. *Compare what Hume said about the apparently universal unanimity of view on basic ethical standards: "It is indeed obvious, that writers of all nations and all ages concur in applauding justice, humanity, magnanimity, prudence, veracity; and in blaming the opposite qualities. . . . This great unanimity is usually ascribed to the influence of plain reason; which, in all these cases, maintains similar sentiments in all men, and prevents those controversies, to which the abstract sciences are so much exposed. So far as the unanimity is real, this account may be admitted as satisfactory: but we must also allow that some part of the seeming harmony in morals may be accounted for from the very nature of language. The word 'virtue,' with its equivalent in every tongue, implies praise; as that of 'vice' does blame; and no one, without the most obvious and grossest impropriety, could affix reproach to a term, which in general acceptation is understood in a good sense; or bestow applause, where the idiom requires disapprobation." Hume, "Of the Standard of Taste," in Essays Moral, Political and Literary (1741).*

d. *Does the passage from Hume suggest a way in which you might define what is at stake in the passage from The Republic?*

4. *Regard Thrasymachus now as a writer: how does he define himself as a mind and a person? To what activities is the mind expressed here naturally suited, and to what activities not?*

   a. *Do you ever hear arguments made today like those Thrasymachus makes here? Make a list of remarks heard in your law classes or seen in the newspaper which you think Thrasymachus might have made.*

   b. *Suppose Thrasymachus were a law school student called upon to criticize a judicial opinion or statute; how might he do so? What standards or values might he invoke, in what vocabulary? What criteria of excellence would he bring to his evaluation of a judicial judgment or a proposed rule? Now ask the correlative question: how would he function as a judge himself? How would he make and explain his decision?*

   Pursue these questions with respect to an actual case you have studied.

   c. *Now examine what Socrates says, and ask the same questions about him. Do you think he could do better than Thrasymachus at the activity we call judicial criticism? At making and explaining decisions? Why?*

   d. *Does the very process of criticism, of thought and judgment, in which you engage every day imply the sorts of connections that Socrates asserts between justice and virtue and wisdom and happiness? How does this process of implication work?*

5. *Of course Socrates' assertions are most incomplete, and he in fact concludes the passage given above by raising an inquiry into the nature of justice. Do you know how this inquiry ends up? Is it conceivable that Socrates will conclude that justice can be stated in a set of legal rules? If*

justice can not be expressed or defined by a set of rules, what is it and how can it be talked about? What is the art by which it can be achieved, and how can that art be attained?

6. *Look back over these three passages from Plato and ask how you respond to him now.*
   a. *Are you willing to dispute his connections between justice and happiness and virtue? Do you say that less than this is at stake in the right working of a legal system?*
   b. *Or do you say that Plato was wrong in his earlier conclusion that the form we call the rule is inadequate to the expression of the arts of justice, wisdom, and happiness?*
   c. *Or is there some lawyer's art by which the language of rules, the materials of our law, can be mastered and controlled, some understanding or skill by which it can be made not only tolerable but the best language for social organization, for judgment and for explanation?*

2. *The Process of Judgment and the Rule*

In the passage you read from *The Statesman, supra* page 625, Socrates claims that the wise and good ruler does not decide what is right and wrong (or expedient and inexpedient) on the basis of rules, which are instruments inadequate to the process of wise judgment; but Socrates does not tell us how such a one does make his judgments. Is this a subject about which nothing more can be said, or is it possible to give some expression, and perhaps some guidance, to the process of responsible and intelligent judgment? Is it ever possible — despite what Socrates says — to make decisions that are wise and just by simply following a set of rules? If not that way, how can such decisions be made, and what place, if any, can rules have in that process? What does one do when, like the lawyer or judge, one finds oneself confronted with rules that are meant to govern one's judgment? However such judgments are to be made, how can they be expressed and guided — and does the rule perhaps have a more important role here? These are your questions, first stated in the introduction to this chapter and (I hope) made more troubling and more meaningful by what you have read so far. What follows is meant to complicate them further. While we shall soon examine some of the ways in which the law has responded to these difficulties, we begin with some questions that may lend a slightly different perspective.

QUESTIONS: Making and Expressing Judgments

1. *Start by thinking back to your work on the sentencing judgment in Chapter 3. Is the process of making wise and just sentencing judgments one that can be guided by or expressed in rules? If not that way, how?*
2. *In Sophocles' play, Antigone buries her dead brother, notwithstanding the*

contrary decree of Creon, the ruler of Thebes. In justification she says that she followed "the unwritten and unfailing statutes of heaven," which she believed no "mortal could override." The problem is apparently expressed as a conflict between rules: she made a choice to follow "the higher law."

a. *Is that how you would characterize a similar choice in your own life — for example, if you were ordered to obey Nazi laws of the worst kind?*
b. *How else might you possibly express such a choice?*
c. *What do you suppose Sophocles is saying when he has Antigone express the matter thus?*
d. *Consider the explanation given in an Icelandic saga: when a man had unwittingly acted as host to the killer of his brother, and was accordingly subjected to two inconsistent rules of that society — to avenge the death and to protect the guest — he chose to defend the guest against his father and family, explaining afterwards, "It seemed to me to be the only fitting thing to do." Quoted in Hallberg, The Icelandic Saga 106* (1962).

3. *How would you describe or explain the choice made below?*

". . . The iridescent, brilliant blue spots in the red darkness of the dorsal fin play a special role when the female jewel fish is putting her babies to bed. She jerks her fin rapidly up and down, making the jewels flash like a heliograph. At this, the young congregate under the mother and obediently descend into the nesting hole. The father, in the meantime, searches the whole tank for stragglers. He does not coax them along but simply inhales them into his roomy mouth, swims to the nest, and blows them into the hollow. The baby sinks at once heavily to the bottom and remains lying there. By an ingenious arrangement of reflexes, the swim-bladders of young 'sleeping' cichlids contract so strongly that the tiny fishes become much heavier than water and remain, like little stones, lying in the hollow, just as they did in their earliest childhood before their swim-bladder was filled with gas. The same reaction of 'becoming heavy' is also elicited when a parent fish takes a young one in its mouth. Without this reflex mechanism it would be impossible for the father, when he gathers up his children in the evening, to keep them together.

"I once saw a jewel fish, during such an evening transport of strayed children, perform a deed which absolutely astonished me. I came, late one evening, into the laboratory. It was already dusk and I wished hurriedly to feed a few fishes which had not received anything to eat that day; amongst them was a pair of jewel fishes who were tending their young. As I approached the container, I saw that most of the young were already in the nesting hollow over which the mother was hovering. She refused to come for the food when I threw pieces of earthworm into the tank. The father, however, who, in great excitement, was dashing backwards and forwards searching for truants, allowed himself to be diverted from his duty by a nice hind-end of earthworm (*for some unknown reason this end is preferred by all worm-eaters to the front one*). *He swam up and seized the worm, but, owing to its size, was unable to swallow it. As he was in the act of chewing this mouthful, he saw a baby fish swimming by itself across the tank; he started as though stung, raced after the baby and took it into his already filled mouth. It was a thrilling moment. The*

fish had in its mouth two different things of which one must go into the stomach and the other into the nest. What would he do? I must confess that, at that moment, I would not have given twopence for the life of that tiny jewel fish. But wonderful what really happened! The fish stood stock still with full cheeks, but did not chew. If ever I have seen a fish think, it was in that moment! What a truly remarkable thing that a fish can find itself in a genuine conflicting situation and, in this case, behave exactly as a human being would; that is to say, it stops, blocked in all directions, and can go neither forward nor backward. For many seconds the father jewel fish stood riveted and one could almost see how his feelings were working. Then he solved the conflict in a way for which one was bound to feel admiration: he spat out the whole contents of his mouth: the worm fell to the bottom, and the little jewel fish, becoming heavy in the way described above, did the same. Then the father turned resolutely to the worm and ate it up, without haste but all the time with one eye on the child which 'obediently' lay on the bottom beneath him. When he had finished, he inhaled the baby and carried it home to its mother.

"Some students, who had witnessed the whole scene, started as one man to applaud." K. Lorenz, King Solomon's Ring 37–38 (1961).

4. What is the place of the rule (or other direction) in the following two instances?
   a. You must have used a combination lock at some time. At first you memorized the numbers, repeated them to yourself, and made appropriate turns of the dial. Did a time come when you no longer repeated the directions but just turned the dial? Perhaps you have even "forgotten" the combination to a very familiar lock, though you could reconstruct it when you next turned the dials.
   b. I asked a pianist why people always play without music at recitals. The answer was: "It is easier, once you know the music, not to have the sheets of music. The written notes stand in your way."
   c. Are legal rules likewise to be regarded as aids to an education, to be discarded as soon as mastered?
5. If you have a child, you have no doubt had to decide whether to call the doctor in the night. How did you make these decisions? By the use of rules? If you look at Spock, Baby and Child Care (1966 ed.), you will see that he very frequently gives directions to this important decision, and that what he says is often cast in the form of rules. "If he has a frequent cough or a deep cough or a wheezy cough, he should be examined by a doctor, even if he has no fever." (Page 461.) "If your child has hoarseness with fever or tightness of breathing with fever, he must be put under the close, continuous supervision of a doctor without delay. If you cannot reach your doctor right away, call another doctor. If a doctor cannot reach you, you should take the child to the hospital." (Page 471.) What connection has there been – or, if you have no children, can you imagine there being – between such rules and an actual judgment of your own?
6. So far in this chapter we have concerned ourselves mainly with the inadequacy or insufficiency of the rule to achieve justice. It is worth thinking as well about the positive harm that the rule can do.
   a. Do we so venerate the form of the rule, and glorify the use of rules to organize experience, that we disregard the state of affairs the system

of rules is meant to bring about? Does our engineer's fascination with the system lead us to forget its purposes of justice or fairness?

(1) *Is it true for us as lawyers that the only question is what the rules say? If so, is that any way to play golf? To run a railroad? To live as a family? To live as a community?*

(2) *What other questions are there for us as lawyers, then?*

b. *Does the use of the rule lead to argument of a bickering kind, a kind of specious intellectual trickery? Your friend at the cocktail party, for example, might say so, and in fact attribute what he sees as your "sophistic skill" to "devotion to rules."*

c. *Exactly what place can a rule of the classical sort have in the life of a good and intelligent person? When would an excellent person use a rule to regulate his life? To explain himself?*

(1) Compare 1 Timothy 1:9–10: "[T]he law is not made for a righteous man, but for the lawless and disobedient, for the ungodly and for sinners, for unholy and profane, for murderers of fathers and murderers of mothers, for manslayers, for whoremongers, for them that defile themselves with mankind, for menstealers, for liars, for perjured persons . . ."

(2) *If the rule has no function for the good and intelligent man, it may have occurred to you to ask: has the good and intelligent man any function in the law? What function: to subvert it at every opportunity?*

d. *Who then is the Good Lawyer, the Man of Good Judgment, and what relationship does he establish and maintain with the rules that are intended to direct his judgment?*

SPEECH TO THE ELECTORS OF BRISTOL*
Edmund Burke

Certainly, Gentlemen, it ought to be the happiness and glory of a representative to live in the strictest union, the closest correspondence, and the most unreserved communication with his constituents. Their wishes ought to have great weight with him; their opinions high respect; their business unremitted attention. It is his duty to sacrifice his repose, his pleasure, his satisfactions, to theirs, — and above all, ever, and in all cases, to prefer their interest to his own.

But his unbiased opinion, his mature judgment, his enlightened conscience, he ought not to sacrifice to you, to any man, or to any set of men living. These he does not derive from your pleasure, — no, nor from the law and the Constitution. They are a trust from Providence, for the abuse of which he is deeply answerable. Your representative owes you, not his industry only, but his judgment; and he betrays, instead of serving you, if he sacrifices it to your opinion.

My worthy colleague says, his will ought to be subservient to yours. If that be all, the thing is innocent. If government were a matter of will

* Nov. 3, 1774, in *Works*, II, 95 (1790; Beaconsfield ed. 1901).

upon any side, yours, without question, ought to be superior. But government and legislation are matters of reason and judgment, and not of inclination; and what sort of reason is that in which the determination precedes the discussion, in which one set of men deliberate and another decide, and where those who form the conclusion are perhaps three hundred miles distant from those who hear the arguments?

To deliver an opinion is the right of all men; that of constituents is a weighty and respectable opinion, which a representative ought always to rejoice to hear, and which he ought always most seriously to consider. But *authoritative* instructions, *mandates* issued, which the member is bound blindly and implicitly to obey, to vote, and to argue for, though contrary to the clearest conviction of his judgment and conscience,— these are things utterly unknown to the laws of this land, and which arise from a fundamental mistake of the whole order and tenor of our Constitution.

QUESTIONS

1. *Do you believe that Burke would approve of a judge or lawyer who adopted a similarly independent attitude towards the instructions and directions meant to regulate his judgment? Would you approve?*
2. *How do you suppose the law has in fact addressed itself to the defects of the rule as an instrument of justice?*

a. Judgment and the Rule in the Law: The Nature of Equity

When you were asked in Chapter 3 to consider how you would make and explain the judgment by which you sentenced another person, you no doubt felt all too acutely the inadequacy of the rule to the process in which you were engaged. Here your situation is somewhat different: you are asked not how you would decide what to do with a person or event if it all were up to you — if you were both legislator and judge — but how you would decide a case as a judge under a rule or set of rules passed by a legislature or other rule-maker. How should the judge read and use the rules and other directions that tell him what to do? How does the good judge figure out who should win and explain why, and what place does the legal rule have in this process? What is there beyond or beside the rule itself to which a judge can look for guidance, or which he can use to explain what he has done?

You know that rules are not self-executing, and that after they are passed they still depend upon the judge and lawyer for any effect they may have in the world. As we saw in Chapter 2, the issue must be stated in terms that invoke the rule; the terms of the rule must be defined; and the often unresolvable tensions between the apparent meaning of the terms — of the label or category of convenience — and the purposes of the rule must somehow be faced. How is all this to be done?

Socrates says that rules are by their nature always subject to exception — even such an obviously just rule as that one should pay one's debts. Is this the beginning of the definition of judicial art, that the task is not to apply rules but to draw exceptions to them? How is the process by which exceptions are made to be talked about and regulated? And if rules really are subject to exceptions all the time, what good are they?

NICOMACHEAN ETHICS*

Aristotle

The same thing, then, is just and equitable, and while both are good the equitable is superior. What creates the problem is that the equitable is just, but not the legally just but a correction of legal justice. The reason is that all law is universal but about some things it is not possible to make a universal statement which shall be correct. In those cases, then, in which it is necessary to speak universally, but not possible to do so correctly, the law takes the usual case, though it is not ignorant of the possibility of error. And it is none the less correct; for the error is not in the law nor in the legislator but in the nature of the thing, since the matter of practical affairs is of this kind from the start. When the law speaks universally, then, and a case arises on it which is not covered by the universal statement, then it is right, where the legislator fails us and has erred by over-simplicity, to correct the omission — to say what the legislator himself would have said had he been present, and would have put into his law if he had known. Hence the equitable is just, and better than one kind of justice — not better than absolute justice but better than the error that arises from the absoluteness of the statement. And this is the nature of the equitable, a correction of law where it is defective owing to its universality.

QUESTIONS

1. *Aristotle seems to say that to establish a system of justice one must provide for "equitable" powers to modify legal rules or make exceptions to them – to "correct" legal justice – and that this is a necessary consequence of the use of the form we call the rule.*
   a. *If this is so, why use rules at all? Or, in Aristotle's terms, why is it ever "necessary" to speak in universals, especially when it is not possible to do so "correctly"?*

* Book 5, Chapter 10 (Oxford Translation of Aristotle, printed in *Basic Works of Aristotle,* R. McKeon ed. 1941).

b. *If we can "correct" legal justice satisfactorily, why can we not do without it entirely?*

2. *Here is a passage of more recent date, asserting that a special set of powers is automatically given to anyone who is asked to apply a rule:*

"[No lawmaker] can enact a completely comprehensive code to take care of every possible contingency that may affect his arrangement, even if he is accorded a theoretically complete power to do so. In some degree, therefore, he is inescapably dependent upon some agency of authoritative application – usually the courts – to fill in some of the details for him." H. Hart and A. Sacks, The Legal Process 252 (1958).

3. *How are the processes of "correcting" legal justice and "filling in" details to go on? According to what standards or values, on what occasions, and by whom?*
   a. *Should we establish a set of rules governing the exercise of equitable powers and the interpretation of rules?*
   b. *To what powers of equity, how expressed, should these rules be subject?*
   c. *Or should we do without rules on these matters? If on these, then on all other matters too, on the theory that whatever guides the correction of legal justice can substitute for it?*

4. *How do you suppose real legal systems have answered these questions?*

EQUITY*

F. W. Maitland

We ought not to think of common law and equity as of two rival systems. Equity was not a self-sufficient system, at every point it presupposed the existence of common law. Common law was a self-sufficient system. I mean this: that if the legislature had passed a short act saying "Equity is hereby abolished," we might still have got on fairly well; in some respects our law would have been barbarous, unjust, absurd, but still the great elementary rights, the right to immunity from violence, the right to one's good name, the rights of ownership and of possession would have been decently protected and contract would have been enforced. On the other hand had the legislature said, "Common Law is hereby abolished," this decree if obeyed would have meant anarchy. At every point equity presupposed the existence of common law. Take the case of the trust. It's of no use for Equity to say that A is a trustee of Blackacre for B, unless there be some court that can say that A is the owner of Blackacre. Equity without common law would have been a castle in the air, an impossibility.

For this reason I do not think that any one has expounded or ever will expound equity as a single, consistent system, an articulate body of law. It is a collection of appendixes between which there is no very close connexion. If we suppose all our law put into systematic order, we shall

* Lecture 2 (1909).

find that some chapters of it have been copiously glossed by equity, while others are quite free from equitable glosses. Since the destruction of the Star Chamber we have had no criminal equity. The Court of Chancery kept very clear of the province of crime, and since the province of crime and the province of tort overlap, it kept very clear of large portions of the province of tort. For example, before 1875 it would grant no injunction to restrain the publication of a libel, for normally the libel which is a tort is also a crime and it was thought, and rightly thought, that such a matter should not be brought before a court where a judge without any jury tried both fact and law. Indeed if you will look at your books on tort you will find that on the whole — if we except the province of fraud — equity has had little to do with tort, though it has granted injunctions to restrain the commission of nuisances and the like. The law of contract has been more richly provided with equitable appendixes. The power of the Chancery to compel specific performance, and its power to decree the cancellation or rectification of agreements brought numerous cases of contract before it, and then it had special doctrines about mortgages, and penalties, and stipulations concerning time. Property law was yet more richly glossed. One vast appendix was added to it under the title of trusts. The bond which kept these various appendixes together under the head of Equity was the jurisdictional and procedural bond. All these matters were within the cognizance of courts of equity, and they were not within the cognizance of the courts of common law. That bond is now broken by the Judicature Acts. Instead of it we find but a mere historical bond — "these rules used to be dealt with by the Court of Chancery" — and the strength of that bond is being diminished year by year. The day will come when lawyers will cease to inquire whether a given rule be a rule of equity or a rule of common law: suffice it that it is a well-established rule administered by the High Court of Justice.

Certainly I should have liked at the outset of my course to have put before you some map, some scheme of equity. But for the reasons that I have endeavoured to state I do not think that such a map, such a scheme can be drawn. Attempts at classification have been made, but they have never been pushed very far and are now of little, if any, service to us. The scheme adopted by the great American judge, Story, and which found very general acceptation, was this — Equity is (1) exclusive, (2) concurrent, (3) auxiliary. You see the basis of this scheme — it is one on which we can no longer build. Equity has an exclusive cognizance of certain subjects, e.g. trusts, a cognizance that is exclusive of courts of law. Then it has a concurrent jurisdiction, a jurisdiction that is concurrent with the jurisdiction of courts of law over certain other subjects, e.g. fraud. Finally men sometimes go to equity merely in order to obtain its assistance in proceedings which they are taking or are about to take in courts of law, e.g. the plaintiff in an action at law goes to the Chancery in order that he may obtain discovery of the documents on which his opponent will rely. Here equity exercises an auxiliary jurisdiction. Then under each of these titles Story and other writers will give a string of sub-titles. Thus the concurrent jurisdiction deals with account, mistake, actual or positive fraud, constructive fraud, administration, legacies, confusion of boundaries, dower, and so forth. But you will at once see that this string is a mere string and not a logical scheme — observe for example the leap from legacies to boundaries, and from boundaries to dower. I am not complaining of Story's procedure; on the contrary it seems to me the only procedure open to him. In my opinion he had to deal not with a single connected system, but with a number of disconnected doctrines, disconnected appendixes to or glosses on the common law. And you will observe that such classification as he could make is no longer useful. It presupposes that there is one set of courts administering law, another set administering equity. That is no longer the case in England. No court, no division of a court, can now say these or those rules are my exclusive property; for every division of the High Court is capable of administering whatever rules are applicable to the case that is before it, whether they be rules of the common law or rules of equity.

QUESTIONS

1. *If equity has never been a "single, consistent system, an articulate body of law," how can that circumstance be explained?*
   a. *Is it that equity by its nature could not have become such a system, or simply that for historical reasons it did not?*
   b. *If it was not such a system, what was it?*
2. *At the beginning of his book, Maitland defines equity: "Thus we are driven to say that Equity is now that body of rules administered by our English courts of justice which, were it not for the operation of the Judicature Acts, would be administered only by those courts which would be known as Courts of Equity."*
   a. *If equity was just a separate set of rules administered by a separate set of courts, why is it that the rules and courts of equity were separated in this fashion from their legal counterparts?*
   b. *If it was something else, what was it?*
   c. *Turn now to the present. Have we any rules that can be called "equitable" rather than "legal"? How, except by their historical origins, can they be distinguished from legal rules? Are they now part of the same "logical scheme" as the rules of law, or is there some substantive or formal difference in the kind of rule we call equitable?*
3. *How do you suppose the irregular powers of equity described by Maitland were exercised and controlled?*

ANCIENT LAW*
H. Maine

[Maine begins his study of what he calls Roman Equity with the passage in Justinian's *Institutes* which says that all nations are governed partly by their own particular laws and partly by laws that are common to all mankind. "The law which a people enacts is called the Civil Law of that people, but that which natural reason appoints for all mankind is called the Law of Nations, because all nations use it."

What are the origins of this law of nations, and what are its relations to natural law and to equity? Maine explains that because the civil law applied only to Roman citizens, another law, called the jus gentium, was applied by the praetor to the many foreigners under Roman jurisdiction. Despite what Justinian seems to say, this was called the law of all the nations not because it was regarded as a universal law of reason or as natural law, but because it applied to all foreigners alike. Originally Roman lawyers had no special respect for this law — "it was the fruit in part of their disdain for all foreign law, and in part of their disinclination to give the foreigner the advantages of their own indigenous Jus Civile." But when the Stoic ethical doctrines (based upon the precept to live in all ways according to the universal law of Nature) became current, the jus gentium attracted attention of a different kind, for it was suddenly seen as a sort of actual natural law, a law of universal justice, an approximation of the ideal from which all legal systems were said to have fallen away.]

. . . After Nature had become a household word in the mouths of the Romans, the belief gradually prevailed among the Roman lawyers that the old Jus Gentium was in fact the lost code of Nature, and that the Praetor in framing an Edictal jurisprudence on the principles of the Jus Gentium was gradually restoring a type from which law had only departed to deteriorate. The inference from this belief was immediate that it was the Praetor's duty to supersede the Civil Law as much as possible by the Edict, to revive as far as might be the institutions by which Nature had governed man in the primitive state. Of course there were many impediments to the amelioration of law by this agency. There may have been prejudices to overcome even in the legal profession itself, and Roman habits were far too tenacious to give way at once to mere philosophical theory. The indirect methods by which the Edict combated certain technical anomalies, show the caution which its authors were compelled to observe, and down to the very days of Justinian there was some part of the old law which had obstinately resisted its influence.

* Chapter 3 (1861).

But on the whole, the progress of the Romans in legal improvement was astonishingly rapid as soon as stimulus was applied to it by the theory of Natural Law. The ideas of simplification and generalization had always been associated with the conception of Nature; simplicity, symmetry, and intelligibility came therefore to be regarded as the characteristics of a good legal system, and the taste for involved language, multiplied ceremonials, and useless difficulties disappeared altogether. The strong will and unusual opportunities of Justinian were needed to bring the Roman law into its eixsting shape, but the ground plan of the system had been sketched long before the imperial reforms were effected. . . .

Something must be said of the formal instrumentality by which the principles and distinctions associated, first with the Law common to all Nations, and afterwards with the Law of Nature, were gradually incorporated with the Roman law. At the crisis of primitive Roman history which is marked by the expulsion of the Tarquins, a change occurred which has its parallel in the early annals of many ancient states, but which had little in common with those passages of political affairs which we now term revolutions. It may best be described by saying that the monarchy was put into commission. The powers heretofore accumulated in the hands of a single person were parcelled out among a number of elective functionaries, the very name of the kingly office being retained and imposed on a personage known subsequently as the Rex Sacrorum or Rex Sacrificulus. As part of the change, the settled duties of the supreme judicial office devolved on the Praetor, at the time the first functionary in the commonwealth, and together with these duties was transferred the undefined supremacy over law and legislation which always attached to ancient sovereigns, and which is not obscurely related to the patriarchal and heroic authority they had once enjoyed. . . .[O]ne precaution of the Roman people against the revival of oppression, had consisted in obliging every magistrate whose duties had any tendency to expand their sphere, to publish, on commencing his year of office, an Edict or proclamation, in which he declared the manner in which he intended to administer his department. The Praetor fell under the rule with other magistrates; but as it was necessarily impossible to construct each year a separate system of principles, he seems to have regularly republished his predecessor's Edict with such additions and changes as the exigency of the moment or his own views of the law compelled him to introduce. The Praetor's proclamation, thus lengthened by a new portion every year, obtained the name of the Edictum Perpetuum, that is, the *continuous* or *unbroken* edict. The immense length to which it extended, together perhaps with some distaste for its necessarily disorderly texture, caused the practice of increasing it to be stopped in the year of Salvius Julianus, who occupied the magistracy in the reign of the Emperor Hadrian. The edict of that

Praetor embraced therefore the whole body of equity jurisprudence, which it probably disposed in new and symmetrical order, and the perpetual edict is therefore often cited in Roman law merely as the Edict of Julianus.

Perhaps the first inquiry which occurs to an Englishman who considers the peculiar mechanism of the Edict is, what were the limitations by which these extensive powers of the Praetor were restrained? How was authority so little definite to be reconciled with a settled condition of society and law? The answer can only be supplied by careful observation of the conditions under which our own English law is administered. The Praetor, it should be recollected, was a jurisconsult himself, or a person entirely in the hands of advisers who were jurisconsults, and it is probable that every Roman lawyer waited impatiently for the time when he should fill or control the great judicial magistracy. In the interval, his tastes, feelings, prejudices, and degree of enlightenment were inevitably those of his own order, and the qualifications which he ultimately brought to office were those which he had acquired in the practice and study of his profession.

An English Chancellor goes through precisely the same training, and carries to the woolsack the same qualifications. It is certain when he assumes office that he will have, to some extent, modified the law before he leaves it; but until he has quitted his seat, and the series of his decisions in the Law Reports has been completed, we cannot discover how far he has elucidated or added to the principles which his predecessors bequeathed to him. The influence of the Praetor on Roman jurisprudence differed only in respect of the period at which its amount was ascertained. As was before stated, he was in office but for a year, and his decisions rendered during his year, though of course irreversible as regarded the litigants, were of no ulterior value. The most natural moment for declaring the changes he proposed to effect, occurred therefore at his entrance on the praetorship; and hence, when commencing his duties, he did openly and avowedly that which in the end his English representative does insensibly and sometimes unconsciously. The checks on his apparent liberty are precisely those imposed on an English judge. Theoretically there seems to be hardly any limit to the powers of either of them, but practically the Roman Praetor, no less than the English Chancellor, was kept within the narrowest bounds by the prepossessions imbibed from early training, and by the strong restraints of professional opinion, restraints of which the stringency can only be appreciated by those who have personally experienced them. It may be added that the lines within which movement is permitted, and beyond which there is to be no travelling, were chalked with as much distinctness in the one case as in the other. In England the judge follows the analogies of reported decisions on insulated groups of facts.

At Rome, as the intervention of the Praetor was at first dictated by simple concern for the safety of the state, it is likely that in the earliest times it was proportioned to the difficulty which it attempted to get rid of. Afterwards, when the taste for principle had been diffused by the Responses, he no doubt used the Edict as the means of giving a wider application to those fundamental principles which he and the other practising jurisconsults, his contemporaries, believed themselves to have detected underlying the law. Latterly he acted wholly under the influence of Greek philosophical theories, which at once tempted him to advance and confined him to a particular course of progress.

The nature of the measures attributed to Salvius Julianus has been much disputed. Whatever they were, their effects on the Edict are sufficiently plain. It ceased to be extended by annual additions, and henceforward the equity jurisprudence of Rome was developed by the labours of a succession of great jurisconsults who fill with their writings the interval between the reign of Hadrian and the reign of Alexander Severus. A fragment of the wonderful system which they built up survives in the Pandects of Justinian, and supplies evidence that their works took the form of treatises on all parts of Roman law, but chiefly that of commentaries on the Edict. Indeed, whatever be the immediate subject of a jurisconsult of this epoch, he may always be called an expositor of Equity. The principles of the Edict had, before the epoch of its cessation, made their way into every part of Roman jurisprudence. The Equity of Rome, it should be understood, even when most distinct from the Civil Law, was always administered by the same tribunals. The Praetor was the chief equity judge as well as the great common law magistrate, and as soon as the Edict had evolved an equitable rule the Praetor's court began to apply it in place of or by the side of the old rule of the Civil Law, which was thus directly or indirectly repealed without any express enactment of the legislature. The result, of course, fell considerably short of a complete fusion of law and equity, which was not carried out till the reforms of Justinian. The technical severance of the two elements of jurisprudence entailed some confusion and some inconvenience, and there were certain of the stubborner doctrines of the Civil Law with which neither the authors nor the expositors of the Edict had ventured to interfere. But at the same time there was no corner of the field of jurisprudence which was not more or less swept over by the influence of Equity. It supplied the jurist with all his materials for generalisation, with all his methods of interpretation, with his elucidations of first principles, and with that great mass of limiting rules which are rarely interfered with by the legislator, but which seriously control the application of every legislative act.

The period of jurists ends with Alexander Severus. From Hadrian to that emperor the improvement of law was carried on, as it is at the present moment in most continental countries, partly by approved commentaries and partly by direct legislation. But in the reign of Alexander Severus the power of growth in Roman Equity seems to be exhausted, and the succession of jurisconsults comes to a close. The remaining history of the Roman law is the history of the imperial constitutions, and, at the last, of attempts to codify what had now become the unwieldy body of Roman jurisprudence. We have the latest and most celebrated experiment of this kind in the *Corpus Juris* of Justinian.

It would be wearisome to enter on a detailed comparison or contrast of English and Roman Equity; but it may be worth while to mention . . .[that each] of them tended, and all such systems tend, to exactly the same state in which the old common law was when Equity first interfered with it. A time always comes at which the moral principles originally adopted have been carried out to all their legitimate consequences, and then the system founded on them becomes as rigid, as unexpansive, and as liable to fall behind moral progress as the sternest code of rules avowedly legal. Such an epoch was reached at Rome in the reign of Alexander Severus; after which, though the whole Roman world was undergoing a moral revolution, the Equity of Rome ceased to expand. The same point of legal history was attained in England under the chancellorship of Lord Eldon, the first of our equity judges who, instead of enlarging the jurisprudence of his court by indirect legislation, devoted himself through life to explaining and harmonizing it.

QUESTIONS

1. *During its years of growth and health, what contribution did Roman equity make to the life of the law? When its powers of growth decayed?*
2. *In both Rome and England the powers of the equity court seem to have been theoretically unlimited, not governed by any set of legal rules. Upon what force, if not that of the rule, did these systems rely to guide and control the powers of equity?*
3. *Maine says that the progress of the law has been from fiction, through equity, to legislation. Is that where it stops, or does it go on? What is the modern analog to equity in the United States?*
4. *Let me suggest that a modern analog to equity is constitutional law.*
   a. *How much of what Maine says about equity could be said about constitutional law?*
   b. *Upon what do we rely to guide and control the powers of the Supreme Court, which may also seem theoretically unlimited? A set of rules? Something else?*
   c. *If you cannot find a set of rules that govern these powers, how do you explain that circumstance? Would you recommend the adoption of a wise and comprehensive set of rules telling the Justices how to exercise their powers?*

b. Judgment and the Rule: Outside the Law

I hope you consider that you have been presented with a real puzzle: the Greeks, the Romans, and the English all recognized that the sort of justice expressible in legal rules is inadequate and should be subject to "correction" by a judge. Yet if this is so, no one has told us why we should bother to have rules at all (unless for "inferior" communities and people) or how these powers of equity and correction ought to be exercised and controlled. What standards or rules or values should govern this process? How can they be expressed? Exactly what is excellence in judicial judgment, and what place has the rule in that activity?

There follow some passages showing how people outside the law have made judgments and how, in doing so, they have dealt with rules which they have faced. As you read these passages, ask what art you see the writers exercise, what excellence they display. Does this process of comparison with the law lead you to ask new sorts of questions about what judges and lawyers do? Be sure to ask, in each case, what point there is in having rules if people are always making exceptions to them or disregarding them.

The following passage deals with the process of judgment under a rule plainly meant to govern our conduct. How would you define the process of judgment here exemplified and recommended? What relationship does this writer establish with the rule he addresses, and how does he justify or explain what he does?

DICTIONARY OF MODERN ENGLISH USAGE*
H. W. Fowler

Split infinitive. The English-speaking world may be divided into (1) those who neither know nor care what a split infinitive is; (2) those who do not know, but care very much; (3) those who know and condemn; (4) those who know and approve; and (5) those who know and distinguish.

1. Those who neither know nor care are the vast majority, and are a happy folk, to be envied by most of the minority classes. "To really understand" comes readier to their lips and pens than "really to understand"; they see no reason why they should not say it (small blame to them, seeing that reasons are not their critics' strong point), and they do say it, to the discomfort of some among us, but not to their own.

2. To the second class, those who do not know but do care, who would as soon be caught putting their knives in their mouths as splitting

* (1926; Gowers ed. 1965.)

an infinitive but have only hazy notions of what constitutes that deplorable breach of etiquette, this article is chiefly addressed. These people betray by their practice that their aversion to the split infinitive springs not from instinctive good taste, but from tame acceptance of the misinterpreted opinion of others; for they will subject their sentences to the queerest distortions, all to escape imaginary split infinitives. "To really understand" is a s.i.; "to really be understood" is a s.i.; "to be really understood" is not one; the havoc that is played with much well-intentioned writing by failure to grasp that distinction is incredible. Those upon whom the fear of infinitive-splitting sits heavy should remember that to give conclusive evidence, by distortions, of misconceiving the nature of the s.i. is far more damaging to their literary pretentions than an actual lapse could be; for it exhibits them as deaf to the normal rhythm of English sentences. No sensitive ear can fail to be shocked, if the following examples are read aloud, by the strangeness of the indicated adverbs. Why on earth, the reader wonders, is that word out of its place? He will find, on looking through again, that each has been turned out of a similar position, viz. between the word *be* and a passive participle. Reflection will assure him that the cause of dislocation is always the same — all these writers have sacrificed the run of their sentences to the delusion that "to be really understood" is a split infinitive. It is not; and the straitest non-splitter of us all can with a clear conscience restore each of the adverbs to its rightful place: He was proposed at the last moment as a candidate likely *generally* to be accepted. / When the record of this campaign comes *dispassionately* to be written, and in just perspective, it will be found that . . . / New principles will have *boldly* to be adopted if the Scottish case is to be met. / This is a very serious matter, which clearly ought *further* to be inquired into. / The Headmaster of a public school possesses very great powers, which ought *most carefully and considerately* to be exercised. / The time to get this revaluation put through is when the amount paid by the State to the localities is *very largely* to be increased.

3. The above writers are bogy-haunted creatures who for fear of splitting an infinitive abstain from doing something quite different, i.e. dividing *be* from its complement by an adverb; see further under POSITION OF ADVERBS. Those who presumably do know what split infinitives are, and condemn them, are not so easily identified, since they include all who neither commit the sin nor flounder about in saving themselves from it — all who combine a reasonable dexterity with acceptance of conventional rules. But when the dexterity is lacking, disaster follows. It does not add to a writer's readableness if readers are pulled up now and again to wonder — Why this distortion? Ah, to be sure, a non-split diehard! That is the mental dialogue occasioned by each of the adverbs in

the examples below. It is of no avail merely to fling oneself desperately out of temptation; one must so do it that no traces of the struggle remain. Sentences must if necessary be thoroughly remodelled instead of having a word lifted from its original place and dumped elsewhere: What alternative can be found which the Pope has not condemned, and which will make it possible *to organize legally* public worship? / It will, when better understood, tend *firmly to establish* relations between Capital and Labour. / Both Germany and England have done ill in not combining *to forbid flatly* hostilities. / Every effort must be made *to increase adequately* professional knowledge and attainments. / We have had *to shorten somewhat* Lord D——'s letter. / The kind of sincerity which enables an author *to move powerfully* the heart would . . . / Safeguards should be provided *to prevent effectually* cosmopolitan financiers from manipulating these reserves.

4. Just as those who know and condemn the s.i. include many who are not recognizable, since only the clumsier performers give positive proof of resistance to temptation, so too those who know and approve are not distinguishable with certainty. When a man splits an infinitive, he may be doing it unconsciously as a member of our class 1, or he may be deliberately rejecting the trammels of convention and announcing that he means to do as he will with his own infinitives. But, as the following examples are from newspapers of high repute, and high newspaper tradition is strong against splitting, it is perhaps fair to assume that each specimen is a manifesto of independence: It will be found possible *to considerably improve* the present wages of the miners without jeopardizing the interests of capital. / Always providing that the Imperialists do not feel strong enough *to decisively assert* their power in the revolted provinces. / But even so, he seems *to still be allowed* to speak at Unionist demonstrations. / It is the intention of the Minister of Transport *to substantially increase* all present rates by means of a general percentage. / The men in many of the largest districts are declared *to strongly favour* a strike if the minimum wage is not conceded.

It should be noticed that in these the separating adverb could have been placed outside the infinitive with little or in most cases no damage to the sentence-rhythm (*considerably* after *miners, decisively* after *power, still* with clear gain after *be, substantially* after *rates,* and *strongly* at some loss after *strike*), so that protest seems a safe diagnosis.

5. The attitude of those who know and distinguish is something like this: We admit that separation of *to* from its infinitive is not in itself desirable, and we shall not gratuitously say either "to mortally wound" or "to mortally be wounded"; but we are not foolish enough to confuse the latter with "to be mortally wounded", which is blameless English, nor "to just have heard" with "to have just heard", which is also blameless. We maintain, however, that a real s.i., though not desirable in itself, is preferable to either of two things, to real ambiguity, and to patent artificiality. For the first, we will rather write "Our object is to further cement trade relations" than, by correcting into "Our object is further to cement . . .", leave it doubtful whether an additional object or additional cementing is the point. And for the second, we take it that such reminders of a tyrannous convention as "in not combining to forbid flatly hostilities" are far more abnormal than the abnormality they evade. We will split infinitives sooner than be ambiguous or artificial; more than that, we will freely admit that sufficient recasting will get rid of any s.i. without involving either of those faults, and yet reserve to ourselves the right of deciding in each case whether recasting is worth while. Let us take an example: "In these circumstances, the Commission, judging from the evidence taken in London, has been feeling its way to modifications intended to better equip successful candidates for careers in India and at the same time to meet reasonable Indian demands." To better equip? We refuse "better to equip" as a shouted reminder of the tyranny; we refuse "to equip better" as ambiguous (*better* an adjective?); we regard "to equip successful candidates better" as lacking compactness, as possibly tolerable from an anti-splitter, but not good enough for us. What then of recasting? "intended to make successful candidates fitter for" is the best we can do if the exact sense is to be kept; it takes some thought to arrive at the correction; was the game worth the candle?

After this inconclusive discussion, in which, however, the author's opinion has perhaps been allowed to appear with indecent plainness, readers may like to settle the following question for themselves. "The greatest difficulty about assessing the economic achievements of the Soviet Union is that its spokesmen try absurdly to exaggerate them; in consequence the visitor may tend badly to underrate them." Has dread of the s.i. led the writer to attach his adverbs to the wrong verbs, and would he not have done better to boldly split both infinitives, since he cannot put the adverbs after them without spoiling his rhythm? Or are we to give him the benefit of the doubt, and suppose that he really meant *absurdly* to qualify *try* and *badly* to qualify *tend?*

It is perhaps hardly fair that this article should have quoted no split infinitives except such as, being reasonably supposed (as in 4) to be deliberate, are likely to be favourable specimens. Let it therefore conclude with one borrowed from a reviewer, to whose description of it no exception need be taken: "A book . . . of which the purpose is thus — with a deafening split infinitive — stated by its author: 'Its main idea is *to* historically, even while events are maturing, and divinely — from the Divine point of view — *impeach* the European system of Church and States'."

QUESTIONS

1. What relationship does Fowler establish with the rule prohibiting the split infinitive? What attitude towards it does he express?
   a. Does he believe the rule ought to be obeyed? That it ought to be disregarded?
   b. What does he think one ought to do? How does he tell you: in a rule?
2. One might put it this way: Fowler merely says that the rule against the split infinitive, like other rules, is subject to exceptions.
   a. What exceptions is it subject to? Does he list them? Does he suggest a rule or standard to define them?
   b. Is Fowler really saying that the user of English should regard himself as an equity judge? How does he define the equity of the split infinitive?
3. Fowler's passage on the split infinitive could be said to define the character of the Person Beyond Rules, the Man of Good English whom they do not bind. As with Plato's pilot and doctor, his art is not defined by the rules in which he tries to express it to inferior people and by which he perhaps once started to learn it. Exactly how does this passage define that character?
   a. How does he define those who "know and distinguish"? After all, anyone could use such a phrase to justify the exceptions he makes to a rule. Does Fowler give you reason to have confidence in his powers of distinction? How does he do so?
   b. Here is another way to put it: exactly what does the reader learn from this passage?
      (1) Does one acquire a new and more refined statement of the rule against the split infinitive? If you are inclined to agree, state the rule you learn.
      (2) What other information, if any, does one obtain from this passage?
      (3) Does one learn merely that good judgment is the ultimate test of good usage? Who needs to be told that?
      (4) If this passage does not impart information, what does it do? If you wish to say that it teaches, explain what it teaches and how it does so.
4. What then is the success of this passage? Is it one a judge might hope to emulate? Compare the following passage.

ETIQUETTE*
Emily Post

[On preparations for a second wedding:]

WIDOW

The marriage of a widow differs from that of a maid in that she cannot wear a bridal veil, orange blossoms, or a myrtle wreath, which are

* Pages 224, 628–629 (1959).

emblems of virginity; nor does she have bridesmaids, though she may have a maid or matron of honor.

If she has not done so long before, she should either remove, or else transfer, her first wedding and engagement rings to the third finger of her right hand as soon as she becomes engaged. When her second engagement ring is given her she of course discards the first engagement ring, and if her second marriage is to take place soon she removes her wedding ring as well. By and by it may be that she will again wear her first engagement ring on her right hand. This, however, depends upon the feelings of her second husband. If she knows that he objects, her future happiness may quite possibly depend upon its permanent discard. . . .

WHEN DIVORCED PARENTS REMAIN FRIENDLY

Because it is obviously happier for the children when friendliness rather than hatred exists between their divorced parents, yesterday's ban against the bad taste of any approach of one to the other is gradually being lifted. According to modern precept, if friendly relationship has been possible, not only Mary's parents but also both of her step-parents are present not only at the church but even possibly at the house. The one unbreakable ban remaining is the sending of a joint wedding invitation by the divorced parents — together!

WHEN THEY ARE NOT FRIENDLY

In the entire subject of etiquette, there is perhaps no situation which brings such unavoidable distress as the wedding of a daughter whose parents are divorced, with both families bitterly estranged. This is especially unhappy for the bride who loves her father and all of his family quite as much as — sometimes even more than — she loves her mother and her family. Yet according to the exactions of chivalry, the wedding of their daughter must be given by her mother.

It is true that she does drive with her father to the church, walks with him up the aisle, and even has him share (very briefly) in the marriage ceremony. But he does not have so much as a glimpse of her after the ceremony, since he does not go to the reception given by his ex-wife and, quite possibly, her present husband.

It is also probable that no member of his family — neither the grandparents nor the aunts or uncles of his daughter — has so much as a glimpse of their granddaughter or their niece on her wedding day, since it is quite possible that those who care most are the very ones who do not go even to the church. . . .

[Our contribution to the beauty of living:]

. . . It should be unnecessary to add that a man and his wife who quarrel before their children or the servants deprive the former of good breeding through example, and publish to the latter that they do not belong to the better class through any qualification except the possession of a bank account.

THE PROBLEMS OF DIVORCE

No rule of propriety has been more completely changed than that which formerly required all divorced people to meet as unspeaking strangers. The reason for the strictness of this convention was that a generation ago a divorce was unthinkable unless there was irreparable injury or such antipathy existed that tranquil encounter could never again be possible.

Experience has, however, made it plain that serious readjustment of many rules must be made — particularly in those cases where conventions and humaneness are in conflict. And as no thinking person could rate the former above the latter, it has been the conventions that have had to be changed. In the thousands of cases where children are involved, it is far, far better that the parents make every effort to remain on friendly terms. Nothing in all the world is so devastating in its destruction of character and of soul as living in an atmosphere infused with hatred. Anything is better for children than that!

The most bitterly unhappy situation that can come to a child is to be the victim of a court decree which condemns it to the continual shifting, like a human shuttlecock, between parents who hate each other, or — even worse in its emotional effect — to feel that one parent has inflicted unmerited cruelty on the other. Emotional disturbance such as this should not be the portion of any child.

There are cases, of course, where divorce is the best — sometimes the only — solution for everyone concerned. If two persons are truly mismated they certainly and perhaps their children too are better off if they part. The only consideration of vital importance is that they shall not part because of a love-for-another attack that might prove to be transient. . . .

TACT

Certainly we've all been thankful — at times — that other people could not read our thoughts — thoughts such as "How very ill you look!" or "How old you've grown!" — thoughts to be locked away quickly in the silence of our own minds. The tactless person seems compelled to say exactly such things as these out loud, even when there can be absolutely nothing to be gained by such brutal frankness.

Of all the qualities that make us likable, none is greater than tact. If there were no tact, there would be little friendship in the world, and social life would revert to the stone-age crudeness. Tact, of course, means quick awareness of the feelings of others, and consideration for them. There is only one flaw in this otherwise most charming of human attributes, the possibility of insincerity. We don't know where we stand with one who diplomatically tells us only what he thinks we'd like to hear, instead of giving us a frank, straightforward answer. The social climber is one who misuses this aspect of tact because he seeks only to please those who can help further his ambitions.

On the other hand the tactless person causes nothing but distress wherever he goes.

QUESTIONS

1. *How would you characterize the relationship this writer establishes with the rules that concern her?*
   a. *Fowler defines a sort of freedom from rules: the Man of Good English. Does Mrs. Post express a similar vision of the Man or Woman of Good Manners? How does she define the process of judgment she recommends?*
   b. *Would you say that according to this passage the master or mistress of rules is one who "knows and distinguishes"? How, by what process and according to what values, are the distinctions defined by this passage to be drawn?*
      (1) *How is the conflict between "convention" and "humaneness" to be resolved?*
      (2) *How is one to distinguish between "tact" and "insincerity" in oneself or others?*
      (3) *How is one to judge whether one's "love-for-another attack" is "transient"? Or whether one is "truly mismated"?*
   c. *Where else do you see rules used and talked about in such a way? (Compare with this passage a paragraph taken at random from American Jurisprudence or Corpus Juris Secundum; or from your own first moot court brief.)*
2. *Ask of this passage what social world it defines: when the author says that a remarried widow's "future happiness may depend upon" discarding her old wedding ring, how does she define the newlyweds? Who are the "intimate friends" who come to such a wedding? Why must the daughter who wishes her divorced father to give her wedding always yield to "the exactions of chivalry"? Why is there an "unbreakable ban" against a wedding given by the divorced parents together?*[1]

   Can what you see here be explained as the manifestation of a relationship between the author and a set of rules? How would you characterize that relationship?
3. *Can you explain how Fowler succeeds and Post fails in their attempts to*

1. In an amusing article, Edmund Wilson shows what happens when *Etiquette* is read as a novel. E. Wilson, "Books of Etiquette and Emily Post," in *A Literary Chronicle: 1920–1950*, at 380 (Anchor ed. 1950).

express an excellence in judgment, an art of life beyond rules? Does it help to ask what each passage teaches you and how it does so?

4. *Below is a selection from Samuel Johnson's Preface to Shakespeare, in which he expresses his judgment of the work of that writer. As you read this, ask what place the rule has in this process of judgment. If Johnson does not judge by rules, how does he judge? It would be a good preparation for reading this material if you first thought for some time about how you yourself would write such an essay.*

PREFACE TO SHAKESPEARE (1765)

Samuel Johnson

[Having praised Shakespeare for his great qualities as a mind and writer, Johnson now considers his defects.]

Shakespeare with his excellencies has likewise faults, and faults sufficient to obscure and overwhelm any other merit. I shall show them in the proportion in which they appear to me, without envious malignity or superstitious veneration. No question can be more innocently discussed than a dead poet's pretensions to renown; and little regard is due to that bigotry which sets candour higher than truth.

His first defect is that to which may be imputed most of the evil in books or in men. He sacrifices virtue to convenience, and is so much more careful to please than to instruct, that he seems to write without any moral purpose. From his writings, indeed, a system of social duty may be selected, for he that thinks reasonably must think morally; but his precepts and axioms drop casually from him; he makes no just distribution of good or evil, nor is always careful to show in the virtuous a disapprobation of the wicked; he carries his persons indifferently through right and wrong, and, at the close, dismisses them without further care, and leaves their examples to operate by chance. This fault the barbarity of his age cannot extenuate; for it is always a writer's duty to make the world better, and justice is a virtue independent on time or place.

The plots are often so loosely formed, that a very slight consideration may improve them, and so carelessly pursued, that he seems not always fully to comprehend his own design. He omits opportunities of instructing or delighting, which the train of his story seems to force upon him, and apparently rejects those exhibitions which would be more affecting, for the sake of those which are more easy.

It may be observed, that in many of his plays the latter part is evidently neglected. When he found himself near the end of his work, and in view of his reward, he shortened the labour to snatch the profit. He, therefore, remits his efforts where he should most vigorously exert them, and his catastrophe is improbably produced or imperfectly represented.

He had no regard to distinction of time or place, but gives to one age or nation, without scruple, the customs, institutions, and opinions of another, at the expense not only of likelihood, but of possibility. These faults Pope has endeavoured, with more zeal than judgment, to transfer to his imagined interpolators. We need not wonder to find Hector quoting Aristotle, when we see the loves of Theseus and Hippolyta combined with the Gothick mythology of fairies. Shakespeare, indeed, was not the only violator of chronology, for in the same age Sidney, who wanted not the advantages of learning, has, in his Arcadia, confounded the pastoral with the feudal times, the days of innocence, quiet, and security, with those of turbulence, violence, and adventure.

In his comick scenes he is seldom very successful, when he engages his characters in reciprocations of smartness and contests of sarcasm; their jests are commonly gross, and their pleasantry licentious; neither his gentlemen nor his ladies have much delicacy, nor are sufficiently distinguished from his clowns by any appearance of refined manners. Whether he represented the real conversation of his time is not easy to determine; the reign of Elizabeth is commonly supposed to have been a time of stateliness, formality and reserve; yet, perhaps, the relaxations of that severity were not very elegant. There must, however, have been always some modes of gaiety preferable to others, and a writer ought to choose the best.

In tragedy his performance seems constantly to be worse, as his labour is more. The effusions of passion, which exigence forces out, are, for the most part, striking and energetick; but whenever he solicits his invention, or strains his faculties, the offspring of his throes is tumour, meanness, tediousness, and obscurity.

In narration he affects a disproportionate pomp of diction, and a wearisome train of circumlocution, and tells the incident imperfectly in many words, which might have been more plainly delivered in few. Narration in dramatick poetry is naturally tedious, as it is unanimated and inactive, and obstructs the progress of the action; it should, therefore, always be rapid, and enlivened by frequent interruption. Shakespeare found it an incumbrance, and instead of lightening it by brevity, endeavoured to recommend it by dignity and splendour.

His declamations or set speeches are commonly cold and weak; for his power was the power of nature; when he endeavoured, like other tragick writers, to catch opportunities of amplification, and instead of inquiring what the occasion demanded, to show how much his stores of knowledge could supply, he seldom escapes without the pity or resentment of his reader.

It is incident to him to be now and then entangled with an unwieldy sentiment, which he cannot well express, and will not reject; he struggles with it a while, and, if it continues stubborn, comprises it in words such as occur, and leaves it to be disentangled and evolved by those who have more leisure to bestow upon it.

Not that always where the language is intricate, the thought is subtile, or the image always great where the line is bulky; the equality of words to things is very often neglected, and trivial sentiments and vulgar ideas disappoint the attention, to which they are recommended by sonorous epithets and swelling figures.

But the admirers of this great poet have most reason to complain when he approaches nearest to his highest excellence, and seems fully resolved to sink them in dejection, and mollify them with tender emotions, by the fall of greatness, the danger of innocence, or the crosses of love. What he does best, he soon ceases to do. He is not long soft and pathetick without some idle conceit, or contemptible equivocation. He no sooner begins to move, than he counteracts himself; and terrour and pity, as they are rising in the mind, are checked and blasted by sudden frigidity.

A quibble is to Shakespeare, what luminous vapours are to the traveller; he follows it at all adventures; it is sure to lead him out of his way, and sure to engulf him in the mire. It has some malignant power over his mind, and its fascinations are irresistible. Whatever be the dignity or profundity of his disquisitions, whether he be enlarging knowledge or exalting affection, whether he be amusing attention with incidents, or enchaining it in suspense, let but a quibble spring up before him, and he leaves his work unfinished. A quibble is the golden apple for which he will always turn aside from his career, or stoop from his elevation. A quibble, poor and barren as it is, gave him such delight, that he was content to purchase it, by the sacrifice of reason, propriety and truth. A quibble was to him the fatal Cleopatra for which he lost the world, and was content to lose it.

It will be thought strange, that, in enumerating the defects of this writer, I have not yet mentioned his neglect of the unities; his violation of those laws which have been instituted and established by the joint authority of poets and of criticks.

For his other deviations from the art of writing, I resign him to critical justice, without making any other demand in his favour, than that which must be indulged to all human excellence; that his virtues be rated with his failings: but, from the censure which this irregularity may bring upon him, I shall, with due reverence to that learning which I must oppose, adventure to try how I can defend him.

His histories, being neither tragedies nor comedies, are not subject to any of their laws; nothing more is necessary to all the praise which they expect, than that the changes of action be so prepared as to be understood; that the incidents be various and affecting, and the characters consistent, natural and distinct. No other unity is intended, and, therefore, none is to be sought.

In his other works he has well enough preserved the unity of action. He has not, indeed, an intrigue regularly perplexed and regularly unravelled: he does not endeavour to hide his design only to discover it, for this is seldom the order of real events, and Shakespeare is the poet of nature: but his plan has commonly what Aristotle requires, a beginning, a middle, and an end; one event is concatenated with another, and the conclusion follows by easy consequence. There are, perhaps, some incidents that might be spared, as in other poets there is much talk that only fills up time upon the stage; but the general system makes gradual advances, and the end of the play is the end of expectation.

To the unities of time and place he has shown no regard; and, perhaps, a nearer view of the principles on which they stand will diminish their value, and withdraw from them the veneration which, from the time of Corneille, they have generally received, by discovering that they have given more trouble to the poet, than pleasure to the auditor.

The necessity of observing the unities of time and place arises from the supposed necessity of making the drama credible. The criticks hold it impossible, that an action of months or years can be possibly believed to pass in three hours; or that the spectator can suppose himself to sit in the theatre, while ambassadors go and return between distant kings, while armies are levied and towns besieged, while an exile wanders and returns, or till he whom they saw courting his mistress, shall lament the untimely fall of his son. The mind revolts from evident falsehood, and fiction loses its force when it departs from the resemblance of reality.

From the narrow limitation of time necessarily arises the contraction of place. The spectator, who knows that he saw the first act at Alexandria, cannot suppose that he sees the next at Rome, at a distance to which not the dragons of Medea could, in so short a time, have transported him; he knows with certainty that he has not changed his place; and he knows that place cannot change itself; that what was a house cannot become a plain; that what was Thebes can never be Persepolis.

Such is the triumphant language with which a critick exalts over the misery of an irregular poet, and exults commonly without resistance or reply. It is time, therefore, to tell him, by the authority of Shakespeare, that he assumes, as an unquestionable principle, a position, which, while his breath is forming it into words, his understanding pronounces to be false. It is false, that any representation is mistaken for reality; that any dramatick fable in its materiality was ever credible, or, for a single moment, was ever credited.

The objection arising from the impossibility of passing the first hour at

Alexandria, and the next at Rome, supposes, that when the play opens, the spectator really imagines himself at Alexandria, and believes that his walk to the theatre has been a voyage to Egypt, and that he lives in the days of Anthony and Cleopatra. Surely he that imagines this may imagine more. He that can take the stage at one time for the palace of the Ptolemies, may take it in half an hour for the promontory of Actium. Delusion, if delusion be admitted, has no certain limitation; if the spectator can be once persuaded, that his old acquaintance are Alexander and Cæsar, that a room illuminated with candles is the plain of Pharsalia, or the bank of Granicus, he is in a state of elevation above the reach of reason, or of truth, and from the heights of empyrean poetry, may despise the circumscriptions of terrestrial nature. There is no reason why a mind thus wandering in ecstacy should count the clock, or why an hour should not be a century in that calenture of the brains that can make the stage a field.

The truth is, that the spectators are always in their senses, and know, from the first act to the last, that the stage is only a stage, and that the players are only players. They come to hear a certain number of lines recited with just gesture and elegant modulation. The lines relate to some action, and an action must be in some place; but the different actions that complete a story may be in places very remote from each other; and where is the absurdity of allowing that space to represent first Athens, and then Sicily, which was always known to be neither Sicily nor Athens, but a modern theatre?

By supposition, as place is introduced, time may be extended; the time required by the fable elapses, for the most part, between the acts; for, of so much of the action as is represented, the real and poetical duration is the same. If, in the first act, preparations for war against Mithridates are represented to be made in Rome, the event of the war may, without absurdity, be represented, in the catastrophe, as happening in Pontus; we know that there is neither war, nor preparation for war; we know that we are neither in Rome nor Pontus; that neither Mithridates nor Lucullus are before us. The drama exhibits successive imitations of successive actions; and why may not the second imitation represent an action that happened years after the first, if it be so connected with it, that nothing but time can be supposed to intervene? Time is, of all modes of existence, most obsequious to the imagination; a lapse of years is as easily conceived as a passage of hours. In contemplation we easily contract the time of real actions, and, therefore, willingly permit it to be contracted when we only see their imitation.

It will be asked, how the drama moves, if it is not credited. It is credited with all the credit due to a drama. It is credited, whenever it moves, as a just picture of a real original; as representing to the auditor what he would himself feel, if he were to do or suffer what is there feigned to be suffered or to be done. The reflection that strikes the heart is not, that the evils before us are real evils, but that they are evils to which we ourselves may be exposed. If there by any fallacy, it is not that we fancy the players, but that we fancy ourselves unhappy for a moment; but we rather lament the possibility than suppose the presence of misery, as a mother weeps over her babe, when she remembers that death may take it from her. The delight of tragedy proceeds from our consciousness of fiction; if we thought murders and treasons real, they would please no more.

Imitations produce pain or pleasure, not because they are mistaken for realities, but because they bring realities to mind.

QUESTIONS

1. *Our general questions are these: how does Samuel Johnson make and explain the judgments he expresses here? What is the place of the rule in that process? How can what he does here be compared with what a judge is asked to do?*
2. *We begin with his response to the contemporary rules for critical judgment. Why does he reject these rules?*
   a. *Is it because they are the wrong rules and need to be replaced by proper ones? Or because the sort of judgment he wishes to make cannot be expressed by any rule?*
   b. *How far does he really reject them?*
      (1) *Does he accept, for example, the requirement of "unity of action"? How does he define that standard of judgment?*
      (2) *He seems to reject the unities of place and time, but one of the faults he finds with Shakespeare is that he "had no regard for distinctions of time and place." Are these consistent positions?*
3. *With what does he supplant the rules he rejects?*
   a. *Does he adopt another set of rules that seem to him more appropriate to the task of literary criticism? (He does not do so expressly, of course, but you can ask whether such a set of rules is implied in the judgments he makes.)*
   b. *If you conclude that he does not employ such a set of rules, implicitly or explicitly, how do you explain that circumstance? Is it that literary criticism was then at a primitive stage of development, or is the process of literary judgment simply not suited to the use of rules?*
   c. *Whether or not you can find a set of rules in this passage, can you yourself begin to work out rules by which the excellence of a work of literature can be judged? Will your rules be subject to some powers of equity, and if so, how can that equity be defined?*
4. *Here is what Samuel Taylor Coleridge had to say about the dramatic unities, in notes written in his copy of Romeo and Juliet. What does he do with these rules? How do you compare what Johnson does and what Plato recommends?*

   "We have had occasion to speak at large on the subject of the three unities, time, place, and action, as applied to the drama in [the] abstract, and to the particular stage for which Shakespeare wrote, as far as he can be said to have written for any stage but that of the universal mind. We

succeeded in demonstrating that the two former, instead of being rules, were mere inconveniences attached to the local peculiarities of the Athenian drama; that the last alone deserved the name of a principle, and that in this Shakespeare stood pre-eminent. Yet instead of unity of action I should great[ly] prefer the more appropriate, tho' scholastic and uncouth words — homogeneity, proportionateness, and totality of interest. The distinction, or rather the essential difference, betwixt the shaping skill of mechanical talent, and the creative, productive life-power of inspired genius: in the former each part separately conceived and then by a succeeding act put together — not as watches are made for wholesale — for here each part presupposes a conception of the whole in some mind — but as the pictures on a motley screen (N.B. I must seek for a happier illustration). Whence the harmony that strikes us in the wildest natural landscapes, — in the relative shapes of rocks, the harmony of colors in the heath, ferns, and lichens, the leaves of the beech and oak, the stems and rich choc[ol]ate brown branches of the birch and other mountain trees, varying from verging autumn to returning spring — compared with the visual effect of the greater number of artificial plantations? The former are effected by a single energy, modified ab intra in each component part. Now as this is the particular excellence of the Shakespearean dramas generally, so it is especially characteristic of the Romeo and Juliet." Coleridge, Shakespearean Criticism, I, 5 (Everyman ed. 1960).

5. *If the process of literary judgment is so subtle or complex that it cannot sensibly be regulated by or expressed in a set of rules, how is it that the process of legal judgment can be so regulated and expressed?*
   a. *Is the judgment of what justice requires in a particular case less subtle or complex than the judgment of excellence in a literary work?*
   b. *Or can our willingness to compromise with justice by imposing the rule on the processes of legal thought and speech be explained by the fact that perfection is less important in legal judgments than literary ones?*
6. *We now return to our original question: what comparison can you draw between the process of literary judgment Johnson expresses here and the process of legal judgment in which the lawyer and judge engage?*
7. *Does it help to ask this question: what does the Johnson passage teach you? How does it do so?*
8. *Below is a far more complicated excerpt dealing with difficulties in judgment and the use of rules.*

OF THE LAWS OF ECCLESIASTICAL POLITY (1593)
Richard Hooker

A Preface to Them That Seek (As They Term It), The Reformation of the Laws and Orders Ecclesiastical in the Church of England

[Hooker's book is a defense of the Church of England against the demands of the Calvinists for radical reform of that institution. The Calvinist position was that there had been a falling away from the true and simple principles of early Christianity, and that questions of church governance, doctrine, and practice should be settled by the plain meaning of the Holy Scriptures without reference to the customs and practices that had evolved over the years. They wanted the end of elaborate ceremony, of government by bishops, and of the implication of the church in a worldly society which it did not control. In Geneva, Calvin had established the sort of theocracy of which they approved; another was to come soon in Massachusetts.

The book as a whole presents a remarkably thorough defense based upon complicated philosophical and theological argument. In the preface Hooker addresses the Calvinists directly, explaining what he thinks is at stake in the dispute and hoping to set the terms by which it will proceed. The several passages together can be taken as expressing a way of responding to and dealing with the views of others, whether expressed in rules or some other form, and as defining a process of argument and reasoning by which differences in judgment and inclination can be addressed. One might even suggest that Hooker's concern here is to define justice itself as a sort of intellectual and social process that these passages exemplify. As you read this material, compare it with the debate between Socrates and Thrasymachus you have already read, page 631 *supra*.]

The wonderful zeal and fervour wherewith ye have withstood the received orders of this Church, was the first thing which caused me to enter into consideration, whether (as all your published books and writings peremptorily maintain) every Christian man, fearing God, stand bound to join with you for the furtherance of that which ye term the *Lord's Discipline*. Wherein I must plainly confess unto you, that before I examined your sundry declarations in that behalf, it could not settle in my head to think, but that undoubtedly such numbers of otherwise right well affected and most religiously inclined minds had some marvellous reasonable inducements, which led them with so great earnestness that way. But when once, as near as my slender ability would serve, I had with travail and care performed that part of the Apostle's advice and counsel in such cases, whereby he willeth to "try all things," and was come at the length so far, that there remained only the other clause to be satisfied, wherein he concludeth that "what good is must be held;" there was in my poor understanding no remedy, but to set down this as my final resolute persuasion: "Surely the present form of church-government which the laws of this land have established is such, as no law of God nor reason of man hath hitherto been alleged of force sufficient to prove they do ill, who to the uttermost of their power withstand the alteration thereof." Contrariwise, "The other, which instead of it we are required to accept, is only by error and misconceit named the ordinance of Jesus Christ, no one proof as yet brought forth whereby it may clearly appear to be so in very deed."

The explication of which two things I have here thought good to offer into your own hands, heartily beseeching you even by the meekness of Jesus Christ, whom I trust ye love; that, as ye tender the peace and quietness of this church, if there be in you that gracious humility which hath ever been the crown and glory of a Christianly-disposed mind, if your own souls, hearts, and consciences (the sound integrity whereof can but hardly stand with the refusal of truth in personal respects) be, as I doubt not but they are, things most dear and precious unto you: let "not the faith which ye have in our Lord Jesus Christ" be blemished "with partialities;" regard not who it is which speaketh, but weigh only what is spoken. Think not that ye read the words of one who bendeth himself as an adversary against the truth which ye have already embraced; but the words of one who desireth even to embrace together with you the self-same truth, if it be the truth; and for that cause (for no other, God he knoweth) hath undertaken the burdensome labour of this painful kind of conference.

[Hooker next addresses the possibility that his argument will be met with an unreasoning rejection, a simple declaration that we know what is right — "our conscience is clear." He tries to show that differences over the proper church government — or any other government — are matters to which that response is not appropriate, and he tries to trace out the implications of that attitude. He then describes the process by which Calvinism makes its appeal, and this can be read as an attempt on his part to define by negation the sort of argument in which he wishes to engage. For what conversation can go on with the mind that knows it is absolutely right?]

The first mean whereby nature teacheth men to judge good from evil, as well in laws as in other things, is the force of their own discretion. Hereunto therefore St. Paul referreth oftentimes his own speech, to be considered of by them that heard him. "I speak as to them which have understanding, judge ye what I say." Again afterward, "Judge in yourselves, is it comely that a woman pray uncovered?" . . . Finally, whatsoever we do, if our own secret judgment consent not unto it as fit and good to be done, the doing of it to us is sin, although the thing itself be allowable. St. Paul's rule therefore generally is, "Let every man in his own mind be fully persuaded of that thing which he either alloweth or doth."

Some things are so familiar and plain, that truth from falsehood, and good from evil, is most easily discerned in them, even by men of no deep capacity. And of that nature, for the most part, are things absolutely unto all men's salvation necessary, either to be held or denied, either to be done or avoided. For which cause St. Augustine acknowledgeth, that they are not only set down, but also plainly set down in Scripture; so that he which heareth or readeth may without any great difficulty understand. Other things also there are belonging (though in a lower degree of importance) unto the offices of Christian men: which, because they are more obscure, more intricate and hard to be judged of, therefore God hath appointed some to spend their whole time principally in the study of things divine, to the end that in these more doubtful cases their understanding might be a light to direct others. "If the understanding power or faculty of the soul be" (saith the grand physician) "like unto bodily sight, not of equal sharpness in all, what can be more convenient than that, even as the dark-sighted man is directed by the clear about things visible; so likewise in matters of deeper discourse the wise in heart do shew the simple where his way lieth?" In our doubtful cases of law, what man is there who seeth not how requisite it is that professors of skill in that faculty be our directors? So it is in all other kinds of knowledge.

But ye will say that if the guides of the people be blind, the common sort of men must not close up their own eyes and be led by the conduct of such: if the priest be "partial in the law," the flock must not therefore depart from the ways of sincere truth, and in simplicity yield to be followers of him for his place sake and office over them. Which thing, though in itself most true, is in your defence notwithstanding weak; because the matter wherein ye think that ye see, and imagine that your ways are sincere, is of far deeper consideration than any one amongst five hundred of you conceiveth. Let the vulgar sort amongst you know, that there is not the least branch of the cause wherein they are so resolute, but to the trial of it a great deal more appertaineth than their conceit doth reach unto. I write not this in disgrace of the simplest that way given, but I would gladly they knew the nature of that cause wherein they think themselves throughly instructed and are not; by means whereof they daily run themselves, without feeling their own hazard, upon the dint of the Apostle's sentence against "evil-speakers as touching things wherein they are ignorant."

Weigh what doth move the common sort so much to favour this innovation, and it shall soon appear unto you, that the force of particular reasons which for your several opinions are alleged is a thing whereof the multitude never did nor could so consider as to be therewith wholly carried; but certain general inducements are used to make saleable your cause in gross; and when once men have cast a fancy towards it, any slight declaration of specialties will serve to lead forward men's inclinable and prepared minds.

The method of winning the people's affection unto a general liking of "the cause" (for so ye term it) hath been this. First, In the hearing of the multitude, the faults especially of higher callings are ripped up with marvellous exceeding severity and sharpness of reproof; which being oftentimes done begetteth a great good opinion of integrity, zeal, and holiness, to such constant reprovers of sin, as by likelihood would never be so much offended at that which is evil, unless themselves were singularly good.

The next thing hereunto is, to impute all faults and corruptions, wherewith the world aboundeth, unto the kind of ecclesiastical government established. Wherein, as before by reproving faults they purchased unto themselves with the multitude a name to be virtuous; so by finding out this kind of cause they obtain to be judged wise above others: whereas in truth unto the form even of Jewish government, which the Lord himself (they all confess) did establish, with like shew of reason they might impute those faults which the prophets condemn in the governors of that commonwealth, as to the English kind of regiment ecclesiastical (whereof also God himself though in other sort is author,) the stains and blemishes found in our state; which springing from the root of human frailty and corruption, not only are, but have been always more or less, yea and (for any thing we know to the contrary) will be till the world's end complained of, what form of government soever take place.

Having gotten this much sway in the hearts of men, a third step is to propose their own form of church-government, as the only sovereign remedy of all evils; and to adorn it with all the glorious titles that may be. And the nature, as of men that have sick bodies, so likewise of the people in the crazedness of their minds possessed with dislike and discontentment at things present, is to imagine that any thing, (the virtue whereof they hear commended,) would help them; but that most, which they least have tried.

The fourth degree of inducement is by fashioning the very notions and conceits of men's minds in such sort, that when they read the scripture, they may think that every thing soundeth towards the advancement of that discipline, and to the utter disgrace of the contrary. Pythagoras, by bringing up his scholars in the speculative knowledge of numbers, made their conceits therein so strong, that when they came to the contemplation of things natural, they imagined that in every particular thing they even beheld as it were with their eyes, how the elements of number gave essence and being to the works of nature. A thing in reason impossible; which notwithstanding, through their misfashioned preconceit, appeared unto them no less certain, than if nature had written it in the very foreheads of all the creatures of God. When they of the "Family of Love" have it once in their heads, that Christ doth not signify any one person, but a quality whereof many are partakers; that to be "raised" is nothing else but to be regenerated, or endued with the said quality; and that when separation of them which have it from them which have it not is here made, this is "judgment:" how plainly do they imagine that the Scripture every where speaketh in the favour of that sect? And assuredly, the very cause which maketh the simple and ignorant to think they even see how the word of God runneth currently on your side, is, that their minds are forestalled and their conceits perverted beforehand, by being taught, that an "elder" doth signify a layman admitted only to the office or rule of government in the Church; a "doctor," one which may only teach, and neither preach nor administer the Sacraments; a "deacon," one which hath charge of the alms-box, and of nothing else: that the "sceptre," the "rod," the "throne" and "kingdom" of Christ, are a form of regiment, only by pastors, elders, doctors, and deacons; that by mystical resemblance Mount Sion and Jerusalem are the churches which admit, Samaria and Babylon the churches which oppugn the said form of regiment. And in like sort they are taught to apply all things spoken of repairing the walls and decayed parts of the city and temple of God, by Esdras, Nehemias, and the rest; as if purposely the Holy Ghost had therein meant to foresignify, what the authors of Admonitions to the Parliament, of Supplications to the Council, of Petitions to her Majesty, and of such other like writs, should either do or suffer in behalf of this their cause.

From hence they proceed to an higher point, which is the persuading of men credulous and over-capable of such pleasing errors, that it is the special illumination of the Holy Ghost, whereby they discern those things in the word, which others reading yet discern them not. "Dearly beloved," saith St. John, "give not credit unto every spirit." . . .

After that the fancy of the common sort hath once throughly apprehended the Spirit to be author of their persuasion concerning discipline; then is instilled into their hearts, that the same Spirit leading men into this opinion doth thereby seal them to be God's children; and that, as the state of the times now standeth, the most special token to know them that are God's own from others is an earnest affection that way. This hath bred high terms of separation between such and the rest of the world; whereby the one sort are named The brethren, The godly, and so forth; the other, worldlings, time-servers, pleasers of men not of God, with such like. . . .

[If] once they have tasted of that cup, let any man of contrary opinion open his mouth to persuade them, they close up their ears, his reasons they weigh not, all is answered with rehearsal of the words of John, " 'We are of God; he that knoweth God heareth us:' as for the rest, ye are of the world; for this world's pomp and vanity it is that ye speak, and the world, whose ye are, heareth you." Which cloak sitteth no less fit on the back of their cause, than of the Anabaptists, when the dignity, authority and honour of God's magistrate is upheld against them. Shew these eagerly-affected men their inability to judge of such matters; their answer is, "God hath chosen the simple." Convince them of folly, and that so plainly, that very children upbraid them with it; they have their bucklers of like defence: "Christ's own apostle was accounted mad: the best men evermore by the sentence of the world have been judged to be out of their right minds."

[Hooker gives a particularly appropriate example of the folly of in transigence in matters of discipline and government, of inflexible devotion to one's own first conclusions. He is discussing the Protestant cities of Switzerland at the time of Calvin's invitation to Geneva:]

It was the manner of those times (whether through men's desire to enjoy alone the glory of their own enterprizes, or else because the quickness of their occasions required present despatch; so it was,) that every particular Church did that within itself, which some few of their own thought good, by whom the rest were all directed. Such number of Churches then being, though free within themselves, yet small, common conference beforehand might have eased them of much after trouble. But a greater inconvenience it bred, that every [one] later endeavoured to be certain degrees more removed from conformity with the Church of Rome, than the rest before had been: whereupon grew marvellous great dissimilitudes, and by reason thereof, jealousies, heartburnings, jars and discords amongst them. Which, notwithstanding, might have easily been prevented, if the orders, which each Church did think fit and convenient for itself, had not so peremptorily been established under the high commanding form, which tendered them unto the people, as things everlastingly required by the law of that Lord of lords, against whose statutes there is no exception to be taken. For by this mean it came to pass, that one Church could not but accuse and condemn another of disobedience to the will of Christ, in those things where manifest difference was between them: whereas the selfsame orders allowed, but yet established in more wary and suspense manner, as being to stand in force till God should give the opportunity of some general conference what might be best for every of them afterwards to do; this I say had both prevented all occasion of just dislike which others might take, and reserved a greater liberty unto the authors themselves of entering into farther consultation afterwards. Which though never so necessary they could not easily now admit, without some fear of derogation from their credit: and therefore that which once they had done, they became for ever after resolute to maintain.

[Hooker goes on to propose a formal disputation, stating what he hopes its premises can be. This is a way of defining an attitude towards disagreement.]

What success God may give unto any such kind of conference or disputation, we cannot tell. But of this we are right sure, that nature,

Scripture, and experience itself, have all taught the world to seek for the ending of contentions by submitting itself unto some judicial and definitive sentence, whereunto neither part that contendeth may under any pretence or colour refuse to stand. This must needs be effectual and strong. As for other means without this, they seldom prevail. I would therefore know, whether for the ending of these irksome strifes, wherein you and your followers do stand thus formally divided against the authorized guides of this church, and the rest of the people subject unto their charge; whether I say ye be content to refer your cause to any other higher judgment than your own, or else intend to persist and proceed as ye have begun, till yourselves can be persuaded to condemn yourselves. If your determination be this, we can be but sorry that ye should deserve to be reckoned with such, of whom God himself pronounceth, "The way of peace they have not known."

Ye will perhaps make answer, that being persuaded already as touching the truth of your cause, ye are not to harken unto any sentence, no not though Angels should define otherwise, as the blessed Apostle's own example teacheth: again, that men, yea councils, may err; and that, unless the judgment given do satisfy your minds, unless it be such as ye can by no further argument oppugn, in a word, unless you perceive and acknowledge it yourselves consonant with God's word; to stand unto it not allowing it were to sin against your own consciences.

Neither wish we that men should do any thing which in their hearts they are persuaded they ought not to do, but this persuasion ought (we say) to be fully settled in their hearts; that in litigious and controversed causes of such quality, the will of God is to have them do whatsoever the sentence of judicial and final decision shall determine, yea, though it seem in their private opinion to swerve utterly from that which is right: as no doubt many times the sentence amongst the Jews did seem unto one part or other contending, and yet in this case, God did then allow them to do that which in their private judgment it seemed, yea and perhaps truly seemed, that the law did disallow. For if God be not the author of confusion but of peace, then can he not be the author of our refusal, but of our contentment, to stand unto some definitive sentence; without which almost impossible it is that either we should avoid confusion, or ever hope to attain peace. To small purpose had the Council of Jerusalem been assembled, if once their determination being set down, men might afterwards have defended their former opinions. When therefore they had given their definitive sentence, all controversy was at an end. Things were disputed before they came to be determined; men afterwards were not to dispute any longer, but to obey. The sentence of judgment finished their strife, which their disputes before judgment could not do. This was ground sufficient for any reasonable man's conscience to build the duty of obedience upon, whatsoever his own opinion were as touching the matter before in question. So full of wilfulness and self-liking is our nature, that without some definitive sentence, which being given may stand, and a necessity of silence on both sides afterward imposed, small hope there is that strifes thus far prosecuted will in short time quietly end.

[In Book 1, which begins his formal argument, Hooker maintains that there are many different kinds of laws, to be read and used and respected differently, and that the great Calvinist error is to confuse one sort of law with another. He concludes with a summing up:]

Thus far therefore we have endeavoured in part to open, of what nature and force laws are, according unto their several kinds; the law which God with himself hath eternally set down to follow in his own works; the law which he hath made for his creatures to keep; the law of natural and necessary agents; the law which angels in heaven obey; the law whereunto by the light of reason men find themselves bound in that they are men; the law which they make by composition for multitudes and politic societies of men to be guided by; the law which belongeth unto each nation; the law that concerneth the fellowship of all; and lastly the law which God himself hath supernaturally revealed.

Easier a great deal it is for men by law to be taught what they ought to do, than instructed how to judge as they should do of law: the one being a thing which belongeth generally unto all, the other such as none but the wiser and more judicious sort can perform. Yea, the wisest are always touching this point the readiest to acknowledge, that soundly to judge of a law is the weightiest thing which any man can take upon him. But if we will give judgment of the laws under which we live; first let that law eternal be always before our eyes, as being of principal force and moment to breed in religious minds a dutiful estimation of all laws, the use and benefit whereof we see; because there can be no doubt but that laws apparently good are (as it were) things copied out of the very tables of that high everlasting law; even as the book of that law hath said concerning itself, "By me kings reign, and" by me "princes decree justice." Not as if men did behold that book and accordingly frame their laws; but because it worketh in them, because it discovereth and (as it were) readeth itself to the world by them, when the laws which they make are righteous. Furthermore, although we perceive not the goodness of laws made, nevertheless sith things in themselves may have that which we peradventure discern not, should not this breed a fear in our hearts, how we speak or judge in the worse part concerning that, the unadvised disgrace whereof may be no mean dishonour to Him, towards whom we profess all submission and awe? Surely there must be very manifest iniquity in laws, against which we shall be able to justify our contumelious invectives. The chiefest root whereof, when we use them without cause, is ignorance how laws inferior are derived from that supreme or highest law. . . .

There are in men operations, some natural, some rational, some supernatural, some politic, some finally ecclesiastical: which if we measure not each by his own proper law, whereas the things themselves are so different, there will be in our understanding and judgment of them confusion.

As that first error sheweth, whereon our opposites in this cause have grounded themselves. For as they rightly maintain that God must be glorified in all things, and that the actions of men cannot tend unto his glory unless they be framed after his law; so it is their error to think that the only law which God hath appointed unto men in that behalf is the sacred Scripture. By that which we work naturally, as when we breathe, sleep, move, we set forth the glory of God as natural agents do, albeit we have no express purpose to make that our end, nor any advised determination therein to follow a law, but do that we do (for the most part) not as much as thinking thereon. In reasonable and moral actions another law taketh place; a law by the observation whereof we glorify God in such sort, as no creature else under man is able to do; because other creatures have not judgment to examine the quality of that which is done by them, and therefore in that they do they neither can accuse nor approve themselves.

Proceed we further; let us place man in some public society with others, whether civil or spiritual; and in this case there is no remedy but we must add yet a further law. For although even here likewise the laws of nature and reason be of necessary use, yet somewhat over and besides them is necessary, namely human and positive law, together with that law which is of commerce between grand societies, the law of nations, and of nations Christian. For which cause the law of God hath likewise said, "Let every soul be subject to the higher powers." The public power of all societies is above every soul contained in the same societies. And the principal use of that power is to give laws unto all that are under it; which laws in such case we must obey, unless there be reason shewed which may necessarily enforce that the law of Reason or of God doth enjoin the contrary. Because except our own private and but probable resolutions be by the law of public determinations overruled, we take away all possibility of sociable life in the world. A plainer example whereof than ourselves we cannot have. How cometh it to pass that we are at this present day so rent with mutual contentions, and that the Church is so much troubled about the polity of the Church? No doubt if men had been willing to learn how many laws their actions in this life are subject unto, and what the true force of each law is, all these controversies might have died the very day they were first brought forth.

It is both commonly said, and truly, that the best men otherwise are not always the best in regard of society. The reason whereof is, for that the law of men's actions is one, if they be respected only as men; and another, when they are considered as parts of a politic body. Many men there are, than whom nothing is more commendable when they are singled; and yet in society with others none less fit to answer the duties which are looked for at their hands. Yea, I am persuaded, that of them with whom in this cause we strive, there are whose betters amongst men would be hardly found, if they did not live amongst men, but in some wilderness by themselves. The cause of which their disposition so unframable unto societies wherein they live, is, for that they discern not aright what place and force these several kinds of laws ought to have in all their actions. Is there question either concerning the regiment of the Church in general, or about conformity between one church and another, or of ceremonies, offices, powers, jurisdictions in our own church? Of all these things they judge by that rule which they frame to themselves with some show of probability, and what seemeth in that sort convenient, the same they think themselves bound to practise; the same by all means they labour mightily to uphold; whatsoever any law of man to the contrary hath determined they weigh it not. Thus by following the law of private reason, where the law of public should take place, they breed disturbance.

For the better inuring therefore of men's minds with the true distinction of laws, and of their several force according to the different kind and quality of our actions, it shall not peradventure be amiss to shew in some one example how they all take place. To seek no further, let but that be considered, than which there is not any thing more familiar unto us, our food.

What things are food and what are not we judge naturally by sense; neither need we any other law to be our director in that behalf than the selfsame which is common unto us with beasts.

But when we come to consider of food, as of a benefit which God of his bounteous goodness hath provided for all things living; the law of Reason doth here require the duty of thankfulness at our hands, towards him at whose hands we have it. And lest appetite in the use of food should lead us beyond that which is meet, we owe in this case obedience to that law of Reason, which teacheth mediocrity in meats and drinks. The same things divine law teacheth also, as at large we have shewed it doth all parts of moral duty, whereunto we all of necessity stand bound, in regard of the life to come.

But of certain kinds of food the Jews sometimes had, and we ourselves likewise have, a mystical, religious, and supernatural use, they of their paschal lamb and oblations, we of our bread and wine in the Eucharist; which use none but divine law could institute.

Now as we live in civil society, the state of the commonwealth wherein we live both may and doth require certain laws concerning food; which laws, saving only that we are members of the commonwealth where they are of force, we should not need to respect as rules of action, whereas now in their place and kind they must be respected and obeyed.

Yea, the selfsame matter is also a subject wherein sometime ecclesiastical laws have place; so that unless we will be authors of confusion in the Church, our private discretion, which otherwise might guide us a contrary way, must here submit itself to be that way guided, which the public judgment of the Church hath thought better. In which case that of Zonaras concerning fasts may be remembered. "Fastings are good, but let good things be done in good and convenient manner. He that transgresseth in his fasting the orders of the holy fathers," the positive laws of the Church of Christ, must be plainly told, "that good things do lose the grace of their goodness, when in good sort they are not performed."

And as here men's private fancies must give place to the higher judgment of that Church which is in authority a mother over them; so the very actions of whole churches have, in regard of commerce and fellowship with other churches, been subject to laws concerning food, the contrary unto which laws had else been thought more convenient for them to observe; as by that order of abstinence from strangled and blood may appear; an order grounded upon that fellowship which the churches of the Gentiles had with the Jews.

Thus we see how even one and the selfsame thing is under divers considerations conveyed through many laws; and that to measure by any one kind of law all the actions of men were to confound the admirable order, wherein God hath disposed all laws, each as in nature, so in degree, distinct from other.

Wherefore that here we may briefly end: of Law there can be no less acknowledged, than that her seat is the bosom of God, her voice the harmony of the world: all things in heaven and earth do her homage, the very least as feeling her care, and the greatest as not exempted from her power, both Angels and men and creatures of what condition soever, though each in different sort and manner, yet all with uniform consent, admiring her as the mother of their peace and joy.

QUESTIONS

1. *How does Hooker define the process of judgment — of argument, reasoning, and conclusion — which he here explains and recommends? What place has the rule in that process? What relationship should an individual attempt to establish with the rules directed to his judgment?*
   a. *According to Hooker, should all rules of a duly constituted authority be followed in all cases? Or should one always follow one's own judgment?*

If sometimes one and sometimes the other, how does Hooker tell his reader to decide in particular instances which it shall be? Does he propose a sort of universal equity by which such questions can be answered, and if so, how is it defined?

b. Who is the Man of Good Judgment, and what is his art?

c. He defines the Man of Bad Judgment rather directly in his description of the Calvinists. Does that description remind you of anyone you know? How is one to become a Man of Good Judgment?

2. What does Hooker teach you in these passages? How does he do it?

3. Does Hooker's complication of the world of rules and judgment help you know what to do with the rules of etiquette or grammar or literary criticism? Of Amherst College (pages 512–514 supra) or the prison (pages 567–583) or the American South (page 507)? Of the law? Explain why an American judge should read this outdated defense of a moribund institution.

4. This passage has particular interest for lawyers in another way: it can be read as a masterful piece of advocacy. In a world torn between Roman Catholicism and Reform, how would you like to be asked to justify the fifty-year-old Church of England, neither Roman nor Reformed?

5. Throughout this work, and especially in the last paragraph reproduced above, Hooker expresses the deepest reverence for the law. How does he prepare for and support this remarkable claim?

   a. Exactly what is the law that Hooker venerates so deeply: a set of legal rules? If not that, what? Is the relationship that Hooker perceives between particular legal rules and the law like the relationship Plato perceives between rules and justice?

   b. Admiration of our law was once a common phenomenon. Blackstone said of the law of England that it was the "best birthright and noblest inheritance of mankind." (Commentaries *443.) Would anyone speak in such a way of our modern law?

   c. One of the great steps towards our modern jurisprudence was the recognition by Holmes and others that the law should be conceived of as a way of expressing social choices, as an instrument of social policy. Is there any other way in which the law might be regarded?

   d. Holmes once said that the law, to be properly understood, must be seen with the eyes of a "bad man"; how would Hooker have responded to that assertion?

6. It might be suggested that both Hooker and Plato define justice not by stating certain rules or doctrines or principles of public life, but by demonstrating certain ways of reasoning and conversing about important matters. Justice is defined by the intellectual processes through which the best men reach conclusions and argue about them.

   a. Do you agree with this interpretation of what Hooker and Plato are saying? How can you define the processes of reasoning and conversation which each one celebrates?

   b. Does the view attributed to Plato and Hooker have any validity as applied to modern law? How would you define the processes of reasoning and conversation which constitute the heart of modern justice?

7. Considering the passages appearing up to this point in this chapter, would you say that the trouble with modern law is that instead of having some other structure it is built upon the rule? Or is the difficulty not the rule

itself, but that we do not know how to use it properly, that we do not understand its proper place in making and explaining judgments? We make the false assumption that justice can be done by rules, and we keep up a furious search for new rules and new laws; but what we need is not a new set of rules — a new medical prescription or Pilot's Guide to the Mississippi or new canons of literary criticism or rules of grammar — but a different attitude towards rules, a new understanding of how they can be used by an intelligent and responsible mind in the enterprise of judgment.

What understanding do we need, and how can it be expressed? Should there be a law school course in Universal Equity? Who is the Man of Good Laws behind or beyond the legal rules with which he must deal, and by what art does he use and control these rules in the judgments he makes?

WRITING ASSIGNMENT 16: Excellence in Judgment and the Use of Rules

In this assignment we approach the general subject of the chapter — "What is the art of legal judgment?" — by examining one important characteristic of the process, namely, that it nearly always involves the use of the form we have called the rule. How is this form of speech to be understood and controlled? What is excellence in legal judgment, and what is the proper place of the rule in that activity?

We have seen that rules of the standard form leave out too much, include too much, encourage trivial and specious argument, lead to unforeseen and harsh results, are so riddled with exceptions and so subject to subversion that they cannot serve as firm and predictable bases for decision, and generally stand in the way of an open and candid inquiry into the truth of our experience. What justification can you find then for their use? Why do we insist upon using them to explain ourselves? With what understanding do you read and use rules? It seems that the tension between rule and nonrule is fundamental to the structure of legal intellectual activity. Can you explain or justify this circumstance? Are rules simply a stumbling block to justice?

Try not to respond to this assignment in the wretched jargon of a poli-sci term paper. This assignment invites you to define and deal with a problem that is important in your own life. When do you use a rule to explain yourself? How do you control that language?

In this assignment you are asked to show what can be meant by excellence both in judgment and in the use of rules, and you can approach the problem from either direction. You might begin, for example, with your own experience with a set of rules, and ask what "good judgment" under them might consist of — taking, say, moral rules or school rules or the rules of a game as your example. Your primary question would then be: how does one function with rules? What relationship can one establish with rules that are meant to direct one's judgment? Or you might begin with a problem or situation (how to decide whom to vote for, whether to call the doctor for your child, what to do about a dishonest classmate), and ask how you would go about making the judgment called for by the situation and what assistance you could hope for from a rule or set of rules. Either approach comes down to the same question: what is the relationship between good judgment and rules? What does the good judge do with the rules that are meant to govern his judgment — cheat, and call it equity? To what beyond the rule does he look, and how does he justify doing so? (Are Plato and Hooker any help here?) It may help you work out your own expectations if you ask how you as a lawyer would try to persuade a judge or juror to decide a case your way: would you be more interested in showing that a rule compels a particular result, or that a particular result is "just" — and how would you do that?

Part One

• Give an account of a real (or imaginary) event in which a person makes and explains a judgment under circumstances where he must deal with a rule or set of rules made by somebody else. Your account should show excellence in judgment and in the use of rules.

Part Two

• Define the excellence you have just demonstrated. How can you do so: in a language of rules or something else? What is the place of the rule in the excellent judgment and its explanation?

As you work out this assignment, study with care the passages from Fowler, Johnson, and Hooker given above. Are you helped if I suggest, as I have done at various times throughout the course, that in some sense good judging is good writing? What relationship does the good judge or lawyer establish with the rules that are meant to govern his judgment? It might be especially useful for you to examine again the assignment in Chapter 1 on good writing and that in Chapter 3 on the sentencing judgment (pages 78 and 407, respectively).

If legal excellence is not in rules, where is it and how is it to be defined? Does it surprise you to be told that Plato's inquiry into that question — into the nature of justice — in The Republic leads him into the study of education? Here you might like to look at your own legal education and ask what place the rule has in that process. What relationship does the good law student or teacher establish with the legal rule?

WRITING ASSIGNMENT 16, ALTERNATIVE A: Are Rules Always Tentative?

Part One

• *Find a legal rule of the classic form, neither too vague nor too specific. Then make a list of all the exceptions you can find to that rule as it might be applied in various cases. Are these exceptions stated in the form of rules? What is their function: are they subversions of the rule? In the interest of what?*

Part Two

• *Show the process of exception at work in a particular case and explain whether you believe the exception is proper, and if so, why. How do you make and explain that judgment? Can you come to some general conclusion as to why we have rules if they are always going to be tentative and subject to exception in this fashion?*

It may be of help if you consider how rules work in some specific fields of law with which you are familiar. What relationship can you perceive between the rule and some other ground of decision?

a. Contracts. What exceptions are there to the familiar rule that says that promises based upon adequate consideration will be enforced by the courts? Are the exceptions stated in the form of rules? Or are they subversions of the contract rules designed to achieve fairness and justice?

b. Criminal Law. We require clear, certain, public prohibitions of specific acts as a condition to the imposition of punishment by the state, and when a rule of this character is broken, the defendant is liable to punishment. What exceptions are there to this description of the system of criminal law rules? Are the exceptions themselves rules, or are they subversions?

c. Domestic Relations. Consider the language of "parental rights" in the law of domestic relations. The law seems to say that a parent has "rights" in a child that can be lost only by consent or by "abandonment." But in most states a court may make an order respecting the child's custody, over the objection of the parent or parents, where a change of custody is in the child's "best interests." So what does "parental right" mean? Is it just a presumption? Are all rules tentative in this way?[2]

2. The idea that rules are always tentative is the subject of detailed exposition and analysis in H. L. A. Hart, "The Ascription of Responsibility and Rights," in *Logic and Language* (1st Ser.) 145 (A. Flew ed. 1955). Hart says that legal rules seem to

WRITING ASSIGNMENT 16, ALTERNATIVE B: The Place of Rules

• *Give an account of a negotiation, an argument, the drafting of a contract or the writing of a judicial opinion in which you show the place of rules in that activity. What is excellence in the use of rules in the situation you describe?*

Let me suggest that in connection with your work in this assignment you read over all your papers in this course to date and ask yourself how your mind has been working. Consider at the same time any other legal writing you may have done — for other courses, advocacy competitions, law review, and the like — as well as your responses and thoughts in your various classes. Are you pleased and satisfied by what you find?

Where is your education taking you? Have you achieved, or are you on your way to achieving, a position from which you can speak? Have you your own voice? Your own style? Your own excellence of thought? Insights? Understanding? Knowledge? Do you see that you are being asked what view you take of yourself and what you are doing?

B. MAKING A LANGUAGE OF JUDICIAL CRITICISM: HOW SHOULD WE TALK ABOUT LEGAL JUDGMENT?

In Section A we asked how an intelligent and responsible mind could work with rules, and especially how such a mind could use rules to guide and explain its judgments. That was the beginning of an inquiry into the judicial mind, which the rest of the book will continue and complicate. There your efforts were given some direction, in that you were asked what sort of relationship you might hope to establish with rules that direct your judgment. We now put the question in its most expanded form: what is it that we expect of the judicial mind, of the mind that makes and explains judgments in the law? What excellence do we hope for and how can it be defined? How can it be attained and taught? What language can we make or find in which to respond to these questions? How, that is, can we criticize the activity of legal judgment?

---

be unqualified, absolute statements, but that actually they are "defeasible," i.e., subject to the perpetual threat of defeat. There is, he says, an unwritten "unless" at the end of every rule, and legal rules cannot be properly understood unless this is appreciated. But what follows that "unless": a set of rules that may defeat the first rule? Or does that word point to the whole world of legal education, thought, and value? What would Plato or Hooker say?

You are asked here to create for your own use a language of judicial criticism, a way of describing and evaluating the processes of legal judgment. The task is enormous, but it is one for which your legal education — centered as it is upon the judicial opinion — should have prepared you. If there is one thing you learn in law school, it is how to evaluate a judicial opinion. What is it that you do when you do that? What is involved in this critical enterprise? I hope you sec that in being asked these questions you are also asked to talk about the action of your own mind, about what it is you do when working with a difficult matter. For — so close is the lawyer to the judge, in all essentials — when you define the judge and explain what is expected of him, you largely define yourself and your own future. And as a quick look at the literature of the law will show (e.g., *American Jurisprudence* or the *North West Reporter* or the bill of fare at a continuing legal education seminar), many people have made very little indeed of their possibilities. How are you to express your awareness of the immense variety that lies before you, how can you define the hopes you have for yourself and others? What language of judicial criticism can you make, and how will you control it?

While you are encouraged to think out this matter as independently and originally as you can (and the directions you can take are numberless), there is one way of talking about what a judge does, to which (because it is both familiar and perplexing) the notes and questions will from time to time refer: the language of "rationality." We all agree that both the judicial judgment and the opinion expressing it should be rational; who could maintain otherwise? But what does "rational" in such a sentence mean? Or — as you know how to read the question — what can it be made to mean? And however you choose to define rationality, is there anything more, anything beyond rationality, that you demand of a judge and his opinion? If so, what is it?

Such are the major questions of the present section, which you will be asked to address in a writing assignment, and their importance should be plain enough. To ask, for example, how rationality can be defined and understood is to examine the great claim of the law to our respect and attention. It is not usually asserted that the law is beautiful or loving or inspired with mystical validity, or that it is an exact science; it is reason, not beauty or truth, that the law serves. But what sort of reason is it that operates in the judicial opinion, how can the rationality that the lawyer demands and admires be defined?

As for the importance of the judicial opinion, that can hardly be exaggerated: a wise judgment may render harmless thousands of false pretenses, omissions, and impossibilities committed in the drafting of a set of rules; a foolish one may make the wisest laws useless. With the judicial opinion the law takes its final stance, utters the last word — and here, if ever, it must be right. The world of the inexpressible is for a moment faced directly, something is said, and the universe moves on. What is said by an excellent judge at such a time? What do you hope and expect of him? The judicial opinion could be said to sum up a civilization; recall the eagerness with which you no doubt turned to the judicial opinions in the law of slavery (in Chapter 3), wondering how the judicial mind could explain itself in such terms, what connections could be drawn between slavery and the law, your own familiar world. Where does the judge look for that which will guide him, for that which will explain what he has done? How are we to criticize what the judge does, and what is the meaning and place of "rationality" in our vocabulary of criticism?

In preparation for the next writing assignment, please read the poem by Alexander Pope entitled *An Essay on Criticism*, which will be discussed at page 728 *infra*.

1. *Talk About the Working Mind: Metaphors, Plain Speech, and the Language of Rationality*

Your work on the insanity defense and the sentencing judgment in Chapter 3 has made you all too familiar, you may say, with the difficulties of talking about the human mind. Now the difficulties are, if anything, increased: it is, in a sense, your own mind that is in question. How can you describe what it is that lawyers and judges do when they make legal judgments? And how can you, as a critic of the process, make and express your judgment that a judge or lawyer has, in a particular case, done well or badly? If you find that you want to talk about "rationality," in what particular vocabulary do you do so, and what do you mean by it?

We shall begin by looking at some ways of talking about excellence of mind outside the law; then we shall examine some actual judicial opinions and some samples of judicial criticism.

a. *Can You Find the Music in the Law?*

A person who both teaches and plays the piano has, in talking to me about how people learn to play that instrument, distinguished between "technique" and "music." Learning "technique" means learning how to move one's fingers fast and accurately, to achieve the manipulative ability that complicated music requires. This can be viewed as a very complicated and difficult sort of touch-typing, and the student who has learned only this cannot make music. He can merely follow directions, not express himself. To make music, he must learn how to have musical ideas and feelings and how to express them by making musical choices and decisions. Such is the musical mind.

QUESTIONS

1. *Can an analogy be drawn between the lawyer and the musician? Or is the law all technique, utterly without music?*
   a. *Can you distinguish between "technique" and "music" in your own activities as a lawyer or law student? Do you know, for example, what it is to have the professional ability to address a difficult problem competently, in accepted ways, yet to feel that something is wrong or missing, that some faculty has failed you, that another mind would make something completely different out of what you have before you?*
   b. *Do you know what it is to have "legal ideas and feelings," to know how to make legal choices and decisions, to express yourself in the law? Where do these capacities come from, and how would you tell another to acquire them?*
2. *Artur Schnabel, one of the great players of the piano music of Beethoven, once produced an edition of Beethoven's piano works in which he tried to show, by fingering directions, pedaling instructions, and metronome markings, exactly how he had played the music. (The metronome markings were particularly detailed, meant to indicate not merely the tempo of a particular section, but also those variations of tempo within such a scheme by which a player will make emphases and distinctions for artistic purposes. The technical term for this sort of speeding up and slowing down is "rubato.")*
   a. *Do you imagine that this edition did in fact show exactly how he had played the music?*
   b. *How might Schnabel have better communicated his sense of how Beethoven should be played, if not by such a system of specific directions? Should he have produced a set of general rules?*
   c. *Is there, in the law, any analogy to what Schnabel could do but could not tell others how to do?*
3. *Do you hope that judges and lawyers, and you yourself, can become musicians in the law? What can you mean by such a remark?*

b. A Famous Metaphor: Plato's Cave

Here is a passage that describes the mind at its best, and explains what its education involves. Why do you suppose Plato chose to express his view of these matters in such peculiar terms?

THE REPUBLIC*
Plato

And now, I said, let me show in a figure how far our nature is enlightened or unenlightened: — Behold! human beings living in an

* Book 7 (Jowett translation).

underground den, which has a mouth open towards the light and reaching all along the den; here they have been from their childhood, and have their legs and necks chained so that they cannot move, and can only see before them, being prevented by the chains from turning round their heads. Above and behind them a fire is blazing at a distance, and between the fire and the prisoners there is a raised way; and you will see, if you look, a low wall built along the way, like the screen which marionette players have in front of them, over which they show the puppets.

I see.

And do you see, I said, men passing along the wall carrying all sorts of vessels, and statues and figures of animals made of wood and stone and various materials, which appear over the wall? Some of them are talking, others silent.

You have shown me a strange image, and they are strange prisoners.

Like ourselves, I replied; and they see only their own shadows, or the shadows of one another, which the fire throws on the opposite wall of the cave?

True, he said; how could they see anything but the shadows if they were never allowed to move their heads?

And of the objects which are being carried in like manner they would only see the shadows?

Yes, he said.

And if they were able to converse with one another, would they not suppose that they were naming what was actually before them?

Very true.

And suppose further that the prison had an echo which came from the other side, would they not be sure to fancy when one of the passers-by spoke that the voice which they heard came from the passing shadow?

No question, he replied.

To them, I said, the truth would be literally nothing but the shadows of the images.

That is certain.

And now look again, and see what will naturally follow if the prisoners are released and disabused of their error. At first, when any of them is liberated and compelled suddenly to stand up and turn his neck round and walk and look towards the light, he will suffer sharp pains; the glare will distress him, and he will be unable to see the realities of which in his former state he had seen the shadows; and then conceive some one saying to him, that what he saw before was an illusion, but that now, when he is approaching nearer to being and his eye is turned towards more real existence, he has a clearer vision, — what will be his reply? And you may further imagine that his instructor is pointing to the objects as they pass and requiring him to name them, — will he not be perplexed? Will he not fancy that the shadows which he formerly saw are truer than the objects which are now shown to him?

Far truer.

And if he is compelled to look straight at the light, will he not have a pain in his eyes which will make him turn away to take refuge in the objects of vision which he can see, and which he will conceive to be in reality clearer than the things which are now being shown to him?

True, he said.

And suppose once more, that he is reluctantly dragged up a steep and rugged ascent, and held fast until he is forced into the presence of the sun himself, is he not likely to be pained and irritated? When he approaches the light his eyes will be dazzled, and he will not be able to see anything at all of what are now called realities.

Not all in a moment, he said.

He will require to grow accustomed to the sight of the upper world. And first he will see the shadows best, next the reflections of men and other objects in the water, and then the objects themselves; then he will gaze upon the light of the moon and the stars and the spangled heaven; and he will see the sky and the stars by night better than the sun or the light of the sun by day?

Certainly.

Last of all he will be able to see the sun, and not mere reflections of him in the water, but he will see him in his own proper place, and not in another; and he will contemplate him as he is.

Certainly.

He will then proceed to argue that this is he who gives the season and the years, and is the guardian of all that is in the visible world, and in a certain way the cause of all things which he and his fellows have been accustomed to behold?

Clearly, he said, he would first see the sun and then reason about him.

And when he remembered his old habitation, and the wisdom of the den and his fellow-prisoners, do you not suppose that he would felicitate himself on the change, and pity them?

Certainly, he would.

And if they were in the habit of conferring honours among themselves on those who were quickest to observe the passing shadows and to remark which of them went before, and which followed after, and which were together; and who were therefore best able to draw conclusions as to the future, do you think that he would care for such honours and glories, or envy the possessors of them? Would he not say with Homer, "Better to be the poor servant of a poor master," and to endure anything, rather than think as they do and live after their manner?

Yes, he said, I think that he would rather suffer anything than entertain these false notions and live in this miserable manner.

Imagine once more, I said, such an one coming suddenly out of the sun to be replaced in his old situation; would he not be certain to have his eyes full of darkness?

To be sure, he said.

And if there were a contest, and he had to compete in measuring the shadows with the prisoners who had never moved out of the den, while his sight was still weak, and before his eyes had become steady (and the time which would be needed to acquire this new habit of sight might be very considerable), would he not be ridiculous? Men would say of him that up he went and down he came without his eyes; and that it was better not even to think of ascending; and if any one tried to loose another and lead him up to the light, let them only catch the offender, and they would put him to death.

No question, he said.

This entire allegory, I said, you may now append, dear Glaucon, to the previous argument; the prison-house is the world of sight, the light of the fire is the sun, and you will not misapprehend me if you interpret the journey upwards to be the ascent of the soul into the intellectual world according to my poor belief, which, at your desire, I have expressed — whether rightly or wrongly God knows. But, whether true or false, my opinion is that in the world of knowledge the idea of good appears last of all, and is seen only with an effort; and, when seen, is also inferred to be the universal author of all things beautiful and right, parent of light and of the lord of light in this visible world, and the immediate source of reason and truth in the intellectual; and that this is the power upon which he who would act rationally either in public or private life must have his eye fixed.

I agree, he said, as far as I am able to understand you.

Moreover, I said, you must not wonder that those who attain to this beatific vision are unwilling to descend to human affairs; for their souls are ever hastening into the upper world where they desire to dwell; which desire of theirs is very natural, if our allegory may be trusted.

Yes, very natural.

And is there anything surprising in one who passes from divine contemplations to the evil state of man, misbehaving himself in a ridiculous manner; if, while his eyes are blinking and before he has become accustomed to the surrounding darkness, he is compelled to fight in courts of law, or in other places, about the images or the shadows of images of justice, and is endeavouring to meet the conceptions of those who have never yet seen absolute justice?

Anything but surprising, he replied.

Any one who has common sense will remember that the bewilderments of the eyes are of two kinds, and arise from two causes, either from coming out of the light or from going into the light, which is true of the mind's eye, quite as much as of the bodily eye; and he who remembers this when he sees any one whose vision is perplexed and weak, will not be too ready to laugh; he will first ask whether that soul of man has come out of the brighter life, and is unable to see because unaccustomed to the dark, or having turned from darkness to the day is dazzled by excess of light. And he will count the one happy in his condition and state of being, and he will pity the other; or, if he have a mind to laugh at the soul which comes from below into the light, there will be more reason in this than in the laugh which greets him who returns from above out of the light into the den.

That, he said, is a very just distinction.

But then, if I am right, certain professors of education must be wrong when they say that they can put a knowledge into the soul which was not there before, like sight into blind eyes.

They undoubtedly say this, he replied.

Whereas, our argument shows that the power and capacity of learning exists in the soul already; and that just as the eye was unable to turn from darkness to light without the whole body, so too the instrument of knowledge can only by the movement of the whole soul be turned from the world of becoming into that of being, and learn by degrees to endure the sight of being, and of the brightest and best of being, or in other words, of the good.

Very true.

And must there not be some art which will effect conversion in the easiest and quickest manner; not implanting the faculty of sight, for that exists already, but has been turned in the wrong direction, and is looking away from the truth?

QUESTIONS

1. *Why does Plato use the story of the cave to talk about excellence in the activity of the mind instead of simply telling us what he means? Is this a mark of the primitive stage of philosophy 2500 years ago?*
2. *Or does he tell us directly what he means, at the end when he says that the story describes "the ascent of the soul into the intellectual world"? Or is that a metaphor too?*
3. *Plato is sometimes spoken of as an apostle of reason. His word for the activity by which one can attain the excellence he describes ("dialegein") is usually translated as "dialectic," and the faculty of mind which engages in this activity is usually referred to as reason. Perhaps "thinking through" and "intellect" would be better terms, but the interesting fact is that we are told by those who know Greek that the terms are really not trans-*

latable at all. How can this be? Surely terms describing such a universal activity as reasoning should be readily translatable. Can it be that reason for the Greeks (or for Plato) was really different from what it is for us? How could that possibly be? And even if it was, why cannot the terms defining it simply be translated into English? What does this apparent fact of untranslatability say about the nature of rationality and of the mind?

4. *One of the subjects of this passage is education, the process by which one goes from a state of darkness and ignorance to one of understanding and light, and of course Plato speaks of that metaphorically too: the critical event is a "turning of the soul in the right direction," or a "conversion." And our own language of education is also metaphorical: "educate" comes from a Latin word meaning to "lead out," for example. And one often hears talk about education as a process of acquiring knowledge or skills, as if the mind came to possess something it did not possess before: a knowledge of Latin, or an understanding of the principles of electricity or of the concepts of grammar or democracy. To learn is to grasp, to get; to know is to possess; to teach is to transfer, so that "I teach them law" is a direct parallel to "I serve them soup." Can you think of any more intelligent ways to talk about learning and education? Are they metaphorical too?*

   Wittgenstein does propose a different version: sometimes, at least, it makes sense to explain understanding by saying that one who understands a proposition "knows how to go on" from that point, that he knows what to say or do next. (Philosophical Investigations ¶¶143–151 (1958).) How is the mind defined here? As a player in a game?

   Which of these ways of describing knowledge (as possession or as a game) would be more helpful to you if you tried to express what you have learned in law school? Or can you think of some third and better way?

5. *Consider now your own ways of talking about what the lawyer and judge do. Do you find that you must use metaphors, or do you talk in direct speech? Certainly you can talk about "rationality" without using metaphors, for that is what law school teaches you, is it not?*

c. *The Language of Rationality: The Mind as Machine?*

Here you are asked to consider how you have in fact been taught to criticize judicial opinions. From your first day in law school you have been given directions to guide you in this process, and have been shown examples of the criticizing mind at work. What is the vocabulary of judicial criticism to which you have been introduced? What is the place of "rationality" in the discourse you have learned, and in what terms is this criterion of excellence expressed? What do these inherited ways of thinking and speaking imply about how the mind works and about the nature of legal judgment?

Look carefully at the critical phrases and terms used in your classes to express approval and disapproval of a judicial opinion. What do you find: direct analytic speech, identifiable criteria of rationality, metaphors, clichés, or what? And in what form do you find it: do you find essays and speeches on How To Criticize a Judicial Opinion? Or must you try to puzzle out what people are doing from the actual critical judgments expressed in your classes and your reading? Why do your teachers not address the enterprise of judicial criticism directly?

Here are some phrases for your consideration: the good judicial opinion "considers all relevant factors"; "takes everything into account"; "balances (or weighs) the real interests"; "reconciles apparent inconsistencies"; and so on. Are those metaphorical or direct statements? Are they of any meaning or assistance to anyone?

Implicit in some of the foregoing and other such phrases are a series of metaphors such as these: a problem has parts which fit together to make a whole; arguments have strengths and weaknesses; interests have bulk or weight, which permit them to be measured, weighed, and balanced; general rules, like boxes, have lots of specific rules inside them; every rule has a reason (or a policy) which determines its proper course, like a tractor driver; conflicts between rules can be harmonized (is that music in the law?); every case presents a problem with a solution; and so on. I urge you to make your own list of inherited phrases and to explicate their metaphorical assumptions. You may have noticed that all the metaphors I have listed derive from the physical world of physics, from the world of measurable weights, sizes, forces, distances, as though everything at last came down to quantities and both the human mind and the difficulties it faces could be spoken of as if they were machines. Is this because the mind and experience of the judge can accurately be expressed in such terms? Or — as the literature of social science might demonstrate — because we have so perfectly accustomed ourselves to the industrial age that we naturally think in no other way? Is the machine our universal metaphor? Can you conceive of other ways of talking about what you do, ways that do more justice to the complexities and frustrations you actually experience, to the hopes and fears you have for yourself?

Consider, for example, the following proposal of a way to guide and evaluate human judgments. What metaphors are implicit in it? Do you know or can you imagine any other way to talk about, to describe and criticize, human judgments?

THE PRINCIPLES OF MORALS AND LEGISLATION (1789)

Jeremy Bentham

[Bentham defines the principle of utility as "that principle which approves or disapproves of every action whatsoever, according to the tendency which it appears to have to augment or diminish the happiness of the party whose interest is in question: or, what is the same thing in other words, to promote or to oppose that happiness." In chapter four he addresses the obvious question this principle raises.]

Chapter 4: Value of a Lot of Pleasure or Pain, How To Be Measured

1. Pleasures then, and the avoidance of pains, are the *ends* which the legislator has in view: it behoves him therefore to understand their *value*. Pleasures and pains are the *instruments* he has to work with: it behoves him therefore to understand their force, which is again, in another point of view, their value.

2. To a person considered *by himself*, the value of a pleasure or pain considered *by itself*, will be greater or less, according to the four following circumstances:

1. Its *intensity*.
2. Its *duration*.
3. Its *certainty* or *uncertainty*.
4. Its *propinquity* or *remoteness*.

3. These are the circumstances which are to be considered in estimating a pleasure or a pain considered each of them by itself. But when the value of any pleasure or pain is considered for the purpose of estimating the tendency of any *act* by which it is produced, there are two other circumstances to be taken into the account; these are,

5. Its *fecundity*, or the chance it has of being followed by sensations of the *same* kind: that is, pleasures, if it be a pleasure: pains, if it be a pain.
6. Its *purity*, or the chance it has of *not* being followed by sensations of the *opposite* kind: that is, pains, if it be a pleasure: pleasures, if it be a pain.

These two last, however, are in strictness scarcely to be deemed properties of the pleasure or the pain itself; they are not, therefore, in strictness to be taken into the account of the value of that pleasure or that pain. They are in strictness to be deemed properties only of the act, or other event, by which such pleasure or pain has been produced; and accordingly are only to be taken into the account of the tendency of such act or such event.

4. To a *number* of persons, with reference to each of whom the value of a pleasure or a pain is considered, it will be greater or less, according to seven circumstances: to wit, the six preceding ones; viz.

1. Its *intensity*.
2. Its *duration*.
3. Its *certainty* or *uncertainty*.
4. Its *propinquity* or *remoteness*.
5. Its *fecundity*.
6. Its *purity*.

And one other; to wit:

7. Its *extent;* that is, the number of persons to whom it *extends;* or (in other words) who are affected by it.

5. To take an exact account then of the general tendency of any act, by which the interests of a community are affected, proceed as follows. Begin with any one person of those whose interests seem most immediately to be affected by it: and take an account,

1. Of the value of each distinguishable *pleasure* which appears to be produced by it in the *first* instance.
2. Of the value of each *pain* which appears to be produced by it in the *first* instance.
3. Of the value of each pleasure which appears to be produced by it *after* the first. This constitutes the *fecundity* of the first *pleasure* and the *impurity* of the first *pain.*
4. Of the value of each *pain* which appears to be produced by it after the first. This constitutes the *fecundity* of the first *pain,* and the *impurity* of the first pleasure.
5. Sum up all the values of all the *pleasures* on the one side, and those of all the *pains* on the other. The balance, if it be on the side of pleasure, will give the *good* tendency of the act upon the whole, with respect to the interests of that *individual* person; if on the side of pain, the *bad* tendency of it upon the whole.
6. Take an account of the *number* of persons whose interests appear to be concerned; and repeat the above process with respect to each. *Sum up* the numbers expressive of the degrees of *good* tendency, which the act has, with respect to each individual, in regard to whom the tendency of it is *good* upon the whole: do this again with respect to each individual, in regard to whom the tendency of it is *bad* upon the whole. Take the *balance;* which, if on the side of *pleasure,* will give the general *good tendency* of the act, with respect to the total number or community of individuals concerned; if on the side of pain, the general *evil tendency,* with respect to the same community.

QUESTIONS

1. *Does Bentham's program for decision-making explain what a good judge or lawyer does? Does it tell him how to do it well?*
   a. *Would it provide an adequate way, for example, for a judge to go about deciding whether or not an earlier decision should be overruled or left undisturbed? Whether a constitutional question should be decided now or deferred? Whether to vote to grant certiorari? How to sentence a defendant?*
   b. *Would it help a young man decide whether or not to accept induction? A citizen how to vote?*

c. *What other ways of describing and evaluating judgments can you think of that might be of greater value in these situations?*

2. *What metaphors are at work in this passage, and what are their implications?*
   a. *There seems to be an assumption that the mind can be regarded as a sort of machine operating in a physical universe, and that its major actions are accordingly those of measuring, weighing, comparing. Is this how you think of your own mind?*[3]
   b. *What other metaphors might describe the mind: is it like a flower, a river, a dancer, a musician?*
3. *This mechanical assumption occurs more or less strongly in a great deal of talk about the mind, not only in the law school clichés given earlier, but in more formal attempts to describe and evaluate the operations of the mind.*
   a. *For example, the logic of classes, which underlies the syllogism and justifies the process we call deduction, operates by a metaphor of inclusion and exclusion: when we say "all men are mortal" and ask what this means about the man Socrates, this logic tells us that all items "included in" or "covered by" the particular term are included in the general. Is this how you normally talk about words, as if they "included" or "covered" demonstrable sets of "objects," tangible and intangible? Is this what the labels in a legal rule do, for example?*
   b. *Compare the following statement about rationality in decision-making. What metaphorical assumptions are at work in this language, and what are their implications?*

THE FORMS AND LIMITS OF ADJUDICATION*
L. Fuller

Must the Decision Be Reached by Applying a Previously Established Rule or Standard?

Here is a point of real difficulty. On the one hand, it would seem that adjudication is meaningless unless the decision is reached by some rational process. (This does not necessarily exclude an "intuitive" or "inarticulate" decision, provided only there is faith that what is "intuited" is something that would appear as rational if it could be brought to adequate expression.)

If a decision is to be rational it must be based upon some rule, principle, or standard. If this rule, principle, or standard is to make any

3. Notice that the language used to describe the mind and its operations also necessarily describes the world in which that mind operates. To say that the mind measures and weighs is to say that the world can be measured and weighed. For two rather different versions of justice as quantitative proportion see Aristotle, *Nicomachean Ethics*, Book 5, Chapter 3 (Oxford Translation of Aristotle, printed in *Basic Works of Aristotle*, R. McKeon ed. 1941); and Calabresi, "Fault, Accidents and the Wonderful World of Blum and Kalven," 75 *Yale L.J.* 216, 223 (1965).

* In H. Hart and A. Sacks, *The Legal Process* 421 (1958).

appeal to the parties it must be something that pre-existed the decision. An explanation in terms of a principle created ad hoc to explain the decision it purports to govern lacks the persuasive power necessary to make adjudication effective.

On the other hand, and in the face of the considerations just advanced, we see a successful resort to adjudication in cases where there appear to be no previously established rules at all, notably in labor law and in international relations. Furthermore, even in the functioning of the ordinary courts of law, often the "rule" that is applied directs nothing more than a "reasonable" or "fair" result.

How are we to explain this contradiction between what occurs in practice and what seems to be demanded in theory? . . .

It is clear, I believe, that any claim of right necessarily implies a principle or rule. If I say, "Give me that, I want it," I do not by implication assert any principle which justifies my demand; I am merely expressing a desire and perhaps a threat to use whatever means are available to me to effectuate that desire.

On the other hand, if I say, "Give that to me, I claim it as a right," or, "I claim it because it is due me, or because it is mine," then by necessary implication I imply some rule or principle by which my claim may be judged.

QUESTIONS

1. *Why is the use of a rule, principle, or standard thought to be essential to "rationality" in judgment? Is the assertion here that rationality in the law is like rationality in mathematics, and that the way a person properly arrives at a conclusory proposition is to deduce it from one or more other propositions which are related tautologically to the conclusion, so that if the givens are accepted the conclusion must (as a matter of definition) be accepted too? Does that describe the process of rational decision-making in the law as you perceive it?*
2. *We might maintain that the process of decision under rules in the law is a direct opposite of the process of deduction from premises: in deduction, we articulate what must, as a matter of definition, be the result if certain givens are accepted; but in the law, the givens, or rules of law, do not require one particular result but authorize a range of results, they permit a multiplicity of acceptable interpretations among which it is the judge's task to choose. If so, what can we mean when we say that this choice should be "rational"?*
3. *If the legal rule does not operate as a basis for deduction, what does it do? Why might one say the rule is essential to rational judgment?*
4. *Is it perhaps useless to speak of rationality as a value in the process of judicial judgment in any way except the most basic (and in some sense unimportant) way, as meaning, for example, that an opinion should not be demonstrably self-contradictory or unintelligible? (I say "unimportant" because, although in saying such things we define necessary conditions to*

the sort of judgment we admire, we do not express the most important or distinguishing qualities of such judgments.)

5. *Is what you most hope of a judge that his judgments be rational? Or do you prefer to express your hopes in terms such as fairness, decency, and wisdom?*
6. *Let us shift our attention to another sort of judgment. Suppose it is decided that a large metropolitan area — London, for example — needs another airport, but it is by no means obvious where that airport ought to be located. A commission is appointed to look into the matter and to make a recommendation as to location. How should such a commission proceed with its work? What sort of decision should it hope to make? What would it mean to say, for example, that the judgment should be made "rationally," especially where there is no preexisting rule or standard to which one could appeal as authority? Would Bentham's system provide a solution?*

   There follows now an excerpt from the report of a commission appointed for exactly this purpose. How do you evaluate its work?

REPORT*

Commission on the Third London Airport

[The commission first prepared a short list of possible sites, and then examined each in great detail. The choice ultimately became one between Cublington — located in the green belt between London and the conurbation of Birmingham and Manchester — and Foulness, an island on the thinly populated east coast just north of the Thames estuary. The Commission chose Cublington, and here is part of its explanation of the problem and of its recommended solution.]

Thus the dilemma arises. The air traveller, the airline operator and the airport authority unite in wanting a site where the airport will be viable, which air travellers will like to use because it is easy of access and from which aircraft can operate without delays caused by congestion. In short the site must be as near as possible to the populations which it is designed to serve and yet also be far enough away from other major airports to avoid conflict with them. To meet the needs of those who travel by air much is sacrificed. Homes will be at worst destroyed and at best subjected to noise. Under the present law those who lose their quiet environment but not their homes will go wholly without compensation. Noise and pollution replace peace. Recuperation from ill health, mental and physical, in the present quietness of hospitals in country areas may be halted. Such ill health instead of being repaired may be aggravated in extent and indeed protracted in duration. In a small country like our own with centuries of history behind it irreparable damage is done to our national heritage by the impact on the country-

* Pages 6–8, 12–13, 131, 137–138 (Roskill, J., Chairman, 1971).

side and the destruction of ancient churches and houses. What has survived over the centuries the ravages of civil war, vandalism, religious reformers, restorers and even foreign foes is to be laid waste in the desire for swift travel by air. On the other hand while to many these are the values of today, they are not the values of all. Further it would be unwise to presume that the values of today will be those of tomorrow. Notwithstanding these environmental drawbacks there are many who positively want the airport because of the benefits which it can bring as a source of employment and wealth. The Commission received eloquent warning of the dangers of viewing the countryside through a townsman's eyes or from a particular class standpoint. We were reminded by the Thurleigh Emergency Committee for Democratic Action that in rural areas there is poverty and hardship as well as peace. We were told that many of those living in the country keenly want the wider job opportunities and scope for improving their social and economic welfare which an airport could bring. Such people are, it was said, perfectly willing to surrender the narrow country lanes if tangible material benefits could result. . . .

Two different approaches have been suggested to us. One may be called the market approach and the other the planning approach. Each helps the understanding and rationalisation of the problem. Each seeks to improve the welfare of society. Neither on its own can provide the answer. The market approach seeks to make the most productive use of the nation's resources and thereby achieve the maximum increase in the nation's wealth. It assumes that that increase will be used for the community's benefit in the way which the community wishes. Alternative courses of action are compared according to their respective contributions to the nation's wealth. The planning approach seeks to identify certain socially desirable aims such as conservation of the countryside and optimum distributions of population and employment. It applies aesthetic and cultural standards to this end. Alternative courses of action are compared according to their respective contributions to the achievement of these aims. There are difficulties in applying both approaches. The market approach assumes that people are economically rational and that authority will spend money to the best advantage of the community. Neither assumption is always valid. For example resources may be most effectively used if people use public transport rather than private cars. But people do not choose to behave that way. Other factors beyond simple least costs enter into their choice to obtain maximum satisfaction. Fear of unpopularity prevents authority encouraging the use of public transport by introducing charges to discourage the use of private cars. Thus both assumptions may not always be true. The market approach can also overlook the impact which changes in one area or community can have on another. It is not always easy to take all consequences into account. The planning approach has to ensure that the identified aims are in fact those to which the community attaches the highest priorities. Planning inquiries for which the law provides can help but this objective cannot always be achieved in the early stages. Perhaps the most important difficulty is that this method does not always inquire whether the same aims could be realised in some other more economical or more acceptable way. Clearly if too little account is taken of cost, air travellers may find the sacrifice in terms of both money and convenience too high. Then both they and the community will be the losers. If air travellers can choose between two airports offering identical levels of service but differing degrees of accessibility, they will prefer the more accessible. If the third London airport site is less attractive than other available airports, travellers will not use it. Demand will build up elsewhere either in this country or even overseas. The American promoter of package tours will cease to include this country on the itinerary of his European tours if the costs and difficulties of getting the tourists to and from the airports become a deterrent; when Paris, Rome and Athens are in the brochure but not London he will be a determined Anglophil who forgoes the journey because London is not included in the itinerary. Those who do continue to travel to and from this country by air will tend to go to some other more convenient airport unless steps are taken to prevent or deter them from exercising that choice. . . .

[The commission explains that its method of decision was cost/benefit analysis.]

We recognised the difficulties of placing money values upon some of the factors which we would need to consider. For example there could be major difficulties in bringing regional planning issues within the cost/benefit framework. . . . Indeed the Town and Country Planning Association has more than once tried to persuade us that we should be wrong even to attempt it. We were alive to the problems of valuing the historic and architectural qualities of Norman or even Victorian churches, open countryside, the unique qualities of the ecology on the shores of Foulness Island and peaceful Sunday afternoons in the garden, to mention but a few of the matters which have been widely canvassed since we began our work.

Two considerations appeared paramount. First, if we were to eschew purely arbitrary and subjective judgments we saw no practical alternative to cost/benefit analysis as a framework for studying the problems. Secondly, we would be able to test the extent to which cost/benefit analysis could be made to embrace some of the factors which we had to consider, while remaining sceptical about the acceptability of some of the results. In some areas we recognised that the reliability of the results would be doubtful. In others the results would be acceptable. At least an attempt would be made to measure and value factors which are external to ordinary market transactions. A common measuring rod could be applied to those factors which proved susceptible to the analysis. This in time would assist though it would not determine the solution of the ultimate and most crucial problem, the assessment of the differences between the four sites. Recognising, as we always have, both the strengths and limitations of cost/benefit analysis, we used it to assist in the short list selection and, as is well known, the Research Team used it in the work which we published in January 1970. Nothing has happened to make us regret our decision. No one has yet suggested a better alternative. . . .

When it became known that we were using cost/benefit analysis there were those, including some who should have known better, who claimed that we were adopting materialistic standards only and ignoring all others. "Money is being preferred to people" may make a rallying cry but betrays ignorance of the underlying purpose of cost/benefit analysis. We have been well aware of the extent and nature of the human problems involved — sacrifice of homes for some, peace and quiet for others, whether in early or middle age or in retirement. Cost/benefit analysis does not ignore them. It seeks so far as it can to assist in bringing all problems into their proper perspective. It provides a logical framework within which to assess all the effects flowing from a particular investment or planning decision. It tries to ensure that decisions are taken on the basis of people's individual values and choices as revealed by their behaviour rather than on the basis of the decision maker's own preferences or standards or of those of vociferous and politically powerful groups. There are formidable technical difficulties in achieving these aims. Quite apart from the difficulty of quantifying certain important matters to which we have already referred, it is rarely easy to observe and draw correct inferences from people's behaviour. In addition there is the problem, shared by other methods of analysis, of finding the correct basis for predicting the repercussions of the alternatives being studied. Finally we have been alerted to the danger of seeing only those consequences with which our own supposed social background makes us familiar and of ignoring those to which importance is attached by the young and by people of different circumstances. . . .

Foulness was on many occasions before and during the final series of public hearings referred to as the public favourite. Indeed if we could base our recommendation upon a counting of heads our task would have been simple and could have ended with the publication of a short list naming that site alone. We do not believe that those who appointed us and devised the procedure for our work — the Government and Opposition of the day — can have contemplated so simple and automatic a solution of the problem, for a decision in favour of Foulness on these grounds could have easily been taken without two and a half years work and expenditure by central government alone of over 1 million pounds. . . .

Our conclusion may be expressed in this way. A third London airport must be able to succeed as an airport. To this end, it must meet the needs of those whom it is designed to serve. But an airport can succeed as an airport and yet fail in some wider social purpose. This in essence is the case made against an airport at Cublington or Thurleigh. Unfortunately the converse is not equally true. An airport cannot serve any social purpose unless it first succeeds as an airport. If an airport does not serve its primary purpose satisfactorily, those who are in consequence denied adequate services will go elsewhere and those who look to the airport for some other purpose — for example as an employment base or for alleviating social conditions in east London — will look in vain for that which they seek. Neither in regional planning terms nor in environmental terms can an ailing airport attain the desired result. We do not believe that an airport at Foulness is as certain of success as an airport at either Cublington or Thurleigh. We cannot therefore be confident that the advantage claimed for Foulness will be achieved with that degree of certainty which justifies its recommendation. It is in every sense a relatively expensive project with relatively uncertain prospects of success. When the choice is between two new investments, one economically advantageous and the other less so, we cannot recommend, especially at this point in the nation's history, that the latter should be preferred to the former solely on the ground that the countryside — everywhere within the southeast — and all that goes with it must forever remain immune from the effects of an airport. We view with abhorrence the disturbance of villages, homes and churches, the disruption of communities and the replacement of the quiet of the countryside by the noise of the jet engine. This will occur to a varying extent whichever site is chosen. If we could overcome the dilemma by saying that no third London airport was required, our task would be easy. But a third London airport is required and is required to open its first runway by 1980. The nation's unsatisfactory economic performance in recent years can at least in part be attributed to a national tendency to forgo economic gains and to prefer other goals. Automatic priority should not be given to economic growth. Yet without that growth to which sound investment decisions must make a major contribution, other benefits are apt to disappear like a will-o'-the-wisp. Without such growth the nation cannot afford to spend what it would wish on its environment and on other benefits.

QUESTIONS

1. So far as you can tell from this excerpt, was the commission's judgment a rational one? What do you mean by "rational"?
   a. Are there rules, principles, or standards implicit in the judgment made by the commission? What are they?
   b. Or is it the absence of any such authoritative declarations of general policy (by reference to which a judgment could be made in a rational way) that constitutes the greatest defect of this report?
   c. What rules, principles, or standards should have governed this judgment?
   d. If the proper use of a preexisting authoritative rule is necessary to any rational judgment, does that mean that no legislative judgment can ever be rational?
   e. Other than by saying it was not rational, how might you criticize this judgment?
2. One possible defense of the commission is to say that the basic standard of its judgment, upon which its rationality depends and by which it can be measured, is a procedural one: the judgment should be made by an accurate and objective evaluation of the social costs and benefits of the competing proposals.
   a. Would this not be a rational way of making a judgment on such a matter? On any matter of public importance? How could anything possibly be said against it?
   b. Should a similar procedure for judgment also be used by courts faced with difficult problems? This would enable judges to escape from the difficulties of the rule that we studied in Section A; perhaps this would be a truly modern equity. Would you approve?
   c. So far as you can assess it from this excerpt, how do you evaluate the commission's actual use of the method of judgment it chose?
3. Can you imagine how a member of the commission might have dissented from its judgment? Here is part of what Professor Buchanan (a commission member) said in his dissent:

   "It is with great regret after the long journey with my colleagues that I find I disagree with their choice of site though not with their forecast of the timing of the need. I believe it would be nothing less than an environmental disaster if the airport were to be built at any of the inland sites, but nowhere more serious than at Cublington where it would lie athwart the critically important belt of open country between London and Birmingham. I have reservations about the cost/benefit analysis and the resulting conclusion that Foulness must be ruled out on economic grounds. From the point of view of national airports policy (which I have found impossible to exclude from my considerations) I believe there is a good case for building the new airport at Foulness in order to provide a better balanced service for Greater London rather than to build it at Cublington where it would inhibit the development of a satisfactory policy for the central regions of Britain. Finally I consider that the development of Foulness would play a vital role in reducing the social imbalances between the eastern and western sides of London, and that no other site has the capability to advance any major social objective. So it is my conclusion that Foulness, in spite of certain undoubted environmental disadvantages, is the best site in the interests of the country as a whole. . . .

"The second confirmatory argument for Foulness springs from the point which I have already touched upon, namely the possibility of using the airport as a means of promoting equality of wealth and opportunity. Looking at the present case from this angle I can see absolutely no convincing reasons for locating the airport at Cublington or indeed at Thurleigh. There are no pressing social or economic problems in these areas that desperately need the airport for their solution, if anything the very reverse is true. On the other hand the location of the airport at Foulness could, in my view, make a powerful contribution to one of the biggest social problems in the country, namely that of east London. It is unnecessary for me to describe at length the historical reasons why London should have developed in the socially lopsided manner that it has done. Suffice it to say that from the moment when the growth provoked by the industrial revolution started in earnest, and when, as a consequence, the wealthier people began to move out from the deteriorating residential environment of the innermost areas, there was a marked tendency for these people to move westwards rather than eastwards. The process resulted, by the beginning of the present century, in a metropolis with a marked polarity: the West End and the East End, corresponding closely to pronounced differences in social status, wealth, housing standards and expectations. Not much has happened since then to change the situation." Report, supra, at 149, 157.

4. If you had been a member of the commission, do you think that you would have agreed with the majority or with Professor Buchanan? Or would you need more information before you could say with certainty what your view would have been? (If so, explain what information you would need, why you would need it, and how you might get it.)
5. If not by the cost/benefit technique actually used, how do you think the commission should have gone about making its recommendation? How would you explain and justify the process you propose?
   a. To start with, what would be your goal: a rational decision, a fair decision, a wise decision, or what? And what do you mean by whatever term you use to characterize it?
   b. How would you know when that goal had been attained?
   c. Suppose you are a member of a legislature that establishes such a commission. What directions to its judgment would you propose that the legislature issue?
6. One of the questions raised by this series of readings is how to talk about the experience of thought and judgment. Does the following passage about language and the mind suggest new possibilities to you?

THE RELATION OF HABITUAL THOUGHT AND BEHAVIOR TO LANGUAGE (1941)*

B. L. Whorf

[Whorf here speaks of the tendency of European languages to speak of intangibles — of ideas, feelings, thoughts — by the metaphorical use of terms whose first meaning is something tangible, physical, real.]

* In *Language, Thought, and Reality* 156–157 (1956).

Much of [this] metaphorical reference to the nonspatial by the spatial was already fixed in the ancient tongues, and more especially in Latin. It is indeed a marked trait of Latin. If we compare, say Hebrew, we find that, while Hebrew has some allusion to not-space as space, Latin has more. Latin terms for nonspatials, like *educo, religio, principia, comprehendo,* are usually metaphorized physical references: lead out, tying back, etc. This is not true of all languages — it is quite untrue of Hopi. The fact that in Latin the direction of development happened to be from spatial to nonspatial (partly because of secondary stimulation to abstract thinking when the intellectually crude Romans encountered Greek culture) and that later tongues were strongly stimulated to mimic Latin, seems a likely reason for a belief, which still lingers on among linguists, that this is the natural direction of semantic change in all languages, and for the persistent notion in Western learned circles (in strong contrast to Eastern ones) that objective experience is prior to subjective. Philosophies make out a weighty case for the reverse, and certainly the direction of development is sometimes the reverse. Thus the Hopi word for "heart" can be shown to be a late formation within Hopi from a root meaning think or remember. Or consider what has happened to the word "radio" in such a sentence as "he bought a new radio," as compared to its prior meaning "science of wireless telephony."

QUESTIONS

1. *Go to a dictionary and see if you can discover the metaphorical roots of the "abstract" terms used to describe and evaluate judicial opinions in your law classes. E.g.: analyze, consider, understand, decide, idea, rules, principles, standards, interests, evaluate. Is all language always metaphorical?*
2. *What do you suppose life was like when an abstract language was first being made up out of a language of physical description? Think, for example, of Plato's definition of justice in The Republic or of love in The Symposium. See J. Lyons, Structural Semantics: An Analysis of Part of the Vocabulary of Plato* (1967).
3. *Can you imagine how different your life would be if the physical world were generally described in terms whose first use was to express or define thoughts and feelings? If there were a direct and nonmetaphorical language of rationality, judgment, and education?*

d. The Language of Judicial Rationality: Two Examples

RATIONALITY IN JUDICIAL DECISIONS*

P. Freund

Some general observations on rationality may tentatively emerge from a study of the judicial process. Rational thinking is to be understood in

* In *On Law and Justice* 78–81 (1968).

the context of an activity or set of practices; relevance and bias are meaningful in that context; and this is true also of creativity. Rational thinking involves respect for roles, not only for the place of a given discipline in society but for the allocation of functions within the discipline.

It has been said (in Paul Diesing's study, *Reason in Society*)[14] that the concept of practical reason has taken one or another of three forms among philosophers from Plato onward: creativity (Plato, Hegel, Whitehead); the discovery and application of rules (natural-law theorists); calculation (Hobbes, the utilitarians). The judicial process, at least, suggests that these are interacting and to a degree interfused.

Sinclair Refining Co. v. Atkinson,[15] decided by the Supreme Court of the United States in 1962, is an interesting and not atypical case presenting problems of rationality in decision-making that may illuminate the meaning and relation of creativity, the application of rules, and calculation.

The facts were not in dispute for purposes of the case. The company and a union of its employees entered into a collective bargaining agreement which provided for arbitration of grievances and renounced strikes or slowdowns over any causes that were arbitrable. In violation of the agreement the union repeatedly engaged in work stoppages on account of arbitrable grievances and did not resort to the arbitration procedure. The company brought suit in a federal court to enjoin such work stoppages. For its defense the union relied on the Norris-LaGuardia Act of 1932, section 7 of which prohibits the federal courts from issuing injunctions against concerted nonviolent activity by a union growing out of a labor dispute.

If this were all, it might appear that the course of decision is plain; that the rule of the Norris-LaGuardia Act compels the Court to refuse an injunction. The "rule" is clear; it need not be extracted from decisions, it is actually codified; and it is not of convenient vagueness like standards ("due process" or "prudent investment") or principles ("no one may profit by his own wrong at the expense of another"). And yet this result might well cause disquiet. Does the Act really fetter the courts in enforcing the obligations of a collective agreement? The background of the Act was a history of federal courts' intervention to restrain strikes and picketing in an era before rights of union organization and bargaining were secured; injunctions served to intensify the inferior position of workers and caused widespread hostility and disrespect on the part of labor toward law and courts. So viewed, would not an application of the Act in the circumstances of the present case be

14. P[age] 224 (1962).
15. 370 U.S. 195.

perverse? Already the neatness of "applying a rule" is becoming blurred. The calculation of consequences and the investigation of purposes suggest the possibility, at least, that the rule is more complex than it seems. Any reformulation must not do violence to the potentialities of the language used; but the term "labor dispute" may be sufficiently protean to exclude cases where there is a breach of an arbitration agreement and of a no-strike clause. Whether this would involve too much creativity on the part of judges is the resulting question. If this were the whole case, the Justices might well have concluded unanimously that on balance this degree of creativity should be left to Congress.

But that was not the whole case. Other data were at hand that bore some relevance to the process of decision. In 1934, without amending the Norris-LaGuardia Act, Congress provided in the Railway Labor Act for compulsory arbitration of certain disputes, and the Court thereafter held that despite Norris-LaGuardia an injunction could be issued against a strike called in violation of the later statutory plan. At this point in the analysis, the present Court might rationally have (a) overruled the railway labor decision as an excess of judicial law making; (b) followed it as a precedent where, as here, a plan of arbitration (though here voluntarily adopted) was in force; or (c) distinguished it as apposite only to a legislative scheme of arbitration. The "rule" of the precedent might have been either (b) or (c), depending on the emphasis placed on the factor of legislative intervention.

But there was in fact additional legislative intervention in the background. In 1947, the Taft-Hartley Act conferred authority on the federal courts to entertain suits for the violation of contracts between employers and employees. This provision, the Court had held, authorized mandatory orders compelling a union or an employer to submit a dispute to arbitration. But did it authorize the kind of negative injunction forbidden generally by the Norris-LaGuardia Act? Now, obviously, the decision could not even in form be rested on "application of a rule." There was at least another coordinate rule to be taken into account, that of the 1947 Act.

In the actual decision, the Court divided. The majority opinion was written by Justice Black, who had been a member of the Senate when the Norris-LaGuardia Act was passed in 1932. The dissent, joined in by Justices Douglas and Harlan, was written by Justice Brennan, who had extensive experience in labor law before going on the bench.

The difference in approach of the two groups loses its significance if it is looked at simply as a difference in the application of a rule. Justice Black took the Norris-LaGuardia Act as the primary datum; held the railway cases inapposite; and stressed what would be the legislative character of a repeal of section 7, which Congress had declined to do.

The calculation of consequences was for Congress; in any event they were not too serious, since an action for damages and a mandatory order to arbitrate were still available. Justice Brennan took as his primary datum a pattern of legislation, and asked not whether the earlier provision had been repealed but whether it could be "accommodated" with the later legislation. This he did because the consequences of the Norris-LaGuardia Act on the beneficent practices of arbitration agreements he regarded as deeply upsetting. And so he essayed a more creative role, seeking to find connections and reconciliation between otherwise discrete legislative provisions, converting inharmonious rules, if you will, into a more refined and comprehensive principle whose touchstone would be the promotion and safeguarding of collective bargaining. This he attempted to achieve by regarding the Norris-LaGuardia Act as a non-rigid direction, to be followed generally but not in the special circumstances of a case falling within the fostering policy of the later Act.

It is not important here to appraise the two opinions in their outcomes. What is of interest, I believe, is the fusion in actual practice of the types of rationality classically described as rule-application, creativity, and calculation. In that fusion each element, while not losing its distinctiveness, takes on some of the qualities of the others. That this is psychologically true, it may be argued, does not establish that it is logically valid or philosophically useful; perhaps the psychological impurities ought to be burned away in the interest of clear and distinct ideas. It is really, I suggest, a matter of pragmatic emphasis: which aspect, the distinctiveness of the types of rationality or their interaction, is it more useful to stress. I can only say that I believe the interaction to be not merely a valid description but a process the receptive awareness of which can enrich the resourcefulness and fruitfulness of the judicial process.[4]

QUESTIONS

1. *Professor Freund's account of judicial rationality is plainly meant to be suggestive, not exhaustive. How would you go on from where he left off? Are there matters here with which you disagree?*
2. *You can see that the writer here describes two ways of deciding a case, and explains the rationality of each; but he does not tell us which he would prefer and why. How would this passage be different if its subject were judicial rightness rather than judicial rationality?*
3. *What metaphors are at work in the following analysis of judicial rationality, and what are their implications? Does this passage define judicial excellence for you?*

4. You may be interested to know that *Sinclair* was overruled by *Boys Markets, Inc. v. Retail Clerks Local* 770, 398 U.S. 235 (1970).

THE NATURE OF THE JUDICIAL PROCESS*

B. Cardozo

My analysis of the judicial process comes then to this, and little more: logic, and history, and custom, and utility, and the accepted standards of right conduct, are the forces which singly or in combination shape the progress of the law. Which of these forces shall dominate in any case must depend largely upon the comparative importance or value of the social interests that will be thereby promoted or impaired. One of the most fundamental social interests is that law shall be uniform and impartial. There must be nothing in its action that savors of prejudice or favor or even arbitrary whim or fitfulness. Therefore in the main there shall be adherence to precedent. There shall be symmetrical development, consistently with history or custom when history or custom has been the motive force, or the chief one, in giving shape to existing rules, and with logic or philosophy when the motive power has been theirs. But symmetrical development may be bought at too high a price. Uniformity ceases to be a good when it becomes uniformity of oppression. The social interest served by symmetry or certainty must then be balanced against the social interest served by equity and fairness or other elements of social welfare. These may enjoin upon the judge the duty of drawing the line at another angle, of staking the path along new courses, of marking a new point of departure from which others who come after him will set out upon their journey.

If you ask how he is to know when one interest outweighs another, I can only answer that he must get his knowledge just as the legislator gets it, from experience and study and reflection; in brief, from life itself. Here, indeed, is the point of contact between the legislator's work and his. The choice of methods, the appraisement of values, must in the end be guided by like considerations for the one as for the other. Each indeed is legislating within the limits of his competence. No doubt the limits for the judge are narrower. He legislates only between gaps. He fills the open spaces in the law. How far he may go without traveling beyond the walls of the interstices cannot be staked out for him upon a chart. He must learn it for himself as he gains the sense of fitness and proportion that comes with years of habitude in the practice of an art. Even within the gaps, restrictions not easy to define, but felt, however impalpable they may be, by every judge and lawyer, hedge and circumscribe his action. They are established by the traditions of the centuries, by the example of other judges, his predecessors and his colleagues, by

* Pages 112–114 (1921).

the collective judgment of the profession, and by the duty of adherence to the pervading spirit of the law.

2. *An Example for Analysis: Griswold v. Connecticut*

As a way of giving you the opportunity to work out for yourself a way of describing and evaluating what a good judge does, we shall here examine the opinions in *Griswold v. Connecticut*. Perhaps your first step should be to inspect the responses you are initially tempted to make as you read these opinions, for this should be good evidence of the sort of education you have so far received. How do your tentative statements of approval and disapproval define judicial excellence and the opposite? How adequate is the language or system of judicial criticism that they exemplify? How do they define you as a law student and judicial critic? Next try to work out a mature judgment of these opinions, one with which you would now be satisfied, expressing the views not of the teachers and writers you have been encouraged to emulate, but of yourself. As you make your way to such a judgment, how do you find yourself elaborating your account of what the judge does and complicating your language for criticizing it? What is the place of rationality in your language of judgment, and what (if anything) do you require of a good opinion beyond that? Do you find yourself speaking directly or in metaphors, and in either case how does your language, your writing, define the activities of judgment and criticism with which you are concerned?

GRISWOLD v. CONNECTICUT
381 U.S. 479 (1965)

DOUGLAS, J., delivered the opinion of the Court. Appellant Griswold is Executive Director of the Planned Parenthood League of Connecticut. Appellant Buxton is a licensed physician and a professor at the Yale Medical School who served as Medical Director for the League at its Center in New Haven — a center open and operating from November 1 to November 10, 1961, when appellants were arrested.

They gave information, instruction, and medical advice to *married persons* as to the means of preventing conception. They examined the wife and prescribed the best contraceptive device or material for her use. Fees were usually charged, although some couples were serviced free.

The statutes whose constitutionality is involved in this appeal are §§53-32 and 54-196 of the General Statutes of Connecticut (1958 rev.). The former provides: "Any person who uses any drug, medicinal article or instrument for the purpose of preventing conception shall be fined not less than fifty dollars or imprisoned not less than sixty days nor more than one year or be both fined and imprisoned."

Section 54-196 provides: "Any person who assists, abets, counsels, causes, hires or commands another to commit any offense may be prosecuted and punished as if he were the principal offender."

The appellants were found guilty as accessories and fined $100 each, against the claim that the accessory statute as so applied violated the Fourteenth Amendment. The Appellate Division of the Circuit Court affirmed. The Supreme Court of Errors affirmed that judgment. 151 Conn. 544, 200 A.2d 479. We noted probable jurisdiction. 379 U.S. 926.

We think that appellants have standing to raise the constitutional rights of the married people with whom they had a professional relationship. *Tileston v. Ullman*, 318 U.S. 44, is different, for there the plaintiff seeking to represent others asked for a declaratory judgment. In that situation we thought that the requirements of standing should be strict, lest the standards of "case or controversy" in Article III of the Constitution become blurred. Here those doubts are removed by reason of a criminal conviction for serving married couples in violation of an aiding-and-abetting statute. Certainly the accessory should have standing to assert that the offense which he is charged with assisting is not, or cannot constitutionally be, a crime.

This case is more akin to *Truax v. Raich*, 239 U.S. 33, where an employee was permitted to assert the rights of his employer; to *Pierce v. Society of Sisters*, 268 U.S. 510, where the owners of private schools were entitled to assert the rights of potential pupils and their parents; and to *Barrows v. Jackson*, 346 U.S. 249, where a white defendant, party to a racially restrictive covenant, who was being sued for damages by the covenantors because she had conveyed her property to Negroes, was allowed to raise the issue that enforcement of the covenant violated the rights of prospective Negro purchasers to equal protection, although no Negro was a party to the suit. And see *Meyer v. Nebraska*, 262 U.S. 390; *Adler v. Board of Education*, 342 U.S. 485; *NAACP v. Alabama*, 357 U.S. 449; *NAACP v. Button*, 371 U.S. 415. The rights of husband and wife, pressed here, are likely to be diluted or adversely affected unless those rights are considered in a suit involving those who have this kind of confidential relation to them.

Coming to the merits, we are met with a wide range of questions that implicate the Due Process Clause of the Fourteenth Amendment. Overtones of some arguments suggest that *Lochner v. New York*, 198 U.S. 45, should be our guide. But we decline that invitation as we did in *West Coast Hotel Co. v. Parrish*, 300 U.S. 379; *Olsen v. Nebraska*, 313 U.S. 236; *Lincoln Union v. Northwestern Co.*, 335 U.S. 525; *William-*

son v. Lee Optical Co., 348 U.S. 483; *Giboney v. Empire Storage Co.*, 336 U.S. 490. We do not sit as a super-legislature to determine the wisdom, need, and propriety of laws that touch economic problems, business affairs, or social conditions. This law, however, operates directly on an intimate relation of husband and wife and their physician's role in one aspect of that relation.

The association of people is not mentioned in the Constitution nor in the Bill of Rights. The right to educate a child in a school of the parents' choice — whether public or private or parochial — is also not mentioned. Nor is the right to study any particular subject or any foreign language. Yet the First Amendment has been construed to include certain of those rights.

By *Pierce v. Society of Sisters, supra*, the right to educate one's children as one chooses is made applicable to the States by the force of the First and Fourteenth Amendments. By *Meyer v. Nebraska, supra*, the same dignity is given the right to study the German language in a private school. In other words, the State may not, consistently with the spirit of the First Amendment, contract the spectrum of available knowledge. The right of freedom of speech and press includes not only the right to utter or to print, but the right to distribute, the right to receive, the right to read (*Martin v. Struthers*, 319 U.S. 141, 143) and freedom of inquiry, freedom of thought, and freedom to teach (see *Wieman v. Updegraff*, 344 U.S. 183, 195) — indeed the freedom of the entire university community. *Sweezy v. New Hampshire*, 354 U.S. 234, 249-250, 261-263; *Barenblatt v. United States*, 360 U.S. 109, 112; *Baggett v. Bullitt*, 377 U.S. 360, 369. Without those peripheral rights the specific rights would be less secure. And so we reaffirm the principle of the *Pierce* and the *Meyer* cases.

In *NAACP v. Alabama*, 357 U.S. 449, 462, we protected the "freedom to associate and privacy in one's associations," noting that freedom of association was a peripheral First Amendment right. Disclosure of membership lists of a constitutionally valid association, we held, was invalid "as entailing the likelihood of a substantial restraint upon the exercise by petitioner's members of their right to freedom of association." *Ibid.* In other words, the First Amendment has a penumbra where privacy is protected from governmental intrusion. In like context, we have protected forms of "association" that are not political in the customary sense but pertain to the social, legal, and economic benefit of the members. *NAACP v. Button*, 371 U.S. 415, 430-431. In *Schware v. Board of Bar Examiners*, 353 U.S. 232, we held it not permissible to bar a lawyer from practice, because he had once been a member of the Communist Party. The man's "association with that Party" was not shown to be "anything more than a political faith in a political party" (*id.*, at 244) and was not action of a kind proving bad moral character. *Id.*, at 245-246.

Those cases involved more than the "right of assembly" — a right that extends to all irrespective of their race or ideology. *De Jonge v. Oregon*, 299 U.S. 353. The right of "association," like the right of belief (*Board of Education v. Barnette*, 319 U.S. 624), is more than the right to attend a meeting; it includes the right to express one's attitudes or philosophies by membership in a group or by affiliation with it or by other lawful means. Association in that context is a form of expression of opinion; and while it is not expressly included in the First Amendment its existence is necessary in making the express guarantees fully meaningful.

The foregoing cases suggest that specific guarantees in the Bill of Rights have penumbras, formed by emanations from those guarantees that help give them life and substance. See *Poe v. Ullman*, 367 U.S. 497, 516-522 (dissenting opinion). Various guarantees create zones of privacy. The right of association contained in the penumbra of the First Amendment is one, as we have seen. The Third Amendment in its prohibition against the quartering of soldiers "in any house" in time of peace without the consent of the owner is another facet of that privacy. The Fourth Amendment explicitly affirms the "right of the people to be secure in their persons, houses, papers, and effects, against unreasonable searches and seizures." The Fifth Amendment in its Self-Incrimination Clause enables the citizen to create a zone of privacy which government may not force him to surrender to his detriment. The Ninth Amendment provides: "The enumeration in the Constitution, of certain rights, shall not be construed to deny or disparage others retained by the people."

The Fourth and Fifth Amendments were described in *Boyd v. United States*, 116 U.S. 616, 630, as protection against all governmental invasions "of the sanctity of a man's home and the privacies of life."* We

* The Court said in full about this right of privacy:

"The principles laid down in this opinion [by Lord Camden in *Entick v. Carrington*, 19 How. St. Tr. 1029] affect the very essence of constitutional liberty and security. They reach farther than the concrete form of the case then before the court, with its adventitious circumstances; they apply to all invasions on the part of the government and its employes of the sanctity of a man's home and the privacies of life. It is not the breaking of his doors, and the rummaging of his drawers, that constitutes the essence of the offence; but it is the invasion of his indefeasible right of personal security, personal liberty and private property, where that right has never been forfeited by his conviction of some public offence, — it is the invasion of this sacred right which underlies and constitutes the essence of Lord Camden's judgment. Breaking into a house and opening boxes and drawers are circumstances of aggravation; but any forcible and compulsory extortion of a man's testimony or of his private papers to be used as evidence to convict him of crime or to forfeit his goods, is within the condemnation of that judgment. In this regard the Fourth and Fifth Amendments run almost into each other." 116 U.S., at 630.

recently referred in *Mapp v. Ohio,* 367 U.S. 643, 656, to the Fourth Amendment as creating a "right to privacy, no less important than any other right carefully and particularly reserved to the people." See Beaney, The Constitutional Right to Privacy, 1962 Sup. Ct. Rev. 212; Griswold, The Right to be Let Alone, 55 Nw. U.L. Rev. 216 (1960).

We have had many controversies over these penumbral rights of "privacy and repose." See, e.g., *Breard v. Alexandria,* 341 U.S. 622, 626, 644; *Public Utilities Comm'n v. Pollak,* 343 U.S. 451; *Monroe v. Pape,* 365 U.S. 167; *Lanza v. New York,* 370 U.S. 139; *Frank v. Maryland,* 359 U.S. 360; *Skinner v. Oklahoma,* 316 U.S. 535, 541. These cases bear witness that the right of privacy which presses for recognition here is a legitimate one.

The present case, then, concerns a relationship lying within the zone of privacy created by several fundamental constitutional guarantees. And it concerns a law which, in forbidding the *use* of contraceptives rather than regulating their manufacture or sale, seeks to achieve its goals by means having a maximum destructive impact upon that relationship. Such a law cannot stand in light of the familiar principle, so often applied by this Court, that a "governmental purpose to control or prevent activities constitutionally subject to state regulation may not be achieved by means which sweep unnecessarily broadly and thereby invade the area of protected freedoms." *NAACP v. Alabama,* 377 U.S. 288, 307. Would we allow the police to search the sacred precincts of marital bedrooms for telltale signs of the use of contraceptives? The very idea is repulsive to the notions of privacy surrounding the marriage relationship.

We deal with a right of privacy older than the Bill of Rights — older than our political parties, older than our school system. Marriage is a coming together for better or for worse, hopefully enduring, and intimate to the degree of being sacred. It is an association that promotes a way of life, not causes; a harmony in living, not political faiths; a bilateral loyalty, not commercial or social projects. Yet it is an association for as noble a purpose as any involved in our prior decisions.

Reversed.

GOLDBERG, J., whom the CHIEF JUSTICE and BRENNAN, J., join, concurring. I agree with the Court that Connecticut's birth-control law unconstitutionally intrudes upon the right of marital privacy, and I join in its opinion and judgment. . . .

This Court, in a series of decisions, has held that the Fourteenth Amendment absorbs and applies to the States those specifics of the first eight amendments which express fundamental personal rights. The language and history of the Ninth Amendment reveal that the Framers of the Constitution believed that there are additional fundamental rights, protected from governmental infringement, which exist alongside those fundamental rights specifically mentioned in the first eight constitutional amendments.

The Ninth Amendment reads, "The enumeration in the Constitution, of certain rights, shall not be construed to deny or disparage others retained by the people." . . .

. . . To hold that a right so basic and fundamental and so deep-rooted in our society as the right of privacy in marriage may be infringed because that right is not guaranteed in so many words by the first eight amendments to the Constitution is to ignore the Ninth Amendment and to give it no effect whatsoever. Moreover, a judicial construction that this fundamental right is not protected by the Constitution because it is not mentioned in explicit terms by one of the first eight amendments or elsewhere in the Constitution would violate the Ninth Amendment, which specifically states that "[t]he enumeration in the Constitution, of certain rights, shall not be *construed* to deny or disparage others retained by the people." (Emphasis added.)

HARLAN, J., concurrring in the judgment. I fully agree with the judgment of reversal, but find myself unable to join the Court's opinion. . . .

In my view, the proper constitutional inquiry in this case is whether this Connecticut statute infringes the Due Process Clause of the Fourteenth Amendment because the enactment violates basic values "implicit in the concept of ordered liberty," *Palko v. Connecticut*, 302 U.S. 319, 325. For reasons stated at length in my dissenting opinion in *Poe v. Ullman, supra,* I believe that it does.[5] While the relevant inquiry may be aided by resort to one or more of the provisions of the Bill of Rights, it is not dependent on them or any of their radiations. The Due Process Clause of the Fourteenth Amendment stands, in my opinion, on its own bottom.

Judicial self-restraint will not, I suggest, be brought about in the "due process" area by the historically unfounded incorporation formula long advanced by my Brother Black, and now in part espoused by my Brother Stewart. It will be achieved in this area, as in other constitutional areas, only by continual insistence upon respect for the teachings of history, solid recognition of the basic values that underlie our society, and wise appreciation of the great roles that the doctrines of federalism and separation of powers have played in establishing and preserving American freedoms.

WHITE, J., concurring in the judgment. In my view this Connecticut law as applied to married couples deprives them of "liberty" without due

5. You are urged to examine Justice Harlan's most impressive opinion in that case. — ED.

process of law, as that concept is used in the Fourteenth Amendment. I therefore concur in the judgment of the Court reversing these convictions under Connecticut's aiding and abetting statute.

It would be unduly repetitious, and belaboring the obvious, to expound on the impact of this statute on the liberty guaranteed by the Fourteenth Amendment against arbitrary or capricious denials or on the nature of this liberty. Suffice it to say that this is not the first time this Court has had occasion to articulate that the liberty entitled to protection under the Fourteenth Amendment includes the right "to marry, establish a home and bring up children," *Meyer v. Nebraska*, 262 U.S. 390, 399, and "the liberty . . . to direct the upbringing and education of children," *Pierce v. Society of Sisters*, 268 U.S. 510, 534-535, and that these are among "the basic civil rights of man." *Skinner v. Oklahoma*, 316 U.S. 535, 541. These decisions affirm that there is a "realm of family life which the state cannot enter" without substantial justification. *Prince v. Massachusetts*, 321 U.S. 158, 166. Surely the right invoked in this case, to be free of regulation of the intimacies of the marriage relationship, "come[s] to this Court with a momentum for respect lacking when appeal is made to liberties which derive merely from shifting economic arrangements." *Kovacs v. Cooper*, 336 U.S. 77, 95 (opinion of Frankfurter, J.).

The Connecticut anti-contraceptive statute deals rather substantially with this relationship. For it forbids all married persons the right to use birth-control devices, regardless of whether their use is dictated by considerations of family planning, *Trubeck v. Ullman*, 147 Conn. 633, 165 A.2d 158, health, or indeed even of life itself. *Buxton v. Ullman*, 147 Conn. 48, 156 A.2d 508. The anti-use statute, together with the general aiding and abetting statute, prohibits doctors from affording advice to married persons on proper and effective methods of birth control. *Tileston v. Ullman*, 129 Conn. 84, 26 A.2d 582. And the clear effect of these statutes, as enforced, is to deny disadvantaged citizens of Connecticut, those without either adequate knowledge or resources to obtain private counseling, access to medical assistance and up-to-date information in respect to proper methods of birth control. *State v. Nelson*, 126 Conn. 412, 11 A.2d 856; *State v. Griswold*, 151 Conn. 544, 200 A.2d 479. In my view, a statute with these effects bears a substantial burden of justification when attacked under the Fourteenth Amendment. *Yick Wo v. Hopkins*, 118 U.S. 356; *Skinner v. Oklahoma*, 316 U.S. 535; *Schware v. Board of Bar Examiners*, 353 U.S. 232; *McLaughlin v. Florida*, 379 U.S. 184, 192.

An examination of the justification offered, however, cannot be avoided by saying that the Connecticut anti-use statute invades a protected area of privacy and association or that it demeans the marriage relationship. The nature of the right invaded is pertinent, to be sure, for statutes regulating sensitive areas of liberty do, under the cases of this Court, require "strict scrutiny," *Skinner v. Oklahoma,* 316 U.S. 535, 541, and "must be viewed in the light of less drastic means for achieving the same basic purpose." *Shelton v. Tucker,* 364 U.S. 479, 488. "Where there is a significant encroachment upon personal liberty, the State may prevail only upon showing a subordinating interest which is compelling." *Bates v. Little Rock,* 361 U.S. 516, 524. See also *McLaughlin v. Florida,* 379 U.S. 184. But such statutes, if reasonably necessary for the effectuation of a legitimate and substantial state interest, and not arbitrary or capricious in application, are not invalid under the Due Process Clause. *Zemel v. Rusk,* 381 U.S. 1.*

As I read the opinions of the Connecticut courts and the argument of Connecticut in this Court, the State claims but one justification for its anti-use statute. Cf. *Allied Stores of Ohio v. Bowers,* 358 U.S. 522, 530; *Martin v. Walton,* 368 U.S. 25, 28 (Douglas, J., dissenting). There is no serious contention that Connecticut thinks the use of artificial or external methods of contraception immoral or unwise in itself, or that the anti-use statute is founded upon any policy of promoting population expansion. Rather, the statute is said to serve the State's policy against all forms of promiscuous or illicit sexual relationships, be they premari-

* Dissenting opinions assert that the liberty guaranteed by the Due Process Clause is limited to a guarantee against unduly vague statutes and against procedural unfairness at trial. Under this view the Court is without authority to ascertain whether a challenged statute, or its application, has a permissible purpose and whether the manner of regulation bears a rational or justifying relationship to this purpose. A long line of cases makes very clear that this has not been the view of this Court. *Dent v. West Virginia,* 129 U.S. 114; *Jacobson v. Massachusetts,* 197 U.S. 11; *Douglas v. Noble,* 261 U.S. 165; *Meyer v. Nebraska,* 262 U.S. 390; *Pierce v. Society of Sisters,* 268 U.S. 510; *Schware v. Board of Bar Examiners,* 353 U.S. 232; *Aptheker v. Secretary of State,* 378 U.S. 500; *Zemel v. Rusk,* 381 U.S. 1.

The traditional due process test was well articulated, and applied, in *Schware v. Board of Bar Examiners, supra,* a case which placed no reliance on the specific guarantees of the Bill of Rights.

"A State cannot exclude a person from the practice of law or from any other occupation in a manner or for reasons that contravene the Due Process or Equal Protection Clause of the Fourteenth Amendment. *Dent v. West Virginia,* 129 U.S. 114. Cf. *Slochower v. Board of Education,* 350 U.S. 551; *Wieman v. Updegraff,* 344 U.S. 183. And see *Ex parte Secombe,* 19 How. 9, 13. A State can require high standards of qualification, such as good moral character or proficiency in its law, before it admits an applicant to the bar, but any qualification must have a rational connection with the applicant's fitness or capacity to practice law. *Douglas v. Noble,* 261 U.S. 165; *Cummings v. Missouri,* 4 Wall. 277, 319–320. Cf. *Nebbia v. New York,* 291 U.S. 502. Obviously an applicant could not be excluded merely because he was a Republican or a Negro or a member of a particular church. Even in applying permissible standards, officers of a State cannot exclude an applicant when there is no basis for their finding that he fails to meet these standards, or when their action is invidiously discriminatory." 353 U.S., at 238–239. Cf. *Martin v. Walton,* 368 U.S. 25, 26 (Douglas, J., dissenting).

tal or extramarital, concededly a permissible and legitimate legislative goal.

Without taking issue with the premise that the fear of conception operates as a deterrent to such relationships in addition to the criminal proscriptions Connecticut has against such conduct, I wholly fail to see how the ban on the use of contraceptives by married couples in any way reinforces the State's ban on illicit sexual relationships. See *Schware v. Board of Bar Examiners*, 353 U.S. 232, 239. Connecticut does not bar the importation or possession of contraceptive devices; they are not considered contraband material under state law, *State v. Certain Contraceptive Materials*, 126 Conn. 428, 11 A.2d 863, and their availability in that State is not seriously disputed. The only way Connecticut seeks to limit or control the availability of such devices is through its general aiding and abetting statute whose operation in this context has been quite obviously ineffective and whose most serious use has been against birth-control clinics rendering advice to married, rather than unmarried, persons. Cf. *Yick Wo v. Hopkins*, 118 U.S. 356. Indeed, after over 80 years of the State's proscription of use, the legality of the sale of such devices to prevent disease has never been expressly passed upon, although it appears that sales have long occurred and have only infrequently been challenged. This "undeviating policy . . . throughout all the long years . . . bespeaks more than prosecutorial paralysis." *Poe v. Ullman*, 367 U.S. 497, 502. Moreover, it would appear that the sale of contraceptives to prevent disease is plainly legal under Connecticut law.

In these circumstances one is rather hard pressed to explain how the ban on use by married persons in any way prevents use of such devices by persons engaging in illicit sexual relations and thereby contributes to the State's policy against such relationships. Neither the state courts nor the State before the bar of this Court has tendered such an explanation. It is purely fanciful to believe that the broad proscription on use facilitates discovery of use by persons engaging in a prohibited relationship or for some other reason makes such use more unlikely and thus can be supported by any sort of administrative consideration. Perhaps the theory is that the flat ban on use prevents married people from possessing contraceptives and without the ready availability of such devices for use in the marital relationship, there will be no or less temptation to use them in extramarital ones. This reasoning rests on the premise that married people will comply with the ban in regard to their marital relationship, notwithstanding total nonenforcement in this context and apparent nonenforcibility, but will not comply with criminal statutes prohibiting extramarital affairs and the anti-use statute in respect to illicit sexual relationships, a premise whose validity has not been demonstrated and whose intrinsic validity is not very evident. At most the broad ban is of marginal utility to the declared objective. A statute limiting its prohibition on use to persons engaging in the prohibited relationship would serve the end posited by Connecticut in the same way, and with the same effectiveness, or ineffectiveness, as the broad anti-use statute under attack in this case. I find nothing in this record justifying the sweeping scope of this statute, with its telling effect on the freedoms of married persons, and therefore conclude that it deprives such persons of liberty without due process of law.

BLACK, J., with whom STEWART, J., joins, dissenting. I agree with my Brother Stewart's dissenting opinion. And like him I do not to any extent whatever base my view that this Connecticut law is constitutional on a belief that the law is wise or that its policy is a good one. In order that there may be no room at all to doubt why I vote as I do, I feel constrained to add that the law is every bit as offensive to me as it is to my Brethren of the majority and my Brothers Harlan, White and Goldberg who, reciting reasons why it is offensive to them, hold it unconstitutional. There is no single one of the graphic and eloquent strictures and criticisms fired at the policy of this Connecticut law either by the Court's opinion or by those of my concurring Brethren to which I cannot subscribe — except their conclusion that the evil qualities they see in the law make it unconstitutional.

The Court talks about a constitutional "right of privacy" as though there is some constitutional provision or provisions forbidding any law ever to be passed which might abridge the "privacy" of individuals. But there is not. There are, of course, guarantees in certain specific constitutional provisions which are designed in part to protect privacy at certain times and places with respect to certain activities. Such, for example, is the Fourth Amendment's guarantee against "unreasonable searches and seizures."

I repeat so as not to be misunderstood that this Court does have power, which it should exercise, to hold laws unconstitutional where they are forbidden by the Federal Constitution. . . . So far as I am concerned, Connecticut's law as applied here is not forbidden by any provision of the Federal Constitution as that Constitution was written, and I would therefore affirm.

STEWART, J., whom BLACK, J., joins, dissenting. Since 1879 Connecticut has had on its books a law which forbids the use of contraceptives by anyone. I think this is an uncommonly silly law. As a practical matter, the law is obviously unenforceable, except in the oblique context of the present case. As a philosophical matter, I believe the use of contraceptives in the relationship of marriage should be left to personal and private choice, based upon each individual's moral, ethical, and religious beliefs. As a matter of social policy, I think professional counsel about methods of birth control should be available to all, so that each individual's choice can be meaningfully made. But we are not asked in this case to say whether we think this law is unwise, or even asinine. We are asked to hold that it violates the United States Constitution. And that I cannot do. . . .

What provision of the Constitution, then, does make this state law invalid? The Court says it is the right of privacy "created by several fundamental constitutional guarantees." With all deference, I can find no such general right of privacy in the Bill of Rights, in any other part of the Constitution, or in any case ever before decided by this Court.

QUESTIONS

1. *How can you describe what you see these judges doing? What metaphors do you use, and what are their implications?*
2. *The possible responses to that question are numberless, and you are encouraged to make and pursue your own. But it may be of some help if we look at a very simple version of what the judge does, one with which you are familiar from your work in Chapter 2 and which – whatever its defects – I suppose no one would call false: "The judge states and resolves the issue according to the applicable principles of law."*
   a. *Make a list of all the ways you can see to state the issue in Griswold. Which of these would you employ as Justice of the United States Supreme Court?*
   b. *How, in what language, would you describe and defend the process by which you chose to state the issue that way?*
   c. *Based on these responses, how would you tell someone else – an innocent man suddenly made judge – to go about stating the issue in cases before him?*
   d. *What principles or standards of judicial criticism are implicit in what you have said? Is it rationality that you call for here – and if so, how defined – or is it something else?*
3. *Ask the same series of questions about the process by which you would define the critical terms of the rule or principle that is implicit in your statement of the issue. Is this a rational process or something else? Can intelligible directions be given to one engaged in it?*
4. *How would you yourself decide this case? What opinion would you write in justification and explanation? How would you describe what you have done?*
5. *What language of judgment and description have you employed in responding to these questions? What metaphors have you used, and what are their implications?*
6. *Now examine the language used by each Justice to explain why he favors one result or another: constitutional "guarantees" have "penumbras" formed by "emanations" that create "zones of privacy"; the Bill of Rights, or "some" of them, are, or are not, "incorporated" in the Fourteenth Amendment; the Bill of Rights "enumerates" specific rights, but the Ninth Amendment establishes "more"; it is not the Ninth Amendment but the due process clause that – does what? establishes*

rights? gives us certain (or uncertain) powers?; we must be careful to ensure that "basic" rights are not "diluted or expanded"; and Justice Stewart looks over the Bill of Rights and says "I can find nothing in them" to invalidate this law. You can, of course, find lots of other examples of the judicial mind expressed in this case.

   a. How do these languages define the judicial process? As a rational one?
   b. Why do the Justices and their bright young clerks not simply tell us what they are doing in plain and direct speech, instead of talking in these sloppy metaphors?

7. As you know, every case has a ratio decidendi, the principle for which it stands. See Goodhart, "Determining the Ratio Decidendi of a Case," 40 Yale L.J. 161 (1930). What is the ratio decidendi of Griswold? For a recent case where that question is relevant, see Eisenstadt v. Baird, 405 U.S. 438 (1972).
8. What are some traditional ways of describing the judicial opinion, and how adequate are they? Here are some possibilities:
   a. What is the traditional anatomy of a judicial opinion: "facts, holding, dictum"? Those terms are second nature to you now, but perhaps an effort of imagination will revive the difficulties you had when first asked to use them. Looking back, who seems more simpleminded: the lawyer who expertly uses these terms of art, or the first-semester student who reiterates his perplexity, claiming that he neither understands the terms nor can discern any intelligible purposes they can be meant to serve?
   b. One metaphor sometimes used in talking about judicial opinions is "completeness." The "perfect" opinion includes all "relevant" arguments and considerations. It is a logical whole. What is more, each argument or consideration must be given just the proper place and force: it is not enough to have all the pieces, they must be arranged properly. So what is it: a machine? A jigsaw puzzle?
   c. Exercise your imagination and think of some new metaphors to describe the perfect judicial opinion: a machine that turns raw experience into law? A translation from one kind of language to another? A picture of life that includes everything? A scientific analysis of material to discover its true elements? Be as extravagant as you can. What language of your own can you use to talk about the perfect judicial opinion?
9. The judicial opinion not only justifies a decision, it is meant to guide others in the future. How does the excellent judicial opinion do that? Is this where rationality comes in?
   a. Consistency and clarity are two radical principles of logic and, one sometimes thinks, of all discourse. Would you advise the new young judge always to be consistent, always to be clear? Why might one have difficulty doing that? What else should he be? Should a judicial opinion ever be inconsistent or unclear?
   b. Does this mean that the good opinion always has a clear and specific rule? How could anyone possibly think otherwise?
   c. Or is this what we demand of an opinion: not a clear rule that will tell us how future cases will be decided, but a full statement of the difficulties the court faced, which will tell us how we should argue — and how we should think — in future cases? What do you think a full and honest statement of a judge's difficulties would look like?

d. Is the difficulty that the effort to be clear and consistent involves an inherently false pretense, with the result that the judge can be clear and consistent only by being dishonest? Should the judge express some of his doubts but not all? How could you tell a judge to do that? What is the place of rationality in the language in which you speak to him?

e. A related question is how the judge should frame his holding: should he confine himself to the specifics of the case before him, or should he attempt to give his case wider significance? How should he make that judgment? You can find examples of both kinds; Griswold is a great example of judicial generalization, and here is an instance of the opposite sort of speech:

"We hold, therefore, that where, as here, the investigation is no longer a general inquiry into an unsolved crime but has begun to focus on a particular suspect, the suspect has been taken into police custody, the police carry out a process of interrogations that lends itself to eliciting incriminating statements, the suspect has requested and been denied an opportunity to consult with his lawyer, and the police have not effectively warned him of his absolute constitutional right to remain silent, the accused has been denied "the Assistance of Counsel" in violation of the Sixth Amendment to the Constitution as "made obligatory upon the States by the Fourteenth Amendment," Gideon v. Wainwright, 372 U.S., at 342, and that no statement elicited by the police during the interrogation may be used against him at a criminal trial." Escobedo v. Illinois, 378 U.S. 478 (1964).

How do you evaluate that statement of a holding? How do you compare it with those in Watts and Miranda (pages 596 and 603 supra)?

10. Think now of some opinions that have interested you, and actually go back and look at one or two. What gives them life and interest? How does a good judge make what he says important to his reader?

11. As you keep asking how the good judge goes about deciding the sorts of questions identified above, do you find yourself working out an ideal pattern or system of judgment, a model to which all judges should conform? To the extent that you do, how do you describe that pattern: in terms of rationality, or something different from or beyond that? What metaphors do you use, and what are their implications?

Is there a sense in which what you look for is not a pattern or system but the expression of the individual mind? In fact, is that one of the great strengths of our judicial system, that it is not yet a total bureaucracy, that behind every judgment is a single person who is responsible for it?

12. One way to approach the problem of explicating the judicial opinion is to ask what its structural tensions, its inherent uncertainties, are, for here may be a source of its life. I have suggested some tensions: between the general and the specific holding, between clarity and honesty, between the official and the individual mind, and so forth. What other such tensions can you find? There follows now a problem that explicates one such tension. Could you construct similar problems for the other tensions you identify?

PROBLEM: CHOICE OF FORM — INTEREST-BALANCING VERSUS RULES OF LAW

One essential task of the judicial mind, necessary to the statement of the issue in all cases to which no statute applies, is the articulation of the rule or principle upon which the result is to depend. Of course the same principle can be stated variously — very generally, very specifically; as a rule, as a set of criteria or factors — all in an attempt to say the "same thing," to express the same notion or idea. But, as you know, it is often the differences that are critical, the choice of form is often a choice of result. How then, when such are the consequences, is the court to go about formulating the principle or rule which it regards as decisive? What should guide or influence this judgment?

There are two fundamentally inconsistent pressures at work here: to build rules which can control and guide decisions, which will maintain the appearance or reality of a rule of law; and to recognize the imperfections of the rule as an instrument of justice by responding to the demands of the particular case for a just result, for a decision based upon what is at stake in the particular case. For example, you saw how judges, faced with the task of making sentencing judgments (upon which virtually no rules bear), struggle to assemble sets of criteria or factors (and in some cases to make rules) to govern these decisions. The history of equity tells the same story. The judicial mind abhors a vacuum, and immediately sets about filling it with rules. But from your first-year courses you also know that no body of rules is secure from change, that rules are perpetually being eroded away. It used to be the nearly universal thesis of law review comments that courts ought to abandon "conceptual thinking" determined by "history" and decide the cases upon an accurate assessment of the issues actually at stake.

The history of the law, then, shows two contrary tendencies: to build rules where there are none, and to tear down rules where there are. Where do these pressures come from: inside the law or outside it? How are they to be addressed and managed by the judge? And how, in what language, are you to talk about this process of judgment?

Here is your problem:

Harold and Wilma execute a separation agreement incident to their divorce, providing that Harold shall pay Wilma $500 per month "until her death or remarriage." Wilma goes through a ceremonial marriage with Jack, but that marriage is annulled. What right to alimony does Wilma have against Harold?[6]

6. This problem is based on a series of cases and questions in H. Clark, *Cases and Problems on Domestic Relations* 167–180 (1965).

1. Can you answer this question on the basis of the information given above? You could propose a rule that "an annulled marriage is a nullity" or that "to go through a ceremonial marriage, whether valid or invalid, is to remarry for the purpose of terminating support obligations" and in either case you would need no more facts, would you? Would you in fact choose one of these rules?

2. What other facts would be relevant and why? As you consider the following questions, ask in each instance how a decision that the answer is relevant would necessarily modify whichever of the rules proposed above appeals to you more. You are here perfecting an imperfect statement: how do you do so?

a. Why were Harold and Wilma divorced? (E.g., for his adultery, for hers, or for incompatibility?)

b. Why was the marriage of Jack and Wilma annulled? (E.g., for his impotence, her fraud, his insanity?)

c. How long did each marriage last?

d. Are there children of either union?

e. How rich is each person?

f. When their marriage was annulled, did Wilma have a legal right to demand alimony? Did she do so?

g. Can she practically enforce such a right at this time?

h. How has Harold responded to his apparent freedom from obligation to Wilma: has he remarried, or perhaps quit his job and moved away? Or is everything much as it was?

i. Did the separation agreement govern property as well as alimony? Was it incorporated into the decree?

You can see here the two pressures at work — the desire to decide by a rule, and the desire to learn all about the particular case and decide it as fairly as possible, whatever that might mean. Notice that the situation can be complicated further: if you want to know, for example, whether Harold has relied on Wilma's remarriage in some way, by committing his assets elsewhere or by quitting a high-paying but boring job, is your real concern whether he has in fact relied or whether husbands generally so rely? Or are you really not engaged in a factual inquiry at all but proposing that husbands ought to be free to rely? *Sefton v. Sefton*, 45 Cal. 2d 872, 291 P.2d 439 (1955) held, on reliance grounds, that alimony rights were extinguished, but did not inquire as to whether this particular husband had relied. *Gaines v. Jacobsen*, 308 N.Y. 218, 124 N.E.2d 290 (1954), did the same thing with another factor: it held that the legal right to alimony from the second husband was enough to warrant extinction of the liability of the first without regard to whether the "legal right" was practically enforceable.

3. Applying the reasoning of these two cases, what would each court

do with a case in which the divorced wife was a mental patient who escaped with another patient and married him, that marriage being annullable by either party for insanity? Assume that alimony can be granted in connection with an annulment. See *Minder v. Minder,* 83 N.J. Super. 159, 199 A.2d 69 (1964).

4. What would the result be under the law of each state if the issue were whether an annulled marriage terminated social security payments available only until the claimant "remarried"? Compare *Folsom v. Pearsall,* 245 F.2d 562 (9th Cir. 1957), with *Nott v. Fleming,* 272 F.2d 380 (2d Cir. 1959).

5. The law could provide several different solutions to this problem. Here are three possibilities, with variations.

a. "[Unless a contrary purpose clearly appears in the agreement,] an annulled remarriage is a remarriage for the purposes of terminating support under a separation agreement."

b. "[Unless a contrary purpose clearly appears in the agreement,] an annulled remarriage is a remarriage for the purposes of terminating support under a separation agreement where either (a) the former husband has in fact relied upon the remarriage by himself remarrying, by committing assets apparently made available by such remarriage, or by taking other actions that reduced his economic worth, [and where such reliance was reasonable]; or (b) the wife obtained a legal right to [an economically adequate source of] support from her second husband."

c. "Whether the annulled remarriage terminates support rights under a separation agreement is to be decided upon consideration of the following factors:

(1) Whether the wife obtained a legal right to support from her second husband;
(2) Whether that support was adequate to her needs;
(3) Whether the wife received any assets as a result of the second marriage, such as gifts, a cause of action for fraud or deceit, and the like;
(4) The amount of any such assets in relation to her needs;
(5) Whether the first husband relied in fact upon the remarriage;
(6) The amount of such reliance in relation to the needs of him and his dependents;
(7) Whether such reliance was induced in any way by the wife and whether it was reasonable;
(8) The reasons for the divorce and annulment, and in particular whether the wife was at fault in any way."

(The number of factors could be increased indefinitely.)

Each of the proposed forms of the rule could be designed to effectuate the same policies and to achieve the same goals. They are "different ways of saying the same thing." Of what consequence are the differences between them, then? How should this choice of form be made?

6. Examine the threc proposed solutions and ask which you would adopt as a judge. Is one more rational than the others? How would you choose among them then, and how give directions to that process of choice by another?

7. Now generalize: how is a judge to choose whether to articulate his basis for a decision in the form of a rule or as a set of factors to be assessed? You are asked to give a guide to choice of form: how do you do so? Is your guide expressed in direct speech? a metaphor? a cliché? Is it a rule? Is it a direction to rationality or something more than that?

8. If you have some difficulty imagining what "more" than rationality could possibly be desired of a judge, perhaps it will be helpful to turn once again to your friend at the cocktail party. What would his response be to the proposition that nothing beyond rationality could possibly be desired of a judge?

3. *Alexander Pope's "Essay on Criticism": A Model for Judicial Criticism?*

Those oft are Stratagems which Errors seem,
Nor is it Homer Nods, but We that Dream.

[179–180]

You are asked to read *An Essay on Criticism* by Alexander Pope in any edition you wish, and to consider the suggestions and questions set forth below.

In this poem Pope speaks to those who would be literary critics — judges of literature — and gives them directions to the task, advice on how to engage in this enterprise. From your own experience you will, I hope, be highly skeptical about what can be achieved by such directions to an activity of judgment, but I also hope that as you read this poem you are surprised by what you find.

One might expect such directions to consist of nothing more than some useless clichés, telling us, for example, not to be narrow-minded or biased or rash, or to attend to important and not trivial matters, or to consider the purpose and context of the work we are judging, and so on, all making up a literature about as interesting as twenty moral rules for happy living. Does Pope here transcend that sort of cliché, and if so, how? What, if anything, does he give us beyond obvious rules? Another way to put it is this: he prefaces his poem with a summary of its contents, in which he lists such earthshaking things as: "Rules for the

Conduct of Manners in a Critic: Candour, v[erse] 563. Modesty, v 566. Good-breeding, v 572. Sincerity, and Freedom of Advice, v 578." Does he give us anything more than this sort of thing in the poem itself? What and how? Or: once he has summed up the message of the poem in the statement of its contents, why does he bother to go on to write the poem itself?

Is literary criticism as Pope describes it a rational process? Or to put it slightly differently, is this poem a rational document — the statement of a position with supporting reasons and arguments — or is it something more than or different from that? Critics sometimes speak of Pope as a master of "ratiocination in verse." What can this mean: that his poems are simply logical or argumentative statements dressed up in verse to look pretty or to be amusing? What else can they be? (For a discussion of this problem see Greene, " 'Logical Structure' in Eighteenth Century Poetry," 31 *Philological Q.* 315 (1952).) If the critical activity to which Pope gives directions in this poem (and which he perhaps enacts in it as well) is not a rational activity, what is it? Is it one the judge or lawyer might emulate? So far as you can tell from this poem, what is the proper place of the rule in the processes of literary composition and criticism?

Let us look now at how the poem begins. In the second paragraph Pope defines excellence in criticism by saying that there is something called "True Taste," which is as rare as "true Genius" and as mysterious:

> Both must alike from Heav'n derive their Light,
> These born to Judge, as well as those to Write.
> Let such teach others who themselves excell,
> And censure freely who have written well.
>
> [13–16]

This sort of statement is scant assistance to us, seeming as it does to say that what concerns us is inexpressible, an accident of birth or nature. Could a judge adopt such a view of himself, or you of a judge? If these lines represent Pope's view, why does he bother to go on?

In the next paragraph he goes on to say that most people, who do not have true taste inborn, do have the "seeds of Judgment in their Mind." But they are often perverted by what he calls "false Learning."

> Some are bewilder'd in the Maze of Schools,
> And some made Coxcombs Nature meant but Fools.
>
> [26–27]

Why does Pope follow these lines with the passage given below? Is his rejection of false learning not plain enough without it?

In search of Wit these lose their common Sense,
And then turn Criticks in their own Defence.
Each burns alike, who can, or cannot write,
Or with a Rival's, or an Eunuch's spite.
All Fools have still an Itching to deride,
And fain wou'd be upon the Laughing Side:
If Mævius Scribble in Apollo's spight,
There are, who judge still worse than he can write.
  Some have at first for Wits, then Poets past,
Turn'd Criticks next, and prov'd plain Fools at last;
Some neither can for Wits nor Criticks pass,
As heavy Mules are neither Horse nor Ass.
Those half-learn'd Witlings, num'rous in our Isle,
As half-form'd Insects on the Banks of Nile;
Unfinish'd Things, one knows not what to call,
Their Generation's so equivocal:
To tell 'em, wou'd a hundred Tongues require,
Or one vain Wit's, that might a hundred tire.

[28–45]

At the end of that passage, Pope addresses the reader directly in a sentence beginning, "But you who seek to give and merit fame . . ." Is this a way of promising to tell us what "true learning" is?

It seems so, for he goes on to state various precepts to criticism: follow nature, observe examples, accept traditional rules. But are these merely precepts or something else? How — by what process, by what art — does Pope in fact define "true learning"? What, for example, is the difference between saying "rules are subject to exception in the interest of good judgment," and writing the passage, familiar to you, that follows:

  Some Beauties yet, no Precepts can declare,
For there's a Happiness as well as Care.
Musick resembles Poetry, in each
Are nameless Graces which no Methods teach,
And which a Master-Hand alone can reach.
If, where the Rules not far enough extend,
(Since Rules were made but to promote their End)
Some Lucky LICENCE answers to the full
Th' Intent propos'd, that Licence is a Rule.
Thus Pegasus, a nearer way to take,
May boldly deviate from the common Track.
Great Wits sometimes may gloriously offend,

And rise to Faults true Criticks dare not mend;
From vulgar Bounds with brave Disorder part,
And snatch a Grace beyond the Reach of Art,
Which, without passing thro' the Judgment, gains
The Heart, and all its End at once attains.

[141–157]

Would you ever speak in such a way of the judge's job?

How is the "learning" with which Pope is concerned defined by these lines:

A little Learning is a dang'rous Thing;
Drink deep, or taste not the Pierian Spring:
There shallow Draughts intoxicate the Brain,
And drinking largely sobers us again.
Fir'd at first Sight with what the Muse imparts,
In fearless Youth we tempt the Heights of Arts,
While from the bounded Level of our Mind,
Short Views we take, nor see the Lengths behind,
But more advanc'd, behold with strange Surprize
New, distant Scenes of endless Science rise!
So pleas'd at first, the towring Alps we try,
Mount o'er the Vales, and seem to tread the Sky;
Th' Eternal Snows appear already past,
And the first Clouds and Mountains seem the last:
But those attain'd, we tremble to survey
The growing Labours of the lengthen'd Way,
Th' increasing Prospect tires our wandring Eyes,
Hills peep o'er Hills, and Alps on Alps arise!

[215–232]

Have these lines any relevance to the "learning" in which a judge or one who criticizes him should engage? How does this passage operate: as the statement of a message or as something else? Compare the passages from Fowler and Hooker, *supra* pages 656 and 670.

The suggestion I am making will be no surprise to you: that the movement of this poem is one of education, that its purpose is not to propound rules or to communicate a lesson, but to offer the reader an experience, to engage him in a process that teaches. How can this process, this experience, be defined? Does this teaching have an affinity with any other teaching you have known? What, for example, do the following lines achieve beyond the statement of the simple idea that the sound should seem an echo to the sense? What do they teach you and how do they do it?

But most by Numbers judge a Poet's Song,
And smooth or rough, with them, is right or wrong;
In the bright Muse tho' thousand Charms conspire,
Her Voice is all these tuneful Fools admire,
Who haunt Parnassus but to please their Ear,
Not mend their Minds; as some to Church repair,
Not for the Doctrine, but the Musick there.
These Equal Syllables alone require,
Tho' oft the Ear the open Vowels tire,
While Expletives their feeble Aid do join,
And ten low Words oft creep in one dull Line,
While they ring round the same unvary'd Chimes,
With sure Returns of still expected Rhymes.
Where-e'er you find the cooling Western Breeze,
In the next Line, it whispers thro' the Trees;
If Chrystal Streams with pleasing Murmurs creep,
The Reader's threaten'd (not in vain) with Sleep.
Then, at the last, and only Couplet fraught
With some unmeaning Thing they call a Thought,
A needless Alexandrine ends the Song,
That like a wounded Snake, drags its slow length along.
Leave such to tune their own dull Rhimes, and know
What's roundly smooth, or languishingly slow;
And praise the Easie Vigor of a Line,
Where Denham's Strength, and Waller's Sweetness join.
True Ease in Writing comes from Art, not Chance,
As those move easiest who have learn'd to dance.
'Tis not enough no Harshness gives Offence,
The Sound must seem an Eccho to the Sense.
Soft is the Strain when Zephyr gently blows,
And the smooth Stream in smoother Numbers flows;
But when loud Surges lash the sounding Shore,
The hoarse, rough Verse shou'd like the Torrent roar.
When Ajax strives, some Rock's vast Weight to throw,
The Line too labours, and the Words move slow;
Not so, when swift Camilla scours the Plain,
Flies o'er th'unbending Corn, and skims along the Main.

[337–373]

Here is how Pope concludes, with a description of the excellent critic. How is excellence in literary judgment defined here? How is one to attain it? Is it in any way analogous to excellence in legal judgment?

But where's the Man, who Counsel can bestow,
Still pleas'd to teach, and yet not proud to know?
Unbiass'd, or by Favour or by Spite;
Not dully prepossest, nor blindly right;
Tho' Learn'd, well-bred; and tho' well-bred, sincere;
Modestly bold, and Humanly severe?
Who to a Friend his Faults can freely show,
And gladly praise the Merit of a Foe?
Blest with a Taste exact, yet unconfin'd;
A Knowledge both of Books and Humankind;
Gen'rous Converse; a Soul exempt from Pride;
And Love to Praise, with Reason on his Side?

[631–642]

As you examine this poem and engage in the process of criticizing it, what do you find you can say about excellence (a) in poetry and (b) in literary criticism? How, for example, can you imagine a conversation going on between two people on the subject of whether or not this is a good poem? Would such a conversation be "rational"? Would it invoke "rules"? What would it do? Return now to the passage from Samuel Johnson, page 664 *supra*, in which he discusses the excellence of Shakespeare; examine it again with these questions in mind. Might one think it useful to suggest that the judge is, in important ways, like the poet, and the student like the critic? How could you elaborate these comparisons beyond what has been done above?

WRITING ASSIGNMENT 17: The Enterprise of Judicial Criticism[7]

Part One

• *Choose a judicial opinion that interests you, and write a brief paper in which you criticize it.*

Part Two

• *Now examine the paper you have written, and write a page or two in which you criticize your criticism. What have you done, and have you done it well or badly? What can you say about the activities of judicial judgment, explanation, and criticism? What metaphors do you use, and what are their implications?*

You may want to analyze more than one opinion, by the same or dif-

7. Supplementary assignments are in the Appendix.

ferent judges. Here are two suggestions: compare the opinions of Justices White, Douglas, and Harlan in United States v. White, reproduced at page 736 infra; or compare the Brandeis dissent in Olmstead v. United States, 277 U.S. 438 (1928), with the Douglas dissent in Osborn v. United States, 385 U.S. 323 (1966).

Can you usefully compare the judicial opinion with Pope's Essay on Criticism?

WRITING ASSIGNMENT 17, ALTERNATIVE A: Excellence in the Judicial Opinion — Rationality and Beyond

Part One

• Explain what you hope and expect from the excellent judicial opinion. What does the judge do, and how does he do it well?

Part Two

• Now explain what place "rationality" has in the language of judicial criticism you have just used. You may do this in any way you wish, of course, but here is a suggestion: first tell us what judicial rationality is; then tell us what, beyond "rationality" so defined, is required of the excellent judicial opinion. What metaphors do you use, and what are their implications?

You are of course responsible for your own statement here: try not to use law school clichés and dead metaphors, but find your own way of speaking, your own way of giving life and interest to what you say. You may find that your explication of judicial excellence is more satisfactory if you proceed by narrative and dialogue rather than presenting a pocket guide to the future judge.

WRITING ASSIGNMENT 17, ALTERNATIVE B: What Do You Approve Of?

You have no doubt often had the experience of disapproving of a judicial opinion which reaches a result with which you agree: as a fellow judge, you would have concurred in the judgment but not the opinion, as the common phrase puts it. You have probably also had the converse experience (though it is perhaps a more complicated one) of approving of an opinion but disagreeing with its result: as a fellow judge, you would have respectfully dissented, rejecting the result but being pleased to have such a colleague on the bench. Something like this happens as well in ordinary life: "Tom? Wonderful fellow — never agreed with him in my life!" It is this paradoxical situation that this assignment asks you to explore.

Part One

• *Explain what it is you approve of when you approve of a judicial opinion which reaches a result with which you agree.*

Part Two

• *Explain what it is you approve of when you approve of a judicial opinion which reaches a result with which you disagree.*

Part Three

• *Based upon your answers to Parts One and Two of this assignment, what is excellence in the judicial opinion?*

Let me make two cautionary suggestions: do not try to answer this assignment in the abstract, but study several actual opinions of both kinds and refer to them in what you write; and remember that in defining judicial excellence you define yourself, both as a future judge and lawyer and as a present writer. Do not make it sound all very simple and obvious unless you really see it that way.

WRITING ASSIGNMENT 17, ALTERNATIVE C:
Explaining a Decision

Part One

• *Give an account of a decision or judgment you have made in your own life.*

Part Two

• *In a page or two, criticize that decision and your account of it.*

Part Three

• *Now criticize your criticism. What can you say about the activities of explaining a decision and criticizing explanations?*

Another way to do this assignment would be to imagine a series of *events, a single true or fictional story, in which several people have to make decisions: first tell the story; then write out each person's explanation of his decision. What can you say about the activity of explaining a decision? As you read the explanations you create, how do you find yourself criticizing them? Write out your criticism of one or more of those explanations, and examine what you have written. What can you now say about the activity of criticizing an explanation?*

Compare the following situations: the curious visitor asks, "Why did you do that?" of a chess player who just moved his bishop; of a lawyer who just objected to a question; of a teacher who just asked a student a question; of a painter who just put a green streak on his canvas. What, in each case, can he properly expect by way of explanation?

UNITED STATES v. WHITE
401 U.S. 745 (1971)

WHITE, J., announced the judgment of the Court and an opinion in which the CHIEF JUSTICE, STEWART, J., and BLACKMUN, J., join. In 1966, respondent James A. White was tried and convicted under two consolidated indictments charging various illegal transactions in narcotics violative of 26 U.S.C. §4705(a) and 21 U.S.C. §174. He was fined and sentenced as a second offender to 25-year concurrent sentences. The issue before us is whether the Fourth Amendment bars from evidence the testimony of governmental agents who related certain conversations which had occurred between defendant White and a government informant, Harvey Jackson, and which the agents overheard by monitoring the frequency of a radio transmitter carried by Jackson and concealed on his person. On four occasions the conversations took place in Jackson's home; each of these conversations was overheard by an agent concealed in a kitchen closet with Jackson's consent and by a second agent outside the house using a radio receiver. Four other conversations — one in respondent's home, one in a restaurant, and two in Jackson's car — were overheard by the use of radio equipment. The prosecution was unable to locate and produce Jackson at the trial and the trial court overruled objections to the testimony of the agents who conducted the electronic surveillance. The jury returned a guilty verdict and defendant appealed.

The Court of Appeals read *Katz v. United States*, 389 U.S. 347 (1967), as overruling *On Lee v. United States*, 343 U.S. 747 (1952), and interpreting the Fourth Amendment to forbid the introduction of the agents' testimony in the circumstances of this case. Accordingly, the court reversed but without adverting to the fact that the transactions at issue here had occurred before *Katz* was decided in this Court. In our view, the Court of Appeals misinterpreted both the *Katz* case and the

Fourth Amendment and in any event erred in applying the *Katz* case to events that occurred before that decision was rendered by this Court.

I

Until *Katz v. United States,* neither wiretapping nor electronic eavesdropping violated a defendant's Fourth Amendment rights "unless there has been an official search and seizure of his person, or such a seizure of his papers or his tangible material effects, or an actual physical invasion of his house 'or curtilage' for the purpose of making a seizure." *Olmstead v. United States,* 277 U.S. 438, 466 (1928); *Goldman v. United States,* 316 U.S. 129, 135-136 (1942). But where "eavesdropping was accomplished by means of an unauthorized physical penetration into the premises occupied" by the defendant, although falling short of a "technical trespass under the local property law," the Fourth Amendment was violated and any evidence of what was seen and heard, as well as tangible objects seized, was considered the inadmissible fruit of an unlawful invasion. *Silverman v. United States,* 365 U.S. 505, 509, 511 (1961); see also *Wong Sun v. United States,* 371 U.S. 471 (1963); *Berger v. New York,* 388 U.S. 41, 52 (1967); *Alderman v. United States,* 394 U.S. 165, 177-178 (1969).

Katz v. United States, however, finally swept away doctrines that electronic eavesdropping is permissible under the Fourth Amendment unless physical invasion of a constitutionally protected area produced the challenged evidence. In that case government agents, without petitioner's consent or knowledge, attached a listening device to the outside of a public telephone booth and recorded the defendant's end of his telephone conversations. In declaring the recordings inadmissible in evidence in the absence of a warrant authorizing the surveillance, the Court overruled *Olmstead* and *Goldman* and held that the absence of physical intrusion into the telephone booth did not justify using electronic devices in listening to and recording Katz' words, thereby violating the privacy on which he justifiably relied while using the telephone in those circumstances.

The Court of Appeals understood *Katz* to render inadmissible against White the agents' testimony concerning conversations that Jackson broadcast to them. We cannot agree. *Katz* involved no revelation to the Government by a party to conversations with the defendant nor did the Court indicate in any way that a defendant has a justifiable and constitutionally protected expectation that a person with whom he is conversing will not then or later reveal the conversation to the police.

Hoffa v. United States, 385 U.S. 293 (1966), which was left undisturbed by *Katz,* held that however strongly a defendant may trust an apparent colleague, his expectations in this respect are not protected by the Fourth Amendment when it turns out that the colleague is a government agent regularly communicating with the authorities. In these circumstances, "no interest legitimately protected by the Fourth Amendment is involved," for that amendment affords no protection to "a wrongdoer's misplaced belief that a person to whom he voluntarily confides his wrongdoing will not reveal it." *Hoffa v. United States*, at 302. No warrant to "search and seize" is required in such circumstances, nor is it when the Government sends to defendant's home a secret agent who conceals his identity and makes a purchase of narcotics from the accused, *Lewis v. United States*, 385 U.S. 206 (1966), or when the same agent, unbeknown to the defendant, carries electronic equipment to record the defendant's words and the evidence so gathered is later offered in evidence. *Lopez v. United States*, 373 U.S. 427 (1963).

Conceding that *Hoffa, Lewis,* and *Lopez* remained unaffected by *Katz*,[3] the Court of Appeals nevertheless read both *Katz* and the Fourth Amendment to require a different result if the agent not only records his conversations with the defendant but instantaneously transmits them electronically to other agents equipped with radio receivers. Where this occurs, the Court of Appeals held, the Fourth Amendment is violated and the testimony of the listening agents must be excluded from evidence.

To reach this result it was necessary for the Court of Appeals to hold that *On Lee v. United States* was no longer good law. In that case, which involved facts very similar to the case before us, the Court first rejected claims of a Fourth Amendment violation because the informer had not trespassed when he entered the defendant's premises and conversed with him. To this extent the Court's rationale cannot survive *Katz*. See 389 U.S., at 352-353. But the Court announced a second and independent ground for its decision; for it went on to say that overruling *Olmstead* and *Goldman* would be of no aid to On Lee since he "was talking confidentially and indiscreetly with one he trusted, and he was overheard. . . . It would be a dubious service to the genuine liberties protected by the Fourth Amendment to make them bedfellows with spurious liberties improvised by farfetched analogies which would liken eavesdropping on a conversation, with the connivance of one of the parties, to an unreasonable search or seizure. We find no violation of the Fourth Amendment here." 343 U.S., at 753-754. We see no indication in *Katz* that the Court meant to disturb that understanding of the Fourth Amendment or to disturb the result reached in the *On Lee* case, nor are we now inclined to overturn this view of the Fourth Amendment.

Concededly a police agent who conceals his police connections may write down for official use his conversations with a defendant and testify

3. It follows from our opinion that we reject respondent's contentions that *Lopez* should be overruled.

concerning them, without a warrant authorizing his encounters with the defendant and without otherwise violating the latter's Fourth Amendment rights. *Hoffa v. United States*, 385 U.S., at 300-303. For constitutional purposes, no different result is required if the agent instead of immediately reporting and transcribing his conversations with defendant, either (1) simultaneously records them with electronic equipment which he is carrying on his person, *Lopez v. United States, supra;* (2) or carries radio equipment which simultaneously transmits the conversations either to recording equipment located elsewhere or to other agents monitoring the transmitting frequency. *On Lee v. United States, supra.* If the conduct and revelations of an agent operating without electronic equipment do not invade the defendant's constitutionally justifiable expectations of privacy, neither does a simultaneous recording of the same conversations made by the agent or by others from transmissions received from the agent to whom the defendant is talking and whose trustworthiness the defendant necessarily risks.

Our problem is not what the privacy expectations of particular defendants in particular situations may be or the extent to which they may in fact have relied on the discretion of their companions. Very probably, individual defendants neither know nor suspect that their colleagues have gone or will go to the police or are carrying recorders or transmitters. Otherwise, conversation would cease and our problem with these encounters would be nonexistent or far different from those now before us. Our problem, in terms of the principles announced in *Katz*, is what expectations of privacy are constitutionally "justifiable" — what expectations the Fourth Amendment will protect in the absence of a warrant. So far, the law permits the frustration of actual expectations of privacy by permitting authorities to use the testimony of those associates who for one reason or another have determined to turn to the police, as well as by authorizing the use of informants in the manner exemplified by *Hoffa* and *Lewis*. If the law gives no protection to the wrongdoer whose trusted accomplice is or becomes a police agent, neither should it protect him when that same agent has recorded or transmitted the conversations which are later offered in evidence to prove the State's case. See *Lopez v. United States*, 373 U.S. 427 (1963).

Inescapably, one contemplating illegal activities must realize and risk that his companions may be reporting to the police. If he sufficiently doubts their trustworthiness, the association will very probably end or never materialize. But if he has no doubts, or allays them, or risks what doubt he has, the risk is his. In terms of what his course will be, what he will or will not do or say, we are unpersuaded that he would distinguish between probable informers on the one hand and probable informers with transmitters on the other. Given the possibility or probability that one of his colleagues is cooperating with the police, it is only speculation to assert that the defendant's utterances would be substantially different or his sense of security any less if he also thought it possible that the suspected colleague is wired for sound. At least there is no persuasive evidence that the difference in this respect between the electronically equipped and the unequipped agent is substantial enough to require discrete constitutional recognition, particularly under the Fourth Amendment which is ruled by fluid concepts of "reasonableness."

Nor should we be too ready to erect constitutional barriers to relevant and probative evidence which is also accurate and reliable. An electronic recording will many times produce a more reliable rendition of what a defendant has said than will the unaided memory of a police agent. It may also be that with the recording in existence it is less likely that the informant will change his mind, less chance that threat or injury will suppress unfavorable evidence and less chance that cross-examination will confound the testimony. Considerations like these obviously do not favor the defendant, but we are not prepared to hold that a defendant who has no constitutional right to exclude the informer's unaided testimony nevertheless has a Fourth Amendment privilege against a more accurate version of the events in question.

It is thus untenable to consider the activities and reports of the police agent himself, though acting without a warrant, to be a "reasonable" investigative effort and lawful under the Fourth Amendment but to view the same agent with a recorder or transmitter as conducting an "unreasonable" and unconstitutional search and seizure. Our opinion is currently shared by Congress and the Executive Branch, Title III, Omnibus Crime Control and Safe Streets Act of 1968, 82 Stat. 212, 18 U.S.C. §2510 *et seq.* (1964 ed., Supp. V), and the American Bar Association. Project on Standards for Criminal Justice, Electronic Surveillance §4.1 (Approved Draft 1971). It is also the result reached by prior cases in this Court. *On Lee, supra; Lopez v. United States, supra.*

No different result should obtain where, as in *On Lee* and the instant case, the informer disappears and is unavailable at trial; for the issue of whether specified events on a certain day violate the Fourth Amendment should not be determined by what later happens to the informer. His unavailability at trial and proffering the testimony of other agents may raise evidentiary problems or pose issues of prosecutorial misconduct with respect to the informer's disappearance, but they do not appear critical to deciding whether prior events invaded the defendant's Fourth Amendment rights.

II

The Court of Appeals was in error for another reason. In *Desist v. United States*, 394 U.S. 244 (1969), we held that our decision in *Katz v. United States* applied only to those electronic surveillances that occurred subsequent to the date of that decision. Here the events in question took place in late 1965 and early 1966, long prior to *Katz*. We adhere to the rationale of *Desist*, see *Williams v. United States, ante*, p. 646. It was error for the Court of Appeals to dispose of this case based on its understanding of the principles announced in the *Katz* case. The court should have judged this case by the pre-*Katz* law and under that law, as *On Lee* clearly holds, the electronic surveillance here involved did not violate White's rights to be free from unreasonable searches and seizures.

The judgment of the Court of Appeals is reversed.

DOUGLAS, J. dissenting.

I

The issue in this case is clouded and concealed by the very discussion of it in legalistic terms. What the ancients knew as "eavesdropping," we now call "electronic surveillance"; but to equate the two is to treat man's first gunpowder on the same level as the nuclear bomb. Electronic surveillance is the greatest leveler of human privacy ever known. How most forms of it can be held "reasonable" within the meaning of the Fourth Amendment is a mystery. To be sure, the Constitution and Bill of Rights are not to be read as covering only the technology known in the 18th century. Otherwise its concept of "commerce" would be hopeless when it comes to the management of modern affairs. At the same time the concepts of privacy which the Founders enshrined in the Fourth Amendment vanish completely when we slavishly allow an all-powerful government, proclaiming law and order, efficiency, and other benign purposes, to penetrate all the walls and doors which men need to shield them from the pressures of a turbulent life around them and give them the health and strength to carry on.

That is why a "strict construction" of the Fourth Amendment is necessary if every man's liberty and privacy are to be constitutionally honored.

When Franklin D. Roosevelt on May 21, 1940, authorized wiretapping in cases of "fifth column" activities and sabotage and limited it "insofar as possible to aliens," he said that "under ordinary and normal circumstances wire-tapping by Government agents should not be carried on for the excellent reason that it is almost bound to lead to abuse of civil rights." See Appendix I to this dissent. Yet as Judge Ferguson said in *United States v. Smith*, 321 F. Supp. 424, 429:

> [T]he government seems to approach these dissident domestic organizations in the same fashion as it deals with unfriendly foreign powers. The government cannot act in this manner when only domestic political organizations

are involved, even if those organizations espouse views which are inconsistent with our present form of government. To do so is to ride roughshod over numerous political freedoms which have long received constitutional protection. The government can, of course, investigate and prosecute criminal violations whenever these organizations, or rather their individual members, step over the line of political theory and general advocacy and commit illegal acts.

Today no one perhaps notices because only a small, obscure criminal is the victim. But every person is the victim, for the technology we exalt today is everyman's master. Any doubters should read Arthur R. Miller's The Assault on Privacy (1971). After describing the monitoring of conversations and their storage in data banks, Professor Miller goes on to describe "human monitoring" which he calls the "ultimate step in mechanical snooping" — a device for spotting unorthodox or aberrational behavior across a wide spectrum. "Given the advancing state of both the remote sensing art and the capacity of computers to handle an uninterrupted and synoptic data flow, there seem to be no physical barriers left to shield us from intrusion." *Id.*, at 46.

When one reads what is going on in this area today, our judicial treatment of the subject seems as remote from reality as the well-known Baron Parke was remote from the social problems of his day. See Chapman, "Big Brother" in the Justice Department, The Progressive, April 1971, p. 27.

II

We held in *Berger v. New York,* 388 U.S. 41, that wiretapping is a search and seizure within the meaning of the Fourth Amendment and therefore must meet its requirements, *viz.*, there must be a prior showing of probable cause, the warrant authorizing the wiretap must particularly describe "the place to be searched, and the persons or things to be seized," and that it may not have the breadth, generality, and long life of the general warrant against which the Fourth Amendment was aimed.

In *Katz v. United States,* 389 U.S. 347, we held that an electronic device, used without trespass onto any given enclosure (there a telephone booth), was a search for which a Fourth Amendment warrant was needed. Mr. Justice Stewart, speaking for the Court, said: "Wherever a man may be, he is entitled to know that he will remain free from unreasonable searches and seizures." *Id.*, at 359.

As a result of *Berger* and of *Katz,* both wiretapping and electronic surveillance through a "bug" or other device are now covered by the Fourth Amendment.

There were prior decisions representing an opposed view. In *On Lee v. United States*, 343 U.S. 747, an undercover agent with a radio transmitter concealed on his person interviewed the defendant whose words were heard over a radio receiver by another agent down the street. The idea, discredited by *Katz*, that there was no violation of the Fourth Amendment because there was no trespass, was the core of the *On Lee* decision. *Id.*, at 751-754.

Lopez v. United States, 373 U.S. 427, was also pre-*Berger* and pre-*Katz*. The government agent there involved carried a pocket wire recorder which the Court said "was not planted by means of an unlawful physical invasion of petitioner's premises under circumstances which would violate the Fourth Amendment." *Id.*, at 439.

Mr. Justice Brennan, dissenting, stated the philosophy of *Katz* soon to be adopted:

> [T]here is a qualitative difference between electronic surveillance, whether the agents conceal the devices on their persons or in walls or under beds, and conventional police stratagems such as eavesdropping and disguise. The latter do not so seriously intrude upon the right of privacy. The risk of being overheard by an eavesdropper or betrayed by an informer or deceived as to the identity of one with whom one deals is probably inherent in the conditions of human society. It is the kind of risk we necessarily assume whenever we speak. But as soon as electronic surveillance comes into play, the risk changes crucially. There is no security from that kind of eavesdropping, no way of mitigating the risk, and so not even a residuum of true privacy. . . .
> . . . Electronic aids add a wholly new dimension to eavesdropping. They make it more penetrating, more indiscriminate, more truly obnoxious to a free society. Electronic surveillance, in fact, makes the police omniscient; and police omniscience is one of the most effective tools of tyranny. [373 U.S., at 465-466.]

It is urged by the Department of Justice that *On Lee* be established as the controlling decision in this field. I would stand by *Berger* and *Katz* and reaffirm the need for judicial supervision[2] under the Fourth Amendment of the use of electronic surveillance which, uncontrolled, promises to lead us into a police state.

These were wholly pre-arranged episodes of surveillance. The first was in the informant's home to which respondent had been invited. The second was also in the informer's home, the next day. The third was four days later at the home of the respondent. The fourth was in the

2. *Osborn v. United States*, 385 U.S. 323, was held to be in that tradition, as the federal district judges, prior to the use of the recording device by the agent and with full knowledge of the alleged law violation involved, "authorized the use of a recording device for the narrow and particularized purpose of ascertaining the truth" of the charge. *Id.*, at 330.

informer's car two days later. Twelve days after that a meeting in the informer's home was intruded upon. The sixth occurred at a street rendezvous. The seventh was in the informer's home and the eighth in a restaurant owned by respondent's mother-in-law. So far as time is concerned there is no excuse for not seeking a warrant. And while there is always an effort involved in preparing affidavits or other evidence in support of a showing of probable cause, that burden was given constitutional sanction in the Fourth Amendment against the activities of the agents of George III. It was designed not to protect criminals but to protect everyone's privacy.

On Lee and *Lopez* are of a vintage opposed to *Berger* and *Katz.* However they may be explained, they are products of the old common-law notions of trespass. *Katz,* on the other hand, emphasized that with few exceptions "searches conducted outside the judicial process, without prior approval by judge or magistrate, are per se unreasonable under the Fourth Amendment. . . ." 389 U.S., at 357. *Camara v. Municipal Court,* 387 U.S. 523, put administrative searches under the Fourth Amendment. We held that administrative actions, like other searches, implicated officials in an invasion of privacy and that the Fourth Amendment was meant to guard against the arbitrariness of any such invasion. We said:

> We simply cannot say that the protections provided by the warrant procedure are not needed in this context; broad statutory safeguards are no substitute for individualized review, particularly when those safeguards may only be invoked at the risk of a criminal penalty. [*Id.,* at 533.]

In *Chimel v. California,* 395 U.S. 752, in considering the constitutionality of a search incident to an arrest we held that, while the area in the immediate reach of an arrestee is "reasonable" though made without a warrant, a search beyond that zone may generally be made "only under the authority of a search warrant." *Id.,* at 763. And in two "stop and frisk" cases, *Terry v. Ohio,* 392 U.S. 1, and *Davis v. Mississippi,* 394 U.S. 721, we held that any restraint of the person, however brief, was subject to judicial inquiry on "reasonableness" (392 U.S., at 19) and that "the Fourth Amendment governs all intrusions by agents of the public upon personal security. . . ." *Id.,* at 18 n.15.

We have moved far away from the rationale of *On Lee* and *Lopez* and only a retrogressive step of large dimensions would bring us back to it.

The threads of thought running through our recent decisions are that these extensive intrusions into privacy made by electronic surveillance make self-restraint by law enforcement officials an inadequate protection, that the requirement of warrants under the Fourth Amendment is essential to a free society.

Monitoring, if prevalent, certainly kills free discourse and spontaneous utterances. Free discourse — a First Amendment value — may be frivolous or serious, humble or defiant, reactionary or revolutionary, profane or in good taste; but it is not free if there is surveillance. Free discourse liberates the spirit, though it may produce only froth. The individual must keep some facts concerning his thoughts within a small zone of people. At the same time he must be free to pour out his woes or inspirations or dreams to others. He remains the sole judge as to what must be said and what must remain unspoken. This is the essence of the idea of privacy implicit in the First and Fifth Amendments as well as in the Fourth.

The philosophy of the value of privacy reflected in the Fourth Amendment's ban on "unreasonable searches and seizures" has been forcefully stated by a former Attorney General of the United States:

> Privacy is the basis of individuality. To be alone and be let alone, to be with chosen company, to say what you think, or don't think, but to say what you will, is to be yourself. Solitude is imperative, even in a high rise apartment. Personality develops from within. To reflect is to know yourself. Character is formed through years of self-examination. Without this opportunity, character will be formed largely by uncontrolled external social stimulations. Americans are excessively homogenized already.
>
> Few conversations would be what they are if the speakers thought others were listening. Silly, secret, thoughtless and thoughtful statements would all be affected. The sheer numbers in our lives, the anonymity of urban living and the inability to influence things that are important are depersonalizing and dehumanizing factors of modern life. To penetrate the last refuge of the individual, the precious little privacy that remains, the basis of individual dignity, can have meaning to the quality of our lives that we cannot foresee. In terms of present values, that meaning cannot be good.
>
> Invasions of privacy demean the individual. Can a society be better than the people composing it? When a government degrades its citizens, or permits them to degrade each other, however beneficent the specific purpose, it limits opportunities for individual fulfillment and national accomplishment. If America permits fear and its failure to make basic social reforms to excuse police use of secret electronic surveillance, the price will be dear indeed. The practice is incompatible with a free society. [R. Clark, Crime in America 287 (1970).]

Now that the discredited decisions in *On Lee* and *Lopez* are resuscitated and revived, must everyone live in fear that every word he speaks may be transmitted or recorded[5] and later repeated to the entire world? I can imagine nothing that has a more chilling effect on people speaking their minds and expressing their views on important matters. The advocates of that regime should spend some time in totalitarian countries and learn firsthand the kind of regime they are creating here.

III

The decision not to make *Katz* retroactive to any electronic surveillance which occurred prior to December 18, 1967 (the day we decided *Katz*), is not, in my view, a tenable one for the reasons stated by Mr. Justice Harlan and me in our dissents in *Desist v. United States*, 394 U.S. 244, 255, 256.

HARLAN, J., dissenting. The uncontested facts of this case squarely challenge the continuing viability of *On Lee v. United States*, 343 U.S. 747 (1952). As the plurality opinion of Mr. Justice White itself makes clear, important constitutional developments since *On Lee* mandate that we reassess that case, which has continued to govern official behavior of this sort in spite of the subsequent erosion of its doctrinal foundations. With all respect, my agreement with the plurality opinion ends at that point.

I think that a perception of the scope and role of the Fourth Amendment, as elucidated by this Court since *On Lee* was decided, and full comprehension of the precise issue at stake lead to the conclusion that *On Lee* can no longer be regarded as sound law. Nor do I think the

5. Senator Edward Long, who intensively investigated wiretapping and "bugging" said:

"You would be amazed at the different ways you can now be 'bugged.' There is today a transmitter the size of an aspirin tablet which can help transmit conversations in your room to a listening post up to 10 miles away.

"An expert can devise a bug to fit into almost any piece of furniture in your room. And even if you find the bug, you will have no evidence of who put it there. A United States Senator was bugged by a transmitter secretly placed into a lamp which his wife was having fixed at the shop. When experts searched for the transmitter, it was gone.

"A leading electronics expert told my Subcommittee last year that wiretapping and bugging in industrial espionage triples every year. He said that new bugging devices are so small and cleverly concealed that it takes search equipment costing over one hundred thousand dollars and an expert with 10 years of field experience to discover them. Ten years ago, the same search for bugs could have been done with equipment costing only one-fourth as much.

"In California we found a businessman who had been so frightened by electronic eavesdropping devices which had been concealed in his office, that he is now spending thousands of dollars having his office searched each day, taking his phone apart every morning, and stationing a special guard outside his office 24 hours a day.

"He is one of a growing number of men in industry who live in constant fear that what they say is being listened to by their competitor." 19 Adm. L. Rev. 442, 444. And see E. Long, The Intruders (1966).

date we decided *Katz v. United States*, 389 U.S. 347 (1967), can be deemed controlling both for the reasons discussed in my dissent in *Desist v. United States*, 394 U.S. 244, 256 (1969), and my separate opinion in *Mackey v. United States* (and companion cases), *ante*, p. 675 (the case before us being here on *direct* review), and because, in my view, it requires no discussion of the holding in *Katz*, as distinguished from its underlying rationale as to the reach of the Fourth Amendment, to comprehend the constitutional infirmity of *On Lee*.

I

Before turning to matters of precedent and policy, several preliminary observations should be made. We deal here with the constitutional validity of instantaneous third-party electronic eavesdropping, conducted by federal law enforcement officers, without any prior judicial approval of the technique utilized, but with the consent and cooperation of a participant in the conversation, and where the substance of the matter electronically overheard[2] is related in a federal criminal trial by those who eavesdropped as direct, not merely corroborative, evidence of the guilt of the nonconsenting party. The magnitude of the issue at hand is evidenced not simply by the obvious doctrinal difficulty of weighing such activity in the Fourth Amendment balance, but also, and more importantly, by the prevalence of police utilization of this technique. Professor Westin has documented in careful detail the numerous devices that make technologically feasible the Orwellian Big Brother. Of immediate relevance is his observation that " 'participant recording,' in which one participant in a conversation or meeting, either a police officer or a co-operating party, wears a concealed device that records the conversation or broadcasts it to others nearby . . . is used tens of thousands of times each year throughout the country, particularly in cases involving extortion, conspiracy, narcotics, gambling, prostitution, corruption by police officials . . . and similar crimes."

Moreover, as I shall undertake to show later in this opinion, the factors that must be reckoned with in reaching constitutional conclusions respecting the use of electronic eavesdropping as a tool of law enforcement are exceedingly subtle and complex. They have provoked sharp differences of opinion both within and without the judiciary, and the entire problem has been the subject of continuing study by various governmental and nongovernmental bodies.

Finally, given the importance of electronic eavesdropping as a technique for coping with the more deep-seated kinds of criminal activity, and the complexities that are encountered in striking a workable consti-

2. In the case at hand agents were also surreptitiously placed in respondent's home at various times. No testimony by these agents was offered at trial.

tutional balance between the public and private interests at stake, I believe that the courts should proceed with specially measured steps in this field. More particularly, I think this Court should not foreclose itself from reconsidering doctrines that would prevent the States from seeking, independently of the niceties of federal restrictions as they may develop, solutions to such vexing problems, see *Mapp v. Ohio*, 367 U.S. 643 (1961) and *Ker v. California*, 374 U.S. 23 (1963), and see also *Berger v. New York*, 388 U.S. 41 (1967); *Baldwin v. New York*, 399 U.S. 66, 117 (1970) (dissenting opinion); *California v. Green*, 399 U.S. 149, 172 (1970) (concurring opinion). I also think that in the adjudication of federal cases, the Court should leave ample room for congressional developments.

II

On these premises I move to the problem of third-party "bugging." To begin by tracing carefully the evolution of Fourth Amendment doctrine in post-*On Lee* decisions has proved useful in several respects. It serves to cast in perspective both the issue involved here and the imperative necessity for reconsidering *On Lee* afresh. Additionally, a full exposition of the dynamics of the decline of the trespass rationale underlying *On Lee* strikingly illuminates the deficiencies of the plurality opinion's retroactivity analysis.

A

On Lee involved circumstances virtually identical to those now before us. There, Government agents enlisted the services of Chin Poy, a former friend of Lee, who was suspected of engaging in illegal narcotics traffic. Poy was equipped with a "minifon" transmitting device which enabled outside Government agents to monitor Poy's conversations with Lee. In the privacy of his laundry, Lee made damaging admissions to Poy which were overheard by the agents and later related at trial. Poy did not testify. Mr. Justice Jackson, writing for five Justices, held the testimony admissible. Without reaching the question of whether a conversation could be the subject of a "seizure" for Fourth Amendment purposes, as yet an unanswered if not completely open question, the Court concluded that in the absence of a trespass, no constitutional violation had occurred.

The validity of the trespass rationale was questionable even at the time the decision was rendered. In this respect *On Lee* rested on common-law notions and looked to a waning era of Fourth Amendment jurisprudence. Three members of the Court refused to join with Justice Jackson, and within 10 years the Court expressly disavowed an approach to Fourth Amendment questions that looked to common-law distinctions. See, e.g., *Jones v. United States*, 362 U.S. 257 (1960); *Silverman v. United States*, 365 U.S. 505 (1961); *Lanza v. New York*, 370 U.S. 139 (1962).

It is, of course, true that the opinion in *On Lee* drew some support from a brief additional assertion that "eavesdropping on a conversation, with the connivance of one of the parties" raises no Fourth Amendment problem. 343 U.S., at 754. But surely it is a misreading of that opinion to view this unelaborated assertion as a wholly independent ground for decision. At the very least, this rationale needs substantial buttressing if it is to persist in our constitutional jurisprudence after the decisions I discuss below. Indeed, the plurality opinion in the present case, in greatly elaborating the point, tacitly recognizes the analytic inability of this bare hypothesis to support a rule of law so profoundly important to the proper administration of justice. Moreover, if this was the true rationale of *On Lee* from the outset, it is difficult to see the relevance of *Desist* to the resolution of the instant case, for *Katz* surely does not speak directly to the continued viability of that ground for decision. See *Katz v. United States*, 389 U.S., at 363 n. (White, J., concurring).

By 1963, when we decided *Lopez v. United States*, 373 U.S. 427, four members of the Court were prepared to pronounce *On Lee* and *Olmstead v. United States*, 277 U.S. 438 (1928), dead. The pyre, they reasoned, had been stoked by decisions like *Wong Sun v. United States*, 371 U.S. 471 (1963), which, on the one hand, expressly brought verbal communication within the sweep of the Fourth Amendment, and, on the other, reinforced our *Silverman* and *Jones* decisions which "refused to crowd the Fourth Amendment into the mold of local property law," 373 U.S., at 460 (Brennan, J., dissenting).

Although the Court's decision in *Lopez* is cited by the Government as a reaffirmation of *On Lee*, it can hardly be thought to have nurtured the questionable rationale of that decision or its much-criticized ancestor, *Olmstead*. To the discerning lawyer *Lopez* could only give pause, not comfort. While the majority opinion, of which I was the author, declined to follow the course favored by the dissenting and concurring Justices by sounding the death knell for *Olmstead* and *On Lee*, our holding, despite an allusion to the absence of "an unlawful . . . invasion of a constitutionally protected area," 373 U.S., at 438-439, was bottomed on two premises: the corroborative use that was made of the tape recordings, which increased reliability in the factfinding process, and the absence of a "risk" not fairly assumed by petitioner. The tape recording was made by a participant in the conversation and the opinion emphasized this absence of a third-party intrusion, expressly noting that there was no "electronic eavesdropping on a private conversation which government agents could not otherwise have overheard." 373 U.S., at

440. As I point out in Part III of this opinion, it is one thing to subject the average citizen to the risk that participants in a conversation with him will subsequently divulge its contents to another, but quite a different matter to foist upon him the risk that unknown third parties may be simultaneously listening in.

While *Lopez* cited *On Lee* without disavowal of its holding, 373 U.S., at 438, it is entirely accurate to say that we did not there reaffirm it. No decision since *Lopez* gives a breath of life to the reasoning that led to the *On Lee* and *Olmstead* results, and it required little clairvoyance to predict the demise of the basic rationale of *On Lee* and *Olmstead* foreshadowed by our subsequent opinons in *Osborn v. United States,* 385 U.S. 323 (1966), and *Berger v. New York,* 388 U.S. 41 (1967).

Only three years after *Lopez,* Mr. Justice Stewart writing for the Court in *Osborn v. United States, supra,* expressly abjured reliance on *Lopez* and, instead, approved identical conduct based on the "circumstances under which the tape recording was obtained in [that] case," facts that involved "using [a recorder] under the most precise and discriminate circumstances, circumstances which fully met the 'requirement of particularity' which the dissenting opinion in *Lopez* found necessary." *Osborn v. United States,* 385 U.S., at 327, 329.

Since *Osborn* our decisions have shown no tolerance for the old dividing lines resting, as they did, on fiction and common-law distinctions without sound policy justification in the realm of values protected by the Fourth Amendment. Thus, in abolishing the "mere evidence rule" we announced that "the principal object of the Fourth Amendment is the protection of privacy rather than property," and once again noted the trend to discard "fictional and procedural barriers [resting] on property concepts." *Warden v. Hayden,* 387 U.S. 294, 304 (1967). That same Term the Court demonstrated the new flexibility in Fourth Amendment doctrine when it held that the warrant protections would be applied to administrative searches. *Camara v. Municipal Court,* 387 U.S. 523 (1967).

Certainly if *Osborn, Warden,* and *Camara* did not plainly draw into question the vigor of earlier precedents, *Berger v. New York,* 388 U.S. 41, did, and expunged any remnants of former doctrine which might have been thought to have survived *Osborn* and *Warden.* There, the Court, following a path opened by Mr. Justice Brandeis' dissent in *Olmstead,* and smoothed in *Osborn* and *Camara,* expressed concern about scientific developments that have put within the reach of the Government the private communications of "anyone in almost any given situation," 388 U.S., at 47; it left no doubt that, as a general principle, electronic eavesdropping was an invasion of privacy and that the Fourth Amendment prohibited unsupervised "bugging." Disturbed by the extent of intrusion which "[b]y its very nature . . . is broad in scope," and noting that "[f]ew threats to liberty exist which are greater than that posed by the use of eavesdropping devices," *id.*, at 63, the Court brought to life the principle of reasonableness adumbrated in *Osborn*. Mr. Justice Clark, writing for the majority, reiterated the new approach:

> [T]he "indiscriminate use of such [bugging] devices in law enforcement raises grave constitutional questions under the Fourth and Fifth Amendments," and imposes "a heavier responsibility on this Court in its supervision of the fairness of procedures . . . ." [388 U.S., at 56, quoting from *Osborn v. United States*, 385 U.S. 323, 329 n.7.]

Nor did the Court waver in resolve in the face of respondent's dire prediction that "neither a warrant nor a statute authorizing eavesdropping can be drawn so as to meet the Fourth Amendment's requirements." It was said that "[i]f that be true then the 'fruits' of eavesdropping devices are barred under the Amendment." 388 U.S., at 63.

If *Berger* did not flatly sound a dirge for *Olmstead*, it articulated principles that led Mr. Justice Douglas, by way of concurrence, to comment on its quiet burial. 388 U.S., at 64. While it was left to *Katz* to perform the last rites, that decision inevitably followed from *Osborn* and *Berger*. The *Berger* majority's affirmative citation of *On Lee* for the principle that "under specific conditions and circumstances" eavesdropping may be lawful, 388 U.S., at 63, serves only to underscore the emerging operative assumptions: that the particular circumstances of each case will be scrutinized to the end of ascertaining the reasonableness of the search, and that will depend in large measure on whether prior judicial authorization, based on a particularized showing, has been obtained. *Katz v. United States, supra.*

Viewed in perspective, then, *Katz* added no new dimension to the law. At most it was a formal dispatch of *Olmstead* and the notion that such problems may usefully be resolved in the light of trespass doctrine, and, of course, it freed from speculation what was already evident, that *On Lee* was completely open to question.

B

But the decisions of this Court since *On Lee* do more than demonstrate that the doctrine of that case is wholly open for reconsideration, and has been since well before *Katz* was decided. They also establish sound general principles for application of the Fourth Amendment that were either dimly perceived or not fully worked out at the time of *On*

Lee. I have already traced some of these principles in Part II-A, *supra:* that verbal communication is protected by the Fourth Amendment, that the reasonableness of a search does not depend on the presence or absence of a trespass, and that the Fourth Amendment is principally concerned with protecting interests of privacy, rather than property rights.

Especially when other recent Fourth Amendment decisions, not otherwise so immediately relevant, are read with those already discussed, the primacy of an additional general principle becomes equally evident: official investigatory action that impinges on privacy must typically, in order to be constitutionally permissible, be subjected to the warrant requirement. Particularly significant in this regard are *Camara v. Municipal Court,* 387 U.S. 523 (1967); *Terry v. Ohio,* 392 U.S. 1 (1968), and *Chimel v. California,* 395 U.S. 752 (1969).

In *Camara* the Court brought under the Fourth Amendment administrative searches that had once been thought to be without its sweep. In doing so the opinion emphasized the desirability of establishing in advance those circumstances that justified the intrusion into a home and submitting them for review to an independent assessor, principles that this Court has always deemed to be at the core of Fourth Amendment protections.[17] In bringing such searches within the ambit of the warrant requirement, *Camara* rejected the notion that the "less hostile" nature of the search relegated this invasion of privacy to the "periphery" of Fourth Amendment concerns. 387 U.S., at 530. The central consideration was, the Court concluded, that these administrative actions, no less than the typical search, involved government officials in an invasion of privacy, and that it was against the possible arbitrariness of invasion that the Fourth Amendment with its warrant machinery was meant to guard. *Berger* and *Katz* built, as noted earlier, on *Osborn v. United States, supra,* and *Camara,* and gave further expression to the principle. It was not enough that government agents acted with restraint, for reasonableness must in the first instance be judged in a detached realm.

17. The classic exposition of the purposes and importance of the warrant requirement is to be found in the opinion of Mr. Justice Jackson in his opinion for the Court in *Johnson v. United States,* 333 U.S. 10, 13-14 (1948):

"The point of the Fourth Amendment, which often is not grasped by zealous officers, is not that it denies law enforcement the support of the usual inferences which reasonable men draw from evidence. Its protection consists in requiring that those inferences be drawn by a neutral and detached magistrate instead of being judged by the officer engaged in the often competitive enterprise of ferreting out crime. . . . The right of officers to thrust themselves into a home is . . . a grave concern, not only to the individual but to a society which chooses to dwell in reasonable security and freedom from surveillance. When the right of privacy must reasonably yield to the right of search is, as a rule, to be decided by a judicial officer, not by a policeman or government enforcement agent."

The scope and meaning of the rule have emerged with even greater clarity by virtue of our holdings setting the boundaries for the exceptions. Recently, in *Chimel v. California*, 395 U.S. 752 (1969), we reiterated the importance of the prior independent determination of a neutral magistrate and underscored its centrality to the reasonableness requirement of the Fourth Amendment, and abandoned the holdings of *Harris v. United States*, 331 U.S. 145 (1947), and *United States v. Rabinowitz*, 339 U.S. 56 (1950). We were concerned by the breadth of searches occasioned by the *Rabinowitz* rule which frequently proved to be an invitation to a hunting expedition. Searches incident to arrest, we held, must be confined to a locus no greater than necessary to prevent injury to the arresting officer or destruction of evidence. 395 U.S. at 763, 767; cf. *Terry v. Ohio*, 392 U.S. 1 (1968).

To complete the tapestry, the strands of doctrine reflected in the search cases must be interwoven with the Court's other contemporary holdings. Most significant are *Terry v. Ohio*, *supra*, and *Davis v. Mississippi*, 394 U.S. 721 (1969), which were also harbingers of the new thrust in Fourth Amendment doctrine. There the Court rejected the contention that only an arrest triggered the "incident-to-arrest" exception to the warrant requirement of the Fourth Amendment, and held that any restraint of the person, however brief and however labeled, was subject to a reasonableness examination. 392 U.S., at 19. The controlling principle is "to recognize that the Fourth Amendment governs all intrusions by agents of the public upon personal security, and to make the scope of the particular intrusion, in light of all the exigencies of the case, a central element in the analysis of reasonableness." 392 U.S., at 18 n.15. See also *Davis v. Mississippi*, 394 U.S., at 727.

III

A

That the foundations of *On Lee* have been destroyed does not, of course, mean that its result can no longer stand. Indeed, the plurality opinion today fastens upon our decisions in *Lopez*, *Lewis v. United States*, 385 U.S. 206 (1966), and *Hoffa v. United States*, 385 U.S. 293 (1966), to resist the undercurrents of more recent cases emphasizing the warrant procedure as a safeguard to privacy. But this category provides insufficient support. In each of these cases the risk the general populace faced was different from that surfaced by the instant case. No surreptitious third ear was present, and in each opinion that fact was carefully noted.

In *Lewis*, a federal agent posing as a potential purchaser of narcotics gained access to petitioner's home and there consummated an illegal sale, the fruits of which were admitted at trial along with the testimony of the agent. Chief Justice Warren, writing for the majority, expressly distinguished the third-party overhearing involved, by way of example, in a case like *Silverman v. United States, supra,* noting that "there, the conduct proscribed was that of eavesdroppers, unknown and unwanted intruders who furtively listened to conversations occurring in the privacy of a house." 385 U.S., at 212. Similarly in *Hoffa,* Mr. Justice Stewart took care to mention that "surreptitious" monitoring was not there before the Court, and so too in *Lopez, supra.*

The plurality opinion seeks to erase the crucial distinction between the facts before us and these holdings by the following reasoning: if A can relay verbally what is revealed to him by B (as in *Lewis* and *Hoffa*), or record and later divulge it (as in *Lopez*), what difference does it make if A conspires with another to betray B by contemporaneously transmitting to the other all that is said? The contention is, in essence, an argument that the distinction between third-party monitoring and *other* undercover techniques is one of form and not substance. The force of the contention depends on the evaluation of two separable but intertwined assumptions: first, that there is no greater invasion of privacy in the third-party situation, and, second, that uncontrolled consensual surveillance in an electronic age is a tolerable technique of law enforcement, given the values and goals of our political system.

The first of these assumptions takes as a point of departure the so-called "risk analysis" approach of *Lewis,* and *Lopez,* and to a lesser extent *On Lee,* or the expectations approach of *Katz.* See discussion in Part II, *supra.* While these formulations represent an advance over the unsophisticated trespass analysis of the common law, they too have their limitations and can, ultimately, lead to the substitution of words for analysis. The analysis must, in my view, transcend the search for subjective expectations or legal attribution of assumptions of risk. Our expectations, and the risks we assume, are in large part reflections of laws that translate into rules the customs and values of the past and present.

Since it is the task of the law to form and project, as well as mirror and reflect, we should not, as judges, merely recite the expectations and risks without examining the desirability of saddling them upon society. The critical question, therefore, is whether under our system of government, as reflected in the Constitution, we should impose on our citizens the risks of the electronic listener or observer without at least the protection of a warrant requirement.

This question must, in my view, be answered by assessing the nature of a particular practice and the likely extent of its impact on the individual's sense of security balanced against the utility of the conduct as a technique of law enforcement. For those more extensive intrusions that significantly jeopardize the sense of security which is the paramount concern of Fourth Amendment liberties, I am of the view that more than self-restraint by law enforcement officials is required and at the least warrants should be necessary. Cf. *Terry v. Ohio, supra; Davis v. Mississippi, supra.*

B

The impact of the practice of third-party bugging, must, I think, be considered such as to undermine that confidence and sense of security in dealing with one another that is characteristic of individual relationships between citizens in a free society. It goes beyond the impact on privacy occasioned by the ordinary type of "informer" investigation upheld in *Lewis* and *Hoffa*. The argument of the plurality opinion, to the effect that it is irrelevant whether secrets are revealed by the mere tattle-tale or the transistor, ignores the differences occasioned by third-party monitoring and recording which insures full and accurate disclosure of all that is said, free of the possibility of error and oversight that inheres in human reporting.

Authority is hardly required to support the proposition that words would be measured a good deal more carefully and communication inhibited if one suspected his conversations were being transmitted and transcribed. Were third-party bugging a prevalent practice, it might well smother that spontaneity — reflected in frivolous, impetuous, sacrilegious, and defiant discourse — that liberates daily life. Much off-hand exchange is easily forgotten and one may count on the obscurity of his remarks, protected by the very fact of a limited audience, and the likelihood that the listener will either overlook or forget what is said, as well as the listener's inability to reformulate a conversation without having to contend with a documented record. All these values are sacrificed by a rule of law that permits official monitoring of private discourse limited only by the need to locate a willing assistant.

It matters little that consensual transmittals are less obnoxious than wholly clandestine eavesdrops. This was put forward as justification for the conduct in *Boyd v. United States*, 116 U.S. 616 (1886), where the Government relied on mitigating aspects of the conduct in question. The Court, speaking through Mr. Justice Bradley, declined to countenance literalism:

> Though the proceeding in question is divested of many of the aggravating incidents of actual search and seizure, yet, as before said, it contains their substance and essence, and effects their substantial purpose. It may be that it is the obnoxious thing in its mildest and least repulsive form; but illegitimate and unconstitutional practices get their first footing in that way, namely, by silent approaches and slight deviations from legal modes of procedure. [116 U.S., at 635.]

Finally, it is too easy to forget — and, hence, too often forgotten — that the issue here is whether to interpose a search warrant procedure between law enforcement agencies engaging in electronic eavesdropping and the public generally. By casting its "risk analysis" solely in terms of the expectations and risks that "wrongdoers" or "one contemplating illegal activities" ought to bear, the plurality opinion, I think, misses the mark entirely. *On Lee* does not simply mandate that criminals must daily run the risk of unknown eavesdroppers prying into their private affairs; it subjects each and every law-abiding member of society to that risk. The very purpose of interposing the Fourth Amendment warrant requirement is to redistribute the privacy risks throughout society in a way that produces the results the plurality opinion ascribes to the *On Lee* rule. Abolition of *On Lee* would not end electronic eavesdropping. It would prevent public officials from engaging in that practice unless they first had probable cause to suspect an individual of involvement in illegal activities and had tested their version of the facts before a detached judicial officer. The interest *On Lee* fails to protect is the expectation of the ordinary citizen, who has never engaged in illegal conduct in his life, that he may carry on his private discourse freely, openly, and spontaneously without measuring his every word against the connotations it might carry when instantaneously heard by others unknown to him and unfamiliar with his situation or analyzed in a cold, formal record played days, months, or years after the conversation. Interposition of a warrant requirement is designed not to shield "wrongdoers," but to secure a measure of privacy and a sense of personal security throughout our society.

The Fourth Amendment does, of course, leave room for the employment of modern technology in criminal law enforcement, but in the stream of current developments in Fourth Amendment law I think it must be held that third-party electronic monitoring, subject only to the self-restraint of law enforcement officials, has no place in our society.

CHAPTER 6

THE IMAGINATION OF THE LAWYER

How simply the fictive hero becomes the real;
How gladly with proper words the soldier dies,
If he must, or lives on the bread of faithful speech.*

We who are born into the world's artificial system can never adequately know how little in our present state and circumstances is natural and how much is merely the interpolation of the perverted mind and heart of man. Art has become a second and stronger Nature; she is a stepmother whose crafty tenderness has taught us to despise the bountiful and wholesome ministrations of our true parent. It is only through the medium of the imagination that we can lessen those iron fetters which we call truth and reality and make ourselves even partially sensible what prisoners we are.†

In asking you to fashion for yourself a language of criticism adequate to the activity of the legal mind, a language in which you could explain and judge what you perceive the legal mind to be doing, the preceding assignment set you a problem (perhaps you felt) not for a week but for life. You have been pushed off, as it were, to make your own way in your own direction. How are you to speak of what you do as a lawyer, how are you to express even to yourself how you regard your professional life? Surely the language that reduces the mind and what it faces to the machine — to the see-saw, or the lever, or the pulley, or the optical glass — cannot do it, but what can? Here your legal education (if it is anything like mine) runs out, and the burden settles upon you alone.

In some sense, then, you may properly feel that we have come to an end, and you may wish for a new beginning. In this chapter you are encouraged to make such a start, to pull together what you have done in this course and in law school, to put it into some sort of order, and move on. The writing assignments will accordingly be less specific than

* Wallace Stevens, "Notes Toward a Supreme Fiction" (1943).
† Nathaniel Hawthorne, "The New Adam and Eve" (1846).

they have been; and even more than before, you will be asked to finish off a particular question in a way that suits you, to make something of your own out of what it offers.

There is an idea in what follows, however (in fact it is the idea that the course has been working out from the beginning); but rather than as a dogmatic restriction on your freedom, it is meant as an invitation, as a thesis for your examination and response: that the activities which make up the professional life of the lawyer and judge constitute an enterprise of the imagination, an enterprise whose central performance is the claim of meaning against the odds: the translation of the imagination into reality by the power of language. Its art is accordingly a literary one, most obviously perhaps in the demand that one master the forces and limits of what we have called the legal language system — speaking, as it does, in a set of official voices, reducing people to institutional identities, insisting on the repetition of inherited patterns of thought and speech (most frustratingly in its use of the rule) and reposing an impossible confidence in its fictional pretenses. The art of the lawyer is perhaps first of all the literary art that controls this language. To say as much, and to ask how that language can be controlled — what the lawyer can do with it — is to say that the lawyer is at heart a writer, one who lives by the power of his imagination. This is not a usual cultural definition of the law — which is often regarded as a subject, not an activity, let alone as an imaginative and literary one — but it is one for which you have been prepared by the work you have done in this course.

The demands on your imagination start outside the legal language system, perhaps outside all language, when you first face a client or a judge or a juror and ask yourself "Who is this person?" in a way that recognizes that he may be different from you. What is called for here is a social and narrative imagination, a capacity to envision different versions of the future. Think back to the Stein problem (page 188 *supra*), for example; what is called for there first of all, and without which nothing will avail, is the capacity to pretend that you are sitting in your office when Stein walks in, to imagine various ways the conversation might go. "Who is this person, and how shall I address him?" is a constant question in the life of the lawyer, and you will not think it a simple one. The imagination here is a faculty of sympathy as well as intellect.[1] Or suppose you are arguing a case: you must imagine ahead of time what the judge might say to this or that, or what the other lawyer might say in objection to the evidence or in refutation of your position, and prepare

1. For an original essay on the limits of the faculty of sympathetic imagination see Baird, "Sympathy: The Broken Mirror," 37 *Am. Scientist* 255 (1949).

to meet it. "If I say this, he may say that; and then I . . ." To argue well, you must imagine another mind and have some sense of how someone else might look at your client and his case. How can you put your case in his terms or get him to see it in yours? Likewise, as a legislator or rule maker, the heart of your task is making a just assessment of what your audience, your judges and lawyers, are likely to do with what you have written. The lawyer must be able to tell himself imaginary stories about the future.

There are other ways, as well, in which it can be said that the lawyer's life is an activity of the imagination. For example, as you learned in the first year of law school, it is not enough to follow the directions of the Speed-Reading Institute and read a case for the main idea; one must read with a literary or archeological imagination, reconstructing the facts, the trial, the argument, asking how a prior case might have been better used, what issues seem omitted or miscast, exactly why things were put just this way or that, and how it all might have been better done. One must engage in a similar process as the auditor of the client's story and as the reader of the documents he provides as a record of his past. The lawyer's imagination, that is, must work in the past as well as the future. "If I had been there . . ."

The imagination of the lawyer is more than a capacity for pretending or for perceiving; it is also a power that organizes what is seen and claims a meaning for it. The lawyer must constantly be ready to express things in an original way, to make an imaginatively organized statement, to speak in a way that meets the occasion and says what it calls for. When he rises in the courtroom to make a closing argument to the jury or to argue on appeal, or when he speaks in a letter or orally to his client, the demand is a literary one: he must organize what he knows about the case, the individuals, and the law, and do so not only for himself but for others, in such a way that his statement, his version of things, can stand the test of comparison with another version, so that it will be taken as the right one. What can he lead his audience to accept and tolerate? What order can he put upon things? "After he killed Caesar, Brutus stood forth to give reasons," says Plutarch; what can Brutus have said? What are the possibilities of thought and expression here? Plutarch does not tell us, "for the people would not hear him." The lawyer fails at his first step.

We return again to Huck and Jim on the raft: Twain cannot imagine how to go on, and neither, I daresay, can anyone else. But what an achievement that would be! And there have been achievements of such a magnitude in the law and elsewhere: think of the very idea of the judge, for example, the judge as someone different from a grumpy old man or a liberal milksop, the judge as a judge; now that is an intellectual and social resource of the first order. And who do you suppose ever came up with the idea that thirteen colonies could be made into one nation, somehow both keeping and losing their status as countries? What do you suppose those people actually thought they were doing? It will not surprise you — you who remember writing about the original intention of the boy on his way to law school, with his hopelessly misconceived expectations (page 44 *supra*) — to learn that no one imagined things the way they worked out, and instead saw questions of constitutional meaning as matters of political dispute or diplomatic negotiation (or so it seems at least from Henry Adams's *History of the United States*). One can look with similar wonder on humbler inventions — the trust, the corporation, the agent — and say that the law is indeed an imaginative activity, its task the constant creation of rhetorical and intellectual resources.

The activities of the lawyer's life are imaginative in still another way: they include a process of self-imagination. For as you work through your life as a lawyer, struggling to put things the right way, to make and defend your claims of meaning — as you choose what you shall say and not say — you work out an identity for yourself, you define a mind and character, very much as the historian or poet or novelist might be said to do. At the end of thirty years you will be able to look at shelves of briefs, think back on negotiations and arguments and interviews, and say, "Here is what I have found it possible to say."

This prospect can certainly be daunting — we can all imagine futures we do not want — but it has been part of the pressure of this course to urge you to try to define it as exhilarating, to try to imagine and express a future you do want. There are many ways to talk about prospective success and failure, and it is not with the idea of excluding other possibilities that I have suggested in this course that one might define success as a matter of the right relationship with language, that one's ultimate claim might be to be an artist, in some sense a master of language. But how does one master the legal language system? By using it with great care to express one's ideas with clarity and precision?

You might sum up the experience this course offers by saying that it is an experience in the collapse of language under strain: the collapse not only of the legal language, but of the other languages you have used (of psychology, of race, of social organization, of explanation, of criticism, of paper-writing, and so on). You have experienced what could be called the central frustration of writer and lawyer, the perpetual breaking down of language in your hands as you try to use it. None of our languages seems to be able to do what it promises, none can bear the stresses of our demands for truth and order and justice. Such, it seems to me, are the conditions of our existence.

How can these conditions be addressed? This has been our question from the beginning, and I offer now no answer, no portable clarification. Perhaps the way in which this chapter works out the analogy that has been our premise from the beginning — that the law can be regarded as an imaginative activity and its art a literary one — should be viewed rather as the making of a metaphor than as, say, a proposal for a solution or a program for a way to face the writer's situation. We start by comparing what the judge does and what the poet does, and ask: is the judge really a poet, his opinion really a poem? What can be learned from the study of poetry and its criticism that will help us understand, engage in, and criticize the arts of lawyer and judge? To put these two forms of expression side by side will not lead to a system of exposition and analysis, of classification and categorization, but it may give us a way of asking new questions and expressing new hopes. To suggest that the judge is like the poet — or the historian or the mathematician — seems more promising than to say he is like a man using a pair of scales or a tape measure or an inclined plane. Perhaps this chapter can best be regarded as my own attempt to begin to meet the responsibilities that the course is meant to uncover and define.

A. *IS THE JUDGE REALLY A POET?*

The philosopher therefore and the historian are they which would win the goal, the one by precept, the other by example. But both, not having both, do both halt. For the philosopher, setting down with thorny argument the bare rule, is so hard of utterance, and so misty to be conceived, that one that hath no other guide but him shall wade in him till he be old before he shall find sufficient cause to be honest. For his knowledge standeth so upon the abstract and general, that happy is that man who may understand him, and more happy that can apply what he doth understand. On the other side, the historian, wanting the precept, is so tied, not to what should be but to what is, to the particular truth of things and not to the general reason of things, that his example draweth no necessary consequence, and therefore a less fruitful doctrine.

Now doth the peerless poet perform both: for whatsoever the philosopher saith should be done, he giveth a perfect picture of it in someone by whom he presupposeth it was done; so as he coupleth the general notion with the particular example. A perfect picture I say, for he yieldeth to the powers of the mind an image of that whereof the philosopher bestoweth but a wordish description: which doth neither strike, pierce, nor possess the sight of the soul so much as that other doth.*

* Sir Philip Sidney, "The Defense of Poesie" (1595).

We are like persons who have come out of a cave or cellar into the open air. This is the effect on us of tropes, fables, oracles, and all poetic forms. Poets are thus liberating gods. Men have really got a new sense, and found within their world another world, or nest of worlds; for, the metamorphosis once seen, we divine that it does not stop. . . .

The poets are thus liberating gods. The ancient British bards had for the title of their order, "Those who are free throughout the world." They are free, and they make free.†

This power [of the imagination in the poet] . . . reveals itself in the balance or reconcilement of opposite or discordant qualities: of sameness, with difference; of the general with the concrete; the idea with the image; the individual with the representative; the sense of novelty and freshness with old and familiar objects; a more than usual state of emotion with more than usual order; judgment ever awake and steady self-possession with enthusiasm and feeling profound or vehement; and while it blends and harmonizes the natural and artificial, still subordinates art to nature; the manner to the matter; and our admiration of the poet to our sympathy with the poetry.‡

1. *The Message and the Rule: What More Do We Find in the Poem and Opinion?*

One way to try to connect these two forms of expression is to realize that a basic question of motive can be asked of both poet and judge: why do you write poems? Why do you write opinions? Presumably the judge could decide his cases and draw his salary without writing opinions if he chose, and in fact it is often a real question for a judge whether to explain a decision or a vote. No doubt the poet could get along well enough without writing poems; it scarcely makes him rich, and no one forces him to do it. Related is the reader's question: why should I read poems? Why should I read opinions? There are, after all, those who would say that neither activity has any value. Why do poets and judges write, then, and why do we read?

Someone might respond: the poet has a message to communicate, the judge a rule to announce, and this explains why they write and why we read. But if this is all there is to it, why do they not satisfy themselves with a simple statement of the rule or message, and why do we read on once we have grasped the main idea? If such were their only motives, nothing could be expected of them beyond rationality in thought and clarity in writing. Why do they go beyond writing of such a kind, one to the poem, the other to the opinion?

† Emerson, "The Poet," in *Essays* (2d ser. 1844).
‡ Coleridge, *Biographia Literaria,* Chapter 14 (1817).

Below is a passage that raises such questions of Burke's *Reflections on the Revolution in France* (1790).

THE LANGUAGE OF POLITICS IN THE AGE OF WILKES AND BURKE*

J. T. Boulton

Not only were numerous opponents quick to proclaim the errors in Burke's facts and question his conclusions, as soon as the *Reflections* was published, but the process has continued ever since. As Raymond Williams observes, "the confutation of Burke on the French Revolution is now a one-finger exercise in politics and history."[1] Yet, in this century at any rate, little has been done thoroughly to account for the continuing impact of the book from 1790 to our own day, except on the level of abstract theory. It is abundantly evident, however, that the response of Burke's contemporaries was not only to a body of ideas but rather to a complete literary achievement, a mode of writing effectively designed to convey a particular manner of thinking; when they attacked or praised the book it was that complete achievement they had in mind. Paine or Mackintosh, for example, were alive to the intimate relationship that exists between Burke's philosophical reflection and his literary techniques, and it is surprising to find critics who examine his political thought without recognising that literary criticism is essential to their purpose. To use John Holloway's remark on the Victorian "sage," what Burke "has to say is not a matter just of 'content' or narrow paraphrasable meaning, but is transfused by the whole texture of his writing as it constitutes an experience for the reader."[2] Burke was not only a great thinker, he was also an imaginative writer who requires a response from the reader as a whole man and not simply as a creature of intellect. Consequently his exposition — the play of imaginative insights as well as the statement of logical argument — itself becomes "proof" in this special sense that it communicates, and affirms while communicating, the rich complexity of a philosophy of life; it does not merely demonstrate the truth of a set of propositions.

Does this passage point the way towards explaining why a judge writes an opinion? Would you say that an excellent opinion has a "play of imaginative insights," that it communicates and "affirms" the "rich complexity of a philosophy of life"? That it requires "a response from the reader as a whole man"? Is this the way in which judges and his-

* Pages 97–98 (1963).
1. *Culture and Society, 1780–1950* (Pelican edn., 1961), p. 24.
2. *The Victorian Sage* (1953), pp. 10–11.

torians alike meet our skeptical reader's familiar query, "Why should I pay any attention to what you say?"

Finding a way to talk about these matters of literary value and purpose is of course most difficult. When asked on the first day of classes why they were reading the *Iliad,* and urged to be honest, freshman humanities students said that they wished to be exposed to our rich classical heritage or to learn about another civilization, or that they hoped to become better and wiser people, or that they did it because it was assigned and they had to, or because they trusted their teachers and felt they ought to, or perhaps because they expected to enjoy it. What their teacher suggested then about the *Iliad,* I suggest now about the judicial opinion: that while all of these responses may be true, none of them begins a valuable conversation, none opens up a line of inquiry and learning of the kind we hope for. What is needed is a literary response — such as, "I read it for its meaning" or "I read it to see what he has done" or perhaps "I read it to learn why one reads" — a response that directs attention away from descriptive or conclusory phrases, away from ulterior motives and hopes, towards the document, the writing; a response that carries us to the activity expressed in the poem or opinion itself.

It is, then, as a way of setting up a question — of making a language in which to carry on an inquiry — that I make the following suggestion: let us agree that the message of a poem ("I am sad"; "I am in love"; "All men must die, including me") is not its meaning; likewise, the message (or rule) of the judicial opinion is not its meaning. Otherwise the poet would simply state the message (as I did) and stop, and the court would state its rule and stop. No need to worry about what rhymes with "obloquy," or what meter to use, or whether the metaphor breaks down and makes everything ridiculous; no need to explain one's decision, to register one's doubts, to cite and reconcile cases and statutes, to open up an argument that could go on forever. As for the reader, if the message really were the meaning, he would stop at the West headnotes; he would skim the poem for its essential wisdom and close the book.

The meaning of a poem is not its paraphrase, but the experience of reading it — not just reading it once, but reading it to learn it, to master it, reading with imaginative engagement and readiness to learn, just as you read an important judicial opinion. Of course the poem may not have a simple statement at all; you may be left with an unresolved ambiguity, an ambivalence or paradox that cannot be put into simple declarative form, or perhaps with just an emotional impression. But some summary can always be made, and you should see that there is always something beyond this summary, beyond the message, in the good poem, and — although you may not in a particular case be able to state with any finality what it is — that it is this which gives the poem value. One has not a sense of solution but the reverse, and this works as an invitation.[2]

Much the same can be said of the judicial opinion: its "rule" (for which it may be cited later in another opinion, in Gilbert's Law Outlines, or on an exam) is not the meaning of that opinion, or the opinion would have consisted of that rule without more. Where the rule is statutory, where the message is given us, the judicial activity would remain wholly unexpressed: the opinion would consist merely of the statement of the rule and the declaration of the judgment. I daresay you know opinions that could be described this way, but we know that at its best the judicial mind does more than this, that its expression defines and exemplifies an education.

The statements of most poems and judicial opinions can alike be reduced to trivial generalization or cliché, to mere message. What is there about these two forms of expression that makes them sometimes so very much more?

That is our question, and it invites a large range of responses. One line of thought was begun in Chapter 1, where it was suggested that the fundamental difficulty of the writer could be put this way: when one writes, one chooses a language, a way of talking, a set of implied interests and relationships; and from the outset the essential task is controlling this language, forcing or adjusting it to one's purposes. We examined three traditional techniques of control — metaphor, irony, and ambiguity — each of which could be said to be a way of using a language and recognizing what it leaves out, a way of writing two ways at once. In this way, success for the artist was defined as a relationship with language, as a way of making his words work to his will, differentiating his statement from all others.

Here, as you see, we begin another line of thought, and I hope you will be interested in seeing whether it can be made to converge in your mind with the first. We start with what one poet has had to say about his art. How much of what you read in the following two essays by Frost could be said of the judicial opinion?

2. These paragraphs should not greatly trouble you. If they do, go back to the poems in Chapters 1 and 2 and paraphrase several of them. Then ask: why did the poet not simply write the paraphrase instead of the poem? See also Cleanth Brooks, "The Heresy of Paraphrase," in *The Well-Wrought Urn* 192 (Harvest ed. 1947); Yvor Winters, "The Morality of Poetry," in *In Defense of Reason* 17 (1937; Swallow ed. 1947).

2. *Reading the Poem: The Education of the Imagination?*

THE CONSTANT SYMBOL*
Robert Frost

There seems to be some such folk saying as that easy to understand is contemptible, hard to understand irritating. The implication is that just easy enough, just hard enough, right in the middle, is what literary criticism ought to foster. A glance backward over the past convinces me otherwise. The *Iliad, Odyssey,* and *Aeneid* are easy. The *Purgatorio* is said to be hard. The Song of Songs *is* hard. There have been works lately to surpass all records for hardness. Some knotted riddles tell what may be worth our trouble. But hard or easy seems to me of slight use as a test either way.

Texture is surely something. A good piece of weaving takes rank with a picture as decoration for the wall of a studio, though it must be admitted to verge on the arty. There is a time of apprenticeship to texture when it shouldn't matter if the stuff is never made up into anything. There may be scraps of repeated form all over it. But form as a whole! Don't be shocking! The title of his first book was *Fragments.* The artist has to grow up and coarsen a little before he looks on texture as not an end in itself.

There are many other things I have found myself saying about poetry, but the chiefest of these is that it is metaphor, saying one thing and meaning another, saying one thing in terms of another, the pleasure of ulteriority. Poetry is simply made of metaphor. So also is philosophy — and science, too, for that matter, if it will take the soft impeachment from a friend. Every poem is a new metaphor inside or it is nothing. And there is a sense in which all poems are the same old metaphor always.

Every single poem written regular is a symbol small or great of the way the will has to pitch into commitments deeper and deeper to a rounded conclusion and then be judged for whether any original intention it had has been strongly spent or weakly lost; be it in art, politics, school, church, business, love, or marriage — in a piece of work or in a career. Strongly spent is synonymous with kept.

We may speak after sentence, resenting judgment. How can the world know anything so intimate as what we were intending to do? The answer is the world presumes to know. The ruling passion in man is not as Viennese as is claimed. It is rather a gregarious instinct to keep

* Printed as the introduction to *The Poems of Robert Frost* (Modern Library ed. 1946).

together by minding each other's business. Grex rather than sex. We *must* be preserved from becoming egregious. The beauty of socialism is that it will end the individuality that is always crying out mind your own business. Terence's answer would be all human business is my business. No more invisible means of support, no more invisible motives, no more invisible anything. The ultimate commitment is giving in to it that an outsider may see what we were up to sooner and better than we ourselves. The bard has said in effect, Unto these forms did I commend the spirit. It may take him a year after the act to confess he only betrayed the spirit with a rhymster's cleverness and to forgive his enemies the critics for not having listened to his oaths and protestations to the contrary. Had he anything to be true to? Was he true to it? Did he use good words? You couldn't tell unless you made out what idea they were supposed to be good for. Every poem is an epitome of the great predicament; a figure of the will braving alien entanglements.

Take the President in the White House. A study of the success of his intention might have to go clear back to when as a young politician, youthfully step-careless, he made the choice between the two parties of our system. He may have stood for a moment wishing he knew of a third party nearer the ideal; but only for a moment, since he was practical. And in fact he may have been so little impressed with the importance of his choice that he left his first commitment to be made for him by his friends and relatives. It was only a small commitment anyway, like a kiss. He can scarcely remember how much credit he deserved personally for the decision it took. Calculation is usually no part in the first step in any walk. And behold him now a statesman so multifariously closed in on with obligations and answerabilities that sometimes he loses his august temper. He might as well have got himself into a sestina royal.

Or he may be a religious nature who lightly gets committed to a nameable church through an older friend in plays and games at the Y.M.C.A. The next he knows he is in a theological school and next in the pulpit of a Sunday wrestling with the angel for a blessing on his self-defensive interpretation of the Creed. What of his original intention now? At least he has had the advantage of having it more in his heart than in his head; so that he should have made shift to assert it without being chargeable with compromise. He could go a long way before he had to declare anything he could be held to. He began with freedom to squander. He has to acknowledge himself in a tighter and tighter place. But his courage asked for it. It would have been the same if he had gone to the North Pole or climbed Everest. All that concerns *us* is whether his story was one of conformance or performance.

There's an indulgent smile I get for the recklessness of the unnecessary commitment I made when I came to the first line in the second stanza of a poem in this book called "Stopping by Woods on a Snowy Evening." I was riding too high to care what trouble I incurred. And it was all right so long as I didn't suffer deflection.

The poet goes in like a rope skipper to make the most of his opportunities. If he trips himself he stops the rope. He is of our stock and has been brought up by ear to choice of two metres, strict iambic and loose iambic (not to count varieties of the latter). He may have any length of line up to six feet. He may use an assortment of line lengths for any shape of stanza like Herrick in "To Daffodils." Not that he is running wild. His intention is of course a particular mood that won't be satisfied with anything less than its own fulfillment. But it is not yet a thought concerned with what becomes it. One thing to know it by: it shrinks shyly from anticipatory expression. Tell love beforehand and, as Blake says, it loses flow without filling the mould; the cast will be a reject. The freshness of a poem belongs absolutely to its not having been thought out and then set to verse as the verse in turn might be set to music. A poem is the emotion of having a thought while the reader waits a little anxiously for the success of dawn. The only discipline to begin with is the inner mood that at worst may give the poet a false start or two like the almost microscopic filament of cotton that goes before the blunt thread-end and must be picked up first by the eye of the needle. He must be entranced to the exact premonition. No mystery is meant. When familiar friends approach each other in the street both are apt to have this experience in feeling before knowing the pleasantry they will inflict on each other in passing.

Probably there is something between the mood and the vocal imagination (images of the voice speaking) that determines a man's first commitment to metre and length of line.

Suppose him to have written down "When in disgrace with Fortune and men's eyes." He has uttered about as much as he has to live up to in the theme as in the form. Odd how the two advance into the open pari passu. He has given out that he will descend into Hades, but he has confided in no one how far before he will turn back, or whether he will turn back at all, and by what jutting points of rock he will pick his way. He may proceed as in blank verse. Two lines more, however, and he has let himself in for rhyme, three more and he has set himself a stanza. Up to this point his discipline has been the self-discipline whereof it is written in so great praise. The harsher discipline from without is now well begun. He who knows not both knows neither. His worldly commitments are now three or four deep. Between us, he was no doubt bent on the sonnet in the first place from habit, and what's the use in pretending he was a freer agent than he had any ambition to be? He had made most of his commitments all in one plunge. The only suspense he asks us to share with him is in the theme. He goes down, for instance, to a depth that must surprise him as much as it does us. But he doesn't even have the say of how long his piece will be. Any worry is as to whether he will outlast or last out the fourteen lines — have to cramp or stretch to come out even — have enough bread for the butter or butter for the bread. As a matter of fact, he gets through in twelve lines and doesn't know quite what to do with the last two.

Things like that and worse are the reason the sonnet is so suspect a form and has driven so many to free verse and even to the novel. Many a quatrain is salvaged from a sonnet that went agley. Dobson confesses frankly to having changed from one form to another after starting: "I intended an Ode and it turned to a Sonnet." But he reverses the usual order of being driven from the harder down to the easier. And he has a better excuse for weakness of will than most, namely, Rose.

Jeremiah, it seems, has had his sincerity questioned because the anguish of his lamentations was tamable to the form of twenty-two stanzas for the twenty-two letters of the alphabet. The Hebrew alphabet has been kept to the twenty-two letters it came out of Egypt with, so the number twenty-two means as much form as ever.

But there they go again with the old doubt about law and order. (The communist looks forward to a day of order without law, bless his merciful heart.) To the right person it must seem naive to distrust form as such. The very words of the dictionary are a restriction to make the best of or stay out of and be silent. Coining new words isn't encouraged. We play the words as we find them. We make them do. Form in language is such a disjected lot of old broken pieces it seems almost as non-existent as the spirit till the two embrace in the sky. They are not to be thought of as encountering in rivalry but in creation. No judgment on either alone counts. We see what Whitman's extravagance may have meant when he said the body was the soul.

Here is where it all comes out. The mind is a baby giant who, more provident in the cradle than he knows, has hurled his paths in life all round ahead of him like playthings given — data so-called. They are vocabulary, grammar, prosody, and diary, and it will go hard if he can't find stepping stones of them for his feet wherever he wants to go. The way will be zigzag, but it will be a straight crookedness like the walking stick he cuts himself in the bushes for an emblem. He will be judged as he does or doesn't let this zig or that zag project him off out of his general direction.

Teacher or student or investigator whose chance on these defenseless lines may seize, your pardon if for once I point you out what ordinarily you would point me out. To some it will seem strange that I have written my verse regular all this time without knowing till yesterday that it was from fascination with this constant symbol I celebrate. To the right person it will seem lucky; since in finding out too much too soon there is danger of arrest. Does anyone believe I would have committed myself to the treason-reason-season rhyme-set in my "Reluctance" if I had been blasé enough to know that these three words about exhausted the possibilities? No rhyming dictionary for me to make me face the facts of rhyme. I may say the strain of rhyming is less since I came to see words as phrase-ends to countless phrases just as the syllables ly, ing, and ation are word-ends to countless words. Leave something to learn later. We'd have lost most of our innocence by forty anyway even if we never went to school a day.

Here is Shakespeare's twenty-ninth sonnet, to which Frost refers in the preceding essay.

When, in disgrace with Fortune and men's eyes,
I all alone beweep my outcast state,
And trouble deaf heaven with my bootless cries,
And look upon myself and curse my fate,
Wishing me like to one more rich in hope,
Featur'd like him, like him with friends possess'd,
Desiring this man's art and that man's scope,
With what I most enjoy contented least;
Yet in these thoughts myself almost despising,
Haply I think on thee, and then my state,
Like to the lark at break of day arising
From sullen earth, sings hymns at heaven's gate;
For thy sweet love remember'd such wealth brings
That then I scorn to change my state with kings.

THE FIGURE A POEM MAKES (1949)*

Robert Frost

Abstraction is an old story with the philosophers, but it has been like a new toy in the hands of the artists of our day. Why can't we have any one quality of poetry we choose by itself? We can have in thought. Then it will go hard if we can't in practice. Our lives for it.

Granted no one but a humanist much cares how sound a poem is if it is only *a* sound. The sound is the gold in the ore. Then we will have the sound out alone and dispense with the inessential. We do till we make

* From *Selected Prose of Robert Frost* (Cox and Lathem ed. 1967).

the discovery that the object in writing poetry is to make all poems sound as different as possible from each other, and the resources for that of vowels, consonants, punctuation, syntax, words, sentences, meter are not enough. We need the help of context — meaning — subject matter. That is the greatest help towards variety. All that can be done with words is soon told. So also with meters — particularly in our language where there are virtually but two, strict iambic and loose iambic. The ancients with many were still poor if they depended on meters for all tune. It is painful to watch our sprung-rhythmists straining at the point of omitting one short from a foot for relief from monotony. The possibilities for tune from the dramatic tones of meaning struck across the rigidity of a limited meter are endless. And we are back in poetry as merely one more art of having something to say, sound or unsound. Probably better if sound, because deeper and from wider experience.

Then there is this wildness whereof it is spoken. Granted again that it has an equal claim with sound to being a poem's better half. If it is a wild tune, it is a poem. Our problem then is, as modern abstractionists, to have the wildness pure; to be wild with nothing to be wild about. We bring up as aberrationists, giving way to undirected associations and kicking ourselves from one chance suggestion to another in all directions as of a hot afternoon in the life of a grasshopper. Theme alone can steady us down. Just as the first mystery was how a poem could have a tune in such a straightness as meter, so the second mystery is how a poem can have wildness and at the same time a subject that shall be fulfilled.

It should be of the pleasure of a poem itself to tell how it can. The figure a poem makes. It begins in delight and ends in wisdom. The figure is the same as for love. No one can really hold that the ecstasy should be static and stand still in one place. It begins in delight, it inclines to the impulse, it assumes direction with the first line laid down, it runs a course of lucky events, and ends in a clarification of life — not necessarily a great clarification, such as sects and cults are founded on, but in a momentary stay against confusion. It has denouement. It has an outcome that though unforeseen was predestined from the first image of the original mood — and indeed from the very mood. It is but a trick poem and no poem at all if the best of it was thought of first and saved for the last. It finds its own name as it goes and discovers the best waiting for it in some final phrase at once wise and sad — the happy-sad blend of the drinking song.

No tears in the writer, no tears in the reader. No surprise for the writer, no surprise for the reader. For me the initial delight is in the surprise of remembering something I didn't know I knew. I am in a place, in a situation, as if I had materialized from cloud or risen out of the ground. There is a glad recognition of the long lost and the rest follows. Step by step the wonder of unexpected supply keeps growing. The impressions most useful to my purpose seem always those I was unaware of and so made no note of at the time when taken, and the conclusion is come to that like giants we are always hurling experience ahead of us to pave the future with against the day when we may want to strike a line of purpose across it for somewhere. The line will have the more charm for not being mechanically straight. We enjoy the straight crookedness of a good walking stick. Modern instruments of precision are being used to make things crooked as if by eye and hand in the old days.

I tell how there may be a better wildness of logic than of inconsequence. But the logic is backward, in retrospect, after the act. It must be more felt than seen ahead like prophecy. It must be a revelation, or a series of revelations, as much for the poet as for the reader. For it to be that there must have been the greatest freedom of the material to move about in it and to establish relations in it regardless of time and space, previous relation, and everything but affinity. We prate of freedom. We call our schools free because we are not free to stay away from them till we are sixteen years of age. I have given up my democratic prejudices and now willingly set the lower classes free to be completely taken care of by the upper classes. Political freedom is nothing to me. I bestow it right and left. All I would keep for myself is the freedom of my material — the condition of body and mind now and then to summons aptly from the vast chaos of all I have lived through.

Scholars and artists thrown together are often annoyed at the puzzle of where they differ. Both work from knowledge; but I suspect they differ most importantly in the way their knowledge is come by. Scholars get theirs with conscientious thoroughness along projected lines of logic; poets theirs cavalierly and as it happens in and out of books. They stick to nothing deliberately, but let what will stick to them like burrs where they walk in the fields. No acquirement is on assignment, or even self-assignment. Knowledge of the second kind is much more available in the wild free ways of wit and art. A school boy may be defined as one who can tell you what he knows in the order in which he learned it. The artist must value himself as he snatches a thing from some previous order in time and space into a new order with not so much as a ligature clinging to it of the old place where it was organic.

More than once I should have lost my soul to radicalism if it had been the originality it was mistaken for by its young converts. Originality and initiative are what I ask for my country. For myself the originality need be no more than the freshness of a poem run in the way I have described: from delight to wisdom. The figure is the same as for love. Like a piece of ice on a hot stove the poem must ride on its own melting. A poem may be worked over once it is in being, but may not be worried into being. Its most precious quality will remain its having run itself and carried away the poet with it. Read it a hundred times; it will forever keep its freshness as a metal keeps its fragrance. It can never lose its sense of a meaning that once unfolded by surprise as it went.

QUESTIONS

1. *How much of what Frost says here about the poem might one say about the judicial opinion?*
   a. *Might the opinion, like the poem, be said to be a constant symbol, a form with a meaning or a figure of its own which one who understood it – like you – might celebrate? Is there a sense in which it is the same old metaphor always?*
   b. *What figure might one say an opinion makes: from delight to wisdom? Has it denouement? What is it a symbol of: the way a mind works out an original intention?*
   c. *Might a judge say with Frost that his effort is to make all opinions "sound as different as possible from each other"? (Or to make them all sound alike?)*
   d. *Might you ask of a judge, as Frost asks of a poet, "Had he anything to be true to? Was he true to it? Did he use good words?"*
2. *Can it be said of the judicial opinion (as Frost says of the poem) that it is metaphor, "saying one thing and meaning another, saying one thing in terms of another"? Is it "simply made of metaphor"?*
   a. *What is to the parties a barroom fight, a dreadful auto accident, or an unsuccessful deal, is spoken of by the lawyers and the courts in terms of other things: cases, statutes, familiar arguments, and so on, and all in the traditional forms of oral and written argument, negotiation, judicial opinion, and the like. This is a way of talking of one thing in terms of another, of life in terms of law, and it could be seen as the central judicial activity. The events – which could be described in ordinary English a thousand ways, and which have a real life of their own outside the law in people's memories and feelings – are converted into a legal matter, and this conversion or metamorphosis is an act of the imagination. There are necessarily at least two languages here, two ways of talking; and in the judge's opinion, as in the poet's metaphor, the life of the expression comes in part from an initial tension, an incompatibility, between them. This tension creates a need that the conversion meets and fulfills. And since every case is different – presenting different material for a different conversion, subject to different strains and tensions – the judge's eye must be for the unique and particular, his imagination must be always ready to deal with this case as a fresh one to be worked through on its own terms. It might indeed be said that every opinion is a "new metaphor inside or it is nothing."*
   b. *The analogy to metaphor, as Frost defines it, can be drawn even more sharply in the case of the lawyer: his immediate concern as an attorney*

is that of his client – to get the money, avoid the judgment, get the divorce – but how does he express this concern? For him, it is usually enough that his client wants it (though what the client "really wants" may be the subject of much thought and conversation), but that is not the view he presses on the court. He speaks instead of the wiser rule or the weight of authority, of sound policy and logic in argument. The rightness of the reasoning he proposes is revelant only as its rightness makes it persuasive. He could function in much the same way in any system, just or unjust, with good rules or bad: his art is learning to speak the language of power, and his function is speaking of his client's situation and wishes in those terms. He plays the words as he finds them, and his skill – if not his pleasure – is in ulteriority.

c. *The judge engages in a similar ulteriority, a pretense of full expression: he certainly has doubts, motives, and fears that find no expression in his opinion. How much of what he says to his clerk ever appears in public? Where has his anger gone, where his worry?*

In writing his opinion the judge speaks of life in terms of the law, and of his true thoughts and feelings in the traditional language of judges: in two senses, then, he speaks of one thing in terms of another, says one thing and means another. One might well say that his opinion is made of metaphor.

d. *The judge engages in metaphor in a third sense too, for the very idea of judicial ritual which lies behind the opinion can be regarded as a sort of social metaphor: the old man who climbs to the bench becomes a judge, and everyone addresses him as such, no matter what they may know or feel about him. The assumption of all courtroom discourse is that the dispute is to be resolved by a disinterested and wise third party upon a showing of all the relevant facts; the truth will be made known and justice done. We say this, but we do not believe it; we have our reasons for saying it, but those who deal with judges had better realize the extent to which this is a deliberate pretense, a way of talking, by which we say one thing and mean another.*

3. *One obvious difference between the judge and the poet, one might have thought, is the poet's freedom to do and say whatever he wishes in the way he wishes. He is a free citizen; the judge is an official bound to apply the law. Is this a real distinction? What does Frost say about the poet's freedom?*

The constant symbol that Frost celebrates is the rigor and discipline of the poetic form, the limits on freedom to which the active will subjects itself as it works out an original intention. The poet starting off on a poem is compared with the young man starting off on his career, which leads through a series of decisions, each taken in partial ignorance, until the form of his life is cast. Potentiality becomes actuality: he is a president, or father, or felon. Like him, the poet must start off without knowing where he will end up; feeling his way, but somehow confident that he is right, that the course is soundly taken; and he must prove to be right. The poetic process is a process of judgment with the whole mind, undertaken in considerable ignorance of where it all will lead. (It may of course be a hopelessly bad start and lead nowhere at all.) Decisions made now must be lived with later. The very notion of poetic form is an important limitation upon the poet's freedom.

Is this not remarkably like the process of judicial thought? The judge, after he has voted in conference or tentatively decided the case for himself, must sit down to work out for himself (and for us) why he did so; and as he complicates what he meant by the choice he has made, he may find that it all works out very differently from what he had expected, that his expectations of clarity or even of intelligibility are frustrated, that he finds himself in a tighter and a tighter place. To be caught between the right to free exercise of religion and the prohibition against establishment may be no better, as Frost might say, than to have started a sestina royal. The activity of putting into order the uncertain array of cases and rules and facts and feelings that he faces can be a process of self-discovery very much like the poet's.

One might want to say that Frost's analogy to the young man setting forth on his career is even more apt for the judge than the poet. For while the poet may be able to dispose of his false starts more easily than the young man can do, the judge has, or may be said to have, an obligation that the poet does not: to reflect in drafts nine and ten what he discovered for the first time in drafts seven and eight, to recognize and express the difficulties he comes to perceive, to tell us what he has learned — and what he has learned may be very uncomfortable. He may even learn that he has to change his vote.[3]

But can the poet really toss off his false starts without cost? Surely if he is to continue with the poem he has begun, he has an obligation like the judge's, and Frost says as much. The poet's freedom is limited by his acceptance of form, his willingness to live with what he discovers as he works out his intention; and the judge's freedom is limited in exactly the same way: he can make his original judgment and choose his direction and his language — indeed he is paid to make such choices, he is one of society's choosers — but he must live with what he discovers, he accepts responsibility for facing what he learns.

Is the poet's freedom more than the judge's then only in this, that he is free from having to vote when he does not know the answer, from having to decide what he cannot decide? Or do you suppose it is exactly these matters — the most puzzling and frustrating — that the poet will conceive it his highest responsibility to address?

3. People sometimes talk rather stupidly about a judge's "gut reactions," as though the choice for a judge were between simple and rational (and proper) application of the law on the one hand, and unleashing some beastly and unlawful instinct on the other. Another way to phrase this common view is that the judge "really" decides a case the way he "wants to," and dresses up the decision in legal language in his opinion. You, of course, know that that view is nonsense. What on earth can "really" and "want" mean in that sentence? And certainly the alternative of the "simple and rational" result does not exist. A judge cannot do his job without a sense of what is right and what not, and in fact he is paid to exercise that faculty of judgment. But on no theory can that be called a "reaction," as if it were a simple and clear impulse. If anyone denies this to you, ask him when the "impulse" occurs: when the judge reads the names of the parties? The facts as stated by the appellant? By the appellee? When he reads their statements of the issue, or their conclusions? When he has pored over both sets of briefs? When he talks about the case with his clerk or colleagues, or asks questions on oral argument? And wherever the person chooses to locate the impulse or decision, ask what he thinks the judge is doing the rest of the time: faking? somnambulating?

4. *How can the shape or movement of the poem and opinion be compared?* In each of his essays, Frost gives an account of the poem as movement, as having life and shape and change and surprise: "The freshness of a poem belongs absolutely to its not having been thought out and then set to verse . . ." "No surprise for the writer, no surprise for the reader." The figure of the poem, he says, is "from delight to wisdom": the reader is first captivated, then enticed along until he is brought up short against a paradox or truth he should have seen but did not. The reader is, as it were, surprised into learning. This is meant as a universal statement about good poems: "it begins in delight, it inclines to the impulse, it assumes direction with the first line laid down, it runs a course of lucky events, and ends in a clarification of life — not necessarily a great clarification, such as sects and cults are founded on, but in a momentary stay against confusion." Can the same be said of a good judicial opinion? If the poem moves from delight to wisdom, how does the opinion move?
   a. Do you want to say that the opinion moves towards the ratio decidendi? How can you describe its movement then?
      (1) From facts to law? From question to answer? From issue to definition? From disagreement to agreement?
      (2) Does it move at all, or is it simply the exposition of facts and reasons?
   b. To put it slightly differently, one might ask (as we did in Chapter 5) how the language game of explaining a judicial decision can be defined: is the activity a simple one of observing something — say, one's reasons or the applicable rule or policy — and telling us about them? Or does the good explanation somehow involve the reader in an activity, a process of some kind? How might you define the experience it offers him? Is it a process of movement from the way things seem at first, through questioning and doubts, to whatever conclusion in the end seems best? Often people speak of the judicial opinion as if it were not a figure at all, as if it had no movement or life, but was simply a description of internal facts. Can you see how one might claim instead that its figure is that of the will "braving alien entanglements"?
   c. Frost defines his sense of the movement of the poem more specifically by pointing out two structural tensions: between the sound or "tune" and its ordering by meter and rhyme; and between the logical statement and the urge to exceed it in some illogical but more meaningful statement of wildness, between the rational and the irrational. Attempts to write poetry without them fail: to write pure music without meter, or pure meter without regard for the "real" sound, are equally impossible; and the utterly illogical poem is a form of nonsense, while pure logic is mathematics. These tensions are sources of life and energy. What structural tensions can you find in the judicial opinion, by which its "figure" can be defined? Obviously it is not these particular tensions that are commonly thought of as central in judicial opinions. There is no meter or rhyme, and the formal ordering of any kind is less obvious. We do not cast opinions in the form of sonnets or anapestic lyrics. But there is a real question here with which you can do something. Can you find ways, beyond the remarks made above, in which the judicial opinion, like the poem, is a constant symbol, a way or pattern

of thinking things through, a model for intellectual engagement? Yvor Winters calls the poem "a technique of contemplation, of comprehension"; could the same be said of the opinion, and if so, how is that technique, that constant symbol, to be defined?

5. It is the purpose of this section as a whole to urge you to suggest your own responses to that question, but I can point to one or two further ways in which the poem and the judicial opinion can be compared.

For example, what Sidney (at the beginning of this section) says about poetry could be said equally well about the law: that its central operation is the connection of the particular with the general, the individual with the representative. Both usually address particular events or experiences, and each does so in a way that is meant to give them a general significance, a representative meaning. Blake's poem, "The Sick Rose" (page 58 supra), is not about a horticultural problem, but much more; Frost's choice of one path over another (page 69) is not merely that, but is converted into an object of contemplation. How do these writers make what they describe involve so much, how do they put so much at stake? Likewise, of course, the opinion makes its events mean much more than $50 or the ownership of Blackacre or the other details of the case; to what are these particulars connected by the judicial opinion, and how does the process of connection work?

There is another side to the paradox: to make a generalization out of a poem or opinion is to be as false to its meaning as to claim that it consists merely of its details. Each has a meaning beyond its message. Where can this meaning – one that is at once more than the particulars of the matter and more than a generalized proposition – be found and how can it be explained?

6. One tension at work in both the opinion and the poem is that between simplicity and complexity. Current critical taste sometimes seems to have made complexity and ambiguity terms of ultimate poetic praise: the good poem includes and includes, complicates and complicates, until it leaves us with a nest of paradoxes, the more tangled the better; complexity is something we cannot have enough of. In this course I have been urging that the judge in the judicial opinion, and the lawyer in his work, ought to include more and more, ought to engage in a process of complication too. But how far can we go? The judge cannot leave us with an intellectual briar patch: he must decide, and he must state his decision in a way that provides some guidance for the future – a rule, perhaps a set of factors or criteria – and in doing so, he must simplify. Is this then a basic difference between the two forms? What does Frost say?

Of course, as you can see from Frost and the poems printed below, complexity run wild is no virtue – Alexander Pope describes the work of one brilliant failure as "one glaring chaos and wild heap of wit" – and the poet, like the judge, must keep what he does in control, must give it shape. If the measure of poetic excellence is not the degree of complexity and ambiguity, but the degree of complexity and ambiguity that the poet can control, how different is the poem in this respect from the judicial opinion?

Related is a matter to which Frost does not refer: the cutting down to the relevant. One can keep up forever one's search for meaning, there is always more to say. As you saw in Chapter 2, any statement seems to leave out volumes. The poet pares possibility down to what enables him to make his statement, and the judge does too; in both forms of expression there is a reduction of possible complexity, yet in both the writer strives for a sense of completeness. Can you say more about how this process works?

7. To what extent do both the poem and the opinion depend upon an inherited language system?

   a. The opinion looks back in time for much of its material of explanation: cases, statutes, and wise words of law professors. Is the same true of the poem? In his famous essay, "Tradition and the Individual Talent," T. S. Eliot presents a view of the relationship between the poem and its intellectual context that is quite like the way in which judicial opinions are often talked about. The poet, he says, must have a feeling that "the whole of the literature of Europe from Homer and within it the literature of his own country has a simultaneous existence and composes a simultaneous order." Can you imagine a similar remark being made about the common law judge? It is this sort of view that underlies the use of allusion as part of poetic structure, and of course Eliot's poetry is full of allusion. How like poetic allusion is the process by which a judge refers to the intellectual past in explaining his decision?

      And the dependence upon inherited language goes even deeper than that. How hard it is for the lawyer to give up the distinction between "privilege" and "right," even after it has been proved meaningless to everyone's satisfaction; how hard for the poet, when he writes about poetry, not to think of a nightingale or skylark. The inherited language in both cases provides a way of working on old expectations. We all know what kind of poem "It is a beauteous evening, calm and free . . ." will lead into; and it is this expectation that Eliot can play against when he begins a poem:

      > "Let us go then, you and I,
      > When the evening is spread out against the sky"
      > [Where now? A simile? "Like the veil of bashful bride"?]
      > Like a patient etherised upon a table."

      Does a judge ever play on inherited language in order to change inherited responses in that fashion? In another fashion?

   b. As you have seen again and again in this course, a legal rule (whether judicial or statutory) almost always uses and depends upon an inherited, professional language. It must speak to a particular intellectual world. But inherited terms can be used for new purposes; consider, for example, the English "Town and Country Planning" acts, which use the device of a new "estate in land" in order to move from private to public control of land use. What other examples can you find? Examine actual statutes and cases, and try to find instances in which inherited terms are used for new purposes. Is one purpose of an inherited language to provide a way of defining new ideas? Compare Terry v. Ohio, 392 U.S. 1 (1968).

      Legal expression of every kind speaks to a community defined by its language, and its task is often to change the language and views of its audience. Is this part of what a poem does? Does this lead to a suggestion of a wholly different way to write opinions?

c. Consider this statement: "The inherited legal language (which so strictly defines a community and its views) seems to provide the assumptions or premises from which reason or logic will take us to the resolution of a particular dispute; but since reason and logic do not operate with certainty but are themselves the subject of constant dispute, the function of this language must be less to justify the present decision (to compel agreement that it is right), than to limit the disagreement as narrowly as possible by affirming that to which we all agree. Dispute is disorder, potentially chaos: the legal language system provides a way by which the disorder is confined, a language in which a conclusion can be stated and understood. We fight about one thing, but at the same time say we agree about thirty others, to keep disorder from spreading. This is a way of saying that the tension that gives life to legal statements is the tension between order and disorder." Does any other language function this way? What are the implications of this statement for the judge and lawyer?

d. The essay by Eliot (Question 7a, supra) can be read another way, with more emphasis on "individual talent" and less on "tradition."[4] That is, the world of past achievement can be regarded as a context for an individual statement – as a body of material, a language – with which each writer must establish and enact for himself his own relationship. The writer does not merely allude to the past, he redefines it, re-creates it, in the use he makes of it. Might such remarks be made about the judge as well as the poet?

8. There will shortly follow a series of poems and questions meant to trace out still more connections and distinctions between these two forms of expression. Some of the questions will be familiar, perhaps complicating lines of thought already begun; others will be new. As you read these poems, you might keep in mind these questions:

a. Is the difference between the poem and the judicial opinion that the former is a personal and emotional statement, the latter rational and professional? The poet is engaged in self-expression, the judge in interpreting the law, and these are utterly different activities?

b. Is the poem meant to be beautiful, lovely, enrapturing, in a way no one ever thought of a judicial opinion as being? One serves beauty, the other serves truth or reason?

9. Reread Frost's "The Road Not Taken," page 69 supra. Is this poem an example of the poetic process as he defines it? Does it move from delight to wisdom? Is he saying one thing in terms of another?

a. What is the message of this poem? What, if anything, beyond that message do you find here? (You may find the comments at pages 69–70 helpful in working out these questions.)

b. Frost says that the meaning of a poem should "unfold by surprise"; John Keats has a famous sentence (to which Frost may be alluding): "I think poetry should surprise by fine excess, and not by singularity; it should strike the reader as a wording of his own highest thoughts, and appear almost a remembrance." Letter to John Taylor, Feb. 27, 1818. Is there a surprise in this poem? Where? Of what kind?

Two great poets say that surprise is essential to poetry. Are you ever

4. See Richard Poirier, *The Performing Self* 45–61 (1971).

surprised by a judicial opinion? Or is "surprise" perhaps a way of distinguishing these two forms of expression?

c. *One might say that the basic tension to which Frost's essays point as a source of the life of poetry is the tension between order and disorder: wild, but controlled; logical, but illogical: metrical, but with a contrasting rhythm; and so on. Can you see such a tension at work in "The Road Not Taken"? In any judicial opinions? Or are judicial opinions all perfectly orderly?*

A suggestion with which you might begin is that we point to such tension, to "order trembling upon disorder," when we speak of the "relevant" and "irrelevant" in the judicial opinion.

DESIGN
Robert Frost

I found a dimpled spider, fat and white,
On a white heal-all, holding up a moth
Like a white piece of rigid satin cloth —
Assorted characters of death and blight
Mixed ready to begin the morning right,
Like the ingredients of a witches' broth —
A snow-drop spider, a flower like a froth,
And dead wings carried like a paper kite.

What had that flower to do with being white,
The wayside blue and innocent heal-all?
What brought the kindred spider to that height,
Then steered the white moth thither in the night?
What but design of darkness to appall? —
If design govern in a thing so small.

QUESTIONS

1. *This poem surprises us, too. Where is the surprise here?*
2. *State the message of this poem. Is it that we don't know what brought the moth and spider together? Do you want to say "So what?" Why not?*
3. *Is this poem about a tension between two ways of talking? What are they? Is this where you are surprised?*

DIRECTIVE
Robert Frost

Back out of all this now too much for us,
Back in a time made simple by the loss
Of detail, burned, dissolved, and broken off

Like graveyard marble sculpture in the weather,
There is a house that is no more a house
Upon a farm that is no more a farm
And in a town that is no more a town.
The road there, if you'll let a guide direct you
Who only has at heart your getting lost,
May seem as if it should have been a quarry —
Great monolithic knees the former town
Long since gave up pretense of keeping covered.
And there's a story in a book about it:
Besides the wear of iron wagon wheels
The ledges show lines ruled southeast-northwest,
The chisel work of an enormous Glacier
That braced his feet against the Arctic Pole.
You must not mind a certain coolness from him
Still said to haunt this side of Panther Mountain.
Nor need you mind the serial ordeal
Of being watched from forty cellar holes
As if by eye pairs out of forty firkins.
As for the woods' excitement over you
That sends light rustle rushes to their leaves,
Charge that to upstart inexperience.
Where were they all not twenty years ago?
They think too much of having shaded out
A few old pecker-fretted apple trees.
Make yourself up a cheering song of how
Someone's road home from work this once was,
Who may be just ahead of you on foot
Or creaking with a buggy load of grain.
The height of the adventure is the height
Of country where two village cultures faded
Into each other. Both of them are lost.
And if you're lost enough to find yourself
By now, pull in your ladder road behind you
And put a sign up CLOSED to all but me.
Then make yourself at home. The only field
Now left's no bigger than a harness gall.
First there's the children's house of make-believe,
Some shattered dishes underneath a pine,
The playthings in the playhouse of the children.
Weep for what little things could make them glad.
Then for the house that is no more a house,

But only a belilaced cellar hole,
Now slowly closing like a dent in dough.
This was no playhouse but a house in earnest.
Your destination and your destiny's
A brook that was the water of the house,
Cold as a spring as yet so near its source,
Too lofty and original to rage.
(We know the valley streams that when aroused
Will leave their tatters hung on barb and thorn.)
I have kept hidden in the instep arch
Of an old cedar at the waterside
A broken drinking goblet like the Grail
Under a spell so the wrong ones can't find it,
So can't get saved, as Saint Mark says they mustn't.
(I stole the goblet from the children's playhouse.)
Here are your waters and your watering place.
Drink and be whole again beyond confusion.

QUESTIONS

1. *What is the message of "Directive"? What more is there in this poem than its message?*
2. *Is "Directive" an expression of what a legal education should involve? (Do you ever hear a judge talk as if he is, or has ever been, "lost enough to find himself"? A law student?)*
3. *"The Road Not Taken," "Design," and "Directive" are expressions of Frost's mind and imagination. Are judicial opinions ever similarly expressive of the mind of the judge? If it seems generally not to be so, does that reflect upon the form or upon the writers?*

   Another way to put it is this: what Frost does here is to make the private public, to draw connections between his own experience and what we all know. Can the judge ever be said to do that? Or have we found a major difference in the possibilities offered by these forms?
4. *Here is a new version of a question we have asked before: to what extent is it true that the poem must be at once particular and representative? In Shakespeare it is said that poetry gives "to airy nothing a local habitation and a name"; but Samuel Johnson, in his Life of Cowley, says "great thoughts are always general." If a poem simply gives us a tiny snip of life, who cares? If it gives us only vague generalities, who cares then? If the poem has a general meaning, how does it avoid the triteness of generalization, how does it avoid the cliché? Do judicial writers avoid triteness in similar ways?*

   The secret may lie in the use of the particular: the choice of path, the spider, the dipper. But how is the particular, the concrete detail, made to mean more? Is the particular object or event just an example of a general idea? "Be specific," as your English teacher used to say. You must recognize that as a hopeless cliché. How is it, then, that the particular events and objects are given the meaning that they have? How is the spider's web or the dipper made to mean what it does in Frost's poems?

Can the judge's written opinion likewise so organize matters that the particular case has a representative meaning and the general principle a particular one? By what process of art and imagination does this creation of meaning, this double metamorphosis, occur? How can it be explained and how performed?

See W. K. Wimsatt, Jr., "The Concrete Universal," in The Verbal Ikon 69 (1967); John Crowe Ransom, "The Concrete Universal: Observations on the Understanding of Poetry," in Poems and Essays 159 (1955).

THE SUN RISING

John Donne

Busy old fool, unruly Sun,
Why dost thou thus,
Through windows, and through curtains, call on us?
Must to thy motions lovers' seasons run?
Saucy pedantic wretch, go chide
Late school-boys and sour prentices,
Go tell court-huntsmen that the King will ride,
Call country ants to harvest offices;
Love, all alike, no season knows nor clime,
Nor hours, days, months, which are the rags of time.

Thy beams so reverend and strong
Why shouldst thou think?
I could eclipse and cloud them with a wink,
But that I would not lose her sight so long.
If her eyes have not blinded thine,
Look, and to-morrow late tell me,
Whether both th' Indias of spice and mine
Be where thou left'st them, or lie here with me.
Ask for those Kings whom thou saw'st yesterday,
And thou shalt hear, All here in one bed lay.

She's all States, and all Princes I;
Nothing else is;
Princes do but play us; compared to this,
All honour's mimic, all wealth alchemy.
Thou, Sun, art half as happy as we,
In that the world's contracted thus;
Thine age asks ease, and since thy duties be
To warm the world, that's done in warming us.
Shine here to us, and thou art everywhere;
This bed thy center is, these walls thy sphere.

QUESTIONS

1. *What is the message of this poem? What more than that do you find here?*
2. *Can you see this poem as movement, as a figure of change from one point to another? Does it work by surprise, by denouement?*
3. *Does this poem talk of one thing in terms of another? Say one thing and mean another?*
4. *Donne here makes a claim, or a set of claims, and of course a judge makes various claims too; how are Donne's claims like and unlike the judge's? (Does not the judge constantly talk as if "nothing else is"?)*
5. *This poem has life; can you locate its life? Is it in surprise, a tension between order and disorder, a conflict between different ways of talking, or what? Does a judicial opinion ever have life of this kind?*
6. *Cleanth Brooks suggests that the poetic statement is by its nature a paradoxical statement, and that what is lost when one reduces a poem to its message ("My love for her is all-important") is the life that comes from paradox. "The language of poetry is the language of paradox." See Brooks, The Well-Wrought Urn 3–21 (Harvest ed. 1947).*
   a. *Do you see a paradox in the Donne poem given above? Explain its elements.*
   b. *Do you ever see a paradox in a judicial opinion? Or does this element distinguish the poem from the opinion?*
7. *In another classic of modern criticism, Seven Types of Ambiguity (1930), William Empson maintains that ambiguity is at the heart of literature, that "the machinations of ambiguity are among the very roots of poetry." Would one ever say the same of a judicial opinion, or is clarity everything there?*[5]
8. *Matthew Arnold despaired of any attempt to make a system or code of criticism, and instead said that one ought to have "always in one's mind lines and expression of the great masters, and to apply them as a touchstone to other poetry. Of course we are not to require this other poetry to resemble them; it may be very dissimilar. But if we have any tact, we shall find them, when we have lodged them well in our minds, an infallible touchstone for detecting the presence or absence of high poetic quality, and also the degree of this quality, in all other poetry which we may place beside them." ("The Study of Poetry," in Essays in Criticism, Second Series (1865).)*

   Do you use excellent judicial opinions thus, as perceived but unexamined standards of excellence? If not, is this because the judicial opinion is by its nature incapable of having such a value? Because few judges realize the possibilities of the form? Or because you do not have the necessary "tact"?

   The closest Arnold comes to a direct definition of poetry and its excellence is to say that it is a "criticism of life" marked at its best by "truth and seriousness," by "high seriousness." Might one hope to say the same of the judicial opinion?

5. One student once said of *Brown v. Board of Education* — "*There* is ambiguity in the law!"

9. *You may have noticed that a line might be drawn connecting Cleanth Brooks's remark that "poetry is paradox" and one of the quotations that head this section, in which Coleridge says that the imagination is the power of reconciling "opposite or discordant qualities." That is not the only possible view of such matters. Dryden, for example, said that "imagination in a poet is a faculty so wild and lawless that like an high-ranging spaniel it must have clogs tied to it, lest it outrun the judgment." Dedication to The Rival Ladies (1664).*

   Does the conflict between imagination and judgment constitute a basic tension in poetry? In the judicial opinion?

10. *The following poem really does have a message, and even an argument.*

TO HIS COY MISTRESS
Andrew Marvell

Had we but world enough, and time,
This coyness, lady, were no crime.
We would sit down, and think which way
To walk, and pass our long love's day.
Thou by the Indian Ganges' side
Should'st rubies find: I by the tide
Of Humber would complain. I would
Love you ten years before the Flood,
And you should, if you please, refuse
Till the conversion of the Jews.
My vegetable love should grow
Vaster than empires, and more slow.
An hundred years should go to praise
Thine eyes, and on thy forehead gaze:
Two hundred to adore each breast:
But thirty thousand to the rest;
An age at least to every part,
And the last age should show your heart.
For, lady, you deserve this state,
Nor would I love at lower rate.
   But at my back I always hear
Time's wingèd chariot hurrying near:
And yonder all before us lie
Deserts of vast eternity.
Thy beauty shall no more be found;
Nor, in thy marble vault, shall sound
My echoing song: then worms shall try
That long-preserved virginity,
And your quaint honor turn to dust,

And into ashes all my lust.
The grave's a fine and private place,
But none, I think, do there embrace.
  Now, therefore, while the youthful hue
Sits on thy skin like morning dew,
And while thy willing soul transpires
At every pore with instant fires,
Now let us sport us while we may;
And now, like amorous birds of prey,
Rather at once our Time devour,
Than languish in his slow-chapt power.
Let us roll all our strength and all
Our sweetness up into one ball,
And tear our pleasures with rough strife
Thorough the iron gates of life.
Thus, though we cannot make our sun
Stand still, yet we will make him run.

QUESTIONS

1. *It has been noticed that this poem takes the form of logical argument: "If A . . . , then . . . B; but A is not the case, and therefore . . ."*
   a. *Is this argument logical in the same way a legal argument is logical?*
   b. *Does the conclusion the poet advances follow from the premises he states? Or does it depend upon still another proposition, not stated but implied? See if you can identify such a proposition and explain why it is unstated.*
2. *How would you describe the movement of this poem? From what point does it take the reader, where does it take him, and how does it do so?*
   a. *Is there a surprise here? Where is it: at the "But at my back . . ."? Or somewhere else?*
   b. *Is this poem a paradox? A metaphor? An ambiguity?*
   c. *Would you say that this epistle to a mistress had "high seriousness"?*
3. *To whom is this poem really addressed? Marvell says that it is to his coy mistress; if that is true, why and how did it ever get published? Do you suppose he dropped it off at her house as part of a sexual adventure? What is he talking about then, and to whom, and why does he talk this way?*

THE PULLEY
George Herbert

  When God at first made man,
Having a glass of blessings standing by —
Let us (said he) pour on him all we can;

Let the world's riches, which dispersed lie,
  Contract into a span.

  So strength first made a way,
Then beauty flow'd, then wisdom, honour, pleasure:
When almost all was out, God made a stay,
Perceiving that, alone of all His treasure,
  Rest in the bottom lay.

  For if I should (said he)
Bestow this jewel also on My creature,
He would adore My gifts instead of Me,
And rest in Nature, not the God of Nature:
  So both should losers be.

  Yet let him keep the rest,
But keep them with repining restlessness;
Let him be rich and weary, that at least,
If goodness lead him not, yet weariness
  May toss him to My breast.

QUESTIONS

1. *What is the message of this poem? What beyond that message do you see here?*
2. *Is the central statement made directly, ironically, or by implication?*
   a. *How is man defined by the way God speaks of him?*
   b. *Why is that definition not made in declarative form?*

UP AT A VILLA — DOWN IN THE CITY
(As Distinguished by an Italian Person of Quality)
Robert Browning

Had I but plenty of money, money enough and to spare,
The house for me, no doubt, were a house in the city-square;
Ah, such a life, such a life, as one leads at the window there!

Something to see, by Bacchus, something to hear, at least!
There, the whole day long, one's life is a perfect feast;
While up at a villa one lives, I maintain it, no more than a beast.

Well now, look at our villa! stuck like the horn of a bull
Just on a mountain-edge as bare as the creature's skull,
Save a mere shag of a bush with hardly a leaf to pull!
— I scratch my own, sometimes, to see if the hair's turned wool.

But the city, oh the city — the square with the houses! Why?
They are stone-faced, white as a curd, there's something to take the eye!
Houses in four straight lines, not a single front awry;
You watch who crosses and gossips, who saunters, who hurries by,
Green blinds, as a matter of course, to draw when the sun gets high;
And the shops with fanciful signs which are painted properly.

What of a villa? Though winter be over in March by rights,
'Tis May perhaps ere the snow shall have withered well off the heights:
You've the brown ploughed land before, where the oxen steam and wheeze,
And the hills over-smoked behind by the faint gray olive-trees.

Is it better in May, I ask you? You've summer all at once;
In a day he leaps complete with a few strong April suns.
'Mid the sharp short emerald wheat, scarce risen three fingers well,
The wild tulip, at end of its tube, blows out its great red bell
Like a thin clear bubble of blood, for the children to pick and sell.

Is it ever hot in the square? There's a fountain to spout and splash!
In the shade it sings and springs; in the shine such foambows flash
On the horses with curling fish-tails, that prance and paddle and pash
Round the lady atop in her conch — fifty gazers do not abash,
Though all that she wears is some weeds round her waist in a sort of sash.

All the year long at the villa, nothing to see though you linger,
Except yon cypress that points like death's lean lifted forefinger.
Some think fireflies pretty, when they mix i' the corn and mingle,
Or thrid the stinking hemp till the stalks of it seem a-tingle.
Late August or early September, the stunning cicala is shrill,
And the bees keep their tiresome whine round the resinous firs on the hill.
Enough of the seasons, — I spare you the months of the fever and chill.

Ere you open your eyes in the city, the blessed church-bells begin:
No sooner the bells leave off than the diligence rattles in:
You get the pick of the news, and it costs you never a pin.

By and by there's the travelling doctor gives pills, lets blood,
draws teeth;
Or the Pulcinello-trumpet breaks up the market beneath.
At the post-office such a scene-picture — the new play, piping hot!
And a notice how, only this morning, three liberal thieves were shot.
Above it, behold the Archbishop's most fatherly of rebukes,
And beneath, with his crown and his lion, some little new law
of the Duke's!
Or a sonnet with flowery marge, to the Reverend Don So-and-so,
Who is Dante, Boccaccio, Petrarca, Saint Jerome, and Cicero,
"And moreover," (the sonnet goes rhyming,) "the skirts of Saint
Paul had reached,
Having preached us those six Lent-lectures more unctuous than
ever he preached."
Noon strikes, — here sweeps the procession! our Lady borne smiling
and smart
With a pink gauze gown all spangles, and seven swords stuck
in her heart!
Bang-whang-whang goes the drum, *tootle-te-tootle* the fife;
No keeping one's haunches still: it's the greatest pleasure in life.

But bless you, it's dear — it's dear! fowls, wine, at double the
rate.
They have clapped a new tax upon salt, and what oil pays passing
the gate
It's a horror to think of. And so, the villa for me, not the city!
Beggars can scarcely be choosers: but still — ah, the pity, the pity!
Look, two and two go the priests, then the monks with cowls
and sandals,
And the penitents dressed in white shirts, a-holding the yellow
candles;
One, he carries a flag up straight, and another a cross with handles,
And the Duke's guard brings up the rear, for the better prevention
of scandals:
Bang-whang-whang goes the drum, *tootle-te-tootle* the fife.
Oh, a day in the city-square, there is no such pleasure in life!

QUESTIONS

1. *Is the message of this poem that the city square is more attractive than a country villa? Do you believe it?*
2. *Does Browning believe it? Then why does he say it? How does Browning express to you his attitude on this matter?*

3. *Does a judge ever do what Browning does here? How does a judge handle statements he disagrees with? (Would you tell him that he should never use irony?)*
4. *Where is the life of this poem: in a tension between two ways of talking? Do you know from the beginning how that tension will be resolved, or are you surprised?*

OUR LITTLE KINSMEN

Emily Dickinson

Our little Kinsmen — after Rain
In plenty may be seen,
A Pink and Pulpy multitude
The tepid Ground upon.

A needless life, it seemed to me
Until a little Bird
As to a Hospitality
Advanced and breakfasted.

As I of He, so God of Me
I pondered may have judged,
And left the little Angle Worm
With Modesties enlarged.

QUESTIONS

1. *Can you see this poem as a movement, a change from one point to another? How does it work: by reasoning, by surprise, or how?*
2. *Does this poem have special relevance to a judge? (Have you ever heard a judge express such an attitude as you see here?)*
3. *I have suggested that the poet and the lawyer or judge have this in common: when they come up against a situation in life, an occasion, their task is to speak to it, to stand up and say "I will say what needs to be said here." So the poet makes of this common event of a bird eating a worm something new, something for which she is responsible; so the lawyer converts what he is told by his client into a new form and language, a statement for which he assumes responsibility. Both may perceive possibilities no one ever saw before, and express a meaning no one else would. At his best, each speaks to a moment in an original way, proposing a new organization of life, and is held to what he says.*

   Compare what the lawyer does with what you saw Euripides do in Alcestis: just like everyone else, he had heard the old stories about the hospitable Admetus, who was saved by his wife's willingness to die, but he saw what the others missed — that there were possibilities for the comic and dramatic here. So Shakespeare read Holinshed's account of the murder of Duncan: "Then Donwald [Macbeth], though he abhorred the act greatly, yet through instigation of his wife he called four of his servants to him . . ." Shakespeare saw possibilities there – how did the wife "instigate" her husband, in what words, by what conduct? How and why did he yield? What relationship explains this? – and so on. He saw, in the occasion, possibilities that other statements obscured, and this is what the lawyer must do too.

FERN HILL

Dylan Thomas

Now as I was young and easy under the apple boughs
About the lilting house and happy as the grass was green,
The night above the dingle starry,
Time let me hail and climb
Golden in the heydays of his eyes,
And honored among wagons I was prince of the apple towns
And once below a time I lordly had the trees and leaves
Trail with daisies and barley
Down the rivers of the windfall light.

And as I was green and carefree, famous among the barns
About the happy yard and singing as the farm was home,
In the sun that is young once only,
Time let me play and be
Golden in the mercy of his means,
And green and golden I was huntsman and herdsman, the calves
Sang to my horn, the foxes on the hills barked clear and cold,
And the sabbath rang slowly
In the pebbles of the holy streams.

All the sun long it was running, it was lovely, the hay-
Fields high as the house, the tunes from the chimneys, it was air
And playing, lovely and watery
And fire green as grass.
And nightly under the simple stars
As I rode to sleep the owls were bearing the farm away,
All the moon long I heard, blessed among stables, the nightjars
Flying with the ricks, and horses
Flashing into the dark.

And then to awake, and the farm, like a wanderer white
With the dew, come back, the cock on his shoulder: it was all
Shining, it was Adam and maiden,
The sky gathered again

And the sun grew round that very day.
So it must have been after the birth of the simple light
In the first, spinning place, the spellbound horses walking warm
Out of the whinnying green stable
On to the fields of praise.

And honored among foxes and pheasants by the gay house
Under the new-made clouds and happy as the heart was long
In the sun born over and over,
I ran my heedless ways,
My wishes raced through the house-high hay
And nothing I cared, at my sky blue trades, that time allows
In all his tuneful turning so few and such morning songs
Before the children green and golden
Follow him out of grace.

Nothing I cared, in the lamb white days, that time would take me
Up to the swallow-thronged loft by the shadow of my hand,
In the moon that is always rising,
Nor that riding to sleep
I should hear him fly with the high fields
And wake to the farm forever fled from the childless land.
Oh as I was young and easy in the mercy of his means,
Time held me green and dying
Though I sang in my chains like the sea.

QUESTIONS

1. *Here, as in the poems by Dickinson and Browning, a statement of positioning is made: the actor or self in each poem is shown to be different in attitude or knowledge from the poet himself as he now is. Does a judge ever position a person or an argument in such a way?*
2. *The positioning here is not simply a matter of articulating differences, for there are also connections between the poet and the self in the poem; in Thomas and Dickinson, at least, it is an earlier self of the poet whose experience is our subject. The movement of the poem is, as Frost saw, the movement of education, from seeing things one way to seeing them another.*

   Does a judge ever establish such a relationship, a sense of sympathy and difference, with a speaker whose views concern him? With a past version of himself? Does he ever regard the movement of what he writes as the movement of an education, carrying his reader from seeing things one way to seeing them another more complete or mature way?
3. *Does this sense of movement tell us more about the life of a poem, its source of energy? For — to connect these remarks with the line of thought*

begun in Chapter 1 – when one writes in a form that moves from one point or attitude or feeling to another, one necessarily writes two ways at once. Is what we have called "writing two ways at once" the heart of what is meant by those who say poetry is metaphor or paradox or ambiguity?

a. *What different ways of talking, what opposed attitudes, can you find in "To His Coy Mistress"? In "Up at a Villa"? In "Our Little Kinsmen"? What is the opposition or conflict that gives these poems life, and how can it be located in the languages that the poet uses?*

b. *If it is a general truth that good writing means writing more than one way – using a language in such a way that one recognizes what it leaves out, saying one thing and meaning another – what hope is there for the judge and lawyer, given a single institutional language in which to speak? Does a judge ever write two ways at once?*

   This is, of course, the question framed by Chapter 1, with which you have been dealing in one way or another ever since, and you can take it as an essential part of your next writing assignment.

4. *In the next two poems, can you find different ways of writing, can you find paradox or metaphor or ambiguity? Or are these just lovely poems, whose beauty nothing we have said can account for?*

UPON WESTMINSTER BRIDGE

William Wordsworth

Earth has not anything to show more fair:
Dull would he be of soul who could pass by
A sight so touching in its majesty:
This City now doth, like a garment, wear
The beauty of the morning; silent, bare,
Ships, towers, domes, theatres, and temples lie
Open unto the fields, and to the sky;
All bright and glittering in the smokeless air.
Never did sun more beautifully steep
In his first splendour valley, rock, or hill;
Ne'er saw I, never felt, a calm so deep!
The river glideth at his own sweet will:
Dear God! the very houses seem asleep;
And all that mighty heart is lying still!

TO AUTUMN

John Keats

Season of mists and mellow fruitfulness,
   Close bosom-friend of the maturing sun;
Conspiring with him how to load and bless

With fruit the vines that round the thatch-eaves run;
To bend with apples the moss'd cottage-trees,
And fill all fruit with ripeness to the core;
To swell the gourd, and plump the hazel shells
With a sweet kernel; to set budding more,
And still more, later flowers for the bees,
Until they think warm days will never cease,
For Summer has o'er-brimmed their clammy cells.

Who hath not seen thee oft amid thy store?
Sometimes whoever seeks abroad may find
Thee sitting careless on a granary floor,
Thy hair soft-lifted by the winnowing wind;
Or on a half-reap'd furrow sound asleep,
Drows'd with the fume of poppies, while thy hook
Spares the next swath and all its twined flowers:
And sometimes like a gleaner thou dost keep
Steady thy laden head across a brook;
Or by a cider-press, with patient look,
Thou watchest the last oozings hours by hours.

Where are the songs of Spring? Ay, where are they?
Think not of them, thou hast thy music too,—
While barred clouds bloom the soft-dying day,
And touch the stubble-plains with rosy hue;
Then in a wailful choir the small gnats mourn
Among the river sallows, borne aloft
Or sinking as the light wind lives or dies;
And full-grown lambs loud bleat from hilly bourn;
Hedge-crickets sing; and now with treble soft
The red-breast whistles from a garden-croft;
And gathering swallows twitter in the skies.

QUESTIONS

1. *What are the messages of these poems? What is there in each beyond its message, and why would anyone be interested in writing or reading the whole poem instead of just its message? Is this just a pretty way to put things?*
2. *Ask of each poem: are there metaphors here? Paradoxes? Ambiguities? What then? A surprise? Is the poet here talking two ways at once?*
3. *In the next poem the poet talks about becoming a poet, he addresses his Muse. How much of what he says about his poetry could be said by a judge of his work?*

OUT OF THE CRADLE ENDLESSLY ROCKING

Walt Whitman

Out of the cradle endlessly rocking,
Out of the mocking-bird's throat, the musical shuttle,
Out of the Ninth-month midnight,
Over the sterile sands, and the fields beyond, where the child, leaving his bed, wander'd alone, bareheaded, barefoot,
Down from the shower'd halo,
Up from the mystic play of shadows, twining and twisting as if they were alive,
Out from the patches of briers and blackberries,
From the memories of the bird that chanted to me,
From your memories, sad brother — from the fitful risings and fallings I heard,
From under that yellow half-moon, late-risèn, and swollen as if with tears,
From those beginning notes of sickness and love, there in the transparent mist,
From the thousand responses of my heart, never to cease,
From the myriad thence-aroused words,
From the word stronger and more delicious than any,
From such, as now they start, the scene revisiting,
As a flock, twittering, rising, or overhead passing,
Borne hither — ere all eludes me, hurriedly,
A man — yet by these tears a little boy again,
Throwing myself on the sand, confronting the waves,
I, chanter of pains and joys, uniter of here and hereafter,
Taking all hints to use them — but swiftly leaping beyond them,
A reminiscence sing.

Once, Paumanok,
When the snows had melted — when the lilac-scent was in the air, and the Fifth-month grass was growing,
Up this sea-shore, in some briers,
Two guests from Alabama — two together,
And their nest, and four light-green eggs, spotted with brown,
And every day the he-bird, to and fro, near at hand,
And every day the she-bird, crouch'd on her nest, silent, with bright eyes,
And every day I, a curious boy, never too close, never disturbing them,
Cautiously peering, absorbing, translating.

Shine! shine! shine!
Pour down your warmth, great Sun!
While we bask — we two together.
Two together!
Winds blow South, or winds blow North,
Day come white, or night come black,
Home, or rivers and mountains from home,
Singing all time, minding no time,
While we two keep together.

Till of a sudden,
May-be kill'd, unknown to her mate,
One forenoon the she-bird crouch'd not on the nest,
Nor return'd that afternoon, nor the next,
Nor ever appear'd again.

And thenceforward, all summer, in the sound of the sea,
And at night, under the full of the moon, in calmer weather,
Over the hoarse surging of the sea,
Or flitting from brier to brier by day,
I saw, I heard at intervals, the remaining one, the he-bird,
The solitary guest from Alabama.

Blow! blow! blow!
Blow up, sea-winds, along Paumanok's shore!
I wait and I wait, till you blow my mate to me.

Yes, when the stars glisten'd,
All night long, on the prong of a moss-scallop'd stake,
Down, almost amid the slapping waves,
Sat the lone singer, wonderful, causing tears.

He call'd on his mate;
He pour'd forth the meanings which I, of all men, know.

Yes, my brother, I know;
The rest might not — but I have treasured every note;
For once, and more than once, dimly, down to the beach gliding,
Silent, avoiding the moonbeams, blending myself with the shadows,
Recalling now the obscure shapes, the echoes, the sounds and sights
after their sorts,
The white arms out in the breakers tirelessly tossing,
I, with bare feet, a child, the wind wafting my hair,
Listen'd long and long.

Listen'd, to keep, to sing — now translating the notes,
Following you, my brother.

Soothe! soothe! soothe!
Close on its wave soothes the wave behind,
And again another behind, embracing and lapping, every one close,
But my love soothes not me, not me.

Low hangs the moon — it rose late;
O it is lagging — O I think it is heavy with love, with love.

O madly the sea pushes, pushes upon the land,
With love — with love.

O night! do I not see my love fluttering out there among the breakers?
What is that little black thing I see there in the white?

Loud! loud! loud!
Loud I call to you, my love!

High and clear I shoot my voice over the waves;
Surely you must know who is here, is here;
You must know who I am, my love.

Low-hanging moon!
What is that dusky spot in your brown yellow?
O it is the shape, the shape of my mate!
O moon, do not keep her from me any longer.

Land! land! O land!
Whichever way I turn, O I think you could give me my mate back again,
if you only would;
For I am almost sure I see her dimly whichever way I look.

O rising stars!
Perhaps the one I want so much will rise, will rise with some of you.

O throat! O trembling throat!
Sound clearer through the atmosphere!
Pierce the woods, the earth;
Somewhere listening to catch you, must be the one I want.

Shake out, carols!
Solitary here — the night's carols!
Carols of lonesome love! Death's carols!
Carols under that lagging, yellow, waning moon!

O, under that moon, where she droops almost down into the sea!
O reckless, despairing carols.

But soft! sink low;
Soft! let me just murmur;
And do you wait a moment, you husky-noised sea;
For somewhere I believe I heard my mate responding to me,
So faint — I must be still, be still to listen;
But not altogether still, for then she might not come immediately to me.

Hither, my love!
Here I am! Here!
With this just-sustain'd note I announce myself to you;
This gentle call is for you, my love, for you.

Do not be decoy'd elsewhere!
That is the whistle of the wind — it is not my voice;
That is the fluttering, the fluttering of the spray;
Those are the shadows of leaves.

O darkness! O in vain!
O I am very sick and sorrowful.

O brown halo in the sky, near the moon, drooping upon the sea!
O troubled reflection in the sea!
O throat! O throbbing heart!
O all — and I singing uselessly, uselessly all the night.

Yet I murmur, murmur on!
O murmurs — you yourselves make me continue to sing, I know not why.
O past! O life! O songs of joy!
In the air — in the woods — over fields;
Loved! loved! loved! loved! loved!
But my love no more, no more with me!
We two together no more.

The aria sinking;
All else continuing — the stars shining,
The winds blowing — the notes of the bird continuous echoing,
With angry moans the fierce old mother incessantly moaning,
On the sands of Paumanok's shore, grey and rustling;
The yellow half-moon enlarged, sagging down, drooping, the face of the sea almost touching;

The boy ecstatic — with his bare feet the waves, with his hair the atmosphere dallying,
The love in the heart long pent, now loose, now at last tumultuously bursting,
The aria's meaning, the ears, the Soul, swiftly depositing,
The strange tears down the cheeks coursing,
The colloquy there — the trio — each uttering,
The undertone — the savage old mother, incessantly crying,
To the boy's Soul's questions sullenly timing — some drown'd secret hissing,
To the outsetting bard of love.

Demon or bird! (said the boy's soul,)
Is it indeed toward your mate you sing? or is it mostly to me?
For I, that was a child, my tongue's use sleeping,
Now I have heard you,
Now in a moment I know what I am for — I awake,
And already a thousand singers — a thousand songs, clearer, louder and more sorrowful than yours,
A thousand warbling echoes have started to life within me,
Never to die.

O you singer, solitary, singing by yourself — projecting me;
O solitary me, listening — never more shall I cease perpetuating you;
Never more shall I escape, never more the reverberations,
Never more the cries of unsatisfied love be absent from me,
Never again leave me to be the peaceful child I was before what there, in the night,
By the sea, under the yellow and sagging moon,
The messenger there aroused — the fire, the sweet hell within,
The unknown want, the destiny of me.

O give me the clue! (it lurks in the night here somewhere;)
O if I am to have so much, let me have more!
O a word! O what is my destination? (I fear it is henceforth chaos;)
O how joys, dreads, convolutions, human shapes, and all shapes, spring as from graves around me!
O phantoms! you cover all the land and all the sea!
O I cannot see in the dimness whether you smile or frown upon me;
O vapour, a look, a word! O well-beloved!
O you dear women's and men's phantoms!
A word then, (for I will conquer it,)
The word final, superior to all,

Subtle, sent up — what is it? — I listen;
Are you whispering it, and have been all the time, you sea-waves?
Is that it from your liquid rims and wet sands?

Whereto answering, the sea,
Delaying not, hurrying not,
Whisper'd me through the night, and very plainly before daybreak,
Lisp'd to me the low and delicious word Death;
And again Death — ever Death, Death, Death,
Hissing melodious, neither like the bird, nor like my aroused child's heart,
But edging near, as privately for me, rustling at my feet,
Creeping thence steadily up to my ears, and laving me softly all over,
Death, Death, Death, Death, Death.

Which I do not forget,
But fuse the song of my dusky demon and brother,
That he sang to me in the moonlight on Paumanok's grey beach,
With the thousand responsive songs, at random,
My own songs, awaked from that hour;
And with them the key, the word up from the waves,
The word of the sweetest song, and all songs,
That strong and delicious word which, creeping to my feet,
The sea whisper'd me.

QUESTIONS

1. *What is the message of this poem, and what more do you see here than that? Is there a movement from one point, one attitude or condition, to another, is there any expression of an education?*
2. *Does a judge ever write this way? In fact, does a judge ever have such an experience, a visitation of his Muse, as is celebrated here?*
3. *Put it this way: here Whitman explains his answer to the question we asked earlier: "Why do you write poetry?" In what terms does he do so? Can you imagine a judge explaining in such a way the springs of his art?*
4. *Compare this poem with Frost's "Directive" (page 780 supra) and Plato's image of the cave (page 689) as other expressions of an education.*

3. *More on the Judicial Opinion and the Poem*

Your next writing assignment will be to do for the judicial opinion what Robert Frost, in the two essays near the beginning of this chapter, did for the poem. There follow now some questions, both familiar and new, which may help you to put into some sort of order your own responses to what you have read and done in this section. You should be prepared to go back and study again the introductory notes and the poems themselves. In fact, you should probably work through in writing several sets of questions asked about particular poems that interest you. The more fully you make this body of imaginative literature your own, the more ready you will be to talk about how the legal imagination expresses itself in the judicial opinion.

Our central question is whether the judicial opinion, like the poem, has a form with its own meaning — its own resources for expression and demands on the reader and writer — and if so, how that form can be defined. Can you tell what figure an opinion makes? What are the structural tensions, the permanent questions each writer must address, that give it life and interest? Can you describe the motion of a judicial opinion? Another way to put it is this: what is there, beyond the message or rule of a judicial opinion, which makes it worth one person's while to write it and another's to read it?

Does the form, when you find it, impose a restraint that makes meaning possible? Consider where we would be, as readers and writers, without our complex expectations of what the judge writes, without standards of inclusion and exclusion, a sense of "ought" in the form of the opinion. Is there a paradox here, that the limitations on freedom provide the occasion for the expression of the individual mind? (Can a comparison be drawn between Massachusetts civil practice and a sestina royal?)

Earlier questions have pointed out some possible tensions in the structure of the opinion — between the particular and the representative, between the logical and the illogical, between the inherited language and the individual mind, between the relevant and the irrelevant, between complexity and simplicity, between honesty and clarity, between legal and nonlegal languages, and so on — and we need not repeat these suggestions in detail. The questions that follow are meant to raise new matters.

QUESTIONS

1. *First I want to ask some questions about the fact that both the judicial opinion and the poem nearly always tell a story. Not all poems are narrative, of course, but most have narrative elements; and the comparison in any event might go to all forms of narrative literature: play, novel, history, short story, etc.*

   What does it mean that the judicial mind tells a story? What kind of story does the judge tell?

   a. *Is there a difference between minds who make the basic assumption that a story has meaning and those who find their meaning elsewhere (in ideas, concepts, theories, rules, and the like)? Of which kind is the judicial mind? Both at once, in a sort of unhappy marriage? Or do you call it a productive tension or a paradox?*

b. *As soon as you start off on a story, you face a choice as to how to tell it. Does this mean the judge and lawyer must always recognize that there are at least two ways to talk, legal ways and other ways? That is, since the whole point of the judicial process is to call a person or event a name, to affix a label, the judge cannot start out by speaking of a person in those terms, he cannot begin by calling him "guilty" or "married" or "insane" or "X"; he must call him something else, if only "he who is to be called X or not-X." Is it then as simple as this: the narrative heart of every judicial opinion provides a way of controlling legal language by requiring the judge to talk two ways at once?*

2. *The preceding question points to a rhetorical difference between judges' stories and lawyers' stories. From the beginning you know where the lawyer wants to come out, and every word points that way. This kind of writing has its own skill and its own interest. (It can be found at its best in Gibbon.) But the judge is bound to keep an open mind, to keep his reader in suspense as long as he can, if he is to express fairly the process of his decision. There is a difference between an opinion that reaches a conclusion and one that is aimed there, one might say. Would a great opinion then have the sort of "surprise" you find in Frost's "Design" or in Emily Dickinson? Have you ever read such an opinion?*

   Let us generalize this way: if it is to express the process by which the original intention is worked out, the judicial narrative must keep the reader in a sort of suspense or open-mindedness, during which he is exposed one by one to the facts and arguments that seem important to the judge, until the reader has them all, at which point he should find himself agreeing with the judgment. Very few opinions do this; the viciousness of the defendant's crime is contained in the statement of facts when the hearsay ruling or instruction is affirmed, but not when it is reversed. In Chambers v. Maroney, 399 U.S. 42 (1970), *a car is searched, and the defendant seeks the exclusion of the evidence; do you not know which way it is coming out when you are told that the evidence seized included a pistol loaded with "dum-dum bullets"? How differently the dissent and majority in case after case tell the story: do they really see it differently, or is this rhetorical writing of a kind improper to a judge?*

One can generalize a degree further and suggest (as I have above) that the movement of the opinion, like that of the poem, ought to be one of education: expressing a change from one attitude, one way of seeing things, to another, by an expansion of understanding. The judge tells you the facts, putting in whatever works either way, maintaining the reader's suspense about the result as long as he can. "That is where I started," he says, "and at first it seemed . . .; but then I wondered . . . ; so I come out . . . Don't you?" To keep the reader's mind open and receptive, undecided, as long as possible is to subject one's opinion to the most severe review: there is a chance, after all, that the reader will respond, "I see all that, and you have done a fine job of tracing out what is involved here. But how can you come out that way? I come out just the reverse!"

The risk is only rhetorical, since the reader in any event follows you only tentatively, and whatever you say, he plans to go back and figure out his differences with you. What this sort of writing achieves, then, can be put in terms of honesty and ease: it opens up for the reader one's doubts, it points out the places of greatest weakness, of most likely difference; it facilitates his judgment and makes it more likely to be sound. It enables one's own opinion to be taken for what it really is, one's range of values to be understood, and what one says to be taken as an expression of what one sees. Does it do even more?

One can claim that it does, and in ways in which the poem does more, too. You have probably noticed that neither the good opinion nor the good poem can be read through once only, that both require reading again and again in light of where they come out. Both must be addressed with the whole mind, both demand all the attention one can give; and one consequence of reading of this sort is not only an increased understanding of what lies outside oneself, but a change in the reader himself, an expansion of sympathy or an opening of a new capacity to perceive. Good writing in the poem or opinion works directly on its reader and changes him.

Take as an example Frost's poem "The Road Not Taken" (page 69 *supra*). One's first reading of that is bound to be wrong, one will read it as a little homily of the kind it actually deplores. One will not catch the tones right, one will miss or misjudge the irony. To work out a satisfactory reading, one must ask over and over how one should respond to this line or that, with what shade of irony should that phrase be taken, and so on. And even after several readings, one's conclusion is tentative. I have given in Chapter 1 a reading of that poem (pages 69–70), but would be happy to have someone show me what I missed or misunderstood. Or look at Browning's "Up at a Villa" (page 787): you may first think that this is Browning being enthusiastically bluff again, and regard this paean of the city square as essentially childish, until perhaps on the second or third reading you realize that is what you are supposed to do. The sense of beauty which provides the dominant value of the poem is expressed in what the speaker rejects: "You've the brown ploughed land before, where the oxen steam and wheeze, / And the hills over-smoked behind by the faint gray olive trees." Or so I say; the premise of such reading is that one is always ready to be corrected, to have what used to be called his taste or judgment improved. We should leave Dickinson's "Our Little Kinsmen," as she leaves the rainy walk, with modesties enlarged.

Do judicial opinions ever work this way? I have suggested that they might, but can you point to any examples? Can you find an opinion that leads to a "clarification of life"? Can the judicial opinion, like the poem, be a technique of self-discovery?

To regard the poem as an instrument of education, as a way of working directly on the reader to change him, may go some way towards explaining what has perplexed literary people forever: why do I read a poem? What is the importance of this literature? Some have tried to put it, as Sidney did, that here we have superior instruction because we have both precept and example; others have regarded the poem as a way of instructing without hurting, as providing a coating of pleasure to the salutary lesson; the general modern view is to regard the poem as pleasure, civilized pleasure. But it can be read and judged as a way of teaching, as a force of education, and this goes some distance, I believe, towards explaining why the poem is taken so seriously, why poetry is felt to be important.

Can one likewise regard the judicial opinion as an instrument of education? If you can find none of which you can say so, can you imagine some? Could you yourself write an opinion that offered an education?

George Eliot said this about art: "The greatest benefit we owe to the artist, whether painter, poet, or novelist, is the extension of our sympathies. Appeals founded on generalizations and statistics require a sympathy ready-made, a moral sentiment already in activity; but a picture of life such as a great artist can give, surprises even the trivial and the selfish into that attention to what is apart from themselves, which may be called the raw material of moral sentiment." *The Natural History of German Life* (1856). Can you say the same of the judicial opinion?

WRITING ASSIGNMENT 18: The Judicial Opinion as a Constant Symbol

• *In a brief essay, do for the judicial opinion what Robert Frost, in the essays at pages 766 and 770 above, has done for the poem.*

You need not come at this question by way of the poem, and you are in fact urged to make whatever response — by comparison or analysis — seems to you best; but I hope that the reading and thinking you have done about the poem has shown you something of what you can do by way of expressing critical understanding and judgment. I do think you can take what Frost says as a model for this sort of statement.

You may find it helpful to draw comparisons and distinctions, not with poetry as I have done, but with something else you know about — mathematics or history or economics or music. Or perhaps you could begin with one of the quotations that head this section; can you say of the judge (as Emerson says of the poet) that he is a liberating god, that he is free and that he makes free? Or take the Coleridge passage: is the judicial imagination, like the poetic, a force that reconciles the discordant or opposite? I am sure that, as you reflect on the poems and questions above, other possible starting points will suggest themselves to you; but the main hope is that you come at this question in your own way, out of your own intellectual experience. Draw on your own studies and reading, express your own thoughts in your own way. Surely you have been perplexed by the judicial opinion ever since you came to law school. What can you say about it? As the poem expresses the mind of the poet, and the opinion that of the judge, let your paper express your mind. Let us hear your own voice.

WRITING ASSIGNMENT 18 (ALTERNATIVE): What Beyond Paraphrase?

Part One

• *Find a good poem, copy it out, and then give a brief paraphrase of it. Now explain what there is in the poem beyond that paraphrase. Why would one person choose to write, and another to read, the poem itself instead of the paraphrase?*

Part Two

• *Find a good judicial opinion and (if it is not too long) reproduce it. Give a brief paraphrase of it, and explain what there is in that opinion beyond the paraphrase. Why would one person choose to write, and another to read, the opinion instead of the paraphrase? Use an opinion of your own composition, if you wish, especially if you cannot find others that meet your standards of excellence.*

Here you are asked to connect several lines of thought that have been started in this chapter and elsewhere. To ask what (beyond its paraphrase or message) there is in the poem or opinion is to ask, among other things, what good writing consists of beyond the clear and precise statement of ideas. How can you respond to that question, and, in doing so, how do you define good writing? Is the reader a vessel ready to receive whatever the writer wishes to pour into his head, the depository at the end of a conveyor belt of ideas? This line of questioning is closely connected to another: one might say that the writer not only states his ideas, he also explains his reasons, he demonstrates the rationality of his *proposition — but what (if anything) does he do beyond that, what besides rationality do you expect of good writing?*

Turn now and look at the writing you yourself have done in this course, and ask whether it is good writing as you have defined it. Look at and study your actual papers. How do you judge what you have done? Can you see to it that your response to this assignment is itself good writing?

B. THE ACTIVITY OF ARGUMENT

Doctor prideaux in his Lectures severall dayes us'd Argumt to prove predestinacōn, att last tells his Auditors, they are damn'd if they doe not beleive it, doeing herein just as schoole boyes when one of them has gott an Apple, or something the rest have a mind to, they use all the Argumts they can to gett some of it from him (I gave you some 'tother day, you shall have some with me another time): when they cannott prevaile they tell him hee's a Jackanapes, a Rogue, & a Raskall.*

Opinion & affeccōn extreamly differr. I may affect a woman best, but it does not follow, I must thinke her the handsomest woman in the world. I love Apples best of any fruitt, it does not follow that I must thinke apples to bee the best of ffruite. Opinion is something wherein I goe about to give reason, why all the world should thinke as I thinke; affeccōn is a thing wherein I onely looke after the pleasing of my selfe.†

In troubled water you cann scarce see yor face, or see it very little till the water bee quiett & stand still; so in troubled times you cann see little truth, when times are quiett & settled then truth appeares.‡

One statement about the legal mind to which even you and your friend at the cocktail party might agree is that it is argumentative. You would mean different things by it, but you would probably both be willing to say that the lawyer is always arguing. Your friend might hold this tendency to be the irritating sign of a partisan pettiness, of a childish desire to turn every conversation into a competition of wits. The judge may be an honorable man — even a poet — he might say, but the lawyer's skill is quickness and plausibility, his art that of the specious, and nothing could be more contemptible to a serious mind. You, on the other hand, speaking in defense of your profession and your life — what would you say?

* John Selden, *Table Talk* (Predestination, 3) (1689).
† *Id.* (Opinion, 1).
‡ *Id.* (Truth, 3).

This question, which sets your next writing assignment, is given special force by the fact that arguing is so close to the center of what we do as lawyers — the capacity for a certain sort of argument very nearly defines us — and if we cannot explain the interest and value of that activity, we do not have much to fall back on. As I said in the introduction to this book, my experience of watching a moot court argument before coming to law school seemed suddenly to expose something essential in the law; before that, I had always thought that the lawyer just looked up the law in a bunch of books where it was all written down and then told the people what it was, and that the only reason for argument and trial was to decide who was lying. Instead I discovered that the lawyer constantly argues, with himself and with others. Why was that such a great discovery, or why might someone think that it was? What is there about legal argument that gives it such fascination and appeal, that makes its mastery a worthy object for a professional life?

You might begin your explanation, your defense, by drawing a distinction between legal argument and ordinary argument, a distinction your friend may have missed: whatever legal argument may look like to him — however trivial and technical — for those who participate, it is an experience that involves everything, that calls upon every perception and capacity. A legal argument is not an open quarrel but something very different, an institution, a way of doing things, a form with opportunities of its own. It is an activity of the imagination that demands every excellence of mind. So you might begin, but how would you go on to justify your claim and explain how it is that legal argument offers such a challenge to the whole mind, such a chance for intellectual life? For not all argument does: think of domestic quarrels, political arguments — even between candidates for the presidency of the United States — and the great art of debating as it was taught at your old college. What is it about legal argument that makes it the occasion not for the inflamed stupidities of most public discourse or the endless contradictions of an ordinary quarrel, but for thinking and speaking well?

In working out your response, you may wish to consider the claim that legal argument can be seen as a remarkable social as well as intellectual achievement. Indeed, your angry client may be disgusted with it (and with you) for exactly this reason, feeling that the process is all too polite and mannered. Opposing parties are often so furious that between them no conversation is possible at all: each thinks he is right, and generous to boot, and as for the other — ! Imagine what two angry litigants might say to one another if they met to discuss their differences, or even to submit them to decision by another. That is what you would call a quarrel, and at least potentially there is such a quarrel, such a complete social and intellectual breakdown, in the background of every legal case. You might draft a page or two of such dialogue. Now imagine the same dispute carried on by two lawyers, in negotiation or trial. There may be forcefulness of expression, there may be emotion, there may even be bad behavior; but there is a form to it all, a sense of what one does and does not do, and this gives the argument shape and motion. Where does this sense of form, this energy for order, come from and how does it operate? Legal argument is a process by which hostility is at once expressed and controlled, at the same time and by the same means. Can you explain how this miracle occurs?

Selden says, "When a protestant & a papist dispute, they talke like two madmen, because they doe not agree upon their principles." Upon what do arguing lawyers agree that keeps them from talking like madmen? What are the conventions of the form, the terms of the invitation extended to one who is asked to argue for a client, and how are they stated? In a particular case we may say that a legal argument has degenerated into bickering, that the lawyers have become quarrelsome rather than argumentative: from what has the degeneration occurred? Precisely what are your hopes and expectations of an argument between lawyers, and from what source do they arise?[6]

One way to work into that question is to say that nearly every legal argument is addressed, actually or potentially, to the judicial mind, and that what is agreed upon is the institution of judicial judgment. One might say then of the argument, as of the opinion, that as it proceeds it defines a civilization: to what does the speaker ask his listener to attend, to what value — what authority, what feeling — does he appeal? How does he get his audience to see things his way, if he does? How, as Henry James might have said, does he put his case?

One might even want to say that the argument is, among other things, a potential judicial opinion — it must show a judge how a favorable judgment can be best explained — and that it has all the possibilities, complexities, and mysteries of that form. But as one works out the relationship between them, it quickly appears that the argument is not just the early stage of the opinion but a fundamentally different form of expression. The judge has the burden of deciding the case and of explaining why he did so; but the lawyer need not decide the case — that critical judgment is made for him — and his task is not to explain what he personally thinks of the case or of the various lines of argument either way. Instead of satisfying himself that the decision is right and

6. Holmes said, "You cannot argue with your neighbor, except on the admission for the moment that he is as wise as you, although you may by no means believe it." *The Common Law*, Lecture 2, pages 43–44 (1881). Is that true of all argument? Of all legal argument?

the explanation rightly put, he must address another mind engaged in that process, and try to catch and turn it. He must provide a range of possible explanations addressed to a range of audiences. In oral argument he must be ready to expand or contract an argument at a touch, to press on or retreat, to take one line rather than another. In his brief he must make available a series of possibilities, a variety of versions of his case, making different appeals to different minds. Yet he cannot sound like a cafeteria worker, offering you cantaloupe if you don't care for cottage cheese. His argument must be formed by his own mind, subjected to a consistent system of organization, yet addressed to a variety of minds.

To say this much is to claim that argument is an art of the greatest subtlety (an art that you may define further in your next paper); but nothing has yet been said of its ultimate object and test, the moment at which one mind persuades another, when argument succeeds or fails. How is it that someone actually makes up his mind or changes it, and what can the words of another have to do with that process? Nothing could be more impossible to talk about, and none more important to the lawyer. You know what value a how-to-do-it book or a course in Persuasive Speaking would have here. A nonlawyer might think that legal argument is simply the demonstration of the logically necessary, that it works by a sort of intellectual compulsion: one shows how a particular result is compelled by logical deduction from a general principle, just as Euclid worked out the implications of his axioms. But you know that this analogy is false: there is no set of fixed rules, and the interpretation of what rules we do have is not a tracing of logical necessity but a choice among possibilities. Imagine a case in which the question is whether two angles are equal, and a dispute between Euclid and another geometer over first principles, definitions, the articulation of the problem, and whether parallel lines do meet at infinity, as well as the process of deduction, and you have some idea of the complexity of ordinary legal argument and the place of deductive logic in it. A legal argument is not an articulation of the logical bearing of a general rule on a particular case, but a complex statement, in several kinds of language, addressed to several matters at once. There is no way to compel your judge or juror into submission; you must persuade him that the view of the case, of life, that you present is the one he wants. And how on earth do you do that?

What other questions can you ask about the form we call the legal argument? What other statements do you make, and in what language do you speak? Obviously no simple outline or mechanical analysis of "The Parts of Legal Argument" can be made, any more than can be done of the opinion or the poem. To draft a set of rules telling someone how to make a good argument is as senseless as to draft directions for good painting. The arguing mind is not a machine, and to talk about its operations in such a language would be foolish. But statements can be made about difficult matters, as you have seen of the opinion and the poem. What can you say about the art of argument? Can the understandings upon which it proceeds be defined and expressed, organized into a sort of logic of legal argument? Or, to put the question in terms now familiar, can you tell us what figure a legal argument makes? Finally, what is to be said for and against the enterprise of argument you define: is this a sensible way for mature minds to deal with serious matters, or is it an inherently trivial activity?

Such are the questions of this section. We begin with a passage by Aristotle on the subject of argument. He writes here about argument as a general matter, not legal argument, but you should be able to ask how what you read here bears on your own experience. What else might be said about legal argument and the activity of mind it entails? What does Aristotle fail to say?

1. *A Classical View of Rhetoric: Ethos, Pathos, and Logos*

RHETORIC*

Aristotle

Rhetoric is useful (1) because things that are true and things that are just have a natural tendency to prevail over their opposites, so that if the decisions of judges are not what they ought to be, the defeat must be due to the speakers themselves, and they must be blamed accordingly. Moreover, (2) before some audiences not even the possession of the exactest knowledge will make it easy for what we say to produce conviction. For argument based on knowledge implies instruction, and there are people whom one cannot instruct. Here, then, we must use, as our modes of persuasion and argument, notions possessed by everybody, as we observed in the *Topics*[5] when dealing with the way to handle a popular audience. Further, (3) we must be able to employ persuasion, just as strict reasoning can be employed, on opposite sides of a question, not in order that we may in practice employ it in both ways (for we must not make people believe what is wrong), but in order that we may see clearly what the facts are, and that, if another man argues unfairly, we on our part may be able to confute him. No other of the arts draws opposite conclusions: dialectic and rhetoric alone do this. Both these

* Book 1, Chapters 1–3 (Oxford Translation of Aristotle, printed in *Basic Works of Aristotle*, McKeon ed., 1941).

5. *Topics* i.2, 101a 30–4.

arts draw opposite conclusions impartially. Nevertheless, the underlying facts do not lend themselves equally well to the contrary views. No; things that are true and things that are better are, by their nature, practically always easier to prove and easier to believe in. Again, (4) it is absurd to hold that a man ought to be ashamed of being unable to defend himself with his limbs, but not of being unable to defend himself with speech and reason, when the use of rational speech is more distinctive of a human being than the use of his limbs. And if it be objected that one who uses such power of speech unjustly might do great harm, *that* is a charge which may be made in common against all good things except virtue, and above all against the things that are most useful, as strength, health, wealth, generalship. A man can confer the greatest of benefits by a right use of these, and inflict the greatest of injuries by using them wrongly.

It is clear, then, that rhetoric is not bound up with a single definite class of subjects, but is as universal as dialectic; it is clear, also, that it is useful. It is clear, further, that its function is not simply to succeed in persuading, but rather to discover the means of coming as near such success as the circumstances of each particular case allow. In this it resembles all other arts. For example, it is not the function of medicine simply to make a man quite healthy, but to put him as far as may be on the road to health; it is possible to give excellent treatment even to those who can never enjoy sound health. Furthermore, it is plain that it is the function of one and the same art to discern the real and the apparent means of persuasion, just as it is the function of dialectic to discern the real and the apparent syllogism. What makes a man a "sophist" is not his faculty, but his moral purpose. In rhetoric, however, the term "rhetorician" may describe either the speaker's knowledge of the art, or his moral purpose. In dialectic it is different: a man is a "sophist" because he has a certain kind of moral purpose, a "dialectician" in respect, not of his moral purpose, but of his faculty.

Let us now try to give some account of the systematic principles of Rhetoric itself — of the right method and means of succeeding in the object we set before us. We must make as it were a fresh start, and before going further define what rhetoric is.

Rhetoric may be defined as the faculty of observing in any given case the available means of persuasion. This is not a function of any other art. Every other art can instruct or persuade about its own particular subject-matter; for instance, medicine about what is healthy and unhealthy, geometry about the properties of magnitudes, arithmetic about numbers, and the same is true of the other arts and sciences. But rhetoric we look upon as the power of observing the means of persuasion on almost any subject presented to us; and that is why we say that, in its technical character, it is not concerned with any special or definite class of subjects.

Of the modes of persuasion some belong strictly to the art of rhetoric and some do not. By the latter I mean such things as are not supplied by the speaker but are there at the outset — witnesses, evidence given under torture, written contracts, and so on. By the former I mean such as we can ourselves construct by means of the principles of rhetoric. The one kind has merely to be used, the other has to be invented.

Of the modes of persuasion furnished by the spoken word there are three kinds. The first kind depends on the personal character of the speaker; the second on putting the audience into a certain[6] frame of mind; the third on the proof, or apparent proof, provided by the words of the speech itself. Persuasion is achieved by the speaker's personal character when the speech is so spoken as to make us think him credible. We believe good men more fully and more readily than others: this is true generally whatever the question is, and absolutely true where exact certainty is impossible and opinions are divided. This kind of persuasion, like the others, should be achieved by what the speaker says, not by what people think of his character before he begins to speak. It is not true, as some writers assume in their treatises on rhetoric, that the personal goodness revealed by the speaker contributes nothing to his power of persuasion; on the contrary, his character may almost be called the most effective means of persuasion he possesses. Secondly, persuasion may come through the hearers, when the speech stirs their emotions. Our judgements when we are pleased and friendly are not the same as when we are pained and hostile. It is towards producing these effects, as we maintain, that present-day writers on rhetoric direct the whole of their efforts. This subject shall be treated in detail when we come to speak of the emotions.[7] Thirdly, persuasion is effected through the speech itself when we have proved a truth or an apparent truth by means of the persuasive arguments suitable to the case in question.

There are, then, these three means of effecting persuasion. The man who is to be in command of them must, it is clear, be able (1) to reason logically, (2) to understand human character and goodness in their various forms, and (3) to understand the emotions — that is, to name them and describe them, to know their causes and the way in which they are excited. It thus appears that rhetoric is an offshoot of dialectic and also of ethical studies. Ethical studies may fairly be called political; and for this reason rhetoric masquerades as political science, and the professors of it as political experts — sometimes from want of education, sometimes from ostentation, sometimes owing to other human failings.

6. i.e. the right, fit, required frame of mind.
7. ii, cc. 2–11.

As a matter of fact, it is a branch of dialectic and similar to it, as we said at the outset.[8] Neither rhetoric nor dialectic is the scientific study of any one separate subject: both are faculties for providing arguments. This is perhaps a sufficient account of their scope and of how they are related to each other. . . .

Rhetoric falls into three divisions, determined by the three classes of listeners to speeches. For of the three elements in speech-making — speaker, subject, and person addressed — it is the last one, the hearer, that determines the speech's end and object. The hearer must be either a judge, with a decision to make about things past or future, or an observer. A member of the assembly decides about future events, a juryman about past events: while those who merely decide on the orator's skill are observers. From this it follows that there are three divisions of oratory — (1) political, (2) forensic, and (3) the ceremonial oratory of display.

Political speaking urges us either to do or not to do something: one of these two courses is always taken by private counsellors, as well as by men who address public assemblies. Forensic speaking either attacks or defends somebody: one or other of these two things must always be done by the parties in a case. The ceremonial oratory of display either praises or censures somebody. These three kinds of rhetoric refer to three different kinds of time. The political orator is concerned with the future: it is about things to be done hereafter that he advises, for or against. The party in a case at law is concerned with the past; one man accuses the other, and the other defends himself, with reference to things already done. The ceremonial orator is, properly speaking, concerned with the present, since all men praise or blame in view of the state of things existing at the time, though they often find it useful also to recall the past and to make guesses at the future.

Rhetoric has three distinct ends in view, one for each of its three kinds. The political orator aims at establishing the expediency or the harmfulness of a proposed course of action; if he urges its acceptance, he does so on the ground that it will do good; if he urges its rejection, he does so on the ground that it will do harm; and all other points, such as whether the proposal is just or unjust, honourable or dishonourable, he brings in as subsidiary and relative to this main consideration. Parties in a law-case aim at establishing the justice or injustice of some action, and they too bring in all other points as subsidiary and relative to this one. Those who praise or attack a man aim at proving him worthy of honour or the reverse, and they too treat all other considerations with reference to this one.

That the three kinds of rhetoric do aim respectively at the three ends

8. i.1. 1354a 1.

we have mentioned is shown by the fact that speakers will sometimes not try to establish anything else. Thus, the litigant will sometimes not deny that a thing has happened or that he has done harm. But that he is guilty of injustice he will never admit; otherwise there would be no need of a trial. So too, political orators often make any concession short of admitting that they are recommending their hearers to take an inexpedient course or not to take an expedient one. The question whether it is not *unjust* for a city to enslave its innocent neighbours often does not trouble them at all. In like manner those who praise or censure a man do not consider whether his acts have been expedient or not, but often make it a ground of actual praise that he has neglected his own interest to do what was honourable. Thus, they praise Achilles because he championed his fallen friend Patroclus, though he knew that this meant death, and that otherwise he need not die: yet while to die thus was the nobler thing for him to do, the expedient thing was to live on.

QUESTIONS

1. *Aristotle says there are three ways of persuading by the spoken word: through the character of the speaker; through the emotions raised in the audience; and through the force of reasoning. The Greek words for these means of persuasion may be respectively transliterated: ethos, pathos, and logos. Without claiming that this is a complete or even an accurate statement, we can use it as a way of framing a series of questions.*
2. *To start with "ethos" (character), Aristotle says that the speaker's appearance of wisdom and decency, of what is called his "personal goodness," is an important mode of persuasion to be mastered.*
   a. *Aristotle may be right with respect to witnesses, who testify on matters of fact and who are believed or disbelieved largely according to their appearance of honesty or the opposite. But how can he be right with respect to the lawyer, whose argument is a legal one, to be accepted or rejected on its merits, not by reference to its source? The lawyer is in fact prevented by the Canons of Ethics from giving his opinion on questions of law or fact. And traditional logic has a term for the fallacy of attacking an argument by attacking its source, the "argumentum ad fontem." Why does the apparent honesty and decency of the lawyer then matter at all? Or is Aristotle just wrong?*
   b. *Compare: "Sir James Johnston happened to say that he paid no regard to the arguments of counsel at the bar of the House of Commons, because they were paid for speaking. Johnson: 'Nay, Sir, argument is argument. You cannot help paying regard to their arguments, if they are good. If it were testimony, you might disregard it, if you knew that it were purchased. There is a beautiful image in Bacon, upon this subject: testimony is like an arrow shot from a long bow; the force of it depends upon the strength of the hand that draws it. Argument is like an arrow from a cross-bow, which has equal force though shot by a child.'" Boswell, The Life of Samuel Johnson, III, 298 (Glover ed. 1901).*

Is Aristotle's answer to Doctor Johnson that, however correct he may be as a matter of right thinking, many people are (like Sir James) more likely to be persuaded by the appearance of character than by the force of argument?

Doctor Johnson, in another vein, recognizes the power of character: "If a man were to go by chance at the same time with Burke under a shed, to shun a shower, he would say, 'This is an extraordinary man.' If Burke should go into a stable to see his horse drest, the ostler would say — 'we have an extraordinary man here.'" Id. at 295. The reverse can happen too: in the second book of the Iliad, Odysseus is trying to persuade the men, who have decided to quit and sail home, to stay and fight; when Thersites, the whining coward, speaks up for the men, they change sides. The advocacy of Thersites, without more, damages his cause.

c. *Assuming that the appearance of personal goodness, kindheartedness, and decency would be of value to one's courtroom career, how is the eager student or young lawyer to acquire it? To fail in the attempt is to occasion disaster — we have all shuddered at a lawyer's expression of sincere concern for the opposing witness — yet what does one do instead? Act natural?*

3. *The idea of "ethos" has another side: instead of referring to the goodness or decency of the speaker, it may refer to his authority. When certain men speak, all obey. "If he says it . . ." What can be asked or said about the phenomenon of personal authority? The idea of social organization depends on it: the policeman can tell you what to do because he is a policeman, because he has authority; so can the judge and the governor. It seems to be part of the notion of authority that it is unquestioned, an obvious fact, not a judgment: "Not all the water in the rough rude sea/ Can wash the balm off from an anointed king," says Shakespeare's Richard II, defining the attitude which regards what happens in that play — the deposition of a king — as unthinkable, impossible.*

   a. *Does a lawyer ever have such authority? Can he somehow manufacture it for himself, or for his arguments?*

   b. *Carlyle speaks to this mystery in the following passage.*

THE FRENCH REVOLUTION*
Carlyle

[The French king is in flight from Paris.]

The Village of Varennes lies dark and slumberous; a most unlevel Village, of inverse saddle-shape, as men write. It sleeps; the rushing of the River Aire singing lullaby to it. Nevertheless from the Golden Arm, *Bras d'Or* Tavern, across that sloping Marketplace, there still comes shine of social light; comes voice of rude drovers, or the like, who have not yet taken the stirrup-cup; Boniface Le Blanc, in white apron, serving them: cheerful to behold. To this *Bras d'Or*, Drouet enters, alacrity looking through his eyes; he nudges Boniface, in all privacy, "*Camarade*,

* Book 11, Chapter 7 (1837).

es-tu bon Patriote, Art thou a good Patriot?" — "*Si je suis!*" answers Boniface. — "In that case," eagerly whispers Drouet — what whisper is needful, heard of Boniface alone.

And now see Boniface Le Blanc bustling, as he never did for the jolliest toper. See Drouet and Guillaume, dexterous Old-Dragoons, instantly down blocking the Bridge, with a "furniture-wagon they find there," with whatever wagons, tumbrils, barrels, barrows their hands can lay hold of; — till no carriage can pass. Then swiftly, the Bridge once blocked, see them take station hard by, under Varennes Archway: joined by Le Blanc, Le Blanc's Brother, and one or two alert Patriots he has roused. Some half-dozen in all, with National muskets, they stand close, waiting under the Archway, till that same Korff Berline rumble up.

It rumbles up: *Alte la!* lanterns flash out from under coat-skirts, bridles chuck in strong fists, two National Muskets level themselves fore and aft through the two Coach-doors: "Mesdames, your Passports?" — Alas, alas! Sieur Sausse, Procureur of the Township, Tallow chandler also and Grocer, is there, with official grocer-politeness; Drouet with fierce logic and ready wit: — The respected Travelling Party, be it Baroness De Korff's, or persons of still higher consequence, will perhaps please to rest itself in M. Sausse's till the dawn strike up!

O Louis; O hapless Marie-Antoinette, fated to pass thy life with such men! Phlegmatic Louis, art thou but lazy semi-animate phlegm, then, to the centre of thee? King, Captain-General, Sovereign Frank! If thy heart ever formed, since it began beating under the name of heart, any resolution at all, be it now then, or never in this world: — "Violent nocturnal individuals, and if it were persons of high consequence? And if it were the King himself? Has the King not the power, which all beggars have, of travelling unmolested on his own Highway? Yes: it is the King; and tremble ye to know it! The King has said, in this one small matter; and in France, or under God's Throne, is no power that shall gainsay. Not the King shall ye stop here under this your miserable Archway; but his dead body only, and answer it to Heaven and Earth. To me, Bodyguards; Postillions, *en avant!*" — One fancies in that case the pale paralysis of these two Le Blanc musketeers, the drooping of Drouet's underjaw; and how Procureur Sausse had melted like tallow in furnace-heat: Louis faring on; in some few steps awakening Young Bouillé, awakening relays and Hussars: triumphant entry, with cavalcading high-brandishing Escort, and Escorts, into Montmedi; and the whole course of French History different!

Alas, it was not *in* the poor phlegmatic man. Had it been in him, French History had never come under this Varennes Archway to decide itself. — He steps out; all step out. Procureur Sausse gives his grocer-arms to the Queen and Sister Elizabeth; Majesty taking the two children by the hand. And thus they walk, coolly back, over the Market-place, to Procureur Sausse's; mount into his small upper story; where straightway his Majesty "demands refreshments." Demands refreshments, as is written; gets bread-and-cheese with a bottle of Burgundy; and remarks, that it is the best Burgundy he ever drank!

QUESTIONS

1. Another kind of authority has a real force in legal argument: the authority not of the lawyer himself, but of the people and writings he refers to — that of the statute or opinion that controls the case, of the "majority rule" or "better reasoned view"; or the personal authority of Justice Traynor or Judge Hand. "Authoritative" can mean "decisive"; and how on earth is it determined what shall be authoritative? How does argument on such a question proceed?

a. These questions apply to argument of every kind, of course: reading Hooker, for example, has given you some exposure to the literature of religious controversy, where much of the dispute is over what shall be authoritative — the Biblical text? church practice and custom? direct revelation? — as well as upon the precise bearing of statements that are accepted as authoritative. In the Renaissance, much literary and philosophical argument proceeded by the compilation and explication of references to the Ancients, whose words were apparently accepted as authoritative. And you are familiar with the moment in ordinary conversation when one person appeals to an authority (a person, a book, a proposition) that the other cannot deny — the moment of victory, when one person silences another.

How is the authority of a proposition, a source, or a person to be established, and once established, how questioned? See M. Gilmore, Argument From Roman Law in Political Thought: 1200–1600 (1941), which tells the story of the making of a language of authority. As you can imagine, when such a language is being made, everything is rethought at once; to question an old authority, an old system of reference and appeal, is to throw everything open. The essence of a language of authority is that it shall not be questioned but accepted as necessary; and, as Shakespeare's Richard II demonstrates, when such a language is taken as open to question, it loses its peculiar force at once. As time passes, a new language — or a new set of people — takes on the character of authority, and there exists a new set of clichés that define what is not to be talked about. This is the story of every revolution, I suppose: Bolingbroke becomes king, Oliver maintains the House of Lords, and so on.

But to say that authority loses its force when it is questioned is too simple: it is not given to any man to destroy a church or government by a question, at his whim; what must happen is that it somehow comes to be agreed that what was unquestioned shall be questioned. How does that process work? How can you, you alone, throw one authority into question and command the acceptance of a new one, or contribute to the process by which that happens? What this requirement of agreement – of an assent underlying the existence of one authority or the making of a new one – means to you as a lawyer is that you must know and master to its very limits the mind that you are addressing, its expectations and fears, its doubts and convictions. You must speak the current language perfectly if you are to effect or to resist its change.

b. Listen to the argument that goes on in your law classes and in moot court competitions, examine opinions and briefs, and ask in each instance what is accepted as authoritative. What appeals are made to what authorities? How are they defined, how questioned? You are looking now at the center of the moment of persuasion: can you learn how to do it?

2. One might say that what is meant by "ethos" in argument is a special case of our familiar problem: how does the writer or speaker meet the basic question of a perpetually busy and distracted audience, "Why should I pay any attention to what you say?"

Look over your papers written for this course, and pick two or three that please you. How have you attempted to answer that question in your opening sentences? Imagine yourself arguing particular cases (chosen from this book or your other courses) at trial or on appeal. How do you tell your audience why attention should be paid to what you say? How will you do so in your next writing assignment?

3. "Pathos," the capacity for arousing emotions in the audience, is Aristotle's second source of power in argument. Obviously most valuable for a lawyer, one might say, but how is it to be achieved? As with "ethos," the danger of failure is enormous, because no one likes to recognize that a speaker is trying to work on his emotions, and if he has that suspicion he may disregard everything you say. "An attempt to use pathos may destroy ethos." But how do you predict success and failure? What can you tell from those twelve faces, from the look of the judge? There you are, there he is; what connections of feeling, of attitude, can you establish? How dare you try?

Every teacher has been told by a student that an apparently successful class was "boring," or that an apparently incoherent class, a dead failure, was "terrific." There is no reason to think that a lawyer knows his jurors and judges better than a teacher knows his students. Yet you know that some speakers, some arguments, stir powerful emotions. You have felt them yourself; how can you in your turn begin to figure out what an appeal to the emotions is and how it is done well?

a. Think of occasions outside the law when you have tried to make others feel one way or another about things – in telling a story with a serious point, perhaps, or in trying to make someone pleased with or ashamed of himself. How, by what skill, and with what success, how measured, have you done such things?

b. A splendid example of pathos as a means of persuasion occurs in the series of speeches in Book 2 of the Iliad. In the ninth year of the war, Agamemnon is deceitfully told by the gods (one night in a dream) that he will win the war the next day. In fact, the divine plan is to incite the Greeks to vigorous action, so that they may feel more sharply the absence of Achilles, who has withdrawn from the battle. As the gods deceive him, Agamemnon deceives his troops: he addresses them, saying it is now time to give up and go home, neither victors nor defeated. He hopes to arouse the contrary emotion, to provoke denial, but the troops respond as one man, preparing to leave on the instant, packing their tents, and dragging their ships to the sea. Odysseus forces the men back to the assembly and addresses them, first shaming them into staying, then exciting them to war. His speech is followed by those of Nestor and Agamemnon; then the troops are ready for battle, their desire to go home having been raised and extinguished. How on earth do you suppose that this is accomplished? Can you see that a legal education would be of value for one asked to speak at such a moment?

c. Whatever the art of "pathos," the law imposes limits on your right to exercise it. Relevant evidence may be excluded from a trial if it is thought too "prejudicial," and remarks likely to "inflame" the jury may be cause for reprimand or mistrial. A judge will frequently give a directed verdict for one side on the grounds that no reasonable jury could find otherwise, when everyone knows that the jury would in fact find otherwise. How can this be explained? If one lawyer can arouse emotions of one kind, surely an equally skilled lawyer can arouse the opposite kind, can he not? And why should emotion, a feeling of what is right, be disfavored as a basis for judgment? What an odd thing the law does to the institution of argument; can you explain it?

4. Aristotle's third source of persuasive power is "logos," a term that will no doubt prove as difficult to deal with as "rationality" has been. As I have already suggested, whatever might be meant by such a term of description and approval, it cannot be the demonstration of the logically necessary: despite the fact that the law is often articulated in rules whose form reminds us of Euclidean postulates and axioms, the process of their use is not one of elucidating logically necessary implications, but of choosing among several logically possible alternatives. The enterprise is not one of compulsion but persuasion. "Logos" cannot refer to the strictest standards of logical validity, or rhetoric would be a form of mathematics. It must point to a complex and nonsystematic excellence, similar to what we mean when we speak of a "good poem" or a "good conversation" or a "good judicial opinion." Aristotle, of course, recognizes all this, and distinguishes between scientific demonstration and rhetorical argument. But he also draws some interesting parallels between them: for example, where scientific demonstration uses the syllogism – under which the result will be a scientific certainty if the premises are demonstrably true and the argument valid in form – rhetoric employs a somewhat similar form, which Aristotle calls in enthymeme, a sort of syllogism of probabilities. Here is one explanation of the distinction:

"Deductive scientific proof takes the form of the syllogism: 'all men are mortal (major premise); Socrates is a man (minor premise); therefore, Socrates is mortal (conclusion).' Deductive rhetorical proof takes the same form, but is called by Aristotle an enthymeme, an argument based on what is true for the most part: 'good men do not commit murder; Socrates is a good man; therefore, Socrates did not commit murder.' This is probably true, and the premises are probably good reasons why Socrates would have been innocent of a charge of murder; but there are individual circumstances when both premises, though generally true, might not *justify the conclusion. The argument would then have formal validity, but would still be false. Brutus and Cassius, for example, were good men too." G. Kennedy, The Art of Persuasion in Greece 97 (1963).*

A similar comparison can be drawn between the scientific process of induction (by which a true conclusion is inferred from a complete or statistically adequate set of samples) and the rhetorical use of an incomplete set of instances, or a single example, which Aristotle calls the paradigm. "It is important to keep the Persian king from acquiring Egypt, for his predecessor did not attack Greece until he controlled Egypt"; "The victory of McGovern over Muskie in 1972 shows that careful organization is far more valuable than publicity and political endorsements."

a. *How far do the remarks of Aristotle help you understand how argument works? How else might the "logic" of argument be talked about?*
b. *Elsewhere in the Rhetoric, and in classes on public speaking and debating ever since, devices of argument have been classified and analyzed. Should we have a course in law school on this subject, in which people are taught the use of the apostrophe and of amplification, how to discern and praise the noble and virtuous, how to move an audience to anger, how to appear wise, and so on?*
c. *As you know, those who came to Athens from Sicily in the fifth century as teachers of argument were greatly distrusted and feared. The feeling was that the skills of rhetoric were fundamentally dishonest — either dangerous or trivial, depending on the circumstances — and that serious men should concern themselves not with persuasion but with truth. Rhetoricians and sophists taught men "how to make the weaker argument the stronger"; one's proper concern is for the truth itself. How does Aristotle meet this objection? Does Aristotle's response have any parallel in contemporary philosophic experience?*

5. *It would be possible to speak of the "logos" of argument quite differently, not trying to articulate the way in which it is rational but trying to identify its typical shape, its structural movements and tensions. The remarks that follow take their direction once more from Robert Frost, and suggest a response to the question: "What figure does an argument make?"*
   a. *To start with, we can observe that in argument, as in the judicial opinion, there is a movement from the facts to the law and back again. The brief begins with a statement of the facts, makes a claim that certain principles of law apply to them, shows how these principles should work in this case, and concludes with a request for an order or judgment — an official effort to change the world, or a decision to leave it alone. But the movement is not just one way, and not a unitary process: the lawyer analyzing the case makes tentative statements of fact and issue, pursues his researches; but all this time he is testing out different versions of the facts, different formulations of the issue, different questions of fact and law. The facts determine what law is relevant; the law, what facts are relevant: the life of legal thought is a motion back and forth between them, a constant translation of one sort of proposition into another.[7] Whatever form his argument finally takes, with whatever assurance the lawyer at last claims that the connection he finds between the facts and the law is plain to see, he must first have gone through this process of doubt — and when he argues,*

7. I owe this observation to H. Hart and A. Sacks, *The Legal Process* 375 (1958).

he addresses a mind that is now doing so. As when a tuning fork is struck, the movement is from oscillation to the true, a vibration narrowing to rest.

b. But that is legal analysis, not argument. In argument there are at least two minds, each advancing its own version of the case, each under a predisposition or duty to contradict, to turn everything one way. A paradigm can be drawn here, I think: where there is real argument, where two minds are engaged with each other, responding and pushing, the movement of argument is from disagreement to agreement, and then (it is hoped) to new agreement on the matter in dispute. The arguer seeks a common ground on which both sides can agree, and then seeks to show that his conclusion flows from it. Socrates was one of the great masters of argument of this kind, as you can see from the passage (page 631 supra) in which he refutes the claims of Thrasymachus that "justice is the interest of the stronger" and that "injustice is of greater value than justice." Thrasymachus first maintains his position with great confidence; under questioning he assents to a set of obviously true statements; he is then led, "red-faced and perspiring," to a recognition that not his conclusion but the opposite flows from the agreed truth. In a case such as this, one might say, the movement of argument is from disagreement to agreement, thence to disagreeable surprise.

c. But this is still too simple an account of argument, because in the usual legal argument one is not in fact hopeful of converting one's adversary — his position and yours are set forever, and you have no adequate intellectual force, no power of logical necessity, to compel him to admit defeat. One seeks instead to persuade a third person, a disinterested observer who participates in the argument mainly by sympathy, at second hand. Perhaps his style is to let himself be carried first one way, then another; more likely, he will silently or orally resist the argument of each speaker, testing the argument by opposing it. And when you do seek to persuade your adversary, as in negotiation, it is often by asking him to imagine he is a judge, to imagine what a judge is likely to do. In both cases, the mind you seek to reach is not the arguing but the judging mind.

How do you reach that mind, how catch and turn it? How on earth do you make out your version of the case, set the terms of argument just so, in order to engage and persuade this other mind? The next writing assignment will ask you to make some progress with these questions. The possibilities are endless, in part because the law is not a closed, coherent system of logic but a mixture of languages, of law and common speech, of substance and procedure, of moral generality and practical detail. To argue well is to organize experience anew, to create for a moment a sufficient language, an account of experience and a statement of value and feeling, a statement that can stand the test of competition. How can this art be spoken of?

"My task which I am trying to achieve is, by the power of the written word, to make you hear, to make you feel — it is, before all, to make you see. That — and no more, and it is everything." In such terms Joseph Conrad speaks of the art of the novel, in his preface to The Nigger of the "Narcissus." Could you say the same of legal argument?

2. *What Is at Stake Here? Argument Over What a Case Involves*

Great argument is a force for meaning; it is a claim that the facts of the case are not just the stated facts, but that they stand for greater facts in the intellectual and moral universe. Every value of civilization, every sound principle of life, is somehow put at stake. Justice itself is involved in every case, and in the argument of the good lawyer its presence is felt — and all on one side. How is this achieved? How is it responded to?

The example we shall study is not legal so much as political argument. It occurs in what Aristotle would have called deliberative argument rather than forensic; but both of the participants were lawyers, and the very question that the parties agreed upon could have been recast in justiciable terms.

Here is one statement of the question: "Shall slavery be allowed to extend into United States territories now legally free?" (Abraham Lincoln, "On Sectionalism," October 1, 1856.) What do you think good lawyers could make argument on that question involve? What could you? One possibility is obvious: any argument on this question involves the morality of slavery, the most detestable institution known to man, and that is the end of it. But in a society in which there were slave states as well as free, under a Constitution expressly protecting the rights of property in slaves, implemented in the Fugitive Slave Law, can that be said by a candidate for the Senate who hopes to be elected? What can be said? The issue of territorial slavery divided Lincoln and Douglas in their campaign, and I urge you to read all the speeches on both sides, as well as the speech by Douglas reproduced below.

It may help with your reading of this speech to be reminded of the background. The Missouri Compromise of 1820 provided that the territories north of a certain line should be permanently free of slavery. In 1854 the Kansas-Nebraska Act, which established the two territories designated in its name, also repealed the Missouri Compromise, leaving the slavery question to the decision of the "people" of each territory at the time statehood was granted. Douglas was chairman of the committee responsible for that bill. In 1856 the Dred Scott case was decided, in which the Supreme Court held (1) that a descendant of African slaves could not become a citizen of the United States, even if he was legally freed and living in a state that purported to accord him full equality; and (2) that the Missouri Compromise was unconstitutional as beyond the powers of Congress. The Lecompton Constitution to which Douglas refers was adopted and proposed by a convention of the Kansas proslavery minority. The "English Bill" was a device by which the Democratic federal administration tried to get the Kansas voters to accept that constitution, whatever their views of its merits, by making special concessions to the state if it were adopted.

The speech by Douglas is not part of their formal debates, but it is given in response to a speech in which Lincoln had said: "A house divided against itself cannot stand. I believe this government cannot endure permanently half slave and half free. I do not expect the Union to be dissolved — I do not expect the house to fall — but I do expect it will cease to be divided. It will become all one thing, or all the other. Either the opponents of slavery will arrest the further spread of it, and place it where the public mind shall rest in the belief that it is in the course of ultimate extinction, or its advocates will push it forward, till it shall become lawful in all the states, old as well as new — North as well as South." (Springfield Convention Speech, accepting the nomination, June 16, 1858.)

What do you suppose an intelligent person, opposed to a federal prohibition of slavery in the territories, would say in response? If you find you cannot even imagine what you might say to such effect (so odious is slavery), then you should imagine what you, as Lincoln or as one of his advisors, would expect Douglas to say in response. What will he claim to be at stake here? How will he cast his argument? And how will you respond to him? It is nothing to say of an argument in support of a detestable position that it is detestable, and rest your case, secure in the absolute knowledge that you are right, for that is where argument begins.

SPRINGFIELD SPEECH*

Stephen A. Douglas

Mr. Chairman and fellow-citizens of Springfield and old Sangamon: My heart is filled with emotions at the allusions which have been so happily and so kindly made in the welcome just extended to me, — a welcome so numerous and so enthusiastic, bringing me to my home among my old friends, that language cannot express my gratitude. I do feel at home whenever I return to old Sangamon and receive those kind and friendly greetings which have never failed to meet me when I have come among you; but never before have I had such occasion to be grateful and to be proud of the manner of the reception as on the present. While I am willing, sir, to attribute a part of this demonstration to those kind and friendly personal relations to which you have referred, I cannot conceal from myself that the controlling and pervad-

* July 17, 1858, in *Complete Works of Abraham* Lincoln, III, 108 (Hay and Nicolay ed. 1894).

ing element in this great mass of human beings is devotion to that principle of self-government to which so many years of my life have been devoted; and rejoice more in considering it an approval of my support of a cardinal principle than I would if I could appropriate it to myself as a personal compliment.

You but speak rightly when you assert that during the last session of Congress there was an attempt to violate one of the fundamental principles upon which our free institutions rest. The attempt to force the Lecompton constitution upon the people of Kansas against their will, would have been, if successful, subversive of the great fundamental principles upon which all our institutions rest. If there is any one principle more sacred and more vital to the existence of a free government than all others, it is the right of the people to form and ratify the constitution under which they are to live. It is the cornerstone of the temple of liberty; it is the foundation upon which the whole structure rests; and whenever it can be successfully evaded, self-government has received a vital stab. I deemed it my duty, as a citizen and as a representative of the State of Illinois, to resist, with all my energies and with whatever of ability I could command, the consummation of that effort to force a constitution upon an unwilling people.

I am aware that other questions have been connected, or attempted to be connected, with that great struggle; but they were mere collateral questions, not affecting the main point. My opposition to the Lecompton constitution rested solely upon the fact that it was not the act and deed of that people, and that it did not embody their will. I did not object to it upon the ground of the slavery clause contained in it. I should have resisted it with the same energy and determination even if it had been a free State instead of a slaveholding State; and as an evidence of this fact I wish you to bear in mind that my speech against the Lecompton act was made on the 9th day of December, nearly two weeks before the vote was taken on the acceptance or rejection of the slavery clause. I did not then know, I could not have known, whether the slavery clause would be accepted or rejected; the general impression was that it would be rejected; and in my speech I assumed that impression to be true; that probably it would be voted down; and then I said to the United States Senate, as I now proclaim to you, my constituents, that you have no more right to force a free State upon an unwilling people than you have to force a slave State upon them against their will. You have no right to force either a good or a bad thing upon a people who do not choose to receive it. And then, again, the highest privilege of our people is to determine for themselves what kind of institutions are good and what kind of institutions are bad; and it may be true that the same people, situated in a different latitude and different climate, and with different productions and different interests, might decide the same question one way in the North and another way in the South, in order to adapt their institutions to the wants and wishes of the people to be affected by them.

You all are familiar with the Lecompton struggle, and I will occupy no more time upon the subject, except to remark that when we drove the enemies of the principle of popular sovereignty from the effort to force the Lecompton constitution upon the people of Kansas, and when we compelled them to abandon the attempt and to refer that constitution to that people for acceptance or rejection, we obtained a concession of the principle for which I had contended throughout the struggle. When I saw that the principle was conceded, and that the constitution was not to be forced on Kansas against the wishes of the people, I felt anxious to give the proposition my support; but when I examined it, I found that the mode of reference to the people and the form of submission, upon which the vote was taken, was so objectionable as to make it unfair and unjust.

Sir, it is an axiom with me that in every free government an unfair election is no election at all. Every election should be free, should be fair, with the same privileges and the same inducements for a negative as for an affirmative vote. The objection to what is called the "English" proposition, by which the Lecompton constitution was referred back to the people of Kansas, was this: that if the people choose to accept the Lecompton constitution they could come in with only 35,000 inhabitants; while if they determined to reject it in order to form another more in accordance with their wishes and sentiments, they were compelled to stay out until they should have 93,420 inhabitants. In other words, it was making a distinction and discrimination between free States and slave States under the Federal Constitution. I deny the justice, I deny the right, of any distinction or discrimination between the States North and South, free or slave. Equality among the States is a fundamental principle of this Government. Hence, while I will never consent to the passage of a law that a slave State may come in with 35,000, while a free State shall not come in unless it have 93,000, on the other hand, I shall not consent to admit a free State with a population of 35,000, and require 93,000, in a slaveholding State.

My principle is to recognize each State of the Union as independent, sovereign, and equal in its sovereignty. I will apply that principle, not only to the original thirteen States, but to the States which have since been brought into the Union, and also to every State that shall hereafter be received, "as long as water shall run, and grass grow." For these reasons I felt compelled, by a sense of duty, by a conviction of principle, to record my vote against what is called the English bill; but yet the bill became a law, and under that law an election has been ordered to be held on the first Monday in August, for the purpose of determining the question of the acceptance or rejection of the proposition submitted by Congress. . . .

. . . I therefore shall only notice those parts of Mr. Lincoln's speech in which he lays down his platform of principles, and tells you what he intends to do if he is elected to the Senate of the United States.

[An old gentleman here arose on the platform and said, "Be particular now, Judge, be particular."]

My venerable friend here says he will be gratified if I will be particular; and in order that I may be so, I will read the language of Mr. Lincoln as reported by himself and published to the country. Mr. Lincoln lays down his main proposition in these words:

> "A house divided against itself cannot stand." I believe this Union cannot endure permanently, half free and half slave. I do not expect the Union will be dissolved, I do not expect the house to fall; but I do expect it to cease to be divided. It will become all one thing or all the other.

Mr. Lincoln does not think this Union can continue to exist composed of half slave and half free States; they must all be free, or all slave. I do not doubt that this is Mr. Lincoln's conscientious conviction. I do not doubt that he thinks it is the highest duty of every patriotic citizen to preserve this glorious Union, and to adopt these measures as necessary to its preservation. He tells you that the only mode to preserve the Union is to make all the States free, or all slave. It must be the one, or it must be the other. Now, that being essential, in his estimation, to the preservation of this glorious Union, how is he going to accomplish it? He says that he wants to go to the Senate in order to carry out this favorite patriotic policy of his, of making all the States free, so that the house shall no longer be divided against itself.

When he gets to the Senate, by what means is he going to accomplish it? By an Act of Congress? Will he contend that Congress has any power under the Constitution to abolish slavery in any State of this Union, or to interfere with it directly or indirectly? Of course he will not contend that. Then what is to be his mode of carrying out his principle, by which slavery shall be abolished in all of the States? Mr. Lincoln certainly does not speak at random. He is a lawyer, — an eminent lawyer, — and his profession is to know the remedy for every wrong. What is his remedy for this imaginary wrong which he supposes to exist? The Constitution of the United States provides that it may be amended by Congress passing an amendment by a two-thirds majority of each house, which shall be ratified by three-fourths of the States; and the inference is that Mr. Lincoln intends to carry this slavery agitation into Congress with the view of amending the Constitution so that slavery can be abolished in all the States of the Union.

In other words, he is not going to allow one portion of the Union to be slave and another portion to be free; he is not going to permit the house to be divided against itself. He is going to remedy it by lawful and constitutional means. What are to be these means? How can he abolish slavery in those States where it exists? There is but one mode by which a political organization, composed of men in the free States, can abolish slavery in the slaveholding States, and that would be to abolish the State legislatures, blot out of existence the State sovereignties, invest Congress with full and plenary power over all the local and domestic and police regulations of the different States of this Union. Then there would be uniformity in the local concerns and domestic institutions of the different States; then the house would be no longer divided against itself; then the States would all be free, or they would all be slave; then you would have uniformity prevailing throughout this whole land in the local and domestic institutions: but it would be a uniformity, not of liberty, but a uniformity of despotism that would triumph. I submit to you, my fellow-citizens, whether this is not the logical consequence of Mr. Lincoln's proposition.

I have called on Mr. Lincoln to explain what he did mean, if he did not mean this, and he has made a speech at Chicago in which he attempts to explain. And how does he explain? I will give him the benefit of his own language, precisely as it was reported in the Republican papers of that city, after undergoing his revision:

> I have said a hundred times, and have now no inclination to take it back, that I believe there is no right and ought to be no inclination in the people of the free States to enter into the slave States and interfere with the question of slavery at all.

He believes there is no right on the part of the free people of the free States to enter the slave States and interfere with the question of slavery, hence he does not propose to go into Kentucky and stir up a civil war and a servile war between the blacks and the whites. All he proposes is to invite the people of Illinois and every other free State to band together as one sectional party, governed and divided by a geographical line, to make war upon the institution of slavery in the slaveholding States. He is going to carry it out by means of a political party that has its adherents only in the free States, — a political party that does not pretend that it can give a solitary vote in the slave States of the Union; and by this sectional vote he is going to elect a president of the United States, form a cabinet, and administer the Government on sectional grounds, being the power of the North over that of the South.

In other words, he invites a war of the North against the South, a warfare of the free States against the slaveholding States. He asks all men in the free states to conspire to exterminate slavery in the Southern States, so as to make them all free, and then he notifies the South that unless they are going to submit to our efforts to exterminate their institutions, they must band together and plant slavery in Illinois and every Northern State. He says that the States must all be free or must all be slave. On this point I take issue with him directly. I assert that Illinois has a right to decide the slavery question for herself. We have decided it, and I think we have done it wisely; but whether wisely or unwisely, it is our business, and the people of no other State have any right to interfere with us, directly or indirectly. Claiming as we do this right for ourselves, we must concede it to every other State, to be exercised by them respectively.

Now, Mr. Lincoln says that he will not enter into Kentucky to abolish slavery there, but that all he will do is to fight slavery in Kentucky from Illinois. He will not go over there to set fire to the match. I do not think he would. Mr. Lincoln is a very prudent man. He would not deem it wise to go over into Kentucky to stir up this strife, but he would do it from this side of the river. Permit me to inquire whether the wrong, the outrage, of interference by one State with the local concerns of another is worse when you actually invade them than it would be if you carried on the warfare from another State? For the purpose of illustration, suppose the British Government should plant a battery on the Niagara River, opposite Buffalo, and throw their shells over into Buffalo, where they should explode and blow up the houses and destroy the town. We call the British Government to an account, and they say, in the language of Mr. Lincoln, we did not enter into the limits of the United States to interfere with you; we planted the battery on our own soil, and had a right to shoot from our own soil; and if our shells and balls fell in Buffalo and killed your inhabitants, why, it is your look-out, not ours.

Thus, Mr. Lincoln is going to plant his Abolition batteries all along the banks of the Ohio River, and throw his shells into Virginia and Kentucky and into Missouri, and blow up the institution of slavery; and when we arraign him for his unjust interference with the institutions of the other States, he says, "Why, I never did enter into Kentucky to interfere with her; I do not propose to do it; I only propose to take care of my own head by keeping on this side of the river, out of harm's way." But yet he says he is going to persevere in this system of sectional warfare, and I have no doubt he is sincere in what he says. He says that the existence of the Union depends upon his success in firing into these slave States until he exterminates them. He says that unless he shall play his batteries successfully, so as to abolish slavery in every one of the States, that the Union shall be dissolved; and he says that a dissolution of the Union would be a terrible calamity. Of course it would. We are all friends of the Union. We all believe — I do — that our lives, our liberties, our hopes in the future, depend upon the preservation and perpetuity of this glorious Union. I believe that the hopes of the friends of liberty throughout the world depend upon the perpetuity of the American Union. But while I believe that my mode of preserving the Union is a very different one from that of Mr. Lincoln, I believe that the Union can only be preserved by maintaining inviolate the Constitution of the United States as our fathers have made it.

That Constitution guarantees to the people of every State the right to have slavery or not have it; to have negroes or not have them; to have Maine liquor laws or not have them; to have just such institutions as they choose, each State being left free to decide for itself. The framers of that Constitution never conceived the idea that uniformity in the domestic institutions of the different States was either desirable or possible. They well understood that the laws and institutions which would be well adapted to the granite hills of New Hampshire would be unfit for the rice plantations of South Carolina; they well understood that each one of the thirteen States had distinct and separate interests, and required distinct and separate local laws and local institutions. And in view of that fact they provided that each State should retain its sovereign power within its own limits, with the right to make just such laws and just such institutions as it saw proper, under the belief that no two of them would be alike. If they had supposed that uniformity was desirable and possible, why did they provide for a separate legislature for each State? Why did they not blot out State sovereignty and State legislatures; and give all the power to Congress, in order that the laws might be uniform? For the very reason that uniformity, in their opinion, was neither desirable nor possible.

We have increased from thirteen States to thirty-two States; and just in proportion as the number of States increases and our territory expands, there will be a still greater variety and dissimilarity of climate, of production, and of interest, requiring a corresponding dissimilarity and variety in the local laws and institutions adapted thereto. The laws that are necessary in the mining regions of California would be totally useless and vicious on the prairies of Illinois; the laws that would suit the lumber regions of Maine or of Minnesota would be totally useless and valueless in the tobacco regions of Virginia and Kentucky; the laws which would suit the manufacturing districts of New England would be totally unsuited to the planting regions of the Carolinas, of Georgia, and of Louisiana. Each State is supposed to have interests separate and distinct from each and every other; and hence must have laws different from each and every other State, in order that its laws shall be adapted to the condition and necessities of the people.

Hence I insist that our institutions rest on the theory that there shall be dissimilarity and variety in the local laws and institutions of the different States, instead of all being uniform; and you find, my friends, that Mr. Lincoln and myself differ radically and totally on the fundamental principles of this Government. He goes for consolidation, for uniformity in our local institutions, for blotting out State rights and State sovereignty, and consolidating all the power in the Federal Government, for converting these thirty-two sovereign States into one empire, and making uniformity throughout the length and breadth of the land. On the other hand, I go for maintaining the authority of the Federal Government within the limits marked out by the Constitution, and then for maintaining and preserving the sovereignty of each and all of the States of the Union, in order that each State may regulate and adopt its own local institutions in its own way, without interference from any power whatsoever. Thus you find there is a distinct issue of principles — principles irreconcilable — between Mr. Lincoln and myself. He goes for consolidation and uniformity in our government; I go for maintaining the confederation of the sovereign States under the Constitution as our fathers made it, leaving each State at liberty to manage its own affairs and own internal institutions.

Mr. Lincoln makes another point upon me, and rests his whole case upon these two points. His last point is, that he will wage a warfare upon the Supreme Court of the United States because of the Dred Scott decision. He takes occasion, in his speech made before the Republican convention, in my absence, to arraign me, not only for having expressed my acquiescence in that decision, but to charge me with being a conspirator with that court in devising that decision three years before Dred Scott ever thought of commencing a suit for his freedom. The object of his speech was to convey the idea to the people that the court could not be trusted, that the late President could not be trusted, that the present one could not be trusted, and that Mr. Douglas could not be trusted; that they were all conspirators in bringing about that corrupt decision, to which Mr. Lincoln is determined he will never yield a willing obedience.

He makes two points upon the Dred Scott decision. The first is that he objects to it because the court decided that negroes descended of slave parents are not citizens of the United States; and, secondly, because they have decided that the Act of Congress passed 8th of March,

1820, prohibiting slavery in all of the Territories north of 36 degrees 30 minutes, was unconstitutional and void, and hence did not have effect in emancipating a slave brought into that Territory. And he will not submit to that decision. He says that he will not fight the judges or the United States marshals in order to liberate Dred Scott, but that he will not respect that decision, as a rule of law binding on this country, in the future. Why not? Because, he says, it is unjust. How is he going to remedy it? Why, he says he is going to reverse it. How? He is going to take an appeal. To whom is he going to appeal? The Constitution of the United States provides that the Supreme Court is the ultimate tribunal, the highest judicial tribunal on earth; and Mr. Lincoln is going to appeal from that! To whom?

I know he appealed to the Republican State convention, of Illinois, and I believe that convention reversed the decision; but I am not aware that they have yet carried it into effect. How are they going to make that reversal effectual? Why, Mr. Lincoln tells us in his late Chicago speech. He explains it as clear as light. He says to the people of Illinois that if you elect him to the Senate he will introduce a bill to reenact the law which the court pronounced unconstitutional. [Shouts of laughter, and voices, "Spot the law."] Yes, he is going to spot the law. The court pronounces that law prohibiting slavery, unconstitutional and void, and Mr. Lincoln is going to pass an act reversing that decision and making it valid. I never heard before of an appeal being taken from the Supreme Court to the Congress of the United States to reverse its decision. I have heard of appeals being taken from Congress to the Supreme Court to declare a statute void. That has been done from the earliest days of Chief Justice Marshall down to the present time.

The Supreme Court of Illinois do not hesitate to pronounce an Act of the legislature void, as being repugnant to the Constitution, and the Supreme Court of the United States is vested by the Constitution with that very power. The Constitution says that that judicial power of the United States shall be vested in the Supreme Court and such inferior courts as Congress shall, from time to time, ordain and establish. Hence it is the province and duty of the Supreme Court to pronounce judgment on the validity and constitutionality of an Act of Congress. In this case they have done so, and Mr. Lincoln will not submit to it, and he is going to reverse it by another Act of Congress of the same tenor. My opinion is that Mr. Lincoln ought to be on the Supreme Bench himself, when the Republicans get into power, if that kind of law knowledge qualifies a man for the bench.

But Mr. Lincoln intimates that there is another mode by which he can reverse the Dred Scott decision. How is that? Why, he is going to appeal to the people to elect a President who will appoint judges who will reverse the Dred Scott decision. Well, let us see how that is going to be done. First, he has to carry on his sectional organization, a party confined to the free States, making war upon the slaveholding States until he gets a Republican president elected. [Voice: "He never will, sir."] I do not believe he ever will. But suppose he should; when that Republican president shall have taken his seat (Mr. Seward, for instance), will he then proceed to appoint judges? No! he will have to wait until the present judges die before he can do that; and perhaps his four years would be out before a majority of these judges found it agreeable to die; and it is very possible, too, that Mr. Lincoln's senatorial term would expire before these judges would be accommodating enough to die. If it should so happen; I do not see a very great prospect for Mr. Lincoln to reverse the Dred Scott decision.

But suppose they should die, then how are the new judges to be appointed? Why, the Republican president is to call upon the candidates and catechise them, and ask them, "How will you decide this case if I appoint you judge?" Suppose, for instance, Mr. Lincoln to be candidate for a vacancy on the Supreme Bench to fill Chief Justice Taney's place, and when he applied to Seward, the latter would say, "Mr. Lincoln, I cannot appoint you until I know how you will decide the Dred Scott case?" Mr. Lincoln tells him, and he then asks him how he will decide Tom Jones's case, and Bill Wilson's case, and thus catechises the judge as to how he will decide any case which may arise before him. Suppose you get a Supreme Court composed of such judges, who have been appointed by a partisan president upon their giving pledges how they would decide a case before it arose, — what confidence would you have in such a court? Would not your court be prostituted beneath the contempt of all mankind? What man would feel that his liberties were safe, his right of person or property was secure, if the Supreme Bench, that august tribunal, the highest on earth, was brought down to that low, dirty pool wherein the judges are to give pledges in advance how they will decide all the questions which may be brought before them? It is a proposition to make that court the corrupt, unscrupulous tool of a political party. But Mr. Lincoln cannot conscientiously submit, he thinks, to the decision of a court composed of a majority of Democrats. If he cannot, how can he expect us to have confidence in a court composed of a majority of Republicans, selected for the purpose of deciding against the Democracy, and in favor of the Republicans? The very proposition carries with it the demoralization and degradation destructive of the judicial department of the Federal Government.

I say to you, fellow-citizens, that I have no warfare to make upon the Supreme Court because of the Dred Scott decision. I have no complaints to make against that Court because of that decision. My private opinions on some points of the case may have been one way; and on other points of the case another; in some things concurring with the Court, and in others dissenting; but what have my private opinions in a question of law to do with the decision after it has been pronounced by the highest judicial tribunal known to the Constitution? You, sir [addressing the chairman], as an eminent lawyer, have a right to entertain your opinions on any question that comes before the court, and to appear before the tribunal and maintain them boldly and with tenacity until the final decision shall have been pronounced; and then, sir, whether you are sustained or overruled, your duty as a lawyer and a citizen is to bow in deference to that decision. I intend to yield obedience to the decisions of the highest tribunal in the land in all cases, whether their opinions are in conformity with my views as a lawyer or not. When we refuse to abide by judicial decisions, what protection is there left for life and property? To whom shall you appeal? To mob law, to partisan caucuses, to town meetings, to revolution? Where is the remedy when you refuse obedience to the constituted authorities? I will not stop to inquire whether I agree or disagree with all the opinions expressed by Judge Taney or any other judge. It is enough for me to know that the decision has been made. It has been made by a tribunal appointed by the Constitution to make it; it was a point within their jurisdiction, and I am bound by it.

But, my friends, Mr. Lincoln says that this Dred Scott decision destroys the doctrine of popular sovereignty, for the reason that the Court has decided that Congress had no power to prohibit slavery in the Territories, and hence he infers that it would decide that the Territorial legislatures could not prohibit slavery there. I will not stop to inquire whether the Court will carry the decision that far or not. It would be interesting as a matter of theory, but of no importance in practice; for this reason, that if the people of a Territory want slavery they will have it, and if they do not want it they will drive it out, and you cannot force it on them. Slavery cannot exist a day in the midst of an unfriendly people with unfriendly laws. There is truth and wisdom in a remark made to me by an eminent Southern senator, when speaking of this technical right to take slaves into the Territories. Said he, "I do not care a fig which way the decision shall be, for it is of no particular consequence; slavery cannot exist a day or an hour in any Territory or State unless it has affirmative laws sustaining and supporting it, furnishing police regulations and remedies; and an omission to furnish them would be as fatal as a constitutional prohibition. Without affirmative legislation in its favor, slavery could not exist any longer than a new-born infant could survive under the heat of the sun, on a barren rock, without protection. It would wilt and die for the want of support."

So it would be in the Territories. See the illustration in Kansas. The Republicans have told you, during the whole history of that Territory, down to last winter, that the pro-slavery party in the legislature had passed a pro-slavery code, establishing and sustaining slavery in Kansas, but that this pro-slavery legislature did not truly represent the people, but was imposed upon them by an invasion from Missouri; and hence the legislature were one way, and the people another. Granting all this, and what has been the result? With laws supporting slavery, but the people against, there are not as many slaves in Kansas to-day as there were on the day the Nebraska bill passed and the Missouri Compromise was repealed. Why? Simply because slave-owners knew that if they took their slaves into Kansas, where a majority of the people were opposed to slavery, that it would soon be abolished, and they would lose their right of property in consequence of taking them there. For that reason they would not take or keep them there. If there had been a majority of the people in favor of slavery, and the climate had been favorable, they would have taken them there; but the climate not being suitable, the interest of the people being opposed to it, and a majority of them against it, the slave-owner did not find it profitable to take his slaves there, and consequently there are not as many slaves there to-day as on the day the Missouri Compromise was repealed. This shows clearly that if the people do not want slavery they will keep it out; and if they do want it, they will protect it.

You have a good illustration of this in the Territorial history of this State. You all remember that by the Ordinance of 1787 slavery was prohibited in Illinois; yet you all know, particularly you old settlers who were here in Territorial times; that the Territorial Legislature, in defiance of that Ordinance, passed a law allowing you to go into Kentucky, buy slaves, and bring them into the Territory, having them sign indentures to serve you and your posterity ninety-nine years, and their posterity thereafter to do the same. This hereditary slavery was introduced in defiance of the Act of Congress. That was the exercise of popular sovereignty, — the right of a Territory to decide the question for itself in defiance of the Act of Congress. On the other hand, if the people of a Territory are hostile to slavery, they will drive it out. Consequently, this theoretical question raised upon the Dred Scott decision is worthy of no consideration whatsoever, for it is only brought into these political discussions and used as a hobby upon which to ride into office, or out of which to manufacture political capital.

But Mr. Lincoln's main objection to the Dred Scott decision I have reserved for my conclusion. His principal objection to that decision is that it was intended to deprive the negro of the rights of citizenship in the different States of the Union. Well, suppose it was, — and there is no doubt that that was its legal effect, — what is his objection to it? Why, he thinks that a negro ought to be permitted to have the rights of citizenship. He is in favor of negro citizenship, and opposed to the Dred Scott decision, because it declares that a negro is not a citizen, and hence is not entitled to vote. Here I have a direct issue with Mr. Lincoln. I am not in favor of negro citizenship. I do not believe that a negro is a citizen or ought to be a citizen. I believe that this Government of ours was founded, and wisely founded, upon the white basis. It was made by white men for the benefit of white men and their posterity, to be executed and managed by white men. I freely concede that humanity requires us to extend all the protection, all the privileges, all the immunities, to the Indian and the negro which they are capable of enjoying consistent with the safety of society.

You may then ask me what are those rights, what is the nature and extent of the rights which a negro ought to have? My answer is that this is a question for each State and each Territory to decide for itself. In Illinois we have decided that a negro is not a slave, but we have at the same time determined that he is not a citizen and shall not enjoy any political rights. I concur in the wisdom of that policy, and am content with it. I assert that the sovereignty of Illinois had a right to determine that question as we have decided it, and I deny that any other State has a right to interfere with us or call us to account for that decision. In the State of Maine they have decided by their constitution that the negro shall exercise the elective franchise and hold office on an equality with the white man. Whilst I do not concur in the good sense or correct taste of that decision on the part of Maine, I have no disposition to quarrel with her. It is her business, and not ours. If the people of Maine desire to be put on an equality with the negro, I do not know that anybody in this State will attempt to prevent it. If the white people of Maine think a negro their equal, and that he has a right to come and kill their vote by a negro vote, they have a right to think so, I suppose, and I have no disposition to interfere with them.

Then, again, passing over to New York, we find in that State they have provided that a negro may vote, provided he holds $250 worth of property, but that he shall not unless he does; that is to say, they will allow a negro to vote if he is rich, but a poor fellow they will not allow to vote. In New York they think a rich negro is equal to a white man. Well, that is a matter of taste with them. If they think so in that State, and do not carry the doctrine outside of it, and propose to interfere with us, I have no quarrel to make with them. It is their business. There is a great deal of philosophy and good sense in a saying of Fridley of Kane. Fridley had a lawsuit before a justice of the peace, and the justice decided it against him. This he did not like; and standing up and looking at the justice for a moment, "Well, Squire," said he, "if a man chooses to make a darnation fool of himself, I suppose there is no law against it." That is all I have to say about these negro regulations and this negro voting in other States where they have systems different from ours. If it is their wish to have it so, be it so. There is no cause to complain. Kentucky has decided that it is not consistent with her safety and her prosperity to allow a negro to have either political rights or his freedom, and hence she makes him a slave. That is her business, not mine. It is her right under the Constitution of the country. The sovereignty of Kentucky, and that alone, can decide that question; and when she decides it, there is no power on earth to which you can appeal to reverse it. Therefore, leave Kentucky as the Constitution has left her, a sovereign, independent State, with the exclusive right to have slavery or not as she chooses; and so long as I hold power I will maintain and defend her rights against any assaults, from whatever quarter they may come.

I will never stop to inquire whether I approve or disapprove of the domestic institutions of a State. I maintain her sovereign rights. I defend her sovereignty from all assault, in the hope that she will join in defending us when we are assailed by any outside power. How are we to protect our sovereign rights, to keep slavery out, unless we protect the sovereign rights of every other State to decide the question for itself? Let Kentucky, or South Carolina, or any other State attempt to interfere in Illinois, and tell us that we shall establish slavery, in order to make it uniform, according to Mr. Lincoln's proposition, throughout the Union; let them come here and tell us that we must and shall have slavery, — and I will call on you to follow me, and shed the last drop of our hearts' blood in repelling the invasion and chastising their insolence. And if we would fight for our reserved rights and sovereign power in our own limits, we must respect the sovereignty of each other State.

Hence, you find that Mr. Lincoln and myself come to a direct issue on this whole doctrine of slavery. He is going to wage a war against it everywhere, not only in Illinois, but in his native State of Kentucky. And Why? Because he says that the Declaration of Independence contains this language: "We hold these truths to be self-evident, that all men are created equal; that they are endowed by their Creator with certain inalienable rights; that among these are life, liberty and the pursuit of happiness;" and he asks whether that instrument does not declare that all men are created equal. Mr. Lincoln then goes on to say that that clause of the Declaration of Independence includes negroes. [Voice, "I say not."] Well, if you say not, I do not think you will vote for Mr. Lincoln. Mr. Lincoln goes on to argue that the language "all men" included the negroes, Indians, and all inferior races.

In his Chicago speech he says, in so many words, that it includes the negroes, that they were endowed by the Almighty with the right of equality with the white man, and therefore that that right is divine, — a right under the higher law; that the law of God makes them equal to the white man, and therefore that the law of the white man cannot deprive them of that right. This is Mr. Lincoln's argument. He is conscientious in his belief. I do not question his sincerity; I do not doubt that he, in his conscience, believes that the Almighty made the negro equal to the white man. He thinks that the negro is his brother. I do not think that the negro is any kin of mine at all. And here is the difference between us. I believe that the Declaration of Independence, in the words, "all men are created equal," was intended to allude only to the people of the United States, to men of European birth or descent, being white men; that they were created equal, and hence that Great Britain had no right to deprive them of their political and religious privileges; but the signers of that paper did not intend to include the Indian or the negro in that declaration; for if they had, would they not have been bound to abolish slavery in every State and colony from that day?

Remember, too, that at the time the Declaration was put forth, every one of the thirteen colonies were slaveholding colonies; every man who signed that Declaration represented slaveholding constituents. Did those signers mean by that act to charge themselves and all their constituents with having violated the law of God, in holding the negro in an inferior condition to the white man? And yet, if they included negroes in that term, they were bound, as conscientious men, that day and that hour, not only to have abolished slavery throughout the land, but to have conferred political rights and privileges on the negro, and elevated him to an equality with the white man. [Voice, "They did not do it."] I know they did not do it; and the very fact that they did not shows that they did not understand the language they used to include any but the white race. Did they mean to say that the Indian, on this continent, was created equal to the white man, and that he was endowed by the Almighty with inalienable rights, — rights so sacred that they could not be taken away by any constitution or law that man could pass? Why, their whole action toward the Indian showed that they never dreamed that they were bound to put him on an equality. I am not only opposed to negro equality, but I am opposed to Indian equality. I am opposed to putting the Coolies, now importing into this country, on an equality with us, or putting the Chinese or any inferior race on an equality with us.

I hold that the white race, the European race, I care not whether Irish, German, French, Scotch, English, or to what nation they belong, so they are the white race, to be our equals. And I am for placing them, as our fathers did, on an equality with us. Emigrants from Europe, and their descendants, constitute the people of the United States. The Declaration of Independence only included the white people of the United States. The Constitution of the United States was framed by the white people; it ought to be administered by them, leaving each State to make such regulations concerning the negro as it chooses, allowing him political rights or not, as it chooses, and allowing *him* civil rights or not, as it may determine for itself.

Let us only carry out those principles, and we will have peace and harmony in the different States. But Mr. Lincoln's conscientious scruples on this point govern his actions, and I honor him for following them, although I abhor the doctrine which he preaches. His conscientious scruples lead him to believe that the negro is entitled by divine right to the civil and political privileges of citizenship on an equality with the white man.

For that reason he says he wishes the Dred Scott decision reversed. He wishes to confer those privileges of citizenship on the negro. Let us see how he will do it. He will first be called upon to strike out of the Constitution of Illinois that clause which prohibits free negroes and slaves from Kentucky or any other State coming into Illinois. When he blots out that clause, when he lets down the door or opens the gate for all the negro population to flow in and cover our prairies, until in midday they will look dark and black as night, — when he shall have done this, his mission will yet be unfulfilled. Then it will be that he will apply his principles of negro equality; that is, if he can get the Dred Scott decision reversed in the meantime. He will then change the Constitution again, and allow negroes to vote and hold office, and will make them eligible to the legislature, so that thereafter they can have the right men for United States senators. He will allow them to vote to elect the legislature, the judges, and the governor, and will make them eligible to the office of judge or governor, or to the legislature. He will put them on an equality with the white man. What then? Of course, after making them eligible to the judiciary, when he gets Cuffee elevated to the bench, he certainly will not refuse his judge the privilege of marrying any woman he may select!

I submit to you whether these are not the legitimate consequences of his doctrine? If it be true, as he says, that by the Declaration of Independence and by divine law, the negro is created the equal of the white man; if it be true that the Dred Scott decision is unjust and wrong, because it deprives the negro of citizenship and equality with the white man, — then does it not follow that if he had the power he would make negroes citizens, and give them all the rights and all the privileges of citizenship on an equality with white men? I think that is the inevitable conclusion. I do not doubt Mr. Lincoln's conscientious conviction on the subject, and I do not doubt that he will carry out that doctrine if he ever has the power: but I resist it because I am utterly opposed to any political amalgamation or any other amalgamation on this continent. We are witnessing the result of giving civil and political rights to inferior races in Mexico, in Central America, in South America, and in the West India Islands. Those young men who went from here to Mexico to fight the battles of their country in the Mexican war can tell you the fruits of negro equality with the white man. They will tell you that the result of that equality is social amalgamation, demoralization, and degradation below the capacity for self-government.

My friends, if we wish to preserve this Government we must maintain it on the basis on which it was established; to-wit, the white basis. We must preserve the purity of the race not only in our politics, but in our domestic relations. We must then preserve the sovereignty of the States, and we must maintain the Federal Union by preserving the Federal Constitution inviolate. Let us do that, and our Union will not only be perpetual, but may extend until it shall spread over the entire continent.

Fellow-citizens, I have already detained you too long. I have exhausted myself and wearied you, and owe you an apology for the desultory manner in which I have discussed these topics. I will have an opportunity of addressing you again before the November election comes off. I come to you to appeal to your judgment as American citizens, to take your verdict of approval or disapproval upon the discharge of my public duty and my principles as compared with those of Mr. Lincoln. If you conscientiously believe that his principles are more in harmony with the feelings of the American people and the interests and honor of the Republic, elect him. If, on the contrary, you believe that my principles are more consistent with those great principles upon which our fathers framed this Government, then I shall ask you to so express your opinion at the polls. I am aware that it is a bitter and severe contest, but I do not doubt what the decision of the people of Illinois will be. I do not anticipate any personal collision between Mr. Lincoln and myself. You all know that I am an amiable, good-natured man, and I take great pleasure in bearing testimony to the fact that Mr. Lincoln is a kind-hearted, amiable, good-natured gentleman, with whom no man has a right to pick a quarrel, even if he wanted one. He is a worthy gentleman. I have known him for twenty-five years, and there is no better citizen and no kinder-hearted man. He is a fine lawyer, possesses high ability, and there is no objection to him, except the monstrous revolutionary doctrines with which he is identified and which he conscientiously entertains, and is determined to carry out if he gets the power.

He has one element of strength upon which he relies to accomplish his object, and that is his alliance with certain men in this State claiming to be Democrats, whose avowed object is to use their power to prostrate the Democratic nominees. He hopes he can secure the few men claiming to be friends of the Lecompton constitution, and for that reason you will find he does not say a word against the Lecompton constitution or its supporters. He is as silent as the grave upon that subject. Behold Mr. Lincoln courting Lecompton votes, in order that he may go to the Senate as the representative of Republican principles! You know that that alliance exists. I think you will find that it will ooze out before the contest is over. It must be a contest of principle. Either the radical Abolition principles of Mr. Lincoln must be maintained, or the strong, constitutional, national Democratic principles with which I am identified must be carried out. I shall be satisfied whatever way you decide. I have been sustained by the people of Illinois with a steadiness, a firmness, and an enthusiasm which makes my heart overflow with gratitude. If I was now to be consigned to private life I would have nothing to complain of. I would even then owe you a debt of gratitude which the balance of my life could not repay.

But, my friends, you have discharged every obligation you owe to me. I have been a thousand times paid by the welcome you have extended to me since I have entered the State on my return home this time. Your reception not only discharges all obligations, but it furnishes inducement to renewed efforts to serve you in the future. If you think Mr. Lincoln will do more to advance the interests and elevate the character of Illinois than myself, it is your duty to elect him; if you think he would do more to preserve the peace of the country and perpetuate the Union than myself, then elect him. I leave the question in your hands, and again tender you my profound thanks for the cordial and heartfelt welcome tendered to me this evening.

QUESTIONS

1. *According to Douglas, what is at stake in the issue which divides him from Lincoln? What does a vote for Lincoln really mean, and what a vote for Douglas? I hope you can see Douglas's expression as a remarkable achievement.*
   a. *The ultimate question is the "principle of self-government," the right of a people to choose the constitution and laws under which they must live, which Douglas affirms and Lincoln denies. How would you respond on behalf of Lincoln?*
   b. *At stake is equality among the states and adherence to our Constitution which gives them equal powers over their own affairs. Lincoln cannot achieve his goal – the extirpation of slavery – without a national despotism utterly destructive of our principles of federalism and*

all sound notions of political democracy. He will achieve a uniformity of law and custom that will be undesirable on the merits and achieved despotically. How would you respond on behalf of Lincoln?

c. Worse, since the slave states cannot be expected to alter at his will, since his despotism will be resisted, his apparently harmless ideal "invites a war of the North against the South." How would you answer on behalf of Lincoln?

d. The choice is between Lincoln, who will destroy the Union in a war, or maintain it by despotism; and Douglas, who proposes keeping the Union by "maintaining inviolate the Constitution of the United States as our fathers have made it." How would you respond on behalf of Lincoln?

e. Lincoln's proposed "resistance" to the decision of the Supreme Court is either a deliberate invitation to lawlessness or a promise of corruption. How would you respond on behalf of Lincoln?

f. Behind the idealistic words of the "sincere" and "conscientious" Lincoln is a revolutionary who promises to involve the entire nation in war and bring the government into total ruin. How would you respond on behalf of Lincoln?

g. Lincoln's view that the clause "all men are created equal" was meant to refer to members of "inferior races" is historically absurd – since all states were at that time slave states – and is a radical statement of general equality between white and black. "He finds the Negro is his brother. I do not think that the Negro is any kin of mine at all." Lincoln's view leads to black votes, black governors, interracial marriages, to a social union of the races. How would you respond on behalf of Lincoln?

h. What else does Douglas say that the issue that divides them involves? What else does he put at stake here? How would you answer him on those points? It would be remarkably instructive for you to draft a complete, argumentative answer. Then look at Lincoln's speech in response, given the same day. It is important, in drafting a response, to write as if you were a person seeking to become senator from Illinois in 1858. There is no difficulty in scribbling down self-righteously the language of equality which, thanks in no small measure to Lincoln's responses to Douglas, is widely accepted today – so widely accepted, in fact, that it is a cliché, a dead language. What was the world like when that language was being made?

It will require the greatest exercise of imagination to put yourself in such a world. I think you will probably agree that one who said at that time what you now believe and feel on the subject of slavery and racial equality could not have hoped to be elected senator from Illinois or president of the United States. What would a decent person say who did hope to be so elected? Your feelings may be that such a compromise of principle for expediency is unthinkable; no concession could be made for a moment to the institution of slavery, and nothing said on the subject except that it should be abolished instantly at absolutely any cost.

It is easy to assume the position of moral superiority that such feelings imply, because the battle against the law of slavery (if not against its consequences) has been won. But let me ask this: do you favor immediate, unilateral destruction of the government of the Union of South Africa by American arms? Why not? Is your position that although you consider her policy heinous, she is a distinct state with power over her own affairs, with which America has not the right to interfere? Or that the cure would be at least as bad as the disease? Or that there are better ways to correct the situation? Who would have talked this way at the time of Lincoln? Whatever your private views, what would you say if you were now running for the United States Senate: would you demand the end of South African apartheid instantly and at any price? Would you have any chance at election?

And how about war? You probably think war is a dreadful institution, yet cannot help thinking it a permanent part of our life. If you were now running for the U.S. Senate, would you advocate a policy of unilateral renunciation of all arms by this country? Would you stand any chance at election if you did so? Yet how would a speech in support of any other view read to those living in that happy future time when war has been abolished? To face this question seriously is to leave it, in Emily Dickinson's phrase, with "modesties enlarged."

2. Douglas defines himself and Lincoln in this speech; how does he do so? What are the two characters he creates? In your proposed response on Lincoln's behalf, what characters do you create for these two roles? You can see that persuasion by the creation of character, or ethos, includes the imaginative definition of one's adversary, and perhaps one's audience, as well as oneself.
3. How do you see Douglas using the powers of pathos and logos in this speech? How would you seek to employ them in your response?
4. I hope that you read Douglas's speech with great excitement, as a challenge, constantly asking yourself: how can I answer that? How can I put that straight? There, he is exposed: how can I make it clear? This sort of competitive reading, this thirst for argument, is an essential element in the lawyer's intellectual and emotional life. You should feel a little like a football player at last given the chance to show what he can do; you must be eager to meet the demands of another mind. Doctor Johnson, when ill, said of Burke: "That fellow calls forth all my powers. Were I to see Burke now it would kill me." Boswell, The Life of Samuel Johnson, II, 205 (Glover ed. 1901).
5. In the Lincoln-Douglas arguments, one side answers another, and is answered itself. The listener or reader asks, at the end of one statement, "How on earth can the other man respond?" yet when the answer comes, he feels that it is complete and carries the day — only to have his mind changed again. Only the most painful thought can enable the reader to resist such pressures and define his own position. The literary question is, "What can he say now?" and the literary experience is surprise and wonder at what he does say. I mean by this to lead you to recognize your feelings at the end of Douglas's speech: do you not ask yourself "What can Lincoln possibly say now?" and at the same time expect that his response will satisfy you?

This literary emotion is not unique to argument, it is central to the act of reading. You believe the death penalty is wrong, and you know, to some extent, why you think so; but what could you say, beyond your conclusion, if asked to rise and speak? Read Darrow's speech in the Loeb-Leopold case and wonder. Much of the experience of reading or watching drama is of this kind: what on earth will Admetus say to his wife, whom he has asked to die for him? What will Troilus say when Cressida is made to leave? We ask the same question in more splendid works: what will Lear say to his rejection by his daughters? What will Odysseus say to Achilles in order to persuade him to return? What will Antigone say when charged with breaking the decree? The failure to speak may be significant too: what could Alcestis say to Admetus when she returns? What possibly?

"What can he say now?" is a radical literary question, a constant pressure in all literature, all expression. The assured speaker, having raised and disposed of every possible question in the clearest and most forceful terms, sits down; his adversary rises. What on earth will he say?

6. Here is another famous moment in the history of argument: suppose you are an inhabitant of the island of Melos during the war between Athens and Sparta. Although Melos is a colony of Sparta, it has remained neutral during the war because it is wholly at the mercy of the sea power of Athens. The Athenians wish to make Melos part of their empire, to exact tribute and allegiance. Arriving with an overwhelming force, they ask for a meeting with the Melian leaders, at which they demand that Melos give up without a fight. They make no pretense of having right on their side but say: "[W]e Athenians will use no fine words; we will not go out of our way to prove at length that we have a right to rule, because we overthrew the Persians; or that we attack you now because we are suffering any injury at your hands. We should not convince you if we did; nor must you expect to convince us by arguing that, although a colony of the Lacedaemonians, you have taken no part in their expeditions, or that you have never done us any wrong. But you and we should say what we really think, and aim only at what is possible, for we both alike know that into the discussion of human affairs the question of justice only enters where the pressure of necessity is equal, and that the powerful exact what they can, and the weak grant what they must." Thucydides, History, V, 89.

   How do you respond? Has argument any function here, or is there simply nothing to be said?

7. Sometimes, however rarely, we see a person who is faced with what seems an impossible situation (e.g. an irrefutable statement) not only find something to say but do so in a way that instantly changes the conditions of discourse irreversibly, a way that puts an end to the argument. Below is a passage of such a dramatic triumph. Can you draw a connection between the sort of wit and force you see at work here and what the lawyer is asked to do? I hope you can admire this as the work of a fellow professional.

NIGGER: AN AUTOBIOGRAPHY*

Dick Gregory

In and out of Roberts in 1960, I had plenty of time to think. I realized that when I started working the white clubs, one of my big problems was going to be hecklers — especially in the beginning when I'd be in honky-tonk white clubs. Handling a heckler just right is very

* Pages 133–135 (1964).

important to a comic. Unless you're well known as an insulting comedian you can't chop hecklers down too hard or the crowd will turn against you. Most hecklers are half drunk anyway, and you will lose a crowd if you get mean with a drunk. On the other hand, you have to put a heckler down. If a heckler gets the best of you, that crowd will start to feel sorry for you. I had worked it out pretty well in the Negro clubs. I'd put a drunken heckler down gently: "Man, I'd rather be your slave than your liver," and that would go even better in a white club. Whenever I got a vicious heckler, I could say something like: "Now how would you like it if I came to *your* job and kicked the shovel out of *your* hand?" That would work fine, too. But some day, somewhere, I'd be in a white club and somebody would get up and call me a nigger.

I worried about that. When that white man calls me nigger, every other white man in that club is going to feel embarrassed. The customers are going to tie in that uncomfortable feeling with that club—even after I'm gone—and the club owner knows this. He would rather keep me out of his club than take a chance on losing customers. It was the same thing when I got kicked in the mouth as a shoeshine boy—the bartender ran me out of the place, even though he felt sorry for me, because he couldn't afford to have the customers fight. But now I'm a man and I have to take care of myself. I need a fast comeback to that word. That split second is all the difference between going on with the show or letting the customers feel pity and a little resentment for the entertainer who got put down.

I used to make Lillian call me a nigger over the dinner table, and I'd practice the fast comeback. Somehow, I couldn't get it right. I'd always come back with something a little bitter, a little evil.

"Nigger."

"Maybe you'd feel more like a man if you lived down South and had a toilet with your name on it."

"No, Greg, that's not right at all."

I was lying around the house one night, watching television and feeling mad at the world. I'd been out of work for three weeks. The snow was so deep I hadn't even been outside the house for four days, Lil was sitting in a corner, so calm and peaceful, reading a book. There was no one else to pick on.

"Hey, Lil."

"Yes, Greg."

"What would you do if from here on in I started referring to you as bitch?"

She jumped out of the chair. "I would simply ignore you."

I fell off the couch and started laughing so hard that old stomach of mine nearly burst. That was it. The quick, sophisticated answer. Cool.

No bitterness. The audience would never know I was mad and mean inside. And there would be no time to feel sorry for me. Now I'd get that comeback.

I got my chance a few weeks later, in a run-down neighborhood club on the outskirts of town. The customers were working-class white men, laborers, factory hands, men whose only marks of dignity were the Negroes they bossed on the job and kept away from on weekends. It happened in the middle of the late show on the second night. Loud and clear.

"Nigger."

The audience froze, and I wheeled around without batting an eye. "You hear what that guy just called me? Roy Rogers' horse: He called me Trigger."

I had hit them so quick that they laughed, and they laughed hard because that was what they really wanted to believe the guy had called me. But I had only bought myself a little time. There was an element in the house that really knew what he had called me. I had the crowd locked up with that fast comeback, so I took a few seconds to look them over and blow out some smoke.

"You know, my contract reads that every time I hear that word, I get fifty dollars more a night. I'm only making ten dollars a night, and I'd like to put the owner out of business. Will everybody in the room please stand up and yell nigger?"

They laughed and they clapped and I swung right back into my show. Afterwards, the owner came over and gave me twenty dollars and shook my hand and thanked me. I had made my test.

3. *The Mystery of Persuasion*

Here we shift attention for a moment from the arguer to his audience, from the persuader to the persuaded. One can analyze arguments indefinitely, showing why this one is good and that one bad, expressing professional admiration or disdain; but one comes at last to a mystery, the mystery of one mind working upon another. Good arguments sometimes fail, bad ones succeed, and lawyers shake their heads. What can be said about the critical moment at which persuasion succeeds or fails, the moment when the auditor shrugs his shoulders and says he has heard enough? What can the words of someone else have to do with the process by which he comes to his conclusion, one way or the other?

Perhaps it would help to think first of your own life, your own experience of making up your mind and changing it. No doubt you have voted for candidates, chosen a doctor, held views about school integration and Black Power and Women's Liberation and the Viet Nam war, and so on — and have often changed your mind on these matters. Time and again your understanding of a legal case or principle (a constitutional doctrine, say) has changed. Think of an actual occasion on which you made up your mind — or better, one on which you changed it: what did you do, and why? Was the process one simply of perceiving reasons or facts you had hitherto not noticed? (Does one "persuade" then simply by pointing to what has not previously been seen by one's audience? If this view seems attractive, be prepared to explain — with reference to the account you have given — why you first missed what was there all along.) In particular, ask yourself what someone else's words may have had to do with the process: are you willing to admit that you yourself have ever been persuaded by someone else?

There follows now a dramatic representation of persuasion: Macbeth, having resolved not to kill Duncan, is persuaded by Lady Macbeth to do it. How would you write such a scene of persuasion? As you read this, ask whether the process of persuasion is fully expressed here or remains a mystery.

MACBETH*

William Shakespeare

Macbeth: If it were done, when 'tis done, then 'twere well
It were done quickly: if th' assassination
Could trammel up the consequence, and catch
With his surcease success; that but this blow
Might be the be-all and the end-all — here,
But here, upon this bank and shoal of time,
We'd jump the life to come. — But in these cases,
We still have judgment here; that we but teach
Bloody instructions, which, being taught, return
To plague th' inventor: this even-handed Justice
Commends th' ingredience of our poison'd chalice
To our own lips. He's here in double trust:
First, as I am his kinsman and his subject,
Strong both against the deed; then, as his host,
Who should against his murtherer shut the door,
Not bear the knife myself. Besides, this Duncan
Hath borne his faculties so meek, hath been
So clear in his great office, that his virtues
Will plead like angels, trumpet-tongu'd, against
The deep damnation of his taking-off;

* Act 1, scene 7.

And Pity, like a naked new-born babe,
Striding the blast, or heaven's Cherubins, hors'd
Upon the sightless couriers of the air,
Shall blow the horrid deed in every eye,
That tears shall drown the wind. — I have no spur
To prick the sides of my intent, but only
Vaulting ambition, which o'erleaps itself
And falls on th' other —

Enter Lady Macbeth.

How now! what news?
Lady M.: He has almost supp'd. Why have you left the chamber?
Macbeth: Hath he ask'd for me?
Lady M.: Know you not, he has?
Macbeth: We will proceed no further in this business:
He hath honor'd me of late; and I have bought
Golden opinions from all sorts of people,
Which would be worn now in their newest gloss,
Not cast aside so soon.
Lady M.: Was the hope drunk,
Wherein you dress'd yourself? Hath it slept since?
And wakes it now, to look so green and pale
At what it did so freely? From this time
Such I account thy love. Art thou afeard
To be the same in thine own act and valour,
As thou art in desire? Would'st thou have that
Which thou esteem'st the ornament of life,
And live a coward in thine own esteem,
Letting "I dare not" wait upon "I would,"
Like the poor cat i' th' adage?
Macbeth: Pr'ythee, peace.
I dare do all that may become a man;
Who dares do more, is none.
Lady M.: What beast was't then,
That made you break this enterprise to me?
When you durst do it, then you were a man;
And, to be more than what you were, you would
Be so much more the man. Nor time, nor place,
Did then adhere, and yet you would make both:
They have made themselves, and that their fitness now
Does unmake you. I have given suck, and know

How tender 'tis to love the babe that milks me:
I would, while it was smiling in my face,
Have pluck'd my nipple from his boneless gums,
And dash'd the brains out, had I so sworn
As you have done to this.

Macbeth: If we should fail?

Lady M.: We fail?
But screw your courage to the sticking-place,
And we'll not fail. When Duncan is asleep
(Whereto the rather shall his day's hard journey
Soundly invite him), his two chamberlains
Will I with wine and wassail so convince,
That memory, the warder of the brain,
Shall be a fume, and the receipt of reason
A limbeck only: when in swinish sleep
Their drenched natures lie, as in a death,
What cannot you and I perform upon
Th' unguarded Duncan? what not put upon
His spongy officers, who shall bear the guilt
Of our great quell?

Macbeth: Bring forth men-children only!
For thy undaunted mettle should compose
Nothing but males. Will it not be receiv'd,
When we have mark'd with blood those sleepy two
Of his own chamber, and us'd their very daggers,
That they have done't?

Lady M.: Who dares receive it other,
As we shall make our griefs and clamour roar
Upon his death?

Macbeth: I am settled, and bend up
Each corporal agent to this terrible feat.
Away, and mock the time with fairest show:
False face must hide what the false heart doth know.

[*Exeunt.*]

QUESTIONS

1. Did Lady Macbeth persuade Macbeth to go on with the plan to kill Duncan? How do you know? If you say she did, how did she do so?

2. Is the process of persuasion fully expressed here, or is something left out? Why would Shakespeare do that?

3. Or is the term "persuade" a necessarily fictional term, never a factual description, always a hope or goal?

4. *Ask the same question of Ulysses' persuasion of Achilles and Agamemnon in Shakespeare's Troilus and Cressida (discussed at page 51 supra).*
5. *See Shakespeare's Richard III, act 1, scene 3, for another instance of persuasion. Richard makes love to Anne, wife and daughter-in-law of two men he has killed, over the bier of one of them. Can you imagine how such a scene as that could ever be written?*
6. *The mystery of persuasion is in part the mystery of force in writing. Here are two passages by Burke which display a certain force of writing. Can you explain the force you perceive?*
   a. *In his Observations on a Late Publication Entitled "The Present State of the Nation" (1769), Burke refutes a pamphlet which painted the most "aggravated, hideous, and deformed picture of the state of this country." At one point he asks why the author has chosen to take this view, suggesting that it is simply a matter of party faction. He goes on:*

      "The author is so conscious of the dangerous effects of that representation [of the state of the nation], that he thinks it necessary, and very necessary it is, to guard against them. He assures us, 'that he has not made that display of the difficulties of his country, to expose her counsels to the ridicule of other states, or to provoke a vanquished enemy to insult her; nor to excite the people's rage against their governors, or sink them in a despondency of the public welfare.' I readily admit this apology for his intentions. God forbid I should think any man capable of entertaining so execrable and senseless a design. The true cause of his drawing so shocking a picture is no more than this; and it ought rather to claim our pity than excite our indignation; he finds himself out of power; and this condition is intolerable to him. The same sun which gilds all nature, and exhilarates the whole creation, does not shine upon disappointed ambition. It is something that rays out of darkness, and inspires nothing but gloom and melancholy. Men in this deplorable state of mind find a comfort in spreading the contagion of their spleen."
   b. *In his Letter to a Noble Lord on the Attacks Upon His Pension (1796), Burke defends his own rather small pension against attacks led by the Duke of Bedford. At one point, Burke compares his own pension with the grants made to the family of his attacker.*

      "The grants to the House of Russell were so enormous as not only to outrage economy, but even to stagger credibility. The Duke of Bedford is the leviathan among all the creatures of the crown. He tumbles about his unwieldy bulk, he plays and frolics in the ocean of the royal bounty. Huge as he is, and whilst 'he lies floating many a rood,' he is still a creature. His ribs, his fins, his whalebone, his blubber, the very spiracle through which he spouts a torrent of brine against his origin, and covers me all over with the spray, everything of him and about him is from the throne. Is it for him to question the disposition of the royal favor?"
7. *What is the force of Burke's writing?*
   a. *Is it merely that the speaker demonstrates considerable skill at insult and vituperation, that he makes himself formidable? The speaker here might, for example, be regarded as a descendant of the Icelandic and Irish bards, whose sarcastic wit was feared almost as if it were magic. Here is an example: Tomas O'Crohan, who lived in the Irish-speaking*

Blasket Islands at the turn of the century, tells of being interrupted in his day's work of cutting turf by the local poet, who stopped and wanted to talk. "I didn't care much for what he had to say, but I was rather shy of refusing to sit down with him. Besides, I knew that if the poet had anything against me, he would make a satire on me that would be very unpleasant, especially as I was just about coming out in the world. So I sat down beside him." The Islandman 108–109 (1934).

b. *Or is this a fine example of what speech teachers tell you never to do, of being carried away in extravagant and irrational assertion?*

c. *How would you expect someone to meet this sort of argument?*

8. *One final passage: the argument in the Burch divorce case, quoted in Donovan, Modern Jury Trials 539–540 (1885):*

Gentlemen of the Jury: The counsel for the defense in this case have assured you in very emphatic terms that they stand here in defense of the innocent. Now, assurances — mere affirmation by counsel — can weigh but little. One thing you will readily believe: Either my client is the most heartless and desperate villain, or the most wronged and oppressed man that ever appeared in a court of justice. He either deserves your warmest sympathies or your deepest execrations. If, as he alleges, his home has been entered by the seducer, and his sacred rights as a husband, his holiest feelings as a parent, invaded and trampled upon, his prospects of domestic happiness blighted and ruined, then he has suffered one of the deepest wrongs that man is capable of suffering or inflicting. And if he cannot ask your sympathy, he may at least demand at your hands that poor justice which the law affords him.

What is this? Gentleman, you are husbands, you are fathers, you know in all their characteristics, you understand and have experienced, and now feel, the full force of all the relations involved in this case; you have each of you a home; by your own firesides a pattern that shall never fail to teach you what a dutiful, affectionate, and virtuous wife is. And you can, by a moment's reflection, by consulting your own hearts, at once understand and feel the justice or injustice of this law, which for the violation of chastity should deprive your wives of the rights and privileges, the happy privileges, the invaluable advantages, which they now enjoy. I cannot explain to you why it is that you could not live for one hour with a woman who had violated her marriage vow. If you do not understand it, I cannot make it clearer.

4. *The Cost of Argument: The Mind of the Sophist*

The power of argument, of analytic and persuasive speech, has been distrusted as much as it has been admired. As you know, the charge was put against the fifth-century sophists — Socrates among them — that they corrupted the youth by teaching them powers of reasoning and argument that could be put to any use, right or wrong, that they taught them to make "the weaker argument the stronger." Plato was obviously troubled by the uses to which the sharpened mind could be put, and in the dialogs he often shows Socrates in opposition to a sophist, his object being to demonstrate that false reasoning and argument cannot stand up against the truth, that the weaker argument cannot be made the stronger. In *The Clouds* Aristophanes wrote a burlesque of the sophists (using Socrates as his example), in which he exposed the teaching of argument as corrupt and ridiculous. The scenario involves a gambler hopelessly in debt who goes to Socrates' Thinking Shop to learn the arguments by which he can avoid his debts, and you can imagine the possibilities for ridicule — although you may also have to recognize some similarities to your own future law practice. In the literature of another era, you have watched Shakespeare's Ulysses at work, making successful but wholly inconsistent and unscrupulous appeals to Agamemnon and Achilles, and have been asked what I hope has been a troubling question: whether you there see your own future self, the manipulator of language and people, reckless of truth and every other decent value.

Sophocles' play *Philoctetes* explores the moral quality of persuasion in a way that might unsettle a modern lawyer. Philoctetes lives alone on an island in the Aegean where, because of a foul-smelling and festering wound in his foot, he was cast off by the Achaeans on their way to Troy. He can survive because he has the bow of Heracles which never misses, and can shoot birds with it. Years later Odysseus and Neoptolemus, the son of dead Achilles, are sent by the Achaeans to obtain the bow, which a soothsayer has told them is necessary to their ultimate victory at Troy. Their end is set for them: they must decide upon the means. When they arrive on the island, Odysseus explains to Neoptolemus that force cannot be used — Philoctetes could easily kill them and would cheerfully do so — and that reasoned arguments will not be listened to. Deceit must then be used: Neoptolemus, pretending to have broken with the Achaeans and to be on his way home, is to offer Philoctetes passage, and to obtain the bow in that way. Neoptolemus at first resists the plan as wrong ("I will fight but not lie") but is easily talked into it by Odysseus, who meets his objections with specious argument ("I have found that words are often the best weapons") and with a reminder that according to the soothsayer he, Neoptolemus, is the one who will destroy Troy once the bow has been obtained. The persuasion and corruption of Neoptolemus is quick and easy — child's play for Odysseus, one might say.

Neoptolemus carries out the deception and obtains the bow. The process of the play is the revelation and articulation of what that course of conduct really means. Philoctetes' sense of outrage at the way the Achaeans had treated him, his generous love for his homeland, his admiration for the heroic Achilles and Nestor, and his gratitude to Neoptolemus all define him as the center of value in the play and make his deception increasingly intolerable. At last, in a remarkably modern decision of renunciation, Neoptolemus returns the bow, giving up Troy and victory, and offers to take Philoctetes home. The movement for Neoptolemus is one of growth by understanding, from a relationship of persuasion — where he is either the lawyer, reckless of honesty, or the dupe — to one of friendship. The life of the play is the exposure of dishonesty, the definition of a conflict not merely between principle and expediency, but between two ways of living, two conditions of humanity, between the heroic and the contemptible.

You need not ask where most people would place the lawyer in such a play, although the lawyer's dishonesty — his pretense that he believes what he says, that he is concerned that the court reach the right result — is perhaps slightly more subtle than that practiced here. We have all had to ask ourselves again and again whether our professional willingness to argue any side of any question, our neutrality on matters of the greatest moment, can possibly be justified. And the common gesture — a declaration of faith in the adversary process as the least of evils — really pleases no one. Can the lawyer be regarded as anything but a hired voice, a man who will say anything for his client, an Odysseus who gets the job done without regard to any values of honesty or decency?[8]

Another kind of cost of legal argument, perhaps less obvious but not less serious than the foregoing, is rooted in its intellectual structure, in its very form. While every genuine inquiry, every careful statement (in the judicial opinion, for example) seems to be an exploration of doubt, a register of uncertainty, the legal argument is a monument of self-assurance. The legal argument does not show how complicated and difficult things are, as the honest and questioning mind does, but the opposite: to the arguing lawyer, everything is simple and obvious; the art of argument seems to be to carry the audience or reader over the difficulties without seeing them. While a good poem or history book or law class or judicial opinion invites speculation and contemplation at every turn, the argument cuts all that off. The pressure is all the other way, sealing the mind into a particular pattern or progression of thought.

8. You may have noticed that Odysseus employs two kinds of persuasion, one rather close to legal argument, the other different from it. In persuading Neoptolemus, he argues much in the way that a lawyer or salesman might do. His deception of Philoctetes by plain lying about matters of fact is not directly parallel to what a good lawyer does, though you are no doubt familiar with problems of legal ethics — how vigorously may one cross-examine the fuzzy-minded but correct witness? how great is the lawyer's obligation to engage in independent inquiry to determine the veracity of his own witnesses? — in which the lawyer's role is not altogether different. And both forms of persuasion here work by a process of exploitation that constitutes the subject of the play. Is legal argument likewise a process of exploitation, or can you distinguish it from what you see here?

How can legal argument be defended then? It may be said, of course, that however much the brief may simplify, may cut off speculation, the writer himself must not do that but the opposite: he must imagine every conceivable argument, every way of organizing the case. Is that true of the good brief writer or arguer? Does this response satisfy you? One difficulty is that what the lawyer is always looking for is arguments, for schemes and systems, for what works in the legal world — and the object of the search determines what is done. Does the college debater's search for argument, for witticism, for the clever and persuasive, carry him closer to the truth? Or consider this suggestion, once made seriously by a teacher of English: a great way to run an English Literature class would be to use the form of legal argument, with different people asked to argue for and against the excellence of a poem or a play. Does that suggestion seem to you to be inspired? Imagine such a class and ask whether it would have any interest for you at all, as teacher or student. For the arguing mind, no question can be asked (or if asked, pursued) which cannot be answered in the terms and form of argumentative statement. How would you like to be asked by a lawyer why it is worth your while to read, for example, *Pride and Prejudice* or *Troilus and Cressida?* Or take this example: could you readily turn from writing a brief to writing a novel or short story? The mind of the lawyer is cast by the forms of legal argument, and the costs — which you have been examining throughout the course — are neither slight nor simple.

Below is an account of a mind too given to argument. As you read it, ask whether it might define a danger for you, perhaps of a kind different from any yet mentioned.

THE LIFE OF CLARENDON BY HIMSELF*

Edward Hyde, First Earl of Clarendon

Mr. Chillingworth was of a stature little superior to Mr. Hales, (and it was an age in which there were many great and wonderful men of that size,) and a man of so great a subtilty of understanding, and so rare a temper in debate, that, as it was impossible to provoke him into any passion, so it was very difficult to keep a man's self from being a little discomposed by his sharpness and quickness of argument, and instances, in which he had a rare facility, and a great advantage over all the men I ever knew. He had spent all his younger time in disputation, and had arrived to so great a mastery, as he was inferior to no man in those skirmishes: but he had, with his notable perfection, in this exercise, contracted such an irresolution and habit of doubting, that by degrees

* Clarendon's autobiography (1759). This passage is printed in *Selections from Clarendon* 42–44 (World's Classics ed. 1953).

he grew confident of nothing, and a sceptic, at least, in the greatest mysteries of faith.

This made him, from first wavering in religion, and indulging to scruples, to reconcile himself too soon and too easily to the church of Rome; and carrying still his own inquisitiveness about him, without any resignation to their authority, (which is the only temper can make that church sure of its proselytes,) having made a journey to St. Omer's, purely to perfect his conversion by the conversation of those who had the greatest name, he found as little satisfaction there; and returned with as much haste from them; with a belief, that an entire exemption from error was neither inherent in, nor necessary to any church: which occasioned that war, which was carried on by the Jesuits with so great asperity and reproaches against him, and in which he defended himself by such an admirable eloquence of language, and clear and incomparable power of reason, that he not only made them appear unequal adversaries, but carried the war into their own quarters; and made the pope's infallibility to be as much shaken, and declined by their own doctors, (and as great an acrimony amongst themselves upon that subject,) and to be at least as much doubted, as in the schools of the reformed, or protestant; and forced them since to defend and maintain those unhappy controversies in religion, with arms and weapons of another nature than were used or known in the church of Rome when Bellarmine died; and which probably will in time undermine the very foundation that supports it.

Such a levity, and propensity to change, is commonly attended with great infirmities in, and no less reproach and prejudice to the person; but the sincerity of his heart was so conspicuous, and without the least temptation of any corrupt end; and the innocence and candour of his nature so evident, and without any perverseness; that all who knew him clearly discerned, that all those restless motions and fluctuations proceeded only from the warmth and jealousy of his own thoughts, in a too nice inquisition for truth. Neither the books of the adversary, nor any of their persons, though he was acquainted with the best of both, had ever made great impression upon him; all his doubts grew out of himself, when he assisted his scruples with all the strength of his own reason, and was then too hard for himself; but finding as little quiet and repose in those victories, he quickly recovered, by a new appeal to his own judgment; so that he was, in truth, upon the matter, in all his sallies and retreats, his own convert; though he was not so totally divested of all thoughts of this world, but that when he was ready for it, he admitted some great and considerable churchmen, to be sharers with him in his public conversion.

Whilst he was in perplexity, or rather some passionate disinclination to the religion he had been educated in, he had the misfortune to have much acquaintance with one Mr. Lugar, a minister of that church; a man of a competency of learning in those points most controverted with the Romanists, but of no acute parts of wit, or judgment; and wrought so far upon him, by weakening and enervating those arguments, by which he found he was governed, (as he had all the logic, and all the rhetoric, that was necessary to persuade very powerfully men of the greatest talents,) that the poor man, not able to live long in doubt, too hastily deserted his own church, and betook himself to the Roman: nor could all the arguments and reasons of Mr. Chillingworth make him pause in the expedition he was using, or reduce him from that church after he had given himself to it; but he had always a great animosity against him, for having (as he said) unkindly betrayed him, and carried him into another religion, and there left him. So unfit are some constitutions to be troubled with doubts, after they are once fixed.

He did really believe all war to be unlawful; and did not think that the parliament (whose proceedings he perfectly abhorred) did in truth intend to involve the nation in a civil war, till after the battle of Edgehill; and then he thought any expedient or stratagem that was like to put a speedy end to it, to be the most commendable: and so having too mathematically conceived an engine, that should move so lightly as to be a breastwork in all encounters and assaults in the field, he carried it, to make the experiment, into that part of his majesty's army, which was only in that winter season in the field, under the command of lord Hopton, in Hampshire, upon the borders of Sussex; where he was shut up in the castle of Arundel; which was forced, after a short, sharp siege, to yield for want of victual; and poor Mr. Chillingworth with it, falling into the rebels' hands; and being most barbarously treated by them, especially by that clergy which followed them; and being broken with sickness, contracted by the ill accommodation, and want of meat, and fire during the siege, which was in a terrible season of frost and snow, he died shortly after in prison. He was a man of excellent parts, and of a cheerful disposition; void of all kind of vice, and endued with many notable virtues; of a very public heart, and an indefatigable desire to do good; his only unhappiness proceeded from his sleeping too little, and thinking too much; which sometimes threw him into violent fevers.

QUESTIONS

1. *Look back at the passage from Billy Budd, page 70 supra, in which Starry Vere explains the arguments that affect him. Can you say that what is exhibited there is the moral paralysis of the arguing mind? Has Melville's passage any parallel in the life of the law as you know it?*

2. Two excellent works on argument in Greece: G. Kennedy, The Art of Persuasion in Greece (1963); J. Finley, Thucydides, Chapter 2 (1942).

WRITING ASSIGNMENT 19: The Legal Argument

• Write a brief paper in which you do for the legal argument what you have already done for the judicial opinion.

The vagueness of this assignment is deliberate, meant as an invitation to pursue your own line of thought in your own way.

WRITING ASSIGNMENT 19, ALTERNATIVE A: The Quarrel and the Argument

Part One

• Draft an account of a dispute between two or more people, not lawyers, in which you show them arguing or quarreling. Write as a novelist with a real style of your own, or perhaps as a playwright.

Part Two

• Now give an account of a legal argument, or a portion of one, bearing on the same dispute.

Part Three

• What conclusions do you now come to about the form of speech and thought we call legal argument? In what ways do you see it as an intellectual and rhetorical resource, in what ways as a form that imprisons the mind?

WRITING ASSIGNMENT 19, ALTERNATIVE B: Argument as a Form That Destroys

Part One

• Give an account of a mind at work on a serious matter. You can show a professional (say, a mathematician, historian, or musician) at work on a matter within his field, or an ordinary citizen thinking about some aspect of his own life. It could be especially valuable to show one mind engaged with another, to show a conversation going on. Try to portray a person or activity you admire.

Part Two

• *Now recast that passage by showing the same mind engaged in argument on the same subject. The argument need not be legal in form, but it should be in some respects like legal argument.*

Part Three

• *What conclusions do you now come to about the form of speech and thought we call legal argument? In what ways do you see it as an intellectual or rhetorical resource, in what ways as a form that imprisons the mind?*

WRITING ASSIGNMENT 19, ALTERNATIVE C: Making Up and Changing Your Mind

Part One

• *Give an account of an event in which you made up your mind about some matter, or, better, one in which you changed your mind. If possible, choose an occasion on which some person's words or actions helped you make up or change your mind.*

Part Two

• *Now explain what happened. Were you persuaded, and if so, how? Do you describe persuasion simply as a pointing to something — a fact, or a reason — or as something else? If persuasion is merely a pointing, can you explain why you never before saw what was pointed to here?*
• *If there was no persuasion here, how do you define the event of which you have just given an account?*

WRITING ASSIGNMENT 19, ALTERNATIVE D: The Art of Argument

Part One

• *Find an argument that interests or impresses you. It can come from any literature, legal or nonlegal, or from your own experience of life. Reproduce the argument, or at least its most important portions.*

Part Two

• *Now criticize the argument, both explaining and evaluating what the arguers do. What is the art of argument you have just defined? What connection can you draw between that art and the art of legal argument?*

C. *THE NARRATIVE IMAGINATION AND THE CLAIM OF MEANING*

The yarns of seamen have a direct simplicity, the whole meaning of which lies within the shell of a cracked nut. But Marlow was not typical (if his propensity to spin yarns be excepted), and to him the meaning of an episode was not inside like a kernel, but outside, enveloping the tale which brought it out only as a glow brings out a haze, in the likeness of one of those misty halos that are sometimes made visible by the spectral illumination of moonshine.*

Presently the course of the Vivonne became choked with water-plants. At first they appeared singly, a lily for instance, which the current, across whose path it had unfortunately grown, would never leave at rest for a moment, so that, like a ferry-boat mechanically propelled, it would drift over to one bank only to return to the other, eternally repeating its double journey. Thrust towards the bank, its stalk would be straightened out, lengthened, strained almost to the breaking point until the current again caught it, its green moorings swung back over their anchorage and brought the unhappy plant to what might fitly be called its starting point, since it was fated not to rest there a moment before moving off once again. I would still find it there, on one walk after another, always in the same helpless state, suggesting certain victims of neurasthenia, among whom my grandfather would have included my aunt Leonie, who present without modification, year after year, the spectacle of their odd and unaccountable habits, which they always imagine themselves to be on the point of shaking off, but which they always retain to the end; caught in the treadmill of their own maladies and eccentricities, their futile endeavors to escape serve only to actuate its mechanism, to keep in motion the clockwork of their strange, ineluctable, fatal daily round. Such as these was the water-lily, and also like one of those wretches whose peculiar torments, repeated indefinitely throughout eternity, aroused the curiosity of Dante, who would have inquired of them at greater length, and in fuller detail from the victims themselves, had not Virgil, striding on ahead, obliged him to hasten after him at full speed, as I must hasten after my parents.†

* Joseph Conrad, *The Heart of Darkness,* Chapter 1 (1902).

† Marcel Proust, *Remembrance of Things Past,* Volume 1, pages 129–130 (1913–1928; Random House ed. 1934).

A fact truly and absolutely stated is taken out of the region of common sense and acquires a mythologic or universal significance.‡

Earlier in this book, a distinction was drawn between the mind that tells a story and the mind that gives reasons: one finds its meaning in representations of events as they occur in time, in imagined experience; the other, in systematic or theoretical explanations, in the exposition of conceptual order or structure. One is given to narrative, the other to analysis. Each works in its own way, and it is hard to imagine a conversation between them (what does the economist really have to say to the novelist, after all, or vice versa?); but however inconsistent these voices seem, the lawyer must recognize both of them within himself. That he must master theoretical and analytic speech is plain enough, for this is the stuff of most legal reasoning and argument, of law texts and classrooms. This is the language in which rules are proposed, holdings defined, distinctions drawn. It should be equally evident that he must know how to tell a story, and how to listen to one: he starts with the story the client tells him, and questions him about it; he then tells the story over and over again to himself and to others, shifting the emphasis as the case proceeds, constantly varying the terms of his narrative but coming at last to a version (or perhaps more than one) cast in terms of legal conclusion. The lawyer, one might say, begins with his client's story and ends in the court of appeals, arguing a point of statutory interpretation or constitutional law. And the judge must take two or more such arguments — two ways of connecting a particular story with a system or theory that will explain and act upon it — and with their aid fashion his own account, a version that concludes with a judgment or order in legal language, with words that work on the world. The endless possibilities for narrative, the retellings of the story in ever more various terms, come to an end at last with a characterization of experience in the terms of the law, a claim of meaning for which the judge must take responsibility. So it is that one story, one set of experiences, can be connected with others; so it is that the law is made. Might it not be suggested that the central act of the legal mind, of judge and lawyer alike, is this conversion of the raw material of life — of the actual experiences of people and the thousands of ways they can be talked about — into a story that will claim to tell the truth in legal terms? To do this, one must master both sorts of discourse (both narrative and analysis) and put them to work, at the same time and despite their inconsistencies, in the service of a larger enterprise. How is this to be done? How can these discordant modes of thought and expression, these incompatible, uncommunicating, sides of oneself, be brought under the

‡ H. D. Thoreau, *Journal*, Nov. 1, 1851.

control of a single active intelligence? How can they be reconciled, if only for a moment, in a single work of the imagination?

This is the central question of this section, and it will not have escaped you that it suggests several lines of connection through a good deal of what you have done in this course. In paper after paper, after all, you have been asked to give an account of an event — to tell a story — and then to relate the story, so told, to the world and language of the law. What is suggested now is that this tension between narrative and theory, between fact and law, is the central literary characteristic of the lawyer's life, defining by its demands a special opportunity for him as a mind and a writer. What I mean by this may perhaps be made clear by asking you to think back to the material in Chapter 1 on controlling a language system (pages 56–77), where it was suggested that the traditional techniques of control — metaphor, irony, and ambiguity — have in common the fact that they are ways of writing more than one way at once, of using a language and recognizing what it leaves out. It then appeared that these techniques are generally not available to the lawyer, that he must look elsewhere for his means of control, for the mechanism of his art. But may it not be that the tension between story and theory, between the lawyer's two basic kinds of language, his two modes of expression, affords a similar opportunity for the exercise of a similar art? Can you organize the thinking you have done in this course about the situation of the lawyer — his plight and his art — and address that question? I have only pointed to an incompatibility of language and claimed that it is fundamental; can you work out for yourself your own sense of that incompatibility, if it is one, and of its importance? Can you perhaps demonstrate the art that addresses this tension between narrative and theory, that achieves a momentary reconciliation of these inconsistent modes of thought and expression?

Such are the concerns of the material that follows. We will first attempt to expose some of the complexities and difficulties of narrative by elaborating the distinction between narrative and analysis, between story and theory. The particular form our question takes is this: how can the tensions between a story one tells and the meaning one claims for it, between the narrative and its message, be understood and defined? How do these tensions manifest themselves as one starts out on a story, as one tells and concludes it, and how are they to be managed? We then shift our ground slightly to investigate the particular form that this structural incompatibility of discourse takes in narratives about events in the real world. We compare law with history, and put the question this way: in literatures of reality such as these, how, by what art, can one reconcile the demands of reality — the pressure for the plain statement of narrative fact — with those of the imagination, with the need to find or create meaning in experience? One or two instances of success at this enterprise will be described or exemplified, as a way of asking you whether you can do what the historian does. In fact, in one of the alternative writing assignments you will be encouraged to find and examine a passage of history with respect to which that question can be asked.

Your general assignment, however, will be to demonstrate excellence in the way a mind addresses the tension between narrative and analysis — or between reality and imagination — especially in a story about the real world for which a particular meaning is claimed and stated. You will be free to address this topic as you wish, but one suggestion is that you consider rewriting one of your earlier assignments (in many of which you were asked for a narrative) for this one; to do this may show, perhaps better than anything else, the place of the present assignment in the course as a whole.

1. *Telling a Story and Saying What It Means: Addressing an Incompatibility of Discourse*

> None of [these stories] are stories of experience in the absolute sense of the word. Experience in them is but the canvas of the attempted picture. Each of them has its more than one intention.*

The distinction between narrative and theory, which it is the purpose of the following material to expose and complicate, is not an absolute one: there are narratives (as you well know from reading law cases and exams) that are nothing more than translations of analytic problems into the form of a story, narratives in which almost none of the possibilities of the form are realized. There are also passages of analytic reasoning that have some of the suggestiveness, some of the sense of qualification, that marks a narrative at its best; I think here especially of Darwin's *Origin of Species*, though that can hardly be said to be without narrative. But that there are two distinct directions and styles of thought here, two kinds of expression, will not be a surprising suggestion to you, who have worked through the relationship between a poem and its meaning and have told complicated narratives of your own. Although you must work out for yourself your own sense of the relationship between these two modes of thought and expression — maybe even to conclude at the end that there are no fundamental differences, no essential incompatibilities — I hope that you will find the following suggestions of some interest and assistance.

* Joseph Conrad, *Preface* to *Typhoon and Other Stories* (1919).

a. Narrative and Analysis: The Differences Elaborated

One might be tempted to say that telling stories is the mark of the primitive mind. It is a way of explaining experience, perhaps, but one that we have left far behind: it is magical, not rational; it is of the world of myth, not science. When spring comes, with warmth and flowers, the event is explained as the return of Persephone from her annual imprisonment in the underworld, not as a change in the earth's posture towards the sun. When a warrior is especially brave and successful, when he has a marvelous day, it is not his diet or the adrenalin in his system that is spoken of, but the presence and blessing of a god. This sort of mind apparently does not demand what we would call scientific explanations of things; instead, it tells a story. The narrative cast of the primitive mind is no doubt related to that concern with the externals of events, with sensory detail, which has so interested Lévi-Strauss in his study of the possibilities and limits of primitive thought, and which, he says, survives in the way even modern man appreciates works of art and music.

Let me give a modern example of one sort of narrative mind. Fridjonson's "The Vanished Heroine"[9] tells of a young woman compelled by emergency to cross an Icelandic mountain range on skis during a winter storm. How is the sense of peril expressed? At each stage of the journey she remembers a fatal or near-fatal accident that had occurred exactly there. "It was here that poor Sigga froze to death in a sleet storm . . ." She did not think of the likelihood of avalanche or how to guard against loss of body heat, but of stories of what had happened there. "A story told by one of her lodgers runs through her mind. He was riding past Enbui one night . . ." The narrative mind can be regarded as a child's mind, which mankind has outgrown, just as each of us has outgrown the fairy tale.

Another way to explore the differences between narrative and conceptual thought, between the primitive and the analytic mind, might be to look at fifth-century Athens, whose intellectual history could be said to involve a movement from one to the other.[10] Take the subject of justice, for example. The century begins with Aeschylus' play *The Oresteia,* which tells the story of retaliatory justice in the house of Atreus — the chain of vengeance continues through the generations

9. In *Icelandic Poems and Stories* (Beck ed. 1943).

10. Chapter 2 of John H. Finley, Jr., *Thucydides* (1942), is the best treatment of this period of intellectual history that I know. Another classic is F. M. Cornford, *From Religion to Philosophy* (1912).

without end — and celebrates the foundation of a public institution for trial and punishment, a way in which the community can bring the narrative of perpetual destruction to a close. The judgment of the court and jury will satisfy the same deep need to set things right that underlay the old obligation of revenge, but without giving rise to a new wrong that must be itself avenged. Aeschylus puts all this in the form of a drama, and we participate in the story imaginatively, through our capacity to understand what experience is like for others. Shortly after the end of the century, Plato writes *The Republic,* an altogether different inquiry into the nature of justice: while written in the form of a dialog, most of it is actually expository, and in it Plato analyzes different forms of political organization and the sorts of life each encourages, making an expository and theoretical statement of a modern kind. We end in the world of theory and analysis.

But you know that the language of analysis has not replaced the narrative, that Aeschylus and Homer are still to be read, and that one who believes that everything can be said in a language of theory and system is an impossible fool. We still read stories and tell them, finding a meaning there that we find nowhere else. The novel is read by millions, "Barbara Allen" is a popular song, Shakespeare is still admired, and so on. The story is still alive; nothing can compete with its hold on the attention. Can you explain why this is so? What is there about narrative that gives it such fascination, that makes it such a resource for speech and thought? You might start by asking exactly why mankind has not simply given up stories in favor of purely rational discourse. Is it simply a matter of inadequate education? What is it that narrative offers us, what possibilities of meaning, what resources for speech and thought? As you work out a response in general terms, shift your focus to the law and ask what the narrative offers the lawyer, what it offers the law.

b. The Force of Narrative: A Pressure Towards the Inexpressible

Of many possible lines of response, I want to deal with just one, suggested in the subhead immediately above: that the process of telling a story generates a pressure towards the inexpressible, the inexplicable; that whatever one's original intentions, the story creates a life and meaning of its own as it goes along. As Frost suggested of the poem, one simply cannot work out every detail of a story ahead of time, and it is a bad mistake to try to do so; "no surprise for the writer, no surprise for the reader." Consider, for instance, the process of drafting a question for a law school examination, which could be considered the extreme case of a fabricated story, a made-up story that can be completely explained, no story at all. My own experience has been that even if one tries, it is by no means easy to keep the story merely an example, an examination problem; somehow the narrative has a tendency to complicate matters, to set its own direction, to take over and pose difficulties of its own. The problem with which one began is, at the end, out of focus or missing entirely, and a new arrangement of life has occurred. Of course, as you might suppose, it is generally thus that the best examination questions are framed. It is a failure, I tell myself, if in reading the blue-books I learn nothing new about the story I have told.

Can the experience that the examination maker has, of watching his story move and grow beyond his control, serve as something of a paradigm for all storytelling? Imagine yourself, for example, starting a story of the opposite kind, a story that is merely a story, meant to have no general or theoretical significance. Suppose it is the story of the adventures of a soldier making his way home from the wars after years away. As you tell more and more adventures of various kinds, might you not find that you have begun to express oppositions in feeling and attitude — say between the side of life that is adventuresome, explorative, full of challenge, and the side that is domestic and peaceful, an opposition between action and reflection, perhaps between life and death? Some such meanings work their way into the fabric of the *Odyssey*, which was at one stage almost certainly just a collection of tales. Or take the *Iliad*, composed over decades (and perhaps centuries) from an earlier tradition of heroic poetry. One poet decides to focus upon the wrath of Achilles, his anger at being deprived of his war prize, and tells the story of his withdrawal and return to battle; perhaps the same poet, perhaps another, finds a new meaning in the battles fought in Achilles' absence — a brutality, a sense of loss — and the opposition of Achilles becomes an opposition not merely to Agamemnon, on account of an insult, but to the enterprise of heroic war. When Achilles returns to battle, it must be on different terms, for motives different from those that begin the poem. This is just a sketch of course, but perhaps it is enough to permit the suggestion that much of this must have been a surprise for the writer or writers, some of it indeed perhaps not recognized at all. If you have read stories to children, you may have been surprised on occasion by an achievement that seems to surpass intention: Peter Rabbit, alone in Mr. MacGregor's garden, afraid of being caught, frightened by the cat, asks a field mouse scurrying under the gate how he can get out; "But she had such a large pea in her mouth that she could not answer. She only shook her head at him." To write a story is very often to find that one has written more than one knew.

To turn to a more direct analogy to the law school exam, how completely do you suppose an allegory — which is expressly meant to be a representation of ideas — can be controlled? Will not the people and animals and objects take on a meaning of their own? Take the three beasts that confront Dante in the forest as his poem begins: are the leopard, the lion, and the wolf beasts in a forest or are they ideas? Or somehow partly one and partly the other? Is this uncertainty, this mixture of meaning, indeed part of the achievement of the poem?

Perhaps I can give an illustration of narrative working in ordinary conversation and argument as a force against theory, against what we call rational discourse. Take a discussion of war, for example; the Viet Nam War or the Six-Day War or the Indo-Pakistan War. We all know how to talk about war and can carry on the arguments for and against a particular one, balancing costs and benefits, rights and wrongs. But when the story of a single wartime death is told — how it happens and what it means to the victim, to his family, to the killer — it fills the mind, and who can then go on to justify a war with words and reasons? You have perhaps seen conversations come to an end at such a point, one side consumed by the story, the other resisting it as irrelevant or emotional, neither satisfied with his response. Much the same can be said of our recognition of what poverty means — the reports of the Hundred Neediest Families affect us every year, though they say nothing new — and of the meaning of racial oppression, sickness, and other common conditions of life. Courage too, and self-sacrifice and gentleness, and other qualities of spirit and feeling, live for us almost exclusively in narrative; analytic or expository talk about such matters is seldom more than sermonizing of the worst kind.

Whenever a story is told, there is a possibility that it will take on a life of its own, a life beyond the intentions — and perhaps beyond the understanding and control — of the writer, a life so compelling that the auditor, whatever his wishes, cannot shake it off. You can see how important this force of narrative would be to the lawyer, at least if he could master it and claim its power for his own; you can imagine the tremendous pressure of a masterfully told story in trial or negotiation. The law recognizes this force in the courtroom — in the jury speech, in the processes of jury decision-making — but it does so with ambivalence, aware of the capacity of the story to undermine the plans and ideas of the law, half approving, half fearful.[11] Can the conflict between narrative and analysis, between story and theory, be regarded as defining

11. What I mean by the role of the story in the processes of jury judgment is this: when the judge asks the jury to decide what a reasonably prudent man would have done or foreseen, what he really asks is that each juror tell himself a story — if I had been there, on that night, what would I have done? If I had seen someone do what the defendant did, what would I have thought of it? — and see how it comes out.

an extraordinary opportunity for the lawyer? For the law? Turning briefly again to a question asked above about early Athens, you can perhaps now more fully imagine what the literature is like — how full of resonance and life — in which a conceptual language is made up for the first time out of the materials of ordinary talk, of story and description; when the metaphors of reason, of society, still have life and ambiguity. Do you suppose such a moment in history can come again, created in part by you?

In the following material we expose in somewhat greater detail the difficulties the narrator must face as he begins his story and carries it through to conclusion. What risks, what possibilities are there for him?

c. *How the Story Begins: The Complicating Choices of Shape and Direction*

It may give you a clearer sense of how the very process of telling a story subjects the writer (and hence the reader) to pressures towards complexity, ultimately towards the inexpressible, if you imagine yourself beginning a narrative, say a short story or novel. What difficulties do you face, what questions must you address? You know a good deal about the complexities involved in choosing a way to talk about your characters (Chapter 3 addresses that subject), but other far simpler choices force themselves upon you in surprising numbers. What physical universe will you create, for example, what landscape, or cityscape, or room or furnishings? What clothing, what wallpaper, what sky? And why will you do what you do? In a world of the movie and TV — which sometimes seem to reproduce segments of the real world without selection or omission — these questions are perhaps rather more surprising than they might othewise be, since we are not trained to imagine how much background and detail a novelist might choose to leave out. But how much description of countryside was there in Jane Austen's *Pride and Prejudice?* Do you know the architectural plan of Mr. Bennett's house or Mr. Bingley's? What can you tell us of clothing, furniture, or personal appearance, of garden or landscape? And what was the weather like, say on the day that Darcy and Elizabeth met in the garden at Pemberly?[12] Compare Conrad's beginning of *Nostromo* (1904):

> In the time of Spanish rule, and for many years afterward, the town of Sulaco — the luxuriant beauty of the orange gardens bears witness to its

12. You do know that it rained the day that Jane walked to Netherfield, but that rain does not define a physical universe, it is not a gesture of meaning; it merely explains how she got a cold, and hence how it was that she remained as a guest and that Elizabeth visited her.

antiquity — had never been commercially anything more important than a coasting port with a fairly large local trade in ox-hides and indigo. The clumsy deep-sea galleons of the conquerors that, needing a brisk gale to move at all, would lie becalmed, where your modern ship built on clipper lines forges ahead by the mere flapping of her sails, had been barred out of Sulaco by the prevailing calms of its vast gulf. Some harbours of the earth are made difficult of access by the treachery of sunken rocks and the tempests of their shores. Sulaco had found an inviolable sanctuary from the temptations of a trading world in the solemn hush of the deep Golfo Placido as if within an enormous and semicircular and unroofed temple open to the ocean, with its walls of lofty mountains hung with the mourning draperies of cloud.

Examine this passage with care, asking what physical universe Conrad creates, what sort of meaning he begins to make. Why do you suppose that he refers to the orange gardens at all, and why in particular as witnesses of antiquity? What is the effect of the great calmness, which has made Sulaco a sanctuary from the temptations of a trading world, and why speak of them as temptations? Why is the bay called a temple? And see what becomes of the clouds on the mountain tops: they are mourning draperies. Would someone actually speak or think that way, do you suppose? This description of the physical world is not just a movie, a travelog, nor does it pretend to be: it is a way of imagining, of giving meaning, of starting a story. One already has the sense that the narrative will be charged with a meaning not easily translatable into other terms, that the materials of this universe will constitute a metaphor in its way as impenetrable as Blake's *Rose.*

You may be interested in Erich Auerbach's *Mimesis* (1946), which takes as its subject the way that a writer imagines and creates a world of his own. His first essay addresses the moment in the *Odyssey* when the disguised Odysseus has arrived at last in Ithaca and is visiting his own house: when his feet are washed by his old nurse, he realizes that she will recognize him by the scar on his thigh, and he attempts to hide it; but she sees it — and the poem goes off on a long digression, telling in every detail the story of the boar hunt where Odysseus had been wounded, describing the hunt itself, the ancestry of the host, and so on. It then returns to the main narrative. Auerbach uses this as an example of the Homeric narrative style: everything is explained and accounted for, all is exposed to the light of day, everything is in the foreground.[13] He contrasts the narrative style of the Old Testament, using the story of

13. A somewhat similar account of Homeric narrative is given by the late Adam Parry in "The Language of Achilles," most easily available in G. S. Kirk (ed.), *The Language and Background of Homer* (1964). He points to a moment in the early battles where the watchfires of the Trojans are seen shining on the plain not far from

Abraham and Isaac as his example: these people are purely moral beings, with no physical characteristics whatever, located neither in time nor space, in no physical universe. All is background. They do go to a mountain, but not a named mountain, not a real place but a symbolic one, a place of sacrifice; they leave "early in the morning," but as Auerbach observes, that remark has not a temporal but an ethical significance, as an expression of their willingness. Which kind of story do you find in the law? Or is that a matter of choice?

Another way to realize the forces at work when one begins a story is to imagine what it would be like to try to make a play or a novel out of a story one has inherited. This was the practice of both Shakespeare and the Greek tragedians, who often seem to have started with very simple stories — from mythology, from Holinshed's *Chronicles,* from Plutarch's *Lives* — in which they sensed possibilities that others had missed, a complication or puzzle. Thus Euripides seems to have started off with a conflict between two traditional stories about Admetus, and to have made his *Alcestis* out of that. Shakespeare very often begins a play with a situation that is explained very little or not at all, a sort of narrative cliché, and sees what he can make up out of these rudiments of story, as the characters and their activities are more fully imagined. *King Lear* starts with the unexplained division of the kingdom, the old man's oddly trusting imperiousness; *Macbeth* starts with the witches' prophecies and the murder of Duncan, the effect of which on the murderer himself is the real subject of the play; *Antony and Cleopatra,* with the simple idea that he chooses her and Egypt over Rome; *Julius Caesar,* with the assassination; and so on. Sometimes — as in *Measure for Measure* or *The Merchant of Venice* — he finds he cannot do what he wants with the story; it all comes out as a mistake. But one way to read these plays is to ask whether you can feel the force of an imagination working out the implications of a story.

---

the Greek camp: they are compared with stars, regarded as beautiful, as part of a universe in which each thing, each event, has its own way of being looked at. There is no threat or malevolence here; the narrator expresses hospitality to every claim of excellence. Parry connects this facet of narrative style with the structure of the poem, saying that this in part explains why Achilles cannot express in words — in a great rhetorical speech — the disillusionment he experiences. Language is simply not used to state that sort of qualification.

Of course the poem as a whole does exactly that. It is a great example of statement and qualification. But Parry is right in saying that this is not achieved through the direct speech of the hero, but through a juxtaposition of the inconsistent: the events of battle are compared with falling snow, or flies humming over a pail of milk, or sheep or goats on a hill; the farewell of Hector to Andromache is contrasted with the battles on the field; the comic world of the gods with the human tragedy; and so on.

Turn now and imagine yourself starting a narrative, say a novel or a short story: how are you going to define your physical world? Will it have weather and sky and landscape? Will it have places we can recognize, actual named places, such as New York City, or 112th Street? Or will it be a sort of make-believe universe, like that of *Troilus and Cressida,* or the *Morte Darthur,* or *Waiting for Godot?* How will you decide such things?

Sometimes a writer seems to pretend that he is simply reporting the real world, saying what anyone would say, just adding to our common experience as a TV documentary might do — that he is not there at all in fact, that there is no imagination at work. Of course you know that you are constantly present in your writing, that it expresses and defines you. Two narrators — even of the "same" story — can be as different as two travelers looking at the same cathedral in France, two people seeing the same lily pulled by the current of the Vivonne. The pretense that the narrator is just a reporter is a false one; everything he does defines him. Each of us has his own experience. We are not able to see into each other's minds, and say "Of course."[14] Imagine yourself on a summer day in 1870 looking across the dense Maryland forest at the United States Capitol. What might you say or think?

> Adams astonished himself by remarking what a purified charm was lent to the Capitol by the greatest possible distance as one caught glimpses of the dome over miles of forest foliage. At such moments he pondered on the distant beauty of St. Peter's and the steps of Ara Coeli.*

There follows now a narrative beginning that might usefully be compared with the passage from *Nostromo* which you read a few pages earlier. What similarities and differences can you perceive? What physical universe is created here, what meaning is given the sea and the sun and the buildings? What choices can you see that the writer has made, why has he done so, and where do they carry you? What questions does he invite the reader to ask about what he will do next? You might put it this way: can you imagine Conrad carrying on from the point where Dickens leaves off, or Dickens finishing *Nostromo?* If not, what does that mean about the nature of narrative?

Can you see the process of narrative working here as a pressure towards the inexpressible?

14. If you have trouble with this paragraph, read two articles by Theodore Baird: "The World Turned Upside Down," 27 *Am. Scholar* 215 (1958); and "Sympathy: The Broken Mirror," 37 *Am. Scientist* 255 (1949).

* Henry Adams, *The Education of Henry Adams,* Chapter 18 (1918).

LITTLE DORRIT*

Charles Dickens

Sun and Shadow

Thirty years ago, Marseilles lay burning in the sun, one day.

A blazing sun upon a fierce August day was no greater rarity in southern France then, than at any other time, before or since. Everything in Marseilles, and about Marseilles, had stared at the fervid sky, and been stared at in return, until a staring habit had become universal there. Strangers were stared out of countenance by staring white houses, staring white walls, staring white streets, staring tracts of arid road, staring hills from which verdure was burnt away. The only things to be seen not fixedly staring and glaring were the vines drooping under their load of grapes. These did occasionally wink a little, as the hot air barely moved their faint leaves.

There was no wind to make a ripple on the foul water within the harbour, or on the beautiful sea without. The line of demarcation between the two colours, black and blue, showed the point which the pure sea would not pass; but it lay as quiet as the abominable pool, with which it never mixed. Boats without awnings were too hot to touch; ships blistered at their moorings; the stones of the quays had not cooled, night or day, for months. Hindoos, Russians, Chinese, Spaniards, Portuguese, Englishmen, Frenchmen, Genoese, Neapolitans, Venetians, Greeks, Turks, descendants from all the builders of Babel, come to trade at Marseilles, sought the shade alike — taking refuge in any hiding-place from a sea too intensely blue to be looked at, and a sky of purple, set with one great flaming jewel of fire.

The universal stare made the eyes ache. Towards the distant line of Italian coast, indeed, it was a little relieved by light clouds of mist, slowly rising from the evaporation of the sea; but it softened nowhere else. Far away the staring roads, deep in dust, stared from the hill-side, stared from the hollow, stared from the interminable plain. Far away the dusty vines overhanging wayside cottages, and the monotonous wayside avenues of parched trees without shade, drooped beneath the stare of earth and sky. So did the horses with drowsy bells, in long files of carts, creeping slowly towards the interior; so did their recumbent drivers, when they were awake, which rarely happened; so did the exhausted labourers in the fields. Everything that lived or grew, was oppressed by the glare; except the lizard, passing swiftly over rough

* Chapter 1 (1857).

stone walls, and the cicala, chirping his dry hot chirp, like a rattle. The very dust was scorched brown, and something quivered in the atmosphere as if the air itself were panting.

Blinds, shutters, curtains, awnings, were all closed and drawn to keep out the stare. Grant it but a chink or keyhole, and it shot in like a white-hot arrow. The churches were the freest from it. To come out of the twilight of pillars and arches — dreamily dotted with winking lamps, dreamily peopled with ugly old shadows piously dozing, spitting, and begging — was to plunge into a fiery river, and swim for life to the nearest strip of shade. So, with people lounging and lying wherever shade was, with but little hum of tongues or barking of dogs, with occasional jangling of discordant church bells, and rattling of vicious drums, Marseilles, a fact to be strongly smelt and tasted, lay broiling in the sun one day.

In Marseilles that day there was a villainous prison. In one of its chambers, so repulsive a place that even the obtrusive stare blinked at it, and left it to such refuse of reflected light as it could find for itself, were two men. Besides the two men, a notched and disfigured bench, immoveable from the wall, with a draught-board rudely hacked upon it with a knife, a set of draughts, made of old buttons and soup bones, a set of dominoes, two mats, and two or three wine bottles. That was all the chamber held, exclusive of rats and other unseen vermin, in addition to the seen vermin, the two men.

It received such light as it got, through a grating of iron bars, fashioned like a pretty large window, by means of which it could be always inspected from the gloomy staircase on which the grating gave. There was a broad strong ledge of stone to this grating, where the bottom of it was let into the masonry, three or four feet above the ground. Upon it, one of the two men lolled, half sitting and half lying, with his knees drawn up, and his feet and shoulders planted against the opposite sides of the aperture. The bars were wide enough apart to admit of his thrusting his arm through to the elbow; and so he held on negligently, for his greater ease.

A prison taint was on everything there. The imprisoned air, the imprisoned light, the imprisoned damps, the imprisoned men, were all deteriorated by confinement. As the captive men were faded and haggard, so the iron was rusty, the stone was slimy, the wood was rotten, the air was faint, the light was dim. Like a well, like a vault, like a tomb, the prison had no knowledge of the brightness outside; and would have kept its polluted atmosphere intact, in one of the spice islands of the Indian Ocean.

The man who lay on the ledge of the grating was even chilled. He jerked his great cloak more heavily upon him by an impatient movement of one shoulder, and growled, "To the devil with this Brigand of a Sun that never shines in here!"

Now turn to your life as lawyer or judge. What stories will you tell and how will you tell them? As you begin the statement of facts in a brief, an account of a client's troubles to an associate, a summation to a jury, or a judicial opinion, what world will you create? What physical universe will you define, filled with what objects, inhabited by what people, imbued with what meaning? How will you address the possibility that as you tell your story it will take on a meaning, have a force or significance, beyond your original intention? What relationship can you establish between your deeply opposing tendencies to talk on forever about the facts of your case and to dispose of it in a language of legal conclusion, to tell the story and analyze it?

d. *The Ending as Cliché: Controlling Narrative Conclusion*

If to begin a narrative is to subject oneself to enormous pressures towards complexity, towards the inexpressible — to find oneself swamped with choices of style and meaning — at the end of a story the situation is reversed: the pressure changes direction, from complication to simplification, from opening the reader's attention to the material of life to closing it off. For here doubts are resolved, loose ends tidied up, here the whole picture comes clear at last. If the narrative has run on suspense, we finally learn what we have been eager to know — that they are to be married, or that Little Nell is dead — and the book by its own terms has come to an end. (Where the ending is obvious or known, the narrative may work by dramatic irony; we are horrified to watch the victorious Agamemnon returning to his death, to see him enticed into treading the gorgeous carpet, because we know what he does not: how it all will end. When a narrative of this kind closes, it is with an equal sense of finality, what was known having come to pass.) The ending of the narrative is the completion of a metaphor. At the end of *Pride and Prejudice*, Darcy and Elizabeth are to "marry": what that means, we are not to inquire. Alcestis is saved and returns to Admetus: what the future holds is not a question in a play about salvation. One might say that at the end of a narrative we move — or there is a danger that we move — from the literature of story, with its pressures towards complication and the inexpressible, to a disposition of it in other terms, in a language of conclusion, of theory.

The emotions upon which the narrative has proceeded from the beginning are satisfied, and everything can now be put in simple terms. "Elizabeth *does* marry Darcy, isn't that nice!" The author has a comic vision, says the critic, or a tragic one, depending on the outcome of the tale. The assumption seems to be that the narrative is a mirror of life, that what it describes is an estimate of the future fate of mankind — "overweening ambition brings its own punishment" — and at the end the author finally lets us know what party he belongs to, Hope or Despair. The experience of reading is converted into a message. You know from your own education what things can be done to *Macbeth* or *Oedipus Tyrannos* by interpretation of such a kind.

For the lawyer or judge, the danger that his narrative will become at the end a cliché of this kind (or that it will be regarded as such) is especially severe because his stories end in a decision, in a reduction of experience to system, a conversion of character into label. The judicial opinion is reduced to a headnote. How is the mind that tells a story, whether a lawyer or another, to address the danger of conclusion, the risk that his reader will at last be able to dispose of his story as if it were merely an example of a theory or an idea?

One way in which a writer can put a qualification on his ending, a complication on his conclusion, is to make it clear that things could have gone the other way. In *Pride and Prejudice*, you remember, Lady Catherine poses at moments a real threat, and the danger of failure for Elizabeth is made plain in the fate of Charlotte Lucas. In Molière's *Miser*, Harpagon (the monster of avarice) is of course finally brought down, the object of ridicule, but much of the force of the play — indeed much of the energy for its comedy — comes from one's sense that Harpagon might prevail, that there is a genuine danger there. The genial Noddy Boffin in Dickens's *Our Mutual Friend* is turned by his wealth into a grasping and cold-hearted person; then we learn that it was all a ruse, his way of teaching a young friend the dangers of greed, and that he is the same good-hearted old fellow after all. One is left with both possibilities — the former, if anything, predominating.[15] In *The Winter's Tale* Shakespeare qualifies the sense of ending by writing two plays with inconsistent endings: in the first half of the play we are told the story of the jealous rage of Leontes, which causes the death of his wife and the exile of his child; in the second, the child is found and

15. Monroe Engel has pointed out that the triumph of good in *Oliver Twist* is similarly qualified by the fact that the good characters never actually confront the bad ones; the reason is that the bad (e.g., Sikes and Fagin) have so much more force and vitality that one cannot imagine such a confrontation ending as Dickens ends his book. Engel, " 'A Kind of Allegory' — The Old Curiosity Shop," 1 *Harv. English Studies* 135 (1970). Compare what is said by Agnes in *David Copperfield* (Chapter 35): "I hope that real love and truth are stronger in the end than any evil or misfortune in the world."

the wife miraculously restored. Which is the "real" ending? The ambivalence is deliberate and makes such a question impossible.

Compare the marvelous ending of Brendan Behan's play *The Hostage,* which tells the story of a young British soldier held in a brothel by the IRA, under the sentence of death. There are two strains of meaning and feeling in the play as it proceeds: concern for the serious, indeed melodramatic plight of the soldier; and a bawdy and raucous comedy of life in the brothel, full of drinking and singing and love of life. Throughout the play there is an alternation between concern for the hostage and a forgetful hilarity. How is such a play possibly to end? It seems as if Behan did not know which sort of play he wanted to write and got hopelessly mixed up. Neither a tragic nor a comic ending can be appropriate. As the end approaches, the play becomes wilder in every way: the danger is more real, the comedy more funny; at last the brothel is raided, pandemonium breaks out, and the hostage is killed, apparently by an accidental shot. The action freezes, people mourn; a girl who had earlier refused to save him makes a sentimental farewell. The audience is embarrassed by this, and by the remembrance of its own earlier laughter. It was a tragedy after all. The hostage then rises and slowly sings:

> The bells of hell
> Go ting-a-ling-a-ling
> For you but not for me.
> Oh Death where is thy
> Sting-a-ling-a-ling,
> Or grave thy victory?
> If you meet the undertaker
> Or the man from the Pru
> Get a pint of what's left over,
> Now I'll say goodbye to you.

The balance has been righted, the comic love of life has been restated as part of the play; the threat is not dispelled but accepted as fact. Behan gets his audience to see things two ways at once.

Is such control of the conclusion of narrative possible in the law, or does every legal case and problem and argument end in an unqualified assertion of legal meaning? Could you as judge or lawyer do what Dickens, Shakespeare, Behan, and Molière do? If not that, is there some other way you can control the implications of ending, the sense of finality, in your legal narratives? Or is that sense of finality, of an impossible and fictional simplicity, in fact your very object as lawyer or judge? Does that please you? Perhaps it can be put this way: when you are a lawyer, will you be able to manage your lawsuits so that they operate with the richness of meaning, the constant qualification and surprise, of great drama? (Does not every rural murder or small-time burglary have within it possibilities of meaning like those that Sophocles found in the Oedipus story or Aeschylus in the *The Oresteia?*) Or will you regard only the ending of your trials as significant, only the outcome, so that the more apt analogy to what you do is not the drama but the horse race or the batting average? Suppose you are a judge: can you write opinions that people must read in their entirety, that cannot be reduced to headnotes?

e. *The Force of Narrative: A Pressure Towards Falsehood?*

You have just seen that there are pressures at work on the teller of a story towards simplification as well as complication, towards narrative clichés as well as ever-expanding metaphors. Below is an example of a storyteller who succumbs to the pressure to convert his experience into the accepted language of a narrative cliché. Does this passage define a danger for the lawyer?

WAR AND PEACE*
Leo Tolstoy

"With God's help, lads," rang out Denisov's voice, "forward, quick, gallop!"

The horses' haunches began moving in the front line. Rook pulled at the reins and set off of himself.

On the right Rostov saw the foremost lines of his own hussars, and still further ahead he could see a dark streak, which he could not distinguish clearly, but assumed to be the enemy. Shots could be heard, but at a distance.

"Quicker!" rang out the word of command, and Rostov felt the drooping of Rook's hindquarters as he broke into a gallop. He felt the joy of the gallop coming, and was more and more lighthearted. He noticed a solitary tree ahead of him. The tree was at first in front of him, in the middle of that border-land that had seemed so terrible. But now they had crossed it and nothing terrible had happened, but he felt more lively and excited every moment. "Ah, won't I slash at him!" thought Rostov, grasping the hilt of his sabre tightly. "Hur . . . r . . . a . . . a!" roared voices.

"Now, let him come on, whoever it may be," thought Rostov, driving the spurs into Rook, and outstripping the rest, he let him go at full gallop. Already the enemy could be seen in front. Suddenly something

* Pages 168–170; 219–220 (1864–1869; Garnett trans., Modern Library ed.).

swept over the squadron like a broad broom. Rostov lifted his sabre, making ready to deal a blow, but at that instant the soldier Nikitenko galloped ahead and left his side, and Rostov felt as though he were in a dream being carried forward with supernatural swiftness and yet remaining at the same spot. An hussar, Bandartchuk, galloped up from behind close upon him and looked angrily at him. Bandartchuk's horse started aside, and he galloped by.

"What's the matter? I'm not moving? I've fallen, I'm killed . . ." Rostov asked and answered himself all in one instant. He was alone in the middle of the field. Instead of the moving horses and the hussars' backs, he saw around him the motionless earth and stubblefield. There was warm blood under him.

"No, I'm wounded, and my horse is killed." Rook tried to get up on his forelegs, but he sank again, crushing his rider's leg under his leg. Blood was flowing from the horse's head. The horse struggled, but could not get up. Rostov tried to get up, and fell down too. His sabretache had caught in the saddle. Where our men were, where were the French, he did not know. All around him there was no one.

Getting his leg free, he stood up. "Which side, where now was that line that had so sharply divided the two armies?" he asked himself, and could not answer. "Hasn't something gone wrong with me? Do such things happen, and what ought one to do in such cases?" he wondered as he was getting up. But at that instant he felt as though something superfluous was hanging on his benumbed left arm. The wrist seemed not to belong to it. He looked at his hand, carefully searching for blood on it. "Come, here are some men," he thought joyfully, seeing some men running towards him. "They will help me!" In front of these men ran a single figure in a strange shako and a blue coat, with a swarthy sunburnt face and a hooked nose. Then came two men, and many more were running up behind. One of them said some strange words, not Russian. Between some similar figures in similar shakoes behind stood a Russian hussar. He was being held by the arms; behind him they were holding his horse too.

"It must be one of ours taken prisoner. . . . Yes. Surely they couldn't take me too? What sort of men are they?" Rostov was still wondering, unable to believe his own eyes. "Can they be the French?" He gazed at the approaching French, and although only a few seconds before he had been longing to get at these Frenchmen and to cut them down, their being so near seemed to him now so awful that he could not believe his eyes. "Who are they? What are they running for? Can it be to me? Can they be running to me? And what for? To kill me? *Me*, whom every one's so fond of?" He recalled his mother's love, the love of his family and his friends, and the enemy's intention of killing him seemed impossible. "But they may even kill me." For more than ten seconds he stood, not moving from the spot, nor grasping his position. The foremost Frenchman with the hook nose was getting so near that he could see the expression of his face. And the excited, alien countenance of the man, who was running so lightly and breathlessly towards him, with his bayonet lowered, terrified Rostov. He snatched up his pistol, and instead of firing with it, flung it at the Frenchman and ran to the bushes with all his might. Not with the feeling of doubt and conflict with which he had moved at the Enns bridge, did he now run, but with the feeling of a hare fleeing from the dogs. One unmixed feeling of fear for his young, happy life took possession of his whole being. Leaping rapidly over the hedges with the same impetuosity with which he used to run when he played games, he flew over the field, now and then turning his pale, good-natured, youthful face, and a chill of horror ran down his spine. "No, better not to look," he thought, but as he got near to the bushes he looked round once more. The French had given it up, and just at the moment when he looked round the foremost man was just dropping from a run into a walk, and turning round to shout something loudly to a comrade behind. Rostov stopped. "There's some mistake," he thought; "it can't be that they meant to kill me." And meanwhile his left arm was as heavy as if a hundred pound weight were hanging on it. He could run no further. The Frenchman stopped too and took aim. Rostov frowned and ducked. One bullet and then another flew hissing by him; he took his left hand in his right, and with a last effort ran as far as the bushes. In the bushes there were Russian sharpshooters. . . .

[Some time later, Rostov is visiting Boris.] Boris, seeing that Rostov was disposed to make fun of Berg, skilfully turned the conversation. He begged Rostov to tell them how and where he had been wounded. That pleased Rostov, and he began telling them, getting more and more eager as he talked. He described to them his battle at Schöngraben exactly as men who have taken part in battles always do describe them, that is, as they would have liked them to be, as they have heard them described by others, and as sounds well, but not in the least as it really had been. Rostov was a truthful young man; he would not have intentionally told a lie. He began with the intention of telling everything precisely as it had happened, but imperceptibly, unconsciously, and inevitably he passed into falsehood. If he had told the truth to his listeners, who, like himself, had heard numerous descriptions of cavalry charges, and had formed a definite idea of what a charge was like and were expecting a similar description, either they would not have believed him, or worse still, would have assumed that Rostov was himself to blame for not having performed the exploits usually performed by those who describe cavalry charges. He could not tell them simply that they had all been charging full gallop, that he had fallen off his horse, sprained his arm, and run with all his might away from the French into the copse. And besides, to tell everything exactly as it happened, he would have had to exercise considerable self-control in order to tell nothing beyond what happened. To tell the truth is a very difficult thing; and young people are rarely capable of it. His listeners expected to hear how he had been all on fire with excitement, had forgotten himself, had flown like a tempest on the enemy's square, had cut his way into it, hewing men down right and left, how a sabre had been thrust into his flesh, how he had fallen unconscious, and so on. And he described all that. In the middle of his tale, just as he was saying: "You can't fancy what a strange frenzy takes possession of one at the moment of the charge," there walked into the room Prince Andrey Bolkonsky, whom Boris was expecting. Prince Andrey liked to encourage and assist younger men, he was flattered at being applied to for his influence, and well disposed to Boris, who had succeeded in making a favourable impression on him the previous day; he was eager to do for the young man what he desired. Having been sent with papers from Kutuzov to the Tsarevitch, he called upon Boris, hoping to find him alone. When he came into the room and saw the hussar with his soldierly swagger describing his warlike exploits (Prince Andrey could not endure the kind of men who are fond of doing so), he smiled cordially to Boris, but frowned and dropped his eyelids as he turned to Rostov with a slight bow. Wearily and languidly he sat down on the sofa, regretting that he had dropped into such undesirable society. Rostov, perceiving it, grew hot, but he did not care; this man was nothing to him. Glancing at Boris, he saw, however, that he too seemed ashamed of the valiant hussar. In spite of Prince Andrey's unpleasant, ironical manner, in spite of the disdain with which Rostov, from his point of view of a fighting man in the regular army, regarded the whole race of staff-adjutants in general — the class to which the new-comer unmistakably belonged — he yet felt abashed, reddened, and subsided into silence.

2. *Reconciling the Demands of Imagination and Reality: The Historian as Model for the Lawyer?*

I am interested in the nature of poetry and I have stated its nature, from one of the many points of view from which it is possible to state it. It is an interdependence of the imagination and reality as equals.*

* Wallace Stevens, "The Noble Rider and the Sound of Words," in *The Necessary Angel* 3, 27 (1942).

The historian, like the lawyer, engages in at least two sorts of discourse at once: he tells us a story, and then he tells us what it means. Having given us the particulars, he generalizes, sums up and reaches conclusions — and in doing so, he must face a tension very similar to that between story and theory which we have been discussing. Of course few historians are attached to a theory of history as detailed and dogmatic as the law, though something like that might be said of some Christian and Marxist historians. But any historian finds some meaning, some order, in the story he tells, and you can see the difficulty that he therefore faces: what relationship should he, can he, establish between these two sorts of discourse? One danger is that he will fit the story to his theory, that the narrative will become a sort of self-justifying example, a rigged proof; another is that he will obscure with detail, or with needless doubting, the pattern he does see, that he will fail to state a genuine truth. What other dangers do you see?

Below, a historian boldly defines his task. As you read this excerpt, ask how you would like to be asked to carry on from here. If you find yourself disapproving, ask how you would commence a similar history, what problems you would set for yourself, what expectations you would seek to arouse in the reader.

THE HISTORY OF ENGLAND FROM THE ACCESSION OF JAMES II*

T. B. Macaulay

I purpose to write the history of England from the accession of King James the Second down to a time which is within the memory of men still living. I shall recount the errors which, in a few months, alienated a loyal gentry and priesthood from the house of Stuart. I shall trace the course of that revolution which terminated the long struggle between our sovereigns and their Parliaments, and bound up together the rights of the people and the title of the reigning dynasty. I shall relate how the new settlement was, during many troubled years, successfully defended against foreign and domestic enemies; how, under that settlement, the authority of law and the security of property were found to be compatible with a liberty of discussion and of individual action never before known; how, from the auspicious union of order and freedom, sprang a prosperity of which the annals of human affairs had furnished no example; how our country, from a state of ignominious vassalage, rapidly rose to the place of umpire among European powers; how her opulence and her martial glory grew together; how, by wise and resolute good

* Chapter 1 (1848).

faith, was gradually established a public credit fruitful of marvels which to the statesmen of any former age would have seemed incredible; how a gigantic commerce gave birth to a maritime power, compared with which every other maritime power, ancient or modern, sinks into insignificance; how Scotland, after ages of enmity, was at length united to England, not merely by legal bonds, but by indissoluble ties of interest and affection; how, in America, the British colonies rapidly became far mightier and wealthier than the realms which Cortez and Pizarro had added to the dominions of Charles the Fifth; how, in Asia, British adventurers founded an empire not less splendid and more durable than that of Alexander.

Nor will it be less my duty faithfully to record disasters mingled with triumphs, and great national crimes and follies far more humiliating than any disaster. It will be seen that even what we justly account our chief blessings were not without alloy. It will be seen that the system which effectually secured our liberties against the encroachments of kingly power gave birth to a new class of abuses from which absolute monarchies are exempt. It will be seen that, in consequence partly of unwise interference, and partly of unwise neglect, the increase of wealth and the extension of trade produced, together with immense good, some evils from which poor and rude societies are free. It will be seen how, in two important dependencies of the crown, wrong was followed by just retribution; how imprudence and obstinacy broke the ties which bound the North American colonies to the parent state; how Ireland, cursed by the domination of race over race, and of religion over religion, remained, indeed, a member of the empire, but a withered and distorted member, adding no strength to the body politic, and reproachfully pointed at by all who feared or envied the greatness of England.

Yet, unless I greatly deceive myself, the general effect of this checkered narrative will be to excite thankfulness in all religious minds, and hope in the breasts of all patriots; for the history of our country during the last hundred and sixty years is eminently the history of physical, of moral, and of intellectual improvement. Those who compare the age on which their lot has fallen with a golden age which exists only in their imagination, may talk of degeneracy and decay; but no man who is correctly informed as to the past will be disposed to take a morose or desponding view of the present.

I should very imperfectly execute the task which I have undertaken if I were merely to treat of battles and sieges, of the rise and fall of administrations, of intrigues in the palace, and of debates in the Parliament. It will be my endeavor to relate the history of the people as well as the history of the government, to trace the progress of useful and ornamental arts, to describe the rise of religious sects and the changes of literary taste, to portray the manners of successive generations, and not to pass by with neglect even the revolutions which have taken place in drcss, furniture, repasts, and public amusements. I shall cheerfully bear the reproach of having descended below the dignity of history, if I can succeed in placing before the English of the nineteenth century a true picture of the life of their ancestors.

QUESTIONS

1. What meaning does Macaulay claim for the narrative he promises us?
   a. Do you expect that the story as it is told will support that meaning? Could it do so if it were told honestly?
   b. Suppose the opposite meaning were claimed for the story, that the past 160 years were years of decay and degeneration. Can you imagine an honestly told story that would support that meaning?
   c. What then is the problem here?

2. Compare J. A. Froude, History of England From the Fall of Wolsey to the Defeat of the Spanish Armada, I, 39 (1856): "The people, not universally but generally, were animated by a true spirit of sacrifice; by a true conviction that they were bound to think first of England, and only next of themselves; and unless we can bring ourselves to understand this we shall nevcr understand what England was under the reigns of the Plantagenets and Tudors."
   a. Could that statement of historical fact be true? Could its opposite?
   b. Should this sort of statement, this sort of claim, then never be made?

3. How would you yourself describe the spirit of America during World War II? Or of London during the Blitz? If you support and explain your statement by stories, are they true stories or fairy tales, representative facts or monuments to the pathetic fallacy of historical comprehensibility? How do you know?

4. Next are two examples of historical discourse. Where else might you see writing like this?

HISTORY OF ENGLAND*
David Hume

This was the time when genius and capacity of all kinds, freed from the restraint of authority, and nourished by unbounded hopes and projects, began to exert themselves and to be distinguished by the public. Then was celebrated the sagacity of Pym, more fitted for use than ornament; matured, not chilled, by his advanced age and long experience; then was displayed the mighty ambition of Hambden, taught disguise, not moderation, from former constraint; supported by courage, conducted by prudence, embellished by modesty; but whether founded in a love of power or zeal for liberty, is still, from his untimely end, left doubtful and uncertain: then too were known the dark, ardent and dangerous character of St. John; the impetuous spirit of Hollis,

* Volume 5, page 136 (1754).

violent and sincere, open and entire in his enmities and his friendships; the enthusiastic genius of Young Vane, extravagant in the means he employed; united by the appearance of religion, negligent of the duties of morality.

THE HISTORY OF ENGLAND FROM THE ACCESSION OF JAMES II*

T. B. Macaulay

[The Roman Catholic king, James II, has ordered a declaration of religious toleration read in the pulpits of the established church. Seven bishops have refused to read it, and for this refusal have been tried for libel.]

. . . It was soon known that the jury were agreed: but what the verdict would be was still a secret.

At ten the Court met again. The crowd was greater than ever. The jury appeared in their box; and there was a breathless stillness.

Sir Samuel Astry spoke. "Do you find the defendants, or any of them, guilty of the misdemeanour whereof they are impeached, or not guilty?" Sir Roger Langley answered, "Not Guilty." As the words were uttered Halifax sprang up and waved his hat. At that signal, benches and galleries raised a shout. In a moment ten thousand persons who crowded the great hall, replied with a still louder shout, which made the old oaken roof crack; and in another moment the innumerable throng without set up a third huzza, which was heard at Temple Bar. The boats which covered the Thames gave an answering cheer. A peal of gunpowder was heard on the water, and another, and another; and so, in a few moments, the glad tidings went flying past the Savoy and the Friars to London Bridge, and to the forest of masts below. As the news spread, streets and squares, marketplaces and coffeehouses, broke forth into acclamations. Yet were the acclamations less strange than the weeping. For the feelings of men had been wound up to such a point that at length the stern English nature, so little used to outward signs of emotion, gave way, and thousands sobbed for very joy. Meanwhile, from the outskirts of the multitude, horsemen were spurring off to bear along all the great roads intelligence of the victory of our Church and nation. Yet not even that astounding explosion could awe the bitter and intrepid spirit of the Solicitor. Striving to make himself heard above the din, he called on the judges to commit those who had violated, by clamour, the dignity of a court of justice. One of the rejoicing populace was seized. But the tribunal felt that it would be absurd to punish a single individual for an offense common to hundreds of thousands, and dismissed him with a gentle reprimand.

* Chapter 8 (1848).

QUESTIONS

1. *One way to begin to figure out a way to talk about historical narrative might be to ask: what do we want a historian to do? Do we want him to "tell the story" of the past, for example, or to "explain the past," or what? What can we mean by the terms we use to state our expectations?*
2. *What might it mean to ask someone to "explain" the murder of Charles I, for example, or the occurrence of the First Crusade, or the rise of Hitler? Would we be asking for the "story" of these events or for something else – and if the latter, what would it be? The question that requests an "explanation" seems to define no language in which a response is invited; it is apparently not a move from a definable language game. What kind of question is it then, and how do we want the historian to respond?*
3. *Consider the following famous sentence of Thucydides, often pointed to as a claim for predictability in history and hence for the existence of a science of human affairs: "It will be enough for me . . . if these words of mine are judged useful by those who want to understand clearly the events which happened in the past and which (human nature being what it is) will, at some time or other and in much the same ways, be repeated in the future." (History, Book I, Chapter 1.) What can Thucydides mean by "understand" in such a sentence? Isn't that term simply the correlative of "explain" and subject to the same difficulties? And if he is going to explain the past, why does he speak in a narrative form?*[16]
4. *In what follows, we shall consider some of the ambiguities and complexities of the historian's activity when it is regarded as a kind of "storytelling," but I hope you see that a similar analysis could begin equally well by asking questions about the nature of historical explanation.*

THE NATURE OF HISTORICAL NARRATIVE

The Macaulay passage you just read could be said to read like a novel: full of detail and dialog and characterization and feeling and movement. Now imagine a possibility at the other end of the scale: a history consisting of pure fact, of the unarranged and uninterpreted materials of the past, the raw data of historical judgment. Of course such an extreme

16. The nature of historical explanation has been the subject of considerable thought and writing. Professor Isaiah Berlin, in the essays cited at page 239 *supra*, takes the position that the historian properly concerns himself with matters of such variety and complexity that any attempt to account for them by descriptive rules or other systems of analysis is badly mistaken. It is a foolish and destructive fiction to try to reduce history to that sort of meaning, to move (as we might put it) from a universe of many languages to a universe of one. In "Historical Explanation," in *Mind* (1943), Professor Morton White makes a similar point, where he says that there is no unitary language of history in which statements of the "rule" or other theoretical variety can be cast. Let me recommend as well the following: P. Gardiner, *The Nature of Historical Explanation* (1952); W. Dray, *Laws and Explanation in History* (1957); P. Gardiner (ed.), *Theories of History* (1959); E. Carr, *What is History?* (1961); P. Geyl, *Debates With Historians* (1958); A. Momigliano, *Studies in Historiography* (1966).

is impossible as a mechanical matter, and would in any event demand of the reader that he work as a professional historian himself. And the problem is not simply one of excessive data; we know so little that virtually every statement about the past seems, when examined, to have inadequate support.

The historian then operates between two extremes, between fairy tale and data, between an intellectual activity that generalizes (seeks meaning, tells a story) and one that scrutinizes and doubts and says it is not proven, or perhaps rescues a solid fact from the mass of uncertainty. Somehow he must find a way of dealing with these two incompatible processes of thought, these two contradictory languages, he must find a place for himself between them. How is he to do this? And what lesson is there here for the lawyer, who must face a similar tension between two sorts of language?

Can these tensions between story and theory, fact and fiction, particular and general, and so on, be regarded in more general terms, as instances of a conflict at work both in history and in law, between the demands of reality and those of the imagination? With that question in mind let us look again at the task of the historian.

To start with, it is plain that the historian is not right simply to resolve his doubts in favor of the careful, the verifiable, though that is perhaps a modern tendency and (in a scientific age) the safer course. As Professor Berlin observes in his essay "The Concept of Scientific History," discussed above at page 239, to do that is to cut oneself off from statements that are, however unscientific, of the greatest significance. For history can be a way of defining a community by its past, a way of expressing what essentially distinguishes life in different times and places — an art of the creative imagination — and this creation of meaning cannot work by monograph alone. A band of Semitic slaves is expelled into the desert: this becomes Exodus when we agree to it. The death of a political criminal can be that of a squalid spy or of Jesus or Socrates, depending upon the meaning that a writer claims and can sustain. To take another instance, the story of early Britain, as Bede tells it, is the story of the Church: the failing Celtic Church, nearly overwhelmed by the Saxon infidels, is, by the miraculous conversion of the victors, supplanted by the Catholic Church of Gregory and Augustine — victory snatched from the jaws of defeat. The story of this success is the story of God's involvement in the affairs of men, and this presence is made felt in the miracles which recur throughout the narrative, as well as in the shape of the story as a whole. You can imagine how different an account of the same period might be given by a historian of Ireland or Cornwall; and you know something of Malory's *Morte Darthur,* to which the promised Saxon victory is the end of a civilization. What do you think Gibbon would make of this event, as part of the history of Rome? Or Snorri Sturluson, the author of *The Heimskringla* (The History of the Kings of Norway), to whom even the battle of Hastings is just the victory of one Norseman over another?

The suggestion is that the central activity of history is an imaginative claim and defense of meaning for events, an activity very much like that of the drama and the novel and the law. Putting aside for the moment the distinctions that can be drawn using the terms "truth" and "fiction," let us look briefly at one or two examples, beginning with a comparison between Herodotus' *History* and Aeschylus' *Persians*, which deal with the same subject, the second Persian war.

Herodotus sets out in the most leisurely way to tell the story of the hostility between Greece and Asia from its beginnings and in its every aspect. As he proceeds, he excites and satisfies a nearly universal curiosity, seeming to include in his story everything that might be said: mythological explanations of the beginnings of hostility between East and West, the Egyptian view of the Trojan War, comparative religious belief and practice, social description (of Egyptian manners, of the Persian ideal "to ride, to draw the bow, to speak the truth"), geography, accounts of travel and exploration, the circumnavigation of Africa by the Phoenicians, military history, political craft and stratagem, marriage customs (in Babylon brides are auctioned off, the price of the beautiful making a dowry for the plain), natural history, the role of the Delphic oracle as a force for Greek colonization, debates on the merits of various forms of government, a dissertation on the power of a free state over a slave state, careful characterization of individuals — and so on and on, it seems, forever. Nothing is left out.

This world of fact and custom and event is not cast as the example of a theory, but as it unfolds it organizes itself into a meaning of its own: the growth of Persian power is contrasted in a thousand ways with the experience of Greece, and the contrast defines a civilization. Persian opulence and cruelty is contrasted with Greek plainness and humanity, the Persian slave lashed into battle contrasted with the Spartan soldier whose only master is the law, and so on.

The crisis comes when Xerxes, the Persian emperor, organizes an enormous expedition to avenge the loss of the battle of Marathon. The invasion at first succeeds: the Spartan defenders of Thermopylae are killed to the last man, Athens is sacked and burned. The Greeks — Athenians, Corinthians, Spartans, and others — retreat to the small island of Salamis which lies against the Athenian coast, forming a long bay, narrow of entrance. Themistocles, the Athenian leader, forces the Peloponnesians to stay and fight, first by threatening instant departure for Italy if they refuse, and then by tricking the Persians, through a false informer, into circling the island all night to prevent the supposititious or genuine escape of the Greeks. The sea-battle of Salamis takes place at dawn, victory going against the odds to the greater spirit and skill of the Greeks.

This battle, upon which everything turns, is given its meaning by what has gone before. The whole history has been the background to this event, it constitutes a past that is brought to bear on the present to give it meaning. The battle is the moment at which a civilization is saved. Out of the ruins of Athens will be built the city of Pericles.

How would you expect the play of Aeschylus to deal with the same battle? Set in Persia, it tells the story (largely through messengers home from Greece) of preparation for war and of defeat. Its central moment is an eyewitness account of the battle of Salamis. Of course — written within eight years of Salamis and addressed to those who had won the battle — it celebrates the victory of Greek over barbarian, of freedom over despotism. But the spirit of pride that it generates is purified by the forced recognition of what the victory meant in human terms to the losers. And purified as well by a sense of danger to the Athenians, by a warning that the fate of the beaten Persian empire may be that of the rising Athenian one, that the very sense of greatness that the play celebrates may prove fatal.

There are of course differences of emphasis, feeling, and immediate purpose in these two works, but can they be traced to a difference between history and fiction, to a difference in form? Are their major truths, their primary purposes, different in kind?

Aeschylus, it is said, was a soldier at Marathon and an eyewitness of Salamis, while Herodotus was probably not born until after both events: so which work is history and which fiction?

One might be inclined to say that Herodotus is not a fair example of the historian — primitive and unreliable, we are told — but one can see a similar pressure towards the fictional at the center of the work of Thucydides, who used to be called the first scientific historian. He tells us, for example, that in writing the speeches he did not attempt to report word for word what was said, even as best remembered, but what the occasion "called for," a phrase reminiscent of the claim attributed to Sophocles that "Euripides portrays men as they are; I as they ought to be." The sense for the typical, for the generic, that characterizes Greek drama is essential (as Professor Finley observes) to the art of Thucydides and perhaps to the art of history itself.[17] One might generalize even further and say that the element of the fictional, of the ideal, is inherent in the very idea of narrative.

A most far-reaching and provoking claim that Thucydides' *History* is

17. John H. Finley, Jr., *Thucydides* 72–73 (1942).

fictional in structure and conception is made by F. M. Cornford in *Thucydides Mythistoricus* (1907). He begins with the observation that while Thucydides sets out to explain the origins of the Peloponnesian War, a modern reader is not satisfied that he has done so. We do not feel that he "has told us all that we want to know, or all that he knew and, if he had considered it relevant, might have told." Cornford traces the difficulty to Thucydides' failure to distinguish between the true causes of an event and the claims by the participants as to what motivated them. "There is in Thucydidean Greek no word which even approaches the meaning and associations of the English 'cause,' with its correlative 'effect.'" Thucydides simply did not conceive of his task as consisting of the sort of explanation we demand, and the first book "is not an analysis of causes, but the story of a quarrel." "The great contrast, in fact, between ancient and modern history is this: that whereas the moderns instinctively and incessantly seek for the operation of social conditions, of economic and topological factors, and of political forces and processes of evolution, — all of which elements they try to bring under laws, as general and abstract as possible; the ancients looked simply and solely to the feelings, motives, characters of individuals or of cities. These, and (apart from supernatural agencies) these only, appeared to them to shape the course of human history." *Id.* at 66.

Cornford then pursues the two questions he has implicitly raised: what were the true causes of the war? And what did Thucydides think he was doing if it was not what we should call the discovery of causes? In response to the first question, Cornford somewhat tentatively claims that the cause was economic pressure for imperialist expansion, particularly for the conquest of Sicily, coming from the commercial class in the Piraeus upon whom Pericles depended for political support — a conclusion I am not competent to judge. His response to the second is more complex and perhaps more interesting to us: the *History*, says Cornford, is in purpose and structure closer to Aeschylean tragic drama than to what we call history. The theme is the traditional tragic one: the destruction that follows insolent pride. Cornford finds all sorts of evidence of this artistic conception, especially in the highly generic and moral characterization of important figures — *e.g.*, "Cleon, the most violent of the citizens and the first in the people's confidence," whose dramatic function is to persuade the people into rash action by exciting false hopes — and in the Sicilian expedition itself, the final act of tragic madness. The Melian dialogue, of which you have read the beginning (page 843 above), is designed to express the pathological insolence and blindness that leads one on to destruction. This conception of the work is manifest in the speeches too: when Alcibiades urges the Sicilian expedition on the Athenians, he begins his speech with a most boastful defense of his own magnificence and greatness. The significance of this is that the speech is not meant to record what he said or might have said — surely he would not actually have spoken so offensively — but to portray a certain psychology, a frame of mind or motive, a blind confidence, to reveal what he would have hidden. Thucydides uses dramatic irony and prophecy in his speeches very much as a tragic dramatist might.

Whether Cornford's version of Thucydides' *History* is accepted or rejected, it is significant enough for our purposes that the claim outlined above could seriously be made. And such a claim could be made about other histories as well: might one not make a somewhat similar claim that the sort of scientific history of which Cornford approves is also "mythological"? Exactly how are the "economic forces" which Cornford calls the "causes" of the war different from the stated and felt motives of the people who made up the commercial class? (That is, assuming with Cornford that such a class, with such motives, did in fact exist and constitute the group to which Pericles owed his position.) One might well hear it said today that it would be more sensible and valuable, more sophisticated, to attempt to give an accurate "account of the quarrel" that preceded the war than to seek to "discover its causes" and the "laws" under which they operate. Might one go further and say that it is not wholly illegitimate for a historian to seek to find the sort of meaning in events, to express the feelings, that Thucydides does?

Is history then to be regarded as indistinguishable — except perhaps for matters of accident and technique — from the literature of fiction, from the drama and the novel? There are, as we have seen, senses in which each form can be said to be true, and each fictional. Yet surely there is some difference between what might be called historical truth and poetic or philosophical truth. History can be said to have its own standards and aims. It makes sense to say that the inspired representation of "the soul of an age" (as in Carlyle's book, *Past and Present*) has a value less as history than as something else, to distinguish this sort of writing from historical discourse; but how are such distinctions to be expressed? What are the aims and standards of history, and how do they differ from those of fiction and the drama?

Where do we leave the historian, then, faced with his two sorts of language, with the discourses of data and fairy tale? Can he perhaps put them to work together, at once claiming a meaning and expressing a qualification, making a statement that recognizes its limits, that is as self-regarding and self-critical as a poem can be? Can historical narrative make its object the momentary reconciliation of the inconsistent demands of reality and imagination? Can legal narrative do the same?

Can it perhaps be said of the work of the historian and the lawyer what Wallace Stevens says of poetry? "There is, in fact, a world of poetry indistinguishable from the world in which we live, or, I ought to say, no doubt, from the world in which we shall come to live, since what makes the poet the potent figure that he is, or was, or ought to be, is that he creates the world to which we turn incessantly and without knowing it and that he gives to life the supreme fictions without which we are unable to conceive of it." ("The Noble Rider and the Sound of Words," in *The Necessary Angel* 3, 31 (1942).)

3. *The Creative (the Delusive?) Imagination*

As the preceding passage from Wallace Stevens makes clear, any talk about reconciling the demands of the imagination and of reality should somehow recognize that the line between them is at least partially false, that our most important realities are also fictions. But if the language by which we define ourselves and our relations, if the language of the law itself, is fictional in its essence, how — by what terms, what standards — can we distinguish one statement from another, how can we express our admiration and approval and the reverse? There are differences between the constitution of Brook Farm and the Constitution of the United States, between a passage by Dickens and a judicial opinion, but how shall they be articulated?

Following are four passages on the creative and delusive imagination.

THE HISTORY OF THE DECLINE AND FALL OF THE ROMAN EMPIRE*

Edward Gibbon

[The Emperor Pertinax has just been killed by the Praetorian Guard, the picked troops upon whose power the emperor depended. "Such formidable servants are always necessary, but often fatal to the throne of despotism." A near relation, Sulpicianus, has begun to argue for the throne. But "the more prudent of the Praetorians, apprehensive that, in this private contract, they should not obtain a just price for so valuable a commodity, ran out upon the ramparts; and, with a loud voice, proclaimed that the Roman world was to be disposed of to the best bidder by public auction."]

This infamous offer, the most insolent excess of military license, diffused a universal grief, shame, and indignation throughout the city. It reached at length the ears of Didius Julianus, a wealthy senator, who, regardless of the public calamities, was indulging himself in the luxury of the table. His wife and his daughter, his freedmen and his parasites, easily convinced him that he deserved the throne, and earnestly conjured him to embrace so fortunate an opportunity. The vain old man

* Chapter 5 (1776).

hastened to the Praetorian camp, where Sulpicianus was still in treaty with the guards, and began to bid against him from the foot of the rampart. The unworthy negotiation was transacted by faithful emissaries, who passed alternately from one candidate to the other, and acquainted each of them with the offers of his rival. Sulpicianus had already promised a donative of five thousand drachms (above one hundred and sixty pounds) to each soldier; when Julian, eager for the prize, rose at once to the sum of six thousand two hundred and fifty drachms, or upwards of two hundred pounds sterling. The gates of the camp were instantly thrown open to the purchaser; he was declared emperor, and received an oath of allegiance from the soldiers, who retained humanity enough to stipulate that he should pardon and forget the competition of Sulpicianus.

It was now incumbent on the Praetorians to fulfil the conditions of the sale. They placed their new sovereign, whom they served and despised, in the centre of their ranks, surrounded him on every side with their shields, and conducted him in close order of battle through the deserted streets of the city. The senate was commanded to assemble; and those who had been the distinguished friends of Pertinax, or the personal enemies of Julian, found it necessary to affect a more than common share of satisfaction at this happy revolution. After Julian had filled the senate-house with armed soldiers, he expatiated on the freedom of his election, his own eminent virtues, and his full assurance of the affections of the senate. The obsequious assembly congratulated their own and the public felicity; engaged their allegiance, and conferred on him all the several branches of the imperial power. From the senate Julian was conducted by the same military procession to take possession of the palace. The first objects that struck his eyes were the abandoned trunk of Pertinax, and the frugal entertainment prepared for his supper. The one he viewed with indifference; the other with contempt. A magnificent feast was prepared by his order, and he amused himself till a very late hour with dice and the performances of Pylades, a celebrated dancer. Yet it was observed that, after the crowd of flatterers dispersed, and left him to darkness, solitude, and terrible reflection, he passed a sleepless night; revolving most probably in his mind his own rash folly, the fate of his virtuous predecessor, and the doubtful and dangerous tenure of an empire which had not been acquired by merit, but purchased by money.

He had reason to tremble. On the throne of the world he found himself without a friend, and even without an adherent. The guards themselves were ashamed of the prince whom their avarice had persuaded them to accept; nor was there a citizen who did not consider his elevation with horror, as the last insult on the Roman name. The nobility, whose conspicuous station and ample possessions exacted the strictest caution, dissembled their sentiments and met the affected civility of the emperor with smiles of complacency and professions of duty. But the people, secure in their numbers and obscurity, gave a free vent to their passions. The streets and public places of Rome resounded with clamors and imprecations. The enraged multitude affronted the person of Julian, rejected his liberality, and, conscious of the impotence of their own resentment, they called aloud on the legions of the frontiers to assert the violated majesty of the Roman empire.

The public discontent was soon diffused from the centre to the frontiers of the empire. The armies of Britain, of Syria, and of Illyricum lamented the death of Pertinax, in whose company, or under whose command, they had so often fought and conquered. They received with surprise, with indignation, and perhaps with envy, the extraordinary intelligence that the Praetorians had disposed of the empire by public auction, and they sternly refused to ratify the ignominious bargain. Their immediate and unanimous revolt was fatal to Julian, but it was fatal at the same time to the public peace; as the generals of the respective armies, Clodius Albinus, Pescennius Niger, and Septimius Severus, were still more anxious to succeed than to revenge the murdered Pertinax. Their forces were exactly balanced. Each of them was at the head of three legions, with a numerous train of auxiliaries; and however different in their characters, they were all soldiers of experience and capacity.

[Clodius Albinus in Britain and Pescennius Niger in Syria both declared against Julian. But there was a nearer danger, in Pannonia and Dalmatia, the area between the Danube and the Adriatic.]

The Pannonian army was at this time commanded by Septimius Severus, a native of Africa, who, in the gradual ascent of private honors, had concealed his daring ambition, which was never diverted from its steady course by the allurements of pleasure, the apprehension of danger, or the feelings of humanity. On the first news of the murder of Pertinax he assembled his troops, painted in the most lively colors the crime, the insolence, and the weakness of the Praetorian guards, and animated the legions to arms and to revenge. He concluded (and the peroration was thought extremely eloquent) with promising every soldier about four hundred pounds; an honorable donative, double in value to the infamous bribe with which Julian had purchased the empire. The acclamations of the army immediately saluted Severus with the names of Augustus, Pertinax, and Emperor; and he thus attained the lofty station to which he was invited by conscious merit and a long train of dreams and omens, the fruitful offspring either of his superstition or policy.

The new candidate for empire saw and improved the peculiar advantage of his situation. His province extended to the Julian Alps, which gave an easy access into Italy; and he remembered the saying of Augustus, that a Pannonian army might in ten days appear in sight of Rome. By a celerity proportioned to the greatness of the occasion, he might reasonably hope to revenge Pertinax, punish Julian, and receive the homage of the senate and people as their lawful emperor, before his competitors, separated from Italy by an immense tract of sea and land, were apprised of his success, or even of his election. During the whole expedition he scarcely allowed himself any moments for sleep or food; marching on foot, and in complete armor, at the head of his columns, he insinuated himself into the confidence and affection of his troops, pressed their diligence, revived their spirits, animated their hopes, and was well satisfied to share the hardships of the meanest soldier, whilst he kept in view the infinite superiority of his reward.

The wretched Julian had expected, and thought himself prepared, to dispute the empire with the Governor of Syria; but in the invincible and rapid approach of the Pannonian legions he saw his inevitable ruin. The hasty arrival of every messenger increased his just apprehensions. He was successively informed that Severus had passed the Alps; that the Italian cities, unwilling or unable to oppose his progress, had received him with the warmest professions of joy and duty; that the important place of Ravenna had surrendered without resistance, and that the Hadriatic fleet was in the hands of the conqueror. The enemy was now within two hundred and fifty miles of Rome, and every moment diminished the narrow span of life and empire allotted to Julian.

He attempted, however, to prevent, or at least to protract, his ruin. He implored the venal faith of the Praetorians, filled the city with unavailing preparations for war, drew lines round the suburbs, and even strengthened the fortifications of the palace; as if those last intrenchments could be defended, without hope of relief, against a victorious invader. Fear and shame prevented the guards from deserting his standard; but they trembled at the name of the Pannonian legions, commanded by an experienced general, and accustomed to vanquish the barbarians on the frozen Danube. They quitted, with a sigh, the pleasures of the baths and theatres, to put on arms whose use they had almost forgotten, and beneath the weight of which they were oppressed. The unpractised elephants, whose uncouth appearance, it was hoped, would strike terror into the army of the North, threw their unskilful riders; and the awkward evolutions of the marines, drawn from the fleet of Misenum, were an object of ridicule to the populace; whilst the senate enjoyed, with secret pleasure, the distress and weakness of the usurper.

Every motion of Julian betrayed his trembling perplexity. He insisted that Severus should be declared a public enemy by the senate. He entreated that the Pannonian general might be associated to the empire. He sent public ambassadors of consular rank to negotiate with his rival; he despatched private assassins to take away his life. He designed that the Vestal Virgins, and all the colleges of priests, in their sacerdotal habits, and bearing before them the sacred pledges of the Roman religion, should advance in solemn procession to meet the Pannonian legions; and, at the same time, he vainly tried to interrogate, or to appease, the fates, by magic ceremonies and unlawful sacrifices.

Severus, who dreaded neither his arms nor his enchantments, guarded himself from the only danger of secret conspiracy by the faithful attendance of six hundred chosen men, who never quitted his person or their cuirasses, either by night or by day, during the whole march. Advancing with a steady and rapid course, he passed, without difficulty, the defiles of the Apennine, received into his party the troops and ambassadors sent to retard his progress, and made a short halt at Interamna, about seventy miles from Rome. His victory was already secure, but the despair of the Praetorians might have rendered it bloody; and Severus had the laudable ambition of ascending the throne without drawing the sword. His emissaries, dispersed in the capital, assured the guards that, provided they would abandon their worthless prince, and the perpetrators of the murder of Pertinax, to the justice of the conqueror, he would no longer consider that melancholy event as the act of the whole body. The faithless Praetorians, whose resistance was supported only by sullen obstinacy, gladly complied with the easy conditions, seized the greatest part of the assassins, and signified to the senate that they no longer defended the cause of Julian. That assembly, convoked by the consul, unanimously acknowledged Severus as lawful emperor, decreed divine honors to Pertinax, and pronounced a sentence of deposition and death against his unfortunate successor. Julian was conducted into a private apartment of the baths of the palace and beheaded as a common criminal, after having purchased, with an immense treasure, an anxious and precarious reign of only sixty-six days.

REFLECTIONS ON THE REVOLUTION IN FRANCE*

Edmund Burke

I have often been astonished, considering that we are divided from you but by a slender dike of about twenty-four miles, and that the mutual intercourse between the two countries has lately been very great, to find how little you seem to know of us. I suspect that this is owing to your forming a judgment of this nation from certain publications, which do,

* In *Works*, III, 343–348, 356–360 (1790; Beaconsfield ed. 1901).

very erroneously, if they do at all, represent the opinions and dispositions generally prevalent in England. The vanity, restlessness, petulance, and spirit of intrigue of several petty cabals, who attempt to hide their total want of consequence in bustle and noise, and puffing and mutual quotation of each other, makes you imagine that our contemptuous neglect of their abilities is a general mark of acquiescence in their opinions. No such thing, I assure you. Because half a dozen grasshoppers under a fern make the field ring with their importunate chink, whilst thousands of great cattle reposed beneath the shadow of the British oak chew the cud and are silent, pray do not imagine that those who make the noise are the only inhabitants of the field, — that, of course, they are many in number, — or that, after all, they are other than the little, shrivelled, meagre, hopping, though loud and troublesome insects of the hour.

I almost venture to affirm that not one in a hundred amongst us participates in the "triumph" of the Revolution Society. If the king and queen of France and their children were to fall into our hands by the chance of war, in the most acrimonious of all hostilities, (I deprecate such an event, I deprecate such hostility,) they would be treated with another sort of triumphal entry into London. We formerly have had a king of France in that situation: you have read how he was treated by the victor in the field, and in what manner he was afterwards received in England. Four hundred years have gone over us; but I believe we are not materially changed since that period. Thanks to our sullen resistance to innovation, thanks to the cold sluggishness of our national character, we still bear the stamp of our forefathers. We have not (as I conceive) lost the generosity and dignity of thinking of the fourteenth century; nor as yet have we subtilized ourselves into savages. We are not the converts of Rousseau; we are not the disciples of Voltaire; Helvetius has made no progress amongst us. Atheists are not our preachers; madmen are not our lawgivers. We know that *we* have made no discoveries, and we think that no discoveries are to be made, in morality, — nor many in the great principles of government, nor in the ideas of liberty, which were understood long before we were born altogether as well as they will be after the grave has heaped its mould upon our presumption, and the silent tomb shall have imposed its law on our pert loquacity. In England we have not yet been completely embowelled of our natural entrails: we still feel within us, and we cherish and cultivate, those inbred sentiments which are the faithful guardians, the active monitors of our duty, the true supporters of all liberal and manly morals. We have not been drawn and trussed, in order that we may be filled, like stuffed birds in a museum, with chaff and rags, and paltry, blurred shreds of paper about the rights of man. We preserve the whole of our feelings still native and entire, unsophisticated by pedantry and infidelity. We have real hearts of flesh and blood beating in our bosoms. We fear God; we look up with awe to kings, with affection to Parliaments, with duty to magistrates, with reverence to priests, and with respect to nobility. Why? Because, when such ideas are brought before our minds, it is *natural* to be so affected; because all other feelings are false and spurious, and tend to corrupt our minds, to vitiate our primary morals, to render us unfit for rational liberty, and, by teaching us a servile, licentious, and abandoned insolence, to be our low sport for a few holidays, to make us perfectly fit for and justly deserving of slavery through the whole course of our lives.

You see, Sir, that in this enlightened age I am bold enough to confess that we are generally men of untaught feelings: that, instead of casting away all our old prejudices, we cherish them to a very considerable degree; and, to take more shame to ourselves, we cherish them because they are prejudices; and the longer they have lasted, and the more generally they have prevailed, the more we cherish them. We are afraid to put men to live and trade each on his own private stock of reason; because we suspect that the stock in each man is small, and that the individuals would do better to avail themselves of the general bank and capital of nations and of ages. Many of our men of speculation, instead of exploding general prejudices, employ their sagacity to discover the latent wisdom which prevails in them. If they find what they seek, (and they seldom fail,) they think it more wise to continue the prejudice, with the reason involved, than to cast away the coat of prejudice, and to leave nothing but the naked reason; because prejudice, with its reason, has a motive to give action to that reason, and an affection which will give it permanence. Prejudice is of ready application in the emergency; it previously engages the mind in a steady course of wisdom and virtue, and does not leave the man hesitating in the moment of decision, skeptical, puzzled, and unresolved. Prejudice renders a man's virtue his habit, and not a series of unconnected acts. Through just prejudice, his duty becomes a part of his nature.

Your literary men, and your politicians, and so do the whole clan of the enlightened among us, essentially differ in these points. They have no respect for the wisdom of others; but they pay it off by a very full measure of confidence in their own. With them it is a sufficient motive to destroy an old scheme of things, because it is an old one. As to the new, they are in no sort of fear with regard to the duration of a building run up in haste; because duration is no object to those who think little or nothing has been done before their time, and who place all their hopes in discovery. They conceive, very systematically, that all things which give perpetuity are mischievous, and therefore they are at inexpiable war with all establishments. They think that government may vary like modes of dress, and with as little ill effect; that there needs no principle of attachment, except a sense of present conveniency, to any constitution of the state. They always speak as if they were of opinion that there is a singular species of compact between them and their magistrates, which binds the magistrate, but which has nothing reciprocal in it, but that the majesty of the people has a right to dissolve it without any reason but its will. Their attachment to their country itself is only so far as it agrees with some of their fleeting projects: it begins and ends with that scheme of polity which falls in with their momentary opinion.

These doctrines, or rather sentiments, seem prevalent with your new statesmen. But they are wholly different from those on which we have always acted in this country. . . .

[One] of the first and most leading principles on which the commonwealth and the laws are consecrated is lest the temporary possessors and life-renters in it, unmindful of what they have received from their ancestors, or of what is due to their posterity, should act as if they were the entire masters; that they should not think it amongst their rights to cut off the entail or commit waste on the inheritance, by destroying at their pleasure the whole original fabric of their society: hazarding to leave to those who come after them a ruin instead of an habitation,— and teaching these successors as little to respect their contrivances as they had themselves respected the institutions of their forefathers. By this unprincipled facility of changing the state as often and as much and in as many ways as there are floating fancies or fashions, the whole chain and continuity of the commonwealth would be broken; no one generation could link with the other; men would become little better than the flies of a summer.

And first of all, the science of jurisprudence, the pride of the human intellect, which, with all its defects, redundancies, and errors, is the collected reason of ages, combining the principles of original justice with the infinite variety of human concerns, as a heap of old exploded errors, would be no longer studied. Personal self-sufficiency and arrogance (the certain attendants upon all those who have never experienced a wisdom greater than their own) would usurp the tribunal. Of course no certain laws, establishing invariable grounds of hope and fear, would keep the actions of men in a certain course, or direct them to a certain end. Nothing stable in the modes of holding property or exercising function could form a solid ground on which any parent could speculate in the education of his offspring, or in a choice for their future establishment in the world. No principles would be early worked into the habits. As soon as the most able instructor had completed his laborious course of institution, instead of sending forth his pupil accomplished in a virtuous discipline fitted to procure him attention and respect in his place in society, he would find everything altered, and that he had turned out a poor creature to the contempt and derision of the world, ignorant of the true grounds of estimation. Who would insure a tender and delicate sense of honor to beat almost with the first pulses of the heart, when no man could know what would be the test of honor in a nation continually varying the standard of its coin? No part of life would retain its acquisitions. Barbarism with regard to science and literature, unskilfulness with regard to arts and manufactures, would infallibly succeed to the want of a steady education and settled principle; and thus the commonwealth itself would in a few generations crumble away, be disconnected into the dust and powder of individuality, and at length dispersed to all the winds of heaven.

To avoid, therefore, the evils of inconstancy and versatility, ten thousand times worse than those of obstinacy and the blindest prejudice, we have consecrated the state, that no man should approach to look into its defects or corruptions but with due caution; that he should never dream of beginning its reformation by its subversion; that he should approach to the faults of the state as to the wounds of a father, with pious awe and trembling solicitude. By this wise prejudice we are taught to look with horror on those children of their country who are prompt rashly to hack that aged parent in pieces and put him into the kettle of magicians, in hopes that by their poisonous weeds and wild incantations they may regenerate the paternal constitution and renovate their father's life.

Society is, indeed, a contract. Subordinate contracts for objects of mere occasional interest may be dissolved at pleasure; but the state ought not to be considered as nothing better than a partnership agreement in a trade of pepper and coffee, calico or tobacco, or some other such low concern, to be taken up for a little temporary interest, and to be dissolved by the fancy of the parties. It is to be looked on with other reverence; because it is not a partnership in things subservient only to the gross animal existence of a temporary and perishable nature. It is a partnership in all science, a partnership in all art, a partnership in every virtue and in all perfection. As the ends of such a partnership cannot be obtained in many generations, it becomes a partnership not only between those who are living, but between those who are living, those who are dead, and those who are to be born. Each contract of each particular state is but a clause in the great primeval contract of eternal society, linking the lower with the higher natures, connecting the visible and invisible world, according to a fixed compact sanctioned by the inviolable oath which holds all physical and all moral natures each in their appointed place. This law is not subject to the will of those who, by an obligation above them, and infinitely superior, are bound to submit their will to that law. The municipal corporations of that universal kingdom are not morally at liberty, at their pleasure, and on their speculations of a contingent improvement, wholly to separate and tear asunder the bands of their subordinate community, and to dissolve it into an unsocial, uncivil, unconnected chaos of elementary principles. It is the first and supreme necessity only, a necessity that is not chosen, but chooses, a necessity paramount to deliberation, that admits no discussion and demands no evidence, which alone can justify a resort to anarchy. This necessity is no exception to the rule; because this necessity itself is a part, too, of that moral and physical disposition of things to which man must be obedient by consent or force: but if that which is only submission to necessity should be made the object of choice, the law is broken, Nature is disobeyed, and the rebellious are outlawed, cast forth, and exiled, from this world of reason, and order, and peace, and virtue, and fruitful penitence, into the antagonist world of madness, discord, vice, confusion, and unavailing sorrow.

These, my dear Sir, are, were, and, I think, long will be, the sentiments of not the least learned and reflecting part of this kingdom.

QUESTIONS

1. *Burke here tells us what Englishmen believe. How does he know what they believe?*
2. *Look at the substance of the beliefs: are they true? False? How then would you characterize them?*
3. *Burke locates wisdom and value in the past, in the inherited public estate. If you were to try to support Burke's view of the past, where would you look for evidence and proof? What century, what place in English history fits his description? He speaks of the fourteenth century: do you believe that the British Constitution, British values, were then in existence? What does Burke mean when he speaks of the past? Is what he says of it true or false?*
4. *Below is a poem that deals directly with the way imagination works upon the world of public fact and reality, one that addresses the limits of our capacities to understand and to judge. As you read this, ask whether Marvell is expressing approval or disapproval of Cromwell, and why.*[18]

AN HORATIAN ODE UPON CROMWELL'S RETURN FROM IRELAND

Andrew Marvell

The forward youth that would appear
Must now forsake his Muses dear,
    Nor in the shadows sing
    His numbers languishing.

18. A book dealing well with some of the general questions raised here, and with this poem in particular, is T. Edwards, *Imagination and Power* (1971).

'Tis time to leave the books in dust,
And oil the unused armour's rust,
    Removing from the wall
    The corslet of the hall.

So restless Cromwell could not cease
In the inglorious arts of peace,
    But through adventurous war
    Urgèd his active star:

And like the three-fork'd lightning, first
Breaking the clouds where it was nurst,
    Did thorough his own side
    His fiery way divide:

For 'tis all one to courage high,
The emulous, or enemy;
    And with such, to enclose
    Is more than to oppose.

Then burning through the air he went
And palaces and temples rent;
    And Caesar's head at last
    Did through his laurels blast.

'Tis madness to resist or blame
The face of angry Heaven's flame;
    And if we would speak true,
    Much to the man is due,

Who, from his private gardens, where
He lived reservèd and austere
    (As if his highest plot
    To plant the bergamot),

Could by industrious valour climb
To ruin the great work of time,
    And cast the Kingdoms old
    Into another mould;

Though Justice against Fate complain,
And plead the ancient rights in vain —
    But those do hold or break
    As men are strong or weak —

Nature, that hateth emptiness,
Allows of penetration less,
And therefore must make room
Where greater spirits come.

What field of all the civil war
Where his were not the deepest scar?
And Hampton shows what part
He had of wiser art;

Where, twining subtle fears with hope,
He wove a net of such a scope
That Charles himself might chase
To Carisbrook's narrow case;

That thence the Royal actor borne
The tragic scaffold might adorn:
While round the armed bands
Did clap their bloody hands.

He nothing common did or mean
Upon that memorable scene,
But with his keener eye
The axe's edge did try;

Nor call'd the Gods, with vulgar spite,
To vindicate his helpless right;
But bow'd his comely head
Down, as upon a bed.

This was that memorable hour
Which first assured the forced power:
So when they did design
The Capitol's first line,

A Bleeding Head, where they begun,
Did fright the architects to run;
And yet in that the State
Foresaw its happy fate!

And now the Irish are ashamed
To see themselves in one year tamed:
So much one man can do
That does both act and know.

They can affirm his praises best,
And have, though overcome, confest
 How good he is, how just
 And fit for highest trust;

Nor yet grown stiffer with command,
But still in the Republic's hand —
 How fit he is to sway
 That can so well obey!

He to the Commons' feet presents
A Kingdom for his first year's rents,
 And, what he may, forbears
 His fame, to make it theirs:

And has his sword and spoils ungirt
To lay them at the public's skirt.
 So when the falcon high
 Falls heavy from the sky,

She, having kill'd, no more does search
But on the next green bough to perch,
 Where, when he first does lure,
 The falconer has her sure.

What may not then our Isle presume
While victory his crest does plume?
 What may not others fear,
 If thus he crowns each year?

As Caesar he, ere long, to Gaul,
To Italy an Hannibal,
 And to all States not free
 Shall climacteric be.

The Pict no shelter now shall find
Within his particolour'd mind,
 But, from this valour, sad
 Shrink underneath the plaid,

Happy, if in the tufted brake
The English hunter him mistake,
 Nor lay his hounds in near
 The Caledonian deer.

But thou, the War's and Fortune's son,
March indefatigably on;
    And for the last effect,
    Still keep the sword erect:

Besides the force it has to fright
The spirits of the shady night,
    The same arts that did gain
    A power, must it maintain.

QUESTIONS

1. *Does Marvell approve or disapprove of Cromwell? How do you know or decide?*
   a. *Why does Marvell call Cromwell's achievement the "ruin" of the "great work of time"?*
   b. *How does he characterize the death of Charles?*
   c. *Yet can you find phrases and moments here in which he praises Cromwell?*
   d. *Why does he not take a more clearly defined position, and what purpose has his ambiguity?*
2. *Is the power that is celebrated here the power of arms? Or of the imagination? Or are they in some sense indistinguishable? (Which is the power of the "sword"?)*
3. *Following is the fourth passage about the delusive and creative imagination. Has it any parallel in the law?*

THE ALCHEMIST (1612)
Ben Jonson

[Sir Epicure Mammon explains what he will do with the wealth that he has been promised by certain seventeenth-century con men.]

I will have all my beds blown up, not stuffed;
Down is too hard: and then, mine oval room
Filled with such pictures as Tiberius took
From Elephantis, and dull Aretine
But coldly imitated. Then, my glasses
Cut in more subtle angles, to disperse
And multiply the figures, as I walk
Naked between my succubae. My mists
I'll have of perfume, vapoured 'bout the room,
To lose our selves in; and my baths, like pits
To fall into; from whence we will come forth,
And roll us dry in gossamer and roses.—
Is it arrived at ruby? —— Where I spy

A wealthy citizen, or [a] rich lawyer,
Have a sublimed pure wife, unto that fellow
I'll send a thousand pound to be my cuckold.
Face. And I shall carry it?
Mammon. No. I'll have no bawds
But fathers and mothers: they will do it best,
Best of all others. And my flatterers
Shall be the pure and gravest of divines,
That I can get for money. My mere fools,
Eloquent burgesses, and then my poets
The same that writ so subtly of the fart,
Whom I will entertain still for that subject.
The few that would give out themselves to be
Court and town-stallions, and, each-where, bely
Ladies who are known most innocent, for them;
Those will I beg, to make me eunuchs of:
And they shall fan me with ten estrich tails
A-piece, made in a plume to gather wind.
We will be brave, Puffe, now we have the med'cine.
My meat shall all come in, in Indian shells,
Dishes of agat set in gold, and studded
With emeralds, sapphires, hyacinths, and rubies.
The tongues of carps, dormice, and camels' heels,
Boiled in the spirit of sol, and dissolved pearl,
Apicius' diet, 'gainst the epilepsy:
And I will eat these broths with spoons of amber,
Headed with diamond and carbuncle.
My foot-boy shall eat pheasants, calvered salmons,
Knots, godwits, lampreys: I myself will have
The beards of barbel served, instead of salads;
Oiled mushrooms; and the swelling unctuous paps
Of a fat pregnant sow, newly cut off,
Drest with an exquisite and poignant sauce;
For which, I'll say unto my cook, *There's gold,*
Go forth, and be a knight.

4. *Placing the Private Self in a Narrative of the Public World: Clarendon's History of the Rebellion*

There follows now a rather extended account of a historian's mind at work, a detailed demonstration of the ways in which one writer has faced and dealt with the difficulties of making a narrative about the real world. I hope to point to Clarendon's *History* as a success, as an example of what the historian can achieve when he addresses the tensions we have been discussing (between story and theory, between reality and the imagination), of which we can ask: "Can the lawyer do what he does?" But the *History* has an interest for us beyond this, since a primary concern of Clarendon's book (as of this one) is the disparity between one's own experience and the public world. The place of the individual in history, of character in narrative — the tension between private and public ways of talking — is as central to his subject as it has been to ours. The similarities of concern go even further: this is a history of the Civil Wars in England written by a man who had immense experience of the events he speaks of, who was in some ways the chief man in England under both Charles I and his son, and who was by training and in attitude very much a lawyer. Here the man of experience tries to explain what he has seen, to organize his life; and this book is, in its way, just what we have been looking for since the beginning of the course. As you shall see, it is altogether different from the modern self-congratulatory memoir. I know of nothing comparable — it offers its reader an education of its own — and it can serve, if you wish it to, as the occasion for summing up what you have done in this course.

As you read the account of it that follows, compare the *History* with what you know of modern public and historical talk — for example, presidential addresses and debates, books on modern history and society, articles in journals of social criticism, and the like. This is a subject as to which you must make your own perceptions and judgments, but in the next paragraph I sketch my own sense of what I hear around us.

Much of our enormous literature of politics and society seems to be written with an impossible confidence (an "overconfidence") in a simple vocabulary, as though to those who listened and received its truths it would explain all. Standing outside, above, the commentator observes and tells us what he sees — social forces, dynamics, trends, models, interactions, groups — speaking always in the language of social problem and solution, using the ultimate metaphor of the machine, with the constant implication that things can be made to work. Out of such a language a political discourse is made up, a discourse that has at its center an absurd and impossible promise of happiness. If you ask, "What is my place in all this?" you are answered by silence; the question does not fit. Or perhaps you are told that because you are young or black or a student, your place is this or that, you are offered another set of promises in other terms, a revolutionary dream. But you know that to see yourself solely in such terms as those would be a form of madness. As a citizen, of course, one is free to turn away, to have nothing to do with all that, and we have a literature of rejection expressing such a response. The public person — a candidate for office — has another resource, the advertising language of personality, upon which he may draw if he can stand it. But to place the self in the public world, to find a way of talking at once about ourselves as we know ourselves and about our society — that is beyond us all.

Or so it seems; whether you can in fact find or make a literature, a way of talking, that unites public and private experience has been a central question in this course. And whatever your present feelings of optimism or the reverse, I assume you will be eager to see how this man of experience tries, in his account of his times, to reconcile what have seemed to us so often to be hopelessly disparate sides of life.

In what follows we consider first Clarendon's narrative art — the form and meaning he gives his story, the way he addresses the difficulties of historical narrative — and then ask how he combines public and private concerns, what place he makes for the private self in the public world.

a. The Narrative

In his book — whose original title was *A True Historical Narration of the Rebellion and Civil Wars in England* — Edward Hyde, the First Earl of Clarendon, gives an account of his world falling apart and coming together again, of the Civil War and Restoration, in which he expresses quite a different understanding of the world, quite a different sense of the relation between public and private experience, from anything we should expect today. While it is my purpose to show how this achievement can be admired, I should perhaps begin by mentioning a characteristic that modern historians sometimes find disturbingly foreign to their purposes: Clarendon was a constant actor in the struggle he tells us of — first on the side of Parliament against the royalist abuses, then against the Parliament when it assumed sovereign power — and his *History* is that of a partisan, of one who feels the events to be charged with meaning and emotion as only one who had lived through them could do. He writes not to put the facts on the laboratory table for analysis by later historians, but to express his own judgments on the events he speaks of. Not that this is party propaganda; as you can see, Clarendon himself switched sides — in fact, neither side was as thoroughly constitutionalist as he — and his judgments about people and policies are remarkably fair, characterized by a great disposition to find fault on the king's side and an occasional willingness to find merit on the other.[19] But the book is one of judgment, suffused with his feelings

19. You will remember, for example, his fairness towards Essex, who was the chief general of the rebels, both in the account given of his character, page 307 *supra*, and in his readiness to deny a rumor of dishonorable conduct in connection with the treatment of the wounded Lindsey, page 107 *supra*.

of loyalty, of respect for the constitution, and so on. However much these qualities of partisanship may disconcert the professional historian — and whether they should do so at all is not a simple question — you personally may find that they give the work a special appeal, for here Clarendon does what you have been asked to do throughout this course: he looks out upon a world of which he has practical experience and about which he has thought, and he tries to make sense of what he sees. But judgment on this matter should in any event be suspended until the reader knows the author's mind better and understands the terms upon which the *History* it offers us is to be read, until he appreciates the book's purposes and structure.

(*1*) *The Purposes.* Although Clarendon is in method and judgment not a modern scientific historian, he states his purposes in terms that seem familiar to us. He seeks to explain what he regards as an enormous public catastrophe, and tells us very early what sort of explanation he offers:

> [T]hough the hand and judgment of God will be very visible, in the infatuating a people (as ripe and prepared for destruction) into all the perverse actions of folly and madness, making the weak to contribute to the designs of the wicked, and suffering even those by degrees, out of the conscience of their guilt, to grow more wicked than they intended to be; letting the wise to be imposed upon by men of no understanding, and possessing the innocent with laziness and sleep in the most visible article of danger; uniting the ill, though of the most different opinions, divided interests, and distant affections, in a firm and constant league of mischief; and dividing those whose opinions and interests are the same into faction and emulation, more pernicious to the public than the treason of the others; . . . I say, though the immediate finger and wrath of God must be acknowledged in these perplexities and distractions, yet he who shall diligently observe the distempers and conjunctures of time, the ambition, pride, and folly of persons, and the sudden growth of wickedness, from want of care and circumspection in the first impressions, will find all this bulk of misery to have proceeded, and to have been brought upon us, from the same natural causes and means which have usually attended kingdoms swoln with long plenty, pride, and excess, towards some signal mortification, and castigation of heaven. [I, 2.][20]

Clarendon here makes his claim, which will carry both him and us to the end of his book: that the appropriate explanation of the Rebellion lies in an analysis of "natural causes and means" rather than in an understanding of the "hand and judgment of God." This is a scientific

20. References are to the edition of the *History* by W. D. Macray (Oxford 1888). Roman numbers represent Books; arabic numbers, paragraphs.

argument, in its own way, but that it is very different from the social writing of today appears from his definition of what he means by "natural causes and means":

[B]y viewing the temper, disposition, and habit, of that time, of the court and of the country, we may discern the minds of men prepared, of some to do, and of others to suffer, all that hath since happened: the pride of this man, and the popularity of that; the levity of one, and the morosity of another; the excess of the court in the greatest want, and the parsimony and retention of the country in the greatest plenty; the spirit of craft and subtlety in some, and the rude and unpolished integrity of others, too much despising craft or art; like so many atoms contributing jointly to this mass of confusion now before us. [I, 4.]

This sentence tells us to expect an explanation not in terms of groups or classes of men, not in terms of "social forces," but in terms of the characters and qualities of individuals, and we get a sense of the immense variety that this side of the work will give us. But simultaneously the limits of this attempt at explanation are foreseen: all may at last be inexplicable, a "mass of confusion" that successfully resists every attempt at comprehension. At the moment when we are set out on the course of explanation, we are told that it may ultimately fail in an overwhelming complexity and proliferation of detail. And somewhere is at work the hand of God, whatever that may prove to mean. While he explains, Clarendon keeps alive a sense that this, like all explanation, must always be partial, that beyond it there is always what cannot be expressed.

The structure in which he works out these complex purposes is fundamentally a narrative one, and the next stage in understanding the *History* is to understand the experience that the narrative offers the reader, the meaning of the story as it is told.

(2) *The Story*. From the beginning, to the death of Charles, the movement of the narrative is (not surprisingly) one of increasing degeneration in public and private life, of decay and destruction. This is told as the story of the uprooting of all inherited institutions, even the Crown itself, of the demolition of all human order. The movement is in this sense rhetorical, defining for the reader a process of destruction, making him feel a sense of loss.

The narrative begins by marking a point on a scale by which we can measure the collapse as it occurs, a position not of perfection but of tolerable strain: the effective usurpation of royal power by the Duke of Buckingham, the favorite of James I. The consequences were disastrous: out of a jealous whim, Buckingham frustrated the marriage of Charles with Maria, daughter of the king of Spain, precipitating a fruitless and costly war; he led Parliament to exceed its powers and impeach a minister unfriendly to him; and finally, to protect himself, he caused those arbitrary "dissolutions of Parliament" which were so "unseasonable, unskillful, and precipitate" and from which Clarendon says "these waters of bitterness we now taste" have flowed. (I, 6.) But what is remarkable is that all this — even the lengthy dissolution of Parliament — is defined by Clarendon (himself a firm defender of Parliament) as no calamity, but as a sort of normalcy, a deviation that could be sustained with little cost:

> I must be so just as to say, that, during the whole time that these pressures were exercised, and those new and extraordinary ways were run, that is, from the dissolution of the Parliament in the fourth year to the beginning of this Parliament, which was above twelve years, this kingdom and all His Majesty's dominions, (— of the interruption in Scotland somewhat shall be said in its due time and place —) enjoyed the greatest calm and the fullest measure of felicity that any people in any age for so long time together have been blessed with; to the wonder and envy of all the parts of Christendom. [I, 159.]

Parliament of course made proper and lawful resistance to the absolutist claims of the king, and the tragedy that forms the next unit of the narrative is the process by which this movement — in which Clarendon was at first a leader — became, through the plots of revolutionaries and the carelessness of loyalists, a destructive one, culminating in the subversion and corruption of Parliament itself, the end of all legitimate government. This process is explained in the manner promised to us: Clarendon portrays in great detail the attitudes and skills of the rebellious, and the ineptitude and slackness of the friends of the king and of the Constitution, as they work themselves out in event after event. The king's exercise of his power to dissolve the Short Parliament, for example, was a grave mistake: "It could never be hoped that more sober and dispassioned men would ever meet together in that place." (II, 77.) When the next Parliament was called, "There was observed a marvellous elated countenance in most of the members . . ." (III, 3.) Pym told Hyde that this time

> "they must not only sweep the house clean below, but must pull down all the cobwebs which hung in the top and corners, that they might not breed dust and make so foul a house hereafter; that they had now an opportunity to make their country happy, by the removing all grievances and pulling up the causes of them by the roots, if all men would do their duties." [III, 3.]

When Strafford, after acquittal of treason, was made the object of a bill of attainder, the king let it pass on bad advicc, "to preserve his kingdom." (III, 198.) In defense of the irregular procedure used, St. John, who directed it, said, "It was true we give law to hares and deer, because they be beasts of chase; but it was never accounted either cruelty, or foul play, to knock foxes and wolves on the head as they can be found, because they be beasts of prey." (III, 140.)

The king's friends were of uncertain loyalty and many of his ministers ill-chosen. Digby, for example, had just the wrong traits of fanciful ambition and misplaced self-confidence; and "the King himself was the unfittest person alive to be served by such a counsellor, being too easily inclined to sudden enterprises, and as easily amazed when they were entered upon." (IV, 129.) Here is Clarendon's account of Digby. (The three persons mentioned in the first sentence are Hyde, Falkland, and Colepeper, three constitutionalist friends.)

He had been instrumental in promoting the three persons above-mentioned to the King's favour, and had himself, in truth, so great an esteem of them that he did very frequently, upon conference together, depart from his own inclinations and opinions and concurred in theirs; and very few men of so great parts are, upon all occasions, more counsellable than he; so that he would seldom be in danger of running into great errors if he would communicate and expose all his own thoughts and inclinations to such a disquisition; nor is he uninclinable in his nature to such an entire communication in all things which he conceives to be difficult. But his fatal infirmity is, that he too often thinks difficult things very easy; and doth not consider possible consequences when the proposition administers somewhat that is delightful to his fancy, and by pursuing whereof he imagines he shall reap some glory to himself, of which he is immoderately ambitious; so that, if the consultation be upon any action to be done, no man more implicitly enters into that debate, or more cheerfully resigns his own conceptions to a joint determination: but when it is once affirmatively resolved, (besides that he may possibly reserve some impertinent circumstance, as he thinks, the imparting whereof would change the nature of the thing,) if his fancy suggests to him any particular which himself might perform in that action, upon the imagination that every body would approve it if it were proposed to them he chooses rather to do it than to communicate, that he may have some signal part to himself in the transaction in which no other person can claim a share. And by this unhappy temper he did often involve himself in very unprosperous attempts. [IV, 128.]

There were too few men like Falkland, who would dutifully accept an undesirable burden (IV, 124); like Hyde himself, who could engage and defeat the enemy in parliamentary skirmishing (III, 238, 240); or like

Coventry — of whom you have read at page 309 *supra* — who had the skill to be firm without arousing hostility, so that "few departed from him with ill will or ill wishes." (I, 99.) The enemy, however, were masterful:

> Mr. Hambden was a man of much greater cunning [than Pym], and it may be of the most discerning spirit and of the greatest address and insinuation to bring anything to pass which he desired of any man of that time, and who laid the design deepest. . . . He was not a man of many words, and rarely began the discourse, or made the first entrance upon any business that was assumed; but a very weighty speaker, and, after he had heard a full debate and observed how the House was like to be inclined, took up the argument, and shortly and clearly and craftily so stated it that he commonly conducted it to the conclusion he desired; and if he found he could not do that, he never was without the dexterity to divert the debate to another time, and to prevent the determining anything in the negative which might prove inconvenient in the future. He made so great a show of civility and modesty and humility, and always of mistrusting his own judgment and esteeming his with whom he conferred for the present, that he seemed to have no opinions or resolutions but such as he contracted from the information and instruction he received upon the discourse of others, whom he had a wonderful art of governing and leading into his principles and inclinations whilst they believed that he wholly depended upon their counsel and advice. [III, 31.]

It is not surprising that many of good intent were won over by such adept "inventions" and "temptations." (III, 29.) Perhaps you can see from these suggestions — and from the passages you have read earlier in this book — how congenial Clarendon's fascination with the ways in which character finds expression in events is likely to prove to a lawyer, who is forever seeking to understand his colleagues, his opponents, and himself in a similar way.

While no adequate sense of the enormous variety of character and personality this book offers can be achieved either by description or by example,[21] one more passage should be given. The Earl of Portland is shown as a man consumed by dissatisfactions. Although he was lord treasurer, he had "not so much joy in what he had as trouble and agony for what he had not. The truth is, he had so vehement a desire to be the sole favourite, that he had no relish of the power that he had." This of course brought enemies and attack — indeed, "even his vices admitted those contradictions in them that he could hardly enjoy the pleasant fruit of any of them." Not a Catholic, he was believed to be such by all but that church; eager to become rich, he spent so wildly that he con-

21. In addition to the characters of Lindsey (page 107 *supra*), Goring, Wilmott, Essex (pages 307–309), and Chillingworth (page 853), you are referred to two anthologies: *Selections From Clarendon* (World's Classics ed. 1955); and D. Nicol Smith, *Characters From the Histories and Memoirs of the Seventeenth Century* (1918).

tracted debts the king could hardly pay. He had "too much courage" in offending other men; "but after having offended and incensed them, he was of so unhappy a feminine temper that he was always in a terrible fright and apprehension of them." (I, 107–109.)

> [A]fter six or eight years spent in outward opulency, and inward murmur and trouble that it was no greater, after vast sums of money and great wealth gotten, and rather consumed than enjoyed, without any sense or delight in so great prosperity, with the agony that it was no greater, he died unlamented by any, bitterly mentioned by most, who never pretended to love him, and severely censured and complained of by those who expected most from him, and deserved best of him; and left a numerous family, which was in a short time worn out, and yet outlived the fortune he left behind him. [I, 115.]

The self-destructive pathology of Portland is especially important because it is symbolic — although the parallel is not expressly drawn — of the state of the country at large. Having described the happy and peaceful state of the nation under Charles, the envy of other lands, Clarendon goes on to say:

> But all these blessings could but enable, not compel, us to be happy: we wanted that sense, acknowledgement, and value of our own happiness which all but we had, and took pains to make, when we could not find, ourselves miserable. [I, 164.]

The story of the parliamentary struggle is too complex to be retold here in detail, but the ending is plain enough:

> [B]y this means, a handful of men, much inferior in the beginning in number and in interest, came to give laws to the major part and to shew that three diligent persons are a greater number in arithmetic, as well as a more significant number in logic, than ten unconcerned, they, by plurality of voices, in the end converted or reduced the whole body to their opinions. [IV, 74.]

Under such control the Commons dismantled the Constitution: they passed a bill stripping the bishops of their votes in the House of Lords (IV, 33), dissolved the connection between church and government, imprisoned the protesting bishops in the Tower (IV, 142), took over the military establishments at Portsmouth and Hull, and prosecuted those who had advised the king — Digby's rash work — to come to the House in search of Pym and Hampden, in breach of parliamentary privilege. (IV, 152, 205.) The Commons had effectively assumed sovereign power. (IV, 209.)

But even now all was not lost. Even now, says Clarendon, the king could have prevailed: "[Y]et the House of Peers was well disposed, and might have been managed, with a little patience, to have blasted all the extravagances of the Commons." (IV, 217.) But that was not to be, and the parliamentary story continues to be one of subversion and defeat.

The next unit of the narrative is the military conflict between the subverted Parliament and the forces of the king, told as another stage in the story of degeneration. Battles are fought to various conclusions, the military facts never arising with clarity. Clarendon does not tell us the numbers of men, their locations, their arms and movements, but instead puts us in the king's camp where we share the confusion of soldier and commander. Even the rules of warfare degenerate: at the siege of Reading, runaways from the parliamentary army are given up to them, and the terms of surrender are not honored by the rebel army. (VII, 37, 39.) Parliament makes its own Great Seal and hangs a messenger of the king. (VII, 314, 319.) Military successes and failures, like political ones, can be traced to the skill of particular people: Digby's courage secures a victory at Torrington (VII, 196), the flight from Marston Moor by Rupert and Newcastle is inexcusable (VIII, 76), and brave Colonel Gage relieves the siege of Basing House. (VIII, 122–129.) The long and detailed negotiations of the Treaty of Uxbridge, the moment at which skill and industry might have produced a peace, are told in great detail. This is in many ways a lawyer's history of argument, persuasion, and finally failure. (VIII, 209 et seq.)

In London, ministers preach sedition from the pulpit. (VI, 39–42.) A self-denying ordinance, severing members of Parliament from positions in the army, is passed, applying to all but Cromwell. (IX, 5.) The Scots, who had supported the rebels, now begin to fear that the dissenting army will destroy their own religious establishment. (IX, 174.) The king's generals lose in the West, by their carelessness and disloyalty, one general refusing to serve under another. (IX, 54–66; 79–83.) The king goes to the Scots army, under false promises of loyalty, and awaits in vain troops from France. (X, 26–27; 33–34.) When Parliament sends humiliating proposals of peace, the king is advised by the Scots to give himself up and, upon his refusal, is handed over to the Parliament for a cash payment. (X, 60, 68.) Held by Parliament, he is denied his chaplain.

When the army and Parliament fall into an open conflict upon the death of Essex, Cromwell first pretends shock at the army's independence, then escapes Parliament's grasp to lead it. (X, 88.) The army seizes the king from Parliament by force. (X, 90.)

From now on the tale is one of majesty abused that ranks with Shakespeare's *Richard II* and Marlowe's *Edward II*. The king is increasingly ill-treated; he is asked to sign documents proclaiming his own guilt and is dealt with in Parliament "with utmost sauciness and license." (X, 141, 146.) A man is hanged for offering him aid. (X, 145.) The officers of the army resolve upon his death. (X, 147.) On the Isle of Wight, far from his friends, he is bullied into undertaking treaty negotiations alone, without advisers of his choice. (XI, 156.) He assents to some of their proposals, which they refuse to modify in any respect, denies others. At this juncture, concessions having been granted under a false promise of compromise, "the thundering declaration of the Army was published, which declared their full resolution to change the whole frame of government." (XI, 184.) He is moved to a new prison, "situated in so vile and unwholesome an air that the common guards there used to be frequently changed for the preservation of their health." (XI, 203.) A charge of high treason is brought against the king, the officers having decided to proceed with "some appearance of justice" (XI, 218), and they concoct a court. Bradshaw "with great humility accepted the office, which he administered with all the pride, impudence, and superciliousness imaginable." (XI, 220.) The king is led to Windsor by Colonel Harryson, "the son of a butcher near Nantwich." (XI, 221.) Persuaded by cynically practical arguments, the officers reject poison and assassination in favor of public trial. (XI, 224–227.) He is kept from all people but his guard, "some of whom sat up always in his chamber, and drank and took tobacco." (XI, 230.) When the charges are read, the king refuses to take off his hat and says that "he is accountable to none but God," not Parliament; and that they "are not the Parliament, nor had any authority from the Parliament to sit in that matter." (XI, 233.) He is abused, spat upon, and sentenced to death. (XI, 236.) One member of the convicting court was Mildmay, raised to favor by the king — "No man more obsequious to the Court than he whilst it flourished; a great flatterer of all persons in authority" — but who came to be "one of the murderers of his master." (XI, 237.)

The other was Sir John Danvers, . . . who being neglected by his brother, and having by a vain expense in his way of living contracted a vast debt which he knew not how to pay, and being a proud, formal, weak man, between being seduced and a seducer, he became so involved in their counsels that he suffered himself to be applied to their worst offices, taking it to be a high honour to sit upon the same bench with Cromwell, who employed and contemned him at once: nor did that party of miscreants look upon any two men in the Kingdom with that scorn and detestation as they did upon Danvers and Mildmay. [XI, 237.]

Clarendon has created a world of the damned in a tragic universe. The monarchy is abolished with the death of Charles, and the kings and princes of Europe buy up his goods. (XI, 251.)

This account of degeneration, this movement from worse to worse, is a way of expressing the destruction of a world of order and value, a way of making the reader feel something of Clarendon's own sense of ultimate loss. For in his account of the struggle between those bent on destruction and those who resist, in the accounts of crisis in the lives of individual men, Clarendon defines the civilization whose end he is lamenting.

With the regicide, the narrative takes a turn and a new movement begins. Cromwell and his successors fall into autocracy, armed dissension, and finally chaos. Faced with opposition from Presbyterians, Levellers, and the army itself, Cromwell dissolves the Long Parliament and appoints the Barebones Parliament. (XIV, 16.) Here begins an acute narrative irony: having led the rebellion to get rid of monarchy, Cromwell becomes a king in all but name and right. When he gives the Barebones Parliament the supreme authority in a document signed with his seal, they return it "acknowledging their own impotency." His council of officers is "too modest to share with him in this royal authority," and declares him sovereign with the title of Lord Protector. (XIV, 21–22.) He has a council and is required to call a Parliament every three years. (XIV, 23.) He establishes prerogative courts for the trial of political offenses, especially those of the king's friends. (XIV, 34–35.) When Parliament questions his authority and its own, he is forced to resort to arguments of legitimate government, as he has had to resort to its forms: he says that "in the government [are] certain fundamentals which [can] not be altered, to wit, that the government should be in a single person and a Parliament, that Parliaments should not be perpetual and always sitting, that the militia should not be entrusted into one hand or power, but so as the Parliament might have a check on the Protector and the Protector on the Parliament; that in matters of religion there ought to be liberty of conscience, and that persecution in the Church was not to be tolerated. These [are] unalterable fundamentals." (XIV, 46.)

This, to Clarendon, is the one sort of argument Cromwell cannot make, for to him it is clear that when old principles are discarded, and government torn up by the roots, it must be by a force of disorder that will eat away at whatever institutions are substituted. Cromwell's dilemma cannot be resolved: if he admits that the source of his power is rebellious arms, he invites and legitimizes new violence and his own destruction; if he adapts himself to the forms and arguments of the old government, he admits that the only difference between that one and his own is legitimacy. The moral and psychological impossibility of the usurper's position is emblematic of the condition of all the victors. Those who won the wars of rebellion lost what they sought to gain: the first destroyers of the monarchy are now themselves destroyed; the Scots have lost the establishment of the religion they joined the rebellion to preserve; Ireland is brutalized; Cromwell, always in terror of assassination, fears no one more than his supporters. (XV, 1–5.) Clarendon has defined the rebellion, for himself and for us, as a force of universal and irresistible destruction.

Cromwell calls a new Parliament in which no one may sit who does not swear allegiance to him — as formerly to the crown (XV, 28–29) — and he is in fact offered the crown. He turns it down, and accepts the protectorate for life instead. (XV, 36.) The writing is now highly comic: Parliament argues that Cromwell should receive the crown, because "the heart of the nation was devoted to the old form [of government] with which it was acquainted." (XV, 37.) His "inauguration" as protector is nothing less than a coronation. (XV, 47.) He assiduously cultivates the nobles and the bishops, and marries his daughters into noble families. (XV, 51.) "It quickly appeared how unsecure new institutions of government are" (XV, 58): Parliament invites back its expelled members, and doubts the jurisdiction of Cromwell's new House of Lords. Cromwell replies, "The other House were lords, and they should be lords." (XV, 62.) Faced with opposition, Cromwell does what many a good king did before him: he dissolves Parliament. He bullies the judges into subverting the law to his policies, including the suspension of habeas corpus; and when the ancient rights of Englishmen are invoked against this action, by the judges themselves, who "with all humility mentioned the law and Magna Carta," Cromwell — in a most gross and splendidly timed breach of decorum in this most sober and decorous book — tells them "their *magna farta* should not control his actions." (XV, 150.) He dies of an ague. (XV, 146.)

He has been an expressly Satanic figure: a man of greatest ability, strength, and resolution, with an incomprehensible wickedness:

> [W]ickedness as great as his could never have accomplished those trophies without the assistance of a great spirit, an admirable circumspection and sagacity, and a most magnanimous resolution. [XV, 147.]
>
> In a word, as he had all the wickednesses against which damnation is denounced and for which hell-fire is prepared, so he had some virtues, which have caused the memories of some men in all ages to be celebrated: and he will be looked upon by posterity as a brave bad man. [XV, 156.]

At the end of Cromwell's rule, his son Richard takes over. Incompetent for the task, without sufficient friends and unwilling to use those he had, he soon resigns in humiliation. (XVI, 9–16.) Like Oliver, he has no language in which to define new institutions and no theory to support them; but he lacks the personal force that enabled Oliver to carry on nevertheless. There is no legitimate and no logical successor, and Parliament's rule seems secure: "They saw not how their empire could be shaken." (XVI, 20.) They put down a royalist rising. The army grows to oppose them; they reach a standoff and form the compromise Committee of Safety. This is naked power: "And thus having chosen each other, [they] agreed that they should exercise the whole legislative power of the nation, and proclaimed themselves the *Committee of Safety for the Kingdom,* and required all people to pay them obedience and issued out their warrants for all things they thought good for themselves . . ." (XVI, 92.)

If Cromwell was ridiculous in aping the king, this declaration without color or form of right is absurd. Monck, merely a general, declares against it as a denial of Parliament, and marches to London, which submits to him. Monck calls for a Parliament, defeats the army, is given powers like Cromwell's by the Parliament. He manages matters in a high-handed manner, taking the city by arms when it refuses a loan. When abjuration of the king is proposed as a test of office, Monck is offended and calls a new Parliament. (XVI, 127–131.) In the midst of this confusion, some begin to mention the king, and Monck sends to ask the king for a letter to read to Parliament, which is received with joy. A messenger of the king is lauded now who would have been killed three months before. (XVI, 220.)

The mock-heroic tone has been maintained: first Richard, then the committee, then Monck have nominal power but are in fact impotent. The dizzying change of governments, speeches, and claims makes all but the one legitimate government seem increasingly impossible. We float in a comic world where there is no harm and no control. Somehow all the actions of these people lead to the Restoration, but

> there was not one man who bore a part in these changes and giddy revolutions who had the least purpose or thought to contribute towards the King's restoration, or who wished well for his interest; they who did so being so totally suppressed and dispirited, that they were only at gaze what light might break out of this darkness, and what order Providence might produce out of this confusion. [XVI, 111.]

The growing comic sense, as the changes in government occur without reason or excuse, prepares the reader for the marvel of the Restoration itself. This event, unlike the process of degeneration, is not explained by reference to character, skills, errors, and judgment, but is an act of Providence.

> In this wonderful manner, and with this miraculous expedition, did God put an end in one month . . . to a rebellion that had raged near twenty

years, and had been carried on with all the horrid circumstances of parricide, murder, and devastation, that fire and the sword, in the hands of the wickedest men in the world could be ministers of, almost to the desolation of two kingdoms and the exceeding deforming and defacing the third. [XVI, 247.]

This triumph is anchored in reality by the attitude of Charles on his return:

In a word, the joy was so unexpressible and universal, that his majesty said smilingly to some about him, that he doubted it had been his own fault he had been absent so long, for he saw nobody that did not protest he had ever wished his return. [XVI, 246.]

(3) *The Way the Narrative Works.* The force and brilliance of this ending — the miraculous transformation of the world into a providential and comic universe — push into momentary oblivion the questions with which Clarendon began. At the outset, you remember, he said that he would attempt to explain the great rebellion by reference to its natural causes, tracing the chain of responsibility from man to man and attending with particular care to the characters of the principal persons. Yet at the same time he expressed an awareness that such an explanation could not do everything, and might not do enough. It is the poise of this claim against this doubt that generates much of the energy upon which the work as a whole operates. As the narrative progresses from full explanation to full explanation, doubt and confusion paradoxically increase: while any particular event of parliamentary or military conflict may perhaps be explained by reference to the qualities and skills of the men involved, the events multiply and complicate themselves so thoroughly that the chain of causation eludes the grasp of understanding. Sureness becomes hesitancy. As the world of the *History* becomes increasingly tragic, it slips increasingly beyond the powers of the good and skillful to control and of Clarendon to explain. The new system of order — the divine comedy — that emerges from the confusion gives up all attempt at such explanation. Joy at the Restoration fills the mind, and the questions which we have pursued with increasing distress for six volumes are forgot.

The problem of explanation with which Clarendon began, and which he at last deserts, is left without a theoretical answer. Whether the chain of cause and effect binds all events as it binds some, or whether it at last dissolves in random incertitude, is left without an answer. Explanation can be only partial. Beyond the events that can be understood and explained lies either the hand of Providence or an ultimate chaos. Clarendon makes no attempt to cover up this mystery, takes no refuge in a metaphor — such as our familiar view of society as a social machine whose parts imply the whole, where one role or activity can be justified by reference to the larger enterprise it presumably advances. The movement to Providence does not mean that explanation by detail is never possible, or that there is always the hand of God to rescue the virtuous, but that here, in this case at least, just when all seems lost and most incomprehensible, a mysterious order arises in affairs. He brings his reader to face the inexpressible and to share his satisfaction in the historical event; the sharpening sense that all has been done that explanation can do, and that the answer is still remote, generates a pressure to assent to the sense of order providentially emerging out of chaos. The new order saves the nation and the book. Clarendon makes momentary royalists of us all.

Of course anyone can say that life cannot be understood, anyone can set a language of explanation against a language of mystery and leave the conflict unresolved. What matters is how he does so, how far he goes before he quits. And the *History* derives much of its special force from the fact that Clarendon goes farther than we expect, that he can be read again and again with curiosity and surprise. Partly this is the result of his extraordinary fair-mindedness to others, partly of his immense and varied experience of the public world — he speaks with a voice that commands respect — but the greatest credential of all is the record of human variety found here. As Clarendon shows character working itself out in action, as he explains events by articulating the precise combination of skills and the qualities of mind and spirit at work in each, he expresses distinctions — observes and defines capacities, catches peculiarities and makes judgments — that go beyond our expectations and even our experience. Think of the handful of character passages you have read (Coventry, Essex, Portland, Hampden, Goring, Wilmot), and imagine the effect that dozens of such passages would have on the historical narrative. As Clarendon goes through his world, he sees and reports more than we could hope to do. Our minds are filled with new material. He proves his right to leave us in uncertainty.

In doing so, he puts himself in a position to claim attention of a different kind, to ask that his book be regarded in a new way. For Clarendon does not stop with his qualified explanation — or his statement of the defined inexplicability — of the events he recounts, as a philosopher or historian might do. Instead, as he works out his sense of the public world he constantly asks himself, and his reader, how one is to live under such conditions. How he addresses this question — which it could be said to be the purpose of his *History* to enable him to ask — is our next subject.

b. Putting the Question: How to Live in Such a World?

He died in a lucky time, in the beginning of the Rebellion, when neither religion, or loyalty, or law, or wisdom, could have provided for any man's security. [I, 117.]

From time to time and in various ways Clarendon looks upon the world he has defined not only as a historian, as an observer seeking to explain it, but as a person who has actually lived in it, trying to survive, to prevail, to act with force and consequence. These two attitudes, and the activities they entail, are connected by the fact that what makes one impossible does the same to the other. When one looks in from the outside on this world, one finds that it cannot be fully explained, that one must recognize a permanent residue of the incomprehensible; when one looks at it from the inside, one finds that it cannot be adequately understood or mastered, that one cannot know with sureness what to do. It is one of the great achievements of the *History* that it is both an account of public affairs and a way of putting a highly personal question: how to live in a world of such complexity and such consequence. For the difficulties, the impossibilities of success, do not release either the historian or the person from responsibility: much of the explanation does work, especially locally, and the initial premise of the book — that qualities of mind and character have immediate and serious consequence in important events — is demonstrated again and again. The explanation is partial, incomplete, but it is enough to define an obligation of the most serious kind, to state a responsibility for both historian and citizen.

How does Clarendon approach the central matter of meeting the responsibilities he defines? How does he explain the successes and failures he observes? At the most simple level, as we have seen, he points to valuable skills, often (as in the cases of Coventry and Hampden) giving remarkably perceptive accounts of particular capacities. Of the Earl of Lauderdale, for example, who took part in the Treaty of Uxbridge where the lawyer's skills and statesman's labors almost made a peace, we are told: "being a young man, not accustomed to an orderly and decent way of speaking, and having no gracious pronunciation, and full of passion, he made everything more difficult than it was before." (VIII, 224.) But that is an odd passage in the *History* because the "skill" required there is relatively easy to define. In this world of elusive complexity, an ordinary lawyer's skill is not enough, and the failures define a dangerous universe indeed. You remember the account of Essex (page 307 *supra*), for example, in which Clarendon shows a man succumbing to forces he cannot handle. The career of Essex, he said, shows that "a weak judgment, and a little vanity, and as much of pride, will hurry a man into as unwarrantable and violent attempts as the greatest and most unlimited and insatiable ambition will do." Northumberland is led to join and stay with the parliamentary army by, of all things, his pride of rank: "If he had thought the King as much above him as he thought himself above other considerable men, he would have been a good subject." (VI, 398.)

But it does not all go one way: the weak or slightly vicious can achieve great things in a good cause. The Earl of Pembroke, "the most universally loved and esteemed of any man of that age," was both independent and loyal, yet not without vices, indulging "to himself the pleasures of all kinds, almost in all excesses," and being "immoderately given up to women."

> But therein likewise he retained such a power and jurisdiction over his very appetite, that he was not so much transported with beauty and outward allurements, as with those advantages of the mind as manifested an extraordinary wit and spirit and knowledge, and administered great pleasure in the conversation. To these he sacrificed himself, his precious time, and much of his fortune. [I, 123.]

The constant pressure of uncertainty, the final inadequacy of any skill or quality of mind, opens the discourse to talk about every sort of virtue and failure, of excellence and weakness. But at some point, the resources of language run out altogether: some men cannot be understood, just as some events cannot be explained. Consider the account of the career of Holland: after being refused a baronetcy, he stayed with the Parliament, but then left to join the king; he found the terms of reconciliation unsatisfactory and returned again to the rebels (who of course no longer trusted him), and finally on behalf of the crown led an insurrection which resulted in his death. Clarendon finally gives up. Holland simply cannot be explained (although Clarendon does believe that he might have been managed: if his pride had been flattered, he might have remained with the king). (IV, 2; VII, 241–248, 311; XI, 4 et seq.) Likewise, some men are simply evil, such as Cromwell or Hampden, or Savill, a "man of ambitious and restless nature, of parts and wit enough, but in his disposition and inclination so false that he could never be believed or depended upon" and who had a "particular malice to the earl of Strafford, which he had sucked in with his milk. . . ." (VI, 393.) Others, like Grandison, are as simply good:

> He was a young man of so virtuous a habit of mind that no temptation or provocation could corrupt him; so great a lover of justice and integrity that

no example, necessity or even the barbarity of this war could make him swerve from the most precise rules of it; and of that rare piety and devotion that the court or camp could not show a more faultless person, or to whose example young men might reasonably conform themselves. [VII, 133.]

The difficulties of living in this world arise as often from an incomprehensible simplicity as from an elaborate psychological complexity.

What has happened is this: the bewildering awareness that at last the great events cannot be explained is combined with the inconsistent demonstration that at least sometimes character — and by this term in this book we can mean every skill and virtue, every excellence of mind and spirit, as these are defined by Clarendon — is of enormous practical consequence. This frustrating inconsistency generates an urgent moral imperative, in celebration of which the book is written: to govern well. For to live well in this world means to live well in public affairs, as subject or citizen. This is a statesman's epic, in which good government is the heroic enterprise. But we have been carried to the limits of explanation with respect to what constitutes the excellence of character necessary to the process of good government, as well as with respect to the causes of great events. No manual of skills and abilities, or virtues, could answer Clarendon's fundamental question, how to live well in this world. The imperative is urgent, but we are given no defined and adequate response. It is a statement of the creative achievement of the *History* that the art of government which it celebrates can be spoken of only as an art of life.

Clarendon addresses newly appointed ministers in these terms:

The best provision that such men can make for their voyage, besides a stock of innocence that cannot be impaired, and a firm confidence in God Almighty that he will never suffer that innocence be utterly oppressed or notoriously infamed, is, an expectation of those gusts and storms of rumour, detraction, and envy; and a resolution not to be over sensible of all calumnies, unkindness or injustice, but to believe that, by being preferred before other men, they have an obligation upon them to suffer more than other men would do, and that the best way to convince scandals and misreports is, by neglecting them, to appear not to have deserved them. . . . In a word, let no man think, that is once entered into this list, that he can by any skill or comportment prevent these conflicts and assaults, or by any stubborn or impetuous humour that he can suppress and prevail over them: but let him look at it as a purgatory he is unavoidably to pass through, and depend upon Providence and time for a vindication; and by performing all the duties of his place to the end, with justice, integrity, and uprightness, give all men cause to believe he was worthy of it the first hour; which is a triumph very lawful to be affected. [VII, 283.]

But Clarendon does not rest there; he points to successes, to genuine forces of assistance, however inexplicable they may be: in speaking of the king's council, for example, he says one must not, "from the particular infirmities of men, the heaviness of this man, the levity of that, the weakness and simplicity of a third, conclude that their advice and opinions are not requisite to any great design. . . ." "For it is in wisdom as it is in beauty": just as a face, which being considered in its parts, "affords scarce one exact feature," yet altogether "by a gracefulness and vivacity in the whole" may constitute an "excellent beauty, and be more catching than another whose symmetry is more faultless,"

so there are many men, who in this particular argument may be unskillful, in that affected, who may seem to have levity, or vanity, or formality, in ordinary and cursory conversation, (a very crooked rule to measure any man's abilities, and gives a better evidence of the nature than of the understanding,) and yet in formed counsels, deliberations, and transactions, are men of great insight and wisdom, and from whom excellent assistance is contributed. [VII, 280.]

There is a process by which the failing parts form a healthy whole, by which there is brought into play the best of each, not the worst or even an average mixture. This is the mystery of virtuous government. This is an expression of an attitude towards the working of institutions similar to that with which we were made to greet the historical event of the Restoration: beyond the explicable, there is, or may be, a miracle.

What we have come to at last is the center of the book. For Clarendon does say more about the process by which men and societies make themselves safe and whole, he does give directions of a kind. In this world, men change and can be changed; the infinitely various qualities of mind and character that constitute the virtue the book defines can be acquired; and the art of life that this book finally expresses is an art of education. In a startling combination of ideas, the process of government is seen as a process of education. How can this process of education be explained or even identified? Virtues are as numerous as leaves; what is right for one man at one time is wrong later, or for another; and even a sublime virtue alone is not enough in a competitive world dominated by such figures as Cromwell and Hampden. No curriculum for the young man can be recommended, no outline of a good education prepared. The answer Clarendon expresses is not in the content of instruction, but — remarkably — in the nature of the relationship in which the process occurs. The education that is the center of virtue celebrated by this book is defined as education between friends. Where the goal of life is inexpressible, Clarendon can still point to the relationship from which it derives its virtue, its power, and its meaning.

The celebration of friendship recurs at every stage. Of Buckingham, whose erratic and destructive career began the work, Clarendon says:

> His single misfortune was, (which indeed was productive of many greater), that he never made a noble and a worthy friendship with a man so near his equal that he would frankly advise him, for his honour and true interest, against the current, or rather the torrent, of his impetuous passions. . . . Let the fault or misfortune be what or whence it will, it may be very reasonably believed that if he had been blessed with one faithful friend who had been qualified with wisdom and integrity, that great person would have committed as few faults, and done as transcendant worthy actions, as any man who shined in such a sphere in that age in Europe. [I, 70–71.]

But the great expression of educative friendship in this book is Clarendon's account of the life of Falkland, his own friend. He here defines a civilization, an ideal whose loss the *History* as a whole laments. And this civilization is characterized by what we have found to be so elusive or impossible: a merger of private and public language, a union of skill and virtue, a bringing together of two sides of life in a way we can hardly imagine.

> But I must here take leave a little longer to discontinue this narration; and if the celebrating the memory of eminent and extraordinary persons, and transmitting their great virtues for the imitation of posterity, be one of the principal ends and duties of history, it will not be thought impertinent in this place to remember a loss which no time will suffer to be forgotten, and no success or good fortune could repair. In this unhappy battle was slain the lord viscount Falkland: a person of such prodigious parts of learning and knowledge, of that inimitable sweetness and delight in conversation, of so flowing and obliging a humanity and goodness to mankind, and of that primitive simplicity and integrity of life, that if there were no other brand upon this odious and accursed civil war than that single loss, it must be most infamous and execrable to all posterity.
>
> *Turpe mori, post te, solo non posse dolore.* [VII, 217.]

Falkland was educated in Ireland, with the consequence that upon his return he could make a "pure election of his company," since he was not entangled in any acquaintances, "which usually grow up by custom of conversation." He chose as his friends men of "the most eminent and sublime parts, and of untouched reputation in point of integrity." (VII, 218.) His home near Oxford was cultivated indeed, constantly visited by a learned company, "a university bound in a lesser volume." In Parliament he gave trust and credit to all, even to the motives and arguments of Hampden. "But when he grew better informed what was law," no man more "opposed those attempts and gave the adverse party trouble by reason and argumentation." Clarendon refers to the bill to take away the bishop's vote, which he opposed and his friend Falkland supported:

> The House was so marvellously delighted to see the two inseparable friends divided in so important a point, they could not contain from a kind of rejoicing; . . . and therefore they entertained an imagination and a hope that they might work the lord Falkland to a farther concurrence with them. But they quickly found themselves disappointed, and that, as there was not the least interruption of the close friendship between the other two, so, when the same argument came into debate about six months after, the lord Falkland changed his opinion, and gave them all the opposition he could: nor was he reserved in acknowledging that he had been deceived, and by whom, and confessed to his friends, with whom he would deal freely, that Mr. Hambden had assured him that if that bill might pass there would be nothing more attempted to the prejudice of the Church: which he thought, as the world then went, would be no ill composition. [III, 152.]

A man of absolute integrity, Falkland avoided fawning for advancement to the point of rudeness; and when he was prevailed upon to become the king's secretary, he refused to use spies and to open letters, as had been the custom. He was "so severe an adorer of truth, that he could as easily have given himself leave to steal as to dissemble. . . ." (IV, 123.) Brave and almost foolhardy in battle, he constantly longed for peace. The war thrust him into a deep melancholy. He was killed in battle.

> Thus fell that incomparable young man, in the four and thirtieth year of his age, having so much dispatched the business of life, that the oldest rarely attain to that immense knowledge, and the youngest enter not into the world with more innocence: and whosoever leads such a life need not care upon how short warning it be taken from him. [VII, 234.]

In a world of uncertainty, where the most arduous analytical labors produce explanations that are only partial, but where skill and virtue have drastic consequence in action, the obligation to excellence in public life is urgent and its demands are ultimate. The response to this obligation lies in educative friendship, which Clarendon expresses as the central process of life, public and private.

What a view this is for us! The world of morality and public events are one; private and public experience merge; the government is seen to consist of individual men and to operate by their relation. Good government is the sum of all felicity, public and private, the ultimate expression of civilization and of religion. The statesman is the hero of virtue and wisdom. Excellence in public life depends upon excellence in education; and excellence in education is seen as excellence in friendship. Whatever defects Clarendon's *History* may have as scientific history, it succeeds in the central purpose of historical writing: to make another reality, with which we may compare our own, live for us.

What must at last be said is that the most remarkable expression of the ideal of educative friendship is in the writing of the *History*. There are many possible relationships between reader and writer. When one looks at a list of political books and memoirs today, one sees that persuasion, prestige, and money are all involved. When a writer writes to us out of friendship, he is writing from a different world.

WRITING ASSIGNMENT 20: Reconciling the Demands of Reality and Imagination

Part One

- *Draft a narrative of a real event — from your experience, your reading, or from history or law — in which you address the tension between reality and imagination. Try to demonstrate excellence in this writing.*

Part Two

- *Explain the excellence you have demonstrated.*

WRITING ASSIGNMENT 20, ALTERNATIVE A: Telling a Story and Saying What It Means

Part One

- *Give an account of a mind, legal or nonlegal, addressing the tension between story and theory, between narrative and analysis. Try to demonstrate excellence in this writing.*

Part Two

- *What is the excellence you have demonstrated? If you say that it is "writing more than one way," be sure to identify the several ways in which you have written, and the relation you have established between them.*

WRITING ASSIGNMENT 20, ALTERNATIVE B: *Placing the Private Self in the Public World*

Part One

• *Give an account of a real or imaginary event in which you show a mind placing the private self in the public world in a way that you can admire.*

Part Two

• *Explain the excellence you have demonstrated.*

If you wish, the passage that is the subject of your criticism here may be written by someone else.

WRITING ASSIGNMENT 20, ALTERNATIVE C: *Rewriting an Old Assignment*

Part One

• *Rewrite any assignment you have prepared for this course in which you can say that you have addressed either the tension between narrative and analysis, or that between reality and the imagination, or in which you placed the private self in the public world. Your writing should be as good as you can make it.*

Part Two

• *Explain the excellence you have demonstrated.*

WRITING ASSIGNMENT 20, ALTERNATIVE D: *The Historian and the Lawyer*

• *Find and reproduce a passage of history which demonstrates an excellence that you believe should be of interest to a lawyer. Explain why it should be of interest to him. What connections or comparisons between the activities of law and history are you now prompted to draw?*

CHAPTER 7

THE EDUCATION OF THE LAWYER

[A]nd it at once struck me what quality went to form a Man of Achievement, especially in Literature, and which Shakespeare possessed so enormously — I mean *Negative Capability*, that is, when a man is capable of being in uncertainties, mysteries, doubts, without any irritable reaching after fact and reason.*

Sir, he knows nothing; he has made up his mind about nothing.†

In this chapter you are asked to turn from your study of the mature legal mind at work — from the examination of your professional future — to the activity in which you and those around you are immediately engaged, the education of the lawyer. How is one to learn to be a lawyer? How can a teacher best contribute to that process? What is it that goes on in a good class, or in preparing for one? What does one properly expect of a good teacher? Of a good student? The literature that commonly addresses such questions is of course inadequate — think of law school catalogs — and one of our questions is how it might be replaced, at least for one's private purposes.

One thought might be said to be imbedded in much talk about legal education: one person "teaches" something called the "law" to another, who "learns" it. The metaphoric implication is that there is in the world an identifiable thing or body of knowledge called "law" which is transferred from teacher to student. The process of the classroom can be expressed in a transitive verb with a double accusative: "I teach them law" is parallel to "I give them soup." To teach is to know something and to tell others what you know, perhaps to hand over the intellectual equivalent of a road map, to be used when necessary by anybody who understands it enough to read it as a set of directions. "Georgia

* John Keats, Letter to George and Thomas Keats, Dec. 22, 1817.
† Boswell, *The Life of Samuel Johnson*, II, 40 (1791; Glover ed. 1901).

does not permit the spendthrift trust or a right turn on a red light." It is possible for the professor's mind to be as remote from the student's as the mechanic's from the child's — "Don't ever touch that knob" — and for much the same reasons. Of course this is not true of your own education, where mind engages with mind. But how do you view that enterprise of yours, how explain how it works? What are your hopes and expectations?

That is the subject of the chapter as a whole. We test a little further the language we have been speaking of — "I teach and you learn the law." We begin by asking a question this language seems to invite: what is the law? Where is it? One who "teaches" or "learns" "the law" must surely identify and find it first.

A. *DEFINING OUR SUBJECT MATTER — WHAT IS THE LAW AND WHERE CAN YOU FIND IT?*

Below is a judicial opinion which interprets the following statute: "Recrimination is a showing by the defendant of any cause of divorce against the plaintiff, in bar of the plaintiff's cause of divorce." Cal. Civ. Code §122 (enacted 1872).

DE BURGH v. DE BURGH
39 Cal. 2d 858, 250 P.2d 598 (1952)

TRAYNOR, J. — Plaintiff Daisy M. De Burgh and defendant Albert Raymond De Burgh were married in California in October, 1946. They separated in February, 1949, and in the same year plaintiff brought this action for divorce on the ground of extreme cruelty. Defendant filed a cross-complaint for divorce, also on the ground of extreme cruelty. The allegations of cruelty were denied in the answers filed by each party. The trial court found "that each of the parties to this action has been guilty of acts of cruelty towards the other, and that such acts of cruelty by each toward the other, were provoked by the acts of the other." The court decided that "each party has been guilty of recrimination and neither is entitled to a divorce from the other." The court entered judgment that plaintiff take nothing by her complaint and that defendant take nothing by his cross-complaint. Plaintiff appeals "from the judgment signed and entered by the court" and from the order denying her motion for a new trial. Since the latter order is nonappealable, the appeal therefrom must be dismissed.

The evidence regarding cruelty is in conflict; it supports the finding that each party has been cruel to the other. Plaintiff's evidence tended to show that defendant was frequently intoxicated to excess, that he inflicted physical injury upon plaintiff on several occasions, that he boasted of his relations with other women, that he unreasonably criticized plaintiff's daughter, that he unjustly berated plaintiff concerning a former suitor, and that, although he was a lavish spender in other ways, he was penurious with plaintiff. Defendant's evidence indicated that plaintiff had unjustly accused him of dishonesty and homosexuality and had communicated to his business associate similar false and malicious statements.

Since the trial court found that defendant was guilty of acts of cruelty towards plaintiff, it is clear that the judgment denying plaintiff a divorce is not on the ground that plaintiff failed to prove the allegations of cruelty in her complaint. The judgment thus must be based either on the finding that defendant's cruelty was provoked by plaintiff or on the ground that defendant established the defense of recrimination.

The finding that the cruelty of each party was provoked by the other party is inconsistent with the conclusion that recrimination was established. Cruelty that is provoked does not give rise to a cause of action. . . .

The determinative question on this appeal, therefore, is whether the findings and conclusions in this case warrant application of the doctrine of recrimination. It is apparent from the remarks of the trial judge at the close of the trial that he believed that the transgressions of each party necessarily precluded the granting of a divorce to either. On the other hand, the language of section 122 of the Civil Code indicates that the trial court may have abused its discretion in disregarding the requirement therein that the cause of divorce of which one party is found guilty must be "in bar" of that party's ground of divorce against the other party. To resolve this conflict, we have studied the history of the doctrine of recrimination, its objectives, and the wording and legislative background of the applicable statutes.

It has sometimes been assumed that any cause of divorce constitutes a recriminatory defense. The legislative language, however, is ill-adapted to such a broad purpose. Read together, sections 111 and 122 of the Civil Code provide: "Divorces must be denied upon . . . a showing by the defendant of any cause of divorce against the plaintiff, in bar of the plaintiff's cause of divorce." Had the Legislature meant to make every cause of divorce an absolute defense, it could easily have provided that: "Divorces must be denied upon . . . a showing by the defendant of any cause of divorce against the plaintiff." We are bound to consider the additional requirement that such a cause of divorce must be "in bar" of the plaintiff's cause of divorce.

Much of the confusion concerning recrimination in California has proceeded from the erroneous discussion of the subject in *Conant v. Conant,* 10 Cal. 249 [70 Am. Dec. 717], which was decided before recrimination became a part of the statutory law. It was stated in that case that this defense is based on the doctrine that one who violates a contract containing mutual and dependent covenants cannot complain of its breach by the other party. Logically, such a theory would permit the party against whom the first marital offense was committed to ignore thereafter the duties imposed by the marriage "contract," for in contract law a material breach excuses further performance by the innocent party. (Restatement of Contracts, §274; Cal. Civ. Code, §1689(2).) In fact, however, the defense may be asserted without regard to whether the plaintiff or the defendant was the first at fault. (*Pullen v. Pullen & Holding,* 123 L.T.R. 203, 36 T.L.R. 506.)

The deceptive analogy to contract law ignores the basic fact that marriage is a great deal more than a contract. It can be terminated only with the consent of the state. In a divorce proceeding the court must consider not merely the rights and wrongs of the parties as in contract litigation, but the public interest in the institution of marriage. The family is the basic unit of our society, the center of the personal affections that ennoble and enrich human life. It channels biological drives that might otherwise become socially destructive; it ensures the care and education of children in a stable environment; it establishes continuity from one generation to another; it nurtures and develops the individual initiative that distinguishes a free people. Since the family is the core of our society, the law seeks to foster and preserve marriage. But when a marriage has failed and the family has ceased to be a unit, the purposes of family life are no longer served and divorce will be permitted. "[P]ublic policy does not discourage divorce where the relations between husband and wife are such that the legitimate objects of matrimony have been utterly destroyed." . . .

The chief vice of the rule enunciated in the *Conant* case is its failure to recognize that the considerations of policy that prompt the state to consent to a divorce when one spouse has been guilty of misconduct are often doubly present when both spouses have been guilty. The disruption of family relationships, the clandestine associations with third parties, and the oppressive effect upon children and the community are intensified. It is a degradation of marriage and a frustration of its purposes when the courts use it as a device for punishment.

Moreover, the historical discussion of the doctrine of recrimination in the *Conant* case is inaccurate. The court relied mainly on the decisions of the eminent English ecclesiastical jurist, Lord Stowell. It is significant that in his later utterances Lord Stowell viewed with regret the illogical and pernicious consequences of a mechanical application of the doctrine. Even the medieval canon law, upon which Lord Stowell relied, did not carry recrimination to the extreme of the *Conant* case; although permitted as a bar when the plaintiff sought a divorce for adultery, this defense was not accepted against a cause of divorce based on cruelty, for the church lawyers realized that public policy was not served by forcing a wife, even if guilty, to return to a home where her life was in danger. . . . On the question of recrimination in cases of absolute divorce, the *Conant* opinion, necessarily looking for its authority to parliamentary practice, relied exclusively upon *Simmons' Case*, 12 C. & F. 339, 8 Eng. Rep. 1438, in which Parliament denied a divorce, overlooking other cases involving recrimination where Parliament allowed divorce. (See, for example, *Major Campbell's Case*, 42 H. of L. Jour. 141, reprinted in MacQueen, A Practical Treatise on the Appellate Jurisdiction of the House of Lords [1842], p. 590.) Only a year before the *Conant* decision, in fact, Parliament had created jurisdiction in the English courts to grant absolute divorce and in so doing expressly provided for judicial discretion on the issue of recrimination. (Divorce and Matrimonial Causes Act of 1857, 20 & 21 Vict., c. 85, §31.)

The California Legislature, in enacting the Civil Code in 1872, did not follow the principles of the *Conant* case. The code provisions on recrimination made two important departures from the existing law.

First, the code requires that the defendant prove a cause of divorce against the plaintiff to establish this defense. The requirement of the *Conant* case that plaintiff be "without reproach" no longer prevails. . . . The dictum to the contrary in *Shapiro v. Shapiro*, 127 Cal. App. 20, 24 [14 P.2d 1058], is without support even in the textbook authority cited and is clearly opposed to the statute.

Second, as shown by the notes of the commissioners who drafted the code, the Legislature rejected the strict rule of recrimination of the ecclesiastical courts. Significantly neither the *Conant* case nor any other divorce cases appear among the precedents listed by the commissioners as the basis of the statute. It is apparent from the decisions that were listed that the Legislature intended that divorce cases involving recrimination be governed by the same principles that apply generally throughout our jurisprudence. Although the plaintiff's fault has always been regarded as an important element in the decision of any case, our courts have traditionally refused to exalt that element above the public interest. Thus, in *Freeman v. Sedwick*, 6 Gill. (Md.) 28, 40 [46 Am. Dec. 650], a fraudulent conveyance case cited by the commissioners, Mr. Justice Story's Equity Jurisprudence is quoted as follows: "Relief is not granted, where both parties are truly *in pari delicto*, unless in cases where public policy would thereby be promoted." (Vol. I, p. 317, §298;

see, also, 14th ed. [1918], vol. I, pp. 395-398, §421.) This respect for the public interest has formed the basis of a recognized exception to the equitable doctrine of unclean hands, with which the defense of recrimination has become increasingly identified since the enactment of the code. It is clear that the Legislature, in relying upon judicial principles of general application, intended that in divorce litigation the fault of the plaintiff should have no more significance than elsewhere in the law. Apparently with this purpose in mind it worded the statute to require that a cause of divorce shown by defendant must be "in bar" of the plaintiff's cause of divorce. It would have defeated its own purpose had it closed the avenues to divorce when the legitimate objects of matrimony have been destroyed. The perpetuation of an unwholesome relationship would be a mockery of marriage.

The California cases decided since the enactment of the Civil Code contain little analysis or discussion of the principles governing the defense of recrimination. In *Brenot v. Brenot,* 102 Cal. 294, 296 [36 P. 672], this court correctly stated the rule to be that "a court of equity is *authorized* to enter a judgment dismissing an action of divorce, where both parties are seeking a decree, and the evidence discloses them to be equally guilty of the misconduct alleged." (Italics added.) Again, in *Glass v. Glass,* 4 Cal. App. 604, 607 [88 P. 734], the appellate court, in affirming the judgment with regard to property issues, observed without objection that the trial court had found both parties guilty of extreme cruelty but nevertheless had granted the plaintiff a divorce. In some cases, however, it has been assumed, apparently with the acquiescence of the parties themselves, that the mere showing of a cause of divorce against the plaintiff is sufficient. . . . This failure to exercise the discretion authorized by the statute has enabled the thinking engendered by the *Conant* case to survive by default. Important developments of the past several decades have made it increasingly clear that the courts can no longer decline to exercise the discretion inherent in the clean hands doctrine.

The rising divorce rate in the United States has compelled a growing recognition of marriage failure as a social problem and correspondingly less preoccupation with technical marital fault. This trend is strikingly exemplified by the recent amendment of section 92 of the Civil Code designating incurable insanity as a ground for divorce. Formerly, no matter how vicious the conduct of an insane spouse, he could not be divorced, for the law refused to find in him the guilt essential to a marital offense. . . . The Legislature has come to realize, however, that when a union is dominated by insanity, fulfilment of the normal purposes of marriage is hopeless. What was once a bar to divorce is now recognized as a justification for divorce. Still more striking in recognition of this trend has been the enactment of legislation in many states authorizing divorce when the spouses have lived apart for a required number of years. Marriage failure, rather than the fault of the parties, is the basis upon which such divorces are granted.

It would be froward indeed for the court, when it is called upon to evaluate an alleged recriminatory defense, to ignore the growing awareness that a marriage in name only is not a marriage in any real sense. In other fields, equity does not deny relief on the ground of plaintiff's unclean hands when to do so would be harmful to the public interest. . . . Such a rule is even more appropriate in marital litigation, where the social consequences of the court's decree are of the utmost importance. . . .

It bears noting how frequently divorces are uncontested. In many cases neither spouse is "innocent," and yet, by agreement, one of them defaults to ensure a divorce. Thus a strict recrimination rule fails in its purpose of denying relief to the guilty. Moreover, it exerts a corrupting influence on the negotiations that precede the entry of such a default. The spouse who more desperately seeks an end to a hopeless union is penalized by the ability of the other spouse to prevent a divorce through the assertion of a recriminatory defense, and the more unscrupulous partner may obtain substantial financial concessions as the price of remaining silent. Were the clean hands doctrine properly applied, it would encourage estranged couples to bring their differences before the chancellor, where the interests of society as a whole can be given proper recognition and where settlement negotiations can be supervised and unfair advantage prevented.

A mechanical application of the doctrine of recrimination is by no means universal. In some states, the defense has been limited by requiring that the plaintiff's offense be of the same type as the defendant's or that it involve equal guilt. . . . Such limitations are not entirely satisfactory, however; even when misconduct is identical the court should be permitted to exercise a sound discretion in the public interest. Several states expressly recognize judicial discretion concerning recrimination. . . .

In examining the doctrine of recrimination, we have given the most serious consideration not only to judicial precedent but also to the work of leading scholars and practitioners. Few rules of law have been more widely condemned by the legal profession. In 1948, a committee of experts of the American Bar Association joined with the representatives of other interested groups in the work of the National Conference on Family Life. The bar association's representatives, acting as the legal section of the conference, strongly recommended the elimination of the defense of recrimination. . . . In view of the statutory provisions on the subject, we are not free to go so far. Moreover, we do not believe that the comparative guilt of the parties will be without significance in every case. We do believe, however, that some of the evils pointed out by the bar association committee can be avoided within the framework of the existing statute if it is kept in mind that the doctrine of recrimination, like the doctrine of unclean hands of which it is a part, is neither puristic nor mechanical, but an equitable principle to be applied according to the circumstances of each case and with a proper respect for the paramount interests of the community at large.

Defendant relies upon *Comfort v. Comfort*, 17 Cal. 2d 736, 745-752 [112 P.2d 259]. The discussion of recrimination in that case, however, was directed entirely to the question whether or not the recriminatory defense there involved had become inoperative owing to lapse of time. The court did not consider the language of section 122 of the Civil Code in the light of the clean hands doctrine, nor was that issue raised in the briefs of the parties. The *Comfort* case therefore does not support the proposition that the doctrine of recrimination precludes the exercise of equitable discretion.

We have concluded that section 122 of the Civil Code imposes upon the trial judge the duty to determine whether or not the fault of the plaintiff in a divorce action is to be regarded as "in bar" of the plaintiff's cause of divorce based upon the fault of the defendant. Tested by the considerations discussed above, the evidence in the present case would have been ample to support a finding that the parties' misconduct should not bar a divorce. Reconciliation appears impossible. The trial judge himself observed that "the marriage here was a failure from the start" and that "there is nothing really to keep them together." There was evidence that defendant more than once inflicted bodily injury upon plaintiff; that after one severe beating plaintiff attempted to commit suicide by an overdose of sleeping pills; that defendant often boasted in the presence of plaintiff and guests of intimate relations with other women and discussed their physical attributes in detail; that defendant was often intoxicated; that defendant frequently told plaintiff that her daughter by a previous marriage had loose morals; that defendant was insanely jealous of a former suitor of plaintiff and on one occasion seized an alarm clock given plaintiff by the suitor and threw it into the toilet; and that defendant lavishly tipped waiters and spent his money freely in public, but in private life refused to give plaintiff sufficient funds to purchase clothes suitable for her station in life. On the other hand, defendant's evidence was to the effect that plaintiff had invented false accusations against him; that plaintiff had deliberately attempted to ruin his business life by writing a letter to his partner falsely accusing defendant of dishonesty and homosexuality; and that plaintiff had announced her intention of writing similar letters to other business associates of defendant. If the foregoing facts are true, it is apparent that there has been a total and [irremediable] breakdown of the marriage. Technical marital fault can play but little part in the face of the unhappy spectacle indicated by this evidence, with its inevitable effect upon the family, friends, neighbors, and business interests of the parties.

Moreover, it is significant that the application of a strict rule of recrimination in the present action does not operate with equal justice. As the spouse entrusted by law with the management and control of the community property (see Civ. Code, §§161a, 172, 172a), defendant is in a position to use that property for his personal benefit. Although he has an obligation to support plaintiff, a large discretion is customarily vested in the husband concerning the manner of performing that obligation; in the present case, disagreement and repeated legal actions to obtain support money are almost certain to ensue.

There can be no precise formula for determining when a cause of divorce shown against a plaintiff is to be considered a bar to his suit for divorce, for the divorce court, as a court of equity (*Sharon v. Sharon*, 67 Cal. 185 [7 P. 456, 635, 8 P. 709]), is clothed with a broad discretion to advance the requirements of justice in each particular case. In general, however, certain major considerations will govern the court's decision:

1. *The prospect of reconciliation.* The court should determine whether the legitimate objects of matrimony have been destroyed or whether there is a reasonable likelihood that the marriage can be saved. It should consider the ages and temperaments of the parties, the length of their marriage, the seriousness and frequency of their marital misconduct proved at the trial and the likelihood of its recurrence, the duration and apparent finality of the separation, and the sincerity of their efforts to overcome differences and live together harmoniously.

2. *The effect of the marital conflict upon the parties.* If a continuation of the marriage would constitute a serious hazard to the health of either party, as in the case of physical brutality, the court should be reluctant to deny divorce. Although financial considerations can play only a minor role in determining the propriety of divorce, even these may not be entirely ignored if the evidence indicates that marital conflicts are destroying the livelihood of the parties.

3. *The effect of the marital conflict upon third parties.* In every divorce case in which children are involved, their interests are of the utmost concern to the court. The disruptive effect of divorce upon children is to be deplored, but in a given case it may be preferable to violence, hatred, or immorality when these are present in the home. The community as a whole also has an interest. Adultery, desertion, or

cruelty, for example, can only discredit marriage; their perpetuation is not lightly to be decreed.

4. *Comparative guilt.* In many ways the guilt of the parties may be unequal — in the gravity of the misconduct involved, in the frequency of its occurrence, or in its effect upon children and others. Moreover, one spouse may demonstrate substantially greater repentance and reform. Marital offenders, therefore, are not necessarily *in pari delicto* before the chancellor. Their comparative guilt may have an important bearing upon whether or not either one or both should be granted relief.

We have concluded that in light of the foregoing discussion the findings and conclusions in the present case are not sufficient to support the determination that recrimination was established. It is essential that findings be made on every material issue raised by the pleadings.

As we have seen, whether or not the cause of action proved against each spouse is to be regarded as in bar of the cause of action proved against the other spouse is a material issue and must be expressly decided by the trial court before it may be said that recrimination has been decided. To decide the issue raised by a plea of recrimination, the court must consider the prospects of reconciliation, the comparative fault of the plaintiff and the defendant, and the effect of the marital strife upon the parties, their children, and the community. . . .

The judgment is reversed. The appeal from the order denying the motion for a new trial is dismissed. Defendant is to bear the costs of this appeal.

QUESTIONS

1. *After De Burgh, what is the law of California with respect to the effect of the existence of a cause of action for divorce by the defendant against the plaintiff in a divorce action? Where can that law be found?*
2. *Was the law the same when the action was begun in 1949? Where could it have been found at that time?*
3. *If you had represented one of the De Burghs, what would you have said the law of California was in 1949? Where would you have found it?*
4. *If you had been teaching law in California in 1949, what would you have told your students the law was with respect to the issue stated in Question 1? Where would you have found it or told them to find it?*
5. *Suppose you had taken a bar examination in California in 1949. What would you have said the law was with respect to that issue? What would your Bar Refresher course have told you? If the examination was in a Domestic Relations course, would your answer have been different?*
6. *Suppose you were a Montana judge asked to decide this question of California law in 1949: what would you have said that law was?*
7. *Was the law of California the same throughout the state in 1949? Or*

was it different in different law offices? In different classrooms? Then how on earth could it possibly have been found?

8. *In 1949, was the law of the De Burgh case to be found in the statute? In the cases? In Justice Traynor's mind? His then future law clerk's mind? Some lawyer's mind? Where?*
9. *If the law is not a set of discoverable and statable rules, what is it?*
10. *Do you want to answer this by saying the law must always be spoken of in the future tense? It never "is," it always "will be"? (This is a little like the famous mathematical puzzle in which it is proven that Achilles can never pass a tortoise because he must always come first to the place the tortoise just was, while the tortoise moves on.) How do you find something that never "is" but only "will be"? Is it no wonder lawyers charge a lot?*
11. *Suppose someone said: "The law is all in there," and pointed to the library. Is there a sense in which that statement is true?*
    a. *Can all of law school then be regarded as a course in "how to use the library"?*
    b. *Does this perhaps explain why your Library Orientation and Legal Research courses were so unsatisfactory?*
12. *How then do you respond when one interested in what you are learning asks: "What is the law? Where do you find it?"*

B. *HOW IS THE LAW TO BE LEARNED? HOW TAUGHT?*

Witt must grow like fingers; if it bee taken from others, tis like plums stuck upon Blackthorne, there they are for a while, but they come to nothing.*

In this course you have examined the activity of the legal mind in several ways: by comparing legal language with other forms of expression; by exploring as best you can what the lawyer does behind the language that he uses; and by analyzing the structure and limits of legal speech and thought as a discrete intellectual system. You have come at the law from the inside and from the outside. Having asked yourself how the "law" could be defined as the subject matter of education — what is it? where can it be found? — you are now asked to explain how it can be taught and learned.

There follows now a brief set of readings and questions; but when you get to the writing assignment, you will see that the burden is upon you to define the question further in your own way. I hope you will welcome this chance to write from your own experience in law school. Perhaps you have felt unsure of yourself when asked to write about the lawyer and the judge; but if you are not the expert on the experience of the student of law, no one is.

* John Selden, *Table Talk* (Wit, 3) (1689).

Perhaps the basic question can best be put this way: can you find a way to express what it is about you that makes you an educated person? Has your experience at law school had anything to do with the process by which you have become such a person? Here are two other possible starting points:

Can you tell your law school and its teachers what they should be doing?

Can you explain why your law school should not shut its doors forever? Why it should? (Do not answer this question by talking about the need for the lawyer in society.)

As you work through this material and write your paper, be careful to avoid the clichés and jargon of the world of education. It will be at least as hard to avoid trivial writing here as it was with respect to the judicial opinion, for example, and perhaps harder.

Below is a proposal for a new law school. How do you respond?

EDUCATING THE LAWYER AS POLICY-MAKER*

Interview with Morris Abram

. . . NOTE: In December 1969, Brandeis University, named after the late Mr. Justice Louis D. Brandeis, announced plans to "build a new law school to train government policy-makers, not practicing lawyers." *Trial* interviewed the then president of the University, Morris Abram, who was for many years a trial lawyer. The resignation of Mr. Abram to enter politics has put "the future of the law school in a state of suspended animation," according to a Brandeis spokesman, but *Trial* is printing the interview nevertheless because of the implications and thoughtfulness of Mr. Abram's observations and their relevance to legal education.

What concept lies behind the planned Brandeis University Law School?

Lawyers are the generalists of today's society — the problem-solvers.

One finds lawyers as advisers and executives in almost any governmental field you can think of, in positions where they pass and advise on economic, fiscal and monetary questions; on welfare questions; on defense and foreign policy questions — fields that are or appear a long way from "law."

Men like George Ball, former Undersecretary of State, Dean Acheson and John Foster Dulles, former Secretaries of State, and William Rogers, present Secretary of State, were all lawyers.

Lawyers are government policymakers out of all proportion to their numbers in the general population.

* *Trial,* Vol. 6, No. 3, 41–42 (1970).

Why out of proportion?

I think there are two principal reasons for this heavy utilization of lawyers in the most sensitive and difficult positions.

1. The people who go to law school seem to have, on the whole, a higher level of ability than those at any other graduate school.

2. The education students receive is an education in problem-solving. They learn to use logic to analyze facts and come to conclusions.

This combination of logic and decision-making skill makes the law school product better suited, in many ways, to governmental policy-making positions.

Part of the lawyer's training is an ability to teach himself new and different fields, and then to work effectively with those fields.

I was a trial lawyer for many years. I remember one case I tried, a medical malpractice case involving a neurosurgeon. To prepare for that trial — to examine and cross-examine some of the most illustrious men in the field — I had to learn a great deal about neurosurgery where previously I had no practical knowledge about it.

And in other cases, I was forced to learn a great deal about tax, a great deal about railroads and their procedures, etc.

The field of trial practice makes it imperative that the lawyer become involved in a kaleidoscope of human experience. He is able to do this because he has been trained to take a new subject and learn it — not just learn about it superficially, but learn enough to be prepared to test, to challenge, and to argue about some of the most difficult problems of a particular field in the live crucible of the courtroom.

Thus it is seen that education has much to do with the reason governments call upon lawyers so much.

Since today, more than ever, there is a disposition for more and more lawyers to go into public life, the question then arises: Is there a better way to educate them?

I believe there is. I believe we can concentrate more heavily on teaching the sorts of things that are relevant to future policy-makers who may also be practicing lawyers.

This is the goal that we have set at Brandeis University Law School. We do not wish to create *just another law school* because of the mere notion that every university should have a law school; we want to do better [what] every first-rate law school has been and is doing almost as an unintentional by-product of its curriculum.

How do you propose to go about it?

There will be a National Organizing Committee of judges, prominent public officials, practicing lawyers, eminent men in the legal academic world, who, I hope, will eventually become a Board of Overseers for the Brandeis University Law School.

Of course, this organizing committee must prepare a great deal of ground work before the school can think of opening its doors.

We have a financial pledge for the building, but we must still raise endowment, library and other necessary funds. We plan to raise this money from people and groups who are not regular supporters of Brandeis University in view of the very difficult financial position faced today by all private institutions of higher education in America.

What are some specific changes from the traditional law school curriculum and approach that are being considered?

We have to analyze each of the traditional subject and curriculum areas to determine whether it produces the effect claimed and consider if these areas are worth the effort in terms of the thrust the school envisions.

For example, we will probably not offer any courses in Agency Law, in the Commercial Code, or in Future Interests, whereas we will certainly offer courses in Administrative Law, Taxation, Government Regulation of Business, Constitutional Law and Jurisprudence.

We will also undoubtedly teach the basic "building block" courses that every lawyer must know: Contracts, Torts, Evidence, Criminal Law.

But I would hope that even in these areas we would take a "policy-maker" approach. For example, in the criminal law, I think the course should not just "teach it," but should analyze the subject in terms of fundamentals:

What is the criminal law supposed to do? Is it any good at what it is supposed to do?

For years I was chairman of the Atlanta Crime Commission, and I came to the conclusion that some very basic questions have to be examined.

To take another example, I hope that the course in Evidence would not just teach things like the hearsay rule and the exceptions to it, but would examine whether there is any real justification for them on the basis of studies of human behavior. For instance, the deathbed admissions exception: Is there really a higher probability that a man facing imminent death will tell the truth or that the person who reports the deathbed statement will do so truthfully?

The thrust of the teaching will be to teach problem-solving and analysis in the context of the law. All subjects in the traditional curriculum can be adapted to this purpose, but it is not worth the time to do this in the context of feudal land-tenure rules or the Institutes of Justinian in Latin. I had to study the latter when I read law at Oxford, and I can attest that it wasn't worth it! It is better to teach in terms of problems in tax law, which is relevant to future policy-makers.

How large will the school be?

It will be a small law school. There are no final plans because there are many unanswered questions. But 50 students in a class would be large.

In addition, the liberal arts faculty may approve undergraduates, taking individual courses in the Brandeis University Law School.

Law students may also find some courses in the liberal arts college or other faculties which are beneficial to them.

We do anticipate cross-listing and registration. In fact, when the ideas for this school were first discussed, we considered whether it should not be a faculty for undergraduate majors or concentrators in legal studies.

It was felt, however, that it would be a great idea only if undergraduates who are would-be lawyers would avoid the program. Since there is no way to guarantee this, it was decided to create a professional school, but to permit undergraduates to take courses with the approval of their own faculty.

If you are keeping so much standard legal education material, although adopting a different approach to teaching it, what other changes do you contemplate?

Many law school deans would like to telescope the traditional three-year law school curriculum into two years on the ground that the third year isn't necessary. For various legal and bureaucratic reasons — chiefly state laws having to do with bar examinations — this is not now possible.

But, why shouldn't a law school substitute some very new things for that one-third of the student's law school experience? We would like to offer other and newer subjects, more closely related to public policy. This might lead to a more productive and better arrangement.

For example, a course in Public Welfare, which could draw upon Brandeis University's Heller School for Advanced Studies in Social Welfare, would be a good curriculum addition. There should be courses aimed at the problems of people who have traditionally avoided the law and who in turn have been avoided by society.

We should teach the law of taxation in conjunction with the problems, proposed changes and studies of national income policy.

Would you graduate practicing lawyers?

No, because it is impossible. No law school in the country does that now and no law school *can* do it.

The best law school graduates who came into my law firm (Paul, Weiss, Rifkind, Garrison & Wharton of New York City) were not ready to do the multiple tasks a practicing lawyer must do in trial work or office work. No amount of additional or different academic training in a university setting would have made them ready. The apprenticeship period for the young lawyer will continue because it is the only way trial lawyers are made.

Our graduates will be as well prepared to become practicing lawyers as those from other first-rank law schools, and our plans call for the school to be appropriately certified and accredited.

As a matter of fact, a policy-maker can be trained in a law school closer to the top-skill level than can a practicing lawyer. The tools of public service can be better learned in law schools than the details of cross-examining a witness. Moot courts and mock trials are useful, yet they can never duplicate the knotted stomach a young lawyer feels in his first courtroom experience.

Will the Brandeis University Law School be a school of government in fact, but a school of law in name?

Definitely not. We will teach to analyze, know and use the law and legal mechanisms as do the best law schools today. In addition, we will go the second mile to teach them to advise and function as policy-makers, using the law's basic educational tenets.

You seem to envision a dynamic law school. Is this really possible, in view of the basically conservative, tradition-bound nature of law and lawyers?

I do not agree with that characterization. Legal institutions like the American Bar Association have been quite conservative. But law itself is not. Law underpins dynamic change.

Of course, law is basically a system of rules. Lawyers occupationally try either to maintain or overthrow one or more of these rules on behalf of a client.

If one wishes to produce change within the legal frame-work, the best instrument is the law. Law is conservative only to those who regard any change within the system, or any orderly change of the system, as conservative.

Law is and can be an instrument of change. For 12 years I worked unsuccessfully to get a one-man, one-vote reapportionment; it was accomplished only after I tried *Sanders v. Gray* in the Supreme Court.

Again, for every lawyer who argues for civil rights or reapportionment or welfare rights, there are lawyers who argue on the other side to keep things as they are.

A healthy society needs both.

While there is an element in law of inflexibility, it should also be recognized that legal institutions are *more* capable of change than some elective instrumentalities.

This capability — in the form of policy-making — is what the Brandeis Law School seeks to expand.

QUESTIONS

1. *Does Mr. Abram's proposal for a new law school say all that needs to be said on this subject?*
2. *How would you yourself set up a law school? Draft a statement of purpose and policy for an ideal law school. (Do not forget your earlier experience of setting up institutions. Consider especially your work in Chapter 4.)*
   a. *As the founder of such a school, how would you explain your educational objectives? Would you talk about the necessity of teaching certain subject areas? Inculcating certain professional skills? Providing and sharpening the basic tools of the lawyer? How would you talk?*
   b. *Suppose you were a teacher being interviewed for a job at the new law school, and were asked what educational (or pedagogical) objectives you pursued in your own teaching. How would you respond?*
   c. *As founder of the new law school, how would you select your students? To answer this you must have some notion of what you hope from them at their best, and how you can estimate the qualities of applicants. Will you rely heavily on the Law School Aptitude Test? On grades earned in undergraduate courses? On the nature of the college attended? On the nature of the courses taken? Why will you do what you do? Is it quickness or brightness that you want above all?*

THE SCHOOLMASTER*

Roger Ascham

I do gladly agree with all good schoolmasters in these points; to have children brought to good perfitness [perfectness] in learning, to all honesty in manners, to have all faults rightly amended, to have every vice severely corrected: but for the order and way, that leadeth rightly to these points, we somewhat differ. For commonly many schoolmasters, some as I have seen, moe [more] as I have heard tell, be of so crooked a nature, as, when they meet with a hard-witted scholar, they rather break him than bow him, rather mar him than mend him. For when the schoolmaster is angry with some other matter, then will he soonest fall to beat his scholar; and though he himself should be punished for his folly, yet must he beat some scholar for his pleasure, though there be no cause for him to do so, nor yet fault in the scholar to deserve so. These, ye will say, be fond schoolmasters, and few they be that be found to be such. They be fond indeed, but surely over many such be found everywhere. But this will I say, that even the wisest of your great beaters, do as oft punish nature as they do correct faults. Yea, many times the better nature is sorer punished. For, if one by quickness of wit take his lesson readily, another by hardness of wit taketh it not so speedily; the first is always commended, the other is commonly punished: when a

* Book 1 (1570; J. A. Giles ed. 1864).

wise schoolmaster should rather discreetly consider the right disposition of both their natures, and not so much weigh what either of them is able to do now, as what either of them is likely to do hereafter. For this I know, not only by reading of books in my study, but also by experience of life abroad in the world, that those which be commonly the wisest, the best learned, and best men also, when they be old, were never commonly the quickest of wit when they were young. The causes why, amongst other, which be many, that move me thus to think, be these few, which I will reckon.

Quick wits commonly be apt to take, unapt to keep; soon hot, and desirous of this and that; as cold, and soon weary of the same again; more quick to enter speedily, than able to pierce far; even like oversharp tools, whose edges be very soon turned. Such wits delight themselves in easy and pleasant studies, and never pass far forward in high and hard sciences. And therefore the quickest wits commonly may prove the best poets, but not the wisest orators; ready of tongue to speak boldly, not deep of judgment, either for good council or wise writing. Also for manners and life, quick wits commonly be, in desire, newfangled; in purpose, unconstant; light to promise anything, ready to forget every thing, both benefit and injury; and thereby neither fast to friend, nor fearful to foe: inquisitive of every trifle, not secret in the greatest affairs; bold with any person; busy in every matter; soothing such as be present, nipping any that is absent: of nature also, always flattering their betters, envying their equals, despising their inferiors; and by quickness of wit, very quick and ready to like none so well as themselves. . . . They be like trees, that show forth fair blossoms and broad leaves in spring-time, but bring out small and not long lasting fruit in harvest-time; and that only such as fall and rot before they be ripe, and so never, or seldom, come to any good at all. For this ye shall find most true by experience, that, amongst a number of quick wits in youth, few be found in the end either very fortunate for themselves, or very profitable to serve the commonwealth, but decay and vanish, men know not which way; except a very few, to whom peradventure blood and happy parentage may perchance purchase a long standing upon the stage. The which felicity, because it cometh by others' procuring, not by their own deserving, and stand by other men's feet, and not by their own, what outward brag soever is borne by them, is indeed of itself, and in wise men's eyes, of no great estimation. . . .

Contrariwise, a wit in youth that is not over-dull, heavy, knotty, and lumpish; but hard, tough, and though somewhat staffish, (as Tully wisheth, *otium quictum non languidum*, and *negotium cum labore, non cum periculo*,) such a wit, I say, if it be at the first well handled by the mother, and rightly smoothed and wrought as it should, not overthwartly, and against the wood, by the school-master, both for learning and whole course of living, proveth always the best. In wood and stone, not the softest, but hardest, be always aptest for portraiture, both fairest for pleasure, and most durable for profit. Hard wits be hard to receive, but sure to keep; painful without weariness, headful without wavering, constant without newfangleness; bearing heavy things, though not lightly, yet willingly; entering hard things, though not easily, yet deeply; and so come to that perfectness of learning in the end, that quick wits seem in hope, but do not indeed, or else very seldom, ever attain unto. Also for manners and life, hard wits commonly are hardly carried, either to desire every new thing, or else to marvel at every strange thing; and therefore they be careful and diligent in their own matters, not curious and busy in other men's affairs: and so they become wise themselves, and also are counted honest by others. They be grave, steadfast, silent of tongue, secret of heart; not hasty in making, but constant in keeping any promise; not rash in uttering, but wary in considering every matter; and thereby not quick in speaking, but deep of judgment, whether they write or give council in all weighty affairs. And these be the men, that become in the end both most happy for themselves, and also always best esteemed abroad in the world.

QUESTIONS

1. *If you were the dean of the school you have hypothetically founded, or a member of its appointments committee, how would you go about selecting teachers?*
   a. *Would you look for those with brilliant records at the most prestigious schools?*
   b. *Would you care whether a candidate had published anything? If he had done so, what would you look for in what he wrote?*
   c. *If he had teaching experience, how would you go about evaluating what he had done: would you ask his former dean, or some of his colleagues you happened to know? Would you ask for recommendations from particular students? What would you be looking for?*
2. *It may help you start working out a statement of what you mean by "good teaching" if you ask in what ways it fails to do justice to the good teacher — or the good class — to say that appropriate information is transferred from professor to student. In thinking about your experience of teaching and learning, do not confine yourself to academic experience, but think of other things you have learned or perhaps taught: how to ski or fly-fish, or paint or play an instrument, or drive a car or choose wine. The painting teacher might be an especially good example: certainly the heart of his teaching is not in the instructions he gives you, the principles he enunciates, the information he transmits. Does not the heart of his teaching come after you have done something of your own — made your own choices of subject, style, and direction — when he responds to your*

attempt? And how does he respond: with a gradc? An instruction? Is there any analog to this experience in law school?

3. If you were a teacher, how would you judge your own work? What would you say to yourself after class, and why?
   a. Suppose you had a class in which the conversation moved quickly, students responding to each other with promptness and intelligence: would that be a good class?
   b. Suppose the opposite: a class in which the conversation moved slowly, in which there were long silences on your part and theirs, in which there was puzzlement and boredom. "It was like pulling teeth," one says in disgust. Would that be a bad class?
   c. To what extent can the teacher properly take credit or responsibility for what happens in his class? Can he know the answer to that question?
   d. What can a teacher then hope or expect about his experience of the classroom? How can he judge it? What can a student hope or expect, and how can he judge the experience he has?
4. Part of the problem you face here is the familiar difficulty of choosing or making a language that will do justice to yourself and your subject. How can you characterize a process of education, other than in the usual mechanical terms of acquiring or possessing knowledge or a skill? The metaphor of growth is another common cliché. What other possibilities are there? As in the assignment on judicial criticism (Chapter 5, Section B), you are urged to be as extravagant as you can: Socrates said his function was that of a midwife or gadfly; what can you say? The teacher is like a cutting horse, that separates a steer from a herd by constantly blocking its attempts to rejoin them? The teacher is a frustrator of students?
5. Here is one suggestion, in familiar terms: the heart of the classroom experience is the process of question and response. Here if anywhere the several educations going on in the room can meet, the different minds can recognize their differences and make a conversation. A good lecture can even be said to proceed by posing questions to which various responses are suggested and examined. The constant symbol of the good class is the good question.

   But what is a good question? We hear people approve of clear, searching, Socratic questions and disapprove of obvious, obscure, meaningless, and trivial questions. But such a vocabulary can be of little help.

   Can you identify various sorts of bad questions you have actually experienced in class — questions that ask a student to state what he already knows, for example, or questions that are false or bullying, to which the student cannot sensibly respond, or to which the professor has his own secret answer which he will reveal ten minutes before the end of the hour? The whole process of the classroom can become an empty game, an intellectual ritual of the sort described by Lévi-Strauss (page 17 supra), an activity no one cares about at all — or worse, an activity about which people really do care, but only as the occasion for intellectual or social competition, where the question becomes the occasion for display.

   How is this to be avoided? What is a good question? It may help you work out a response if you examine the supplementary assignment on what makes a good conversation, page 951 infra.
6. Most of the literature of education is terrible, but there are exceptions.

You may be interested in examining one or more of the following books: Plato, The Republic; W. Jaeger, Paideia (1939); G. Sampson, English for the English (1926); D. Holbrook, English for Maturity (1961); K. Grahame, The Wind in the Willows, Chapter 1 (1908).

WRITING ASSIGNMENT 21: The Lawyer's Education

• *In a brief paper, explain what a legal education should involve: how is law to be learned and taught?*

At the beginning of this section, I suggested three possible ways to start out:

1. Can you tell us what it is about you that makes you an educated person, and what contribution your experience of law school has made towards that end?

2. Can you tell teachers and your fellow students what they should be doing: what does the good teacher do, and what the good student?

3. Can you explain why your law school should not close its doors tomorrow?

4. Here is a fourth suggestion: give an account of a moment or a period of time in your own life which you can say was educative. Does this experience find any parallel in law school?

Here is one last passage on education: "In this time, his house being within ten miles of Oxford, he contracted familiarity and friendship with the most polite and accurate men of that University; who found such an immenseness of wit, and such a solidity of judgment in him, so infinite a fancy bound in by a most logical ratiocination, such a vast knowledge, that he was not ignorant in any thing, yet such an excessive humility as if he had known nothing, that they frequently resorted and dwelt with him, as in a college situated in a purer air, so that his house was a university bound in a lesser volume, whither they came not so much for repose, as study; and to examine and refine those grosser propositions, which laziness and consent made current in vulgar conversation." Edward Hyde, First Earl of Clarendon, History of the Rebellion and Civil Wars in England, Book 7, para. 220 (1702; Macray ed. 1888).

APPENDIX

BIBLIOGRAPHICAL NOTE

INDEX

APPENDIX

SUPPLEMENTARY WRITING ASSIGNMENTS*

2–1: WHAT IS A GOOD CONVERSATION?

"He experienced that irresistible impulse to impart information which is inseparable from gross ignorance. There is always some one thing which the ignorant man knows, and that thing is the only thing worth knowing; it fills the ignorant man's universe." Joseph Conrad, Outcast of the Islands, Chapter 1 (1896).

"In this time, his house being within ten miles of Oxford, he contracted familiarity and friendship with the most polite and accurate men of that University; who found such an immenseness of wit, and such a solidity of judgment in him, so infinite a fancy bound in by a most logical ratiocination, such a vast knowledge that he was not ignorant in any thing, yet such an excessive humility as if he had known nothing, that thcy frequently resorted and dwelt with him, as in a college situated in a purer air; so that his house was a university bound in a lesser volume, whither they came not so much for repose as study, and to examine and refine those grosser propositions which laziness and consent made current in vulgar conversation." Edward Hyde, First Earl of Clarendon, History of the Rebellion and Civil Wars in England, Book 7, para. 220 (1702; Macray ed. 1888).

This assignment might be done in addition to the main assignment, or perhaps by part of the class instead of it; or it might serve simply as additional reading; or it might be done more than once during the course, first now, and again later.

* Problems that might be used as writing assignments appear throughout the text, under the heading of either Questions or, more rarely, Problems. See e.g., pages 188 and 210–213 *supra*.

Part One

• Give an account of a real or imaginary conversation, or part of one, which you regard as a good conversation, a success. Try not to choose an easy success, a mechanical or routine exchange, but a real conversation, an occasion which could be a source of satisfaction or pleasure.

Part Two

• Give an account of a real or imaginary conversation, or part of one, which you regard as a failure. This too should be an important occasion, not a casual one. Make it an occasion of frustration, where people really try but fail to get a talk going.

Part Three

• Explain the judgments you have made about these conversations. What was it that made the first a success and the second a failure?
• In explaining your judgment, be sure to explain your language of criticism as well. For example, if you say that one conversation was a success because it produced genuine communication, you should explain what you mean by that term, and, so far as you can, why communication occurred in one instance and not the other; if you say that one conversation was founded upon a good question, and the other on a poor one, you should explain what makes a good question; and so on.

The following questions and readings may be of some interest to you as you work out this assignment.

1. Take the notion of "communication," for example: this is an extremely common term of approval used to refer to the way in which a business organization works well, to a technique for reducing community tensions in the cities and universities, to the essence of family harmony, and so on. What can be meant by this term? That our minds lie wholly open, one to the other — that you know what I know and I know what you know? How can that be? Yet what does the term mean if not that?

2. To ask what makes a good question is to address a real complexity. For one thing, as you know from your law classes, there is the matter of seriousness: is the question really meant as a question, to elicit a response in which the questioner has an interest? Or is it a fake question, a kind of manipulation or patronization? There is also the matter of its substance: is it cast in a way that invites genuine discussion, is it intellectu-

ally (as opposed to socially) a serious question or a fake one? Here you might think about your experience of LSAT questions, for example — not questions at all, but the occasion for the clever elimination of the improbable — or the questions that consumed evenings of your college life. What conversation could be founded, for example, upon the question of whether reason is superior to emotion, baseball to football, the mountains to the sea, youth to age, work to play?

Compare the following excerpt.

THE ENDLESS ADVENTURE*

F. S. Oliver

The student of politics will not make a beginning till he has realised that in this art there are antinomies everywhere, and that it is no shame to a politician, or to the man who writes about him, if the opinions he utters are often in conflict one with another. The politician or the writer who succeeds in proving his life-long consistency is less an object of admiration than of derision. We know that such a one cannot have penetrated beyond the vestibule, and therefore cannot have arrived at any truth worth telling.

I would not presume to say which of the items in the following list are false and which are true; or which of them are idols and which ideals. They will be regarded differently in different countries, and by different people in the same country. Very often they will be regarded differently by the same man at different periods of his life. And not so rarely as one might think, a pair of these opposites may be believed in quite honestly by the same man at one and the same time. But although there has been and will doubtless continue to be endless debate as to the truth of each one of these opinions, and as to whether it ought to be looked on as an ideal or as an idol, there will be general agreement among most readers of history that hardly one of them is altogether new: —

That the goal of political endeavour is a state in which there will be no rich and no poor: — That the division of mankind into rich and poor is a divine institution, or a law of nature as inevitable as gravitation.

That all wealth should belong to the state: — That the state is a muddler that cannot create wealth, and a spendthrift that cannot save it; so that, if all wealth were taken by the state there would soon be a universal impoverishment.

That religion is the buckler of the poor: — That religion is one of the chief weapons of the oppressor.

* Pages 51–55 (1930).

That minorities must go to the wall: — That only minorities are fit to rule.

That family life and friendship are the foundations of human society: — That family life and friendship are odious ties that prevent a man from realising his highest nature in the service of humanity.

That vast confederate unions are the surest hope of world-peace and of a rapid moral and material development: — That there should be as many free, sovereign and independent nations as there are branches, or even twigs, of the human race; and that when ethnologists or poets have discovered a shade of difference between two sections of a nation, it is contrary to freedom and the principles of self-determination for the smaller to remain united with the larger.

That law should supersede physical force in international disputes: — That a law which does not rest on physical force is an impossibility.

That in wars between nations both are usually in the wrong, though in popular rebellions right is almost always on the side of the rebels: — That of all kinds of war civil war is the most detestable and hardly ever to be justified; but that when two nations go to war it often happens that both are in the right.

That war is a hideous form of insanity and that preparations for defence do but increase the danger of an outbreak: — That a nation which is not at all times ready and willing to fight for its life will assuredly lose its life and its soul too.

That a democracy is distinguished from an oligarchy or a despotism by the fact, among others, that it cannot be founded securely except upon a basis of universal military training; that universal military training will raise the moral tone and improve the physical condition of the people; will safeguard the state, not only against foreign attack, but also against the conspiracies of a would-be tyrant, or of an anarchic or reactionary minority; and will tend to discourage wars of vanity and aggression, owing to the concern most men have for their own skins: — That standing armies and every form of militia are an abomination; that military training and discipline debauch the morals and brutalise the character of a nation; are a provocation rather than a deterrent to potential enemies; are a ready-made weapon in the hands of conspirators; and, owing to the natural pugnacity and over-confidence of mankind, are less likely to diminish than to increase wars of vanity and aggression.

That capital punishment is a crime against human nature: — That everyone who opposes or obstructs a popular revolution should suffer the death penalty.

That the intellectual and the benevolent have too little power in government, the cunning and the greedy too much: — That theorists of exceptional intelligence, and sentimentalists possessed by a passionate faith, cause more suffering in the world (when they happen to engross power) than is caused by able and unscrupulous men seeking their own interests.

That justice should be tempered with mercy: — That justice tempered with mercy is inhumanity.

That there is no place for sentiment in government: — That all government is founded upon sentiment.

That women should take part in business and public affairs on a perfect equality with men: — That woman's sphere is the home or, failing that, a nunnery.

That by the Law of Nature all men are born equal: — That by the Law of Nature men are endowed from their birth with an infinite variety of faculties that produce, without any aid from human institutions, an infinite variety of inferiority and superiority; and that, arrange things how you will, those who are superior will get more of their own way than those who are inferior.

That by the Law of Nature all men are born free: — That no man was ever born free, or in any form of human society ever became free at any period of his life, with the possible exception of Robinson Crusoe on his desert island until Man Friday's arrival, on which day his freedom was curtailed.

That no state is securely founded until every adult has a vote for the choice of his rulers: — That when every adult has a vote there will be such confusion and inconstancy that a dictatorship will be the only way of escape from anarchy — a dictatorship of the proletariat, a dictatorship of virtue and goodwill, or a dictatorship of reaction.

2–2: *STUDENT-TALK AND THE LAWYER*

One of the purposes of this course is to invite you to talk and write not as a student but as an independent mind. Its questions are meant to be taken as real questions — as if your teacher really wanted to know what you thought about them — not as exercises to which there is a right or wrong answer. The subject of this assignment is what it means to write like a student, and what connections (if any) there are between that sort of writing and writing as a lawyer.

Part One

- *Give an example of student writing on a particular subject and explain what marks it as such.*

Part Two

• *Draft another statement on the same subject which is not written as a student, and explain how it differs from the first one. Your statement should be a passage of good writing, one in which you take some satisfaction.*

Part Three

• *Does the lawyer ever write like the student? Does he ever write as an independent mind?*

2–3: METAPHOR AND CLICHÉ

There is a great concern with metaphor in this course. You were asked earlier whether you can make the law and your life in it a metaphor, and if so, how; the materials themselves could be viewed as working out a metaphor, that law is literature; and again and again we uncover hidden metaphors in what at first seems to be plain speech, and try to bring them to life. Is all language metaphorical in all its uses, or does it make sense to isolate a certain activity or event and call that metaphor? Robert Frost said the metaphor was a way of saying one thing and meaning another, of speaking of one thing in terms of another. What is a good metaphor and what is a bad one?

Another critical term that appears throughout the material is "cliché." That is how we do not want to speak and think. What is a cliché? Can a metaphor be a cliché? Obviously the answer is yes. What makes a metaphor live, what removes it from the cliché?

Part One

• *Give an example from your own reading or writing of a successful metaphor, one that seems to you to be alive, to do what writing should do.*

Part Two

• *Give an example from your own reading or writing of a metaphor that seems dead, that is no more than a cliché.*

Part Three

• *Explain the difference between the two passages. What makes a good metaphor?*

2-4: TRANSLATION

For those who have some knowledge of foreign languages, this assignment carries our way of looking at law as a language — as a distinct way of thinking and talking — one step further. On several occasions the question has been raised, why do we not discard the special language of the law and carry on our affairs in plain English; we could simply translate from Law into English. This assignment begins a response to that suggestion by exploring what translation involves.

Part One

• Reproduce a short passage written in a foreign language. Translate that passage into English. Explain what you did when you translated the passage.

Part Two

• Reproduce a short passage written in the language of the law, and translate it into plain English. Explain what you did when you translated that passage.

Part Three

• Are these two acts of translation similar, or different? What, if anything, is lost when each passage is translated? Can you now explain why we cannot translate all legal statements into plain English, or have you shown that we can do so?

One especially illuminating work on translation is W. Frost, Dryden and the Art of Translation (1955). A work which gives interesting and frequently deplorable examples of rewriting English passages is R. Graves and A. Hodge, The Reader Over Your Shoulder (1943). A general essay of some interest is Steiner, "The Retreat from the Word," in Language and Silence 12 (1967).

2-5: PARODY

• Write a parody of a legal speaker — lawyer, judge, legislator, or law teacher — and explain what you have done.

You may find that the best way to expose for analysis (and entertainment) the ways in which lawyers think and speak is to make fun of them. Parody trains the ear as almost nothing else can do, but it is a demanding art and not all of us are equal to it. Your rendition of the legal speaker must be precise if it is to be made funny or illuminating. It may be helpful to look at D. MacDonald, Parodies (1960), an anthology of parodies in English literature. You may find it most congenial to parody the law teacher or law student, and you should feel free to do so.

How do you explain what you have done? Is it a matter of catching a language, a turn of mind, or what? And what do you do when you have caught it: exaggerate it, twist it, isolate it? It may be useful for you to ask whether your parody is fair. Is it conceivable that you could make a parody of a mind or style you admire?

4: GIVING ADVICE

One activity of the lawyer referred to but not adequately explored in the "Stein" assignment (Chapter 2, Section B) is that of giving advice. You could say that everything a lawyer does is either arguing or advising: all briefs, oral argument, and negotiations with officials or other parties are forms of argument; almost all conversations with clients are part of a process of giving advice. What does it mean to give — or get — advice?

Part One

• Give an account of an occasion on which someone gave you advice.
• A. Did you think at the time that this was good advice or bad advice? How did you make that judgment? What did you do about this advice?
• B. If you thought it was good advice at the time, does that mean it was just unnecessary advice?
• C. What do you think now of that advice, and why? If it was bad advice, tell us what would have been good advice.

It is suggested that if you recognized the advice as good when it was given, it was therefore unnecessary. Does this mean that truly good advice, advice that really is necessary, is never listened to? Why does one listen to advice one does not want to hear, and what happens when one does so? It is a perplexing notion that one can recognize as good advice what one disagrees with. If you say that in such a case one trusts the adviser — because of who he is? what he knows? — the next question is how one decides to trust an adviser. For you as a lawyer the question might be: how does an adviser make himself trustable — by radiating confidence, by smiling knowingly, or what?

Part Two

• *Now tell us what good advice is. Does it consist simply in telling another what he ought to do, or in something more or different? Here you are asked to explain the activity of giving and receiving good advice.*

One possibility is that good advice is that which is later seen as correct by the one advised. He looks back thankfully or ruefully and says, yes that was good advice. How else could good advice possibly be defined?

Samuel Johnson wrote on the activity of advising, in the Rambler No. 87 (1751), in a way you might find helpful.

Here are two additional questions on advice:

1. Where else in the law is advice given, other than by the lawyer to the client? Do you want to say that the judge advises the jury, or the appellate court advises the trial court, or the lawyer advises the judge? How are these activities like and unlike the activity of advising as you defined it in your paper?

2. Do you ever give yourself advice? Do you ever give yourself advice that is "good" in the sense that it is what you do not want to hear? How do you explain that process of internal advising?

5–1: *MAKING DIRECTIONS CLEAR AND PRECISE — MORE ON THE STATUTORY RULE*

To some it might seem that the sorts of complication in which you became involved in the assignment on drafting statutes are unnecessary or stupid, and that all that is required is that people write laws plainly and clearly in ordinary English. The function of language, after all, is to express precise ideas in precise terms, and clarity is the greatest single merit speech can have. This seems obvious; who would speak for obscurity in the statute? This assignment is meant to give you the opportunity to examine what clarity has meant in your own experience, and to bring that experience to bear on what you expect of statutes that you write or read.

Part One

• *Give an account of two occasions on which you were given directions as to your behavior, one in which you found the direction unclear, the other in which you found it clear.*

• *A. Explain why the unclear statement was unclear. What made it unclear?*

• *B. In similar fashion, explain why the clear statement was clear.*

• *C. Presumably you followed or refused to follow the clear direction. What did you do about the unclear one?*

Part Two

• *Now give an account of an occasion on which you gave someone else a guide to his conduct.*
• *Was your statement clear or unclear? How do you know? What made it so?*

Part Three

• *Now explain what it is that makes a statement of direction clear. Is clarity the same as precision? Can a statute ever be clear?*

5–2: A JUDICIAL OPINION ON A STATUTE

In the primary assignments given in the body of Chapter 2 you are not asked to write specifically as a judge, though the assignments on the lawyer and the legislator both require an understanding of what the judge does. The reason for this omission is that Chapters 5 and 6 deal with the judicial mind in considerable detail. But it may be valuable to work on a judicial opinion at this stage, and this assignment will give you that opportunity.

Part One

• *Draft a judicial opinion passing upon the constitutionality of a particular abortion statute, death penalty statute, or a conscientious objection provision in a military draft statute.*

If you wish, you need not write the entire opinion; but be sure to include the precise terms of the statute you are considering, a statement of whatever facts are necessary to your decision, and a full statement of the central passage of judgment in your opinion. You can leave out background, and be allusive or descriptive in your treatment of authority, but the passage you reproduce should state and not merely describe your judgment of constitutionality or unconstitutionality. If you do not know what I mean by the phrase "central passage of judgment," read two or three Supreme Court opinions and look for the central paragraph or page. I think it can be done.

Part Two

• *Now explain what you have done, giving an account of the judicial activity as you engaged in it. How can you compare what you have done* as a judge with what a lawyer or legislator does? In characterizing what the judge does, do you:

a. Give your reader some way of evaluating whether the judicial opinion or decision is good or bad?
b. Express something of what the process of judging means to you?

If your account of what you have done as a judge does not carry with it some expression of how it is to be done well or badly, what sort of account is that? Does this mean that judging is a matter that cannot be judged? Think of an account of some other activity you know how to do well — say, sailing or riding or reading poems or doing mathematics or speaking French. Can an account of an instance of that activity which does not express standards of criticism do justice to the activity? Ask of your passage: if this were all that a young person knew about the life of the law, would he enter it or does it sound mechanical and dull? How could you rewrite your account of what you have done in a way that would express something of what you know of the life of the legal mind?

7: EXPLAINING BEHAVIOR

Part One

• Give an account of an event from your own life, or an imaginary event if you prefer, in which you find the conduct of another to be inexplicable.

Part Two

• Now give an account of a similar event in which you find another's conduct to be explicable.

Part Three

• Explain what you mean by "explicable" and "inexplicable."

17–1: THE MIND OF THE JUDGE

Part One

• Read several opinions by a single judge with considerable care. Then write a short paper in which you criticize his work. In what ways is he a good judge, in what ways less than good?

Part Two

• *Now criticize your essay. What have you done? What can you find to say about the activities of judging and criticizing judges?*

17–2: A DOCUMENT THAT TEACHES

Part One

• *Find and reproduce a passage from legal or nonlegal literature that teaches its reader, that offers him an education.*

Part Two

• *Explain how that passage achieves what it does, how it teaches its reader.*

Part Three

• *Can a judicial opinion ever achieve what this passage achieves? Can you find one that does so?*

17–3: DRAFTING AN OPINION IN ROBINSON v. CALIFORNIA

Part One

• *Reproduced below is the opinion of the Court in Robinson v. California. Draft an opinion for this case that does everything you think an opinion should do.*

Part Two

• *Explain and criticize what you have done. As you have demonstrated it, what is excellence in the judicial opinion?*

Part Three

• *Now look at your criticism and explanation. How does what you say here define possibilities for your profession and yourself?*

Of course you could do this assignment with respect to any case of your own choosing.

ROBINSON v. CALIFORNIA
370 U.S. 660 (1963)

Stewart, J., delivered the opinion of the Court. A California statute makes it a criminal offense for a person to "be addicted to the use of narcotics."[1] This appeal draws into question the constitutionality of that provision of the state law, as construed by the California courts in the present case.

The appellant was convicted after a jury trial in the Municipal Court of Los Angeles. The evidence against him was given by two Los Angeles police officers. Officer Brown testified that he had had occasion to examine the appellant's arms one evening on a street in Los Angeles some four months before the trial. The officer testified that at that time he had observed "scar tissue and discoloration on the inside" of the appellant's right arm, and "what appeared to be numerous needle marks and a scab which was approximately three inches below the crook of the elbow" on the appellant's left arm. The officer also testified that the appellant under questioning had admitted to the occasional use of narcotics.

Officer Lindquist testified that he had examined the appellant the following morning in the Central Jail in Los Angeles. The officer stated that at that time he had observed discolorations and scabs on the appellant's arms, and he identified photographs which had been taken of the appellant's arms shortly after his arrest the night before. Based upon more than ten years of experience as a member of the Narcotic Division of the Los Angeles Police Department, the witness gave his opinion that "these marks and the discoloration were the result of the injection of hypodermic needles into the tissue into the vein that was not sterile." He stated that the scabs were several days old at the time of his examination, and that the appellant was neither under the influence of narcotics nor suffering withdrawal symptoms at the time he saw him. This witness also testified that the appellant had admitted using narcotics in the past.

The appellant testified in his own behalf, denying the alleged conver-

1. The statute is §11721 of the California Health and Safety Code. It provides: "No person shall use, or be under the influence of, or be addicted to the use of narcotics, excepting when administered by or under the direction of a person licensed by the State to prescribe and administer narcotics. It shall be the burden of the defense to show that it comes within the exception. Any person convicted of violating any provision of this section is guilty of a misdemeanor and shall be sentenced to serve a term of not less than 90 days nor more than one year in the county jail. The court may place a person convicted hereunder on probation for a period not to exceed five years and shall in all cases in which probation is granted require as a condition thereof that such person be confined in the county jail for at least 90 days. In no event does the court have the power to absolve a person who violates this section from the obligation of spending at least 90 days in confinement in the county jail."

sations with the police officers and denying that he had ever used narcotics or been addicted to their use. He explained the marks on his arms as resulting from an allergic condition contracted during his military service. His testimony was corroborated by two witnesses.

The trial judge instructed the jury that the statute made it a misdemeanor for a person "either to use narcotics, or to be addicted to the use of narcotics. . . . That portion of the statute referring to the 'use' of narcotics is based upon the 'act' of using. That portion of the statute referring to 'addicted to the use' of narcotics is based upon a condition or status. They are not identical. . . . To be addicted to the use of narcotics is said to be a status or condition and not an act. It is a continuing offense and differs from most other offenses in the fact that [it] is chronic rather than acute; that it continues after it is complete and subjects the offender to arrest at any time before he reforms. The existence of such a chronic condition may be ascertained from a single examination, if the characteristic reactions of that condition be found present."

The judge further instructed the jury that the appellant could be convicted under a general verdict if the jury agreed *either* that he was of the "status" *or* had committed the "act" denounced by the statute. "All that the People must show is either that the defendant did use a narcotic in Los Angeles County, or that while in the City of Los Angeles he was addicted to the use of narcotics . . . ."

Under these instructions the jury returned a verdict finding the appellant "guilty of the offense charged." An appeal was taken to the Appellate Department of the Los Angeles County Superior Court, "the highest court of a State in which a decision could be had" in this case. 28 U.S.C. §1257. See *Smith v. California*, 361 U.S. 147, 149; *Edwards v. California*, 314 U.S. 160, 171. Although expressing some doubt as to the constitutionality of "the crime of being a narcotic addict," the reviewing court in an unreported opinion affirmed the judgment of conviction, citing two of its own previous unreported decisions which had upheld the constitutionality of the statute. We noted probable jurisdiction of this appeal, 368 U.S. 918, because it squarely presents the issue whether the statute as construed by the California courts in this case is repugnant to the Fourteenth Amendment of the Constitution.

The broad power of a State to regulate the narcotic drugs traffic within its borders is not here in issue. More than forty years ago, in *Whipple v. Martinson*, 256 U.S. 41, this Court explicitly recognized the validity of that power: "There can be no question of the authority of the State in the exercise of its police power to regulate the administration, sale, prescription and use of dangerous and habit-forming drugs . . . . The right to exercise this power is so manifest in the interest of the public health and welfare, that it is unnecessary to enter upon a discussion of it beyond saying that it is too firmly established to be successfully called in question." 256 U.S., at 45.

Such regulation, it can be assumed, could take a variety of valid forms. A State might impose criminal sanctions, for example, against the unauthorized manufacture, prescription, sale, purchase, or possession of narcotics within its borders. In the interest of discouraging the violation of such laws, or in the interest of the general health or welfare of its inhabitants, a State might establish a program of compulsory treatment for those addicted to narcotics.[7] Such a program of treatment might require periods of involuntary confinement. And penal sanctions might be imposed for failure to comply with established compulsory treatment procedures. Cf. *Jacobson v. Massachusetts,* 197 U.S. 11. Or a State might choose to attack the evils of narcotics traffic on broader fronts also — through public health education, for example, or by efforts to ameliorate the economic and social conditions under which those evils might be thought to flourish. In short, the range of valid choice which a State might make in this area is undoubtedly a wide one, and the wisdom of any particular choice within the allowable spectrum is not for us to decide. Upon that premise we turn to the California law in issue here.

It would be possible to construe the statute under which the appellant was convicted as one which is operative only upon proof of the actual use of narcotics within the State's jurisdiction. But the California courts have not so construed this law. Although there was evidence in the present case that the appellant had used narcotics in Los Angeles, the jury were instructed that they could convict him even if they disbelieved that evidence. The appellant could be convicted, they were told, if they found simply that the appellant's "status" or "chronic condition" was that of being "addicted to the use of narcotics." And it is impossible to know from the jury's verdict that the defendant was not convicted upon precisely such a finding.

The instructions of the trial court, implicitly approved on appeal, amounted to "a ruling on a question of state law that is as binding on us as though the precise words had been written" into the statute. *Terminiello v. Chicago,* 337 U.S. 1, 4. "We can only take the statute as the state courts read it." *Id.,* at 6. Indeed, in their brief in this Court counsel for the State have emphasized that it is "the proof of addiction by circumstantial evidence . . . by the tell-tale track of needle marks and scabs over the veins of his arms, that remains the gist of the section."

This statute, therefore, is not one which punishes a person for the use

7. California appears to have established just such a program in §§5350-5361 of its Welfare and Institutions Code. The record contains no explanation of why the civil procedures authorized by this legislation were not utilized in the present case.

of narcotics, for their purchase, sale or possession, or for antisocial or disorderly behavior resulting from their administration. It is not a law which even purports to provide or require medical treatment. Rather, we deal with a statute which makes the "status" of narcotic addiction a criminal offense, for which the offender may be prosecuted "at any time before he reforms." California has said that a person can be continuously guilty of this offense, whether or not he has ever used or possessed any narcotics within the State, and whether or not he has been guilty of any antisocial behavior there.

It is unlikely that any State at this moment in history would attempt to make it a criminal offense for a person to be mentally ill, or a leper, or to be afflicted with a venereal disease. A State might determine that the general health and welfare require that the victims of these and other human afflictions be dealt with by compulsory treatment, involving quarantine, confinement, or sequestration. But, in the light of contemporary human knowledge, a law which made a criminal offense of such a disease would doubtless be universally thought to be an infliction of cruel and unusual punishment in violation of the Eighth and Fourteenth Amendments.

We cannot but consider the statute before us as of the same category. In this Court counsel for the State recognized that narcotic addiction is an illness. Indeed, it is apparently an illness which may be contracted innocently or involuntarily. We hold that a state law which imprisons a person thus afflicted as a criminal, even though he has never touched any narcotic drug within the State or been guilty of any irregular behavior there, inflicts a cruel and unusual punishment in violation of the Fourteenth Amendment. To be sure, imprisonment for ninety days is not, in the abstract, a punishment which is either cruel or unusual. But the question cannot be considered in the abstract. Even one day in prison would be a cruel and unusual punishment for the "crime" of having a common cold.

We are not unmindful that the vicious evils of the narcotics traffic have occasioned the grave concern of government. There are, as we have said, countless fronts on which those evils may be legitimately attacked. We deal in this case only with an individual provision of a particularized local law as it has so far been interpreted by the California courts.

Reversed.

MAJOR WRITING ASSIGNMENT

As you can tell, I have drawn heavily on my own experience of literature and literary criticism in defining a point of view from which to regard the law. One might even say that this course is an attempt to connect different sides of my own intellectual life, a response to the feeling that the life of the lawyer is somehow set off from all other experience. In drawing the connection, one defines a context: the legal life can be understood by being compared. "How does the lawyer think and write?" can be answered by comparing him with others. And of course the reader of literature is used to asking exactly the sort of questions about the use of language that I, for one, have found most illuminating in application to the law. I hope these materials will express enough of both kinds of intellectual activity to enable you to see the process of connecting and comparing at work. But what I hope above all is that you can do your own connecting and comparing. For that reason, you are asked to write a paper in which you connect some aspects of your own life as a lawyer with some other side of your intellectual life. You might look at your undergraduate major, for example: what can be learned about the way lawyers think and express themselves by comparing their discipline with those of mathematics, or music, or sociology? You may choose to connect law with any other side of your life that you find interesting and valuable. This is an invitation to place your legal experience in the context of your own mind and its concerns.

• *Write a paper about twenty pages long, due on the last class, in which you connect your legal education with some other aspect of your intellectual life.*

BIBLIOGRAPHICAL NOTE

It is possible to talk about the questions raised in this course in many ways; you are urged to find your own way of talking, and not to feel that behind it all there is a system of analysis for you to figure out and repeat, or that you should find and imitate what someone else has done. With that warning, I shall indicate a few of the basic materials which deal with lawyers and their language in ways that might be of interest to you. This is not a comprehensive bibliography, of course. For that I refer you to D. Mellinkoff, *The Language of the Law* 455–478 (1963).

Philosophers sometimes ask, as we do, "What is the structure and logic of legal thought?" The major figure here is H. L. A. Hart, especially *The Concept of Law* (1961) and "Definition and Theory in Jurisprudence," 70 *L. Q. Rev.* 37 (1954). See also Wittgenstein, *Philosophical Investigations* (2d ed. 1958). Less congenial, to me at least, is the field known as semantics. Here the basic book is I. Richards and C. Ogden, *The Meaning of Meaning* (1923). See also Hayakawa, *Language in Action* (1941); Probert, "Law and Persuasion: The Language-Behavior of Lawyers," 108 *U. Penn. L. Rev.* 35 (1959).

A completely different tack is taken by those who write books on writing for lawyers. Though they often present interesting problems, most of these books boil down to the message that clarity and precision are essential to good writing. See R. Dickerson, *The Fundamentals of Legal Drafting* (1965); F. Cooper, *Writing in Law Practice* (1963). Cf. R. Doremus, *Writing College Themes* (1960); R. Graves and A. Hodge, *The Reader Over Your Shoulder* (1943).

There are, in addition, some writers who have attempted to draw connections between law and literature, almost always in a superficial (however entertaining) way. See E. London (ed.), *Law as Literature* and *Law in Literature* (1960). This sentence is, I am afraid, all too typical: "And so the best literature — drama or poetry, philosophy or fiction — must always be an arsenal for the lawyer." J. Wigmore, *Introduction* to J. Gest, *The Lawyer in Literature* at xii (1913).

There is a rather small body of literature dealing with the lawyer's use of language that might be directly useful to you in this course. The best works are: Chafee, "The Disorderly Conduct of Words," 41 *Colum. L.*

Rev. 381 (1941); Williams, "Language and the Law," which appears in five parts in 61 and 62 *L.Q. Rev.* (1945–1946); Gibson, "Literary Minds and Judicial Style," 36 *N.Y.U.L. Rev.* 915 (1961); F. Philbrick, *Language and the Law* 1–113 (1949); Curtis, "A Better Theory of Legal Interpretation," 3 *Vand. L. Rev.* 407 (1950); Cardozo, "Law and Literature," in *Law and Literature and Other Essays and Addresses* (1931). One extremely important article is I. Berlin, "The Concept of Scientific History," 1 *History and Theory* (No. 1) 1–31 (1960). This is an analysis of the way the historian thinks and writes which defines the historian very much as this course tentatively defines the lawyer: as one who must write against a current of misleading expectations of scientific or logical precision. Also let me suggest that the best of legal history and comparative law seems to face questions like ours and to do so in a way you may find interesting and helpful. Especially let me recommend: H. Maine, *Ancient Law* (1861); F. Pollock and F. Maitland, *The History of English Law* (1895); D. Daube, *Studies in Biblical Law* (1947); M. Gilmore, *Humanists and Jurists* (1963); W. Kunkel, *An Introduction to Roman Legal and Constitutional History* (1966).

Finally, there are two books that in different ways have special affinities with what I attempt to do in this one: Richard Poirier, *The Performing Self* (1971); I. A. Richards, *Practical Criticism* (1929). The theoretically-minded may also be interested in C. Perelman and L. Olbrechts-Tyteca, *The New Rhetoric* (1969).

INDEX